WORLD TRAVEL ATLAS

ISBN: 1-902221-79-6

© 2003 Highbury Columbus Publishing

(information for the Skiing & Snowboarding maps on pages 61 and 146 © 2003 Snow24 plc.)

- **Cartographic Editor:** David Burles.

- **Production Editor:** Brian Quinn of Space Design & Production Services Ltd, London EC2.

- **Additional Cartography:** Anderson Geographics Ltd, Berksire.

- **Contributors:** Patrick Fitzgerald, Tony Peisley, Patrick Thorne, Graeme Payne, Jon Gillaspie, Gary Bowerman, Karen Henderson, Ned Middleton, Penny Locke, Sachiko Burles.

- **Continental Introductions:** Brian Quinn.

- **Cover Design:** Warren Evans of Space Design & Productio

- **Printed by:** Resolution Ltd, Sussex.

- **Founding Editor:** Mike Taylor of the University of Brighton.

- **Publisher:** Pete Korniczky.

This publication has been created from a wide range of sources, and where appropriate these have been credited on the relevant maps, charts or articles.The publishers would like to thank all the organisations and individuals who have helped in the preparation of this edition, with particular thanks to Bill Adams of Safari Consultants; Ruth Skipsey of JLA; Tim Best of Tim Best Travel; Tim O'Brien and Keith Wright of Amusement Business; Brad Smith of Foremost West; John Knighton of African Pride; Louis Abramovitc of TIA; Ed Thompson of CTC; Olivia Doxsee of WTO; Maria Hinayon of ACI; John Douglas of Malawi Tourism; John Haycock of Africa Explorer; Adrian McCallister of the CTO; Sean Ford of ATA; David Ezra of the Saltmarsh Partnership; Emma Humphreys of ATC (London); Maria Polk of Tours.com; Ron Erdman of OTTI; Vivek Angra and Guru Sachdev of Indiatourism; Samantha Day of Easy.Jet; Mark Leech of Murray Consultants; Jeff Bertus and Floorjte Bertus of Bertus Leisure; James Cummings of ATC; Patcharin Hongprapat of PATA; Anne-Marie Hansen of Kuoni; Alan Fredericks of Northstar (US); Tineke Ras-Marees of Toerboek; Penny Locke; Leila Carlyle; Anthony Clewes; Dan Josty; Michael Knop; Helen Argent; Chris Clack; Excelprint; and John Doyle and Lisa Wellesley of Resolution Ltd. Apologies to organisations or individuals omitted from this list in error.

Contents

World	4-45
Introduction	4
Physical	8
Prevailing Winds	8
Lithospheric Plates	8
Ocean Currents	9
Political	10
Regions used in this book	10
IATA Regions	11
Climate	12
Time Zones	13
Sun, Earth & Moon	13
Agricultural Land Use	14
Forests	14
Greenhouse Gases	14
Environmental Change	15
Environmental Treaties	15
Population	16
Urbanization	16
Human Development Index	17
Religion	17
National Income	18
Economic Growth	18
Foreign Aid	18
Economic Activity	19
International Arrivals	20
Visitor Receipts	20
Hotel Bedrooms	20
Visitor Expenditure	21
WTO Regions	22
Energy Deposits	22
Energy Production	22
Energy Consumption	23
Renewable Energy	23
Nuclear Energy	23
International Organisations	24
International Business	26
Telecommunications	28
The Internet	29
Media Freedom	29
Health Expenditure	30
Health Indicators	30
Areas of Health Risk	31
Sport	32
Military Spending	33
Weapons of Mass Destruction	33
Airports	34

Flight Times	37
Cruising	38
UNESCO Natural Heritage Sites	40
UNESCO Cultural Heritage Sites	42
Europe	46-101
Introduction	46
Physical	48
Climate	49
Historical	50
Empires	51
European Union	52
Airports & High-Speed Rail	54
Railways & Ferries	56
National Parks	58
Leisure Parks	59
Museums & Art Galleries	60
Skiing & Snowboarding	61
United Kingdom	62
UK Beaches & National Parks	64
UK Airports, Motorways & Ferries	66
London Airport Connections	67
UK Attractions	68
Ireland	69
Benelux	70
Netherlands Attractions	71
Germany	72
Berlin Airport Connections	73
Germany Attractions	75
France	76
French Wine Regions	76
Paris Airport Connections	77
France Attractions	79
Spain & Portugal	80
Iberia Attractions	81
Spain	82
Andorra	82
Strait of Gibraltar	82
Balearics & Canaries	83
Portugal	84
Azores & Madeira	84
Italy	85
Italy Attractions	88
Central Europe: North	89
Bohemia	89
South Central Poland	89
Alpine Countries	90
Switzerland	90

Austria	91
Central Europe: South	92
Croatia	92
Slovenia	92
Black Sea Coast	92
Greece	93
Crete	93
Ionian & Aegean Islands	94
Turkey	95
Mediterranean	96
Malta	96
Cyprus	96
Mediterranean Diving	96
Scandinavia & Iceland	97
Eastern Europe	100
The Baltic Republics	100
Russian Federation	101
Africa	102-113
Introduction	102
Physical	104
Climate	105
Northwest & West Africa	106
Languages	107
Morocco	107
Tunisia	107
Northeast & East Africa	108
Red Sea Diving	109
Egypt	109
Kenya	109
Southern Africa	110
Tanzania	110
Botswana	110
South Africa	111
African Game Parks	112
Réunion	113
Mauritius	113
Seychelles	113
Asia	114-131
Introduction	114
Physical	116
Climate	117
Empires	118
Museums & Art Galleries	119
West Asia	120
Holy Land	120
Central Asia	121
Silk Road	121

Contents

South Asia	122
India	123
Hill Stations & Beach Resorts	124
Sri Lanka	124
Maldives	124
East Asia	125
China	126
Japan	127
South-East Asia	128
Singapore	129
Malaysia	129
Vietnam	129
Thailand	130
Indonesia	131

Australasia & Oceania 132-139

Introduction	132
Physical	134
Australia	135
Australian Railways	136
New Zealand	137
Pacific Ocean	138
Pacific Diving	139

USA & Canada 140-161

Introduction	140
Physical	142
Climate	143
Railways & Airports	144
Museums & Art Galleries	145
Skiing & Snowboarding	146
United States	147
Northwest USA	148
Southwest USA	149
Northeast USA	150
Southeast USA	151
US National Parks	152
United States Focus Maps	154
Indian Reservations	155
NYC Airport Connections	156

US Theme Parks	157
Canada	158
Canadian National Parks	161
The Great Lakes	161

Latin America & the Caribbean 161-174

Introduction	162
Caribbean Languages	164
Bahamas	164
Turks & Caicos Is.	164
Cuba	164
Cayman Is.	165
Jamaica	165
Dominican Republic	165
Haiti	165
Puerto Rico	165
Bermuda	165
Caribbean Diving	166
Anguilla	166
Aruba	166
Bonaire	166
British Virgin Is.	166
Curaçao	166
Grenada	166
Isla de Margarita	166
St-Barthélemy	166
St Martin	166
Trinidad	166
Tobago	166
US Virgin Is.	166
Antigua & Barbuda	167
Barbados	167
Dominica	167
The Grenadines	167
Guadeloupe	167
Martinique	167
Montserrat	167
Saba	167
St Eustatius	167

St Kitts & Nevis	167
St Lucia	167
St Vincent	167
Mexico	168
Central America	170
La Ruta Maya	170
Panama Canal	170
South America – Physical	171
Galapagos Islands	170
South America – Climate	172
South America: Northwest	173
South America: East	174
South America: South	175

The Poles 176

Arctic & Antarctic	176
Polar Cruising	176
Antarctic Research Bases	176

Appendices 177-192

1. Geographical Definitions	177
2. Highest & Lowest	177
3. World's Longest Rivers	177
4. Conversion Chart	177
5. Foreign Geographical Terms	178
6. Climate Terms	181
7. Major Cities & Urban Areas	181
8. US States	182
9. Canadian Provinces	182
10. Australian States	182
11. Russian Republics	182
12. Brazilian States	182
13. French Départements	182
14. World's Tallest Buildings	183
15. World's Longest Bridges	183
16. World's Longest Tunnels	183
17. World Monuments Watch	183
Countries A-Z	184

Index 193-224

Outline Maps X1-X16

KEY TO TOPOGRAPHIC MAPS

Communications

- ✈ Airport *main international gateways and domestic hubs*
- ▬▬ ----- Main road, motorway • Road in tunnel
- ▬◻▬ --- Main passenger railway, with station • Railway in tunnel
- ▬▬▬ Dedicated high-speed rail line *focus maps only*
- ·········· Ferry route *selected passenger routes: focus maps only*

Boundaries & boxes

- ▬ · ▬ · ▬ International boundary
- ▬ ▬ ▬ ▬ Disputed international boundary
- ▬ ▬ ▬ Internal administrative boundary
- ▬▬▬ National park, game reserve
- ▭ Area featured in a focus map

Settlement

- ● ● ○ ○ ○ Towns and cities *size of dot is determined by population; largest symbol indicates a city with over one million inhabitants*
- ■ ■ ◻ ○ ◻ National capital *named in CAPITAL LETTERS*
- Built-up area *larger scale focus maps only*
- ∴ ■ Archaeological site, ancient ruins • Important building/s (e.g castle, temple)
- ◆ Other place of interest (e.g. park, reserve, natural feature, small settlement)

Physical features (see individual map pages for elevation tints)

- △ ▽ Mountain peak • Land depression *with altitude in metres*
- = Pass, canyon *with altitude in metres*
- River, with waterfall, with dam • Seasonal river
- Lake • Seasonal lake
- ▬▬ Canal
- ······· Coral reef

World

Key facts

Number of Countries	227
Area ('000 sq km)	135,477
Population ('000)	6,362,615
Population Density (per sq km)	47
Gross National Income (US$m)	31,319,420
Visitor Arrivals ('000)	679,833
Visitor Receipts (US$m)	457,795
Travel Departures ('000)	652,488
Travel Expenditure (US$m)	411,156

GNI figures relate to 2001. Population figures are taken from the most recent reliable source. Travel figures (WTO) are based on overnight stays, not same-day visitors, and are generally for 2001: where these are unavailable or unreliable, earlier years have been used. Where data for certain countries was not available, this has been regarded as zero. For more information see the Countries A-Z section from page 184. The totals for visitor arrivals and visitor departures, and for visitor receipts and travel expenditure, are not equal, as logic would suggest, because of (a) the different ways these figures are calculated and (b) the fact that not all countries report in every category. The area figure excludes Antarctica, which would add a further 13,661,000 sq km onto the world total. For information on the six continents as defined in this atlas, see the continental introductions – consult the Contents pages for details. Note that the World Tourism Organisation defines continents and regions in a different way: for details of their regions, see page 21.

Opinions differ as to how big the worldwide travel business really is. Like all service-based sectors it has no physical product that can be weighed or counted. Many problems of definition follow from this – an airline pilot or a travel agent is clearly part of the industry; but what about a small-town taxi driver, or the owner of a convenience store that also sells local souvenirs? Different countries will often take different views on such points. Despite such challenges, widely accepted estimates are produced by several respected bodies. On such, the World Travel and Tourism Council, suggests that around 11% of the world's GDP and 8% of the world's jobs depend directly or indirectly on travel and tourism, making it the world's largest industry: in the 1960s it was not even in the top ten. The World Tourism Organisation further suggests that travel is the world's fastest growing, with an annual average increase in receipts of 9% between 1984 and 2000. By any estimate, travel is clearly big business – a multi-trillion dollar industry, driven by people's frequent desire to be somewhere else.

This atlas, now in its ninth edition, provides a unique overview of the travel industry in the early 21st century. The focus maps which complement the conventional regional and country plates offer detailed, travel-specific coverage of the most-visited areas. A large number of themes, ranging from economic indicators to UNESCO World Heritage Sites and from ski resorts to time zones, are covered throughout the book, supplemented with detailed appendices. There are also six continental introductions, which provide an overview of each region, a discussion of some of the key travel-related issues and a summary of the main travel destinations. Themes covered here include low-cost airlines, the African renaissance, the cruise industry, SARS, intra-regional travel patterns, the changing role of the travel agent, the impact of the 11 September attacks, regional economic change, the internet, the problems of the major airlines and niche markets. Overall, the book's aim is to provide a clear, balanced and accurate picture of the world for a wide range of readers in the travel industry and elsewhere.

Past, present and future

Apart from 1982 (due mainly to the Gulf War) and 2001 (due mainly to the 11 September terrorist attacks), visitor numbers and travel receipts have risen in every year since accurate records began in 1950. Aviation figures go back even further than that: in 1926 the US domestic air travel market involved some 8,000 passengers, about the number that took to the skies in America every five minutes in 2002. As for international flights from the USA in 1926, there were none recorded. It was not until 1946 that US international departures broke through the one million mark, and they have increased by an average of about one million per year ever since.

By whatever means of transport, Europe remained comfortably the most-visited continent in 2002. What is encouraging for the global health of the industry is that, while Europe's market is still growing, arrivals to other regions – notably East Asia – are growing at a faster pace. The WTO's Tourism 2020 Vision forecasts that worldwide international arrivals are likely to exceed 1.5 billion by 2020. Under this model, Europe will remain the most-visited region, but with a diminished market share. As regards outbound travel, Europe will continue to dominate, but Asia will, by 2020, be supplying twice the number of international travellers than the Americas, compared to only around 7% more as in 2002.

The world's leading countries in the travel numbers league seem to have their positions assured. By some margin, the French receive the most visitors, the Germans travel the most and the Americans spend and receive the most money; this despite their having only around one third of the annual vacation days of many European countries. The most significant medium-term development is likely to be the emergence of China, not only as a destination but also as a source of travellers.

Travel remains something of an exclusive market: the 10 most visited countries accounted for over 50% of all tourist arrivals in 2001. It is also something of a crowded one: in 47 of the world's countries the annual visiting population in 2001 exceeded the native one, on occasions by a factor of more than 10.

Travel trends

The last quarter of 2001 saw a decline in traffic, profits and confidence. All things considered, it was perhaps remarkable that the year as a whole saw only a 0.4% fall in visitor numbers compared to 2000, and even more so that 2002 should have bounced back with a 3.1% increase. That is not to say that all previous travel patterns were reassumed: perhaps the most significant change was that for the first time international travellers to Asian countries exceeded those to the Americas. In times of financial and political uncertainty, certain destinations will seem more attractive than others, but the desire to travel remains. The term 'replacement destination' – where one country seeks to exploit people's unwillingness to travel to another one, generally in the same region – has become more commonly used. Thailand, for example, benefited at the expense of Indonesia after the Bali bombing.

Another area which has tended to benefit is domestic tourism, the extent of which is much harder to quantify than international journeys. The area is of less interest to the travel trade as, except for large countries where air travel may be needed, most arrangements are made independently. Domestic travel in USA has always been strong (around 85% of all trips taken by Americans are domestic, according to TIA), and this sector has held firm in recent years while the volume of international travel has been declining. Although this generates no new revenue from abroad, it at least keeps money flushing through the national economy and keeps travel-related businesses healthy. By contrast, the foot-and-mouth outbreak in the UK hit many businesses particularly hard, as large areas of the countryside were off-limits to Britons and foreigners alike. Several European countries, such as Spain, Greece and France, benefited, becoming in part replacement destinations for the UK's own domestic travel industry.

■ Visitor arrivals

The world's 25 most visited countries in 2001 (millions)
Source: WTO

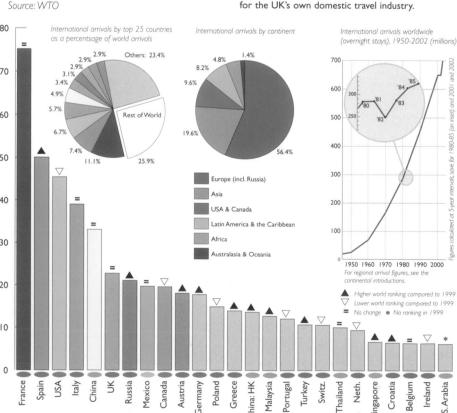

International arrivals by top 25 countries as a percentage of world arrivals

Others: 23.4%
2.9%
2.9%
2.9%
3.1%
3.4%
4.9%
5.7%
6.7%
7.4%
11.1%
25.9%
Rest of World

International arrivals by continent

1.4%
4.8%
8.2%
9.6%
19.6%
56.4%

- Europe (incl. Russia)
- Asia
- USA & Canada
- Latin America & the Caribbean
- Africa
- Australasia & Oceania

International arrivals worldwide (overnight stays), 1950-2002 (millions)

For regional arrival figures, see the continental introductions.

▲ Higher world ranking compared to 1999
▽ Lower world ranking compared to 1999
= No change   * No ranking in 1999

Figures calculated at 5-year intervals, save for 1980-85 (on inset) and 2001 and 2002

- In economic terms, international travel and tourism receipts are classified as exports, and international tourism expenditure as imports. According to the World Tourism Organisation's (WTO's) Tourism Economic Report (1998), travel and tourism is one of the top five export categories for 83% of countries and the main source of foreign currency for 38% of them.
- In June 2003, IATA estimated that the world's airlines had lost US$25 billion in 2001 and 2002. Part of their costs are an estimated US$40 billion for airport charges and air traffic control.
- According to ATW Research, in 2002 the world's airlines flew a total of 1.84 billion passengers and covered 3,920 billion RPKs (Revenue Passenger Kilometres).
- In 2001, Lufthansa carried 29,102,000 international passengers, more than any other carrier. Delta carried the most domestic passengers (85,256,000). Of the ten largest carriers by domestic passenger numbers in 2001, seven were American and three Japanese.
- 19 countries received over 10 million international visitors in 2001. 54 others received over 1 million.
- 18 countries supplied more than 10 million international travellers in 2001. 41 others supplied more than 1 million.
- Nine countries received in excess of US$10billion from international travel in 2001. 53 others received in excess of US$1billion.
- 11 countries spent in excess of US$10billion on international travel in 2001. 37 others spent in excess of US$1billion.
- The biggest travellers, the Germans, have, on average, 35 vacation days a year: Americans have only 13.
- The world's population grew from 1.6 billion to 6.1 billion during the 20th century and is expected to exceed 7 billion by 2015.
- In an average year, Carnival Cruise lines put 10 million chocolate mints on their guests' pillows.
- Nepal is the only country whose flag is not rectangular.
- Denmark is the only country whose foreign aid donations in 2001 exceeded 1% of its GNI.
- 47 countries (including France, Hong Kong (China), Portugal, Greece, Singapore and most of the islands in the Caribbean) receive annually more visitors than their population.
- Over 52% of cruises in 2002 were in the Caribbean or the Mediterranean.
- The first commercial flight took place in 1914.
- More people are killed on the roads of the USA in an average six-month period than have been in all commercial aviation accidents since 1960.
- The WTO predicts that international travel arrivals will exceed 1 billion by 2010 and 1.5 billion by 2020. Of the 2020 arrivals, 1.2 billion will be intra-regional and the remainder long-haul. According to this model, arrivals to Europe and North America will grow at a slower speed than in the rest of the world.
- And finally, a few thoughts from some other travellers:
  'The world is a book, and those who do not travel read only a page.' (St Augustine).
  'I can't think of anything that excites a greater sense of childlike wonder than to be in a country where you are ignorant of almost everything.' (Bill Bryson).
  'Air travel is nature's way of making you look like your passport photo.' (Al Gore).
  'The airplane has unveiled for us the true face of the earth.' (Antoine de Saint-Exupéry).
  'Travel is ninety percent anticipation and ten percent recollection.' (Edward Streeter).
  'We live in a wonderful world that is full of beauty and charm. There is no end to the adventures we can have if only we seek them with our eyes open.' (Jawaharlal Nehru).

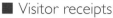

Visitor receipts

The 25 countries that received most from international travel in 2001 (US$ billions)
Source: WTO

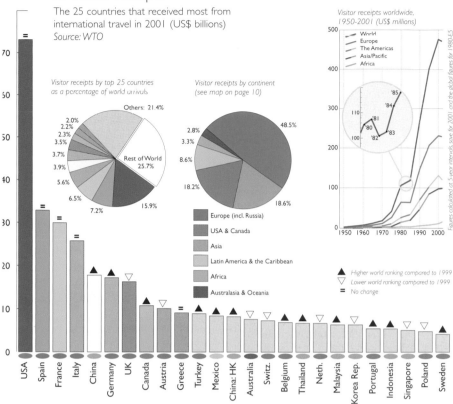

Visitor receipts by top 25 countries as a percentage of world arrivals

Others: 21.4%
2.0%
2.2%
2.3%
3.5%
3.7%
3.9%
5.6%
6.5%
7.2%
15.9%
Rest of World 25.7%

Visitor receipts by continent (see map on page 10)

48.5%
2.8%
3.3%
8.6%
18.2%
18.6%

- Europe (incl. Russia)
- USA & Canada
- Asia
- Latin America & the Caribbean
- Africa
- Australasia & Oceania

▲ Higher world ranking compared to 1999
▽ Lower world ranking compared to 1999
= No change

Visitor receipts worldwide, 1950-2001 (US$ millions)

World
Europe
The Americas
Asia/Pacific
Africa

Special-interest holidays have been growing steadily in recent years and the trend shows no sign of slowing. Adventure holidays, cruising, winter-sports and city-breaks are four of the most important and travel agencies able to offer specialist advice and services in these areas have benefited. Travellers are also becoming more discriminating, demanding and adventurous, a trend fuelled by the internet. In Europe, for example, the low-cost airlines are offering a complete one-stop range of short-break options – flights, hotels, car-hire and insurance – through their web-sites. Many of these involve destinations that ten years ago would have been almost unknown.

The travel trade, like many industries, uses many technical terms. 'Disintermediation' is perhaps one of

the longer ones. To retail travel agents it is also one of the more alarming. The word refers to the practice of a wholesaler, such as a tour operator or airline, selling directly to the consumer rather than via an intermediary, such as a travel agent. Direct-sell tour operators have been around for some time, albeit with a fairly small market share, but the biggest threat to this traditional chain of supply has emerged recently in the shape of the internet. Numerous statistics, some of which are reported elsewhere in this book, testify to the internet's dramatic growth as a medium for travel information and bookings, and appear to suggest an irreversible trend towards direct booking. The reality is rather more complex. The more successful agencies are now making use of the internet as a 24-hour marketing and sales tool, while at the same time ensuring that their levels of knowledge (often in specialist areas) and customer service keep pace with consumers' increasing expectations. In the same way, many on-line companies are looking to provide a human face to their services by using call-centres or even retail outlets. In time, these developments are likely to blur

the distinction between 'on-line' and 'traditional' travel suppliers. Throughout the travel industry, the companies that thrive will do so because they manage to provide the best and most cost-effective service to their customers. For them, the internet is therefore not a rival, but merely another method of conducting business.

The reasons for travelling, the means by which the arrangements are made, the choice of possible destinations and the activities to engage in one arrived are all more numerous than ever before. Business trips or beach holidays, cruises or kayaking, safaris or skiing – they are all available somewhere, as long as one has the necessary leisure time and disposable income.

Travel and wealth

Sadly, many people in the world are currently no more than spectators at this glamorous industry. According to the World Bank, the percentage of the population in developing countries who live on a purchasing power parity of less than US$2 a day (defined as describing what US$2 will actually buy in that country, rather than what it will buy in the USA) was 62.1% in 1990 and had only fallen to 55.6% by 2000. This is over 2.8 billion people. In subsistence economies, leisure time as it is understood in the developed world is virtually non-existent. For such people, international leisure travel is an impossibility.

As beneficiaries, directly or otherwise, of the leisure time and spending of others, however, travel and tourism becomes rather more relevant. For many countries, incoming travel represents a large, if not the largest, source of foreign exchange and jobs. The infrastructure required is generally less damaging or divisive than that needed for an industrial operation, there is less danger of its being sold out to a foreign government or corporation and at least as good a chance of the wealth it creates reaching the local economy. Moreover, the 'product' itself is generally already in place, in the shape of beaches, jungles, temples or local culture. The demands of tourism have in many cases reversed trends of destruction

Flying high

The world's 15 largest airlines, 2002
Source: ATW Research

By passengers (000)		By net profit (US$000s)	
■ Delta	104,943	■ Southwest	511,147
■ American	78,178	■ FedEx	452,950
■ United	75,457	■ Singapore Gp	351,225
■ Southwest	64,647	■ Qantas	216,006
■ US Airways	56,114	■ Air France Gp	134,640
■ Northwest	54,056	■ Ryanair	130,826
■ All Nippon Gp	49,306	■ Emirates	127,467
■ Continental	44,200	■ Cathay Pacific	84,000
■ British Airways	40,004	■ China Eastern	65,409
■ Lufthansa	38,694	■ SkyWest	56,428
■ Air France	39,067	■ EasyJet	55,723
■ JAL	37,183	■ China Airlines	51,769
■ Iberia	24,928	■ South African	50,853
■ Alitalia	24,926	■ Iberia	46,762
■ SAS	23,244	■ Thai Int'l	44,888

Financial data relates to last complete financial year. Gp=Group

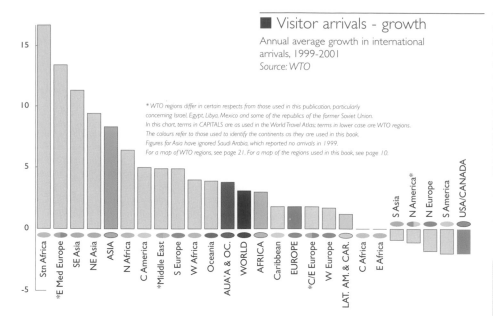

■ Visitor arrivals - growth

Annual average growth in international
arrivals, 1999-2001
Source: WTO

** WTO regions differ in certain respects from those used in this publication, particularly
concerning Israel, Egypt, Libya, Mexico and some of the republics of the former Soviet Union.
In this chart, terms in CAPITALS are as used in the World Travel Atlas; terms in lower case are WTO regions.
The colours refer to those used to identify the continents as they are used in this book.
Figures for Asia have ignored Saudi Arabia, which reported no arrivals in 1999.
For a map of WTO regions, see page 21. For a map of the regions used in this book, see page 10.*

The challenge, as the Travel Foundation recognises, is to encourage tourism that is of a high quality, that respects the environment, that protects natural and cultural resources and that offers economic benefit to destination communities. Travellers and travel companies are becoming more aware of their responsibilities, but the destinations have a job to do, too. A start has already been made: for example, as a result of sustainable tourism projects, hotels in Jamaica now save nearly one billion gallons of water a year, while five of Egypt's Red Sea hotels predict a 25% reduction in electricity usage in 2003. The act of saving resources saves costs. Increasingly, it is also likely to be a way of attracting clients.

■ Big spenders

The 15 countries whose residents spent the most
on international travel in 2001.
Source: WTO

	Expenditure (US$ millions)	GNI (US$ billions)	Expenditure as % of GNI
■ USA	60,117	9,780.80	0.6%
■ Germany	46,222	1,939.60	2.4%
■ UK	36,483	1,476.80	2.5%
■ Japan	26,530	4,523.30	0.6%
■ France	17,718	1,380.70	1.3%
■ Italy	14,215	1,123.80	1.3%
■ China	13,909	1,131.20	1.2%
■ China: HK	12,494	170.30	7.3%
■ Neth.	12,016	390.30	3.1%
■ Canada	11,624	681.60	1.7%
■ Russia	10,360	253.40	4.1%
■ Belgium	9,766	245.30	4.0%
■ Austria	8,886	194.70	4.6%
■ Sweden	6,803	225.90	3.0%
■ Korea, Rep.	6,547	447.60	1.5%

and development; without tourists, many national parks and game reserves would not be financially viable. The world's number-one industry may have its share of faults and cause its share of problems, but it also has much to be proud of.

Sustainable tourism

All forms of travel have an impact on the planet, as do the creation and maintenance of what visitors expect on arrival: while mass tourism can cause change and disruption to the destination societies, and not always for the better. All sectors have been forced to become more aware of the effects of their transient presence. Various 'eco-taxes' have been tried and

have, in general, failed. One of the more promising current initiatives is the UK's Travel Foundation, formed in July 2003, which will raise funds from around 90% of outbound holidays, mainly in the form of voluntary contributions from travellers. The proceeds will be used to find a variety of projects to protect heavily visited areas from social and environmental damage. The development seems to be reflecting public opinion: in a 2002 MORI poll, 85% of UK travellers believed it was important that their holidays preserved the environment of the areas they were visiting, while 94% expressed willingness to pay 1% more on the cost of their trips in order to help make this this happen.

World Pointers

This section provides information or definitions for a selection of the global events, industry trends and technical terms which are directly or indirectly relevant to today's travel business. Many are referred to in the continental introductions (as indicated by a coloured square after the entry) or in the map notes. This list is not intended to be exhaustive, but merely an Editor's selection. More information on these and many other points may be explored in more detail in the World Travel Guide and the World Travel Dictionary, also published by Highbury Columbus, or on the comprehensive internet site which can be found at www.columbustravelguides.com

11 Sept 2001 • The date on which Islamic terrorists hijacked four planes in the USA and destroyed the twin towers of the World Trade Centre in New York and damaged the US Defense Pentagon building in Virginia with the loss of around 3,000 lives. Often referred to as 9/11. For the travel business not least, the scars have been psychological as much as physical and plunged airlines in particular into a sharp decline. On a wider level, the event has served to redefine the nature and focus of US foreign policy. ■

2000 Olympic Games • Hosted by Sydney in Australia between 15 September and 1 October and widely regarded as one of the best-ever modern Olympics. ■

2002 Football World Cup • The 17th such event, and the first to be co-hosted, which took place in Japan and the Republic of Korea between 31 May and 30 June 2002. Brazil defeated Germany 2-0 in the final; the Republic of Korea and Turkey were the losing semi-finalists. ■

2003 Cricket World Cup • The eighth such event, co-hosted by South Africa (where most of the matches were played), Zimbabwe and Kenya between 9 February and 23 March 2003. The competition became mired in controversy due to England and New Zealand refusing to play their matches in Zimbabwe as a protest against the Zimbabwe government. Australia defeated India by 125 runs in the final. ■

Adventure travel • Originally, this was a general terms for a type of holiday, such as trekking, white-water rafting or jungle expeditions, which involved a fairly high level of physical exertion and often an element of danger. Increasingly, the term covers a wider field: skiing, diving, cycling and walking holidays are now often referred to in this way. ■

Afghanistan war • The US-led military action to topple the Taliban regime in Afghanistan – which was widely believed to have been supporting international terrorism and sheltering Osama Bin Laden – was launched on 8 October 2001, less than a month after the 11

September attacks (see above). The last Taliban stronghold, Kandahar, fell on 7 December. Since then, the new government has struggled to extend its control over the whole country.

AIDS • Acquired Immune Deficiency Syndrome, a loss of cellular immunity as a result of viral infection generally through sexual fluids and blood which leaves the body vulnerable to a wide range of infections. The first reported case was in December 1980. Estimates as to how many people are, or will be, infected varies greatly, but many experts predict over 40 million worldwide by 2007. The majority of cases are in sub-Saharan Africa. ■

Bali bombing • A massive car bomb planted by a militant Islamic group which exploded outside a nightclub in Bali, Indonesia on 12 October 2002, killing over 200 people, mostly from Australia. The atrocity showed that Americans were not the only targets of such extremist groups. ■

Balkan war • The conflict in the 1990s between all the constituent republics of the former Yugoslavia (except Slovenia), and the first European war since 1945. Yugoslavia has as a result divided into five independent republics. ■

Climate change • The effects of industrial pollution and in particular the burning of fossil fuels has, according to most estimates, caused measurable increases in average global temperatures and sea levels. Travel and tourism, along with many other industries, is now taking some steps to redress these potentially very serious problems. Most remedies are, however, seemingly incompatible with economic growth.

Concorde • The world's first and to date only supersonic passenger aircraft. An Anglo-French co-operative venture, it made its maiden flight in March 1969: regular trans-Atlantic services started in May 1976. Only 20 were ever built, though the original plan was for over 300. On 25 July 2000, an Air France Concorde crashed on take-off from Paris with the loss of 113 lives. Services were resumed the following November. Its future remains deeply uncertain after a joint British Airways and Air France announcement in April 2003 that all Concordes would be withdrawn from service by November of that year.

Continents • There are anything between five and eight of these depending on which source one consults. The six divisions used in this atlas have been created to make the title easy to use and have no political or other significance.

Cruising • One of the fastest-growing sectors within the travel business, and one of the areas which has shown continued growth throughout the problematic years of the early 21st century. In 1985 there were 2.75 million worldwide cruise passengers: this had risen to 4.5 million in 1990, to 10.1 million in 2000 and to 11.2 million in 2002. ■

European Union expansion • In 1957, there were six founding members of the then-European Economic Community: by mid-2004, the European Union will have 25 members and will, for the first time, have a frontier with Russia. Several other countries are waiting to join. ■

Euro • The common currency of 12 of

World: Introduction

Conclusion

The leading article in the 2002 *Travel Industry World Yearbook* suggested that 'perhaps the only thing that can accurately be predicted about the state of the tourism industry in 2003 is its absolute unpredictability.' The SARS outbreak in Asia, to name but one event unforeseen to the editor of this authoritative publication, rather backs this point up.

Yet looking beyond this, still with SARS and similarly damaging events in mind, it is perhaps the travel industry's resilience and adaptability that makes a more appropriate final thought. After several decades of comparitive peace and economic growth (for the developed world at least), the last few years have seen many unwelcome reverses. Whilst having to cope with these, the travel business has also undergone revolutions of its own. The days of a few destinations offering beach holidays and a few cities attracting business clients, all linked by a few national carriers with monopolistic routes and fare structures, sold via GDS systems to an undiscriminating public by commission-driven travel agents, are long gone. Is what we have now more varied? Certainly. Is it better? Consumers and the travel companies that have survived and thrived would say 'yes'. Will there be disasters, challenges and unforeseen crises to contend with in the future? Sadly, yes. Will everything change again over the next five or ten years? Who can say – but considering the number of changes that the world in general and the travel industry in particular have experienced during the last five or ten years, there would seem to be every chance.

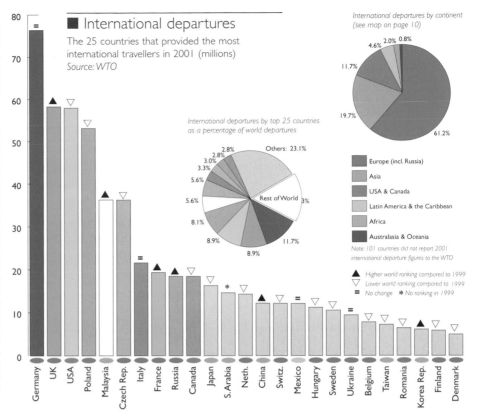

International departures

The 25 countries that provided the most international travellers in 2001 (millions)
Source: WTO

International departures by top 25 countries as a percentage of world departures

Others: 23.1%
Rest of World

2.8% · 2.8% · 3.0% · 3.3% · 5.6% · 5.6% · 3% · 8.1% · 8.9% · 11.7% · 8.9%

International departures by continent (see map on page 10)

0.8% · 2.0% · 4.6% · 11.7% · 19.7% · 61.2%

- Europe (incl. Russia)
- Asia
- USA & Canada
- Latin America & the Caribbean
- Africa
- Australasia & Oceania

Note: 101 countries did not report 2001 international departure figures to the WTO

▲ Higher world ranking compared to 1999
▽ Lower world ranking compared to 1999
= No change * No ranking in 1999

Germany · UK · USA · Poland · Malaysia · Czech Rep. · Italy · France · Russia · Canada · Japan · S. Arabia · Neth. · China · Switz. · Mexico · Hungary · Sweden · Ukraine · Belgium · Taiwan · Romania · Korea Rep. · Finland · Denmark

---

the members of the European Union, introduced in January 2002 and replacing the previously used local currencies. Denmark, Sweden and the UK have so far declined to participate, although none has ruled this out for the future. ■

European City of Culture • An initiative run by the European Union since 1985 to reflect, promote and celebrate Europe's wide cultural diversity. Until 1999, only one city a year was selected, but the millennium year of 2000 there were nine (Avignon, Bergen, Bologna, Brussels, Cracow, Helsinki, Prague, Reykjavik and Santiago de Compostela), and two in 2001 (Oporto and Rotterdam), 2002 (Bruges and Salamanca) and 2004 (Genoa and Lille); Graz was the lone city in 2003. The UK's only representative to date has been Glasgow in 1990, although Liverpool is expected to be nominated for 2008.

Foot-and-mouth disease • A contagious viral disease of cattle. A serious outbreak in 2001 caused great damage to the UK's tourist industry, partly because many rural footpaths were closed to halt the spread of infection.

Golden Jubilee • The 50th anniversary of the accession of Queen Elizabeth II was celebrated throughout 2002 but particularly in the first weekend of June. The occasion provided a welcome boost for the British travel industry after its problems in 2001 (see foot-and-mouth and 11 September, above).

GDP and GNI • In crude terms, GDP (Gross Domestic Product) is the value of the wealth produced by a nation – 'the gross value of all resident producers in the economy' as the part of the World Bank's definition puts it. GNI (Gross National Income) is increasingly used in many publications, including this one. The two measures are broadly comparable: in essence, GNI also includes income derived by residents of the country in question from abroad,

such as from external investments.

High-speed rail • Many countries, particularly in mainland Western Europe and Japan, have invested massive sums in dedicated high-speed lines and trains offering city-to-city services at speeds in excess of 200 kph. The network is constantly expanding and major new projects are being planned in many other countries, including China and the USA. The new Maglev (magnetic levitation) trains represent the new generation, and should run at over 550kph. In Europe, the low-cost airlines have provided considerable competition. ■

Internet • On-line sales and information services have revolutionised the travel business in recent years, and the trend is increasing. There are countless statistics to illustrate this, and the growth in web usage generally. For example, it took radio 38 years and TV 13 years to build an audience of 50 million in the US: the internet achieved this in three and a half years. The internet had over 600 million worldwide users in September 2002. On-line sales in Western Europe increased by over 50% in 2002. 64 million Americans in 2002 plan their travel on-line. ■

Iraq war • After years of diplomatic stand-off and unsuccessful UN attempts to locate Iraq's alleged weapons of mass destruction, US-led coalition forces began attacking the country on 20 March 2003. The photogenic toppling of Saddam Hussein's statue in Baghdad took place on 9 April. The war itself, and in particular its protracted count-down, caused a slump in the travel industry worldwide, although the relatively quick resolution of the initial phase of the conflict saw a fairly quick recovery in airline bookings. The long-term future of Iraq and the nature of its government remains uncertain, as does the question as to whether the intervention will have calmed or inflamed the volatile situation in the Middle East. ■

Long-haul charters • The introduction of medium-sized wide-body

aircraft such as the Boeing 767 and Airbus A300 in the 1990s facilitated the growth of package holidays to destinations further afield such as Goa, Sri Lanka and the Maldives. These areas suddenly became very affordable and, as a consequence, have rapidly developed as a result of the arrival of charter flights from Europe.

Low-cost airlines • The terms 'budget' and 'no-frills' are also often used. The concept began in the USA in 1971 when Southwest Airlines started services between Dallas and San Antonio. Numerous other airlines have since followed suit, including Jet Blue, Ryanair and EasyJet. Their low prices and commercial flexibility result from following very precise and efficient business models. ■

Mega cruise ships • Any ship with a gross registered tonnage of 100,000 is regarded as mega. The first of these arrived in the late 1990s as *Voyager of the Seas* owned by Royal Caribbean Line at GRT 142,000: it took 21 million man-hours to build and is (so far) the only cruise vessel with its own zip-code (33132-2028). These massive ships of up to 22 decks high have become resorts at sea opening the cruise market to a much wider audience. ■

Millennium Celebrations • The various festivities surrounding 31 December 1999, particularly in those countries which use the Christian calendar. Third millennia are nothing new, however: the Jews are on to their sixth and the Chinese their fifth, while the Buddhists saw in their third when Christopher Columbus was still a young boy. ■

Pets Travel Scheme • Introduced in 2000, this allows cats and dogs to travel between the UK and a number of European and long-haul destinations (though currently not North America) without the need for quarantine on arrival back in the UK. Pets must be micro-chipped, be issued with an

appropriate pet passport, and have a valid vet's certificate certifying vaccination against rabies.

SARS • Severe Acute Respiratory Syndrome, an air-borne virus which causes flu-like symptoms and sometimes death. The first reported case was in Hanoi in February 2003 and it rapidly spread to other parts of Asia, and to Canada, causing havoc in the travel industry for several months.

St Petersburg's 300th anniversary • Russia's second city staged a spectacular series of cultural events, attended by global heads of state to mark its 300th birthday in 2003. Founded by Peter the Great, the city was known as Leningrad for most of the 20th century and was blockaded by German troops between 1941 and 1944. This publicity has encouraged the city's position as a flourishing tourist destination and has also helped encourage travel to the rest of Russia.

Travel statistics • There are a multitude of these available. organisations, cities, states, countries and regions all produce their own, for a variety of purposes; while the most authoritative global figures are compiled by the World Tourism Organisation based in Madrid. Statistics concerning movement of people and money as a result of travel can most conveniently be divided into inbound and outbound, of which the former are generally more complete and reliable. Because of the time spent collating and analysing them, many statistics are not published for months or even years after the period to which they refer. Comparisons between figures produced by different organisations may be misleading due to the different methodologies used or time periods covered.

USSR • The Union of Soviet Socialist Republics, dominated by Russia, which fragmented into 15 independent states in Eastern Europe and North and Central Asia in the early 1990s. ■

Thanks to: Patrick Fitzgerald, Gary Bowerman, Graeme Payne

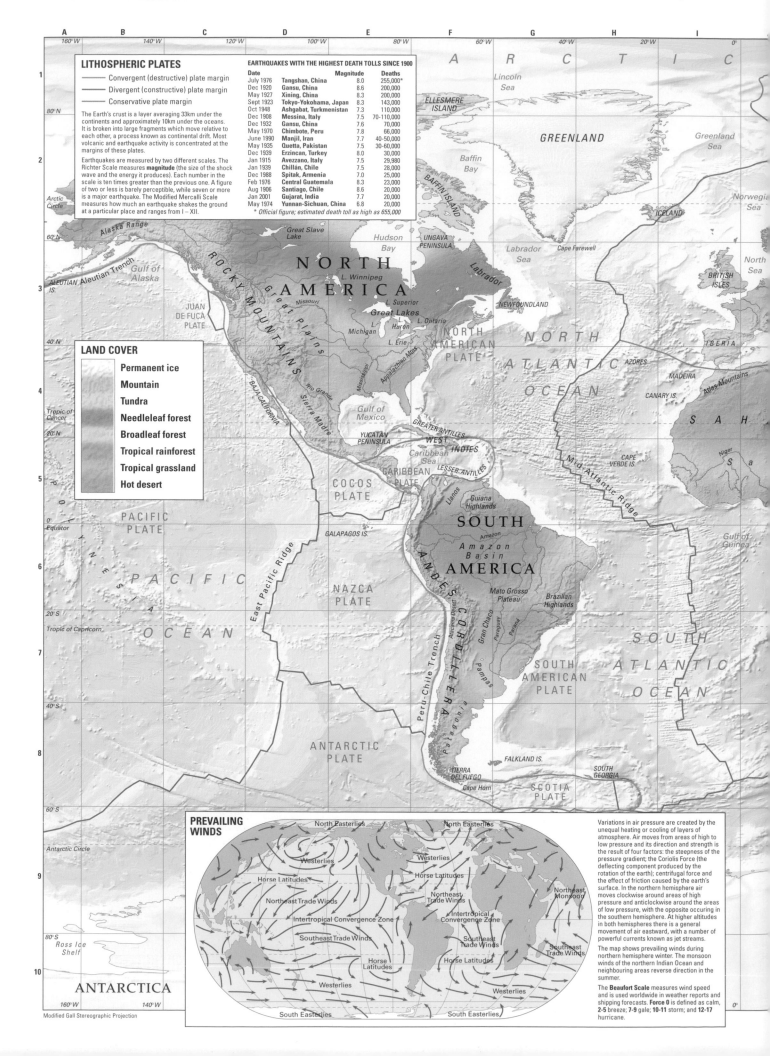

LITHOSPHERIC PLATES

— Convergent (destructive) plate margin
— Divergent (constructive) plate margin
— Conservative plate margin

The Earth's crust is a layer averaging 33km under the continents and approximately 10km under the oceans. It is broken into large fragments which move relative to each other, a process known as continental drift. Most volcanic and earthquake activity is concentrated at the margins of these plates.

Earthquakes are measured by two different scales. The Richter Scale measures **magnitude** (the size of the shock wave and the energy it produces). Each number in the scale is ten times greater than the previous one. A figure of two or less is barely perceptible, while seven or more is a major earthquake. The Modified Mercalli Scale measures how much an earthquake shakes the ground at a particular place and ranges from I – XII.

EARTHQUAKES WITH THE HIGHEST DEATH TOLLS SINCE 1900

Date		Magnitude	Deaths
July 1976	Tangshan, China	8.0	255,000*
Dec 1920	Gansu, China	8.6	200,000
May 1927	Xining, China	8.3	200,000
Sept 1923	Tokyo-Yokohama, Japan	8.3	143,000
Oct 1948	Ashgabat, Turkmenistan	7.3	110,000
Dec 1908	Messina, Italy	7.5	70-110,000
Dec 1932	Gansu, China	7.6	70,000
May 1970	Chimbote, Peru	7.8	66,000
June 1990	Manjil, Iran	7.7	40-50,000
May 1935	Quetta, Pakistan	7.5	30-60,000
Dec 1939	Erzincan, Turkey	8.0	30,000
Jan 1915	Avezzano, Italy	7.5	29,980
Jan 1939	Chillán, Chile	7.5	28,000
Dec 1988	Spitak, Armenia	7.0	25,000
Feb 1976	Central Guatemala	8.3	23,000
Aug 1906	Santiago, Chile	8.6	20,000
Jan 2001	Gujarat, India	7.7	20,000
May 1974	Yunnan-Sichuan, China	6.8	20,000

* Official figure; estimated death toll as high as 655,000

LAND COVER

- Permanent ice
- Mountain
- Tundra
- Needleleaf forest
- Broadleaf forest
- Tropical rainforest
- Tropical grassland
- Hot desert

PREVAILING WINDS

Variations in air pressure are created by the unequal heating or cooling of layers of atmosphere. Air moves from areas of high to low pressure and its direction and strength is the result of four factors: the steepness of the pressure gradient; the Coriolis Force (the deflecting component produced by the rotation of the earth); centrifugal force and the effect of friction caused by the earth's surface. In the northern hemisphere air moves clockwise around areas of high pressure and anticlockwise around the areas of low pressure, with the opposite occuring in the southern hemisphere. At higher altitudes in both hemispheres there is a general movement of air eastward, with a number of powerful currents known as jet streams.

The map shows prevailing winds during northern hemisphere winter. The monsoon winds of the northern Indian Ocean and neighbouring areas reverse direction in the summer.

The **Beaufort Scale** measures wind speed and is used worldwide in weather reports and shipping forecasts. **Force 0** is defined as calm, **2-5** breeze; **7-9** gale; **10-11** storm; and **12-17** hurricane.

Modified Gall Stereographic Projection

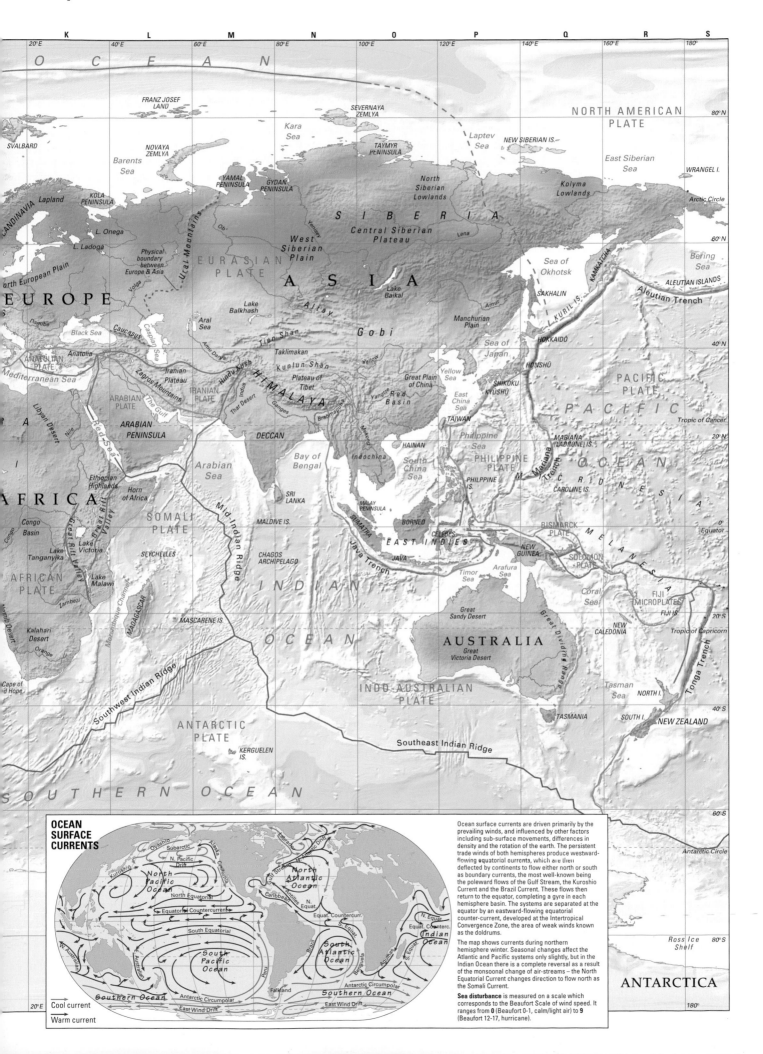

OCEAN SURFACE CURRENTS

Ocean surface currents are driven primarily by the prevailing winds, and influenced by other factors including sub-surface movements, differences in density and the rotation of the earth. The persistent trade winds of both hemispheres produce westward-flowing equatorial currents, which are then deflected by continents to flow either north or south as boundary currents, the most well-known being the poleward flows of the Gulf Stream, the Kuroshio Current and the Brazil Current. These flows then return to the equator, completing a gyre in each hemisphere basin. The systems are separated at the equator by an eastward-flowing equatorial counter-current, developed at the Intertropical Convergence Zone, the area of weak winds known as the doldrums.

The map shows currents during northern hemisphere winter. Seasonal changes affect the Atlantic and Pacific systems only slightly, but in the Indian Ocean there is a complete reversal as a result of the monsoonal change of air-streams – the North Equatorial Current changes direction to flow north as the Somali Current.

Sea disturbance is measured on a scale which corresponds to the Beaufort Scale of wind speed. It ranges from **0** (Beaufort 0-1, calm/light air) to **9** (Beaufort 12-17, hurricane).

Cool current

Warm current

ALB.	- ALBANIA
AUS.	- AUSTRIA
AZ.	- AZERBAIJAN
B.H.	- BOSNIA-HERZEGOVINA
BELG.	- BELGIUM
CRO.	- CROATIA
HUNG.	- HUNGARY
LIE.	- LIECHTENSTEIN
LUX.	- LUXEMBOURG
MAC.	- FORMER YUGOSLAV REPUBLIC OF MACEDONIA
NETH.	- THE NETHERLANDS
PAL.	- PALESTINE NATIONAL AUTHORITY REGION (West Bank & Gaza)
S.	- SAN MARINO
SLOV.	- SLOVENIA
SWITZ.	- SWITZERLAND
UAE	- UNITED ARAB EMIRATES
V.	- VATICAN CITY
S&M	- SERBIA & MONTENEGRO

REGIONS USED IN THIS ATLAS

Europe & the Russian Federation
Africa
Asia
Australasia & Oceania
United States & Canada
Latin America & the Caribbean

Modified Gall Stereographic Projection

Political

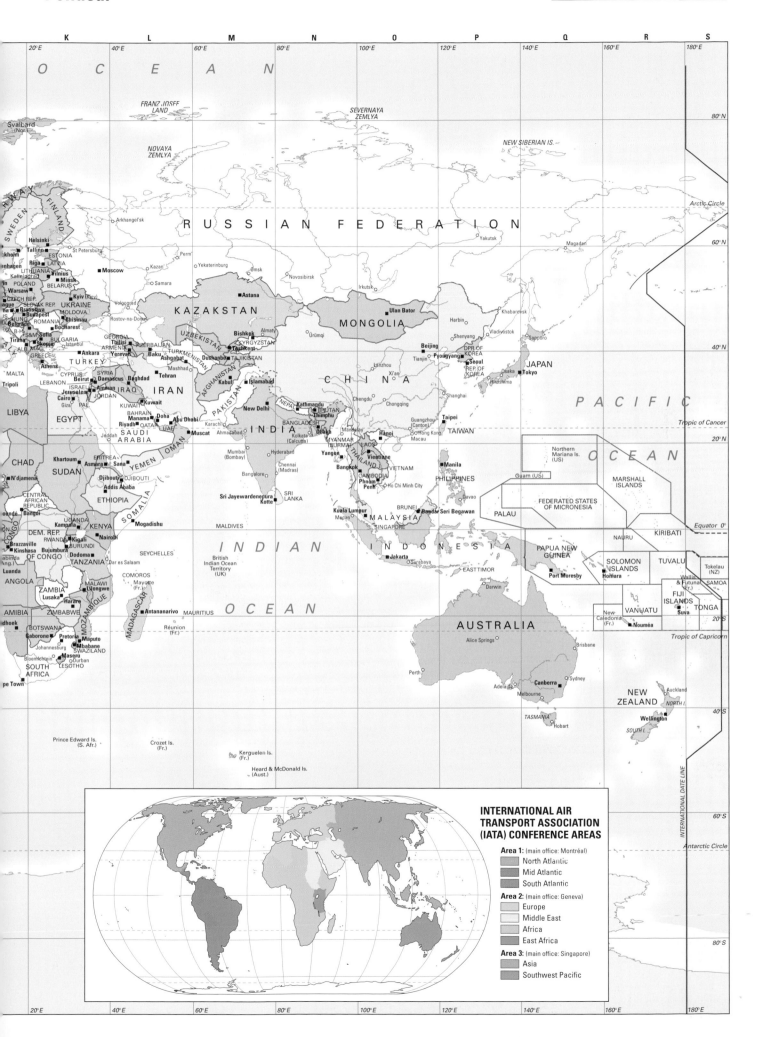

O C E A N

FRANZ JOSEF LAND

SEVERNAYA ZEMLYA

Svalbard (Nor.)

80° N

NEW SIBERIAN IS.

NOVAYA ZEMLYA

Arctic Circle

60° N

ckholm
enhagen
in
Helsinki
St Petersburg
Tallinn
ESTONIA
Riga
LATVIA
LITHUANIA Vilnius
Kaliningrad Minsk
POLAND
BELARUS
Warsaw
Kyiv (Kiev)
CZECH REP.
ague
SLOVAK REP.
na
Bratislava
HUNG
Budapest
UKRAINE
Belgrade
ROMANIA
Chisinau
MOLDOVA
Bucharest
Rostov-na-Donu
BULGARIA
Tirana
S&M Sofia
ALB. MAC. Skopje
GEORGIA
Tbilisi
GREECE
ARMENIA
Athens
Ankara
AZERBAIJAN
Yerevan
Baku
TURKEY
TURKMENISTAN
Ashgabat
Arkhangel'sk
Perm'
Kazan'
Yekaterinburg
Omsk
Novosibirsk
Samara
Volgograd

R U S S I A N   F E D E R A T I O N

Yakutsk

Magadan

60° N

Moscow
Astana
Irkutsk
Khabarovsk
KAZAKSTAN
MONGOLIA
Ulan Bator
Harbin
Vladivostok
UZBEKISTAN
Bishkek
Almaty
KYRGYZSTAN
Ürümqi
Shenyang
Sapporo
Tashkent
Beijing
DPR OF KOREA
Dushanbe TAJIKISTAN
Pyongyang
JAPAN
Lanzhou
Tianjin
Seoul
Osaka
Tokyo
40° N
REP OF KOREA
Hiroshima

MALTA
Tripoli
GREECE
Athens
CYPRUS
LEBANON
Beirut
Damascus
SYRIA
Baghdad
IRAQ
Tehran
IRAN
AFGHANISTAN
Kabul
Islamabad
C H I N A
Xi'an
Chengdu
Chongqing
Shanghai

LIBYA
EGYPT
ISRAEL
Amman
Jerusalem
JORDAN
Cairo
Giza
PAL.
KUWAIT
Kuwait
BAHRAIN
Manama
Riyadh
Doha
QATAR
UAE
Abu Dhabi
PAKISTAN
Karachi
Mashhad
New Delhi
NEPAL
Kathmandu
BHUTAN
Thimphu
BANGLADESH
Dhaka
Mandalay
Guangzhou (Canton)
Hong Kong
Macau
TAIWAN
Taipei
Tropic of Cancer

SAUDI ARABIA
Jeddah
OMAN
Muscat
Ahmadabad
I N D I A
Mumbai (Bombay)
Hyderabad
Kolkata (Calcutta)
MYANMAR (BURMA)
Yangon
LAOS
Vientiane
Hanoi
VIETNAM
Manila
PACIFIC
OCEAN
20° N
Northern Mariana Is. (US)

CHAD
N'djamena
SUDAN
Khartoum
ERITREA
Asmara
Sana
YEMEN
Chennai (Madras)
Bangalore
THAILAND
Bangkok
CAMBODIA
Phnom Penh
Ho Chi Minh City
PHILIPPINES
Davao
Guam (US)
MARSHALL ISLANDS

CENTRAL AFRICAN REPUBLIC
Bangui
Djibouti
DJIBOUTI
Addis Ababa
ETHIOPIA
SOMALIA
Sri Jayewardenepura Kotte
SRI LANKA
MALDIVES
BRUNEI
Bandar Seri Begawan
FEDERATED STATES OF MICRONESIA
PALAU

CONGO
DEM. REP. OF CONGO
UGANDA
Kampala
KENYA
Nairobi
RWANDA Kigali
BURUNDI
Bujumbura
Dodoma
TANZANIA
Kuala Lumpur
Medan
MALAYSIA
SINGAPORE
Singapore
I N D O N E S I A
NAURU
KIRIBATI
Equator 0°

Brazzaville
Kinshasa
Dar es Salaam
SEYCHELLES
I N D I A N
British Indian Ocean Territory (UK)
Jakarta
Surabaya
EAST TIMOR
PAPUA NEW GUINEA
Port Moresby
SOLOMON ISLANDS
Honiara
TUVALU
Tokelau (NZ)

abinda
Ang.)
Luanda
ANGOLA
AMIBIA
dhoek
ZAMBIA
Lusaka
MALAWI
Lilongwe
COMOROS
Mayotte (Fr.)
Antananarivo
MAURITIUS
O C E A N
Darwin
Wallis & Futuna (Fr.)
SAMOA
FIJI ISLANDS
Suva
TONGA

Harare
ZIMBABWE
MOZAMBIQUE
MADAGASCAR
Réunion (Fr.)
New Caledonia (Fr.)
Nouméa
VANUATU
20° S

BOTSWANA
Gaborone
Pretoria
Maputo
Johannesburg
Mbabane
SWAZILAND
Maseru
LESOTHO
AUSTRALIA
Alice Springs
Brisbane
Tropic of Capricorn

SOUTH AFRICA
Bloemfontein
Durban
pe Town
Perth
Adelaide
Canberra
Sydney
Melbourne
NEW ZEALAND
NORTH I.
Auckland

Prince Edward Is. (S. Afr.)
Crozet Is. (Fr.)
Kerguelen Is. (Fr.)
TASMANIA
Hobart
SOUTH I.
Wellington
40° S

Heard & McDonald Is. (Aust.)

INTERNATIONAL AIR TRANSPORT ASSOCIATION (IATA) CONFERENCE AREAS

60° S

Area 1: (main office: Montréal)
North Atlantic
Mid Atlantic
South Atlantic

Area 2: (main office: Geneva)
Europe
Middle East
Africa
East Africa

Area 3: (main office: Singapore)
Asia
Southwest Pacific

Antarctic Circle

80° S

Climate

Legend

Polar: no warm season (warmest month below 10°C)
Ice cap (perpetual frost: all months below 0°C) and Tundra (warmest month between 0°C and 10°C)

Cooler humid: rainy climates with severe winters (coldest month below 0°C, warmest month above 10°C)
Subarctic (less than four months over 10°C), Continental cool summer (warmest month below 22°C) and
Continental warm summer (warmest month above 22°C)

Warmer humid: rainy climates with mild winters (coolest month between 0°C and 18°C, warmest month above 10°C)
Temperate (warmest month below 22°C), Humid Subtropical (warmest month above 22°C) and
Mediterranean (dry season in summer)

Dry Steppe/semi-arid and Desert/arid

Tropical humid: rainy climates with no winter (coolest month above 18°C) and
Savannah (with a dry season, either in summer or winter) and
Rainforest (constantly moist or monsoon rain with only a short dry season)

WEATHER EXTREMES

Highest temperature in the shade: Al 'Azīzīyah, Libya
57.8°C (136.0°F) on 13th Sept 1922

Hottest place: Dalol, Ethiopia
average annual temperature of 34.4°C (94.0°F)

Lowest temperature: Vostok Base, Antarctica
–89.2°C (–128.6°F) on 21st July 1983

Coldest place: Pole of Cold, Antarctica
average annual temperature of –58°C (–72°F)

Coldest inhabited place: Noril'sk, Russian Federation
average annual temperature of –10.9°C (12.4°F)

Greatest snowfall: Mt Rainier, Washington, USA
31,102 mm (1,224.5 inc³es) over a 12-month period, 1972-73

Most sunshine: Yuma, Arizona, USA
averages 4,127 hours of sunshine per year

Least sunshine: South Pole
no sunshine for 182 days a year

Driest place: Atacama Desert, Chile
virtually no rain throughout the year

Wettest place: Mawsynram, Meghalaya, India
11,873 mm (467.4 inches) during a 12-month period

Most rainy days: Mt Waialeale, Hawaii
up to 350 rainy days per year

Most thunder days: Tororo, Uganda
up to 251 days per year

Highest surface wind speed
• Tornado: Oklahoma City, Oklahoma, USA
512 km per hour (318 miles per hour) per year
• High altitude: Mt Washington, New Hampshire, USA
372 km per hour (231 miles per hour) on 12th Apr 1934
• Low altitude: Qaanaaq (Thule), Greenland
333 km per hour (207 miles per hour) on 8th Mar 1972

Windiest place: Commonwealth Bay, Antarctica
322 km per hour (200 miles per hour) in gales

Heaviest hailstones: Gopalganj, Bangladesh
weighing up to one kilogram (2.2 lb) on 14th Apr 1986

TEMPERATURE CONVERSION

Celsius	–10	0	10	20	30	40
Fahrenheit	14	32	50	68	86	104

RAINFALL CONVERSION

Millimetres	102	203	305	406	508	610
Inches	4	8	12	16	20	24

The Tropics of Cancer and Capricorn are lines of latitude, 23° 28' N and S, where the sun appears directly overhead at noon during the summer solstice in the respective northern and southern hemispheres.

The Arctic Circle marks the northernmost point at which the sun can be seen during the northern hemisphere's winter solstice. Positioned at 66° 30' N.

The Antarctic Circle marks the southernmost point at which the sun can be seen during the southern hemisphere's winter solstice. Positioned at 66° 30' S.

Time

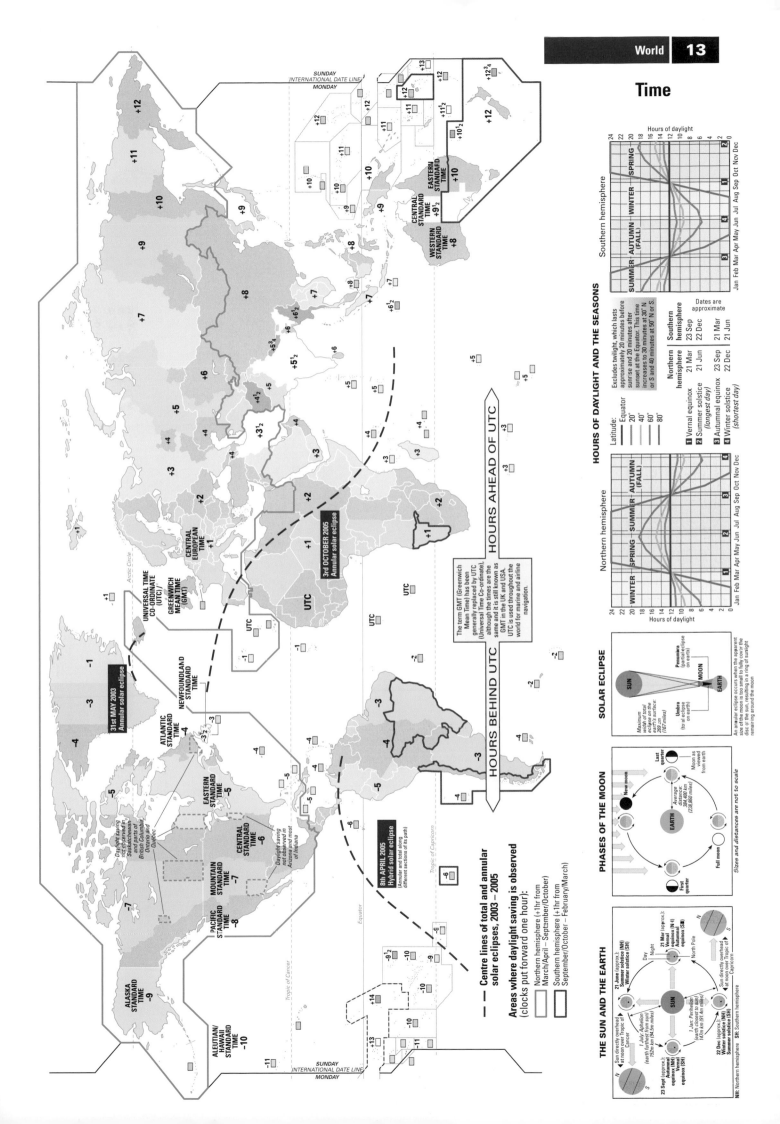

HOURS OF DAYLIGHT AND THE SEASONS

Southern hemisphere

Hours of daylight

SUMMER · AUTUMN (FALL) · WINTER · SPRING

Jan Feb Mar Apr May Jun Jul Aug Sep Oct Nov Dec

Northern hemisphere

WINTER · SPRING · SUMMER · AUTUMN (FALL)

Jan Feb Mar Apr May Jun Jul Aug Sep Oct Nov Dec

Hours of daylight

Excludes twilight, which lasts approximately 20 minutes before sunrise and 20 minutes after sunset at the Equator. This time increases to 30 minutes at 30° N or S and 40 minutes at 50° N or S.

Latitude:
Equator
20°
40°
60°
80°

Dates are approximate

	Northern hemisphere	Southern hemisphere
1 Vernal equinox	21 Mar	23 Sep
2 Summer solstice (longest day)	21 Jun	22 Dec
3 Autumnal equinox	23 Sep	21 Mar
4 Winter solstice (shortest day)	22 Dec	21 Jun

HOURS AHEAD OF UTC

HOURS BEHIND UTC

The term GMT (Greenwich Mean Time) has been generally replaced by UTC (Universal Time Co-ordinate), although the times are the same and it is still known as GMT in the UK and USA. UTC is used throughout the world for marine and airline navigation.

3rd OCTOBER 2005 Annual solar eclipse

31st MAY 2003 Annular solar eclipse

8th APRIL 2005 Hybrid solar eclipse (Annular and total along different sections of its path)

— — — Centre lines of total and annular solar eclipses, 2003 – 2005

Areas where daylight saving is observed (clocks put forward one hour):
Northern hemisphere (+1hr from March/April – September/October)
Southern hemisphere (+1hr from September/October – February/March)

UNIVERSAL TIME CO-ORDINATE (UTC) / GREENWICH MEAN TIME (GMT)

CENTRAL EUROPEAN TIME

Arctic Circle

NEWFOUNDLAND STANDARD TIME

ATLANTIC STANDARD TIME

EASTERN STANDARD TIME

CENTRAL STANDARD TIME

MOUNTAIN STANDARD TIME

PACIFIC STANDARD TIME

ALASKA STANDARD TIME

ALEUTIAN/ HAWAII STANDARD TIME

Daylight saving not observed in Saskatchewan and parts of British Columbia, Ontario and Québec

Daylight saving not observed in Arizona and most of Indiana

WESTERN STANDARD TIME

CENTRAL STANDARD TIME

EASTERN STANDARD TIME

SUNDAY INTERNATIONAL DATE LINE MONDAY

Tropic of Cancer

Equator

Tropic of Capricorn

SOLAR ECLIPSE

SUN

MOON

EARTH

Penumbra (partial eclipse on earth)

Umbra (total eclipse on earth)

Maximum width of total eclipse on the earth's surface: 269 km (167 miles)

An annular eclipse occurs when the apparent size of the moon is too small to fully cover the disc of the sun, resulting in a ring of sunlight remaining around the moon

PHASES OF THE MOON

New moon

First quarter

Full moon

Last quarter

EARTH

Moon as viewed from earth

Average distance: 384,400 km (238,860 miles)

Sizes and distances are not to scale

THE SUN AND THE EARTH

SUN

21 June (approx.): Summer solstice (NH) Winter solstice (SH)

1 July Aphelion (earth furthest from sun) 152m km (94.5m miles)

1 Jan Perihelion (earth closest to sun) 147m km (91.4m miles)

21 Mar (approx.): Vernal equinox (NH) Autumnal equinox (SH)

23 Sept (approx.): Autumnal equinox (NH) Vernal equinox (SH)

22 Dec (approx.): Winter solstice (NH) Summer solstice (SH)

Sun directly overhead at noon over Tropic of Cancer

Sun directly overhead at noon over Tropic of Capricorn

Day
Night
North Pole

NH: Northern hemisphere   SH: Southern hemisphere

SUNDAY INTERNATIONAL DATE LINE MONDAY

Environment: Land Use & Greenhouse Gases

AGRICULTURAL LAND & FORESTS

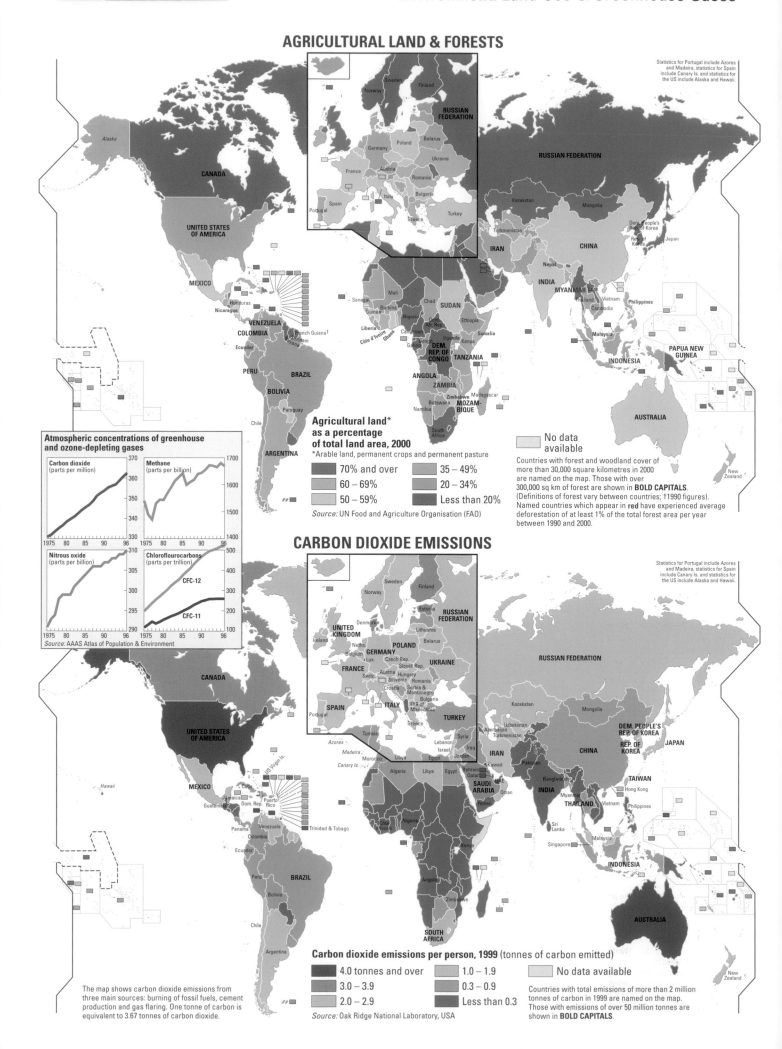

Statistics for Portugal include Azores and Madeira, statistics for Spain include Canary Is. and statistics for the US include Alaska and Hawaii.

Agricultural land* as a percentage of total land area, 2000

*Arable land, permanent crops and permanent pasture

- 70% and over
- 60 – 69%
- 50 – 59%
- 35 – 49%
- 20 – 34%
- Less than 20%

Source: UN Food and Agriculture Organisation (FAO)

No data available

Countries with forest and woodland cover of more than 30,000 square kilometres in 2000 are named on the map. Those with over 300,000 sq km of forest are shown in **BOLD CAPITALS**. (Definitions of forest vary between countries; †1990 figures). Named countries which appear in **red** have experienced average deforestation of at least 1% of the total forest area per year between 1990 and 2000.

Atmospheric concentrations of greenhouse and ozone-depleting gases

Carbon dioxide (parts per million)

Methane (parts per billion)

Nitrous oxide (parts per billion)

Chloroflourocarbons (parts per trillion)

CFC-12

CFC-11

Source: AAAS Atlas of Population & Environment

CARBON DIOXIDE EMISSIONS

Statistics for Portugal include Azores and Madeira, statistics for Spain include Canary Is. and statistics for the US include Alaska and Hawaii.

Carbon dioxide emissions per person, 1999 (tonnes of carbon emitted)

- 4.0 tonnes and over
- 3.0 – 3.9
- 2.0 – 2.9
- 1.0 – 1.9
- 0.3 – 0.9
- Less than 0.3
- No data available

Source: Oak Ridge National Laboratory, USA

The map shows carbon dioxide emissions from three main sources: burning of fossil fuels, cement production and gas flaring. One tonne of carbon is equivalent to 3.67 tonnes of carbon dioxide.

Countries with total emissions of more than 2 million tonnes of carbon in 1999 are named on the map. Those with emissions of over 50 million tonnes are shown in **BOLD CAPITALS**.

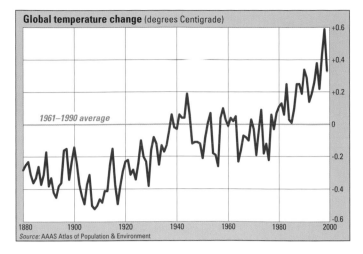

Global temperature change (degrees Centigrade)

1961–1990 average

Source: AAAS Atlas of Population & Environment

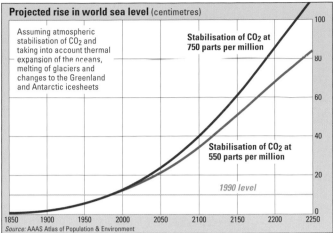

Projected rise in world sea level (centimetres)

Assuming atmospheric stabilisation of CO_2 and taking into account thermal expansion of the oceans, melting of glaciers and changes to the Greenland and Antarctic icesheets

Stabilisation of CO_2 at 750 parts per million

Stabilisation of CO_2 at 550 parts per million

1990 level

Source: AAAS Atlas of Population & Environment

PRINCIPAL ENVIRONMENTAL TREATIES

All the themes addressed on these pages, and many others besides, are the subject of a range of international conventions and treaties. Within some of these, various protocols also exist to provide action plans in specific areas. The list below is a selection of the most important of these various agreements. In their various ways, they all seek to encourage environmental awareness and protection, thereby addressing the effects of mankind's impact on the planet.
This information was compiled largely by Greenpeace. For more information on the work Greenpeace is doing in these areas, visit www.greenpeace.org. For more information on the various treaties, conventions and protocols themselves, see the web-site address within each entry.

23/6/61 Date treaty in force   **44** Ratifications (at June '03)

Principal Areas of Responsibility

🐾   Wildlife protection   ♻   Pollution control
≈   Marine protection   ✿   Bio-diversity
✕   Ozone depletion/climate change

Antarctic Treaty 🐾 ✿ ♻ **23/6/61** 44
The treaty is designed to protect the Antarctic continent from the exploitation of its raw materials and to ensure the use of its territory for peaceful purpose only, such as scientific research. In addition to several other objectives, the treaty also prescribes the preservation and conservation of Antarctic living resources.

ASCOBANS 🐾 ≈ ♻ **29/3/94** 8
Agreement on the Conservation of Small Cetaceans of the Baltic and North Seas
www.ascobans.org
With the establishment of this environmental treaty, Northern European countries such as Denmark, Germany and the UK sought to secure long-term protection of small cetaceans in the Baltic and North Seas from hazards such as high bycatch rates and habitat deterioration.

Barcelona Convention 🐾 ≈ ♻ 21
The Barcelona Convention for the Protection of the Mediterranean Sea
www.unepmap.gr
Established in 1976 for the protection of the Mediterranean as part of the UNEP Regional Seas Programme. Its objective is to achieve international co-operation for a co-ordinated and comprehensive approach to the protection and enhancement of the Mediterranean marine environment.

Basel Convention ♻ **5/5/92** 149
Basel Convention on the Control of Transboundary Movements of Hazardous Wastes and their Disposal
www.unep.ch/basel
The Basel Convention provides targets for the reduction of hazardous wastes and the creation of adequate disposal facilities; since 1998, it has also instituted a ban on waste exports from OECD to non-OECD countries.

CBD 🐾 ✿ **29/12/93** 187
Convention on Biological Diversity
www.biodiv.org
The Convention's objectives are 'the conservation of biological diversity, the sustainable use of its components and the fair and equitable sharing of the benefits arising out of the utilization of genetic resources.' It is the first comprehensive agreement to address all aspects of biological diversity. Its objectives have led to a broad work plan, involving all primary sectors (forests, oceans, and agriculture) and cross-cutting issues such as genetic engineering, indigenous peoples, technology transfer and intellectual property rights.

CCAMLR 🐾 ≈ ✿ ♻ **7/4/82** 31
Convention on the Conservation of Antarctic Marine Living Resources
www.ccamlr.org
The convention focuses on the conservation of Antarctic marine living resources by attempting to minimise the risk of irreversible changes to the Antarctic marine ecosystem and ensuring an increase in the populations of exploited species.

CITES 🐾 **1/7/75** 155
Convention on International Trade in Endangered Species of Wild Fauna and Flora
www.cites.org
This is the only treaty whose focus is the global protection of plant and animal species from unregulated international trade. A classification of endangered species is constantly monitored and updated to co-ordinate protection measures.

HELCOM 🐾 ≈ ✿ ♻ **17/1/00** 10
Convention on the Protection of the Marine Environment of the Baltic Sea Area, 1992
www.helcom.fi
This is the first convention to take into account all aspects of the Baltic marine environment and its protection. It deals with all aspects of pollution, including land-based, from ships, from dumping, and resulting from the exploration and exploitation of the sea-bed and its subsoil. The convention also regulates co-operation in combating marine pollution by oil and other harmful substances.

London Convention ≈ ♻ **30/8/75** 77
London Convention on the Prevention of Marine Pollution by Dumping of Wastes and Other Matter
www.marine.gov.uk/london_convention.htm
This Convention is the principal international instrument to limit marine pollution and ocean contamination by dumping of wastes and other harmful matter.

OSPAR ≈ ♻ **25/3/98** 16
Convention for the Protection of the Marine Environment of the North-East Atlantic
www.ospar.org
In 1992, this Commission replaced, and combined the aims of, the Oslo Convention on the Prevention of Marine Pollution by Dumping of Ships & Aircraft (1972) and the Paris Convention for the Prevention of Marine Pollution from Land-Based Sources (1974).

Ramsar 🐾 ≈ **2/2/71** 136
Ramsar Convention on Wetlands
www.ramsar.org
This convention, signed in Ramsar, Iran, in 1971, is an intergovernmental treaty which provides the framework for international cooperation for the conservation and prudent use of wetlands and their resources. There are presently 1,283 wetland sites, totaling 108.7 million hectares, designated for inclusion in the Ramsar List of Wetlands of International Importance.

Stockholm Convention ♻ **22/5/01** 20
Stockholm Convention on Persistent Organic Pollutants
www.pops.int
This Convention focuses on the elimination of a priority list of 12 of the most hazardous persistent organic pollutants (POPs), the elimination of other existing POPs and the prevention of the marketing of new chemicals with POP's characteristics.

UNCLOS ≈ ♻ **16/11/94** 142
United Nations Convention on the Law of the Sea
www.un.org/depts/los/index.htm
This Convention addresses protection and preservation of the marine environment to reflect customary international law with respect to maritime navigation. In addition, it provides basic obligations to prevent and reduce pollution from land-based sources, from sea-bed activities subject to national jurisdiction and from ocean dumping.

UNFCCC & Kyoto Protocol ✕ **21/3/94** 31 (Kyoto)
United Nations Framework Convention on Climate Change
www.unfccc.org
The objective of the Convention is to achieve stabilisation of greenhouse gas concentrations in the atmosphere at a level that would prevent dangerous anthropogenic interference with the climate system. Such a level should be achieved within a time frame sufficient to allow ecosystems to adapt naturally to climate change, to ensure that food production is not threatened and to enable economic development to proceed in a sustainable manner. As part of the UNFCCC, the widely discussed Kyoto Protocol commits its signatories to targets in the reduction and limitation of their national greenhouse gas emission. To date, the Protocol has yet to receive the 55 national ratifications necessary for it to come into force.

Vienna Convention & Montréal Protocol ✕ **1/1/89** 184
Montreal Protocol on Substances that Deplete the Ozone Layer
www.unep.org/unep/secretar/ozone
The Montréal Protocol operates within the framework of the 1985 Vienna Convention, which seeks to protect human health and the environment against adverse effects resulting from depletion of the ozone layer. The Montréal Protocol is specifically concerned with the protection of the ozone layer by taking precautionary measures to control global emissions of substances that deplete it, such as CFCs and Halons. It also seeks to promote the exchange of appropriate technological research.

POPULATION

The **population density** of the states, provinces and territories of Australia, Brazil, Canada, China and the USA are shown individually. The Azores and Madeira are treated separately from mainland Portugal, the Canary Islands separately from mainland Spain.

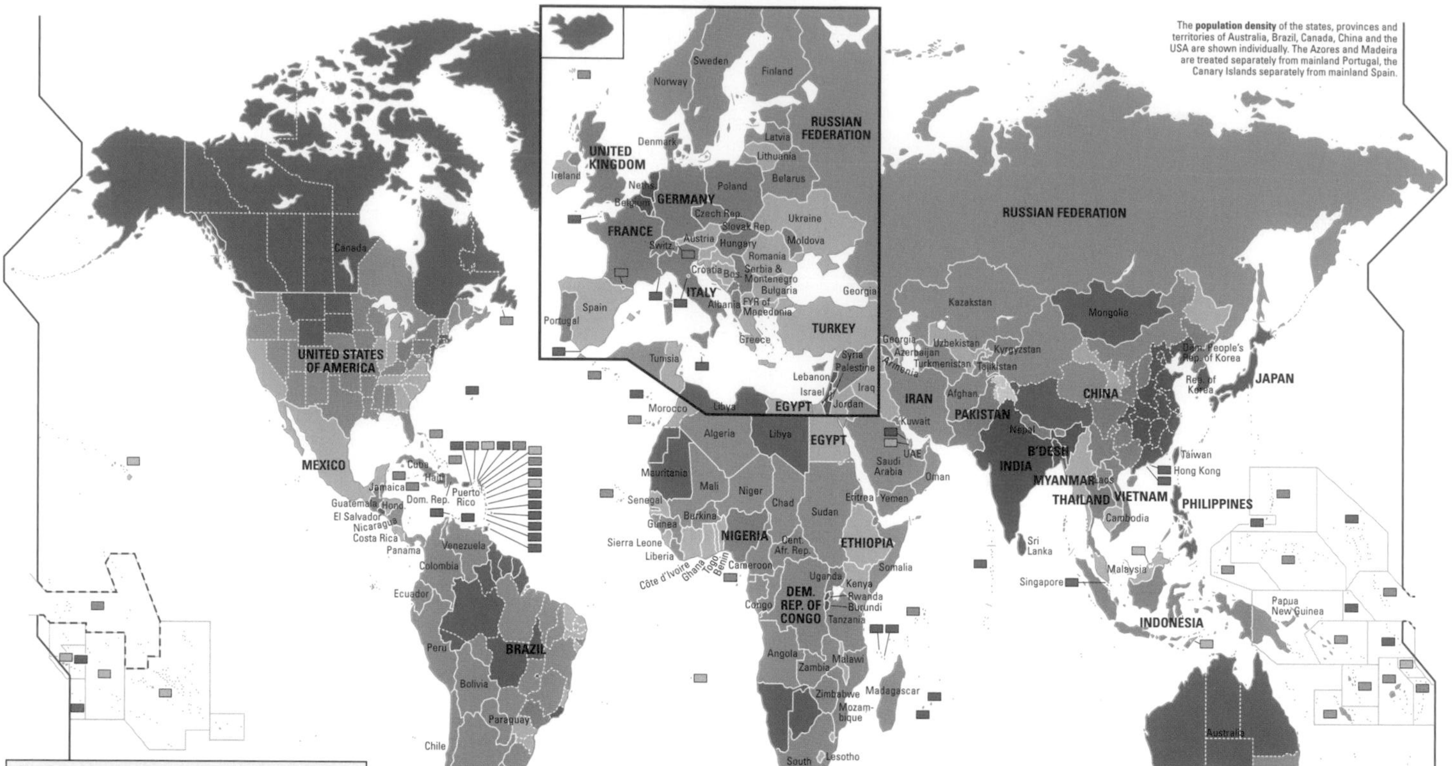

Total world population since 1910 (millions)

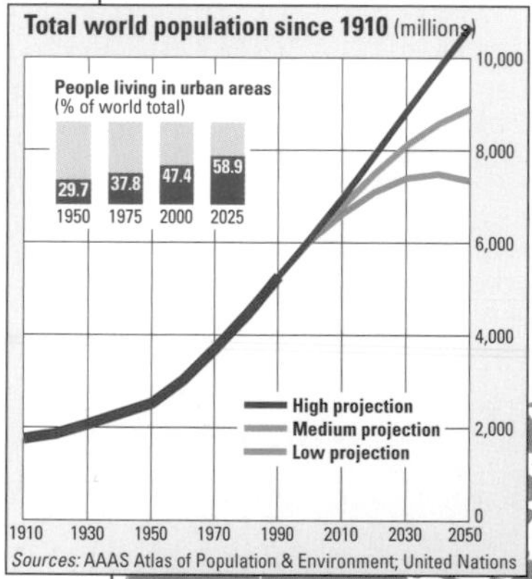

People living in urban areas
(% of world total)

29.7	37.8	47.4	58.9
1950	1975	2000	2025

— High projection
— Medium projection
— Low projection

Sources: AAAS Atlas of Population & Environment; United Nations

Population density, 2003
(people per square kilometre)

■ 250 and over	■ 20 – 49	☐ No data available
■ 100 – 249	■ 5 – 19	
■ 50 – 99	■ Less than 5	

Source: www.world-gazetteer.com

Countries with a total population of more than two million in 2003 are named on the map. Those with an population of over 50 million are shown in **BOLD CAPITALS**.

URBANIZATION

Statistics for Portugal include Azores and Madeira, statistics for Spain include Canary Is. and statistics for the US include Alaska and Hawaii.

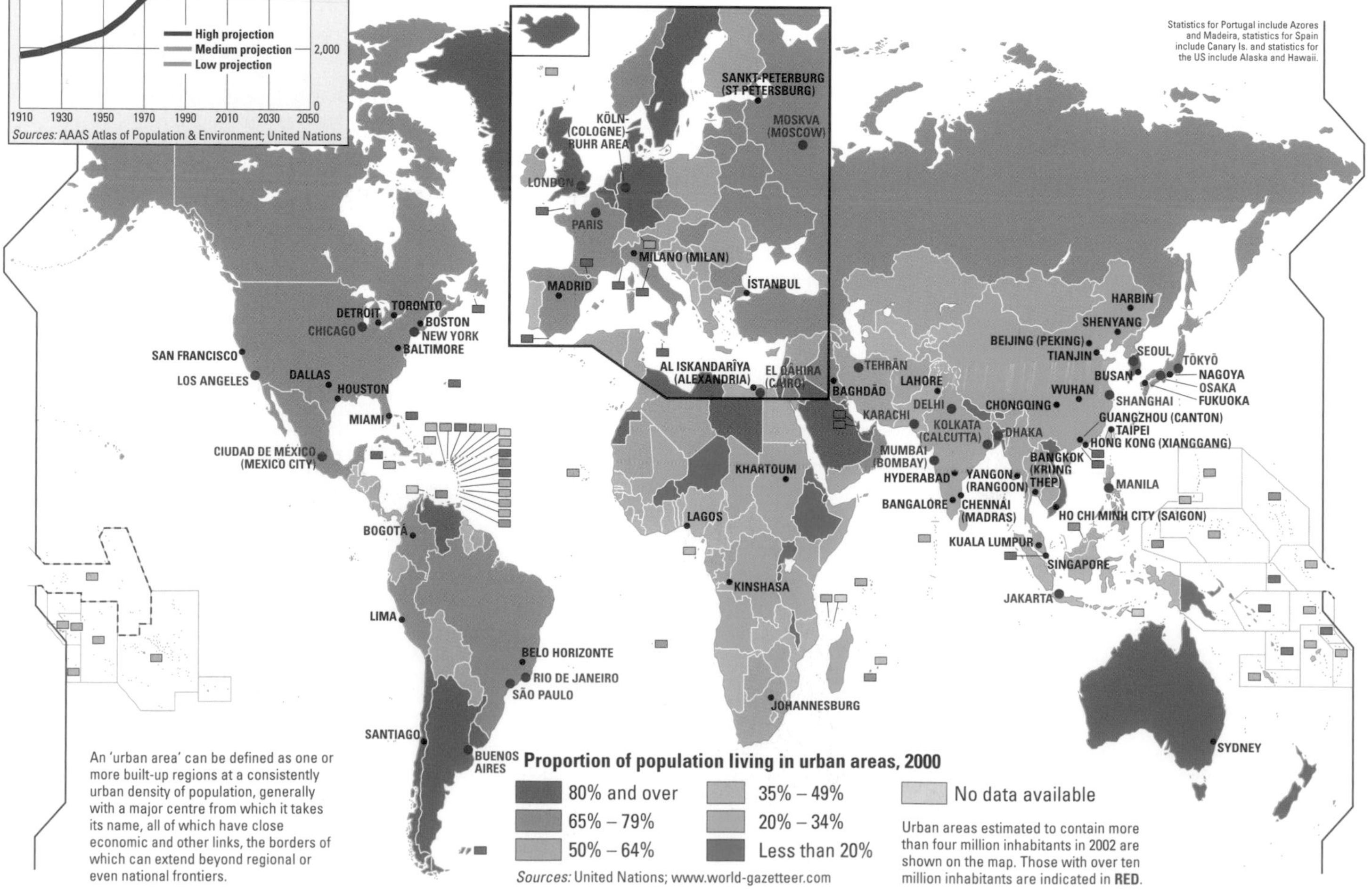

An 'urban area' can be defined as one or more built-up regions at a consistently urban density of population, generally with a major centre from which it takes its name, all of which have close economic and other links, the borders of which can extend beyond regional or even national frontiers.

Proportion of population living in urban areas, 2000

■ 80% and over	■ 35% – 49%	☐ No data available
■ 65% – 79%	■ 20% – 34%	
■ 50% – 64%	■ Less than 20%	

Sources: United Nations; www.world-gazetteer.com

Urban areas estimated to contain more than four million inhabitants in 2002 are shown on the map. Those with over ten million inhabitants are indicated in **RED**.

People: Development & Religion

HUMAN DEVELOPMENT INDEX

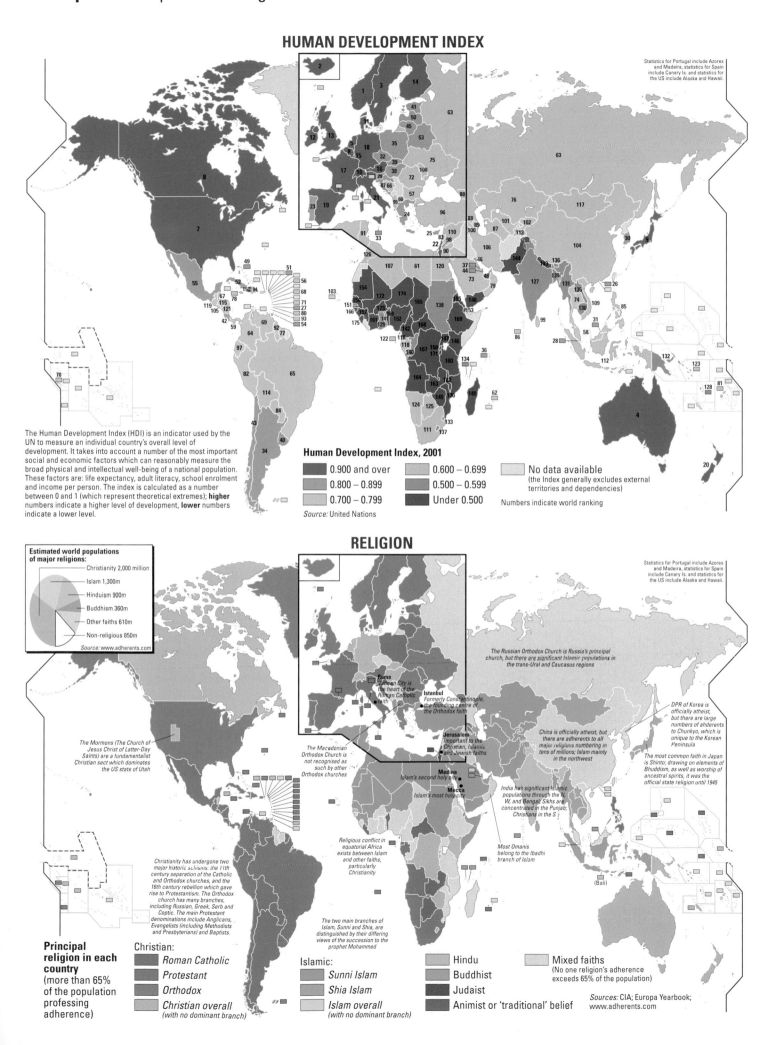

Statistics for Portugal include Azores and Madeira, statistics for Spain include Canary Is. and statistics for the US include Alaska and Hawaii.

The Human Development Index (HDI) is an indicator used by the UN to measure an individual country's overall level of development. It takes into account a number of the most important social and economic factors which can reasonably measure the broad physical and intellectual well-being of a national population. These factors are: life expectancy, adult literacy, school enrolment and income per person. The index is calculated as a number between 0 and 1 (which represent theoretical extremes); **higher** numbers indicate a higher level of development, **lower** numbers indicate a lower level.

Human Development Index, 2001

- 0.900 and over
- 0.800 – 0.899
- 0.700 – 0.799
- 0.600 – 0.699
- 0.500 – 0.599
- Under 0.500
- No data available (the Index generally excludes external territories and dependencies)

Numbers indicate world ranking

Source: United Nations

RELIGION

Estimated world populations of major religions:

- Christianity 2,000 million
- Islam 1,300m
- Hinduism 900m
- Buddhism 360m
- Other faiths 610m
- Non-religious 850m

Source: www.adherents.com

Statistics for Portugal include Azores and Madeira, statistics for Spain include Canary Is. and statistics for the US include Alaska and Hawaii.

The Russian Orthodox Church is Russia's principal church, but there are significant Islamic populations in the trans-Ural and Caucasus regions

Rome Vatican City is the heart of the Roman Catholic faith

Istanbul Formerly Constantinople, the founding centre of the Orthodox faith

Jerusalem Important to the Christian, Islamic and Jewish faiths

The Macedonian Orthodox Church is not recognised as such by other Orthodox churches

Medina Islam's second holy city

Mecca Islam's most holy city

The Mormons (The Church of Jesus Christ of Latter-Day Saints) are a fundamentalist Christian sect which dominates the US state of Utah

Christianity has undergone two major historic schisms: the 11th century separation of the Catholic and Orthodox churches, and the 16th century rebellion which gave rise to Protestantism. The Orthodox church has many branches, including Russian, Greek, Serb and Coptic. The main Protestant denominations include Anglicans, Evangelists (including Methodists and Presbyterians) and Baptists.

Religious conflict in equatorial Africa exists between Islam and other faiths, particularly Christianity

The two main branches of Islam, Sunni and Shia, are distinguished by their differing views of the succession to the prophet Mohammed

China is officially atheist, but there are adherents to all major religions numbering in tens of millions; Islam mainly in the northwest

India has significant Islamic populations through the N, W, and Bengal; Sikhs are concentrated in the Punjab; Christians in the S

Most Omanis belong to the Ibadhi branch of Islam

DPR of Korea is officially atheist, but there are large numbers of adherents to Chunkyo, which is unique to the Korean Peninsula

The most common faith in Japan is Shinto; drawing on elements of Bhuddism, as well as worship of ancestral spirits, it was the official state religion until 1945

(Bali)

Principal religion in each country
(more than 65% of the population professing adherence)

Christian:
- Roman Catholic
- Protestant
- Orthodox
- Christian overall (with no dominant branch)

Islamic:
- Sunni Islam
- Shia Islam
- Islam overall (with no dominant branch)

- Hindu
- Buddhist
- Judaist
- Animist or 'traditional' belief

- Mixed faiths (No one religion's adherence exceeds 65% of the population)

Sources: CIA; Europa Yearbook; www.adherents.com

INCOME

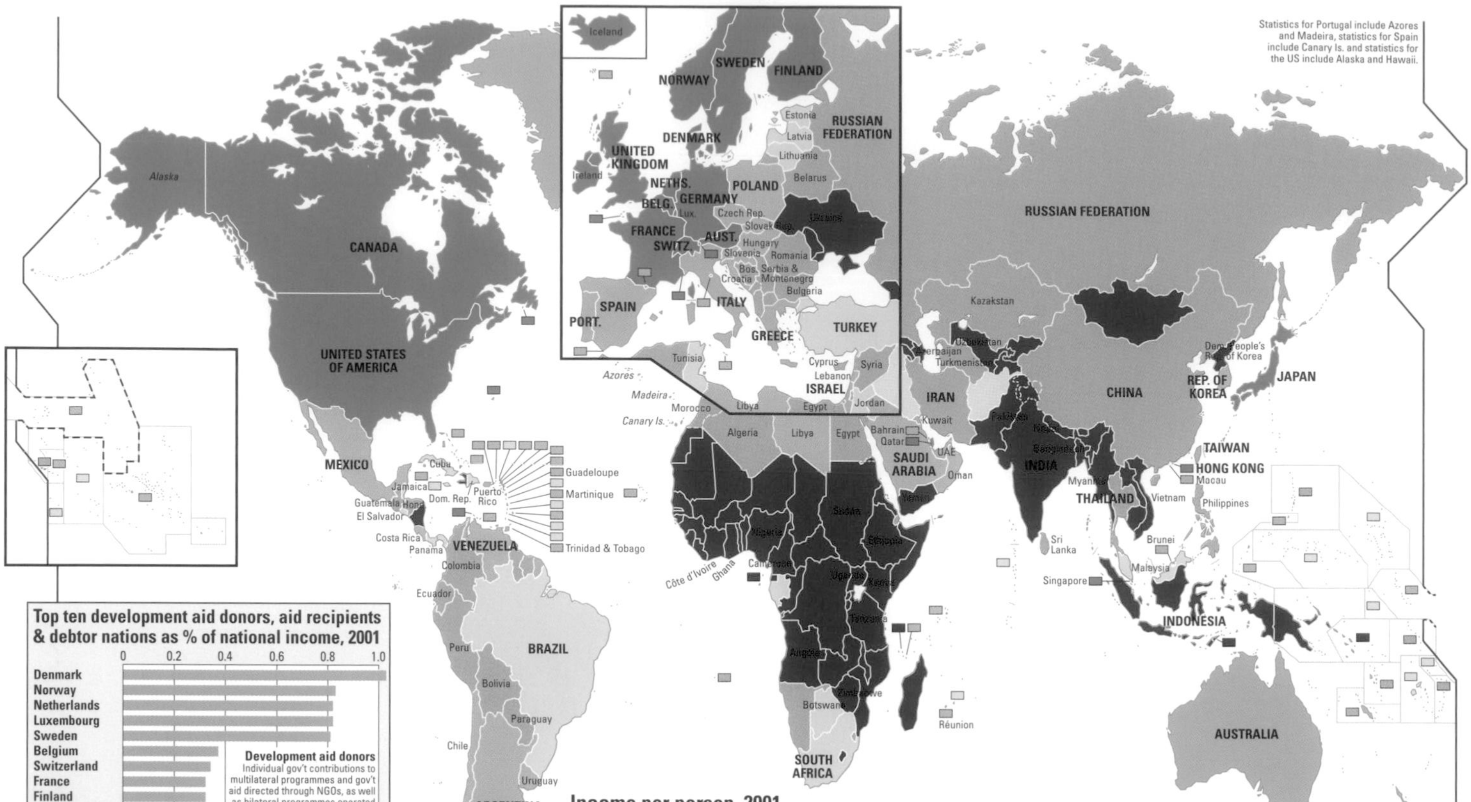

Statistics for Portugal include Azores and Madeira, statistics for Spain include Canary Is. and statistics for the US include Alaska and Hawaii.
Iceland
NORWAY
SWEDEN
FINLAND
DENMARK
UNITED KINGDOM
Ireland
NETHS.
BELG.
GERMANY
Lux.
POLAND
FRANCE
SWITZ.
AUST.
Czech Rep.
Slovakia
Hungary
Slovenia
Romania
Croatia
Bos. Serbia & Montenegro
Bulgaria
ITALY
SPAIN
PORT.
GREECE
TURKEY
Estonia
Latvia
Lithuania
Belarus
Ukraine
RUSSIAN FEDERATION
Tunisia
Cyprus
Lebanon
Syria
ISRAEL
Jordan
Egypt
Libya
Morocco
Algeria
Azores
Madeira
Canary Is.
Alaska
CANADA
UNITED STATES OF AMERICA
MEXICO
Cuba
Jamaica
Dom. Rep.
Puerto Rico
Guadeloupe
Martinique
Trinidad & Tobago
Guatemala
Honduras
El Salvador
Costa Rica
Panama
VENEZUELA
Colombia
Ecuador
Peru
BRAZIL
Bolivia
Paraguay
Chile
Uruguay
ARGENTINA
Côte d'Ivoire
Ghana
Cameroon
Nigeria
Sudan
Ethiopia
Uganda
Kenya
Tanzania
Angola
Zimbabwe
Botswana
SOUTH AFRICA
Réunion
SAUDI ARABIA
Bahrain
Qatar
UAE
Oman
Kuwait
Yemen
IRAN
Kazakstan
Uzbekistan
Azerbaijan
Turkmenistan
Pakistan
INDIA
Nepal
Bangladesh
Sri Lanka
Myanmar
THAILAND
Vietnam
RUSSIAN FEDERATION
CHINA
Dem. People's Rep. of Korea
REP. OF KOREA
JAPAN
TAIWAN
HONG KONG
Macau
Philippines
Brunei
Malaysia
Singapore
INDONESIA
AUSTRALIA
New Zealand

Income per person, 2001

- US$20,000 and over
- US$10,000 – $19,999
- US$4,000 – $9,999
- US$2,000 – $3,999
- US$800 – $1,999
- Less than US$800
- No data available

Source: World Bank

Countries with a total income of more than $5 billion in 2001 are named on the map. Those with an income of over $100bn are shown in **BOLD CAPITALS**.

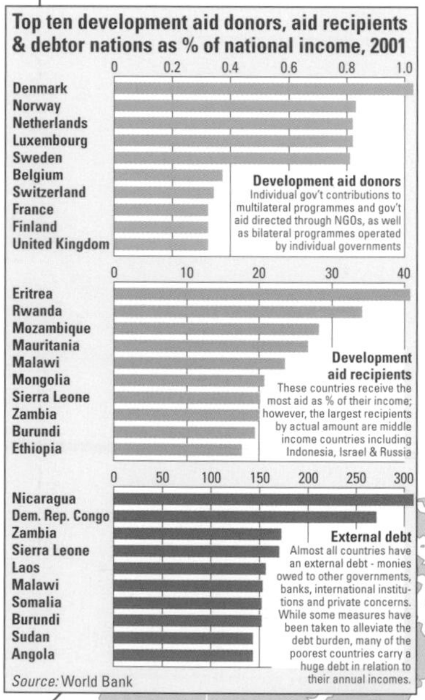

Top ten development aid donors, aid recipients & debtor nations as % of national income, 2001
0
0.2
0.4
0.6
0.8
1.0
Denmark
Norway
Netherlands
Luxembourg
Sweden
Belgium
Switzerland
France
Finland
United Kingdom
Development aid donors
Individual gov't contributions to multilateral programmes and gov't aid directed through NGOs, as well as bilateral programmes operated by individual governments
0
10
20
30
40
Eritrea
Rwanda
Mozambique
Mauritania
Malawi
Mongolia
Sierra Leone
Zambia
Burundi
Ethiopia
Development aid recipients
These countries receive the most aid as % of their income; however, the largest recipients by actual amount are middle income countries including Indonesia, Israel & Russia
0
50
100
150
200
250
300
Nicaragua
Dem. Rep. Congo
Zambia
Sierra Leone
Laos
Malawi
Somalia
Burundi
Sudan
Angola
External debt
Almost all countries have an external debt - monies owed to other governments, banks, international institutions and private concerns. While some measures have been taken to alleviate the debt burden, many of the poorest countries carry a huge debt in relation to their annual incomes.
Source: World Bank

GROWTH

Statistics for Portugal include Azores and Madeira, statistics for Spain include Canary Is. and statistics for the US include Alaska and Hawaii.
Estonia
LATVIA
Lithuania
Belarus
Russian Federation
Ireland
Ukraine
Slovak Rep.
Hungary
MOLDOVA
Romania
Croatia
Bos.
Serbia & Montenegro
Bulgaria
Albania
Greece
Georgia
TURKEY
Canada
Russian Federation
KAZAKSTAN
Mongolia
Georgia
AZER.
ARMENIA
Iran
TAJIKISTAN
CHINA
REP. OF KOREA
Pakistan
BHUTAN
Bangladesh
India
Taiwan
Myanmar
Laos
Thailand
Vietnam
Cambodia
Philippines
Sri Lanka
Malaysia
Maldives
Indonesia
Morocco
Algeria
Jordan
Bahrain
Mauritania
MALI
CHAD
Sudan
Yemen
Cape Verde
Gambia
Guinea
Burkina
Benin
SIERRA LEONE
Ethiopia
Ghana
Cameroon
São Tomé e Príncipe
EQ. GUINEA
Congo
UGANDA
RWANDA
Burundi
Tanzania
ANGOLA
MOZAMBIQUE
Mauritius
Lesotho
Belize
Dom. Rep.
Trinidad & Tobago
Peru
Australia
Fiji Is.
New Zealand

Growth in Gross Domestic Product (GDP), 1995–2004

- 7.5% and over
- 5.0% – 7.4%
- 4.0% – 4.9%
- 3.0% – 3.9%
- 2.0% – 2.9%
- Less than 2.0%
- Negative growth
- No data available

Annual average growth over 10 years (2003 & 04 estimated)

Sources: World Bank; IMF

Countries with a 2001–2002 GDP growth of more than 3% are named on the map. Those with growth of over 6% are shown in **BOLD CAPITALS**.

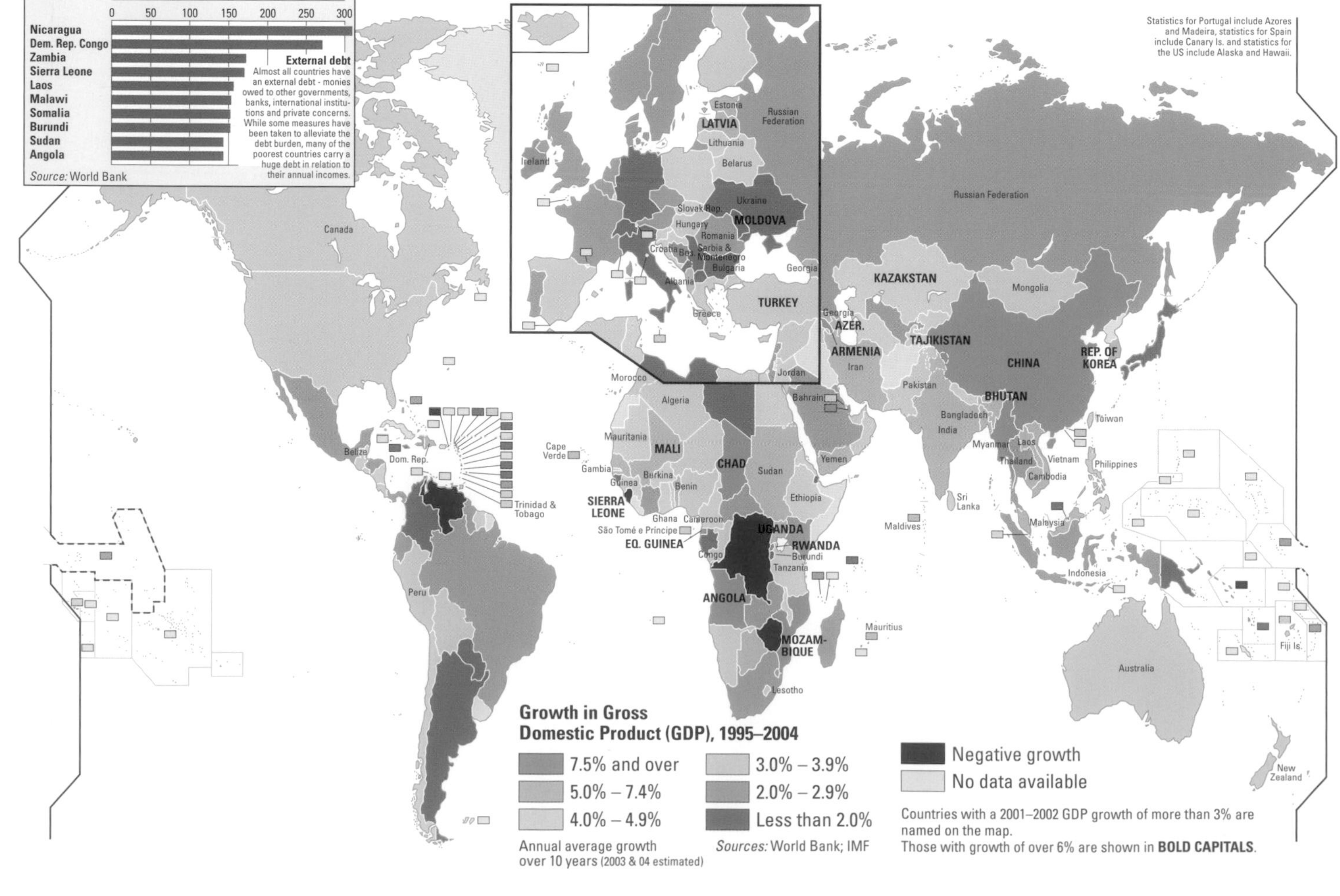

Wealth: Economic Activity

Income from each sector as a percentage of GDP, 2001

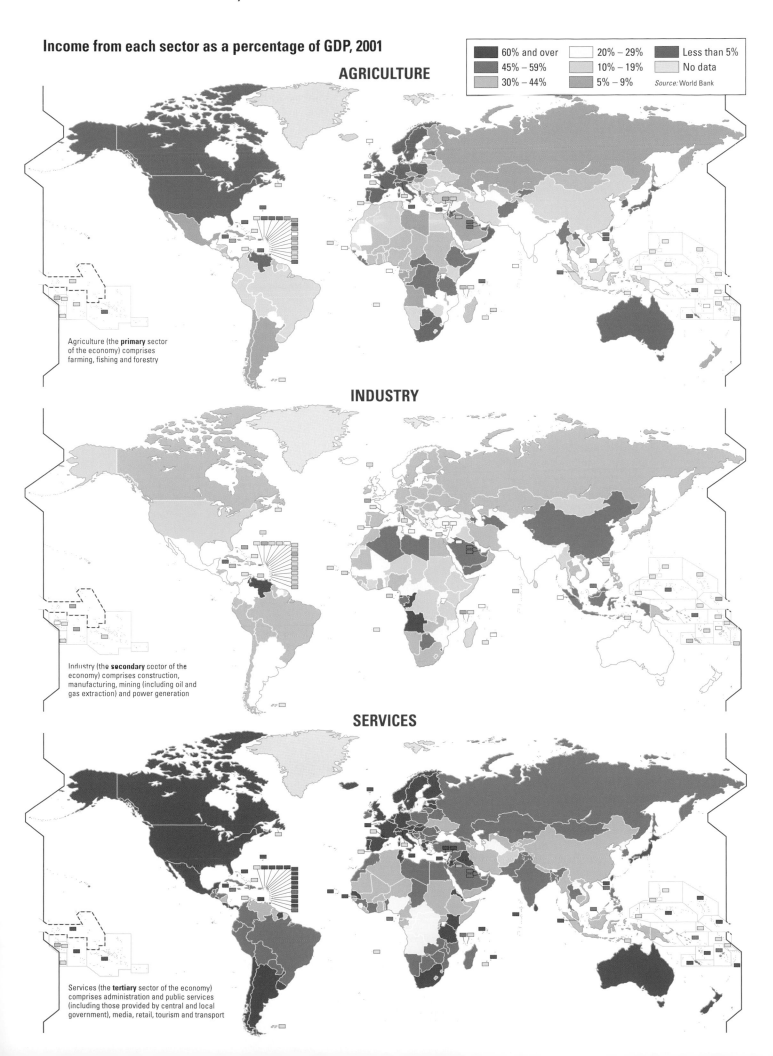

60% and over	20% – 29%	Less than 5%
45% – 59%	10% – 19%	No data
30% – 44%	5% – 9%	*Source:* World Bank

AGRICULTURE

Agriculture (the **primary** sector of the economy) comprises farming, fishing and forestry

INDUSTRY

Industry (the **secondary** sector of the economy) comprises construction, manufacturing, mining (including oil and gas extraction) and power generation

SERVICES

Services (the **tertiary** sector of the economy) comprises administration and public services (including those provided by central and local government), media, retail, tourism and transport

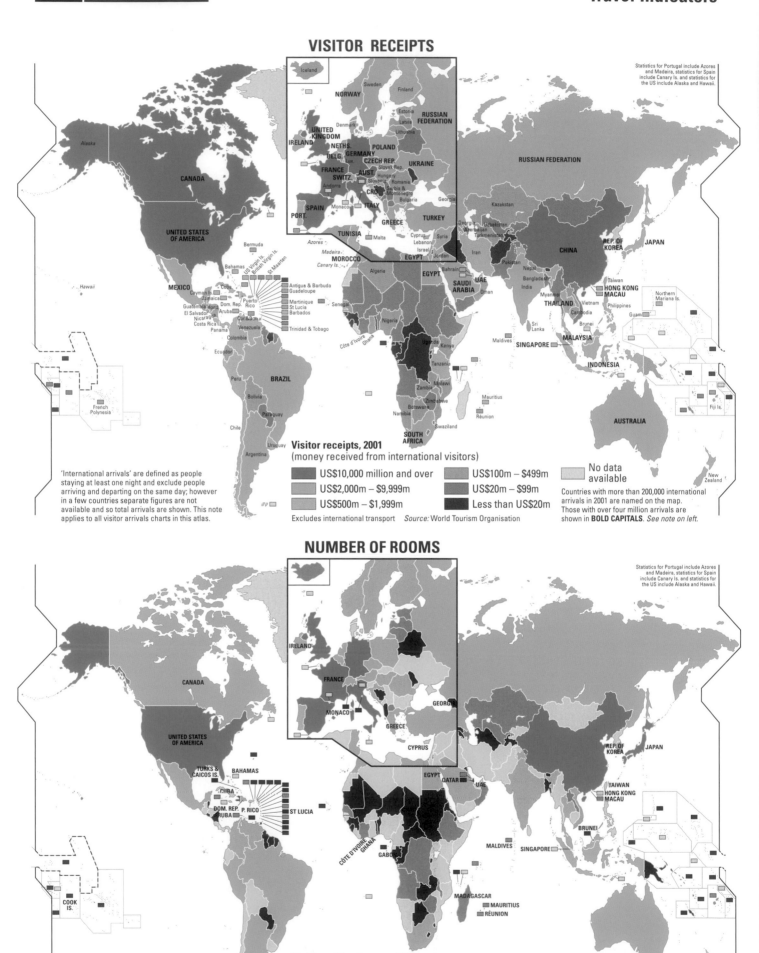

VISITOR RECEIPTS

Statistics for Portugal include Azores and Madeira, statistics for Spain include Canary Is. and statistics for the US include Alaska and Hawaii.

Visitor receipts, 2001
(money received from international visitors)

- US$10,000 million and over
- US$2,000m – $9,999m
- US$500m – $1,999m
- US$100m – $499m
- US$20m – $99m
- Less than US$20m
- No data available

'International arrivals' are defined as people staying at least one night and exclude people arriving and departing on the same day; however in a few countries separate figures are not available and so total arrivals are shown. This note applies to all visitor arrivals charts in this atlas.

Countries with more than 200,000 international arrivals in 2001 are named on the map. Those with over four million arrivals are shown in **BOLD CAPITALS**. *See note on left.*

Excludes international transport · *Source:* World Tourism Organisation

NUMBER OF ROOMS

Statistics for Portugal include Azores and Madeira, statistics for Spain include Canary Is. and statistics for the US include Alaska and Hawaii.

Number of hotel rooms, 2001

- 500,000 and over
- 100,000 – 499,999
- 50,000 – 99,999
- 10,000 – 49,999
- 5,000 – 9,999
- Less than 5,000
- No data available

Countries where the occupancy rate exceeded 60% in 2001 are named on the map.

Rooms in hotels and similar establishments · *Source:* World Tourism Organisation

Travel Indicators

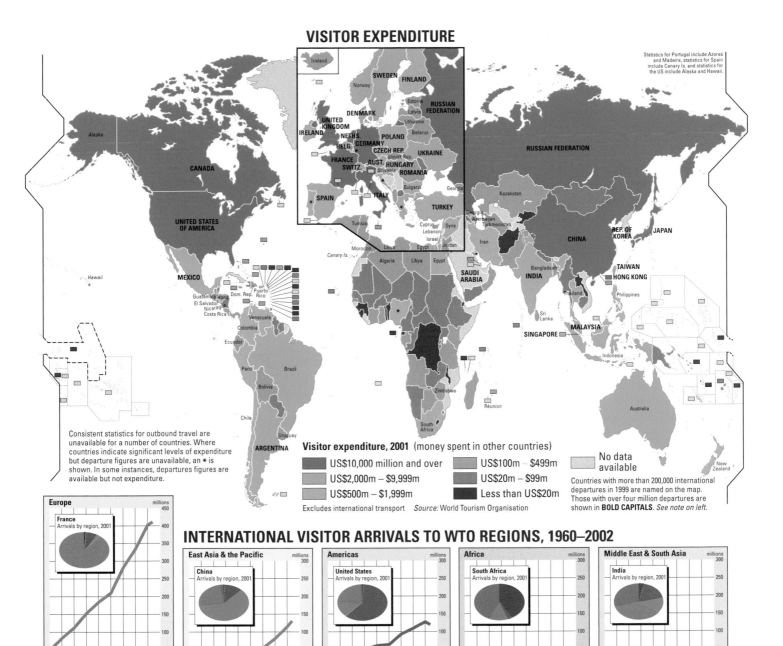

VISITOR EXPENDITURE

Statistics for Portugal include Azores and Madeira, statistics for Spain include Canary Is. and statistics for the US include Alaska and Hawaii.

Consistent statistics for outbound travel are unavailable for a number of countries. Where countries indicate significant levels of expenditure but departure figures are unavailable, an * is shown. In some instances, departures figures are available but not expenditure.

Visitor expenditure, 2001 (money spent in other countries)

US$10,000 million and over	US$100m – $499m
US$2,000m – $9,999m	US$20m – $99m
US$500m – $1,999m	Less than US$20m

No data available

Excludes international transport   *Source:* World Tourism Organisation

Countries with more than 200,000 international departures in 1999 are named on the map. Those with over four million departures are shown in **BOLD CAPITALS**. *See note on left.*

INTERNATIONAL VISITOR ARRIVALS TO WTO REGIONS, 1960–2002

Europe — millions
France — Arrivals by region, 2001

East Asia & the Pacific — millions
China — Arrivals by region, 2001

Americas — millions
United States — Arrivals by region, 2001

Africa — millions
South Africa — Arrivals by region, 2001

Middle East & South Asia — millions
India — Arrivals by region, 2001

The World Tourism Organisation, based in Madrid, is an intergovernmental organisation vested by the United Nations with a central and decisive role in promoting the development of responsible, sustainable and universally accessible tourism. It is the industry's leading international body and serves as a global forum for tourism policy issues and a practical source of tourism know-how and statistics. Through tourism, the WTO aims to stimulate economic growth and job creation, provide incentives for protecting the environment and cultural heritage, and promote peace, prosperity and respect for human rights.

Its membership includes 139 countries, seven territories and some 350 affiliate members representing regional and local promotion boards, tourism trade associations, educational institutions and private sector companies, including airlines, hotel groups and tour operators. One of its main functions is to help its members maximize the positive impacts of tourism, such as job creation, new infrastructure and foreign exchange earnings, while at the same time minimizing negative environmental or social impacts. The WTO also helps to develop national and regional tourism policies in conjunction with its members, and to address specific areas or problems such as ecotourism and safety and security. Specific projects include the promotion of the Silk Road in Central Asia and the Slave Route in West Africa.

For statistical and administrative purposes, the WTO divides the world into several regions and sub-regions (see map on right) which do not correspond to the continental divisions used in this publication. The tourist arrival charts on this page refer to the WTO's regions: those used elsewhere (for example in the continental introductions) refer to the regions as defined in this book.

For more information on the World Tourism Organisation, visit www.world-tourism.org

WORLD TOURISM ORGANISATION (WTO) REGIONS

01 Africa:
Northern Africa
Western Africa
Middle Africa
Eastern Africa
Southern Africa

02 Americas:
Northern America
Central America
Caribbean
Southern America

03 East Asia & the Pacific:
Northeastern Asia
Southeastern Asia
Australasia
Melanesia
Micronesia
Polynesia
(Oceania)

04 Europe:
Northern Europe
Western Europe
Southern Europe
Central/East Europe
East Mediterranean Europe

05 Middle East:

06 South Asia:

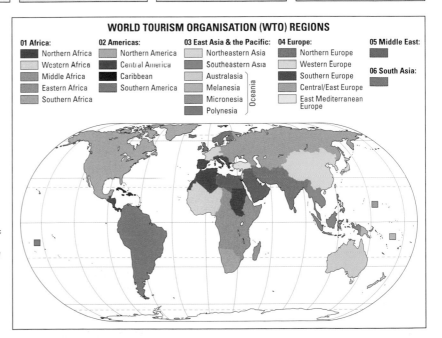

MAJOR FOSSIL FUEL DEPOSITS & HYDROELECTRIC SCHEMES

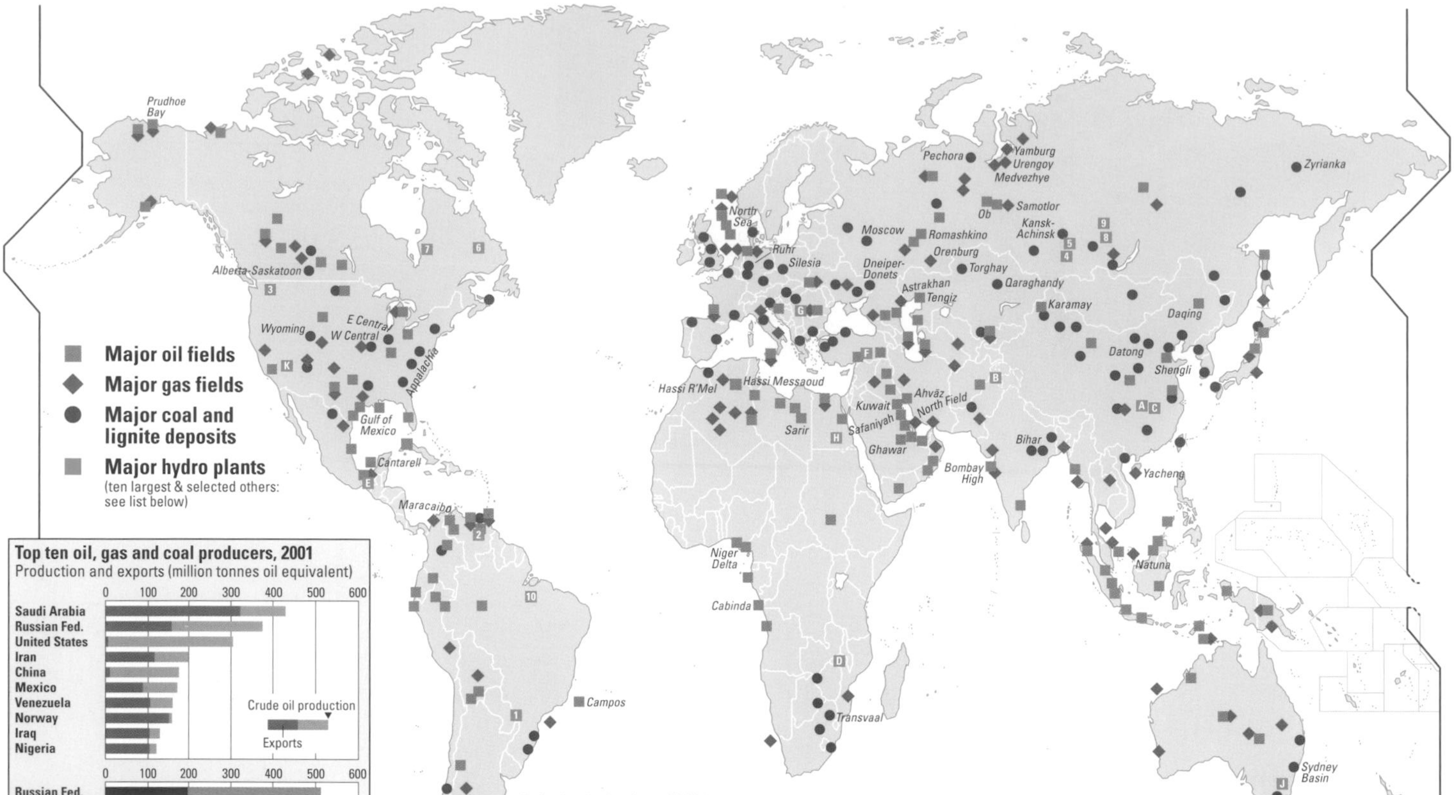

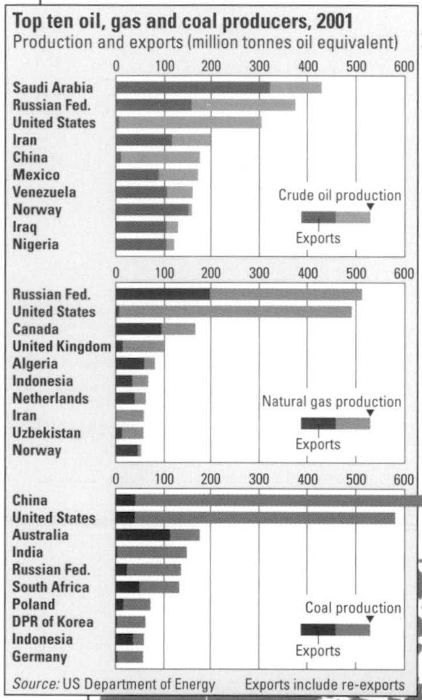

- ■ **Major oil fields**
- ◆ **Major gas fields**
- ● **Major coal and lignite deposits**
- ■ **Major hydro plants**
  (ten largest & selected others: see list below)

Map labels: Prudhoe Bay, Alberta-Saskatoon, Wyoming, E Central, W Central, Appalachia, Gulf of Mexico, Cantarell, Maracaibo, Campos, North Sea, Ruhr, Silesia, Moscow, Dneiper-Donets, Orenburg, Astrakhan, Tengiz, Torghay, Qaraghandy, Karamay, Daqing, Datong, Shengli, Pechora, Yamburg, Urengoy, Medvezhye, Ob, Samotlor, Kansk-Achinsk, Romashkino, Zyrianka, Hassi R'Mel, Hassi Messaoud, Sarir, Kuwait, Safaniyah, Ahvāz, North Field, Ghawar, Bihar, Bombay High, Yacheng, Natuna, Niger Delta, Cabinda, Transvaal, Aswān, Sydney Basin

Top ten oil, gas and coal producers, 2001
Production and exports (million tonnes oil equivalent)

Crude oil production / Exports:
Saudi Arabia, Russian Fed., United States, Iran, China, Mexico, Venezuela, Norway, Iraq, Nigeria

Natural gas production / Exports:
Russian Fed., United States, Canada, United Kingdom, Algeria, Indonesia, Netherlands, Iran, Uzbekistan, Norway

Coal production / Exports:
China (668.6), United States, Australia, India, Russian Fed., South Africa, Poland, DPR of Korea, Indonesia, Germany

Source: US Department of Energy   Exports include re-exports

Hydroelectric plant / year of initial operation / current rated capacity (megawatts)

1 Itaipú, Brazil/Paraguay	1983 12,600	8 Bratsk, Russian Fed.	1961 4,500
2 Guri, Venezuela	1986 10,000	9 Ust-Ilim, Russian Fed.	1977 4,320
3 Grand Coulee, WA, USA	1942 6,494	10 Tucurui, Brazil	1984 4,245
4 Sayano-Shushensk, Russian Fed.	1989 6,400	A Three Gorges, China (u/c, 18,200 by 2009)	
5 Krasnoyarsk, Russian Fed.	1968 6,000	B Tarbela, Pakistan	1977 3,478
6 Churchill Falls, QU, Canada	1971 5,428	C Gezhouba, China	1981 2,715
7 La Grande 2, QU, Canada	1979 5,328	D Cahora Bassa, Mozambique 1975 2,425	

E Chicoasén, Mexico	1980 2,400
F Atatürk, Turkey	1992 2,400
G Iron Gates I, Romania/Yugo.	1970 2,136
H Aswān High, Egypt	1967 1,815
J Talbingo (Tumut 3), Australia 1972 1,500	
K Hoover, AZ/NV, USA	1936 1,434

ENERGY PRODUCTION

Statistics for Portugal include Azores and Madeira, statistics for Spain include Canary Is. and statistics for the US include Alaska and Hawaii.

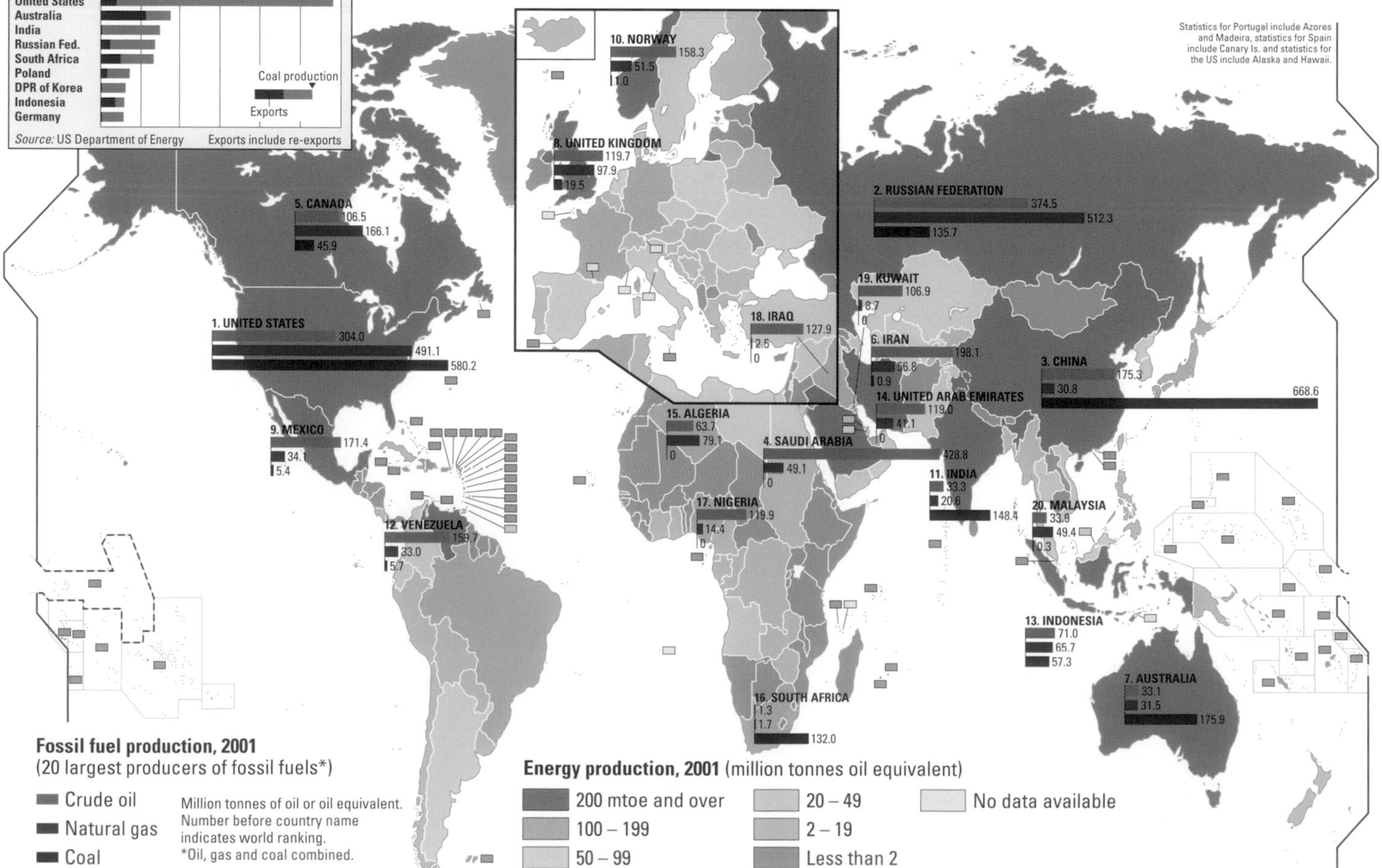

Country values (million tonnes oil equivalent) — Crude oil / Natural gas / Coal:

- **10. NORWAY** 158.3 / 51.5 / 1.0
- **8. UNITED KINGDOM** 119.7 / 97.9 / 19.5
- **5. CANADA** 106.5 / 166.1 / 45.9
- **2. RUSSIAN FEDERATION** 374.5 / 512.3 / 135.7
- **19. KUWAIT** 106.9 / 8.7 / 0
- **1. UNITED STATES** 304.0 / 491.1 / 580.2
- **18. IRAQ** 127.9 / 2.5 / 0
- **6. IRAN** 198.1 / 56.8 / 0.9
- **3. CHINA** 175.3 / 30.8 / 668.6
- **9. MEXICO** 171.4 / 34.1 / 5.4
- **14. UNITED ARAB EMIRATES** 119.0 / 41.1 / 0
- **15. ALGERIA** 63.7 / 79.1 / 0
- **4. SAUDI ARABIA** 428.8 / 49.1 / 0
- **11. INDIA** 33.3 / 20.6 / 148.4
- **20. MALAYSIA** 33.8 / 49.4 / 0.3
- **12. VENEZUELA** 159.7 / 33.0 / 5.7
- **17. NIGERIA** 119.9 / 14.4 / 0
- **13. INDONESIA** 71.0 / 65.7 / 57.3
- **7. AUSTRALIA** 33.1 / 31.5 / 175.9
- **16. SOUTH AFRICA** 1.3 / 1.7 / 132.0

Fossil fuel production, 2001
(20 largest producers of fossil fuels*)

- ■ Crude oil
- ■ Natural gas
- ■ Coal

Million tonnes of oil or oil equivalent. Number before country name indicates world ranking.
*Oil, gas and coal combined.

Source: US Department of Energy

Energy production, 2001 (million tonnes oil equivalent)

- 200 mtoe and over
- 100 – 199
- 50 – 99
- 20 – 49
- 2 – 19
- Less than 2
- No data available

Source: US Department of Energy

Energy: Consumption & Renewables

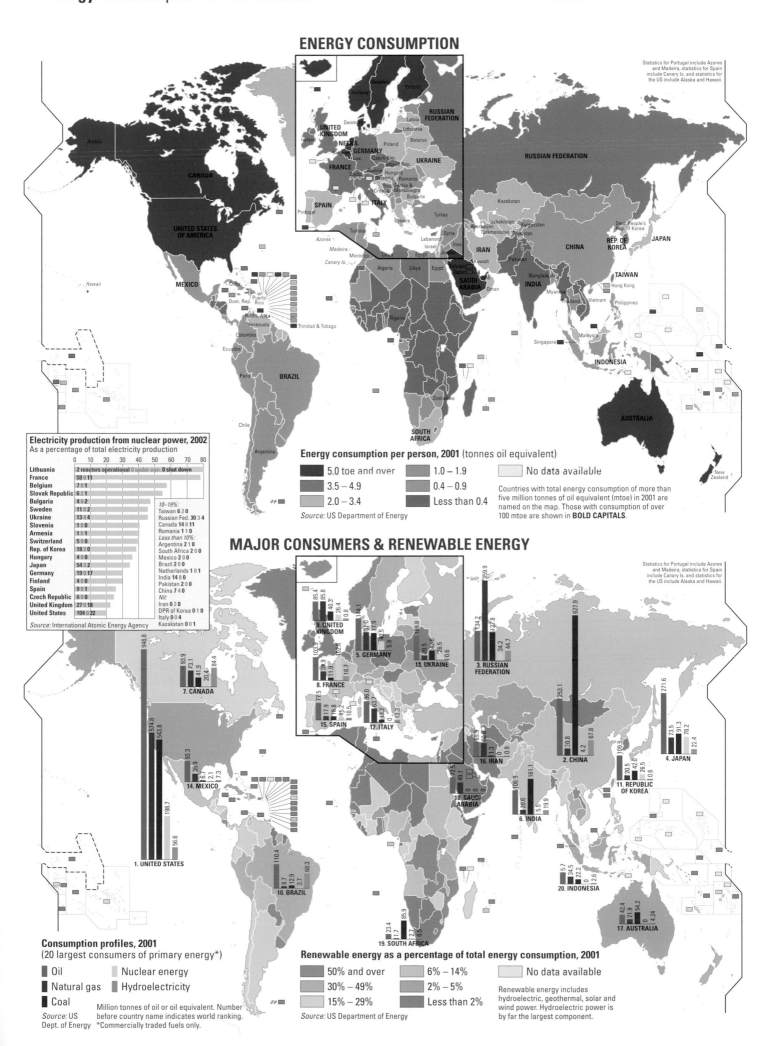

ENERGY CONSUMPTION

Electricity production from nuclear power, 2002
As a percentage of total electricity production

	2 reactors operational 0 under con. 0 shut down
Lithuania	
France	59 0 11
Belgium	7 0 1
Slovak Republic	6 2 1
Bulgaria	4 0 2
Sweden	11 0 2
Ukraine	13 4 4
Slovenia	1 0 0
Armenia	1 0 1
Switzerland	5 0 0
Rep. of Korea	18 2 0
Hungary	4 0 0
Japan	54 3 2
Germany	19 0 17
Finland	4 0 0
Spain	9 0 1
Czech Republic	6 0 0
United Kingdom	27 0 18
United States	104 0 22

10–19%:
Taiwan 6 2 0
Russian Fed. 30 3 4
Canada 14 0 11
Romania 1 1 0
Less than 10%:
Argentina 2 1 0
South Africa 2 0 0
Mexico 2 0 0
Brazil 2 0 0
Netherlands 1 0 1
India 14 8 0
Pakistan 2 0 0
China 7 4 0
Nil:
Iran 0 2 0
DPR of Korea 0 1 0
Italy 0 0 4
Kazakstan 0 0 1

Source: International Atomic Energy Agency

Energy consumption per person, 2001 (tonnes oil equivalent)

- 5.0 toe and over
- 3.5 – 4.9
- 2.0 – 3.4
- 1.0 – 1.9
- 0.4 – 0.9
- Less than 0.4
- No data available

Source: US Department of Energy

Countries with total energy consumption of more than five million tonnes of oil equivalent (mtoe) in 2001 are named on the map. Those with consumption of over 100 mtoe are shown in **BOLD CAPITALS**.

Statistics for Portugal include Azores and Madeira, statistics for Spain include Canary Is. and statistics for the US include Alaska and Hawaii.

MAJOR CONSUMERS & RENEWABLE ENERGY

Statistics for Portugal include Azores and Madeira, statistics for Spain include Canary Is. and statistics for the US include Alaska and Hawaii.

Consumption profiles, 2001
(20 largest consumers of primary energy*)

- Oil
- Natural gas
- Coal
- Nuclear energy
- Hydroelectricity

Million tonnes of oil or oil equivalent. Number before country name indicates world ranking.

Source: US Dept. of Energy *Commercially traded fuels only.

Renewable energy as a percentage of total energy consumption, 2001

- 50% and over
- 30% – 49%
- 15% – 29%
- 6% – 14%
- 2% – 5%
- Less than 2%
- No data available

Renewable energy includes hydroelectric, geothermal, solar and wind power. Hydroelectric power is by far the largest component.

Source: US Department of Energy

International Organisations

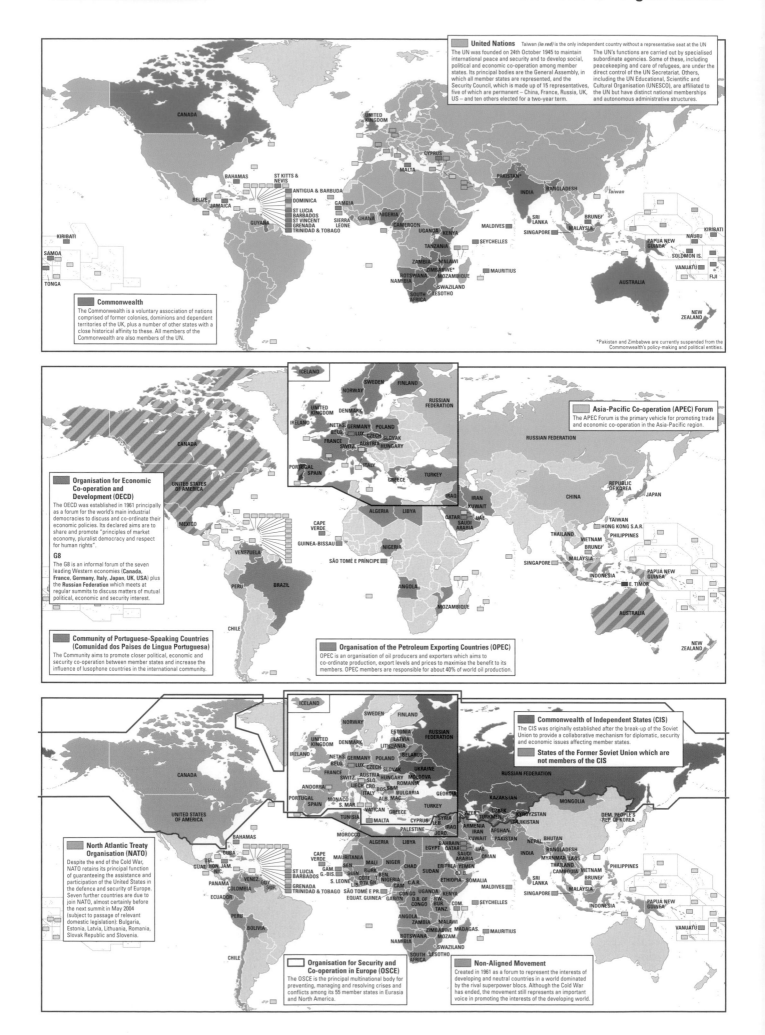

United Nations Taiwan (*in red*) is the only independent country without a representative seat at the UN

The UN was founded on 24th October 1945 to maintain international peace and security and to develop social, political and economic co-operation among member states. Its principal bodies are the General Assembly, in which all member states are represented, and the Security Council, which is made up of 15 representatives, five of which are permanent – China, France, Russia, UK, US – and ten others elected for a two-year term.

The UN's functions are carried out by specialised subordinate agencies. Some of these, including peacekeeping and care of refugees, are under the direct control of the UN Secretariat. Others, including the UN Educational, Scientific and Cultural Organisation (UNESCO), are affiliated to the UN but have distinct national memberships and autonomous administrative structures.

Commonwealth

The Commonwealth is a voluntary association of nations comprised of former colonies, dominions and dependent territories of the UK, plus a number of other states with a close historical affinity to these. All members of the Commonwealth are also members of the UN.

*Pakistan and Zimbabwe are currently suspended from the Commonwealth's policy-making and political entities.

Organisation for Economic Co-operation and Development (OECD)

The OECD was established in 1961 principally as a forum for the world's main industrial democracies to discuss and co-ordinate their economic policies. Its declared aims are to share and promote "principles of market economy, pluralist democracy and respect for human rights".

G8

The G8 is an informal forum of the seven leading Western economies (**Canada, France, Germany, Italy, Japan, UK, USA**) plus the **Russian Federation** which meets at regular summits to discuss matters of mutual political, economic and security interest.

Asia-Pacific Co-operation (APEC) Forum

The APEC Forum is the primary vehicle for promoting trade and economic co-operation in the Asia-Pacific region.

Community of Portuguese-Speaking Countries (Comunidad dos Paises de Lingua Portuguesa)

The Community aims to promote closer political, economic and security co-operation between member states and increase the influence of lusophone countries in the international community.

Organisation of the Petroleum Exporting Countries (OPEC)

OPEC is an organisation of oil producers and exporters which aims to co-ordinate production, export levels and prices to maximise the benefit to its members. OPEC members are responsible for about 40% of world oil production.

Commonwealth of Independent States (CIS)

The CIS was originally established after the break-up of the Soviet Union to provide a collaborative mechanism for diplomatic, security and economic issues affecting member states.

States of the Former Soviet Union which are not members of the CIS

North Atlantic Treaty Organisation (NATO)

Despite the end of the Cold War, NATO retains its principal function of guaranteeing the assistance and participation of the United States in the defence and security of Europe. Seven further countries are due to join NATO, almost certainly before the next summit in May 2004 (subject to passage of relevant domestic legislation): Bulgaria, Estonia, Latvia, Lithuania, Romania, Slovak Republic and Slovenia.

Organisation for Security and Co-operation in Europe (OSCE)

The OSCE is the principal multinational body for preventing, managing and resolving crises and conflicts among its 55 member states in Eurasia and North America.

Non-Aligned Movement

Created in 1961 as a forum to represent the interests of developing and neutral countries in a world dominated by the rival superpower blocs. Although the Cold War has ended, the movement still represents an important voice in promoting the interests of the developing world.

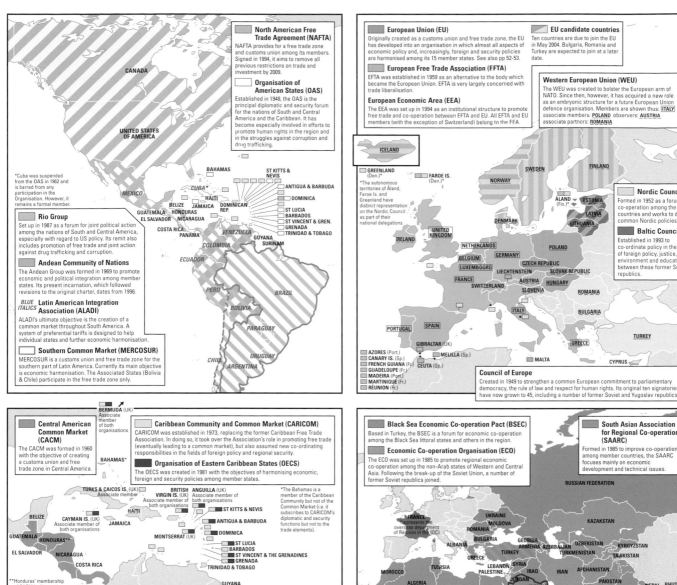

North American Free Trade Agreement (NAFTA)

NAFTA provides for a free trade zone and customs union among its members. Signed in 1994, it aims to remove all previous restrictions on trade and investment by 2009.

Organisation of American States (OAS)

Established in 1948, the OAS is the principal diplomatic and security forum for the nations of South and Central America and the Caribbean. It has become especially involved in efforts to promote human rights in the region and in the struggles against corruption and drug trafficking.

*Cuba was suspended from the OAS in 1962 and is barred from any participation in the Organisation. However, it remains a formal member.

Rio Group

Set up in 1987 as a forum for joint political action among the nations of South and Central America, especially with regard to US policy. Its remit also includes promotion of free trade and joint action against drug trafficking and corruption.

Andean Community of Nations

The Andean Group was formed in 1969 to promote economic and political integration among member states. Its present incarnation, which followed revisions to the original charter, dates from 1996.

BLUE ITALICS **Latin American Integration Association (ALADI)**

ALADI's ultimate objective is the creation of a common market throughout South America. A system of preferential tariffs is designed to help individual states and further economic harmonisation.

Southern Common Market (MERCOSUR)

MERCOSUR is a customs union and free trade zone for the southern part of Latin America. Currently its main objective is economic harmonisation. The Associated States (Bolivia & Chile) participate in the free trade zone only.

European Union (EU)

Originally created as a customs union and free trade zone, the EU has developed into an organisation in which almost all aspects of economic policy and, increasingly, foreign and security policies are harmonised among its 15 member states. See also pp 52-53.

European Free Trade Association (EFTA)

EFTA was established in 1959 as an alternative to the body which became the European Union. EFTA is very largely concerned with trade liberalisation.

European Economic Area (EEA)

The EEA was set up in 1994 as an institutional structure to promote free trade and co-operation between EFTA and EU. All EFTA and EU members (with the exception of Switzerland) belong to the EEA

EU candidate countries

Ten countries are due to join the EU in May 2004. Bulgaria, Romania and Turkey are expected to join at a later date.

Western European Union (WEU)

The WEU was created to bolster the European arm of NATO. Since then, however, it has acquired a new role as an embryonic structure for a future European Union defence organisation. Members are shown thus: ITALY associate members: POLAND observers: AUSTRIA associate partners: ROMANIA

Nordic Council

Formed in 1952 as a forum for co-operation among the Nordic countries and works to develop common Nordic policies.

*The autonomous territories of Aland, Faroe Is. and Greenland have distinct representation on the Nordic Council as part of their national delegations.

Baltic Council

Established in 1993 to co-ordinate policy in the areas of foreign policy, justice, environment and education between these former Soviet republics.

AZORES (Port.)
CANARY IS. (Sp.)
FRENCH GUIANA (Fr.)
GUADELOUPE (Fr.)
MADEIRA (Port.)
MARTINIQUE (Fr.)
RÉUNION (Fr.)
MELILLA (Sp.)
CEUTA (Sp.)

Council of Europe

Created in 1949 to strengthen a common European commitment to parliamentary democracy, the rule of law and respect for human rights. Its original ten signatories have now grown to 45, including a number of former Soviet and Yugoslav republics.

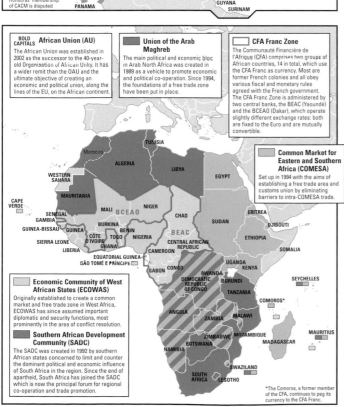

Central American Common Market (CACM)

The CACM was formed in 1960 with the objective of creating a customs union and free trade zone in Central America.

Caribbean Community and Common Market (CARICOM)

CARICOM was established in 1973, replacing the former Caribbean Free Trade Association. In doing so, it took over the Association's role in promoting free trade (eventually leading to a common market), but also assumed new co-ordinating responsibilities in the fields of foreign policy and regional security.

Organisation of Eastern Caribbean States (OECS)

The OECS was created in 1981 with the objectives of harmonising economic, foreign and security policies among member states.

*The Bahamas is a member of the Caribbean Community but not of the Common Market (i.e. it subscribes to CARICOM's diplomatic and security functions but not to the trade elements).

**Honduras' membership of CACM is disputed

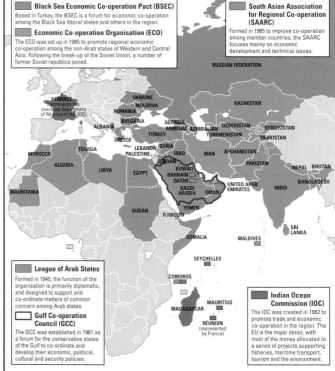

Black Sea Economic Co-operation Pact (BSEC)

Based in Turkey, the BSEC is a forum for economic co-operation among the Black Sea littoral states and others in the region.

Economic Co-operation Organisation (ECO)

The ECO was set up in 1985 to promote regional economic co-operation among the non-Arab states of Western and Central Asia. Following the break-up of the Soviet Union, a number of former Soviet republics joined.

South Asian Association for Regional Co-operation (SAARC)

Formed in 1985 to improve co-operation among member countries, the SAARC focuses mainly on economic development and technical issues.

FRANCE represents the overseas department of Reunion in the IOC

League of Arab States

Formed in 1945, the function of the organisation is primarily diplomatic, and designed to support and co-ordinate matters of common concern among Arab states.

Gulf Co-operation Council (GCC)

The GCC was established in 1981 as a forum for the conservative states of the Gulf to co-ordinate and develop their economic, political, cultural and security policies.

Indian Ocean Commission (IOC)

The IOC was created in 1982 to promote trade and economic co-operation in the region. The EU is the major donor, with most of the money allocated to a series of projects supporting fisheries, maritime transport, tourism and the environment.

RÉUNION (represented by France)

BOLD CAPITALS **African Union (AU)**

The African Union was established in 2002 as the successor to the 40-year-old Organisation of African Unity. It has a wider remit than the OAU and the ultimate objective of creating an economic and political union, along the lines of the EU, on the African continent.

Union of the Arab Maghreb

The main political and economic bloc in Arab North Africa was created in 1989 as a vehicle to promote economic and political co-operation. Since 1994, the foundations of a free trade zone have been put in place.

CFA Franc Zone

The Communauté Financière de l'Afrique (CFA) comprises two groups of African countries, 14 in total, which use the CFA Franc as currency. Most are former French colonies and all obey various fiscal and monetary rules agreed with the French government. The CFA Franc Zone is administered by two central banks, the BEAC (Yaoundé) and the BCEAO (Dakar), which operate slightly different exchange rates: both are fixed to the Euro and are mutually convertible.

Common Market for Eastern and Southern Africa (COMESA)

Set up in 1994 with the aims of establishing a free trade area and customs union by eliminating barriers to intra-COMESA trade.

Economic Community of West African States (ECOWAS)

Originally established to create a common market and free trade zone in West Africa, ECOWAS has since assumed important diplomatic and security functions, most prominently in the area of conflict resolution.

Southern African Development Community (SADC)

The SADC was created in 1992 by southern African states concerned to limit and counter the dominant political and economic influence of South Africa in the region. Since the end of apartheid, South Africa has joined the SADC which is now the principal forum for regional co-operation and trade promotion.

*The Comoros, a former member of the CFA, continues to peg its currency to the CFA Franc.

South Pacific Forum (SPF)

The Forum was created primarily to promote economic and social co-operation amongst member states. However, it has also become the Pacific islands' principal voice in the context of a number of vital regional issues such as nuclear testing and global warming.

Association of South-East Asian Nations (ASEAN)

Although its founding charter envisaged economic and social functions for the organisation, ASEAN was primarily an anti-communist strategic body from its establishment in 1967 to the end of the Cold War. During the 1990s, however, its wider role has come into play.

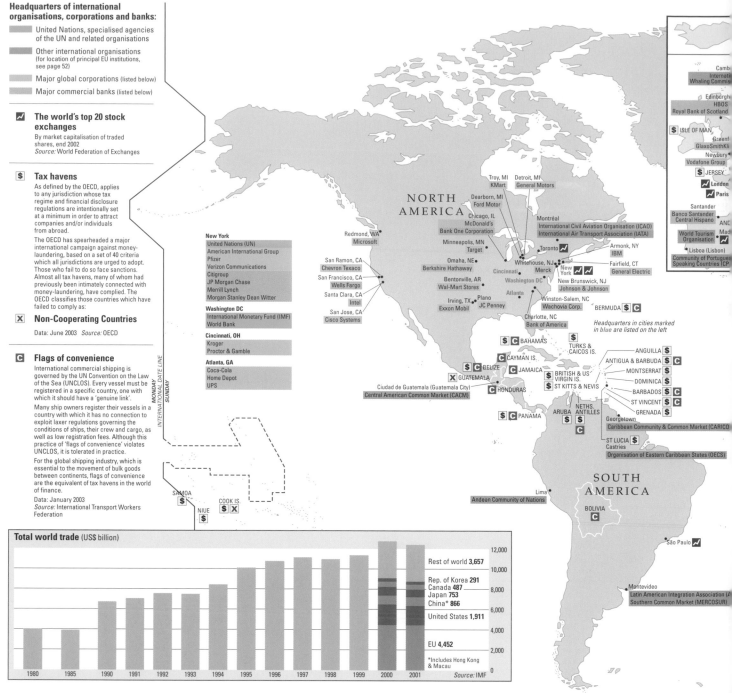

Headquarters of international organisations, corporations and banks:

■ United Nations, specialised agencies of the UN and related organisations

■ Other international organisations (for location of principal EU institutions, see page 52)

■ Major global corporations (listed below)

■ Major commercial banks (listed below)

☑ **The world's top 20 stock exchanges**
By market capitalisation of traded shares, end 2002
Source: World Federation of Exchanges

$ **Tax havens**
As defined by the OECD, applies to any jurisdiction whose tax regime and financial disclosure regulations are intentionally set at a minimum in order to attract companies and/or individuals from abroad.

The OECD has spearheaded a major international campaign against money-laundering, based on a set of 40 criteria which all jurisdictions are urged to adopt. Those who fail to do so face sanctions. Almost all tax havens, many of whom had previously been intimately connected with money-laundering, have complied. The OECD classifies those countries which have failed to comply as:

☒ **Non-Cooperating Countries**
Data: June 2003 *Source:* OECD

C **Flags of convenience**
International commercial shipping is governed by the UN Convention on the Law of the Sea (UNCLOS). Every vessel must be registered in a specific country, one with which it should have a 'genuine link'.

Many ship owners register their vessels in a country with which it has no connection to exploit laxer regulations governing the conditions of ships, their crew and cargo, as well as low registration fees. Although this practice of 'flags of convenience' violates UNCLOS, it is tolerated in practice.

For the global shipping industry, which is essential to the movement of bulk goods between continents, flags of convenience are the equivalent of tax havens in the world of finance.
Data: January 2003
Source: International Transport Workers Federation

New York
United Nations (UN)
American International Group
Pfizer
Verizon Communications
Citigroup
JP Morgan Chase
Merrill Lynch
Morgan Stanley Dean Witter

Washington DC
International Monetary Fund (IMF)
World Bank

Cincinnati, OH
Kroger
Proctor & Gamble

Atlanta, GA
Coca-Cola
Home Depot
UPS

Headquarters in cities marked in blue are listed on the left

Total world trade (US$ billion)

Rest of world **3,657**
Rep. of Korea **291**
Canada **487**
Japan **753**
China* **866**
United States **1,911**
EU **4,452**
*Includes Hong Kong & Macau
Source: IMF

(Bar chart years: 1980, 1985, 1990, 1991, 1992, 1993, 1994, 1995, 1996, 1997, 1998, 1999, 2000, 2001)

THE WORLD'S TOP 20 GLOBAL CORPORATIONS (excluding banks)

By annual turnover (US$ million):		By number of employees (thousands):		By market capitalisation (US$ million):	
Wal-Mart Stores	244,524	Wal-Mart Stores	1,342	General Electric	286,098
General Motors	186,763	Siemens	426	Microsoft	263,990
Royal Dutch/Shell	179,431	McDonald's	413	Exxon Mobil	244,932
Exxon Mobil	178,909	UPS	366	Pfizer	244,886
BP	178,721	Daimler Chrysler	366	Wal-Mart Stores	232,219
Ford Motor	162,586	General Motors	356	Johnson & Johnson	161,359
Daimler Chrysler	140,777	Hitachi	340	Royal Dutch/Shell	158,475
General Electric	131,698	Ford Motor	335	BP	153,240
Toyota Motor	131,616	Volkswagen	322	American Internat.	150,974
Mitsubishi	109,271	IBM	318	IBM	148,975
Mitsui	108,517	General Electric	313	Vodafone Group	147,992
Allianz	101,466	Kroger	288	Intel	136,038
Total	96,504	Matsushita	288	Merck	124,808
Chevron Texaco	91,685	Target	280	GlaxoSmithKline	118,955
NTT DoCoMo	89,550	Deutsche Post	276	Proctor & Gamble	118,879
Itochu	85,787	Unilever	265	Cisco Systems	115,165
Volkswagen	84,707	JC Penney	260	Novartis	113,087
IBM	81,186	Verizon Communications	240	Coca-Cola	112,973
Siemens	77,013	KMart	234	Berkshire Hathaway	108,981
Marubeni	72,089	Home Depot	221	NTT DoCoMo	105,306

Data: 2002/03 *Source:* Business Week   Data: 2002/03 *Source:* Forbes   Data: 1st June 2003 *Source:* Business Week

THE WORLD'S TOP 20 BANKS

By Tier One capital (US$ million):		By assets (US$ million):		By market capitalisation (US$ million):	
Citigroup	58,448	Mizuho Group	1,178,285	Citigroup	210,862
Bank of America	41,972	Citigroup	1,051,450	HSBC Holdings	126,972
Mizuho Group	40,498	Sumitomo Bank	840,281	Bank of America	111,055
JP Morgan Chase	37,713	Deutsche Bank	809,220	Wells Fargo	81,718
HSBC Holdings	35,074	Bk of Tokyo-Mitsub.	751,480	Royal Bk of Scotland	75,134
Sumitomo Bank	29,952	UBS	747,211	UBS	67,635
Crédit Agricole	28,876	BNP Paribas	727,325	JP Morgan Chase	66,707
Bk of Tokyo-Mitsub.	25,673	HSBC Holdings	696,381	Wachovia Corp.	54,042
UFJ Holdings	23,815	JP Morgan Chase	693,575	Morgan Stanley DW	49,667
I & C Bank of China	23,107	HypoVereinsBank	641,729	Barclays Bank	46,186
Bank of China	22,085	Bank of America	621,764	HBOS	44,114
Deutsche Bank	21,859	UFJ Holdings	616,485	Bank One Corp.	43,510
Royal Bk of Scotland	21,830	Crédit Suisse Group	609,618	BNP Paribas	44,325
Bank One Corp.	21,749	ABN-AMRO	526,450	Lloyds TSB	40,933
BNP Paribas	21,748	I & C Bank of China	524,235	Merrill Lynch	40,283
HypoVereinsBank	19,154	Royal Bk of Scotland	519,991	Banco Santander CH	38,585
Wachovia Corp.	18,999	Barclays Bank	505,408	Deutsche Bank	36,407
Wells Fargo	18,247	Crédit Agricole	496,421	National Australian Bk	33,003
HBOS	18,086	Norinchukin Bank	462,593	ING Bank	32,407
Barclays Bank	18,046	Société Générale	451,660	Crédit Suisse Group	32,307

Data: August 2002 *Source:* The Banker   Data: August 2002 *Source:* The Banker   Data: 1st June 2003 *Source:* Business Week

Headquarters in cities marked in **red** are listed on the right

Basel (Basle)
Bank for International Settlements (BIS)
Novartis

Bruxelles/Brussel (Brussels)
European Union (EU)
North Atlantic Treaty Organisation (NATO)
Western European Union (WEU)
World Customs Organisation

Genève (Geneva)
International Labour Organisation (ILO)
International Telecommunications Union (ITU)
World Health Organisation (WHO)
European Broadcasting Union (EBU)
European Free Trade Association (EFTA)
International Air Transport Association (IATA)
International Committee for the Red Cross
International Organisation for Standardisation (ISO)
World Council of Churches
World Trade Organisation

Gland
World-Wide Fund for Nature /
World Wildlife Fund (WWF)

Den Haag/'s-Gravenhage (The Hague)
International Court of Justice
Royal Dutch/Shell Group

Lausanne
International Olympic Committee (IOC)

London
International Maritime Organisation (IMO)
Amnesty International
The Commonwealth
European Bank for Reconstruction
& Development (EBRD)
International Maritime Satellite
Organisation (INMARSAT)
BP
Unilever PLC
Barclays Bank
HSBC Holdings
Lloyds TSB

München (Munich)
Allianz
Siemens
HypoVereinsBank

Paris
UN Educational, Scientific &
Cultural Organisation (UNESCO)
CFA Franc Zone
Organisation for Economic
Co-operation & Development (OECD)
Total
BNP Paribas
Crédit Agricole
Société Générale

Strasbourg
Council of Europe

Stuttgart
Daimler Chrysler

Vernier
International Road Federation (IRF)

Zürich
Fédération International de
Football Association (FIFA)
Crédit Suisse Group
UBS

Map labels

EUROPE

AFRICA

ASIA

AUSTRALIA

Amsterdam ABN-AMRO / ING Bank
Rotterdam Unilever NV
Helsinki (Helsingfors)
Stockholm
GERMANY
København (Copenhagen)
Nordic Council
Wolfsburg Volkswagen
Minsk Commonwealth of Independent States (CIS)
Bonn Deutsche Post
UKRAINE
Frankfurt am Main Deutsche Bank
München (Munich) Wien (Vienna) International Atomic Energy Agency (IAEA) UN Industrial Development Organisation (UNIDO)
Stuttgart
Lausanne Basel (Basle)
Zürich LIECHTENSTEIN
Genève (Geneva) Milano (Milan)
MONACO
Lyons Interpol
Roma (Rome) Food & Agriculture Organisation (FAO)
İstanbul Black Sea Economic Co-operation Pact
GIBRALTAR
MALTA
LEBANON
CYPRUS

Rabat Union of the Arab Maghreb
El Qâhira (Cairo) League of Arab States
EGYPT
Tehrän
BAHRAIN
Ar Riyäd (Riyadh) Gulf Co-operation Council (GCC)
Economic Co-operation Organisation (ECO)
Kathmandu South Asian Association for Regional Co-operation
Beijing (Peking) Bank of China Industrial & Commercial Bank of China
Seoul
Tökyö Hitachi Itochu Marubeni Mitsubishi Mitsui NTT DoCoMo Bank of Tokyo-Mitsubishi Mizuho Financial Group Norinchukin Bank
Toyota Toyota Motor
Shanghai
Ösaka Matsushita Electrical Industries Sumitomo Bank UFJ Holdings
Taipei
Shenzhen
Xianggang (Hong Kong)
MYANMAR
Mumbai (Bombay)
Manila Asian Development Bank
MARSHALL IS.
Abuja Economic Community of West African States (ECOWAS)
Abidjan African Development Bank
NIGERIA
Ädis Äbeba (Addis Ababa) African Union (AU)
SRI LANKA
CAMBODIA
PHILIPPINES
LIBERIA
SÃO TOMÉ E PRINCIPE
EQUATORIAL GUINEA
MALDIVES
Singapore Asia-Pacific Economic Co-operation (APEC) Forum International Air Transport Association (IATA)
NAURU
SEYCHELLES
COMOROS
INDONESIA
Jakarta Association of South-East Asian Nations (ASEAN)
VANUATU
Lusaka Common Market for Eastern & Southern Africa (COMESA)
MAURITIUS
Quatre Bornes Indian Ocean Commission (IOC)
Nouméa Pacific Community (SPC)
Suva
TONGA
South Pacific Forum (SPF)
Gaborone Southern African Development Community (SADC)
Sydney
Melbourne National Australian Bank

MONDAY / INTERNATIONAL DATE LINE / SUNDAY

Stock market charts

NEW YORK _Dow Jones Industrial Average_
(12,000 / 10,000 / 8,000 / 6,000 / 4,000 / 2,000 / 0)
1993 94 95 96 97 98 99 2000 01 02 03

NASDAQ (New York) _NASDAQ-100_
(5,000 / 4,000 / 3,000 / 2,000 / 1,000 / 0)
1993 94 95 96 97 98 99 2000 01 02 03

TOKYO _Nikkei-225_
(30,000 / 25,000 / 20,000 / 15,000 / 10,000 / 5,000 / 0)
1993 94 95 96 97 98 99 2000 01 02 03

LONDON _FTSE-100_
(7,000 / 6,000 / 5,000 / 4,000 / 3,000 / 2,000 / 1,000 / 0)
1993 94 95 96 97 98 99 2000 01 02 03

PARIS _CAC-40_
The Amsterdam, Brussels and Paris stock exchanges amalgamated in Sept 2000 to form Euronext
(7,000 / 6,000 / 5,000 / 4,000 / 3,000 / 2,000 / 1,000 / 0)
1993 94 95 96 97 98 99 2000 01 02 03

FRANKFURT _DAX_
(8,000 / 7,000 / 6,000 / 5,000 / 4,000 / 3,000 / 2,000 / 1,000 / 0)
1993 94 95 96 97 98 99 2000 01 02 03

TORONTO _TSE-300_
(12,000 / 10,000 / 8,000 / 6,000 / 4,000 / 2,000 / 0)
1993 94 95 96 97 98 99 2000 01 02 03

HONG KONG _Hang Seng_
(20,000 / 16,000 / 12,000 / 8,000 / 4,000)
1993 94 95 96 97 98 99 2000 01 02 03

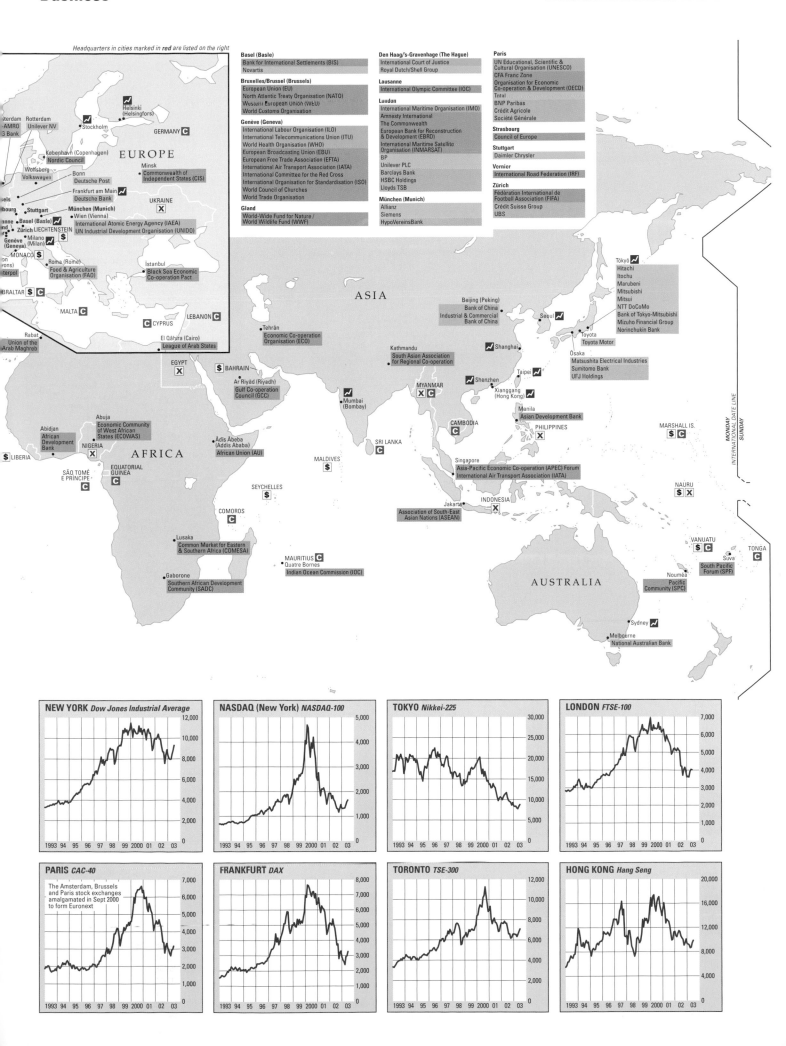

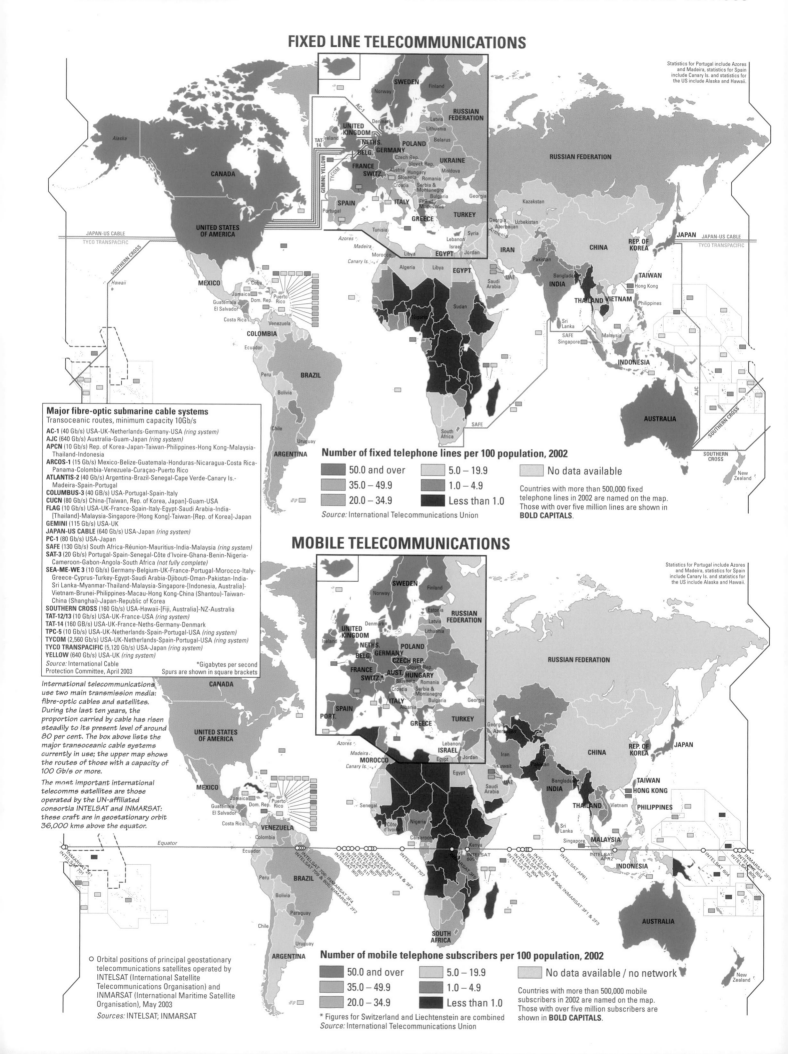

FIXED LINE TELECOMMUNICATIONS

Statistics for Portugal include Azores and Madeira, statistics for Spain include Canary Is. and statistics for the US include Alaska and Hawaii.

Major fibre-optic submarine cable systems
Transoceanic routes, minimum capacity 10Gb/s

AC-1 (40 Gb/s) USA-UK-Netherlands-Germany-USA *(ring system)*
AJC (640 Gb/s) Australia-Guam-Japan *(ring system)*
APCN (10 Gb/s) Rep. of Korea-Japan-Taiwan-Philippines-Hong Kong-Malaysia-Thailand-Indonesia
ARCOS-1 (15 Gb/s) Mexico-Belize-Guatemala-Honduras-Nicaragua-Costa Rica-Panama-Colombia-Venezuela-Curaçao-Puerto Rico
ATLANTIS-2 (40 Gb/s) Argentina-Brazil-Senegal-Cape Verde-Canary Is.-Madeira-Spain-Portugal
COLUMBUS-3 (40 GB/s) USA-Portugal-Spain-Italy
CUCN (80 Gb/s) China-[Taiwan, Rep. of Korea, Japan]-Guam-USA
FLAG (10 Gb/s) USA-UK-France-Spain-Italy-Egypt-Saudi Arabia-India-[Thailand]-Malaysia-Singapore-[Hong Kong]-Taiwan-[Rep. of Korea]-Japan
GEMINI (115 Gb/s) USA-UK
JAPAN-US CABLE (640 Gb/s) USA-Japan *(ring system)*
PC-1 (80 Gb/s) USA-Japan
SAFE (130 Gb/s) South Africa-Réunion-Mauritius-India-Malaysia *(ring system)*
SAT-3 (20 Gb/s) Portugal-Spain-Senegal-Côte d'Ivoire-Ghana-Benin-Nigeria-Cameroon-Gabon-Angola-South Africa *(not fully complete)*
SEA-ME-WE 3 (10 Gb/s) Germany-Belgium-UK-France-Portugal-Morocco-Italy-Greece-Cyprus-Turkey-Egypt-Saudi Arabia-Djibouti-Oman-Pakistan-India-Sri Lanka-Myanmar-Thailand-Malaysia-Singapore-[Indonesia, Australia]-Vietnam-Brunei-Philippines-Macau-Hong Kong-China (Shantou)-Taiwan-China (Shanghai)-Japan-Republic of Korea
SOUTHERN CROSS (160 Gb/s) USA-Hawaii-[Fiji, Australia]-NZ-Australia
TAT-12/13 (10 Gb/s) USA-UK-France-USA *(ring system)*
TAT-14 (160 GB/s) USA-UK-France-Neths-Germany-Denmark
TPC-5 (10 Gb/s) USA-UK-Netherlands-Spain-Portugal-USA *(ring system)*
TYCOM (2,560 Gb/s) USA-UK-Netherlands-Spain-Portugal-USA *(ring system)*
TYCO TRANSPACIFIC (5,120 Gb/s) USA-Japan *(ring system)*
YELLOW (640 Gb/s) USA-UK *(ring system)*

Source: International Cable Protection Committee, April 2003

*Gigabytes per second
Spurs are shown in square brackets

International telecommunications use two main transmission media: fibre-optic cables and satellites. During the last ten years, the proportion carried by cable has risen steadily to its present level of around 80 per cent. The box above lists the major transoceanic cable systems currently in use; the upper map shows the routes of those with a capacity of 100 Gb/s or more.

The most important international telecomms satellites are those operated by the UN-affiliated consortia INTELSAT and INMARSAT: these craft are in geostationary orbit 36,000 kms above the equator.

Number of fixed telephone lines per 100 population, 2002

- 50.0 and over
- 35.0 – 49.9
- 20.0 – 34.9
- 5.0 – 19.9
- 1.0 – 4.9
- Less than 1.0
- No data available

Countries with more than 500,000 fixed telephone lines in 2002 are named on the map. Those with over five million lines are shown in **BOLD CAPITALS**.

Source: International Telecommunications Union

MOBILE TELECOMMUNICATIONS

Statistics for Portugal include Azores and Madeira, statistics for Spain include Canary Is. and statistics for the US include Alaska and Hawaii.

○ Orbital positions of principal geostationary telecommunications satellites operated by INTELSAT (International Satellite Telecommunications Organisation) and INMARSAT (International Maritime Satellite Organisation), May 2003

Sources: INTELSAT; INMARSAT

Number of mobile telephone subscribers per 100 population, 2002

- 50.0 and over
- 35.0 – 49.9
- 20.0 – 34.9
- 5.0 – 19.9
- 1.0 – 4.9
- Less than 1.0
- No data available / no network

Countries with more than 500,000 mobile subscribers in 2002 are named on the map. Those with over five million subscribers are shown in **BOLD CAPITALS**.

* Figures for Switzerland and Liechtenstein are combined
Source: International Telecommunications Union

INTERNET SUBSCRIBERS

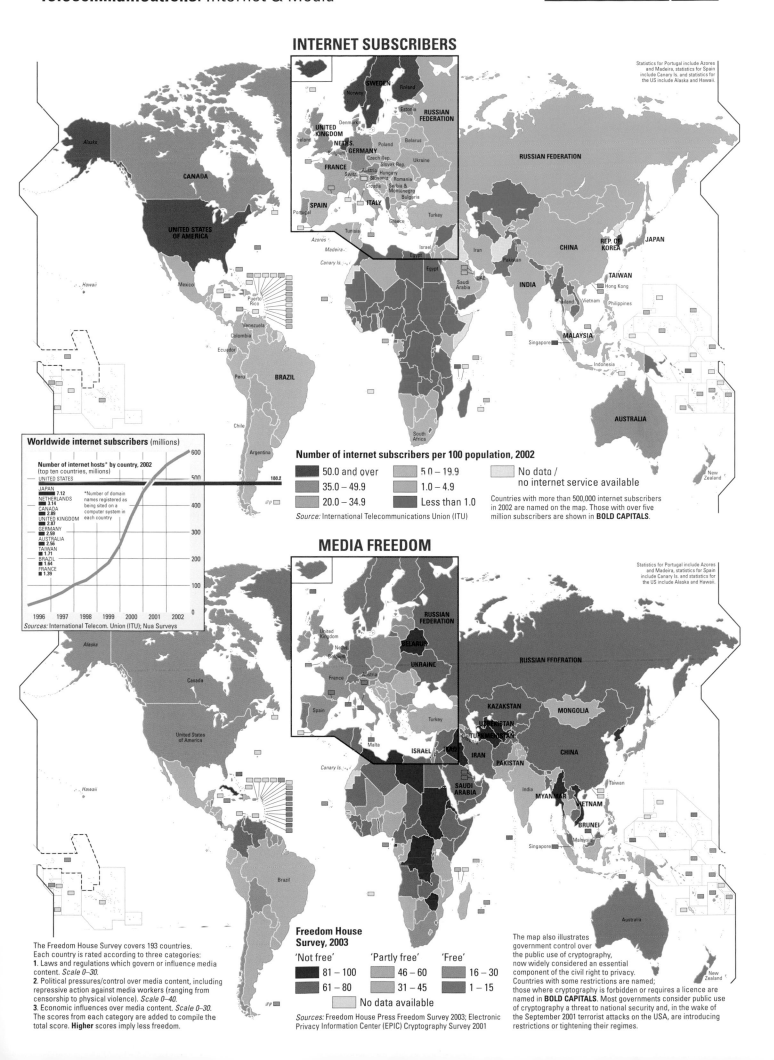

Statistics for Portugal include Azores and Madeira, statistics for Spain include Canary Is. and statistics for the US include Alaska and Hawaii.

Worldwide internet subscribers (millions)

Number of internet hosts* by country, 2002
(top ten countries, millions)

UNITED STATES	100.1
JAPAN	7.12
NETHERLANDS	3.14
CANADA	2.89
UNITED KINGDOM	2.87
GERMANY	2.59
AUSTRALIA	2.56
TAIWAN	1.71
BRAZIL	1.64
FRANCE	1.39

*Number of domain names registered as being sited on a computer system in each country

1996 1997 1998 1999 2000 2001 2002

Sources: International Telecom. Union (ITU); Nua Surveys

Number of internet subscribers per 100 population, 2002

- 50.0 and over
- 35.0 – 49.9
- 20.0 – 34.9
- 5.0 – 19.9
- 1.0 – 4.9
- Less than 1.0
- No data / no internet service available

Source: International Telecommunications Union (ITU)

Countries with more than 500,000 internet subscribers in 2002 are named on the map. Those with over five million subscribers are shown in **BOLD CAPITALS**.

MEDIA FREEDOM

Statistics for Portugal include Azores and Madeira, statistics for Spain include Canary Is. and statistics for the US include Alaska and Hawaii.

The Freedom House Survey covers 193 countries. Each country is rated according to three categories:
1. Laws and regulations which govern or influence media content. *Scale 0–30.*
2. Political pressures/control over media content, including repressive action against media workers (ranging from censorship to physical violence). *Scale 0–40.*
3. Economic influences over media content. *Scale 0–30.* The scores from each category are added to compile the total score. **Higher** scores imply less freedom.

Freedom House Survey, 2003

'Not free'	'Partly free'	'Free'
81 – 100	46 – 60	16 – 30
61 – 80	31 – 45	1 – 15

No data available

Sources: Freedom House Press Freedom Survey 2003; Electronic Privacy Information Center (EPIC) Cryptography Survey 2001

The map also illustrates government control over the public use of cryptography, now widely considered an essential component of the civil right to privacy. Countries with some restrictions are named; those where cryptography is forbidden or requires a licence are named in **BOLD CAPITALS**. Most governments consider public use of cryptography a threat to national security and, in the wake of the September 2001 terrorist attacks on the USA, are introducing restrictions or tightening their regimes.

SPENDING ON HEALTH

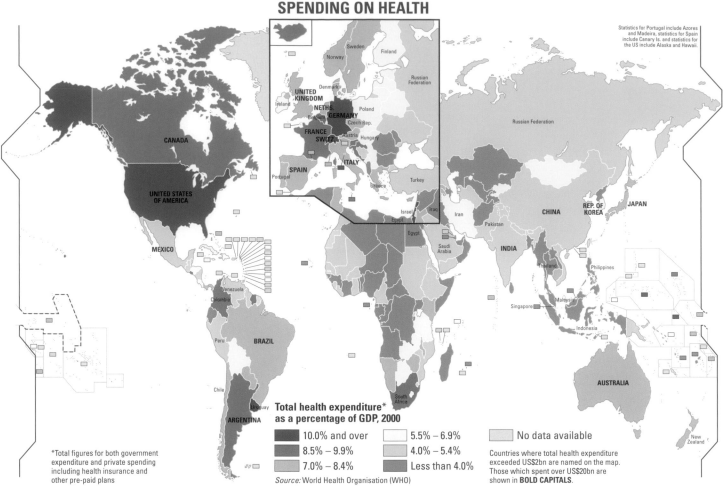

Statistics for Portugal include Azores and Madeira, statistics for Spain include Canary Is. and statistics for the US include Alaska and Hawaii.

Total health expenditure* as a percentage of GDP, 2000

- 10.0% and over
- 8.5% – 9.9%
- 7.0% – 8.4%
- 5.5% – 6.9%
- 4.0% – 5.4%
- Less than 4.0%
- No data available

*Total figures for both government expenditure and private spending including health insurance and other pre-paid plans

Source: World Health Organisation (WHO)

Countries where total health expenditure exceeded US$2bn are named on the map. Those which spent over US$20bn are shown in **BOLD CAPITALS**.

HEALTH INDICATORS

Male life expectancy, 2001 (years)

EUROPE & THE RUSSIAN FEDERATION	69.6
AFRICA	50.2
ASIA	64.7
AUSTRALASIA & OCEANIA	71.8
UNITED STATES & CANADA	74.5
LATIN AMERICA & THE CARIBBEAN	67.0
OECD COUNTRIES *(see p.24)*	74.2
NON-OECD COUNTRIES	61.8
WORLD	**64.1**

TOP TEN COUNTRIES

ICELAND	78.2
JAPAN	77.9
SAN MARINO	77.6
AUSTRALIA	77.4
SWITZERLAND	77.3
CANADA	76.6
MONACO	76.5
SINGAPORE	76.5
ANDORRA	76.2
ITALY	76.2

BOTTOM TEN COUNTRIES

SWAZILAND	40.2
LESOTHO	40.1
BOTSWANA	39.3
RWANDA	38.9
BURUNDI	38.4
ZIMBABWE	37.1
ZAMBIA	36.7
MALAWI	35.7
ANGOLA	34.1
SIERRA LEONE	32.7

Averages weighted by population
Source: WHO

Female life expectancy, 2001 (years)

EUROPE & THE RUSSIAN FEDERATION	77.5
AFRICA	52.8
ASIA	67.7
AUSTRALASIA & OCEANIA	76.4
UNITED STATES & CANADA	79.7
LATIN AMERICA & THE CARIBBEAN	73.1
OECD COUNTRIES *(see p.24)*	80.0
NON-OECD COUNTRIES	65.3
WORLD	**68.1**

TOP TEN COUNTRIES

JAPAN	84.7
MONACO	84.0
SAN MARINO	83.9
FRANCE	82.9
ANDORRA	82.9
SWITZERLAND	82.8
AUSTRALIA	82.6
SPAIN	82.6
SWEDEN	82.3
ITALY	82.2

BOTTOM TEN COUNTRIES

NIGER	43.2
RWANDA	42.8
BURUNDI	42.3
SWAZILAND	40.1
BOTSWANA	38.6
ANGOLA	38.3
ZAMBIA	37.0
MALAWI	36.9
ZIMBABWE	36.5
SIERRA LEONE	35.9

Averages weighted by population
Source: WHO

Mortality* in childbirth, 2000 (per 10,000 births)

EUROPE & THE RUSSIAN FEDERATION	3.0
AFRICA	67.7
ASIA	26.6
AUSTRALASIA & OCEANIA	7.3
UNITED STATES & CANADA	0.8
LATIN AMERICA & THE CARIBBEAN	12.6
OECD COUNTRIES *(see p.24)*	2.0
NON-OECD COUNTRIES	31.7
WORLD	**26.0**

Averages weighted by population
Source: UNDP

*Death of mother during childbirth

Infant* mortality, 2001 (per 1,000 live births)

EUROPE & THE RUSSIAN FEDERATION	14.1
AFRICA	143.5
ASIA	61.6
AUSTRALASIA & OCEANIA	20.2
UNITED STATES & CANADA	7.9
LATIN AMERICA & THE CARIBBEAN	32.7
OECD COUNTRIES *(see p.24)*	10.8
NON-OECD COUNTRIES	77.2
WORLD	**64.2**

Averages weighted by population
Source: UNICEF

*Child under five years old

Number of people per doctor, 2001

EUROPE & THE RUSSIAN FEDERATION	308
AFRICA	2,593
ASIA	977
AUSTRALASIA & OCEANIA	529
UNITED STATES & CANADA	364
LATIN AMERICA & THE CARIBBEAN	626
OECD COUNTRIES *(see p.24)*	375
NON-OECD COUNTRIES	954
WORLD	**720**

Averages weighted by population
Source: WHO

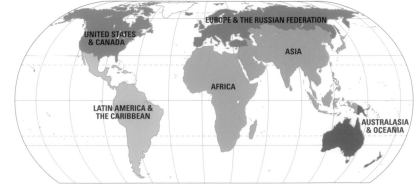

UNITED STATES & CANADA

EUROPE & THE RUSSIAN FEDERATION

ASIA

AFRICA

LATIN AMERICA & THE CARIBBEAN

AUSTRALASIA & OCEANIA

Health: Areas of Risk

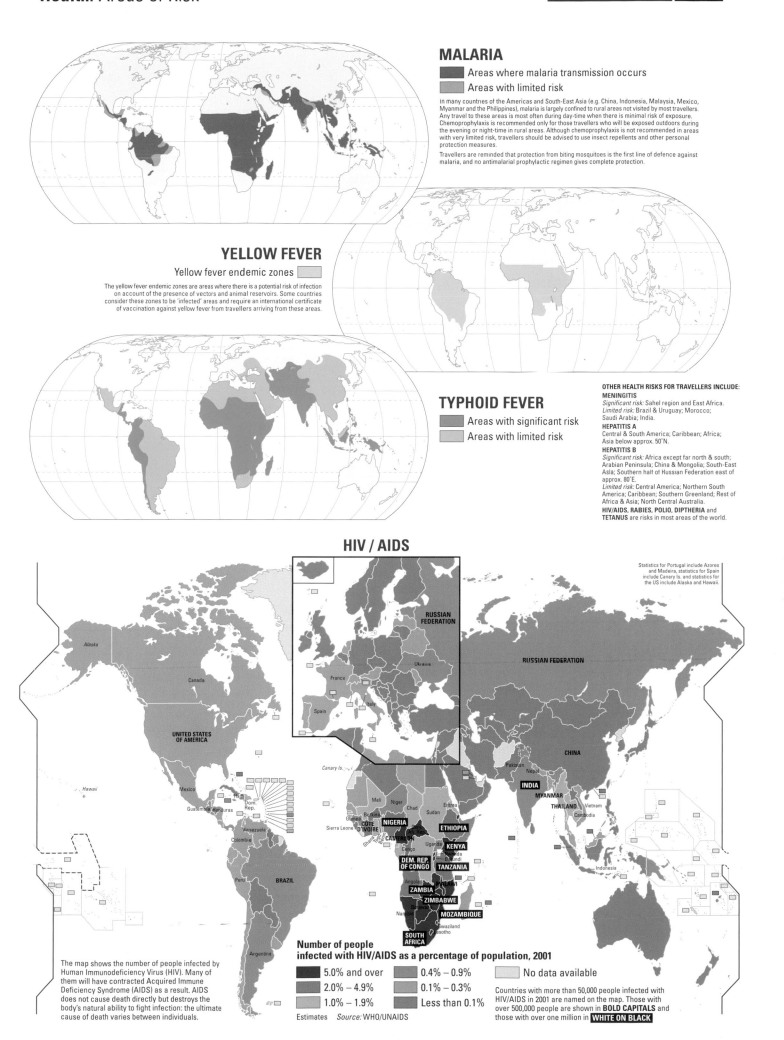

MALARIA

- Areas where malaria transmission occurs
- Areas with limited risk

In many countries of the Americas and South-East Asia (e.g. China, Indonesia, Malaysia, Mexico, Myanmar and the Philippines), malaria is largely confined to rural areas not visited by most travellers. Any travel to these areas is most often during day-time when there is minimal risk of exposure. Chemoprophylaxis is recommended only for those travellers who will be exposed outdoors during the evening or night-time in rural areas. Although chemoprophylaxis is not recommended in areas with very limited risk, travellers should be advised to use insect repellents and other personal protection measures.

Travellers are reminded that protection from biting mosquitoes is the first line of defence against malaria, and no antimalarial prophylactic regimen gives complete protection.

YELLOW FEVER

Yellow fever endemic zones

The yellow fever endemic zones are areas where there is a potential risk of infection on account of the presence of vectors and animal reservoirs. Some countries consider these zones to be 'infected' areas and require an international certificate of vaccination against yellow fever from travellers arriving from these areas.

TYPHOID FEVER

- Areas with significant risk
- Areas with limited risk

OTHER HEALTH RISKS FOR TRAVELLERS INCLUDE:
MENINGITIS
Significant risk: Sahel region and East Africa.
Limited risk: Brazil & Uruguay; Morocco; Saudi Arabia; India.
HEPATITIS A
Central & South America; Caribbean; Africa; Asia below approx. 50°N.
HEPATITIS B
Significant risk: Africa except far north & south; Arabian Peninsula; China & Mongolia; South-East Asia; Southern half of Russian Federation east of approx. 80°E.
Limited risk: Central America; Northern South America; Caribbean; Southern Greenland; Rest of Africa & Asia; North Central Australia.
HIV/AIDS, RABIES, POLIO, DIPTHERIA and **TETANUS** are risks in most areas of the world.

HIV / AIDS

Statistics for Portugal include Azores and Madeira, statistics for Spain include Canary Is. and statistics for the US include Alaska and Hawaii.

The map shows the number of people infected by Human Immunodeficiency Virus (HIV). Many of them will have contracted Acquired Immune Deficiency Syndrome (AIDS) as a result. AIDS does not cause death directly but destroys the body's natural ability to fight infection: the ultimate cause of death varies between individuals.

Number of people infected with HIV/AIDS as a percentage of population, 2001

- 5.0% and over
- 2.0% – 4.9%
- 1.0% – 1.9%
- 0.4% – 0.9%
- 0.1% – 0.3%
- Less than 0.1%
- No data available

Estimates   *Source:* WHO/UNAIDS

Countries with more than 50,000 people infected with HIV/AIDS in 2001 are named on the map. Those with over 500,000 people are shown in **BOLD CAPITALS** and those with over one million in WHITE ON BLACK

Sport

MAJOR INTERNATIONAL SPORTING EVENTS

SUMMER OLYMPICS
The first modern Olympic Games, founded by Frenchman Baron de Coubertin, were held at Athens in 1896. They are held every four years. An extra Olympics were held in 1906 to celebrate the tenth anniversary of the 1896 games. The next Games are due to be held in Athens in 2004 and Beijing in 2008.

WINTER OLYMPICS
The first separate Winter Games took place in 1924 at Chamonix, France. The games originally took place in the same year as the Summer Olympics, but beginning in 1994, are now held in between the Summer Games. The next Winter Olympics are due to be held in Turin in 2006 and Vancouver in 2010.

COMMONWEALTH GAMES
Originally the British Empire Games and first held in 1930 at Hamilton, Ontario. Renamed the British Empire and Commonwealth Games in 1954, the British Commonwealth Games in 1970 and the Commonwealth Games in 1978. Held every four years, the next Games are due to be held in Melbourne in 2006.

WORLD ATHLETICS CHAMPIONSHIPS
The World Athletics Championships were first held in Helsinki in 1983, and at four-year intervals until 1991. They are now held every two years. The next Championships are due to be held in Helsinki in 2005 and Osaka in 2007.

FOOTBALL WORLD CUP
Association Football's premier event. Brazil kept the Jules Rimet Trophy after winning it for the third time in 1970. The teams now compete for the FIFA World Cup. Held every four years, the next competition is due to be hosted by Germany in 2006.

CRICKET WORLD CUP
The venue of the first Cricket World Cup in 1975 was England. Played every three to five years, it was not until 1987 that the competition was held outside England. The next World Cup is due to be held in the West Indies in 2007.

RUGBY UNION WORLD CUP
The first Rugby Union World Cup was held in 1987 and is now held every four years, with the next competition in France in 2007.

FOOTBALL WORLD CUP FINAL RESULTS

1930	Uruguay 4	Argentina 2
1934	Italy 2	Czechoslovakia 1
1938	Italy 4	Hungary 2
1950	Uruguay 2	Brazil 1
1954	FR Germany 3	Hungary 2
1958	Brazil 5	Sweden 2
1962	Brazil 3	Czechoslovakia 1
1966	England 4	FR Germany 2
1970	Brazil 4	Italy 1
1974	FR Germany 2	Netherlands 1
1978	Argentina 3	Netherlands 1
1982	Italy 3	FR Germany 1
1986	Argentina 3	FR Germany 2
1990	FR Germany 1	Argentina 0
1994	Brazil 0	Italy 0
	(Brazil won 3–2 on penalties)	
1998	France 3	Brazil 0
2002	Brazil 2	Germany 0

RUGBY UNION WORLD CUP FINAL RESULTS

1987	New Zealand 29	France 9
1991	Australia 12	England 6
1995	South Africa 15	New Zealand 12
1999	Australia 35	France 12

FIFA WORLD RANKINGS

	May1996	1997	1998	1999	2000	2001	2002	2003
Brazil	1	1	1	4	3	2	=2	1
France	5	4	17	2	1	1	=2	2
Spain	5	6	15	8	4	4	6	3
Germany	2	2	2	3	11	9	11	4
Argentina	8	21	6	9	2	3	5	5
Netherlands	13	7	25	21	8	5	7	6
England	24	13	5	11	12	14	12	7
Turkey	30	42	53	34	29	22	8	8
Mexico	12	12	4	13	=8	7	9	9
United States	14	26	11	24	19	15	13	=10
Denmark	11	3	27	18	13	20	20	=10
Italy	7	6	14	7	6	4	4	12
Czech Rep.	10	8	3	5	5	5	15	13
Portugal	18	16	39	15	15	5	14	14
Ireland	44	44	46	38	39	27	15	15
Belgium	40	31	36	27	30	30	54	16
Costa Rica	87	53	58	65	69	38	29	17
Cameroon	33	41	42	38	27	37	17	18

CRICKET WORLD CUP FINAL RESULTS

1975	West Indies (291-8) beat Australia (274) by 17 runs
1979	West Indies (286-9) beat England (194) by 92 runs
1983	India (183) beat West Indies (140) by 43 runs
1987	Australia (253-5) beat England (246-8) by 7 runs
1992	Pakistan (249-6) beat England (227) by 22 runs
1996	Sri Lanka (245-3) beat Australia (241) by 7 wickets
1999	Australia (133-2) beat Pakistan (132) by 8 wickets
2003	Australia (359-2) beat India (234) by 125 runs

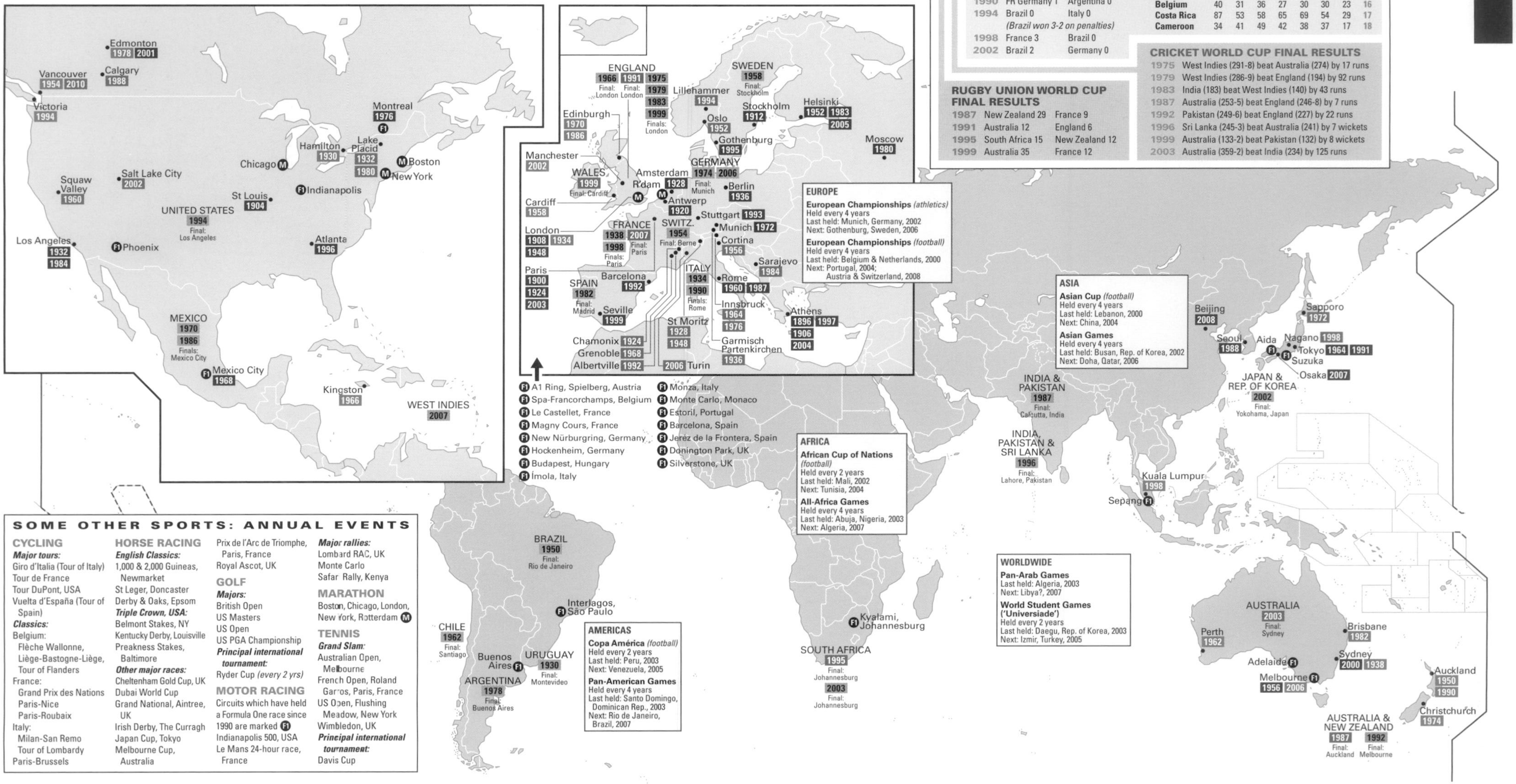

SOME OTHER SPORTS: ANNUAL EVENTS

CYCLING
Major tours:
Giro d'Italia (Tour of Italy)
Tour de France
Tour DuPont, USA
Vuelta d'España (Tour of Spain)
Classics:
Belgium:
Flèche Wallonne,
Liège-Bastogne-Liège,
Tour of Flanders
France:
Grand Prix des Nations
Paris-Nice
Paris-Roubaix
Italy:
Milan-San Remo
Tour of Lombardy
Paris-Brussels

HORSE RACING
English Classics:
1,000 & 2,000 Guineas, Newmarket
St Leger, Doncaster
Derby & Oaks, Epsom
Triple Crown, USA:
Belmont Stakes, NY
Kentucky Derby, Louisville
Preakness Stakes, Baltimore
Other major races:
Cheltenham Gold Cup, UK
Dubai World Cup
Grand National, Aintree, UK
Irish Derby, The Curragh
Japan Cup, Tokyo
Melbourne Cup, Australia

GOLF
Prix de l'Arc de Triomphe, Paris, France
Royal Ascot, UK
Majors:
British Open
US Masters
US Open
US PGA Championship
Principal international tournament:
Ryder Cup (every 2 yrs)

MOTOR RACING
Circuits which have held a Formula One race since 1990 are marked Ⓕ
Indianapolis 500, USA
Le Mans 24-hour race, France

MARATHON
Boston, Chicago, London, New York, Rotterdam Ⓜ

TENNIS
Grand Slam:
Australian Open, Melbourne
French Open, Roland Garros, Paris, France
US Open, Flushing Meadow, New York
Wimbledon, UK
Principal international tournament:
Davis Cup

Major rallies:
Lombard RAC, UK
Monte Carlo
Safari Rally, Kenya

Map location labels

- Auckland 1950 1990
- Christchurch 1974
- Brisbane 1982
- Sydney 2000 1938
- Adelaide Ⓕ
- Melbourne Ⓕ 1956 2006
- Perth 1962
- **AUSTRALIA**
- **AUSTRALIA & NEW ZEALAND** Final: Auckland Final: Melbourne
- Sapporo 1972
- Aida Ⓕ
- Nagano 1998 1991
- Tokyo 1964 2007
- Suzuka Ⓕ
- Osaka 2007
- **JAPAN & REP. OF KOREA** 2002 Final: Yokohama, Japan
- Seoul 1988
- Beijing 2008
- Kuala Lumpur 1998
- Sepang Ⓕ
- **INDIA & PAKISTAN** 1987 Final: Calcutta, India
- **INDIA, PAKISTAN & SRI LANKA** 1996 Final: Lahore, Pakistan
- Kyalami, Johannesburg Ⓕ
- **SOUTH AFRICA** 1995 Final: Johannesburg
- 2003 Final: Johannesburg
- Moscow 1980
- Helsinki 1952 1983 2005
- Stockholm 1912 Final: Stockholm
- **SWEDEN** 1958
- Gothenburg 1995
- Oslo 1952
- Lillehammer 1994
- **GERMANY** 1974 2006
- Berlin 1936 Final: Munich
- Amsterdam 1928
- R'dam 1920 Ⓜ Final: Rotterdam
- Antwerp 1920
- Stuttgart 1993
- Munich 1972
- Cortina 1956
- **SWITZ.** 1954 Final: Berne
- Sarajevo 1984
- **ITALY** 1934 1990 Final: Rome
- Rome 1960 1987
- Innsbruck 1964 1976
- Garmisch Partenkirchen 1936
- Athens 1896 1906 2004
- St Moritz 1928 1948
- 2006 Turin
- **FRANCE** 1938 1998 Final: Paris
- Paris 1900 1924 2003
- Chamonix 1924
- Grenoble 1968
- Albertville 1992
- Barcelona 1992
- **SPAIN** 1982 Final: Madrid
- Seville 1999
- **ENGLAND** 1966 1991 1975 Final: London
- London 1908 1948 Final: London
- Edinburgh 1970 1986
- Manchester 2002
- **WALES** 1999 Final: Cardiff
- Cardiff 1958
- Ⓕ A1 Ring, Spielberg, Austria
- Ⓕ Spa-Francorchamps, Belgium
- Ⓕ Le Castellet, France
- Ⓕ Magny Cours, France
- Ⓕ Nürburgring, Germany
- Ⓕ New Nürburgring, Germany
- Ⓕ Hockenheim, Germany
- Ⓕ Budapest, Hungary
- Ⓕ Imola, Italy
- Ⓕ Monza, Italy
- Ⓕ Monte Carlo, Monaco
- Ⓕ Estoril, Portugal
- Ⓕ Barcelona, Spain
- Ⓕ Jerez de la Frontera, Spain
- Ⓕ Donington Park, UK
- Ⓕ Silverstone, UK
- Edmonton 1978 2001
- Calgary 1988
- Vancouver 1954 2010
- Victoria 1994
- Montreal 1976 Ⓕ
- Lake Placid 1932 1980
- Hamilton 1930
- Chicago Ⓜ
- Indianapolis Ⓕ
- St Louis 1904
- Atlanta 1996
- Boston Ⓜ
- New York Ⓜ
- Salt Lake City 2002
- Squaw Valley 1960
- Los Angeles 1932 1984
- Phoenix
- **UNITED STATES** 1994 Final: Los Angeles
- Mexico City 1968
- **MEXICO** 1970 1986 Final: Mexico City
- Kingston 1966
- **WEST INDIES** 2007
- InterLagos, São Paulo Ⓕ
- **BRAZIL** 1950 Final: Rio de Janeiro
- **CHILE** 1962 Final: Santiago
- Buenos Aires Ⓕ
- **URUGUAY** 1930 Final: Montevideo
- **ARGENTINA** 1978 Final: Buenos Aires

Regional panels

ASIA
Asian Cup (football)
Held every 4 years
Last held: Lebanon, 2000
Next: China, 2004
Asian Games
Held every 4 years
Last held: Busan, Rep. of Korea, 2002
Next: Doha, Qatar, 2006

WORLDWIDE
Pan-Arab Games
Last held: Algeria, 2003
Next: Libya?, 2007
World Student Games ('Universiade')
Held every 2 years
Last held: Daegu, Rep. of Korea, 2003
Next: Izmir, Turkey, 2005

EUROPE
European Championships (athletics)
Held every 4 years
Last held: Munich, Germany, 2002
Next: Gothenburg, Sweden, 2006
European Championships (football)
Held every 4 years
Last held: Belgium & Netherlands, 2000
Next: Portugal, 2004;
Austria & Switzerland, 2008

AFRICA
African Cup of Nations (football)
Held every 2 years
Last held: Tunisia, 2004
Next: Mali, 2002
All-Africa Games
Held every 4 years
Last held: Abuja, Nigeria, 2003
Next: Algeria, 2007

AMERICAS
Copa América (football)
Held every 2 years
Last held: Peru, 2003
Next: Venezuela, 2005
Pan-American Games
Held every 4 years
Last held: Santo Domingo, Dominican Rep. 2003
Next: Rio de Janeiro, Brazil, 2007

MILITARY SPENDING

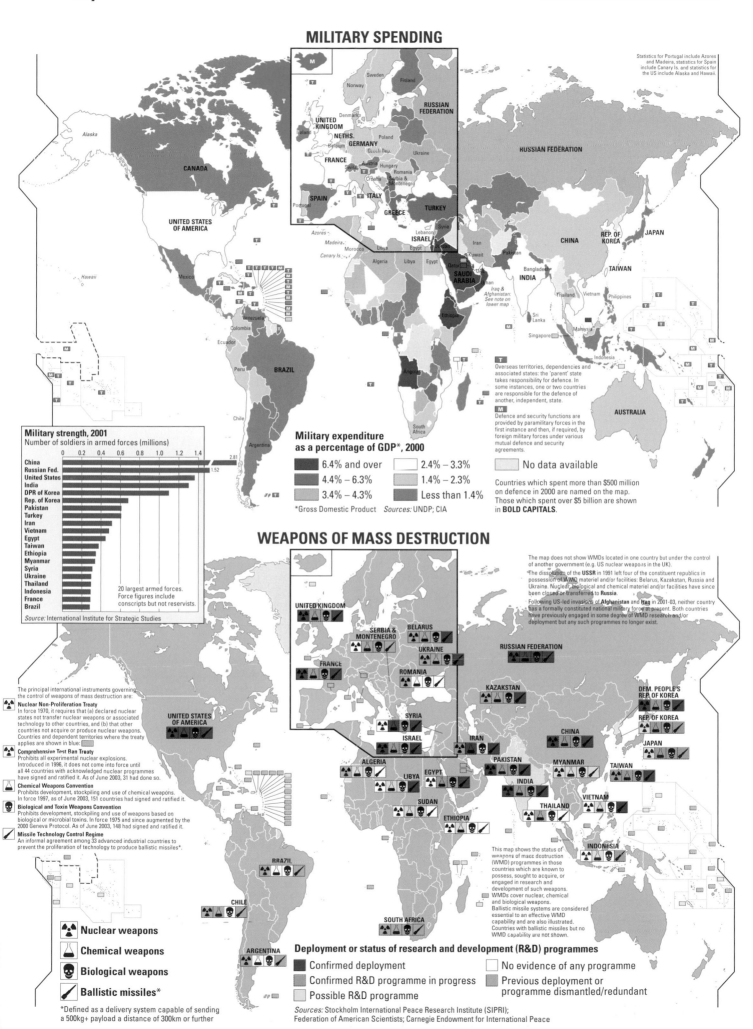

Statistics for Portugal include Azores and Madeira, statistics for Spain include Canary Is. and statistics for the US include Alaska and Hawaii.

T Overseas territories, dependencies and associated states: the 'parent' state takes responsibility for defence. In some instances, one or two countries are responsible for the defence of another, independent, state.

M Defence and security functions are provided by paramilitary forces in the first instance and then, if required, by foreign military forces under various mutual defence and security agreements.

Military expenditure as a percentage of GDP*, 2000

- 6.4% and over
- 4.4% – 6.3%
- 3.4% – 4.3%
- 2.4% – 3.3%
- 1.4% – 2.3%
- Less than 1.4%
- No data available

*Gross Domestic Product   *Sources:* UNDP; CIA

Countries which spent more than $500 million on defence in 2000 are named on the map. Those which spent over $5 billion are shown in **BOLD CAPITALS**.

Military strength, 2001
Number of soldiers in armed forces (millions)

	0	0.2	0.4	0.6	0.8	1.0	1.2	1.4	
China									2.81
Russian Fed.								1.52	
United States									
India									
DPR of Korea									
Rep. of Korea									
Pakistan									
Turkey									
Iran									
Vietnam									
Egypt									
Taiwan									
Ethiopia									
Myanmar									
Syria									
Ukraine									
Thailand									
Indonesia									
France									
Brazil									

20 largest armed forces. Force figures include conscripts but not reservists.

Source: International Institute for Strategic Studies

WEAPONS OF MASS DESTRUCTION

The map does not show WMDs located in one country but under the control of another government (e.g. US nuclear weapons in the UK).

The dissolution of the USSR in 1991 left four of the constituent republics in possession of WMD materiel and/or facilities: Belarus, Kazakstan, Russia and Ukraine. Nuclear, biological and chemical materiel and/or facilities have since been closed or transferred to Russia.

Following US-led invasions of Afghanistan and Iraq in 2001-03, neither country has a formally constituted national military force at present. Both countries have previously engaged in some degree of WMD research and/or deployment but any such programmes no longer exist.

The principal international instruments governing the control of weapons of mass destruction are:

Nuclear Non-Proliferation Treaty
In force 1970, it requires that (a) declared nuclear states not transfer nuclear weapons or associated technology to other countries, and (b) that other countries not acquire or produce nuclear weapons. Countries and dependent territories where the treaty applies are shown in blue:

Comprehensive Test Ban Treaty
Prohibits all experimental nuclear explosions. Introduced in 1996, it does not come into force until all 44 countries with acknowledged nuclear programmes have signed and ratified it. As of June 2003, 31 had done so.

Chemical Weapons Convention
Prohibits development, stockpiling and use of chemical weapons. In force 1997, as of June 2003, 151 countries had signed and ratified it.

Biological and Toxin Weapons Convention
Prohibits development, stockpiling and use of weapons based on biological or microbial toxins. In force 1975 and since augmented by the 2000 Geneva Protocol. As of June 2003, 148 had signed and ratified it.

Missile Technology Control Regime
An informal agreement among 33 advanced industrial countries to prevent the proliferation of technology to produce ballistic missiles*.

This map shows the status of weapons of mass destruction (WMD) programmes in those countries which are known to possess, sought to acquire, or engaged in research and development of such weapons. WMDs cover nuclear, chemical and biological weapons. Ballistic missile systems are considered essential to an effective WMD capability and are also illustrated. Countries with ballistic missiles but no WMD capability are not shown.

Nuclear weapons
Chemical weapons
Biological weapons
Ballistic missiles*

*Defined as a delivery system capable of sending a 500kg+ payload a distance of 300km or further

Deployment or status of research and development (R&D) programmes

- Confirmed deployment
- Confirmed R&D programme in progress
- Possible R&D programme
- No evidence of any programme
- Previous deployment or programme dismantled/redundant

Sources: Stockholm International Peace Research Institute (SIPRI); Federation of American Scientists; Carnegie Endowment for International Peace

The world's main airports are shown here with their IATA international three-letter codes.

Many cities have more than one airport, and a separate code for the city itself. The codes shown here are for each city's principal airport or airports.

International Air Transport Association (IATA) Conference Areas

Area 1:
North Atlantic
Mid Atlantic
South Atlantic
Main office: Montréal

Area 2:
Europe
Middle East
Africa
East Africa
Main office: Geneva

Area 3:
Asia
SW Pacific
Main office: Singapore

World airline traffic

Billion passenger-kilometres (international & domestic passenger services)

World total
United States

1990 92 94 96 98 2000 02 04

Sources: International Civil Aviation Organisation; ATA

ABJ Abidjan, Côte d'Ivoire
ABQ Albuquerque, NM, USA
ABV Abuja, Nigeria
ACA Acapulco, Mexico
ACC Accra, Ghana
ADD Adis Abeba (Addis Ababa), Ethiopia
ADE Adan (Aden), Yemen
ADL Adelaide, Australia
AKL Auckland, New Zealand
ALA Almaty, Kazakstan
ALB Albany, NY, USA
ANC Anchorage, AK, USA
ANU Antigua
APW Apia, Samoa
ARI Arica, Chile
ASB Ashgabat, Turkmenistan
ASM Asmara, Eritrea
ASU Asunción, Paraguay
ATL Atlanta, GA, USA
AUH Abu Zaby (Abu Dhabi), UAE
BAH Bahrain
BAK Baki (Baku), Azerbaijan
BAQ Barranquilla, Colombia
BDA Bermuda
BDL Hartford-Springfield, CT, USA
BEL Belém, Brazil
BEW Beira, Mozambique
BGF Bangui, Central African Republic
BGI Barbados
BGW Baghdad, Iraq
BIL Billings, MT, USA
BJL Banjul, The Gambia
BJM Bujumbura, Burundi
BKI Kota Kinabalu, Malaysia
BKK Bangkok (Krung Thep), Thailand
BKO Bamako, Mali
BNA Nashville, TN, USA
BNE Brisbane, Australia
BOG Bogotá, Colombia
BOI Boise, ID, USA
BOM Mumbai (Bombay), India
BOS Boston, MA, USA
BSB Brasilia, Brazil
BUF Buffalo, NY, USA
BWI Baltimore-Washington International, MD, USA
BWN Bandar Seri Begawan, Brunei
BZE Belize City, Belize
BZV Brazzaville, Congo
CAN Guangzhou (Canton), China
CAY Cayenne, French Guiana
CBR Canberra, Australia

CBU Cebu, the Philippines
CCS Caracas, Venezuela
CCU Kolkata (Calcutta), India
CGK Jakarta, Indonesia
CHC Christchurch, New Zealand
CKY Conakry, Guinea
CLE Cleveland, OH, USA
CLT Charlotte, NC, USA
CMB Colombo, Sri Lanka
CMM Columbus, OH, USA
CNS Cairns, Australia
CNX Chiang Mai, Thailand
COO Cotonou, Benin
COR Córdoba, Argentina
CPT Cape Town, South Africa
CTU Chengdu, China
CUU Chihuahua, Mexico
CVG Cincinnati-N Kentucky, OH-KY, USA
DAC Dhaka, Bangladesh
DAR Dar es Salaam, Tanzania
DCA Washington Ronald Reagan, VA, USA
DEL Delhi, India
DEN Denver, CO, USA
DFW Dallas-Fort Worth, TX, USA
DIL Dili, East Timor
DKR Dakar, Senegal
DLA Douala, Cameroon
DMM Ad Dammam, Saudi Arabia
DOH Ad Dawhah (Doha), Qatar
DPS Denpasar, Bali, Indonesia
DRW Darwin, Australia
DTW Detroit, MI, USA
DUR Durban, South Africa
DXB Dubayy (Dubai), UAE
DYU Dushanbe, Tajikistan
EBB Entebbe, Uganda
EVN Yerevan, Armenia

EWR Newark, NJ, USA
EZE Buenos Aires, Argentina
FIH Kinshasa, Democratic Republic of Congo
FLL Fort Lauderdale-Hollywood, FL, USA
FNA Freetown, Sierra Leone
FNC Funchal, Madeira
FNJ P'yongyang, Democratic People's Republic of Korea
FPO Freeport, Bahamas
FRU Bishkek, Kyrgyzstan
FUK Fukuoka, Japan
GBE Gaborone, Botswana
GDL Guadalajara, Mexico
GDX Magadan, Russian Federation
GEG Spokane, WA, USA
GEO Georgetown, Guyana
GIG Rio de Janeiro, Brazil
GND Grenada
GOH Nuuk (Godthåb), Greenland
GRU São Paulo-Guarulhos, Brazil
GUA Ciudad de Guatemala (Guatemala City), Guatemala
GUM Guam
GYE Guayaquil, Ecuador
HAN Hanoi, Vietnam
HAV La Habana (Havana), Cuba
HBA Hobart, Tasmania, Australia
HIR Honiara, Solomon Is.
HKG Hong Kong (Xianggang), China
HKT Phuket, Thailand
HND Tokyo Haneda, Japan
HNL Honolulu, HI, USA
HRE Harare, Zimbabwe
IAD Washington Dulles, VA, USA
IAH Houston, TX, USA
ICN Seoul Incheon, Republic of Korea

IKT Irkutsk, Russian Federation
IND Indianapolis, IN, USA
IPC Easter Island
ISB Islamabad, Pakistan
ITM Osaka Itami, Japan
JAX Jacksonville, FL, USA
JED Jiddah (Jeddah), Saudi Arabia
JFK New York John F. Kennedy, NY, USA
JIB Djibouti
JNB Johannesburg, South Africa
JRO Kilimanjaro, Tanzania
KAN Kano, Nigeria
KBL Kabul, Afghanistan
KCH Kuching, Malaysia
KEF Reykjavík, Iceland
KGL Kigali, Rwanda
KHH Kaohsiung, Taiwan
KHI Karachi, Pakistan
KHV Khabarovsk, Russian Federation
KIN Kingston, Jamaica
KIX Osaka Kansai, Japan
KJA Krasnoyarsk, Russian Federation
KRT Khartoum, Sudan
KTM Kathmandu, Nepal
KUF Samara, Russian Federation
KUL Kuala Lumpur, Malaysia
KWI Al Kuwayt (Kuwait)
LAD Luanda, Angola
LAS Las Vegas, NV, USA
LAX Los Angeles, CA, USA
LBV Libreville, Gabon
LFW Lomé, Togo
LGA New York LaGuardia, NY, USA
LHE Lahore, Pakistan
LIM Lima, Peru
LLW Lilongwe, Malawi
LOS Lagos, Nigeria

LPA Las Palmas de Gran Canaria, Canary Is.
LPB La Paz, Bolivia
LUN Lusaka, Zambia
LXA Lhasa, China
LXR Luxor, Egypt
MAA Chennai (Madras), India
MAO Manaus, Brazil
MBA Mombasa, Kenya
MCI Kansas City, MO, USA
MCO Orlando, FL, USA
MCT Masqat (Muscat), Oman
MEL Melbourne, Australia
MEM Memphis, TN, USA
MES Medan, Indonesia
MEX Ciudad de México (Mexico City), Mexico
MGA Managua, Nicaragua
MGQ Muqdisho (Mogadishu), Somalia
MIA Miami, FL, USA
MKE Milwaukee, WI, USA
MLE Malé, Maldives
MMK Murmansk, Russian Federation
MNL Manila, the Philippines
MPM Maputo, Mozambique

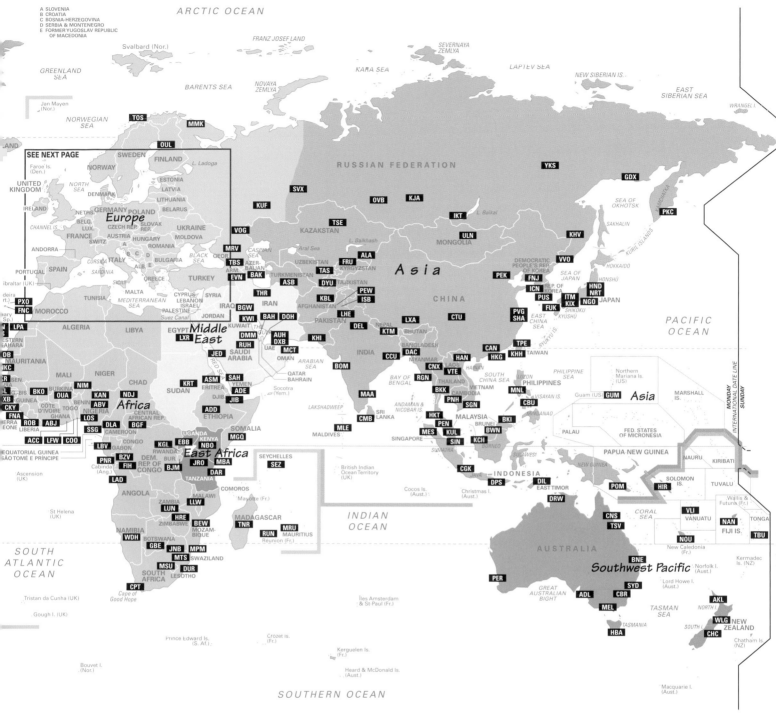

MRU	Mauritius		**PBM**	Paramaribo, Surinam		**RAI**	Praia, Cape Verde		**SJU**	San Juan, Puerto Rico		**UIO**	Quito, Ecuador
MRV	Mineral'nyye Vody, Russian Federation		**PDL**	Ponta Delgada, São Miguel, Azores		**RAR**	Rarotonga, Cook Is.		**SKB**	St Kitts		**ULN**	Ulaanbaatar (Ulan Bator), Mongolia
MSP	Minneapolis-St Paul, MN, USA		**PDX**	Portland, OR, USA		**RDU**	Raleigh-Durham, NC, USA		**SLC**	Salt Lake City, UT, USA		**UVF**	Hewanorra, St Lucia
MSU	Maseru, Lesotho		**PEK**	Beijing (Peking), China		**REC**	Recife, Brazil		**SMA**	Santa Maria, Azores		**VLI**	Port-Vila, Vanuatu
MSY	New Orleans, LA, USA		**PEN**	Pinang (Penang), Malaysia		**RGL**	Río Gallegos, Argentina		**SRZ**	Santa Cruz, Bolivia		**VOG**	Volgograd, Russian Federation
MTS	Manzini, Swaziland		**PER**	Perth, Australia		**RGN**	Yangon (Rangoon), Myanmar		**SSA**	Salvador, Brazil		**VTE**	Viangchan (Vientiane), Laos
MTY	Monterrey, Mexico		**PEW**	Peshawar, Pakistan		**ROB**	Monrovia, Liberia		**SSG**	Malabo, Equatorial Guinea		**VVO**	Vladivostok, Russian Federation
MVD	Montevideo, Uruguay		**PHL**	Philadelphia, PA, USA		**RSW**	Southwest Florida, FL, USA		**STL**	St Louis, MO, USA		**WDH**	Windhoek, Namibia
NAN	Nadi, Fiji Is.		**PHX**	Phoenix, AZ, USA		**RUH**	Ar Riyad (Riyadh), Saudi Arabia		**SVD**	St Vincent		**WLG**	Wellington, New Zealand
NAS	Nassau, Bahamas		**PIT**	Pittsburgh, PA, USA		**RUN**	Réunion		**SVX**	Yekaterinburg, Russian Federation		**YEG**	Edmonton, AL, Canada
NBO	Nairobi, Kenya		**PKC**	Petropavlovsk-Kamchatskiy, Russian Federation		**SAH**	Sana'a (Sana), Yemen		**SYD**	Sydney, Australia		**YFB**	Iqaluit, NU, Canada
NDB	Nouadhibou, Mauritania		**PNH**	Phnom Penh, Cambodia		**SAL**	San Salvador, El Salvador		**TAS**	Toshkent (Tashkent), Uzbekistan		**YHM**	Hamilton, OT, Canada
NDJ	N'djamena, Chad		**PNR**	Pointe-Noire, Congo		**SAN**	San Diego, CA, USA		**TBS**	T'bilisi, Georgia		**YHZ**	Halifax, NS, Canada
NGO	Nagoya, Japan		**POM**	Port Moresby, Papua New Guinea		**SCL**	Santiago, Chile		**TBU**	Tongatapu, Tonga		**YKX**	Yakutsk, Russian Federation
NIM	Niamey, Niger					**SDQ**	Santo Domingo, Dominican Republic		**TER**	Terceira, Azores		**YMX**	Montréal Mirabel, QU, Canada
NKC	Nouakchott, Mauritania		**POP**	Puerto Plata, Dominican Republic		**SEA**	Seattle-Tacoma, WA, USA		**TFN**	Tenerife North, Canary Is.		**YOW**	Ottawa, OT, Canada
NOU	Nouméa, New Caledonia		**POS**	Port of Spain, Trinidad		**SEZ**	Mahé, Seychelles		**TFS**	Tenerife South, Canary Is.		**YQB**	Québec, QU, Canada
NRT	Tokyo Narita, Japan		**PPT**	Papeete, Tahiti, French Polynesia		**SFJ**	Kangerlussuaq, Greenland		**TGU**	Tegucigalpa, Honduras		**YQX**	Gander, NF, Canada
ORD	Chicago, IL, USA		**PTY**	Ciudad de Panamá (Panama City), Panama		**SFO**	San Francisco, CA, USA		**THR**	Tehran, Iran		**YUL**	Montréal Dorval, QU, Canada
OUA	Ouagadougou, Burkina					**SGN**	Ho Chi Minh City (Saigon), Vietnam		**TNR**	Antananarivo, Madagascar		**YVR**	Vancouver, BC, Canada
OUL	Oulu, Finland		**PUS**	Busan, Republic of Korea					**TOS**	Tromsø, Norway		**YWG**	Winnipeg, MN, Canada
OVB	Novosibirsk, Russian Federation		**PVG**	Shanghai Pudong, China		**SHA**	Shanghai Hongqiao, China		**TPA**	Tampa, FL, USA		**YXE**	Saskatoon, SA, Canada
			PXO	Porto Santo, Madeira		**SIN**	Singapore		**TPE**	Taipei, Taiwan		**YYC**	Calgary, AL, Canada
OXB	Bissau, Guinea-Bissau					**SJD**	San José del Cabo, Mexico		**TSE**	Astana, Kazakstan		**YYT**	St John's, NF, Canada
PAP	Port-au-Prince, Haiti					**SJO**	San José, Costa Rica		**TSV**	Townsville, Australia		**YYZ**	Toronto, OT, Canada
									UAK	Narsarsuaq, Greenland		**YZF**	Yellowknife, NT, Canada

Key (inset, top left):

A SLOVENIA
B CROATIA
C BOSNIA-HERZEGOVINA
D SERBIA & MONTENEGRO
E FORMER YUGOSLAV REPUBLIC OF MACEDONIA

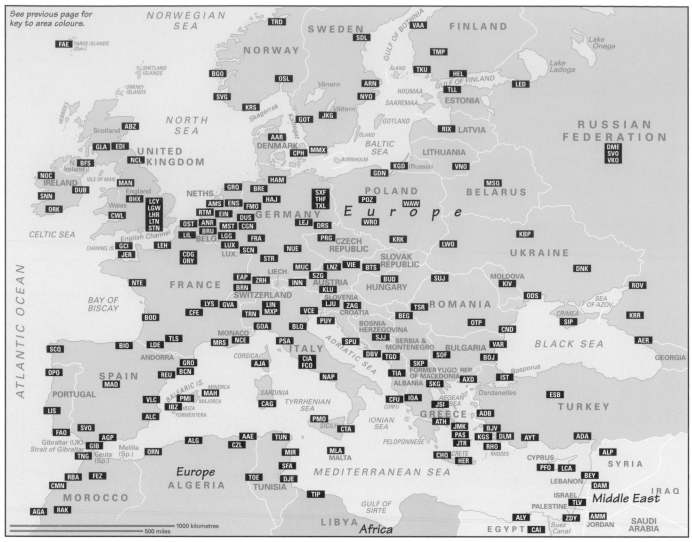

See previous page for key to area colours.

Europe and North Africa's main airports are shown here with their IATA international three-letter code.
Many cities have more than one airport, and a separate code for the city itself. The codes shown here are for each city's principal airport or airports.

AAE	Annaba, Algeria	BTS	Bratislava, Slovak Republic	GOT	Göteborg (Gothenburg), Sweden	MAN	Manchester, England
AAR	Århus, Denmark	BUD	Budapest, Hungary	GRO	Girona, Spain	MIR	Monastir, Tunisia
ABZ	Aberdeen, Scotland	CAG	Cágliari, Italy	GRQ	Groningen, The Netherlands	MLA	Malta
ADA	Adana, Russian Federation	CAI	El Qâhira (Cairo), Egypt	GVA	Genève (Geneva), Switzerland	MMX	Malmö, Sweden
ADB	Izmir (Smyrna), Turkey	CDG	Paris Roissy-Charles de Gaulle, France	HAJ	Hannover (Hanover), Germany	MRS	Marseille (Marseilles), France
AER	Adler-Sochi, Russian Federation	CFE	Clermont-Ferrand, France	HAM	Hamburg, Germany	MSQ	Minsk, Belarus
AGA	Agadir, Morocco	CFU	Kérkira (Corfu), Greece	HEL	Helsinki (Helsingfors), Finland	MST	Maastricht, The Netherlands
AGP	Málaga, Spain	CGN	Köln (Cologne)-Bonn, Germany	HER	Iráklio (Herakleion), Greece	MUC	München (Munich), Germany
AJA	Ajaccio, France	CHQ	Haniá (Canea), Greece	IBZ	Eivissa (Ibiza), Spain	MXP	Milano (Milan) Malpensa, Italy
ALC	Alacant (Alicante), Spain	CIA	Roma (Rome) Ciampino, Italy	INN	Innsbruck, Austria	NAP	Nápoli (Naples), Italy
ALG	Alger (Algiers), Algeria	CMN	Casablanca, Morocco	IOA	Ioánina, Greece	NCE	Nice, France
ALP	Halab (Aleppo), Syria	CND	Constanta, Romania	IST	Istanbul, Turkey	NCL	Newcastle, England
ALY	El Iskandarîya (Alexandria), Egypt	CPH	København (Copenhagen), Denmark	JER	Jersey	NOC	Horan (Knock), Ireland
AMM	Amman, Jordan	CTA	Catánia, Italy	JKG	Jönköping, Sweden	NTE	Nantes, France
AMS	Amsterdam, The Netherlands	CWL	Cardiff, Wales	JMK	Míkonos, Greece	NUE	Nürnberg (Nuremberg), Germany
ANR	Antwerpen (Antwerp), Belgium	CZL	Constantine, Algeria	JSI	Skíathos, Greece	NYO	Stockholm Skavsta, Sweden
ARN	Stockholm Arlanda, Sweden	DAM	Dimashq (Damascus), Syria	JTR	Thíra, Greece	ODS	Odesa (Odessa), Ukraine
ATH	Athína (Athens), Greece	DBV	Dubrovnik, Croatia	KBP	Kyiv (Kiev), Ukraine	OPO	Porto (Oporto), Portugal
AXD	Alexandroúpoli, Greece	DJE	Jerba, Tunisia	KGD	Kaliningrad, Russian Federation	ORK	Cork, Ireland
AYT	Antalya, Turkey	DLM	Dalaman, Turkey	KGS	Kós (Cos), Greece	ORN	Oran, Algeria
BCN	Barcelona, Spain	DME	Moskva (Moscow) Domodedovo, Russian Federation	KIV	Chisinau (Kishinev), Moldova	ORY	Paris Orly, France
BEG	Beograd (Belgrade), Serbia & Montenegro	DNK	Dnipropetrovs'k, Ukraine	KLU	Klagenfurt, Austria	OSL	Oslo, Norway
BEY	Bayrut (Beirut), Lebanon	DRS	Dresden, Germany	KRK	Kraków (Cracow), Poland	OST	Oostende (Ostend), Belgium
BFS	Belfast, Northern Ireland	DUB	Dublin, Ireland	KRR	Krasnodar, Russian Federation	OTP	Bucuresti (Bucharest), Romania
BGO	Bergen, Norway	DUS	Düsseldorf, Germany	KRS	Kristiansand, Norway	PAS	Páros, Greece
BHX	Birmingham, England	EAP	EuroAirport [Basel (BSL)-Mulhouse (MLH)-Freiburg], France/Germany/Switzerland	LCA	Larnaca, Cyprus	PFO	Pafos (Paphos), Cyprus
BIO	Bilbao, Spain	EDI	Edinburgh, Scotland	LCY	London City, England	PMI	Palma de Mallorca, Spain
BJV	Bodrum-Milas, Turkey	EIN	Eindhoven, The Netherlands	LDE	Lourdes-Tarbes, France	PMO	Palermo, Italy
BLQ	Bologna, Italy	ENS	Enschede, The Netherlands	LED	Sankt-Peterburg (St Petersburg), Russian Federation	POZ	Poznan, Poland
BOD	Bordeaux, France	ESB	Ankara, Turkey	LEH	Le Havre, France	PRG	Praha (Prague), Czech Republic
BOJ	Burgas, Bulgaria	FAE	Vágar, Faroe Islands	LEJ	Leipzig-Halle, Germany	PSA	Pisa, Italy
BRE	Bremen, Germany	FAO	Faro, Portugal	LGG	Liège, Belgium	PUY	Pula, Croatia
BRN	Bern (Berne), Switzerland	FCO	Roma (Rome) Fiumicino/Leonardo da Vinci, Italy	LGW	London Gatwick, England	RAK	Marrakech, Morocco
BRU	Bruxelles/Brussel (Brussels), Belgium	FEZ	Fès, Morocco	LHR	London Heathrow, England	RBA	Rabat, Morocco
		FMO	Münster-Osnabrück, Germany	LIL	Lille, France	REU	Reus, Spain
		FRA	Frankfurt am Main, Germany	LIN	Milano (Milan) Linate, Italy	RHO	Ródos (Rhodes), Greece
		GCI	Guernsey	LIS	Lisboa (Lisbon), Portugal	RIX	Riga, Latvia
		GDN	Gdansk, Poland	LJU	Ljubljana, Slovenia	ROV	Rostov-na-Donu, Russian Federation
		GIB	Gibraltar	LNZ	Linz, Austria	RTM	Rotterdam, The Netherlands
		GLA	Glasgow, Scotland	LTN	London Luton, England	SCN	Saarbrücken, Germany
		GOA	Génova (Genoa), Italy	LUX	Luxembourg	SCQ	Santiago de Compostela, Spain
				LWO	L'viv (L'vov), Ukraine	SDL	Sundsvall, Sweden
				LYS	Lyon (Lyons), France	SFA	Sfax, Tunisia
				MAD	Madrid, Spain	SIP	Simferopol, Ukraine
				MAH	Maó (Mahón), Spain	SJJ	Sarajevo, Bosnia-Herzegovina

SKG	Thessaloníki (Salonika), Greece
SKP	Skopje, Former Yugoslav Republic of Macedonia
SNN	Shannon, Ireland
SOF	Sofiya (Sofia), Bulgaria
SPU	Split, Croatia
STN	London Stansted, England
STR	Stuttgart, Germany
SUJ	Satu Mare, Romania
SVG	Stavanger, Norway
SVO	Moskva (Moscow) Sheremetyevo, Russian Federation
SVQ	Sevilla (Seville), Spain
SXF	Berlin Schönefeld, Germany
SZG	Salzburg, Austria
TGD	Podgorica, Serbia & Montenegro
THF	Berlin Tempelhof, Germany
TIA	Tiranë (Tirana), Albania
TIP	Tarabulus (Tripoli), Libya
TKU	Turku (Åbo), Finland
TLL	Tallinn, Estonia
TLS	Toulouse, France
TLV	Tel Aviv-Yafo, Israel
TMP	Tampere, Finland
TNG	Tanger (Tangier), Morocco
TOE	Tozeur, Tunisia
TRD	Trondheim, Norway
TRN	Torino (Turin), Italy
TSR	Timisoara, Romania
TUN	Tunis, Tunisia
TXL	Berlin Tegel, Germany
VAA	Vaasa (Vasa), Finland
VAR	Varna, Bulgaria
VCE	Venézia (Venice), Italy
VIE	Wien (Vienna), Austria
VKO	Moskva (Moscow) Vnukovo, Russian Federation
VLC	Valencia, Spain
VNO	Vilnius, Lithuania
WAW	Warszawa (Warsaw), Poland
WRO	Wroclaw, Poland
ZAG	Zagreb, Croatia
ZDY	Gaza, Palestine National Authority Region
ZRH	Zürich, Switzerland

Flight Times

Average flight times from London, New York and Singapore to other major destinations. Hours do not include stopover time, when necessary, from one destination to another.

Less than 2 hours
2 hours – 4 hours 59 mins
5 hours – 8 hours 59 mins
9 hours – 14 hours 59 mins
15 hours – 24 hours 59 mins
25 hours and over

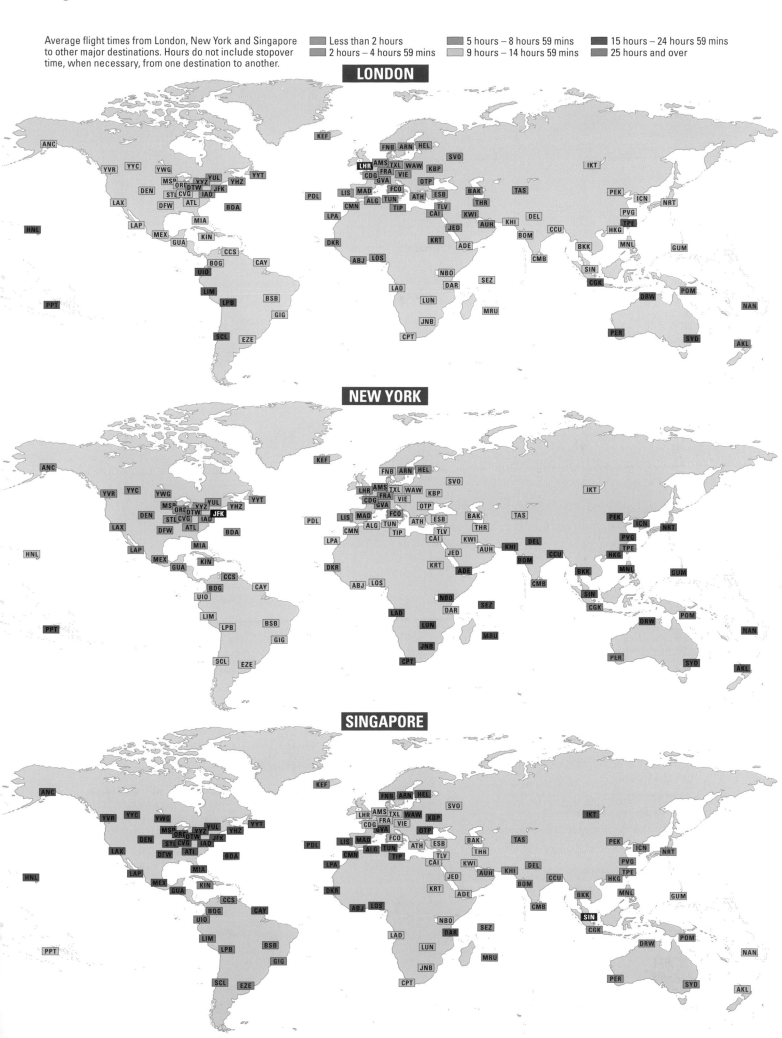

Cruising

The main ocean and river cruise areas are highlighted along with the most visited ports (red dots). Follow the green line for a typical three-month world cruise route. The Mediterranean and the Caribbean, the two most popular cruising regions, are shown in extra detail below.

Not all ships can dock alongside all ports. On these occasions, ship's launches are used to tender passengers ashore. In some remote regions such as Antarctica, passengers can only travel ashore by Zodiac boats.

Cruises are year-round except in the following regions, where climate or sea conditions limit the season:
Alaska: cruises scheduled between May and September;
US East Coast May – Sep;
Baltic May – Sep;
South Africa Nov – Mar;
Antarctica & South America (Cape Horn) Nov – Feb

Cruise passengers (millions)

Estimated regional breakdown, 2002 (thousands)

Caribbean/Florida (incl. Panama Canal) **5,500**
Mediterranean Sea/Black Sea/Red Sea **1,300**
Alaska/Canada **870**
Norwegian Fjords/Baltic **800**
Asia **650**
Mexican Riviera **580**
US East Coast **380**
Hawaiian Is. **220**
South America/Antarctica **220**
Bermuda **180**
Other regions **510**

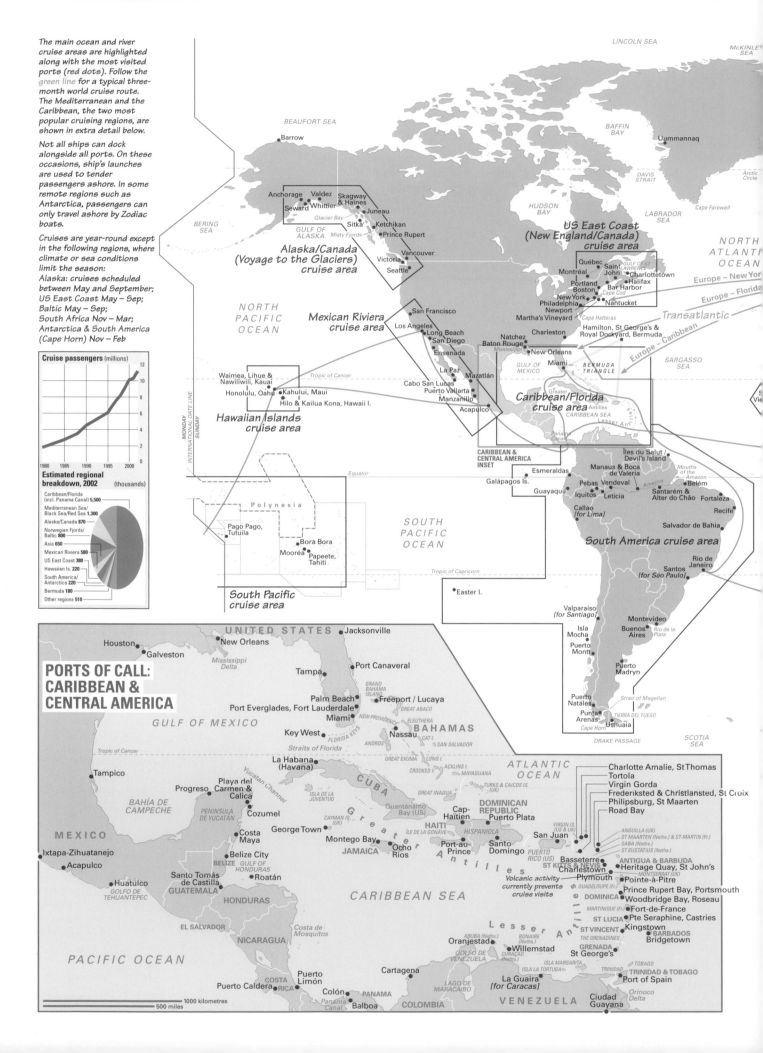

PORTS OF CALL: CARIBBEAN & CENTRAL AMERICA

Cruising

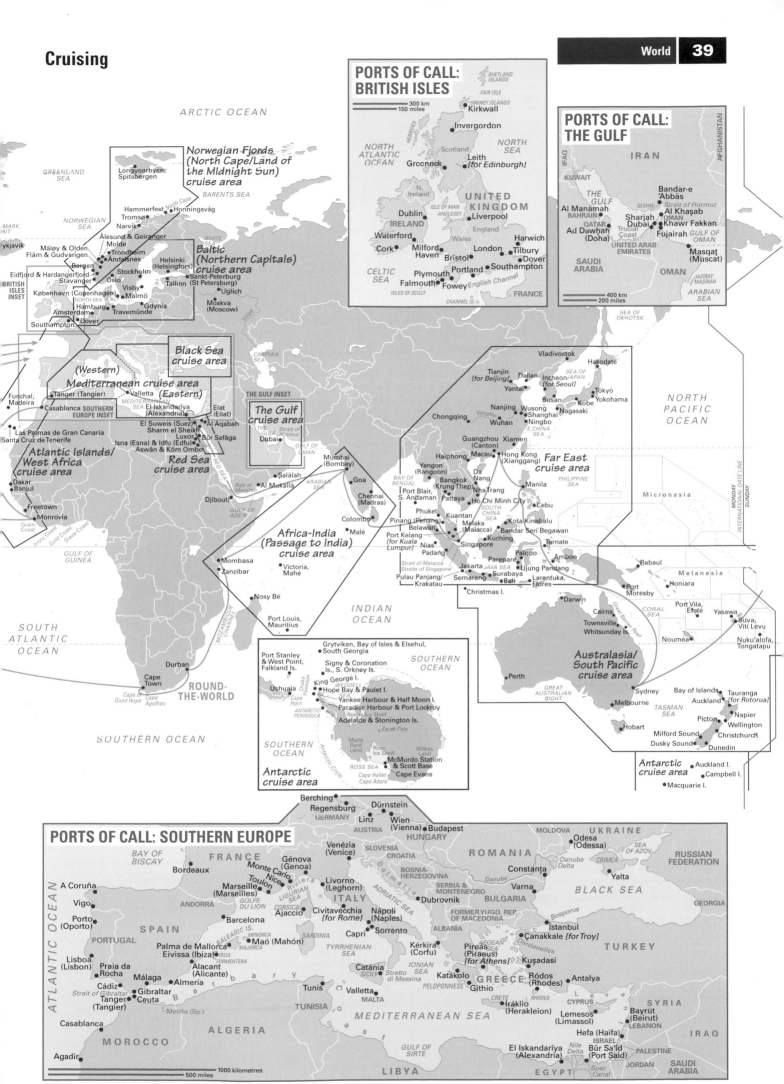

The UNESCO World Heritage List consists of sites considered to be of global importance either because of their natural heritage or their significant man-made contribution to world culture. Countries which are signatories to the World Heritage Convention can submit potential sites to UNESCO, which considers each proposal under strict criteria and lists each site where one or more natural or cultural criteria have been met. Some sites satisfy both natural and cultural criteria; these appear on both maps.

The natural sites shown here are either: significant natural features, areas which constitute the habitat of threatened species of outstanding value, or areas of outstanding scientific or conservation value or natural beauty.

Sites nominated should fulfil one or more of the following criteria. They should:
(i) be outstanding examples representing major stages in earth's history; or
(ii) be outstanding examples representing significant on-going ecological and biological processes; or
(iii) contain superlative natural phenomena or areas of outstanding natural beauty and aesthetic importance; or
(iv) contain the most important habitats for conservation of biological diversity, including significant threatened species.

Properties named in red are included on the list of World Heritage in Danger.
Those shown in italics are joint natural and cultural sites.

For further information, contact:

UNESCO World Heritage Centre,
7 place de Fontenoy,
75352 Paris 07 SP,
France.
Tel: +33 (0)1 45 68 15 71.
www.unesco.org/whc/

Sites marked with an asterisk (*) are featured in Columbus Travel Guides' *Tourist Attractions and Events of the World*

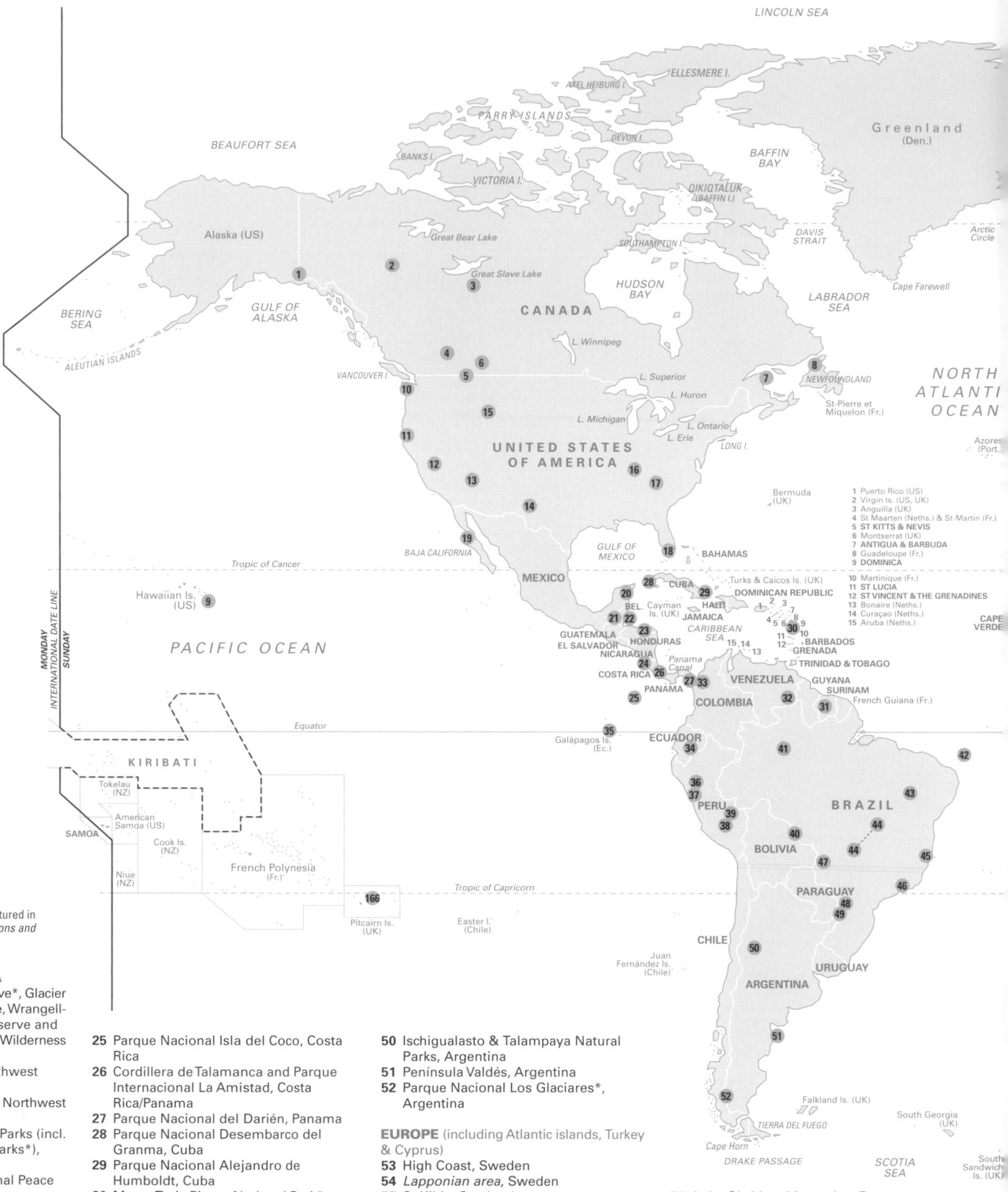

UNITED STATES & CANADA

1 Kluane National Park & Reserve*, Glacier Bay National Park & Preserve, Wrangell-St Elias National Park & Preserve and Tatshenshini-Alsek Provincial Wilderness Park, Alaska/Yukon
2 Nahanni National Park, Northwest Territories
3 Wood Buffalo National Park, Northwest Territories/Alberta
4 Canadian Rocky Mountains Parks (incl. Banff and Jasper National Parks*), British Columbia/Alberta
5 Waterton-Glacier International Peace Park, Alberta/Montana
6 Dinosaur Provincial Park, Alberta
7 Miguasha Provincial Park, Québec
8 Gros Morne National Park, Newfoundland
9 Hawaii Volcanoes National Park*, Hawaii
10 Olympic National Park, Washington
11 Redwood National Park, California
12 Yosemite National Park*, California
13 Grand Canyon National Park*, Arizona
14 Carlsbad Caverns National Park, New Mexico
15 Yellowstone National Park*, Wyoming
16 Mammoth Cave National Park, Kentucky
17 Great Smoky Mountains National Park, Tennessee/North Carolina
18 **Everglades National Park***, Florida

LATIN AMERICA & THE CARIBBEAN

19 El Vizcaíno whale sanctuary, Mexico
20 Reserva de la Biósfera Sian Ka'an, Mexico
21 *Parque Nacional Tikal**, Guatemala
22 Barrier Reef Reserve System, Belize
23 **Reserva de la Biósfera Río Plátano**, Honduras
24 Area de Conservación Guanacaste, Costa Rica
25 Parque Nacional Isla del Coco, Costa Rica
26 Cordillera de Talamanca and Parque Internacional La Amistad, Costa Rica/Panama
27 Parque Nacional del Darién, Panama
28 Parque Nacional Desembarco del Granma, Cuba
29 Parque Nacional Alejandro de Humboldt, Cuba
30 Morne Trois Pitons National Park*, Dominica
31 Central Surinam Nature Reserve, Surinam
32 Parque Nacional Canaima, Venezuela
33 Parque Nacional Los Katios, Colombia
34 **Parque Nacional Sangay**, Ecuador
35 Parque Nacional Galápagos*
36 *Parque Nacional Río Abiseo*, Peru
37 Parque Nacional Huascarán, Peru
38 *Santuario histórico Machu Picchu**, Peru
39 *Parque Nacional del Manú*, Peru*
40 Parque Nacional Noel Kempff Mercado, Bolivia
41 Parque Nacional Jaú, Brazil
42 Fernando de Noronha and Atol das Rocas, Brazil
43 Parque Nacional da Serra da Capivara, Brazil
44 Parque Nacional da Chapada dos Veadeiros and Parque Nacional das Emas, Brazil
45 Discovery Coast Atlantic forest reserves, Brazil
46 Southeast Atlantic forest reserves, Brazil
47 Pantanal conservation area, Brazil
48 Parque Nacional do Iguaçu*, Brazil
49 Parque Nacional de Iguazú*, Argentina

50 Ischigualasto & Talampaya Natural Parks, Argentina
51 Península Valdés, Argentina
52 Parque Nacional Los Glaciares*, Argentina

EUROPE (including Atlantic islands, Turkey & Cyprus)

53 High Coast, Sweden
54 *Lapponian area*, Sweden
55 St Kilda, Scotland
56 Giant's Causeway* and its coast, Northern Ireland
57 Dorset and East Devon coast, England
58 Messel Pit fossil site, Germany
59 Paris: banks of the Seine, France
60 Mont-St-Michel* and its bay, France
61 Golfe de Girolata, Golfe de Porto, Piana Calanches and Réserve naturelle Scandola, Corsica, France
62 *Mont Perdu/Monte Perdido*, France/Spain
63 *Ibiza: biodiversity and culture*, Spain
64 Parque Nacional Doñana, Spain
65 Laurisilva of Madeira
66 Parque Nacional de Garajonay, Gomera, Canary Is.
67 Jungfrau-Aletsch-Bietschhorn, Switzerland
68 *Ísole Eólie (Lipari)*, Italy
69 Bialowieza Forest & Belovezhskaya Pushcha, Poland/Belarus
70 Aggtelek Caves and the Slovak karst, Hungary/Slovak Republic
71 Skocjan Caves, Slovenia
72 Plitvice Lakes National Park*, Croatia
73 Durmitor National Park, Serbia & Montenegro

74 *Lake Ohrid and its region*, Former Yugoslav Republic of Macedonia
75 Danube Delta, Romania
76 Srebarna Nature Reserve, Bulgaria
77 Pirin National Park, Bulgaria
78 *Metéora*, Greece
79 *Athos*, Greece
80 *Hierapolis-Pamukkale*, Turkey
81 *Göreme National Park* and Cappadocia rock sites*, Turkey

RUSSIAN FEDERATION

82 Western Caucasus
83 Komi virgin forests
84 Golden Mountains of Altay
85 Lake Baikal
86 Central Sikhote-Alin mountain range
87 Kamchatka volcanoes

AFRICA

88 **Ichkeul National Park**, Tunisia
89 Tassili n'Ajjer, Algeria
90 *Bandiagara Cliffs: Land of the Dogons*, Mali
91 Banc d'Arguin National Park, Mauritania
92 **Parc national des Oiseaux du Djoudj (Djoudj Nat. Bird Sanctuary)**, Senegal
93 Parc national du Niokolo Koba, Senegal

UNESCO: Natural Heritage

A SLOVENIA
B CROATIA
C BOSNIA-HERZEGOVINA
D SERBIA & MONTENEGRO
E FORMER YUGOSLAV REPUBLIC
OF MACEDONIA

2003 UPDATES
In July 2003 the World Heritage Committee inscribed five new natural sites on the World Heritage List:
Australia Purnululu National Park
China Three Parallel Rivers, Yunnan: upper reaches of the Yangtze, Mekong and Salween
Mongolia/Russian Federation Uvs Nuur Basin
Switzerland Monte San Giorgio
Vietnam Phong Nha-Ke Bang National Park
In addition the Committee extended one natural site: The Central Amazon Conservation Complex, which includes Jaú National Park (**41**), now protects over 6m hectares.

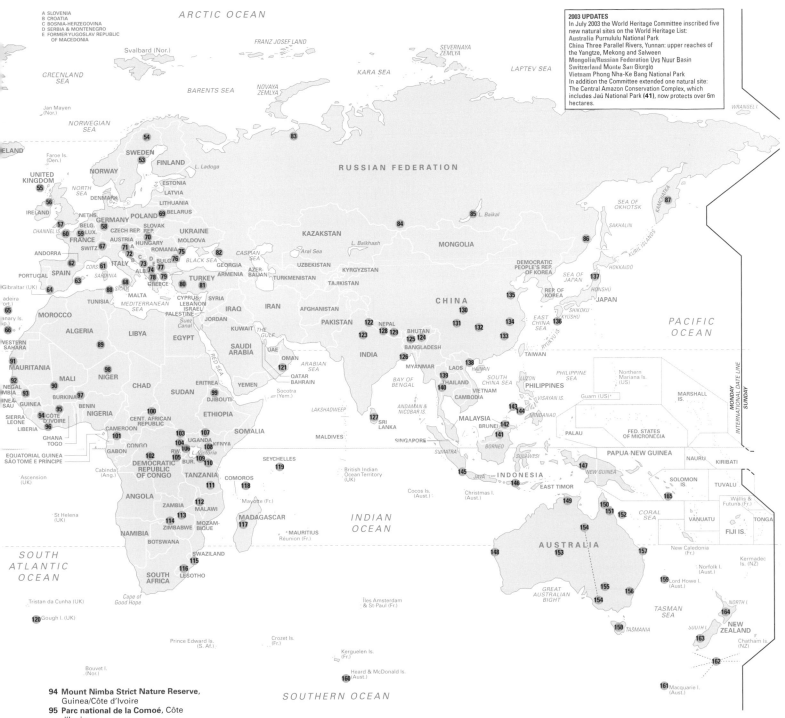

94 **Mount Nimba Strict Nature Reserve**, Guinea/Côte d'Ivoire
95 **Parc national de la Comoé**, Côte d'Ivoire
96 Parc national de Taï, Côte d'Ivoire
97 Parc national du "W", Niger
98 **Aïr and Ténéré Natural Reserves**, Niger
99 **Simien Mountains National Park**, Ethiopia
100 **Parc national du Manovo-Gounda-St-Floris**, Central African Republic
101 Réserve du Dja, Cameroon
102 **Parc national de la Salonga**, Dem. Rep. of Congo
103 **Parc national de la Garamba**, Dem. Rep. of Congo
104 Réserve du Okapi, Dem. Rep. of Congo; **Parc national des Virunga**, Dem. Rep. of Congo
105 **Parc national du Kahuzi-Biega**, Dem. Rep. of Congo
106 **Ruwenzori Mountains National Park**, Uganda; Bwindi Impenetrable Forest National Park*, Uganda
107 Lake Turkana national parks, Kenya
108 Mount Kenya National Park* and forest, Kenya
109 Serengeti National Park*, Tanzania
110 Ngorongoro Conservation Area, Tanzania; Kilimanjaro National Park*, Tanzania

111 Selous Game Reserve, Tanzania
112 Lake Malawi National Park*, Malawi
113 Mana Pools National Park and Sapi & Chewore safari areas, Zimbabwe
114 Mosi-oa-Tunya – Victoria Falls*, Zambia/Zimbabwe
115 Greater St Lucia Wetland Park, South Africa
116 uKhahlamba-Drakensberg Park, South Africa
117 Réserve naturelle intégrale de Tsingy de Bemaraha, Madagascar
118 Groupe d'Aldabra, Seychelles
119 Vallée de Mai Nature Reserve, Seychelles
120 Gough Island Wildlife Reserve

ASIA
121 Arabian Oryx Sanctuary, Oman
122 Nanda Devi National Park, India
123 Keoladeo National Park, India
124 **Manas Wildlife Sanctuary**, India
125 Kaziranga National Park*, India
126 Sundarbans National Park, India; Sundarbans, Bangladesh
127 Dambulla Golden Rock Temple, Sri Lanka; Sinharaja Forest Reserve, Sri Lanka

128 Royal Chitwan National Park, Nepal
129 Sagarmatha National Park, Nepal
130 Jiuzhaigou Valley Scenic and Historic Interest Area, Sichuan, China; Huanglong Scenic and Historic Interest Area, Sichuan, China
131 Emei Shan and Leshan Giant Buddha, Sichuan, China
132 Wulingyuan Scenic and Historic Interest Area, Hunan, China
133 Wuyi Shan, Fujian, China
134 Huang Shan, Anhui, China
135 Tai Shan, Shandong, China
136 Yaku-shima, Japan
137 Shirakami-Sanchi, Japan
138 Ha Long Bay, Vietnam
139 Sukhothai and its region: historic towns, Thailand
140 Thung Yai-Huai Kha Khaeng Wildlife Sanctuaries, Thailand
141 Gunung Mulu National Park, Malaysia
142 Kinabalu Park, Malaysia
143 Puerto-Princesa Subterranean River National Park, the Philippines
144 Tubbataha Reef Marine Park, the Philippines
145 Ujung Kulon National Park and Krakatau Nature Reserve, Indonesia

146 Komodo National Park, Indonesia
147 Lorentz National Park, Indonesia

AUSTRALASIA & OCEANIA
148 Shark Bay, Australia
149 Kakadu National Park*, Australia
150 Queensland wet tropics, Australia
151 Central eastern rainforest reserves, Australia
152 Great Barrier Reef*, Australia
153 Uluru-Kata Tjuta National Park*, Australia
154 Naracoorte & Riversleigh: fossil mammal sites, Australia
155 Willandra Lakes region, Australia
156 Greater Blue Mountains area, Australia
157 Fraser Island, Australia
158 Tasmanian wilderness, Australia
159 Lord Howe island group, Australia
160 Heard and McDonald Islands
161 Macquarie Island
162 New Zealand sub-antarctic islands
163 Southwest New Zealand parks (Fiordland*, Aoraki/Mount Cook* and Westland National Parks)
164 Tongariro National Park*, New Zealand
165 East Rennell, Solomon Islands
166 Henderson Island, Pitcairn Islands

UNESCO: Cultural Heriatge

The UNESCO World Heritage List consists of sites considered to be of global importance either because of their natural heritage or their significant man-made contribution to world culture. Countries which are signatories to the World Heritage Convention can submit potential sites to UNESCO, which considers each proposal under strict criteria and lists each site where one or more natural or cultural criteria have been met. Some sites satisfy both natural and cultural criteria; these appear on both maps.

The cultural sites are either:
(a) monuments (architectural works, works of monumental sculpture and painting or archaeological sites; or
(b) groups of buildings which are of outstanding universal value from the point of view of history, art or science; or
(c) works of man or the combined works of nature and man which are of outstanding universal value.

Sites nominated should fulfil one or more of the following criteria. They should:
(i) represent a masterpiece of human creative genius; or
(ii) exhibit an important interchange of human values on developments in architecture or technology, monumental arts, town planning and landscape design; or
(iii) bear exceptional testimony to a cultural tradition or civilisation; or
(iv) be an outstanding example of building or architecture which illustrates a significant stage or stages in human history; or
(v) be an outstanding example of traditional human settlement and land-use, especially when it has become vulnerable; or
(vi) be associated with events, traditions, ideas, beliefs or artistic and literary works of outstanding universal significance.

Properties named in red are included on the list of World Heritage in Danger. Those shown in italics are joint natural and cultural sites.

The Organisation of World Heritage Cities (OWHC) was established in 1993 with the aim of assisting member cities adapt and improve their management methods in relation to the specific requirements of having a site inscribed on the UNESCO World Heritage List.

World Heritage Cities are named on the map.

For further information on Heritage Sites and Heritage Cities, contact:

UNESCO World Heritage Centre,
7 place de Fontenoy,
75352 Paris 07 SP,
France.
Tel: +33 (0)1 45 68 15 71.
www.unesco.org/whc/

Sites marked with an asterisk (*) are featured in Columbus Travel Guides' *Tourist Attractions and Events of the World*

UNITED STATES & CANADA
1 Anthony Island, British Columbia
2 Head-Smashed-In Buffalo Jump, Alberta
3 Québec: historic area*
4 Lunenburg: old city, Nova Scotia
5 L'Anse aux Meadows Historic Park, Newfoundland
6 Mesa Verde National Park, Colorado
7 Chaco Culture National Historical Park, New Mexico
8 Pueblo de Taos, New Mexico
9 Cahokia Mounds State Historic Site, Illinois
10 Charlottesville: Monticello and University of Virginia, Virginia
11 Philadelphia: Independence Hall*, Pennsylvania
12 Statue of Liberty*, New York

LATIN AMERICA & THE CARIBBEAN
13 Sierra de la San Francisco: rock paintings, Mexico
14 Paquimé Casas Grandes: archaeological site, Mexico
15 Zacatecas: historic centre, Mexico
16 Guadalajara: Hospicio Cabañas, Mexico
17 Guanajuato: historic town and adjacent mines, Mexico
18 Querétaro: historic monuments, Mexico
19 Teotihuacán: pre-Hispanic city*, Mexico
20 El Tajin: pre-Hispanic city, Mexico
21 Morelia: historic centre, Mexico
22 Ciudad de México (Mexico City): historic centre and Xochimilco, Mexico; Xochicalco: archaeological site, Mexico
23 Popocatépetl: monasteries, Mexico; Puebla: historic centre, Mexico

24 Tlacotalpán: historic monuments, Mexico
25 Monte Albán: archaeological site*, and Oaxaca: historic centre, Mexico
26 Palenque: pre-Hispanic city and national park*, Mexico
27 Campeche: historic fortified town, Mexico
28 Uxmal: pre-Hispanic city, Mexico
29 Chichén-Itzá: pre-Hispanic city*, Mexico
30 Calakmul: pre-Hispanic city, Mexico
31 Parque Nacional Tikal*, Guatemala
32 Quiriguá: archaeological park, Guatemala
33 Antigua, Guatemala
34 Copán: Maya site, Honduras
35 Joya de Cerén: archaeological site, El Salvador
36 León Viejo: ruins, Nicaragua
37 Portobelo and San Lorenzo: fortifications, Panama
38 Ciudad de Panamá (Panama City): historic district and the Salón Bolívar, Panama
39 St George: historic town and related fortifications, Bermuda
40 Viñales valley, Cuba; La Habana (Havana): old town and its fortifications*, Cuba
41 Trinidad and Valley de los Ingenios, Cuba
42 Santiago de Cuba: San Pedro de la Roca castle, Cuba; First coffee plantations in southeast Cuba: archaeological landscape
43 La Citadelle, Sans Souci and Ramiers: National Historic Park, Haiti
44 Santo Domingo: colonial city, Dominican Rep.
45 La Fortaleza and San Juan: historic sites, Puerto Rico
46 Brimstone Hill Fortress National Park, St Kitts and Nevis
47 Willemstad: historic area, inner city and harbour, Curaçao
48 Paramaribo: historic inner city, Surinam
49 Caracas: university campus, Venezuela
50 Coro: town and its port, La Vela, Venezuela
51 Cartagena: port, fortress and monuments, Colombia
52 Mompós: historic centre, Colombia
53 Parque Arqueológico Nacional Tierradentro, Colombia; Parque Arqueológico San Agustín, Colombia
54 Quito: old city, Ecuador
55 Cuenca: historic centre, Ecuador
56 Parque Nacional Río Abiseo, Peru
57 **Chan Chan: archaeological area**, Peru

58 Chavin: archaeological site, Peru
59 Lima: historic centre, Peru
60 Santuario Histórico Machu Picchu*, Peru; Cusco: old city, Peru
61 Nazca: geoglyphs and Pampas de Juma, Peru
62 Arequipa: historic centre, Peru
63 Tiwanaku: pre-Hispanic city, Bolivia
64 Potosí, Bolivia
65 Sucre: historic city, Bolivia
66 El Fuerte de Samaipata, Bolivia; Chiquitos Jesuit missions, Bolivia
67 Jesús and Trinidad: Jesuit missions, Paraguay
68 Goiás: historic centre, Brazil
69 Brasília, Brazil
70 Parque Nacional da Serra da Capivara, Brazil
71 São Luís: historic centre, Brazil
72 Olinda: historic centre, Brazil
73 Salvador de Bahia: historic centre, Brazil
74 Diamantina: historic centre, Brazil
75 Ouro Prêto: historic town, Brazil
76 Congonhas: Sanctuary of Bom Jesus, Brazil
77 São Miguel: Jesuit mission ruins, Brazil; Loreto, San Ignacio Miní, Santa Ana & Santa Maria Mayor: Guaraní Jesuit missions, Argentina
78 Colonia del Sacramento: historic quarter, Uruguay
79 Córdoba: Jesuit Block and estancias, Argentina
80 Cueva de las Manos, Río Pinturas, Argentina
81 Isla de Chiloé, Chile
82 Parque Nacional Rapa Nui, Easter Island

EUROPE† (including Atlantic islands)
83 Angra do Heroísmo: central area, Terceira, Azores
84 San Cristóbal de la Laguna, Tenerife, Canary Is.
85 Urnes: stave church, Norway
86 Røros: mining town, Norway
87 Alta: rock drawings, Norway
88 Lapponian area, Sweden
89 Luleå: Gammelstad church town, Sweden
90 Rauma: old town, Finland; Sammallahdenmäki: Bronze Age burial site, Finland
91 Petäjävesi: old church, Finland
92 Verla: groundwood and board mill, Finland

RUSSIAN FEDERATION†
93 Solovetskiye Ostrova: cultural and historic ensemble
94 Khizi Pogost
95 Kazan: Kremlin

AFRICA†
96 St Catherine (Jebel Musa) area, Egypt
97 Thebes: ancient city and necropolis (incl. Hatshepsut's Temple*, Karnak*, Luxor, Valley of the Kings*, Valley of the Queens*), Egypt
98 Abu Simbel* to Philae: Nubian monuments, Egypt
99 Aksum: archaeological site, Ethiopia; Fasil Ghebbi & Gonder monuments, Ethiopia
100 Lalibela: rock-hewn churches, Ethiopia
101 Awash lower valley, Ethiopia
102 Tiya: carved steles, Ethiopia; Omo lower valley, Ethiopia
103 Tadrart Acacus: rock-art sites, Libya
104 Tassili n'Ajjer, Algeria
105 Chinguetti, Ouadane, Oualata and Tichitt: trading and religious centres, Mauritania
106 **Tombouctou (Timbuktu)**, Mali
107 *Bandiagara Cliffs: Land of the Dogons*, Mali
108 Djenné: old towns, Mali
109 Île de St Louis, Senegal
110 Île de Gorée, Senegal
111 Ashante traditional buildings, Ghana
112 Accra and Volta areas: forts and castles, Ghana
113 **Abomey: royal palaces**, Benin
114 Sukur: cultural landscape, Nigeria
115 Kasubi: tombs of Buganda kings, Uganda
116 Lamu old town, Kenya
117 Zanzibar: stone town*, Tanzania
118 Kilwa Kisiwani and Songo Mnara: ruins, Tanzania
119 Ilha de Moçambique, Mozambique
120 Great Zimbabwe National Monument*, Zimbabwe
121 Khami Ruins National Monument, Zimbabwe

UNESCO: Cultural Heritage

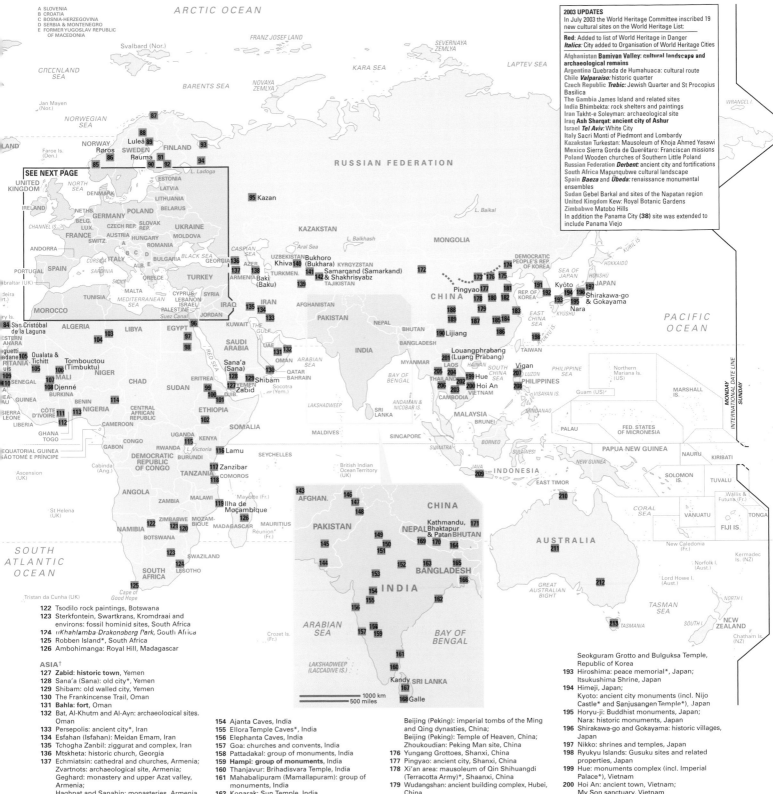

A SLOVENIA
B CROATIA
C BOSNIA-HERZEGOVINA
D SERBIA & MONTENEGRO
E FORMER YUGOSLAV REPUBLIC OF MACEDONIA

2003 UPDATES
In July 2003 the World Heritage Committee inscribed 19 new cultural sites on the World Heritage List:

Red: Added to list of World Heritage in Danger
Italics: City added to Organisation of World Heritage Cities

Afghanistan Bamiyan Valley: cultural landscape and archaeological remains
Argentina Quebrada de Humahuaca: cultural route
Chile *Valparaiso:* historic quarter
Czech Republic *Trebic:* Jewish Quarter and St Procopius Basilica
The Gambia James Island and related sites
India Bhimbetka: rock shelters and paintings
Iran Takht-e Soleyman: archaeological site
Iraq Ash Sharqat: ancient city of Ashur
Israel *Tel Aviv:* White City
Italy Sacri Monti of Piedmont and Lombardy
Kazakstan Turkestan: Mausoleum of Khoja Ahmed Yasawi
Mexico Sierra Gorda de Querétaro: Franciscan missions
Poland Wooden churches of Southern Little Poland
Russian Federation *Derbent:* ancient city and fortifications
South Africa Mapunqubwe cultural landscape
Spain *Baeza* and *Úbeda:* renaissance monumental ensembles
Sudan Gebel Barkal and sites of the Napatan region
United Kingdom Kew: Royal Botanic Gardens
Zimbabwe Matobo Hills
In addition the Panama City (**38**) site was extended to include Panama Viejo

---

122 Tsodilo rock paintings, Botswana
123 Sterkfontein, Swartkrans, Kromdraai and environs: fossil hominid sites, South Africa
124 *uKhahlamba-Drakensberg Park*, South Africa
125 Robben Island*, South Africa
126 Ambohimanga: Royal Hill, Madagascar

ASIA†
127 **Zabid: historic town**, Yemen
128 **Sana'a (Sana): old city***, Yemen
129 **Shibam: old walled city**, Yemen
130 The Frankincense Trail, Oman
131 **Bahla: fort**, Oman
132 Bat, Al-Khutm and Al-Ayn: archaeological sites, Oman
133 Persepolis: ancient city*, Iran
134 Esfahan (Isfahan): Meidan Emam, Iran
135 Tchogha Zanbil: ziggurat and complex, Iran
136 Mtskheta: historic church, Georgia
137 Echmiatsin: cathedral and churches, Armenia; Zvartnots: archaeological site, Armenia; Geghard: monastery and upper Azat valley, Armenia; Haghpat and Sanahin: monasteries, Armenia
138 **Baki (Baku): walled city**, Azerbaijan
139 Mary: Merv State Historical and Cultural Park, Turkmenistan
140 Itchan Kala, Uzbekistan
141 **Bukhoro (Bukhara): historic centre**, Uzbekistan
142 **Samarqand (Samarkand)**, Uzbekistan; **Shakhrisyabz: historic centre**, Uzbekistan
143 **Jam: minaret and archaeological remains**, Afghanistan
144 Thatta: historical monuments, Pakistan
145 Mohenjodaro: archaeological site, Pakistan
146 Takht-i-Bahi: Buddhist ruins, Pakistan; Sahr-i-Bahlol: remains of city, Pakistan; Taxila: archaeological site, Pakistan
147 **Rohtas: fort**, Pakistan
148 **Lahore: fort and Shalimar gardens**, Pakistan
149 Delhi: Humayun's tomb, India; Delhi: Qutb Minar and its monuments, India
150 Agra Fort, India; Taj Mahal*, Agra, India
151 Fatehpur Sikri: Mongol city, India
152 Khajuraho: group of monuments*, India
153 Sanchi: Buddhist monastery, India

154 Ajanta Caves, India
155 Ellora Temple Caves*, India
156 Elephanta Caves, India
157 Goa: churches and convents, India
158 Pattadakal: group of monuments, India
159 **Hampi: group of monuments**, India
160 Thanjavur: Brihadisvara Temple, India
161 Mahabalipuram (Mamallapuram): group of monuments, India
162 Konarak: Sun Temple, India
163 Bodhgaya: Mahabodi Temple complex, India
164 Darjiling Himalayan railway, India
165 Paharpur: ruins of the Buddhist Vihara, Bangladesh
166 Bagerhat: historic city, Bangladesh
167 Anuradhapura: sacred city, Sri Lanka; Sigiriya: ancient city*, Sri Lanka; Polonnaruwa: ancient city, Sri Lanka; Dambulla Golden Rock Temple, Sri Lanka; Kandy: sacred city (incl. Temple of the Sacred Tooth*), Sri Lanka
168 Galle: old town and its fortifications, Sri Lanka
169 Lumbini: birthplace of Lord Buddha, Nepal
170 **Kathmandu valley**, Nepal
171 Lhasa: Potala Palace*, Norbulinka and Jokhang Temple Monastery, Tibet, China
172 Mogao Caves, Gansu, China
173 Great Wall of China*
174 Chengde: mountain resort and outlying temples, Hebei, China
175 Beijing (Peking): imperial palace of the Ming and Qing dynasties (Forbidden City)*, China; Beijing (Peking): Summer Palace*, China;

Beijing (Peking): imperial tombs of the Ming and Qing dynasties, China; Beijing (Peking): Temple of Heaven, China; Zhoukoudian: Peking Man site, China
176 Yungang Grottoes, Shanxi, China
177 Pingyao: ancient city, Shanxi, China
178 Xi'an area: mausoleum of Qin Shihuangdi (Terracotta Army)*, Shaanxi, China
179 Wudangshan: ancient building complex, Hubei, China
180 Longmen Grottoes, Henan, China
181 Tai Shan, Shandong, China
182 Qufu: temple & cemetery of Confucius and Kong family mansion, Shandong, China
183 Suzhou: classical gardens, Jiangsu, China
184 Hongcun and Xidi: ancient villages, Anhui, China; *Huang Shan*, Anhui, China
185 Lu Shan, Jiangxi, China
186 Wuyi Shan, Fujian, China
187 Dazu rock carvings, Chongqing, China
188 Qincheng Shan and Dujiangyan irrigation system, Sichuan, China
189 *Emei Shan and Leshan giant buddha*, Sichuan, China
190 Lijiang: old town, Yunnan, China
191 Hwasun, Ganghwa and Gochang: Megalithic cemeteries, Republic of Korea; Seoul: Changdeokgung Palace complex, Republic of Korea; Seoul: Jongmyo Shrine, Republic of Korea; Suwon: Hwaseong Fortress, Rep. of Korea;
192 Haeinsa Temple*, Republic of Korea; Gyeongju: historic areas*, Republic of Korea;

Seokguram Grotto and Bulguksa Temple, Republic of Korea;
193 Hiroshima: peace memorial*, Japan; Itsukushima Shrine, Japan
194 Himeji, Japan; Kyoto: ancient city monuments (incl. Nijo Castle* and Sanjusangen Temple*), Japan
195 Horyu-ji: Buddhist monuments, Japan; Nara: historic monuments, Japan
196 Shirakawa-go and Gokayama: historic villages, Japan
197 Nikko: shrines and temples, Japan
198 Ryukyu Islands: Gusuku sites and related properties, Japan
199 Hue: monuments complex (incl. Imperial Palace*), Vietnam
200 Hoi An: ancient town, Vietnam; My Son sanctuary, Vietnam
201 Louangphrabang (Luang Prabang), Laos
202 Champasak cultural landscape, including Vat Phou Temple complex, Laos
203 Angkor*, Cambodia
204 Ban Chiang: archaeological site, Thailand
205 Sukhothai and its region: historic towns, Thailand
206 Ayutthaya and its region: historic towns, Thailand
207 Vigan: historic town, the Philippines; **Cordilleras Central: rice terraces***, the Philippines
208 Manila: Baroque churches, the Philippines
209 Borobudur: temple compound, Indonesia; Prambanan: temple compound*, Indonesia; Sangiran: early man site, Indonesia

AUSTRALASIA & OCEANIA
210 *Kakadu National Park*, Australia
211 *Uluru-Kata Tjuta National Park*, Australia
212 *Willandra Lakes region*, Australia
213 *Tasmanian wilderness*, Australia

†See next page for other sites in these areas

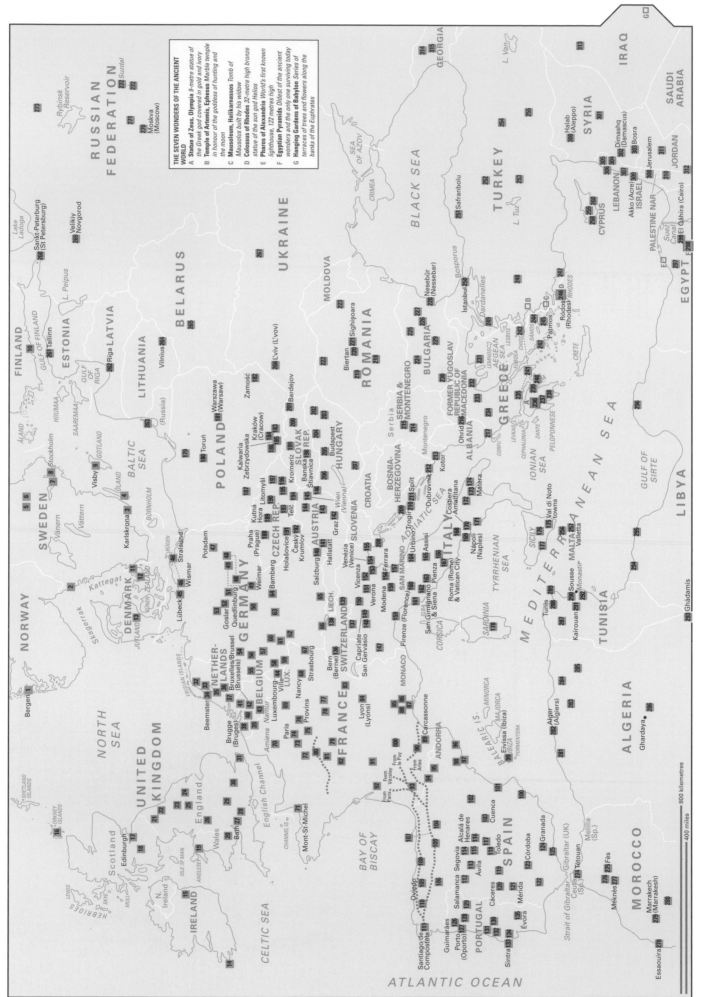

THE SEVEN WONDERS OF THE ANCIENT WORLD

A **Statue of Zeus**, Olympia 9-metre statue of the Greek god covered in gold and ivory

B **Temple of Artemis**, Ephesus Marble temple in honour of the goddess of hunting and the moon

C **Mausoleum, Halikarnassos** Tomb of Mausolus built by his widow

D **Colossus of Rhodes** 32-metre high bronze statue of the sun god Helios

E **Pharos of Alexandria** World's first known lighthouse, 122 metres high

F **Egyptian Pyramids** Oldest of the ancient wonders and the only one surviving today

G **Hanging Gardens of Babylon** Series of terraces of trees and flowers along the banks of the Euphrates

Properties named in **red** *are included on the list of World Heritage in Danger. Those shown in italics are joint natural and cultural sites. Cities named on the map are members of the Organisation of World Heritage Cities (OWHC), see previous page for explanation. Observer members are shown in grey italics.*

Sites marked with an asterisk (*) are featured in Columbus Travel Guides' *Tourist Attractions and Events of the World*

EUROPE (including Turkey & Cyprus)

1 Bergen: Bryggen*, Norway
2 Tanum: rock carvings, Sweden
3 Karlskrona: naval city, Sweden
4 Öland: agricultural landscape of the southern part of the island, Sweden
5 Falun: mining area of the Great Copper Mountain, Sweden
6 Engelsberg: ironworks, Sweden
7 Birka and Hovgården: archaeological sites, Sweden
8 Stockholm: Skogskyrkogarden, Sweden; Drottningholms Slot (Drottningholm Royal Palace)*, Sweden
9 Visby: Hanseatic town and former Viking site, Sweden
10 Helsinki (Helsingfors): Suomenlinna Sea Fortress*, Finland
11 Helsingør (Elsinore): Kronborg Slot (Kronborg Castle)*, Denmark
12 Roskilde: cathedral, Denmark
13 Jelling: mounds, runic stones and church, Denmark
14 Skellig Michael: monastic complex, Ireland
15 Brú Na Bóinne: archaeological ensemble at the bend of the Boyne, Ireland
16 Neolithic Orkney, Scotland
17 Edinburgh: old and new towns (incl. Castle*, Royal Botanic Garden*, Royal Museum & Museum of Scotland*, Scotch Whisky Heritage Centre & Royal Mile*), Scotland
18 New Lanark: industrial village, Scotland
19 Castles and town walls of King Edward (incl. Caernarfon Castle*), northwest Wales
20 Blaenavon: industrial landscape, Wales
21 Hadrian's Wall*, England
22 Durham: castle and cathedral*, England
23 Studley Royal Park and Fountains Abbey ruins, England
24 Derwent Valley mills, England
25 Saltaire: industrial village, England
26 Ironbridge Gorge, England
27 Bath (incl. Roman baths and pumproom*), England
28 Stonehenge*, Avebury and associated Megalithic sites, England
29 Blenheim Palace, England
30 London: Tower of London*, England; London: Westminster Palace (Big Ben and the Houses of Parliament)*, Westminster Abbey* and St Margaret's Church, England; London: Maritime Greenwich*, England
31 Canterbury: cathedral*, St Augustine's Abbey and St Martin's Church, England
32 D.F. Wouda steam pumping station, The Netherlands
33 Schokland: prehistoric settlements, The Netherlands
34 Droogmakerij de Beemster (Beemster Polder), The Netherlands
35 Amsterdam: defence line, The Netherlands
36 Utrecht: Rietveld Schröderhuis, The Netherlands
37 Kinderdijk-Elshout: mill network, The Netherlands
38 Brugge (Bruges): historic centre, Belgium
39 Tournai: Cathédrale Notre-Dame, Belgium
40 Belfries of Flanders and Wallonia (incl. Onze Lieve Vrouwekathedraal, Antwerpen (Antwerp)*), Belgium
41 Flemish Béguinages, Belgium
42 Bruxelles/Brussel (Brussels): Grand-Place*, Belgium; Bruxelles/Brussel (Brussels): four town houses of architect Victor Horta, Belgium
43 Canal du Centre: four boat-lifts and environs, La Louvière and Le Rœulx, Belgium; Mons: Spiennes Neolithic flint mines, Belgium
44 Luxembourg-Ville: old quarters and fortifications
45 Lübeck: Hanseatic city, Germany
46 Stralsund and Wismar: historic centres, Germany
47 Berlin: Museumsinsel (incl. Pergamonmuseum*), Germany; Potsdam and SW Berlin: palaces and parks (incl. Schloss Sanssouci*), Germany
48 Eisleben and Wittenberg: Luther memorials, Germany
49 Dessau-Wörlitz: Garden Kingdom, Germany; Dessau and Weimar: Bauhaus buildings, Germany; Weimar: classical city, Germany
50 Wartburg: castle, Germany
51 Quedlinburg: collegiate church, castle and old town, Germany
52 Goslar: historic town and Rammelsberg mines, Germany
53 Hildesheim: cathedral and St Michaeliskirche, Germany
54 Essen: Zollverein coal mine industrial complex, Germany
55 Aachen (Aix-la-Chapelle): cathedral, Germany
56 Köln (Cologne): cathedral*, Germany; Brühl: Schloss Augustusburg and Jagdschloss Falkenlust, Germany
57 Upper Middle Rhine Valley, Germany
58 Trier: Roman monuments, cathedral and Liebfrauenkirche, Germany
59 Völklingen: ironworks, Germany
60 Lorsch: abbey and Altenmünster, Germany
61 Speyer: cathedral, Germany
62 Maulbronn: Cistercian monastery complex, Germany
63 Würzburg: Residenz with the court gardens and square, Germany
64 Bamberg, Germany
65 Wies: pilgrimage church, Germany
66 Reichenau: Benedictine monastery remains, Germany
67 Strasbourg: Grand Île, France
68 Nancy: Place Stanislas, Place de la Carrière and Place d'Alliance, France
69 Reims: Cathédrale Notre-Dame, Abbaye St Remi and Palais du Tau, France
70 Amiens: cathedral, France
71 Mont-St-Michel* and its bay, France
72 Chartres: cathedral*, France
73 Versailles: palace and park*, France
74 Paris: banks of the Seine (incl. Tour Eiffel*, Musée du Louvre*, Musée d'Orsay*, Cathédrale de Notre-Dame*), France
75 Fontainebleau: palace and park, France
76 Provins: fortified medieval town, France
77 Fontenay: Cistercian abbey, France
78 Vézelay: basilica and hill, France
79 Bourges: cathedral, France
80 Loire Valley between Chalonnes and Sully-sur-Loire
81 Chambord: château and estate, France
82 St-Savin-sur-Gartempe: church, France
83 Arc-et-Senans: royal saltworks, France
84 Lyon (Lyons): historic city, France
85 Orange: Roman theatre and its surroundings and the triumphal arch, France
86 Avignon: historic centre (incl. Palais des Papes*, Pont St-Bénézet*), France
87 Arles: Roman and Romanesque monuments (incl. Roman amphitheatre*), France
88 Remoulins: Pont du Gard Roman aqueduct*, France
89 Carcassonne: historic fortified city*, France
90 Canal du Midi, France
91 Vallée du Vézère: Lascaux* and other decorated grottoes, France
92 St-Émilion: vineyard landscape, France
93 Way of St James pilgrimage route: 4 routes through France
94 *Mont Perdu/Monte Perdido*, France/Spain
95 Vall de Boí: Catalan Romanesque churches, Spain
96 Barcelona: Parque and Palacio Güell* and Casa Milá, Spain; Barcelona: Palau de la Música Catalaña and the Hospital de Sant Pau, Spain
97 Tarragona: Roman city of Tárraco, Spain
98 Poblet: monastery, Spain
99 *Eivissa (Ibiza): biodiversity and culture*, Spain
100 Elx (Elche): Palmeral (date palm) landscape, Spain
101 Valencia: La Lonja de la Seda, Spain
102 Aragón: Mudejar architecture, Spain
103 Cuenca: historic walled town, Spain
104 San Millán: Suso and Yuso monasteries, Spain
105 Burgos: cathedral, Spain; Cuevas de Atapuerca: archaeological site, Spain
106 Las Médulas, Spain
107 Camino de Santiago: the Way of St James pilgrimage route, Spain
108 Cuevas de Altamira: archaeological site, Spain
109 Oviedo: churches of the Asturias Kingdom, Spain
110 Lugo: Roman walls, Spain
111 Santiago de Compostela: old town (incl. cathedral*), Spain
112 Salamanca: old city, Spain
113 Ávila: old town with extra-muros churches, Spain
114 Segovia: old town and aqueduct*, Spain
115 El Escorial: monastery*, Spain
116 Alcalá de Henares: university and historic precinct, Spain
117 Aranjuez: cultural landscape, Spain
118 Toledo: historic city, Spain
119 Guadalupe: Real Monasterio de Santa María, Spain
120 Cáceres: old town, Spain
121 Mérida: archaeological ensemble, Spain
122 Sevilla (Seville): cathedral*, Alcazar and Archivo de Indias, Spain
123 Córdoba: mosque and historic centre, Spain
124 Granada: Alhambra*, Generalife & Albaicín quarter, Spain
125 Mediterranean seaboard prehistoric rock-art sites, Spain
126 Guimarães: historic centre, Portugal
127 Porto (Oporto): historic centre, Portugal
128 Alto Douro wine region, Portugal
129 Vale do Côa: prehistoric rock-art sites, Portugal
130 Tomar: Convent of Christ, Portugal
131 Batalha: monastery, Portugal
132 Alcobaça: monastery, Portugal
133 Sintra: historic city, Portugal
134 Lisboa (Lisbon): Mosteiro dos Jerónimos* and Torre de Belém*, Portugal
135 Évora: historic centre, Portugal
136 Bern (Berne): old city, Switzerland
137 Bellinzona: group of fortifications, Switzerland
138 St Gallen (St Gall): convent, Switzerland
139 Müstair: Benedictine convent of St John, Switzerland
140 Salzburg: historic centre (incl. Mozart's birthplace and residence*), Austria
141 Hallstatt-Dachstein-Salzkammergut: cultural landscape, Austria
142 Graz: historic centre, Austria
143 Semmering Railway, Austria
144 Wachau: cultural landscape, Austria
145 Wien (Vienna): historic centre, Austria; Wien (Vienna): Schloss Schönbrunn and gardens*, Austria
146 Neusiedlersee, Austria / Fertö, Hungary: cultural landscape
147 Torino (Turin): Residences of the Royal House of Savoy, Italy
148 Milano (Milan): church and convent of Santa Maria delle Grazie with 'The Last Supper' by Leonardo da Vinci, Italy
149 Crespi d'Adda: industrial workers' town, Italy
150 Val Camónica: rock drawings, Italy
151 Verona: historic city, Italy
152 Vicenza: city and the Palladian villas of the Veneto, Italy
153 Pádova (Padua): botanical garden, Italy
154 Venézia (Venice) and lagoon (incl. Basilica di San Marco*, Palazzo Ducale*), Italy
155 Aquileia: archaeological site including Patriarchal Basilica, Italy
156 Ferrara: Renaissance city, Italy
157 Ravenna: early Christian monuments and mosaics, Italy
158 Modena: cathedral, Torre Civica and Piazza Grande, Italy
159 Portovénere, Cinque Terre (Corníglia, Manarola, Monterosso, Riomaggiore, Vernazza), Ísola Palmária, Í. del Tino and Í. del Tinetto, Italy
160 Firenze (Florence): historic centre (incl. Duomo Santa Maria del Fiore*, Galleria degli Uffizi*, Ponte Vecchio*), Italy
161 Pisa: Piazza del Duomo (incl. Torre Pendente*), Italy
162 San Gimignano: historic centre, Italy; Siena: historic centre (incl. Piazza del Campo*), Italy
163 Pienza: historic centre, Italy
164 Urbino: historic centre, Italy
165 Assisi: Basilica di San Francesco and other Franciscan sites, Italy
166 Tivoli: Villa d'Este, Italy; Villa Adriana (Hadrian's Villa), Italy
167 Vatican City (incl. Basilica di San Pietro*, Musei Vaticani & Capella Sistina*); Roma (Rome): historic centre and extraterritorial properties of the Holy See & San Paolo fuori le Mura (incl. Colosseo*, Fontana di Trevi*, Foro Romano*, Pantheon*, Spanish Steps & Keats-Shelley Memorial House*), Italy
168 Caserta: Palazzo Reale & gardens, Vanvitelli aqueduct & San Leucio complex, Italy
169 Nápoli (Naples): historic centre, Italy; Herculaneum, Pompeii* and Torre Annunziata: archaeological areas, Italy
170 Costiera Amalfitana, Italy
171 Cilento area: cultural landscape including Parco Nazionale del Cilento e Vallo di Diano, Certosa di San Lorenzo in Padula and the archaeological sites of Paestum and Vélia, Italy
172 Castel del Monte: medieval castle, Italy
173 Matera: I Sassi di Matera troglodyte settlement, Italy
174 Alberobello: Trulli houses, Italy
175 Val di Noto: late Baroque towns (Caltagirone, Catánia, Militello in Val di Catánia, Módica, Noto, Palazzolo, Ragusa, Scicli), Sicily, Italy
176 Villa Romana del Casale, Sicily, Italy
177 Agrigento: archaeological area, Sicily, Italy
178 Su Nuraxi di Barúmini, Sardinia, Italy
179 Malbork: Teutonic castle, Poland
180 Torun: medieval town, Poland
181 Warszawa (Warsaw): historic centre (incl. Warsaw Royal Castle*), Poland
182 Zamosc: old city, Poland
183 Wieliczka: salt mines, Poland
184 Kraków (Cracow): historic centre (incl. Market Sq.*, Wawel Royal Castle*), Poland
185 Kalwaria Zebrzydowska: Mannerist architectural and park landscape complex and pilgrimage park, Poland
186 Oswiecim (Auschwitz): Auschwitz-Birkenau concentration camp*, Poland
187 Jawor and Swidnica: Churches of Peace, Poland
188 Praha (Prague): historic centre (incl. Charles Bridge*, Castle & St Vitus Cathedral*, Old Town Square*), Czech Republic
189 Kutná Hora*: historical centre, Church of Santa Barbara and Cathedral of Our Lady at Sedlec, Czech Republic
190 Litomysl Castle, Czech Republic
191 Holasovice: historical village reservation, Czech Republic
192 Cesky Krumlov: historic centre, Czech Republic
193 Telc: historic centre, Czech Republic
194 Lednice-Valtice: cultural landscape, Czech Republic
195 Brno: Tugendhat Villa, Czech Republic
196 Zelená Hora: St John of Nepomuk, Czech Republic; Kromeríz: castle and gardens, Czech Republic
197 Olomouc: Holy Trinity column, Czech Republic
198 Banská Stiavnica, Slovak Republic
199 Vlkolínec, Slovak Republic
200 Spisské Pohradie: Spissky Hrad* and associated monuments, Slovak Republic
201 Bardejov: fortified medieval town, Slovak Republic
202 Tojaki wine region: cultural landscape, Hungary
203 Hortobágyi National Park, Hungary
204 Hollokö: traditional village, Hungary
205 Budapest: banks of the Danube, Buda Castle* area (incl. Fisherman's Bastion*) Andrássy Avenue and the Millennium Underground, Hungary
206 Pannonhalma: millenary Benedictine abbey and its natural environment, Hungary
207 Pécs: early Christian cemetery, Hungary
208 Porec: Episcopal complex, Croatia
209 Sibenik: St James cathedral, Croatia
210 Trogir: historic city, Croatia
211 Split: historic centre with Diocletian palace, Croatia
212 Dubrovnik: old city*, Croatia
213 Kotor and its gulf, Serbia & Montenegro
214 Studenica: monastery, Serbia & Montenegro
215 Stari Ras: medieval buildings and monuments; Sopocani Monastery, Serbia & Montenegro
216 *Lake Ohrid and its region*, FYR of Macedonia
217 **Butrint (Buthrotum): archaeological site**, Albania
218 Horezu: monastery, Romania
219 Orastie mountains: Dacian fortresses, Romania
220 Biertan: town and fortified church, Romania
221 Sighisoara: historic centre, Romania
222 Maramures: wooden churches, Romania
223 Moldavian churches, Romania
224 Boyana: church, Bulgaria
225 Sveshtari: Thracian tomb, Bulgaria
226 Ivanovo: rock chapels, Bulgaria
227 Madara: horseman stone relief, Bulgaria
228 Nesebur (Nessebar): ancient city, Bulgaria
229 Kazanluk: Thracian tomb, Bulgaria
230 Rila: monastery*, Bulgaria
231 *Athos*, Greece
232 Thessaloniki (Salonika): Palaeochristian and Byzantine monuments, Greece
233 Vergina: archaeological site, Greece
234 *Metéora*, Greece
235 Delfí (Delphi): archaeological site*, Greece
236 Olimbía (Olympia): archaeological site*, Greece
237 Bassae: Temple of Apollo Epicurius, Greece
238 Mistrás, Greece
239 Mycenae* and Tiryns: archaeological sites, Greece
240 Epídavros (Epidaurus): archaeological site*, Greece
241 Athina (Athens): Acropolis*, Greece
242 Delos, Greece
243 Daphni, Hossios Luckas and Néa Moni monasteries, Greece
244 Sámos: Pythagoreion and Heraion, Greece
245 Pátmos: historic centre (chorá) with the monastery of St John the Theologian and Cave of the Apocalypse, Greece
246 Ródos (Rhodes): medieval city, Greece
247 Xanthos-Letoon, Turkey
248 *Hierapolis-Pamukkale*, Turkey
249 Truva (Troy): archaeological site*, Turkey
250 Istanbul: historic areas (incl. Blue Mosque*, Hagia Sophia*, Topkapi Palace*), Turkey
251 Safranbolu, Turkey
252 Hattusha: Hittite city, Turkey
253 *Göreme National Park* and Cappadocia rock sites*, Turkey
254 Divrigi: Great Mosque and hospital, Turkey
255 Nemrut Dagi: archaeological site, Turkey
256 Ggantija: Megalithic temples, Malta
257 Valletta: old city, Malta; Hal Saflieni Hypogeum, Malta
258 Paphos: archaeological site*, Cyprus
259 Troodos region: painted churches, Cyprus
260 Choirokoitia: archaeological site, Cyprus
261 Tallinn: historic centre (incl. Town Hall Square*), Estonia
262 Riga: historic centre, Latvia
263 Curonian Spit, Lithuania/Russian Federation
264 Vilnius: old city, Lithuania
265 Mir: castle complex, Belarus
266 L'viv (L'vov): historic centre, Ukraine
267 Kyiv (Kiev): St Sophia Cathedral, related monastic buildings and Lavra of Kyiv-Pechersk, Ukraine

RUSSIAN FEDERATION

268 Sankt-Peterburg (St Petersburg): historic centre (incl. State Hermitage Museum*)
269 Velikiy Novgorod: historic monuments and surroundings
270 Moskva (Moscow): Kremlin*, Red Square* and St Basil's Cathedral*; Moskva (Moscow): Church of the Ascension at Kolomenskoye
271 Sergiyev Posad: architectural ensemble of the Trinity Sergius Lavra
272 Vladimir and Suzdal: White Monuments
273 Ferapontov Monastery

AFRICA

274 Tétouan: medina, Morocco
275 Fès: medina*, Morocco
276 Volubilis: archaeological site, Morocco
277 Meknès: historic city, Morocco
278 Essaouira: medina, Morocco
279 Marrakech (Marrakesh): medina, Morocco
280 Aït Benhaddou: fortified village, Morocco
281 **Tipasa: archaeological park**, Algeria
282 Alger (Algiers): kasbah, Algeria
283 Benî Hammâd: Al Qal'a, Algeria
284 Djemila: Roman ruins, Algeria
285 Timgad: Roman ruins, Algeria
286 M'Zab Valley, Algeria
287 Dougga (Thugga), Tunisia
288 Tunis: medina*, Tunisia; Carthage: archaeological site*, Tunisia
289 Kerkouane: Punic town and its necropolis, Tunisia
290 Sousse: medina, Tunisia
291 Kairouan, Tunisia
292 El Jem: amphitheatre, Tunisia
293 Ghadamis: old town, Libya
294 Sabratha: archaeological site, Libya
295 Leptis Magna: archaeological site, Libya
296 Cyrene: archaeological site, Libya
297 **Abu Mena: Christian ruins**, Egypt
298 Memphis: Pyramid fields from Giza to Dahshur and its necropolis*, Egypt
299 El Qâhira (Cairo): Islamic city (incl. Egyptian Antiquities Museum*), Egypt

ASIA

300 Halab (Aleppo): ancient city of Aleppo*, Syria
301 Tadmur: archaeological site of Palmyra*, Syria
302 Dimashq (Damascus): ancient city, Syria
303 Bosra: ancient city, Syria
304 Anjar: archaeological site, Lebanon; Baalbek, Lebanon
305 Holy Valley and Forest of the Cedars of God, Lebanon
306 Byblos, Lebanon
307 Soûr (Tyre): archaeological site of Tyre*, Lebanon
308 **Jerusalem: old city and walls** (incl. Temple Mount*, Wailing Wall*) *site proposed by Jordan*
309 Akko: old city of Acre, Israel
310 Masada National Park, Israel
311 Qasr Amra, Jordan
312 Petra*, Jordan
313 Hatra, Iraq
314 Upper Svaneti area, Georgia
315 K'ut'aisi: Bagrati Cathedral and Gelati Monastery, Georgia

Europe

Europe is comfortably the world's most visited continent. It has numerous natural and man-made attractions, a generally excellent transport network and a wide range of cities, landscapes and climates. These factors helped draw over 383 million international visitors in 2001, 56.4% of the world's total and an increase of 12% over 1997. Global recession and the struggle against terrorism depressed the industry in 2001, but many European travel patterns – several of which are regional and thus less reliant on air travel – are well established and impervious to all but the very worst catastrophes. Stability has been vital to this.

That is not to say that Europe has not changed. Since 1989, the Warsaw Pact, the USSR and Yugoslavia have disappeared and the Berlin Wall been torn down; 14 new countries have emerged; the European Union is about to expand to 25 members, including three former Soviet republics, and rivals the USA as the world's largest economy; and 12 of the continent's most powerful nations have voluntarily abandoned their own currencies in favour of a common one. Above all, except for the Balkan wars, these changes have been effected without significant bloodshed. Given Europe's violent and divisive history between 1914 and 1945, this is a considerable achievement.

In general, European states are wealthy, stable, secular, liberal democracies. Despite linguistic differences, national economies and societies are closely integrated and intra-regional trade is high. Apart from some separatist movements, there is little violent conflict. This inter-dependence, security and stability has underpinned Europe's vast travel and tourism industry.

After years of steady growth, Europe saw a 0.3% fall in visitors in 2001 against 2000, slightly better than the world average of -0.5%. 2002 saw some recovery – up 2.4% (3.1% globally), thanks in part to the intra-regional market. With so many attractions within easy reach, it is not surprising so many Europeans holiday in their own continent. 17 out of 20 of journeys which start in Europe also finish there. Indeed, trips made by Europeans within Europe account for over half of all international journeys worldwide.

Although many of these intra-regional journeys are by car or train, there are parts of Europe where flying is often more practical. Air travel of all kinds is encouraged by a country being wealthy, being physically separated from its neighbours, having a large number of airports and being part of a larger international community which makes visits necessary or desirable. Outbound leisure travel is further boosted if the country does not enjoy particularly good weather. The country most closely matching these conditions is the UK; and it is the UK that provides the best examples of two of the most significant European travel trends – the rush to the sun and the rise of the low-cost airlines.

The rush to the sun

The movement from northern to southern Europe, traditionally in the summer but increasingly at other times, has been happening for decades. In 2001, nationals of the UK, Ireland, Germany, Benelux and Scandinavia took 185 million foreign trips, an average of slightly less than one per person. Over 50% trips taken by Britons were to the same five European countries.

■ Heading south

European sunshine destinations ex-UK (000s)
Source: BTA

	1997	2001
to Spain	8,281	11,790
to France	11,149	11,959
to Greece	1,512	3,215
to Italy	1,801	2,471
to Portugal	1,304	1,598
TOTAL	24,047	31,033
% of all outbound trips	52.3%	52.9%

There are other countries that Britons visit more – the USA and Ireland would both make it into the top five – but these five draw the traditional sun-seekers. Spain and Greece were also the fastest growing destinations for Britons between 1997 and 2001, followed by the USA (partly due to winter-sun trips to Florida), France, Cyprus and Italy.

To add to the variety, activities such as camping, city-breaks, skiing and rural holidays are also increasing. Many provide separate holiday options, but sometimes are combined with traditional beach holidays on packages: even skiing, which can be enjoyed in Spain's Sierra Nevada only an hour's drive from the Costa del Sol. Many now take more than one holiday a year to experience more of these ever-increasing alternatives.

Increasingly affordable travel has led to a constant demand for new destinations. Most of the northern Mediterranean coastal region is now seen as a holiday area. To the long-established favourites, one must add Turkey, Croatia, Slovenia and Cyprus, all of which saw double-digit growth in 1997-2001.

UK outbound

Some other trends concerning holidays taken by Britons – the second biggest outbound market in the world – are worth noting. In 1981, 8% of foreign trips were to the USA, 84% to Europe and 8% to the rest of the world: in 2001 (by which time three times as many Britons were travelling), the figures were almost unchanged – 8%, 82% and 10% respectively. In 1981, around 60% of overseas trips were by air: by 2001, this had risen to 75%. One-third of all foreign trips in 2001 took place in July, August or September, as was the case in 1997. 53% of trips in 1997 were package holidays: 2001 saw only a small increase. Visits to European countries grew by an annual average of 7.4% a year between 1997 and 2001, compared to 5.5% for visits to North America and 9% to the rest of the world. 15.5% of trips abroad in 1997 were for business: in 2001, this had fallen slightly to 14.1%. Between 1997 and 2001, usage of the Channel Tunnel grew by 8.2% and that of ferries fell by 4.3%; but collectively these two took the same number of people – 15 million – to Europe in both years. The length of time Britons stayed abroad remained unchanged over this period, with an average of 10 days for each of the five years.

Key facts

Number of Countries	48
Area ('000 sq km)	25,926
Population ('000)	795,682
Population Density (per sq km)	31
Gross National Income (US$m)	9,533,090
Visitor Arrivals ('000)	383,708
Visitor Receipts (US$m)	222,892
Travel Departures ('000)	399,121
Travel Expenditure (US$m)	210,689

GNI figures relate to 2001. Population figures are taken from the most recent reliable source. Travel figures (WTO) are based on overnight stays, not same-day visitors, and are generally for 2001: where these are unavailable or unreliable, earlier years have been used. Where data for certain countries was not available, this has been regarded as zero. For more information see the Countries A–Z section from page 184.

■ Big spenders

Expenditure on foreign travel (excluding international transport), 2001 – top ten countries (US$ billions) *Source: WTO*

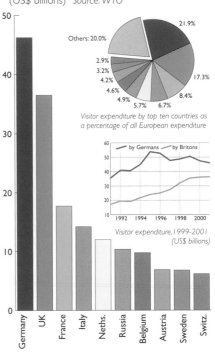

Visitor expenditure by top ten countries as a percentage of all European expenditure

Visitor expenditure, 1999-2001 (US$ billions)

All this suggests that British travel patterns are well-established, and that travellers are looking for, and finding, new holiday options within a familiar range of destinations. Outbound travel growth should also be seen in an economic context. Between 1997 and 2001, the UK's GDP grew by an average of 2.6% a year, while foreign travel increased by 6.2%. The effect is even more marked in Germany: 1.7% and 8.5% respectively. Factors such as the Channel Tunnel and intra-EU freedom of travel have also encouraged this growth: but one factor which cannot be ignored is the rise of the low-cost airlines, particularly in the UK and Ireland.

Low-cost airlines

The term 'low-cost' is slightly arbitrary: 'no-frills' and 'budget' are also used; while 'full-service' is often employed to describe other carriers. In reality, the distinction is starting to blur, for most other airlines now compete on cost. The picture is further complicated by established airlines starting their own low-cost operations, some of which (like Buzz and Go) have since been taken over by the very companies with which these were designed to compete.

Low-cost airlines have continued the job started by airline deregulation by providing competition, and thus lower fares, on many routes. To do this, they had to build a radically different kind of airline. The ones that have succeeded best – principally Ireland's Ryanair and the UK's EasyJet – entered the market afresh, adapting the model of USA's Southwest: 'low-cost' thus applies as much to their overheads as to their prices. Their main distinctive features, and areas of cost-saving, are:

■ Economies

The region's 10 largest economies
Source: World Bank/International Monetary Fund

	GNI (US$ bn)	Annual GDP growth rate (%)			
	2001	2001	2002	est2003	est2004
Germany	1,939.6	0.6	0.2	0.5	1.9
UK	1,476.8	2.2	1.6	2.0	2.5
France	1,380.7	1.8	1.2	1.2	2.4
Italy	1,123.8	1.8	0.4	1.1	2.3
Spain	588.0	2.7	2.0	2.2	3.1
Netherlands	390.3	1.1	0.3	0.6	1.8
Switzerland	227.3	1.3	1.9	1.6	2.1
Russia	253.4	5.0	4.3	4.0	3.5
Belgium	245.3	0.8	0.7	1.1	2.2
Sweden	225.9	1.2	1.9	1.6	2.1

Europe: Introduction

- Europe occupies 19.1% of the world's land area and is home to 12.9% of the world's population. 66% of the area and 18.3% of the population is provided by Russia.
- Europe's combined GDI is US$9,553,090 million, just over 30.5% of the world's total.
- Europe accounts for 61.2% of global travel departures and 56.4% of arrivals.
- International travel and tourism contributed over US$222 billion to Europe's economy in 2001.
- Of the 25 countries in the world with a Gross National Income per head of over US$20,000, 17 are in Europe.
- 12 countries in Europe received more than US$5 billion from travel and tourism in 1999 and six received more than US$10 billion.
- Europe has six of the ten most visited countries in the world; seven of the top ten travel earners; seven of the ten countries that produce the outbound travellers; and five of the top ten travel spenders.
- Germans continue to spend more money on foreign travel than any other nationality.
- 12 European countries received more than 10 million visitors in 2001.
- The most popular destination, France, on its own received almost one in nine of the world's international travellers.
- There were 383 million international tourist arrivals in Europe in 2001, an increase of 12.3% over 1997.
- Nine countries, including Poland and the UK, have seen visitor numbers fall between 1997 and 2001, although these countries only accounted for 12% of Europe's visitors. Of the countries attracting over 5 million visitors in 2001, the biggest increases in this period were seen by Croatia, Greece and Spain.
- In 2003, the 15 countries of the European Union occupied 12.5% of the land area of Europe (including Russia), had 47.5% of its population and 85.7% of its GNI. The 10 new EU members will add 20.1% to the EU's area and 20.3% to its population but only 4.3% to its wealth.
- The most significant growth in tourist arrivals in 2002 compared to 2001 was in Central and Eastern Europe which showed a rise of 3.9%.
- Europe had about 5,365,000 hotel rooms in 2001.
- Tourism employs more people in Scotland than do the whisky, gas and oil industries combined.
- Visitors to Malta in 2001 each spent an average of US$2,195, the highest expenditure per head in Europe.
- Russia spans 11 time zones.
- Measured by GNI per sq km, Monaco is comfortably the richest country in the world.

- Flying from or to under-used airports, so reducing landing fees.
- Tending to use one kind of aircraft, so reducing training and maintenance costs;
- Cutting back on free meals, so reducing purchases;
- Operating in general point-to-point, so reducing the risk of unprofitable empty legs;
- Selling flights over the internet, so avoiding agency commissions.

The first four factors also reduce delays and turn-around time, so offering further advantages. This combination, together with bold marketing and the commercial flexibility that so often accompanies low overheads, saw the new airlines prosper even through the dark days of late 2001. European low-cost traffic grew by 38% in the first four months of 2002 compared to the same period the year before, with over 24,000 new flights being added. In the UK, 16% of travellers flew low-cost in April 2003, against 9% in April 2001. (Their success partly explains the slower growth in high-speed rail travel in recent years. Channel Tunnel services in particular have failed to capitalise on the the major airlines' problems to the extent widely predicted after 11 September.) The EU-applicant countries are likely to provide the next wave of growth, particularly given the tradionally high air fares and lower standards and speed of rail travel.

There are drawbacks, however, particularly for business travellers, for whom out-of-the-way airports and inflexible ticket conditions are generally impractical. Travel managers also had the problem of being unable to use the airline or agency to help provide historical analyses of employees' flight details and costs, although this has now started to change. With agencies now more comfortable with charging clients fees, increased agency sales of non-commissionable low-cost tickets has also increased.

Finally, could the days of the 'no-cost' airline be round the corner? In June 2003, Ryanair's CEO Michael O'Leary suggested that airports and their shops and services might one day pay airlines to bring customers to them on zero-priced tickets. The idea is entrancing to travellers: what the traditional airlines think about it is another matter.

Travel trends
The more extreme tastes in adventure holidays are best satisfied in other continents but, that aside, Europe has something for everyone, from castles to clubs, scuba-diving to ski resorts and golf courses to art galleries. Major patterns or possible future trends, in addition to those discussed above, are as follows.

- With so many countries with different attractions, histories and cultures in such close proximity, touring by car, caravan and campervan remains popular. Drivers can cover huge swathes of Europe by utilising the continent's integrated motorway network.
- The growth in low-cost airlines has led to the opening up of several previously under-visited areas of Europe.
- The sun-migration pattern reverses into a dash to the mountains for winter sports. The central Alps remain ever-popular, but Slovenia, Romania and Bulgaria are emerging destinations.
- City breaks are increasingly popular. Urban fashions come and go, but the main capitals are ever-popular, as are cities such as Bruges, St Petersburg, Istanbul, Tallinn, Venice, Barcelona, Munich, Milan and Cracow.
- Short-breaks to beach destinations are increasing, such as to Majorca, the Côte d'Azur and the Algarve.
- The recent opening up of eastern Europe has led to a dramatic increase of travel not only between these countries but also from other parts of Europe. Poland, Hungary and the Czech Republic have been in the forefront.
- Health and spa holidays are also on the increase: again, eastern Europe is helping to lead the way.
- Golf holidays in Spain and Portugal, have long been popular, while France's uncrowded courses make it a strengthening force in the market.
- The Mediterranean and the Baltic are, after the Caribbean, the most popular cruise areas in the world.

◼ Big earners
Receipts from Foreign Travel (excluding international transport), 2001 – top ten countries (US$ billions) Source: WTO

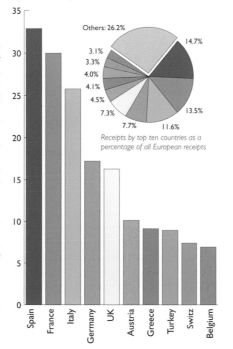

Receipts by top ten countries as a percentage of all European receipts

- No-frills hotels are now competing with the deluxe brands for the attention of the business traveller.
- EU enlargement is likely to lead to the ten new members being further assimilated into Europe's travel patterns. They are also likey to be cheaper than many traditional destinations.

Problem areas
- Major terrorist attacks in Europe cannot be ruled out.
- Until the UK adopts the euro (if it does), imports and exports, including travel, will remain at the mercy of euro/sterling exchange rate fluctuations.
- Although away from the European mainstream, instability is a risk in Russia and some of the former Russian republics. The newly expanded EU's relations with these countries will be of great importance.
- Traffic congestion in some major cities has reduced average driving speeds to near walking-pace.
- Air travel has increased more quickly than the investment in air traffic control and airport infrastructure, which can cause delays at peak times.
- Europe's wealth is attracting migrants from poorer parts of the world, which is fuelling social tensions and the growth of right-wing political parties.

◼ Visitors
Visitor arrivals 2001 Source: WTO

	Visitors (thousands)	Change since 1997
France	75,202	12.9%
Spain	50,093	26.6%
Italy	39,055	12.6%
United Kingdom	22,835	-10.5%
Russian Federation	21,169	21.2%
Austria	18,180	9.2%
Germany	17,861	12.8%
Poland	15,000	-23.2%
Greece	14,033	39.4%
Portugal	12,167	19.6%
Turkey	10,783	19.3%
Switzerland	10,700	0.9%
Netherlands	9,500	21.2%
Croatia	6,544	56.6%
Belgium	6,452	6.9%
Ireland	6,448	15.4%
Ukraine	5,791	-23.4%
Czech Rep.	5,194	4.4%
Norway	4,243	57.0%
Andorra	3,516	49.8%
Romania	3,300	11.6%
Bulgaria	3,186	6.9%
Hungary	3,070	6.3%
Sweden	2,894	21.2%
Finland	2,826	54.3%
Cyprus	2,697	29.2%
Denmark	2,028	-6.0%
Estonia	1,320	80.8%
Lithuania	1,271	25.6%
Slovenia	1,219	25.2%
Slovak Rep.	1,219	49.8%
Malta	1,180	6.2%
Luxembourg	812	4.4%
Latvia	591	-6.9%
Serbia & Montenegro	351	17.8%
Iceland	303	50.0%
Monaco	270	4.2%
Macedonia, FYR	99	-18.2%
Bosnia-Herzegovina	90	18.4%
Belarus	61	-76.0%
Liechtenstein	56	-1.8%
San Marino	49	75.0%
Albania	34	78.9%
Moldova	16	-23.8%

(Figures not available for the Channel Islands, the Faroe Islands, Greenland or Gibraltar)

Thanks to: Patrick Fitzgerald, Danny McDowell, Gary Bowerman, Graeme Payne

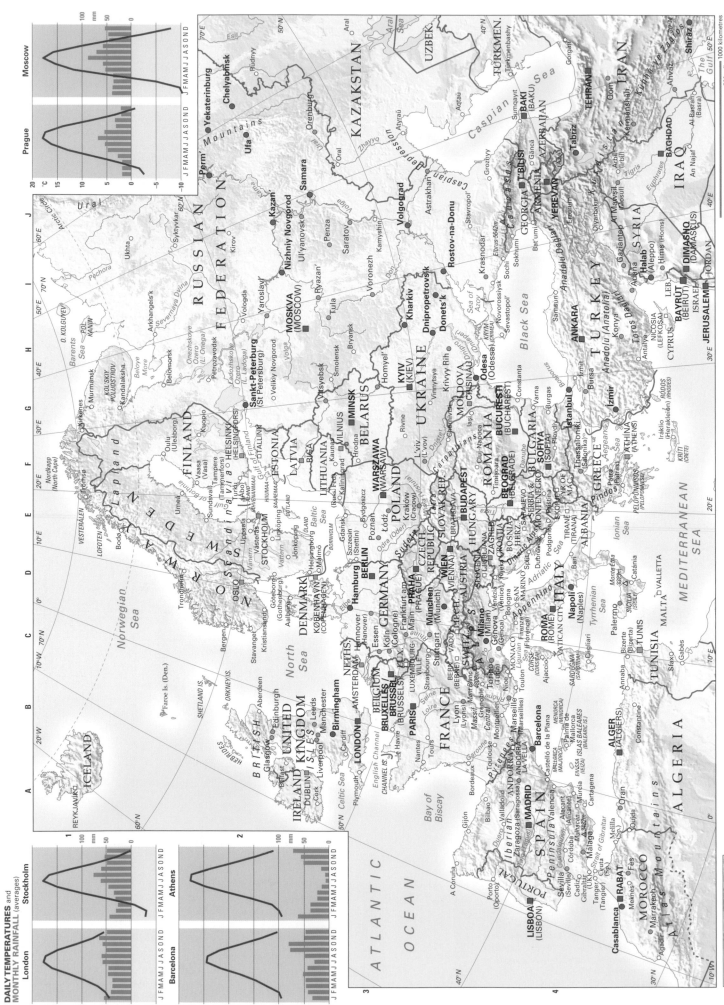

DAILY TEMPERATURES and
MONTHLY RAINFALL (averages)

London   Stockholm

Barcelona   Athens

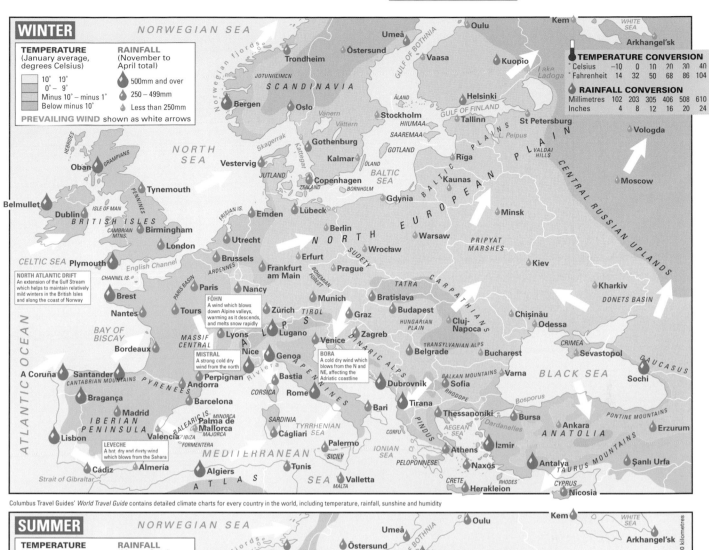

WINTER

TEMPERATURE
(January average, degrees Celsius)
- 10° – 19°
- 0° – 9°
- Minus 10° – minus 1°
- Below minus 10°

RAINFALL
(November to April total)
- 500mm and over
- 250 – 499mm
- Less than 250mm

PREVAILING WIND shown as white arrows

TEMPERATURE CONVERSION

Celsius	−10	0	10	20	30	40
Fahrenheit	14	32	50	68	86	104

RAINFALL CONVERSION

Millimetres	102	203	305	406	508	610
Inches	4	8	12	16	20	24

NORTH ATLANTIC DRIFT
An extension of the Gulf Stream which helps to maintain relatively mild winters in the British Isles and along the coast of Norway

FÖHN
A wind which blows down Alpine valleys, warming as it descends, and melts snow rapidly

MISTRAL
A strong cold dry wind from the north

BORA
A cold dry wind which blows from the N and NE, affecting the Adriatic coastline

LEVECHE
A hot dry and dusty wind which blows from the Sahara

Columbus Travel Guides' *World Travel Guide* contains detailed climate charts for every country in the world, including temperature, rainfall, sunshine and humidity

SUMMER

TEMPERATURE
(July average, degrees Celsius)
- 30° and over
- 20° – 29°
- 10° – 19°
- 0° – 9°

RAINFALL
(May to October total)
- 500mm and over
- 250 – 499mm
- Less than 250mm

PREVAILING WIND shown as white arrows

SIROCCO
A hot dusty wind which blows from north Africa; after crossing the Mediterranean the wind is often very humid

ETESIAN WIND / MELTEMI
A wind blowing from the N and NW, often creating rough seas

This map shows selected aspects of European history between the end of the Roman Empire in the 5th century and the Peace of Westphalia in 1648. Modern equivalents of important cities are included in parentheses. No historical boundaries are indicated apart from the maximum extent of Roman and Islamic conquests. The present-day coastline is shown and current international boundaries are marked in grey.

Northern limit of the Roman Empire at its greatest extent

Northern limit of Islamic conquests in Europe between the 7th and 11th centuries

Trieste Cities and regions which came under Venetian influence in any period prior to 1648.
Venice acquired many trading posts at various times during its period of commercial expansion in the late Middle Ages

✕ Sites of major battles in the period 476–1648, with date
In general, battles have only been marked which had important political consequences

The Hanseatic League
A commercial union of northern European cities, designed to create economic security in an age of political chaos, which flourished in the 14th and 15th centuries
● Principal cities
◆ Principal foreign trading posts (kontore)

Principal cities of the Lombard League
A shifting political alliance of northern Italian cities designed to combat the territorial ambitions of the Holy Roman Emperors (principally Frederick I and Frederick II) between 1153 and 1268

The Cinque Ports
A loose confederation of towns in southern England whose defensive obligations were first established in the 11th century and subsequently redefined by many royal charters, principally that of 1278. At one time there were over 30 towns and villages in the Cinque Ports Confederation; the original five are shown here

○ Universities founded prior to 1600, with year of foundation
In some cases, particularly for the oldest universities, precise dates are open to debate

Major ecclesiastical centres, 16th century:
Roman Catholic
(Patriarchal and Archiepiscopal Sees)
Orthodox
(Patriarchal Sees and other major centres)

Camino de Santiago
(the Way of St James)
A medieval pilgrimage route which developed after the discovery of the tomb of St James the Apostle in Galicia in about 812; the pilgrimage's popularity was at its height in the 11th and 12th centuries, resulting in the legacy of many churches and chapels along its various routes

VIKING AND ISLAMIC CONQUESTS AND THE CAROLINGIAN EMPIRE

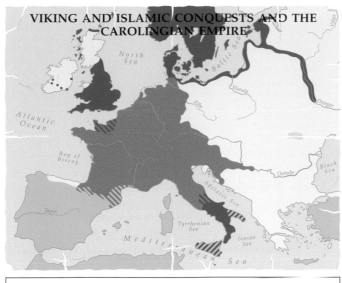

Maximum extent of Islamic conquests, 7th – 11th centuries	Areas ruled by the Vikings or Normans, 9th – 12th centuries	Carolingian Empire at the death of Charlemagne in 814

THE ANGEVIN AND HOHENSTAUFEN EMPIRES AND THE IBERIAN KINGDOMS

The Angevin Empire at the death of Henry II in 1189	The Hohenstaufen Empire at the death of Frederick II in 1250	The Christian Kingdoms of Iberia in the mid 13th century

THE HABSBURG AND OTTOMAN EMPIRES

The European Habsburg Empire at the abdication of Charles V in 1556

The Ottoman Empire, c1560

THE EMPIRE OF NAPOLEON

Area under direct rule of Napoleon in 1812

Dependent states in 1812

EVE OF WORLD WAR ONE

Triple Alliance, 1914 (Austria-Hungary, Germany, Italy)

Triple Entente, 1914 (France, Russia, United Kingdom)

THE COLD WAR

North Atlantic Treaty Organisation (NATO), 1962   [other members: Iceland, Canada, USA]

Warsaw Pact, 1962

European Union

Greenland exercised its autonomy under the Danish Crown and withdrew from the EEC in 1985. The territory now has an Association Agreement with the EU.

The European Union has its origin in the European Coal and Steel Community, established in 1951. It was originally designed to ensure peace in Europe by combining the essential economic interests of its six member countries. These countries became the founding members of the European Economic Community (EEC) in 1957 under the Treaty of Rome. A gradual process of expansion and economic and political integration led in November 1993 to the creation of the 12-member European Union (EU).

The EU has developed far beyond its original design of trade co-operation, embracing not only a single currency and a European Central Bank, but also common measures in justice, policing, immigration, transport, environment, security and foreign policy. The EU is also the world's single largest provider of aid to developing countries. As a result, the EU has a complicated structure, in which both individual national governments and pan-EU bodies play a role. The most important of the latter are: the Council of the EU, which comprises senior representatives of the constituent national governments; the European Commission which operates, in effect, as the 'government' or executive of the EU; and the elected European Parliament which serves as its legislature.

The Åland Is. are exempted from certain EU taxes

The Baltic port of Kaliningrad and its hinterland form an enclave of the Russian Federation. After the scheduled expansion of the EU in May 2004, it will be completely surrounded by EU territory. The EU Commission and the Russian government have agreed special arrangements to allow travel between the enclave and Russia proper. There are, at present, no special economic or trade agreements between the enclave and the EU although these may be negotiated at a later date.

The Channel Is. and the Isle of Man are not officially part of the UK, but as dependencies of the British Crown they maintain certain connections with the EU

Turkey has had an Association Agreement with the EU since 1963. A formal application to join was lodged in 1987 but has since been in abeyance. This is a result of the attitude of existing EU members towards Turkey's poor human rights record, continuing support of northern Cyprus, perceived lack of democratic credentials and state-controlled economic system. It is also believed in some quarters that Turkey's Moslem character disqualifies it from EU membership. However, following recent political and economic reforms in Turkey, the EU has agreed to reconsider Turkey's full application for membership, beginning in December 2004. If all proceeds smoothly, the Turkish government hopes to join in 2012/13.

Liechtenstein is not a member of the EU

Andorra is not a member of the EU

Monaco, San Marino and Vatican City maintain connections with the EU due to their close relationships with France and Italy respectively

Gibraltar, as a dependency of the UK, is part of the EU

Ceuta and Melilla are integral parts of Spain

Since the 1974 Turkish invasion, Cyprus has been partitioned between the southern, mainly Greek-populated 'Republic of Cyprus' and the Turkish-controlled northern sector. Only the Republic of Cyprus, which enjoys full international recognition, has been admitted to the EU. The 'Turkish Republic of Northern Cyprus' is not recognised by the EU.

Legend

█ **Founder members** (1957)

░ **Other members**

Denmark, Ireland & the UK joined on 1st Jan 1973; Greece on 1st Jan 1981; Portugal & Spain on 1st Jan 1986; Austria, Finland & Sweden on 1st Jan 1995. Following the reunification of Germany in 1990, the former German Democratic Republic was automatically admitted to the EEC.

░ **Candidate countries**

░ **Other candidate countries**

Bulgaria & Romania (due to join 2007) Turkey (may join 2012/13)

The ten candidate countries marked have been accepted to join the EU on 1st May 2004. The final decision depends on favourable votes in the European parliament (which has already concurred), the national parliaments of existing members (a formality) and in national referenda in each of the candidate countries. As of 1st July 2003, the peoples of eight of the ten – Estonia and Latvia will hold their polls in September 2003 – had endorsed membership.

Membership applications from three additional countries have been provisionally accepted. Accession negotiations for Bulgaria and Romania are already in progress; negotiations with Turkey will begin at the end of 2004.

There are no formal limits on the ultimate boundaries of the EU and other nations may apply to join in future. These include countries which have previously opted out (Norway, Iceland, Switzerland), the Balkan states (the former Yugoslav republics, Albania) and perhaps others beyond Europe in the former Soviet Union, the Levant and North Africa.

The process of joining the EU begins with the signing of an Association Agreement, essentially a free trade accord. Then, once a formal application for membership has been lodged and provisionally accepted, the candidate country must fulfil three main sets of conditions: democratic government, guaranteeing human rights and the rule of law; a market economy; and adoption of the EU's acquis. The 31 acquis lay down the basic principles and standards to which all member states must subscribe and cover almost every aspect of government.

ITALY **Members which have adopted monetary union**

The single European currency, the Euro, came into being on 1st January 1999. It is supervised by the European Central Bank which was created at the same time and is also responsible for setting interest rates throughout the Euro-zone. For its first three years the Euro was used only for transactions between banks, companies and organisations. Since January 2002, it has been the sole legitimate currency in the 12 states which have adopted it. (The initial 11 member countries were joined by Greece at the beginning of 2001).

Three existing EU members (Denmark, Sweden, UK) have so far eschewed it for various political and economic reasons.

The candidate countries will be able to adopt the Euro provided their economies meet the requisite criteria: these impose limits on inflation, interest and exchange rates and on government finances.

░ **Schengen countries**

The Schengen Agreement allows for the removal of most frontier controls and the harmonisation of procedures governing the movement of people and goods between signatory countries. It also provides for co-operation between law enforcement agencies in specified areas including immigration, terrorism and serious crime. Two non-EU countries, Iceland and Norway, are associate members of the Schengen Agreement.

Britain and Ireland subscribe only to some parts of the Schengen Agreement.

Most of the Schengen conditions have now been incorporated into the acquis which comprise the basic conditions for entry into the EU. As such, all new EU members will necessarily adopt the Schengen measures in due course.

█ **Principal EU institutions**

■ **Capital cities**

SUMMARY TABLE

For more country statistics, including tourism, energy and health, see the Countries A-Z section in the Appendices

The provisions and conditions of EU membership apply to the following territories which are integral parts of member states: Canary Is., Ceuta and Melilla (Spain); French Guiana, Guadeloupe, Martinique and Réunion (France); Faroe Is. (Denmark); Azores and Madeira (Portugal).

	Country	Exchange rate, 1st Jun 2003 One euro equals:	Currency	Central Bank interest rate, 1st Jun 2003 (%)	Normal VAT rate (%)	Inflation, 2002 average (%)	Unemployment, 2002 average (% of workforce)	Balance of payments, 2002 (m euros)	GDP growth, 2002 (%)	Gov't debt, 2001 (% of GDP)	Gov't expenditure, 2000 (% of GDP)
EURO ZONE	Austria	1		2.50	20 [1]	1.7	4.3	+1,632	1.2	67.3	40.4
	Belgium	1		2.50	21	1.6	7.3	+12,876	1.2	108.5	45.6
	Finland	1		2.50	22 [2]	2.0	9.1	+1,051	2.2	43.8	33.4
	France	1		2.50	19.6 [3]	1.9	8.7	+30,170	1.1	56.8	46.2
	Germany	1		2.50	16 [4]	1.3	8.6	+51,138	0.4	59.5	32.7
	Greece	1		2.50	18 [5]	3.9	9.9	−9,540	3.6	107.0	30.7
	Ireland	1		2.50	21	4.7	4.4	−189	3.3	36.8	33.0
	Italy	1		2.50	20 [6]	2.6	9.0	−7,326	1.0	109.5	41.9
	Luxembourg	1		2.50	15	2.1	2.8	+1,976	1.1	5.6	38.2
	Netherlands	1		2.50	19	3.9	2.7	+9,890	0.5	52.8	45.9
	Portugal	1		2.50	17 [7]	3.7	5.1	−8,836	0.5	55.6	38.5
	Spain	1		2.50	16 [8]	3.6	11.3	−17,394	2.0	56.9	32.7
OTHER EU	Denmark	7.43	Krone	2.65	25 [9]	2.4	4.5	+5,694	1.5	45.4	34.9
	Sweden	9.13	Krona	3.50	25	2.0	4.9	+11,111	1.4	54.4	39.3
	United Kingdom	0.72	Sterling	3.75	17.5 [10]	1.3	5.1	−14,463	2.2	39.0	36.0
CANDIDATE COUNTRIES	Cyprus	0.59	Cyprus Pound	4.50	13	2.8	3.8	−441	4.0	na	36.9
	Czech Republic	31.30	Koruna	2.50	22	1.4	8.0	−2,930	3.2	23.7	36.8
	Estonia	15.65	Kroon	2.70	18	3.6	12.4	−378	4.7	4.8	31.4
	Hungary	249.50	Forint	6.50	25	5.2	5.7	−1,239	4.5	53.1	40.2
	Latvia	0.66	Lats	3.00	18	0.4	13.1	−825	5.5	16.0	31.6
	Lithuania	3.45	Litas	5.90	18	2.0	16.5	−640	3.5	23.1	27.6
	Malta	0.48	Maltese Lira	3.50	15	2.4	7.4	−190	3.4	65.7	42.3
	Poland	4.39	Zloty	5.50	22	1.9	18.4	−5,916	3.2	38.7	34.6
	Slovak Republic	41.18	Koruna	7.00	25	7.5	19.4	+32	3.9	44.1	40.5
	Slovenia	239.17	Tolar	8.00	20	3.3	5.7	−1,950	3.6	27.5	40.2

[1] 16% in Jungholz & Mittelberg. [2] Excluding Åland Is. [3] 8.5% in Guadeloupe, Martinique & Réunion. [4] Not applicable in Helgoland. [5] 13% on many of the Greek islands. No VAT applies to Mount Athos. [6] Excluding Livigno, the Italian enclave of Campione d'Italia & territorial waters of Lake Lugano. [7] 12% in the Azores & Madeira. [8] Excluding Canary Is., Ceuta & Melilla. [9] Not applicable in Faroe Is. or Greenland. [10] Excluding Channel Is.

Sources: Eurostat; Central banks; IMF; oanda.com; OECD; World Bank;

Map labels

ICELAND

FAROE IS. (Den.)

NORWAY
SWEDEN
Stockholm
FINLAND
Helsinki (Helsingfors)
ÅLAND
Tallinn
ESTONIA
Riga
LATVIA
LITHUANIA
Vilnius

DENMARK
København (Copenhagen)
EUROPEAN ENVIRONMENT AGENCY

Scotland
N. Ire.
UNITED KINGDOM
I.O.M.
IRELAND
Dublin
Wales England
London
CH. IS.

(German Dem. Rep.)
Warszawa (Warsaw)
POLAND
Berlin
NETHS.
Amsterdam
GERMANY
Bonn
BELG.
Bruxelles/Brussel (Brussels)
COUNCIL OF THE EUROPEAN UNION
EUROPEAN COMMISSION
EUROPEAN PARLIAMENT
COMMITTEE OF PERMANENT REPRESENTATIVES
EU ECONOMIC AND SOCIAL COMMITTEE
EU COMMITTEE OF THE REGIONS
LUX.
Frankfurt am Main
EUROPEAN CENTRAL BANK
Praha (Prague)
CZECH REP.
SLOVAK REP.
Strasbourg
EUROPEAN PARLIAMENT
Bratislava
Paris
LIECH.
Wien (Vienna)
Budapest
AUSTRIA
HUNGARY
Luxembourg
EUROPEAN COURT OF JUSTICE
EUROPEAN COURT OF AUDITORS
EUROPEAN INVESTMENT BANK
EUROSTAT
FRANCE
Ljubljana
SLOVENIA
ROMANIA
Bucureşti (Bucharest)

MONACO
ANDORRA
S.M.
ITALY
VAT Roma (Rome)
BULGARIA
Sofiya (Sofia)

PORTUGAL
Lisboa (Lisbon)
Madrid
SPAIN
Ankara
TURKEY

GIBRALTAR (UK)
CEUTA (Sp.)
MELILLA (Sp.)

GREECE
Athína (Athens)

CYPRUS
Nicosia

Valletta
MALTA

European Union

POPULATION DENSITY

Statistics for Denmark include the Faroe Is.

People per square kilometre, 1999

- 400 and over
- 250 – 399
- 150 – 249
- 80 – 149
- 30 – 79
- Less than 30

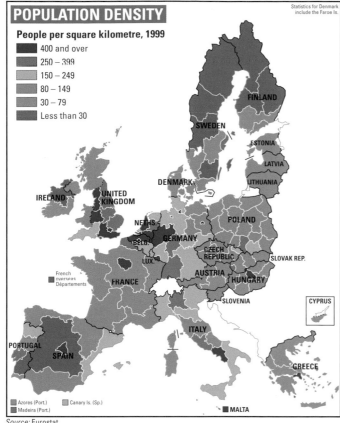

- Azores (Port.)
- Madeira (Port.)
- Canary Is. (Sp.)
- MALTA

Source: Eurostat

THE EU'S LARGEST URBAN AREAS, 2002

Estimated populations in thousands
Source: www.world-gazetteer.com

Köln (Cologne)–Ruhr area	**11,298**	Hamburg	**3,261**	Budapest	**2,598**
[incl. Dortmund, Duisburg, Düsseldorf, Essen, Wuppertal]		Athens	**3,216**	Manchester	**2,482**
		Birmingham area	**3,203**	*[incl. Bolton, Oldham, Stockport]*	
Paris	**11,293**	*[incl. Dudley, Sutton Coldfield, Walsall,*		München (Munich)	**2,342**
Greater London	**11,231**	*West Bromwich, Wolverhampton]*		Stuttgart	**2,330**
Milano (Milan)	**4,052**	Frankfurt am Main	**2,717**	Warszawa (Warsaw)	**2,202**
Berlin	**3,943**	*[incl. Darmstadt, Offenbach am Main,*		Wien (Vienna)	**2,038**
Barcelona	**3,871**	*Wiesbaden]*		Lille	**1,728**
Liverpool *[incl. St Helens]*	**3,630**	Katowice	**2,657**	Lyon *[incl. Villeurbanne]*	**1,666**
Nápoli (Naples)	**3,620**	*[incl. Bytom, Gliwice, Sosnowiec,*		Stockholm	**1,622**
Roma (Rome)	**3,553**	*Zabrze]*		Torino (Turin)	**1,618**
		Lisboa (Lisbon)	**2,612**		

THE EU BUDGET

EU budget receipts, 2001
(Total budget: 94,289 million euros, of which 80,718 million euros from member states)

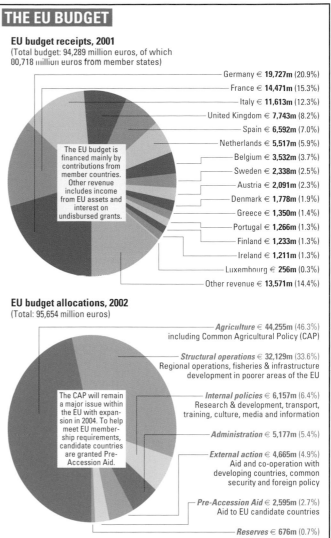

The EU budget is financed mainly by contributions from member countries. Other revenue includes income from EU assets and interest on undisbursed grants.

- Germany € **19,727m** (20.9%)
- France € **14,471m** (15.3%)
- Italy € **11,613m** (12.3%)
- United Kingdom € **7,743m** (8.2%)
- Spain € **6,592m** (7.0%)
- Netherlands € **5,517m** (5.9%)
- Belgium € **3,532m** (3.7%)
- Sweden € **2,338m** (2.5%)
- Austria € **2,091m** (2.3%)
- Denmark € **1,778m** (1.9%)
- Greece € **1,350m** (1.4%)
- Portugal € **1,266m** (1.3%)
- Finland € **1,233m** (1.3%)
- Ireland € **1,211m** (1.3%)
- Luxembourg € **256m** (0.3%)
- Other revenue € **13,571m** (14.4%)

EU budget allocations, 2002
(Total: 95,654 million euros)

The CAP will remain a major issue within the EU with expansion in 2004. To help meet EU membership requirements, candidate countries are granted Pre-Accession Aid.

- *Agriculture* € **44,255m** (46.3%) including Common Agricultural Policy (CAP)
- *Structural operations* € **32,129m** (33.6%) Regional operations, fisheries & infrastructure development in poorer areas of the EU
- *Internal policies* € **6,157m** (6.4%) Research & development, transport, training, culture, media and information
- *Administration* € **5,177m** (5.4%)
- *External action* € **4,665m** (4.9%) Aid and co-operation with developing countries, common security and foreign policy
- *Pre-Accession Aid* € **2,595m** (2.7%) Aid to EU candidate countries
- *Reserves* € **676m** (0.7%)

Source: EU

INCOME

Statistics for Denmark include the Faroe Is.

Gross domestic product per person, 2000

- 25,000 euros (€) and over
- € 20,000 – 24,999
- € 15,000 – 19,999
- € 12,000 – 14,999
- € 10,000 – 11,999
- Less than € 10,000

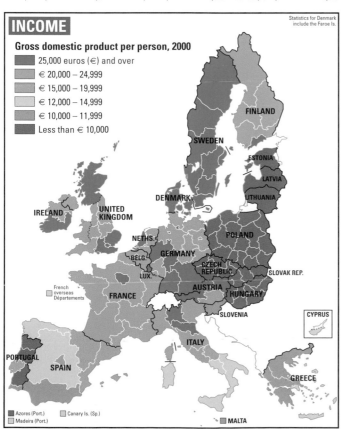

- Azores (Port.)
- Madeira (Port.)
- Canary Is. (Sp.)
- MALTA

Source: Eurostat

UNEMPLOYMENT

Statistics for Denmark include the Faroe Is.

Unemployed as a percentage of the workforce, 2001

- 20% and over
- 15.0% – 19.9%
- 11.0% – 14.9%
- 8.0% – 10.9%
- 5.0% – 7.9%
- Less than 5.0%

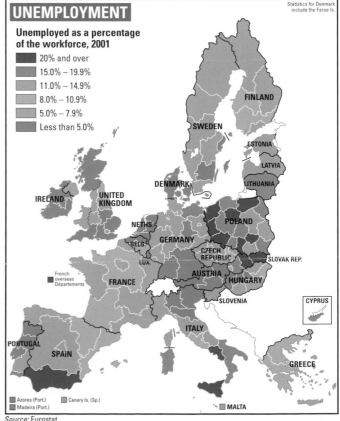

- Azores (Port.)
- Madeira (Port.)
- Canary Is. (Sp.)
- MALTA

Source: Eurostat

Faced with stern competition from the ever-increasing high-speed rail services and the need to utilise precious runway slots for the more lucrative long-haul routes, several European airlines have been forced into co-operation with rail companies. As a result, many previously prestigious air routes, such as Air France's Paris–Brussels and Lufthansa's Stuttgart–Frankfurt, are now run by, or in conjunction with, high-speed rail operators offering city-centre to city-centre services. As the European rail network expands, as its standards of safety, speed and comfort improve and as the continent's airports become more overcrowded, this development is likely to become more widespread. Increasingly, a consideration of Europe's air routes thus also requires an appreciation of these complementary high-speed rail services.

Note: the airports shown are selected, on the basic of international passenger movements, from those which report to Airports Council International (ACI). Some airports in some countries are therefore not shown.

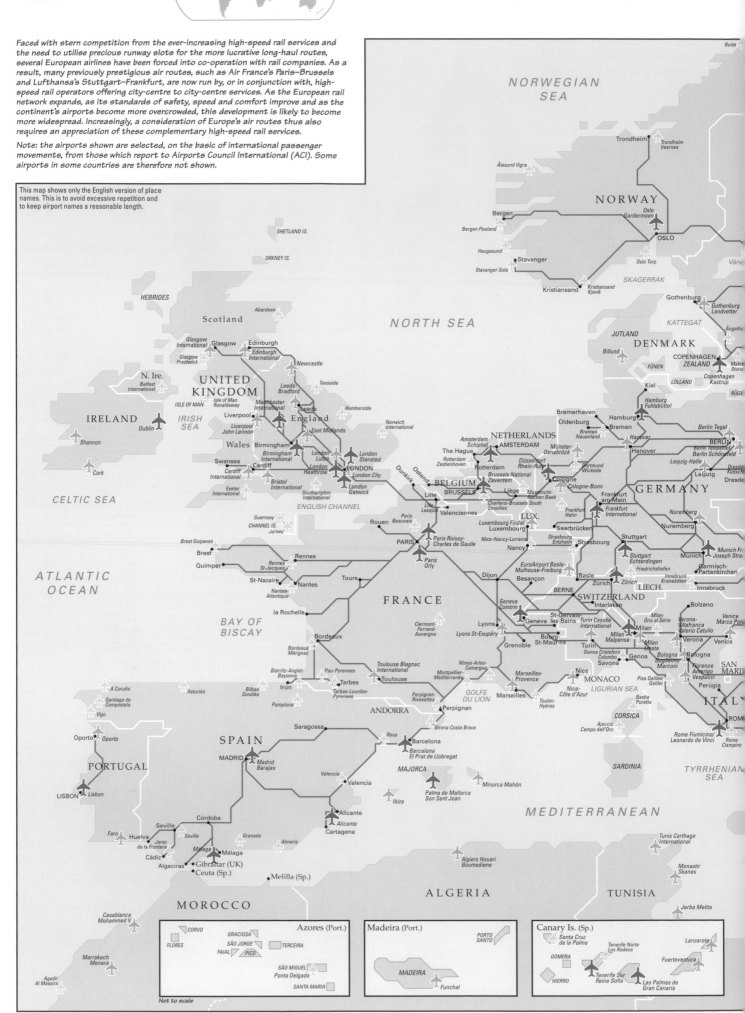

This map shows only the English version of place names. This is to avoid excessive repetition and to keep airport names a reasonable length.

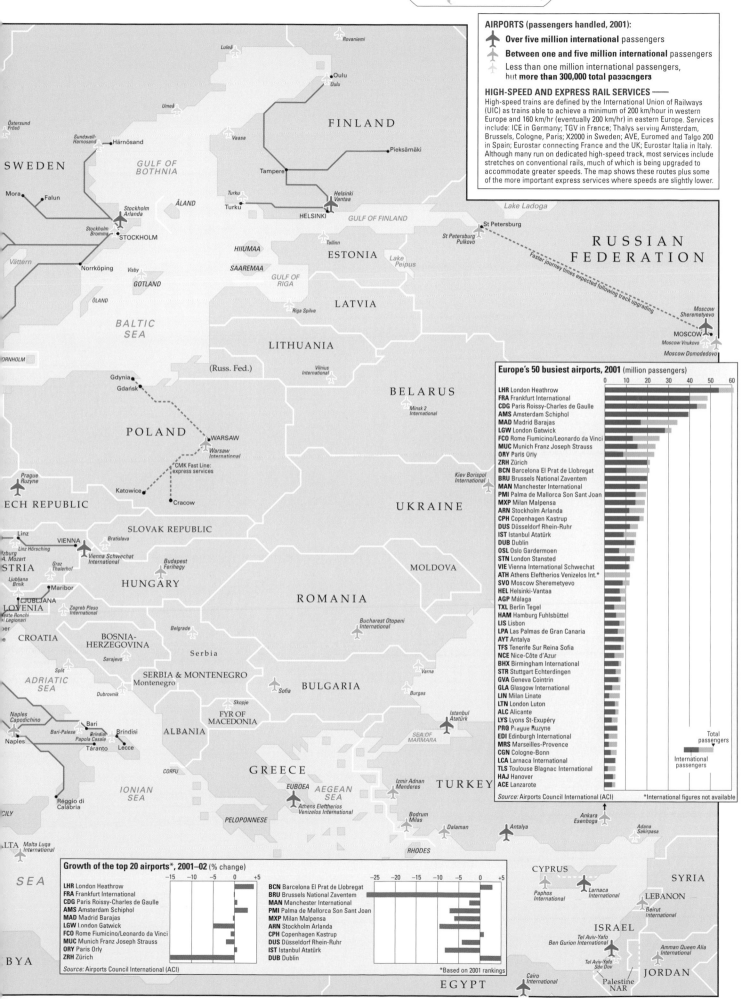

AIRPORTS (passengers handled, 2001):

✈ Over five million **international** passengers

✈ Between one and five million **international** passengers

✈ Less than one million international passengers, but **more than 300,000 total passengers**

HIGH-SPEED AND EXPRESS RAIL SERVICES ——

High-speed trains are defined by the International Union of Railways (UIC) as trains able to achieve a minimum of 200 km/hour in western Europe and 160 km/hr (eventually 200 km/hr) in eastern Europe. Services include: ICE in Germany; TGV in France; Thalys serving Amsterdam, Brussels, Cologne, Paris; X2000 in Sweden; AVE, Euromed and Talgo 200 in Spain; Eurostar connecting France and the UK; Eurostar Italia in Italy. Although many run on dedicated high-speed track, most services include stretches on conventional rails, much of which is being upgraded to accommodate greater speeds. The map shows these routes plus some of the more important express services where speeds are slightly lower.

Europe's 50 busiest airports, 2001 (million passengers)

LHR London Heathrow
FRA Frankfurt International
CDG Paris Roissy-Charles de Gaulle
AMS Amsterdam Schiphol
MAD Madrid Barajas
LGW London Gatwick
FCO Rome Fiumicino/Leonardo da Vinci
MUC Munich Franz Joseph Strauss
ORY Paris Orly
ZRH Zürich
BCN Barcelona El Prat de Llobregat
BRU Brussels National Zaventem
MAN Manchester International
PMI Palma de Mallorca Son Sant Joan
MXP Milan Malpensa
ARN Stockholm Arlanda
CPH Copenhagen Kastrup
DUS Düsseldorf Rhein-Ruhr
IST Istanbul Atatürk
DUB Dublin
OSL Oslo Gardermoen
STN London Stansted
VIE Vienna International Schwechat
ATH Athens Eleftherios Venizelos Int.*
SVO Moscow Sheremetyevo
HEL Helsinki-Vantaa
AGP Málaga
TXL Berlin Tegel
HAM Hamburg Fuhlsbüttel
LIS Lisbon
LPA Las Palmas de Gran Canaria
AYT Antalya
TFS Tenerife Sur Reina Sofia
NCE Nice-Côte d'Azur
BHX Birmingham International
STR Stuttgart Echterdingen
GVA Geneva Cointrin
GLA Glasgow International
LIN Milan Linate
LTN London Luton
ALC Alicante
LYS Lyons St-Exupéry
PRG Prague Ruzyne
EDI Edinburgh International
MRS Marseilles-Provence
CGN Cologne-Bonn
LCA Larnaca International
TLS Toulouse Blagnac International
HAJ Hanover
ACE Lanzarote

Total passengers ▼
International passengers

Source: Airports Council International (ACI) *International figures not available

Growth of the top 20 airports*, 2001–02 (% change)

LHR London Heathrow
FRA Frankfurt International
CDG Paris Roissy-Charles de Gaulle
AMS Amsterdam Schiphol
MAD Madrid Barajas
LGW London Gatwick
FCO Rome Fiumicino/Leonardo da Vinci
MUC Munich Franz Joseph Strauss
ORY Paris Orly
ZRH Zürich

BCN Barcelona El Prat de Llobregat
BRU Brussels National Zaventem
MAN Manchester International
PMI Palma de Mallorca Son Sant Joan
MXP Milan Malpensa
ARN Stockholm Arlanda
CPH Copenhagen Kastrup
DUS Düsseldorf Rhein-Ruhr
IST Istanbul Atatürk
DUB Dublin

Source: Airports Council International (ACI) *Based on 2001 rankings

This map shows principal passenger rail and shipping routes in Europe. Some of the railways marked have limited services but are included because of their significance (such as connection to resort or international crossing).

A number of European rail passes are available, offering free travel on many rail and ferry services.

The Eurail pass is valid for first-class rail travel in the countries shown on the map. For those under 26, the Eurail Youthpass is valid in the same countries for second-class rail travel. The pass is not available to European residents or to visitors from Algeria, Morocco, Tunisia, Turkey or the former Soviet Union.

European residents are eligible for the Inter-Rail pass, offering train travel in the area shown on the map, excluding the country of purchase. Passes are available for one or more zones within the validity area.

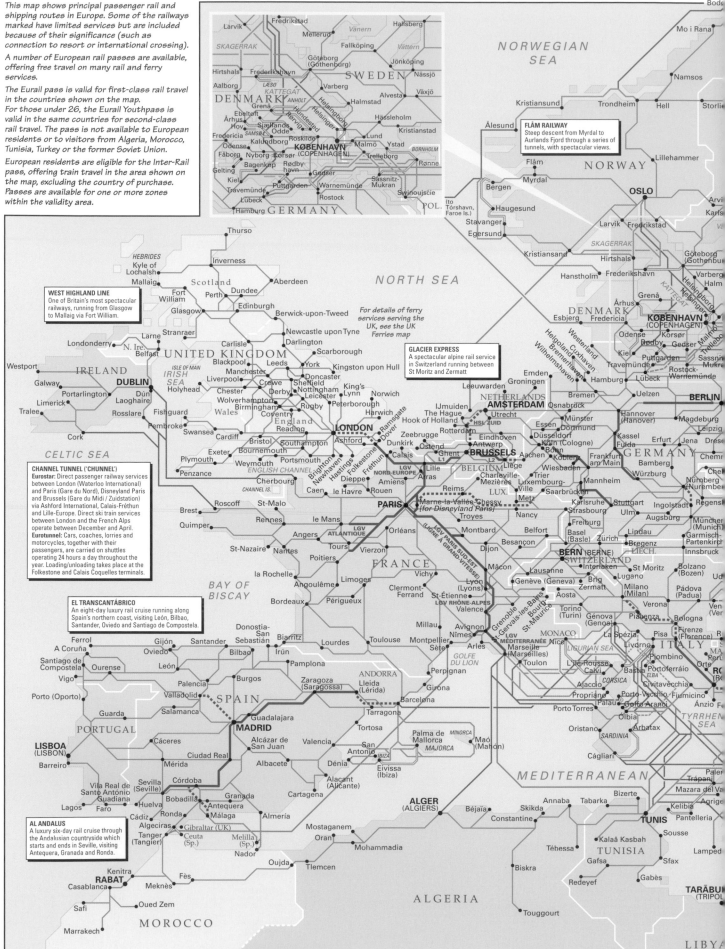

FLÅM RAILWAY
Steep descent from Myrdal to Aurlands Fjord through a series of tunnels, with spectacular views.

WEST HIGHLAND LINE
One of Britain's most spectacular railways, running from Glasgow to Mallaig via Fort William.

GLACIER EXPRESS
A spectacular alpine rail service in Switzerland running between St Moritz and Zermatt.

For details of ferry services serving the UK, see the UK Ferries map

CHANNEL TUNNEL ('CHUNNEL')
Eurostar: Direct passenger railway services between London (Waterloo International) and Paris (Gare du Nord), Disneyland Paris and Brussels (Gare du Midi / Zuidstation) via Ashford International, Calais-Fréthun and Lille-Europe. Direct ski train services between London and the French Alps operate between December and April.
Eurotunnel: Cars, coaches, lorries and motorcycles, together with their passengers, are carried on shuttles operating 24 hours a day throughout the year. Loading/unloading takes place at the Folkestone and Calais Coquelles terminals.

EL TRANSCANTÁBRICO
An eight-day luxury rail cruise running along Spain's northern coast, visiting León, Bilbao, Santander, Oviedo and Santiago de Compostela.

AL ANDALUS
A luxury six-day rail cruise through the Andalusian countryside which starts and ends in Seville, visiting Antequera, Granada and Ronda.

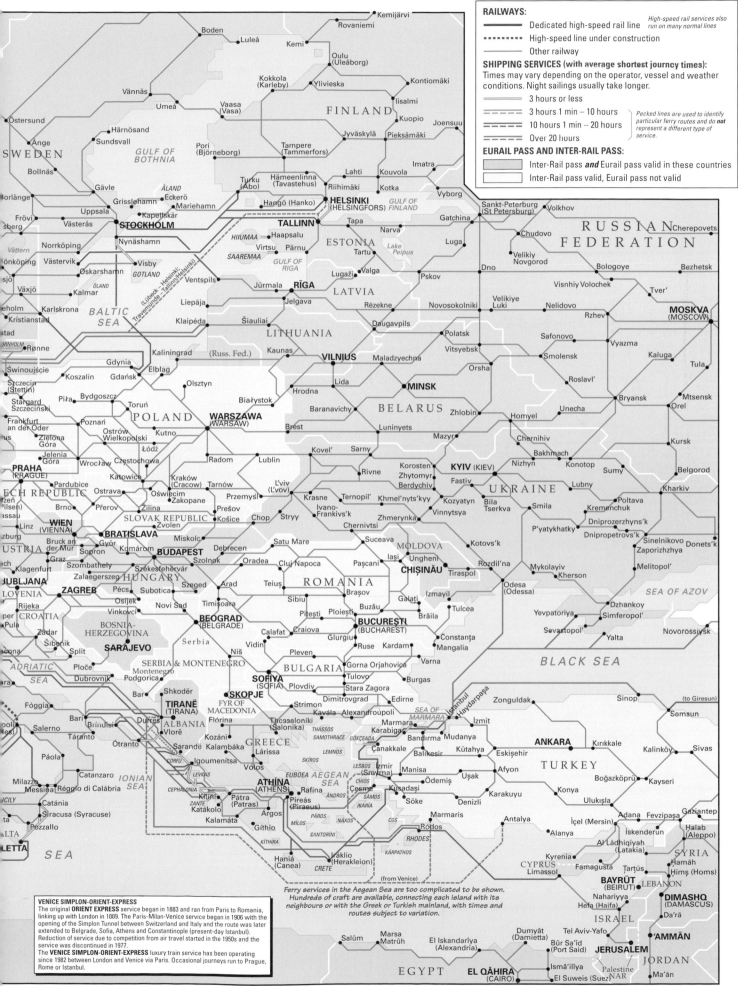

RAILWAYS:

— Dedicated high-speed rail line — High-speed rail services also run on many normal lines
- - - High-speed line under construction
— Other railway

SHIPPING SERVICES (with average shortest journey times):
Times may vary depending on the operator, vessel and weather conditions. Night sailings usually take longer.

3 hours or less
3 hours 1 min – 10 hours — Pecked lines are used to identify particular ferry routes and do **not** represent a different type of service.
10 hours 1 min – 20 hours
Over 20 hours

EURAIL PASS AND INTER-RAIL PASS:

Inter-Rail pass **and** Eurail pass valid in these countries
Inter-Rail pass valid, Eurail pass not valid

Ferry services in the Aegean Sea are too complicated to be shown. Hundreds of craft are available, connecting each island with its neighbours or with the Greek or Turkish mainland, with times and routes subject to variation.

VENICE SIMPLON-ORIENT-EXPRESS
The original **ORIENT EXPRESS** service began in 1883 and ran from Paris to Romania, linking up with London in 1889. The Paris-Milan-Venice service began in 1906 with the opening of the Simplon Tunnel between Switzerland and Italy and the route was later extended to Belgrade, Sofia, Athens and Constantinople (present-day Istanbul). Reduction of service due to competition from air travel started in the 1950s and the service was discontinued in 1977.
The **VENICE SIMPLON-ORIENT-EXPRESS** luxury train service has been operating since 1982 between London and Venice via Paris. Occasional journeys run to Prague, Rome or Istanbul.

This map shows the most important areas that have been designated as National Parks throughout Western and Central Europe.

Sites marked with an asterisk (*) are featured in Columbus Travel Guides' *Tourist Attractions and Events of the World*

Iceland
1 **Jökulsárgljúfur** Spectacular glacial canyon landscape
2 **Skaftafell** Example of active glacial landscape
3 **Thingvellir** Broad forested plain, home of historic Iceland parliament

Norway
4 **Øvre Pasvik** Forest & tundra
5 **Stabbursdalen** Arctic landscape: tundra, lakes, gravel plains & forest
6 **Øvre Anarjokka** Undulating tundra with woodland & lakes
7 **Reisa** Mixed mountain country
8 **Øvre Divdal** Mountainous country with tundra & woodland
9 **Ånderdalen** Mixed mountain country
10 **Saltfjellet-Svartisen** Varied landscape; fjords, mountains & glacier
11 **Børgefjell** Remote mountain area with varied habitats
12 **Gressåmoen** Mountainous country & spruce forest
13 **Dovrefjell** Mountainous tundra & snowfields; famous for its flora
14 **Rondane** Mountain country with varied landscapes
15 **Jotunheimen** Mountainous area with tundra, bogs & forest
16 **Hardangervidda** Large mountain plateau, a popular walking area

Sweden
17 **Vadvetjåkka** Wild terrain with karst caves
18 **Abisko** Mountain & forest with tundra, lakes & rivers
19 **Muddus** Forest, tundra & bog
20 **Padjelanta, Sarek and Stora Sjöfallet** 3 parks protect Europe's largest wilderness area; mixed landscape
21 **Pieljekaise** Wooded mountainous country with tundra, open water & bogs
22 **Skuleskogen** Coastal forest landscape
23 **Töfsingdalen** Woodland, tundra & bog
24 **Sånfjället** Woodland, tundra & bog
25 **Hamra** Woodland, tundra & bog, noted for its insects
26 **Garphyttan** Forest & meadows
27 **Tiveden** Hilly forest, lakes & bogs
28 **Store Mosse** Predominantly boggy, with lakes & forest
29 **Gotska Sandön** Sand & gravel island

Finland
30 **Pallas-Ounastunturi** Upland plateau & taiga, with lakes, tundra, gorges & forest
31 **Lemmenjoki** Wilderness mountain area; gold rush in 1940's
32 **Urho Kekkonen** Large wilderness area with fells, forest & peatlands
33 **Pyhätunturi** Mountainous area with tundra, bogs & forest
34 **Oulanka** Varied tundra landscape
35 **Petkeljärvi** Typical Finnish lakeland scenery
36 **Linnansaari** Lake & islands
37 **Pyhä-Häkki** Mainly forest & bog
38 **Seitseminen** Typical S Finland landscape with forest & bog
39 **Liesjärvi** Lakes, previously cultivated land & forest
40 **Saaristomeri** Extensive island group with mixed habitats

Denmark
41 **Rebild Bakker** Glacial valleys, hills & woodland; home to largest 4th July celebrations outside US

Ireland
42 **Glenveagh** Mixed upland area
43 **Connemara** Typical W Ireland mountain area
44 **Killarney*** Ancient woodland with moorland, lakes, bogs, wetland & mountains
45 **Wicklow Mountains** Partly wooded mountains with upland moorland & grassland

United Kingdom
46 **Cairngorms** Mountain region with ski resorts
47 **Loch Lomond & the Trossachs** Lakes & wooded valley with literary associations
48 **Northumberland** Mainly upland grassy moorland; Hadrian's Wall in S
49 **Lake District** Mountain & lakeland; very popular all year
50 **Yorkshire Dales** Varied upland country
51 **North York Moors** Hilly uplands with heather moorland
52 **Peak District** Limestone in the south, with many caves; high peat moors in the north
53 **Snowdonia*** Mountain country with lakes, moorland, grassland & woodland
54 **Pembrokeshire Coast** Scenic coastline; varied seabird habitats
55 **Brecon Beacons*** Mainly grass-covered mountain area
56 **Exmoor** High heather moorland & wooded valleys, with dramatic coastline
57 **Dartmoor** Granite uplands with heather & grassland

Netherlands
58 **Dwingelderveld** Heathland, fen & woodland with lakes
59 **De Hoge Veluwe** Variety of habitats: heathland, dunes, fens, wet heath & woodland
Veluwezoom Heath & mixed woodland
60 **De Biesbosch** Confluence of Maas & Waal

Germany
61 **Niedersächsisches Wattenmeer** East Frisan Islands; mudflats & saltmarsh
62 **Hamburgisches W'meer** Mudflats & saltmarsh
63 **Schleswig-Holsteinisches W'meer** Mudflats & saltmarsh
64 **Vorpommersche Boddenlandschaft** Mudflats & saltmarsh with dunes, lagoons, lakes & woodland
65 **Jasmund** Varied landscape with cliffs, lakes & woodland
66 **Müritz** Woodland & lakes with heath, marsh & pasture
67 **Unteres Odertal** Floodplain of the Oder; park shared with Poland
68 **Sächsische Schweiz** Numerous rock towers; lower slopes wooded; deep valleys
69 **Hoch Harz** Wooded mountains with moorland, bogs & lakes
70 **Bayerischer Wald** Wooded mountain area
71 **Berchtesgaden** Mountain landscape with Alpine pastures, small glaciers, cliffs, lakes & varied woodland

France
72 **Vanoise** High mountain scenery
73 **Écrins** High mountain scenery with glaciers
74 **Mercantour** Some of the best parts of the Maritime Alps
75 **Port-Cros** Small wooded island
76 **Cévennes** Varied mountain & forest
77 **Pyrénées-Occidentales** Diverse mountain landscape; snowfields, pastures & woodland

Spain
78 **Aigües Tortes-Sant Maurici** Characteristic glacial landscape of high Pyrenees
79 **Ordesa** Spectacular mountain & gorge scenery; forests & Alpine pastures
80 **Covadonga** Mountain area with mixed woodlands, pasture & glacial lakes
81 **Tablas de Daimiel** Small wetland
82 **Doñana** Guadalquivir delta; important wildlife site
83 **Caldera de Taburiente** Volcanic landscape
84 **Garajonay** Sub-tropical forests
85 **Cañadas del Teide** Volcanic landscapes
86 **Timanfaya** Volcanic landscapes

Portugal
87 **Peneda-Gerês** Mountain & forest area; cliffs & rock formations

Switzerland
88 **The Swiss National Park** Strictly controlled mountainous area; forests, pastures, lakes, cliffs & snowfields

Austria
89 **Hohe Tauern** High Alpine scenery; forests in lower areas
90 **Nockberge** Forested mountain area with bogs & moors
91 **Donau-auen** Danube flood plain E of Vienna

Neusiedler See Europe's largest steppe lake, over half is thick reedbeds

Italy
92 **Stelvio** Typical Alpine scenery & large glacier
93 **Gran Paradiso** High Alpine country; famous for the Ibex
94 **Monti Sibillini** Upspoilt mountain area with folklore connections
95 **Gran Sasso e Monti della Laga** Varied landscape of mountains, rivers & lakes
96 **Abruzzo** Wooded mountainous area
Maiella Group of high peaks with karst plains
97 **Circeo** Coastal marsh & rocky promontory
98 **Calábria** Three areas of wooded mountainous landscape

Poland
99 **Wolinski** Woodland, lakes and sea cliffs; white-tailed sea eagle the main attraction
100 **Slowinski** Coastal landscape with shifting sand dunes
101 **Kampinoski** Varied landscape nr. Warsaw
102 **Mazurski & Wigierski** Numerous lakes and extensive forests
103 **Biebrzanski** Central Europe's largest area of natural peat bogs
104 **Bialowieski** Europe's largest original lowland forest; principal attraction the European bison

105 **Bieszczadzki** Remote wooded mountain area in E Carpathians
106 **Babiogórski, Tatrzanski, Gorczanski & Pieninski** Four parks in the spectacular High Tatra mountains
107 **Ojcówski** Hilly landscape with many rock pinnacles
108 **Gory Stolowe & Karkonoski** Dramatic mountain scenery of the Sudety Mountains

Czech Republic
109 **Krkonose** Wooded mountain area with Alpine pastures, meadows, bogs & lakes
110 **Sumava** Forested slopes, ancient mountains & peat bogs

Slovak Republic
111 **Vysoké Tatry*** (High Tatras) **Nízke Tatry*** (Low Tatras) Spectacular mtn area: forests, lakes, grassland & bogs
112 **Pieninsky** Limestone mountains with mixed forests
113 **Slovenská raj** Karst plateau with extensive caves

Hungary
114 **Aggtelek** Important karst scenery
Bukk Hilly forested region
115 **Hortobágyi** Varied steppe landscape with rich birdlife
116 **Kiskunság** Wide range of lowland habitats

Slovenia
117 **Triglav** Limestone mountain scenery & mixed forest

Croatia
118 **Risnjak** Limestone mountain scenery & mixed forest
119 **Plitvice Lakes*** Scenic lakes linked by waterfalls formed by limestone deposition
Paklenica Limestone peaks, gorges & mixed forest
120 **Kornati** Limestone islands, karst scenery
121 **Krka** Park follows the route of the Krka river; lakes, dams, gorges, falls & woodland
122 **Mljet** Western part of island

Bosnia-Herzegovina
123 **Sutjeska** Wooded mountainous area; mixed landscape & reserve of virgin forest

Serbia & Montenegro
124 **Fruska Gora** Wooded hilly valley
125 **Djerdap** Gorge of the Danube; dam has created a long thin lake
126 **Tara** Mixed upland scenery
127 **Durmitor** Mountain area in the west, Tara Gorge in east; mixed landscape & karst
Biogradska Gora Mountain area with high grasslands & five lakes
128 **Lovcen** Wooded limestone mountains

Skadarsko jezero Montenegran part of Lake Scutari

Former Yugoslav Rep. of Macedonia
129 **Mavrovo** Mountain area, partly wooded
130 **Galicica** S end of Dinaric Alps; mostly natural forest
Pelister Wooded mountain area with Alpine pastures

Albania
131 **Divjaka** Dunes & coastal woodland with rich birdlife on neighbouring lagoon

Romania
132 **Retezat** Mountain country with extensive forest

Bulgaria
133 **Rusenski Lom** Deciduous woodland
134 **Central Balkan** Widely varied landscape; thick forests
135 **Vitosa** Varied mountain area
136 **Pirin** High mountains; forest & mixed landscape
Rila Alpine peaks & many small lakes the 'Eyes of the Rila'

Greece
137 **Préspa** Shallow lakes with reed- & sedge-beds
138 **Olimbos (Olympus)** Mountain area with maquis & forest; home of the gods in ancient Greek mythology

139 **Pindos** Wooded mountain area
Vikos-Aóos Wooded mountain area; Vikos & Aóos gorges
140 **Ainos** Area around Mt Aínos
141 **Iti Óros** Wooded mountain area
Parnassós Wilderness mountain area; mixed habitats
142 **Párnitha** Limestone area; maquis
Soúnion Typical Greek coastline

Turkey
143 **Manyas-Kuscenneti** Part of large lake

Estonia
144 **Lahemaa** Wooded area & scenic coast
145 **Vilsandi** Exposed coastline with shifting dunes
146 **Soomaa** Marsh & forest, severe annual flooding
147 **Karula** Forested area with glacial debris

Latvia
148 **Gauja** River & gorge scenery; the 'Switzerland of Latvia'

Lithuania
149 **Kursiv Nerija** Long sand spit with popular beaches; ice fishing in winter
150 **Zemaitija** Forest with popular Lake Platelai
151 **Aukstaitija (Ignalina)** Forest & lakes; great diversity of wildlife
152 **Trakai** 5 lakes; Trakai Castle as centrepiece
153 **Dzukija** Confluence of Nemunas & Merkys rivers

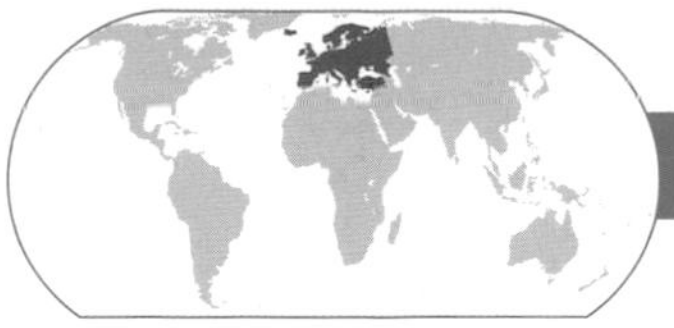

Leisure Parks

This map shows major theme parks and amusement parks in Europe. Most of those shown are members of either the International Association of Amusement Parks and Attractions (IAAPA) or the European Federation of Amusement and Leisure Parks (Europarks). Most parks which primarily attract visitors from the local area have been excluded.

Parks marked with an asterisk (*) are featured in Columbus Travel Guides' *Tourist Attractions and Events of the World.*

Thanks to Jeff Bertus Leisure for help in compiling this section.

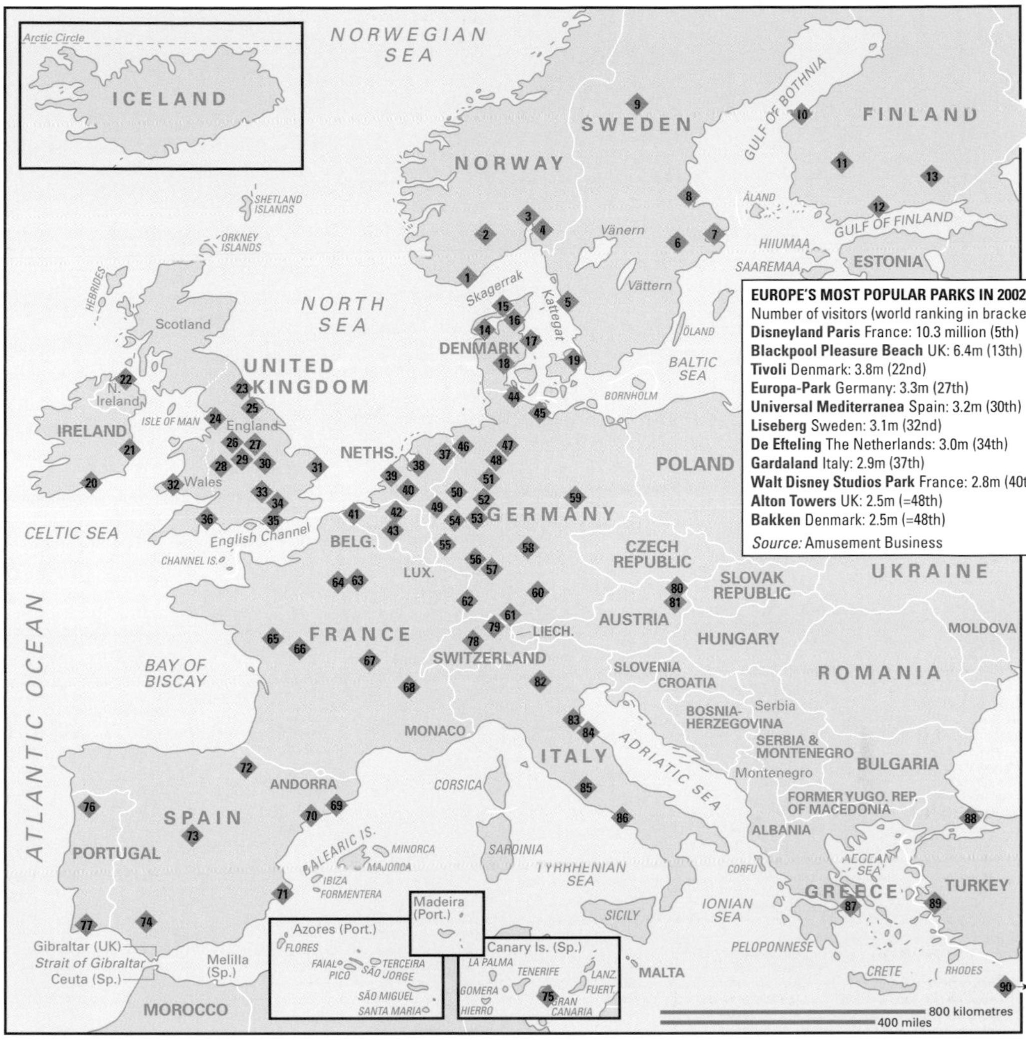

EUROPE'S MOST POPULAR PARKS IN 2002
Number of visitors (world ranking in brackets)
Disneyland Paris France: 10.3 million (5th)
Blackpool Pleasure Beach UK: 6.4m (13th)
Tivoli Denmark: 3.8m (22nd)
Europa-Park Germany: 3.3m (27th)
Universal Mediterranea Spain: 3.2m (30th)
Liseberg Sweden: 3.1m (32nd)
De Efteling The Netherlands: 3.0m (34th)
Gardaland Italy: 2.9m (37th)
Walt Disney Studios Park France: 2.8m (40th)
Alton Towers UK: 2.5m (=48th)
Bakken Denmark: 2.5m (=48th)
Source: Amusement Business

Norway

1 **Kristiansand Dyrepark**
Norway's largest zoo and amusement park
2 **Telemark Sommarland**, Bø
Combined waterpark and theme park
3 **Lunds Tivoli**, Oslo
Amusement park
4 **TusenFryd & VikingLandet**, Vinterbro
Theme park and a small water park; VikingLandet is a re-enactment of the Viking Age

Sweden

5 **Liseberg**, Gothenburg
Large theme park with convention facilities and harbour
6 **Parken Zoo i Eskilstuna**
Zoo, amusement park and waterpark
7 **Gröna Lunds Tivoli**, Stockholm
Amusement park in the centre of Stockholm, founded 1883
8 **Furuviksparken**, Gavle
Amusement park and zoo
9 **Jamtli Historieland**, Östersund
Combined indoor and outdoor museum

Finland

10 **Wasalandia**, Vaasa
Family theme park with Tropical Spa Tropiclandia
11 **Tampereen Sarkanniemi Oy**, Tampere
City-centre amusement park and entertainment centre; includes an art museum, dolphinarium and planetarium
12 **Linnanmäki**, Helsinki
Finland's most popular amusement park with live stage shows and a Sea Life Centre
13 **Tykkimäki**, Kouvola
Large amusement park with reptile zoo and dance pavilion

Denmark

14 **Jesperhus Blomstherpark**, Nykøbing, Mors
Amusement park, family entertainment centre and zoo
15 **Fårup Aquapark & Sommerland**, Saltum
Amusement park with more than 30 activities and Scandinavia's largest waterpark
16 **Tivoliland**, Aalborg
Large amusement park
17 **Djurs Sommerland**, Nimtofte
Amusement park with more than 60 activities and shows and a waterpark
18 **LEGOLAND Billund***
Theme park based on LEGO toy products; interactive attractions, building challenges, *Driving School* & *Miniland*
19 **Dyrehavsbakken ('Bakken')**, Klampenborg
The world's oldest amusement park, over 100 attractions
Tivoli*, Copenhagen
Large amusement park in the centre of Copenhagen, opened in 1843; a mixture of new and old rides; the famous Copenhagen Christmas Market is held here in Nov & Dec

Ireland

20 **Perks Pleasure Park**, Youghal
Seaside amusement park with neighbouring wildlife park
21 **Clara Lara Fun Park**, Wicklow
Park and amusement centre plus a junior playground

United Kingdom

22 **Barry's Amusement Park**, Portrush
Family amusement park with rides for all ages
23 **The New Metroland**, Gateshead
Europe's largest indoor funfair with many rides
24 **Blackpool Pleasure Beach***
Opened in 1896, over 145 attractions and rides classified according to their 'terror factor'; one of the biggest collections of white-knuckle rides in the world, plus spectacular shows & Ripley's Believe It or Not! Odditorium
Camelot Theme Park, Chorley, Lancashire
A medieval world with over 100 attractions and rides
25 **Flamingo Land and Holiday Village**, Malton
Amusement park and zoo with eight coaster rides and many extreme rides in White Knuckle Valley
Lightwater Valley, Ripon
Theme park with unique attractions including the world's first suspended hang-glider ride and the world's longest rollercoaster
26 **Alton Towers***, near Stoke-on-Trent
One of the UK's most popular theme parks with 125 rides and attractions in a number of different kingdoms: *Ugland, Forbidden Valley, Towers Street* and *Cred Street*
Gullivers Kingdom, Matlock Bath
Theme park with over 35 rides and hot-air balloon flights
27 **American Adventure World**, Ilkeston
Adventure park with a American theme
28 **West Midland Safari Park**, Bewdley
Drive-around safari park; leisure area with over 25 rides
29 **Drayton Manor Park**, Tamworth
Theme park with over 100 rides and attractions, plus a zoo, parkland, lakes and walks
30 **Wicksteed Park**, Kettering
UK's oldest theme park, opened in 1921
31 **Pleasurewood Hills**, Lowestoft
50 rides, sea lion and parrot shows, a castle and theatre
32 **Oakwood Adventure**, Narberth
Theme park with over 40 attractions including stage shows
33 **LEGOLAND Windsor***
Over 50 interactive rides, building workshops and driving schools in beautiful parkland
34 **Chessington World of Adventures***
Zoo includes gorillas and large cats; amusement park with many rides
Thorpe Park, Chertsey
The UK's fastest changing thrill park with many white-knuckle rides
35 **Harbour Park**, Littlehampton
Seaside amusement park with extensive undercover facilities and arcades
36 **Crealy Adventure Park**, Exeter
A re-creation of a country childhood; with six different realms combining magic, adventure, action, animals, farming and nature

The Netherlands

37 **Attractiepark Slagharen**, Slagharen
Theme park with Wild West shows and over 40 rides
Avonturenpark Hellendoorn
Amusement park with many rides and animal attractions
38 **Dolfinarium Harderwijk**
Europe's largest marine theme park featuring six different shows with animals plus a dolphin rehabilitation centre, an open-air dolphin lagoon and a research centre
Six Flags Holland, Dronten
Family amusement park famous for its rollercoasters
39 **Drievliet**, Rijswijk
Family park with over 30 major attractions, shows and playgrounds
Duinrell, Wassenaar
Family park with educational exhibitions; over 50 rides and water attractions
40 **De Efteling**, Kaatsheuvel
One of Europe's leading family leisure parks with a full range of attractions including spectacular shows and PandaVision, an educational 3D journey through the world of nature

Belgium

41 **Bellewaerde Park**, Ypres
Mix of attractions and exotic animals in a natural setting
Boudewijnpark, Bruges
Family park, famous for its dolphinarium; with rides, skating, boating, Seal Island and other animals
Plopsaland, De Panne
Theme park for families with children up to 12 years old
42 **Bobbejaanland**, Lichtaart
Amusement and theme park with 45 major rides, including *The Revolution* and *Arcade 2000*; also includes *Kinderland*, a covered children's play area with 20 rides
43 **Six Flags Belgium**, Wavre
Over 50 attractions and shows; includes Aqualibi, a tropical waterpark

Germany

44 **Familien-Freizeitpark Tolk-Schau**, Tolk
Amusement park situated in a scenic landscape
45 **Hansapark**, Sierksdorf
Theme park with many rides and attractions including water circus and 3,000-seat Hansapark Theatre
46 **Ferienzentrum Schloss Dankern**, Haren
Family entertainment centre with many water facilities
47 **Heide-Park**, Soltau
Amusement park with shows and 40 major rides
Serengeti Safaripark, Hodenhagen
Animal park over 1,000 animals and three themed areas: *Monkey Land, Leisure Land* and *Water Land*
48 **Dinosaurier Park Münchehagen**, Rehburg-Loccum
Dinosaur park
49 **Kernwasser Wunderland**, Kalkar
Unique amusement park for children up to 12 years old on the site of a former nuclear power station
50 **Warner Brothers Movie World**, Bottrop
Movie theme park with over 40 attractions and shows including stunt shows and a free-fall tower
51 **Safari & Hollywood-Park**, Schloss Holte-Stukenbrock
Combined safari park and amusement park
52 **Fort Fun Abenteuerland**, Bestwig
Amusement park with a Western theme
53 **Panoramapark Sauerland**, Kirchhundem
Wild animal park and amusement park with its own 500-kilowatt windpower station
54 **Phantasialand**, Brühl
Theme park divided into six areas: *China Town, Old Berlin, Fantasy, Mystery, Mexico* and *Silver City*; attractions include shows and culinary delicacies
55 **Eifelpark**, Gondorf bei Bitburg
Wild animal park and amusement park with open-air theatre
56 **Holiday-Park**, Hassloch
Theme park with many attractions and rides including a 180-degree cinema and a live show parade
57 **Erlebnispark Tripsdrill**, Cleebronn
Germany's oldest amusement park with rides and animals
58 **Freizeit-Land**, Geiselwind
Theme park and zoo, including four rollercoasters
59 **BELANTIS**, Leipzig
Attractions and live shows in six BELANTIS Worlds: *Castle BELANTIS, Beach of the Gods, Valley of the Pharoahs, Country of the Counts, Island of the Knights* and *Coast of the Discoverers*
60 **LEGOLAND Deutschland**, Günzburg
Unique blend of entertainment and learning by play for families with children up to 13 years old
61 **Ravensberger Spieleland**, Meckenbeuren
Largest playground in the world with over 40 attractions
62 **Europa-Park**, Rust
One of Europe's major parks, close to France & Switzerland

France

63 **Disneyland Resort Paris***, Marne-la-Vallée
Disneyland Paris is divided into five areas: *Main Street USA, Frontierland, Adventure-land, Fantasyland* and *Discoveryland*. ***Walt Disney Studios Park***, opened in 2002, takes visitors back to the golden age of Hollywood and also behind the scenes of movie-making. ***Disney Village*** is Europe's largest entertainment complex.
La Mer de Sable, Ermenonville
Amusement park developed into themed areas: *China, Wild West* and *Morocco*; includes *Babagattau Village*
Parc Astérix*, Plailly
Theme park offering visitors a 3D trip into comic strip Asterix's universe, spread out over six neighbourhoods
64 **Le Jardin d'Acclimatation**, Paris
Amusement park with family rides and a zoo
65 **Grand Parc du Puy du Fou**, Les Espesses
Historical park with live shows and other attractions
66 **Futuroscope***, Jaunay-Clan, near Poitiers
Space-age park with advanced visual-image technology including an IMAX screen, virtual reality and Cyberspace
67 **Le Pal**, Dompierre sur Besbre
Animal and amusement park; shows feature sea lions, parrots and birds
68 **Walibi Rhône-Alpes**, Les Avenières
Regional amusement park with more than 30 rides and a waterpark area

Spain

69 **Parc d'Atraccions Tibidabo**, Barcelona
Urban amusement park, founded 1899, renovated 1988
70 **Universal Mediterranea***, Salou
Europe's only Universal Studios Theme Park; also Costa Caribe waterpark, Zona de Playa beach, Port Aventura resort
71 **Terra Mítica***, Benidorm
Five areas: *Egypt, Iberia, Greece, Rome* and *The Islands*, illustrate the past, present and future of Mediterranean culture
72 **Txiki Park**, Pamplona
Family entertainment centre designed for children
73 **Parque de Atracciones Casa de Campo**, Madrid
Urban amusement park, Madrid's main entertainment centre
Warner Brothers Movie World, Madrid
Movie theme park with live shows and numerous attractions including Superman and Batman rides
74 **Parque Isla Magica**, Seville
Theme park based upon exploration of the New World by 16th century Spanish adventurers
75 **Sioux City**, San Agustin, Gran Canaria
Western-themed park with stage shows and concerts

Portugal

76 **Bracalândia**, Braga
Theme park with various themed areas and attractions
77 **Zoomarine**, Albufeira
Zoo and marine park taking its theme from the Algarve's links with the sea

Switzerland

78 **Mystery Park**, Interlaken
Theme parks presenting unexplained mysteries of the world
79 **Conny-Land**, Lipperswil
Amusement park with underwater and animal shows

Austria

80 **Safari- und Abenteuerpark**, Gänserndorf
Adventure park and drive-through safari park
81 **Wiener Prater**, Vienna
Amusement park for over 100 years

Italy

82 **Gardaland**, Castelnuovo del Garda
Huge multiufunctional amusement park with many attractions; four themed villages; profusion of plants and flowers
83 **Mirabilandia**, Sàvio
Amusement park with rides, stage shows and concerts
84 **Fiabilandia**, Rimini
Amusement park and funfair
85 **Luneur**, Rome
Traditional amusement park and funfair, 30 years old
86 **Edenlandia**, Naples
One of Italy's largest amusement parks

Greece

87 **Luna Park 'Ta Aidonakia'**, Athens
20 family and children's rides

Turkey

88 **Tatilya Turizm**, Avcilar, Istanbul
Largest indoor entertainment centre in Europe and the Middle East, Tatilya is a holiday and amusement republic with its own president, citizens and constitution
89 **Aqua Fantasy***, Selçuk
Turkey's largest water park

Cyprus

90 **WaterWorld**, Ayia Napa
Cyprus' largest waterpark and most popular attraction

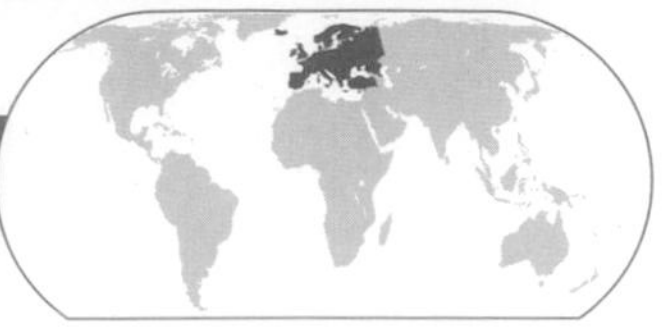

Museums & Art Galleries

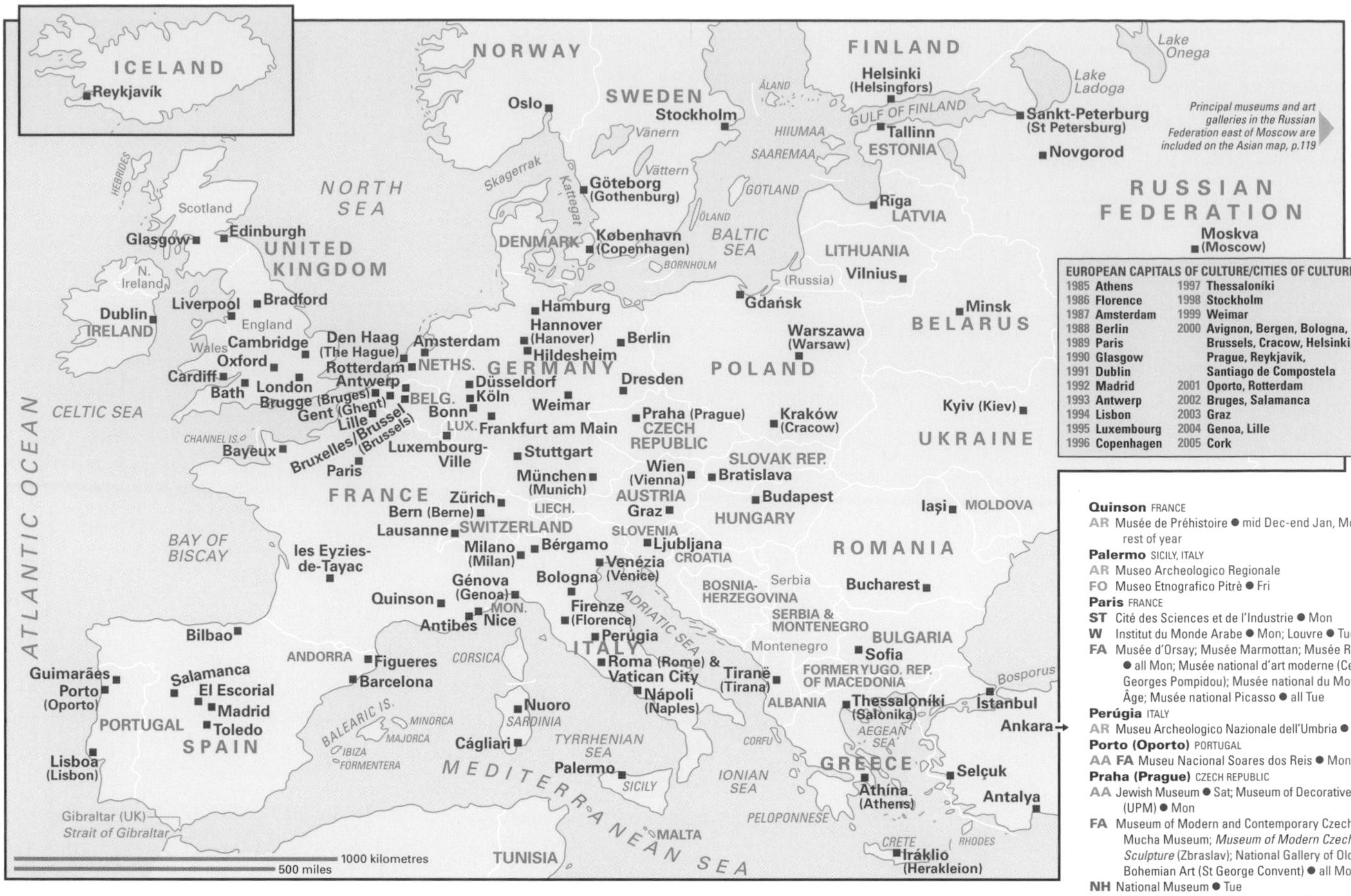
ICELAND
Reykjavík
NORWAY
Oslo
SWEDEN
Stockholm
Vänern
Vättern
Göteborg (Gothenburg)
Skagerrak
Kattegat
FINLAND
Helsinki (Helsingfors)
ÅLAND
GULF OF FINLAND
HIIUMAA
SAAREMAA
Tallinn
ESTONIA
Lake Ladoga
Lake Onega
Sankt-Peterburg (St Petersburg)
Novgorod
Principal museums and art galleries in the Russian Federation east of Moscow are included on the Asian map, p.119
RUSSIAN FEDERATION
Moskva (Moscow)
GOTLAND
ÖLAND
Riga
LATVIA
LITHUANIA
Vilnius
(Russia)
BORNHOLM
BALTIC SEA
København (Copenhagen)
DENMARK
NORTH SEA
HEBRIDES
Scotland
Glasgow
Edinburgh
UNITED KINGDOM
N. Ireland
England
Dublin
IRELAND
Liverpool
Bradford
Wales
Cambridge
Oxford
Cardiff
Bath
London
Den Haag (The Hague)
Amsterdam
Rotterdam
NETHS.
Antwerp
Brugge (Bruges)
Gent (Ghent)
BELG.
Lille
Bruxelles/Brussel (Brussels)
Hamburg
Hannover (Hanover)
Hildesheim
Berlin
GERMANY
Düsseldorf
Köln
Bonn
Dresden
Weimar
LUX.
Frankfurt am Main
Luxembourg-Ville
Stuttgart
München (Munich)
Gdańsk
POLAND
Warszawa (Warsaw)
Minsk
BELARUS
Kraków (Cracow)
Praha (Prague)
CZECH REPUBLIC
SLOVAK REP.
Bratislava
Wien (Vienna)
AUSTRIA
Graz
Kyiv (Kiev)
UKRAINE
CELTIC SEA
CHANNEL IS.
Bayeux
Paris
FRANCE
Zürich
LIECH.
Bern (Berne)
Lausanne
SWITZERLAND
SLOVENIA
Ljubljana
CROATIA
HUNGARY
Budapest
Iaşi
MOLDOVA
ROMANIA
ATLANTIC OCEAN
BAY OF BISCAY
les Eyzies-de-Tayac
Milano (Milan)
Bérgamo
Venézia (Venice)
Génova (Genoa)
Bologna
Quinson
MON.
Antibes
Nice
Firenze (Florence)
Perúgia
BOSNIA-HERZEGOVINA
Serbia
SERBIA & MONTENEGRO
Montenegro
Bucharest
BULGARIA
Sofia
ADRIATIC SEA
ITALY
Roma (Rome) & Vatican City
Nápoli (Naples)
Tiranë (Tirana)
ALBANIA
FORMER YUGO. REP. OF MACEDONIA
Thessaloníki (Salonika)
Bosporus
İstanbul
Ankara
Bilbao
ANDORRA
Figueres
Barcelona
CORSICA
Nuoro
SARDINIA
Guimarães
Porto (Oporto)
Salamanca
El Escorial
Madrid
Toledo
PORTUGAL
SPAIN
BALEARIC IS.
MINORCA
MAJORCA
IBIZA
FORMENTERA
Cágliari
TYRRHENIAN SEA
Palermo
SICILY
CORFU
IONIAN SEA
AEGEAN SEA
GREECE
Athína (Athens)
Selçuk
Antalya
PELOPONNESE
Lisboa (Lisbon)
Gibraltar (UK)
Strait of Gibraltar
MEDITERRANEAN SEA
MALTA
TUNISIA
CRETE
RHODES
Iráklio (Herakleion)
1000 kilometres
500 miles

EUROPEAN CAPITALS OF CULTURE/CITIES OF CULTURE			
1985	Athens	1997	Thessaloniki
1986	Florence	1998	Stockholm
1987	Amsterdam	1999	Weimar
1988	Berlin	2000	Avignon, Bergen, Bologna, Brussels, Cracow, Helsinki, Prague, Reykjavík, Santiago de Compostela
1989	Paris		
1990	Glasgow		
1991	Dublin		
1992	Madrid	2001	Oporto, Rotterdam
1993	Antwerp	2002	Bruges, Salamanca
1994	Lisbon	2003	Graz
1995	Luxembourg	2004	Genoa, Lille
1996	Copenhagen	2005	Cork

Europe's most important museums and art galleries are listed here. Selection is based on importance and depth of the collection and its cultural diversity within a geographic spread.
Most cities named will also offer the visitor a number of smaller museums of specialist interest. Many single great works of art may also be housed in local cathedrals and churches.
Data compiled by Jon A. Gillaspie email: let@sarastro.com

Principal contents of institution:
AA Applied & decorative art
AR Archaeology / ancient art
FA Fine art (paintings, sculpture)
FO Folk art & culture / ethnology
H History / historical site / reconstruction
NH Natural history
ST Science / technology
W Wide range of subjects

Opening times:
Days or months preceded by a red circle (●) indicate when the institution is closed.
Many close on national holidays and other special days. Some museums and galleries have shorter opening hours at certain days of the week or in certain months.

Admission charges:
All charge for admission except those shown in *italics*, where entry is free (although charges for special exhibitions may apply).
Some institutions allow free entry or reduce their admission charges on certain days.

Amsterdam THE NETHERLANDS
W Rijksmuseum
FA Stedelijk Museum; Van Gogh Museum
Ankara TURKEY
AR Museum of Anatolian Civilizations ● Mon
Antalya TURKEY
AR Archaeological Museum ● Mon
Antibes FRANCE
FA Musée Picasso ● Mon
Antwerpen (Antwerp) BELGIUM
FA Museum voor Schone Kunsten ● Mon
Athína (Athens) GREECE
AR *Acropolis Museum*; Nat. Archaeological Mus.
W Benáki Museum ● Tue
AR Museum of Cycladic and Ancient Greek Art ● Tue & Sun
Barcelona SPAIN
AR Museu Arqueològic ● Mon
FA Museu d'Art Contemporani; Museu Nac. d'Art de Catalunya; Museu Picasso ● all Mon
Bath ENGLAND
AA Museum of Costume
AR Roman Baths and Museum
Bayeux FRANCE
AA Bayeux Tapestry
Bérgamo ITALY
FA Accademia Carrara ● Mon
Berlin GERMANY
AR Ägyptisches Museum ● Mon; Antiken Museum ● Fri
W Dahlem museums ● Mon
ST Deutsches Teknikmuseum ● Mon
W Kulturforum ● Mon includes:
FA Gemäldegalerie
AA Kunstgewerbemuseum
NH Museum für Naturkunde ● Mon
W Museumsinsel ● Mon includes:
FA Alte Nationalgalerie
AR Bodemuseum; Pergamonmuseum
Bern (Berne) SWITZERLAND
FA Kunstmuseum ● Mon
Bilbao SPAIN
FA Mus. de Bellas Arte; Mus. Guggenheim ● Mon
Bologna ITALY
AR Museo Civico Archeologico ● Mon
Bonn GERMANY
NH Alexander-Koenig-Museum ● Mon
FA Kunstmuseum ● Mon
Bradford UNITED KINGDOM
ST *Nat. Mus. of Photography, Film & TV* ● Mon
Bratislava SLOVAK REPUBLIC
FA National Gallery ● Mon
W National Museum ● Mon
Brugge (Bruges) BELGIUM
FA Groeningemuseum ● Tue (Oct-Mar)
Bruxelles/Brussel (Brussels) BELGIUM
FA Musées Royaux des Beaux-Arts ● Mon
Bucharest ROMANIA
FA National Art Museum ● Mon & Tue
AR H National History Museum ● Mon & Tue
Budapest HUNGARY
FA National Gall.; Mus. of Fine Arts ● both Mon
AA National Jewish Museum ● Sat
W National Museum ● Mon
Cágliari SARDINIA, ITALY
AR Museo Nazionale Archeologico
Cambridge ENGLAND
W *Fitzwilliam Museum* ● Mon
Cardiff WALES
FO Museum of Welsh Life, St Fagans
W *National Museum & Gallery of Wales* ● Mon
Den Haag (The Hague) THE NETHERLANDS
W Gemeentemuseum ● Mon
FA Mauritshuis ● Mon
Dresden GERMANY
AA Gemäldegalerie Alte Meister ● Mon
Dublin IRELAND
FA *National Gallery*
AR *National Museum* ● Mon
Düsseldorf GERMANY
W Kunstmuseum ● Mon
FA Kunstsammlung Nordrhein-Westfalen ● Mon
Edinburgh SCOTLAND
W *Royal Museum & Museum of Scotland*
FA *National Gallery of Scotland; Gall. of Modern Art (GOMA); Scottish National Portrait Gall.*
El Escorial SPAIN
FA Monasterio de El Escorial ● Mon
Les Eyzies-de-Tayac FRANCE
AR Musée national de Préhistoire ● Tue
Figueres SPAIN
FA Teatre-Museu Dalí ● Mon (Oct-Jun)
Firenze (Florence) ITALY
FA Uffizi ● Mon; Bargello ● Mon (& 1st+3rd Sun)
AR Museo Archeologico ● Mon
Frankfurt am Main GERMANY
FA Museum für Moderne Kunst ● Mon
W Museumsufer ● Mon & Thu includes:
AA FA Städel; Museum für Kunsthandwerk
Gdansk POLAND
W National Art Museum ● Mon
Génova (Genoa) ITALY
FA Galleria Nazionale di Palazzo Spinola; Palazzo Bianco; Palazzo Rosso ● all Mon
Gent (Ghent) BELGIUM
FA *Museum voor Schone Kunsten*
Glasgow SCOTLAND
W *Burrell Collection*
FA *Hunterian Art Gallery and Museum* ● Sun
Göteborg (Gothenburg) SWEDEN
FA Konstmuseet ● Mon (Sep-Apr)
AA Röhsska Konstlöjdmuseet ● Mon (Sep-Apr)
Graz AUSTRIA
FA Alte Galerie ● Mon
W Landesmuseum Joanneum
Guimarães PORTUGAL
AA Museu Alberto Sampaio ● Mon
AR Museu Martins Sarmiento ● Mon
AA Sé (Cathedral museum), Braga
Hamburg GERMANY
FA Kunsthalle ● Mon
AA Museum für Kunst und Gewerbe ● Mon
Hannover (Hanover) GERMANY
FA Sprengel Museum ● Mon
Helsinki (Helsingfors) FINLAND
FA Helsinki kaupingin museo ● Mon & Tue
W Kansallismuseo; Kiasma
Hildesheim GERMANY
AR Roemer-Pelizaeus Museum ● Mon
Iasi ROMANIA
W Palace of Culture ● Mon
Iráklio (Herakleion) CRETE, GREECE
AR Archaeological Museum
Istanbul TURKEY
W Museum of Turkish and Islamic Art ● Mon
København (Copenhagen) DENMARK
AR Nationalmuseet ● Mon
W Ny Carlsberg Glyptotek ● Mon
FA Statens Museum for Kunst ● Mon
Köln (Cologne) GERMANY
AR Römisch-Germanisches Museum ● Mon
FA Wallraf-Richartz/Ludwig Museum ● Mon
Kraków (Cracow) POLAND
W Czartoryski Museum ● Mon
FO Museum of Ethnography ● Tue
Kyiv (Kiev) UKRAINE
W Historical Treasures Museum
FA Russian Art Museum ● Thu
Lausanne SWITZERLAND
W Musée Olympique ● Mon (Oct-Apr)
Lille FRANCE
FA Musée des Beaux-Arts
Lisboa (Lisbon) PORTUGAL
FA Museu Nacional de Arte Antiga ● Mon
W Museu Calouste Gulbenkian ● Mon
Liverpool ENGLAND
FA *Walker Art Gallery*
Ljubljana SLOVENIA
FA National Gallery ● Sun & Mon
W National Museum ● Sun & Mon
London ENGLAND
W *British Museum; Museum of London*
FA *National Gallery; National Portrait Gallery; Tate Britain; Tate Modern*
NH *Natural History Museum*
ST *Science Museum*
AA *Victoria and Albert Museum*
Luxembourg-Ville LUXEMBOURG
W *Musée national* ● Mon
Madrid SPAIN
FA Centro de Arte Reina Sofia ● Tue; Museo del Prado; Museo Thyssen-Bornemisza ● both Mon
AR Museo Arqueológico Nacional ● Mon
W Museo de América ● Mon
Milano (Milan) ITALY
FA *Civico Museo di Arte Contemporanea*; Pinacoteca Ambrosiana; Pinacoteca di Brera ● all Mon
AR *Museo Civico di Archeologico* ● Mon
Minsk BELARUS
FA Belarusian State Art Museum ● Tue
W National Mus. of History and Culture ● Wed
Moskva (Moscow) RUSSIAN FEDERATION
AA Kremlin ● Thu
FA Museum of Private Collections ● Mon & Tue; Tretyakov Gallery ● Mon
W Pushkin Museum of Fine Arts ● Mon
München (Munich) GERMANY
FA Alte Pinakothek; Neue Pinakothek; Pinakothek der Moderne ● all Mon
AA Bayerisches Nationalmuseum ● Mon
ST Deutsches Museum
AR Glyptothek und Antikensammlungen ● Mon
Nápoli (Naples) ITALY
AR Museo Archeologico Nazionale
Nice FRANCE
FA Musée Marc-Chagall; Mus. Matisse ● both Tue
Novgorod RUSSIAN FEDERATION
AA Museum of History, Architecture and Art ● Tue
Nuoro SARDINIA, ITALY
FO Museo Etnografico ● Mon (Oct-Easter)
Oslo NORWAY
FA *Nasjonalgalleriet*
FO Norsk Folkemuseum
AR Vikingskiphuset ● Mon (Sep-May)
Oxford ENGLAND
W *Ashmolean Museum* ● Mon
FA *Museum of Modern Art (MOMA)* ● Mon
Quinson FRANCE
AR Musée de Préhistoire ● mid Dec-end Jan, Mon rest of year
Palermo SICILY, ITALY
AR Museo Archeologico Regionale
FO Museo Etnografico Pitrè ● Fri
Paris FRANCE
ST Cité des Sciences et de l'Industrie ● Mon
W Institut du Monde Arabe ● Mon; Louvre ● Tue
FA Musée d'Orsay; Musée Marmottan; Musée Rodin ● all Mon; Musée national d'art moderne (Centre Georges Pompidou); Musée national du Moyen-Âge; Musée national Picasso ● all Tue
Perúgia ITALY
AR Museu Archeologico Nazionale dell'Umbria ● Mon
Porto (Oporto) PORTUGAL
AA FA Museu Nacional Soares dos Reis ● Mon
Praha (Prague) CZECH REPUBLIC
AA Jewish Museum ● Sat; Museum of Decorative Arts (UPM) ● Mon
FA Museum of Modern and Contemporary Czech Art; Mucha Museum; *Museum of Modern Czech Sculpture* (Zbraslav); National Gallery of Old Bohemian Art (St George Convent) ● all Mon
NH National Museum ● Tue
ST National Museum of Technology ● Mon
Reykjavík ICELAND
W *Thjódminjasafn Íslands (National Museum)*
Riga LATVIA
AA Museum of Decorative and Applied Arts ● Mon
Roma (Rome) ITALY **& Vatican City**
W Capitoline museums ● Mon includes:
AR Museo Capitolino
W Museo del Palazzo del Conservatori
AR Museo Nazionale di Villa Giulia; Museo Nazionale Romano ● Mon
FA Galleria Borghese; Palazzo Barberini ● both Mon; Galleria Doria Pamphili ● Thu
W Musei Vaticani ● Sun
Rotterdam THE NETHERLANDS
FA Museum Boymans-van Beuningen ● Mon
Salamanca SPAIN
AA Museo Art Nouveau y Art Deco ● Mon
Sankt-Peterburg (St Petersburg) RUSSIAN FED.
W Hermitage ● Mon
FO Museum of Anthropology and Ethnography ● Mon
FA Russian Museum ● Tue
Selçuk TURKEY
AR Archaeological Museum
Sofia BULGARIA
FO Ethnographic Museum ● Mon & Tue
FA National Art Gallery ● Mon & Tue
AR H National Historical Museum ● Mon
Stockholm SWEDEN
FA Modernamuséet ● Mon
AA Nationalmuseum ● Mon
AR Vasamuseet
Stuttgart GERMANY
FA Staatsgalerie ● Mon
Tallinn ESTONIA
FA National Art Museum ● Tue
Thessaloníki (Salonlka) GREECE
AR Archaeological Museum
FO Folklore Museum ● Tue (summer), Thu (winter)
Tiranë (Tirana) ALBANIA
AR National Archaeology Museum
FA National Art Gallery
W National Historical Museum
Toledo SPAIN
AR Museo de Arte Visigótico ● Mon
FA Museo de Santa Cruz
Venézia (Venice) ITALY
FA Coll. Guggenheim ● Tue; Galleria dell'Accademia
W Museo Correr
AA Museo Vitrario di Murano ● Wed
Vilnius LITHUANIA
AA Lithuanian History and Ethnographic Museum ● Mon & Tue
Warszawa (Warsaw) POLAND
W National Museum ● Mon
Weimar GERMANY
FA Schlossmuseum ● Mon
Wien (Vienna) AUSTRIA
FA Albertina; Kunsthistorisches Museum ● both Mon Österrischische Galerie, Belvedere ● Tue
W MuseumsQuartier, includes:
FA MUMOK (Museum moderner Kunst); Leopold Museum ● both Mon
Zürich SWITZERLAND
FA Kunsthaus ● Mon
W *Schweizerisches Landesmuseum* ● Mon

Winter Sports

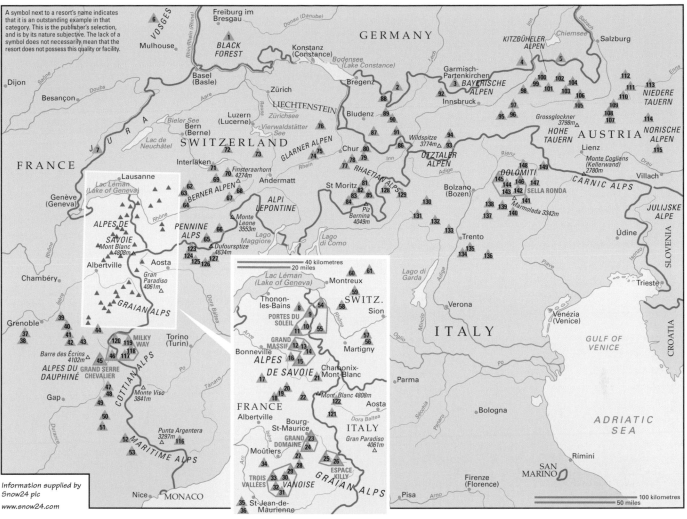

A symbol next to a resort's name indicates that it is an outstanding example in that category. This is the publisher's selection, and is by its nature subjective. The lack of a symbol does not necessarily mean that the resort does not possess this quality or facility.

Information supplied by
Snow24 plc
www.snow24.com

▲ **THE MOST BEAUTIFUL RESORTS**
Ski areas with spectacular scenery

❄ **SNOWSURE**
The best reputations for season-long snow cover

▲ **SUMMER SKIING DESTINATIONS**
Resorts where lifts stay open for skiing or boarding during the summer

◆ **EXPERT**
Best of the black diamond destinations

■ **BEGINNER SKI AREAS**
Best choices for first timers

♠ **FAMILY FRIENDLY**
Ideal choices for family ski holidays

● **PARTY TOWNS**
Après ski centres

▼ **SNOWBOARDER HEAVEN**
Best bets for boarders

★ **NOT JUST SKIING**
Plenty to do if you don't want to slide

THE LARGEST SKI AREAS △

Portes du Soleil *France/Switzerland*
9   Châtel
10 Avoriaz
11 Morzine
11 les Gets
54 Torgon
55 Champéry-Planachaux / Val-d'Illiez / Les Crosets

Grand Massif *France*
12 Morillon les Essert
13 Samoëns
14 Sixt
15 Flaine

Grand Domaine *France*
23 les Arcs
24 Peisey / Nancroix-Vallandry

Espace Killy *France*
25 Tignes
26 Val d'Isère

Trois Vallées *France*
29 la Tania
29 Courchevel
30 Méribel

31 Val Thorens
32 les Menuires
33 St-Martin-de-Belleville

Grand Serre-Chevalier *France*
45 Serre-Chevalier
45 Briançon

Milky Way *France/Italy*
46 Montgenèvre
117 San Sicário / Cesana
117 Clavière
118 Sestriere
119 Sàuze d'Oulx

Sella Ronda *Italy*
142 Arabba
143 Campitello di Fassa
143 Canazei
144 Santa Cristina / Pranauron
144 Selva Gardena (Wolkenstein)
145 Ortisei (St Ulrich)
146 Alta Badia [Colfosco / Corvara / La Villa (Stern) / San Cassiano (St Kassian) / Pedráces / San Leonardo (St Leonhard)]

Germany
1 Feldberg ■★
2 Oberstdorf ▲◆■
3 Garmisch-Partenkirchen ▲❄■▲◆●★
4 Bayrischzell ▲◆■
5 Reit im Winkl ▲■♠★

France
6 la Bresse-Hohneck ■❄▼
7 Métabief / le Mont d'Or ♠★
8 Abondance / la Chapelle d'Abondance ▲■♠■
9 Châtel ▲
10 Avoriaz ❄◆■♠●▼
11 Morzine ▲◆♠●★
    les Gets ▲■♠
12 Morillon les Essert ▲■
13 Samoëns ▲■
15 Flaine ❄▲■
16 les Carroz ▼
17 la Clusaz ●▼
18 Notre-Dame-de-Bellecombe ▲❄
19 Praz-sur-Arly ♠
20 Megève ▲●★
21 Chamonix-Mont-Blanc ▲❄◆●▼

22 St-Nicolas-de-Véroce ▲■
    les Contamines-Montjoie ▲❄♠◆■
23 les Arcs ❄◆■♠▼
25 Tignes ❄▲♠▼
26 Val d'Isère ❄▲♠◆●▼
27 la Plagne / les Coches / Montchavin / Plagne Montalbert ❄▲♠▼★
28 Champagny-en-Vanoise ▲❄▼
29 la Tania ❄▲♠
    Courchevel ❄❄◆●▼
30 Méribel ▲♠●▼♠★
31 Val Thorens ❄▲♠■▼
32 les Menuires ▲◆❄■▼
33 St-Martin-de-Belleville ▲❄
34 Valmorel ■♠▼
35 la Toussuire ▲❄
    le Corbier ■
36 St-Jean d'Arves ▲
37 Villard-de-Lans / Cote 2000 ▲■
38 Corrençon-en-Vercors ▲
39 les Sept Laux (le Pleiney / Prapoutel) ▲■
40 Vaujany / Oz-en-Oisans ▲◆
41 Alpe d'Huez / Auris-en-Oisans / Villard-Reculas ▲❄▲◆♠●▼
42 les Deux Alpes ❄▲■♠●▼★
43 la Grave ▲◆▼
44 Valloire ❄▲★
45 Serre-Chevalier ▲■♠▼★
    Briançon ▲★
46 Montgenèvre ❄■♠▼
47 Risoul ❄■♠
48 Vars ❄
49 les Orres ▲♠▼
50 Pra-Loup ■★
51 Val d'Allos-la Foux ▲■
52 Auron / St-Étienne-de-Tinée ●
53 Valberg ▲
    Beuil-les-Launes ▲

Switzerland
55 Champéry-Planachaux / Val-d'Illiez / Les Crosets ▲■♠★
56 Verbier ❄■♠▼
57 La Tzoumas (Mayens-de-Riddes) ❄♠
58 Villars-sur-Ollon / Gryon ❄▲■♠▼
59 les Diablerets ▲■♠▼
60 Château-d'Oex ▲■▼
61 Gstaad-Saanenland ▲❄♠●▼♠
62 Adelboden ▲❄■♠▼
63 Lenk ▲■♠●▼♠▼★
64 Crans-Montana ▲▼★
65 Zermatt ▲❄▲◆●▼★

66 Saas Fee ▲❄▲◆■♠▼★
67 Bettmeralp ▲♠
    Mörel-Breiten ■
    Fiesch ★
68 Sörenberg ▲
69 Wengen ▲♠●▼
    Mürren / Stechelberg ■♠
70 Riederalp ♠
71 Interlaken / Wilderswil bei Interlaken ■●★
72 Grindelwald ▲■♠▼
73 Engelberg ❄▲♠●▼★
74 Laax ▲❄◆■♠▼
75 Flims ❄▲♠▼
76 Flumserberg ■♠
77 Lenzerheide-Valbella ❄♠◆●▼
    Parpan ▲■
78 Arosa ▲❄♠●★
79 Davos ▲❄■♠▼★
80 Klosters / Fideris ▲❄◆●▼
81 Celerina ❄
    Samedan ❄■
82 St Moritz ❄❄◆●▼★
83 Sils-Maria ▲❄
84 Maloja ▲
85 Pontresina ❄▼
86 Samnaun ❄●★

Austria
87 St Gallenkirch ■▼
88 Kleinwalsertal [Hirschegg /Mittelberg / Riezlern] ■●
89 Lech / Oberlech ❄❄■♠▼
    Zürs ❄◆
90 St Anton am Arlberg / St Jakob am Arlberg ▲❄♠●▼
    St Christoph am Arlberg ❄◆
91 Ischgl / Silvretta ❄◆●▼♠
92 Lermoos ▲■♠
    Ehrwald ❄▲■
93 Obergurgl / Hochgurgl ▲❄♠
94 Sölden ▲▲♠●▼
95 Hintertux ▲▲▼
96 Mayrhofen ❄▲♠●▼
97 Zell am Ziller ▲■♠●
98 Alpbach ▲■
99 Hopfgarten im Brixental ■♠▼
100 Söll ■♠▼
101 Kitzbühel ▲❄♠●▼
102 Fieberbrunn ◆●▼
103 Saalbach Hinterglemm ◆■♠▼
104 Leogang ▲■♠▼
105 Kaprun ▲❄■♠▼

106 Zell am See ■♠●★
107 Badgastein ❄■♠●▼★
108 Bad Hofgastein ●♠★
109 Grossarl ▼
110 Flachau ◆▼
111 Altenmarkt-Zauchensee ★
112 Annaberg im Lammertal ▲
113 Ramsau am Dachstein ▲❄♠■
    Schladming ▲❄▲♠●▼♠
114 St Michael im Lungau ▲★
115 Bad Kleinkirchheim ▲▼★

Italy
116 Limone Piemonte ■●
117 Clavière ▲■♠
118 Sestriere ▲◆●▼
119 Sàuze d'Oulx ▲■●
120 Bardonécchia ■●
121 la Thuile ❄❄♠
122 Courmayeur ▲♠
123 Breuil-Cervínia ▲❄▲
124 Valtournenche ❄
125 Champoluc / Antagnod ❄■
126 Gressoney-la-Trinité / Gressoney-St Jean ●
127 Alagna-Valsésia ▲▲◆
128 Livigno ❄■♠●▼
129 Bormio ❄▼
130 Folgárida ●▼
131 Passo Tonale ❄▲■♠★
132 Madonna di Campiglio ▲❄♠●▼★
133 Andalo ●
134 Folgaria ♠
135 Lavarone / Luserna ▲
136 Asiago / Canove ★
137 Cavalese ▲★
138 Obereggen ▼
139 Bellamonte ■●
140 San Martino di Castrozza ▲★
141 Alleghe ♠
142 Arabba ▲❄▼
143 Campitello di Fassa ▲
    Canazei ♠
144 Santa Cristina / Pranauron ●
    Selva Gardena (Wolkenstein) ▲●
146 Alta Badia [Colfosco / Corvara / La Villa (Stern) / San Cassiano (St Kassian) / Pedráces / San Leonardo (St Leonhard)] ▲❄■
147 Cortina ▲❄▲♠●★
148 San Vigilio di Marebbe ■●
149 Versciaco (Vierschach) ❄♠■

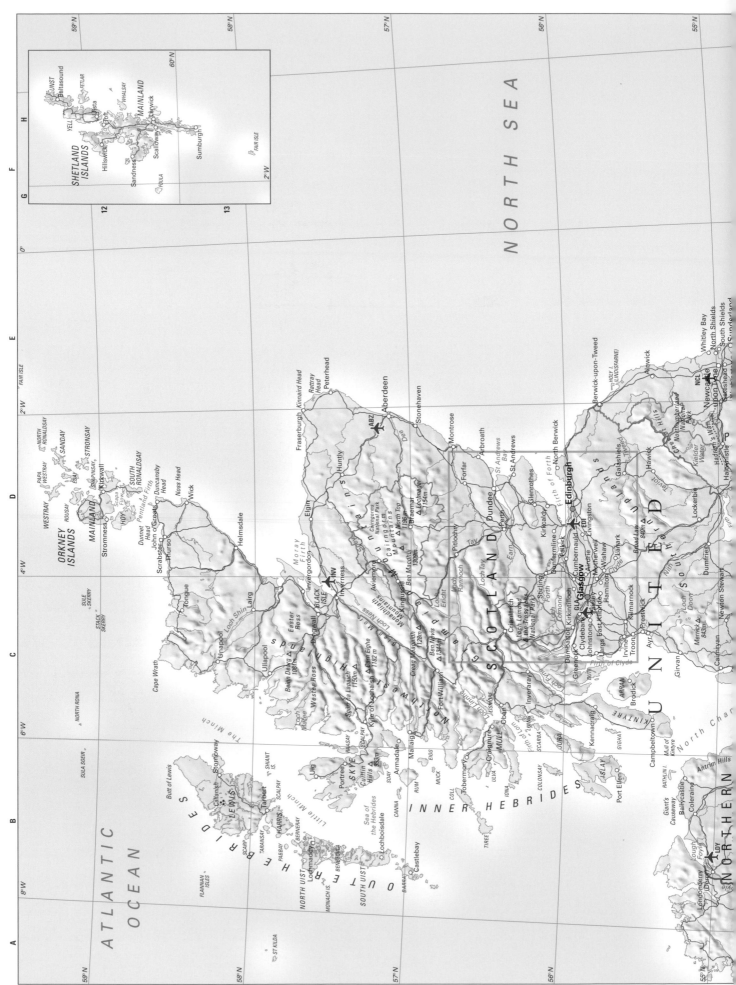

SHETLAND ISLANDS

UNST
Baltasound
FETLAR
WHALSAY
YELL
Toft
MAINLAND
Lerwick
Hillswick
Sandness
Scalloway
FOULA
Sumburgh
FAIR ISLE

12
13

ATLANTIC OCEAN

NORTH SEA

SULA SGEIR

NORTH RONA

ST KILDA

FLANNAN ISLES

Butt of Lewis
Stornoway
LEWIS
Callanich
Tarbert
HARRIS
SCALPAY
SCARP
TARANSAY
PABBAY
BERNERAY
NORTH UIST
Lochmaddy
BENBECULA
MONACH IS.
Lochboisdale
SOUTH UIST
Castlebay
BARRA

OUTER HEBRIDES

The Minch
Little Minch
SHIANT IS.
Sea of the Hebrides

Uig
Portree
SKYE
RAASAY
SCALPAY
Cuillin Hills 993m
SOAY
RUM
EIGG
MUCK
CANNA
COLL
TIREE
ULVA
MULL
IONA
Tobermory
COLONSAY
JURA
ISLAY
Port Ellen
GIGHA I.

Kennacraig
KINTYRE
Campbeltown
Mull of Kintyre

RATHLIN I.
Giant's Causeway
Ballycastle
Coleraine
ANTRIM Hills

Londonderry
Lough Foyle
LDY

NORTHERN

North Channel

FAIR ISLE

ORKNEY ISLANDS
NORTH RONALDSAY
PAPA WESTRAY
WESTRAY
SANDAY
EDAY
ROUSAY
STRONSAY
SOUTH RONALDSAY
Kirkwall
MAINLAND
HOY
Stromness
Scapa Flow
Pentland Firth
Duncansby Head
John o' Groats
Dunnet Head
Thurso
Scrabster
Helmsdale
Wick
Noss Head

STACK SKERRY
SULE SKERRY

Cape Wrath
Tongue
Loch Shin
Lairg
Unapool
Ullapool
Beinn Dearg 1084m
EASTER ROSS
WESTER ROSS
Loch Maree
Beinn Eighe 1182m
Sgurr na Lapaich 1150m

Kinnaird Head
Fraserburgh
Rattray Head
Peterhead
Aberdeen
ABZ
Stonehaven
Montrose
Arbroath

Huntly
Elgin
Invergordon
BLACK ISLE
Inverness
INV
Aviemore
Kingussie
Monadhliath Mountains
Cairngorms National Park
North Top 1196m
Ben Macdhui 1309m
Braemar
Lochnagar 1154m
Pitlochry

SUTHERLAND

GRAMPIAN MOUNTAINS

Loch Morar
Ben Nevis 1344m
Fort William
Armadale
Mallaig
Kyle of Lochalsh

Dee
Don
Spey
Tay
Dundee
Forfar
St Andrews
St Andrews
Glenrothes
Kirkcaldy
Dunfermline
Firth of Forth
Edinburgh
EDI
Livingston
Falkirk
Stirling
Loch Tay
Loch Rannoch
Loch Ericht
Rannoch
Loch Lomond
The Trossachs National Park
Crianlarich
Loch Earn
Earn
Forth

SCOTLAND

Oban
Craignure
Inveraray
Loch Linnhe
Loch Fyne
Loch Awe
LISMORE
LUING
SCARBA

Clydebank
Glasgow
GLA
Cumbernauld
Airdrie
Motherwell
Wishaw
Lanark
Hamilton
Clyde
East Kilbride
Kilmarnock
Irvine
Troon
Prestwick
Ayr
Firth of Clyde
Kirkintilloch
Paisley
Dumbarton
Johnstone
Greenock
Gourock
Largs
ARRAN
Brodick
Kennacraig
Newton Stewart
Merrick 843m
Cairnryan
Girvan
Loch Doon
North Berwick
Berwick-upon-Tweed
HOLY I. (LINDISFARNE)
Alnwick
Whitley Bay
North Shields
South Shields
Gateshead
Sunderland
Newcastle upon Tyne
NCL
Northumberland National Park
Cheviot Hills
The Cheviot 815m
Haltwhistle
Galashiels
Hawick
Kielder Water
Tweed
Tyne
Nith
Broad Law 840m
Lockerbie
Dumfries
UNITED

UNITED KINGDOM

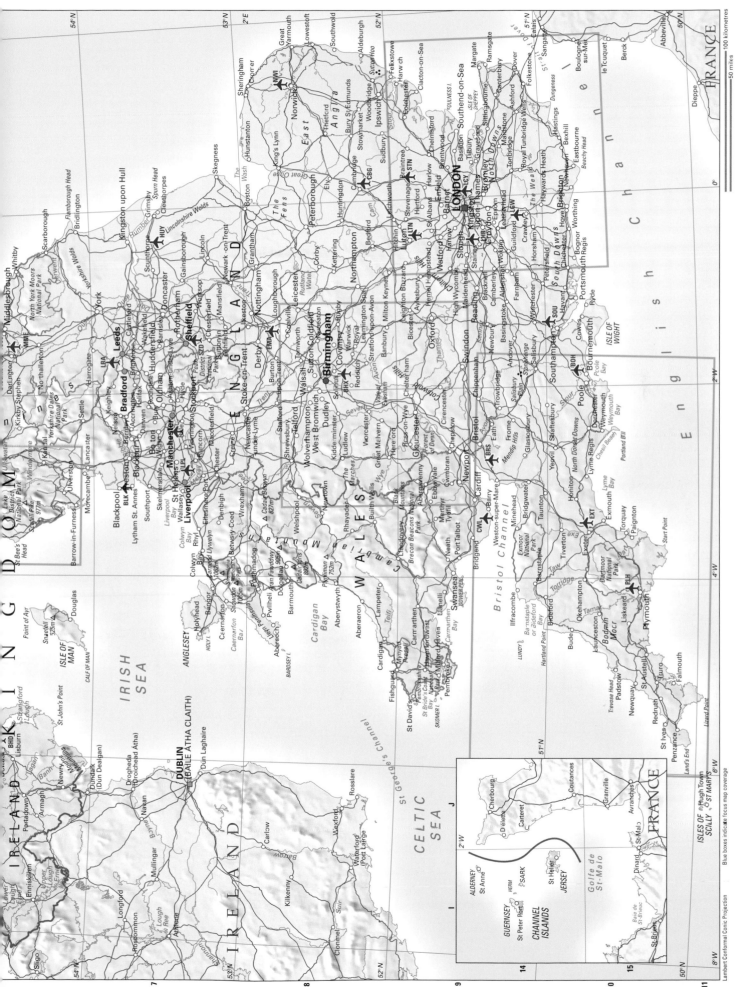

The European Blue Flag Campaign is an environmental awareness raising activity by the Foundation for Environmental Education in Europe (FEEE).

To qualify for a Blue Flag, a beach has to fulfil a number of strict criteria regarding water quality (compliance with the EU Bathing Water Directive), environmental education and information, environmental management and safety and services. The Blue Flag is awarded annually and is valid for one year. The map shows beaches awarded the Blue Flag in 2003. For more information visit: www.seasideawards.org.uk

The map shows geographical counties, and not the administrative counties and unitary authorities which have, for administrative purposes, replaced them. Geographical counties give a more familiar picture of the divisions of the UK: they are also of a more consistent size, as they do not reflect the growth of urban populations over the last 200 years. For more information on geographical countries, visit: www.abcounties.co.uk

Scotland
1 St Andrews: West Sands
2 Elie Harbour
3 Burntisland
4 Aberdour: Silver Sands
Northumbria
5 Tynemouth: Cullercoats
Tynemouth: King Edwards Bay
Tynemouth: Longsands South
6 South Shields: Sandhaven
Whitburn North: Seaburn
Whitburn South: Roker
Yorkshire
7 Whitby: West Cliff
8 Scarborough: North Bay
9 Bridlington North
10 Cleethorpes Central
Heart of England
11 Mablethorpe Central
Sutton on Sea Central
12 Skegness: Tower Esplanade

13 Keynes Country Park (inland beach)
East of England
14 Sheringham
15 Cromer
16 Mundesley
17 Sea Palling
18 Great Yarmouth: Gorleston
19 Lowestoft North
Lowestoft South
20 Southwold Pier
21 Felixstowe South
22 Dovercourt Bay
23 Shoeburyness East
Shoebury Common
Southend-on-Sea: Three Shells
South East England
24 Sheerness: Beach Street
25 Herne Bay Central
26 Birchington: Minnis Bay
Westgate-on-Sea: West Bay
27 Margate: Westbrook Bay

28 Ramsgate: Main Sands
29 Camber
30 Littlehampton: Coastguards
31 West Wittering
Southern England
32 Hayling Island: Beachlands Central
Hayling Island: Beachlands West
33 Bournemouth: Alum Chine
Bournemouth: Durley Chine
Bournemouth: Fisherman's Walk
34 Poole: Branksome Chine
Poole: Sandbanks
Poole: Shore Road
35 Swanage Central
Isle of Wight
36 Ryde East
37 Sandown
Shanklin
Ventnor
South West
38 Dawlish Warren
39 Torquay: Oddicombe
Torquay: Meadfoot
40 Broadsands
Brixham: Shoalstone Breakwater
41 Blackpool Sands
42 Bigbury-on-Sea
43 Falmouth: Gyllyngvase
44 Sennen Cove
45 St Ives: Porthmeor
St Ives: Porthminster
46 Polzeath
47 Croyde Bay
Woolacombe
Wales
48 Swansea: Bracelet Bay
Swansea: Langland Bay
Swansea: Caswell Bay
49 Port-Eynon
50 Pembrey Country Park: Cefn Sidan
51 Amroth
Saundersfoot
52 Tenby North
Tenby Castle
Tenby South
53 Lydstep
54 Newgale
55 St David's: Whitesands
56 Cardigan: Poppit Sands
57 Aberporth
Tresaith
58 New Quay: Traeth yr Harbwr
59 Aberystwyth South: Traeth y De
60 Fairbourne: Ffriog
61 Barmouth: Abermaw
62 Criccieth
63 Pwllheli: Marian y De
64 Abersoch
65 Dinas Dinlle
66 Llandudno: West Shore
Llandudno: North Shore
67 Rhos-on-Sea
Anglesey
68 Newborough: Llanddwyn
69 Holy Island: Trearddur Bay
70 Benllech
71 Llanddona
Northern Ireland
72 Magilligan: Benone Strand
73 Portrush: West Strand
74 Ballycastle
75 Tyrella
76 Cranfield West

International arrivals (millions)
Source: World Tourism Organisation

Geographical county boundary
English Tourism Council boundary
National Park

100 kilometres
50 miles

Blue boxes indicate focus map coverage

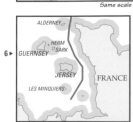

United Kingdom

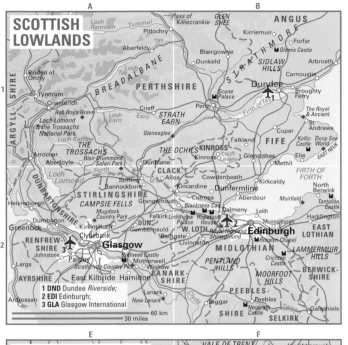

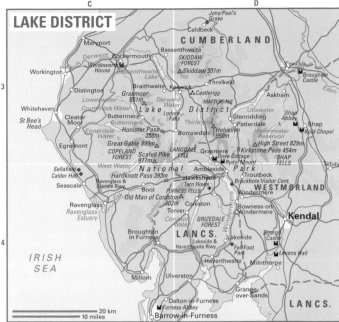

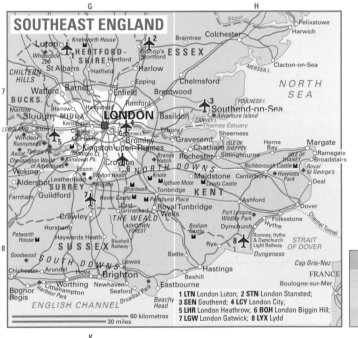

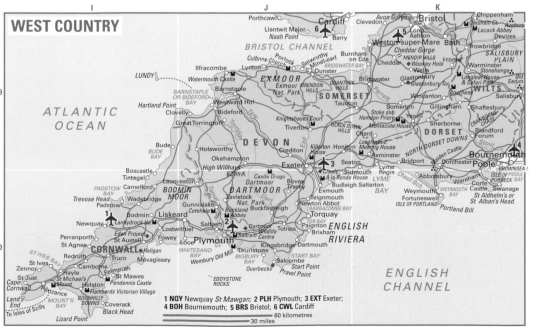

JAN 1st New Year's Day Parade (London)
JAN Up Helly Aa (Lerwick, Shetland)
JAN Celtic Connections (Glasgow)
JAN 25th Burns Night (Scotland)
APR Oxford-Cambridge Boat Race (River Thames, London)
APR Edinburgh International Science Festival
MAY 1st Hobby Horse: May Day celebrations (Padstow)
MAY Flora Day Furry Dance (Helston)
MAY Mayfest (Glasgow)
end MAY Chelsea Flower Show (London)
MAY-JUN Bath International Festival
MAY-AUG Glyndebourne Festival
early JUN Trooping The Colour (London)
JUN Royal Highland Show (Ingliston)
JUN Aldeburgh Festival
late JUN Glastonbury Festival
JUN-JUL York Mystery Plays; 2004 and every four years
JUN-JUL Lawn Tennis Championships (Wimbledon)
JUN-AUG Riding of the Marches (Eng-Scot borders)
JUL Henley Royal Regatta
JUL Llangollen International Music Eisteddfod
JUL/AUG WOMAD World Music Festival (Reading)
JUL/AUG Highland Games (various places in Scotland)
JUL-AUG Cardiff Festival
JUL-SEP Promenade Concerts 'Proms' (London)
early AUG Royal National Eisteddfod (Wales: venue changes)
AUG Three Choirs Festival (Gloucester/Hereford/Worcester)
AUG Edinburgh International Festival & Fringe; Military Tattoo
AUG Brecon Jazz Festival
AUG Great British Beer Festival (London)
AUG Bank Holiday Notting Hill Carnival (London)
SEP Royal Highland Gathering (Braemar)
SEP-NOV Blackpool Illuminations
NOV 5th Guy Fawkes Night
early NOV London-Brighton Veteran Car Rally
NOV London Film Festival; London Jazz Festival
NOV State Opening of Parliament (London)
NOV Lord Mayor's Procession and Show (London)

UK: Airports, Motorways & Ferries

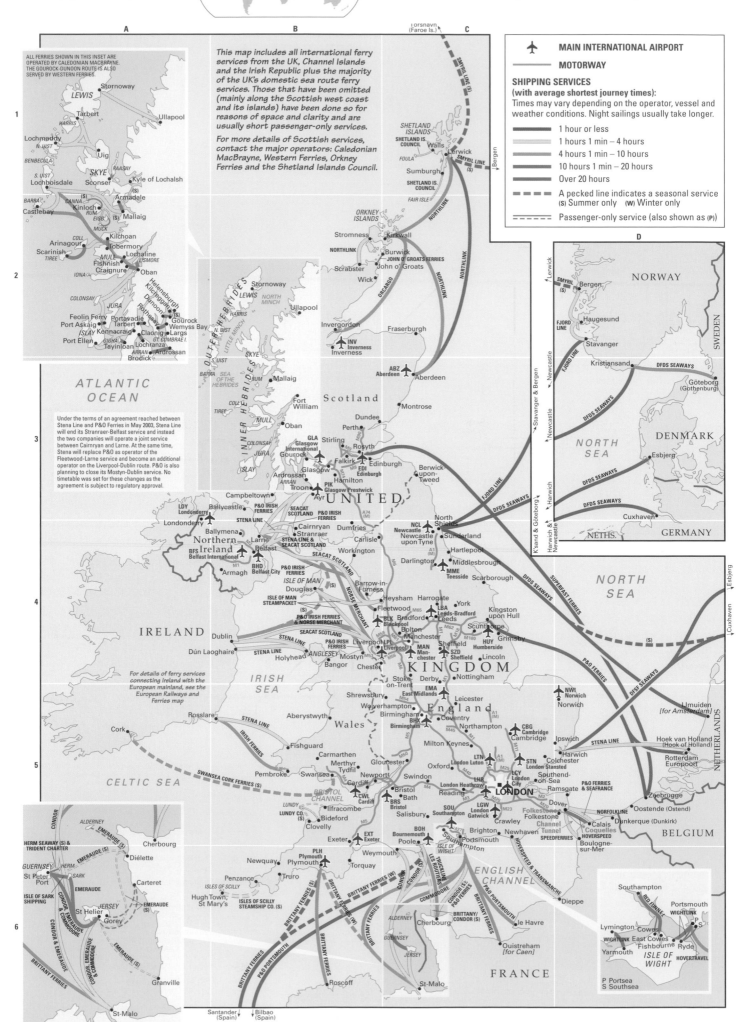

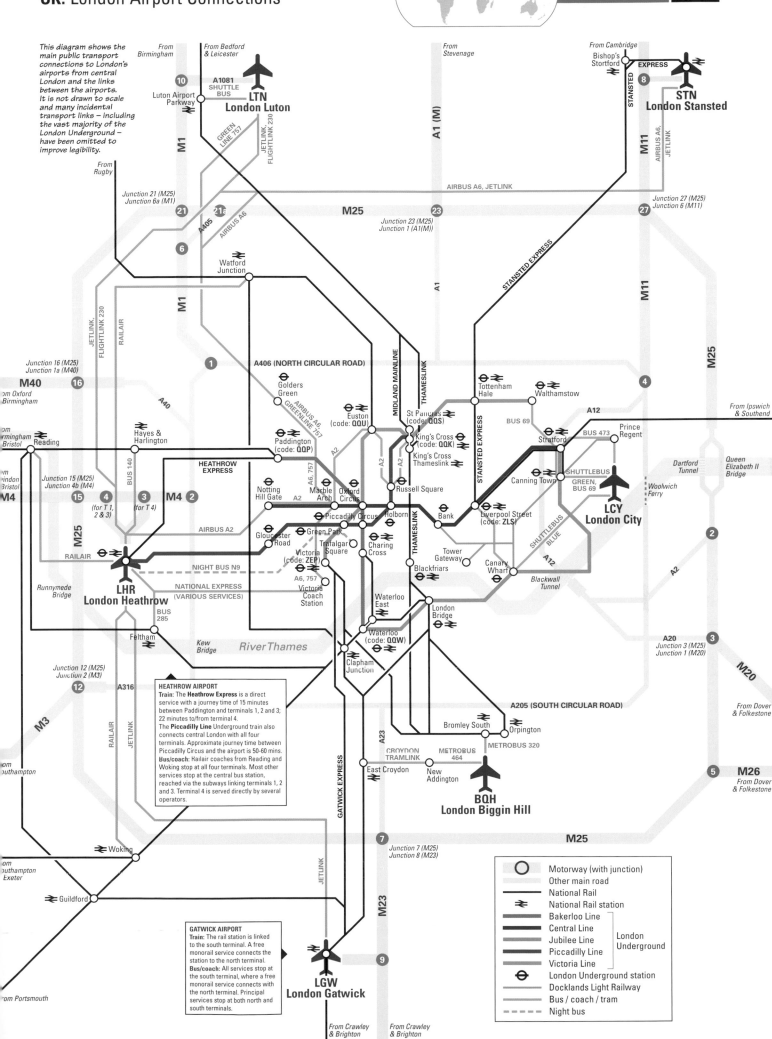

This diagram shows the main public transport connections to London's airports from central London and the links between the airports. It is not drawn to scale and many incidental transport links – including the vast majority of the London Underground – have been omitted to improve legibility.

HEATHROW AIRPORT
Train: The **Heathrow Express** is a direct service with a journey time of 15 minutes between Paddington and terminals 1, 2 and 3; 22 minutes to/from terminal 4.
The **Piccadilly Line** Underground train also connects central London with all four terminals. Approximate journey time between Piccadilly Circus and the airport is 50-60 mins.
Bus/coach: Railair coaches from Reading and Woking stop at all four terminals. Most other services stop at the central bus station, reached via the subways linking terminals 1, 2 and 3. Terminal 4 is served directly by several operators.

GATWICK AIRPORT
Train: The rail station is linked to the south terminal. A free monorail service connects the station to the north terminal.
Bus/coach: All services stop at the south terminal, where a free monorail service connects with the north terminal. Principal services stop at both north and south terminals.

	Legend
	Motorway (with junction)
	Other main road
	National Rail
	National Rail station
	Bakerloo Line
	Central Line
	Jubilee Line
	Piccadilly Line
	Victoria Line
	London Underground station
	Docklands Light Railway
	Bus / coach / tram
	Night bus

London Underground

UK: Attractions

Legend

- Theme park, leisure park
- Museum, gallery
- Religious building
- Park, reserve, zoo, etc.
- Historic building
- Water-related attraction
- Other place of interest

Attractions in cities marked in **red** are listed around the edge of the map

100 kilometres
50 miles

Edinburgh

- Gallery of Modern Art (GOMA)
- National Gallery of Scotland
- Royal Museum & Museum of Scotland
- Scottish National Portrait Gallery
- Our Dynamic Earth
- St Giles' Cathedral
- Royal Botanic Gardens
- Edinburgh Castle
- Holyroodhouse
- Royal Yacht Britannia, Leith
- Calton Hill
- Charlotte Square
- Royal Mile

London

- British Museum
- Courtauld Institute Galleries
- Imperial War Museum
- London Dungeon
- London Planetarium
- Madame Tussaud's
- Museum of London
- National Gallery
- National Portrait Gallery
- Natural History Museum
- Science Museum
- Tate Britain
- Tate Modern
- Victoria & Albert Museum
- Wallace Collection
- St Paul's Cathedral
- Westminster Abbey
- London Zoo
- Hampstead Heath
- Buckingham Palace
- Palace of Westminster & Big Ben
- Tower of London
- Keats House
- Kensington Palace
- Kenwood House
- London Aquarium
- British Airways London Eye
- Whitehall & Downing Street
- Lords Cricket Ground & Museum
- Piccadilly Circus

Glasgow

- Burrell Collection
- Glasgow School of Art
- Hunterian Art Gallery & Museum
- Kelvingrove Art Gallery & Museum
- Museum of Transport
- Cathedral

Liverpool

- The Beatles Story
- Walker Art Gallery
- Liverpool Anglican Cathedral
- Metropolitan Cathedral
- Speke Hall
- Albert Dock
- Port Sunlight

Newcastle upon Tyne

- The New Metroland, Gateshead
- Baltic Centre for Contemporary Art
- Tyne bridges
- Angel of the North

York

- Jorvik Viking Centre
- National Railway Museum
- Minster
- City walls
- The Shambles

Manchester

- Granada Studios
- Imperial War Museum North
- John Ryland's Library
- Lowry Centre
- Museum of Science & Industry
- Urbis
- Heaton Park, Prestwich

Birmingham

- Barber Institute of Fine Arts
- Birmingham Museum & Art Gallery
- Aston Hall

Bristol

- Industrial Museum
- Cathedral of St Peter & St Paul
- St Mary Redcliffe Church
- Bristol Zoological Gardens
- Georgian House
- Clifton Suspension Bridge

Bath

- Museum of Costume
- Roman Baths & Pumproom
- The King's Circus
- Royal Crescent

Oxford

- Ashmolean Museum
- Museum of Modern Art (MOMA)
- University

Map labels

Scotland

Thurso, Wick, Stornoway, LEWIS, GREAT BERNERA, Callanish, FLANNAN ISLES, St Kilda, TARANSAY, HARRIS, NORTH UIST, BENBECULA, SOUTH UIST, BARRA, Ullapool, Inverewe Garden, Loch Maree, SKYE, RAASAY, SCALPAY, Cuillin Hills, SDAY, CANNA, RUM, EIGG, MUCK, COLL, TIREE, ULVA, MULL, LISMORE, Isle of Iona, LUING, SCARBA, JURA, COLONSAY, ISLAY, Oban, Inverary Castle, Glen Coe, Fort William, Blair Castle, Aviemore, Cairngorms National Park, Loch Ness, Inverness, Banff, Duff House, Pitmedden Gardens, Archaeolink Prehistory Park, Crathes Castle, Aberdeen, Aberdeen Art Gallery, King's College Chapel, St Machar's Cathedral, Marischal College, Balmoral Castle, Dunottar Castle, Montrose, Scotland, Perth, Scone Castle, Dundee, Discovery Point, St Andrews, Cathedral, University, Stirling Castle, Loch Lomond & the Trossachs National Park, Dunfermline, Deep Sea World, North Berwick, Mugdock Country Park, Greenock, Glasgow, Falkirk, Edinburgh, Berwick-upon-Tweed, East Kilbride, Strathclyde Country Park, Hamilton, New Lanark, Mellerstain House, HOLY I., FARNE IS., Brodick Castle, ARRAN, Ayr, Melrose, Abbey, Lindisfarne Castle, Alnwick Castle, Northumberland National Park, Drumlanrig Castle, Dumfries, Gretna Green, Old Blacksmith's Shop, Hadrian's Wall, Beamish Open Air Museum

Northern Ireland

Portrush, Barry's Amusement Park, Giant's Causeway, RATHLIN I., Londonderry (Derry), City walls, Ballymena, Larne, Omagh, Ulster American Folk Park, Northern Ireland, Bangor, Lough Neagh, Belfast, Golden Mile, Loch Erne, Armagh, BANN

England / Wales

Stranraer, Carlisle, Workington, Durham, Cathedral, Castle, Hartlepool, Middlesbrough, Sunderland, Newcastle upon Tyne, Lake District National Park, Darlington, Whitby, Ripon, Lightwater Valley, Fountains Abbey, Studley Royal Park, North York Moors National Park, Scarborough, Windermere, Barrow-in-Furness, Lancaster, Harrogate, Flamingo Land, Castle Howard, Beningbrough Hall, Yorkshire Dales National Park, National Museum of Photography, Film & Television, Blackpool, Pleasure Beach, Brontë Parsonage, Saltaire, Leeds, Royal Armouries, Beverley, Minster, Kingston upon Hull, Preston, Blackburn, Bradford, Huddersfield, Doncaster, Scunthorpe, Grimsby, Bolton, Oldham, Southport, Camelot, St Helens, Wigan, Manchester, Rotherham, Sheffield, Peak District National Park, Lincoln, Cathedral, Skegness, Holyhead, Beaumaris Castle, ANGLESEY, HOLY I., Birkenhead, Conwy Castle, Dunham Massey, Chatsworth, Gulliver's Kingdom, Clumber Park, Bangor, Plas Newydd, Caernarfon Castle, Snowdonia National Park, Chester, Cathedral, Zoo, Crewe, Stoke-on-Trent, American Adventure World, THE WASH, Cromer, Portmeirion, The Rows, Alton Towers, Derwent Valley mills, Nottingham, Grantham, Belton House, King's Lynn, Blickling Hall, Harlech Castle, Stafford, Derby, England, Great Yarmouth, Norwich, Cathedral, Norfolk Broads, Lowestoft, Powys Castle, Telford, Ironbridge, Sutton Coldfield, Drayton Manor Park, Leicester, Peterborough, Cathedral, Celtica, Wolverhampton, West Bromwich, Birmingham, Coventry, Cathedral, Pleasurewood Hills, Aberystwyth, Wales, Elan Valley, W. Midlands Safari Park, Stratford-upon-Avon, Royal Leamington Spa, Northampton, Cambridge, Fitzwilliam Museum, University, Wickstead Park, Ely, Cathedral, Ipswich, Sutton Hoo, Worcester, Warwick Castle, Milton Keynes, Bedford, Felixstowe, Harwich, Hereford, Hidcote Manor Garden, Woburn Abbey, Colchester, Clacton-on-Sea, St David's, Bishop's Palace Cathedral, Fishguard, Carmarthen, Brecon Beacons National Park, Gloucester, Cathedral, Cheltenham, The Cotswolds, Blenheim Palace, Oxford, Luton, Hatfield House, Enfield, Southend-on-Sea, Greenwich, National Maritime Museum, Old Royal Observatory, Cutty Sark, Oakwood Adventure, Blaenavon, Wye Valley, Chepstow, Swindon, Reading, LONDON, Chatham, Dockyard, Ramsgate, Pembrokeshire Coast National Park, Pembroke, Swansea, Caerphilly Castle, Isca, Newport, Bristol, Bath, Avebury, Windsor, LEGOLAND, Thorpe Park, Chessington, Kew Gardens, Canterbury, Cathedral, St Augustine's Abbey, Dover, Museum of Welsh Life, St Fagans National Museum & Gallery, Techniquest, Cardiff Castle, Cardiff, Barry, Weston-super-Mare, Cheddar Gorge, Longleat, Stonehenge, Eton College, Hampton Court, Ightham Mote, Knole, Leeds Castle, Royal Tunbridge Wells, Uffington White Horse, Exmoor National Park, Wells, Cathedral, Salisbury, Cathedral, Winchester, Cathedral, Crawley, The Pantiles, Rye, Hastings, Barnstaple, Stourhead, Glastonbury, Abbey, Tor, Southampton, Portsmouth, Dockyard, Battle Abbey, Brighton, Beachy Head, Clovelly, Taunton, New Forest, National Motor Museum, Bognor Regis, Brighton Pavilion, Palace Pier, Tintagel, Exeter, Dartmoor National Park, Creaty Adventure Park, Exmouth, Weymouth, Bournemouth, Russell-Cotes Art Gallery & Museum, Compton Acres, Poole, Littlehampton, Harbour Park, ISLE OF WIGHT, Newquay, Eden Project, Plymouth, Torquay, St Ives, Tate Gallery, Trewithen, Lost Gardens of Heligan, Barbara Hepworth Museum, Penzance, Truro, Falmouth, St Michael's Mount, ISLES OF SCILLY, LUNDY

Shetland Islands

SHETLAND ISLANDS, UNST, YELL, FETLAR, WHALSAY, MAINLAND, BRESSAY, Lerwick, FOULA, Mousa Broch, Jarlshof

Orkney Islands

ORKNEY ISLANDS, FAIR ISLE, NORTH RONALDSAY, WESTRAY, SANDAY, ROUSAY, STRONSAY, EDAY, MAINLAND, SHAPINSAY, Skara Brae, Maes Howe, Kirkwall, St Magnus Cathedral, HOY, SOUTH RONALDSAY, Thurso

Same scale as main map

Channel Islands

ALDERNEY, GUERNSEY, St Peter Port, HERM, SARK, CHANNEL ISLANDS, Little Chapel, German Military Underground Hospital, JERSEY, St Helier, German Underground Hospital, Jersey Zoo

Isle of Man

ISLE OF MAN, Peel, House of Mananan, Douglas

Tay, Clyde, Tees, Trent, Severn, Thames, Great Ouse

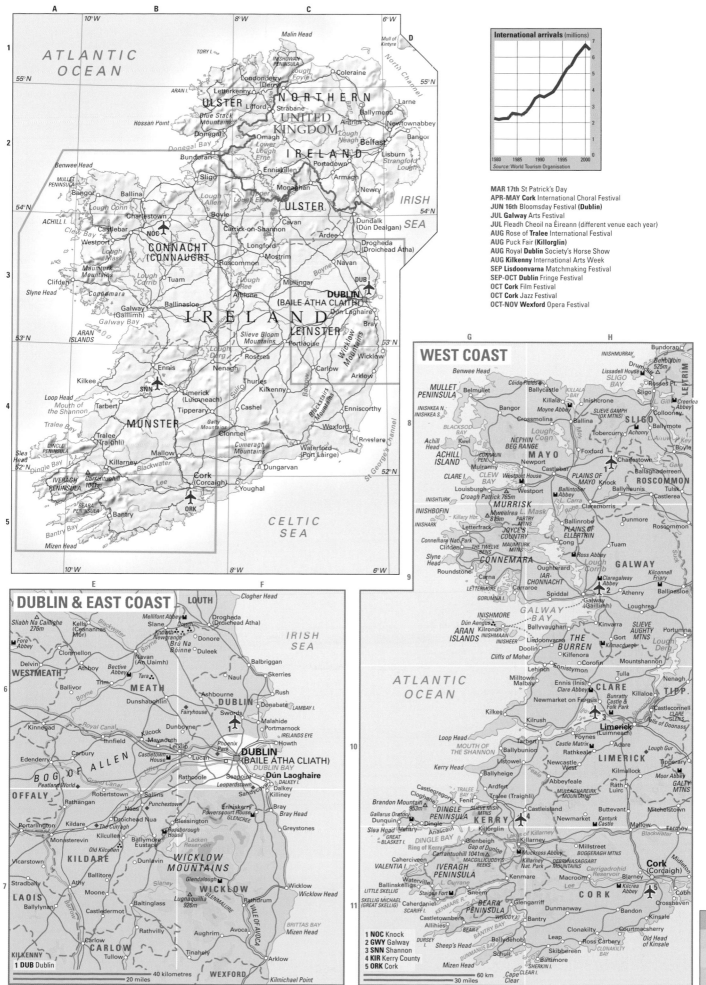

International arrivals (millions)

Source: World Tourism Organisation

MAR 17th St Patrick's Day
APR-MAY Cork International Choral Festival
JUN 16th Bloomsday Festival (**Dublin**)
JUL Galway Arts Festival
JUL Fleadh Cheoil na Éireann (different venue each year)
AUG Rose of **Tralee** International Festival
AUG Puck Fair (**Killorglin**)
AUG Royal **Dublin** Society's Horse Show
AUG Kilkenny International Arts Week
SEP Lisdoonvarna Matchmaking Festival
SEP-OCT Dublin Fringe Festival
OCT Cork Film Festival
OCT Cork Jazz Festival
OCT-NOV Wexford Opera Festival

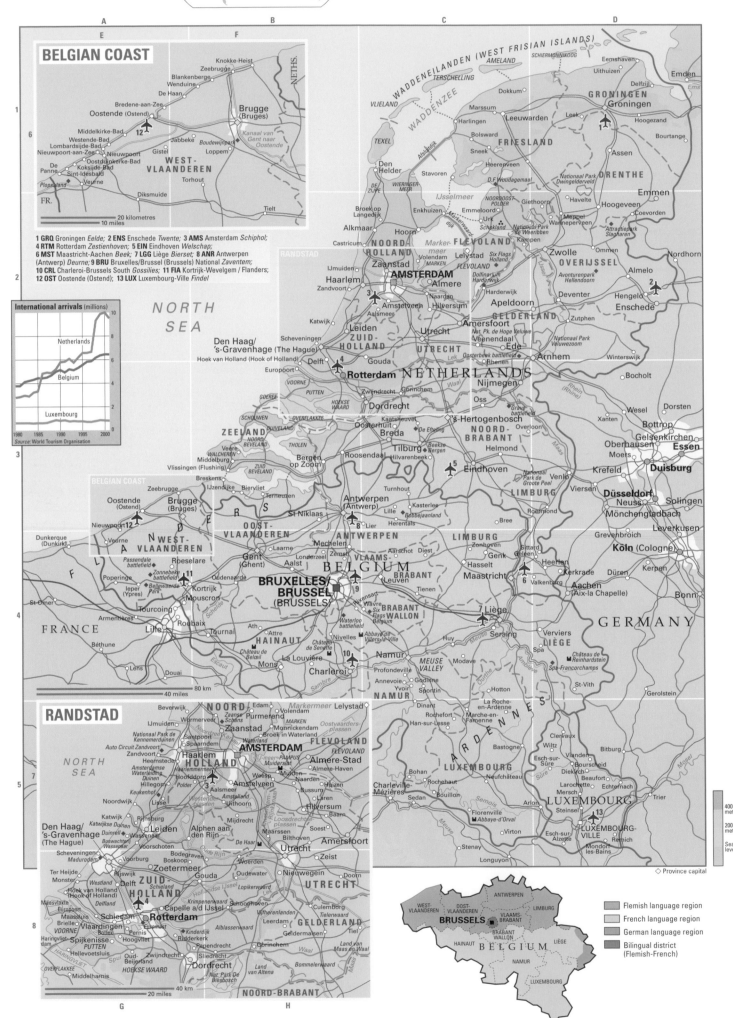

Legend

- Theme park, leisure park
- Museum, gallery
- Religious building
- Park, reserve, zoo, etc.
- Historic building
- Water-related attraction
- Other place of interest

Attractions in cities marked in **red** are listed on the left of the map

Amsterdam
Museum Amstelkring
Amsterdams Historisch Museum
Anne Frankhuis
Joods Historisch Museum
Madame Tussaud Scenerama
Museum Het Rembrandthuis
Nederlands Scheepvaart Museum
NeMo (New Metropolis)
Rijksmuseum
Stedelijk Museum
Tropenmuseum
Van Gogh Museum
Nieuwe Kerk
Westerkerk
Artis
Bloemenmarkt
Begijnhof
Koninklijk Paleis
Amsterdam canals (grachten)

Haarlem
Frans Halsmuseum
Teylers Museum
St Bavokerk
Vleeshal
Grote Markt

Leiden
Museum Boerhaave
Molenmuseum De Valk
Naturalis
Stedelijk Museum De Lakenhal
Rijksmuseum van Oudheden
Rijksmuseum voor Volkenkunde
De Burcht

Den Haag (The Hague)
Madurodam
Museum voor Communicatie
Gemeentemuseum
Mauritshuis
Museum Mesdag; Panorama Mesdag
Museon
Schilderijengalerij Prins Willem V
Binnenhof
Paleis Noordeinde

Gouda
Stedelijk Mus. Het Catharina Gasthuis
Sint Jan
Stadhuis

Delft
Koninklijk Nederlands
Leger- en Wapenmuseum
Prinsenhof
Nieuwe Kerk
Oude Kerk

Rotterdam
Museum Boymans-Van Beuningen
Museum De Dubbelde Palmboom
Historisch Museum
Het Schielandshuis
Nederlands Architectuurinstituut
Diergaarde Blijdorp
Boat trips to the port
Erasmusbrug
Euromast

Utrecht
Centraal Museum
Museum Het Catharijneconvent
Nationaal Museum van
Speelklok Tot Pierement
Nederlands Spoorwegmuseum
Domkerk; Domtoren
Pieterskerk
Rietveld Schröderhuis

Festivals and events

FEB/MAR Carnaval (**Breda, Maastricht & 's-Hertogenbosch**)
MAR Stille Ommegang: silent procession (**Amsterdam**)
MAR-MAY National Floral Exhibition (**Keukenhof**)
APR Floral Procession (**Haarlem to Noordwijk**)
APR 30th Koninginnedag: Queen's Birthday
MAY National Windmill & Pumping Station Day
MAY-SEP Passion Plays (**Tegelen**); 2005 and every five years
JUN Holland Festival (**Amsterdam**)
JUL North Sea Jazz Festival (**The Hague**)
AUG International Fireworks Festival (**Scheveningen**)
AUG Boekenmarkt (**Deventer**)
AUG Amsterdam Gay Pride
AUG-SEP Festival of Ancient Music (**Utrecht**)
SEP Bloemen Corso: floral procession (**Aalsmeer to Amsterdam**)
SEP Jordaan Festival (**Amsterdam**)
OCT 3rd Leidens Ontzet: historical procession (**Leiden**)
mid NOV St Nicholas' official entrance (**Amsterdam**)
DEC Candle Festival (**Gouda**)

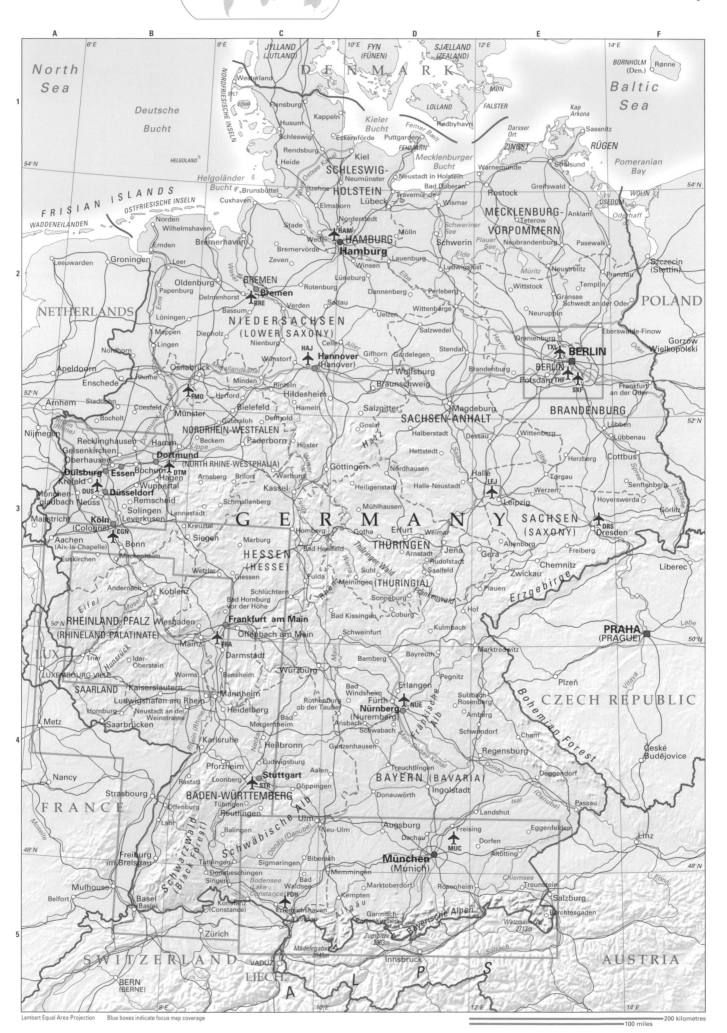

Lambert Equal Area Projection   Blue boxes indicate focus map coverage

200 kilometres
100 miles

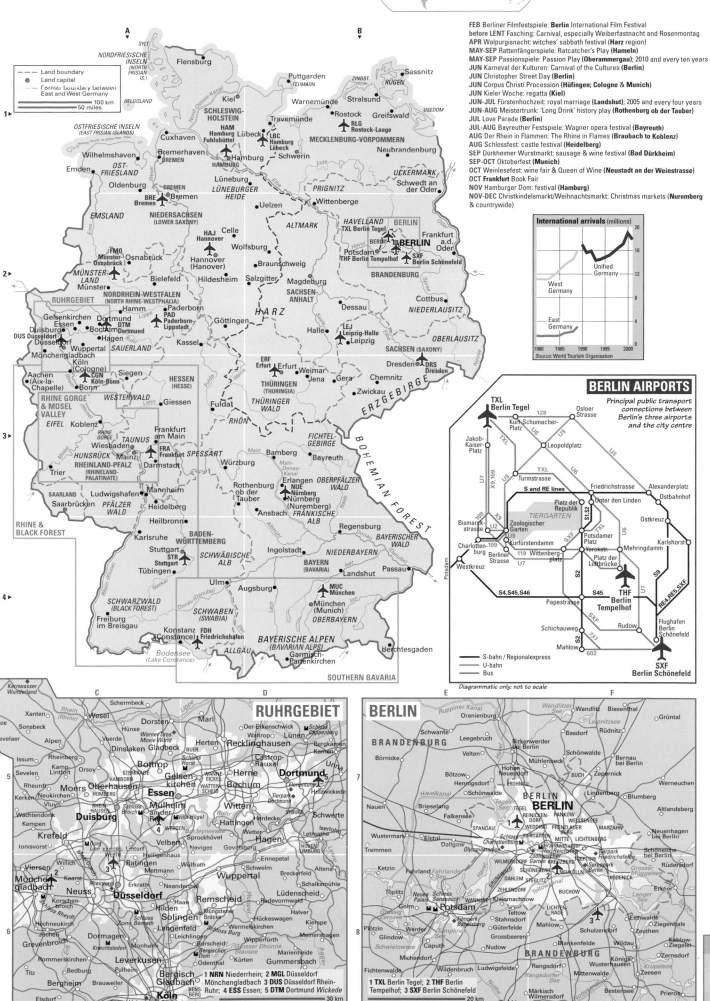

FEB Berliner Filmfestspiele: **Berlin** International Film Festival
before LENT Fasching: Carnival, especially Weiberfastnacht and Rosenmontag
APR Walpurgisnacht: witches' sabbath festival (**Harz** region)
MAY-SEP Rattenfängerspiele: Ratcatcher's Play (**Hameln**)
MAY-SEP Passionspiele: Passion Play (**Oberammergau**); 2010 and every ten years
JUN Karneval der Kulturen: Carnival of the Cultures (**Berlin**)
JUN Christopher Street Day (**Berlin**)
JUN Corpus Christi Procession (**Hüfingen**; **Cologne** & **Munich**)
JUN Kieler Woche: regatta (**Kiel**)
JUN-JUL Fürstenhochzeit: royal marriage (**Landshut**); 2005 and every four years
JUN-AUG Meistertrunk: 'Long Drink' history play (**Rothenburg ob der Tauber**)
JUL Love Parade (**Berlin**)
JUL-AUG Bayreuther Festspiele: Wagner opera festival (**Bayreuth**)
AUG Der Rhein in Flammen: The Rhine in Flames (**Braubach to Koblenz**)
AUG Schlossfest: castle festival (**Heidelberg**)
SEP Dürkheimer Wurstmarkt: sausage & wine festival (**Bad Dürkheim**)
SEP-OCT Oktoberfest (**Munich**)
OCT Weinlesefest: wine fair & Queen of Wine (**Neustadt an der Weinstrasse**)
OCT Frankfurt Book Fair
NOV Hamburger Dom: festival (**Hamburg**)
NOV-DEC Christkindelsmarkt/Weihnachtsmarkt: Christmas markets (**Nuremberg** & countrywide)

International arrivals (millions)

BERLIN AIRPORTS
Principal public transport connections between Berlin's three airports and the city centre

Diagrammatic only: not to scale

— S-bahn / Regionalexpress
— U-bahn
— Bus

RUHRGEBIET

1 **NRN** Niederrhein; 2 **MGL** Düsseldorf Mönchengladbach 3 **DUS** Düsseldorf Rhein-Ruhr; 4 **ESS** Essen; 5 **DTM** Dortmund *Wickede*

BERLIN

1 **TXL** Berlin Tegel; 2 **THF** Berlin Tempelhof; 3 **SXF** Berlin Schönefeld

ROMANTIC ROAD

Germany has a well-developed network of tourist routes passing through areas of scenic or historic interest. They include the Coastal Road, the Lakes Road (in Mecklenburg-Vorpommern), the Harz Mountains Road, the Martin Luther Road (Leipzig, Magdeburg, Erfurt), the Saxon Road, the Fairy-Tale Road (Bremen, Hameln, Kassel), the River Road (Rhine & Mosel), the Black Forest Road, the Castle & Thuringia Road, the Alpine Road and the Alpine-Baltic Road.

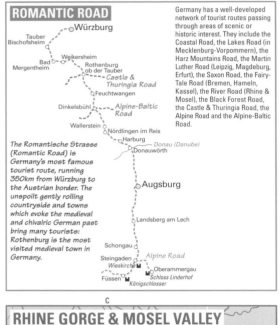

The Romantische Strasse (Romantic Road) is Germany's most famous tourist route, running 350km from Würzburg to the Austrian border. The unspoilt gently rolling countryside and towns which evoke the medieval and chivalric German past bring many tourists: Rothenburg is the most visited medieval town in Germany.

RHINE & BLACK FOREST

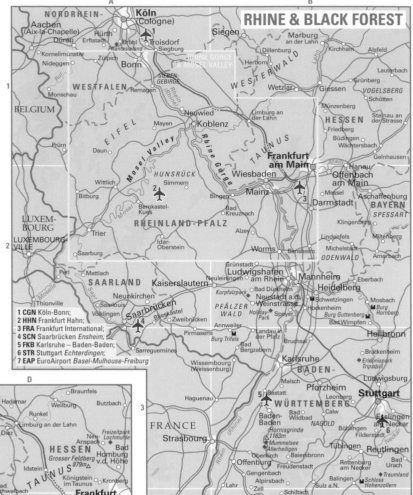

1 CGN Köln-Bonn;
2 HHN Frankfurt Hahn;
3 FRA Frankfurt International;
4 SCN Saarbrücken Ensheim;
5 FKB Karlsruhe – Baden-Baden;
6 STR Stuttgart Echterdingen;
7 EAP EuroAirport Basel-Mulhouse-Freiburg

RHINE GORGE & MOSEL VALLEY

1 HHN Frankfurt Hahn;
2 FRA Frankfurt International;

40 kilometres
20 miles

80 kilometres
40 miles

SOUTHERN BAVARIA

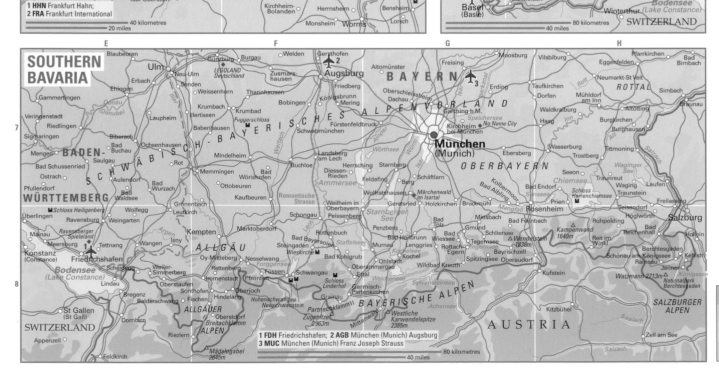

1 FDH Friedrichshafen; 2 AGB München (Munich) Augsburg
3 MUC München (Munich) Franz Joseph Strauss

40 kilometres
80 miles

1000 metres
500 metres
Sea level

Germany: Attractions

Legend:
- Theme park, leisure park
- Museum, gallery
- Religious building
- Park, reserve, zoo, etc.
- Historic building
- Water-related attraction
- Other place of interest

Attractions in cities marked in **red** are listed around the edge of the map

100 kilometres
50 miles

Bonn
- Alexander-Koenig Museum
- Haus der Geschichte der BRD
- Kunstmuseum
- Münster

Düsseldorf
- Kunstmuseum
- Kunstsammlung Nordrhein-Westfalen
- Schloss Jägerhof
- Altstadt
- Königsallee

Frankfurt am Main
- Goethe-Haus
- Jüdisches Museum
- Museum für Moderne Kunst
- Museumsufer
- Zoo
- Römerberg

Hamburg
- Altonaer Museum
- Kunsthalle
- Museum für Kunst & Gewerbe
- Hauptkirche St Michaelis
- Tierpark Hagenpark (zoo)
- Hafen (port)
- Altstadt
- Fernsehturm
- Reeperbahn

Köln (Cologne)
- Museum für Ostasiatische Kunst
- Römisch-Germanisches Museum
- Schnütgen Museum
- Wallraf-Richartz/Ludwig Museum
- Dom
- St Gereonskirche
- Fernsehturm

Berlin
- Ägyptisches Museum
- Antiken Museum
- Bauhaus Archiv
- Dahlem Museums
- Deutsches Teknikmuseum
- Jüdisches Museum
- Kulturforum
- Kunstgewerbemuseum
- Museum für Naturkunde
- Museumsinsel
- Botanischer Garten
- Zoologischer Garten
- Brandenburger Tor
- Bundestag (Reichstag)
- Haus am Checkpoint Charlie
- Schloss Charlottenburg
- Fernsehturm
- Gendarmenmarkt
- Kurfürstendamm
- Nikolaiviertel
- Potsdamer Platz
- Unter den Linden

Dresden
- Albertinum
- Dom
- Japanisches Palais
- Semperoper
- Schloss Pillnitz
- Zwinger

München (Munich)
- Alte & Neue Pinakothek
- Antikensammlungen
- Bayerisches Nationalmuseum
- Deutsches Museum
- Glyptothek
- Pinakothek der Moderne
- Dom
- Englischer Garten
- Residenz
- Schloss Nymphenburg
- Marienplatz
- Olympiaturm

France

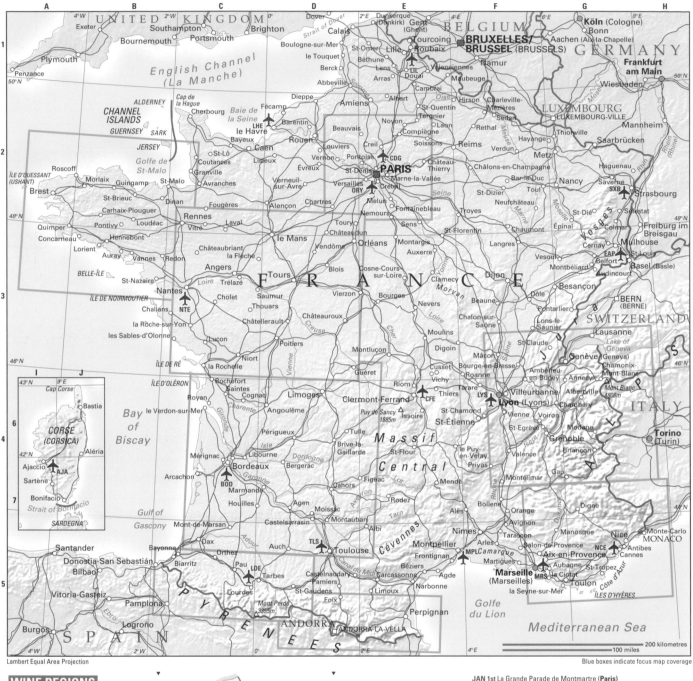

Lambert Equal Area Projection

Blue boxes indicate focus map coverage

WINE REGIONS

Some of the more important vin de pays areas are shown in *BLUE TYPE*. Numbers indicate the month when important wine festivals occur in each region (1=Jan., 12=Dec., E=Easter)

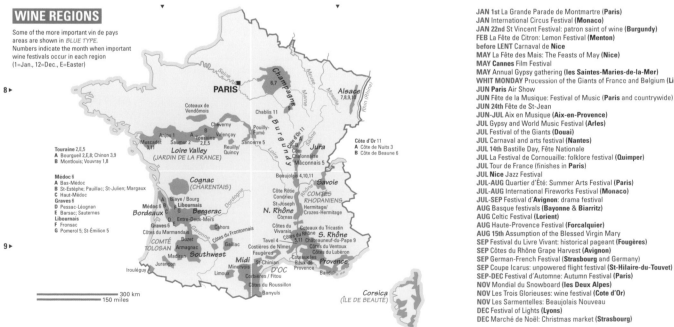

JAN 1st La Grande Parade de Montmartre (**Paris**)
JAN International Circus Festival (**Monaco**)
JAN 22nd St Vincent Festival: patron saint of wine (**Burgundy**)
FEB La Fête de Citron: Lemon Festival (**Menton**)
before LENT Carnaval de Nice
MAY La Fête des Mais: The Feasts of May (**Nice**)
MAY Cannes Film Festival
MAY Annual Gypsy gathering (**les Saintes-Maries-de-la-mer**)
WHIT MONDAY Procession of the Giants of France and Belgium (**Lille**)
JUN Paris Air Show
JUN Fête de la Musique: Festival of Music (**Paris** and countrywide)
JUN 24th Fête de St-Jean
JUN-JUL Aix en Musique (**Aix-en-Provence**)
JUL Gypsy and World Music Festival (**Arles**)
JUL Festival of the Giants (**Douai**)
JUL Carnaval and arts festival (**Nantes**)
JUL 14th Bastille Day, Fête Nationale
JUL La Festival de Cornouaille: folklore festival (**Quimper**)
JUL Tour de France (finishes in **Paris**)
JUL Nice Jazz Festival
JUL-AUG Quartier d'Été: Summer Arts Festival (**Paris**)
JUL-AUG International Fireworks Festival (**Monaco**)
JUL-SEP Festival d'Avignon: drama festival (**Avignon**)
AUG Basque festivals (**Bayonne** & **Biarritz**)
AUG Celtic Festival (**Lorient**)
AUG Haute-Provence Festival (**Forcalquier**)
AUG 15th Assumption of the Blessed Virgin Mary
SEP Festival du Livre Vivant: historical pageant (**Fougères**)
SEP Côtes du Rhône Grape Harvest (**Avignon**)
SEP German-French Festival (**Strasbourg** and Germany)
SEP Coupe Icarus: unpowered flight festival (**St-Hilaire-du-Touvet**)
SEP-DEC Festival d'Automne: Autumn Festival (**Paris**)
NOV Mondial du Snowboard (**les Deux Alpes**)
NOV Les Trois Glorieuses: wine festival (**Cote d'Or**)
NOV Les Sarmentelles: Beaujolais Nouveau
DEC Festival of Lights (**Lyons**)
DEC Marché de Noël: Christmas market (**Strasbourg**)

France

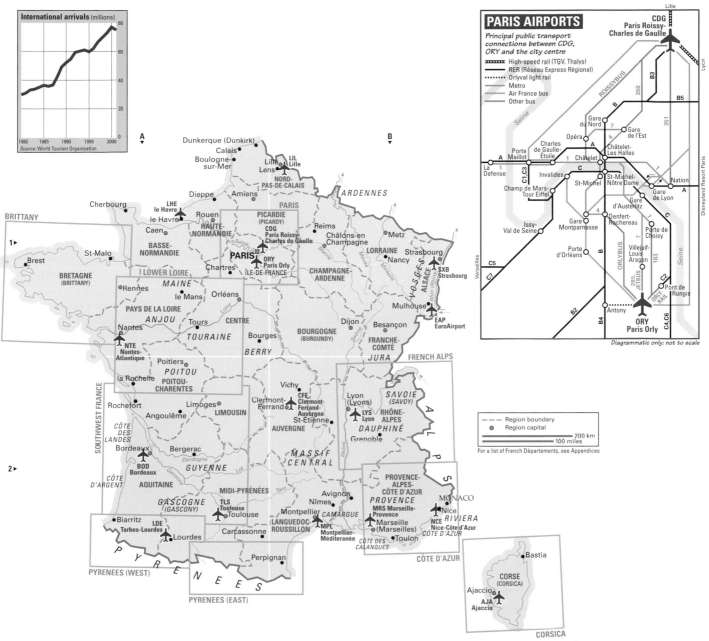

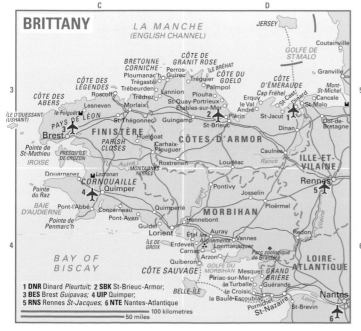

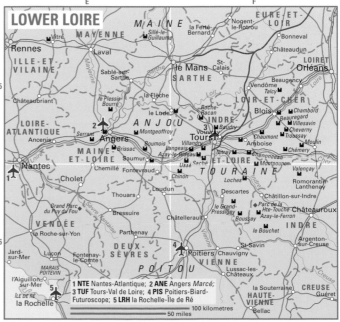

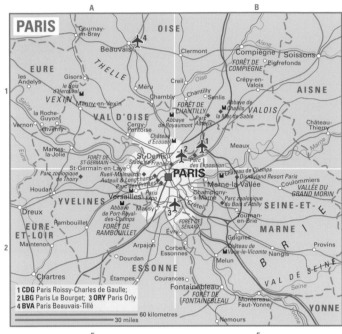

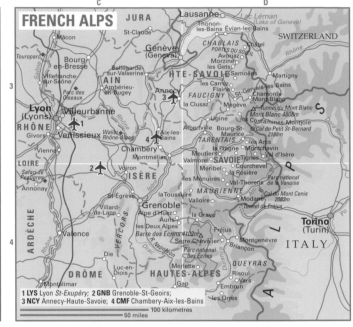

France: Attractions

Legend:
- Theme park, leisure park
- Museum, gallery
- Religious building
- Park, reserve, zoo, etc.
- Historic building
- Water-related attraction
- Other place of interest

Attractions in cities marked in **red** are listed above and below the map

200 kilometres
100 miles

Paris
- Le Jardin d'Acclimatation
- Centre Georges-Pompidou
- Cité des Sciences et de l'Industrie
- Institut du Monde Arabe
- Louvre
- Musée d'Orsay
- Musée Marmottan
- Musée national du Jeu de Paume
- Musée national du Moyen-Âge
- Musée national de l'Orangerie
- Musée national Picasso
- Musée Rodin
- Cathédrale St-Denis
- Cathédrale de Notre-Dame
- Église du Dôme
- Panthéon
- Sacré-Cœur
- Ste-Chapelle
- Jardin de Luxembourg
- La Grande Arche de la Défense
- Hôtel des Invalides
- Opéra Garnier
- Palais de Chaillot
- Arc de Triomphe
- Champs-Élysées
- Cimetière de Montmartre
- Cimetière du Père-Lachaise
- Le Marais
- Montmartre
- Place de la Concorde
- Place des Vosges
- Tour Eiffel

Orange
- Théâtre Antique
- Arc de Triomphe

Avignon
- Musée Calvet
- Musée du Petit Palais
- Palais des Papes
- Pont St-Bénézet

Nîmes
- Jardin de la Fontaine
- Arènes
- Maison Carrée

Lyon (Lyons)
- Musée d'Art contemporain
- Musée des Beaux-Arts
- Musée de la Civilisation Gallo-Romaine
- Musée Henri-Malartre
- Centre d'histoire de la Résistance
- Musée historique des Tissus
- Basilique du Fourvière
- Maison des Canuts
- Quartier St-Jean

Spain & Portugal

SPAIN

JAN 5th Cabalgata de los Reyes Magos: Three Kings Festival (**Barcelona**)
JAN Festividad de **San Sebastián**: drum parades
before Lent Carnaval (**Cádiz, Madrid** and countrywide)
MAR Las Fallas de **Valencia**
EASTER Semana Santa: Holy Week
APR La Feria de **Sevilla**
APR Moros y Cristianos mock battle: St George's Festival (**Alcoy**)
APR 23rd La Diada de Sant Jordi: Day of St George 'Day of Lovers' (**Barcelona**)
MAY Cruces de Mayo and national flamenco competition (**Córdoba**)
MAY Feria del Caballo: horse fair (**Jeréz de la Frontera**)
MAY-JUN Fiestas de San Isidro (**Madrid**)
MAY/JUN Corpus Christi
WHIT SUNDAY Romería del Rocío: pilgrimage (near **Huelva**)
JUN SONAR: electronic music festival (**Barcelona**)
JUN Haro: Wine war (**La Rioja**)
JUN 23-24th Festes de Sant Joan (**Barcelona** and Catalonia)
JUN 24th Xiquets de Valls: human towers (**Valls**)
JUN-JUL GREC: **Barcelona** Summer Festival
JUN-JUL International Festival of Music and Dance (**Granada**)
JUL Los Sanfermines: running of the bulls (**Pamplona**)
JUL Santa Marta de Ribarteme: 'near-death' pilgrimage (**Las Nieves, Pontevadra**)
JUL 22nd Cuesta de los Danzadores: stilt dancers (**Anguiano**, La Rioja)
JUL 25th Feast of St James (**Santiago de Compostela**)
AUG Semana Grande, includes Basque Herri Kilorak: traditional sports (**Bilbao**)
AUG Moros y Cristianos mock battle and mystery play (**Elx**)
AUG La Tomatina: Tomato Battle (**Buñol**)
SEP 19th Americas Day (**Oviedo**)
SEP 24th Festa de la Mercé: Our Lady of Mercy Festival (**Barcelona**)
OCT-NOV Madrid Autumn Festival

PORTUGAL

before Lent Lisbon Carnival
MAY 13th Pilgrimage to the Shrine of Our Lady of **Fátima**
MAY Queimade Fitas: academic celebrations (**Coimbra**)
JUN Festas de Lisboa: festivities in honour of three saints (**Lisbon**)
JUL Festa do Colete Encarnado: Festival of the Red Waistcoat (**Vila Franca de Xira**)
AUG Romaria de Nossa Senhora de Agonia: fair & pilgrimage (**Viana do Castelo**)
OCT Fiera de Outabro: October Festival (**Vila Franca de Xira**)
OCT 13th Pilgrimage to the Shrine of Our Lady of **Fátima**
NEW YEAR'S EVE Noite Mágica: Magic Night (**Lisbon**)

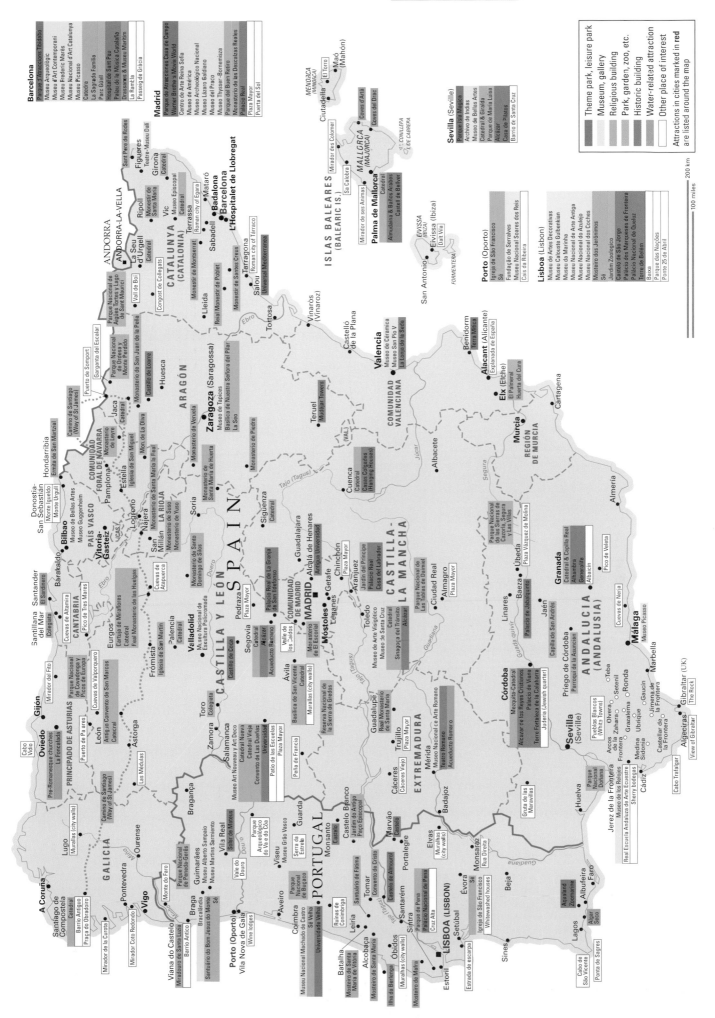

Spain, Andorra & Gibraltar

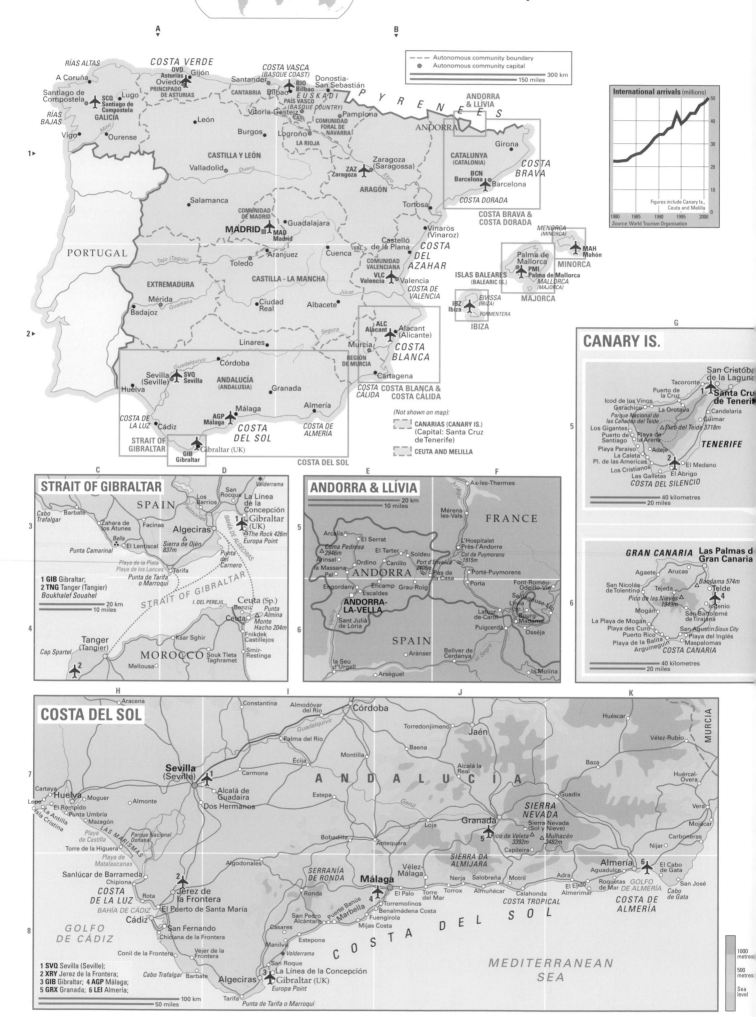

- - - Autonomous community boundary
- Autonomous community capital

300 km
150 miles

International arrivals (millions)

Figures include Canary Is.,
Ceuta and Melilla
Source: World Tourism Organisation

RÍAS ALTAS
COSTA VERDE
COSTA VASCA (BASQUE COAST)

A Coruña
SCQ Santiago de Compostela
Santiago de Compostela
GALICIA
RÍAS BAJAS
Vigo
Ourense
Lugo
Gijón
OVD Asturias Oviedo
PRINCIPADO DE ASTURIAS
CANTABRIA
Santander
BIO Bilbao
Donostia-San Sebastián
EUSKADI
PAÍS VASCO (BASQUE COUNTRY)
Vitoria-Gasteiz
PYRENEES
León
Burgos
CASTILLA Y LEÓN
Pamplona
COMUNIDAD FORAL DE NAVARRA
LA RIOJA
Logroño
ANDORRA & LLÍVIA
ANDORRA
CATALUNYA (CATALONIA)
Girona
COSTA BRAVA
Valladolid
Duero
ZAZ Zaragoza
Zaragoza (Saragossa)
ARAGÓN
Ebro
Barcelona
BCN Barcelona
COSTA DORADA
PORTUGAL
Salamanca
COMUNIDAD DE MADRID
MADRID
MAD Madrid
Guadalajara
Tortosa
COSTA BRAVA & COSTA DORADA
Vinaròs (Vinaroz)
MENORCA (MINORCA)
MAH Mahón
Castelló de la Plana
COSTA DEL AZAHAR
Palma de Mallorca
PMI Palma de Mallorca
MINORCA
Tajo (Tagus)
Toledo
Aranjuez
VAL Cuenca
COMUNIDAD VALENCIANA
ISLAS BALEARES (BALEARIC IS.)
MALLORCA (MAJORCA)
EXTREMADURA
CASTILLA - LA MANCHA
Júcar
VLC Valencia
Valencia
COSTA DE VALENCIA
MAJORCA
Mérida
Guadiana
Ciudad Real
Albacete
IBZ Ibiza
EIVISSA (IBIZA)
FORMENTERA
Badajoz
Segura
ALC Alacant
Alacant (Alicante)
IBIZA
Linares
Murcia
REGIÓN DE MURCIA
COSTA BLANCA
Córdoba
SVQ Sevilla
Sevilla (Seville)
ANDALUCÍA (ANDALUSIA)
Granada
Cartagena
COSTA CÁLIDA
COSTA BLANCA & COSTA CÁLIDA
Huelva
Málaga
Almería
COSTA DE LA LUZ
AGP Málaga
COSTA DEL SOL
Cádiz
COSTA DE ALMERÍA
STRAIT OF GIBRALTAR
GIB Gibraltar
Gibraltar (UK)
COSTA DEL SOL

(Not shown on map):
CANARIAS (CANARY IS.) (Capital: Santa Cruz de Tenerife)
CEUTA AND MELILLA

CANARY IS.

San Cristóbal de la Laguna
Tacoronte
Puerto de la Cruz
1 Santa Cruz de Tenerife
Icod de los Vinos
Garachico
La Orotava
Candelaria
Parque Nacional de las Cañadas del Teide
Güímar
Los Gigantes
Pico del Teide 3718m
Puerto de Santiago
Playa de la Arena
Playa Paraíso
Adeje
2 El Medano
La Caleta
Pl. de las Américas
TENERIFE
Los Cristianos
El Abrigo
Las Galletas
COSTA DEL SILENCIO

40 kilometres
20 miles

GRAN CANARIA
Las Palmas de Gran Canaria
Agaete
Arucas
Bandama 574m
San Nicolás de Tolentino
Tejeda
Telde
Pico de las Nieves 1949m
4 Ingenio
Mogán
San Bartolomé de Tirajana
La Playa de Mogán
Playa des Cura
San Agustín Sioux City
Puerto Rico
Playa del Inglés
Playa de la Balita
Maspalomas
Arguineguín
COSTA CANARIA

40 kilometres
20 miles

STRAIT OF GIBRALTAR

SPAIN
Cabo Trafalgar
Barbate
Zahara de los Atunes
Los Barrios
San Roque
Valderrama
La Línea de la Concepción
Gibraltar (UK)
1 GIB Gibraltar
The Rock 426m
Europa Point
Bella
El Lentiscal
Facinas
Algeciras
Sierra de Ojén 837m
BAHÍA DE ALGECIRAS
Punta Camarinal
Tarifa
Punta del Carnero
Playa de la Plata
Playa de los Lances
Punta de Tarifa o Marroquí

1 GIB Gibraltar;
2 TNG Tanger (Tangier) Boukhalef Souahel

20 km
10 miles

STRAIT OF GIBRALTAR
I. DEL PEREJIL
Ceuta (Sp.)
Benzú
Punta Almina
Ceuta
Monte Hacho 204m
Tanger (Tangier)
Cap Spartel
2
Ksar Sghir
Fnidek Castillejos
Smir-Restinga
MOROCCO
Souk Tleta Taghramet
Mellousa

ANDORRA & LLÍVIA

20 km
10 miles

Ax-les-Thermes
Arcalís
El Serrat
Mérens-les-Vals
FRANCE
Coma Pedrosa 2946m
El Tarter
Soldeu
L'Hospitalet Près-l'Andorre
Arinsal
Ordino
Canillo
Port d'Envalira 2408m
Col de Puymorens 1915m
la Massana
Pal
ANDORRA
Pas de la Casa
Porté-Puymorens
Engordany
Encamp
Grau-Roig
Porta
Font-Romeu-Odeillo-Via
Escaldes
ANDORRA-LA-VELLA
Llívia
Saillagouse-Llo
Sant Julià de Lòria
Latour-de-Carol
Bourg-Madame
Ossèja
Puigcerdà
SPAIN
la Seu d'Urgell
Aránser
Bellver de Cerdanya
el Segre
Arsèguel
la Molina

COSTA DEL SOL

Aracena
Constantina
Almodóvar del Río
Córdoba
Huéscar
MURCIA
Cartaya
Huelva
Moguer
Almonte
Guadalquivir
Palma del Río
Torredonjimeno
Jaén
Vélez-Rubio
Lepe
La Antilla
Punta Umbría
Mazagón
Écija
Montilla
Baena
Baza
Isla Cristina
Parque Nacional de Doñana
Écija
Bobadilla
Loja
Alcalá la Real
Guadix
Vera
LAS MARISMAS
Playa de Castilla
1 Sevilla (Seville)
Alcalá de Guadaira
Dos Hermanos
Carmona
Estepa
Genil
Granada
SIERRA NEVADA
Sierra Nevada (Sol y Nieve)
Pico de Veleta 3392m
Mulhacén 3482m
Huércal-Overa
Torre de la Higuera
Playa de Matalascañas
Sanlúcar de Barrameda
Chipiona
Rota
2 Jerez de la Frontera
El Puerto de Santa María
Algodonales
SERRANÍA DE RONDA
Antequera
Capileira
SIERRA DA ALMIJARA
Mojácar
COSTA DE LA LUZ
BAHÍA DE CÁDIZ
Cádiz
San Fernando
Ronda
Vélez-Málaga
Málaga
4 El Palo
Nerja
Salobreña
Motril
Almería
6 El Cabo de Gata
Aguadulce
Carboneras
Níjar
GOLFO DE CÁDIZ
Chiclana de la Frontera
San Pedro Alcántara
Puerto Banús
Marbella
Benalmádena Costa
Fuengirola
Mijas Costa
Torremolinos
Torrox
Almuñécar
Calahonda
El Ejido
Roquetas de Mar
Almerimar
Adra
GOLFO DE ALMERÍA
San José
Cabo de Gata
COSTA DE ALMERÍA
Conil de la Frontera
Vejer de la Frontera
Casares
Estepona
Manilva
Valderrama
San Roque
La Línea de la Concepción
COSTA TROPICAL
COSTA DEL SOL
Cabo Trafalgar
Barbate
Algeciras
3 Gibraltar (UK)
Europa Point
Tarifa
Punta de Tarifa o Marroquí
MEDITERRANEAN SEA

1 SVQ Sevilla (Seville);
2 XRY Jerez de la Frontera;
3 GIB Gibraltar; 4 AGP Málaga;
5 GRX Granada; 6 LEI Almería;

100 km
50 miles

1000 metres
500 metres
Sea level

Spain

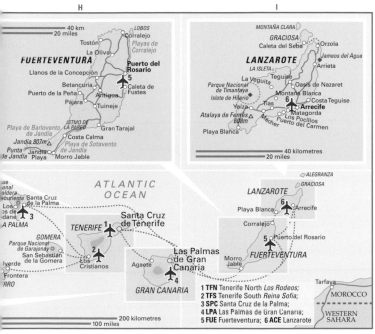

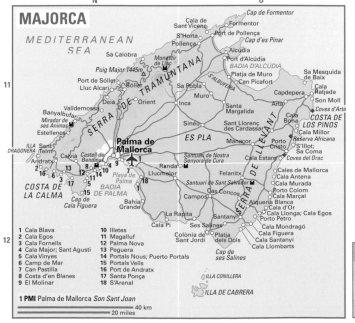

Portugal

District boundary
District capital
100 km
50 miles

AZORES

B | C
200 kilometres
100 miles

1 **FLW** Flores; 2 **HOR** Horta; 3 **PIX** Pico;
4 **TER** Terceira; 5 **PDL** Ponta Delgada; 6 **SMA** Santa Maria

CORVO
1 Santa Cruz das Flores
FLORES

ATLANTIC OCEAN

Santa Cruz da Graciosa
GRACIOSA

4 TERCEIRA
Angra do Heroísmo

FAIAL
Horta 3 Velas SÃO JORGE
2 Lajes do Pico PICO

20 km
10 miles

SÃO MIGUEL
Ponta da Ferraria
Caldeiras das Sete Cidades
Ribeira Grande
Pico da Vara 1105m
Nordeste
Ponta do Arnel
5 Ponta Delgada
Lagoa
Furnas
Povoação
Vila Franca do Campo

SÃO MIGUEL
5 Ponta Delgada
FORMIGAS

SANTA MARIA 6
Vila do Porto

International arrivals (millions)

Figures include Azores and Madeira
Source: World Tourism Organisation

Monção
SERRA DA PENEDA
VIANA DO CASTELO
Viana do Castelo
SERRA DO GERÊS
Braga
BRAGA
Bragança
VILA REAL
Vila Real
TRÁS OS MONTES
BRAGANÇA
Póvoa de Varzim
OPO Porto
Porto (Oporto)
PORTO
Espinho
Douro
MONTANHAS
AVEIRO
VISEU
Aveiro
Viseu
GUARDA
Guarda
Figueira da Foz
Coimbra
SERRA DA ESTRELA
COIMBRA
Covilhã
CASTELO BRANCO
Castelo Branco
Leiria
LEIRIA
Fátima
Nazaré
Tejo (Tagus)
SANTARÉM
Portalegre
Peniche
Santarém
PORTALEGRE
RIBATEJO
LISBOA
LIS Lisboa
LISBOA (LISBON)
Elvas
COSTA DE LISBOA (COSTA DO SOL)
Setúbal
ÉVORA
Évora
Barragem de Alqueva
LISBON
PLANÍCIES
SETÚBAL
COSTA DA GALÉ
Beja
Moura
Sines
COSTA DOURADA (COSTA DE OURO)
BEJA
Odemira
Portimão
FARO
FAO Faro
Faro
ALGARVE
ALGARVE

COSTA VERDE
COSTA DE PRATA

(Not shown on map) AUTONOMOUS REGIONS OF:
AÇORES (AZORES) (Capital: Ponta Delgada)
MADEIRA (Capital: Funchal)

MADEIRA

D | E

ATLANTIC OCEAN

PORTO SANTO
I. DE FERRO
I. DE CENOURAS
Camacha
2 Pico de Facho 517m
I. DE BAIXO
Vila Baleira
I. DE CIMA

Porto Moniz
Ponta do Pargo
Seixal
São Vicente
Boaventura
São Jorge
Santana
Faial
PAUL DA SERRA
Prazeres
Pico Ruivo 1862m
Porto da Cruz
BAIA DE ZARCO
Ponta do Castelo
Calheta
Pico de Arieiro 1818m
MADEIRA
Curral das Freiras
Portela
Caniçal
ILHÉU DE AGOSTINHO
Prainha
ILHÉU DE FORA
Ponta do Sol
Santo da Serra
Machico
1 Agua de Pena
Terreiro da Luta
Santa Cruz
Cabo Girão
Funchal
Quinta do Palheiro Ferreiro
Câmara de Lobos
Caniço

1 **FNC** Funchal;
2 **PXO** Porto Santo

30 kilometres
15 miles

LISBON

F | G

Alenquer
Ericeira
Mafra
LISBOA
Vila Franca de Xira
Benavente
Coruche
Rio Tagus
Sorraia
SANTARÉM
Azenhas do Mar
Praia das Maçãs
Colares
Sintra
Reserva Natural do Estuário do Tejo
Infantado
Praia Grande
SERRA DE SINTRA
Cacém
Amadora
Alcochete
Cabo da Roca
Malveira da Serra
Queluz
Praia do Guincho
Cabo Raso
Estoril
Belém
LISBOA (LISBON)
SETÚBAL
Cascais
Oeiras
Almada
Montijo
COSTA DO ESTORIL
Praia Parede
Barreiro
Aguas de Moura
Praia da Carparica
Seixal
Palmela
Mataceca
Costa da Caparica
ATLANTIC OCEAN
COSTA DE LISBOA (COSTA DO SOL)
Vila Nogueira de Azeitão
Setúbal
Lagoa de Albufeira
SERRA DA ARRÁBIDA
Outão
Tróia
Sado
1 **LIS** Lisboa (Lisbon)
Sesimbra
Portinho da Arrábida
30 kilometres
15 miles
Cabo Espichel
COSTA BELA

ALGARVE

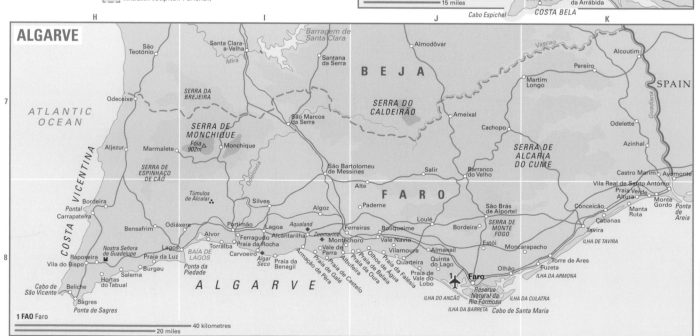

H | I | J | K

Barragem de Santa Clara
Santa Clara-a-Velha
Santana da Serra
Almodôvar
Alcoutim
São Teótonio
Mira
BEJA
Pereiro
Odeceixe
SERRA DA BREJEIRA
São Marcos da Serra
SERRA DO CALDEIRÃO
Martim Longo
SPAIN
ATLANTIC OCEAN
Ameixal
Cachopo
Odelette
SERRA DE MONCHIQUE
Foia 902m
Monchique
Guadiana
Azinhal
SERRA DE ESPINHAÇO DE CÃO
Odelouca
São Bartolomeu de Messines
Salir
Barranco do Velho
SERRA DE ALCARIA DO CUME
Castro Marim
Ayamonte
Bordeira
Túmulos de Alcalar
Silves
Algoz
Alte
FARO
São Brás de Aportel
SERRA DE MONTE FOGO
Vila Real de Santo António
Pontal
Bensafrim
Odiáxere
Portimão
Lagoa
Aqualand
Ferreiras
Boliqueime
Loulé
Estói
Moncarapacho
Praia Verde
Altura
Monte Gordo
Ponta de Areia
Carrapateira
Alvor
Torralba
Praia da Rocha
Alcantarilha
Zeemarine
Montechoro
Vilamoura
Almansil
Conceição
Cabanas
Tavira
Ráposeira
Lagos
Ferragudo
Carvoeiro
Vale de Parra
Albufeira
Quarteira
Quinta do Lago
Torre de Ares
ILHA DE TAVIRA
Vila do Bispo
Praia da Luz
Burgau
Algar Seco
Praia da Benagil
Armação de Pêra
Praia de Galé
Praia da Oura
Praia da Falésia
Vale do Lobo
Fuzeta
ILHA DA ARMONA
Cabo de São Vicente
Beliche
Hortas do Tabual
Salema
Ponta da Piedade
Praia da Marinha
Olhos de Água
Praia da Água
1 Faro
Olhão
Sagres
Ponta de Sagres
BAÍA DE LAGOS
ALGARVE
Reserva Natural da Ria Formosa
ILHA DA CULATRA
ILHA DO ANCÃO
ILHA DA BARRETA
Cabo de Santa Maria
COSTA VICENTINA

1 **FAO** Faro
40 kilometres
20 miles

500 metres
200 metres
Sea level

Italy

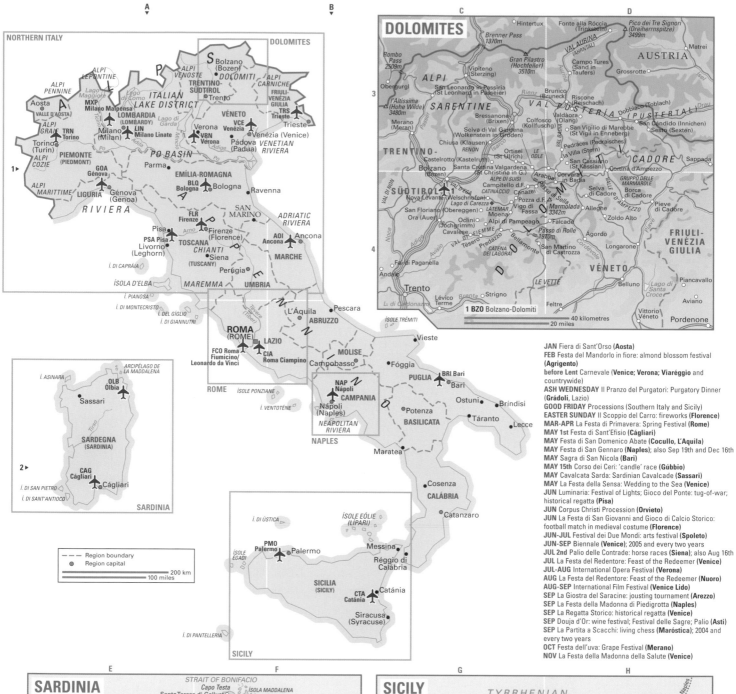

JAN Fiera di Sant'Orso (**Aosta**)

FEB Festa del Mandorlo in fiore: almond blossom festival (**Agrigento**)

before Lent Carnevale (**Venice; Verona; Viaréggio** and countrywide)

ASH WEDNESDAY Il Pranzo del Purgatori: Purgatory Dinner (**Grádoli**, Lazio)

GOOD FRIDAY Processions (Southern Italy and Sicily)

EASTER SUNDAY Il Scoppio del Carro: fireworks (**Florence**)

MAR-APR La Festa di Primavera: Spring Festival (**Rome**)

MAY 1st Festa di Sant'Efisio (**Cágliari**)

MAY Festa di San Domenico Abate (**Cocullo, L'Aquila**)

MAY Festa di San Gennaro (**Naples**); also Sep 19th and Dec 16th

MAY Sagra di San Nicola (**Bari**)

MAY 15th Corso dei Ceri: 'candle' race (**Gúbbio**)

MAY Cavalcata Sarda: Sardinian Cavalcade (**Sassari**)

MAY La Festa della Sensa: Wedding to the Sea (**Venice**)

JUN Luminaria: Festival of Lights; Gioco del Ponte: tug-of-war; historical regatta (**Pisa**)

JUN Corpus Christi Procession (**Orvieto**)

JUN La Festa di San Giovanni and Gioco di Calcio Storico: football match in medieval costume (**Florence**)

JUN-JUL Festival dei Due Mondi: arts festival (**Spoleto**)

JUN-SEP Biennale (**Venice**); 2005 and every two years

JUL 2nd Palio delle Contrade: horse races (**Siena**); also Aug 16th

JUL La Festa del Redentore: Feast of the Redeemer (**Venice**)

JUL-AUG International Opera Festival (**Verona**)

AUG La Festa del Redentore: Feast of the Redeemer (**Nuoro**)

AUG-SEP International Film Festival (**Venice Lido**)

SEP La Giostra del Saracino: jousting tournament (**Arezzo**)

SEP La Festa della Madonna di Piedigrotta (**Naples**)

SEP La Regatta Storico: historical regatta (**Venice**)

SEP Douja d'Or: wine festival; Festival delle Sagre; Palio (**Asti**)

SEP La Partita a Scacchi: living chess (**Maróstica**); 2004 and every two years

OCT Festa dell'uva: Grape Festival (**Merano**)

NOV La Festa della Madonna della Salute (**Venice**)

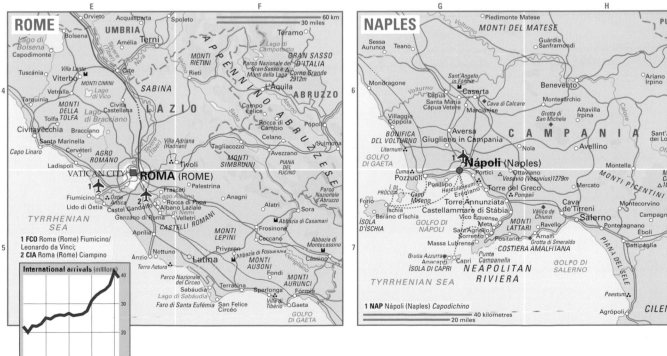

Italy: Attractions

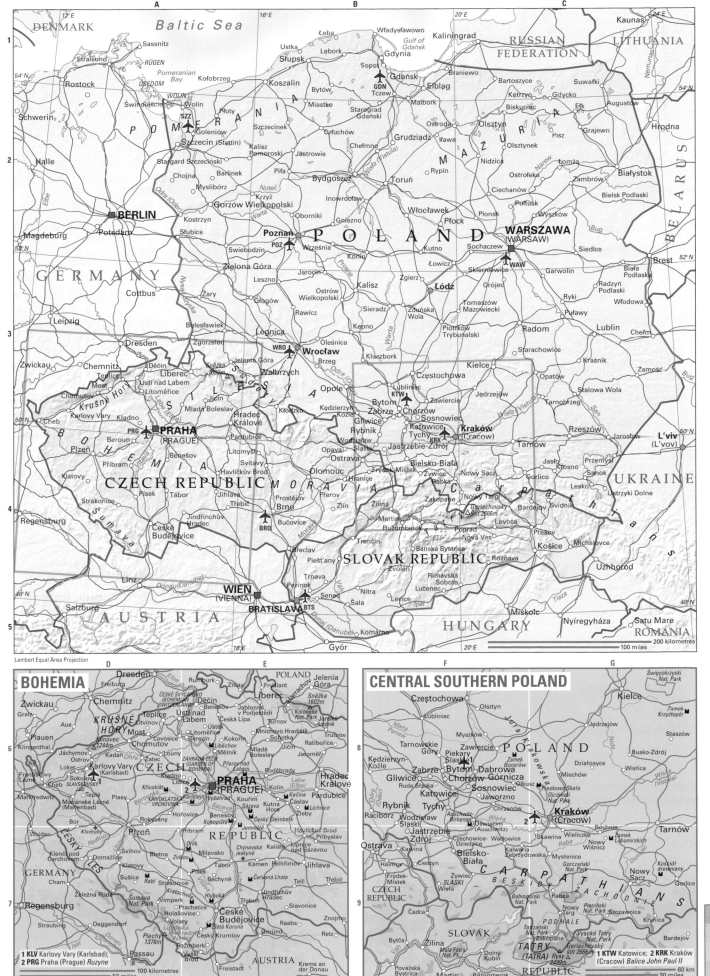

Lambert Equal Area Projection

BOHEMIA

1 KLV Karlovy Vary (Karlsbad);
2 PRG Praha (Prague) *Ruzyne*

CENTRAL SOUTHERN POLAND

1 KTW Katowice; 2 KRK Kraków
(Cracow) *Balice John Paul II*

1000 metres
500 metres
Sea level

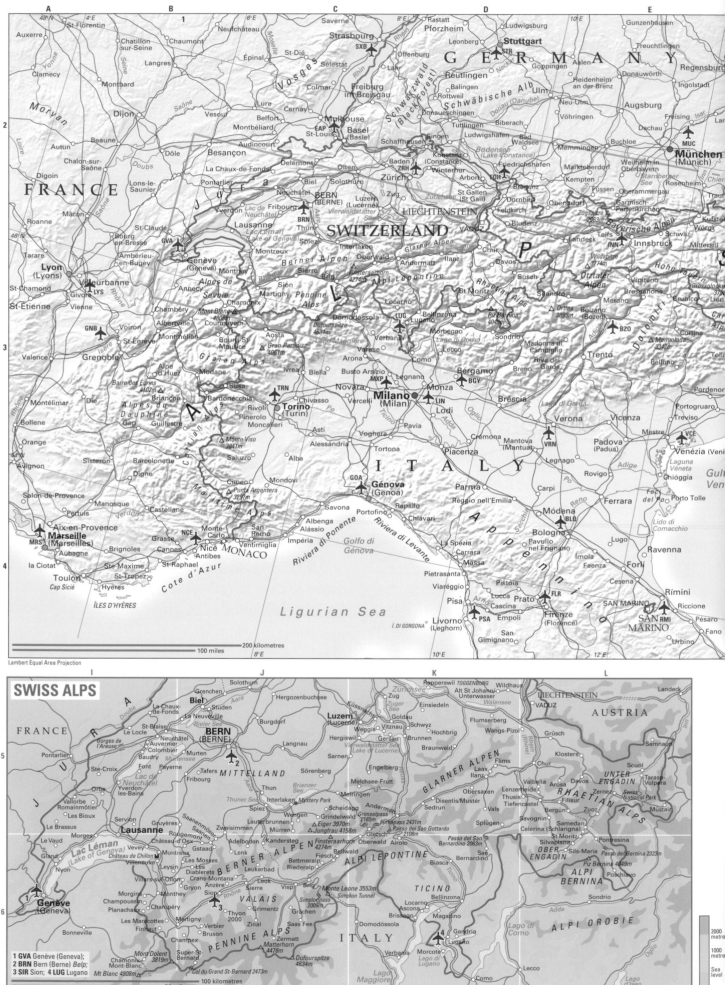

The Alps

Central Europe: South

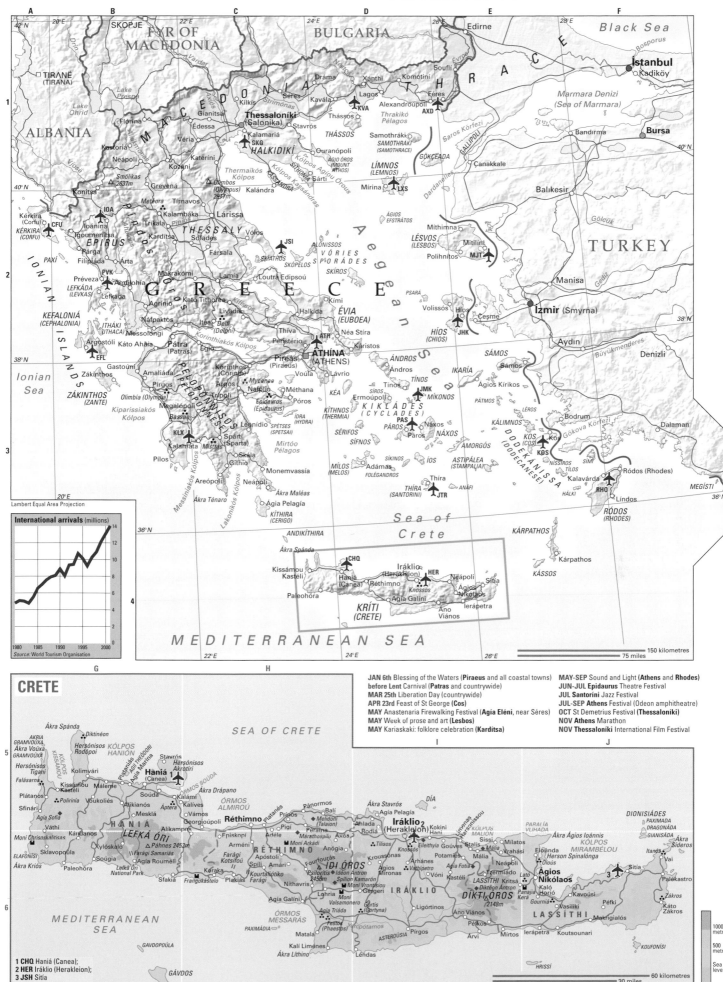

International arrivals (millions)

Lambert Equal Area Projection

Source: World Tourism Organisation

CRETE

JAN 6th Blessing of the Waters (**Piraeus** and all coastal towns)
before Lent Carnival (**Patras** and countrywide)
MAR 25th Liberation Day (countrywide)
APR 23rd Feast of St George (**Cos**)
MAY Anastenaria Firewalking Festival (**Agía Eléni**, near **Séres**)
MAY Week of prose and art (**Lesbos**)
MAY Kariaskaki: folklore celebration (**Karditsa**)

MAY-SEP Sound and Light (**Athens** and **Rhodes**)
JUN-JUL Epidaurus Theatre Festival
JUL Santoríni Jazz Festival
JUL-SEP Athens Festival (Odeon amphitheatre)
OCT St Demetrius Festival (**Thessaloníki**)
NOV Athens Marathon
NOV Thessaloníki International Film Festival

1 CHQ Haniá (Canea);
2 HER Iráklio (Herakleion);
3 JSH Sitía

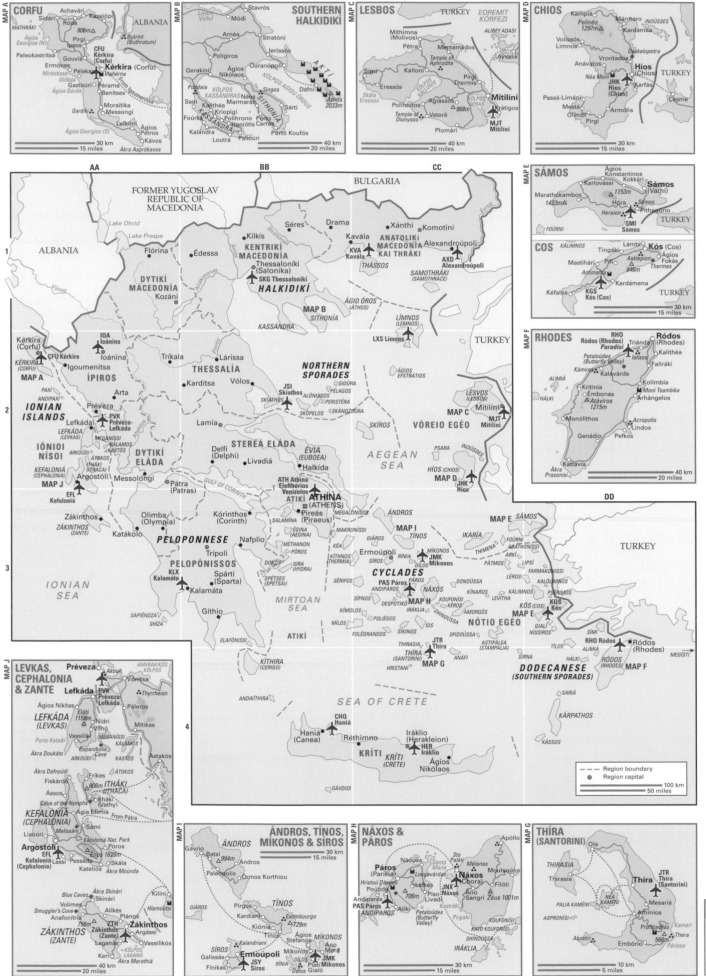

Turkey

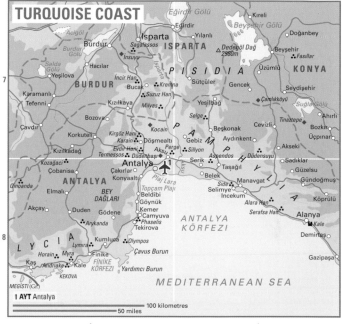

AEGEAN COAST

TURQUOISE COAST

EASTERN MEDITERRANEAN COAST

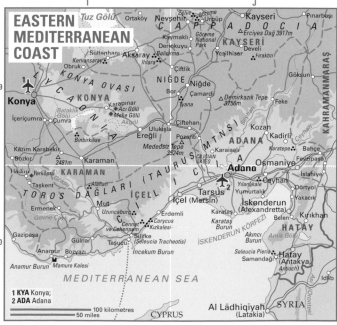

International arrivals (millions)
Source: World Tourism Organisation

This map shows the principal diving destinations in the Mediterranean Sea and the main underwater attractions including the existence of soft corals or sea fans, cliffs and caves and shipwrecks (including submerged aircraft). The diver may encounter turtle and dolphin at any time, shark and rays less often, but only those places where regular sightings occur are indicated here. Whales are now exceedingly rare.

Diving facilities for each destination, including availability of scuba diving equipment and related support services, are graded as limited, good or excellent. It must be emphasised that these grades are a general reflection on the overall availability of everything required by the visiting scuba diver and are not an interpretation of the standards found within any one facility or organisation.

Each diving destination provides every level of depth from the very shallow to the extremely deep.

FRANCE: SOUTH COAST
1 2 3 4 D S T W ★
Dive sites all along the coast; main facilities in Marseilles, Nice and Toulon
Shipwreck 'Liban' off Cap Croisette and submarine 'Rubis' off Cap Camarat are outstanding; the diving infrastructure on mainland France is rather limited, largely because French divers favour the club system for diving; PADI is, however, opening up new shops and facilities all the time and it is worth requesting a PADI Centre List before departure

FRANCE: CORSICA
1 2 3 4 D S T W ★
Dive sites all around the island; main facilities in Ajaccio, Calvi and Sagone
British Vickers Viking, Canadian CL215 and US B17 bomber provide three very unusual aircraft wrecks off the west coast

ITALY: MAINLAND
1 2 3 4 D S T W ★★★
Dive sites all along the coast; facilities in all major towns, especially Genoa and Portofino
Diving is very popular in Italy; there are numerous shipwrecks, both ancient and modern, although many lie in very deep waters; cave systems on the Adriatic coast and steep underwater cliffs everywhere; away from the busy industrial ports, water clarity is very good

ITALY: SARDINIA
1 2 3 4 D S T W ★★
Dive sites all around the island; facilities centred on Bosa, Cágliari, Orosei and Palau
Several shipwrecks including 'Romagna'; at least one aircraft plus several cave systems including the Nereo Caves off Cape Caccia

ITALY: WESTERN ISLANDS
(Capráia, Elba, Giannutri, Gíglio, Montecristo)
1 2 3 4 D S T W ★
Dive sites all around the islands; some facilities on Elba but generally very limited on the islands – best nearby mainland facilities at Portofino
Spectacular vertical cliffs with outstanding seafans, red coral and large shoals of tuna; a few very exciting shipwrecks, such as the vehicle ferry 'Nasim II' off Giannutri

ITALY: SICILY
1 2 3 4 D S T W ★★
Dive sites all around the island; facilities centred on Catánia, Messina and Palermo
Shipwreck 'Amerique' on the northern tip of the island; Sicily attracts large pelagics and large shoals of tuna at certain times of the year

Lambert Equal Area Projection

SPAIN
1 2 3 4 D S T W ★★★
Main dive areas Balearic Islands and Costa Brava; best facilities at l'Estartit and Roses (Costa Brava), Almeria, Majorca, Minorca
Submarine cave system 'Pont en Gill' holds outstanding examples of submerged stalactites and stalagmites; the Medes Islands (off l'Estartit) are a protected marine reserve where the flora and fauna is quite prolific

GIBRALTAR
1 2 3 4 D S T W ★★★
Main dive sites off the western and southern coastlines; facilities in Gibraltar town
Shipwrecks 'Excellent' and 'Rosslyn' just outside Gibraltar Harbour are outstanding; there is also ongoing artificial reef programme which involves the sinking of small vessels near Rosia Bay

MALTA
1 2 3 4 D S T W ★★★
Dive sites all around the islands; facilities in all resort towns
Diving is very popular here although a valid medical certificate and proof of diving experience/qualifications are required; outstanding submarine arches, walls, reefs, tunnels and caves plus some new and very exciting shipwrecks deliberately sunk for divers

Dive sites:
1 Soft corals / sea fans
2 Steep underwater cliffs
3 Cave diving
4 Shipwrecks
White square: not present

Regular sightings of:
D Dolphins
S Sharks / rays / pelagics
T Turtles
W Whales
White square: not regularly seen

Facilities for the diver:
★ Limited ★★ Good ★★★ Excellent

GREECE
1 2 3 4 D S T W ★★
Main dive areas Corfu, Crete, Náxos and Rhodes; best facilities on Crete
Until recently, Greece frowned upon scuba divers; today, however, new centres are opening all the time and there are several sites of ancient amphora where the diver is allowed to look but not touch; there are also spectacular submarine cave systems

CYPRUS
1 2 3 4 D S T W ★★★
Main dive sites off the southern and western coastlines; facilities centred on Larnaca, Limassol and Paphos
12,000 tonne ro-ro ferry 'Zenobia' sank off Larnaca in 1980 and is the largest shipwreck in the Mediterranean; the seas are very warm but Cyprus suffers from severe over-fishing
The Turkish Republic of Northern Cyprus has less opportunities for divers and limited facilities

TURKEY
1 2 3 4 D S T W ★★★
Dive sites all along the coast; facilities centred on the southwest coast, in particular at Bodrum, Fetihye and Marmaris
Many ancient amphora wrecks available for inspection and new diving areas are being explored all the time before being opened to visitors

EGYPT: NORTH COAST
1 2 3 4 D S T W ★
Main dive sites and facilities at Alexandria
Not as popular as Egypt's Red Sea coast and often overlooked; the remains of Cleopatra's Palace were recently found in Alexandria Harbour
For Egypt's Red Sea dive sites, see page 109

Data compiled by Ned Middleton, all rights reserved
email: ned.middleton@which.net

600 kilometres
300 miles

Sea level
-200 metres
-1000 metres
-2000 metres

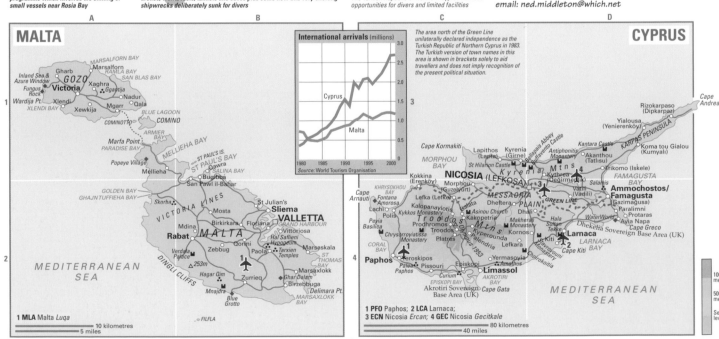

MALTA

International arrivals (millions)

Cyprus
Malta

Source: World Tourism Organisation

The area north of the Green Line unilaterally declared independence as the Turkish Republic of Northern Cyprus in 1983. The Turkish version of town names in this area is shown in brackets and does not imply recognition of the present political situation.

CYPRUS

1 MLA Malta Luqa

10 kilometres
5 miles

1 PFO Paphos; 2 LCA Larnaca;
3 ECN Nicosia Ercan; 4 GEC Nicosia Gecitkale

80 kilometres
40 miles

1000 metre
500 metre
Sea level

Scandinavia

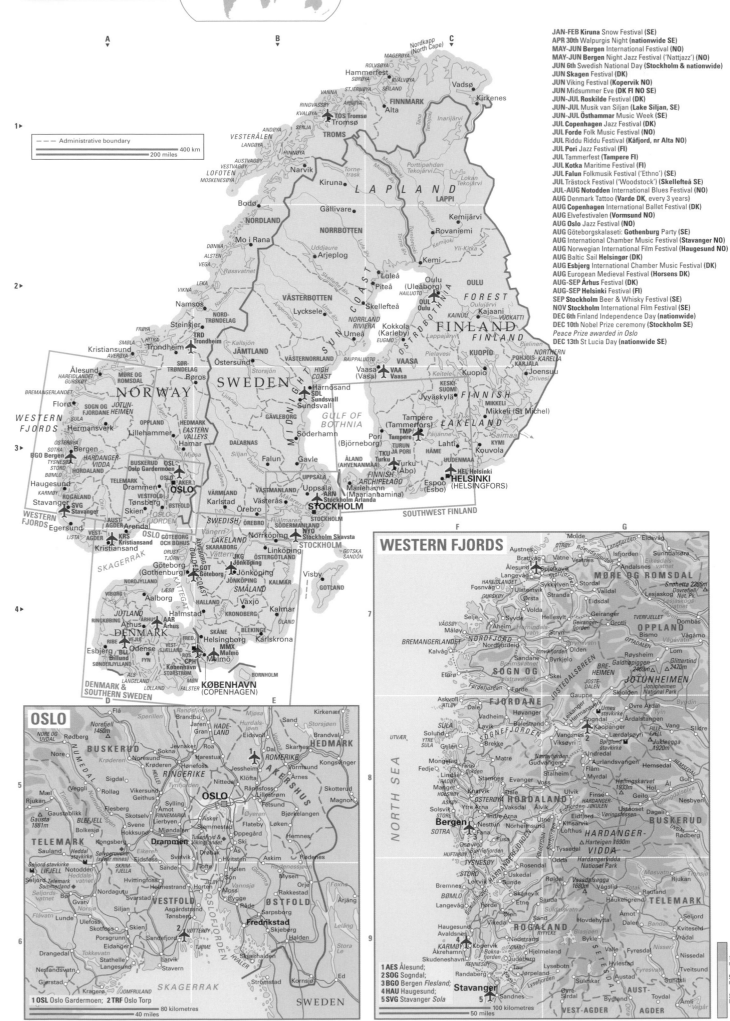

JAN-FEB **Kiruna** Snow Festival **(SE)**
APR 30th **Walpurgis Night (nationwide SE)**
MAY-JUN **Bergen** International Festival **(NO)**
MAY-JUN **Bergen** Night Jazz Festival ('Nattjazz') **(NO)**
JUN 6th **Swedish National Day (Stockholm & nationwide)**
JUN **Skagen** Festival **(DK)**
JUN **Viking** Festival **(Kopervik NO)**
JUN **Midsummer Eve (DK FI NO SE)**
JUN-JUL **Roskilde** Festival **(DK)**
JUN-JUL **Musik van Siljan (Lake Siljan, SE)**
JUN-JUL **Östhammar** Music Week **(SE)**
JUL **Copenhagen** Jazz Festival **(DK)**
JUL **Forde** Folk Music Festival **(NO)**
JUL **Riddu Riddu** Festival **(Kåfjord, nr Alta NO)**
JUL **Pori** Jazz Festival **(FI)**
JUL **Tammerfest (Tampere FI)**
JUL **Kotka** Maritime Festival **(FI)**
JUL **Falun** Folkmusik Festival ('Ethno') **(SE)**
JUL **Trästock** Festival ('Woodstock') **(Skellefteå SE)**
JUL-AUG **Notodden** International Blues Festival **(NO)**
AUG **Denmark** Tattoo **(Varde DK, every 3 years)**
AUG **Copenhagen** International Ballet Festival **(DK)**
AUG **Elvefestivalen (Vormsund NO)**
AUG **Oslo** Jazz Festival **(NO)**
AUG **Göteborgskalaseti: Gothenburg** Party **(SE)**
AUG International Chamber Music Festival **(Stavanger NO)**
AUG **Norwegian** International Film Festival **(Haugesund NO)**
AUG **Baltic Sail Helsingør (DK)**
AUG **Esbjerg** International Chamber Music Festival **(DK)**
AUG **European** Medieval Festival **(Horsens DK)**
AUG-SEP **Århus** Festival **(DK)**
AUG-SEP **Helsinki** Festival **(FI)**
SEP **Stockholm** Beer & Whisky Festival **(SE)**
NOV **Stockholm** International Film Festival **(SE)**
DEC 6th **Finland** Independence Day **(nationwide)**
DEC 10th **Nobel** Prize ceremony **(Stockholm SE)**
Peace Prize awarded in Oslo
DEC 13th **St Lucia** Day **(nationwide SE)**

WESTERN FJORDS

OSLO

1 **OSL** Oslo Gardermoen; 2 **TRF** Oslo Torp

1 **AES** Ålesund;
2 **SOG** Sogndal;
3 **BGO** Bergen *Flesland*;
4 **HAU** Haugesund;
5 **SVG** Stavanger *Sola*

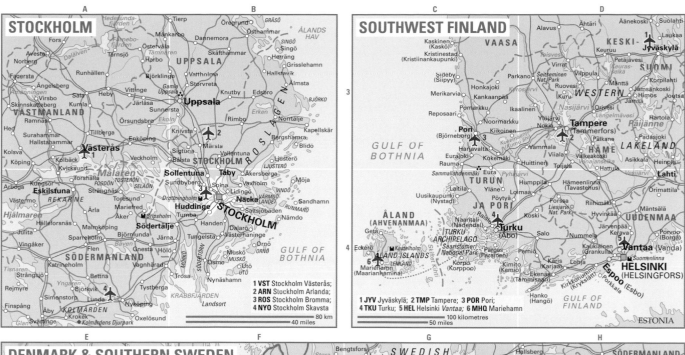

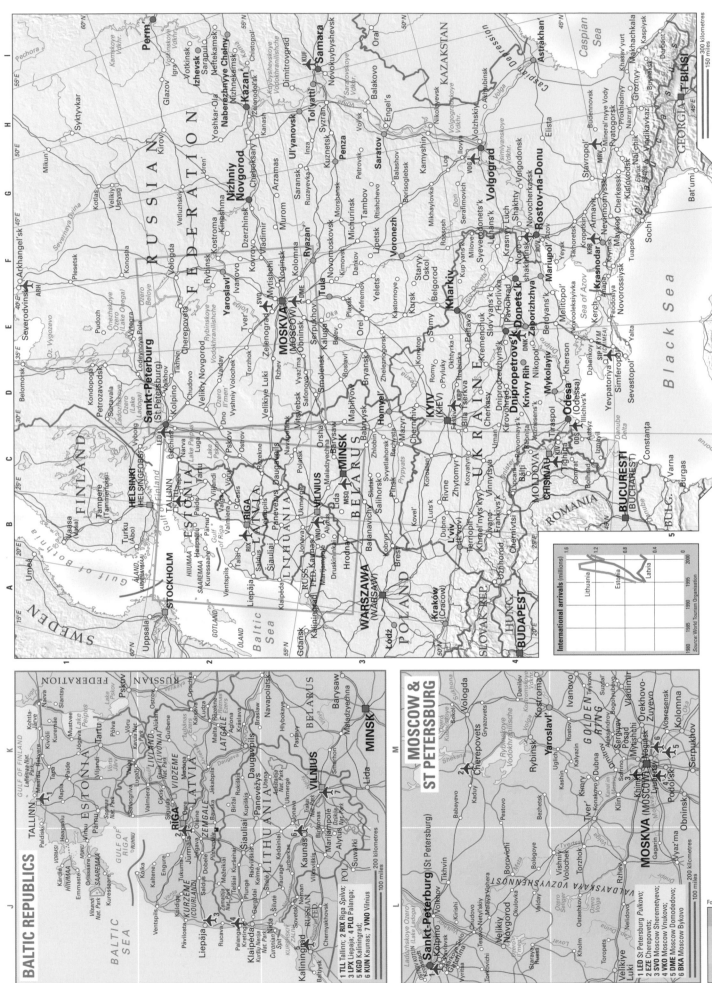

International arrivals (millions)
Source World Tourism Organisation

BALTIC REPUBLICS

1 TLL Tallinn; 2 RIX Riga Spilva; 3 LPX Liepāja; 4 PLQ Palanga; 5 KGD Kaliningrad; 6 KUN Kaunas; 7 VNO Vilnius

MOSCOW & ST PETERSBURG

1 LED St Petersburg Pulkovo; 2 EZE Cherepovets; 3 SVO Moscow Sheremetyevo; 4 VKO Moscow Vnukovo; 5 DME Moscow Domodedovo; 6 BKA Moscow Bykovo

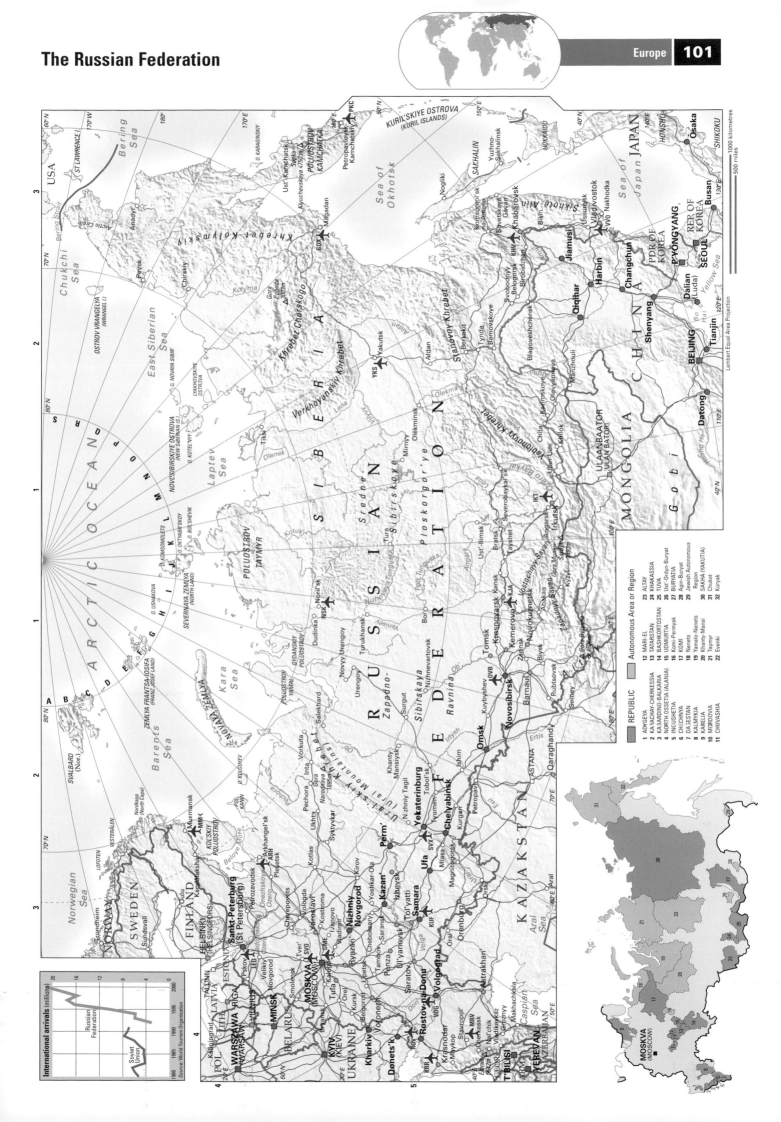

The Russian Federation

International arrivals (millions)

Russian Federation

Soviet Union

Source: World Tourism Organisation

REPUBLIC

1 ADYGEYA
2 KARACHAY-CHERKESSIA
3 KABARDINO-BALKARIA
4 NORTH OSSETIA (ALANIA)
5 INGUSHETIA
6 CHECHNYA
7 DAGESTAN
8 KALMYKIA
9 KARELIA
10 MORDOVIA
11 CHUVASHIA

12 MARI-EL
13 TATARSTAN
14 BASHKORTOSTAN
15 UDMURTIA
16 KOMI-PERMYAK
17 KOMI
18 NENETS
19 YAMALO-NENETS
20 KHANTY-MANSI
21 TAYMYR
22 EVENKI

Autonomous Area or Region

23 ALTAY
24 KHAKASSIA
25 TUVA
26 UST'-ORDYN-BURYAT
27 BURYATIA
28 AGIN-BURYAT
29 Jewish Autonomous Region
30 SAKHA (YAKUTIA)
31 CHUKOT
32 KORYAK

Africa

'There is always something new from Africa,' Pliny the Elder remarked in the first century AD. Sadly, 20 centuries later, much of this is bad news. The continent's potential has, with some exceptions, yet to be developed to any satisfactory or lasting extent. Africa occupies nearly 25% of the earth's landmass and is home to over 13% of its population, yet accounts for less than 2% of its Gross National Income. Although tourism is Africa's third largest industry, performance is just as out of step with its size: 32 million international visitors, less than half the total for France, and US$15 billion in receipts, slightly less than that spent in the UK.

Key facts

Number of Countries	57
Area ('000 sq km)	30,211
Population ('000)	879,848
Population Density (per sq km)	29
Gross National Income (US$m)	558,920
Visitor Arrivals ('000)	32,318
Visitor Receipts (US$m)	15,225
Travel Departures ('000)	13,331
Travel Expenditure (US$m)	7,201

GNI figures relate to 2001. Population figures are taken from the most recent reliable source. Travel figures (WTO) are based on overnight stays, not same-day visitors, and are generally for 2001: where these are unavailable or unreliable, earlier years have been used. Where data for certain countries was not available, this has been regarded as zero. For more information see the Countries A-Z section from page 184.

Africa registered a growth in tourist arrivals of 1.3% in 2001 compared to 2000: hardly spectacular, but well above the world average. The two main regions for tourism traffic, North and Southern Africa, saw a fall of 1.7% and a rise of 2.4% respectively: other regions all experienced growth. Travel receipts were up by 2.7%. On a wider economic level, Africa was, according to the IMF, the only continent where 2001 growth exceeded that for 2000 (3.5% compared to 3.0%). However, these statistical positives conceal some grim realities. It should also be said that small size of many African economies, both generally and in terms of their travel sectors, makes year-on-year statistics volatile and sometimes misleading.

Major problems

A major tenet of capitalism is the 'trickle-down effect', by which wealth created by the richest members of society will, in time and with many deductions, filter down to everyone else, to the long-term benefit of all. Africa has more impediments to this vital process than most regions of the world.

The less reliant an economy is on agriculture and commodities, and the larger its educated, professional base is, the more successful and stable it is likely to be. Agricultural and commodity-based economies are less efficient than manufacturing and services at creating and distributing wealth. They are also tend to have a small GNI, and are vulnerable to international market prices, the distorting effects of subsidies and, in the case of agriculture, the weather. The concentration of power in the hands of a few people can lead towards a number of misfortunes, including corruption, poor government and divisive inequalities of opportunity and wealth.

For Africa, these problems operate against a background of numerous complex ethnic conflicts – which colonialism obscured or complicated but rarely solved – and an often acrimonious religious divide, broadly between a Muslim north and a Christian south. Over 30 wars since 1970 and up to 10 million refugees are the result. Global terrorism has also left its mark, both as an alleged base (Somalia) and as a target (Kenya).

Africa also suffers heavily from two of the world's most serious diseases, HIV/AIDS and malaria. HIV has been described as a demographic time-bomb. 80% of global AIDS deaths are in Africa, and in some countries 25% of the population is believed to be infected. Malaria – which by some estimates has caused half of all human deaths since the Stone Age – is, due to the mosquitoes' immunity to drugs, inadequate precautions and global warming, fast becoming more prevalent. These and other diseases are more likely to be fatal amongst populations already weakened by war, malnutrition and poverty. All are clearly also risks for foreign visitors.

■ Economies

The region's five largest economies
Source: World Bank/International Monetary Fund

	GNI (US$ bn) 2001	Annual GDP growth rate (%) 2001	2002	est2003	est2004
South Africa	121.9	2.8	3.0	2.8	3.2
Egypt	99.6	3.5	2.0	3.0	3.5
Algeria	51.0	2.1	3.1	3.5	4.3
Nigeria	37.1	2.8	0.5	6.7	4.2
Morocco	34.7	6.5	4.5	5.5	3.4

None of these problems are conducive to either internal or external investment on a scale necessary to cure them. As a result, governments mortgage assets or borrow money, leading to increased poverty and debt. Deforestation, whether for timber sales or to create land for growing cash crops, has been one solution. This briefly solves some problems, but creates others by threatening the delicate eco-systems on which both Africa's agriculture and tourism products depend.

All these challenges lead to several travel-safety concerns for foreign visitors. These include gun-related crime, particularly on public transport, at border crossings and in urban areas; and exposure to dangerous and unfamiliar diseases. Specialist advice should be sought before travelling, and local advice followed once arrived.

Opportunities for change

There are, however, several areas of optimism. Banks and corporations in the developed world are adopting a less top-heavy approach to their investments and are actively seeking to encourage sustainable private enterprise. Attempts are being made to redress some of the trading inequalities with the EU and the USA. Newly revitalised regional organisations, such as the African Union, hope to give the continent a more powerful and united international voice. An upsurge in international environmental concerns and signs of more ethical corporate practices are already starting to lead to a more restrained and equitable development of Africa's resources. The internet and other communications technologies are empowering their users, in Africa and worldwide: mobile phones, for example, helped people co-ordinate opposition to electoral fraud in recent elections in Kenya, Senegal and Ghana. Many obstacles remain; but several are being overcome. The term 'African Renaissance' was first voiced by no less a person than the then South African President Nelson Mandela in 1994. His country's rebirth has been relatively successful. How many others will follow?

Travel overview

In travel terms, Africa paradoxically possesses many of the advantages of its drawbacks. It is a vast, largely pristine and staggeringly beautiful continent, rich in wildlife, teeming with a diverse cultural vibrancy, and utterly different from Europe or North America. The desire for adventure has long attracted visitors, and today's range of travel options is vast. Most travel companies have long been sensitive of striking the delicate balance between demand and responsibility. Increasingly, they are also becoming involved in projects whereby local organisations, such as schools and hospitals, benefit from local tourism expenditure. Visitors may therefore find that some of their money filters down to those who need it more directly than in many other parts of the world.

Africa's imbalances persist in its travel patterns. If one were to exclude the five countries of North Africa and the three of the Indian Ocean, all key travel indicators would fall by between 40% and 60%. More than half of Africa's countries received less than 200,000 visitors in 2001, and 19 received less than 100,000. A mere four countries – Egypt, Morocco, South Africa and Tunisia –

■ Big spenders

Expenditure on foreign travel (excluding international transport), 2001 – top ten countries (US$ billions)   *Source: WTO*

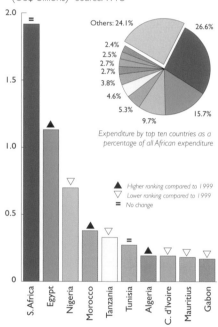

Expenditure by top ten countries as a percentage of all African expenditure

▲ Higher ranking compared to 1999
▽ Lower ranking compared to 1999
= No change

accounted for over two-thirds of Africa's US$15.2 billion travel receipts and nearly two-thirds of Africa's 32.2 million visitor arrivals in 2001.

Until recently, Zimbabwe would have been the fifth major contributor, but its travel business has largely collapsed. This is not immediately obvious from the 2001 WTO figures, which show a growth from 2000 to over two million international visitors. These visitors were, however, spending a good deal less money. In neighbouring Botswana, receipts per head increased by a third between 1997 and 2001. In the same period in Zimbabwe, they declined by a factor of four. Botswana – with high growth, social and political stability and the second highest GDP/head south of the Sahara – is admittedly one of Africa's economic success stories: as Zimbabwe was once.

Travel trends

Adventure is the key feature of African holidays. Although many safaris are not budget options, an increasing number of overland and adventure holidays offer a similar experience at a fraction of the cost.

Many countries such as South Africa and Kenya have well-administered game parks which enable them to count safari holidays as a major foreign currency earner. These offer a fairly sanitised version of adventure. Africa's rivers, waterfalls, mountains, deserts, reefs and jungles provide closer brushes with nature.

Although internal and regional air and rail services are improving in many areas, coach travel is often the most practical choice. All tastes and budgets and budgets are

- Africa occupies 23.3% of the world's land area and is home to 13.3% of the world's population.
- Africa's combined GDI is US$559 billion, 1.8% of the world's total.
- Africa accounts for 4.8% of global travel arrivals and 2.0% of departures.
- International travel and tourism contributed over US$15 billion to Africa's economy in 2001.
- The most-visited country in Africa, South Africa, ranked 26th in the world in 2001. Tunisia was 29th and Egypt 36th.
- Libya saw an increase in tourist arrivals of nearly 250% between 1997 and 2001, from 50,000 to 174,000.
- Botswana is the world's third largest producer of diamonds, from which it derives 80% of its export earnings. This helped the country's economy grow by an average of 5.7% between 1995 and 2002.
- Africa has a total of around 564,000 hotel rooms. 62% of these are in countries south of the Sahara.
- South Africans are Africa's most frequent travellers, accounting for over a quarter of Africa's total recorded international departures.
- The highest temperature in the shade ever recorded was at Al'Aziziyah in Libya in 1922 – 57.8°C (136°F).
- 17 out of the world's 40 largest countries are in Africa.
- Lest anyone doubt the economic, as well as environmental, importance of the species, the research institute Panos Media has calculated that a Kenyan elephant is worth £560,000 in tourism revenue if it is allowed to realise its full lifespan.
- The *Cathédrale Notre-Dame de la Paix* in Yamoussoukro in the Côte d'Ivoire has more stained glass than in all the churches in France combined.
- The UK is slightly larger than Uganda and slightly smaller than Guinea.
- South Africa has three capital cities.
- The Pyramids in Egypt are the only one of the seven wonders of the ancient world still standing.
- Botswana's Fish River Canyon is the second largest in the world, after the Grand Canyon in the USA
- At the height of the flood season, up to 550 million litres of water plummet over the edge of the Victoria Falls every minute.

catered for, and vehicles include modern 9-16 seaters. Self-drive is also an increasingly popular option in many countries.

Luxury holidays are a growing niche. Options include lodges in the game parks, secure country club accommodation and the Blue Train and Rovos rail journeys in Southern Africa. Beach holidays, often combined with remarkable diving opportunities or spectacular safaris, also remain popular.

Established favourites

At the centre of the sub-Saharan market is South Africa. It has stunning natural attractions (including some of the continent's most celebrated national parks), an excellent infrastructure and vibrant cities, a combination which supports a thriving travel industry.

The North African states of Egypt, Morocco and Tunisia have the advantage of being able to market themselves as both African and Mediterranean destinations.

Aside from South Africa, and Zimbabwe, five sub-Saharan countries – Nigeria, Kenya, Botswana, Namibia and Tanzania – attracted more than 500,000 international visitors in 2001, with Zambia and Ghana not far behind. Most have numerous excellent game parks. All seem better placed than most African states to capitalise on their existing strengths. South African Airways' recent acquisition of a controlling interest in Air Tanzania, with the promise not only of significant investment but also of the creation of a high-quality air network linking Western, Eastern and Southern Africa, is the kind of initiative that bodes well for the futures both of the countries concerned and of pan-African economic co-operation in general.

The major attractions of the top five travel destinations are, apart from their year-round sunshine:

- South Africa – A modern infrastructure with a range of products including beach holidays, safaris, luxury train journeys, touring and golf.

■ African adventures

Game parks in Sub-Saharan Africa, 2003
Source: Safari Consultants Ltd

Most visited...

1 Kruger, SA	6 Serengeti, Tanz.
2 Hluhluwe-Umfolozi, SA	7 Ngorogoro, Tanz.
3 Tsavo, Ken.	8 Etosha, Nam.
4 Masai Mara, Ken.	9 Amboseli, Ken
5 Samburu, Ken.	10 Luangwe, Zam.

Up-and-coming...

1 Selous, Tanz.	4 Kafue, Zam.
2 Ruaha, Tanz.	5 Limpopo Valley, Bots.
3 Tarangire, Tanz.	6 Katavi, Tanz.

- Kenya – Safaris and beach holidays are the dominant travel themes with, respectively, Nairobi and Mombasa being principally gateways for these activities. Political stability is likely to increase since the recent elections. The country's travel industry suffered badly in 2002 and 2003 as a result of the reality and threat of terrorist activity.

- Egypt – Thousands of years of history to explore, with modern hotels in many cities and the chance to cruise the River Nile. Cairo is a popular European short-break destination. The Red Sea resorts provide some of the world's best diving opportunities.

- Morocco – The closest African country to Europe. Attractions include golf, the Sahara, fine Atlantic beaches and its exotic and historic imperial cities.

- Tunisia – Several developed resorts to suit European tastes and a growing inventory of excellent golf courses. 65% of international visitors are from Europe.

The Indian Ocean islands of the Seychelles, Réunion and Mauritius have avoided many of the continent's problems. All are in different ways exceedingly beautiful and ecologically unique, and have used these advantages to create a viable tourism industry. Travel receipts from these three states combined is exceeded only by South Africa, Morocco, Tunisia and Egypt. The economies here are in general heavily dependent on travel and tourism: the sector contributes nearly 60% of the GDP in Mauritius and is responsible for around 30% of jobs in the Seychelles. Several cruises operate between Kenya and Zanzibar and the Indian Ocean Islands.

■ Big earners

Receipts from Foreign Travel (excluding international transport), 2001 – top ten countries (US$ billions) *Source: WTO*

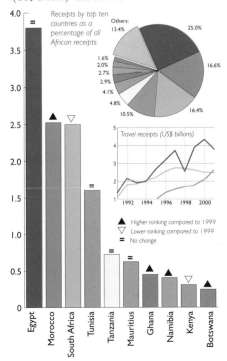

Receipts by top ten countries as a percentage of all African receipts

Others: 13.4%

25.0%

1.6%
2.0%
2.7%
2.9%
4.1%
4.8%
10.5%

16.6%
16.4%

Travel receipts (US$ billions)

1992 1994 1996 1998 2000

▲ Higher ranking compared to 1999
▽ Lower ranking compared to 1999
= No change

Egypt · Morocco · South Africa · Tunisia · Tanzania · Mauritius · Ghana · Namibia · Kenya · Botswana

Developing areas

Africa is still developing its travel and tourism potential, and even the countries leading the way still have much to do to realise their ambitions. The challenges of climate, geography, politics and economics are vast.

Many countries, including Namibia, Zambia, Botswana, Mozambique, Tanzania, Ghana, Cape Verde, Lesotho, Malawi and (perhaps surprisingly) Libya offer, in different ways and for different reasons, hopes for future travel and tourism growth. Political stability and international perceptions will remain key to progress here, and elsewhere in the continent.

Despite all its problems, Africa remains a uniquely fascinating and rewarding continent for all kinds of travellers, particularly those seeking adventure. It is to be hoped that responsible tourism policies, both by suppliers and consumers, can help the continent break the vicious cycles that have haunted it for so long.

■ Visitors

Visitor arrivals 2001 *Source: WTO*

	Visitors (thousands)	Change since 1997
South Africa	5,908	14.3%
Tunisia	5,387	26.4%
Egypt	4,357	19.2%
Morocco	4,223	37.5%
Zimbabwe	2,068	61.4%
Algeria	901	41.9%
Kenya	841	-7.3%
Nigeria	831	36.0%
Botswana	796	31.1%
Namibia	670	33.5%
Mauritius	660	23.1%
Tanzania	501	44.4%
Zambia	492	44.3%
Ghana	439	35.1%
Réunion	424	13.4%
Senegal	396	26.1%
Côte d'Ivoire	301	9.9%
Swaziland	283	5.2%
Malawi	266	28.5%
Uganda	205	17.1%
Lesotho	186	29.2%
Libya	174	248.0%
Madagascar	170	68.3%
Gabon	169	1.2%
Ethiopia	148	6.5%
Seychelles	130	0.0%
Burkina	129	-6.5%
Cape Verde	115	155.6%
Rwanda	113	8.7%
Eritrea	113	-72.4%
Congo, Dem. Rep.	103	243.3%
Benin	96	-35.1%
Mali	89	18.7%
Gambia, The	75	-11.8%
Angola	67	48.9%
Cameroon	59	40.5%
Togo	57	-38.0%
Chad	57	111.1%
Niger	52	18.2%
Sudan	50	66.7%
Guinea	38	123.5%
Burundi	36	227.3%
Mauritania	30	25.0%
Sierra Leone	24	4.3%
Comoros	24	-7.7%
Djibouti	21	5.0%
Congo	19	-29.6%
Central African Rep.	10	-41.2%
Guinea-Bissau	8	n/a
São Tomé e Príncipe	8	58.3%

(Figures not available for Liberia, Mayotte, Mozambique, Somalia, Western Sahara or Equatorial Guinea)

Thanks to: Bill Adams of Safari Consultants; Tim Best of Tim Best Travel; John Haycock of Africa Explorer; John Douglas of Malawi Tourism; John Knighton of African Pride; Patrick Fitzgerald; Gary Bowerman; Graeme Payne

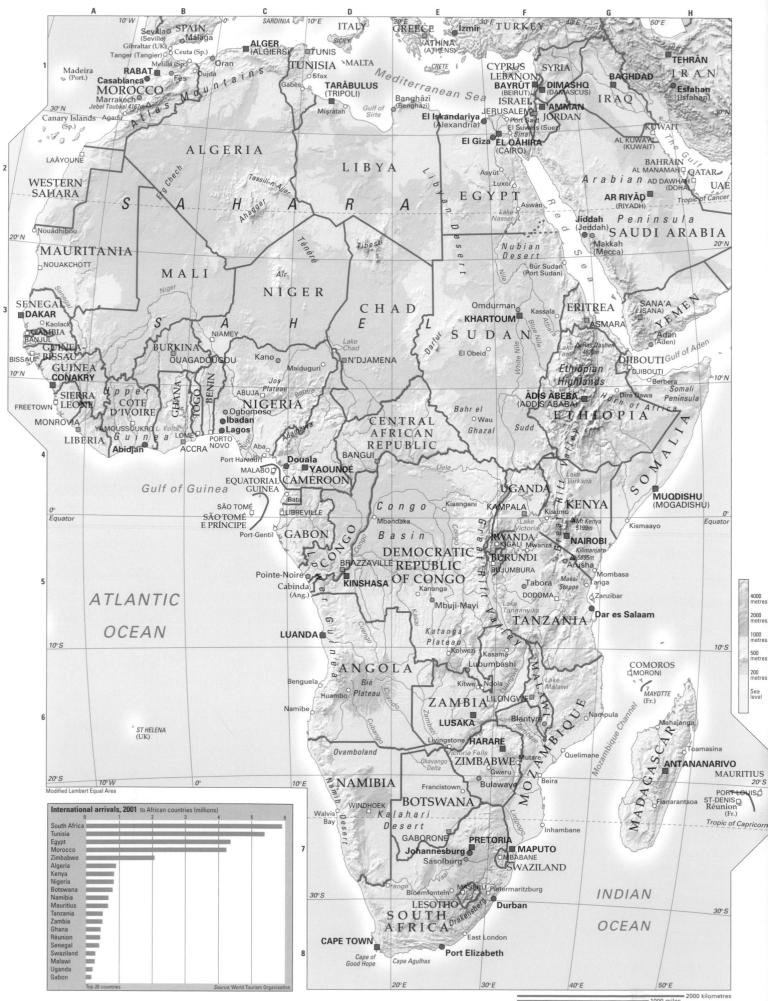

International arrivals, 2001 to African countries (millions)

0 1 2 3 4 5 6

South Africa
Tunisia
Egypt
Morocco
Zimbabwe
Algeria
Kenya
Nigeria
Botswana
Namibia
Mauritius
Tanzania
Zambia
Ghana
Réunion
Senegal
Swaziland
Malawi
Uganda
Gabon

Top 20 countries   Source: World Tourism Organisation

Modified Lambert Equal Area

4000 metres
2000 metres
1000 metres
500 metres
200 metres
Sea level

2000 kilometres
1000 miles

Climate

NOVEMBER TO APRIL

TEMPERATURE
(January average, degrees Celsius)

- 30° and over
- 20° – 29°
- 10° – 19°
- 0° – 9°
- Below 0°

PREVAILING WIND
shown as white arrows

RAINFALL
(November to April total)

- 500mm and over
- 250 – 499mm
- Less than 250mm

DAILY TEMPERATURES and MONTHLY RAINFALL (averages)

Dakar   Algiers   Cairo

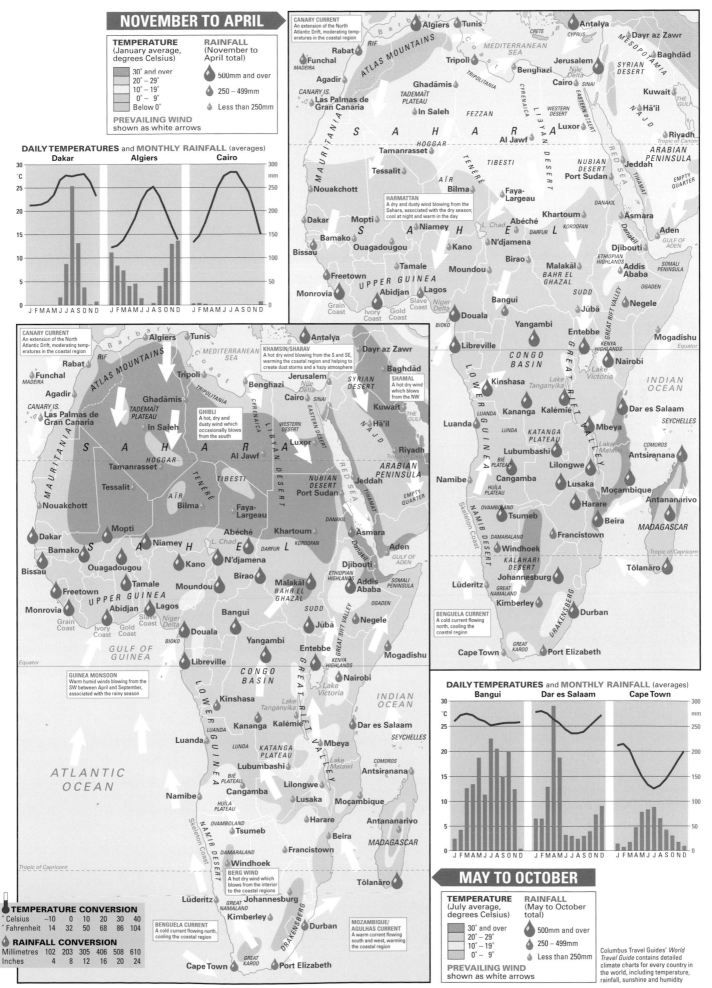

CANARY CURRENT
An extension of the North Atlantic Drift, moderating temperatures in the coastal region

HARMATTAN
A dry and dusty wind blowing from the Sahara, associated with the dry season; cool at night and warm in the day

KHAMSIN/SHARAV
A hot dry wind blowing from the S and SE, warming the coastal region and helping to create dust storms and a hazy atmosphere

SHAMAL
A hot dry wind which blows from the NW

GHIBLI
A hot, dry and dusty wind which occasionally blows from the south

GUINEA MONSOON
Warm humid winds blowing from the SW between April and September, associated with the rainy season

BERG WIND
A hot dry wind which blows from the interior to the coastal regions

BENGUELA CURRENT
A cold current flowing north, cooling the coastal region

MOZAMBIQUE/AGULHAS CURRENT
A warm current flowing south and west, warming the coastal region

DAILY TEMPERATURES and MONTHLY RAINFALL (averages)

Bangui   Dar es Salaam   Cape Town

MAY TO OCTOBER

TEMPERATURE
(July average, degrees Celsius)

- 30° and over
- 20° – 29°
- 10° – 19°
- 0° – 9°

PREVAILING WIND
shown as white arrows

RAINFALL
(May to October total)

- 500mm and over
- 250 – 499mm
- Less than 250mm

Columbus Travel Guides' *World Travel Guide* contains detailed climate charts for every country in the world, including temperature, rainfall, sunshine and humidity

TEMPERATURE CONVERSION

°Celsius	–10	0	10	20	30	40
°Fahrenheit	14	32	50	68	86	104

RAINFALL CONVERSION

Millimetres	102	203	305	406	508	610
Inches	4	8	12	16	20	24

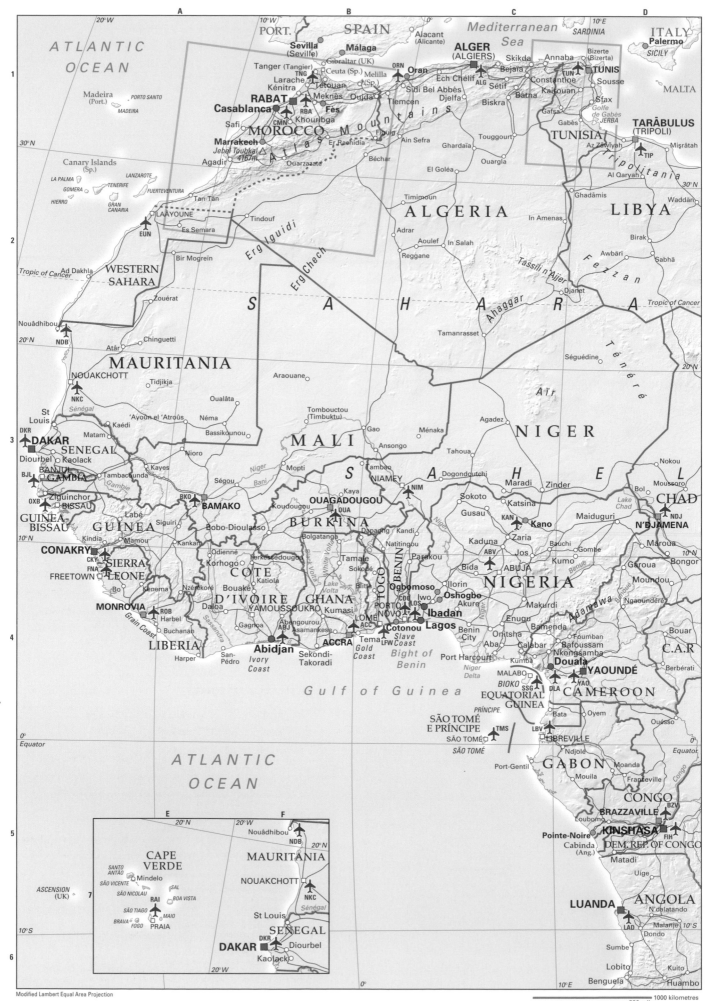

Morocco, Tunisia & African Languages

MOROCCO

Strait of Gibraltar
Cap Spartel
Gibraltar (UK)
Ceuta (Sp.)
Tanger (Tangier)
Mdiq
Smir-Restinga
Cabo Negro
MEDITERRANEAN SEA
Asilah
Tamuda
Martil
Cap des Trois Fourches
Tétouan
Et Tleta de Oued Laou
Luxus
Chaouên
Melilla (Sp.)
Larache
Ksar el Kebir
Torres de Alcala
Nador
Spidia
Arbaoua
Ouezzane
Al Hoceima
Ahfir
Moulay Bousselham
Taounate
Oujda
Souk el Arba du Rharb
Mehdiya Plage
Kénitra
Taourirt
Plage des Nations
Sidi
Taza
Jerada
Mohammedia
RABAT
Salé
Fès
Dar Bouazza
Meknès
Sefrou
Casablanca
Tiflet
Adrar Bou Nasser 3340m
El Jadida
Azemmour
Berrechid
Oulmès
Ifrane
MOYEN ATLAS
Settat
Azrou
Sidi Moussa
Khouribga
Oued Zem
Khenifra
Tendrara

200 kilometres
100 miles

ATLANTIC OCEAN

SPAIN
Gibraltar (UK)
Tanger
Ceuta (Sp.)
MEDITERRANEAN SEA
Asilah
Tétouan
Melilla (Sp.)
Kénitra
RIF
Al Hoceima
Oujda
RABAT
Fès
Taza
Casablanca
Meknès
El Jadida
Oued Zem
Khenifra
MOYEN ATLAS
Safi
Beni Mellal
Cirque de Jáffar
Bouârfa
Benguerir
Gorges du Dadès
Er Rachidia
Figuig
Marrakech
HAUT ATLAS
Gorges du Todra
Meski
Essaouira
Asni
Tinerhir
Béchar
Jebel Toubkal 4167m
Aït Benhaddou
Erfoud
Ouarzazate
Cap Rhir
Oukaïmeden
Vallée du Drâa
Zagora
Agadir
TAFILALT
Taroudannt
ANTI ATLAS
Tamegroute
Beni Abbès
Tiznit
Mhamid
Sidi Ifni
Tafraoute
Tabelbala
Goulimine
Cap Drâa
Tan-Tan
Drâa
ALGERIA
Tarfaya
Tindouf
WESTERN SAHARA
Es Semara
MAURITANIA

1 TNG Tanger (Tangier) Boukhalef Souahel;
2 AHU Al Hoceïma; 3 OUD Oujda; 4 FEZ Fès Saïs;
5 RBA Rabat Salé; 6 CMN Casablanca Mohammed V;
7 RAK Marrakech Menara; 8 AGA Agadir Inezgane

400 kilometres
200 miles

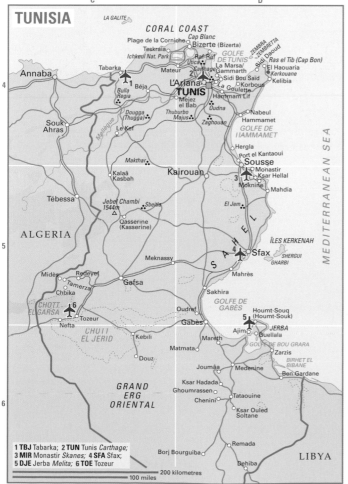

TUNISIA

LA GALITE
CORAL COAST
Plage de la Corniche
Cap Blanc
Bizerte (Bizerta)
Teskraïa
ZEMBRA
Ichkeul Nat. Park
Raf-Raf
ZEMBRETTA
Utica
Ras el Tib (Cap Bon)
Tabarka
Mateur
Sidi Daoud
Annaba
Béja
Carthage
El Haouaria
Bulla Regia
La Marsa/Gammarth
Kerkouane
L'Ariana
Sidi Bou Saïd
Kelibia
TUNIS
La Goulette
Mejez el Bab
Hammam Lif
Dougga (Thugga)
Oudna
Nabeul
Souk Ahras
Le Kef
Thuburbo Majus
Hammamet
Zaghouan
GOLFE DE HAMMAMET
Makthar
Hergla
Port el Kantaoui
Kalaâ Kasbah
Kairouan
Sousse
Tébessa
Monastir
Ksar Hellal
Jebel Chambi 1544m
Sbeïtla
Moknine
Mahdia
Qasserine (Kasserine)
El Jem
ALGERIA
S A H E L
Meknassy
ÎLES KERKENAH
Mides
Redeyef
Sfax
SHERGUI GHARBI
Tamerza
Mahrès
Chbika
Gafsa
Sakhira
MEDITERRANEAN SEA
CHOTT EL GARSA
Tozeur
Oudref
GOLFE DE GABÈS
Nefta
Gabès
Houmt-Souq (Houmt-Souk)
CHOTT EL JERID
Kebili
Ajim
JERBA
Guellala
Mareth
GOLFE DE BOU GRARA
Douz
Matmata
Zarzis
BIRHET EL BIBANE
Joumâa
Medenine
Ben Gardane
GRAND ERG ORIENTAL
Ksar Hadada
Ghoumrassen
Tataouine
Chenini
Ksar Ouled Soltane
Remada
Borj Bourguiba
Dehiba
LIBYA

1 TBJ Tabarka; 2 TUN Tunis Carthage;
3 MIR Monastir Skanes; 4 SFA Sfax;
5 DJE Jerba Melita; 6 TOE Tozeur

100 miles
200 kilometres

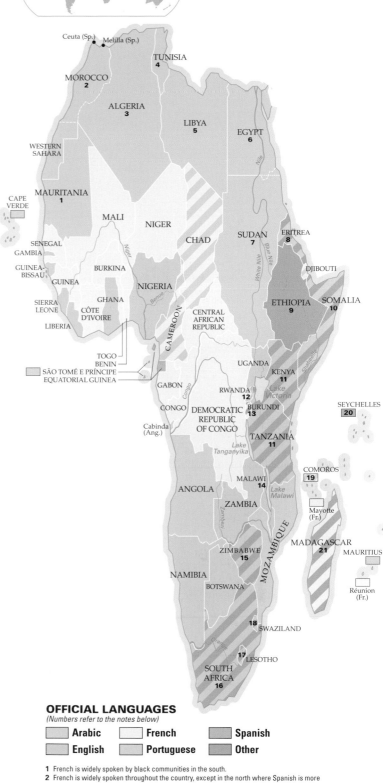

Ceuta (Sp.)
Melilla (Sp.)
TUNISIA 4
MOROCCO 2
ALGERIA 3
LIBYA 5
EGYPT 6
WESTERN SAHARA
MAURITANIA 1
MALI
NIGER
CHAD
SUDAN 7
ERITREA 8
CAPE VERDE
SENEGAL
GAMBIA
GUINEA-BISSAU
GUINEA
BURKINA
DJIBOUTI
SIERRA LEONE
NIGERIA
GHANA
CÔTE D'IVOIRE
CENTRAL AFRICAN REPUBLIC
ETHIOPIA 9
SOMALIA 10
LIBERIA
TOGO
BENIN
CAMEROON
UGANDA
KENYA 11
SÃO TOMÉ E PRÍNCIPE
EQUATORIAL GUINEA
GABON
CONGO
DEMOCRATIC REPUBLIC OF CONGO
RWANDA 12
BURUNDI 13
Lake Victoria
SEYCHELLES 20
Cabinda (Ang.)
TANZANIA 11
Lake Tanganyika
COMOROS 19
ANGOLA
MALAWI 14
Lake Malawi
ZAMBIA
Mayotte (Fr.)
ZIMBABWE 15
MADAGASCAR 21
MAURITIUS
NAMIBIA
MOZAMBIQUE
BOTSWANA
Réunion (Fr.)
SWAZILAND 18
LESOTHO 17
SOUTH AFRICA 16

OFFICIAL LANGUAGES
(Numbers refer to the notes below)

Arabic	French	Spanish
English	Portuguese	Other

1 French is widely spoken by black communities in the south.
2 French is widely spoken throughout the country, except in the north where Spanish is more predominant. Berber is spoken by a large minority.
3 Arabic is compulsory for all official business. English has replaced French as the official second language. Berber is spoken by a large minority.
4 French is used for most business transactions. English is spoken in major cities and resorts. Berber is spoken by a large minority.
5 English is normally understood in hotels, restaurants and shops.
6 English and French are widely spoken in urban centres.
7 English is widely spoken throughout the country.
8 The official languages are Arabic and Tigrinya. English and Italian are the most common foreign languages.
9 The official language is Ahmaric, and English is widely understood. Italian and French are still widely spoken.
10 The official languages are Arabic and Somali. Some English and Italian are also spoken.
11 The official languages are English and Kiswahili.
12 The official languages are English, French and Kinyarwanda.
13 The official languages are French and Kirundi.
14 Chichewa is widely spoken and is regarded as the national language by Malawi's largest ethnic group, the Chewa.
15 The official languages are English, Ndebele and Shona.
16 The official languages are Afrikaans, English, Ndebele, Pedi, Sesotho, Siswati, Tsonga, Tswana, Venda, Xhosa and Zulu.
17 The official languages are English and Sesotho.
18 The official languages are English and Siswati.
19 The official languages are English, French and Comorian (a blend of Arabic and Swahili).
20 The official language is Creole, but English and French are widely spoken.
21 The official languages are French and Malagasy. Very little English is spoken.

2000 metres
1000 metres
Sea level

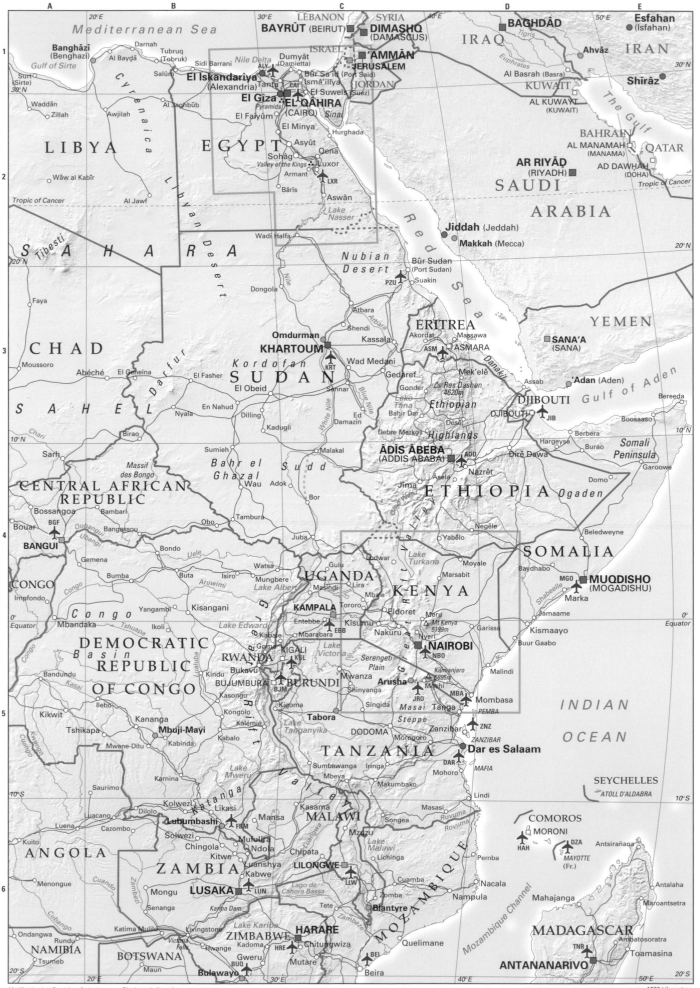

Mediterranean Sea

Banghâzî
(Benghazi)
Gulf of Sirte
Surt (Sirte)
Darnah
Al Baydâ
Tubruq
(Tobruk)
Sidi Barrani
Salûm

BAYRÛT (BEIRUT)
DIMASHQ
(DAMASCUS)
LEBANON
SYRIA
BAGHDÂD
IRAQ
Tigris
Esfahan
(Isfahan)
ISRAEL
'AMMÂN
JERUSALEM
JORDAN
Ahvâz
IRAN
Al Basrah (Basra)
Euphrates
KUWAIT
AL KUWAYT
(KUWAIT)
Shîrâz
The Gulf

Waddân
Zillah
Awjilah
Al Jaghbûb
Dumyât
(Damietta)
Bûr Sa'îd
(Port Said)
Ismâ'ilîya
El Suweis (Suez)
El Iskandarîya
(Alexandria)
Tanta
El Gîza
Pyramids
EL QÂHIRA
(CAIRO)
El Faiyûm
El Minya
Asyût
Sohâg
Valley of the Kings
Luxor
Armant
Bâris
Aswân
Sinai
Hurghada
Qena
Lake Nasser

LIBYA
Wâw al Kabîr
Al Jawf
Tropic of Cancer
EGYPT

Faya

S A H A R A
Tibesti
Libyan Desert
Cyrenaica

Wadi Halfa

Nubian Desert

Red Sea

Jiddah (Jeddah)
Makkah (Mecca)
AR RIYÂD
(RIYADH)
SAUDI
ARABIA
AD DAWHAH
(DOHA)
AL MANAMAH
(MANAMA)
BAHRAIN
QATAR
Tropic of Cancer

CHAD
Moussoro
Abéché
El Geneina
Birao
Sarh
Massif des Bongo
Bossangoa
Bambari

C H A D

Dongola

Omdurman
KHARTOUM
Kordofan
El Fasher
El Obeid
En Nahud
Nyala
Dilling
Kadugli
Sumieh
S U D A N
Darfur
Atbara
Shendi
Wad Medani
Sennar
Ed Damazin
White Nile
Blue Nile
Kassala
Gedaref
ERITREA
Akordat
Massawa
ASMARA
Mek'elê
Danakil
Assab
SANA'A
(SANA)
YEMEN
'Adan (Aden)
Gulf of Aden
Bereeda
Gonder
Lake Tana
Bahir Dar
△ Ras Dashen
4620m
DJIBOUTI
DJIBOUTI
Boosaaso
Ethiopian
Debre Markos
Highlands
Hargeysa
Berbera
Burao
Somali Peninsula
Garoowe

SAHEL
Chari
Bûr Sudan
(Port Sudan)
Suakin

S A H E L

CENTRAL AFRICAN
REPUBLIC
Bouar
BANGUI
Bangassou
Gemena
Obo
Tambura
Wau
Adok
Bor
Juba
ÂDÎS ÂBEBA
(ADDIS ABABA)
Jima
Âsela
Nazrêt
Negêle
Yabêlo
E T H I O P I A
Ogaden
Dirê Dawa
Beledweyne
Oubangui
Ubangi
Bangui

CONGO
Impfondo
Mbandaka
Bumba
Buta
Kisangani
Yangambi
Ikoli
Congo
Bondo
Watsa
Mungbere
Isiro
Aruwimi
Gulu
Masindi
Lira
Mbale
Lake Albert
UGANDA
Tororo
KAMPALA
Entebbe
Kabale
Mbarabara
Lake Edward
Lodwar
Lake Turkana
Moyale
Marsabit
Meru
△ Mt Kenya
5199m
K E N Y A
Eldoret
Nakuru
Kisumu
Nyeri
NAIROBI
Garissa
Jamaame
Kismaayo
Buur Gaabo
Malindi
Baydhabo
Marka
MUQDISHO
(MOGADISHU)
S O M A L I A
Shabeelle

DEMOCRATIC
REPUBLIC
OF CONGO
Congo Basin
Bandundu
Tshuapa
Kasai
Kikwit
Ilebo
Kananga
Mbuji-Mayi
Mwene-Ditu
Kabinda
Kindu
Bukavu
Goma
KIGALI
RWANDA
BUJUMBURA
BURUNDI
Kigoma
Lake Tanganyika
Uvira
Kongolo
Kalemié
Kabalo
Kamina
Kasongo
Lake Victoria
Mwanza
Shinyanga
Singida
Arusha
Moshi
△ Kilimanjaro
5895m
Mombasa
PEMBA
Tanga
Masai Steppe
Tabora
DODOMA
Morogoro
Zanzibar
ZANZIBAR
Dar es Salaam
MAFIA
INDIAN
OCEAN
Serengeti Plain
Mbeya

Kikwit
Tshikapa
Kwango
Cuango
Saurimo
Kwilu
Kasai
Kabinda
Lake Mweru
Lualaba
Kolwezi
Katanga
Likasi
Lubumbashi
Mufulira
Chingola
Kitwe
Ndola
Luanshya
Kabwe
Mansa
Kasama
Mzuzu
Lake Malawi
Lichinga
Pemba
Nacala
Nampula

A N G O L A
Menongue
Kuito
Ondangwa
Rundu
NAMIBIA
Tsumeb
Cubango
Cuando
Katima Mulilo
Livingstone
Victoria Falls
BOTSWANA
Maun
Hwange
Kadoma
ZIMBABWE
Chitungwiza
HARARE
Mutare
Gweru
Bulawayo
Lake Kariba
Kariba Dam
Zambezi
Chipata
Z A M B I A
Solwezi
Mongu
Senanga
LUSAKA
Tete
MALAWI
Mzuzu
LILONGWE
Blantyre
Zomba
Quelimane
Beira
Lago de Cahora Bassa
Cuamba
M O Z A M B I Q U E
Mozambique Channel
Mahajanga
Antsirañana
Antalaha
MADAGASCAR
Ambatosoratra
Toamasina
ANTANANARIVO
Maroantsetra

SEYCHELLES
ATOLL D'ALDABRA
COMOROS
MORONI
MAYOTTE
(Fr.)
DZA

Equator
0°
Equator

10°S
10°S

20°S
20°S

20°E
30°E
40°E
50°E

Modified Lambert Equal Area Projection   Blue boxes indicate focus map coverage

1000 kilometres
500 miles

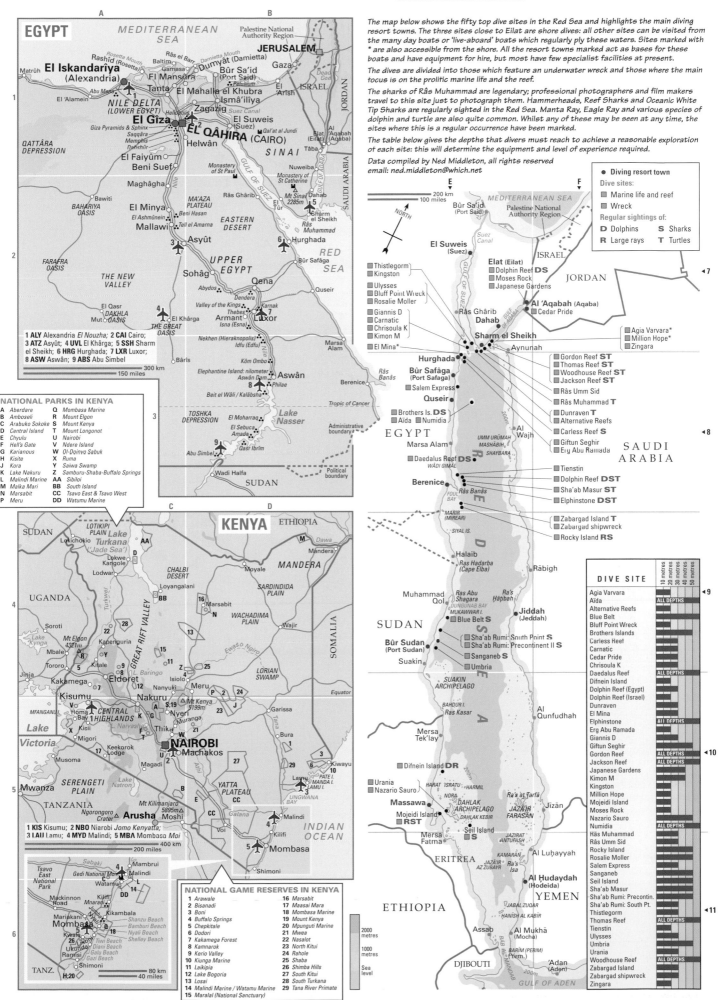

The map below shows the fifty top dive sites in the Red Sea and highlights the main diving resort towns. The three sites close to Eilat are shore dives: all other sites can be visited from the many day boats or 'live-aboard' boats which regularly ply these waters. Sites marked with * are also accessible from the shore. All the resort towns marked act as bases for these boats and have equipment for hire, but most have few specialist facilities at present.

The dives are divided into those which feature an underwater wreck and those where the main focus is on the prolific marine life and the reef.

The sharks of Râs Muhammad are legendary; professional photographers and film makers travel to this site just to photograph them. Hammerheads, Reef Sharks and Oceanic White Tip Sharks are regularly sighted in the Red Sea. Manta Ray, Eagle Ray and various species of dolphin and turtle are also quite common. Whilst any of these may be seen at any time, the sites where this is a regular occurrence have been marked.

The table below gives the depths that divers must reach to achieve a reasonable exploration of each site: this will determine the equipment and level of experience required.

Data compiled by Ned Middleton, all rights reserved
email: ned.middleton@which.net

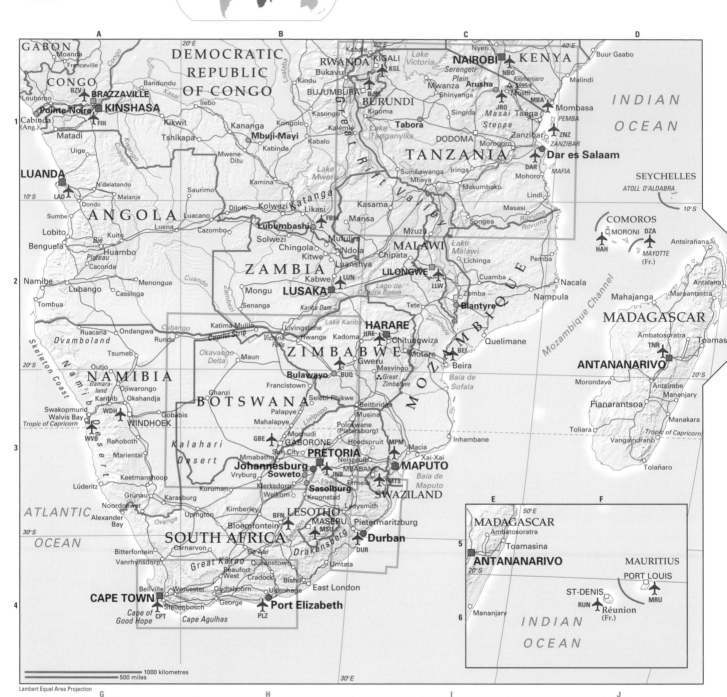

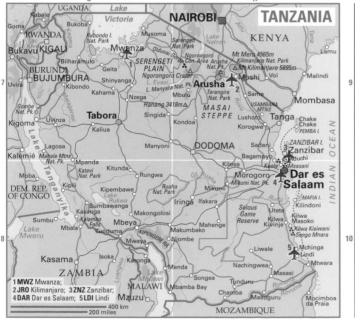

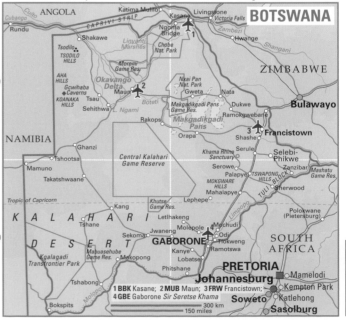

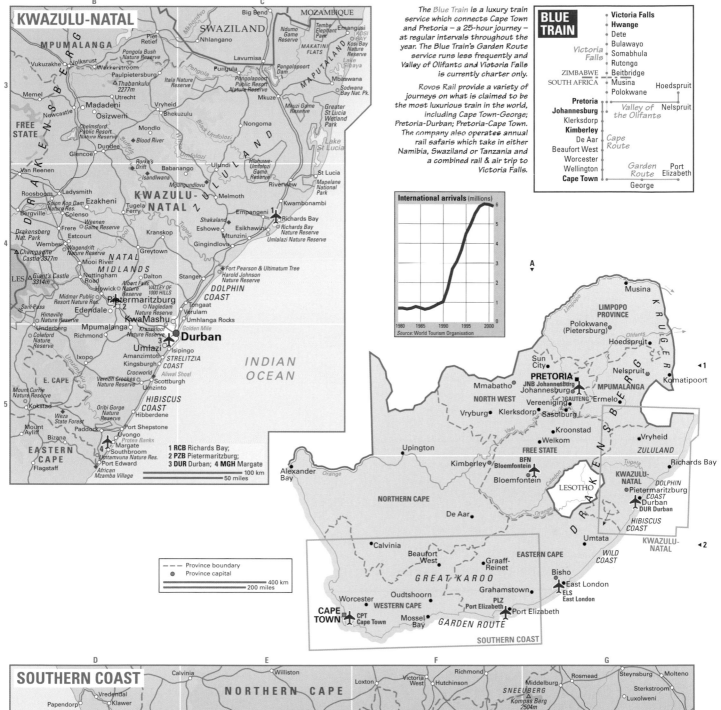

KWAZULU-NATAL

SOUTHERN COAST

The *Blue Train* is a luxury train service which connects Cape Town and Pretoria – a 25-hour journey – at regular intervals throughout the year. The Blue Train's Garden Route service runs less frequently and Valley of Olifants and Victoria Falls is currently charter only.

Rovos Rail provide a variety of journeys on what is claimed to be the most luxurious train in the world, including Cape Town–George; Pretoria–Durban; Pretoria–Cape Town. The company also operates annual rail safaris which take in either Namibia, Swaziland or Tanzania and a combined rail & air trip to Victoria Falls.

BLUE TRAIN

- Victoria Falls
- Hwange
- Dete
- Bulawayo
- Somabhula
- Rutengo
- Beitbridge
- Musina
- Polokwane
- Hoedspruit

Victoria Falls
ZIMBABWE
SOUTH AFRICA

- Pretoria
- Johannesburg — *Valley of the Olifants* — Nelspruit
- Klerksdorp
- Kimberley — *Cape Route*
- De Aar
- Beaufort West
- Worcester
- Wellington — *Garden Route* — Port Elizabeth
- Cape Town — George

International arrivals (millions)

Source: World Tourism Organisation

1 RCB Richards Bay; 2 PZB Pietermaritzburg; 3 DUR Durban; 4 MGH Margate

--- Province boundary
● Province capital

1 CPT Cape Town; 2 GRJ George;
1 PBZ Plettenberg Bay; 2 PLZ Port Elizabeth

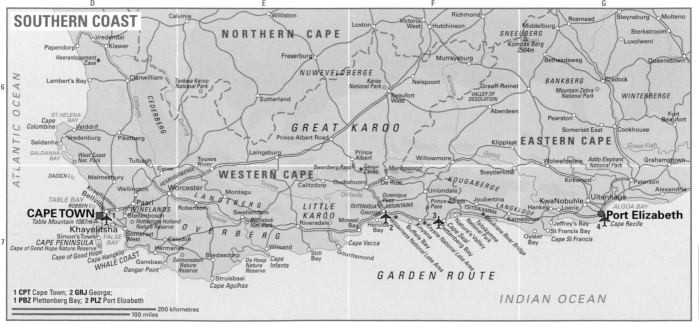

Wildlife Parks

Africa is a prime destination for wildlife holidays: its national parks, game reserves and wildlife sanctuaries feature prominently in package holidays and tourist itineraries. Many parks, such as the Masai Mara, Serengeti and Kruger, are well-known throughout the world and a number of them have been recognised by both UNESCO and the WWF for their unique and important character.

The area of Africa south of the Sahara is featured here. Although there are areas of wildlife interest in northern Africa, particularly on the Mediterranean coast, these are generally on a much smaller scale and do not usually provide the primary motivation for travel to these countries.

The map and table features the major parks and reserves used by tour operators and visited by overseas tourists. Some lesser-known parks are also included to give a broader geographical spread; access to many of these may be difficult due to poor infrastructure or political problems.

The table lists the major species most likely to be seen while visiting each park or those animals for which the park is famous, according to government literature and independent reports. Quality of information varies considerably from country to country and the following table should be regarded as a rough guide only. Poaching is a serious problem in some countries, particularly where wildlife tourism is less developed or where wars or civil unrest have diverted resources and personnel away from park administration.

Coloured symbols indicate the main vegetation and habitat in each park or reserve. In some areas, particularly in mountain regions, there is a wide range of habitats and the colour shown is where the majority of wildlife is to be found.

Tropical rainforest
Heavy rainfall and constant heat promote rapid growth and luxuriant vegetation; dense undergrowth and a wide diversity of plant and animal species develops under a high tree canopy

Savannah
Transitional areas which have a long dry season, preventing widespread tree growth except around watercourses; grass grows very rapidly during the wet season and can reach a height of two metres

Grassland
Extensive short lush grasses indispersed with trees and clumps of bushes; an excellent habitat for the main browsing species and their predators

Scrub
The boundary between grassland and desert; usually flat with thorn bushes and often featuring cacti

Desert / semi-arid
Characterised by little or no vegetation; it can vary from extensive stretches of sand to areas of baked clay to rocks and pebbles

Marine / wetland
Mangrove forests, coastal swamps and inland lakes, rivers and pools provide a rich and varied habitat for many different species

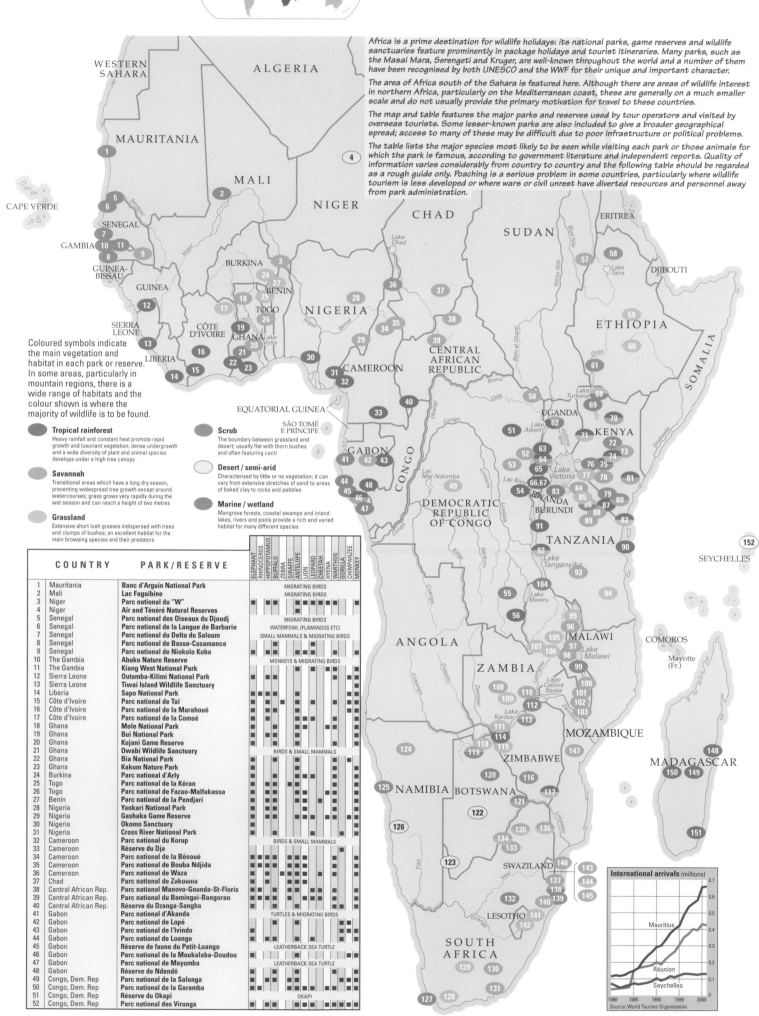

Species columns: ELEPHANT · RHINOCEROS · HIPPOPOTAMUS · BUFFALO · ZEBRA · GIRAFFE · ANTELOPE · LION · LEOPARD · CHEETAH · HYENA · WARTHOG · GORILLA · CHIMPANZEE · MONKEY

No	COUNTRY	PARK/RESERVE	Notes
1	Mauritania	Banc d'Arguin National Park	MIGRATING BIRDS
2	Mali	Lac Faguibine	MIGRATING BIRDS
3	Niger	Parc national du "W"	
4	Niger	Aïr and Ténéré Natural Reserves	
5	Senegal	Parc national des Oiseaux du Djoudj	MIGRATING BIRDS
6	Senegal	Parc national de la Langue de Barbarie	WATERFOWL (FLAMINGOS ETC)
7	Senegal	Parc national du Delta du Saloum	SMALL MAMMALS & MIGRATING BIRDS
8	Senegal	Parc national de Basse-Casamance	
9	Senegal	Parc national de Niokolo Koba	
10	The Gambia	Abuko Nature Reserve	MONKEYS & MIGRATING BIRDS
11	The Gambia	Kiang West National Park	
12	Sierra Leone	Outamba-Kilimi National Park	
13	Sierra Leone	Tiwai Island Wildlife Sanctuary	
14	Liberia	Sapo National Park	
15	Côte d'Ivoire	Parc national de Taï	
16	Côte d'Ivoire	Parc national de la Marahoué	
17	Côte d'Ivoire	Parc national de la Comoé	
18	Ghana	Mole National Park	
19	Ghana	Bui National Park	
20	Ghana	Kujani Game Reserve	
21	Ghana	Owabi Wildlife Sanctuary	BIRDS & SMALL MAMMALS
22	Ghana	Bia National Park	
23	Ghana	Kakum Nature Park	
24	Burkina	Parc national d'Arly	
25	Togo	Parc national de la Kéran	
26	Togo	Parc national de Fazao-Malfakassa	
27	Benin	Parc national de la Pendjari	
28	Nigeria	Yankari National Park	
29	Nigeria	Gashaka Game Reserve	
30	Nigeria	Okomo Sanctuary	
31	Nigeria	Cross River National Park	BIRDS & SMALL MAMMALS
32	Cameroon	Parc national du Korup	
33	Cameroon	Réserve du Dja	
34	Cameroon	Parc national de la Bénoué	
35	Cameroon	Parc national de Bouba Ndjida	
36	Cameroon	Parc national de Waza	
37	Chad	Parc national de Zakouma	
38	Central African Rep.	Parc national Manovo-Gounda-St-Floris	
39	Central African Rep.	Parc national du Bamingui-Bangoran	
40	Central African Rep.	Réserve du Dzanga-Sangha	TURTLES & MIGRATING BIRDS
41	Gabon	Parc national d'Akanda	
42	Gabon	Parc national de Lopé	
43	Gabon	Parc national de l'Ivindo	
44	Gabon	Parc national de Loango	
45	Gabon	Réserve de faune du Petit-Loango	LEATHERBACK SEA TURTLE
46	Gabon	Parc national de la Moukalaba-Doudou	
47	Gabon	Parc national de Mayumba	LEATHERBACK SEA TURTLE
48	Gabon	Réserve de Ndendé	
49	Congo, Dem. Rep	Parc national de la Salonga	
50	Congo, Dem. Rep	Parc national de la Garamba	
51	Congo, Dem. Rep	Réserve du Okapi	OKAPI
52	Congo, Dem. Rep	Parc national des Virunga	

International arrivals (millions)

Mauritius · Réunion · Seychelles

1980 · 1985 · 1990 · 1995 · 2000

Source: World Tourism Organisation

152 · SEYCHELLES

Wildlife Parks; Indian Ocean Islands

	COUNTRY	PARK/RESERVE	ELEPHANT	RHINOCEROS	HIPPOPOTAMUS	BUFFALO	ZEBRA	GIRAFFE	ANTELOPE	LION	LEOPARD	CHEETAH	HYENA	WARTHOG	GORILLA	CHIMPANZEE	MONKEY
53	Congo, Dem. Rep.	Parc national de la Maiko															
54	Congo, Dem. Rep.	Parc national du Kahuzi-Biega															
55	Congo, Dem. Rep.	Parc national de l'Upemba															
56	Congo, Dem. Rep.	Parc national de Kundelungu															
57	Sudan	Dinder National Park															
58	Ethiopia	Simien Mountains National Park	BABOONS & SMALL MAMMALS														
59	Ethiopia	Awash National Park															
60	Ethiopia	Bale Mountains National Park	ANTELOPE, SMALL MAMMALS & BIRDS														
61	Ethiopia	Omo National Park															
62	Uganda	Murchison Falls National Park															
63	Uganda	Ruwenzori Mountains National Park															
64	Uganda	Queen Elizabeth National Park															
65	Uganda	Bwindi Impenetrable Forest National Park*															
66	Rwanda	Parc des Volcans															
67	Rwanda	Parc national de l'Akagera	BIRDS														
68	Kenya	Sibiloi National Park															
69	Kenya	Central Island National Park	FLAMINGOS & CROCODILES														
70	Kenya	Marsabit National Reserve															
71	Kenya	Mount Elgon National Park															
72	Kenya	Samburu-Shaba-Buffalo Springs Nat. Park															
73	Kenya	Meru National Park															
74	Kenya	Mount Kenya National Park*															
75	Kenya	Aberdare National Park															
76	Kenya	Lake Nakuru National Park	FLAMINGOS & MANY OTHER ANIMALS														
77	Kenya	Maasai Mara National Reserve*															
78	Kenya	Nairobi National Park															
79	Kenya	Amboseli National Park*															
80	Kenya	Tsavo National Parks (East & West)															
81	Kenya	Tana River Primate National Reserve															
82	Kenya	Shimba Hills National Reserve															
83	Tanzania	Rubondo Island National Park	WETLAND BIRDS														
84	Tanzania	Serengeti National Park*															
85	Tanzania	Ngorongoro Conservation Area															
86	Tanzania	Lake Manyara National Park															
87	Tanzania	Kilimanjaro National Park*															
88	Tanzania	Arusha National Park															
89	Tanzania	Tarangire National Park															
90	Tanzania	Jozani Reserve, Zanzibar															
91	Tanzania	Gombe National Park															
92	Tanzania	Mahale Mountains National Park															
93	Tanzania	Ruaha National Park															
94	Tanzania	Selous Game Reserve															
95	Malawi	Nyika National Park															
96	Malawi	Vwaza Marsh Wildlife Reserve															
97	Malawi	Nkhotakota Wildlife Reserve															
98	Malawi	Kasungu National Park															
99	Malawi	Lake Malawi National Park*															
100	Malawi	Liwonde National Park*															
101	Malawi	Majete Wildlife Reserve															
102	Malawi	Lengwe National Park															
103	Malawi	Mwabvi Wildlife Reserve															
104	Zambia	Nsumbu National Park															
105	Zambia	North Luangwa National Park															
106	Zambia	South Luangwa National Park															
107	Zambia	Kasanka National Park															
108	Zambia	Kafue National Park															
109	Zambia	Lochinvar National Park															
110	Zambia	Lower Zambezi National Park															
111	Zambia	Mosi-oa-Tunya National Park															
112	Zimbabwe	Mana Pools National Park															
113	Zimbabwe	Matusadona National Park															
114	Zimbabwe	Zambezi National Park															
115	Zimbabwe	Hwange National Park															
116	Zimbabwe	Matobo National Park															
117	Zimbabwe	Gonarezhou National Park															
118	Botswana	Chobe National Park															
119	Botswana	Moremi Game Reserve*															
120	Botswana	Makgadikgadi Pans Game Reserve	FLAMINGOS														
121	Botswana	Tuli Block safari reserves															
122	Botswana	Central Kalahari Game Reserve															
123	Botswana / S. Africa	Kgalagadi Transfrontier Park															
124	Namibia	Etosha National Park*															
125	Namibia	Cape Cross Reserve	SEALS														
126	Namibia	Namib-Naukluft National Park	JACKALS & ORYX														
127	South Africa	Cape of Good Hope Nature Reserve	ANTELOPE & BABOON														
128	South Africa	Bontebok National Park															
129	South Africa	Karoo National Park															
130	South Africa	Mountain Zebra National Park															
131	South Africa	Addo Elephant National Park															
132	South Africa	Willem Pretorius Game Reserve															
133	South Africa	Pilanesberg National Park															
134	South Africa	Madikwe Game Reserve															
135	South Africa	Marakele National Park															
136	South Africa	Kruger National Park*															
137	South Africa	Ndumo Game Reserve															
138	South Africa	Mkuzi Game Reserve															
139	South Africa	Greater St Lucia Wetland Park															
140	South Africa	Hluhluwe-Umfolozi Game Reserve															
141	South Africa	Giant's Castle Game Reserve															
142	Lesotho	Sehlabathebe National Park	BIRDS														
143	Swaziland	Hlane Royal National Park															
144	Swaziland	Mlawula Nature Reserve															
145	Swaziland	Milwane Game Reserve															
146	Mozambique	Maputo Elephant Reserve															
147	Mozambique	Parque Nacional da Gorongosa	BIRDS														
148	Madagascar	Réserve de Perinet-Mantadia															
149	Madagascar	Parc national de Ranomafana															
150	Madagascar	Réserve naturelle de Tsingy de Bemaraha															
151	Madagascar	Réserve de Berenty															
152	Seychelles	Cousin Island Nature Reserve	BIRDS														

Thanks to the following for their help in compiling this section:
Wintana Tsegai of the Kenyan Tourist Board, London
Patricia D'Arcy of the South African Tourism Board, London
Warren Green of Kartagener Associates Inc, New York
John Haycock of Africa Explorer: john@africa-explorer.co.uk
Bill Adams of Safari Consultants: bill@safariconsultantuk.com
Tim Best of Tim Best Travel: info@timbesttravel.com
John Knighton of African Pride: info@African-pride.co.uk
John Douglas of Malawi Tourism: enquiries@malawitourism.com
Any errors or omissions remain the responsibility of the publishers.

Parks and reserves marked with an asterisk (*) are featured in Columbus Travel Guides' *Tourist Attractions and Events of the World*

SEYCHELLES

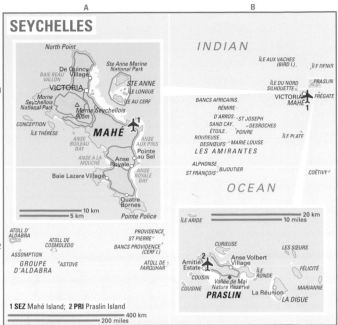

1 SEZ Mahé Island; 2 PRI Praslin Island

RÉUNION

1 RUN Réunion St-Denis Roland-Garros

MAURITIUS

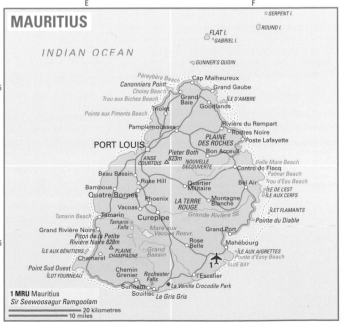

1 MRU Mauritius Sir Seewoosagur Ramgoolam

Asia

Asia offers arguably more variety than any other continent. It stretches from the Mediterranean to the Pacific, from the exotic cultures of the Middle East to the mysteries of China, and from the arid expanse of the Gobi Desert to the rain forests of New Guinea. There are other varieties, too: command economies and free-market capitalism, dictatorships and well-established democracies. Asia has 60% of the world's population, five of the world's eight most populous countries and six of the its ten largest cities.. It is, by far, the most densely populated continent. It has given the world its most important civilizations and religions, and three of its most potent inventions: paper, gunpowder and Arabic numerals. As several recent events have shown, this sophistication, vibrancy and diversity has brought its share of problems as well as advantages.

Asia has recently experienced political and economic volatility. War, terrorism and recession, or the threat of them, have caused or reawakened problems, and also served to complicate their solutions. Ethnic and religious affinities often bridge national frontiers, and this tends to export unrest and to undermine nation states. Although many conflicts, such as those in Sri Lanka and East Timor, appear to have been resolved, tensions elsewhere, principally in Israel/Palestine, remain high. Some argue that enforced regime changes in Afghanistan and Iraq have intensified these problems; others claim that they were necessary to build more stable societies.

Influences

Any view of Asia is meaningless without an awareness of the influence of the three main faiths, Buddhism, Hinduism and Islam. Each provides distinct solutions for human problems, and not all are compatible with the Christian separation between church and state that is the bedrock of most western societies. Islam – the dominant religion in around half of Asia's countries – has recently become increasingly politicised, challenging existing conceptions of governance and, partly as a consequence, polarising views of Islam globally. Whether these developments have been a cause or a result of problems in Asia and elsewhere is debateable: what is not, is that Islam's relationship with the non-Islamic world (Christian or otherwise) is now the central issue in global affairs. As with other divisions, travel and tourism perhaps has a vital role to play here. UNESCO's constitution asserts that 'since wars begin in the minds of men, it is in the minds of men that defences of peace must be constructed'. Each foreign visitor has the potential to help this process.

Recent decades have also seen spectacular economic growth, particularly in the so-called 'tiger economies' of East Asia. Although this has now slowed (especially in Japan) many countries still match North America and Western Europe in prosperity, albeit with a less even distribution of wealth. Asian adaptations of Western capitalism have generally been achieved without political liberalisation, the pursuit of which is currently a major goal of US global foreign policy. China is the most important country to pursue this split-level path. As the

global economy moves into a services- and information-based phase, this contradiction is likely to become more acute. The full economic and social benefits of this revolution are unlikely to felt wherever the state has widespread control over the content of or access to the internet and other information sources.

Travel trends

Visitors to Asian countries increased by 37% between 1997 and 2001, far more than to any other continent. 2002 and early 2003 saw similar growth for all the countries in the Asia-Pacific region apart from Indonesia and Nepal. This was largely driven by visitors from within Asia. With the threat of war in Iraq at that time hanging over travel plans, European and North American markets were performing less impressively.

In the midst of this uncertainty, a thunderbolt arrived from an unexpected direction in the shape of the mysterious SARS virus. Initial official statements were confusing and evasive and public reaction briefly reached panic levels. Travel to affected destinations plummeted, as did the profits of many airlines. One, China Southern, even offered free flights for life to anyone who developed a cure. By July, the situation had stabilised and most official travel warnings had been withdrawn, although travel bargains are likely to persist for some time as visitors are wooed back.

The crisis demonstrated both the short-term vulnerability and the long-term resilience of the travel business (as well as the value of effective and honest public relations). As in North America and Europe, the large airlines were the hardest hit, enabling smaller, more flexible low-cost carriers such as Silk Air to take advantage.

Established favourites

Five countries accounted for 57% of visitor arrivals in 2001 (figures include the considerable travel between mainland China, Hong Kong and Macau).

- China retains great mystique but the 'Bamboo Curtain' is now parting. Beijing will host the 2008 Olympics, and a US$22 billion infrastructure programme is under way. As the completion of the Three Gorges Dam approaches, Yangtze River cruises are selling fast. The Terracotta Army in Xi'an and the Great Wall are hugely popular attractions.

- Hong Kong was, until SARS, recovering well from a downturn following return of sovereignty to China. US$2.3 billion will have been spent by 2007 on upgrading tourist attractions and facilities.

- Malaysia's main attractions are the beaches in Penang and Langkawi, but efforts are being made to promote dual-centre trips that also take in the country's vibrant cultural heritage, particularly in Malacca. Areas with future potential include Sabah, Sarawak, Tioman and Redang.

- Thailand has recently sustained dramatic tourism growth. Its exceptional beaches and resorts such as Patong in Phuket have enjoyed an environmental

■ Big spenders

Expenditure on foreign travel (excluding international transport), 2001 – top ten countries (US$ billions)   Source: WTO

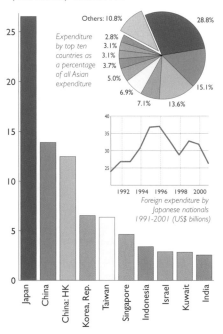

clean-up. Up-and-coming areas include the island of Ko Samui, the resorts of Hua Hin and Krabi and the spectacular scenery of the country's many national parks.

- Singapore is an established city-break, stopover and business/convention destination, and a major boarding point for Asian cruises. It is looking to attract a younger clientele and to increase lengths of stay. The islands south-west of Sentosa are being developed as eco-tourism destinations.

Other destinations – South & East

- Japan and the Republic of Korea's successful joint-hosting of the 2002 Football World Cup helped to increase visitors and to shake off their 'business-only' tags. Japan has begun an ambitious plan to double overseas arrivals by 2007, while Seoul's new airport should cement its position as a regional hub and encourage stop-over and dual-centre business. Five of the world's ten most visited theme parks in 2002 are in Korea or Japan.

■ Asian leaders

Top 10 Asian destinations (Kuoni holidays, ex-UK), 2003 Source: Kuoni

	'01	'02		'01	'02
Thailand	1	1	Hong Kong	4	5
Maldives	2	2	Malaysia	7	6
Sri Lanka	4	3	Singapore	6	7
Dubai (UAE)	5	4	Indonesia	8	8

■ Economies

The region's 10 largest economies
Source: World Bank/International Monetary Fund

	GNI (US$ bn) 2001	Annual GDP growth rate (%) 2001	2002 est	2003 est	2004 est
Japan	4,523.3	0.4	0.3	0.8	1.0
China	1,131.2	7.3	8.0	7.5	7.5
India	477.4	4.2	4.9	5.1	5.9
Korea, Rep.	447.6	3.0	6.1	5.0	5.3
Taiwan	281.9	-2.2	3.5	3.2	3.7
Saudi Arabia	181.1	1.2	2.1	4.0	3.1
China: HK	170.3	0.6	2.3	3.0	3.3
Indonesia	144.7	3.4	3.7	3.5	4.0
Thailand	118.5	1.9	5.2	4.2	4.3
Iran	108.7	5.7	6.0	6.5	5.9

- Asia occupies 22.8% of the world's land area and is home to 59.5% of the world's population.
- Asia's combined GDI is US$8,374,740 million, 26.7% of the world's total.
- Asia accounts for 19.7% of global travel departures and 19.6% of arrivals.
- International travel and tourism contributed US$85.5 billion to Asia's economy in 2001.
- The most visited country in Asia in 2001 was China (not including Hong Kong or Macau), which received 33.2 million visitors: worldwide, only France, the USA, Spain and Italy received more.
- 21 Asian countries received over one million visitors in 2001.
- Although visitors to Israel fell by 40% in 2001 compared to 2000, average spending per head was, at US$1,811, the highest in Asia.
- There were 133.5 million international tourist arrivals in Asia in 2001, an increase of 22% over 1999.
- Visitors to countries in north east Asia (which includes China, Hong Kong, Korea and Japan) increased by 11.9% in 2002 compared to 2001, nearly four times the world average. Much of this, however, was intra-regional: over 90% of visitors to China came from this area.
- 16 countries (including Hong Kong and Macau) received in excess of US$1 billion from travel and tourism in 2001.
- Of the 34 countries that experienced annual GDP growth of over 5% in 2002, 14 are in Asia: by contrast, Europe can muster only five.
- Macau's gambling taxes provided 60% of its government's revenue in 2001.
- Malaysians are Asia's most frequent travellers, recording over 36 million overseas journeys in 1999, 28% of Asia's total. Worldwide, only four nationalities travelled more.
- Asia has 3.9 million hotel rooms, 24% of the world's total.
- Asian carriers filled the top four places in the Best Leisure Airline category of the 2003 Observer Travel Awards.
- The Japanese continue to top the Asian big spenders' league, although with a reduced share compared to 1999. Their expenditure on travel in 2001 was US$26.5 billion, 29% of Asia's total. Worldwide, only the Americans, the Germans and the British spent more.
- With around 22,000 people per sq km, Macau is the most densely populated state in the world.
- 60% of the world's population increase between 2000 and 2003 was in Asian countries.
- The Republic of Korea finished fourth in the 2002 World Cup, the best ever performance by an Asian country.
- Armenia's spectacular increase in visitor arrivals in 2001 (the highest in the world at 435%) was largely due to celebrations marking the 1700th anniversary of the adoption of Christianity as the official religion.
- The Chinese government has set a target of all police officers in Beijing being conversant in Russian, Japanese, Arabic and English by the time of the 2008 Olympics.
- Nine of the 14 tallest mountains in the world can be reached via Nepal.

- India is a country of staggering diversity, with one of the world's oldest civilizations. The Golden Triangle, Goa and the major cities have long been popular. Growth areas include Ayurveda and spa resorts in Kerala, wildlife sanctuaries and heritage tourism.

- The Maldives offers glorious beaches with excellent diving and water-sports and is a wedding and honeymoon favourite. Partly with this market in mind, many resort islands have recently been renovated to the highest standards of luxury.

- Sri Lanka is slowly recovering after severe political troubles, and is keen to advance from being an add-on destination as part of longer trips. Most holidays combine temple and hill-country tours with time on one of the island's magnificent beaches.

- Vietnam and Cambodia have seen increased stability, rapidly normalising relations with the USA and co-ordinated marketing activities with neighbouring countries. All have helped combined visitor arrivals grow by 71% between 1997 and 2001.

- Macau has taken steps to reform and modernise its gambling businesses, on which so much of its revenue depends.

- Taiwan has traditionally been viewed as a business destination. The long-running dispute with China shows some signs of relenting with a relaxation of trade and transport restrictions: this may increase stability and encourage more leisure travellers.

Other destinations – West & Central

- The Middle East attracts many of its visitors from within the Arab world, particularly since September 2001. Lebanon has been a major beneficiary of this trend. Its upheavals have now been resolved and the economy and infrastructure largely rebuilt. It is now seeking to reclaim its 1970's tag of 'the Paris of the Middle East'. In 2003 Lebanaon's airline, MEA, took delivery of its first new aircraft for 30 years. Jordan, despite its proximity to Israel and Palestine, has a successful tourism industry, with Petra as its main attraction. Many hotels have recently been opened or upgraded. Syria also has several cultural attractions, including the ancient city of Damascus, and has the capacity to attract more visitors than it currently does. Indeed, Lebanon, Jordan and Syria's 2001 hotel occupancy rates were all under 30%. All three are undertaking co-ordinated tourism marketing campaigns as 'three countries, one destination'.

- In the Arabian Peninsula, Dubai (part of the UAE) has invested billions of dollars in airports, leisure facilities, hotels and shops to make it the Middle East's most popular short-break destination. Other Gulf States such as Kuwait, Qatar and Bahrain also have ambitions to be more than shopping stopovers. Saudi Arabia reported arrival figures to the WTO for the first time in 2001, with pilgrimages and business travel being the main reason for visiting, although it has recently put plans in place to encourage a more broadly-based visitor profile.

- Israel built a highly successful tourism product based on a combination of biblical tours and diving and beach holidays, but ongoing conflict has severely damaged this.

- The Central Asian economies rely heavily on their oil and gas reserves, and many visitors are connected with these industries. The WTO's Silk Road project may in time encourage more leisure travellers: political stability will be another key factor.

Problem areas

- Political unrest and terrorism may at any time cause decline. Long-running disputes in Kashmir, Taiwan and Korea have generally produced only localised stand-offs, but risk escalation in the current geo-political climate.

- The aftermaths of the wars in Afghanistan and Iraq are currently uncertain.

Big earners

Receipts from Foreign Travel (excluding international transport), 2001 – top ten countries (US$ billions) Source: WTO

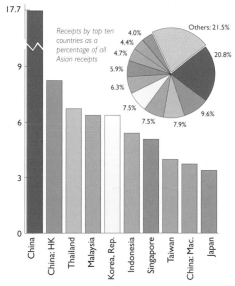

Receipts by top ten countries as a percentage of all Asian receipts

Others: 21.5%
20.8%
9.6%
7.9%
7.5%
7.5%
6.3%
5.9%
4.7%
4.4%
4.0%

- Further outbreaks of SARS or similar diseases such as the West Nile virus cannot be ruled out.

- Indonesia is struggling to recover from the effects of the Bali bombing and the perception of other security and human-rights problems.

- Iran's complex relations with the USA could provide another regional flashpoint – a long-standing travel ban was lifted in 1997 but trade sanctions were imposed in 2001.

- The Philippines, Yemen and Nepal have all experienced considerable security problems in recent years.

- Myanmar (Burma) remains accused of widespread human rights abuses and attracts little international tourism as a result.

- China's human rights record remains a concern to many.

- Israel's tourism industry, once thriving, is currently in crisis as a result of the ongoing conflict with Palestine.

- Some countries are major sources of illegal drugs, which often causes social, political and economic instability.

Visitors

Visitor arrivals 2001 Source: WTO

	Visitors (thousands)	Change since 1997
China	33,167	39.5%
China: Hong Kong	13,725	21.8%
Malaysia	12,775	105.7%
Thailand	10,133	38.9%
Singapore	6,726	3.0%
Saudi Arabia	6,296	n/a
China: Macau	5,842	52.3%
Indonesia	5,153	-0.6%
Korea, Rep. (South)	5,147	31.7%
Japan	4,772	13.1%
United Arab Emirates	4,134	67.0%
Taiwan	2,617	10.3%
India	2,537	6.9%
Bahrain	2,420	50.2%
Kazakstan	1,845	25.4%
Philippines	1,797	-19.2%
Vietnam	1,599	43.5%
Jordan	1,478	31.1%
Iran	1,402	83.5%
Syria	1,318	47.9%
Israel	1,196	-40.5%
Brunei	984	53.0%
Lebanon	837	50.0%
Azerbaijan	676	120.9%
Cambodia	605	176.3%
Oman	562	49.5%
Pakistan	500	33.3%
Maldives	461	26.0%
Nepal	361	-14.5%
Uzbekistan	345	-64.1%
Sri Lanka	337	-7.9%
Georgia	302	-3.5%
Turkmenistan	300	16.7%
Bangladesh	207	13.7%
Myanmar (Burma)	205	8.5%
Laos	173	-10.4%
Mongolia	166	102.4%
Armenia	123	434.8%
Kuwait	78	-1.3%
Yemen	76	-5.0%
Qatar	76	-82.5%
Kyrgyzstan	69	-20.7%
Palestine NAR	7	-96.5%
Bhutan	6	18.5%
Tajikistan	4	118.8%

(Figures not available for Afghanistan, East Timor, Iraq or Korea DPR.)

Thanks to: Anne-Marie Hansen of Kuoni Travel, Indiatourism, Tourism Malaysia, Tourism Authority of Thailand, Patrick Fitzgerald, Jon Gillaspie, Gary Bowerman, Graeme Payne

[Bar chart x-axis labels: China, China: HK, Thailand, Malaysia, Korea, Rep., Indonesia, Singapore, Taiwan, China: Mac., Japan; y-axis values: 17.7, 9, 6, 3, 0]

Physical

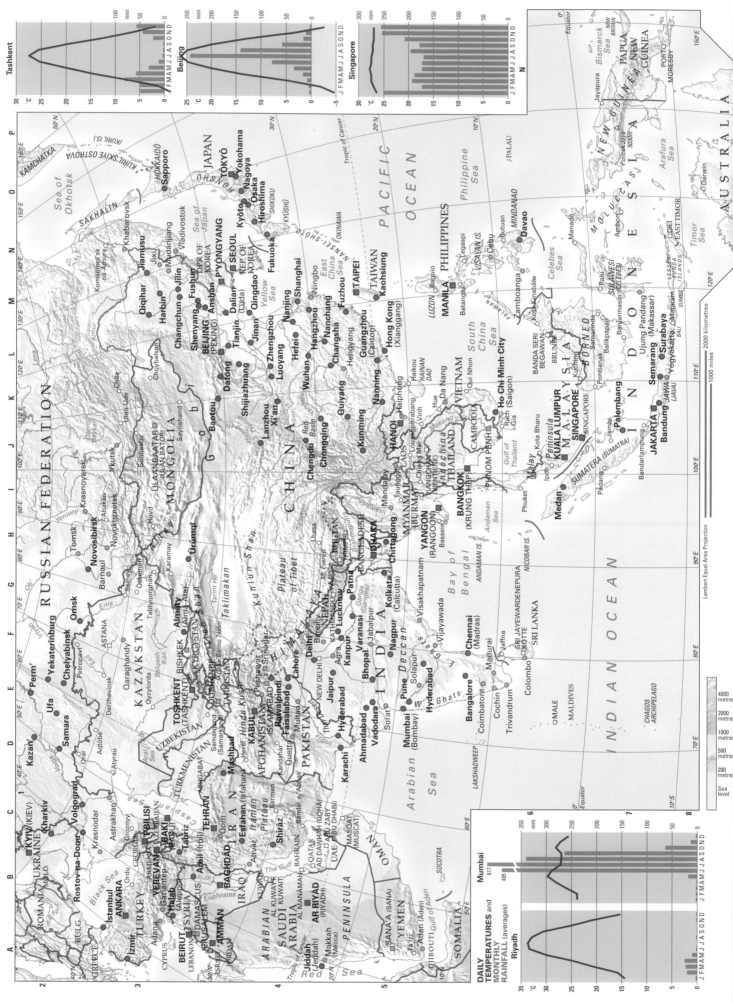

Climate

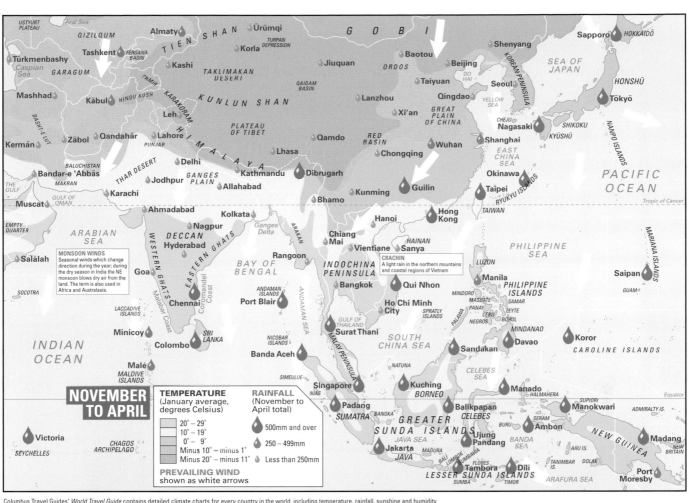

NOVEMBER TO APRIL

TEMPERATURE (January average, degrees Celsius)
- 20° – 29°
- 10° – 19°
- 0° – 9°
- Minus 10° – minus 1°
- Minus 20° – minus 11°

RAINFALL (November to April total)
- 500mm and over
- 250 – 499mm
- Less than 250mm

PREVAILING WIND shown as white arrows

MONSOON WINDS
Seasonal winds which change direction during the year; during the dry season in India the NE monsoon blows dry air from the land. The term is also used in Africa and Australasia.

CRACHIN
A light rain in the northern mountains and coastal regions of Vietnam.

Columbus Travel Guides' *World Travel Guide* contains detailed climate charts for every country in the world, including temperature, rainfall, sunshine and humidity

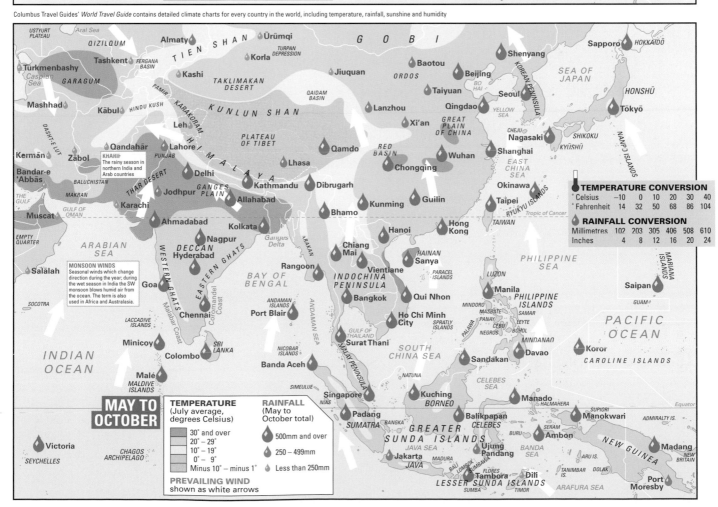

MAY TO OCTOBER

TEMPERATURE (July average, degrees Celsius)
- 30° and over
- 20° – 29°
- 10° – 19°
- 0° – 9°
- Minus 10° – minus 1°

RAINFALL (May to October total)
- 500mm and over
- 250 – 499mm
- Less than 250mm

PREVAILING WIND shown as white arrows

MONSOON WINDS
Seasonal winds which change direction during the year; during the wet season in India the SW monsoon blows humid air from the ocean. The term is also used in Africa and Australasia.

KHARIF
The rainy season in northern India and Arab countries.

TEMPERATURE CONVERSION

°Celsius	-10	0	10	20	30	40
°Fahrenheit	14	32	50	68	86	104

RAINFALL CONVERSION

Millimetres	102	203	305	406	508	610
Inches	4	8	12	16	20	24

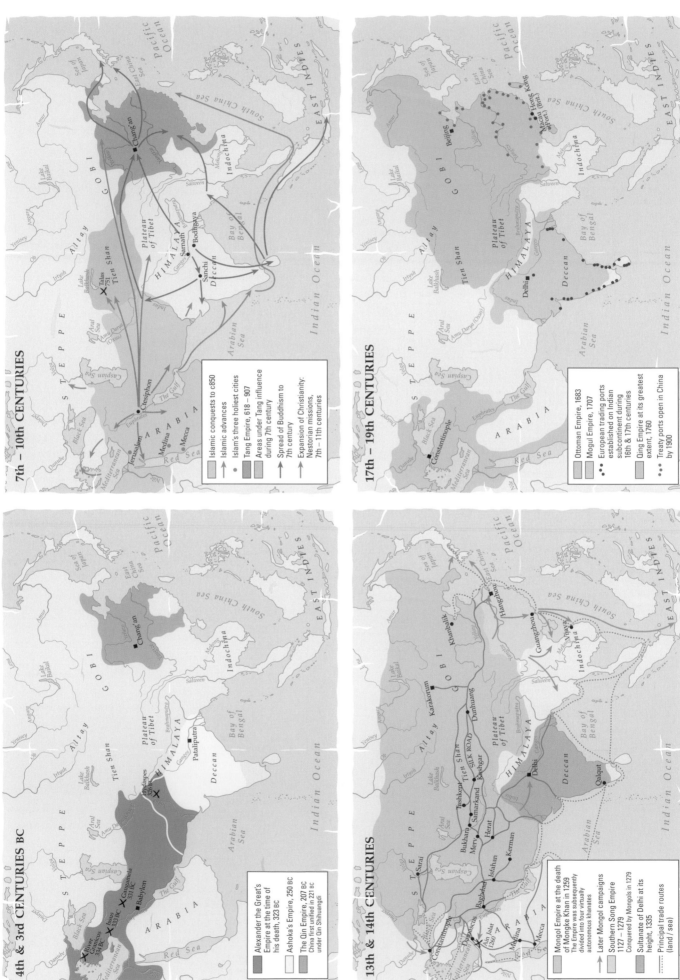

7th – 10th CENTURIES

- Islamic conquests to c850
- Islamic advances
- Islam's three holiest cities
- Tang Empire, 618 – 907
- Areas under Tang influence during 7th century
- Spread of Buddhism to 7th century
- Expansion of Christianity: Nestorian missions, 7th – 11th centuries

Chang'an
Talas 751
Sarnath
Bodhgaya
Sanchi
Ctesiphon
Jerusalem
Medina
Mecca

17th – 19th CENTURIES

- Ottoman Empire, 1683
- Mogul Empire, 1707
- European trading ports established on Indian subcontinent during 16th & 17th centuries
- Qing Empire at its greatest extent, 1760
- Treaty ports open in China by 1900

Beijing
Hong Kong
Macau (Port.)
Delhi
Constantinople

4th & 3rd CENTURIES BC

- Alexander the Great's Empire at the time of his death, 323 BC
- Ashoka's Empire, 250 BC
- The Qin Empire, 207 BC China first unified in 221 BC under Qin Shihuangdi

Chang'an
Pataliputra
Hydaspes 326 BC
Gaugamela 331 BC
Issus 333 BC
River Granicus 334 BC
Babylon

13th & 14th CENTURIES

- Mongol Empire at the death of Mongke Khan in 1259 The Empire was subsequently divided into four virtually autonomous khanates
- Later Mongol campaigns
- Southern Song Empire 1127 – 1279 Conquered by Mongols in 1279
- Sultanate of Delhi at its height, 1335
- Principal trade routes (land / sea)

Khanbalik
Karakorum
Dunhuang
SILK ROAD
Kashgar
Tashkent
Samarkand
Bukhara
Merv
Herat
Isfahan
Kerman
Sarai
Baghdad
Constantinople
Damascus
Ain Jalut 1260
Medina
Mecca
Delhi
Hangzhou
Guangzhou
Qalqut

Museums & Art Galleries

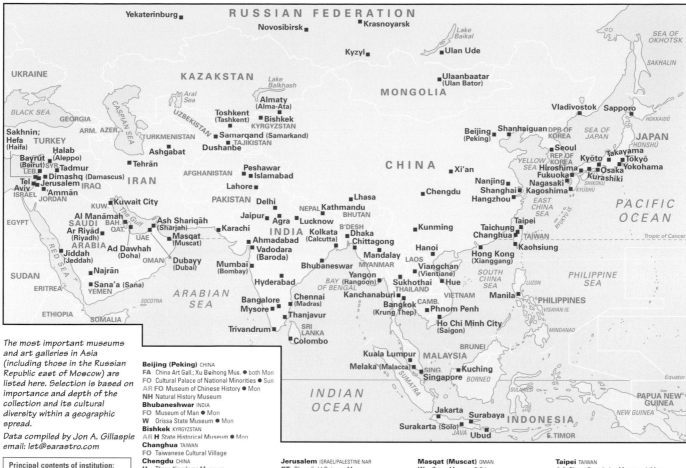

The most important museums and art galleries in Asia (including those in the Russian Republic east of Moscow) are listed here. Selection is based on importance and depth of the collection and its cultural diversity within a geographic spread.

Data compiled by Jon A. Gillaspie email: let@sarastro.com

Principal contents of institution:

AA	Applied & decorative art
AR	Archaeology / ancient art
FA	Fine art (paintings, sculpture)
FO	Folk art & culture / ethnology
H	History / historical site / reconstruction
NH	Natural history
ST	Science / technology
W	Wide range of subjects

Opening times:

Days or months preceded by a red circle (●) indicate when the institution is closed.

Many close on national holidays and other special days. Some museums and galleries have shorter opening hours at certain days of the week or in certain months.

Admission charges:

All charge for admission except those shown in *italics*, where entry is free (although charges for special exhibitions may apply).

Some institutions allow free entry or reduce their admission charges on certain days.

Ad Dawhah (Doha) QATAR
FO *Ethnographic Museum* ● Sat
W *Qatar National Museum* ● Sat

Agra INDIA
H Taj Mahal Museum

Ahmadabad INDIA
FA *NC Mehta Gallery (Indology Institute)* ● Mon
FO *Tribal Art Museum* ● Sun

Al Manamah BAHRAIN
W National Museum ● Fri

Almaty KAZAKSTAN
AR H Central State Museum ● Tue
FA Kasteyev Museum of Fine Arts ● Mon

Amman JORDAN
FO Jordanian Mus. of Popular Traditions ● Tue
AR National Archaeology Museum ● Tue
FA National Gallery of Fine Art

Ar Riyad (Riyadh) SAUDI ARABIA
AR FO *Riyadh Museum* ● Thu & Fri

Ashgabat TURKMENISTAN
FO NH Brunei Museum ● Mon
FO *Malay Technology Museum* ● Mon

Ash Shariqah (Sharjah) UNITED ARAB EM.
AR Sharjah Archaeology Museum
FA Sharjah Art Museum ● Fri
ST Sharjah Science Museum ● Sun

Bangalore INDIA
W *Government Museum* ● Wed

Bangkok (Krung Thep) THAILAND
AR National Museum ● Mon & Tue
AA FA Thai Houses of Jim Thompson ● Sun

Bayrut (Beirut) LEBANON
AR National Museum of Beirut ● Mon

Beijing (Peking) CHINA
FA China Art Gall.; Xu Beihong Mus. ● both Mon
FO Cultural Palace of National Minorities ● Sun
AR FO Museum of Chinese History ● Mon
NH Natural History Museum

Bhubaneshwar INDIA
FO Museum of Man ● Mon
W Orissa State Museum ● Mon

Bishkek KYRGYZSTAN
AR H State Historical Museum ● Mon

Changhua TAIWAN
FO Taiwanese Cultural Village

Chengdu CHINA
H Three Kingdoms Museum

Chennai (Madras) INDIA
AR FO Government Museum ● Fri

Chittagong BANGLADESH
FO Ethnological Museum ● Sat

Colombo SRI LANKA
H Dutch Period Museum ● Fri
FA National Art Gallery
AR H National Museum ● Fri

Delhi INDIA
FA National Gallery of Modern Art
W National Museum ● Mon

Dhaka BANGLADESH
W National Museum ● Thu

Dimashq (Damascus) SYRIA
W National Museum ● Tue

Dubayy (Dubai) UNITED ARAB EMIRATES
W Dubai Museum

Dushanbe TAJIKISTAN
AA FO Museum of Ethnography ● Sun
W Tajikistan Unified Museum ● Sun

Fukuoka JAPAN
FA Fukuoka Art Museum

Halab (Aleppo) SYRIA
FO Museum of Popular Tradition ● Tue
W National Museum of Aleppo ● Tue

Hangzhou CHINA
AR Zhejiang Provincial Museum ● Mon

Hanoi VIETNAM
AR H History Museum ● Mon
H Ho Chi Minh Museum; Museum of the Vietnamese Revolution ● both Mon
FA FO National Fine Arts Museum ● Mon

Hefa (Haifa) ISRAEL
FA Haifa Museum of Art
ST National Museum of Science & Technology

Hiroshima JAPAN
H Hiroshima Peace Memorial Museum

Ho Chi Minh City (Saigon) VIETNAM
W History Museum ● Mon
H Revolut. Mus.; War Crimes Mus. ● both Mon

Hong Kong (Xianggang) CHINA
ST Hong Kong Space Museum ● Tue
AR FA Museum of Art ● Thu
H Museum of History ● Fri
AR H Sam Tung Uk Museum ● Tue
W University Museum ● Sun

Hue VIETNAM
AA AR Hue Museum of Antique Objects

Hyderabad INDIA
AR Archaeology Museum ● Mon
W Salar Jung Museum ● Fri

Islamabad PAKISTAN
W Lok Virsa Museum ● Fri
FO *Islamabad Museum* ● Wed

Jaipur INDIA
W Central Museum ● Fri; Museum of Indology

Jakarta INDONESIA
AA FA Adam Malik Museum; Balai Seni Rupa ● both Mon
W National Museum ● Mon
W Taman Mini Indonesia Indah, includes: Asmat Museum; Museum Indonesia; Komodo Museum; Science Museum

Jerusalem ISRAEL/PALESTINE NAR
ST Bloomfield Science Museum
AR *Islamic Museum* ● Fri; Museum of the History of Jerusalem; Wohl Archaeology Museum (& Burnt House) ● Sat
W Israel Museum ● Sun
FA L.A. Mayer Memorial Museum of Islamic Art
AR H Rockerfeller Museum

Jiddah (Jeddah) SAUDI ARABIA
AR FO *Reg. Mus. of Archaeol. & Ethnology* ● Thu

Kagoshima JAPAN
FA Museum of Fine Arts
W Reimeikan – Prefectural Museum of Culture

Kanchanaburi THAILAND
H JEATH War Museum (River Kwai Bridge)

Kaohsiung TAIWAN
FA Fine Arts Museum ● Mon
ST Science & Technology Museum ● Mon

Karachi PAKISTAN
W National Museum

Kathmandu NEPAL
W Biheswari – National Museum ● Tue

Kolkata (Calcutta) INDIA
FA Academy of Fine Arts ● Mon
H Ashutosh Museum of Indian History ● Sun
FA FO Birla Academy of Art & Culture ● Mon
ST Birla Industrial & Technological Mus. ● Mon
AR H Indian Museum ● Mon

Krasnoyarsk RUSSIAN FEDERATION
FA Surikov Art Museum ● Mon

Kuala Lumpur MALAYSIA
AR FA Muzium Negara
FA *National Art Gallery*
W National Museum of Islamic Arts ● Mon

Kuching MALAYSIA
W *Islamic Museum*; Sarawak Museum

Kunming CHINA
W Kunming City Museum ● Mon

Kurashiki JAPAN
FA Ohara New Art Museum ● Mon

Kuwait City KUWAIT
FA *Tareq Rajab Museum* ● Fri

Kyoto JAPAN
AR *Archaeological Museum* ● Mon
AA FA Kyoto Municipal Museum of Art ● Mon
H Kyoto National Museum; National Museum of Modern Art ● both Mon

Kyzyl RUSSIAN FEDERATION
W Tuva National Museum ● Mon

Lahore PAKISTAN
W Lahore Central Museum ● Sat & 1st Wed

Lhasa CHINA
AR H Potala Palace

Lucknow INDIA
FO *Kaisarbagh's Folk Art Museum* ● Sat & Sun
FA Muhammad Ali Shah Art Gallery
AR State Museum ● Mon

Mandalay MYANMAR
W National Museum & Library

Manila THE PHILIPPINES
AR FA Metropolitan Museum ● Sun
ST Museo Pambata ● Mon
AR *Museum of the Filipino People* ● Mon
W Nayong Pilipino, includes: Museum of Ethnology; Museo ng Buhag; Torogan House

Masqat (Muscat) OMAN
W *Oman Museum* ● Fri

Melaka (Malacca) MALAYSIA
W Istana Ke Sultanan
FO Museum of Ethnology ● Tue

Mumbai (Bombay) INDIA
AA FA Jehangir Art Gallery ● Sat & Sun
W Prince of Wales Museum of W. India ● Mon

Mysore INDIA
FA Jayachamarahendra Art Gallery

Nagasaki JAPAN
H Atomic Bomb Museum

Najran SAUDI ARABIA
W *Najran Museum* ● Thu & Fri

Nanjing CHINA
AR H Municipal Museum; Nanjing Mus. ● Mon; Taiping Heavenly Kingdom History Museum

Novosibirsk RUSSIAN FEDERATION
AR FO Russian Inst. of Archaeology & Ethnography

Osaka JAPAN
FO Japanese Folk Art Museum; National Ethnology Museum ● both Wed
FA National International Art Museum ● Wed
FA AR Osaka Municipal Art Museum ● Mon

Pengosekan INDONESIA
FA Agung Rai Museum of Art (ARRIA)

Peshawar PAKISTAN
AR FO *Peshawar Museum* ● Wed

Phnom Penh CAMBODIA
W National Museum ● Mon

Sakhnin ISRAEL
FO Museum of Palestinian Folk Heritage

Samarqand (Samarkand) UZBEKISTAN
AR Historical Mus. of Uzbek Culture & Art ● Wed

Sana'a (Sana) YEMEN
AA FA Museum of Arts & Crafts ● Fri
W National Museum ● Fri

Sapporo JAPAN
FA Hokkaido Museum of Modern Art; Migishio Kotaro Museum of Art ● both Mon

Seoul REP. OF KOREA
FO National Folk Museum ● Tue
W National Museum ● Mon
FA National Museum of Contemporary Art ● Mon

Shanghai CHINA
FA Art Museum
W Shanghai Museum ● Sun

Shanhaiguan CHINA
AR H Great Wall Museum

Singapore
AR H Asian Civilization Museum ● Mon
H Changi Prison Museum ● Sun
FA Singapore Art Museum ● Mon
ST Singapore Science Centre ● Mon

Sukhothai THAILAND
AR Ramkhamhaeng Museum ● Mon & Tue

Surabaya INDONESIA
FO H Museum Negeri Propinsi Jawa Timur

Surakarta (Solo) INDONESIA
W Radya Pustaka Museum

Tadmur SYRIA
AR Palmyra Archaeological Museum ● Tue

Taichung TAIWAN
FA Taiwan Museum of Art ● Mon
ST National Science Museum

Taipei TAIWAN
AA Chang Foundation Museum ● Mon
FA Fine Arts Museum ● Mon
W National Palace Museum
FO Taiwan Folk Arts Museum

Takayama JAPAN
AA AR Hida Minzuko Kukuokan
FA Hida Minzuko Mura

Tehran IRAN
AA FA Islamic Arts Museum ● Mon
AR *National Museum* ● Mon
FA Tehran Mus. of Contemporary Art ● Fri am

Tel Aviv ISRAEL
AR Eretz Yisra'el Museum (HaAretz Museum)
FA Tel Aviv Museum of Art

Thanjavur INDIA
AR Nayak Durbar Hall Art Museum
AR Rajaraja Cholan Museum

Tokyo JAPAN
FA National Museum of Modern Art; National Museum of Western Art; Tokyo Central Museum of Arts; Tokyo Metropolitan Fine Art Museum ● all Mon
NH Natural Science Museum ● Mon
ST Science & Technology Museum ● Mon
H Shitamachi History Museum ● Mon
AA FA *Suntory Bijutsukan* ● Mon
AR FA Tokyo National Museum ● Mon

Toshkent (Tashkent) UZBEKISTAN
AR H Amur Timur Museum ● Mon
AA Museum of Applied Arts ● Tue
AA AR Museum of the History of the People of Uzbekistan ● Sun
FA State Fine Arts Museum ● Tue

Trivandrum INDIA
FO *Government (Napier) Museum* ● Mon
FA Shri Chitra Art Gallery ● Mon

Ubud BALI, INDONESIA
FA Neka Museum

Ulaanbaatar (Ulan Bator) MONGOLIA
FA Mongolian National Modern Art Gallery; Zanabazar Museum of Fine Arts
AR H National Museum of Mongolian History

Ulan Ude RUSSIAN FEDERATION
AR FO Ethnographical Museum ● Mon
FA Fine Arts Museum ● Mon
AR Mus. of Oriental Art & Buryat History ● Mon

Vadodara (Baroda) INDIA
W Baroda Museum & Picture Gallery

Viangchan (Vientiane) LAOS
AR FA Haw Pha Kaew ● Mon

Vladivostok RUSSIAN FEDERATION
W Arsenev Regional Museum ● Mon
FA Primorsky Art Museum ● Sun & Mon

Xi'an CHINA
H Shaanxi History Museum
W Tang Dynasty Arts Museum

Yangon (Rangoon) MYANMAR
AR FO National Museum ● Fri

Yekaterinburg RUSSIAN FEDERATION
AA FA Fine Arts Museum
AR H History & Local Studies Museum

Yokohama JAPAN
AR Kanagawa Kenritsu Hakubutsukan ● Mon
AA Silk Centre Museum

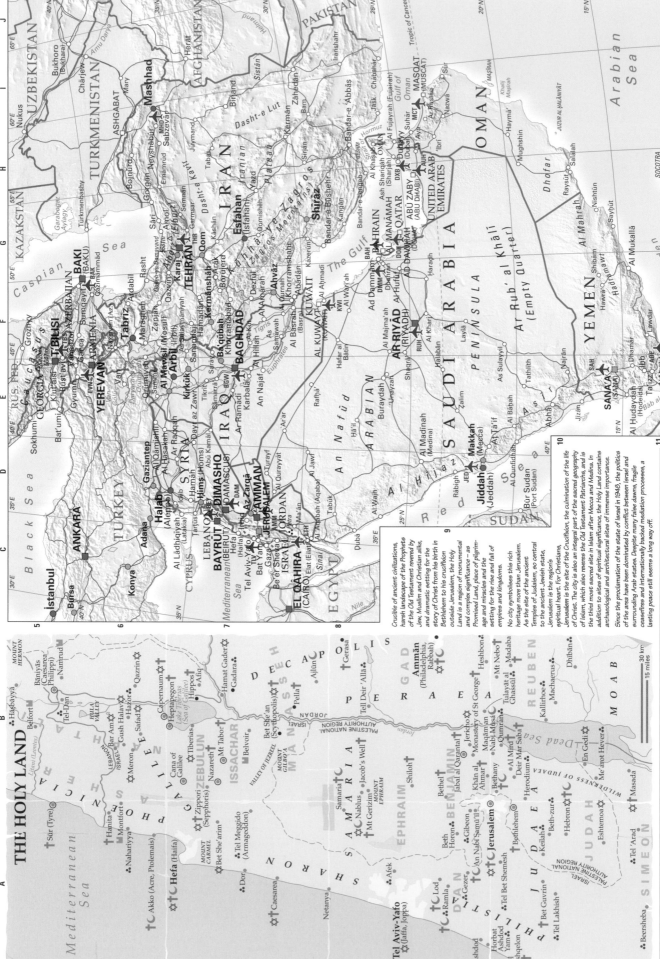

Crucible of ancient civilizations, harsh landscape of the Prophets of the Old Testament revered by Jew, Muslim and Christian alike, and dramatic setting for the story of Christ from his birth in Bethlehem to his crucifixion outside Jerusalem, the Holy Land is a region of monumental and complex significance – as Promised Land, place of pilgrimage and miracles and the setting for the rise and fall of empires and kingdoms.

No city symbolizes the region's spiritual heart. For Christians, Jerusalem is the site of the Crucifixion, the culmination of the life of Christ. The city is also an integral part of the sacred geography of Islam, which also reveres the Old Testament Patriarchs, and is the third most sacred site in Islam after Mecca and Medina. In addition to sites of spiritual significance, the Holy Land contains archaeological and architectural sites of immense importance.

No city epitomizes more than Jerusalem. As the site of the ancient Temples of Judaism, so central to the ancient Jewish state, Jerusalem is the region's spiritual heart.

Since the proclamation of the state of Israel in 1948, the politics of the area have been dominated by conflict between Israel and surrounding Arab states. Despite many false dawns, fragile ceasefires and internationally-backed mediation processes, a lasting peace still seems a long way off.

Legend

☆ Site significant in Judaism
☾ Site significant in Islam
✝ Site significant in Christianity
◎ Important location relating to the life of Jesus
⛫ Crusader castle or fortifications
⚒ Other important historical site
● City of the Decapolis
DAN The Twelve Tribes of Israel
• Other important historical site

Present-day boundaries shown as grey lines

Lambert Equal Area Projection

0 — 400 miles
0 — 800 kilometres

Central Asia & the Silk Road

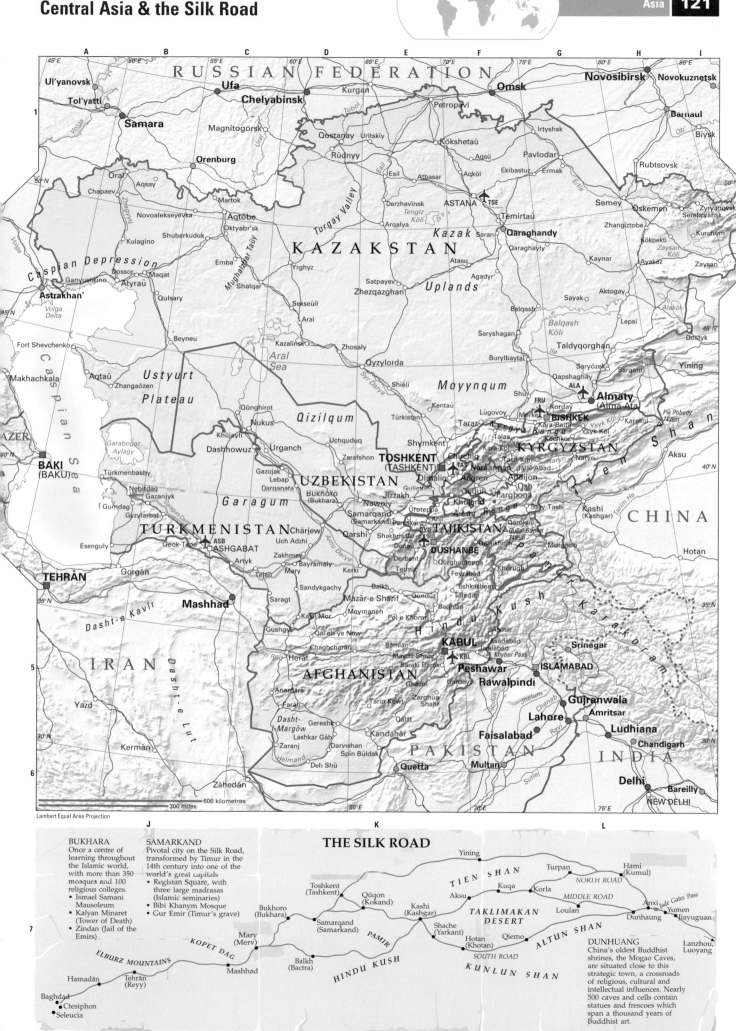

RUSSIAN FEDERATION

KAZAKSTAN

UZBEKISTAN

TURKMENISTAN

IRAN

AFGHANISTAN

PAKISTAN

KYRGYZSTAN

TAJIKISTAN

CHINA

INDIA

Lambert Equal Area Projection

300 miles
600 kilometres

BUKHARA
Once a centre of learning throughout the Islamic world, with more than 350 mosques and 100 religious colleges.
• Ismael Samani Mausoleum
• Kalyan Minaret (Tower of Death)
• Zindan (Jail of the Emirs)

SAMARKAND
Pivotal city on the Silk Road, transformed by Timur in the 14th century into one of the world's great capitals
• Registan Square, with three large madrasas (Islamic seminaries)
• Bibi Khanym Mosque
• Gur Emir (Timur's grave)

THE SILK ROAD

TIEN SHAN

TAKLIMAKAN DESERT

NORTH ROAD

MIDDLE ROAD

SOUTH ROAD

PAMIR

HINDU KUSH

KUNLUN SHAN

ALTUN SHAN

KOPET DAG

ELBURZ MOUNTAINS

DUNHUANG
China's oldest Buddhist shrines, the Mogao Caves, are situated close to this strategic town, a crossroads of religious, cultural and intellectual influences. Nearly 500 caves and cells contain statues and frescoes which span a thousand years of Buddhist art.

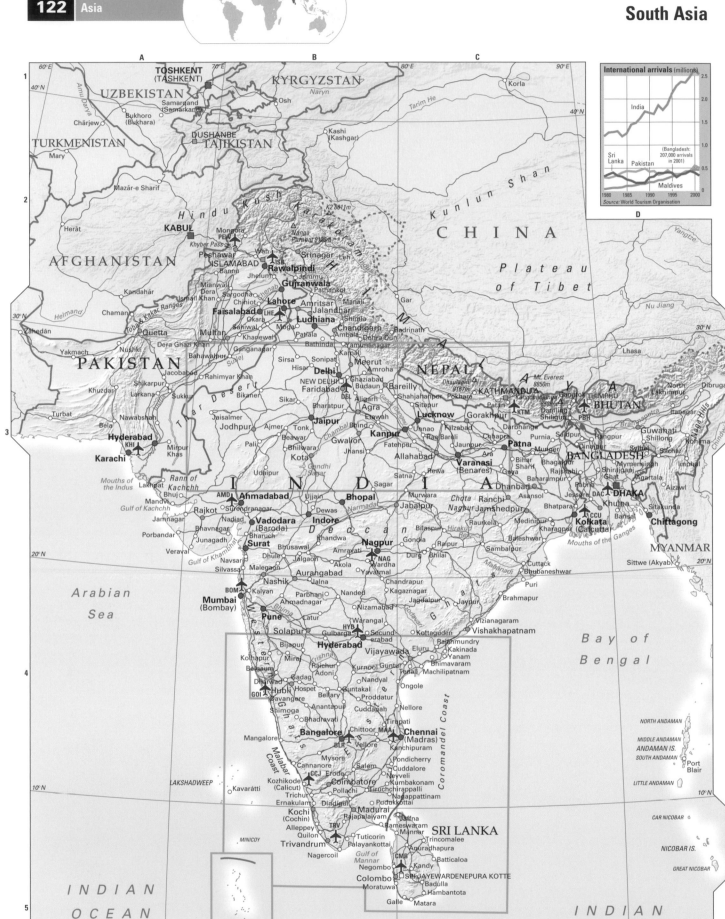

International arrivals (millions)

India

Sri Lanka

Pakistan

Maldives

1980 1985 1990 1995 2000

(Bangladesh: 207,000 arrivals in 2001)

Source: World Tourism Organisation

Lambert Equal Area Projection   Blue boxes indicate focus map coverage

800 kilometres

400 miles

India

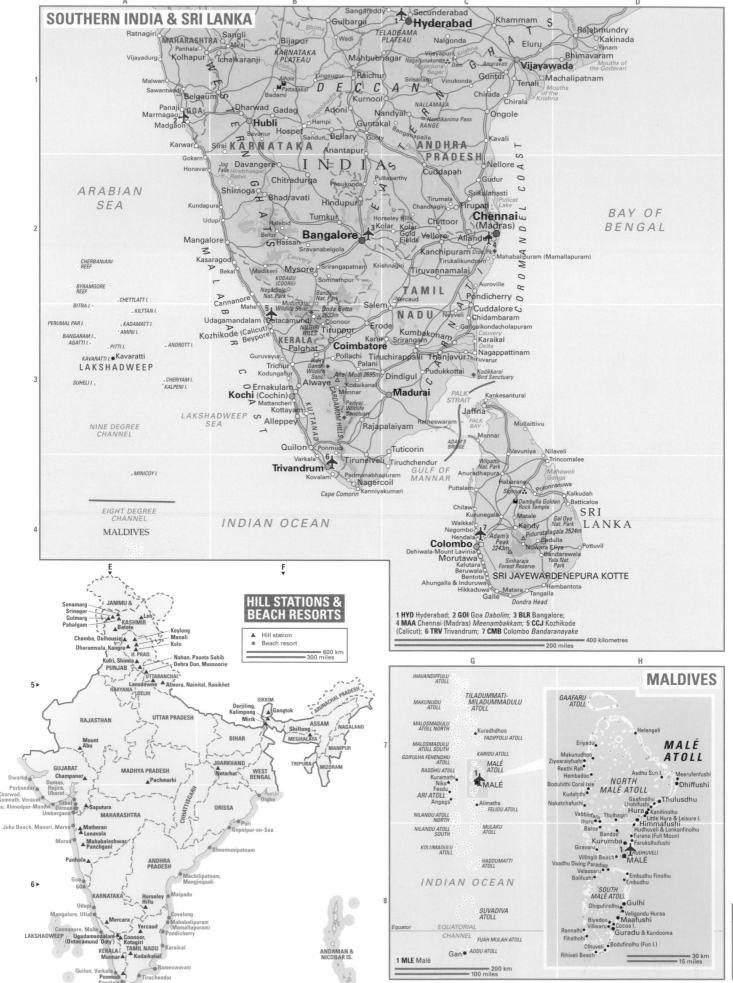

SOUTHERN INDIA & SRI LANKA

ARABIAN SEA

MAHARASHTRA

KARNATAKA PLATEAU

DECCAN

TELADGAMA PLATEAU

KARNATAKA

INDIA

ANDHRA PRADESH

BAY OF BENGAL

Hyderabad

Vijayawada

Bangalore

Chennai (Madras)

TAMIL NADU

KERALA

Coimbatore

Madurai

Kochi (Cochin)

Trivandrum

LAKSHADWEEP

LAKSHADWEEP SEA

NINE DEGREE CHANNEL

EIGHT DEGREE CHANNEL

INDIAN OCEAN

MALDIVES

PALK STRAIT

PALK BAY

GULF OF MANNAR

Jaffna

Colombo

SRI LANKA

SRI JAYEWARDENEPURA KOTTE

1 HYD Hyderabad; 2 GOI Goa *Dabolim*; 3 BLR Bangalore;
4 MAA Chennai (Madras) *Meenambakkam*; 5 CCJ Kozhikode
(Calicut); 6 TRV Trivandrum; 7 CMB Colombo *Bandaranayake*.

200 miles / 400 kilometres

HILL STATIONS & BEACH RESORTS

▲ Hill station
● Beach resort

300 miles / 600 km

JAMMU & KASHMIR

H. PRAD.

PUNJAB

UTTARANCHAL

HARYANA

DELHI

RAJASTHAN

UTTAR PRADESH

SIKKIM

ARUNACHAL PRADESH

ASSAM

NAGALAND

MEGHALAYA

MANIPUR

GUJARAT

MADHYA PRADESH

BIHAR

JHARKHAND

WEST BENGAL

TRIPURA

MIZORAM

MAHARASHTRA

CHHATTISGARH

ORISSA

ANDHRA PRADESH

KARNATAKA

TAMIL NADU

KERALA

LAKSHADWEEP

ANDAMAN & NICOBAR IS.

INDIAN OCEAN

EQUATORIAL CHANNEL

MALDIVES

IHAVANDIFFULU ATOLL

TILADUMMATI-MILADUMMADULU ATOLL

MAKUNUDU ATOLL

MALOSMADULU ATOLL NORTH

FADIFFOLU ATOLL

MALOSMADULU ATOLL SOUTH

GOIFULHA FEHENDHU ATOLL

KARIDU ATOLL

RASDHU ATOLL

MALÉ ATOLL

ARI ATOLL

FELIDU ATOLL

NILANDU ATOLL NORTH

MULAKU ATOLL

NILANDU ATOLL SOUTH

KOLUMADULU ATOLL

HADDUMMATI ATOLL

SUVADIVA ATOLL

FUAH MULAH ATOLL

ADDU ATOLL

MALÉ ATOLL

GAAFARU ATOLL

NORTH MALÉ ATOLL

SOUTH MALÉ ATOLL

MALÉ

1 MLE Malé

1000 metres / 500 metres / Sea level

15 miles / 30 km

100 miles / 200 miles

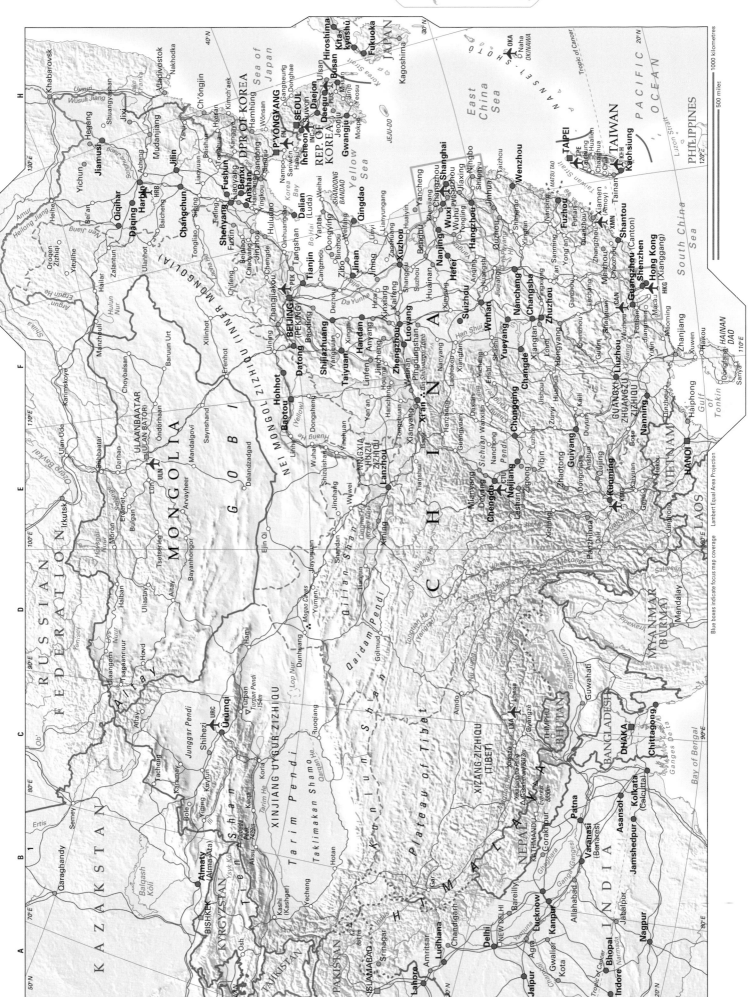

China

Japan

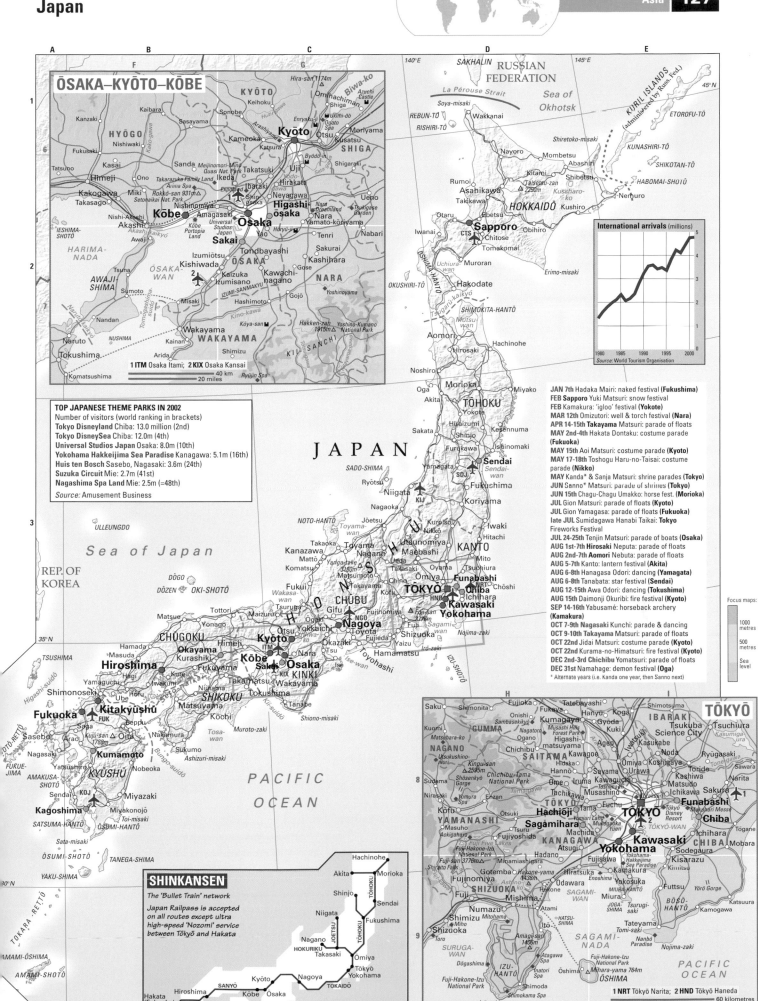

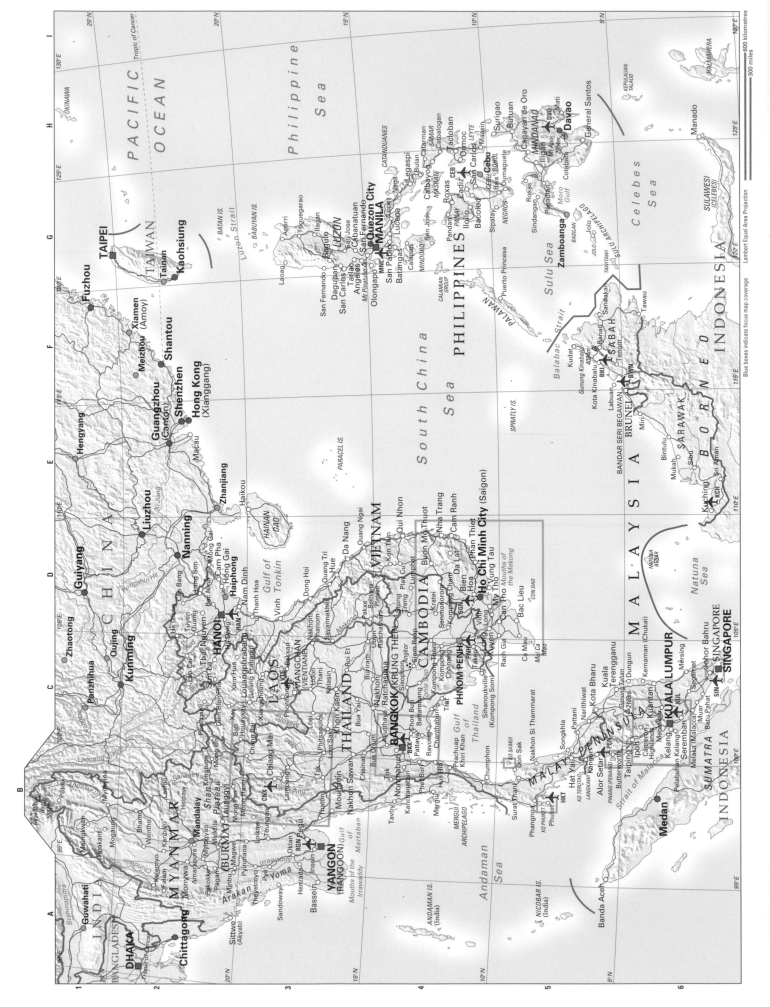

PACIFIC OCEAN

Philippine Sea

South China Sea

Celebes Sea

Sulu Sea

Gulf of Thailand

Andaman Sea

Natuna Sea

INDIA

BANGLADESH

MYANMAR (BURMA)

CHINA

LAOS

THAILAND

VIETNAM

CAMBODIA

PHILIPPINES

MALAYSIA

INDONESIA

BORNEO

SUMATRA

TAIWAN

TAIPEI

Kaohsiung
Tainan

Fuzhou
Xiamen (Amoy)
Meizhou
Shantou
Shenzhen
Guangzhou (Canton)
Hong Kong (Xianggang)
Macau
Zhanjiang
Haikou

Hengyang
Guiyang
Panzhihua
Kunming
Qujing
Zhaotong
Liuzhou
Nanning

HANOI
Haiphong
Nam Dinh
Vinh

VIENTIANE

Chiang Mai

BANGKOK KRUNG THEP

PHNOM PENH

Ho Chi Minh City (Saigon)

Da Nang

YANGON (RANGOON)

Mandalay

KUALA LUMPUR

SINGAPORE

Medan

Banda Aceh

MANILA
Quezon City
Baguio

Davao

MINDANAO

Zamboanga

LUZON

Cebu

DHAKA

Chittagong

Guwahati

BANDAR SERI BEGAWAN

BRUNEI

SABAH

SARAWAK

Kuching

MALAY PENINSULA

Strait of Malacca

Mouths of the Mekong

Gulf of Tonkin

Luzon Strait

Mouths of the Irrawaddy

Gulf of Martaban

Tropic of Cancer

Blue boxes indicate focus map coverage

Lambert Equal Area Projection

600 kilometres

300 miles

Indochina

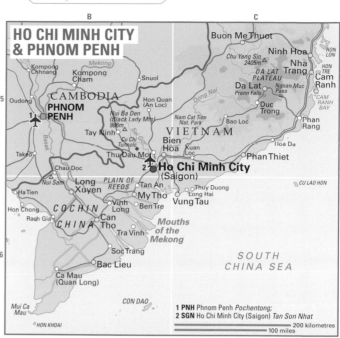

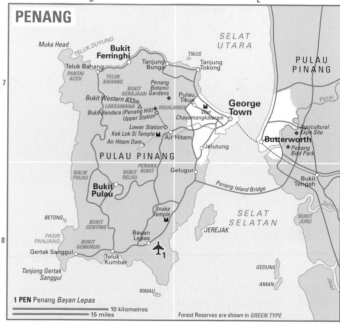

Thailand

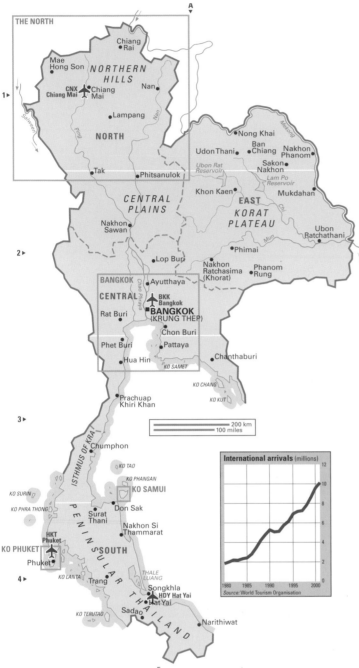

THE NORTH

Chiang Rai, Mae Hong Son, Chiang Mai, CNX, Nan, Lampang, NORTHERN HILLS, NORTH, Silween, Ping, Nong Khai, Ban Chiang, Nakhon Phanom, Udon Thani, Tak, Phitsanulok, Sakon Nakhon, Mekong, Ubon Rat Reservoir, CENTRAL PLAINS, Khon Kaen, Mukdahan, EAST KORAT PLATEAU, Lam Po Reservoir, Nakhon Sawan, Phimai, Mun, Ubon Ratchathani, Lop Buri, Ayutthaya, Nakhon Ratchasima (Khorat), Phanom Rung, BANGKOK, BKK Bangkok, BANGKOK (KRUNG THEP), CENTRAL, Rat Buri, Chon Buri, Phet Buri, Pattaya, Hua Hin, Chanthaburi, KO SAMET, KO CHANG, KO KUT, Prachuap Khiri Khan, ISTHMUS OF KRA, Chumphon, KO TAO, KO PHANGAN, KO SAMUI, KO SURIN, Don Sak, KO PHRA THONG, Surat Thani, Nakhon Si Thammarat, HKT Phuket, KO PHUKET, PENINSULAR SOUTH, Phuket, KO LANTA, Trang, THALE LUANG, KO TERUTAO, Songkhla, HDY Hat Yai, Hat Yai, Sadao, Narithiwat

200 km / 100 miles

International arrivals (millions)
Source: World Tourism Organisation
1980 1985 1990 1995 2000

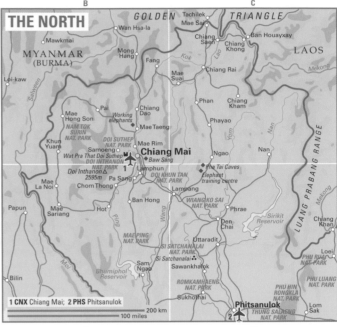

THE NORTH

GOLDEN TRIANGLE, Tachilek, Mae Sai, Mawkmai, Wan Hsa-la, Ban Houayxay, MYANMAR (BURMA), Mong Hang, Chiang Saen, Chiang Khong, LAOS, Loi-kaw, Fang, Mae Suai, Chiang Rai, Mekong, Pai, Chiang Dao, Phan, Chiang Kham, Mae Hong Son, Working elephants, NAM TOK SURIN NAT. PARK, Mae Taeng, Phayao, Nan, Khun Yuam, DOI SUTHEP NAT. PARK, Mae Rim, Samoeng, Wat Pra That Doi Suthep, Chiang Mai, Baw Sang, Ngao, DOI INTHANON NAT. PARK, Lamphun, Tha Tai Caves, Doi Inthanon 2595m, Pa Sang, Elephant training centre, Mae La Noi, Chom Thong, Ban Hong, Lampang, DOI KHUN TAN NAT. PARK, Phrae, LUANG PRABANG RANGE, Chiang Khan, Loei, Papun, Mae Sariang, Hot, WIANG KO SAI NAT. PARK, Den Chai, Sirikit Reservoir, MAE PING NAT. PARK, Uttaradit, SI SATCHANALAI NAT. PARK, Si Satchanalai, Sawankhalok, PHU RUA NAT. PARK, PHU LUANG NAT. PARK, Bilin, Moei, Bhumiphol Reservoir, Sam Ngao, ROMKAMHAENG NAT. PARK, Sukhothai, PHU HIN RONGKLA NAT. PARK, Lom Sak, Phitsanulok, THUNG SALAENG NAT. PARK

1 CNX Chiang Mai; 2 PHS Phitsanulok
200 km / 100 miles

BANGKOK

Phra Phutthabat, KHAO YAI NAT. PARK, Suphan Buri, Sara Buri, Khao Laem 1351m, KHAO KHEAW NAT. PARK, Wat Phai Rong Wua, Aisawan Tippaya Asna, Ayutthaya, WANG TAKHRAI NAT. PARK, Bang Pa-in, Nakhon Nayok, River Kwai Bridge, Kanchanaburi, Tha Chin, Chao Phraya, Wang Takhrai Gardens, Prachin Buri, Mae Klong, Phra Pathom Chedi, Kabin Buri, Ban Pong, Nakhon Pathom, Nonthaburi, BANGKOK (KRUNG THEP), Khok Pip, Thon Buri, Rose garden, Floating market, Sa Keo, Phra Buddha Sothorp, Rat Buri, Damnoan Saduak floating market, Samut Prakan, Chachoengsao, Phanat Nikhom, Samut Sakhon, Crocodile farm, Ancient City, Chon Buri, Samut Songkhram, Bang Saen, Khao Kheaw Zoo, Luang Po Ban Laem, Ban Laem, Ocean World Water Park, KO SICHANG, Si Racha, Wat Phra Sriratana Mahathat, Phet Buri, Laem Chabang, Bira International Racing Circuit, Wang Phetburi Mountain, Ha-ad Chao Samran, BIGHT OF BANGKOK, KO PHOI, KO LAN, Pattaya, Elephant Village, KHAO CHAMAO NAT. PARK, Ban Tah, Jomtien, KANG KRA CHAN NAT. PARK, Cha-Am, KO KHRAM, Nong Nooch Garden, Soontornpoo Monument, Klaeng, Hua Hin, KO SAMAE SAN, Sattahip, Rayong, Ban Klaeng, Samae San, Ban Pae, KO SAMET, KO CHUANG

1 BKK Bangkok Don Muang
100 kilometres / 50 miles

KO PHUKET

PHANG NGA BAY, Sarasin Bridge, KO PANUG, AO TO NONG, Laem Saum, KO LAVAYAI, Mai Khao Beach, KUNG BAY, Bo Sai, Muang Mai, KO NGUM, Nai Yang Beach, Phara, KO RAD, Nai Yang, Wat Phra Thong, ANDAMAN SEA, Thalang, KO NAKA YAI, Tonesai Falls, Heroines monument, KO NAKA NOI, LE PHANG BAY, Bang Kaong Beach, Bang Thao Beach, Saon Beach, Bang Thao, Tha Rua, Laem Yabu, Surin Beach, SAPAM BAY, Singh Beach, KO RUNG, Nam Tok, Katu, Laem Nga, KO MAPOU, PATONG BAY, Patong Beach, Patong, 516m, Phuket, Laem Lumjiag, Karon, KO SIRE, MAKHAM BAY, Karon Beach, Wat Chalong, Makham Beach, KO TAPHAO NOI, Kata, Makham, KO TAPHAO YAI, TANG KEM BAY, Kata Yai Beach, Chalong, Aquarium, Kata Noi Beach, CHALONG BAY, Rawai, Nai Harn Beach, Laem Ka, KO LON, KO PHI PHI, Laem Promthep, Rawai Beach, KO MUN, KO VAO, KO HAE, KO KAEW YAI, KO KAEW NOI, KO RAJA NOI, KO RAJA YAI

1 HKT Phuket
20 kilometres / 10 miles

EASTERN & ORIENTAL EXPRESS

	Distance from Bangkok	
	Kilometres	Miles
Chiang Mai	751	467
Lampang	642	390
Phitsanulok	389	242
Ayutthaya	71	44
Bangkok	0	0
Kanchanaburi	(138)	(86)
Hua Hin	229	142
Hat Yai	945	587
Butterworth	1161	721
Kuala Lumpur	1552	964
Singapore	1946	1209

The Eastern & Oriental Express is a luxury train service operating on two routes: an overnight service between Bangkok and Chiang Mai and a service between Bangkok to Singapore which takes three days and includes guided tours of Kanchanaburi, River Kwai and Penang.

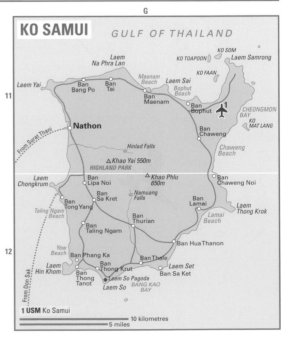

KO SAMUI

GULF OF THAILAND, KO SOM, Laem Na Phra Lan, KO TOAPOON, Laem Samrong, KO FAAN, Laem Yai, Maenam Beach, Maenam, Laem Sai, Bophut Beach, Ban Bang Po, Ban Tai, Ban Bophut, From Surat Thani, Nathon, CHEONGMON BAY, KO MAT LANG, Hinlad Falls, Khao Yai 550m, HIGHLAND PARK, Chaweng Beach, Laem Chongkrum, Ban Lipa Noi, Ban Sa Kret, Khao Phlu 650m, Ban Chaweng, Namuang Falls, Taling Ngam Beach, Ban Tong Yang, Ban Thurian, Ban Lamai, Lamai Beach, Laem Thong Krok, Yow Beach, Ban Phang Ka, Ban Taling Ngam, Ban Hua Thanon, From Don Sak, Laem Hin Khom, Ban Thong Krut, Laem Set, Ban Thong Tanot, Ban Thale, BANG KAO BAY, Laem So Pagoda, Ban Sa Ket, Laem So

1 USM Ko Samui
10 kilometres / 5 miles

1000 metr / 500 metr / Sea level

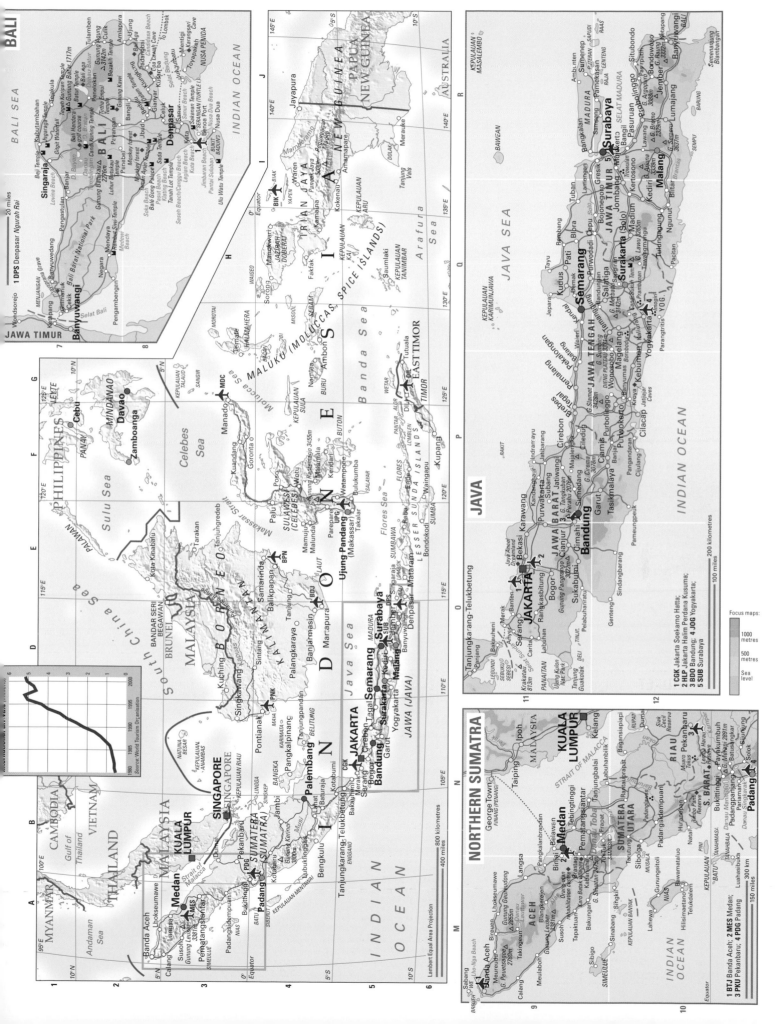

Australasia & Oceania

istance is probably what best characterises Australasia & Oceania: vast distances must be covered to get there and, once arrived, intra-regional distances are often formidable too. This obvious point explains both the region's strengths and its weaknesses as economies and, particularly, as travel destinations. The major weakness is that travel costs, though now falling, are still high (but, on a mile-for-mile basis, far cheaper than many short-haul journeys elsewhere). The major advantage is that many global problems tend to pass the region by. Modern communications have made Australasia & Oceania a seamless part of the 21st century, but physical distance helps protect it from the century's worst problems.

Key facts

Number of Countries	22
Area ('000 sq km)	8,505
Population ('000)	31,516
Population Density (per sq km)	4
Gross National Income (US$m)	454,630
Visitor Arrivals ('000)	9,490
Visitor Receipts (US$m)	12,735
Travel Departures ('000)	5,102
Travel Expenditure (US$m)	7,292

GNI figures relate to 2001. Population figures are taken from the most recent reliable source. Travel figures (WTO) are based on overnight stays, not same-day visitors, and are generally for 2001: where these are unavailable or unreliable, earlier years have been used. Where data for certain countries was not available, this has been regarded as zero. For more information see the Countries A-Z section from page 184.

The regional power-house is Australia, a country over 30 times the size of the UK but with less than one-third of its population. New Zealand, more European in scale, runs it a respectable second by most indicators. Together they account for 97% of the region's GNI and over 70% of its visitors (Guam, with a mainly American clientele, receives 12%). In 2001, the region saw a 6.4% growth in international visitors since 1997. Of the 11 economies in the region that report data to the World Bank, all but two saw GDP growth rise in 2001 against 2000. Australia and New Zealand saw rises of 2.7% and 2.4% respectively. Australia is the world's 15th largest economy: of the other 14, only China, India and Korea grew faster in 2001.

Travel highlights

Of all the many factors which influence travel, three predominate – cost, safety and the desire for new or exciting experiences. The order of importance will depend on personal or international circumstances, but all will be carefully considered before planning any trip, particularly a long-haul one.

On all three measures, Australasia and Oceania scores highly. For new and exciting experiences, the region can hardly be matched. From cosmopolitan cities to sun-drenched Pacific beaches, from the awesome emptiness of the Outback to the staggering landscapes of New Zealand or the wonders of the Great Barrier Reef, there truly is something for everyone. The unspoiled quality is also a major selling point. '100% Pure' is Tourism New Zealand's current strap-line, and it could justly be applied to most of the other countries in the region.

Although travel costs are high, there are more bargains to be had than ever before. The 'holiday of a lifetime' appeal is still strong, but it is no longer necessary to write out the cheque of a lifetime to pay for it. Most travellers agree: the repeat-visitor figure is on the increase – 57% of 2002 visitors to Australia were making at least their second trip. Moreover an increasing number, including nearly a third of those from the UK, were seeing themselves as 'budget travellers' in 2002. For Australia, the good news was that most were prepared, on arrival, to spend a bit of what they saved on their air fares: average visitor expenditure increased by over 25% between 1999 and 2003.

Just as importantly, the region is regarded as being safe in a way that large parts of the world are currently not. Crime levels are lower than those in most of the countries from which visitors come. Now that Fiji's recent tensions have eased, there are no wars. As for terrorism, the countries have neither the

■ Economies

The region's two largest economies, 2001
Source: World Bank/International Monetary Fund

	GNI (US$ bn) 2001	Annual GDP growth rate (%) 2001	2002	est 2003	est 2004
Australia	385.9	2.7	3.8	3.0	3.7
New Zealand	51.0	2.4	4.2	2.7	3.0

■ Aussie rules

International visitor arrivals, 2002 (millions)
Sources: WTO/ATC

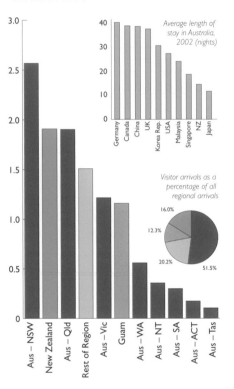

internal problems to encourage it, nor the external policies to attract it from elsewhere. The Bali bombing of 2002 claimed many Australian lives, but there is little evidence to suggest similar attacks within the region are likely. Most foreign interventions, such as Australia's in East Timor, have been uncontroversial. Australia and New Zealand have had an uneasy relationship with their pasts, but generally equitable settlements with the Aborigines and Maoris have been achieved without serious conflict. In general, Australasian influence on world affairs has been conciliatory rather than aggressive.

The same cannot be said for the sports in which they excel. Visitor figures from the UK, in particular, are seasonally boosted by sports enthusiasts making the long journey to witness generally resounding defeats on the cricket and rugby fields of the Antipodes.

If the Australians play sports well, they also know how to organise them. The 2000 Sydney Olympics were widely regarded as the best ever and inspired interest in the country and – more, importantly – boosted visitor arrivals and spending. Australian GDP attributed to inbound tourism increased by A$1.5 billion (24%) in 2000. These figures have been more or less maintained in 2001 and 2002. Across the Tasman Sea, the stunning cinematography of *The Lord of the Rings* films is likely to give a significant, though less quantifiable, boost to New

Zealand's tourism. The positive impact of both these different showcases is likely to be felt for some time. The 2003 Rugby World Cup in Australia and the 2006 Melbourne Commonwealth Games seem set to stimulate further growth.

An additional motivation is visiting friends and relations. In 2002, 18% of trips to Australia and New Zealand were mainly for this reason. Between the two countries, the figure is higher still.

Both countries are supportive of each other's travel product: New Zealanders make up 33% of visitors to Australia, and Australians 16% of visitors to New Zealand. Other major markets – mainly the USA, the UK and Japan – are spread widely across the world, thus minimising the effects of regional downturns. Both see themselves as being part of the Asian region, as well as members of the far-flung English-speaking world, and both have been quick to develop travel links with the vast and fast-growing Chinese market. Varied travel products – in each case a unique blend of the exotic, the untamed and the familiar – are clearly and effectively marketed worldwide. On the face of it, the situation appears healthy.

Airline problems

The one cloud on the horizon, however, is the crisis amongst the world's major airlines. Route cutbacks have been one result, and Asia-Pacific services have been heavily hit. This will have a particularly serious effect on the Pacific islands, which are generally visited *en route* to somewhere else. As some islands derive up to 80% of their GDP from tourism, and as many rely on a fairly small number of visitors and markets to produce this revenue, the effects of the reduction of even a few air services can be deeply problematic. As in other areas of the world, the current pace is being set by the budget airlines. In June 2003, Virgin Blue announced a proposed service linking Australia and New Zealand with Fiji and Vanuatu (although probably under a new brand name). Many Pacific islands will hope this development will be the first of many.

The collapse of Ansett in mid-September 2001 (for reasons unconnected with the terrorist attacks in the USA) disrupted internal Australian travel patterns, particularly to remote areas. Although many routes were soon taken up by other operators, total capacity took time to return to August 2001 levels.

Travel trends

Adventure holidays have long been popular in Australia and New Zealand. There is a wide range of

■ Best customers

Australia's top ten international markets by average per-day spending in 2002 (A$) *Source: ATC*

1	Singapore	147	6	Taiwan	105
2	Japan	122	7	Malaysia	104
3	Indonesia	118	8	Thailand	103
	USA	118		Korea, Rep.	103
5	China – HK	112	10	China	95

- Australasia & Oceania (A&O) occupies 6.3% of the world's land area and is home to 0.5% of the world's population.
- A&O's combined GDI is US$454.6 billion, 1.5% of the world's total.
- A&O accounts for 1.4% of global travel arrivals and 0.8% of departures.
- International travel and tourism contributed US$12.6 billion to A&O's economy in 2001.
- Australia dominates the travel economy of the region, accounting for 50% of all international visitors, 60% of all international travel receipts, 70% of all international departures and 80% of all international expenditure.
- If the UK had the same population density as Australia it would have about 600,000 people, rather than about 59 million.
- If Western Australia were a country, it would be the tenth largest in the world.
- Sydney spent over A$3.3 billion of public and private money on infrastructure and facilities prior to hosting the 2000 Olympics. Over 35 new hotels opened in the run-up to the event.
- New Zealand's receipts from international travel and tourism doubled between 1997 and 2002.
- 26% of 2002 visitors to Australia researched their trip on the internet before departure: 13% did so in 2000.
- The longest straight stretch of rail track in the world — 478 kilometres — is between Nurina in Western Australia and Ooldea in South Australia.
- An estimated 3.5 million British nationals were living in Australia in 2001, an increase of some 300,000 compared to 1997.
- British visitors to Australia on average stay twice as long than Singaporean ones, but the Singaporeans spend nearly twice as much per day while they're there.
- Australia has won the Cricket World Cup three times (1987, 1999 & 2003), more than any other country.
- In 1893, New Zealand became the first country in the world to extend the vote to women.
- Caroline Island in Kiribati (pronounced 'Kiribass') was renamed Millennium Island after it became the first place on earth to see the sun rise on the 21st century. To do this, that part of the island republic redefined its time as being 14 hours ahead of GMT.
- The islands of French Polynesia are spread over an area of ocean about the size of Western Europe; yet, put together, they would comfortably fit inside the US state of Connecticut.

landscapes, many comparatively close to major centres. Touring is also a major growth area in the form of self-drive cars, coach tours and, increasingly, motorhomes. Rail travel is also increasing, particularly on the scenic routes.

The cities are among the most cosmopolitan in the world, each with a unique blend of Asian, European, American and native ingredients.

The region features on an increasing number of world cruises. With longer cruises becoming more attractive, many ports in the area are visited by ships originating from South-East Asia.

Australia
Around 80% of visitors do not spend a night away from the key attractions of the six main cities, the Gold Coast and Tropical North Queensland. 60% of all visitors spent some time in Sydney. The average length of stay is 27 days, but for some markets, such as Canada and the UK, this is closer to 40. About 33% of travellers are on a tour or package.

- New South Wales is Australia's most visited state. The state capital, Sydney, is Australia's main gateway. The state has superb surfing conditions as well as skiing in the Blue Mountains.

- Queensland's main attractions are its state capital

■ Leading gateways
Top-selling gateway destinations, ex-UK, 2003
Source: Travel2

| 1 Sydney | 3 Brisbane | 5 Perth |
| 2 Auckland | 4 Melbourne | 6 Christchurch |

of Brisbane, the Gold Coast, the Great Barrier Reef and the tropical north. The Whitsunday Islands are becoming popular, as is the area around Cape Tribulation.

- Western Australia occupies the western third of the country, with cosmopolitan Perth as its capital. It is famed for the unique Wave Rock and Pinnacles geological formations.

- Victoria is home to Australia's second largest city, Melbourne, and many national parks. The Great Southern Touring Route is growing in popularity.

- Northern Territory was made famous by the *Crocodile Dundee* films. Top attractions are the Outback, the town of Alice Springs and Australia's greatest icon, Uluru (Ayers Rock). The rail extension from Alice Springs to Darwin is expected to boost travel to the region.

New Zealand
The Northern/Auckland district is visited by 74% of travellers. 25% of visitors also go to Australia in the same trip. House rentals and stays in farms and family homes have increased by around 125% since 1997. Only 20% of visitors are on a tour or package.

- New Zealand's scenery is exceptional, and includes some of the best wilderness walking itineraries in the world. Touring routes include the Caitlins in South Island.

- The major cities, though small by European and American standards, are cosmopolitan and sophisticated. Specific attractions include Auckland's Sky Tower, the southern hemisphere's tallest structure.

- Luxury lodge-style accommodation is attracting an increasing number of guests.

- Geo-thermal sites remain the most popular single type of attraction, closely followed by beaches.

Pacific islands
As discussed above, these are mainly stop-over destinations. They offer some of the most idyllic and unspoiled beaches in the world, providing a welcome break on many long-haul and round-the-world trips. Top island destinations include:

- Fiji — watersports and hiking are the main attractions. The country is recovering from recent unrest, and indeed benefitted from being seen by many Australians as a safe post-Bali replacement destination. Remoter islands such as Treasure Island and Castaway Island are increasing in popularity.

- French Polynesia — a tropical taste of France, although in 1999 American visitors exceeded French ones for the first time. The economy is one of the most tourism-reliant in the world: a French-backed plan is currently in place to address this.

- Guam — the island has long been both a popular travel destination, particularly from the American and Asian markets, and is the site of an important US military base. A combination of a decline in visitors from Japan (Guam's biggest market) and US military cutbacks have led to a decline in its fortunes. None the less, the island is making significant investment in its tourism and other infrastructures.

- Northern Mariana Islands — a compact group roughly half-way between Australia and Japan, and popular with the American market. There are many shipwrecks dating back to the Pacific conflict in the Second World War, some of which can be dived.

Problem areas
- The biggest challenge for the Pacific island states is that of developing sustainable and diverse

■ Top earners
Receipts from foreign travel, 2001 (millions)
Sources: WTO/ATC

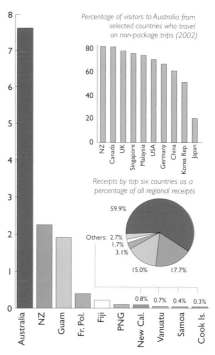

Percentage of visitors to Australia from selected countries who travel on non-package trips (2002)

Receipts by top six countries as a percentage of all regional receipts

economies. These generally low-lying countries also face the threats posed by rising sea levels.

- From most of the world, the flying times to the region are considerable. Much of the publicity surrounding deep vein thrombosis (DVT) has centred on ultra-long haul flights as experienced by travellers to the Antipodes.

- Australia has many species of highly venomous plant, reptile, insect and marine life.

- For water-sports enthusiasts and divers, sea-rescue facilities in some of the Pacific islands may not be comprehensive. Medical facilities may also be basic.

- The return of political problems in Fiji cannot be ruled out. Sporadic unrest, often due to ethnic conflicts, is also a risk in the Solomon Islands.

■ Visitors
Visitor arrivals 2001.
Source: WTO

	Visitors (thousands)	Change since 1997
Australia	4,856	12.5%
New Zealand	1,910	27.6%
Guam	1,160	-16.1%
Northern Mariana Is.	438	-36.1%
Fiji Is.	348	-3.1%
French Polynesia	228	26.7%
New Caledonia	101	-3.8%
Samoa	88	29.4%
Cook Is.	75	50.0%
Palau	54	-27.0%
Papua New Guinea	54	-18.2%
Vanuatu	53	6.0%
American Samoa	44	69.2%
Tonga	32	23.1%
Solomon Is.	21	31.3%
Micronesia, Fed. States	15	-11.8%
Marshall Is.	5	-15.6%
Kiribati	5	-9.8%
Niue	2	16.7%
Tuvalu	1	20.0%
(Figures not available for Nauru or Wallis & Futuna.)		

Thanks to: David Ezra of the Saltmarsh Partnership; Travel2; James Cummings of ATC (Australia); Emma Humphreys of ATC (London); Penny Locke; Graeme Payne; Gary Bowerman.

Oceania

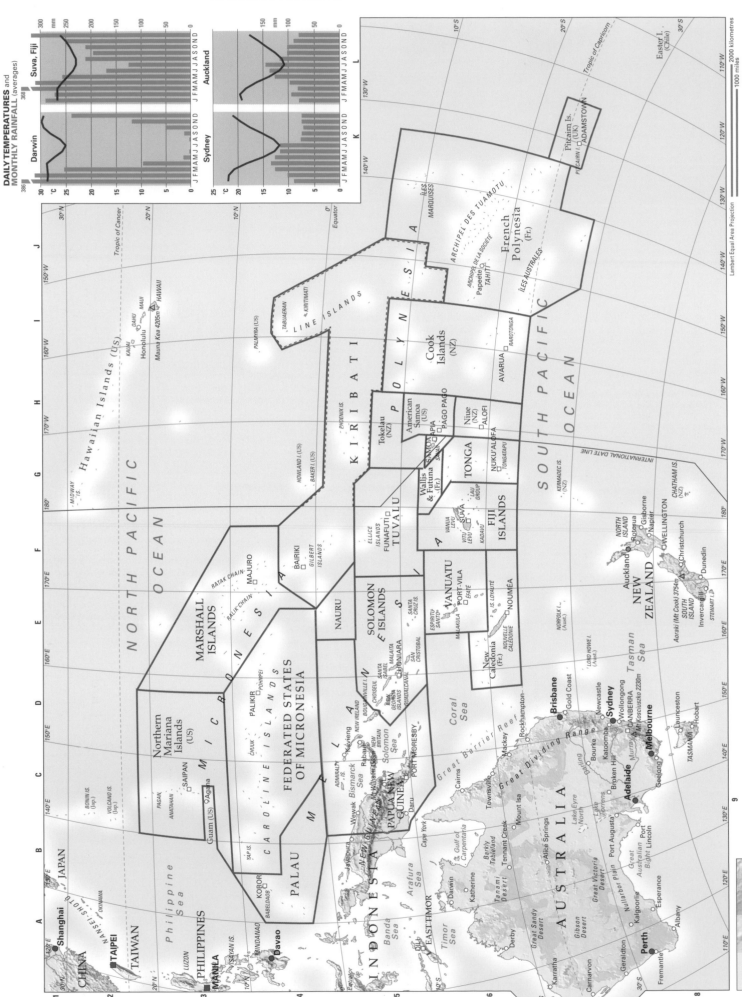

DAILY TEMPERATURES and MONTHLY RAINFALL (averages)

Australia

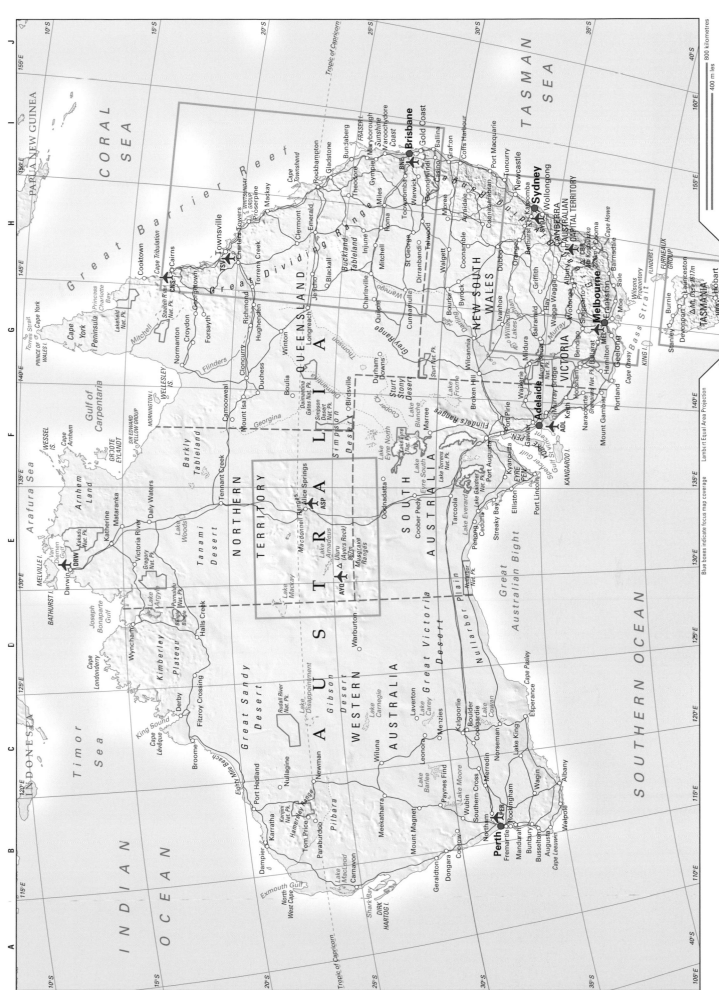

JAN Australian Tennis Open (**Melbourne**)
JAN Sydney Festival
JAN Montsalvet Jazz Festival (**Eltham** *NE Melbourne*)
JAN 26th Australia Day (**Sydney & nationwide**)
JAN-FEB Perth International Arts Festival
FEB/MAR Sydney Gay and Lesbian Mardi Gras
MAR Adelaide Arts Festival; biennial, even years
APR Barossa Valley Vintage Festival; biennial, odd years (**SA**)
APR 25th ANZAC Day
JUN Melbourne International Film Festival

JUN Barunga Sports Festival (**Beswick Aboriginal Land NT** *near Katherine*)
JUL Camel Cup: camel racing (**Alice Springs NT**)
AUG Shinju Matsuri: oriental festival (**Broome WA**)
AUG Mount Isa Rodeo (**QL**)
SEP Bathurst 1000 Road Races (**NS**)
SEP Birdsville Races (**QL**)
SEP Warana Arts Festival (**Brisbane**)
SEP Melbourne International Festival of the Arts
NOV Melbourne Cup: horse race
DEC 26th Sydney-Hobart Yacht Race

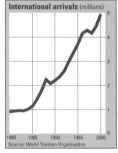

International arrivals (millions)

Source: World Tourism Organisation

LONG-DISTANCE RAIL SERVICES

In addition to the services shown here, Australia has its own version of the Orient Express – the Great South Pacific Express – offering various services between Sydney, Canberra, Brisbane & Cairns, including Barrier Reef, vineyard and other guided tours

Diagrammatic only: not to scale

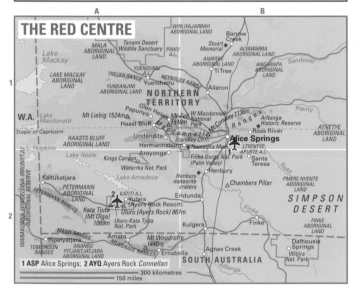

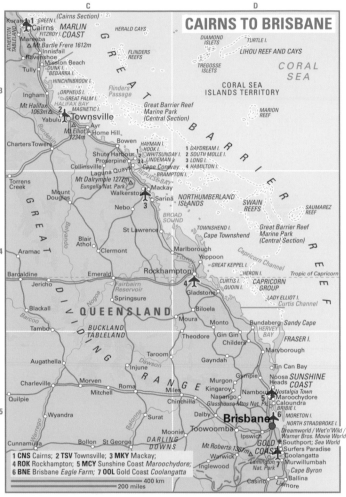

CAIRNS TO BRISBANE

1 **CNS** Cairns; 2 **TSV** Townsville; 3 **MKY** Mackay;
4 **ROK** Rockhampton; 5 **MCY** Sunshine Coast *Maroochydore*;
6 **BNE** Brisbane *Eagle Farm*; 7 **OOL** Gold Coast *Coolangatta*

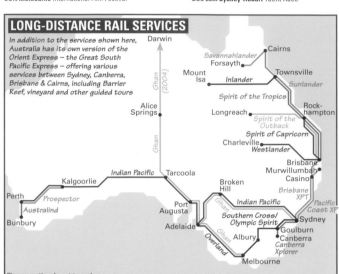

THE RED CENTRE

1 **ASP** Alice Springs; 2 **AYQ** Ayers Rock *Connellan*

300 kilometres
150 miles

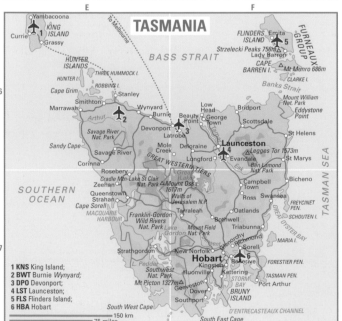

TASMANIA

1 **KNS** King Island;
2 **BWT** Burnie *Wynyard*;
3 **DPO** Devonport;
4 **LST** Launceston;
5 **FLS** Flinders Island;
6 **HBA** Hobart

150 km
75 miles

SYDNEY TO MELBOURNE

1 **SYD** Sydney *Kingsford Smith*; 2 **CBR** Canberra;
3 **ABX** Albury; 4 **MEL** Melbourne *Tullamarine*

300 kilometres
150 miles

1000 metres
500 metres
Sea level

New Zealand

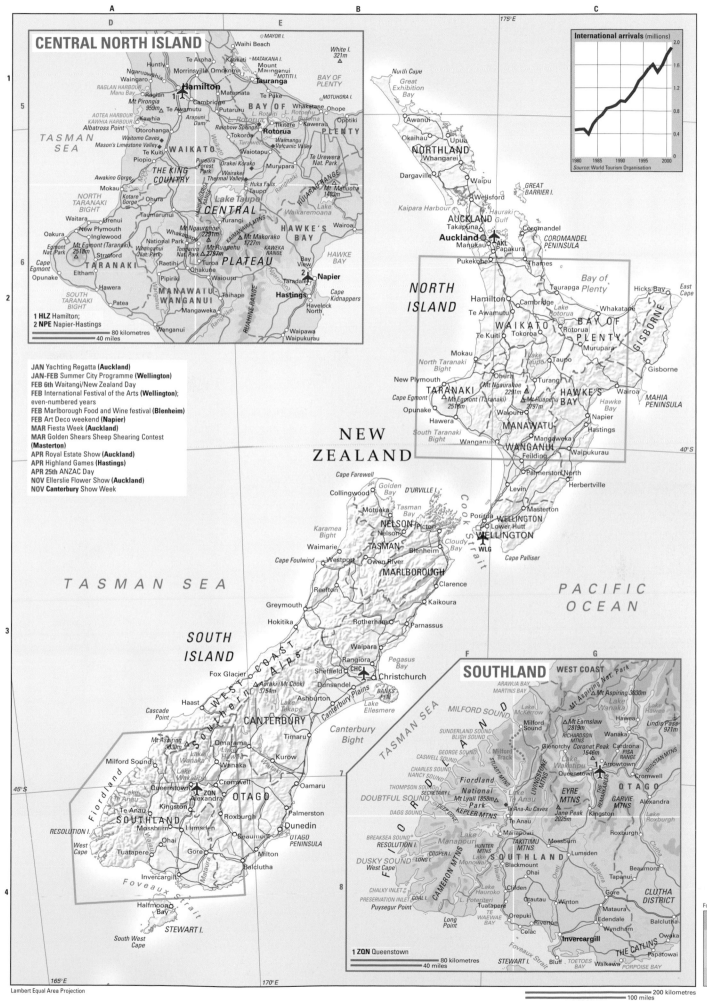

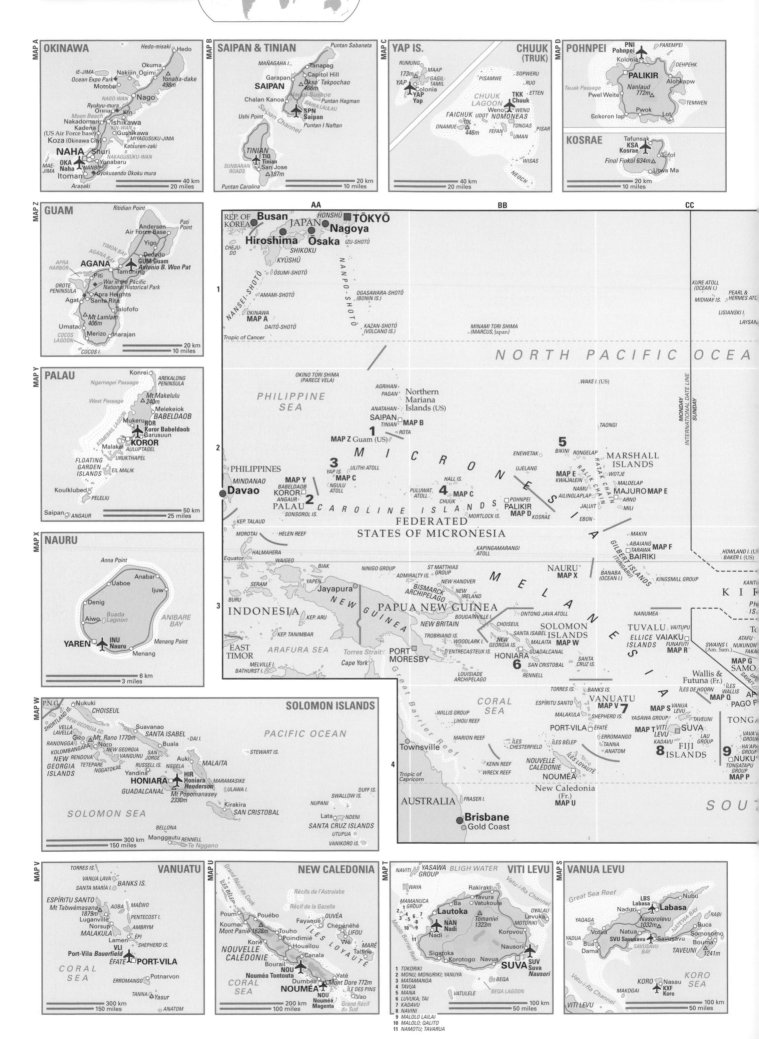

MAP E

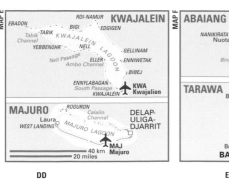

KWAJALEIN
EBADON · ROI-NAMUR · NELL · BIGI · EDGIGEN · TABIK *Tabik Channel* · YEBBENOHR · NELL · *Nell Passage Ambo Channel* · KWAJALEIN LAGOON · GELLINAM · ENNIWETAK · ELLER · BIGEJ · ENNYLABAGAN · *South Passage KWAJALEIN* · ✈ KWA Kwajalein

MAJURO
ROGURON · *Calalin Channel* · Laura · WEST LANDING · MAJURO LAGOON · DELAP-ULIGA-DJARRIT · ✈ MAJ Majuro

40 km / 20 miles

MAP F

ABAIANG
Takarano · NANIKIRATA · Nuotoea · Koinaa · ABF Abaiang · *LAGOON* · TEIRIO-*Bingham Channel* · Tuarabu · Tabontebike · Tebanga

TARAWA
30 km / 15 miles
Buariki · Notoue · Kainaba · TRW Tarawa Bonriki ✈ · *LAGOON* · Bonriki · Betio · BAIRIKI · Teaoraereke

MAP G

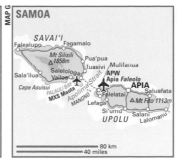

SAMOA
SAVAI'I · Falealupo · Fagamalo · Mt Silisili △1858m · Pua'pua · Tuasivi · Mulifanua · Sala'ilua · Salelologa · Vailoa · APW · *Apolima-Strait* · APIA · Apia *Faleolo* · Cape Asuisui · PALAULI BAY · MXS Maota · MANONO · *Falelatai* · Saluafata · Si'umu · Lefaga · △Mt Fito 1113m · Salani · Lalomanu · *UPOLU*

80 km / 40 miles

MAP H

AMERICAN SAMOA
Nat. Park of American Samoa · Cape Matatula · Fagasa · PAGO PAGO · Alolau · Tula · Cape Taputapu · 653m△ · Uttulei · AUNU'U · *TUTUILA* · Leone · PPG Pago Pago · Coconut Point · *LEONE BAY* · Futiga · *PAGO PAGO HARBOR* · Vaitogi · Steps Point

Tumu Mtn 494m△ · Piamafua Mtn 639m · Lata Mtn 966m · *MANU'A GROUP* · *OFU* · *OLOSEGA* · *TA'U* · Maia · Luma · TAV Tau ✈ · Nat. Park of American Samoa · Siufaalele Point

20 km / 10 miles

MAP I

TABUAERAN (FANNING I.)
North Cape · Canoe Passage · Nabari · Rapa Passage · Paelau · *LAGOON* · TNV Tabuaeran ✈

KIRITIMATI (CHRISTMAS I.)
XCH Kiritimati ✈ · London · North-East Point · Paris · NORMANS LAGOON · Banana · BAY OF WRECKS · Poland · *The Isles Lagoon* · Fresh Water Lagoons

30 km / 15 miles

MAP DD / EE / FF

The names of some South Pacific islands have become synonymous with unspoilt, pristine coral reefs and an exciting, vibrant fish life whereas others have become the very byword for shipwrecks. Many of these destinations already have a well-established diving infrastructure.

The Pacific's premier diving sites:

GUAM (1)
In addition to numerous wrecks from WW2, Guam has a reputation for drift dives along a wide choice of reefs with outstanding marine life. Two historic shipwrecks lie together: Japanese *Tokai Maru* & German *SMS Cormoran*.

PALAU (2)
Information is limited but Palau claims one of Micronesia's largest collections of WW2 shipwrecks. Reef walls, coral gardens and stunning drop-offs all teeming with marine life and an abundance of large pelagics.

YAP (3)
Famous amongst divers for its large population of resident manta rays, Yap also boasts more than 200 species of coral in addition to some exciting underwater cave systems. The outer coral reefs teem with tropical fish and invertebrates where shark and turtle are common.

CHUUK LAGOON (4) (formerly Truk Lagoon)
World-famous ship graveyard of approx. 70 Japanese support vessels sunk in 1944 by US forces. Probably the world's no. 1 shipwreck destination for scuba divers.

BIKINI ATOLL (5)
Outstanding wreck diving; a US aircraft carrier, US submarine and Japanese battleship were used in 1946 when the US detonated an atomic bomb to test the effects of a nuclear explosion on a naval fleet. The resultant radioactive fallout left Bikini untouched for almost 50 years. With marine life virtually untouched during that time, there are outstanding examples of shark, manta ray, marlin, tuna and turtle.

GUADALCANAL (6)
The scene of fierce WW2 naval battles and today, 'Iron Bottom Sound' contains hundreds of wrecked aeroplanes and ships, providing an exciting selection of dive sites. The rest of the Islands have excellent natural underwater terrain & marine life.

VANUATU (7)
The many ship and aeroplane wrecks from WW2 include the 22,288 tonne *President Coolidge* - one of the largest accessible shipwrecks in the Pacific. Elsewhere there are spectacular coral reefs, prolific marine life, cave diving and a genuine 'blue hole'

FIJI ISLANDS (8)
Hundreds of small islands where the underwater environment is largely unvisited and unspoilt. Well known for abundant 'soft corals', there are also a number of historic shipwrecks in addition to spectacular walls, caves and large pelagics such as shark, manta ray, turtle, pilot whale and dolphin.

TONGA (9)
Known for its caves, drop-offs and pinnacles, as well as opportunities for diving with whales at certain times of the year, but facilities are limited.

HAWAII (10)
Known for passing migratory whales, Hawaii boasts an almost unique underwater terrain formed by volcanic action with lava formations, walls, caves, archways and lava-tubes - all with abundant marine life. Night diving with manta rays.

Hawaiian Islands (US)
SEE USA SECTION
FRENCH FRIGATE SHOALS · NECKER I. · NIHOA · KAUAI · NIIHAU · OAHU · MOLOKAI · MAUI · Honolulu · **10** · LANAI · HAWAII

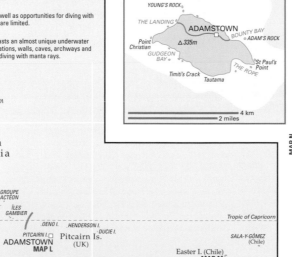

UNITED STATES OF AMERICA · Los Angeles · CHANNEL IS. · San Diego · Phoenix · GUADALUPE · Hermosillo · BAJA CALIFORNIA · MEXICO · Culiacán · *Tropic of Cancer*

HOWLAND REEF (US) · PALMYRA ATOLL (US) · TERAINA · TABUAERAN (FANNING I.) · **MAP I** · KIRITIMATI (CHRISTMAS I.) · JARVIS I. (US) · LINE ISLANDS · MALDEN I. · STARBUCK I. · PENRHYN · RAKAHANGA · MANIHIKI · PUKAPUKA ATOLL · NASSAU · SUWARROW · VOSTOK I. · MILLENNIUM I. (CAROLINE I.) · FLINT I. · American Samoa (US) · MANU'A GROUP · Cook Islands (NZ) · RAROTONGA · AVARUA · MAUKE · MANGAIA · PALMERSTON · AITUTAKI ATOLL · **MAP N**

NUKU HIVA · **MAP J** · ÎLES MARQUISES · HIVA OA · FATU HIVA · UA HUKA · ÎLES DU DÉSAPPOINTEMENT · MANIHI · RANGIROA · ARCHIPEL DES TUAMOTU · French Polynesia (Fr.) · HUAHINE · BORA BORA · RAIATEA · **MAP K** · MOOREA · PAPEETE · Tahiti · ARCHIPEL DE LA SOCIÉTÉ · GROUPE ACTÉON · ÎLES DU DUC DE GLOUCESTER · ÎLES GAMBIER · ÎLES AUSTRALES · MARIA · RURUTU · RIMATARA · TUBUAI · RAIVAVAE · ÎLOTS DE BASS · OENO I. · HENDERSON I. · DUCIE I. · PITCAIRN I. · ADAMSTOWN · **MAP L** · Pitcairn Is. (UK) · SALA-Y-GÓMEZ (Chile) · Easter I. (Chile) · **MAP M**

PACIFIC OCEAN

Scale at Equator
3000 kilometres / 1500 miles

MAP K

TAHITI & MOOREA
MOZ Moorea ✈ · *Pointe Vénus* · Papenoo · Mt Tohiea △1207m · Afareaitu · PAPEETE · Faaa · *TAHITI* · Haapiti · Mont Orohena △2241m · Tiarei · Taapuna · PPT Papeete Faaa ✈ · *MOOREA* · Punaauia · *Isthme de Taravao* · Taravao · Maraa · Papeari · Mataiea · Papeari · *PRESQU'ÎLE DE TAIARAPU* · Tautira · Teahupoo · △Mont Mairepui 1306m

40 km / 20 miles

MAP J

NUKU HIVA
NHV Nuku Hiva ✈ · Aakapa · Cap Matautoa · *TERRE DÉSERTE* · △Mont Tekao 1224m · Hatiheu · Hooumi · Taiohae · Cap Tikapo · Hakaui

HIVA OA
Hanamenu · Hanaiapa · AUQ Atuona ✈ · Puamau · Cap Balguerie · Pointe Kiukiu · Mont Temetiu △1276m · Atuona · Hekeani · BAIE TAAOA · △Mont Mairepui 1306m · Taaoa · Pointe Teaehoa

30 km / 15 miles

MAP L

PITCAIRN ISLAND
YOUNG'S ROCK · THE LANDING · ADAMSTOWN · BOUNTY BAY · ADAM'S ROCK · Point Christian · △335m · GUDGEON BAY · St Paul's Point · Timiti's Crack · THE ROPE · Tautama

4 km / 2 miles

MAP M

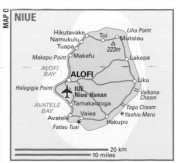

EASTER ISLAND (RAPA NUI / ISLA DE PASCUA)
Cabo Norte · Anakena · Ovahe · Te Pito Kura · △Terevaka 510m · Rano Raraku quarry · Puakatiki △400m · *POIKE* · Cabo Roggeveen · Puna Pau quarry · Tongariki · CALETA HOTUITI · Hanga Piko · Hanga Roa · Punta Cuidado · Orongo · Mataveri · CALETA OVAHE · Vaihu · △ · IPC Vinapu · △ Easter I. *Mataveri* · Cabo Sur · MOTU NUI · Rano Kau 410m · MOTU TAUTARA

10 km / 5 miles

MAP N

AITUTAKI ATOLL
Maungapu 124m△ · Arutanga Passage · AITUTAKI · Arutanga · EE · Nikaupara · Tautu · MAINA · *LAGOON* · AKAIAMI · TEKOPUA · TAPUAETAI

RAROTONGA
RAR Rarotonga ✈ · AVARUA · Nika · Avatiu · Matavera · Arorangi · Te Manga 652m · NGONEROA · Titikaveka · Muri

20 km / 10 miles

MAP R

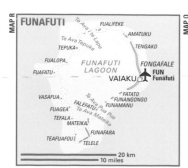

FUNAFUTI
Te Ava i te Lape · FUALIFEKE · AMATUKU · Te Ava Tepuka · TENGAKO · TEPUKA · *FUNAFUTI LAGOON* · FUALOPA · FONGAFALE · FUAFATU · FUN Funafuti ✈ · VAIAKU · VASAFUA · FATATO · FUNANGONGO · FUNAMANU · FUAGEA · Te Ava Matelua · TEFALA · MATEIKA · FUNAFARA · TEAFUAFOU · TELELE

20 km / 10 miles

MAP Q

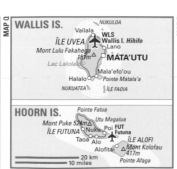

WALLIS IS.
NUKULOA · Vailala · Vailala · ÎLE UVEA · WLS Wallis I. Hihifo ✈ · Lano · Mont Lulu Fakahega △151m · MÁTA'UTU · Lac Lalolalo · Mala'efo'ou · Halalo · Pointe Matala'a · NUKUATEA · ÎLE FAIOA

HOORN IS.
Pointe Fatua · Mont Puke △524m · Utu Magalua · Nuku Poi · FUT Futuna ✈ · ÎLE FUTUNA · Taoa · Alo · ÎLE ALOFI · Mont Kolofau △417m · Alofitai · Pointe Afaga

20 km / 10 miles

MAP P

TONGATAPU
Niu Aunofo · ATATA · *Lahi Passage* · Kolovai · *Piha Passage* · 'EUAIKI · NUKU'ALOFA · Kolonga · Ha'amonga · Mui Hopohoponga · Houma · Pea · Mu'a · Lapaha · Lángi tombs · *blow holes* · TBU Nuku'alofa ✈ · Vaini · Fua'amotu · Houma Toloa

20 km / 10 miles

MAP O

NIUE
Hikutavake · Toi · Liha Point · Namukulu · Mutalau · Tuapa · △223m · Makapu Point · Makefu · Lakepa · ALOFI BAY · Hanan · ALOFI · IUE Niue Hanan ✈ · Liku · Tamakautoga · Togo Chasm · Vaikona Chasm · *AVATELE BAY* · Vaiea · Yashio Maru · Avatele · Fatiau Tuai · Hakupu

20 km / 10 miles

1000 metres / 500 metres / Sea level / 200 metres

USA & Canada

Three major sets of events have dominated North America in recent years: the terrorist attacks of 11 September 2001 and the consequent military actions in Afghanistan and Iraq; the economic downturn and blue-chip corporate failures; and, perhaps less obviously, the seemingly insatiable growth of the internet. These have touched every aspect of American life, but have had a particularly dramatic effect on the travel industry, and the airlines in particular.

Although there were clear signs of downturn in the American economy from late 2000, 11 September 2001 was a defining moment after which the world suddenly seemed a grimmer place. For the travel business, which relies so heavily on confidence, this was a particularly hard time. The long-term significance, however, lies less in the tragic events of the day itself than in the way in which it accelerated trends already in place, and in how North American travellers and travel professionals have reacted.

Challenges

The airline industry had problems before September 2001, and these have continued since. In mid-2003, industry experts were still talking about the worst crisis in its history, with passenger numbers, revenues and profitability all down. As elsewhere, the larger carriers have generally been hardest hit. Filings for creditor protection, staff lay-offs, wage reductions and capacity cuts by the majors have become commonplace, and new security requirements have added to their costs. Recent marketing partnerships, such as that between Continental, Delta and NorthWest, may help redress the problems, but many observers predict no significant recovery until later in the decade. One bonus for travellers has been increased flexibility, such as relaxations of cancellation and flight-change penalties, although some in-flight service cutbacks have also taken effect. Low-cost airlines like JetBlue, JetsGo and Southwest have benefited from the majors' problems, but the unavoidable fact is that many Americans have, for the time being at least, abandoned their taste for flying. In early April 2003, US bookings were down one-sixth against the same period in 2002, while on some international routes the decline was over 40%. Overall, revenues in the first half of 2003 were running at 1995 levels. In this climate, further cutbacks and economies seem inevitable. In 1987, American Airlines reportedly saved $40,000 a year by eliminating one olive from each first-class meal. With 2002 airline losses standing at US$9 billion (post-federal subsidy), something a bit more drastic is called for.

War and terrorism, or the threat of them, are not wholly to blame for the airline's problems. A 2003 survey by TIA (Travel Industries of America) revealed that lack of disposable income is a greater deterrent to travel. Economic recovery is not evenly spread across all sectors, and consumer confidence (reported in early 2003 to be at a seven-year low) remains uncertain. Until that returns, travel – particularly international air travel – is seen as being non-essential, despite there being more bargains to be had than ever before.

The internet has contributed to this last development. On-line bookings are, by almost every estimate, on the increase. The sector rebounded more quickly than the 'off-line' agencies, recording a 70% sales increase in the first quarter of 2002 compared to 2001. On the web, it is easier for consumers to shop around for the best rates – seen by 90% of the respondents to YPB's 2002 National Travel Monitor survey as being their most

Economies

The region's economies, 2001 *Source: World Bank/IMF*

	GNI (US$ bn) 2001	Annual GDP growth rate (%) 2001	2002	est2003	est2004
USA	10,472.5	0.9	1.8	1.9	2.9
Canada	681.6	1.5	3.4	2.8	3.2

■ Top states

Top ten US states and Canadian provinces by overseas visitors, 2002 (millions) *Source: OTTI/CTC*

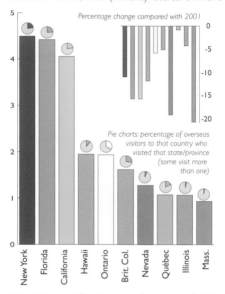

Percentage change compared with 2001

Pie charts: percentage of overseas visitors to that country who visited that state/province (some visit more than one)

important consideration – and easier to find last-minute deals. On-line companies like Orbitz, Travelocity and Expedia have been quick to exploit this new market. They now provide a direct, though sometimes controversial, supplier-to-consumer link that since the 1980s has been monopolised by retail agents and the GDS suppliers.

Agencies

At first glance, this looks like bad news for the conventional ('off-line') agencies. The terms 'on-line' and 'off-line' suggest opposite and conflicting priorities, but the reality is more complex. The on-lines are increasingly 'humanising' their services with call centres and retail outlets, while traditional firms, initially wary of the web, are now exploiting it to create an interactive and 24/7 service. As Travel Weekly's 2002 *Travel Industry Survey* observed, 'both are using the same strategy: dealing with the customer across multiple channels' to create a marriage of personal attention and technology. The moral is clear: 'be where your customers want to do business.' This trend is likely to make the on-line/off-line distinction more blurred and, in time, irrelevant.

A few other trends are worth noting. Although there are fewer agencies now than in 1999, on average these are more profitable. Revenue based on commission from high sales volumes is no longer enough. Specialisation in fields like cruising, packages and business travel is increasing, as is the charging of fees to clients. Agencies are fast becoming adept at positioning themselves as experts who can help save their clients money. In general, the more complex the product, the more likely a travel agent is to be involved: they currently sell 90% of cruises, for example. Many people reseach complex options on-line, but far fewer book them that way. The next challenge for agencies may come as this starts to change.

Change and recovery

All these issues need to be seen in the context of North America's staggering achievements during the

Key facts

Number of Countries	2
Area ('000 sq km)	19,343
Population ('000)	323,367
Population Density (per sq km)	17
Gross National Income (US$m)	10,462,470
Visitor Arrivals ('000)	65,170
Visitor Receipts (US$m)	83,893
Travel Departures ('000)	76,322
Travel Expenditure (US$m)	71,741

GNI figures relate to 2001. Population figures are taken from the most recent reliable source. Travel figures (WTO) are based on overnight stays, not same-day visitors, and are generally for 2001: where these are unavailable or unreliable, earlier years have been used. Where data for certain countries was not available, this has been regarded as zero. For more information see the Countries A-Z section from page 184.

late 20th century. The USA is the richest and most powerful country the world has ever seen, while Canada has long been the standard by which the world's quality of life is judged. The two countries rank third and ninth respectively in terms of visitor arrivals, accounting for nearly 10% of the world's total. Their combined expenditure on foreign travel is 50% more than second-placed Germany's, and their combined receipts two and a half times greater than that of second-placed Spain. North American surveys indicate a continued desire to travel and, as the economies recover, an increasing ability to do so.

Above all, this pre-eminence was not achieved by standing still. Without doubt, travel and booking patterns are changing. The results have been painful for several sectors, destinations and companies but have provided opportunities for others. In this light, two headlines from respected industry publications are worth considering: 'The Struggle Continues and Intensifies' from the Canadian Tourism Commission's (CTC) May 2003 *Tourism Intelligence Bulletin;* and 'New Markets, New Rules, New Power' from Travel Weekly's 2002 *Travel Industry Survey.* Together, they eloquently sum up the challenges and opportunities that lie ahead.

Canada

In Canada, the 2003 picture was further clouded by the SARS outbreak in Toronto, which only relented after causing several months of short-term havoc and, perhaps, longer-term damage to travel patterns. In April 2003 the situation was certainly bad enough, with hotel occupancy levels down one-third. Canada depends greatly on the currently air-wary US market, although areas within easy reach of the USA by surface transport are likely to benefit. The CTC has identified several areas for growth. They include sharpening Canada's marketing message, positioning it as a 'replacement' destination for the USA, pushing the

■ Comings and goings

Inbound and outbound travel to and from the USA and Canada, 2002 *Source: OTTI/CTC*

Visitor arrivals to USA and Canada, by country of origin

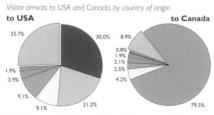

to USA **to Canada**

Travel departures from USA and Canada, by country of destination

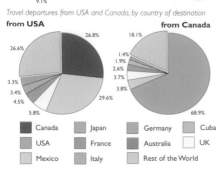

from USA **from Canada**

■ Canada	■ Japan
■ USA	■ France
■ Mexico	■ Italy

■ Germany	■ Cuba
■ Australia	□ UK
■ Rest of the World	

- The USA and Canada (USA&C) occupies 14.3% of the world's land area and is home to 5.1% of the world's population.
- USA&C's combined GNI is US$10,462,470 million, 33.4% of the world's total.
- USA&C accounts for 11.7% of global travel departures and 9.6% of arrivals.
- International travel and tourism contributed US$ 84.9 billion to USA&C's economy in 2001, compared to US$85.3 billion in 1999.
- 54% of international visitors to the USA in 2002 were from Canada (12.9 million) and Mexico (9.8 million). 20% came from Europe: and 40% of these European visitors were from the UK.
- 24% of Canadian and 14% of Mexican visitors to the US in 2002 arrived by air, a decline of 11% and 5% respectively over 2001.
- In 2002, New York overtook California as being the most popular state amongst overseas visitors..
- Europeans spent US$23.7 billion in the USA in 2001 (not including international transport), a fall of 14% compared to 2000. Britons accounted for nearly 39% of this.
- 79% of all international visitors to Canada in 2001 were from the USA (15.6 million). 49% of these US visitors were residents of the states of New York, Michigan, Washington, California or Ohio.
- Of the non-US visitors to Canada in 2002, 20% were from the UK. Visitors from the UK, Japan, France and Germany accounted for half of all non-US visitors to Canada.
- The USA spends more on, and receives more from, international travel than any other country. Only France received more foreign visitors in 2001, and only the Germans and the British made more foreign trips.
- 12% of all US travel receipts in 2002 were from nationals of Japan. The two countries which supplied the most visitors, Canada and Mexico, contributed 9% and 7% respectively to US travel receipts.
- Travel and tourism is responsible directly or indirectly for over 12% of jobs in the USA.
- In 2001, the USA received US$4.6 billion more from international travel and tourism than it spent: it has recorded a surplus every year since 1989. In 2001, Canada recorded a deficit of US$880 million.
- Overseas visitors to the US (excluding those from Canada and Mexico) spend an average of $90 a day.
- Over a third of US residents who travel abroad are from New York or California. New Yorkers are at least three times more likely to travel abroad than the inhabitants of any other US city.
- 36% of overseas visitors to the USA in 2002 entered via New York, Miami or Los Angeles.
- 885,000 Britons visited New York City in 2001, down 17% compared to 2000.
- The total impact of 2001 visitor spending in New York City is estimated to be US$22 billion, over US$2,730 for every city resident. This is down 12% compared to 2000.
- 83% of overseas visitors to the USA in 2002 were independent travellers, rather than on packages.
- More than five times as many US and Canadian residents went on a cruise in 2002 than in 1980.
- 14% of overseas trips by US nationals in 2001 involved visits to two countries, and 8% to three or more.
- Of the USA's 25 most visited states in 2002, only Utah (1%) registered an increase in visitors compared to 2001.
- 43% of Canada's foreign visitors in 2001 visited Ontario.
- The UK is comfortably the most popular non-North American and Mexican destination for US and Canadian residents.
- In May 2003, an average of nearly 15,000 planes a day took off from US airports.
- If Manhatten had the same population density as Alaska, 14 people would live there.
- The Statue of Liberty's index finger is eight feet long.

Holiday trends

Most travel promotion in the USA (and, to a lesser extent, in Canada) is conducted at state or regional, rather than national, level, creating the confusing illusion of over 60 separate destinations. This is perhaps justified, given that 80% of visitors to the USA take in only one state. Whichever state, province or territory is chosen, all tastes are catered for. The appeal lingers, too: 75% of 2002 visits to the USA were repeats, only slightly down compared to 1999.

North America has some of the most unique and dynamic cities in the world, including New York, Las Vegas, Chicago, Miami, New Orleans, San Francisco, Los Angeles, Toronto, Québec and Vancouver.

Over a third of international leisure travellers to the USA in 2002 made a visit to an amusement or theme park, and this trend is increasing. Seven of the 15 most visited theme parks in the world are in Florida. In 2002 these attracted a total of some 58 million visitors – roughly the population of the UK.

Major beach destinations are Florida and California, although every state with a coastline has something to offer. A third of all international visitors spent at least part of their holiday in, on or by the ocean. 'Soft adventure' opportunities include skiing, white-water rafting, canoeing and national park trekking in the wilderness areas that both the USA and Canada have diligently preserved. There were over 60 million domestic and international visitors to US national parks in 2002: nearly one in five international tourists went to at least one.

USA established favourites

- New York, Florida and California dominate the US inbound travel market. Nearly 70% of international visitors visit at least one, and the USA's five most-visited cities are all in these states.
- California, the USA's most populous state, has myriad attractions, including not only beaches and theme parks but also city visits and touring.
- Florida's image is mainly one of sun-drenched pleasure centring on beaches and theme parks. Another strength is golf: the state has over 1,000 courses.
- New York offers probably the world's most intense urban experience, as well as spectacular up-state countryside. Neighbouring New Jersey includes the famous gaming resort of Atlantic City.
- Hawaii is a firm favourite with the USA's Far East market. Tourism is the state's main industry, and its tourism promotion budget is traditionally the highest in the country.
- Nevada, where tourism accounts for over a third of all state employment, is home to the comparison-defying city of Las Vegas.
- Washington DC, Virginia and Maryland are strongly associated with some of the country's historic events and have a strong 'heritage' appeal.

Top cities

Top ten US cities by overseas visitors, 2002 (millions) Source: OTTI/CTC

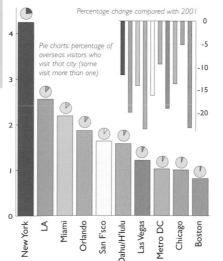

Percentage change compared with 2001

Pie charts: percentage of overseas visitors who visit that city (some visit more than once)

New York, LA, Miami, Orlando, San F'sco, Oahu/H'lulu, Las Vegas, Metro DC, Chicago, Boston

Airline uncertainty

Performance of ATA US-member airlines, January 2001 to April 2003 (Revenue Passenger emplanements, 000s) Source: Air Transport Association

— All flights
— Domestic flights

Jan'01 Apr Jul Oct Jan'02 Apr Jul Oct Jan'03 Apr

- The New England states of Vermont, Connecticut, Rhode Island, New Hampshire, Massachusetts and Maine are popular for family touring and skiing.
- Leading adventure destinations are California, Washington and Arizona, for activities ranging from rafting and trekking to mountain climbing and cycling.

Canada established favourites

- Traditionally, tours took in the east or the west and skipped the wilderness in-between. This imbalance is now being redressed, and an increasing number of visits now take in one of Canada's many national parks. Skiing has long been a popular attraction.
- Eastern Canada's highlights include the Niagara Falls, and Ontario and Québec, large provinces with excellent variety for touring and city visiting. Many visitors to Vancouver combine a self-drive tour of British Columbia with Alberta on the eastern side of the Rockies, or with the Pacific US States.

Up and coming in the USA

- The Deep South is attracting ever-increasing interest, particularly New Orleans for its Cajun culture and jazz; and Georgia, one of the country's fastest growing economies. Only Las Vegas, Orlando and Los Angeles have more hotel rooms than Atlanta, and no airport in the world receives more passengers.
- The Rocky Mountain states of Montana, Wyoming and Idaho are cashing in on the lifestyles sector and offering adventure activities.
- The vast and diverse state of Texas has recently been targeting overseas markets.
- The cruise market, in- and outbound, continues to grow, particularly in Alaska and Hawaii.

Up and coming in Canada

- The Atlantic coast provinces, particularly with the US short-break market.
- Ecotourism.
- The Western and Northern Canadian wildernesses.
- Theme-based holidays, such as cultural heritage, wildlife and gastronomy.

Challenges ahead

A number of factors could derail any recovery in the travel business. These include lack of sustained economic growth, further wars or terrorist actions, fluctuations in the value of the dollar, continued airline-industry turmoil and the further spread of SARS or similar diseases. In addition, the outcome of the next US presidential elections in 2004 is likely to influence all but the last of these.

Visitors

Visitor arrivals 2001 Source: WTO

	Visitors (thousands)	Change since 1997
USA	43,491	-4.7%
Canada	19,679	11.4%

(Figures not available for St Pierre et Miquelon.)

hard-adventure market and attracting more Mexican visitors. These measures seem necessary in the light of, amongst other indicators, a fall of 7% in overnight stays in the first quarter of 2003 compared to 2002 and Air Canada's loss of 10% of its RPMs (revenue passenger miles) in the same period.

Thanks to: Ed Thompson of CTC; Maria Polk of tours.com; Sean Ford of ATA; Tim O'Brien and Keith Wright of Amusement Business; Tony Peisley; Maria Hinayon of ACI; Louis Abramovitc of TIA; Penny Locke; Alan Fredericks of Northstar Travel Media (US); Graeme Payne; Gary Bowerman; Patrick Fitzgerald.

Climate

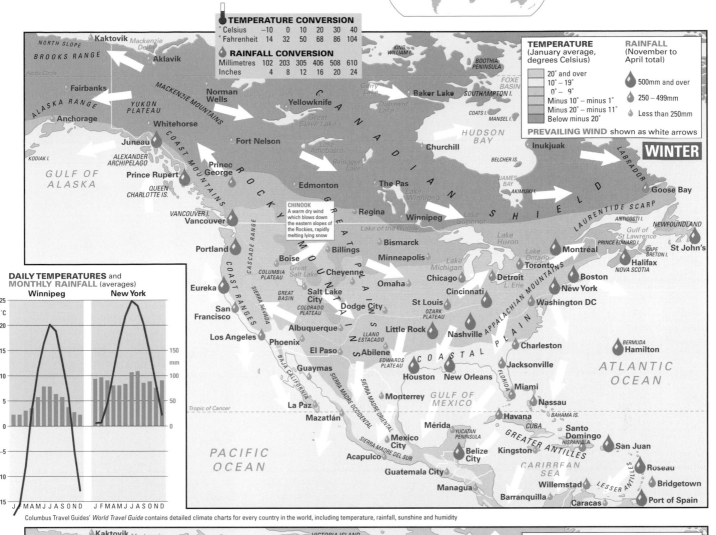

Columbus Travel Guides' *World Travel Guide* contains detailed climate charts for every country in the world, including temperature, rainfall, sunshine and humidity

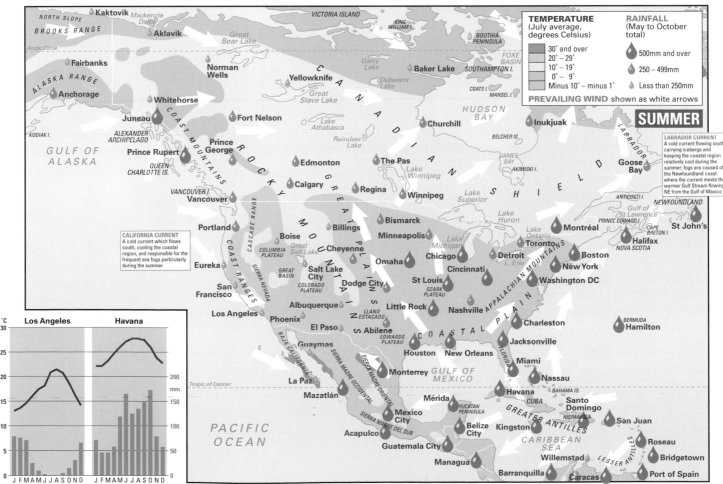

Railways & Airports

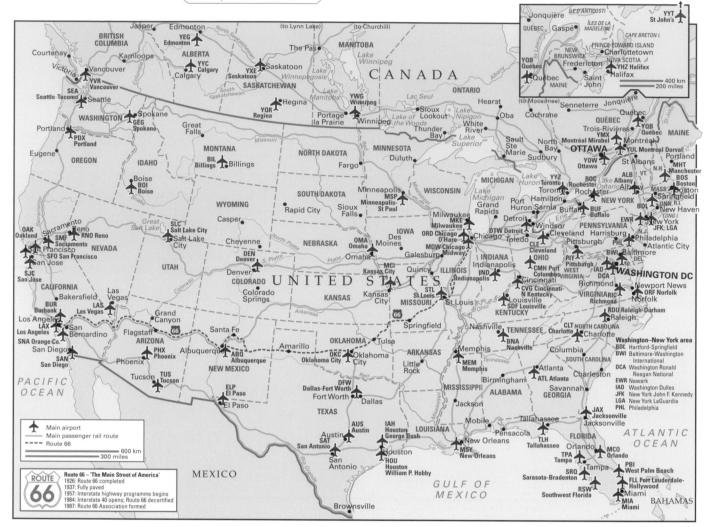

Legend
- Main airport
- Main passenger rail route
- - - Route 66

600 km / 300 miles

ROUTE 66 – 'The Main Street of America'
- 1926: Route 66 completed
- 1937: Fully paved
- 1957: Interstate highway programme begins
- 1984: Interstate 40 opens; Route 66 decertified
- 1987: Route 66 Association formed

The 50 busiest airports in the USA & Canada, 2001 (million passengers)

Total passengers
International passengers

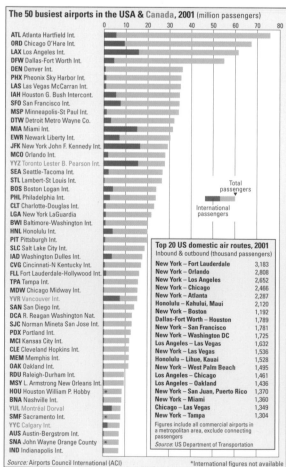

- ATL Atlanta Hartfield Int.
- ORD Chicago O'Hare Int.
- LAX Los Angeles Int.
- DFW Dallas-Fort Worth Int.
- DEN Denver Int.
- PHX Phoenix Sky Harbor Int.
- LAS Las Vegas McCarran Int.
- IAH Houston G. Bush Intercont.
- SFO San Francisco Int.
- MSP Minneapolis-St Paul Int.
- DTW Detroit Metro Wayne Co.
- MIA Miami Int.
- EWR Newark Liberty Int.
- JFK New York John F. Kennedy Int.
- MCO Orlando Int.
- YYZ Toronto Lester B. Pearson Int.
- SEA Seattle-Tacoma Int.
- STL Lambert-St Louis Int.
- BOS Boston Logan Int.
- PHL Philadelphia Int.
- CLT Charlotte-Douglas Int.
- LGA New York LaGuardia
- BWI Baltimore-Washington Int.
- HNL Honolulu Int.
- PIT Pittsburgh Int.
- SLC Salt Lake City Int.
- IAD Washington Dulles Int.
- CVG Cincinnati-N Kentucky Int.
- FLL Fort Lauderdale-Hollywood Int.
- TPA Tampa Int.
- MDW Chicago Midway Int.
- YVR Vancouver Int.
- SAN San Diego Int.
- DCA R. Reagan Washington Nat.
- SJC Norman Mineta San Jose Int.
- PDX Portland Int.
- MCI Kansas City Int.
- CLE Cleveland Hopkins Int.
- MEM Memphis Int.
- OAK Oakland Int.
- RDU Raleigh-Durham Int.
- MSY L. Armstrong New Orleans Int.
- HOU Houston William P. Hobby
- BNA Nashville Int.
- YUL Montréal Dorval
- SMF Sacramento Int.
- YYC Calgary Int.
- AUS Austin-Bergstrom Int.
- SNA John Wayne Orange County
- IND Indianapolis Int.

Source: Airports Council International (ACI)

*International figures not available

Top 20 US domestic air routes, 2001
Inbound & outbound (thousand passengers)

Route	Passengers
New York – Fort Lauderdale	3,183
New York – Orlando	2,808
New York – Los Angeles	2,652
New York – Chicago	2,466
New York – Atlanta	2,287
Honolulu – Kahului, Maui	2,120
New York – Boston	1,192
Dallas-Fort Worth – Houston	1,789
New York – San Francisco	1,781
New York – Washington DC	1,725
Los Angeles – Las Vegas	1,632
New York – Las Vegas	1,536
Honolulu – Lihue, Kauai	1,528
New York – West Palm Beach	1,495
Los Angeles – Chicago	1,461
Los Angeles – Oakland	1,436
New York – San Juan, Puerto Rico	1,370
New York – Miami	1,360
Chicago – Las Vegas	1,349
New York – Tampa	1,304

Figures include all commercial airports in a metropolitan area, exclude connecting passengers

Source: US Department of Transportation

- LIH Lihue
- HNL Honolulu
- OGG Kahului
- KOA Kona

NIIHAU, KAUAI, OAHU, MOLOKAI, MAUI, LANAI, HAWAII

300 km / 150 miles

RUSSIAN FED. · ALASKA · CANADA
- Fairbanks
- ANC Anchorage
- Whittier
- Seward
- Juneau
- YXY Whitehorse

BERING SEA, ST LAWRENCE I., NUNIVAK I., KODIAK I., ALEUTIAN ISLANDS, ALEXANDER ARCHIPELAGO, Yukon, Mackenzie

1000 km / 500 miles

LONG-DISTANCE RAIL SERVICES

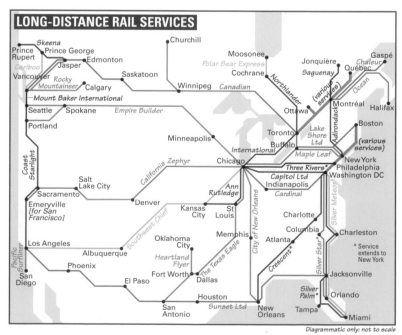

* Service extends to New York

Diagrammatic only: not to scale

Museums & Art Galleries

The most important museums and art galleries in the United States and Canada are listed here. Selection is based on importance and depth of the collection and its cultural diversity within a geographic spread.

Data compiled by Jon A. Gillaspie
email: let@sarastro.com

Principal contents of institution:

AA Applied & decorative art
AR Archaeology / ancient art
FA Fine art (paintings, sculpture)
FO Folk art & culture / ethnology
H   History / historical site / reconstruction
NH Natural history
ST Science / technology
W   Wide range of subjects

Opening times:

Days or months preceded by a red circle (●) indicate when the institution is closed.
Many close on national holidays and other special days. Some museums and galleries have shorter opening hours at certain days of the week or in certain months.

Admission charges:

All charge for admission except those shown in *italics*, where entry is free (although charges for special exhibitions may apply).
Some institutions allow free entry or reduce their admission charges on certain days.

Albuquerque NEW MEXICO
W   Indian Pueblo Cultural Center
Atlanta GEORGIA
FA High Museum of Art ● Mon
W   Michael C. Carlos Museum (Emory Univ.)
Baltimore MARYLAND
FA Baltimore Museum of Art ● Mon & Tue
W   Walters Art Gallery ● Mon
Banff ALBERTA
NH Whyte Museum of Rockies ● Mon (Oct-May)
Baraboo WISCONSIN
H   Circus World Museum ● no shows Oct-Apr
Baton Rouge LOUISIANA
W   LSU Rural Life Museum
Boston MASSACHUSETTS
FA Isabella Stewart Gardner Museum ● Mon
W   Museum of Fine Arts
Bozeman MONTANA
W   Museum of the Rockies
Buffalo NEW YORK
FA Albright-Knox Art Gallery ● Mon
Burlington VERMONT
W   Shelburne Museum ● tours only Nov-May
Calgary ALBERTA
W   Glenbow Museum ● Mon (Sep-May)
Cedar Rapids IOWA
FA Museum of Art ● Mon

Charlotte NORTH CAROLINA
ST Discovery Place ●
W   Mint Museum of Art ● Mon
Chicago ILLINOIS
FA Art Institute of Chicago; Museum of Contemporary Art ● Mon
W   Field Museum of Chicago
ST Museum of Science and Technology
Cincinnati OHIO
FA Cincinnati Art Museum ● Mon; Contemporary Arts Center ● Sun; Taft Museum
Cleveland OHIO
ST Great Lakes Science Center
FA *Museum of Art* ● Mon
NH Museum of Natural History
H   Rock and Roll Hall of Fame
Cody WYOMING
H   Buffalo Bill Hist. Center ● Tue & Wed (Nov-Apr) includes: Plains Ind. Mus., Witney Gall.
Columbus OHIO
FA Columbus Museum of Art ● Mon
Corpus Christi TEXAS
FA Art Museum of South Texas ● Mon
Dallas TEXAS
FO African-American Museum ● Mon
AR FA *Dallas Museum of Art* ● Mon
NH Dallas Museum of Natural History
H   Sixth Floor Museum (School Book Depository)
Denver COLORADO
H   Black Amer. West Mus. ● Mon & Tue (winter)
W   *Art Museum* ● Mon; Mus. of Natural History
Des Moines IOWA
FA Des Moines Art Center ● Mon
Detroit OHIO
FA Detroit Institute of Art ● Mon & Tue
H   Museum of Afro-American History ● Mon
Drumheller ALBERTA
NH Royal Tyrrell Museum of Paleontology ● Mon (Oct-May)
Durham NORTH CAROLINA
W   *Duke University Museum of Art* ● Mon
Edmonton ALBERTA
ST Edmonton Space and Science Center ● Mon
Flagstaff ARIZONA
FO Museum of Northern Arizona
Fort Steele BRITISH COLUMBIA
H   Fort Steele Heritage Town
Fort Worth TEXAS
FA *Amon Carter Museum; Kimbell Art Museum; Modern Art Museum; Sid Richardson Collection of Western Art* ● Mon
W   Museum of Science and History ● Mon
Fredericton NEW BRUNSWICK
FA Beaverbrook Art Gallery ● Mon (winter)
Halifax NOVA SCOTIA
H   Atlantic Maritime Museum ● Mon (Oct-May)
NH NS Natural History Museum ● Mon (Oct-May)
Houston TEXAS
FA Museum of Fine Arts ● Mon
NH Museum of Natural Science
ST Space Center Houston
Huntsville ALABAMA
ST Space and Rocket Center
Indianapolis INDIANA
FO Eiteljorg Museum ● Mon (Sep-Jun)
FA *Indianapolis Museum of Art* ● Sun & Mon
FA *Children's Mus. of Indianap.* ● Mon (winter)
Kansas City MISSOURI
FA Nelson-Atkins Museum of Art ● Mon
Kingston ONTARIO
W   Agnes Ethrington Art Center ● Mon
Los Angeles CALIFORNIA
AA FA *Getty Center* ● Mon
FA Armand Hammer Museum of Art; Museum of Contemporary Art (MOCA) ● Mon

AR FA LA County Museum of Art (LACMA)
W   Natural History Museum of LA County ● Mon
H   Museum of Tolerance ● Sat & Jewish hols
Louisville KENTUCKY
FA *J.B. Speed Art Museum* ● Mon
Macon GEORGIA
W   Tubman African-American Museum
Manchester NEW HAMPSHIRE
AA FA *Currier Gallery of Art* ● Tue
Memphis TENNESSEE
W   National Civil Rights Museum ● Tue
Merritt Island FLORIDA
ST *Kennedy Space Center*
Mesa Verde National Park COLORADO
AR Archaeological Museum
Miami FLORIDA
FA Bass Mus.; Center for Fine Arts ● both Mon
FA *Lowe Art Museum (Univ. of Miami)* ● Mon
AA *Wolfsonian Museum* ● Mon
Milwaukee WISCONSIN
FA Milwaukee Art Gallery ● Mon
W   Museum Center
Minneapolis and St Paul MINNESOTA
W   *Minneapolis Institute of Arts* ● Mon; Minnesota Children's Museum ● Mon (winter)
ST Science Museum of Minnesota
W   Walker Art Cent. and Sculpture Gdn. ● Mon
Montgomery ALABAMA
FA *Montgomery Museum of Fine Art* ● Mon
Montréal QUÉBEC
NH Montréal Biodôme
AA Centre Canadien d'Architecture ● Mon & Tue (Oct-May); Chât. Ramezay ● Mon (Oct-May)
AR Mus. d'archéologie et d'histoire de Mont. ● Mon
FA Musée des beaux-arts de Montréal; Musée d'art contemporain de Montréal ● both Mon
H   Musée McCord d'histoire Canadienne
Morrisburg ONTARIO
FO Upper Canada Village ● Oct-May
Mystic CONNECTICUT
H   Mystic Seaport
Nashville TENNESSEE
H   Country Music Hall of Fame
W   Tennessee State Museum ● Mon
New Haven CONNECTICUT
FA *Center for British Art* ● Mon; *Yale University Library* ● Mon (Jul-Aug)
NH Peabody Museum of Natural History
New Orleans LOUISIANA
W   Louisiana State Museum ● Mon includes: Cabildo; Presbytere; 1850 House; Jazz Mus.
FA New Orleans Museum of Art ● Mon
New York NEW YORK
W   American Mus. of Nat. History; Brooklyn Mus. of Art ● both Mon & Tue; Metropolitan Mus. of Art; NY Historical Society ● both Mon
AA Cooper-Hewitt National Design Mus. ● Mon
FA Frick Collection ● Mon; Guggenheim Mus. ● Thu; Whitney Mus. of American Art ● Mon & Tue
AA FA Museum of Modern Art (MoMA) ● Wed
FO *National Museum of the American Indian*
Norfolk VIRGINIA
FA Chrysler Museum ● Mon
Oberlin OHIO
W   *Allen Memorial Art Museum* ● Mon

Oklahoma City OKLAHOMA
FA FO National Cowboy Hall of Fame
Omaha NEBRASKA
H   Great Plains Black Museum ● Sat & Sun
Orlando FLORIDA
ST EPCOT Center
Ottawa QUÉBEC
NH Canadian Museum of Nature
W   Can. Museum of Civilization ● Mon (Oct-Apr)
FA FO *National Gallery* ● Mon & Tue (Sep-Apr)
ST National Aviation Museum ● Mon (Sep-Apr)
ST National Museum of Science ● Mon (Sep-Apr)
Pasadena CALIFORNIA
FA Huntington Museum and Library ● Mon; Norton Simon Museum ● Mon, Tue & Wed
Philadelphia PENNSYLVANIA
H   Afro-American Hist. & Cultural Mus. ● Mon
AR FO Museum of Archaeology and Anthropology (University of Pennsylvania) ● Mon
FA Philadelphia Museum of Art; Rodin Museum ● both Mon
Phoenix ARIZONA
FO Heard Museum
Pittsburgh PENNSYLVANIA
FA Andy Warhol Museum ● Mon; Museum of Art (Carnegie Center) ● Mon (Sep-Jun)
AA FA Frick Art Museum ● Mon
Portland OREGON
ST Oregon Museum of Science and Industry ● Mon (winter)
W   Portland Art Museum ● Mon
Princeton NEW JERSEY
ST Carnegie Science Center
NH Natural History Museum ● Mon (Sep-Jun)
FA *University Art Museum* ● Mon
Québec QUÉBEC
W   Musée de la civilisation ● Mon (Sep-Jun)
FA Musée du Québec ● Mon (Sep-May)
Raleigh NORTH CAROLINA
FA North Carolina Museum of Art ● Mon
ST North Carolina Museum of Natural Sciences
Rapid City SOUTH DAKOTA
H   Sioux Indian Museum ● Mon
Richmond VIRGINIA
W   Virginia Museum of Fine Arts ● Mon
Rochester NEW YORK
AA International Museum of Photography ● Mon
Saint John NEW BRUNSWICK
W   New Brunswick Museum
St Louis MISSOURI
H   Museum of Western Expansion
W   *St Louis Art Museum* ● Mon
St Petersburg FLORIDA
FA Museum of Fine Arts ● Mon
FA Salvador Dalí Museum ● Mon
Salem MASSACHUSETTS
W   Peabody Essex Museum
H   Plimoth Plantation
San Diego CALIFORNIA
FA Museum of Contemporary Art, La Jolla ● Mon
San Francisco CALIFORNIA
FA California Palace of the Legion of Honor; Yerba Buena Gardens; San Francisco Art Institute ● all Mon; San Francisco Museum of Modern Art ● Wed

Santa Fe NEW MEXICO
W   Museum of New Mexico ● Mon includes:
FA   Georgia O'Keeffe Mus.; Mus. of Fine Arts
FO   Mus. of Indian Arts; Mus. of Internat. Folk Art
Sarasota FLORIDA
FA Ringling Museum Complex
Saskatoon SASKATCHEWAN
FA Mendel Art Gallery
Seattle WASHINGTON
FA Henry Art Gallery ● Mon
ST Museum of Flight; Pacific Science Center
FO Thomas Burke Memorial Museum
Sudbury ONTARIO
ST Science North
Tallahassee FLORIDA
W   Black Archives Research Center ● Sat & Sun
Tampa FLORIDA
ST Museum of Science and Industry ● varies
W   Tampa Museum of Art ● Fri
Toronto ONTARIO
FA Art Gallery of Ontario (AGO) ● Mon, ● Tue (Oct-May); McMichael Canadian Art Collection ● Mon (Oct-May); Thomson Gallery ● Sun
FO Toronto Dominion Gallery of Inuit Art
ST Ontario Science Centre
W   Royal Ontario Museum (ROM)
Tucson ARIZONA
NH Arizona-Sonora Desert Museum
FO Arizona State Museum
AR FA Tucson Museum of Art ● Mon (Jun-Aug)
Vancouver BRITISH COLUMBIA
FO UBC Museum of Anthropology ● Mon (Sep-May)
Victoria BRITISH COLUMBIA
W   Royal British Columbia Museum
Virginia Beach VIRGINIA
ST Virginia Marine Museum
Washington DC
FA Corcoran Gallery ● Tue; National Gall. of Art; National Mus. of Women in the Arts; Phillips Coll.
H   US Holocaust Memorial Museum
W   Smithsonian Institution includes:
AA FA *Freer Gallery of Art*
FA   *Hirshhorn Museum; National Museum of American Art; National Portrait Gallery*
ST   *National Air and Space Museum*
FO   *National Museum of African Art; Sackler Gallery*
H   *National Museum of American History*
NH   *National Museum of Natural History*
Wichita KANSAS
FA Wichita Art Museum ● Mon
Williamsburg VIRGINIA
H   Colonial Williamsburg; Jamestown Settlement
Wilmington DELAWARE
AA Nemours Mansion
AA FO Winterthur Museum, Winterthur
Windsor ONTARIO
FA *Art Gallery of Windsor* ● Mon
Winnipeg MANITOBA
NH Manit. Museum of Man & Nature ● Mon (Sep-Jun)
FA Winnipeg Art Gallery ● Mon (Sep-May)
Winston-Salem NORTH CAROLINA
FA Reynolda House Museum of American Art ● Mon

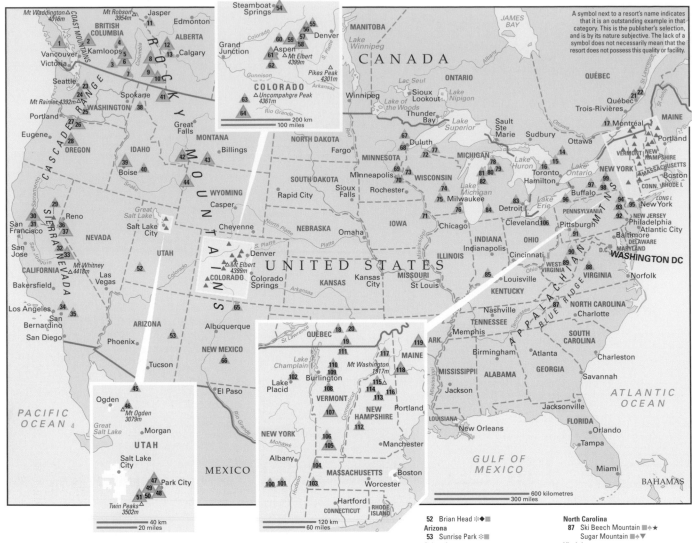

A symbol next to a resort's name indicates that it is an outstanding example in that category. This is the publisher's selection, and is by its nature subjective. The lack of a symbol does not necessarily mean that the resort does not possess this quality or facility.

KEY

▲ THE MOST BEAUTIFUL RESORTS
Ski areas with spectacular scenery

❄ SNOWSURE
The best reputations for season-long snow cover

◆ EXPERT
Best of the black diamond destinations

■ BEGINNER SKI AREAS
Best choices for first timers

♣ FAMILY FRIENDLY
Ideal choices for family ski holidays

● PARTY TOWNS
Après ski centres

▼ SNOWBOARDER HEAVEN
Best bets for boarders

★ NOT JUST SKIING
Plenty to do if you don't want to slide

THE LARGEST SKI AREAS △

1 Mount Washington, BC
2 Whistler & Blackcomb, BC
5 Silver Star, BC
6 Big White, BC
8 Panorama, BC
9 Kimberley, BC
10 Fernie Snow Valley, BC
11 Lake Louise (Banff), AL
12 Sunshine Village (Banff), AL
24 Crystal Mountain, WA
26 Mount Hood Meadows, OR
28 Mount Bachelor, OR
30 Squaw Valley, CA
33 Mammoth Mountain, CA
37 Heavenly, NV
39 Bogus Basin, ID
41 Big Mountain, MT
42 Big Sky, MT
43 Red Lodge Mountain, MT
44 Jackson Hole, Teton, WY
47 The Canyons, UT
48 Deer Valley, UT
48 Park City, UT
49 Solitude, UT
51 Snowbird, UT
54 Steamboat, CO
56 Winter Park (Mary Jane), CO
56 Loveland, CO
56 Keystone, CO
58 Breckenridge, CO
59 Copper Mountain, CO
59 Vail, CO
61 Snowmass, CO
61 Aspen, CO
64 Durango Mountain Resort, CO
105 Mount Snow (Haystack / Carinthia), VT
107 Killington, VT
118 Sunday River, ME
119 Sugarloaf USA, ME

Canada

British Columbia
1 Mount Washington ❄▼
2 Whistler & Blackcomb ❄◆■♣●▼★
3 Apex ❄■♣▼
4 Sun Peaks ❄■♣▼
5 Silver Star ❄■♣▼
6 Big White ❄◆♣●▼
7 Red Mountain ❄◆♣▼
8 Panorama ❄■♣▼
9 Kimberley ❄■♣●▼
10 Fernie Snow Valley ❄▼

Alberta
11 Marmot Basin (Jasper) ▲❄■♣●▼★
12 Lake Louise (Banff) ▲❄◆■♣●▼
    Sunshine Village (Banff) ❄■♣●▼★
13 Fortress Mountain (Banff) ❄■
    Nakiska ▲❄▼

Ontario
14 Sir Sam's ■♣★
15 Mount St Louis / Moonstone ■♣▼★
16 Blue Mountain ❄■♣▼

Québec
17 Mont Gabriel ❄♣
    Mont Ste-Sauveur ■♣▼★
    Ski Morin Heights ■♣▼
    Mont Blanc ♣▼★
    Tremblant ❄■♣●▼★
18 Bromont ■♣▼
19 Owl's Head ■♣▼
20 Mont Orford ■♣▼
21 Mont Ste-Anne ▲❄■♣●▼★
22 Stoneham ❄♣▼★

United States

Washington
23 Stevens Pass ♣
24 Crystal Mountain ▲❄◆▼
25 White Pass Village ❄▼

Oregon
26 Mount Hood Meadows ▲❄◆▼
27 Timberline ❄■♣●▼
28 Mount Bachelor ▲❄◆▼

California
29 Donner Ski Ranch ▲▼
    Boreal ■▼
30 Squaw Valley ❄■♣▼★
31 Alpine Meadows ▲❄◆▼
    Sierra-at-Tahoe ▲❄■♣▼
    Kirkwood ▲❄■♣▼
32 Dodge Ridge ▼
    June Mountain ▲■♣▼
33 Mammoth Mountain ▲❄◆♣●▼
34 Mountain High ▲■♣▼
35 Snow Summit ■▼

Nevada
36 Diamond Peak ▲♣
    Mount Rose ◆▼
37 Heavenly ▲❄◆■♣●▼

Idaho
38 Silver Mountain ❄■♣▼
40 Sun Valley ▲❄◆■♣▼★

Montana
41 Big Mountain ◆■♣▼★
42 Big Sky ▲❄◆■♣▼
43 Red Lodge Mountain ▲◆♣●▼

Wyoming
44 Jackson Hole, Teton ▲❄◆■♣●▼★

Utah
45 Powder Mountain ❄■♣▼
46 Snowbasin ▲❄♣
47 The Canyons ❄■♣▼★
48 Deer Valley ❄■♣●▼★
    Park City ❄■●▼★
49 Solitude ▲❄■♣
50 Alta ▲❄◆■♣
51 Snowbird ▲❄◆■♣●▼

Colorado (continued right column)

52 Brian Head ▲◆■
Arizona
53 Sunrise Park ❄■
Colorado
54 Steamboat ▲❄■♣●▼★
55 Eldora Mountain ❄
56 Winter Park (Mary Jane) ❄◆■♣●▼★
    Loveland ▲❄◆
    Keystone ❄■♣●▼
57 Arapahoe Basin ❄◆
58 Breckenridge ❄■♣●▼★
59 Copper Mountain ▲❄◆■♣●▼★
    Vail ❄♣●▼
60 Beaver Creek ▲❄♣■▼★
61 Snowmass ❄◆■♣●▼★
    Aspen ▲❄■♣●▼★
62 Crested Butte ▲❄◆■♣▼★
63 Telluride ▲❄■♣●▼★
64 Durango Mountain Resort ▲❄■♣▼

New Mexico
65 Taos ▲▼■
66 Ski Apache ●▼★

Minnesota
67 Giants Ridge ■★
68 Spirit Mountain ■▼
69 Afton Alps ■▼
70 Buck Hill ■▼

Iowa
71 Sundown Mountain ▼★

Wisconsin
72 Whitecap Mountains ■▼★
73 Trollhaugen ■♣▼
74 Nordic Mountain ■♣▼
75 Cascade Mountain ◆■♣▼
    Devils Head ◆■♣▼
76 Wilmot Mountain ■▼

Michigan
77 Big Powderhorn Mountain ❄■▼
    Indianhead Mountain & Bear Creek ◆★
78 Boyne Mountain ■♣▼★
    Boyne Highlands ■♣▼★
    Nub's Nob ■▼
79 Treetops / Sylvan ♣
80 Shanty Creek / Schuss Mountain ■
81 Caberfae Peaks ■★
82 Sugar Loaf ▼
83 Alpine Valley ■
84 Timber Ridge ■

Indiana
85 Paoli Peaks ■♣▼

Ohio
86 Boston Mills / Brandywine ■♣

North Carolina

87 Ski Beech Mountain ■♣★
    Sugar Mountain ■♣▼
Virginia
88 Wintergreen ▲■★
West Virginia
89 Snowshoe ▲■♣▼★
90 Canaan Valley ▲■♣★
Pennsylvania
91 Hidden Valley ▲■♣★
    Seven Springs ■♣▼
92 Doe Mountain ▲♣
93 Big Boulder ❄■♣▼
    Camelback ■♣▼
94 Shawnee Mountain ■▼
New Jersey
95 Mountain Creek ■♣▼★
New York
96 Holiday Valley ■♣●▼
97 Bristol Mountain ★
98 Greek Peak ■
99 Labrador Mountain ■♣
100 Belleayre ▲♣
101 Hunter Mountain ❄■♣▼
102 Whiteface Mountain ▼★
Massachusetts
103 Butternut Basin ■♣
104 Jiminy Peak ■♣
Vermont
105 Mount Snow (Haystack / Carinthia) ❄■♣●▼★
106 Stratton ▲❄◆■♣▼★
107 Killington ❄◆■♣●▼★
108 Sugarbush ■♣▼
109 Stowe (Mount Mansfield) ▲❄◆■♣▼★
110 Smugglers' Notch ▲❄◆■♣●▲
111 Jay Peak ▲❄▼
New Hampshire
112 Mount Sunapee ▲■
113 Waterville Valley ▲▼★
114 Loon ▲♣
    Cannon ▲■
115 Bretton Woods ♣
116 Attitash-Bear Peak ▼★
117 The Balsams ▲♣●★
Maine
118 Sunday River ❄◆■♣▼
119 Sugarloaf USA ❄■♣♣▼

Information supplied by Snow24 plc
www.snow24.com

Map labels (partial)

Mt Waddington △ 4016m — COAST MOUNTAINS — BRITISH COLUMBIA — Mt Robson △ 3954m — Jasper — Edmonton — ALBERTA — Calgary — ROCKY RANGE — Vancouver — Kamloops — Victoria — Seattle — Mt Rainier 4392m — WASHINGTON — Spokane — Portland — Eugene — OREGON — Great Falls — MONTANA — Billings — IDAHO — Boise — WYOMING — Casper — Cheyenne — NEVADA — Reno — San Francisco — SIERRA NEVADA — San Jose — CALIFORNIA — Mt Whitney △ 4418m — Las Vegas — Bakersfield — Los Angeles — San Bernardino — San Diego — Phoenix — ARIZONA — Tucson — NEW MEXICO — Albuquerque — El Paso — UTAH — Salt Lake City — Great Salt Lake — △Mt Elbert 4399m — COLORADO — Denver — Colorado Springs — KANSAS — Kansas City — NEBRASKA — Omaha — IOWA — Des Moines — MISSOURI — St Louis — ARKANSAS — OKLAHOMA — TEXAS — MEXICO

CANADA — MANITOBA — Winnipeg — Lake Winnipeg — ONTARIO — Lac Seul — Lake Nipigon — Thunder Bay — Sault Ste Marie — Sudbury — Ottawa — QUÉBEC — Québec — Trois-Rivières — Montréal — MAINE — Portland — VERMONT — NEW HAMPSHIRE — NEW YORK — Boston — MASSACHUSETTS — CONN. — RHODE I. — Buffalo — New York — PENNSYLVANIA — Philadelphia — Atlantic City — NEW JERSEY — Pittsburgh — Cleveland — OHIO — WEST VIRGINIA — WASHINGTON DC — MARYLAND — DELAWARE — VIRGINIA — Norfolk — NORTH CAROLINA — Charlotte — Charleston — SOUTH CAROLINA — TENNESSEE — Nashville — Memphis — KENTUCKY — Louisville — Cincinnati — Indianapolis — INDIANA — ILLINOIS — Chicago — Milwaukee — WISCONSIN — Minneapolis — MINNESOTA — Fargo — NORTH DAKOTA — SOUTH DAKOTA — Rapid City — Sioux Falls — Rochester — MICHIGAN — Detroit — Toronto — Hamilton — Lake Ontario — Lake Erie — Lake Huron — Lake Michigan — Lake Superior — APPALACHIAN MTNS — BLUE RIDGE — ALABAMA — GEORGIA — Atlanta — Birmingham — MISSISSIPPI — Jackson — LOUISIANA — New Orleans — GULF OF MEXICO — FLORIDA — Orlando — Tampa — Miami — Jacksonville — Savannah — ATLANTIC OCEAN — BAHAMAS — PACIFIC OCEAN — JAMES BAY

Inset maps

COLORADO inset: Steamboat Springs 54 — Grand Junction — Denver — Aspen 63 60 59 57 58 61 — △Mt Elbert 4399m — 62 — Pikes Peak △ 4301m — △Uncompahgre Peak 4361m — 64 — Gunnison — Rio Grande — Arkansas — 100 miles / 200 km

UTAH inset: Ogden 46 — Mt Ogden △ 3079m — Morgan — Great Salt Lake — UTAH — Salt Lake City — Park City 47 — 49 50 48 — 51 — Twin Peaks △ 3502m — 45 — 20 miles / 40 km

Northeast inset: QUÉBEC — St Lawrence — Lake Champlain — 18 20 19 — 111 — 110 109 — Mt Washington 1917m — MAINE — 117 119 — 118 — 102 — Lake Placid — Burlington — VERMONT — 108 115 114 116 — 113 — NEW HAMPSHIRE — 112 — Portland — 107 — 106 — 105 — NEW YORK — 104 — Albany — Mohawk — Hudson — MASSACHUSETTS — 100 101 — 103 — Boston — Worcester — Hartford — CONNECTICUT — RHODE ISLAND — 60 miles / 120 km

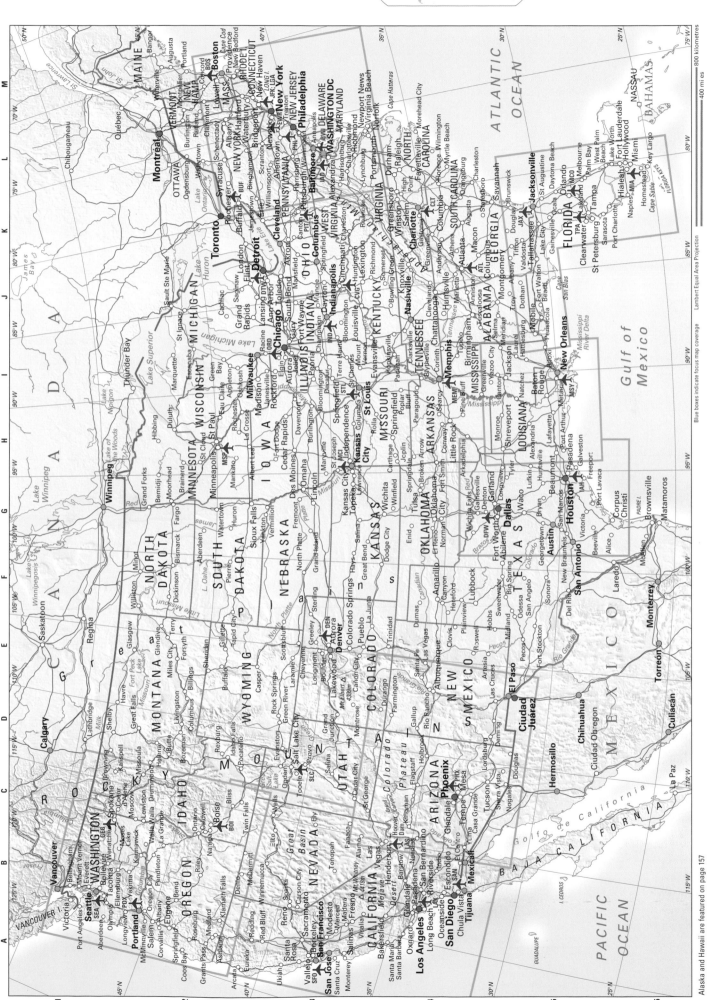

Alaska and Hawaii are featured on page 157

Blue boxes indicate focus map coverage

Lambert Equal Area Projection

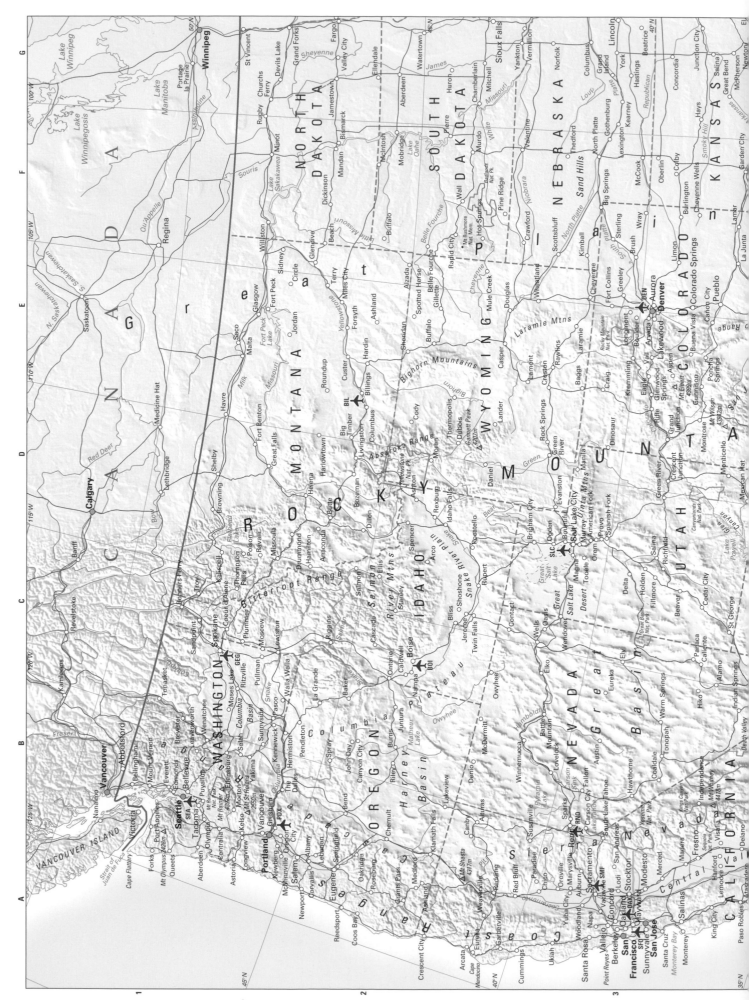

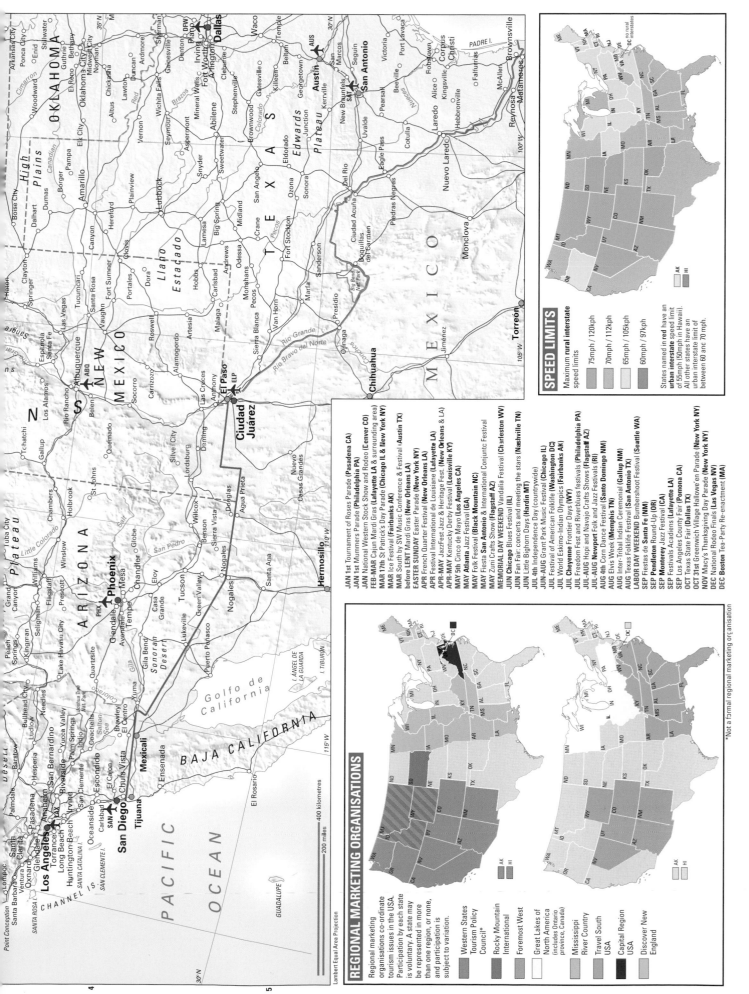

SPEED LIMITS

Maximum rural interstate speed limits

- 75mph / 120kph
- 70mph / 112kph
- 65mph / 105kph
- 60mph / 97kph
- no rural interstates

States named in **red** have an **urban interstate** speed limit of 55mph (50mph in Hawaii). All other states have an urban interstate limit of between 60 and 70 mph.

AK HI

JAN 1st **Tournament of Roses Parade (Pasadena CA)**
JAN 1st **Mummers Parade (Philadelphia PA)**
JAN **National Western Stock Show and Rodeo (Denver CO)**
FEB–MAR **Cajun Mardi Gras (Lafayette LA & surrounding area)**
MAR 17th **St Patrick's Day Parade (Chicago IL & New York NY)**
MAR **Ice Festival (Fairbanks AK)**
MAR **South by SW Music Conference & Festival (Austin TX)**
before LENT **Mardi Gras (New Orleans LA)**
EASTER SUNDAY **Easter Parade (New York NY)**
APR **French Quarter Festival (New Orleans LA)**
APR **Festival International de Louisiane (Lafayette LA)**
APR–MAY **JazzFest Jazz & Heritage Fest. (New Orleans & LA)**
APR–MAY **Kentucky Derby Festival (Louisville KY)**
MAY 5th **Cinco de Mayo (Los Angeles CA)**
MAY **Atlanta Jazz Festival (GA)**
MAY **Folk Festival (Black Mountain NC)**
MAY **Fiesta San Antonio & International Conjunto Festival**
MAY **Zuni Crafts Show (Flagstaff AZ)**
MEMORIAL DAY WEEKEND **Vandalia Festival (Charleston WV)**
JUN **Chicago Blues Festival (IL)**
JUN **Fan Fair: concerts and meeting the stars (Nashville TN)**
JUN **Little Bighorn Days (Hardin MT)**
JUL 4th **Independence Day (countrywide)**
JUN–AUG **Grant Park Music Festival (Chicago IL)**
JUL **Festival of American Folklife (Washington DC)**
JUL **World Eskimo-Indian Olympics (Fairbanks AK)**
JUL **Cheyenne Frontier Days (WY)**
JUL **Freedom Fest and Riverblues festivals (Philadelphia PA)**
JUL–AUG **Newport Folk and Jazz Festivals (RI)**
JUL–AUG **Hopi and Navajo Crafts Shows (Flagstaff AZ)**
AUG 4th **Corn Dance Festival (Santo Domingo NM)**
AUG **Elvis Week (Memphis TN)**
AUG **Inter-Tribal Indian Ceremonial (Gallup NM)**
AUG **Texas Folklife Festival (San Antonio TX)**
LABOR DAY WEEKEND **Bumbershoot Festival (Seattle WA)**
SEP **Fiestas de Santa Fe (NM)**
SEP **Pendleton Round-Up (OR)**
SEP **Monterey Jazz Festival (CA)**
SEP **Festivals Acadiens (Lafayette LA)**
SEP **Los Angeles County Fair (Pomona CA)**
OCT **Texas State Fair (Dallas TX)**
OCT 31st **Greenwich Village Hallowe'en Parade (New York NY)**
NOV **Macy's Thanksgiving Day Parade (New York NY)**
DEC **National Rodeo Finals (Las Vegas NV)**
DEC **Boston Tea-Party Re-enactment (MA)**

REGIONAL MARKETING ORGANISATIONS

Regional marketing organisations co-ordinate tourism issues in the USA. Participation by each state is voluntary. A state may be represented in more than one region, or none, and participation is subject to variation.

- Western States Tourism Policy Council*
- Rocky Mountain International
- Foremost West
- Great Lakes of North America (includes Ontario province, Canada)
- Mississippi River Country
- Travel South USA
- Capital Region USA
- Discover New England

*Not a formal regional marketing organisation

AK HI

AK HI

Lambert Equal Area Projection

200 miles
400 kilometres

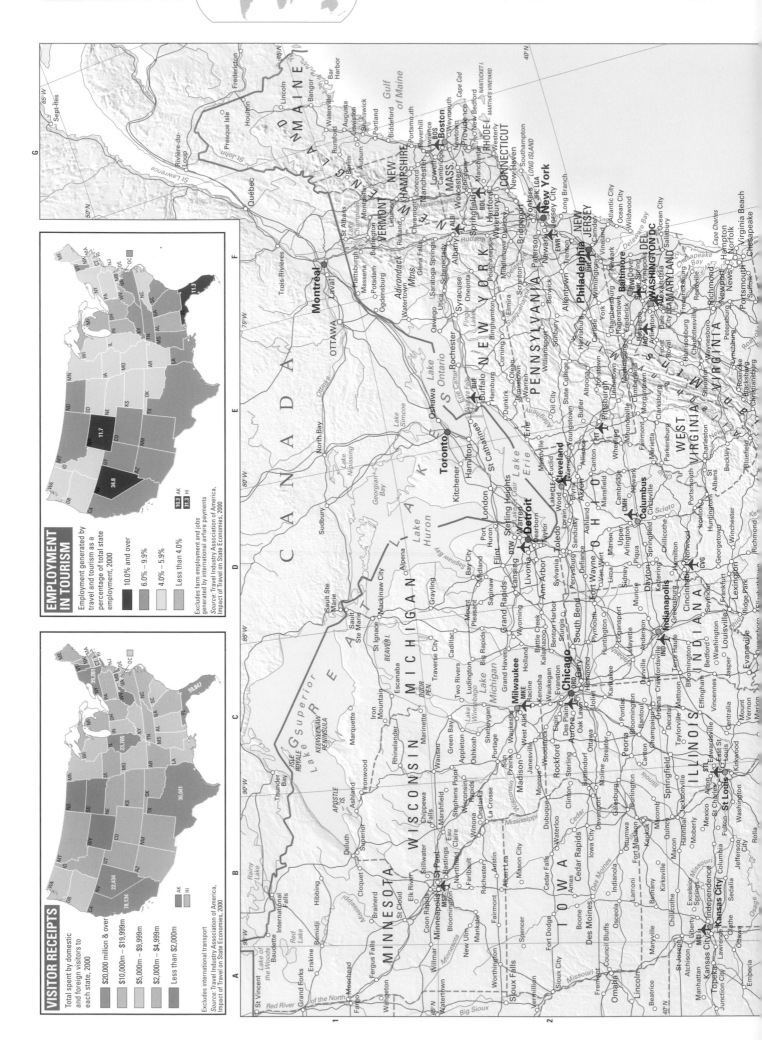

VISITOR RECEIPTS

Total spent by domestic and foreign visitors to each state, 2000

- $20,000 million & over
- $10,000m – $19,999m
- $5,000m – $9,999m
- $2,000m – $4,999m
- Less than $2,000m

AK HI

Excludes international transport

Source: Travel Industry Association of America, Impact of Travel on State Economies, 2000

EMPLOYMENT IN TOURISM

Employment generated by travel and tourism as a percentage of total state employment, 2000

- 10.0% and over
- 6.0% – 9.9%
- 4.0% – 5.9%
- Less than 4.0%

AK HI

Excludes farm employment and jobs generated by international airfare payments

Source: Travel Industry Association of America, Impact of Travel on State Economies, 2000

US National Parks

Legend

■ **National Park / Preserve**
NATIONAL PARKS contain a variety of resources protected by large areas of land or water; National Preserves permit activities not permitted in National Parks, such as hunting, fishing and mineral extraction

▲ **National Memorial**
Commemorate a historical subject or person

● **National Monument**
National Monuments administered by the US National Parks Service tend to focus on one site or on a feature of national significance

♣ **National Recreation Area / Seashore / Lakeshore**
National Recreation Areas are set aside for purely recreational use and are often near major cities; National Seashores and Lakeshores provide water-oriented recreation whilst preserving shorelines and islands

◆ **National Battlefield / Battlefield Park / Battlefield Site / Military Park**
All associated with US military history

▼ **National Historic Site / Historical Park**
National Historic Sites preserve locations and commemorate persons or events important in the nation's history; National Historical Parks are similar but larger and more complex

✪ **National Parkways**
Roadways that have been preserved for their scenic value.

Other protected areas managed by the National Park Service include National Rivers, Wild & Scenic Rivers and National Scenic & Historic Trails. Affiliated areas include National Heritage Areas which are managed by government-private partnerships.

THE TEN MOST VISITED NATIONAL PARKS [■] IN THE USA IN 2002

Number of recreational visitors (total for all National Parks [■]: 64,509,866)

		Number in list ▼
1	**Great Smoky Mountains** Tenn/N Car: 9,316,420 *(www.nps.gov/grsm)*	226
2	**Grand Canyon** Arizona: 4,001,974 *(www.nps.gov/grca)*	101
3	**Olympic** Washington: 3,691,310 *(www.nps.gov/olym)*	25
4	**Yosemite** California: 3,361,867 *(www.nps.gov/yose)*	48
5	**Cuyahoga Valley** Ohio: 3,217,935 *(www.nps.gov/cuva)*	185
6	**Rocky Mountain** Colorado: 2,988,475 *(www.nps.gov/romo)*	88
7	**Yellowstone** Wyoming/Montana: 2,973,677 *(www.nps.gov/yell)*	72
8	**Grand Teton** Wyoming: 2,612,629 *(www.nps.gov/grte)*	73
9	**Zion** Utah: 2,592,545 *(www.nps.gov/zion)*	77
10	**Acadia** Maine: 2,558,572 *(www.nps.gov/acad)*	295

Source: National Park Service

Sites marked with an asterisk (*) are featured in Columbus Travel Guides' *Tourist Attractions and Events of the World.*

Alaska
1 ▼ Aleutian World War II National Historic Area
2 ■ Bering Land Bridge National Preserve
3 ● Cape Krusenstern National Monument
4 ■ KOBUK VALLEY NATIONAL PARK
5 ■ Noatak National Preserve
6 ■ GATES OF THE ARCTIC NATIONAL PARK and Preserve
7 ■ Yukon-Charley Rivers National Preserve
8 ■ DENALI NATIONAL PARK and Preserve
9 ■ LAKE CLARK NATIONAL PARK and Preserve
10 ■ KATMAI NATIONAL PARK and Preserve
11 ● Aniakchak National Monument and Preserve
12 ■ KENAI FJORDS NATIONAL PARK
13 ■ WRANGELL-ST ELIAS NATIONAL PARK and Preserve
14 ▼ Klondike Gold Rush National Historical Park (also in Seattle, WA)
15 ■ GLACIER BAY NATIONAL PARK and Preserve
16 ▼ Sitka National Historical Park

Hawaii
17 ▲ USS Arizona Memorial
18 ▼ Kalaupapa National Historical Park
19 ■ HALEAKALA NATIONAL PARK
20 ▼ Puukohola Heiau National Historic Site
21 ▼ Kaloko-Honokohau National Historical Park
22 ▼ Pu'uhonua o Honaunau National Historical Park
23 ■ HAWAII VOLCANOES NATIONAL PARK*

Washington
24 ▼ San Juan Island National Historical Park
25 ■ OLYMPIC NATIONAL PARK
26 ▼ Ebey's Landing National Historical Reserve
27 ■ NORTH CASCADES NATIONAL PARK
28 ♣ Ross Lake National Recreation Area
29 ♣ Lake Chelan National Recreation Area
30 ♣ Lake Roosevelt National Recreation Area
31 ▼ Whitman Mission National Historic Site
32 ■ MOUNT RAINIER NATIONAL PARK
33 ▼ Fort Vancouver National Historic Site

Oregon
34 ▲ Fort Clatsop National Memorial
35 ● John Day Fossil Beds National Monument
36 ■ CRATER LAKE NATIONAL PARK
37 ● Oregon Caves National Monument

California
38 ■ REDWOOD NATIONAL PARK
39 ● Lava Beds National Monument
40 ♣ Whiskeytown-Shasta-Trinity National Recreation Area
41 ■ LASSEN VOLCANIC NATIONAL PARK
42 ♣ Point Reyes National Seashore
43 ♣ Golden Gate National Recreation Area (incl. Alcatraz Island*)
   ▼ Fort Point National Historic Site
   ● Muir Woods National Monument
   ▼ San Francisco Maritime National Historical Park
44 ▼ Rosie the Riveter WWII Home Front National Historical Park
45 ▲ Port Chicago Naval Magazine National Memorial
   ▼ John Muir National Historic Site

46 ▼ Eugene O'Neill National Historic Site
47 ● Pinnacles National Monument
48 ■ YOSEMITE NATIONAL PARK*
49 ● Devils Postpile National Monument
50 ■ SEQUOIA AND KINGS CANYON NATIONAL PARKS
51 ▼ Manzanar National Historic Site
52 ■ DEATH VALLEY NATIONAL PARK* (also in Nevada)
53 ■ CHANNEL ISLANDS NATIONAL PARK
54 ♣ Santa Monica Mountains National Recreation Area
55 ● Cabrillo National Monument
56 ■ JOSHUA TREE NATIONAL PARK
57 ■ Mojave National Preserve

Nevada
58 ♣ Lake Mead National Recreation Area (also in Arizona, includes Hoover Dam*)
59 ■ GREAT BASIN NATIONAL PARK

Idaho
60 ■ City of Rocks National Reserve
61 ● Minidoka Internment National Monument
62 ● Hagerman Fossil Beds National Monument
63 ● Craters of the Moon National Monument
64 ▼ Nez Perce National Historical Park

Montana
65 ■ GLACIER NATIONAL PARK
66 ▼ Grant-Kohrs Ranch National Historic Site
67 ◆ Big Hole National Battlefield
68 ● Little Bighorn Battlefield National Monument

Wyoming
69 ♣ Bighorn Canyon National Recreation Area (also in Montana)
70 ● Devils Tower National Monument
71 ▼ Fort Laramie National Historic Site
72 ■ YELLOWSTONE NATIONAL PARK* (also in Montana)
73 ✪ John D. Rockefeller, Jr. Memorial Parkway
   ■ GRAND TETON NATIONAL PARK
74 ● Fossil Butte National Monument

Utah
75 ▼ Golden Spike National Historic Site
76 ● Timpanogos Cave National Monument

77 ■ ZION NATIONAL PARK
78 ● Cedar Breaks National Monument
79 ■ BRYCE CANYON NATIONAL PARK
80 ■ CAPITOL REEF NATIONAL PARK
81 ● Rainbow Bridge National Monument
82 ● Natural Bridges National Monument
83 ■ CANYONLANDS NATIONAL PARK
84 ■ ARCHES NATIONAL PARK
85 ● Hovenweep National Monument (also in Colorado)

Colorado
86 ● Dinosaur National Monument (also in Utah)
87 ■ ROCKY MOUNTAIN NATIONAL PARK
88 ● Colorado National Monument
89 ■ BLACK CANYON OF THE GUNNISON NATIONAL PARK
90 ♣ Curecanti National Recreation Area
91 ● Yucca House National Monument
92 ■ MESA VERDE NATIONAL PARK
93 ● Great Sand Dunes National Monument
94 ● Florissant Fossil Beds National Monument
95 ▼ Bent's Old Fort National Historic Site

Arizona
96 ● Parashant National Monument
97 ● Pipe Spring National Monument
98 ■ GRAND CANYON NATIONAL PARK*
99 ♣ Glen Canyon National Recreation Area (also in Utah)
100 ● Navajo National Monument
101 ● Canyon de Chelly National Monument
102 ▼ Hubbell Trading Post National Historic Site
103 ■ PETRIFIED FOREST NATIONAL PARK
104 ● Wupatki National Monument
   ● Sunset Crater Volcano National Monument
105 ● Walnut Canyon National Monument
106 ● Tuzigoot National Monument
107 ● Montezuma Castle National Monument
108 ● Tonto National Monument
109 ● Hohokam Pima National Monument
110 ● Casa Grande Ruins National Monument
111 ● Organ Pipe Cactus National Monument
112 ▼ Tumacacori National Historical Park
113 ▲ Coronado National Memorial

114 ■ SAGUARO NATIONAL PARK
115 ▼ Fort Bowie National Historic Site
116 ● Chiricahua National Monument

New Mexico
117 ● Gila Cliff Dwellings National Monument
118 ● White Sands National Monument
119 ■ CARLSBAD CAVERNS NATIONAL PARK
120 ● Salinas Pueblo Missions National Monument
121 ● Aztec Ruins National Monument
122 ▼ Chaco Culture National Historical Park
123 ● El Morro National Monument
124 ● El Malpais National Monument
125 ● Petroglyph National Monument
126 ● Bandelier National Monument
127 ▼ Pecos National Historical Park
128 ▼ Fort Union National Monument
129 ● Capulin Volcano National Monument

Texas
130 ♣ Lake Meredith National Recreation Area
131 ● Alibates Flint Quarries National Monument
132 ▲ Chamizal National Memorial
133 ■ GUADALUPE MOUNTAINS NATIONAL PARK
134 ▼ Fort Davis National Historic Site
135 ■ BIG BEND NATIONAL PARK
136 ♣ Amistad National Recreation Area
137 ▼ Lyndon B. Johnson National Historical Park
138 ▼ San Antonio Missions National Historical Park
139 ▼ Palo Alto Battlefield National Historic Site
140 ♣ Padre Island National Seashore
141 ■ Big Thicket National Preserve

Oklahoma
142 ♣ Chickasaw National Recreation Area
143 ▲ Oklahoma City National Memorial
144 ▼ Washita Battlefield National Historic Site

North Dakota
145 ▼ Fort Union Trading Post National Historic Site
146 ■ THEODORE ROOSEVELT NATIONAL PARK
147 ▼ Knife River Indian Villages National Historic Site

South Dakota
148 ● Jewel Cave National Monument
   ▲ Mount Rushmore National Memorial*
149 ■ WIND CAVE NATIONAL PARK
150 ■ BADLANDS NATIONAL PARK

US National Parks

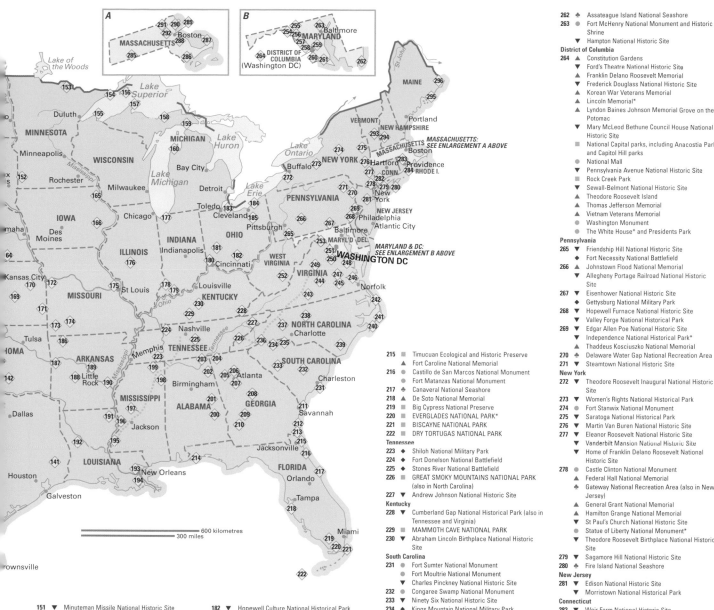

262 ⚓ Assateague Island National Seashore
263 ▲ Fort McHenry National Monument and Historic Shrine
　 ▼ Hampton National Historic Site
District of Columbia
264 ▲ Constitution Gardens
　 ▼ Ford's Theatre National Historic Site
　 ▲ Franklin Delano Roosevelt Memorial
　 ▲ Frederick Douglass National Historic Site
　 ▲ Korean War Veterans Memorial
　 ▲ Lincoln Memorial*
　 ▲ Lyndon Baines Johnson Memorial Grove on the Potomac
　 ▼ Mary McLeod Bethune Council House National Historic Site
　 ■ National Capital parks, including Anacostia Park and Capitol Hill parks
　 ■ National Mall
　 ▲ Pennsylvania Avenue National Historic Site
　 ■ Rock Creek Park
　 ▼ Sewall-Belmont National Historic Site
　 ▲ Theodore Roosevelt Island
　 ▲ Thomas Jefferson Memorial
　 ▲ Vietnam Veterans Memorial
　 ● Washington Monument
　 ▼ The White House* and Presidents Park
Pennsylvania
265 ▼ Friendship Hill National Historic Site
　 ▼ Fort Necessity National Battlefield
266 ▼ Johnstown Flood National Memorial
　 ▼ Allegheny Portage Railroad National Historic Site
267 ▼ Eisenhower National Historic Site
　 ◆ Gettysburg National Military Park
268 ▼ Hopewell Furnace National Historic Site
　 ▼ Valley Forge National Historical Park
269 ▼ Edgar Allen Poe National Historic Site
　 ▲ Independence National Historical Park*
　 ▲ Thaddeus Kosciuszko National Memorial
270 ■ Delaware Water Gap National Recreation Area
271 ▼ Steamtown National Historic Site
New York
272 ▼ Theodore Roosevelt Inaugural National Historic Site
273 ▼ Women's Rights National Historical Park
274 ▼ Fort Stanwix National Monument
275 ◆ Saratoga National Historical Park
276 ▼ Martin Van Buren National Historic Site
277 ▼ Eleanor Roosevelt National Historic Site
　 ▼ Vanderbilt Mansion National Historic Site
　 ▼ Home of Franklin Delano Roosevelt National Historic Site
278 ▲ Castle Clinton National Monument
　 ▲ Federal Hall National Memorial
　 ⚓ Gateway National Recreation Area (also in New Jersey)
　 ▲ General Grant National Memorial
　 ▲ Hamilton Grange National Memorial
　 ● St Paul's Church National Historic Site
　 ● Statue of Liberty National Monument*
　 ▼ Theodore Roosevelt Birthplace National Historic Site
279 ▼ Sagamore Hill National Historic Site
280 ⚓ Fire Island National Seashore
New Jersey
281 ▼ Edison National Historic Site
　 ▼ Morristown National Historical Park
Connecticut
282 ▼ Weir Farm National Historic Site
Rhode Island
283 ▲ Roger Williams National Memorial
284 ▼ Touro Synagogue National Historic Site
Massachusetts
285 ▼ Springfield Armory National Historic Site
286 ▼ New Bedford Whaling National Historical Park
287 ⚓ Cape Cod National Seashore
288 ▲ Adams National Historic Park
289 ▼ Boston African American National Historical Site
　 ⚓ Boston Harbor Islands National Recreation Area
　 ▼ Boston National Historical Park
　 ▼ Frederick Law Olmsted National Historic Site
　 ▼ John F. Kennedy National Historic Site
　 ▼ Longfellow National Historic Site
290 ▼ Saugus Iron Works National Historic Site
　 ▼ Salem Maritime National Historic Site
291 ▼ Lowell National Historical Park
292 ▼ Minute Man National Historical Park
Vermont
293 ▼ Marsh-Billings-Rockefeller National Historical Park
New Hampshire
294 ▼ St-Gaudens National Historic Site
Maine
295 ■ ACADIA NATIONAL PARK
296 ▼ St Croix Island International Historic Site

The following are not shown on the map:
Puerto Rico
　 ● San Juan National Historic Site
US Virgin Islands
　 ● Buck Island Reef National Monument
　 ▼ Christiansted National Historic Site
　 ▼ Salt River Bay National Historical Park and Ecological Preserve
　 ■ VIRGIN ISLANDS NATIONAL PARK
American Samoa
　 ■ NATIONAL PARK OF AMERICAN SAMOA
Guam
　 ▼ War in the Pacific National Historical Park

151 ▼ Minuteman Missile National Historic Site
Minnesota
152 ● Pipestone National Monument
153 ■ VOYAGEURS NATIONAL PARK
154 ● Grand Portage National Monument
Wisconsin
155 ⚓ Apostle Islands National Lakeshore
Michigan
156 ■ ISLE ROYALE NATIONAL PARK
157 ▼ Keweenaw National Historical Park
158 ⚓ Pictured Rocks National Lakeshore
159 ▲ Father Marquette National Memorial
160 ⚓ Sleeping Bear Dunes National Lakeshore
Nebraska
161 ● Agate Fossil Beds National Monument
162 ● Scotts Bluff National Monument
163 ▼ Chimney Rock National Historic Site
164 ● Homestead National Monument of America
Iowa
165 ● Effigy Mounds National Monument
166 ▼ Herbert Hoover National Historic Site
Kansas
167 ▼ Nicodemus National Historic Site
168 ▼ Fort Larned National Historic Site
169 ■ Tallgrass Prairie National Preserve
170 ▼ Brown v. Board of Education National Historic Site
171 ▼ Fort Scott National Historic Site
Missouri
172 ▼ Harry S. Truman National Historic Site
173 ● George Washington Carver National Monument
174 ▼ Wilson's Creek National Battlefield
175 ◆ Ulysses S. Grant National Historic Site
　 ▲ Jefferson National Expansion Memorial
Illinois
176 ▼ Lincoln Home National Historic Site
Indiana
177 ⚓ Indiana Dunes National Lakeshore
178 ▼ George Rogers Clark National Historical Park
179 ▲ Lincoln Boyhood National Memorial
Ohio
180 ▼ William Howard Taft National Historic Site
181 ▼ Dayton Aviation National Historical Park
182 ▼ Hopewell Culture National Historical Park
183 ▲ Perry's Victory and International Peace Memorial
184 ▼ James A. Garfield National Historic Site
185 ■ CUYAHOGA VALLEY NATIONAL PARK
Arkansas
186 ▼ Pea Ridge National Military Park
187 ▼ Fort Smith National Historic Site
188 ■ HOT SPRINGS NATIONAL PARK
189 ▼ Central High School National Historic Site
190 ▼ Arkansas Post National Memorial
Louisiana
191 ● Poverty Point National Monument
192 ▼ Cane River Creole National Historical Park
193 ▼ New Orleans Jazz National Historical Park
194 ▼ Jean Lafitte National Historical Park & Preserve
Mississippi
195 ▼ Natchez National Historical Park
196 ▼ Vicksburg National Military Park
197 ⊘ Natchez Trace Parkway (also in Alabama & Tennessee)
198 ▼ Tupelo National Battlefield
199 ▼ Brices Cross Roads National Battlefield Site
Alabama
200 ▼ Tuskegee Airman National Historic Site
　 ▼ Tuskegee Institute National Historic Site
201 ▼ Horseshoe Bend National Military Park
202 ■ Little River Canyon National Preserve
203 ▼ Russell Cave National Monument
Georgia
204 ▼ Chickamauga & Chattanooga National Military Park
205 ◆ Kennesaw Mountain National Battlefield Park
206 ● Chattahoochee River National Recreation Area
207 ▼ Martin Luther King Jr. National Historic Site
208 ● Ocmulgee National Monument
209 ▼ Andersonville National Historic Site
210 ▼ Jimmy Carter National Historic Site
211 ▲ Fort Pulaski National Monument
212 ▼ Fort Frederica National Monument
213 ⚓ Cumberland Island National Seashore
Florida
214 ⚓ Gulf Islands National Seashore (also in Mississippi)

215 ■ Timucuan Ecological and Historic Preserve
　 ▲ Fort Caroline National Memorial
216 ● Castillo de San Marcos National Monument
　 ● Fort Matanzas National Monument
217 ⚓ Canaveral National Seashore
218 ▲ De Soto National Memorial
219 ■ Big Cypress National Preserve
220 ■ EVERGLADES NATIONAL PARK*
221 ■ BISCAYNE NATIONAL PARK
222 ■ DRY TORTUGAS NATIONAL PARK
Tennessee
223 ◆ Shiloh National Military Park
224 ◆ Fort Donelson National Battlefield
225 ◆ Stones River National Battlefield
226 ■ GREAT SMOKY MOUNTAINS NATIONAL PARK (also in North Carolina)
227 ▼ Andrew Johnson National Historic Site
Kentucky
228 ▼ Cumberland Gap National Historical Park (also in Tennessee and Virginia)
229 ■ MAMMOTH CAVE NATIONAL PARK
230 ▼ Abraham Lincoln Birthplace National Historic Site
South Carolina
231 ▲ Fort Sumter National Monument
　 ● Fort Moultrie National Monument
　 ▼ Charles Pinckney National Historic Site
232 ● Congaree Swamp National Monument
233 ▼ Ninety Six National Historic Site
234 ◆ Kings Mountain National Military Park
235 ◆ Cowpens National Battlefield
North Carolina
236 ▼ Carl Sandburg Home National Historic Site
237 ⊘ Blue Ridge Parkway (also in Virginia)
238 ◆ Guilford Courthouse National Military Park
239 ◆ Moores Creek National Battlefield
240 ⚓ Cape Lookout National Seashore
241 ⚓ Cape Hatteras National Seashore
242 ▼ Fort Raleigh National Historic Site
　 ▲ Wright Brothers National Memorial
Virginia
243 ● Booker T. Washington National Monument
244 ▼ Appomattox Court House National Historical Park
245 ◆ Petersburg National Battlefield
246 ▼ Colonial National Historical Park
247 ▼ Maggie L. Walker National Historic Site
　 ◆ Richmond National Battlefield Park
248 ● George Washington Birthplace National Monument
249 ■ SHENANDOAH NATIONAL PARK
250 ◆ Fredericksburg and Spotsylvania County Battlefields Memorial National Military Park
　 ■ Prince William Forest Park
251 ▼ Manassas National Battlefield Park
　 ⚓ Wolf Trap National Park for the Performing Arts
　 ⊘ George Washington Memorial Parkway
　 ▲ Arlington House, The Robert E. Lee Memorial
West Virginia
252 ● Gauley River National Recreation Area
253 ▼ Harpers Ferry National Historical Park
Maryland
254 ▼ Antietam National Battlefield
255 ■ Catoctin Mountain Park
256 ▼ Monocacy National Battlefield
257 ▼ Chesapeake and Ohio Canal National Historical Park
258 ▼ Clara Barton National Historic Site
259 ■ Greenbelt Park
260 ▼ Fort Washington Park
　 ■ Piscataway Park
261 ▼ Thomas Stone National Historic Site

United States of America

Map (main)

A   B   C   D

Seattle · Olympia · Portland · Salem · Eugene — WASHINGTON · OREGON
Spokane · Great Falls · Helena · MONTANA · Billings · Boise · IDAHO
CASCADE RANGE · Columbia · Missouri · Missouri Breaks
NORTH DAKOTA · Bismarck · Fargo · Duluth
Lake of the Woods · Lake Superior · Great Lakes · Lake Huron
MINNESOTA · St Paul · Minneapolis · Rochester · WISCONSIN · Madison · Milwaukee
MICHIGAN · Bay City · Lake Michigan · Lake Ontario · Lake Erie
Rochester · Buffalo · NEW YORK · MAINE · Augusta · Portland
Montpelier · VERMONT · NEW HAMPSHIRE · Concord · MASSACHUSETTS · Boston
Albany · Hartford · CONNECTICUT · RHODE ISLAND · Providence · LONG I. · New York
SOUTH DAKOTA · Pierre · Rapid City · WYOMING · Casper · Cheyenne
ROCKY MOUNTAINS · GREAT PLAINS · BADLANDS · GREAT SALT LAKE
SIERRA NEVADA · GREAT BASIN · NEVADA · Reno · Carson City
Sacramento · San Francisco · San Jose · CALIFORNIA
Salt Lake City · UTAH · COLORADO · Denver · Colorado Springs
NEBRASKA · Lincoln · Omaha · North Platte · South Platte · Platte
IOWA · Des Moines · ILLINOIS · Chicago · Springfield · INDIANA · Indianapolis
OHIO · Columbus · Cleveland · Toledo · Detroit · Lansing
PENNSYLVANIA · Pittsburgh · Harrisburg · Philadelphia · NEW JERSEY · Trenton · Atlantic City
Baltimore · MARYLAND · Dover · DELAWARE · WASHINGTON DC · Annapolis
Bakersfield · Los Angeles · San Bernardino · San Diego · CHANNEL IS.
Las Vegas · GRAND CANYON · COLORADO PLATEAU · ARIZONA · Phoenix · Tucson
Santa Fe · Albuquerque · NEW MEXICO · El Paso
KANSAS · Topeka · MISSOURI · Kansas City · Jefferson City · St Louis
OZARK PLATEAU · Branson · Amarillo · Lubbock · LLANO ESTACADO
OKLAHOMA · Oklahoma City · Tulsa · ARKANSAS · Little Rock
Memphis · TENNESSEE · Nashville · KENTUCKY · Frankfort · Louisville
WEST VIRGINIA · Charleston · VIRGINIA · Richmond · Norfolk
APPALACHIAN MTNS · BLUE RIDGE · NORTH CAROLINA · Raleigh · Charlotte
SOUTH CAROLINA · Columbia · Charleston · GEORGIA · Atlanta · Savannah
ALABAMA · Montgomery · Birmingham · MISSISSIPPI · Jackson
TEXAS · Fort Worth · Dallas · Austin · Houston · Galveston · San Antonio
EDWARDS PLATEAU · Rio Grande · Red · LOUISIANA · Baton Rouge · New Orleans
MISSISSIPPI RIVER DELTA · Jacksonville · Tallahassee · FLORIDA · Orlando · Tampa · Miami · FLORIDA KEYS
Brownsville · EAST TEXAS

BOSTON–NEW YORK WASHINGTON
CALIFORNIA & NEVADA
WEST OF THE RIO GRANDE

Legend:
- — — State boundary
- ● State capital
- 800 km / 400 miles
- For an alphabetical list of US states, see Appendices

HAWAII (E)
NIIHAU · KAUAI · OAHU · Honolulu · MOLOKAI · LANAI · MAUI · HAWAII · HAWAII
300 km / 150 miles

ALASKA (F)
1000 km / 500 miles
ST LAWRENCE I. · NUNIVAK I. · ALASKA · Anchorage · Juneau · KODIAK I. · ALEUTIAN ISLANDS · ALEXANDER ARCHIPELAGO · Yukon

Airport codes
1 SMF Sacramento
2 OAK Oakland
3 SFO San Francisco
4 SJO San Jose *Norman Mineta*
5 MRY Monterey *Peninsula*
6 FCH Fresno
7 BUR Burbank-Glendale-Pasadena
8 LAX Los Angeles
9 SNA Orange County *John Wayne*
10 SAN San Diego *Lindbergh Field*
11 PSP Palm Springs
12 LAS Las Vegas *McCarran*
13 RNO Reno *Cannon*

1 SEA Seattle-Tacoma
2 GEG Spokane
3 PDX Portland
4 EUG Eugene
5 BOI Boise

CALIFORNIA & NEVADA
I   J

OREGON · IDAHO · Twin Falls · SNAKE RIVER PLAIN
Medford · Klamath Falls · Upper Klamath Lake · Lava Beds Nat. Mon.
Crescent City · Redwood Nat. Park · KLAMATH MOUNTAINS · Mt Shasta 4317m · Alturas
JARBIDGE WILDERNESS AREA · Granite Peak 2966m · BLACK ROCK DESERT
Eureka · Punta Gorda · Redding · Red Bluff · Lassen Volcanic National Park
Susanville · Winnemucca · GREAT COWBOY COUNTRY · Wells · Elko · Wendover · BONNEVILLE SALT FLATS
Mackerricher State Park · Fort Bragg · Chico · Quincy
Battle Mountain · RUBY MTNS · Lovelock · Pyramid Lake · BASIN
Mendocino · Nevada City · Grass Valley · Reno · Sparks · Carson Sink · PONY EXPRESS TERRITORY
Fort Ross State Historic Park · Healdsburg · Napa Valley · Auburn · Coloma · Virginia City · Carson City · Gabbs · Austin · Eureka · Ely
Santa Rosa · Petaluma · Sonoma · Vallejo · Sacramento · Lake Tahoe · Walker Lake · SHOSHONE MTNS · BIG SMOKY · Wheeler Pk 3982m · Great Basin National Park
San Francisco · Sausalito · Berkeley · Oakland · Stockton · Modesto · Hawthorne · PIONEER TERRITORY
BAY AREA · San Mateo · Fremont · SILICON VALLEY · Yosemite National Park · Mono Lake · Tonopah
Paramount's Great America · San Jose · Santa Cruz · San Juan Bautista · Merced · Mariposa · Mammoth Lakes · Devils Postpile Nat. Mon. · Caliente · Alamo
Monterey · Carmel · Salinas · Big Sur · MONTEREY BAY · San Joaquin · Fresno · Visalia · Kings Canyon Nat. Park · Bishop · Beatty
Pfeiffer Big Sur State Park · Hanford · Porterville · Mt Whitney 4418m · Sequoia Nat. Park · Death Valley National Park
San Miguel · Delano · Badwater −86m · Valley of Fire State Park · Overton
Hearst San Simeon State Hist. Mon. · Bakersfield · Las Vegas · Lake Mead Nat. Rec. Area · Hoover Dam
Morro Bay State Park · San Luis Obispo · MOJAVE DESERT · Calico Ghost Town · Needles
La Purísima Mission State Historic Park · Santa Maria · Mojave National Preserve · Lake Havasu City
Point Conception · Santa Barbara · Oxnard · Six Flags Magic Mtn · San Bernardino · Barstow
SANTA ROSA I. · Ventura · Hollywood · Pasadena · Big Bear Lake · Joshua Tree Nat. Park
Channel Is. National Park · Malibu · Los Angeles · Disneyland · Palm Springs
SANTA CRUZ I. · SANTA BARBARA I. · Torrance · Long Beach · Santa Ana · COLORADO DESERT
SAN NICOLAS I. · Huntingdon Beach · Mission San Luis · Oceanside · Salton Sea
SAN MIGUEL I. · LEGOLAND · Escondido · Anza-Borrego Desert State Park
SeaWorld California · Capistrano · SAN CLEMENTE I. · San Diego · Chula Vista · Mexicali
CHANNEL ISLANDS · PACIFIC OCEAN · Tijuana · MEXICO · Ensenada · Yuma · ARIZ.
DIABLO RANGE · CALIFORNIA · SIERRA NEVADA

2000 metr / 1000 metr / Sea level
300 kilometres / 150 miles

WASHINGTON & OREGON
G   H

CANADA · Waterton Lakes National Park*
VANCOUVER ISLAND · Victoria · Blaine · Bellingham · Trail · Glacier National Park
Cape Flattery · Port Angeles · San Juan Island Nat. Hist. Park · Mt Baker 3285m · Bonners Ferry · Troy · Kalispell
Forks · Edmonds · N. Cascades Nat. Pk · Ross Lake Nat. Rec. Area · Franklin D. Roosevelt Lake · Flathead Lake · MT
Mt Olympus 2428m · Everett · L. Chelan Nat. Rec. Area · Grand Coulee Dam · Pend Oreille Lake · Polson
Olympic National Park · Queets · Seattle · Bellevue · Alpental · Wenatchee · Silverwood · Coeur d'Alene · Kellogg · CABINET MTNS · Battlesnake N.R.A.
Aberdeen · Tacoma · Puyallup · WASHINGTON · Ellensburg · Moscow · Missoula · BITTERROOT
GRAYS HARBOR · Mt Rainier 4392m · Mt Rainier Nat. Pk · Yakima · Pullman · Lolo Pass 1598m
WILLAPA BAY · Morton · Richland · COLUMBIA BASIN · Pasco · Lewiston · Nez Perce Nat. Hist. Park · Lost Trail Pass 2138m
Astoria · Mt St Helens 2550m · Mt St Helens Nat. Vol. Mon. · Walla Walla · Whitman Mission Nat. Hist. Site
Fort Clatsop Nat. Mem. · Longview · Pendleton · WALLOWA MTNS · Hells Canyon Nat. Rec. Area
Seaside · Cannon Beach · Vancouver · COLUMBIA GORGE · The Dalles · La Grande · Baker · SALMON RIVER MOUNTAINS
PACIFIC OCEAN · Portland · Gresham · Mt Hood 3425m · CASCADE RANGE · BLUE MTNS · McCall · IDAHO
McMinnville · Oregon City · Salem · Deschutes · John Day Fossil Beds Nat. Mon. · Sawtooth Nat. Rec. Area
Lincoln City · Newport · Albany · Springfield · Bend · Mt Batchelor 2763m · Ontario · Nampa · Sun Valley
Corvallis · Eugene · OREGON · Mt Bachelor 1563m · John Day · Caldwell · Boise
Florence · Oregon Dunes Nat. Rec. Area · Riley · Burns · SNAKE RIVER PLAIN · Shoshone
Coos Bay · Winston · Chemult · HARNEY BASIN · Hagerman Fossil Beds Nat. Mon. · Salmon Falls · Twin Falls
Bandon · GREAT SANDY DESERT · Harney Lake · Malheur Lake · Bliss · Gooding
Cape Blanco · Crater Lake Nat. Park · Upper Klamath Lake · Lake Abert · City of Rocks Nat. Reserve
Gold Beach · Grants Pass · Medford · Klamath Falls · WARNER MTNS · WARNER VALLEY · Overton
Oregon Caves Nat. Mon. · Ashland · Altamont · Lakeview · COLUMBIA PLATEAU · NEVADA

300 kilometres / 150 miles

*Combined as the Waterton-Glacier International Peace Park

United States of America

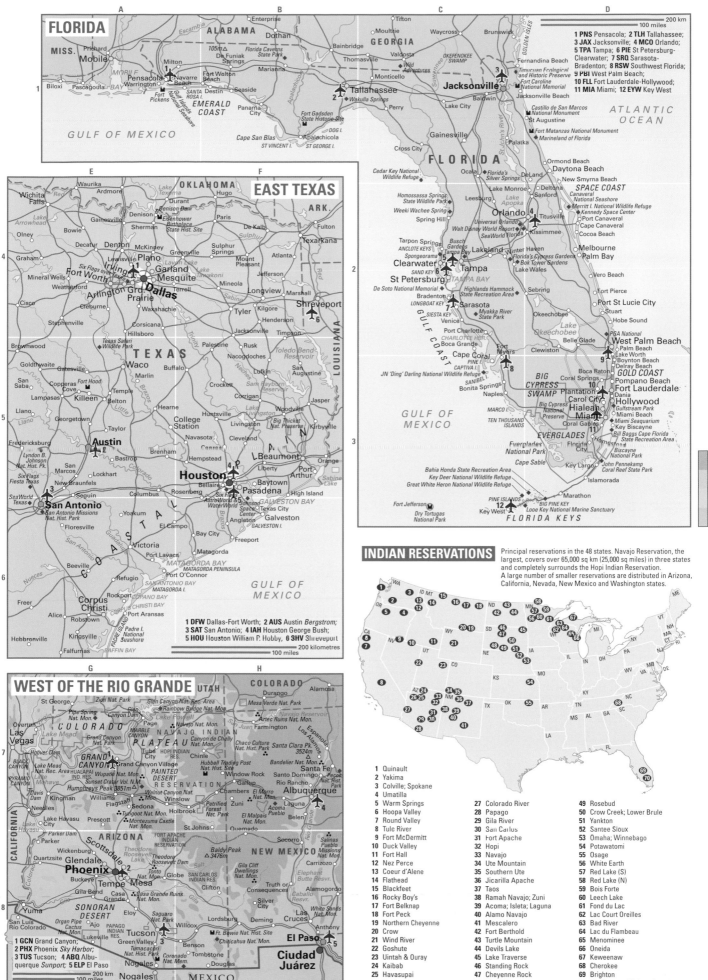

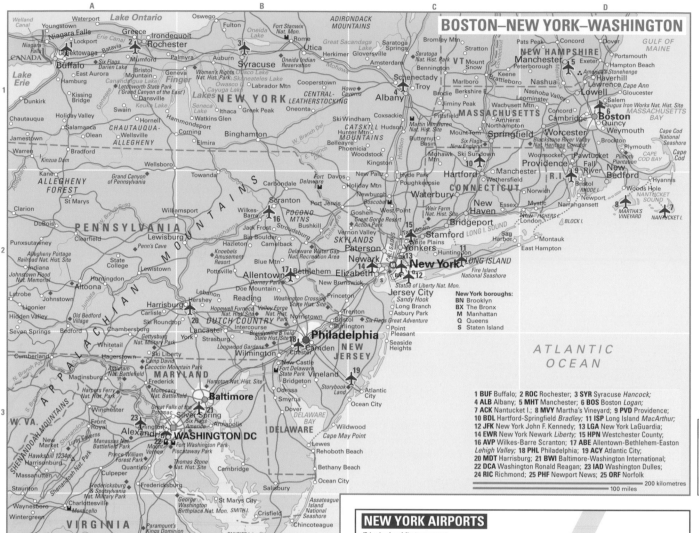

BOSTON–NEW YORK–WASHINGTON

New York boroughs:
BN Brooklyn
BX The Bronx
M Manhattan
Q Queens
S Staten Island

1 BUF Buffalo; 2 ROC Rochester; 3 SYR Syracuse *Hancock*;
4 ALB Albany; 5 MHT Manchester; 6 BOS Boston *Logan*;
7 ACK Nantucket I.; 8 MVY Martha's Vineyard; 9 PVD Providence;
10 BDL Hartford-Springfield *Bradley*; 11 ISP Long Island *MacArthur*;
12 JFK New York John F. Kennedy; 13 LGA New York LaGuardia;
14 EWR New York Newark *Liberty*; 15 HPN Westchester County;
16 AVP Wilkes-Barre Scranton; 17 ABE Allentown-Bethlehem-Easton
Lehigh Valley; 18 PHL Philadelphia; 19 ACY Atlantic City;
20 MDT Harrisburg; 21 BWI Baltimore-Washington International;
22 DCA Washington Ronald Reagan; 23 IAD Washington Dulles;
24 RIC Richmond; 25 PHF Newport News; 25 ORF Norfolk

2000 metres
1000 metres
Sea level

200 kilometres
100 miles

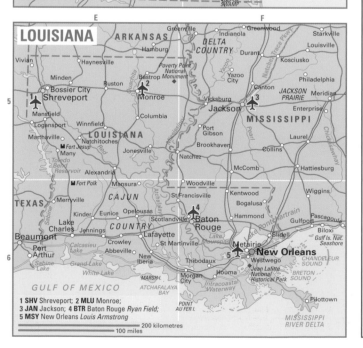

LOUISIANA

1 SHV Shreveport; 2 MLU Monroe;
3 JAN Jackson; 4 BTR Baton Rouge *Ryan Field*;
5 MSY New Orleans *Louis Armstrong*

200 kilometres
100 miles

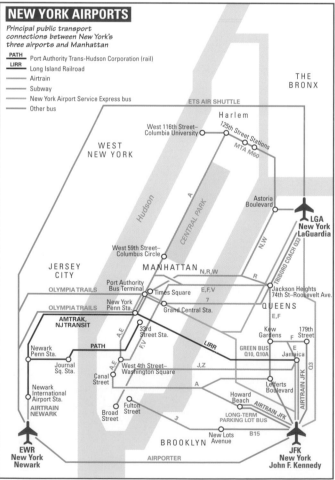

NEW YORK AIRPORTS

Principal public transport connections between New York's three airports and Manhattan

PATH — Port Authority Trans-Hudson Corporation (rail)
LIRR — Long Island Railroad
— Airtrain
— Subway
— New York Airport Service Express bus
— Other bus

Diagrammatic only: not to scale

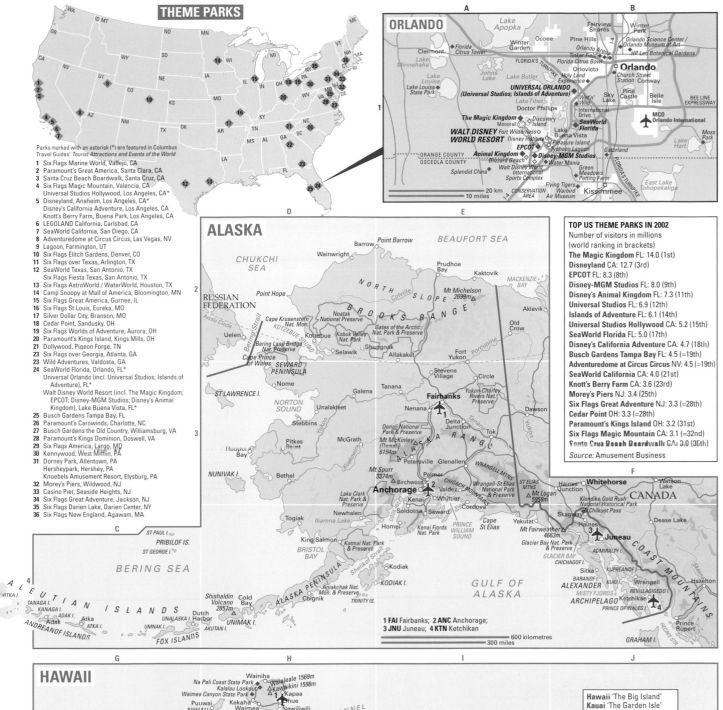

THEME PARKS

Parks marked with an asterisk (*) are featured in Columbus Travel Guides' *Tourist Attractions and Events of the World*

1 Six Flags Marine World, Vallejo, CA
2 Paramount's Great America, Santa Clara, CA
3 Santa Cruz Beach Boardwalk, Santa Cruz, CA
4 Six Flags Magic Mountain, Valencia, CA
  Universal Studios Hollywood, Los Angeles, CA*
5 Disneyland, Anaheim, Los Angeles, CA*
  Disney's California Adventure, Los Angeles, CA
  Knott's Berry Farm, Buena Park, Los Angeles, CA
6 LEGOLAND California, Carlsbad, CA
7 SeaWorld California, San Diego, CA
8 Adventuredome at Circus Circus, Las Vegas, NV
9 Lagoon, Farmington, UT
10 Six Flags Elitch Gardens, Denver, CO
11 Six Flags over Texas, Arlington, TX
12 SeaWorld Texas, San Antonio, TX
   Six Flags Fiesta Texas, San Antonio, TX
13 Six Flags AstroWorld / WaterWorld, Houston, TX
14 Camp Snoopy at Mall of America, Bloomington, MN
15 Six Flags Great America, Gurnee, IL
16 Six Flags St Louis, Eureka, MO
17 Silver Dollar City, Branson, MO
18 Cedar Point, Sandusky, OH
19 Six Flags Worlds of Adventure, Aurora, OH
20 Paramount's Kings Island, Kings Mills, OH
21 Dollywood, Pigeon Forge, TN
22 Six Flags over Georgia, Atlanta, GA
23 Wild Adventures, Valdosta, GA
24 SeaWorld Florida, Orlando, FL*
   Universal Orlando (incl. Universal Studios; Islands of Adventure), FL*
   Walt Disney World Resort (incl. The Magic Kingdom; EPCOT; Disney-MGM Studios; Disney's Animal Kingdom), Lake Buena Vista, FL*
25 Busch Gardens Tampa Bay, FL
26 Paramount's Carowinds, Charlotte, NC
27 Busch Gardens the Old Country, Williamsburg, VA
28 Paramount's Kings Dominion, Doswell, VA
29 Six Flags America, Largo, MD
30 Kennywood, West Mifflin, PA
31 Dorney Park, Allentown, PA
   Hersheypark, Hershey, PA
   Knoebels Amusement Resort, Elysburg, PA
32 Morey's Piers, Wildwood, NJ
33 Casino Pier, Seaside Heights, NJ
34 Six Flags Great Adventure, Jackson, NJ
35 Six Flags Darien Lake, Darien Center, NY
36 Six Flags New England, Agawam, MA

TOP US THEME PARKS IN 2002
Number of visitors in millions (world ranking in brackets)

The Magic Kingdom FL: 14.0 (1st)
Disneyland CA: 12.7 (3rd)
EPCOT FL: 8.3 (8th)
Disney-MGM Studios FL: 8.0 (9th)
Disney's Animal Kingdom FL: 7.3 (11th)
Universal Studios FL: 6.9 (12th)
Islands of Adventure FL: 6.1 (14th)
Universal Studios Hollywood CA: 5.2 (15th)
SeaWorld Florida FL: 5.0 (17th)
Disney's California Adventure CA: 4.7 (18th)
Busch Gardens Tampa Bay FL: 4.5 (=19th)
Adventuredome at Circus Circus NV: 4.5 (=19th)
SeaWorld California CA: 4.0 (21st)
Knott's Berry Farm CA: 3.6 (23rd)
Morey's Piers NJ: 3.4 (25th)
Six Flags Great Adventure NJ: 3.3 (=28th)
Cedar Point OH: 3.3 (=28th)
Paramount's Kings Island OH: 3.2 (31st)
Six Flags Magic Mountain CA: 3.1 (=32nd)
Santa Cruz Beach Boardwalk CA: 3.0 (36th)

Source: Amusement Business

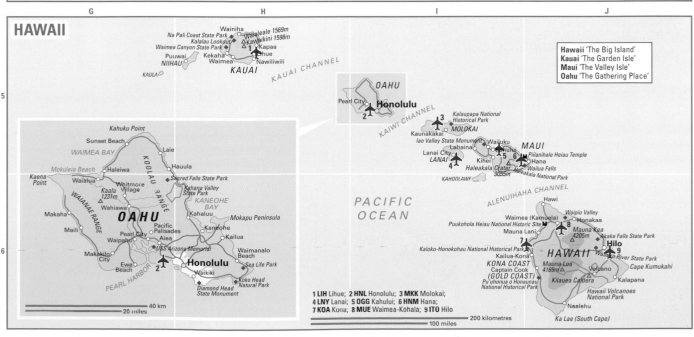

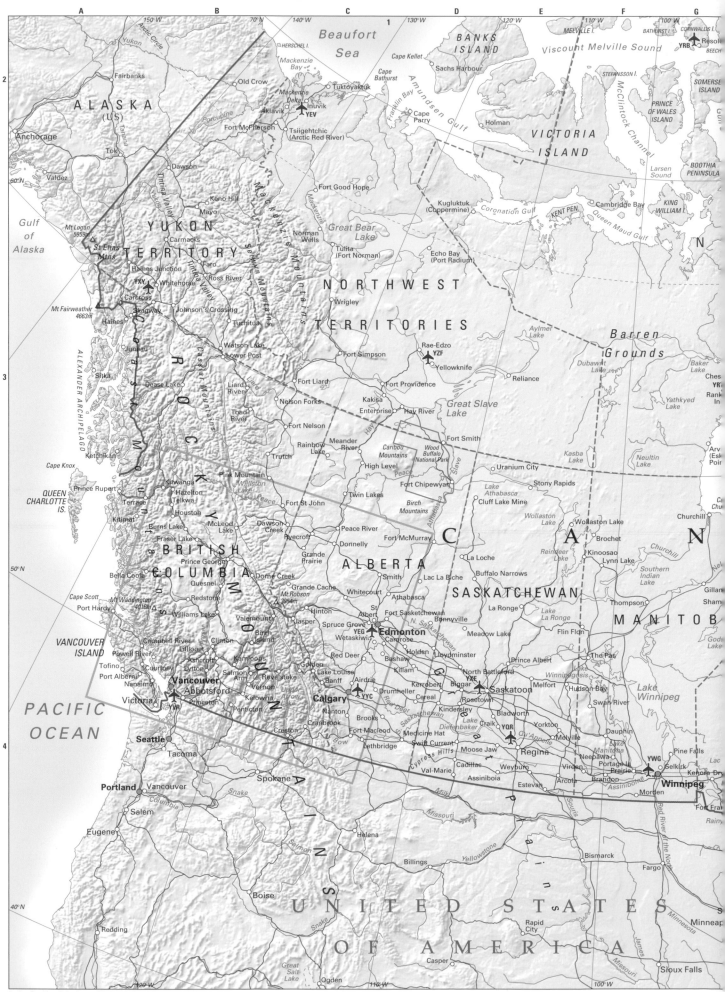

A | B | C | 1 | D | E | F | G

150° W   70° N   140° W   130° W   120° W   110° W   100° W

Beaufort Sea

HERSCHEL I.

Mackenzie Bay

MELVILLE I.

BATHURST I.

CORNWALLIS I.

YRB

Resol

BEECH

BANKS ISLAND

Cape Kellet

Sachs Harbour

Viscount Melville Sound

STEFANSSON I.

SOMERSET ISLAND

Fairbanks

Old Crow

Tuktoyaktuk

Cape Bathurst

Franklin Bay

Amundsen Gulf

Holman

McClintock Channel

PRINCE OF WALES ISLAND

A L A S K A (US)

Mackenzie Delta

Inuvik YEV

Aklavik

Cape Parry

Coronation Gulf

Kugluktuk (Coppermine)

VICTORIA ISLAND

Cambridge Bay

KING WILLIAM I.

BOOTHIA PENINSULA

Anchorage

Fort McPherson

Tsiigehtchic (Arctic Red River)

Larsen Sound

Tok

60° N

Valdez

Dawson

Keno Hill

Fort Good Hope

KENT PEN.

Queen Maud Gulf

Mayo

Norman Wells

Great Bear Lake

Echo Bay (Port Radium)

Uranium City

Gulf of Alaska

Mt Logan 5959m

St Elias Mtns

Carmacks

Y U K O N

Tulita (Fort Norman)

Stony Rapids

Arv (Esk Poir

Haines Junction

YXY

Whitehorse

Faro

Ross River

T E R R I T O R Y

Wrigley

N O R T H W E S T

Rae-Edzo YZF

Yellowknife

Aylmer Lake

Barren Grounds

Dubawnt Lake

Baker Lake

Ches

YR

Mt Fairweather 4663m

Carcross

Johnson's Crossing

T E R R I T O R I E S

Fort Simpson

Reliance

Kasba Lake

Neultin Lake

Rank in

Skagway

Haines

Tuchitua

Fort Liard

Fort Providence

Enterprise

Great Slave Lake

Hay River

Fort Smith

Yathkyed Lake

Arv

Sham

Juneau

Watson Lake

Lower Post

Nelson Forks

Kakisa

Churchill

50° N

Sitka

Liard River

Toad River

Fort Nelson

Meander River

Caribou Mountains

Wood Buffalo National Park

Fort Chipewyan

Lake Athabasca

Cluff Lake Mine

Wollaston Lake

Wollaston Lake

Reindeer Lake

Kinoosao

Churchill

N

Chu

Dease Lake

Rainbow Lake

High Level

Birch Mountains

Brochet

Cape Knox

QUEEN CHARLOTTE IS.

Pink Mountain

Williston Lake

Trutch

Twin Lakes

Fort McMurray

La Loche

Buffalo Narrows

Lynn Lake

Southern Indian Lake

Churchill

Prince Rupert

Kitwanga

Hazelton

Telkwa

Terrace

Houston

Fort St John

Peace

Peace River

Smith

Athabasca

S A S K A T C H E W A N

Lac La Biche

La Ronge

Lake La Ronge

Meadow Lake

Flin Flon

Thompson

M A N I T O B

Kitimat

Burns Lake

Fraser Lake

McLeod Lake

Dawson Creek

Pouce Coupe

Donnelly

Fort McMurray

C A N

Gillam

Prince George

B R I T I S H

Grande Prairie

Grande Cache

A L B E R T A

Whitecourt

Edmonton

Fort Saskatchewan

Bonnyville

Lloydminster

Prince Albert

The Pas

Lake Winnipeg

Bella Coola

C O L U M B I A

Dome Creek

Mt Robson 3954m

Hinton

Jasper

Spruce Grove

YEG

Wetaskiwin

Holden

North Battleford

YXE

Melfort

Hudson Bay

Lake Winnipeg

God's Lake

Cape Scott

Port Hardy

Mt Waddington 4016m

Quesnel

Redstone

Williams Lake

Valemount

Birch Island

Red Deer

Bashaw

Killam

Kerrobert

Biggar

Saskatoon

Swan River

Dauphin

VANCOUVER ISLAND

Powell River

Campbell River

Lillooet

Clinton

Kamloops

Golden

Lake Louise

Banff

Airdrie

Drumheller

Cereal

Rosetown

Kindersley

Bladworth

Craik

Yorkton

Melville

Pine Falls

Tofino

Courtenay

Ashcroft

Lytton

Salmon Arm

Revelstoke

Vernon

Calgary

YYC

Nanton

Brooks

Medicine Hat

Craik

YQR

Regina

Dauphin

Port Alberni

Nanaimo

Powell River

Vancouver

Abbotsford

Kelowna

Penticton

Creston

Cranbrook

Fort Macleod

Lethbridge

Swift Current

Lake Diefenbaker

Moose Jaw

Qu'Appelle

YWG

Pine Falls

Selkirk

Kenora

Victoria

YVR

Princeton

Cypress Hills

Cadillac

Assiniboia

Weyburn

Virden

Brandon

Portage la Prairie

Winnipeg

Morden

Fort Frat

Seattle

Tacoma

Spokane

Val-Marie

Estevan

Arcola

Assiniboine

Souris

Red River of the North

Portland

Vancouver

Salem

Snake

Columbia

Helena

Billings

Yellowstone

Bismarck

Fargo

Eugene

Missouri

U N I T E D   S T A T E S

Minnea

40° N

Redding

Boise

Snake

Salmon

O F   A M E R I C A

Rapid City

Minnesota

Great Salt Lake

Ogden

Casper

Missouri

James

Sioux Falls

120° W   110° W   100° W

2

3

4

PACIFIC OCEAN

ALEXANDER ARCHIPELAGO

Ketchikan

Arctic Circle

Yukon

Porcupine

Tanana

Tinina Valley

Mackenzie Mountains

Selwyn Mountains

Cassiar Mountains

Coast Mountains

R O C K Y   M O U N T A I N S

Peace

Athabasca

Slave

Hay

N. Saskatchewan

S. Saskatchewan

Red Deer

Bow

Milk

Lambert Equal Area Projection   Blue boxes indicate focus map coverage

Canada

Baffin Bay

Lancaster Sound

VON ISLAND

BYLOT I.

Arctic Bay
BORDEN
PENINSULA

Pond Inlet

Clyde River

Uummannaq

Qeqertarsuaq (Disko)

Qeqertarsuaq (Godhavn)

Kangerlussuaq (Søndre Strømfjord)

Sisimiut

Davis Strait

Arctic Circle

G r e e n l a n d (Den.)

Q I K I Q T A A L U K

BAFFIN ISLAND

Hall Beach

PRINCE CHARLES I.

MELVILLE PENINSULA

Committee Bay

se Bay

N A V U T

Foxe Basin

CUMBERLAND PENINSULA

Pangnirtung

Cumberland Sound

Amadjuak Lake

FOXE PENINSULA

Iqaluit (Frobisher Bay)
YFB

HALL PENINSULA

Frobisher Bay

META INCOGNITA PENINSULA

Cape Dorset

SALISBURY I.

NOTTINGHAM I.

RESOLUTION I.

Labrador Sea

NUUK (GODTHÅB)

Paamiut (Frederikshåb)

Narsarsuaq

Qaqortoq (Julianehåb)

Nunap Isua (Cape Farewell)

ATLANTIC OCEAN

Coral Harbour

SOUTHAMPTON I.

Roes Welcome Sound

Evans Strait

Fisher Strait

COATS I.

MANSEL I.

Hudson Strait

Ivujivik

Salliut

Quaqtaq

AKPATOK I.

Cape Chidley

Mont d'Iberville (Mt Caubvick) 1652m

Hebron

Ungava Bay

Aupaluk

Kuujjuaq (Fort Chimo)
YVP

Nain

Hudson Bay

PÉNINSULE D'UNGAVA

Inukjuak (Port Harrison)

L'Ape Harrison

Makkovik

Rigolet

Port Hope Simpson
Battle Harbour

BELLE ISLE

Cape Bauld

L'Anse aux Meadows

C A N A D A

BELCHER IS.

Cape Henrietta Maria

Winisk

Réservoir Caniapiscau

Kuujjuarapik (Poste de la Baleine)

Schefferville

Smallwood Reservoir

NEWFOUNDLAND AND LABRADOR

Churchill Falls

Churchill

Happy Valley-Goose Bay

Esker

Harrington Harbour

Blanc Sablon

Port Saunders

Springdale

Gander

St John's
YYT

NEWFOUNDLAND

Strait of Belle Isle

Deer Lake

Corner Brook

Stephenville

Cape Race

Q U É B E C

Réservoir La Grande 2

Sakami

Réservoir La Grande 3

Chisasibi (Fort George)

Radisson

Labrador City

Fermont

Natashquan

Cape Henrietta Maria

AKIMISKI I.

Attawapiskat

James Bay

Eastmain

Eastmain

Rupert

Lake Mistassini

Gagnon

Réservoir Manicouagan

Sept-Îles

Havre-St-Pierre

ÎLE D'ANTICOSTI

Channel-Port-aux-Basques

St-Pierre et Miquelon (Fr.)
St-Pierre

Fortune

Gulf of St Lawrence

Cabot Strait

Cape North

CAPE BRETON I.

Sydney

Glace Bay

T A R I O

Pickle Lake

Fort Albany

Moosonee

Albany

Chibougamau

Jonquière Chicoutimi

Alma

Roberval

Réservoir Cabonga

Baie-Comeau

Matane

Rimouski

Campbellton

Bathurst

Gaspé

Cap Gaspé

ÎLES DE LA MADELEINE

Natre Dame

Cap Chat

PRINCE EDWARD ISLAND

Charlottetown

Chatham

Moncton
YQM

New Glasgow

SABLE I.

Savant Lake

Armstrong

Pagwa River

Hearst

Fraserdale

Matagami

Senneterre

Miquelon

La Tuque

Rivière-du-Loup

Grand Falls

Edmundston

NEW BRUNSWICK

Fredericton

Riverview

Truro
YHZ

Dartmouth

NOVA SCOTIA

Halifax

Nakina

Lake Nipigon

Cochrane

Timmins

Kirkland Lake

Noranda

Rouyn

Val-d'Or

Roberval

Trois-Rivières

Victoriaville

Thetford Mines

St-Georges

Lévis

Québec
YQB

Montmagny

Saint John

St John (St Jean)

Lunenburg

Bay of Fundy

Shelburne

Terrace Bay

White River

Wawa

Chapleau

Gogama

New Liskeard

Maniwaki

St-Jérôme

Joliette

Drummondville

Sherbrooke

Sorel

Mons

Yarmouth

Cape Sable

Thunder Bay

Red Rock

Lake Superior

Sudbury

North Bay

Pembroke

Mont-Laurier

Lachute
YMX

Laval

Montréal

Gatineau
YUL

OTTAWA

Nepean
YOW

St Albans

Portland

Manchester

Bay of Fundy

G R E A T

Sault Ste Marie

MANITOULIN I.

Georgian Bay

Parry Sound

Huntsville

Bancroft

Kingston

Brockville

Boston

Cape Cod

LONG I.

ATLANTIC OCEAN

Green Bay

Grand Rapids

Lansing

Lake Michigan

Owen Sound

Collingwood

Orillia

Lindsay

Trenton

Lake Ontario

Hudson

Albany

Syracuse

Springfield

Hartford

New Haven

Providence

LAKES

Lake Huron

Brampton
YYZ

Kitchener

Hamilton

Oshawa

Toronto

St Catharines

Niagara Falls

Buffalo

London

Sarnia

Lake Claire

Lake Erie

Madison

Milwaukee

Chicago

Detroit

Cleveland

Toledo

Windsor

New York

Mississippi

300 miles

600 kilometres

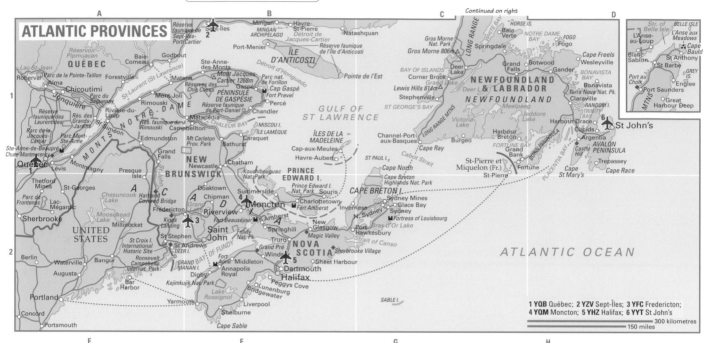

Continued on right

ATLANTIC PROVINCES

1 YQB Québec; 2 YZV Sept-Îles; 3 YFC Fredericton;
4 YQM Moncton; 5 YHZ Halifax; 6 YYT St John's

300 kilometres
150 miles

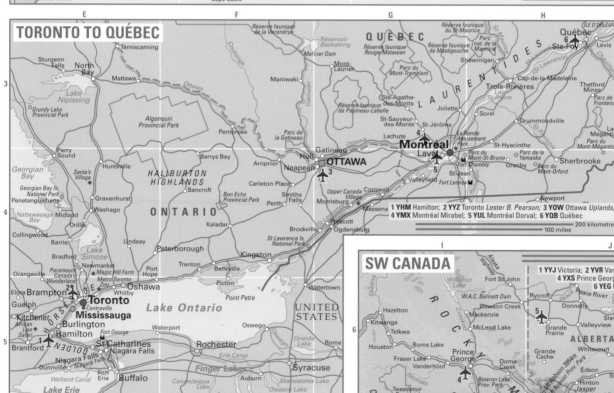

TORONTO TO QUÉBEC

1 YHM Hamilton; 2 YYZ Toronto *Lester B. Pearson*; 3 YOW Ottawa *Uplands*;
4 YMX Montréal Mirabel; 5 YUL Montréal Dorval; 6 YQB Québec

200 kilometres
100 miles

SW CANADA

1 YYJ Victoria; 2 YVR Vancouver; 3 YLW Kelowna;
4 YXS Prince George; 5 YQU Grande Prairie;
6 YEG Edmonton; 7 YYC Calgary

400 kilometres
200 miles

*Combined as the Waterton-Glacier International Peace Park

2000 metr
1000 metr
Sea level

FEB Carnaval de **Québec (QU)**
FEB Winterlude **(Ottawa OT)**
FEB Winterfest **(Toronto OT)**
FEB Sourdough Rendezvous **(Whitehorse YT)**
MAY Canadian Tulip Festival **(Ottawa OT)**
MAY-JUN **Vancouver** International Children's Festival **(BC)**
MAY-OCT Shakespeare Festival **(Stratford OT)**
JUN Festival d'Été **(Québec City QU)**
JUN Metro International Caravan **(Toronto OT)**
JUN Nova Scotia International Tattoo **(Halifax NS)**
JUN 24th St-Jean Baptiste Day **(Québec City QU)**
JUN-JUL International Jazz Festival **(Montréal OT)**
JUN-SEP Harbourfront Centre Summerfete **(Toronto OT)**
JUL 1st Canada Day **(Ottawa OT** & countrywide**)**
JUL International Freedom Festival **(Windsor OT)**
JUL Stampede **(Williams Lake BC)**
JUL Sea Festival **(Vancouver BC)**
JUL Loyalist Days Festival **(Saint John NB)**
JUL Klondike Days **(Edmonton AL)**
JUL **Calgary** Exhibition & Stampede **(AL)**
JUL Folklorama **(Winnipeg MN)**
JUL Manitoba Stampede & Exhibition **(Morris MN)**
JUL Manitoba Threshermen's Reunion **(Austin MN)**
JUL New Brunswick Highland Games & Scottish Festival
(Fredericton NB)
JUL-AUG Caribana **(Toronto OT)**
AUG Regatta Day **(St John's NF)**
AUG **Abbotsford** International Air Show **(BC)**

AUG Folklorama **(Winnipeg MN)**
AUG Gaelic Mod: Scottish festival **(St Ann's NS)**
AUG Fringe Festival **(Edmonton AL)**
AUG Six Nations Native Pageant **(Brantford OT)**
AUG Nova Scotia Fisheries Exhibition & Fishermen's
Reunion **(Lunenburg NS)**
AUG Discovery Day **(Dawson City YT)**
AUG-SEP Canadian National Exhibition **(Toronto OT)**
OCT Oktoberfest **(Kitchener-Waterloo OT)**
NOV Canadian Rodeo Finals **(Edmonton AL)**

International arrivals (millions)

20

15

10

5

1980 1985 1990 1995 2000
Source: World Tourism Organisation

Parks Canada administers Canada's National Parks and marine conservation areas. Parks Canada also administers a large number of the country's many National Historic Sites.

Parks marked with an asterisk (*) are featured in Columbus Travel Guides' *Tourist Attractions and Events of the World*

- - - Province boundary
◇ National Park of Canada

1000 km
500 miles

Yukon Territory
1 Ivvavik National Park
2 Vuntut National Park
3 Kluane National Park & Reserve*

Northwest Territories
4 Nahanni National Park
5 Tuktut Nogait National Park (also in NU)
6 Aulavik National Park

Nunavut
7 Quttinirpaaq (Ellesmere Island) National Park
8 Sirmilik National Park

9 Auyuittuq National Park

British Columbia
10 Gwaii Haanas National Park Reserve and Haida Heritage Site
11 Pacific Rim National Park Reserve
12 Gulf Islands National Park Reserve
13 Mount Revelstoke National Park; Glacier National Park
14 Yoho National Park
15 Kootenay National Park

Alberta
16 Wood Buffalo National Park (also in NT)

17 Elk Island National Park
18 Jasper National Park*
19 Banff National Park*
20 Waterton Lakes National Park

Saskatchewan
21 Prince Albert National Park
22 Grasslands National Park

Manitoba
23 Wapusk National Park
24 Riding Mountain National Park

Ontario
25 Pukaskwa National Park

26 Bruce Peninsula National Park, Fathom Five National Marine Park
27 Georgian Bay Islands National Park
28 Point Pelee National Park
29 St Lawrence Islands National Park

Québec
30 Parc national de la Mauricie
31 Parc marin du Saguenay-St-Laurent

32 Réserve du Parc national de l'Archipel-de-Mingan
33 Parc national de Forillon

New Brunswick
34 Kouchibouguac National Park
35 Fundy National Park

Prince Edward Island
36 Prince Edward Island National Park

Nova Scotia
37 Kejimkujik National Park
38 Cape Breton Highlands National Park

Newfoundland and Labrador
39 Gros Morne National Park
40 Terra Nova National Park

GREAT LAKES

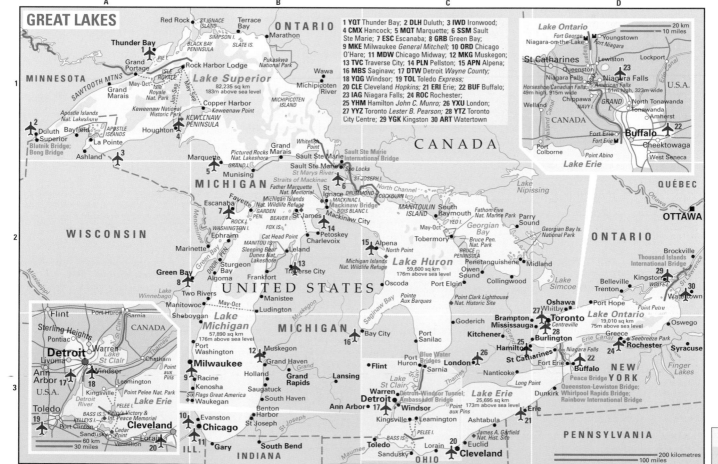

1 **YQT** Thunder Bay; 2 **DLH** Duluth; 3 **IWD** Ironwood;
4 **CMX** Hancock; 5 **MQT** Marquette; 6 **SSM** Sault
Ste Marie; 7 **ESC** Escanaba; 8 **GRB** Green Bay;
9 **MKE** Milwaukee *General Mitchell*; 10 **ORD** Chicago
O'Hare; 11 **MDW** Chicago Midway; 12 **MKG** Muskegon;
13 **TVC** Traverse City; 14 **PLN** Pellston; 15 **APN** Alpena;
16 **MBS** Saginaw; 17 **DTW** Detroit *Wayne County*;
18 **YQG** Windsor; 19 **TOL** Toledo *Express*;
20 **CLE** Cleveland *Hopkins*; 21 **ERI** Erie; 22 **BUF** Buffalo;
23 **IAG** Niagara Falls; 24 **ROC** Rochester;
25 **YHM** Hamilton *John C. Munro*; 26 **YXU** London;
27 **YYZ** Toronto *Lester B. Pearson*; 28 **YTZ** Toronto
City Centre; 29 **YGK** Kingston 30 **ART** Watertown

Latin America & the Caribbean

Key facts

Number of Countries	48
Area ('000 sq km)	20,567
Population ('000)	541,450
Population Density (per sq km)	26
Gross National Income (US$m)	1,915,670
Visitor Arrivals ('000)	55,607
Visitor Receipts (US$m)	39,511
Travel Departures ('000)	29,806
Travel Expenditure (US$m)	22,091

GNI figures relate to 2001. Population figures are taken from the most recent reliable source. Travel figures (WTO) are based on overnight stays, not same-day visitors, and are generally for 2001: where these are unavailable or unreliable, earlier years have been used. Where data for certain countries was not available, this has been regarded as zero. For more information see the Countries A-Z section from page 184.

Latin America, despite occupying only 15% of the world's land area, has a greater latitudinal range than any other continent. It stretches from the southern temperate zone of the northern hemisphere to the edge of the Antarctic and offers a similarly broad range of activities and attractions. Although many areas have recently become accessible – and not just to the adventurous traveller – much remains to be explored. The Caribbean, by contrast, is firmly established as a sunshine holiday destination. Many of the islands are heavily dependent on visitors from United States and, increasingly, on the cruise market.

Reconstruction and recession has recently hit many aspects of Latin America's economies, including the travel business. After a decade of steady growth, 2001 visitor arrivals rose slightly in Central America (up 1.6% v 2000), but fell in the Caribbean (down 1.9%) and South America (down 5.1%). More of the same followed in 2002: a rise of 9.7% in Central America, but further falls of 3% in the Caribbean and 7% in South America. First-half figures for 2003 suggest that recovery is underway, but that it unevenly spread. Of the major Caribbean destinations, the biggest rises in early 2003 were seen in the Dominican Republic and Cuba (19.3% and 19.1% respectively), two countries which are comparitively unreliant on the US market.

The Caribbean and South American travel industries have thus recently been through volatile times. Of the two, the Caribbean now appears better placed to achieve stable growth. Firstly, the cruise market is booming, with arrivals up by around 10% in 2002. Secondly, Caribbean countries have launched expensive but effective marketing campaigns, as well as a large programme of infrastructure improvement involving over 20% of the region's investment. By contrast, travel and tourism promotion is a less high priority for many South American countries. Thirdly, the Caribbean needs the travel business more. It is estimated that about 25% of all jobs directly or indirectly depend on it: in a few cases the figure is closer to 80%. Some islands derive more than half their foreign earnings from this source. This compares with Mexico which, despite receiving more foreign visitors than the whole of the Caribbean, relies upon them to provide only 1.5% of its GDP. Finally, a rather obvious point: the Caribbean is closer to Europe and North America than the rest of the region. Jamaica can be reached in five hours from New York; journeys to South America can take up to three times as long.

South America's biggest opportunity may be the growing perception – unforeseeable just a decade ago – that it is a 'safe' destination. This is likely to appeal to the US market, which currently supplies only around 12% of South America's visitors. If so, the message has yet to be received, for US visitors to South America were down 8% in 2002. By contrast, specialist operators out of the UK are reporting no slump in sales to the region. With the region's three largest visitor recipients, Mexico, Brazil and Puerto Rico, all experiencing falling hotel occupancy rates between

1997 and 2001, it is clear that Latin America can accommodate many more visitors than it currently receives. The question, perhaps, is how much effort the countries are prepared to spend in attracting them.

64% of visitors to the Caribbean, 77% of visitors to South America and 85% of visitors to Central America come from within the Americas. For some countries, including Mexico and Puerto Rico, the figure is over 90%. Little suggests that this will change significantly in the near future.

Economic change

The 1990s saw political and economic change in Latin America, with democracy, free trade and privatisation replacing military dictatorship, protectionism and state control. To date, the results have been mixed, and opinions vary as to how suitable these often painful remedies are for Latin America's problems. Critics point to currency devaluations in Brazil, fiscal crises in Argentina and industrial and social unrest in Venezuela. Others argue that political and economic liberalisation are good things, regardless of any teething problems, and it seems likely that this trend will continue. Central America so far appears to have had a slightly smoother ride than South America, content – for the time being – to seek the rewards of US-sponsored democracy.

Largely due to this increasing American influence, the dollar is fast becoming the favoured means of exchange in the region. This too has brought some benefits – particularly for visitors from hard-currency countries – but also some problems, not least the reality and perception of loss of national economic independence.

This trend towards globalisation has shown itself in other areas. Over the last decade Iberia airlines has gained control of several Latin American carriers, so helping improve access from other continents. Many local airlines are now concentrating on providing local services from Iberia's regional hubs.

Travel trends

The typical visitor to Latin America might once have been a backpacker, prepared to rough it on a low budget, but the picture is now more diverse. The growth in the 1990s was fuelled partly by an increase in family package holidays, such as to beach destinations in Brazil; partly by a growth in intraregional travel; and partly by the appetite for adventure holidays, a taste Latin America is well able to satisfy. This has helped open up many previously unknown destinations, especially around the Amazon river and in the Andes.

Traditional low-budget destinations such as the Mayan trail from Mexico to Honduras and the Inca paths through Peru are seeking a more upmarket and ecologically-minded clientele. Interest in all aspects of Latin American culture, indigenous and Iberian, is on the rise, and holiday options increasingly seek to satisfy this. South America's major cities are amongst the most vibrant in the world, with the attendant advantages and disadvantages, and attract leisure and business travellers alike. Events such as the Rio Carnival are celebrated with a verve that draws visitors from all over the world.

■ Big spenders

Expenditure on foreign travel (excluding international transport), 2001 – top ten countries (US$ billions) Source: WTO

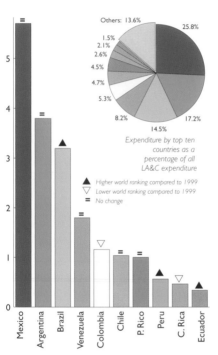

Others: 13.6%

25.8%
1.5%
2.1%
2.6%
4.5%
4.7%
5.3%
8.2%
14.5%
17.2%

Expenditure by top ten countries as a percentage of all LA&C expenditure

▲ Higher world ranking compared to 1999
▽ Lower world ranking compared to 1999
= No change

Mexico / Argentina / Brazil / Venezuela / Colombia / Chile / P. Rico / Peru / C. Rica / Ecuador

Central America has capitalised on its indigenous culture, beaches, diving destinations and colonial heritage. Its comparative proximity to the USA, its Caribbean coastline, greater economic stability and more effective international marketing strategies help explain why its visitor numbers have risen since 2000, while those of South America have fallen.

Throughout the mainland region, overland travel and tailor-made holidays are proving enduringly popular, and specialist operators are offering an ever-increasing range of options.

The Caribbean

The Caribbean islands, with high average temperatures, year-round warm waters of around 24°C and idyllic palm-fringed coastlines, are principally beach and water-sports destinations. They pioneered the 'all-inclusive holiday' and are very popular stop-off points

■ Economies

The region's 10 largest economies
Source: World Bank/International Monetary Fund

	GNI (US$ bn)	Annual GDP growth rate (%)			
	2001	2001	2002	est2003	est2004
Mexico	550.2	-0.3	0.9	2.3	3.7
Brazil	528.9	1.4	1.5	2.8	3.5
Argentina	260.3	-4.4	-11.0	3.0	4.5
Venezuela	117.2	2.7	-8.9	-17.0	13.4
Colombia	81.6	1.4	1.6	2.0	3.3
Chile	70.6	2.8	2.0	3.1	4.8
Peru	52.2	0.2	5.2	4.0	4.5
Puerto Rico	42.1	5.6	n/a	n/a	n/a
Guatemala	19.6	2.1	2.0	2.8	3.5
Uruguay	19.2	-3.1	-10.6	-2.0	4.5

■ Latin leapers

Fastest growing destinations and holiday types, 2003
Source: Journey Latin America

Fastest growing destinations...

1	Peru	2=	Ecuador	5	Guatemala
2=	Chile	2=	Mexico	6	Cuba

Fastest growing holiday types...

1	Luxury travel	3	Adventure travel
2	Honeymoons	4	Language courses

- Latin America and the Caribbean (LA&C) occupies 15.2% of the world's land area and is home to 8.5% of the world's population.
- LA&C's combined GDI is US$1,915,570 million, 6.1% of the world's total.
- LA&C accounts for 4.6% of global travel departures and 8.2% of arrivals.
- International travel and tourism contributed US$39.5 billion to LA&C's economy in 2001, compared to US$37.3 billion in 1999.
- 11 LA&C countries – four in South America, five in the Caribbean, one in Central America, and Mexico – received over 1 million visitors in 2001. Mexico alone accounted for over a third of all regional arrivals.
- The most-visited country in LA&C, Mexico, ranked 8th in the world in 2001 with 19 million visitors: over 90% of these were from the USA.
- Five countries – Mexico, Brazil, Puerto Rico, Dominican Rep. and Argentina – accounted for 50% of LA&C's earnings from international travel and tourism in 2001.
- There were 55.6 million international tourist arrivals in LA&C in 2001, an increase of 9.5% over 1997 but a fall of 4% compared to 2000. 38.7 million of these were to the mainland and 16.9 million to the Caribbean.
- South American countries have won the Football World Cup nine times, compared to eight wins by Europe.
- Visitors to the US Virgin Islands in 2001 each spent an average of over US$2,000.
- Central America's European visitors have doubled since 1990.
- In 2002, ten Caribbean countries received more cruise visitors than overnight visitors.
- The WTO estimates that there are 1.5 million hotel rooms in the region in 2001. Of the 34 countries which reported occupancy rates, the highest were Turks & Caicos Islands (78%) and Aruba (74%): the lowest were Peru (25%) and Bolivia (23%).
- Mexicans are LA&C's most frequent travellers, accounting for over 38% of the region's recorded international departures. Around 90% of these departures were to the USA.
- Citizens of the USA accounted for over 22% of all arrivals to the region (not including Mexico) in 2001.
- Each day, three cargo planes fly from Colombia to the USA loaded with flowers for shops and markets.
- Many experts believe that south-eastern Peru has more diversity of birdlife than any other place on earth.

for cruises. Improved inter-island air services are assisting the development of island-hopping and multi-centre holidays.

The recent fall in visitors has highlighted the dangers of over-reliance on tourism, and many states are taking urgent steps to diversify their economies.

Cruising

Cruise passengers provide a vital part of the tourism industry in the Caribbean and a major source of income for the Panama Canal. Some countries receive more than twice as many cruise passengers on shore trips as they do arrivals by air. Hoteliers can take comfort from this, for such day-trip visitors often return for a longer holiday.

Newer ships in the Caribbean are amongst the world's largest, carrying up to 4,000 passengers. Operators are now forced to be more environmentally friendly and there is strict control on the number of vessels entering each port each day. Cruise lines provide valuable employment for many Latin Americans.

Established favourites

- Mexico – One of the world's major destinations, especially for North Americans. Attractions range from Mayan sites to beach resorts such as Cancun, Acapulco and Puerto Vallarta. The Baja California area is also becoming popular.
- Brazil – Beach holidays around Salvador de Bahia, Recife and Natal have benefited from the introduction of charter flights from Europe. Brazil accommodates the majority of the vast Amazon rainforest. Rio de Janeiro's attractions include the carnival, Corcovado Mountain with its statue of Christ the Redeemer and the world-famous Ipanema and Copacabana beaches.

- Peru – ever-popular with adventure-seeking tourists, attractions include dramatic mountains and jungles, Lake Titicaca and Inca sites such as Machu Picchu, the Nasca Lines and Cusco.
- Puerto Rico – long popular with North Americans, the island has undergone revitalisation and is now popular with Europeans for pre- and post-cruise stays.
- Dominican Republic – this country offers some of the Caribbean's best beaches. Hotel standards have improved in recent years and each season sees an increase in the number of charter flights from Europe.
- Jamaica – dominated by all-inclusive resorts, but also well known for golfing, beach and activity holidays.
- Cayman Islands – one of the world's top diving locations that has been a pioneer in the ecological efforts to protect reefs.
- Barbados – perhaps the most British of the Caribbean islands and popular with those seeking a luxury beach holiday or a shorter visit either side of a cruise.
- The Bahamas – a country of over 700 islands, the most important of which are Grand Bahama and Nassau, the main port for hundreds of cruise ships. The tourist industry has long relied on visitors from the nearby USA.

Growth areas

- Cuba – tourism has developed rapidly in this communist outpost. 'Tour and stay' options are popular, with visits to historical and cultural sites, especially Havana, being followed by time spent in beach resorts such as Varadero.
- Central America – in visitor-arrival terms, the region's success story. Lush jungles, ancient monuments and spectacular diving (Belize, for instance, has the world's second largest reef) all form part of a successful and varied eco-tourism product.
- Chile – a diverse and fast-growing destination, and voted favourite long-haul country in the 2003 *Observer* travel awards. The Patagonian region is proving increasingly popular, while skiing holidays are starting to feature on operator's programmes.
- Galapagos Islands – featured on many expedition cruise itineraries and popular with those interested in wildlife. They have benefited from improved transport connections with Europe and USA via Ecuador.
- Antarctica – although not part of South America, the

seasonally accessible parts of this vast, icebound continent are becoming a popular destination for adventure travel and expedition cruises.

- Foreign-language holidays – many tour operators are featuring Spanish and Portuguese language courses throughout the region.
- Weddings & honeymoons – many resorts, particularly in the Caribbean, are promoting themselves as romantic destinations with this market in mind.

Problem areas

- Seasonal hurricanes occur in parts of Central America and the Caribbean.
- The rain forests in Central and South America continue to be depleted, affecting the local and global environment.
- Street crime and kidnapping has increased in South America in recent years, as it has worldwide, and continues to be a risk for business and leisure travellers.
- Colombia remains a trading post for illegal drugs.
- Industrial and social unrest in some countries, such as Venezuela and Bolivia, can disrupt travel plans.
- The recurring El Niño climate pattern is likely to have a disruptive effect on weather throughout the region in the coming years.

▦ Visitors

Visitor arrivals 2001. *Source: WTO*

	Visitors (thousands)	Change since 1997
Mexico	19,810	2.4%
Brazil	4,773	67.5%
Puerto Rico	3,551	9.5%
Dominican Republic	2,882	30.3%
Argentina	2,620	-5.2%
Uruguay	1,892	-18.3%
Cuba	1,736	50.6%
Chile	1,723	4.8%
Bahamas	1,538	-4.9%
Jamaica	1,277	7.1%
Costa Rica	1,131	39.5%
Guatemala	835	45.0%
Peru	798	23.0%
El Salvador	735	89.9%
Aruba	691	6.3%
Netherlands Antilles	677	-4.0%
Ecuador	641	21.2%
Colombia	616	-3.6%
US Virgin Islands	592	44.0%
Venezuela	584	-28.3%
Guadeloupe (not St Mart.)	521	-21.1%
Panama	519	23.3%
Honduras	518	68.7%
Barbados	507	7.4%
Nicaragua	483	34.9%
Martinique	460	-10.3%
Trinidad & Tobago	383	18.2%
Cayman Islands	334	-12.3%
Bolivia	308	-13.2%
British Virgin Islands	296	21.3%
Paraguay	295	-25.3%
Bermuda	278	-26.8%
St Lucia	250	0.8%
Antigua & Barbuda	237	-1.3%
Belize	196	34.2%
Turks & Caicos Islands	165	77.4%
Haiti	142	-4.7%
Grenada	123	10.8%
Guyana	95	25.0%
St Kitts & Nevis	75	-14.8%
St Vincent & the Gren.	71	9.2%
Dominica	68	4.6%
French Guiana	65	-4.4%
Surinam	58	-4.9%
Anguilla	48	11.6%
Montserrat	10	100.0%

(Figures not available for Falkland Islands or St Helena.)

▦ Big earners

Receipts from Foreign Travel (excluding international transport), 2001
(US$ billions) *Source: WTO*

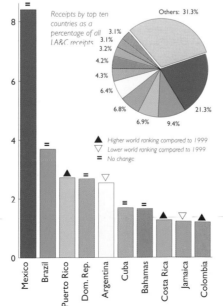

Receipts by top ten countries as a percentage of all LA&C receipts

Others: 31.3%

3.1%
3.1%
3.2%
4.2%
4.3%
6.4%
6.8%
6.9%
9.4%
21.3%

▲ Higher world ranking compared to 1999
▽ Lower world ranking compared to 1999
= No change

Mexico, Brazil, Puerto Rico, Dom. Rep., Argentina, Cuba, Bahamas, Costa Rica, Jamaica, Colombia

Thanks to: Ruth Skipsey of Journey Latin America; Adrian McCallister of the Caribbean Tourism Organisation; Graeme Payne; Gary Bowerman; Patrick Fitzgerald.

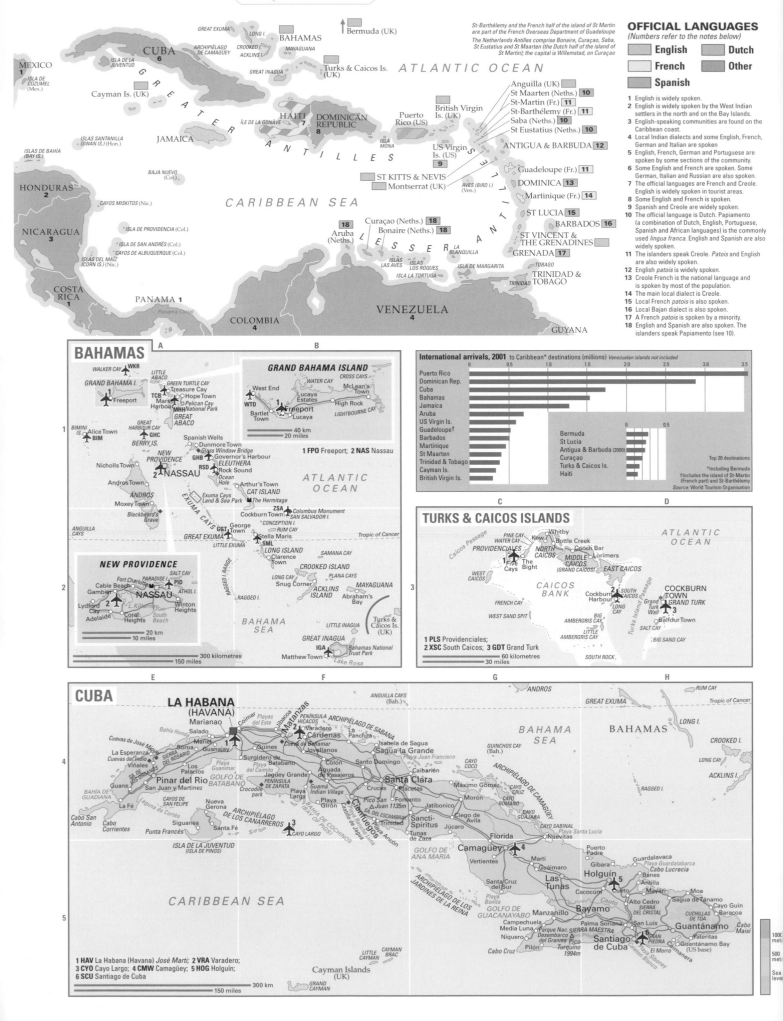

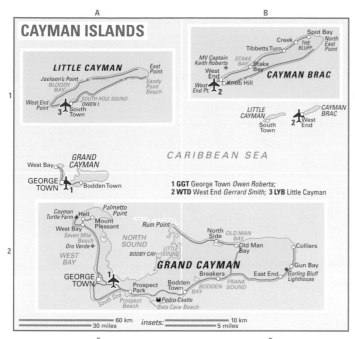

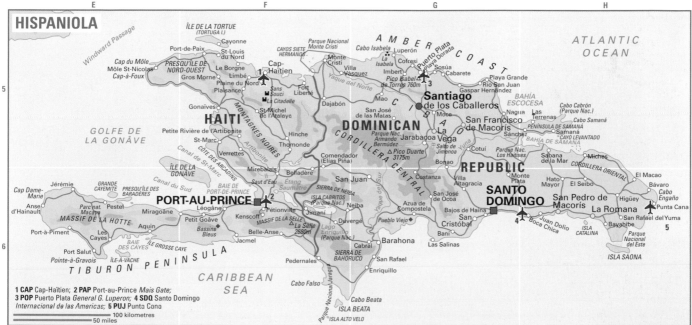

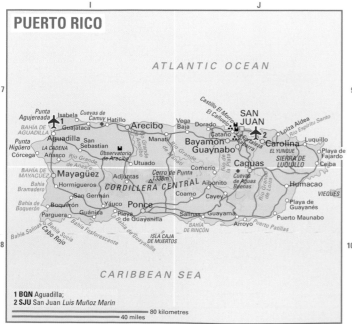

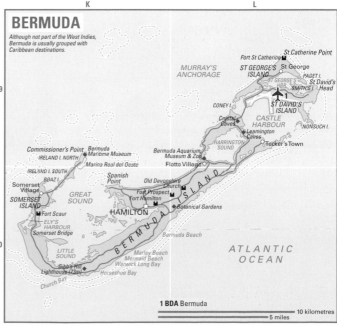

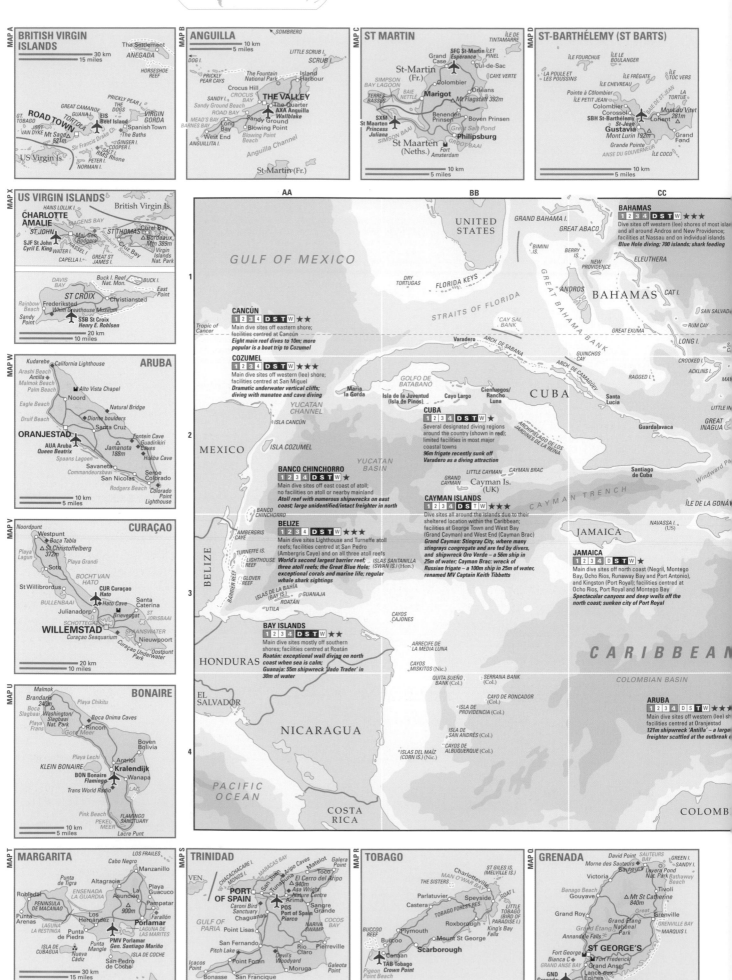

Caribbean: Dive Sites & the Lesser Antilles

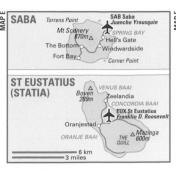

SABA
Torrens Point — SAB Saba Juancho Yrausquin
Mt Scenery 870m △ — SPRING BAY
Hell's Gate
The Bottom — Windwardside
Fort Bay — Corner Point

ST EUSTATIUS (STATIA)
VENUS BAAI
Boven 289m △ — Zeelandia
CONCORDIA BAAI
EUX St Eustatius Franklin D. Roosevelt
Oranjestad
ORANJE BAAI — THE QUILL — Mazinga 600m
6 km / 3 miles

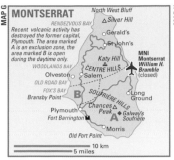

ST KITTS & NEVIS
St Paul's — Dieppe Bay
Sandy Point — Mt Liamuiga △1156m — Cayon
PUMP BAY — Brimstone Hill Fortress — Old Road Town — SKB St Kitts Robert L Bradshaw
ST KITTS (ST CHRISTOPHER)
BASSETERRE — North Frigate Bay — Frigate Bay
South Frigate Bay
Nag's Head — The Narrows — GREAT SALT POND
NEV Nevis — Newcastle
Pinney's Beach — NEVIS — Nevis Peak △985m
Charlestown — Nelson Museum
Dogwood Point
10 km / 5 miles

MONTSERRAT
North West Bluff — Silver Hill
RENDEZVOUS BAY
Recent volcanic activity has destroyed the former capital, Plymouth. The area marked A is an exclusion zone, the area marked B is open during the daytime only.
Gerald's
St John's
Katy Hill — MNI Montserrat William H. Bramble (closed)
WOODLANDS BAY — CENTRE HILLS — Olveston — Salem
OLD ROAD BAY — FOX'S BAY — Bransby Bay — B — SOUFRIÈRE HILLS — Long Ground
Plymouth — Chances Peak — A — Galway's Soufrière
Fort Barrington — Morris
Old Fort Point
10 km / 5 miles

BARBUDA
Goat Point
Cedar Tree Point — GOAT — RABBIT I. — KID I.
CODRINGTON LAGOON
Codrington — THE HIGHLANDS
BBQ Barbuda
Palmetto Point
Cocoa Point
Spanish Point
10 km / 5 miles

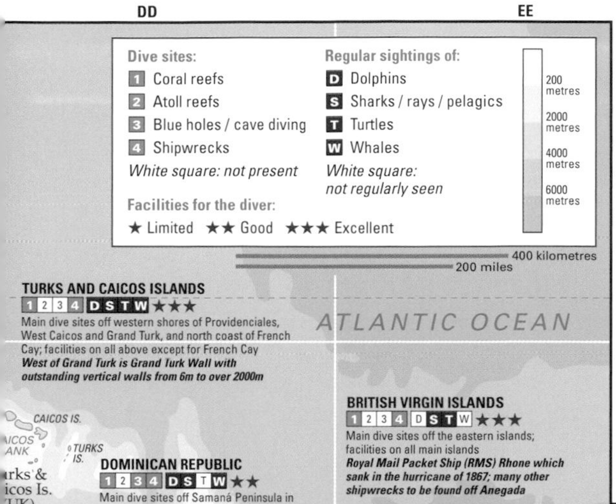

This map shows the Caribbean's principal diving destinations and the main underwater attractions they have to offer. Details include the existence of coral reefs; atoll reefs (of which there are only four in the entire Caribbean); blue hole and cave diving plus the existence of shipwrecks (including wrecked aircraft). Whilst the diver may encounter turtle, shark, large rays and dolphin at any time – and whales occasionally – only those places where these are featured and regular sightings occur are indicated here.

Diving facilities for each destination, including availability of scuba diving equipment and related support services, are graded as limited, good or excellent. It must be emphasised that these grades are a general reflection on the overall availability of everything required by the visiting scuba diver and are not an interpretation of the standards found within any one facility or organisation.

Each diving destination provides every level of depth from the very shallow to the extremely deep.

Data compiled by Ned Middleton, all rights reserved.
email: ned.middleton@which.net

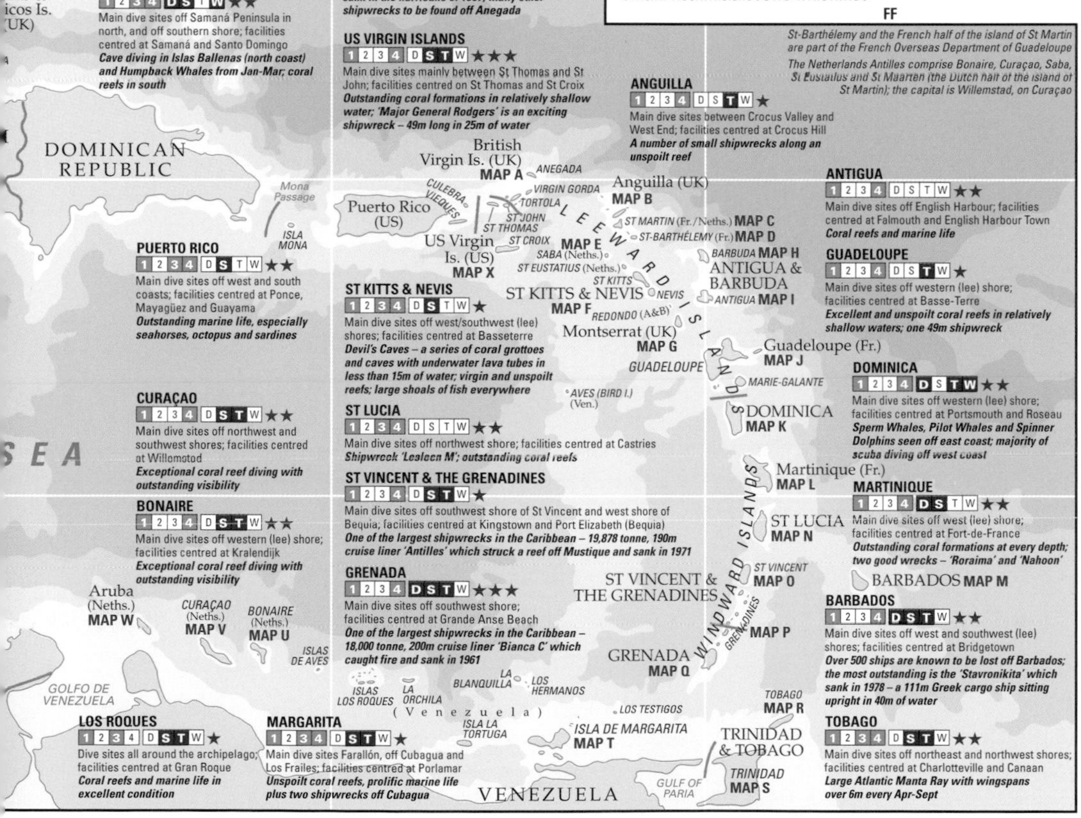

Legend
Dive sites:
1 Coral reefs
2 Atoll reefs
3 Blue holes / cave diving
4 Shipwrecks
White square: not present

Regular sightings of:
D Dolphins
S Sharks / rays / pelagics
T Turtles
W Whales
White square: not regularly seen

Facilities for the diver:
★ Limited ★★ Good ★★★ Excellent

200 metres / 2000 metres / 4000 metres / 6000 metres
400 kilometres / 200 miles

ANTIGUA
DICKENSON BAY — Cedar Grove — LONG ISLAND — GREAT BIRD I.
Fort James — ANU Antigua V.C. Bird — PARHAM HARBOUR — GUIANA I.
Fort Barrington — ST JOHN'S — Parham — Indian Town Point
FIVE ISLANDS HBR. — All Saints — Devil's Bridge
Bolans — GREEN I.
Boggy Peak 402m △ — SHEKERLEY MTNS — Potworks Dam — Falmouth — English Harbour Town — Freetown
Nelson's Dockyard — Shirley Heights — Cape Shirley — HORSE SHOE REEF
CADES REEF — ENGLISH HARBOUR
10 km / 5 miles

TURKS AND CAICOS ISLANDS
1 2 3 4 D S T W ★★★
Main dive sites off western shores of Providenciales, West Caicos and Grand Turk, and north coast of French Cay; facilities on all above except for French Cay.
West of Grand Turk is Grand Turk Wall with outstanding vertical walls from 6m to over 2000m

BRITISH VIRGIN ISLANDS
1 2 3 4 D S T W ★★★
Main dive sites off the eastern islands; facilities on all main islands
Royal Mail Packet Ship (RMS) Rhone which sank in the hurricane of 1867; many other shipwrecks to be found off Anegada

DOMINICAN REPUBLIC
1 2 3 4 D S T W ★★
Main dive sites off Samaná Peninsula in north, and off southern shore; facilities centred at Samaná and Santo Domingo
Cave diving in Islas Ballenas (north coast) and Humpback Whales from Jan–Mar; coral reefs in south

US VIRGIN ISLANDS
1 2 3 4 D S T W ★★★★
Main dive sites off St Thomas and St John; facilities centred on St Thomas and St Croix
Outstanding coral formations in relatively shallow water; 'Major General Rodgers' is an exciting shipwreck – 49m long in 25m of water

ANGUILLA
1 2 3 4 D S T W ★
Main dive sites between Crocus Valley and West End; facilities centred at Crocus Hill
A number of small shipwrecks along an unspoilt reef

St-Barthélemy and the French half of the island of St Martin are part of the French Overseas Department of Guadeloupe. The Netherlands Antilles comprise Bonaire, Curaçao, Saba, St Eustatius and St Maarten (the Dutch half of the island of St Martin); the capital is Willemstad, on Curaçao.

PUERTO RICO
1 2 3 4 D S T W ★★
Main dive sites off west and south coasts; facilities centred at Ponce, Mayagüez and Guayama
Outstanding marine life, especially seahorses, octopus and sardines

CURAÇAO
1 2 3 4 D S T W ★★
Main dive sites off northwest and southwest shores; facilities centred at Willomotod
Exceptional coral reef diving with outstanding visibility

BONAIRE
1 2 3 4 D S T W ★★
Main dive sites off western (lee) shore; facilities centred at Kralendijk
Exceptional coral reef diving with outstanding visibility

LOS ROQUES
1 2 3 4 D S T W ★
Dive sites all around the archipelago; facilities centred at Gran Roque
Coral reefs and marine life in excellent condition

MARGARITA
1 2 3 4 D S T W ★
Main dive sites Farallón, off Cubagua and Los Frailes; facilities centred at Porlamar
Unspoilt coral reefs, prolific marine life plus two shipwrecks off Cubagua

ANTIGUA
1 2 3 4 D S T W ★★
Main dive sites off English Harbour; facilities centred at Falmouth and English Harbour Town
Coral reefs and marine life

GUADELOUPE
1 2 3 4 D S T W ★★
Main dive sites off western (lee) shore; facilities centred at Basse-Terre
Excellent and unspoilt coral reefs in relatively shallow waters; one 49m shipwreck

DOMINICA
1 2 3 4 D S T W ★★
Main dive sites off western (lee) shore; facilities centred at Portsmouth and Roseau
Sperm Whales, Pilot Whales and Spinner Dolphins seen off east coast; majority of scuba diving off west coast

MARTINIQUE
1 2 3 4 D S T W ★★
Main dive sites off western (lee) shore; facilities centred at Fort-de-France
Outstanding coral formations at every depth; two good wrecks – 'Roraima' and 'Nahoon'

ST KITTS & NEVIS
1 2 3 4 D S T W ★★
Main dive sites off west/southwest (lee) shores; facilities centred at Basseterre
Devil's Caves – a series of coral grottoes and caves with underwater lava tubes in less than 15m of water; virgin and unspoilt reefs; large shoals of fish everywhere

ST LUCIA
1 2 3 4 D S T W ★★
Main dive sites off northwest shore; facilities centred at Castries
Shipwreck 'Lesleen M'; outstanding coral reefs

ST VINCENT & THE GRENADINES
1 2 3 4 D S T W ★★
Main dive sites off southwest shore of St Vincent and west shore of Bequia; facilities centred at Kingstown and Port Elizabeth (Bequia)
One of the largest shipwrecks in the Caribbean – 19,878 tonne, 190m cruise liner 'Antilles' which struck a reef off Mustique and sank in 1971

GRENADA
1 2 3 4 D S T W ★★★
Main dive sites off southwest shore; facilities centred at Grande Anse Beach
One of the largest shipwrecks in the Caribbean – 18,000 tonne, 200m cruise liner 'Bianca C' which caught fire and sank in 1961

BARBADOS
1 2 3 4 D S T W ★★
Main dive sites off west and southwest (lee) shores; facilities centred at Bridgetown
Over 500 ships are known to be lost off Barbados; the most outstanding is the 'Stavronikita' which sank in 1978 – a 111m Greek cargo ship sitting upright in 40m of water

TOBAGO
1 2 3 4 D S T W ★★
Main dive sites off northeast and northwest shores; facilities centred at Charlotteville and Canaan
Large Atlantic Manta Ray with wingspans over 6m every Apr–Sept

ATLANTIC OCEAN
CAICOS IS. — TURKS IS.
DOMINICAN REPUBLIC
Mona Passage — ISLA MONA
Puerto Rico (US) — British Virgin Is. (UK) MAP A — ANEGADA
CULEBRA — VIRGIN GORDA — VIEQUES — TORTOLA — ST JOHN — ST THOMAS — ST CROIX
US Virgin Is. (US) MAP E — Anguilla MAP B — ST MARTIN (Fr./Neths.) MAP C — ST-BARTHÉLEMY (Fr.) MAP D
SABA (Neths.) — ST EUSTATIUS (Neths.) — BARBUDA MAP H — ANTIGUA & BARBUDA — ANTIGUA MAP I
ST KITTS & NEVIS MAP F — REDONDO (A&B) — GUADELOUPE MAP J
Montserrat (UK) MAP G — GUADELOUPE — MARIE-GALANTE — DOMINICA MAP K
AVES (BIRD I.) (Ven.) — Martinique (Fr.) MAP L
ST LUCIA MAP N — ST VINCENT MAP O — BARBADOS MAP M
ST VINCENT & THE GRENADINES — GRENADINES
GRENADA MAP Q — TOBAGO MAP R — TRINIDAD & TOBAGO — TRINIDAD MAP S
LEEWARD ISLANDS — WINDWARD ISLANDS
Aruba (Neths.) MAP W — CURAÇAO (Neths.) MAP V — BONAIRE (Neths.) MAP U
ISLAS DE AVES
GOLFO DE VENEZUELA
LA BLANQUILLA — LOS HERMANOS — LA ORCHILA — LOS ROQUES — ISLA LA TORTUGA — ISLA DE MARGARITA MAP T — LOS TESTIGOS
ISLAS LOS ROQUES (Venezuela)
GULF OF PARIA
VENEZUELA
SEA

GUADELOUPE
Pointe de la Grande Vigie
Anse-Bertrand — Port-Louis — GRANDE-TERRE
Ste-Rose — PTP Point-à-Pitre Le Raizet — Moule — LA DÉSIRADE
Pointe-Noire — Pointe-à-Pitre — St-François — Pointe des Châteaux
Gosier — Ste-Anne — ÎLES DE LA PETITE TERRE
BASSE-TERRE — Parc naturel — Capesterre-Belle-Eau
Soufrière 1467m — St-Claude — BASSE-TERRE — Trois-Rivières — MARIE-GALANTE
LES SAINTES — Terre-de-Haut — Grand-Bourg
60 km / 30 miles

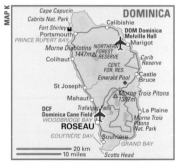

DOMINICA
Cape Capucin — Cabrits Nat. Park — Calibishie
Fort Shirley — DOM Dominica Melville Hall
PRINCE RUPERT BAY — Portsmouth — Marigot
Morne Diablotins 1447m — NORTHERN FOREST RESERVE — Carib Reserve
Colihaut — CENT. FOR. RES. — Castle Bruce
St Joseph — Emerald Pool
Mahaut — Morne Trois Pitons 1387m — La Plaine
DCF Dominica Cane Field — Trafalgar Falls — Morne Trois Pitons Nat. Park
WOODBRIDGE BAY — ROSEAU
SOUFRIÈRE BAY — Soufrière — GRAND BAY
Scotts Head
20 km / 10 miles

MARTINIQUE
Grand' Rivière — Basse-Pointe
Montagne Pelée 1397m — Plantation Leyritz — Gorges de la Falaise
le Prêcheur — Ste-Marie
St-Pierre — Château Dubuc — PRESQU'ÎLE LA CARAVELLE
la Carbet — Parc naturel — la Trinité
Schœlcher — FDF Fort-de-France — le Vauclin
BAIE DE FORT-DE-FRANCE — FORT-DE-FRANCE — Lamentin
Pointe du Bout — les Trois-Ilets — Rivière-Pilote
les Anses-d'Arlets — le Diamant
ROCHER DU DIAMANT — Ste-Anne
Pointe d'Enfer
30 km / 15 miles

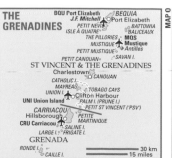

THE GRENADINES
BQU Port Elizabeth — BEQUIA
J.F. Mitchell — Port Elizabeth
PETIT NEVIS — ISLE À QUATRE — BATTOWIA
THE PILLORIES — BALICEAUX
MUSTIQUE — MQS Mustique — Mustique Antilles
PETIT MUSTIQUE — SAVAN I.
PETIT CANOUAN — Charlestown — CANOUAN
ST VINCENT & THE GRENADINES
CATHOLIC I. — MAYREAU — TOBAGO CAYS — Clifton Harbour — UNION I. — UNI Union Island — PALM I. (PRUNE I.) — PETIT ST VINCENT ('PSV')
CARRIACOU — CRU Carriacou — PETITE MARTINIQUE — Hillsborough — SALINE I. — LARGE I. — FRIGATE I.
GRENADA — RONDE I. — CAILLE I.
30 km / 15 miles

ST VINCENT
Fancy — Cow and Calves
Falls of Baleine — Sandy Bay
La Soufrière 1234m — Georgetown
Wallibou Beach — Richmond Beach — Crater Lake
CHATEAUBELAIR — Chateaubelair — MORNE GARU MOUNTAINS
Barrouallie — Greiggs — Biabou
Layou — Argyle Beach
Botanic Gardens — Fort Charlotte — KINGSTOWN — Stubbs
KINGSTOWN BAY — YOUNG I. — SVD St Vincent E.T. Joshua — Fort Duvernette
20 km / 10 miles

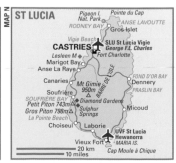

ST LUCIA
Pigeon I. Nat. Park — Pointe du Cap
RODNEY BAY — ANSE LAVOUTTE
Gros Islet
Vigie Beach — SLU St Lucia Vigie George F.L. Charles
CASTRIES — Fort Charlotte
Lesleen M — Marigot Bay
Anse La Raye — FOND D'OR BAY
Canaries — Dennery — PRASLIN BAY
Soufrière — Mt Gimie 950m — Diamond Gardens
Petit Piton 743m — Sulphur Springs — Micoud
Gros Piton 798m — La Pointe Beach
Choiseul — Laborie — UVF St Lucia Hewanorra — MARIA IS.
Vieux Fort — Cap Moule à Chique
20 km / 10 miles

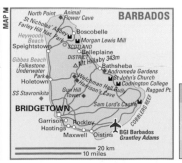

BARBADOS
North Point — Animal Flower Cave
St Nicholas Abbey — Farley Hill Nat. Park — SCOTLAND DISTRICT
Heywoods — Morgan Lewis Mill
Speightstown — Belleplaine
Gibbes Beach — Folkestone Underwater Park — Mt Hillaby 343m — Bathsheba
Holetown — Andromeda Gardens — St John's Church
Welchman Hall Gully — Codrington College
SS Stavronikita — Gun Hill Tower — Sam Lord's Castle
BRIDGETOWN — Garrison — Rockley — Gun Hill — Ragged Pt.
Hastings — Maxwell — Oistins — BGI Barbados Grantley Adams
COBBLER'S REEF
1000 metres / 500 metres / Sea level
20 km / 10 miles

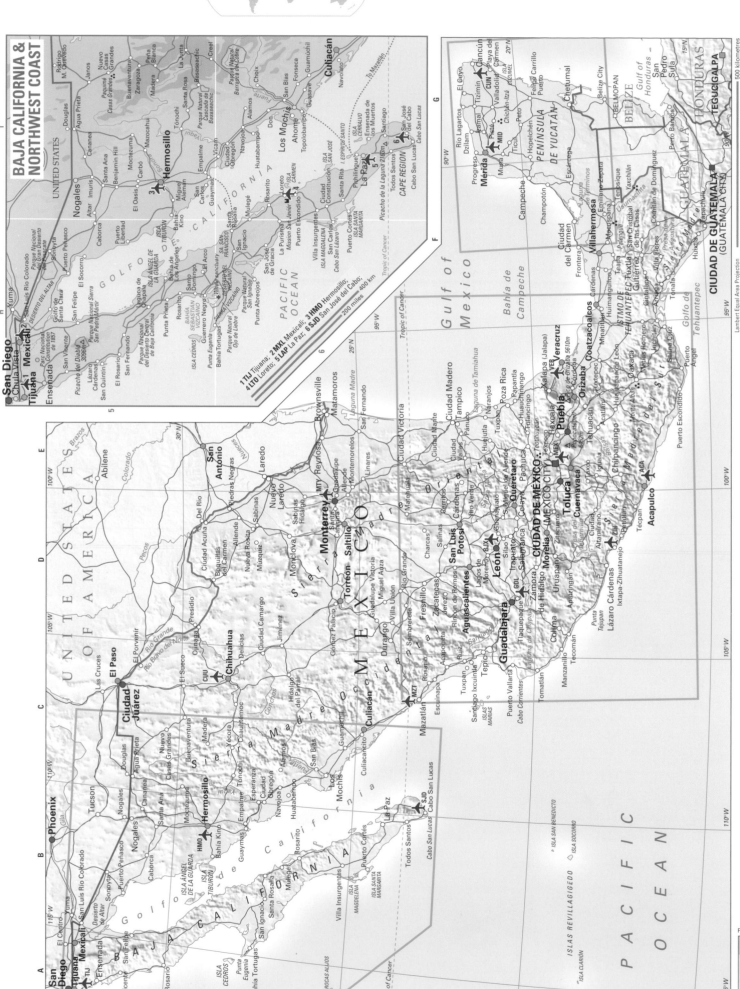

BAJA CALIFORNIA & NORTHWEST COAST

1 TIJ Tijuana; 2 MXL Mexicali; 3 HMO Hermosillo;
4 LTO Loreto; 5 LAP La Paz; 6 SJD San José del Cabo;

1 TIJ Tijuana, 2 MXL Mexicali, 3 HMO Hermosillo;
4 LTO Loreto, 5 LAP La Paz, 6 SJD San José del Cabo;

Lambert Equal Area Projection

500 kilometres
250 miles

Focus map:

2000 metres

1000 metres

Sea level

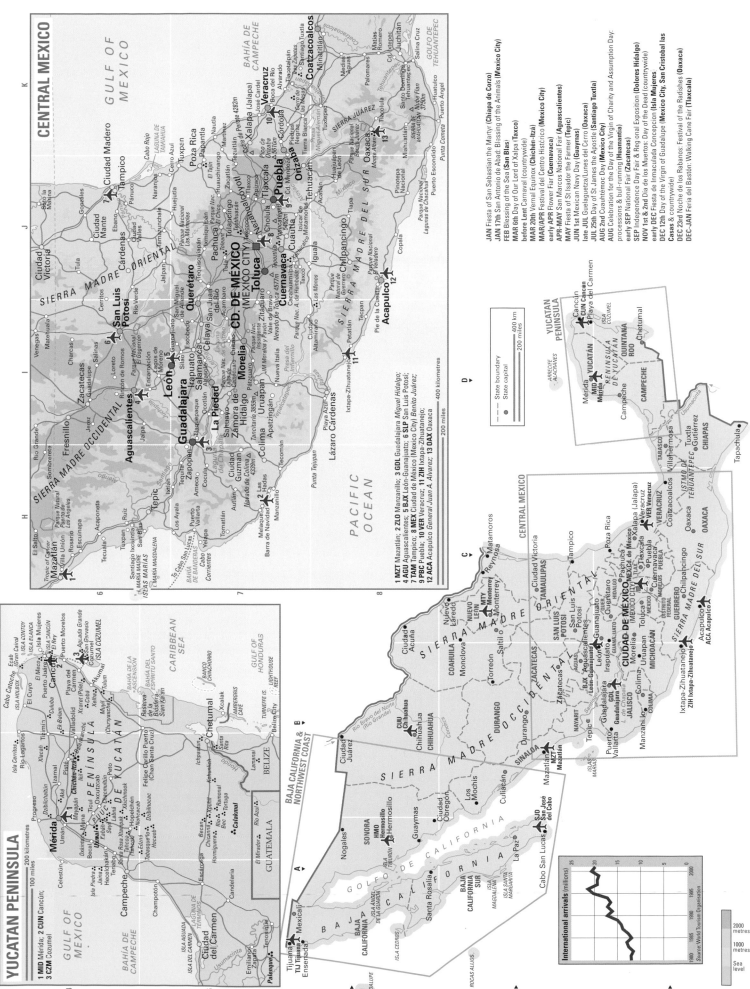

YUCATAN PENINSULA

1 MID Mérida; 2 CUN Cancún;
3 CZM Cozumel

CENTRAL MEXICO

1 MZT Mazatlán; 2 ZLO Manzanillo; 3 GDL Guadalajara *Miguel Hidalgo*;
4 AGU Aguascalientes; 5 BJX León-Guanajuato; 6 SLP San Luis Potosí;
7 TAM Tampico; 8 MEX Ciudad de México (Mexico City) *Benito Juárez*;
9 PBC Puebla; 10 VER Veracruz; 11 ZIH Ixtapa-Zihuatanejo;
12 ACA Acapulco *General Juan A. Álvarez*; 13 OAX Oaxaca

JAN Fiesta of San Sebastian the Martyr (**Chiapa de Corzo**)
JAN 17th San Antonio de Abad: Blessing of the Animals (**Mexico City**)
FEB Blessing of the Sea (**San Blas**)
MAR 6th Day of Our Lord of Xalpa (**Taxco**)
before Lent Carnaval (countrywide)
MAR 20th Vernal Equinox (**Chichén-Itza**)
MAR/APR Festival del Centro Histórico (**Mexico City**)
early APR Flower Fair (**Cuernavaca**)
APR–MAY San Marcos National Fair (**Aguascalientes**)
MAY Fiesta of St Isador the Farmer (**Tepic**)
JUN 1st Mexican Navy Day (**Guaymas**)
late JUL Guelaguetza/Lunes del Cerro (**Oaxaca**)
JUL 25th Day of St James the Apostle (**Santiago Tuxtla**)
AUG 2nd Cuauhtémoc Day (**Mexico City**)
AUG Celebration for the Day of the Virgin of Charity and Assumption Day:
processions & bull-running (**Huamantla**)
early SEP National Fair (**Zacatecas**)
SEP Independence Day Fair & Reg[i]onal Exposition (**Dolores Hidalgo**)
NOV 1st & 2nd Día de los Muertos: Day of the Dead (countrywide)
early DEC Fiesta de Inmaculada Concepcion (**Isla Mujeres**)
DEC 12th Day of the Virgin of Guadalupe (**Mexico City, San Cristobal las
Casas** & countrywide)
DEC 23rd Noche de los Rabanos: Festival of the Radishes (**Oaxaca**)
DEC–JAN Feria del Bastón: Walking Cane Fair (**Tlaxcala**)

International arrivals (millions)

Source: World Tourism Organisation

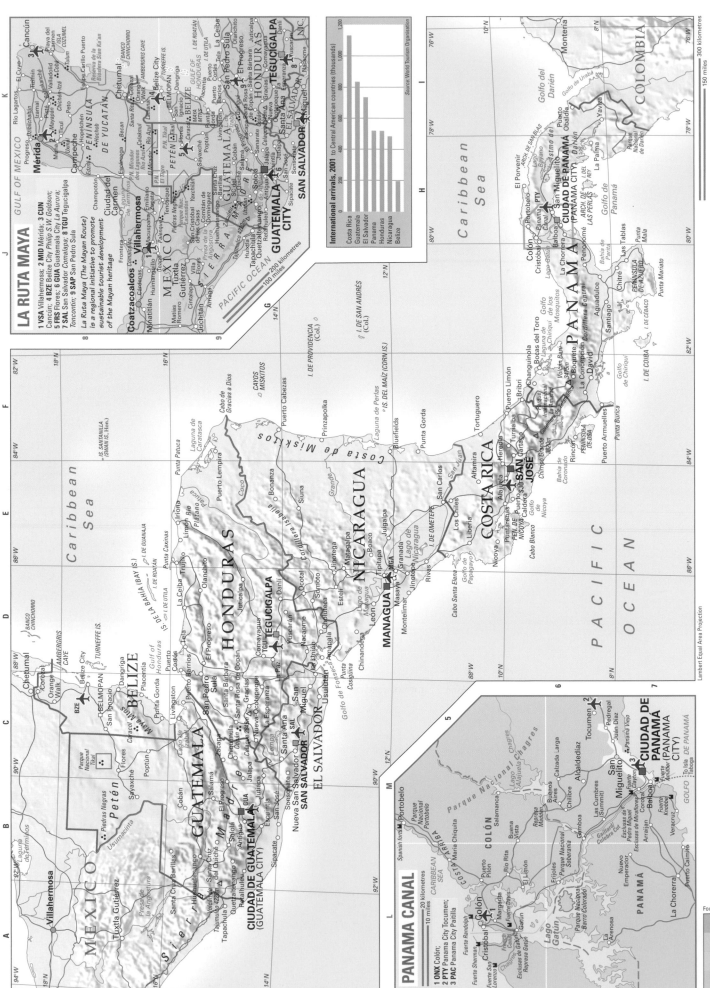

LA RUTA MAYA

1 VSA Villahermosa; 2 MID Mérida; 3 CUN Cancún; 4 BZE Belize City Philip S.W. Goldson; 5 FRS Flores; 6 GUA Guatemala City La Aurora; 7 SAL San Salvador Comalapa; 8 TGU Tegucigalpa Toncontín; 9 SAP San Pedro Sula

La Ruta Maya (The Mayan Route) is a regional initiative to promote sustainable tourist development of the Mayan heritage

International arrivals, 2001 to Central American countries (thousands)

Source: World Tourism Organisation

Costa Rica
Guatemala
El Salvador
Panama
Honduras
Nicaragua
Belize

PANAMA CANAL

1 ONX Colón; 2 PTY Panama City Tocumen; 3 PAC Panama City Paitilla

Lambert Equal Area Projection

Focus map

2000 metres
1000 metres
Sea level

South America: Physical

International arrivals, 2001 to South American countries (millions)

Brazil
Argentina
Uruguay
Chile
Peru
Ecuador
Colombia
Venezuela
Bolivia
Paraguay
Guyana
French Guiana
Surinam

Source: World Tourism Organisation

GALÁPAGOS ISLANDS

GPS Galápagos Is.
1 Baltra (South Seymour)
2 Puerto Baquerizo Moreno

Lambert Equal Area Projection

1000 kilometres
500 miles

South America: Climate

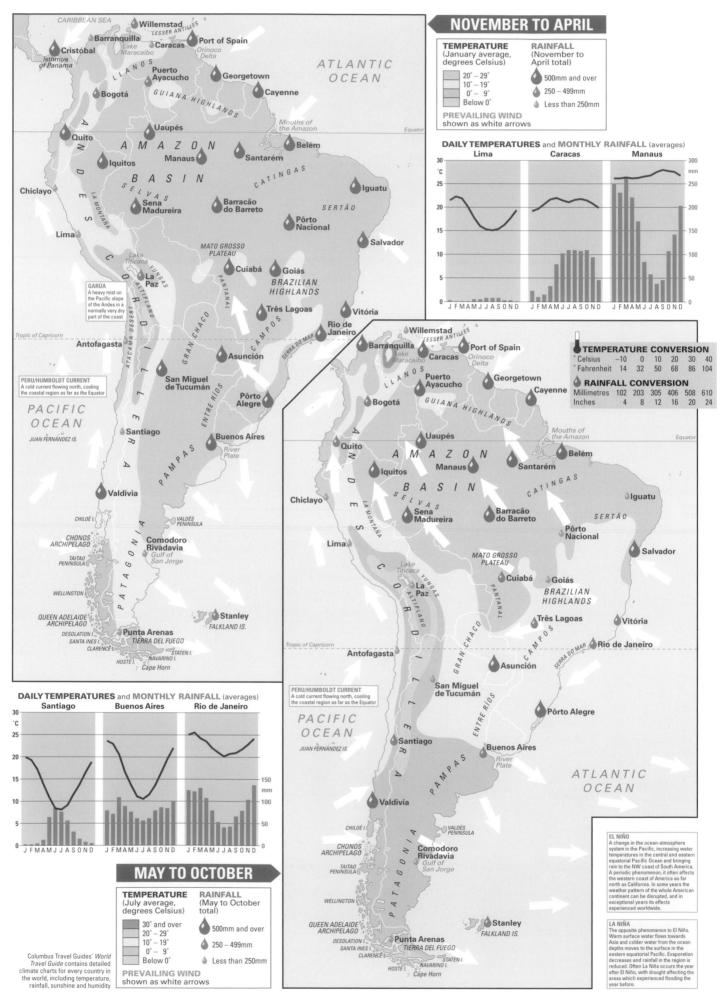

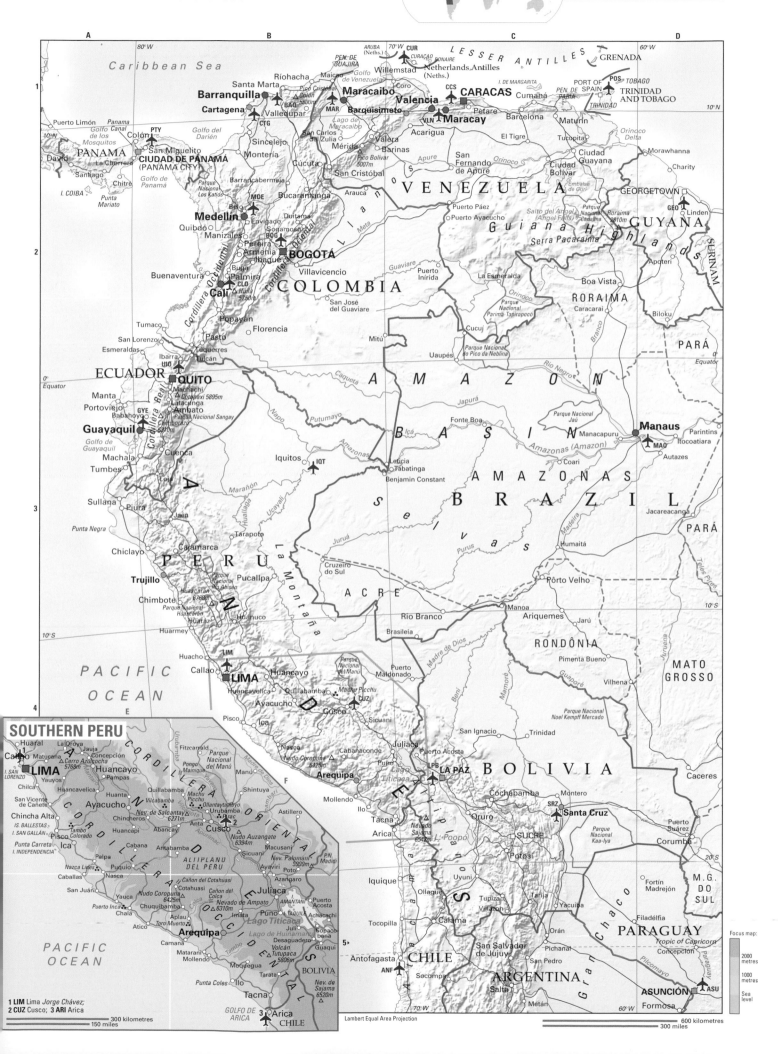

SOUTHERN PERU

1 LIM Lima *Jorge Chávez*;
2 CUZ Cusco; 3 ARI Arica

300 kilometres
150 miles

Lambert Equal Area Projection

600 miles
300 miles

Focus map:
2000 metres
1000 metres
Sea level

South America: East

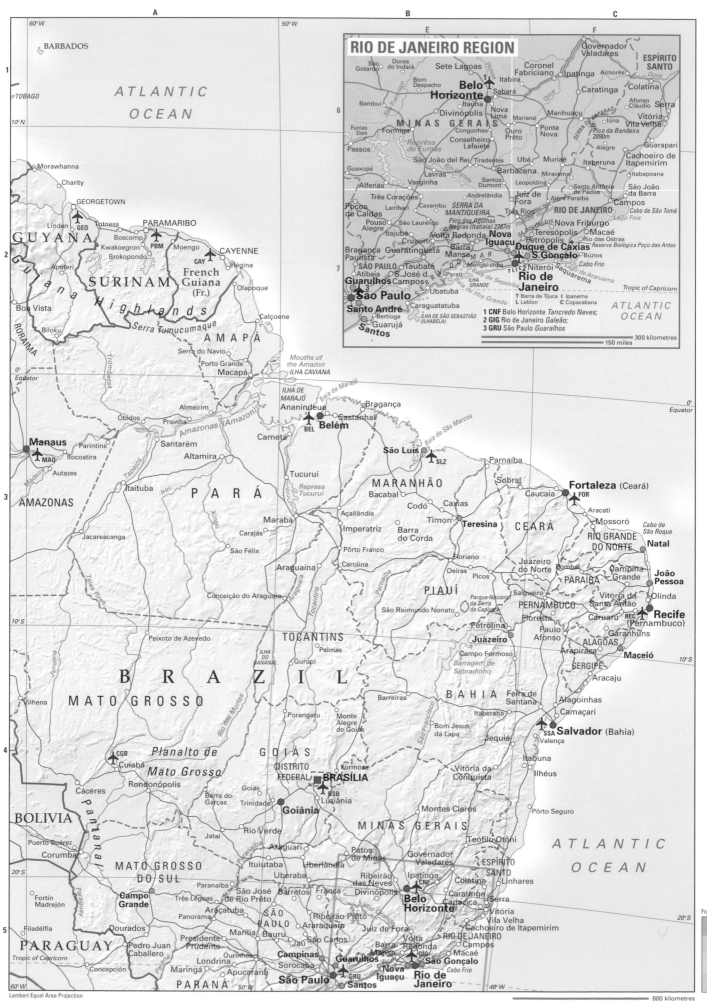

RIO DE JANEIRO REGION

São Gotardo · Dores do Indaiá · Sete Lagoas · Coronel Fabriciano · Governador Valadares · **ESPÍRITO SANTO**
Bom Despacho · Itabira · Ipatinga · Aimorés
Bambuí · **Belo Horizonte** · Sabará · Caratinga · Colatina
MINAS GERAIS · Itaúna · Nova Lima · Manhuaçu · Afonso Cláudio · Serra
Furnas Dam · Divinópolis · Mariana · Ponte Nova · Iúna · Vitória · Vila Velha
Formiga · Congonhas · Ouro Prêto · SERRA DO CAPARAÓ · Pico da Bandeira 2890m
Passos · Conselheiro Lafaiete · Guarapari
São João del Rei · Tiradentes · Ubá · Muriaé · Itaperuna · Cachoeiro de Itapemirim
Guaxupé · Lavras · Barbacena · Miracema · Itabapoana
Alfenas · Varginha · Santos Dumont · Leopoldina · Santo Antônio de Pádua · São João da Barra
Poços de Caldas · Três Corações · Lambari · Caxambu · Andrelândia · Juiz de Fora · Além Paraíba · **RIO DE JANEIRO** · Campos
Pouso Alegre · São Lourenço · SERRA DA MANTIQUEIRA · Três Rios · Cabo de São Tomé
Itajubá · Pico das Agulhas Negras (Itatiaia) 2787m · Nova Friburgo · Lago Feia
Bragança Paulista · Guaratinguetá · Volta Redonda · **Nova Iguaçu** · Teresópolis · Macaé
SÃO PAULO · Cruzeiro · Petrópolis · Rio das Ostras · Reserva Biológica Poço das Antas
Atibaia · Taubaté · Barra Mansa · **Duque de Caxias** · **S. Gonçalo** · Búzios
Guarulhos · S. José d. Campos · Mangaratiba · **Niterói** · Cabo Frio · Saquarema
São Paulo · Parati · **Rio de Janeiro** · Tropic of Capricorn
Santo André · Ubatuba · BAÍA DE SEPETIBA · ILHA GRANDE · Barra de Tijuca · Ipanema
Bertioga · Caraguatatuba · Leblon · Copacabana
Guarujá · ILHA DE SÃO SEBASTIÃO (ILHABELA) · **ATLANTIC OCEAN**
Santos

1 CNF Belo Horizonte *Tancredo Neves*;
2 GIG Rio de Janeiro *Galeão*;
3 GRU São Paulo *Guaralhos*

300 kilometres
150 miles

BARBADOS

TOBAGO

ATLANTIC OCEAN

10° N

Morawhanna
Charity
GEORGETOWN · GEO
Linden · Totness · PARAMARIBO
GUYANA · Kwakoegron · PBM · Moengo · **CAYENNE** · CAY
Apoteri · Boscomp · Brokopondo · Régina
Boa Vista · **SURINAM** · French Guiana (Fr.)
Biloku · *Guiana Highlands* · Oiapoque
RORAIMA · *Serra Tumucumaque* · Calçoene

0° · Equator

AMAPÁ
Serra do Navio
Porto Grande
Óbidos · Almeirim · Macapá · *Mouths of the Amazon* · ILHA CAVIANA
Prainha · ILHA DE MARAJÓ · *Baía de Marajó*
Amazonas (Amazon) · Bragança
Manaus · MAO · Parintins · Ananindeua · Castanhal
Itacoatiara · Santarém · Cametá · BEL · **Belém** · *Baía de São Marcos*
Autazes · **São Luís** · SLZ · Parnaíba
AMAZONAS · Altamira · Tucuruí · *Represa Tucuruí* · Sobral
Itaituba · **P A R Á** · Açailândia · Bacabal · Caxias · Caucaia · **Fortaleza** (Ceará) · FOR
Marabá · Codó · Timon · Aracati
Carajás · Imperatriz · **Teresina** · **CEARÁ** · Mossoró · *Cabo de São Roque*
Jacareacanga · São Félix · Barra do Corda · **RIO GRANDE DO NORTE**
Araguaína · Carolina · Floriano · Juàzeiro do Norte · Pombal · **Natal**
Conceição do Araguaia · Oeiras · Picos · Campina Grande · **João Pessoa**
PIAUÍ · **PARAÍBA** · Vitória de Santa Antão · Olinda
Parque Nacional da Serra da Capivara · Salgueiro · Caruaru · **Recife** (Pernambuco) · REC
Peixoto de Azevedo · São Raimundo Nonato · **PERNAMBUCO** · Floresta · Garanhuns
Palmas · Petrolina · Paulo Afonso · **ALAGOAS**
TOCANTINS · ILHA DO BANANAL · Gurupi · Arapiraca · **Maceió**
Vilhena · Campo Formoso · **SERGIPE**
Barragem de Sobradinho · Aracaju
B R A Z I L · Barreiras · **BAHIA** · Alagoinhas
MATO GROSSO · Porangatu · Bom Jesus da Lapa · Feira de Santana · Camaçari
Cáceres · Monte Alegre de Goiás · Itaberaba · **Salvador** (Bahia) · SSA
CGB · *Planalto de Mato Grosso* · **GOIÁS** · Jequié · Valença
Cuiabá · Formosa · Vitória da Conquista · Itabuna
Rondonópolis · **DISTRITO FEDERAL** · **BRASÍLIA** · BSB · Ilhéus
Barra do Garças · Luziânia
BOLIVIA · Goiás · Trinidade · Pôrto Seguro
Puerto Suárez · **Goiânia** · Montes Claros
Corumbá · Rio Verde · Teófilo Otôni
Pantanal · Jataí · **MINAS GERAIS** · *ATLANTIC OCEAN*
Fortín Madrejón · Araguari · Patos de Minas · Governador Valadares
MATO GROSSO DO SUL · Ituiutaba · Ipatinga · **ESPÍRITO SANTO**
Paranaíba · Uberlândia · CNF · Colatina · Linhares
Campo Grande · Três Lagoas · Ribeirão das Neves · Caratinga · Serra
Filadélfia · São José do Rio Prêto · Uberaba · **Belo Horizonte** · Cariacica · Vitória
Dourados · Araçatuba · Barretos · Franca · Divinópolis · Vila Velha
Pedro Juan Caballero · Panorama · **SÃO PAULO** · Ribeirão Prêto · Juiz de Fora · Cachoeiro de Itapemirim
Tres Lagoas · Araraquara · São Carlos · **RIO DE JANEIRO** · Campos
PARAGUAY · Marília · Bauru · Jaú · Barra · Macaé
Filadélfia · Presidente Prudente · **Campinas** · **Volta Redonda** · Cabo Frio
Concepción · Maringá · Ourinhos · Sorocaba · **Guarulhos** · **São Gonçalo**
Apucarana · Londrina · **São Paulo** · GRU · **Nova Iguaçu**
PARANÁ · **Santos** · **Rio de Janeiro**

60° W · 50° W · 40° W

Tropic of Capricorn

Lambert Equal Area Projection

600 kilometres
300 miles

Focus map

2000 metres
1000 metres
Sea level

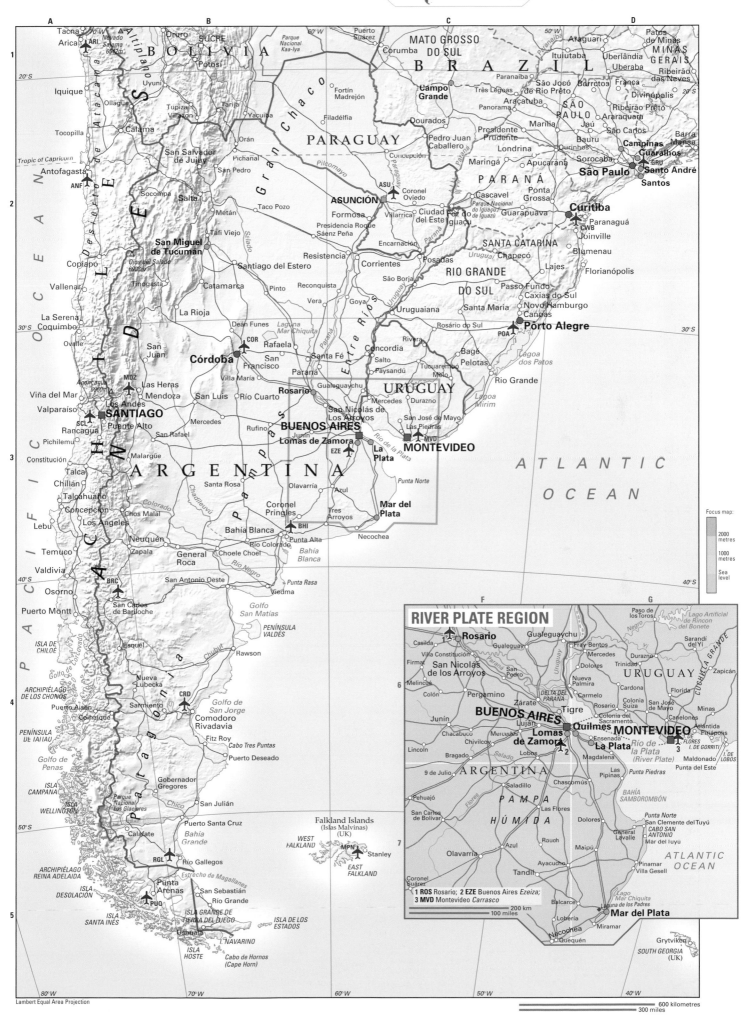

South America: South

Main map labels:

BOLIVIA · PARAGUAY · BRAZIL · MATO GROSSO DO SUL · SÃO PAULO · PARANÁ · SANTA CATARINA · RIO GRANDE DO SUL · MINAS GERAIS · ARGENTINA · CHILE · URUGUAY · Gran Chaco · Patagonia · Pampas

ATLANTIC OCEAN · PACIFIC OCEAN

Tacna · Arica · Iquique · Tocopilla · Antofagasta · Copiapó · Vallenar · La Serena · Coquimbo · Ovalle · Viña del Mar · Valparaíso · Santiago · Rancagua · Pichilemu · Constitución · Talca · Chillán · Talcahuano · Concepción · Los Ángeles · Lebu · Temuco · Valdivia · Osorno · Puerto Montt · Coihaique · Puerto Aisén · Punta Arenas · Ushuaia

Oruro · Sucre · Potosí · Uyuni · Tupiza · Villazón · Tarija · Yacuiba · Orán · San Salvador de Jujuy · Pichanal · San Pedro · Salta · Metán · Socompa · Taco Pozo · Tafí Viejo · San Miguel de Tucumán · Santiago del Estero · Catamarca · La Rioja · Pinto · Deán Funes · Rafaela · San Francisco · Córdoba · Villa María · San Juan · Las Heras · Mendoza · Los Andes · Puente Alto · San Luis · Río Cuarto · Mercedes · San Rafael · Rufino · Rosario · Junín · San Nicolás de Los Arroyos · Buenos Aires · Lomas de Zamora · La Plata · Santa Rosa · Olavarría · Azul · Coronel Pringles · Tres Arroyos · Mar del Plata · Necochea · Bahía Blanca · Punta Alta · Río Colorado · Choele Choel · Neuquén · Zapala · General Roca · Malargüe · Chos Malal · San Antonio Oeste · Viedma · San Carlos de Bariloche · Esquel · Nueva Lubecka · Sarmiento · Comodoro Rivadavia · Fitz Roy · Cabo Tres Puntas · Puerto Deseado · Gobernador Gregores · San Julián · Calafate · Puerto Santa Cruz · Río Gallegos · San Sebastián · Río Grande

Puerto Suárez · Corumba · Campo Grande · Dourados · Pedro Juan Caballero · Concepción · Coronel Oviedo · ASUNCIÓN · Formosa · Villarrica · Ciudad del Este · Foz do Iguaçu · Presidencia Roque Sáenz Peña · Resistencia · Corrientes · Posadas · Encarnación · Vera · Reconquista · Goya · San Borja · Paraná · Santa Fé · Concordia · Salto · Paysandú · Rosário do Sul · Rivera · Bagé · Pelotas · Río Grande · Melo · Durazno · Mercedes · San José de Mayo · Las Piedras · MONTEVIDEO

Araguari · Ituiutaba · Uberlândia · Uberaba · Ribeirão das Neves · Paranaíba · Três Lagoas · São José do Rio Prêto · Barretos · Franca · Divinópolis · Araçatuba · Panorama · Marília · Jaú · Araraquara · Ribeirão Prêto · São Carlos · Barra Mansa · Presidente Prudente · Bauru · Sorocaba · Campinas · Guarulhos · São Paulo · Santo André · Santos · Londrina · Maringá · Apucarana · Cascavel · Ponta Grossa · Guarapuava · Curitiba · Paranaguá · Joinville · Blumenau · Chapecó · Lajes · Florianópolis · Passo Fundo · Caxias do Sul · Novo Hamburgo · Canoas · Santa Maria · Pôrto Alegre

Nevado Sajama 6542m · Ojos del Salado 6908m · Aconcagua 6960m · Altiplano · Desierto de Atacama · Cordillera de los Andes · Laguna Mar Chiquita · Salado · Pilcomayo · Paraguay · Paraná · Uruguay · Río de la Plata · Colorado · Chadileuvú · Río Negro · Chubut · Chico · Lagoa dos Patos · Lagoa Mirim · Punta Norte · Punta Rasa · Golfo San Matías · PENÍNSULA VALDÉS · Golfo San Jorge · Bahía Grande · Estrecho de Magallanes · ISLA DE CHILOÉ · ARCHIPIÉLAGO DE LOS CHONOS · PENÍNSULA DE TAITAO · Golfo de Corcovado · Golfo de Penas · ISLA CAMPANA · ISLA WELLINGTON · ARCHIPIÉLAGO REINA ADELAIDA · ISLA DESOLACIÓN · ISLA SANTA INÉS · ISLA GRANDE DE TIERRA DEL FUEGO · ISLA HOSTE · NAVARINO · Cabo de Hornos (Cape Horn) · ISLA DE LOS ESTADOS · Parque Nacional Los Glaciares

Falkland Islands (Islas Malvinas) (UK) · WEST FALKLAND · EAST FALKLAND · Stanley · SOUTH GEORGIA (UK) · Grytviken

Parque Nacional Kaa-Iya · Fortín Madrejón · Filadélfia · Parque Nacional do Iguaçu · Parque Nacional Iguazú

Airport codes: ARI · ANF · MDZ · SCL · COR · EZE · MVD · POA · GRU · CWB · BHI · BRC · CRD · RGL · PUQ · ASU · MPN

Tropic of Capricorn · 20°S · 30°S · 40°S · 50°S · 80°W · 70°W · 60°W · 50°W · 40°W

Lambert Equal Area Projection

600 kilometres
300 miles

Focus map:
2000 metres
1000 metres
Sea level

RIVER PLATE REGION

Rosario · Casilda · Villa Constitución · Firmat · Melincué · San Nicolás de los Arroyos · Colón · Pergamino · San Pedro · Zárate · Junín · Chacabuco · Tigre · BUENOS AIRES · Luján · Lomas de Zamora · Quilmes · Ensenada · La Plata · Mercedes · Chivilcoy · Lobos · 9 de Julio · Bragado · Saladillo · Las Flores · Lincoln · Pehuajó · San Carlos de Bolívar · Azul · Olavarría · Coronel Suárez · Tandil · Balcarce · Necochea · Miramar · Mar del Plata

Gualeguaychu · Gualeguay · Fray Bentos · Mercedes · Dolores · Trinidad · Nueva Palmira · Carmelo · Colonia Suiza · Rosario · Colonia del Sacramento · Cardona · San José de Mayo · Florida · Canelones · MONTEVIDEO · I. DE FLORES · I. DE GORRITI · Minas · Maldonado · Punta del Este · I. DE LOBOS · Atlántida · Magdalena · Las Pipinas · Punta Piedras · Chascomús · Punta Norte · San Clemente del Tuyú · CABO SAN ANTONIO · Mar del Tuyú · General Lavalle · Dolores · Maipú · Ayacucho · Rauch · Pinamar · Villa Gesell · General Madariaga · Lobería · Quequén · Laguna Mar Chiquita · Laguna de los Padres

URUGUAY · ARGENTINA · PAMPA HÚMIDA · Paso de los Toros · Lago Artificial de Rincón del Bonete · Sarandí del Yí · Durazno · Zapicán · CUCHILLA GRANDE · DELTA DEL PARANÁ · BAHÍA SAMBOROMBÓN · ATLANTIC OCEAN · Negro · Salado · Flores · Río de la Plata (River Plate)

1 ROS Rosario; 2 EZE Buenos Aires Ezeiza;
3 MVD Montevideo Carrasco

200 km
100 miles

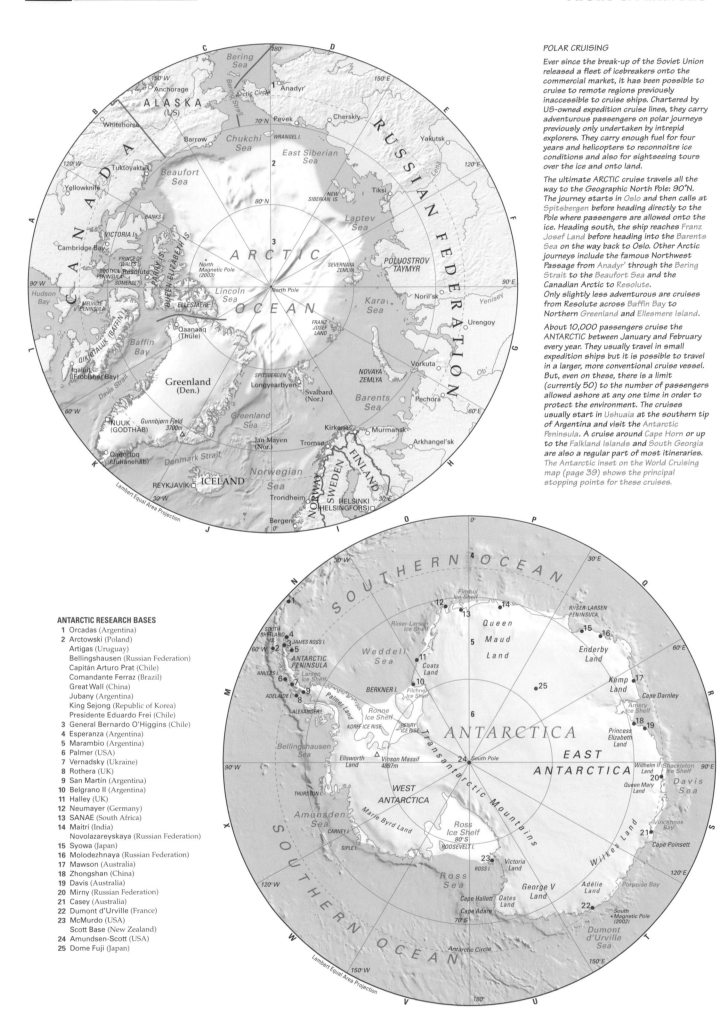

POLAR CRUISING

Ever since the break-up of the Soviet Union released a fleet of icebreakers onto the commercial market, it has been possible to cruise to remote regions previously inaccessible to cruise ships. Chartered by US-owned expedition cruise lines, they carry adventurous passengers on polar journeys previously only undertaken by intrepid explorers. They carry enough fuel for four years and helicopters to reconnoitre ice conditions and also for sightseeing tours over the ice and onto land.

The ultimate ARCTIC cruise travels all the way to the Geographic North Pole: 90°N. The journey starts in Oslo and then calls at Spitsbergen before heading directly to the Pole where passengers are allowed onto the ice. Heading south, the ship reaches Franz Josef Land before heading into the Barents Sea on the way back to Oslo. Other Arctic journeys include the famous Northwest Passage from Anadyr' through the Bering Strait to the Beaufort Sea and the Canadian Arctic to Resolute.
Only slightly less adventurous are cruises from Resolute across Baffin Bay to Northern Greenland and Ellesmere Island.

About 10,000 passengers cruise the ANTARCTIC between January and February every year. They usually travel in small expedition ships but it is possible to travel in a larger, more conventional cruise vessel. But, even on these, there is a limit (currently 50) to the number of passengers allowed ashore at any one time in order to protect the environment. The cruises usually start in Ushuaia at the southern tip of Argentina and visit the Antarctic Peninsula. A cruise around Cape Horn or up to the Falkland Islands and South Georgia are also a regular part of most itineraries. The Antarctic inset on the World Cruising map (page 39) shows the principal stopping points for these cruises.

ANTARCTIC RESEARCH BASES
1. Orcadas (Argentina)
2. Arctowski (Poland)
   Artigas (Uruguay)
   Bellingshausen (Russian Federation)
   Capitán Arturo Prat (Chile)
   Comandante Ferraz (Brazil)
   Great Wall (China)
   Jubany (Argentina)
   King Sejong (Republic of Korea)
   Presidente Eduardo Frei (Chile)
3. General Bernardo O'Higgins (Chile)
4. Esperanza (Argentina)
5. Marambio (Argentina)
6. Palmer (USA)
7. Vernadsky (Ukraine)
8. Rothera (UK)
9. San Martín (Argentina)
10. Belgrano II (Argentina)
11. Halley (UK)
12. Neumayer (Germany)
13. SANAE (South Africa)
14. Maitri (India)
    Novolazareyskaya (Russian Federation)
15. Syowa (Japan)
16. Molodezhnaya (Russian Federation)
17. Mawson (Australia)
18. Zhongshan (China)
19. Davis (Australia)
20. Mirny (Russian Federation)
21. Casey (Australia)
22. Dumont d'Urville (France)
23. McMurdo (USA)
    Scott Base (New Zealand)
24. Amundsen-Scott (USA)
25. Dome Fuji (Japan)

1600 kilometres
800 miles

Appendices 1–4

1: GEOGRAPHICAL DEFINITIONS

The following list includes names and abbreviations which appear in this atlas, together with other terms that are commonly used in the travel industry. Various authorities differ on the exact definitions of some of these entries; the definitions given here are those which are generally understood within the travel trade. *For principal world and regional organisations, see pages 24-25.*

Arabian Peninsula
Geographical region comprising: Bahrain, Kuwait, Oman, Qatar, Saudi Arabia, United Arab Emirates, Yemen.

Australasia
Geographical region comprising: Australia, New Caledonia, New Zealand, Solomon Islands, Vanuatu and the island of New Guinea including all of Papua New Guinea. Often described as equivalent to all of Oceania between the Equator and 47ûS. The term is not commonly used in Australia and New Zealand because of confusion with Australia itself.

Bahama Islands
Group of islands in the Atlantic comprising the Commonwealth of The Bahamas and the Turks and Caicos Islands.

Balkans, The
The Balkan Peninsula, which is bordered by the Adriatic and Ionian Seas to the west, the Aegean and Black Seas to the east and the Mediterranean Sea to the south. The countries occupying this peninsula are described as Balkan states: Albania, Bosnia-Herzegovina, Bulgaria, Croatia, Greece, Former Yugoslav Republic of Macedonia, Romania, Serbia & Montenegro, Slovenia and the European part of Turkey.

Borneo
Island in the Malay Archipelago (qv) divided between Brunei, Indonesia (the provinces of Central, East, South and West Kalimantan) and Malaysia (the states of Sabah and Sarawak).

British Isles
Geographical region comprising: United Kingdom (qv), Republic of Ireland, Isle of Man, Channel Islands.

Caribbean
General tourist term used to describe the West Indies (qv).

Caroline Islands
Archipelago in the west Pacific Ocean. Islands comprise the Federated States of Micronesia and Palau.

Celebes
Island in the Malay Archipelago (qv), Sulawesi in Indonesian.

Central America
Geographical region comprising: Belize, Costa Rica, El Salvador, Guatemala, Honduras, Nicaragua, Panama. Usually considered part of the North American (qv) continent.

Ceylon
Island off the southeast coast of India, officially Sri Lanka.

Channel Islands
Group of islands comprising Jersey, Guernsey, Alderney, Sark and Herm, situated off the northwest coast of France. They are possessions of the British Crown and not officially part of the United Kingdom (qv).

East Indies
General geographical term sometimes applied loosely to India, Indochina and the Malay Archipelago (qv). Often used as alternative to the Malay Archipelago or the Republic of Indonesia itself. The term is now rarely used.

Europe
Continent. Northern boundary formed by Arctic Ocean. Eastern boundary formed by Ural Mountains, Ural River and Caspian Sea. Southern boundary formed by Caucasus Mountains, Black Sea, Bosporus, Aegean Sea and Mediterranean Sea. Western boundary formed by Atlantic Ocean. Includes Iceland, Svalbard and area of Turkey west of the Bosporus.

Far East
General geographical term describing east and South-East Asia: Brunei, Cambodia, China, Indonesia, Japan, Democratic People's Republic of Korea (North Korea), Republic of Korea (South Korea), Laos, Malaysia, Myanmar, the Philippines, Singapore, Taiwan, Thailand, Vietnam. Sometimes extended to include Mongolia and the eastern Siberian region of the Russian Federation.

Formosa
Island off the southeast coast of the People's Republic of China, known variously as the Republic of China or Taiwan.

Great Britain
Geographical region comprising: England, Scotland, Wales.

Greater Antilles
Group of Caribbean islands comprising: Cayman Islands, Cuba, Hispaniola, Jamaica, Puerto Rico.

Hispaniola
Island in the Greater Antilles (qv) divided between the Dominican Republic and Haiti.

Iberia
Peninsula in southwest Europe occupied by Spain, Portugal, Andorra and Gibraltar.

Indochina
Geographical region comprising: Cambodia, Laos, Peninsular Malaysia, Myanmar, Singapore, Thailand, Vietnam.

International Air Transport Association (IATA)
An association which acts as a governing body of the major airlines, responsible for establishing fare levels and for rules and regulations concerning international passenger and cargo services. It has over 100 tariff members and a further 100 trade associate airlines.

Latin America
Defined either as: the Spanish- and Portuguese-speaking speaking countries of the Americas (sometimes also including French-speaking Haiti); or all of the Americas south of the United States. This latter, more general, definition is the one used in this atlas.

Lesser Antilles
Group of Caribbean islands comprising: Leeward Islands (qv), Windward Islands (qv), Aruba, Barbados, Bonaire, Cura≤ao, Trinidad and Tobago. Also includes the chain of small Venezuelan islands east of Bonaire.

Leeward Islands
Group of Caribbean islands comprising: Anguilla, Antigua & Barbuda, Dominica, Guadeloupe, Montserrat, Saba, St Eustatius, St Kitts & Nevis, St Maarten/St Martin, Virgin Islands.

Low Countries
Geographical region comprising: Belgium, Luxembourg, The Netherlands.

Maghreb
Arabic name for northwest Africa and, during the Moorish period, Spain. Algeria, Morocco and Tunisia are described as Maghreb countries.

Malay Archipelago
The largest island group in the world, off the southeast coast of Asia and between the Indian and Pacific Oceans. Major islands include Borneo (qv), Sulawesi (Celebes, qv), Jawa (Java), New Guinea and Sumatera (Sumatra). Countries within this archipelago: Brunei, Indonesia, East Malaysia, Papua New Guinea, the Philippines.

Mediterranean
General tourist destination term used to describe the islands of the Mediterranean Sea and the countries bordering it.

Melanesia
Collective name for the islands in the southwest Pacific Ocean, south of the Equator and northeast of Australia. Includes: Fiji Islands, Nauru, New Caledonia, Papua New Guinea (excluding New Guinea mainland), Solomon Islands, Vanuatu.

Micronesia
Collective name for the islands in the west Pacific Ocean, north of the Equator and east of the Philippines. Includes: Guam, Kiribati (west), Marshall Islands, Federated States of Micronesia, Northern Mariana Islands, Palau.

Middle East
General geographical term describing a loosely defined area comprising: countries of the Arabian Peninsula, Egypt, Iran, Iraq, Israel, Jordan, Lebanon, Syria. Sometimes extended to include Algeria, Cyprus, Libya, Morocco, Sudan, Tunisia and Turkey.

Near East
Rarely used general geographical term describing an area of SW Asia: the Arabian Peninsula, Cyprus, Israel, Jordan, Lebanon, Syria, Turkey. Often extended to Egypt and Sudan.

Netherlands Antilles
Islands of the West Indies administered by The Netherlands, comprising: Bonaire, Curaçao, Saba, St Eustatius, St Maarten. Aruba, formerly part of the Netherlands Antilles is now administered from The Netherlands separately.

New Guinea
Island in the Malay Archipelago (qv) divided between Papua New Guinea and the Indonesian province of Irian Jaya.

North America
Continent comprising: USA, Canada, Mexico, Bermuda, West Indies (qv). Usually considered to also include Central America and Greenland.

Oceania
General geographical term describing the islands of the central and south Pacific Ocean, including Melanesia, Micronesia and Polynesia. Sometimes extended to include Australia, New Zealand and the Malay Archipelago (qv).

Polynesia
Collective name for the islands of the central and south Pacific Ocean. Includes: American Samoa, Cook Islands, Easter Island, French Polynesia, Hawaii, Kiribati (east), New Zealand, Niue, Pitcairn Islands, Samoa, Tokelau, Tonga, Tuvalu, Wallis & Futuna.

Scandinavia
Geographical region comprising: Denmark, Norway, Sweden. Often extended to include Finland and Iceland.

South America
Continent comprising: countries on mainland south of Panama, Falkland Islands, Galapagos Islands.

South-East Asia
Geographic region comprising Maynmar, Laos, Thailand, Vietnam, Cambodia, Malaysia, Singapore, Brunei and the Philippines. Sometimes taken to include Indonesia, Taiwan, Macau, Hong Kong and the southern coastal areas of China.

Ulster
Geographical region comprising Northern Ireland plus the counties of Cavan, Donegal and Monaghan in the Republic of Ireland. It is often used (incorrectly) as an unofficial term to describe Northern Ireland.

United Kingdom
Country comprising Great Britain (qv) and Northern Ireland. The Isle of Man and the Channel Islands are Crown dependencies and not officially part of the UK.

West Indies
Islands enclosing the Caribbean Sea, comprising: Bahama Islands (qv), Greater Antilles (qv), Lesser Antilles (qv).

Windward Islands
Group of Caribbean islands comprising: Grenada, Martinique, St Lucia, St Vincent and The Grenadines.

2: HIGHEST & LOWEST

Name	*Metres*	*Feet*	*Country*
AFRICA			
Kilimanjaro (Kibo)	5,895	19,340	Tanzania
Lake Assal	–155	–509	Djibouti
ANTARCTICA			
Vinson Massif	4,897	16,066	Antarctica
(ice covered)	–2,538	–8,327	Antarctica
ASIA			
Everest (Qomolangma Feng/ Sagarmatha)	8,850	29,035	China-Nepal
Dead Sea	–411	–1,349	Israel-Jordan-Palestine NAR
AUSTRALASIA & OCEANIA			
Aoraki (Cook)	3,754	12,315	New Zealand
Lake Eyre	–16	–52	Australia
EUROPE & RUSSIAN FEDERATION			
Elbrus	5,642	18,510	Russian Fed.
Caspian Sea	–28	–92	Russia-C. Asia-Caucasus
NORTH AMERICA			
McKinley (Denali)	6,194	20,321	Alaska, USA
Death Valley	–86	–282	California, USA
SOUTH AMERICA			
Aconcagua	6,960	22,834	Argentina
G. Bajo de S. Julián	–105	–344	Argentina

Name	*Metres*	*Feet*	*Country*
SOME OTHER NOTABLE MOUNTAINS			
K2 (Chogori/ Qogir Feng)	8,611	28,250	China-Kashmir
Kangchenjunga	8,586	28,170	India-Nepal
Makalu	8,463	27,766	China-Nepal
Dhaulagiri	8,167	26,795	Nepal
Nanga Parbat	8,126	26,660	Kashmir
Annapurna	8,091	26,545	Nepal
Gosainthan (Xixabangma Feng)	8,013	26,289	China
Qullai Garmo	7,495	24,590	Tajikistan
Ojos del Salado	6,908	22,664	Argentina-Chile
Huascarán	6,768	22,205	Peru
Logan	5,959	19,550	Yukon, Canada
Damavand	5,681	18,638	Iran
Citlaltépetl (Orizaba)	5,610	18,405	Mexico
Kenya (Kirinyaga)	5,199	17,057	Kenya
Ararat	5,165	16,946	Turkey
Mont Blanc	4,808	15,774	France-Italy
Ras Dashen	4,533	14,872	Ethiopia
Whitney	4,418	14,495	California, USA
Kinabalu	4,094	13,432	Malaysia
Fuji	3,776	12,388	Japan

3: THE WORLD'S LONGEST RIVERS

Local names are shown in square brackets: [ ]

River	*Length: (km)*	*(miles)*	*Source(s) and outflow*
Nile Luvironza-Ruvuvu-Kagera-White Nile	6,825	4,240	Lake Victoria region – Mediterranean Sea
Amazon Apurimac-Ene-Tambo-Ucayali	6,516	4,049	Peruvian Andes – Atlantic Ocean
Chang Jiang (Yangtze) [Tuotuo-Tongtian-Jinsha]	6,380	3,964	Tanggula Shan, China – East China Sea
Mississippi-Missouri Red Rock-Beaverhead	5,969	3,709	SW Montana – Gulf of Mexico
Ob-Irtysh [Ertix]	5,568	3,459	Altay Mountains, China – Kara Sea
Yenisey Selenga-Angara	5,550	3,448	Western Mongolia – Kara Sea
Huang He (Yellow)	5,464	3,395	Bayan Har Shan, China – Yellow Sea
Congo Lualaba	4,667	2,900	Katanga Plateau, Congo D.R. – Atlantic Ocean
Paraná Río de la Plata	4,500	2,796	Serra da Mantiquera, Brazil – Atlantic Ocean
Mekong [Za-Lancang]	4,425	2,749	Tanggula Shan, China – South China Sea
Amur Kerulen-Argun	4,416	2,744	Eastern Mongolia – Sea of Japan
Lena Kirenga	4,400	2,734	Baikal Mtns, Russian Fed., – Laptev Sea
Mackenzie Finlay-Peace-Slave	4,241	2,635	Omineca Mtns, BC, Canada – Beaufort Sea
Niger [Joliba/Kworra]	4,184	2,599	Guinea/Sierra Leone border – Gulf of Guinea
Murray-Darling	3,750	2,330	Gt. Dividing Range, Australia – Southern Ocean

4: CONVERSIONS

Kilometres	**10**	**20**	**30**	**40**	**50**	**60**	**70**	**80**	**90**	**100**
Miles	6.2	12.4	18.6	24.9	31.1	37.3	43.5	49.7	55.9	62.1
Metres	**10**	**20**	**30**	**40**	**50**	**60**	**70**	**80**	**90**	**100**
Feet	33	66	98	131	164	197	230	262	295	328

Centimetres	**10**	**20**	**30**	**40**	**50**	**60**	**70**	**80**	**90**	**100**
Inches	3.9	7.9	11.8	15.7	19.7	23.6	27.6	31.5	35.4	39.4
ºCentigrade	**-10**	**-5**	**0**	**5**	**10**	**15**	**20**	**25**	**30**	**35**
ºFahrenheit	14	23	32	41	50	59	68	77	86	95

5: GLOSSARY OF FOREIGN GEOGRAPHICAL TERMS

The following list provides the English equivalents for some of the most common foreign geographical terms used in this atlas and other international atlases.

Å, -å	Danish, Norwegian	Stream
Abar, Abyar	Arabic	Wells
Açude	Portuguese	Reservoir
Adalar	Turkish	Islands
Adasi	Turkish	Island
Agía, Ágios	Greek	Saint
Aiguille(s)	French	Peak(s)
Ain, Aïn	Arabic	Spring, well
-air	Indonesian	Stream
Ákra, Akrotírion	Greek	Cape, point
Ala-	Finnish	Lower
A'lá	Arabic	Upper
Alt-	German	Old
Alta, Alto	Italian, Portug., Spanish	Upper
Altiplanicie	Spain	High plain, mesa
Älv, -älven	Swedish	River
am, an	German	On, upon
Áno	Greek	Upper
Anse	French	Bay
Ao	Chinese, Thai	Bay
'Aqabat	Arabic	Pass
Arrecife	Spanish	Reef
Arroio/Arroyo	Portuguese/Spanish	Watercourse
Archipiélago	Spanish	Archipelago
Aust-	Norwegian	East, eastern
Austral	Spanish	Southern
'Ayn	Arabic	Spring, well
Baai	Afrikaans	Bay
Bab	Arabic	Strait
Bach	German	Stream
Bad	German	Spa
Badiyat	Arabic	Desert
Bælt	Danish	Strait
Baharu	Malay	New
Bahía	Spanish	Bay
Bahiret	Arabic	Lagoon
Bahr	Arabic	Bay, canal, lake
Bahra/Bahrat	Arabic	Lagoon/Lake
Baía/Baie	Portuguese/French	Bay
Baixo	Portuguese	Lower
Baja, Bajo	Spanish	Lower
Bala	Persian	Upper
Ban	Cambodian, Laotian, Thai	Village
-bana	Japanese	Cape, point
Bañado	Spanish	Marshy land
Banc/Banco	French/Spanish	Sandbank
Bandao	Chinese	Peninsula
Bandar	Arabian, Malay, Persian	Inlet, port
-bando	Korean	Peninsula
Baraj, Baraji	Turkish	Dam
Barat	Indonesian, Malay	West, western
Barqa	Arabic	Hill
Barra	Portuguese	Sandbank
Barracão	Portuguese	Dam, weir
Barragem	Portuguese	Reservoir
Baruun	Mongolian	Western
Bas, Basse	French	Lower
Bassin	French	Basin
Batin, Batn	Arabic	Depression
Becken	German	Basin
Beek	Flemish	Stream
bei	German	At, near
Bei	Chinese	North, northern
Beinn, Ben	Gaelic	Mountain
Belogor'ye	Russian	Mountain
Bereg	Russian	Bank, shore
-berg	Norwegian, Swedish	Mountain
Berg(e)	German	Mountain(s)
Besar	Indonesian, Malay	Big, great
Bir, Bîr/Bi'ar	Arabic	Well/Wells
Birkat, Birket	Arabic	Pool, well
-bjerg	Danish	Hill
Boca	Portuguese, Spanish	Mouth
Bocche	Italian	Estuary, mouths
Bodden	German	Bay, gulf
Bogazi	Turkish	Strait
Bogen	Norwegian	Bay
Bois	French	Woods
Boloto	Russian	Bog, marsh
Bol'sh-aya, -iye, -oy, -oye	Russian	Big
-bong	Korean	Mountain
Boquerón	Spanish	Pass
Bor	Polish	Forest
-botn/-botten	Norwegian/Swedish	Valley floor
Bouche	French	Estuary, mouth
-bre, -breen	Norwegian	Glacier
Bredning	Danish	Bay
Bron	Afrikaans	Spring, well
-brønn	Norwegian	Spring, well
Bucht/Bugt	German/Danish	Bay
Buhayrat, Buheirat	Arabic	Lake
Bukhta	Russian	Bay
Bukit	Malay	Hill
Bukt, Bukten	Norwegian, Swedish	Bay
Bulag	Mongolian	Spring
Bulak	Russian, Uighur	Spring
Burg	German	Castle
Burun, Burnu	Turkish	Cape, point
Büyük	Turkish	Big
Cabeço	Portuguese	Summit
Cabeza	Spanish	Summit
Cabo	Portuguese, Spanish	Cape, headland
Cachoeira	Portuguese	Waterfall
Cala/Caleta	Catalan/Spanish	Inlet
Cañada	Spanish	Ravine
Cañadón	Spanish	Gorge
Canal	Portuguese, Spanish	Channel
Cañe	Spanish	Stream
Cañon	Spanish	Canyon
Cap/Capo	Catalan, French/Italian	Cape, headland
Catarata	Spanish	Waterfall
Cayo(s)	Spanish	Islet(s), rock(s)
Cerro	Spanish	Hill, peak
Chaco	Spanish	Plain
Chaîne	French	Mountain chain
Chalb	Arabic	Watercourse
Chapada	Portuguese	Hills, uplands
Chebka	Arabic	Hill
-chedo	Korean	Archipelago
Chenal	French	Channel
Chiang	Thai	Town
-ch'on	Korean	River
Chong	Thai	Bay
Chott	Arabic	Marsh, salt lake
Chuluu	Mongolian	Mountain
Chute	French	Waterfall
Ci	Indonesian	Stream
Ciénaga	Spanish	Marshy lake
Cima/Cime	Italian/French	Summit
Città/Ciudad	Italian/Spanish	City, town
Co	Tibetan	Lake
Col	French	High pass
Collado	Spanish	Hill, saddle
Colle	Italian	Pass
Collina	Italian	Hill
Colline(s)	French	Hill(s)
Combe	French	Valley
Conca	Italian	Hollow
Cordillera	Spanish	Mountain chain
Corne/Corno	French/Italian	Peak
Costa	Italian, Portug., Spanish	Coast, shore
Côte	French	Coast, slope
Coteau(x)	French	Hill(s)
Cove	Catalan	Cave
Cuchilla	Spanish	Mountain chain
Cuenca	Spanish	River basin
Cueva	Spanish	Cave
Cun	Chinese	Village
Da	Chinese	Big
Dag/Dagh	Turkish/Persian	Mountain
Daglar	Turkish	Mountain
-dake	Japanese	Peak
-dal	Afrikaans, Danish, Norwegian, Swedish	Valley
Danau	Indonesian	Lake
Dao	Chinese	Island
Darreh	Persian	Valley
Daryacheh	Persian	Lake
Dasht	Persian, Urdu	Desert
Davaa	Mongolian	Pass
Denizi	Turkish	Sea
Dhar	Arabic	Hills, mountain
-diep	Flemish	Channel
Djebel/Djibâl	Arabic	Mountain/Mtns.
-do	Korean	Island
Dolina	Russian	Valley
Dolna/Dolní	Bulgarian/Czech	Lower
Dolny	Polish	Lower
Dong	Chinese	East, eastern
Dong	Thai	Mountain
-dong	Korean	Village
Donja, Donji	Serbo-Croat	Lower
Dorf	German	Village
-dorp	Afrikaans	Village
Dûr	Arabic	Mountains
Dzüün	Mongolian	East, eastern
Eiland(en)	Afrikaans, Flemish	Island(s)
-elv, -elva	Norwegian	River
Embalse	Spanish	Reservoir
Embouchure	French	Estuary
Ensenada	Spanish	Bay
Erg	Arabian	Desert & dunes
Eski	Turkish	Old
Estero	Spanish	Inlet, estuary, swamp
Estrecho	Spanish	Strait
Estreito	Portuguese	Strait
Étang	French	Lake, lagoon
Fajj	Arabic	Watercourse
Fels	German	Rock
Feng	Chinese	Peak
Fiume	Italian	River
-fjäll, -fjället	Swedish	Mountain
-fjärden	Swedish	Fjord
-fjell, -fjellet	Norwegian	Mountain
-fjord, -fjorden	Danish, Norwegian	Fjord, lagoon
Fleuve	French	River
Foce	Italian	River-mouth
-fonn	Norwegian	Glacier
Förde	German	Inlet
Forêt/Forst	French/German	Forest
-foss	Norwegian	Waterfall
Fuente	Spanish	Source, well
-gan	Japanese	Rock
Gang	Chinese	Harbour
Garet	Arabic	Hill
Gardaneh	Persian	Pass
Gat	Flemish	Channel
-gata	Japanese	Inlet, lagoon
Gau	German	District
Gave	French	Torrent
-gawa	Japanese	River
Gebel	Arabic	Mountain
Gebergte	Afrikaans	Mountain range
Gebiet	German	District, region
Gebirge	German	Mountains
Gedigi	Turkish	Pass
Gezîret/Gezâir	Arabic	Island/Islands
Ghadfat	Arabic	Watercourse
Ghadir	Arabic	Well
Ghard	Arabic	Sand dunes
Ghubbat	Arabic	Bay
Gipfel	German	Peak
Gletscher	German	Glacier
Gobi	Mongolian	Desert
Gol	Mongolian	River
Göl, Gölü	Turkish	Lake
Golfe	French	Bay, gulf
Golfete	Spanish	Bay
Golfo	Italian, Spanish	Bay, gulf
Gora	Bulgarian	Forest
Gora/Góra	Russian, Serbo-Croat/ Polish	Mountain
Górka	Polish	Hill
Gornja, Gornji	Serbo-Croat	Upper
Gory/Góry	Russian/Polish	Mountains
Goulet	French	Narrow entrance
Grabean	German	Ditch, trench
-grad	Bulgarian, Russian, Serbo-Croat	Town, castle
Grand, Grands	French	Big
Grat	German	Crest, ridge
Greben'	Russian	Ridge
-gród	Polish	Town, castle
Groot	Afrikaans	Big
Gross, -e, -en, -er	German	Big
Grotta/Grotte	Italian/French	Cave, grotto
Grund	German	Ground, valley
Gryada	Russian	Ridge
Guan	Chinese	Pass
Guba	Russian	Bay
Guelta	Arabic	Well
-gunto	Japanese	Island group
Gunung	Indonesian, Malay	Mountain
Hadabat	Arabic	Plain
Hadh, Hadhat	Arabic	Sand dunes
-haehyop	Korean	Strait
Hafar	Arabic	Wells
Hafen	German	Harbour, port
Haff	German	Bay
Hai	Chinese	Sea
Halbinsel	German	Peninsula
-halvøya	Norwegian	Peninsula
Hamad-a, -et	Arabic	Plateau
Hammad-ah, -at	Arabic	Plain, rocky plateau
-hamn	Norwegian, Swedish	Harbour
Hamun	Persian	Marsh
-hanto	Japanese	Peninsula
Hardt	German	Wooded hills
Harrat	Arabic	Lava fields
Hassi, Hasy	Arabic	Well
-haug	Norwegian	Hill
Haut, -e	French	Upper
Hawr	Arabic	Lake
-havn	Danish, Norwegian	Harbour
Hazm	Arabic	Plateau
He	Chinese	River
-hede	Danish, Norwegian	Heath
-hegység	Hungarian	Mountains
-hei/Heide	Norwegian/German	Heath, moor
Hersónisos	Greek	Peninsula
Higashi-	Japanese	East, eastern
-hisar	Turkish	Castle

Term	Language	Meaning
Hisn	Arabic	Fort
-hø	Norwegian	Peak
Hoch/Hoë	German/Afrikaans	High
Hoek	Flemish	Cape, point
Hög/-høg(d)	Swedish/Norwegian	High, height
Höhe, Hohen-	German	Height
Hoog	Flemish	High
-høoj	Danish	Hill
Hora/Hory	Czech	Mountain/Mtns
Horn	German	Peak, summit
Horní	Czech	Upper
Hot	Mongolian	Town
-høy	Norwegian	Height
-hrad	Czech	Castle
Hu	Chinese	Lake
Hügel	German	Hill
Idd	Arabic	Well
Idhan	Arabic	Sand dunes
'Idwet	Arabic	Mountain
Île(s)/Ilha(s)	French/Portuguese	Island(s)
Illa, Illes	Catalan	Island, islands
im, in	German	In
Inférieur, -e	French	Lower
Insel(n)	German	Island(s)
Irmak	Turkish	Large river
'Irq	Arabic	Sand dunes
Isla(s)/Isle	Spanish/French	Island(s)
Islote	Spanish	Small island
Iso	Finnish	Big
Ísola, Isole	Italian	Island, islands
Istmo	Spanish	Isthmus
Jabal	Arabic	Mountain
-järvi	Finnish	Lake
-jaure, -javrre	Lappish	Lake
Jazirat/Jaza'ir	Arabic	Island/Islands
Jbel, Jebel	Arabic	Mountain
Jezero/Jezioro	Serbo-Croat/Polish	Lake
Jiang	Chinese	River
Jiao	Chinese	Point, reef
Jibal	Arabic	Mountains
-jima	Japanese	Island
-joki/-jokka	Finnish/Lappish	River
-jøkulen	Norwegian	Glacier
-jökull	Icelandic	Glacier
Jun	Arabic	Bay
Kaap	Afrikaans	Cape
-kai	Japanese	Sea, bay, inlet
Kali	Indonesian	River
Kamm	German	Crest, ridge
Kampung	Indonesian, Malay	Village
Kanaal/Kanal	Flemish/German, Russian	Canal
-kapp	Norwegian	Cape
Karif	Arabic	Well
Kathib	Arabic	Sand dunes
Káto	Greek	Lower
-kawa	Japanese	River
Kecil	Indonesian, Malay	Small
Kepulauan	Indonesian	Archipelago
Kereb	Arabic	Hill, ridge
Keski-	Finnish	Central, middle
Khalîg, Khalij	Arabic	Bay, gulf
Khao	Thai	Peak
Khashm	Arabic	Mountain
Khawr, Khor/Khowr	Arabic/Persian	Inlet
Khrebet	Russian	Mountain range
Kis-	Hungarian	Small
Kita-	Japanese	North, northern
Klamm	German	Ravine
Klein	Afrikaans, German	Small
Klint/Klit	Danish	Cliff/Dunes
Klong	Thai	Canal, creek
Kloof	Afrikaans	Gorge
Ko/Koh	Thai/Cambodian	Island
-ko	Japanese	Lake, inlet
Kólpos	Greek	Gulf
Koog	German	Polder
Kop/Kopf	Afrikaans/German	Hill
Körfezi	Turkish	Bay, gulf
Kotlina	Czech, Polish	Basin, depression
Kotlovina	Russian	Depression
-köy	Turkish	Village
Kraj	Czech, Polish, Serbo-Croat	Region
Kray	Russian	Region
Kreis	German	District
Kryazh	Russian	Ridge
Kuala	Malay	Estuary
Küçük	Turkish	Small
Kuduk	Russian	Spring, well
Kuh	Persian	Mountain
Kul'	Russian	Lake
Kület	Arabic	Hill
Kum	Russian	Sandy desert
-kundo	Korean	Island group
-kylä	Finnish	Village
Lac	French	Lake
Laem	Thai	Point
Lago	Italian, Portug., Spanish	Lake
Lagoa	Portuguese	Lagoon
Laguna	Spanish	Lagoon, lake
Lam	Thai	Stream

Term	Language	Meaning
Län	Swedish	Province
Land	German	Province, area
Lande	French	Heath, sandy moor
Las/Les	Polish/Czech, Russian	Forest, wood
Laut	Indonesia	Sea
Lednik	Russian	Glacier
lès, lez	French	Beside, near
Liedao	Chinese	Island group
Lille	Danish, Norwegian	Small
Liman	Russian	Bay, gulf
Liman, Limani	Turkish	Harbour, port
Límni	Greek	Lake, lagoon
Ling	Chinese	Mountain range
Llano	Spanish	Plain, prairie
Loma	Spanish	Hill
-luoto	Finnish	Rocky island
-lyng	Danish	Heath
Macizo	Spanish	Massif
Madinat	Arabic	City, town
Mae Nam	Thai	River
Mala/Malé	Serbo-Croat/Czech	Small
Malaya, -oye, -yy	Russian	Small
-man	Korean	Bay
Manâqir	Arabic	Hills
Mar	Portuguese, Spanish	Sea
Marais	French	Marsh, swamp
Mare	Italian/Romanian	Sea/Big
Marsá	Arabic	Anchorage, inlet
Marsch	German	Fen, marsh
Masabb	Arabic	Estuary
Mashâsh	Arabic	Well
Massif	French	Mountains, upland
Mayor	Spanish	Higher, larger
Meer	Afrikaans, Flemish, German	Lake, sea
Méga, Megál-a, -i, -o	Greek	Big
Menor	Portuguese, Spanish	Lesser, smaller
Mer	French	Sea
Mersa	Arabic	Anchorage, inlet
Mesa, Meseta	Spanish	Tableland
Mesto	Czech, Serbo-Croat	Town
Mezzo	Italian	Middle, mid-
Miasto	Polish	Town
Mic/Mikr-í, ón	Romanian/Greek	Small
Mina'	Arabic	Harbour, port
Minami-	Japanese	South, southern
Minqâr	Arabic	Hill
-misaki	Japanese	Cape, point
Mishâsh, Mushâsh	Arabic	Well
Miti	Greek	Cape
Mittel-, Mitten-	German	Central, middle
Mjesto	Serbo-Croat	Town
Monasterio/Moni	Spanish/Greek	Monastery
Mont/Monte	French/Italian, Portuguese, Spanish	Mountain
Montagne(s)	French	Mountain(s)
Monti	Italian	Mountains
Moor	German	Bog, moor, swamp
Moos	German	Bog, moss
More	Russian	Sea
Mörön	Mongolian	River
Morro	Portuguese	Hill, mountain
-mose	Danish	Bog, moor
Moyen, -ne	French	Middle, mid-
Muara	Indonesian	Estuary
Mudiriyat	Arabic	Province
Muntii	Romanian	Mountains
-myr	Norwegian, Swedish	Moor, swamp
Mys	Russian	Cape
na	Bulgarian, Russian, Serbo-Croat	On
nad	Czech, Polish, Russian	Above, over
-nada	Japanese	Gulf, sea
Nádrz	Czech	Reservoir
-naes	Danish	Cape, point
Nafud	Arabic	Desert, dune
Nagor'ye	Russian	Highland, uplands
Nagy-	Hungarian	Big, great
Nahr	Arabic	River
Nakhon	Thai	Town
Nam	Korean, Vietnamese	South, southern
Nam	Burmese, Thai, Vietnamese	River
Nan	Chinese	South, southern
Naqb	Arabic	Pass
Nasb	Arabic	Hill, mountain
Né-a, -on, -os	Greek	New
Neder-	Flemish	Lower
Nehri	Turkish	River
Nei	Chinese	Inner
-nes	Icelandic, Norwegian	Cape, point
Neu-/Neuf, Neuve	German/French	New
Nevado	Spanish	Peak
-ni	Korean	Village
Nieder-	German	Lower
Nieu	Afrikaans	New
Nieuw, -e, -en, -er	Flemish	New
Nishi	Japanese	West, western
-nísi	Greek	Island
Nizhn-eye, -iy, -iye, -yaya	Russian	Lower

Term	Language	Meaning
Nízina/Nízni	Czech	Lowland/Lower
Nizmennost'	Russian	Lowland
Noord-	Flemish	North, northern
Nord	Danish, French, German	North, northern
Nordre, Nørre	Danish	Northern
Norra	Swedish	Northern
Norte	Portuguese, Spanish	North
Nos	Bulgarian, Russian	Point, spit
Nótios	Greek	Southern
Nou	Romanian	New
Nouv-eau, -elle	French	New
Nova	Italian	New
Nova, Novi	Bulgarian, Serbo-Croat	New
Nova, Novo	Portuguese	New
Nová, Nové, Novy	Czech	New
Nov-aya, -o, -oye, -yy, -yye	Russian	New
Nowa, Nowe, Nowy	Polish	New
Nudo	Spanish	Mountain
Nueva, Nuevo	Spanish	New
Nuruu	Mongolian	Mountains
Nusa	Indonesian	Island
Nuur	Mongolian	Lake
Ny-	Danish, Norweg., Swedish	New
-ö, -ön/-ø	Swedish/Danish	Island
-oaivi, -oaivve	Lappish	Hill, mountain
Ober-	German	Upper
Oblast'	Russian	Province
Occidental	Spanish	Western
-odde	Danish, Norwegian	Cape, point
Ogla, Oglet	Arabic	Well
Okrug	Russian	District
Ömnö-	Mongolian	South, southern
Onder	Flemish	Lower
Öndör-	Mongolian	Upper
-oog	German	Island
Oost, -er, -elijk	Flemish	East, eastern
Orasu	Romanian	Town
Oriental, -e	French, Romanian, Spanish	Eastern
Ormani	Turkish	Forest
Órmos	Greek	Bay
Óros/Óri	Greek	Mountain/Mtns.
Ost-/Öster-	German/Danish, Norweg.	East, eastern
Ostan	Persian	Province
Östra-	Swedish	East, eastern
Ostrov(a)	Russian	Island(s)
Otok/Otoci	Serbo-Croat	Island/Islands
Oud, -e, -en, -er	Flemish	Old
Oued	Arabic	Dry river-bed
Ovasi	Turkish	Plain
Over-	Danish, Flemish	Upper
Över-, Övre-	Norwegian, Swedish	Upper
-øy, -a	Norwegian	Island
Ozero, Ozera	Russian	Lake, lakes
-pää	Finnish	Hill
Palai-á, -ó, Palió	Greek	Old
Parbat	Urdu	Mountain
Parc	French	Park
Pas	French	Low pass, strait
Paso	Spanish	Pass, strait
Pass/Passo	Spanish/Italian	Pass
Pays	French	Region
Pegunungan	Indonesian	Mountain range
Pélagos	Greek	Sea
Peña(s)	Spanish	Cliff(s), rocks(s)
Pendi	Chinese	Basin
Penisola	Italian	Peninsula
Peñon	Spanish	Cliff
Pereval	Russian	Pass
Perv-o, -yy	Russian	First
Peski	Russian	Sands, desert
Petit, -e, -es	French	Little
Pic	French, Spanish	Peak, summit
Pico/Picacho	Portuguese, Spanish	Peak, summit
Pik	Russian	Peak, summit
Pingyuan	Chinese	Plain
Pizzo	Italian	Peak, summit
-plaat	Dutch	Sandbank, shoal
Plage	French	Beach
Plaine/Planicie	French/Spanish	Plain
Plaj(i)	Turkish	Beach(es)
Planalto	Portuguese	Plateau
Planina	Bulgarian, Serbo-Croat	Mountains
Platja/Playa	Catalan/Spanish	Beach
Plato	Afrikaans, Bulg., Russian	Plateau
Platte	German	Plateau, plain
Plosina	Czech	Tableland
Ploskogor'ye	Russian	Plateau
pod	Czech, Russian	Under
Pohor-í, -ie	Czech	Mountain range
Pointe	French	Cape, point
Poluostrov	Russian	Peninsula
Pólwysep	Polish	Peninsula
Pongo	Spanish	Water gap
Ponta, Pontal	Portuguese	Point
Portile	Romanian	Gate
Portillo	Spanish	Gap, pass
Porto	Catalan, Italian, Portug.	Harbour, port
Pradesh	Hindi	State
Praia	Portuguese	Beach, shore

Term	Language	Meaning
près	French	Near
Presqu'île	French	Peninsula
Pri-	Russian	Near
Proliv	Russian	Strait
Protoka	Russian	Channel
Prusmyk	Czech	Pass
Przelecz	Polish	Pass
Pubu	Chinese	Waterfall
Pueblo	Spanish	Village
Puente	Spanish	Bridge
Puerta	Spanish	Narrow pass
Puerto	Spanish	Harbour, port
Puk-	Korean	North, northern
Pulau	Indonesian, Malay	Island
Puna	Spanish	Desert plateau
Punta	Catalan, Italian, Spanish	Cape, point
Puntjak	Indonesian	Mountain
Puy	French	Peak
Qa	Arabic	Depression
Qalamat, Qalib	Arabic	Well
Qanat	Arabic, Persian	U'ground conduit
Qararat	Arabic	Depression
Qâret	Arabic	Hill
Qiao	Chinese	Bridge
Qiuling	Chinese	Hills
Qoz	Arabic	Hill
Qu	Tibetan	Stream
Quan	Chinese	Spring
Quedas	Portuguese	Rapids
Qulban	Arabic	Wells
Qum	Persian	Sand
Qundao	Chinese	Archipelago
Qûr, Qurayyat	Arabic	Hills
Qurnat	Arabic	Peak
Quwayrat/Qurûn	Arabic	Hill/Hills
Ramlat	Arabic	Sands
Râs/Ra's	Arabic/Arabic, Persian	Cape, point
Raso	Portuguese	Upland
Ravnina/Razlivy	Russian	Plain
Região	Portuguese	Region
Reprêsa	Portuguese	Dam
Reshteh	Persian	Mountain range
-retto	Japanese	Island chain
-rev	Norwegian	Cliff, reef
Ri	Tibetan	Mountain
-ri	Korean	Village
Ria/Ría	Portuguese/Spanish	River-mouth
Ribeirão	Portuguese	River
Ribeiro	Portuguese	Stream
Rio/Río	Portuguese/Spanish	River
Rivier/Rivière	Afrikaans/French	River
Rocher	French	Cliff, rock
Rocque	French	Rock
Rt	Serbo-Croat	Cape, point
Rücken	German	Ridge
Rud, Rudkhaneh	Persian	River
Rudohorie	Czech	Mountains
-saari	Finnish	Island
Sabkhat	Arabic	Salt-flat
Sagar, Sagara	Hindi	Lake
Sahl	Arabic	Plain
Sahra	Arabic	Desert
-saki	Japanese	Cape, point
Salada/Salar, Salina	Spanish	Salt lake/Salt pan
Salto	Portuguese, Spanish	Waterfall
-san	Japanese, Korean	Mountain
-sanchi	Japanese	Mountainous area
Saniyat	Arabic	Well
Sanmaek	Korean	Mountain range
-sanmyaku	Japanese	Mountain range
San	Italian, Portug., Spanish	Saint
Sankt/Sant	German/Catalan	Saint
Santa, Santo	Italian, Portug., Spanish	Saint
São	Portuguese	Saint
Satu	Romanian	Village
Schloss	German	Castle, mansion
Schutzgebiet	German	Reserve
Sebkra	Arabic	Salt-flat
See	German	Lake
-sehir	Turkish	Town
Selat	Indonesian	Channel, strait
Selatan	Indonesian, Malay	South, southern
-selkä	Finnish	Open water, ridge
Selo	Russian, Serbo-Croat	Village
Selva	Spanish	Forest, wood
-sen	Japanese	Mountain
Serra/Serrania	Catalan, Portug. /Span.	Mountain range
-seto	Japanese	Channel, strait
Sever-naya, -noye, -nyy, -o	Russian	North, northern
Sfîntu	Romanian	Saint
Shahr	Persian	Town
Sha'ib, -an	Arabic	Watercourse
Shamo	Chinese	Desert
Shan	Chinese	Mountain(s)
Shandi	Chinese	Mountainous area
Shang	Chinese	Upper
Shankou	Chinese	Pass
Shanmai	Chinese	Mountain range
Sharm	Arabic	Cove, inlet
Shatt	Arabic	River, river-mouth
-shima/-shoto	Japanese	Island/Island group
Shuiku	Chinese	Reservoir
Sierra	Spanish	Mountain range
Silsilesi	Turkish	Mountain range
Sint	Afrikaans, Flemish	Saint
-sjø/sjön	Norwegian/Swedish	Lake
Skala, Skaly	Czech	Cliff, rock
-skog	Norwegian	Woods
-slette	Norwegian	Plain
Sliabh, Slieve	Gaelic	Mountain, upland
Sloboda	Russian	Suburb, large village
Sø	Danish, Norwegian	Lake
Söder-, Södra	Swedish	Southern
Solonchak	Russian	Salt lake
Sommet	French	Peak, summit
Sønder-	Danish	Southern
Søndre	Danish, Norwegian	Southern
Sopka	Russian	Hill
Sør	Norwegian	Southern
sous	French	Under
Spitze	German	Peak
Sredn-a, -i	Bulgarian	Central, middle
Sredn-e, -eye, -iy, -yaya	Russian	Central, middle
-stad	Afrikaans, Norwegian, Swedish	Town
-stadt	German	Town
Stara, Stari	Serbo-Croat	Old
Stará, Staré	Czech	Old
Star-aya, oye, -yy, -yye	Russian	Old
Stausee	German	Reservoir
Stenó	Greek	Pass, strait
Step'	Russian	Steppe
Stít	Czech	Peak
Stor-, Stora/Store	Swedish/Danish	Big
Strand	Gaelic, German	Beach
-strand	Danish, Norweg., Swedish	Beach
Strasse	German	Road
-strede	Norwegian	Passage, strait
Strelka	Russian	Spit
Stretto	Italian	Strait
Sud	French	South
Süd(er)	German	South (southern)
Suhul	Arabic	Plain
Suid	Afrikaans	South
-suido	Japanese	Channel, strait
Sul	Portuguese	South
sul, sull'	Italian	On
Sund	Swedish	Sound, strait
Sungai	Indonesian, Malay	River
-suo	Finnish	Marsh, swamp
Supérieur/Superior	French/Spanish	Upper
Sur	Spanish	South
sur	French	On
Sveti	Serbo-Croat	Saint
Szent-	Hungarian	Saint
-take	Japanese	Peak
Tal	German	Valley
Tall(ât)	Arabic	Hill(s)
Tang	Persian	Pass, strait
Tanjung	Indonesian, Malay	Cape, point
Taraq	Arabic	Hills
Tasek	Malay	Lake
Tau	Russian	Mountain(s)
Tekojärvi	Finnish	Reservoir
Tell	Arabic	Hill
Teluk	Indonesian	Bay
Tengah	Indonesian	Middle
Teniet	Arabic	Pass
Tepe, Tepesi	Turkish	Hill, peak
Tepeler, Tepeleri	Turkish	Hills, peaks
Terre/Tierra	French/Spanish	Land
Thale	Thai	Lake
Tilat	Arabic	Hill
Timur	Indonesian	East, eastern
-tind, -tinderne	Norwegian	Peak, peaks
Tir'at	Arabic	Canal
-tji	Indonesian	Stream
-to	Japanese	Island
-toge	Japanese	Pass
-tong	Korean	Village
Tonle	Cambodian	Lake
-topp	Norwegian	Peak
Torrente	Spanish	Rapids
Travesía	Spanish	Desert
Tulul	Arabic	Hills
Túnel	Spanish	Tunnel
über	German	Above
-udden	Swedish	Cape, point
Új-	Hungarian	New
Ujung	Indonesian	Cape, point
-umi	Japanese	Inlet
Unter-	German	Lower
'Uqlat	Arabic	Well
-ura	Japanese	Inlet
'Urayq	Arabic	Sand ridge
'Uruq	Arabic	Area of dunes
Ust'ye	Russian	Estuary
Utara	Indonesian	North, northern
Uttar	Hindi	Northern
Uul	Mongolian	Mountains
Uval	Russian	Hill
'Uyun	Arabic	Springs
-vaara(t)	Finnish	Hill(s)
-vaart	Flemish	Canal
-våg	Norwegian	Bay
Val, Vall	Italian, Spanish	Valley
Vale	Portuguese, Romanian	Valley
Valle/Vallée	Italian, Spanish/French	Valley
Vallon	French	Small valley
-vann	Norwegian	Lake
-város	Hungarian	Town
-varre	Norwegian	Mountain
Väster, Västra	Swedish	Western
-vatn	Icelandic, Norwegian	Lake
-vatnet	Norwegian	Lake
-vatten, vattnet	Swedish	Lake
Vaux	French	Valleys
Vecchio	Italian	Old
Vechi	Romanian	Old
Velha, Velho	Portuguese	Old
Velik-a, -i	Serbo-Croat	Big
Velik-aya, -iy, -iye	Russian	Big
Vel'k-á, -é, -y	Czech	Big
Verkhn-e, -eye, -iy, -yaya	Russian	Upper
-vesi	Finnish	Lake, water
Vester	Danish	Western
Vest, Vestre	Norwegian	West, western
-vidda	Norwegian	Plateau
Vieja, Viejo/ Vieux	Spanish/French	Old
Vig/-vik	Danish/Norwegian	Bay
Vila	Portuguese	Small town
Ville	French	Town
Víztároló	Hungarian	Reservoir
Vodokhranilishche	Russian	Reservoir
Volcán	Spanish	Volcano
Vorota	Russian	Channel, strait
Vostochn-aya, -oye, -yy	Russian	Eastern
Vozvyshennost'	Russian	Uplands
Vpadina	Russian	Depression
Vrch(y)	Czech	Mountain(s)
Vrchovina	Czech	Mountainous area
Vysocina	Czech	Upland
Vysok-aya, -oye	Russian	Upper
Wad	Flemish	Sand-flat
Wâdi, Wadi	Arabic	Watercourse
Wahat	Arabic	Oasis
Wai	Chinese	Outer
Wald	German	Forest
Wan/-wan	Chinese/Japanese	Bay
Wand	German	Cliff
Wasser	German	Lake, water
Wes-	Afrikaans	West
West, Wester	Flemish, German	West
Wielk-a, -i, -ie, -o	Polish	Big
Wysok-a, -i, -ie	Polish	Upper
Xi	Chinese	Stream, west
Xia	Chinese	Gorge, lower
Xian	Chinese	County
Xiao	Chinese	Small
Xu	Chinese	Islet
-yama	Japanese	Mountain(s)
Yang	Chinese	Ocean
Yarimadasi	Turkish	Peninsula
Yeni	Turkish	New
Yli-	Finnish	Upper
Ytre-	Norwegian	Outer
Ytter-	Norwegian, Swedish	Outer
Yuan	Chinese	Spring
Yugo-	Russian	Southern
Yunhe	Chinese	Canal
Yuzhn-aya, -o, -oye, -yy	Russian	South, southern
-zaki	Japanese	Cape, point
Zalew	Polish	Bay, inlet, lagoon
Zaliv	Russian	Bay
-zan	Japanese	Mountain
Zapadn-aya, -o, -oye, -yy	Russian	West, western
Zatoka	Polish	Gulf
-zee	Flemish	Sea
Zemlya	Russian	Land
-zhen	Chinese	Town
Zhong	Chinese	Middle
Zhou	Chinese	Islet
Zui	Chinese	Point, spit
Zuid	Flemish	South
Zuid-elijk, er	Flemish	Southern

6: GLOSSARY OF CLIMATE TERMS

An alphabetical list of all the terms featured on the regional climate maps.

Benguela Current *Africa maps*
A cold current flowing north along the west coast of South Africa, cooling the coastal region.

Berg Wind *Africa May–October map*
A hot dry wind which blows from the interior to the coastal regions of Namibia and South Africa.

Bora *Europe Winter map*
A cold dry wind which blows from the N and NE, affecting the Adriatic coastlines of Croatia, Italy and Slovenia.

California Current *North America Summer map*
A cold current which flows south along the west coast of California and Mexico, cooling the coastal region, and responsible for the frequent sea fogs particularly during the summer.

Canary Current *Africa maps*
An extension of the North Atlantic Drift (qv), flowing south along the NW Africa coast and moderating temperatures in the coastal region.

Chinook *North America Winter map*
A warm dry wind which blows down the eastern slopes of the Rockies, rapidly melting lying snow.

Crachin *Asia November–April map*
Light rain in the northern mountains and coastal regions of Vietnam.

El Niño *South America maps*
A change in the ocean-atmosphere system in the Pacific, increasing water temperatures in the central and eastern equatorial Pacific Ocean and bringing rain to the NW coast of South America. A periodic phenomenon, it often affects the western coast of America as far north as California. In some years the weather pattern of the whole American continent can be disrupted, and in exceptional years its effects experienced worldwide.

Etesian Wind / Meltemi *Europe Winter map*
A wind blowing from the N and NW in the eastern Mediterranean and the Aegean, often creating rough seas.

Föhn *Europe Winter map*
A wind which blows down Alpine valleys, warming as it descends, and melts snow rapidly.

Garúa *South America November–April map*
A heavy mist on the Pacific slope of the Andes in a normally very dry part of the coast.

Ghibli *Africa May–October map*
Local name for the Sirocco (qv) in Libya.

Guinea Monsoon *Africa May–October map*
Warm humid winds blowing from the SW in West Africa between April and September, associated with the rainy season.

Gulf Stream
North America Summer map (mentioned in 'Labrador current' box)
A warm current which flows NE from the Gulf of Mexico. After passing Newfoundland, it divides and follows three separate routes: 1. northwest towards Europe (the North Atlantic Drift (qv)); 2. southeast; 3. recirculating around an area north of Bermuda.

Harmattan *Africa November–April map*
A dry and dusty NE wind in West Africa blowing from the Sahara, associated with the dry season; cool at night and warm in the day. Opposite of the Guinea Monsoon (qv).

Kharif *Asia May–October map*
The rainy season in northern India and Arab countries.

Khamsin / Sharav *Africa May–October map*
A hot dry wind blowing from the S and SE in the eastern Mediterranean, warming the coastal region and helping to create dust storms and a hazy atmosphere.

Labrador Current *North America Summer map*
A cold current flowing south along the east coast of Canada, carrying icebergs and keeping the coastal region relatively cool druing the summer; fogs are caused off the Newfoundland coast where the current meets the warmer Gulf Stream flowing NE from the Gulf of Mexico.

La Niña *South America maps*
The opposite phenomenon to El Niño. Warm surface water flows towards Asia and colder water from the ocean depths moves to the surface in the eastern equatorial Pacific. Evaporation decreases and rainfall in the region is reduced. Often La Niña occurs the year after El Niño, with drought affecting the areas which experienced flooding the year before.

Leveche *Europe Winter map*
A hot, dry and dusty wind in southern Spain which blows from the Sahara.

Mistral *Europe Winter map*
A strong cold dry wind blowing from the north in southern France; known as Cers in Aude département.

Monsoon Winds *Asia maps*
Seasonal winds which change direction during the year; during the dry season in India the NE monsoon blows dry air from the land and during the wet season the SW monsoon blows wet air from the ocean. The term is also used in Africa and Australasia.

Mozambique Current / Agulhas Current *Africa May–October map*
A warm current flowing south and west along the coast of Mozambique and eastern South Africa, warming the coastal region.

North Atlantic Drift *Europe Winter map*
An extension of the Gulf Stream (qv) which helps to maintain relatively mild winters in the British Isles and along the Norwegian coast.

Peru Current / Humboldt Current *South America maps*
A cold current flowing north along the west coast of South America and cooling the coastal region as far as the Equator.

Shamal *Africa May–October map*
A hot dry wind which blows from the NW in Iraq and The Gulf.

Sirocco *Europe Summer map*
A hot dusty wind blowing towards Europe from north Africa. Known as the Ghibli (qv) in Libya and Leveche (qv) in Spain. Its origins are the same as the Khamsin (qv) or Sharav (qv). On the northern Mediterranean coast, particularly in southern Italy, the wind is moist after crossing the Mediterranean.

7: THE WORLD'S MAJOR CITIES & URBAN AREAS

The list shows the world's largest cities (left column) and urban areas (right column) with estimates of their population in 2003 as supplied by www.world-gazetteer.com. An 'urban area' can be defined as one or more built-up regions at a consistently urban density of population, generally with a major centre from which it takes its name, all of which have close economic and other links, the borders of which can extend beyond regional or even national frontiers. A 'city' can be defined as an urban area contained within a defined administrative boundary.

The ten biggest cities in 1900 and in 1800 are listed at the foot of the page.

City & country	Population	Urban area & country	Population
Mumbai (Bombay), India	12,147,100	**Tokyo**, Japan	31,036,900
Buenos Aires, Argentina	11,655,100	**New York**, USA	29,881,200
Seoul, Rep. of Korea	11,153,200	**Mexico City**, Mexico	21,027,200
Jakarta, Indonesia	10,810,400	**Seoul**, Rep. of Korea	19,844,500
Karachi, Pakistan	10,272,500	**São Paulo**, Brazil	18,505,100
Manila, the Philippines	10,133,200	**Osaka**, Japan	17,592,400
São Paulo, Brazil	10,057,700	**Jakarta**, Indonesia	17,369,200
Delhi, India	10,009,200	**Delhi**, India	16,713,200
Istanbul, Turkey	9,216,400	**Los Angeles**, USA	16,584,700
Shanghai, China	9,031,200	**Cairo**, Egypt	15,546,100
Mexico City, Mexico	8,589,600	**Manila**, the Philippines	13,503,200
Dhaka, Bangladesh	8,539,500	**Buenos Aires**, Argentina	12,923,800
Moscow, Russia	8,376,000	**Mumbai (Bombay)**, India	12,147,100
New York, USA	8,103,700	**Moscow**, Russia	12,100,100
Lagos, Nigeria	8,029,200	**Shanghai**, China	12,005,300
Tokyo, Japan	8,027,500	**Kolkata (Calcutta)**, India	11,387,400
Cairo, Egypt	7,764,700	**Köln-Ruhr Area**, Germany	11,297,800
Tehran, Iran	7,722,900	**Paris**, France	11,293,200
Lima, Peru	7,603,500	**Rio de Janeiro**, Brazil	11,246,600
London, UK	7,393,800	**London**, UK	11,230,500
Beijing, China	7,129,500	**Tehran**, Iran	10,978,500
Bogotá, Colombia	6,680,500	**Chicago**, USA	10,894,200
Bangkok, Thailand	6,513,100	**Karachi**, Pakistan	10,272,500
Kinshasa, Dem. Rep. of Congo	6,301,100	**Dhaka**, Bangladesh	10,168,600
Rio de Janeiro, Brazil	6,029,300	**Istanbul**, Turkey	9,640,500
Lahore, Pakistan	5,611,500	**Deijing**, China	9,349,300
Santiago, Chile	5,034,500	**Lagos**, Nigeria	9,123,200
Baghdad, Iraq	4,948,300	**Bangkok**, Thailand	8,707,900
Kolkata (Calcutta), India	4,670,000	**Nagoya**, Japan	8,595,400
St Petersburg, Russia	4,619,800	**Hong Kong**, China	8,208,200
Bangalore, India	4,376,100	**Bogotá**, Colombia	7,798,000
Tianjin, China	4,344,500	**Taipei**, Taiwan	7,728,300
Chennai (Madras), India	4,298,600	**Baltimore**, USA	7,610,600
Sydney, Australia	4,280,900	**Lima**, Peru	7,603,500
Singapore, Singapore	4,154,500	**Kinshasa**, Dem. Rep. of Congo	7,527,500
Busan, Rep. of Korea	4,085,300	**Chongqing**, China	7,161,100
Yangon (Rangoon), Myanmar	4,016,000	**San Francisco**, USA	7,108,600
Wuhan, China	3,957,500	**Boston**, USA	7,025,000
Alexandria, Egypt	3,806,300	**Tianjin**, China	6,927,200
Los Angeles, USA	3,805,400	**Chennai (Madras)**, India	6,550,100
Riyadh, Saudi Arabia	3,627,700	**Baghdad**, Iraq	6,492,200
Ahmadabad, India	3,584,000	**Shenyang**, China	6,422,700
Yokohama, Japan	3,552,300	**Detroit**, USA	5,959,000
Hyderabad, India	3,517,300	**Khartoum**, Sudan	5,862,500
Shenyang, China	3,452,900	**Bangalore**, India	5,797,900
Guangzhou, China	3,433,700	**Ho Chi Minh City**, Vietnam	5,728,900
Ho Chi Minh City, Vietnam	3,378,500	**Hyderabad**, India	5,641,700
Melbourne, Australia	3,353,300	**Santiago**, Chile	5,636,800
Casablanca, Morocco	3,344,300	**Lahore**, Pakistan	5,611,500
Ankara, Turkey	3,329,400	**Toronto**, Canada	5,462,100
Abidjan, Côte d'Ivoire	3,310,500	**Guangzhou**, China	5,370,800
Berlin, Germany	3,289,500	**Madrid**, Spain	5,078,100
Kano, Nigeria	3,248,700	**Dallas**, USA	5,077,300
Ibadan, Nigeria	3,078,400	**Johannesburg**, South Africa	5,014,000
Chicago, USA	2,934,900	**Miami**, USA	4,923,200
Madrid, Spain	2,905,100	**St Petersburg**, Russia	4,891,100
Bandung, Indonesia	2,884,300	**Singapore**, Singapore	4,876,000
Harbin, China	2,765,400	**Houston**, USA	4,647,300
Surabaya, Indonesia	2,729,300	**Wuhan**, China	4,574,200
Pyongyang, DPR of Korea	2,724,700	**Harbin**, China	4,457,800

1900:		*1800:*	
London, United Kingdom	6,500	**Peking**, China	1,100
New York, USA	4,200	**London**, Great Britain	900
Paris, France	3,300	**Canton**, China	800
Berlin, Germany	2,700	**Tokyo (Edo)**, Japan	700
Chicago, USA	1,700	**Constantinople**, Ottoman Empire	600
Vienna, Austro-Hungarian Empire	1,700	**Paris**, France	550
Tokyo, Japan	1,500	**Naples**, Kingdom of Naples	450
St Petersburg, Russia	1,400	**Hangchow**, China	400
Manchester, United Kingdom	1,400	**Osaka**, Japan	380
Philadelphia, USA	1,400	**Kyoto**, Japan	380

8: US STATES

ISO* Abbr.	State	Nickname	Date of admission to the Union	State Capital
AL	Alabama	Heart of Dixie	14th Dec 1819	Montgomery
AK	Alaska	The Last Frontier	3rd Jan 1959	Juneau
AZ	Arizona	Grand Canyon State	14th Feb 1912	Phoenix
AR	Arkansas	The Natural State	15th June 1836	Little Rock
CA	California	Golden State	9th Sept 1850	Sacramento
CO	Colorado	Centennial State	1st Aug 1876	Denver
CT	Connecticut	Constitution State	9th Jan 1788 †	Hartford
DE	Delaware	First State / Diamond State	7th Dec 1787 †	Dover
DC	District of Columbia	(Federal District, coextensive with the city of Washington)		
FL	Florida	Sunshine State	3rd Mar 1845	Tallahassee
GA	Georgia	Empire State of the South / Peach State	2nd Jan 1788 †	Atlanta
HI	Hawaii	Aloha State	21st Aug 1959	Honolulu
ID	Idaho	Gem State	3rd July 1890	Boise
IL	Illinois	Land of Lincoln	3rd Dec 1818	Springfield
IN	Indiana	Hoosier State	11th Dec 1816	Indianapolis
IA	Iowa	Hawkeye State	28th Dec 1846	Des Moines
KS	Kansas	Sunflower State	29th Jan 1861	Topeka
KY	Kentucky	Bluegrass State	1st June 1792	Frankfort
LA	Louisiana	Pelican State	30th Apr 1812	Baton Rouge
ME	Maine	Pine Tree State	15th Mar 1820	Augusta
MD	Maryland	Old Line State	28th Apr 1788 †	Annapolis
MA	Massachusetts	Bay State	6th Feb 1788 †	Boston
MI	Michigan	Great Lakes State	26th Jan 1837	Lansing
MN	Minnesota	Gopher State / North Star State	11th May 1858	St Paul
MS	Mississippi	Magnolia State	10th Dec 1817	Jackson
MO	Missouri	Show Me State	10th Aug 1821	Jefferson City
MT	Montana	Treasure State	8th Nov 1889	Helena
NE	Nebraska	Cornhusker State	1st Mar 1867	Lincoln
NV	Nevada	Silver State	31st Oct 1864	Carson City
NH	New Hampshire	Granite State	21st June 1788 †	Concord
NJ	New Jersey	Garden State	18th Dec 1787 †	Trenton
NM	New Mexico	Land of Enchantment	6th Jan 1912	Santa Fe
NY	New York	Empire State	26th July 1788 †	Albany
NC	North Carolina	Tar Heel State	21st Nov 1789 †	Raleigh
ND	North Dakota	Flickertail State / Peace Garden State	2nd Nov 1889	Bismarck
OH	Ohio	Buckeye State	1st Mar 1803	Columbus
OK	Oklahoma	Sooner State	16th Nov 1907	Oklahoma City
OR	Oregon	Beaver State	14th Feb 1859	Salem
PA	Pennsylvania	Keystone State	12th Dec 1787 †	Harrisburg
RI	Rhode Island	Ocean State	29th May 1790 †	Providence
SC	South Carolina	Palmetto State	23rd May 1788 †	Columbia
SD	South Dakota	Mount Rushmore State	2nd Nov 1889	Pierre
TN	Tennessee	Volunteer State	1st June 1796	Nashville
TX	Texas	Lone Star State	29th Dec 1845	Austin
UT	Utah	Beehive State	4th Jan 1896	Salt Lake City
VT	Vermont	Green Mountain State	4th Mar 1791	Montpelier
VA	Virginia	Old Dominion State	25th June 1788 †	Richmond
WA	Washington	Evergreen State	11th Nov 1889	Olympia
WV	West Virginia	Mountain State	20th June 1863	Charleston
WI	Wisconsin	Badger State	29th May 1848	Madison
WY	Wyoming	Cowboy State / Equality State	10th July 1890	Cheyenne

International Organisation for Standardisation. † Original 13 states: date of ratification of the Constitution.

9: CANADIAN PROVINCES & TERRITORIES

ISO Abbr.	State	Language*	Date of admission to the Dominion	State Capital
AL	Alberta	English	1st Sept 1905	Edmonton
BC	British Columbia	English	20th July 1871	Victoria
MN	Manitoba	English	15th July 1870	Winnipeg
NB	New Brunswick	English †	1st July 1867	Fredericton
NF	Newfoundland and Labrador	English	31st March 1949	St John's
NT	Northwest Territories	English	1870	Yellowknife
NS	Nova Scotia	English	1st July 1867	Halifax
NU	Nunavut (Territory)	Inuktitut **	1st April 1999	Iqaluit
OT	Ontario	English	1st July 1867	Toronto
PE	Prince Edward Island	English	1st July 1873	Charlottetown
QU	Québec	French	1st July 1867	Québec
SA	Saskatchewan	English	1st Sept 1905	Regina
YT	Yukon Territory	English	13th June 1898	Whitehorse

*Although Canada is officially bilingual (English & French), this column indicates the most commonly-spoken language in each region. † Approx. 35% of the population are French-speaking. ** The language of the Inuit.*

10: AUSTRALIAN STATES & TERRITORIES

ISO Abbr.	State	Nickname	Date of granting of responsible gov't	State Capital
AC	Australian Capital Territory	Nation's Capital	1911	Canberra *
CL	Coral Sea Territory	(External Territory bordering the Queensland coast and Gt. Barrier Reef)		
NS	New South Wales	Premier State	1788 †	Sydney
NT	Northern Territory	Outback Australia	1911 **	Darwin
QL	Queensland	Sunshine State	1859	Brisbane
SA	South Australia	Festival State	1856	Adelaide
TS	Tasmania	Holiday Isle	1856	Hobart
VI	Victoria	Garden State	1855	Melbourne
WA	Western Australia	State of Excitement	1890	Perth

*Canberra became the seat of the Australian government on 9th May 1927. † Date of first settlement: New South Wales originally covered the whole island with the exception of Western Australia. ** Transferred to Commonwealth from South Australia in 1911, self-government within the Commonwealth granted 1978.*

11: RUSSIAN REPUBLICS

State	Capital	State	Capital
Adygeya	Maykop	Sakha (Yakutia)	Yakutsk
Altay	Gorno-Altaysk	Tatarstan	Kazan'
Bashkortostan	Ufa	Tuva	Kyzyl
Buryatia	Ulan-Ude	Udmurtia	Izhevsk
Chechnya	Groznyy		
Chuvashia	Cheboksary	*AUTONOMOUS AREAS & REGIONS:*	
Dagestan	Makhachkala	Agin-Buryat	Aginskoye
Ingushetia	Nazran'	Chukot	Anadyr
Kabardino-Balkaria	Nal'chik	Evenki	Tura
Kalmykia	Elitsa	Khanty-Mansi	Khanty-Mansiysk
Karachay-Cherkessia	Cherkessk	Komi-Permyak	Kudymkar
Karelia	Petrozavodsk	Koryak	Palana
Khakassia	Abakan	Nenets	Nar'yan-Mar
Komi	Syktyvkar	Taymyr	Dudinka
Mari-El	Yoshkar-Ola	Ust'-Ordyn-Buryat	Ust'-Ordynskiy
Mordovia	Saransk	Yamalo-Nenets	Salekhard
North Ossetia (Alania)	Vladikavkaz	Jewish Autonomous Region	Birobidzhan

12: BRAZILIAN STATES

State	Capital	State	Capital
North:		**South-East:**	
Acre	Rio Branco	Espírito Santo	Vitória
Amapá	Macapá	Minas Gerais	Belo Horizonte
Amazonas	Manaus	Rio de Janeiro	Rio de Janeiro
Pará	Belém	São Paulo	São Paulo
Rondônia	Pôrto Velho	**South:**	
Roraima	Boa Vista	Paraná	Curitiba
Tocantins	Palmas	Rio Grande do Sul	Pôrto Alegre
North-East:		Santa Catarina	Florianópolis
Alagoas	Maceió	**Central West:**	
Bahia	Salvador	Distrito Federal*	Brasília
Ceará	Fortaleza	Goiás	Goiânia
Maranhão	São Luís	Mato Grosso	Cuiabá
Paraíba	João Pessoa	Mato Grosso do Sul	Campo Grande
Pernambuco	Recife	* Federal District	
Piauí	Teresina		
Rio Grande do Norte	Natal		
Sergipe	Aracaju		

13: FRENCH DEPARTEMENTS

Dept. no.	Département	Capital	Dept. no.	Département	Capital
01	Ain	Bourg-en-Bresse	48	Lozère	Mende
02	Aisne	Laon	49	Maine-et-Loire	Angers
03	Allier	Moulins	50	Manche	St-Lô
04	Alpes-de-Hte-Provence	Digne	51	Marne	Châlons-sur-Marne
05	Hautes-Alpes	Gap	52	Haute-Marne	Chaumont
06	Alpes-Maritimes	Nice	53	Mayenne	Laval
07	Ardèche	Privas	54	Meurthe-et-Moselle	Nancy
08	Ardennes	Charleville-Mézières	55	Meuse	Bar-le-Duc
09	Ariège	Foix	56	Morbihan	Vannes
10	Aube	Troyes	57	Moselle	Metz
11	Aude	Carcassonne	58	Nièvre	Nevers
12	Aveyron	Rodez	59	Nord	Lille
13	Bouches-du-Rhône	Marseille	60	Oise	Beauvais
14	Calvados	Caen	61	Orne	Alençon
15	Cantal	Aurillac	62	Pas-de-Calais	Arras
16	Charente	Angoulême	63	Puy-de-Dôme	Clermont-Ferrand
17	Charente-Maritime	La Rochelle	64	Pyrénées-Atlantiques	Pau
18	Cher	Bourges	65	Hautes-Pyrénées	Tarbes
19	Corrèze	Tulle	66	Pyrénées-Orientales	Perpignan
20	Corse-du-Sud (2A)	Ajaccio	67	Bas-Rhin	Strasbourg
	Haute-Corse (2B)	Bastia	68	Haut-Rhin	Colmar
21	Côte-d'Or	Dijon	69	Rhône	Lyon
22	Côtes-d'Armor	St-Brieuc	70	Haute-Saône	Vesoul
23	Creuse	Guéret	71	Saône-et-Loire	Mâcon
24	Dordogne	Périgueux	72	Sarthe	Le Mans
25	Doubs	Besançon	73	Savoie	Chambéry
26	Drôme	Valence	74	Haute-Savoie	Annecy
27	Eure	Évreux	75	Paris	Paris
28	Eure-et-Loir	Chartres	76	Seine-Maritime	Rouen
29	Finistère	Quimper	77	Seine-et-Marne	Melun
30	Gard	Nîmes	78	Yvelines (canton)	Versailles
31	Haute-Garonne	Toulouse	79	Deux-Sèvres	Niort
32	Gers	Auch	80	Somme	Amiens
33	Gironde	Bordeaux	81	Tarn	Albi
34	Hérault	Montpellier	82	Tarn-et-Garonne	Montauban
35	Ille-et-Vilaine	Rennes	83	Var	Toulon
36	Indre	Châteauroux	84	Vaucluse	Avignon
37	Indre-et-Loire	Tours	85	Vendée	La Roche-sur-Yon
38	Isère	Grenoble	86	Vienne	Poitiers
39	Jura	Lons-le-Saunier	87	Haute-Vienne	Limoges
40	Landes	Mont-de-Marsan	88	Vosges	Épinal
41	Loir-et-Cher	Blois	89	Yonne	Auxerre
42	Loire	St-Étienne	90	Territoire-de-Belfort	Belfort
43	Haute-Loire	Le Puy	91	Essonne (canton)	Évry
44	Loire-Atlantique	Nantes	92	Hauts-de-Seine (canton)	Nanterre
45	Loiret	Orléans	93	Seine-St-Denis (canton)	Bobigny
46	Lot	Cahors	94	Val-de-Marne (canton)	Créteil
47	Lot-et-Garonne	Agen	95	Val-d'Oise (canton)	Cergy

Appendices 14-17

14: THE WORLD'S TALLEST BUILDINGS

Height is measured from the street level of the main entrance to the structural or architectural top of the building, including spires but excluding antennae and flag poles. The list shows the world's tallest traditional buildings (structures intended primarily for human habitation with the great majority of their height divided into occupiable levels). Buildings under construction, TV-tower hybrids and other structures not recognised as traditional buildings are excluded. The world's tallest freestanding structure is Toronto's CN Tower (553m).

Name & location	*Height (m)*	*Date*	*Name & location*	*Height (m)*	*Date*	*Name & location*	*Height (m)*	*Date*
Petronas Towers 1 & 2, Kuala Lumpur, Malaysia	452	1998	**Emirates Hotel Tower**, Dubai, UAE	309	2000	**The Trump Building**, New York City, USA	283	1930
Sears Tower, Chicago, USA	442	1974	**AT&T Corporate Center**, Chicago, USA	307	1989	**Bank of America Plaza**, Dallas, USA	281	1985
Jin Mao Tower, Shanghai, China	421	1998	**JPMorganChase Tower**, Houston, USA	305	1982	**OUB Centre**, Singapore	280	1986
Two International Finance Centre, Hong Kong, China	415	2003	**Baiyoke Tower II**, Bangkok, Thailand	304	1997	**Republic Plaza**, Singapore	280	1995
CITIC Plaza, Guangzhou, China	391	1997	**Two Prudential Plaza**, Chicago, USA	303	1990	**UOB Plaza One**, Singapore	280	1992
Shun Hing Square, Shenzhen, China	384	1996	**Kingdom Centre**, Riyadh, Saudi Arabia	302	2002	**Citigroup Center**, New York City, USA	279	1977
Empire State Building, New York City, USA	381	1931	**Ryugyong Hotel**, Pyongyang, DPR of Korea	300	1991	**Hong Kong New World Tower**, Shanghai, China	278	2002
Central Plaza, Hong Kong, China	374	1992	**First Canadian Place**, Toronto, Canada	298	1975	**Scotia Plaza**, Toronto, Canada	275	1988
Bank of China Tower, Hong Kong, China	367	1990	**Yokohama Landmark Tower**, Yokohama, Japan	296	1993	**Williams Tower**, Houston, USA	275	1983
Emirates Office Tower, Dubai, UAE	355	2000	**Wells Fargo Plaza**, Houston, USA	296	1983	**Wuhan World Trade Tower**, Wuhan, China	273	1998
Tuntex Sky Tower, Kaohsiung, Taiwan	348	1997	**Bank of America Tower**, Seattle, USA	295	1985	**Renaissance Tower**, Dallas, USA	270	1974
Aon Center, Chicago, USA	346	1973	**311 South Wacker Drive**, Chicago, USA	293	1990	**Dapeng International Plaza**, Guangzhou, China	269	2003
The Center, Hong Kong, China	346	1998	**SEG Plaza**, Shenzhen, China	292	2000	**Al Faisaliah Centre**, Riyadh, Saudi Arabia	267	2000
John Hancock Center, Chicago, USA	344	1969	**American International Building**, New York City, USA	290	1932	**900 North Michigan**, Chicago, USA	265	1989
Burj Al Arab, Dubai, UAE	321	1999	**Key Tower**, Cleveland, USA	289	1991	**Bank of America Corp. Center**, Charlotte, USA	265	1992
Chrysler Building, New York City, USA	319	1930	**Plaza 66**, Shanghai, China	288	2001	**SunTrust Plaza**, Atlanta, USA	265	1992
Bank of America Plaza, Atlanta, USA	312	1992	**One Liberty Place**, Philadelphia, USA	288	1987	**Bocom Financial Towers**, Shanghai, China	265	2002
US Bank Tower, Los Angeles, USA	310	1990	**Tomorrow Square**, Shanghai, China	285	2003	**120 Collins Street**, Melbourne, Australia	264	1991
Menara Telekom, Kuala Lumpur, Malaysia	310	2001	**Cheung Kong Centre**, Hong Kong, China	283	1999	**Tower Palace Three, Tower G**, Seoul, Rep. of Korea	264	2004

15: THE WORLD'S LONGEST BRIDGES

Name & location (measurement is of longest span, not length of bridge)	*Type*	*Length (m)*	*Date*
Akashi Kaikyo, Kobe–Akashi Island, Japan	Suspension	1,991	1998
Storebælt East, Fyn (Fünen)–Sjælland (Zealand), Denmark	Suspension	1,624	1998
Humber, England, UK	Suspension	1,410	1981
Jiangyin, Yangtze River, Jiangsu, China	Suspension	1,385	1999
Tsing Ma, Lantau Island–Tsing Yi Island, Hong Kong, China	Suspension	1,377	1997
Verrazano Narrows, Brooklyn–Staten Island, NY, USA	Suspension	1,298	1964
Golden Gate, San Francisco Bay, CA, USA	Suspension	1,280	1937
Höga Kusten (High Coast), Ångermanälven River, Sweden	Suspension	1,210	1997
Mackinac Straits, Mackinaw City–St Ignace, MI, USA	Suspension	1,158	1957
Minami Bisan-Seto, Kojima–Sakaide [Honshu–Shikoku], Japan	Suspension	1,100	1988
Bosporus II (Fatih Sultan Mehmet), Turkey	Suspension	1,090	1988
Bosporus I (Atatürk), Turkey	Suspension	1,074	1973
George Washington, Hudson River, NJ-NY, USA	Suspension	1,067	1931
Kurushima Kaikyo III; II, Onomichi–Imabari [Honshu–Shikoku], Japan	Suspension	1,020/1,030	1999
25 de Abril, Tagus River, Lisboa (Lisbon), Portugal	Suspension	1,013	1966
Forth Road, Edinburgh, UK	Suspension	1,006	1964
LONGEST BRIDGE SPANS OF OTHER TYPES:			
Tatara, Onomichi–Imabari [Honshu–Shikoku], Japan	Cable-stayed	890	1999
Pont de Normandie, Seine River, Le Havre, France	Cable-stayed	856	1995
Pont de Québec, St Lawrence River, QU, Canada	Cantilever Truss	549	1917
Forth Rail, Scotland, UK	Cantilever Truss	521	1890
Lupu, Shanghai, China	Steel Arch	550	2003
New River Gorge, Fayetteville, WV, USA	Steel Arch	518	1977
Bayonne (Kill van Kull), New Jersey – Staten Island, NY, USA	Steel Arch	504	1931

16: THE WORLD'S LONGEST TUNNELS

Name & location	*Type*	*Length (km)*	*Date*
Seikan, Tsugaru Strait [Honshu–Hokkaido], Japan	Rail	53.9	1988
Channel Tunnel, Strait of Dover [England–France]	Rail	50.5	1994
Moscow Metro, Belyaevo–Bitsevsky, Moscow, Russian Fed.	Metro	37.9	1979
Northern Line, East Finchley–Morden, London, UK	Metro	27.8	1939
Iwate, Tohoku Shinkansen, Japan	Rail	25.8	2002
Lærdal, Lærdal–Aurland, Sogn og Fjordane, Norway	Road	24.5	2000
Shimizu, Joetsu Shinkansen, Honshu, Japan	Rail	22.2	1982
Simplon II; I, Brig, Switzerland–Iselle, Italy	Rail	19.8; 19.8	1922; 1906
Vereina, Selfranga–Sagliains, Switzerland	Rail	19.1	1999
Shin-Kanmon, Sanyo Shinkansen [Honshu–Kyushu], Japan	Rail	18.7	1975
Appennino, 'Direttissima', Bologna–Firenze (Florence), Italy	Rail	18.5	1934
Gotthard (Road), Göschenen–Airolo, Switzerland	Road	16.9	1980
Rokko, Sanyo Shinkansen [Osaka–Kobe], Honshu, Japan	Rail	16.2	1971
Furka Base, Oberwald–Realp, Switzerland	Rail	15.4	1982
Haruna, Joetsu Shinkansen, Honshu, Japan	Rail	15.4	1982
Severomuysk, Baikal-Amur Line, Russian Federation	Rail	15.3	1984
Gorigamine, Hokuriku Shinkansen, Honshu, Japan	Rail	15.2	1997
Monte Santomarco, Páola–Cosenza, Italy	Rail	15.0	1987
Gotthard (Rail), Andermatt–Airolo, Switzerland	Rail	15.0	1882
Nakayama, Joetsu Shinkansen, Japan	Rail	14.9	1982
Lötschberg, Kandersteg–Goppenstein, Switzerland	Rail	14.6	1913
Mount Macdonald, Rogers Pass, BC, Canada	Rail	14.6	1989
Romeriksporten, Oslo–Gardermoen Airport, Norway	Rail	14.6	1999
Dayaoshan, Hengyang–Guangzhou Line, China	Rail	14.3	1987

17: WORLD MONUMENTS WATCH

*The World Monuments Fund is a New York-based non-profit organisation dedicated to the conservation of culturally and historically significant works of art and architecture around the world. WMF's World Monuments Watch, launched in 1995, calls attention to imperiled cultural heritage sites by publishing a list every two years of the world's 100 most endangered sites. The 2002 list is shown below. Following the terrorist attack on New York in September 2001, a 101st site was added**

UNITED STATES & CANADA
Schindler Kings Road House and Studio, West Hollywood, CA
San Luis Capistrano Mission Church, San Luis Capistrano, CA
San Esteban del Ray Mission, Acoma Pueblo, NM
A. Conger Goodyear House, Old Westbury, NY
St Ann and the Holy Trinity Church, Brooklyn, New York, NY
Historic Lower Manhattan, New York, NY*

LATIN AMERICA & THE CARIBBEAN
Immaculada Concepción Chapel, Nurio, Michoacán, Mexico
San Juan de Ulúa Fort, Veracruz, Mexico
Yaxchilán archaeological site, Chiapas, Mexico
Piedras Negras archaeological site, Guatemala
San Lorenzo and San Gerónimo Forts, Colón & Portobelo, Panama
Whylly Plantation, Clifton Point, Bahamas
National Schools of Art, La Habana (Havana), Cuba
Falmouth historic town, Jamaica
Los Pinchudos archaeological site, Parque Nac. Río Abiseo, Peru
Caral archaeological site, Supe, Peru
Oyón Valley Missionary Chapels, near Lima, Peru
Santuario de Nuestra Señora de Cocharcas, Chincheros, Peru
Cuzco historic centre, Peru
San Pedro de Morropé Chapel, Morropé, Peru
Vila de Paranapiacaba, Santo André, Brazil
Ruedas de Agua, Larmahue, Chile

EUROPE (including Turkey)
Sinclair and Girnigoe Castles, near Wick, Scotland
Greenock Sugar Warehouses, Scotland
Selby Abbey, North Yorkshire, England
Stowe House, Buckingham, England
St George's Church, Bloomsbury, London, England
Brading Roman Villa, Isle of Wight, England
Karl-Theodor Brücke, Heidelberg, Germany
Cathédrale St Pierre, Beauvais, France
Château de Chantilly, Chantilly, France
Cinque Terre, Liguria, Italy
Port of Trajan archaeological park, Fiumicino, Italy
Bridge of Chains, Bagni di Lucca, Italy
Wislica archaeological site, Poland
Terezin Fortress, Czech Republic
Vukovar city centre, Croatia
Maritime Quarantine-Lazareti, Dubrovnik, Croatia
Mostar historic centre, Bosnia-Herzegovina
Subotica Synagogue, Vojvodina, Serbia & Montenegro
Pec and Decani monasteries, Kosovo, Serbia & Montenegro
Prizren historic centre, Kosovo, Serbia & Montenegro
Voskopojë churches, Albania
Palékastro archaeological site, Crete, Greece
Little Hagia Sophia Mosque, Istanbul, Turkey
Temple of Augustus, Ankara, Turkey
Tepebasi district, Gaziantep, Turkey
Ani archaeological site, Ocarli Köyü, Kars, Turkey
Mnajdra prehistoric temples, Malta
Pervomaisk Church, Uzda, Belarus
Church of Our Saviour of Berestove, Kyiv (Kiev), Ukraine
Ancient Chersonesos, Sevastopol', Ukraine
Barbary-Bosia monastery complex, Butuceni, Moldova

RUSSIAN FEDERATION
Karelian petroglyphs, Belomorsk and Pudozh districts
Assumption Church, Kondopoga
Viipuri Library, Vyborg
Resurrection New Jerusalem Monastery, Istra
Arkhangel'skoye State Museum, Moscow
Narcomfin Building, Moscow
Rostov Veliky historic centre and Church of Our Saviour
Oranienbaum State Museum, Lomonosov, Sankt-Peterburg (St Petersburg)

AFRICA
Sultan El-Muayyad Hospital, El Qâhira (Cairo), Egypt
White and Red Monasteries, Sohâg, Egypt
Valley of the Kings, Luxor, Egypt
Temple of Khasekhemwy, Nekhen (Hierakonopolis), Egypt
Médine Fort, Mali
Larabanga Mosque, Ghana
Benin City earthworks, Nigeria
Thimlich Ohinga cultural landscape, Migori, Kenya
Bagamoyo historic town, Tanzania

ASIA
Citadel of Aleppo, Halab (Aleppo), Syria
Old City and Saddle Souk, Dimashq (Damascus), Syria
Enfeh archaeological site, near Tripoli, Lebanon
Bet She'arim archeaological site, Kiryat Tiv'on, Israel
Petra archaeological site, Jordan
Art Nouveau buildings, Bat'umi, K'ut'aisi and T'bilisi, Georgia
T'bilisi historical district, Georgia
Bodbe Cathedral, Qedeli, Georgia
Ninevah and Nimrud Palaces, near Al Mawsil (Mosul), Iraq
Arbil (Erbil) Citadel, Iraq
Tarim historic city, Yemen
Merv archaeological site, Mary, Turkmenistan
Uch monument complex, near Bahawalpur, Pakistan
Maitreya Temples of Basgo, Leh, India
Nako Temples, Himachal Pradesh, India
Lutyens bungalow zone, Delhi, India
Dwarka Dheesh Mandir Temple, Ahmadabad, India
Osmania Women's College, Hyderabad, India
Anagundi historic settlement, Karnataka, India
Itum Baha Monstery, Kathmandu, Nepal
Teku Thapatali Monastery, Kathmandu, Nepal
Da Qin Christian Pagoda and Monastery, Shaanxi, China
Great Wall of China cultural landscape, Beijing (Peking), China
Ohel Rachel Synagogue, Shanghai, China
Shaxi market area, Jianchuan, Yunnan, China
Tomo port town, Fukuyama, Kyushu, Japan
Sri-Ksetra Temples, Hmawa, Myanmar
Banteay Chhmar Temple of Jayavarman VII, Thmar Puok, Cambodia
Kampung Cina river frontage, Kuala Terengganu, Malaysia
George Town historic enclave, Pinang (Penang), Malaysia
Omo Hada, Nias, Indonesia

This chart provides exact data relevant to many of the thematic maps which appear elsewhere in this atlas: over 8,000 figures in all. Attention in drawn to the notes at the foot of page 192. Many sources have been used in the compilation of these statistics and these are specified on the maps themselves, as are the year/s to which the information relates.

The matter of deciding what is and what is not a country is by no means clear-cut, but no political or other subjective stance has been adopted. Many countries have dependencies, overseas possessions and the like; for various reasons (mainly connected with the availability, reliability or relevance of statistical data) some have been listed separately, some have had their figures amalgamated with those for their mother country and some have been excluded. Figures for enclaves (such as Cabinda) have been included in those for the countries to which they politically belong. For more information on countries worldwide, consult the latest edition of the Highbury Columbus World Travel Guide.

The data figures have been rounded up or down to either a whole number, or to one or to two decimal places. The only exception is Population Density, which has been rounded to the nearest whole number for figures above 9.5, the nearest single decimal place for those under 9.49 and to two decimal places for those under 0.99.

The italic numbers in the second row for each country (preceded by •) give the country's world ranking for that category. These are in descending order (i.e. highest figure ranked number 1) with the exceptions of Infant Mortality where ascending order is used. The top 10 countries in each category have their ranking figure in bold. Countries whose figures are equal are ranked according to whatever rounding has been employed have been ranked equally. As data is not always available for all 226 countries, the figures at the bottom of the chart give the lowest ranking figure in that category; as this can be shared by two or more countries, it may therefore not always represent the total number of countries covered.

Throughout, n/a means that, at the time of going to press, data was not available, not reliable or not relevant. In the case of mobile telephone lines and internet usage, it may in a few instances also mean that the country did not have a network or service.

Country (Map Ref.)	Capital	Area '000 sq km	Population '000	Pop. Density people/sq km	Intl Arrivals '000	Visitor Receipts US$ m	Intl Departs '000	Visitor Expend. US$ m	Hotel Bedrooms	Gross Nat'l Income US$ m	GNI per Person US$	GDP Growth % 1995-2004	Energy Prod. Mt oil eq.	Energy Consump. Mt oil eq.	Energy Consump. t oil eq./pers	Fixed Tel Lines /100	Mobile Subscr. /100	Internet Subscr. /100	Agricultural Land %	Total Health Spend. % GNI	Military Spend. % GNI	Infant Mortality <5yrs/'000	Life Expect. Years
Afghanistan (M4)	Kabul	652.10 •41	25,089.8 •44	38 •155	n/a –	n/a –	n/a –	n/a –	n/a –	n/a –	n/a –	n/a –	0.26 •122	0.49 •156	0.02 •206	n/a –	n/a –	n/a –	58.4 •47	1.0 •191	n/a –	257 •186	42.4 •187
Albania (J3)	Tirana	28.70 •142	3,079.1 •134	107 •88	34 •187	n/a –	n/a –	258 •72	3,881 •132	4.20 •122	$1,327 •141	5.7 •22	1.70 •102	2.78 •111	0.88 •120	5.46 •131	19.85 •79	0.25 •169	39.9 •157	3.4 •90	1.2 •116	30 •91	69.8 •90
Algeria (J4)	Algiers	2,381.70 •11	33,577.5 •34	14 •192	901 •76	100 •127	1,190 •58	193 •84	32,837 •57	51.00 •48	$1,654 •130	3.2 •97	154.34 •15	32.48 •44	1.05 •112	6.10 •129	0.96 •156	1.60 •132	16.7 •162	3.6 •151	3.5 •34	49 •117	69.4 •97
American Samoa (A6)	Pago Pago	0.20 •211	60.1 •204	301 •36	44 •184	n/a –	41 •97	n/a –	n/a –	0.38 •195	$5,461 •78	n/a –	0.00 •164	0.20 •174	2.81 •63	n/a –	n/a –	n/a –	25.0 •145	n/a –	T –	n/a –	n/a –
Andorra (J3)	Andorra la Vella	0.45 •196	71.8 •199	160 •66	3,516 •41	n/a –	n/a –	n/a –	n/a –	1.01 •167	$14,386 •41	n/a –	0.00 •164	n/a –	n/a –	43.83 •39	30.18 •60	8.97 •66	57.8 •49	7.9 •38	T –	7 •31	79.6 **•8**
Angola (J6)	Luanda	1,246.70 •23	13,036.3 •65	10 •199	67 •169	22 •169	n/a –	136 •98	6,157 •110	6.70 •103	$496 •175	7.8 **•8**	39.81 •38	2.31 •117	0.17 •170	0.61 •176	0.93 •158	0.29 •162	46.0 •80	3.6 •151	21.2 **•2**	260 •187	36.2 •195
Anguilla (F5)	The Valley	0.16 •215	12.3 •219	77 •111	48 •183	61 •141	n/a –	9 •144	1,069 •171	0.03 •220	$2,341 •108	n/a –	0.00 •164	n/a –	n/a –	n/a –	n/a –	n/a –	n/a –	n/a –	T –	n/a –	n/a –
Antigua & Barbuda (F5)	St John's	0.44 •197	70.1 •201	159 •67	237 •130	272 •101	n/a –	31 •132	3,185 •137	0.63 •183	$9,221 •61	1.4 •155	0.00 •164	0.18 •179	2.72 •65	48.13 •30	32.29 •58	9.04 •65	27.3 •137	5.5 •90	M –	14 •49	71.1 •74
Argentina (F7)	Buenos Aires	2,780.40 **•8**	36,993.0 •32	13 •195	2,620 •49	2,547 •42	4,762 •28	3,800 •25	168,012 •19	260.30 •18	$6,944 •24	0.3 •169	90.13 •24	65.96 •29	1.76 •85	21.88 •77	17.76 •84	11.20 •55	60.9 •37	8.6 •20	1.3 •102	19 •74	73.9 •49
Armenia (L3)	Yerevan	29.80 •141	3,912.6 •126	131 •74	123 •147	123 •116	110 •91	40 •126	3,600 •133	2.20 •147	$578 •170	7.6 **•10**	1.03 •105	2.55 •85	0.67 •132	13.98 •93	1.17 •152	1.84 •125	46.8 •79	7.5 •49	4.4 •20	35 •99	69.6 •93
Aruba (F5)	Oranjestad	0.18 •213	69.2 •202	384 •24	691 •85	890 •65	n/a –	158 •92	7,783 •99	3.04 •139	$33,764 **•9**	n/a –	0.00 •164	0.33 •165	3.70 •42	35.03 •51	50.00 •41	22.64 •38	11.1 •181	n/a –	T –	n/a –	n/a –
Australia (P7)	Canberra	7,682.30 **•6**	19,978.1 •52	2.6 •220	4,856 •33	7,625 •14	3,498 •36	5,812 •21	198,133 •16	385.90 •15	$19,905 •26	3.7 •77	248.11 **•9**	123.12 •21	6.35 •19	53.86 •26	63.97 •32	42.72 •15	59.3 •41	8.3 •24	1.7 •81	6 •17	80.0 **•5**
Austria (J3)	Vienna	83.90 •115	8,037.4 •89	96 •94	18,180 **•10**	10,118 **•9**	4,207 •31	8,886 •13	310,412 •13	194.70 •22	$23,942 •19	2.1 •143	13.71 •60	35.13 •41	4.32 •33	46.81 •32	82.85 •15	40.94 •18	40.4 •93	8.0 •35	0.8 •141	5 **•6**	78.9 •16
Azerbaijan (L3)	Baku	86.60 •113	8,239.2 •88	95 •96	676 •87	43 •151	1,130 •59	109 •103	5,259 •118	5.30 •114	$653 •164	6.9 •12	21.94 •53	13.99 •68	1.72 •99	12.14 •99	10.68 •102	3.68 •103	51.6 •65	2.7 •50	2.1 •53	105 •143	63.7 •133
Bahamas (F4)	Nassau	13.90 •159	320.0 •175	23 •176	1,538 •62	1,665 •53	n/a –	297 •66	15,105 •79	4.53 •121	$14,623 •39	2.8 •115	0.00 •164	1.22 •132	3.92 •39	40.56 •43	39.03 •49	6.80 •79	0.9 •208	8.0 •35	0.7 •148	16 •52	71.9 •63
Bahrain (L4)	Manama	0.71 •187	730.5 •161	1,029 **•8**	2,420 •52	630 •75	n/a –	250 •75	7,618 •100	7.25 •102	$11,131 •54	4.3 •57	10.31 •69	9.73 •76	14.95 **•6**	26.31 •65	58.33 •38	24.75 •37	14.1 •171	4.1 •132	4.0 •24	16 •52	72.8 •55
Bangladesh (N4)	Dhaka	148.40 •93	138,906.0 **•9**	936 •10	207 •132	48 •146	1,075 •60	166 •91	4,550 •125	48.60 •51	$364 •189	5.1 •32	8.90 •74	12.69 •70	0.95 •119	0.51 •180	0.81 •164	0.15 •182	61.2 •36	3.8 •144	1.3 •102	77 •132	61.8 •141
Barbados (F5)	Bridgetown	0.43 •198	264.3 •178	615 •14	507 •100	687 •72	n/a –	94 •106	6,781 •106	2.61 •142	$9,754 •58	1.9 •146	0.09 •135	0.59 •151	2.21 •76	48.06 •31	19.80 •80	5.59 •84	44.2 •86	6.4 •67	0.8 •141	14 •49	74.4 •46
Belarus (K3)	Minsk	207.60 •85	10,044.8 •81	48 •143	61 •171	82 •130	1,386 •54	263 •71	800 •178	12.90 •82	$1,294 •143	4.3 •57	2.18 •95	29.87 •47	3.00 •59	29.94 •57	4.69 •127	8.19 •71	44.6 •83	5.7 •87	1.3 •102	20 •65	68.6 •107
Belgium (J3)	Brussels	30.50 •139	10,339.3 •77	339 •28	6,452 •23	6,917 •16	7,775 •20	9,766 •12	61,769 •37	245.30 •20	$23,848 •20	2.1 •143	11.86 •63	68.65 •28	6.67 •21	49.61 •28	78.63 •21	32.86 •26	49.9 •69	8.7 •19	1.4 •97	6 •17	78.0 •27
Belize (E5)	Belmopan	23.00 •150	257.4 •180	11 •198	196 •135	121 •117	n/a –	24 •135	4,463 •130	0.73 •176	$2,943 •101	4.5 •50	0.02 •151	0.27 •170	1.08 •110	12.51 •94	20.75 •74	8.70 •68	6.0 •197	4.6 •116	1.6 •84	40 •108	70.2 •87
Benin (J5)	Porto Novo	112.60 •100	6,738.6 •96	60 •131	96 •154	77 •133	n/a –	12 •142	2,733 •143	2.40 •146	$373 •188	5.4 •27	0.10 •132	0.73 •143	0.11 •179	0.92 •170	1.94 •142	0.39 •154	24.6 •146	3.2 •164	1.3 •102	158 •166	52.2 •161

Countries A-Z: Bermuda-Congo, Republic of

Values are shown as *figure* followed by *•world ranking*.

Country (Map Ref. gdp 10-11)	Capital	Area '000 sq km	Population '000	Pop. Density people/sq km	Int'l Arrivals '000	Visitor Receipts US$m	Int'l Depart's '000	Visitor Expenditure US$m	Hotel Bedrooms	Gross Nat'l Income US$m	GNI per Person US$	GDP Growth Av.% 1995-2004	Energy Production Mtoe	Energy Consumption Mtoe	Energy Cons. toe/person	Fixed Tel Lines /100	Mobile Subscribers /100	Internet Subscribers /100	Agricultural Land %	Total Health Spending % GNI	Military Spending % GNI	Infant Mortality /000	Life Expectancy yrs
Bermuda F4	Hamilton	0.05 •221	64.5 •203	1,290 •6	278 •126	351 •92	n/a	n/a	3,234 •136	2.55 •143	$42,417 •1	n/a	0.00 •164	0.20 •174	3.38 •50	86.92 •1	20.64 •76	46.44 •12	n/a	n/a	T	n/a	n/a
Bhutan N4	Thimphu	46.50 •131	1,745.5 •147	38 •155	6 •202	6 •176	n/a	n/a	1,215 •169	0.53 •190	$639 •166	6.8 •13	0.50 •114	0.56 •154	0.67 •132	2.84 •148	n/a	1.45 •137	9.9 •184	4.1 •132	1.9 •70	95 •139	61.6 •143
Bolivia F8	note 8	1,098.60 •28	8,676.0 •85	7.9 •207	308 •118	156 •112	240 •81	118 •101	16,810 •71	8.10 •97	$951 •152	3.3 •94	6.35 •78	4.00 •96	0.47 •146	6.76 •125	10.46 •105	2.18 •119	32.8 •117	6.7 •62	1.5 •90	77 •132	62.7 •137
Bosnia-Herzegovina J3	Sarajevo	51.10 •127	4,207.3 •120	82 •105	90 •156	14 •171	n/a	n/a	4,546 •126	5.00 •118	$1,232 •144	15.7 •2	4.49 •82	5.48 •89	1.35 •99	11.96 •101	9.17 •111	2.44 •115	36.2 •108	4.5 •119	4.0 •24	18 •58	72.9 •54
Botswana K7	Gaborone	581.70 •47	1,762.1 •146	3.0 •216	796 •83	245 •102	n/a	143 •96	2,400 •150	5.30 •114	$3,127 •99	5.3 •30	0.61 •112	1.71 •123	1.01 •114	8.48 •118	24.13 •71	2.97 •109	44.7 •82	6.0 •76	3.7 •30	110 •149	39.0 •191
Brazil G6	Brasília	8,547.40 •5	179,712.5 •5	21 •179	4,773 •34	3,701 •32	2,269 •44	3,199 •28	212,580 •15	528.90 •11	$3,068 •100	2.5 •130	153.56 •16	217.38 •10	1.26 •101	22.32 •76	20.06 •78	8.22 •78	29.3 •129	8.3 •24	1.3 •102	36 •88	68.8 •104
British Virgin Is. F5	Road Town	0.13 •217	22.0 •214	169 •63	296 •123	337 •93	n/a	n/a	1,688 •164	0.25 •203	$13,013 •47	n/a	0.00 •164	0.02 •205	1.11 •109	n/a	n/a	n/a	69.2 •18	n/a	T	n/a	n/a
Brunei O5	Bandar Seri Begawan	5.80 •169	362.7 •173	63 •124	984 •75	n/a	n/a	n/a	2,412 •149	6.37 •105	$18,504 •32	1.9 •146	21.68 •54	2.01 •121	5.84 •21	25.86 •68	40.06 •47	10.23 •61	2.2 •202	3.1 •167	7.6 •9	6 •17	74.6 •45
Bulgaria K3	Sofia	111.00 •102	7,917.6 •91	71 •118	3,186 •43	1,201 •59	2,730 •40	569 •54	n/a	13.20 •79	$1,646 •131	1.5 •153	12.13 •62	22.97 •53	2.86 •62	37.46 •48	19.12 •82	7.46 •75	56.3 •51	3.9 •139	3.0 •42	16 •52	71.6 •67
Burkina H5	Ouagadougou	274.10 •74	11,862.6 •68	43 •148	129 •146	34 •159	n/a	n/a	227 •191	2.50 •144	$216 •211	4.9 •37	0.02 •149	0.44 •159	0.04 •197	0.49 •181	0.64 •168	0.16 •181	35.9 •109	4.2 •129	1.6 •84	197 •177	42.9 •184
Burundi K6	Bujumbura	27.80 •145	7,596.7 •92	273 •43	36 •186	1 •188	35 •101	20 •138	1,132 •170	0.70 •178	$101 •223	0.2 •171	0.04 •144	0.19 •177	0.03 •204	0.29 •188	0.45 •173	0.09 •185	79.0 •7	3.1 •167	5.4 •12	190 •176	40.4 •189
Cambodia O5	Phnom Penh	181.00 •89	13,382.4 •64	74 •115	605 •92	304 •98	49 •96	35 •130	10,804 •86	3.30 •134	$269 •203	5.9 •20	0.01 •154	0.20 •174	0.02 •206	0.25 •190	1.66 •145	0.22 •175	29.3 •129	8.1 •30	2.4 •58	138 •159	56.2 •154
Cameroon J5	Yaoundé	475.40 •53	16,341.0 •57	34 •165	59 •172	39 •154	n/a	n/a	13,980 •82	8.70 •93	$572 •171	4.6 •45	5.02 •81	2.02 •120	0.13 •177	0.66 •175	3.57 •135	0.29 •162	19.3 •161	9.1 •14	1.3 •102	155 •165	49.7 •167
Canada D2	Ottawa	9,970.60 •2	31,720.4 •36	3.2 •215	19,679 •9	10,774 •8	18,359 •10	11,624 •10	367,271 •10	681.60 •8	$21,929 •24	3.4 •91	450.59 •5	309.73 •7	9.96 •11	63.55 •11	37.72 •51	48.38 •10	7.5 •192	2.6 •178	1.2 •116	7 •31	79.3 •9
Cape Verde H5	Praia	4.00 •172	456.3 •167	114 •81	115 •149	23 •167	n/a	41 •124	2,489 •145	0.60 •185	$1,336 •139	6.4 •16	0.00 •164	0.10 •188	0.23 •166	15.99 •89	9.78 •108	3.64 •104	16.5 •166	2.9 •172	1.3 •102	38 •101	68.9 •102
Cayman Is. E5	George Town	0.26 •205	46.8 •208	180 •59	334 •117	585 •78	n/a	n/a	5,428 •117	0.68 •181	$19,400 •27	n/a	0.00 •164	0.12 •184	3.49 •44	n/a	n/a	n/a	7.7 •191	3.1 •167		n/a	n/a
Central African Rep. K5	Bangui	622.40 •43	3,986.4 •123	6.4 •209	10 •197	n/a	n/a	n/a	719 •181	1.00 •168	$265 •205	2.5 •130	0.02 •148	0.14 •182	0.04 •197	0.24 •191	0.29 •176	0.08 •187	8.3 •187	2.9 •172	2.2 •62	180 •171	42.7 •185
Chad J5	N'djamena	1,284.00 •21	7,210.2 •95	5.6 •210	57 •174	n/a	39 •100	n/a	n/a	1.46 •157	$202 •213	10.3 •4	0.00 •164	0.08 •192	0.01 •211	0.14 •194	0.43 •175	0.05 •189	37.8 •101	3.1 •167	1.0 •130	200 •179	48.6 •172
Channel Is. I3	note 9	0.20 •212	151.0 •190	755 •11	n/a	n/a	n/a	n/a	n/a	4.14 •126	$27,768 •12	n/a	n/a	n/a	n/a	85.20 •2	61.90 •35	18.65 •41	n/a	n/a	T	n/a	n/a
Chile F7	Santiago	736.90 •39	15,265.6 •59	21 •179	1,723 •60	788 •69	1,608 •53	1,040 •48	49,895 •46	70.60 •44	$4,584 •83	4.4 •52	7.79 •76	26.24 •52	1.70 •88	23.04 •74	42.83 •46	20.14 •39	20.7 •156	7.2 •54	3.3 •36	12 •46	76.4 •36
China O4	Beijing	9,536.70 •3	1,319,132.5 •1	138 •70	33,167 •5	17,732 •5	12,133 •14	13,909 •7	816,260 •5	1,131.20 •6	$889 •155	8.2 •6	946.95 •3	981.81 •2	0.77 •127	16.69 •88	16.09 •88	4.60 •90	56.2 •53	5.3 •96	2.1 •63	39 •105	71.3 •69
China: Hong Kong SAR[1] O4	—	1.10 •180	6,725.0 •97	6,114 •4	13,725 •14	8,241 •13	4,799 •27	12,494 •8	35,999 •55	170.30 •24	$25,323 •16	3.1 •105	0.00 •164	21.48 •57	3.19 •54	56.74 •19	92.98 •4	43.09 •14	n/a	n/a	T	n/a	78.8 •17
China: Macau SAR[1] O4	—	0.02 •222	440.0 •170	22,000 •1	5,842 •27	3,745 •31	192 •85	1,160 •46	9,030 •91	6.33 •106	$14,384 •42	1.8 •149	0.00 •164	0.61 •150	1.39 •97	40.23 •44	63.00 •33	26.3 •35	n/a	n/a	T	n/a	n/a
Colombia F5	Bogotá	1,141.70 •26	44,533.3 •28	39 •154	616 •91	1,209 •58	1,382 •55	1,160 •46	53,970 •43	81.60 •41	$1,896 •123	2.4 •137	75.08 •30	28.06 •48	0.65 •134	17.94 •86	10.62 •104	4.58 •91	39.8 •95	9.6 •11	2.3 •60	23 •75	70.8 •80
Comoros L6	Moroni	1.90 •177	628.5 •163	331 •30	24 •190	15 •170	n/a	3 •158	389 •184	0.22 •205	$383 •187	2.4 •137	0.04 •162	0.04 •199	0.06 •192	1.35 •162	0.42 •153	n/a	75.3 •14	4.4 •121	3.0 •42	75 •130	61.8 •141
Congo, Republic of J6	Brazzaville	341.80 •63	3,362.2 •130	9.8 •204	19 •194	12 •174	n/a	60 •116	2,522 •144	2.00 •151	$645 •165	3.2 •98	14.45 •59	0.43 •160	0.14 •175	0.67 •174	6.74 •117	0.03 •191	29.9 •127	2.2 •184	2.8 •47	108 •146	52.8 •160

*: Ranking (top 10 in **bold**).   **n/a**: Not available, not relevant or not reliable.   **M**: See note on page 33.   **T**: See note on page 33.   For more information, see pages 134 & 192.

Values shown as: figure (ranking). Ranking top 10 shown in **bold**.

Country (Map Ref)	Capital	Life Expectancy (years)	Infant Mortality (Deaths <5yrs/000)	Military Spending (% of GNI)	Total Health Spending (% of GNI)	Agricultural Land (% of national area)	Internet Subscribers (Users/100)	Mobile Subscribers (Users/100)	Fixed Tel Lines (Lines/100)	Energy Consumption (t oil equiv/person)	Energy Consumption (Mt oil equiv)	Energy Production (Mt oil equiv)	GDP Growth (Av. annual % 1995-2004)	GNI per Person (US$)	Gross Nat'l Income (US$ bn)	Hotel Bedrooms	Visitor Expenditure (US$ m)	International Departs (000)	Visitor Receipts (US$ m)	International Arrivals (000)	Population Density (people/sq km)	Population (000)	Area (000 sq km)
Congo, Dem. Rep. K6	Kinshasa	43.8 (182)	205 (181)	n/a (193)	1.5 (189)	9.8 (185)	0.01 (193)	0.29 (176)	0.04 (195)	0.04 (197)	1.93 (122)	2.66 (91)	-0.7 (176)	$80 (224)	4.20 (122)	6,000 (111)	n/a	50 (95)	n/a	80 (159)	24 (175)	56,861.1 (22)	2,344.90 (12)
Cook Is. A6	Avarua	72.0 (61)	n/a	T	4.7 (112)	30.4 (124)	n/a	n/a	n/a	1.15 (107)	0.02 (205)	0.00 (164)	n/a	$2,396 (107)	0.05 (215)	783 (179)	n/a	9 (106)	38 (157)	75 (163)	77 (111)	17.6 (217)	0.23 (210)
Costa Rica E5	San José	76.2 (38)	11 (44)	n/a	6.4 (67)	55.7 (56)	9.33 (64)	12.75 (94)	25.05	0.98 (115)	3.81 (99)	2.03 (98)	3.7 (78)	$4,054 (87)	15.70 (75)	31,706 (56)	467 (58)	361 (73)	1,278 (56)	1,131 (74)	81 (108)	4,148.5 (121)	51.10 (128)
Côte d'Ivoire I5	note 10	46.0 (178)	175 (170)	1.3 (102)	2.7 (176)	63.4 (28)	0.55 (150)	6.23 (119)	2.04 (155)	0.18 (169)	2.96 (108)	2.22 (94)	2.6 (127)	$628 (167)	10.30 (87)	7,786 (98)	192 (85)	n/a	48 (146)	301 (121)	57 (136)	18,301.2 (55)	320.80 (68)
Croatia J3	Zagreb	73.0 (53)	8 (34)	3.0 (42)	8.6 (20)	55.9 (55)	16.29 (43)	47.03 (44)	38.79 (46)	2.42 (72)	10.62 (74)	5.13 (80)	4.2 (64)	$4,542 (84)	19.90 (65)	74,107 (22)	606 (53)	n/a	3,335 (35)	6,544 (22)	78 (110)	4,397.4 (116)	56.50 (126)
Cuba F4	Havana	77.0 (32)	9 (37)	n/a	6.8 (59)	60.1 (39)	1.07 (142)	0.08 (184)	5.11 (133)	0.86 (121)	9.66 (77)	3.66 (86)	n/a	$2,140 (114)	24.03 (61)	40,158 (51)	n/a	121 (90)	1,692 (52)	1,736 (59)	107 (89)	11,822.8 (69)	110.90 (103)
Cyprus 2 K4	Nicosia	76.9 (33)	6 (17)	3.2 (38)	7.9 (38)	15.8 (168)	30.00 (32)	59.70 (37)	61.06 (14)	3.46 (47)	2.63 (113)	0.00 (164)	3.8 (74)	$12,315 (50)	9.37 (91)	45,058 (48)	283 (69)	589 (66)	1,981 (48)	2,697 (48)	101 (92)	935.4 (156)	9.30 (166)
Czech Republic J3	Prague	75.4 (40)	**5 (6)**	2.0 (69)	7.2 (54)	54.2 (59)	14.67 (50)	84.88 (8)	37.76 (47)	3.71 (41)	37.89 (40)	26.46 (49)	2.5 (130)	$5,311 (79)	54.30 (46)	91,490 (30)	1,388 (42)	**36,224 (6)**	3,106 (37)	5,194 (30)	130 (76)	10,290.0 (79)	78.90 (117)
Denmark J3	Copenhagen	77.2 (30)	**4 (2)**	1.5 (90)	8.3 (24)	61.4 (34)	46.52 (11)	83.33 (14)	69.58 (7)	5.08 (24)	22.16 (56)	27.61 (48)	2.3 (139)	$37,623 (5)	164.00 (26)	40,181 (50)	4,684 (21)	4,946 (25)	3,923 (28)	2,028 (54)	125 (78)	5,387.3 (107)	43.10 (133)
Djibouti L5	Djibouti	49.2 (168)	143 (162)	4.4 (20)	5.0 (104)	56.0 (54)	0.69 (141)	2.29 (141)	1.54 (159)	0.96 (118)	0.62 (148)	0.00 (164)	0.7 (164)	$888 (156)	0.57 (187)	360 (185)	n/a	n/a	n/a	21 (192)	35 (164)	820.6 (158)	23.20 (149)
Dominica F5	Roseau	73.8 (50)	15 (51)	M	6.1 (74)	22.7 (152)	16.03 (45)	11.99 (98)	32.58 (54)	0.54 (140)	0.04 (164)	0.01 (155)	0.3 (169)	$3,194 (97)	0.23 (204)	937 (175)	9 (144)	n/a	47 (148)	68 (168)	94 (98)	70.5 (200)	0.75 (184)
Dominican Republic F5	Santo Domingo	67.3 (115)	47 (116)	1.1 (124)	6.3 (70)	76.4 (9)	2.15 (120)	14.65 (92)	11.02 (105)	0.79 (125)	6.76 (83)	0.19 (126)	5.4 (27)	$2,234 (109)	19.00 (69)	54,302 (42)	286 (68)	310 (76)	2,689 (41)	2,882 (46)	190 (56)	9,219.8 (83)	48.40 (130)
East Timor P6	Dili	n/a	124 (153)	n/a	n/a	15.8 (168)	n/a	n/a	n/a	n/a	n/a	n/a	n/a	$519 (174)	0.39 (194)	n/a	n/a	n/a	n/a	n/a	66 (120)	965.3 (155)	14.60 (158)
Ecuador F6	Quito	70.4 (85)	30 (91)	3.4 (35)	2.4 (181)	29.4 (128)	3.89 (101)	12.09 (96)	11.02 (105)	0.65 (134)	8.38 (79)	24.62 (50)	2.4 (137)	$1,087 (148)	14.00 (77)	36,620 (53)	340 (64)	562 (68)	430 (85)	641 (90)	45 (144)	12,471.6 (66)	275.80 (73)
Egypt K4	Cairo	66.6 (117)	41 (105)	2.3 (60)	3.8 (144)	3.3 (200)	0.93 (147)	6.72 (118)	10.36 (109)	0.81 (123)	52.79 (32)	65.73 (33)	4.3 (57)	$1,528 (133)	99.60 (38)	120,720 (23)	1,132 (47)	3,074 (39)	3,800 (29)	4,357 (36)	69 (119)	69,296.0 (17)	997.70 (30)
El Salvador E5	San Salvador	69.5 (95)	39 (105)	0.7 (148)	8.8 (16)	76.4 (9)	4.65 (89)	13.76 (93)	10.34 (110)	0.44 (151)	2.84 (110)	0.78 (110)	3.1 (104)	$2,031 (118)	13.00 (80)	4,996 (121)	195 (83)	933 (61)	235 (105)	735 (84)	294 (41)	6,178.7 (101)	21.00 (152)
Equatorial Guinea J5	Malabo	53.7 (158)	153 (164)	2.5 (52)	3.4 (157)	11.9 (180)	0.35 (158)	5.53 (122)	1.80 (156)	0.26 (161)	0.12 (184)	8.98 (73)	**28.2 (1)**	$697 (162)	0.33 (197)	n/a	8 (149)	n/a	2 (187)	n/a	17 (185)	476.2 (165)	28.10 (144)
Eritrea K5	Asmara	53.7 (158)	111 (150)	**22.9 (1)**	4.3 (123)	79.7 (6)	0.23 (172)	0.23 (172)	0.90 (171)	0.07 (189)	0.31 (167)	0.00 (164)	4.1 (70)	$167 (218)	0.70 (178)	4,509 (129)	n/a	n/a	74 (136)	113 (150)	43 (149)	3,991.8 (122)	93.70 (109)
Estonia K3	Tallinn	71.1 (74)	12 (46)	1.6 (84)	6.1 (74)	31.7 (120)	41.33 (17)	65.02 (29)	35.06 (50)	1.74 (86)	2.37 (115)	0.00 (159)	5.5 (26)	$3,886 (90)	5.30 (114)	8,452 (96)	191 (86)	1,658 (51)	507 (81)	1,320 (65)	28 (170)	1,268.3 (152)	45.20 (132)
Ethiopia L5	Addis Ababa	48.0 (173)	172 (169)	9.4 (7)	4.6 (116)	27.8 (134)	0.07 (188)	0.07 (185)	0.55 (179)	0.44 (206)	1.64 (125)	0.44 (117)	4.9 (37)	$102 (222)	6.70 (104)	9,676 (89)	44 (121)	n/a	75 (135)	148 (143)	63 (124)	69,981.8 (16)	1,104.30 (27)
Falkland Is. G8	Stanley	n/a	n/a	n/a	n/a	**92.6 (1)**	n/a	n/a	n/a	n/a	n/a	0.00 (164)	n/a	$8,704 (64)	0.03 (219)	n/a	n/a	n/a	n/a	n/a	0.19 (225)	2.3 (225)	12.20 (160)
Faroe Is. I2	Tórshavn	n/a	n/a	T	2.1 (204)	2.1 (204)	n/a	n/a	n/a	5.03 (25)	0.25 (171)	0.02 (152)	n/a	$18,900 (30)	0.95 (171)	n/a	n/a	n/a	n/a	n/a	34 (166)	47.6 (207)	1.40 (179)
Fiji Is. R6	Suva	69.8 (90)	21 (70)	1.5 (90)	3.9 (139)	25.1 (144)	2.64 (112)	10.78 (101)	11.23 (103)	0.49 (145)	0.40 (161)	0.11 (131)	3.0 (107)	$2,148 (113)	1.76 (154)	5,520 (116)	78 (111)	85 (93)	217 (107)	348 (114)	45 (144)	818.1 (159)	18.30 (155)
Finland K2	Helsinki	77.9 (28)	**5 (6)**	1.3 (102)	6.6 (64)	6.5 (195)	50.89 (7)	84.50 (9)	54.73 (20)	7.84 (15)	32.82 (43)	11.08 (67)	3.6 (81)	$29,465 (10)	123.40 (30)	55,268 (41)	1,854 (38)	5,824 (24)	1,441 (55)	2,826 (47)	15 (187)	5,215.1 (111)	338.10 (64)
France 3 J3	Paris	**79.3 (9)**	**5 (6)**	2.6 (51)	9.5 (12)	54.1 (60)	31.38 (28)	64.70 (30)	56.89 (18)	4.40 (32)	260.43 (8)	127.14 (21)	2.2 (140)	$23,326 (22)	1,380.70 (5)	600,492 (7)	17,718 (5)	19,265 (8)	29,979 (3)	**75,202 (1)**	108 (87)	59,303.8 (20)	549.10 (49)
French Guiana G5	Cayenne	**79.3 (9)**	n/a	T	n/a	0.3 (210)	n/a	n/a	n/a	2.01 (81)	0.35 (163)	0.00 (164)	n/a	$12,422 (49)	2.15 (148)	1,255 (167)	n/a	n/a	42 (152)	65 (170)	2.2 (222)	188.2 (184)	85.50 (114)

*: Ranking (top 10 in **bold**). n/a: Not available, not relevant or not reliable. T: See note on page 33. M: See note on page 33. For more information, see pages 184 & 192.

Countries A-Z: French Polynesia-Israel

Country (Map Ref.)	Capital	Life Expectancy (years)	Infant Mortality (deaths <5yr/'000)	Military Spending (% of GNI)	Total Health Spending (% of GNI)	Agricultural Land (% of national area)	Internet Subscribers (users/100)	Mobile Subscribers (users/100)	Fixed Tel Lines (lines/100)	Energy Consumption (tonnes oil equiv./person)	Energy Consumption (million tonnes oil equiv.)	Energy Production (million tonnes oil equiv.)	GDP Growth (av. annual % 1995–2004)	GNI per Person (US$)	Gross Nat'l Income (US$ million)	Hotel Bedrooms	Visitor Expenditure (US$ million)	International Depart's ('000)	Visitor Receipts (US$ million)	International Arrivals ('000)	Population Density (people/sq km)	Population ('000)	Area ('000 sq km)
French Polynesia (B7)	Papeete	n/a –	n/a –	T	n/a –	10.2 •182	10.41 •60	37.49 •53	21.88 •77	1.22 •103	0.29 •168	0.04 •142	n/a –	$17,140 •35	4.06 •127	2,943 •138	n/a –	n/a –	394 •89	228 •131	60 •131	253.7 •181	4.20 •171
Gabon (J6)	Libreville	59.3 •149	90 •135	0.3 •158	3.0 •170	19.3 •160	1.92 •122	20.45 •77	2.95 •147	0.71 •130	0.89 •139	16.24 •58	1.3 •157	$3,172 •98	4.00 •128	2,450 •146	170 •90	n/a –	7 •182	169 •140	5.0 •212	1,345.3 •151	267.70 •76
Gambia, The (H5)	Banjul	58.6 •150	126 •155	1.1 •124	4.1 •132	64.9 •24	1.35 •139	4.12 •132	2.62 •149	0.07 •189	0.10 •188	0.00 •164	4.6 •45	$298 •196	0.40 •193	2,015 •155	16 •140	n/a –	49 •145	75 •163	142 •69	1,522.7 •148	10.70 •164
Georgia (L3)	Tbilisi	68.9 •102	29 •88	0.9 •137	7.1 •56	43.0 •89	1.49 •136	10.21 •106	13.14 •94	1.02 •113	4.35 •94	1.67 •103	5.6 •24	$724 •159	3.10 •137	—	158 •92	306 •78	442 •84	302 •120	77 •111	5,334.8 •109	69.70 •121
Germany (J3)	note8	78.1 •25	5 •6	1.5 •90	10.6 •8	47.8 •74	42.37 •16	71.67 •25	65.04 •10	4.31 •34	355.24 •4	128.92 •20	1.4 •155	$23,558 •21	1,939.60 •3	884,534 •4	46,222 •2	76,400 •1	17,225 •6	17,861 •11	229 •52	81,904.1 •12	357.00 •62
Ghana (I5)	Accra	57.1 •153	100 •141	1.0 •130	4.2 •129	59.4 •40	0.19 •177	0.93 •158	1.16 •165	0.22 •167	4.24 •95	2.53 •92	4.4 •52	$289 •197	5.70 •112	15,453 •78	100 •104	n/a –	448 •83	439 •107	83 •103	19,850.8 •52	238.50 •81
Gibraltar (I4)	Gibraltar	n/a –	n/a –	T	n/a –	n/a –	n/a –	n/a –	n/a –	87.66 •2	2.37 •115	0.00 •164	n/a –	$17,510 •34	0.47 •192	730 •180	n/a –	n/a –	300 •99	n/a –	2,940 •5	29.4 •212	0.01 •225
Greece (K4)	Athens	78.2 •24	5 •6	4.9 •15	8.3 •24	64.6 •25	18.15 •42	83.86 •12	52.92 •22	3.26 •51	34.49 •42	10.36 •68	3.5 •90	$11,425 •53	121.00 •32	316,668 •12	4,181 •24	n/a –	9,121 •10	14,033 •13	84 •102	11,100.2 •73	132.00 •96
Greenland (G2)	Nuuk	77.2 •30	n/a –	M	—	0.1 •211	35.66 •24	29.86 •61	46.74 •33	3.23 •52	0.19 •177	0.19 •177	n/a –	$11,948 •51	0.72 •177	1,734 •163	n/a –	n/a –	n/a –	123 •147	0.03 •226	56.5 •205	2,166.10 •14
Grenada (F5)	St George's	67.3 •115	n/a –	T	4.8 •110	35.3 •111	6.13 •81	7.13 •116	31.65 •55	0.47 •148	0.05 •196	0.00 •164	4.3 •57	$3,630 •92	0.36 •196	—	8 •149	n/a –	53 •139	n/a –	276 •42	94.0 •196	0.34 •202
Guadeloupe (F5)	note 11	n/a –	n/a –	M	n/a –	28.8 •131	4.35 •95	69.72 •27	45.65 •37	1.57 •89	0.67 •145	0.00 •164	n/a –	$13,327 •45	5.66 •113	8,019 •97	n/a –	n/a –	418 •86	521 •97	259 •46	440.4 •169	1.70 •178
Guam (Q5)	Agana	n/a –	n/a –	T	n/a –	37.0 •104	30.53 •29	20.74 •75	50.89 •24	6.67 •16	1.05 •135	0.00 •164	n/a –	$18,717 •31	2.94 •141	9,002 •93	n/a –	n/a –	1,908 •49	1,160 •73	300 •37	162.1 •187	0.54 •191
Guatemala (E5)	Guatemala City	66.3 •119	58 •120	0.8 •141	4.7 •112	41.4 •112	1.71 •127	9.70 •109	6.47 •127	0.34 •156	3.93 •97	1.91 •100	3.5 •86	$1,678 •129	19.60 •66	16,595 •72	196 •82	579 •67	493 •82	835 •79	131 •74	14,223.4 •62	108.90 •104
Guinea (I5)	Conakry	52.0 •162	169 •168	1.5 •90	3.4 •157	49.6 •71	0.20 •176	0.73 •167	0.34 •187	0.07 •189	0.57 •153	0.11 •130	4.3 •57	$409 •186	3.10 •137	3,533 •134	15 •141	n/a –	14 •171	38 •185	33 •167	8,011.2 •90	245.90 •78
Guinea-Bissau (I5)	Bissau	47.3 •174	211 •182	1.3 •102	3.9 •139	39.6 •96	0.33 •160	n/a –	0.98 •169	0.11 •179	0.13 •183	0.00 •164	0.7 •164	$163 •219	0.20 •207	—	n/a –	n/a –	n/a –	8 •199	37 •160	1,346.8 •150	36.10 •137
Guyana (G5)	Georgetown	64.0 •130	72 •127	5.1 •103	5.1 •103	8.0 •189	10.92 •57	9.93 •107	9.15 •114	0.75 •129	0.58 •152	0.00 •161	2.8 •116	$837 •158	0.64 •182	730 •180	n/a –	n/a –	59 •142	95 •155	4.0 •214	865.2 •157	215.00 •84
Haiti (F5)	Port-au-Prince	50.2 •166	123 •152	M	4.9 •107	50.4 •67	0.96 •145	1.69 •144	1.57 •157	0.08 •187	0.62 •148	0.06 •138	2.5 •130	$480 •179	3.90 •129	1,758 •160	37 •129	n/a –	54 •144	142 •144	305 •35	8,490.2 •86	27.80 •146
Honduras (E5)	Tegucigalpa	67.4 •114	38 •101	0.6 •154	6.8 •59	26.2 •138	2.98 •107	4.86 •126	4.80 •134	0.33 •158	2.14 •119	0.48 •116	2.9 •109	$896 •154	5.90 •109	15,906 •73	157 •94	279 •80	275 •100	518 •99	59 •134	6,606.1 •98	112.10 •101
Hungary (J3)	Budapest	71.7 •66	9 •37	1.5 •90	6.8 •59	62.9 •29	15.76 •46	64.64 •31	36.12 •49	2.66 •68	27.06 •49	11.28 •66	3.6 •82	$4,830 •80	49.20 •50	59,897 •40	1,309 •44	11,167 •17	3,933 •27	3,070 •44	109 •86	10,164.1 •80	93.00 •110
Iceland (I2)	Reykjavik	79.8 •7	4 •2	M	8.9 •15	22.1 •153	60.76 •6	90.28 •1	66.39 •8	11.82 •7	3.33 •105	2.39 •93	3.2 •101	$28,908 •7	8.15 •96	6,174 •109	416 •61	283 •79	335 •94	303 •119	2.9 •217	294.3 •176	103.00 •105
India (M4) [19]	New Delhi	60.9 •145	93 •137	2.4 •58	4.9 •107	58.9 •43	1.59 •134	1.22 •150	3.98 •139	0.31 •160	316.75 •6	231.82 •11	5.8 •21	$462 •181	477.40 •12	82,181 •31	2,567 •32	4,067 •33	3,042 •38	2,537 •51	348 •26	1,067,421.1 •2	3,065.00 •7
Indonesia (O6)	Jakarta	65.9 •122	45 •115	1.1 •124	2.7 •176	23.3 •151	1.90 •123	5.52 •123	3.60 •143	0.55 •139	114.60 •19	200.94 •13	2.8 •117	$692 •163	144.70 •19	259,450 •13	3,406	n/a –	5,411 •22	5,153 •31	113 •82	217,825.4 •4	1,919.40 •16
Iran (L4)	Tehran	68.8 •105	42 •110	3.8 •28	5.5 •90	36.6 •105	1.56 •135	3.23 •137	19.95 •82	1.99 •82	128.30 •16	259.82 •7	5.0 •35	$1,684 •128	108.70 •36	27,889 •62	918 •50	2,400 •42	920 •64	1,402 •64	40 •151	66,469.1 •18	1,648.00 •18
Iraq (L4)	Baghdad	60.8 •146	33 •157	3.7 •147	3.7 •147	21.8 •154	n/a –	n/a –	n/a –	1.12 •108	26.61 •51	131.36 •19	n/a –	n/a –	n/a –	26,691 •63	n/a –	n/a –	n/a –	n/a –	60 •131	26,298.9 •40	438.30 •58
Ireland (I3)	Dublin	76.5 •35	6 •17	0.7 •148	6.7 •62	62.6 •30	27.09 •34	75.53 •23	48.45 •29	3.93 •38	15.08 •67	0.96 •106	7.8 •8	$22,844 •23	87.70 •40	61,230 •38	2,767 •31	4,250 •30	3,547 •33	6,448 •24	56 •137	3,968.1 •124	70.30 •120
Israel (K4)	Jerusalem	78.5 •19	6 •17	8.0 •8	10.9 •5	25.5 •143	30.14 •30	95.45 •3	46.72 •34	3.08 •57	19.60 •62	0.02 •150	2.9 •111	$16,753 •36	106.60 •37	46,143 •47	2,896 •29	3,562 •35	2,166 •46	1,196 •71	299 •38	6,556.0 •99	21.90 •151

•: *Ranking* (top 10 in **bold**). **n/a:** Not available, not relevant or not reliable. **T:** See note on page 33. **M:** See note on page 33. For more information, see pages 184 & 192.

Country / Map Ref. (pp10-11)	Capital	Life Expectancy Years	Infant Mortality Deaths <5yrs/'000	Military Spending % of GNI	Total Health Spending % of GNI	Agricultural Land % of national area	Internet Subscribers Users/100	Mobile Subscribers Users/100	Fixed Tel Lines /100	Energy Consumption Tonnes oil equiv./person	Energy Consumption Million tonnes oil equiv.	Energy Production Million tonnes oil equiv.	GDP Growth Av. annual % 1995-2004	GNI per Person US$	Gross Nat'l Income US$ billion	Hotel Bedrooms	Visitor Expenditure US$ million	International Departs '000	Visitor Receipts US$ million	International Arrivals '000	Population Density People/sq km	Population '000	Area 000 sq km
Italy J3	Rome	79.2 •14	6 •17	2.1 •63	8.1 •30	50.7 •66	30.11 •31	92.65 •5	48.62 •28	3.46 •46	200.76 •11	33.62 •42	1.8 •149	$19,393 •28	1,123.80 •7	975,601 •20	14,215 •6	21,502 •7	25,787 •4	39,055 •4	187 •57	56,209.9 •23	301.30 •71
Jamaica F5	Kingston	72.8 •55	20 •65	0.5 •156	5.5 •90	44.1 •87	3.85 •102	24.43 •70	20.47 •81	1.41 •95	3.64 •100	0.05 •139	0.7 •164	$2,819 •104	7.30 •101	20,220 •66	206 •80	n/a •–	1,233 •57	1,277 •67	243 •49	2,772.9 •137	11.40 •162
Japan P4	Tokyo	81.3 •1	5 •6	1.0 •130	7.8 •41	13.9 •173	44.93 •13	62.11 •34	58.58 •16	2.52 •71	319.85 •5	111.19 •23	1.2 •160	$35,607 •7	4,523.30 •2	1,572,131 •2	26,530 •4	16,216 •11	3,401 •34	4,772 •35	338 •29	127,708.0 •10	377.80 •61
Jordan K4	Amman	71.1 •74	33 •98	9.5 •6	8.1 •30	13.0 •176	4.52 •94	16.71 •86	12.76 •96	1.42 •94	5.71 •88	0.28 •121	4.2 •64	$2,183 •110	8.80 •92	19,247 •67	420 •60	1,755 •49	700 •71	1,478 •63	61 •127	5,612.2 •105	91.90 •111
Kazakstan	note 12	63.0 •136	76 •130	0.7 •148	3.7 •147	76.1 •12	0.93 •147	3.62 •134	12.05 •100	2.88 •61	42.93 •37	81.26 •27	4.9 •37	$1,349 •138	20.10 •63	9,124 •90	474 •57	2,294 •43	396 •88	1,845 •57	5.2 •211	14,168.3 •63	2,717.30 •9
Kenya K5	Nairobi	48.9 •170	122 •151	1.8 •74	8.3 •24	44.3 •85	1.60 •132	4.15 •131	1.03 •168	0.11 •179	3.47 •102	0.42 •118	2.1 •143	$348 •193	10.70 •84	n/a •–	143 •96	n/a •–	308 •77	841 •77	56 •137	32,499.1 •35	582.60 •46
Kiribati A6	Bairiki	63.8 •132	69 •125	M •–	8.1 •30	n/a •–	2.32 •116	0.58 •170	4.21 •137	0.11 •179	0.01 •208	0.00 •164	2.7 •121	$8,280 •66	0.77 •174	158 •192	2 •160	n/a •–	3 •186	5 •203	135 •72	97.0 •195	0.72 •186
Korea, DPR (North) P3	Pyongyang	66.2 •119	55 •119	n/a •–	2.1 •187	16.7 •162	n/a •–	n/a •–	n/a •–	3.14 •55	70.36 •27	66.06 •32	n/a •–	$465 •180	10.41 •86	n/a •–	n/a •–	n/a •–	n/a •–	n/a •–	205 •54	25,191.7 •43	122.80 •98
Korea, Rep. (South) P4	Seoul	75.0 •44	5 •6	2.8 •47	6.0 •76	19.8 •158	55.19 •3	67.95 •28	48.86 •27	4.21 •35	199.46 •12	28.98 •47	5.4 •27	$9,454 •60	447.60 •13	53,478 •44	6,547 •15	6,084 •23	6,373 •20	5,147 •32	471 •20	46,852.3 •26	99.40 •107
Kuwait L4	Kuwait City	75.4 •40	10 •43	5.2 •13	3.0 •170	8.2 •188	8.79 •67	38.59 •50	20.77 •80	11.19 •9	22.87 •54	120.07 •22	2.7 •121	$18,297 •33	37.40 •55	1,988 •157	2,843 •30	n/a •–	104 •124	78 •160	113 •82	2,014.1 •143	17.80 •156
Kyrgyzstan M3	Bishkek	64.2 •127	61 •121	1.9 •70	6.0 •76	53.7 •61	2.98 •107	1.04 •154	7.75 •120	1.23 •102	6.09 •85	3.47 •88	4.2 •64	$283 •200	1.40 •161	12 •143	12 •143	32 •102	104 •124	69 •167	26 •176	5,218.9 •110	199.90 •86
Laos O5	Vientiane	64.2 •127	100 •141	4.2 •22	3.4 •157	7.8 •190	0.27 •165	1.00 •155	1.12 •166	0.11 •179	0.47 •158	0.34 •120	6.2 •18	$363 •191	1.60 •157	8,797 •94	8 •149	n/a •–	120 •118	173 •138	23 •176	5,559.2 •106	236.80 •82
Latvia K3	Riga	70.6 •82	21 •70	1.0 •130	5.9 •82	38.5 •98	13.31 •51	39.38 •48	30.11 •56	2.16 •75	5.10 •108	0.80 •108	5.7 •22	$3,222 •96	7.60 •99	7,034 •105	224 •78	2,697 •41	120 •118	591 •94	35 •163	2,290.1 •141	64.60 •124
Lebanon K4	Beirut	69.8 •90	32 •95	3.6 •32	11.8 •2	33.1 •116	11.71 •53	22.70 •72	19.88 •83	1.37 •98	6.00 •86	0.05 •141	2.8 •118	$4,014 •88	17.60 •70	15,687 •76	n/a •–	1,650 •52	837 •66	837 •78	417 •22	4,376.9 •117	10.50 •165
Lesotho K7	Maseru	44.1 •181	132 •156	3.1 •39	6.3 •70	76.5 •8	0.23 •172	4.25 •130	1.57 •157	0.04 •197	0.09 •191	0.00 •164	3.6 •84	$533 •173	1.10 •165	1,027 •173	9 •144	n/a •–	23 •167	186 •136	83 •104	2,523.4 •139	30.40 •140
Liberia I5	Monrovia	46.3 •177	235 •185	1.3 •102	4.0 •138	26.2 •138	n/a •–	0.23 •172	n/a •–	0.05 •194	0.16 •181	0.00 •164	n/a •–	$156 •221	0.50 •191	n/a •–	n/a •–	n/a •–	n/a •–	n/a •–	28 •170	2,844.3 •136	99.10 •108
Libya J4	Tripoli	70.7 •81	19 •59	3.9 •27	3.3 •163	8.7 •186	0.36 •156	0.90 •160	10.93 •107	3.65 •43	16.08 •64	79.39 •28	1.7 •152	$7,739 •67	34.14 •59	11,815 •85	150 •95	650 •65	28 •160	174 •137	4.1 •213	7,250.8 •94	1,775.50 •17
Liechtenstein J3	Vaduz	n/a •–	11 •44	T •–	n/a •–	56.3 •52	n/a •–	n/a •–	n/a •–	n/a •–	n/a •–	n/a •–	n/a •–	$39,302 •3	1.18 •164	n/a •–	n/a •–	n/a •–	n/a •–	56 •176	216 •53	34.6 •210	0.16 •216
Lithuania K3	Vilnius	72.8 •55	9 •37	1.3 •102	6.0 •76	53.4 •62	6.79 •80	47.16 •43	27.05 •62	2.34 •74	8.15 •81	3.46 •89	4.8 •41	$3,360 •93	11.70 •83	5,649 •114	218 •79	3,390 •38	383 •90	1,271 •68	53 •140	3,491.5 •128	65.30 •123
Luxembourg J3	Luxembourg	78.4 •22	5 •6	0.7 •148	5.8 •86	48.1 •72	36.75 •22	101.34 •2	77.99 •3	11.40 •8	5.03 •92	0.05 •140	4.4 •52	$39,844 •2	17.57 •71	7,568 •101	1,467 •41	n/a •–	1,782 •50	812 •81	174 •62	451.7 •168	2.60 •174
Macedonia, FYR J3	Skopje	71.9 •63	26 •83	2.1 •63	6.0 •76	46.8 •78	3.42 •105	10.92 •100	26.35 •64	1.52 •90	3.10 •107	1.91 •99	1.9 •146	$1,712 •127	3.50 •132	6,726 •108	38 •127	n/a •–	99 •153	170 •139	82 •107	2,114.5 •142	25.70 •148
Madagascar L8	Antananarivo	54.9 •157	136 •158	1.2 •116	3.5 •154	46.8 •78	0.23 •172	0.95 •157	0.38 •186	0.05 •194	0.81 •141	0.14 •128	2.9 •108	$263 •206	4.20 •122	7,356 •103	115 •102	n/a •–	170 •121	170 •121	26 •172	15,243.1 •60	587.00 •45
Malawi K6	Lilongwe	36.3 •183	183 •172	0.8 •141	7.6 •45	34.5 •112	0.26 •166	0.82 •163	0.70 •173	0.05 •194	0.48 •157	0.19 •125	4.6 •45	$162 •220	1.70 •155	5,170 •119	45 •120	28 •160	331 •95	266 •128	95 •96	11,255.5 •71	118.50 •99
Malaysia O5	Kuala Lumpur	71.8 •65	8 •34	2.5 •52	2.5 •179	23.9 •149	27.31 •33	34.88 •56	19.79 •84	2.37 •73	56.31 •30	88.21 •25	5.0 •35	$3,332 •94	79.30 •43	130,757 •22	2,052 •36	36,248 •5	6,374 •19	12,775 •15	73 •117	24,014.2 •45	329.80 •66
Maldives M6	Malé	64.2 •129	77 •132	M •–	7.6 •45	13.3 •174	5.37 •85	15.02 •90	10.27 •112	0.60 •180	0.17 •180	0.07 •164	6.3 •17	$2,007 •112	0.56 •188	8,503 •118	41 •124	n/a •–	331 •95	461 •105	955 •9	286.4 •177	0.30 •204
Mali I5	Bamako	45.2 •179	231 •184	2.5 •52	4.9 •107	27.8 •135	0.29 •162	0.44 •174	0.48 •183	0.02 •206	0.27 •169	0.07 •137	5.1 •32	$225 •209	2.50 •144	2,816 •141	41 •124	n/a •–	71 •138	89 •157	8.4 •205	10,441.3 •75	1,248.60 •22

•: *Ranking (top 10 in **bold**)*. **n/a:** Not available, not relevant or not reliable. **M:** See note on page 33. **T:** See note on page 33. For more information, see pages 184 & 192.

Countries A-Z: Malta-Niue

Country (Map Ref pp10-11)	Capital	Area '000 sq km	Population '000	Population Density /sq km	International Arrivals '000	Visitor Receipts US$m	International Departs '000	Visitor Expenditure US$m	Hotel Bedrooms	Gross Nat'l Income US$m	GNI per Person US$	GDP Growth % 1995-2004	Energy Production Mtoe	Energy Consumption Mtoe	Energy Consumption toe/person	Fixed Tel Lines /100	Mobile Subscribers /100	Internet Subscribers /100	Agricultural Land %	Total Health Spending % GNI	Military Spending % GNI	Infant Mortality /'000	Life Expectancy yrs
Malta J4	Valletta	0.32 (203)	383.0 (172)	1,197 (7)	1,180 (72)	579 (79)	200 (82)	180 (88)	n/a	3.64 (131)	$9,208 (63)	3.7 (79)	0.00 (164)	1.27 (130)	3.22 (53)	52.34 (23)	69.91 (26)	25.26 (36)	28.1 (133)	8.8 (16)	0.8 (141)	5 (6)	78.1 (25)
Marshall Is. R5	Majuro	0.18 (214)	53.8 (206)	299 (40)	5 (203)	4 (185)	n/a	n/a	305 (188)	0.12 (211)	$2,170 (111*)	n/a	0.01 (157)	0.11 (187)	2.05 (79)	7.67 (122)	0.90 (160)	1.65 (131)	16.7 (162)	9.4 (13)	T	66 (122)	62.5 (139)
Martinique F5	Fort-de-France	1.10 (181)	391.0 (171)	355 (25)	460 (106)	245 (102)	n/a	n/a	6,766 (107)	5.98 (108)	$15,583 (37)	n/a	0.00 (164)	0.70 (144)	1.84 (83)	43.00 (40)	78.99 (19)	10.00 (62)	30.0 (125)	n/a	T	n/a	79.3 (9)
Mauritania I5	Nouakchott	1,030.70 (29)	2,754.4 (138)	2.7 (219)	30 (189)	28 (160)	n/a	55 (117)	2,000 (156)	1.00 (168)	$362 (190)	4.7 (43)	0.01 (158)	1.25 (131)	0.45 (149)	1.19 (163)	9.16 (112)	0.37 (155)	38.6 (97)	4.3 (123)	3.7 (30)	183 (172)	52.0 (162)
Mauritius L7	Port Louis	2.00 (176)	1,243.0 (153)	622 (13)	660 (89)	625 (77)	161 (88)	182 (87)	9,024 (92)	4.60 (120)	$3,833 (91)	5.1 (32)	0.03 (146)	1.16 (133)	0.97 (117)	27.03 (63)	28.91 (62)	14.87 (49)	56.5 (50)	3.4 (157)	0.2 (159)	19 (59)	71.2 (72)
Mayotte L6	Dzaoudzi	0.37 (200)	183.4 (185)	496 (18)	n/a	n/a	n/a	n/a	n/a	0.83 (172)	$5,71E (75)	n/a	n/a	n/a	n/a	6.98 (123)	14.66 (91)	n/a	n/a	n/a	T	n/a	n/a
Mexico D4	Mexico City	1,967.20 (15)	101,457.2 (11)	52 (142)	19,810 (8)	8,401 (12)	12,075 (16)	5,702 (20)	452,116 (9)	550.20 (10)	$5,534 (77)	2.8 (120)	237.32 (10)	148.61 (14)	1.49 (91)	14.67 (90)	25.45 (69)	4.58 (91)	54.5 (58)	5.4 (93)	0.5 (156)	29 (88)	74.2 (47)
Micronesia, Fed. States Q5	Palikir	0.70 (188)	161.8 (188)	231 (51)	15 (196)	n/a	n/a	n/a	n/a	0.26 (201)	$2,150 (112)	n/a	n/a	0.02 (205)	4.01 (37)	8.67 (116)	n/a	4.30 (96)	65.7 (23)	10.5 (9)	T	24 (76)	66.2 (120)
Moldova K3	Chisinău	33.70 (138)	4,229.7 (118)	126 (77)	16 (195)	n/a	30 (103)	88 (108)	2,905 (139)	1.50 (160)	$351 (192)	1.1 (161)	0.08 (136)	3.33 (105)	0.78 (126)	14.56 (91)	5.13 (124)	1.37 (138)	76.2 (11)	3.5 (154)	0.7 (148)	32 (95)	68.0 (110)
Monaco J3	Monaco-Ville	0.00 (226)	33.8 (211)	16,900 (2)	270 (127)	n/a	n/a	n/a	2,240 (152)	0.82 (173)	$27,467 (14)	n/a	n/a	1.65 (124)	0.68 (131)	5.18 (132)	8.12 (114)	1.67 (130)	83.4 (3)	7.4 (51)	T	5 (6)	80.3 (3)
Mongolia O3	Ulan Bator	1,565.00 (19)	2,511.4 (140)	1.6 (223)	166 (141)	39 (154)	n/a	55 (117)	2,352 (151)	1.00 (168)	$413 (184)	3.5 (87)	1.13 (104)	0.80 (142)	0.45 (149)	6.43 (128)	8.00 (115)	2.46 (114)	47.1 (76)	6.6 (64)	2.5 (52)	76 (130)	64.8 (126)
Montserrat F5	note 13	0.10 (219)	7.3 (222)	73 (116)	10 (197)	9 (177)	n/a	2 (160)	243 (190)	0.02 (221)	$4,121 (86)	n/a	0.00 (164)	0.02 (196)	4.97 (26)	1.41 (161)	0.09 (183)	0.26 (166)	30.0 (125)	11.3 (4)	M	30 (91)	62.5 (139)
Morocco I4	Rabat	458.70 [21] (55)	30,456.9 [21] (37)	66 (120)	4,223 (38)	2,526 (43)	1,887 (47)	380 (62)	67,968 (35)	34.70 (58)	$1,190 (145)	3.2 (99)	0.24 (123)	11.83 (71)	0.41 (152)	3.80 (140)	20.91 (73)	1.69 (128)	67.0 (21)	4.5 (119)	4.2 (22)	44 (114)	69.4 (97)
Mozambique K7	Maputo	799.40 (35)	18,151.1 (56)	23 (176)	n/a	n/a	n/a	n/a	n/a	3.80 (130)	$210 (212)	8.7 (5)	1.85 (101)	2.30 (118)	0.13 (177)	0.51 (181)	0.86 (162)	0.17 (178)	60.2 (38)	4.3 (123)	2.5 (52)	197 (177)	44.8 (180)
Myanmar (Burma) N4	note 14	676.60 (40)	51,853.1 (24)	77 (111)	205 (133)	45 (150)	27 (136)	n/a	15,752 (74)	12.99 (81)	$269 (204)	7.5 (11)	8.66 (75)	5.07 (94)	0.10 (184)	0.61 (176)	0.03 (186)	0.02 (192)	16.0 (167)	2.84 (184)	T	109 (147)	57.3 (152)
Namibia J7	Windhoek	824.30 (34)	1,923.8 (145)	2.3 (221)	670 (88)	404 (97)	88 (108)	88 (108)	2,441 (148)	3.50 (132)	$1,953 (121)	3.5 (88)	0.00 (164)	0.80 (142)	0.45 (149)	6.43 (128)	8.00 (115)	2.46 (114)	47.1 (76)	7.1 (56)	3.3 (36)	67 (123)	48.7 (171)
Nauru R6	Yaren District	0.02 (223)	11.5 (220)	575 (15)	n/a	n/a	n/a	n/a	n/a	0.03 (217)	$2,909 (102)	n/a	0.00 (164)	0.05 (196)	4.97 (26)	n/a	n/a	n/a	n/a	11.3 (4)	M	30 (91)	62.5 (139)
Nepal N4	Kathmandu	140.80 (95)	25,836.1 (41)	183 (58)	361 (112)	140 (114)	200 (83)	80 (110)	18,880 (68)	5.80 (111)	$246 (208)	4.2 (64)	0.42 (119)	1.53 (127)	0.06 (192)	1.41 (161)	0.26 (166)	0.09 (183)	33.6 (114)	5.4 (93)	0.9 (137)	91 (136)	58.3 (151)
Netherlands J3	Amsterdam [15]	41.50 (134)	16,258.3 (58)	392 (23)	9,500 (20)	6,723 (18)	14,220 (13)	12,016 (9)	133,593 (21)	390.30 (14)	$24,334 (18)	2.6 (127)	65.24 (34)	104.73 (21)	6.53 (18)	62.11 (13)	72.24 (24)	53.04 (6)	47.1 (75)	8.1 (30)	1.6 (84)	6 (17)	78.3 (23)
Netherlands Antilles F5	Willemstad	0.80 (183)	262.6 (179)	328 (31)	677 (86)	821 (67)	—	199 (81)	7,445 (102)	2.03 (150)	$9,214 (62)	0.4 (168)	0.00 (164)	20.89 (59)	94.97 (1)	n/a	n/a	n/a	10.0 (183)	n/a	T	n/a	n/a
New Caledonia R7	Nouméa	18.60 (154)	222.9 (182)	12 (196)	101 (152)	93 (128)	68 (94)	68 (94)	2,441 (148)	3.20 (136)	$14,829 (38)	n/a	0.10 (133)	0.67 (145)	3.11 (56)	23.12 (73)	35.71 (55)	11.35 (54)	12.3 (179)	n/a	T	n/a	n/a
New Zealand R7	Wellington	270.50 (75)	3,785.6 (64)	14 (192)	1,910 (55)	2,252 (45)	1,287 (57)	1,340 (43)	26,679 (64)	51.00 (48)	$13,250 (46)	3.0 (106)	17.12 (57)	20.89 (59)	5.43 (23)	44.81 (38)	61.84 (36)	48.44 (9)	61.3 (35)	8.0 (35)	1.0 (130)	6 (17)	78.5 (19)
Nicaragua E5	Managua	130.70 (97)	5,777.7 (103)	44 (147)	483 (104)	109 (123)	499 (71)	76 (112)	3,442 (135)	2.06 (149)	$490 (176)	4.3 (57)	0.14 (127)	1.44 (129)	0.34 (156)	3.20 (146)	4.47 (128)	1.68 (129)	57.9 (48)	4.4 (121)	1.1 (124)	43 (112)	69.6 (93)
Niger J5	Niamey	1,186.40 (25)	12,241.7 (67)	10 (199)	52 (180)	24 (165)	10 (105)	28 (135)	1,233 (168)	2.00 (151)	$179 (215)	3.5 (85)	0.10 (134)	0.38 (162)	0.03 (193)	0.19 (193)	0.11 (184)	0.11 (187)	13.9 (172)	3.9 (139)	1.4 (97)	265 (188)	42.6 (186)
Nigeria J5	Abuja	923.80 (32)	150,539.7 (7)	163 (65)	831 (80)	156 (112)	700 (51)	700 (51)	n/a	37.10 (56)	$286 (198)	3.3 (95)	135.78 (18)	22.68 (55)	0.17 (170)	0.58 (178)	1.36 (147)	0.17 (178)	75.8 (13)	2.2 (184)	0.9 (137)	183 (172)	51.6 (165)
Niue A6	Alofi	0.26 (206)	1.7 (226)	6.5 (208)	2 (206)	1 (188)	n/a	n/a	72 (193)	0.004 (224)	$2,130 (115)	n/a	0.00 (164)	0.00 (211)	0.50 (143)	n/a	n/a	n/a	30.8 (121)	7.6 (45)	T	n/a	70.6 (82)

*: Ranking (top 10 in bold). n/a: Not available, not relevant or not reliable. T: See note on page 33. M: See note on page 33. For more information, see pages 184 & 192.

Values shown as: figure • rank. n/a = not available/not relevant/not reliable; – = no rank; T and M = see note on page 33.

Country (Map Ref.)	Capital	Area '000 sq km	Population '000	Pop. Density /sq km	Intl. Arrivals '000	Visitor Receipts US$m	Intl. Departs '000	Visitor Expenditure US$m	Hotel Bedrooms	Gross Nat'l Income US$m	GNI per Person US$	GDP Growth %	Energy Production Mtoe	Energy Consumption Mtoe	Energy Consumption toe/person	Fixed Tel. Lines /100	Mobile Subscribers /100	Internet Subscribers /100	Agricultural Land %	Total Health Spending %	Military Spending %	Infant Mortality /000	Life Expectancy yrs
Northern Mariana Is. / Saipan (Q5)	Saipan	0.46 •194	76.3 •198	166 •64	438 •108	n/a	n/a	n/a	4,521 •128	0.11 •213	$1,336 •140	n/a	n/a	n/a	n/a	39.59 •45	n/a	n/a	26.1 •140	n/a	n/a	n/a	n/a
Norway (J2)	Oslo	323.80 •67	4,551.1 •115	14 •192	4,243 •37	2,037 •47	753 •63	4,305 •23	66,428 •36	160.80 •28	$35,630 •6	2.9 •110	253.00 •8	47.18 •35	10.45 •10	72.98 •5	84.33 •11	50.48 •8	3.2 •201	7.8 •41	1.8 •74	4 •2	78.5 •19
Oman (L5)	Muscat	309.50 •70	3,100.3 •133	10 •199	562 •96	118 •119	n/a	367 •63	5,729 •112	14.90 •76	$6,011 •73	3.8 •75	63.66 •36	8.53 •78	3.44 •48	8.97 •115	12.37 •95	4.57 •93	3.5 •198	2.8 •174	9.7 •5	13 •48	72.0 •61
Pakistan (M4)	Islamabad	796.10 •36	153,124.8 •6	192 •55	500 •102	92 •129	n/a	255 •73	36,483 •54	60.00 •45	$424 •183	3.9 •73	29.21 •46	46.29 •36	0.33 •158	2.48 •150	0.56 •171	0.34 •159	33.9 •113	4.1 •132	4.5 •18	109 •147	61.3 •144
Palau (P5)	Koror	0.51 •192	20.4 •215	40 •151	54 •177	n/a	9 •106	n/a	973 •174	0.13 •210	$6,600 •71	n/a	n/a	n/a	n/a	8.64 •117	9.26 •110	2.32 •116	27.5 •136	6.4 •67	T	29 •88	68.7 •106
Palestine NAR [4] (K4)	Jerusalem [16]	6.20 •168	3,328.3 •131	537 •17	7 •201	9 •177	n/a	n/a	5,703 •113	4.20 •122	$1,359 •137	n/a	n/a	n/a	n/a	n/a	n/a	n/a	61.5 •33	n/a	n/a	24 •76	72.5 •59
Panama (E5)	Panama City	75.50 •118	2,991.0 •135	40 •151	519 •98	626 •76	200 •84	176 •89	14,246 •81	9.50 •89	$3,279 •95	2.5 •130	0.65 •111	3.43 •103	1.18 •104	12.99 •95	16.40 •87	4.14 •99	28.2 •132	7.6 •45	1.2 •116	25 •80	75.1 •42
Papua New Guinea (Q6)	Port Moresby	462.80 •54	4,813.6 •114	10 •199	54 •177	101 •126	93 •92	38 •127	1,976 •158	3.00 •140	$705 •161	0.7 •164	3.70 •85	1.08 •134	0.25 •163	1.17 •164	0.20 •180	0.94 •146	2.75 •202	4.1 •132	0.8 •141	94 •138	59.9 •147
Paraguay (G7)	Asunción	406.80 •59	6,028.9 •102	15 •187	295 •124	77 •133	170 •87	91 •107	4,866 •122	7.60 •99	$1,639 •132	0.8 •163	11.56 •64	2.75 •112	0.59 •138	4.73 •135	28.83 •63	1.73 •126	59.2 •42	7.9 •38	1.0 •130	30 •91	70.6 •82
Peru (F6)	Lima	1,285.20 •175	27,083.4 •38	21 •179	798 •58	817 •68	661 •64	566 •55	106,715 •24	52.20 •47	$1,981 •120	3.6 •83	9.85 •71	13.62 •69	0.52 •141	7.75 •120	8.60 •113	7.66 •74	24.4 •147	4.8 •110	1.8 •74	39 •105	68.6 •107
Philippines (P5)	Manila	300.00 •72	81,636.0 •14	272 •44	1,797 •48	1,723 •51	1,787 •48	1,224 •45	28,971 •61	80.80 •42	$1,032 •151	3.9 •72	9.48 •72	31.05 •46	0.40 •153	4.17 •138	17.77 •83	2.56 •113	37.8 •102	3.4 •157	1.2 •116	38 •101	67.9 •111
Poland (J3)	Warsaw	312.70 •69	38,576.7 •30	123 •80	15,000 •12	4,815 •24	53,122 •4	3,500 •26	60,658 •39	163.60 •27	$4,234 •85	4.2 •64	76.13 •29	87.53 •23	2.27 •75	29.51 •58	36.26 •54	9.84 •63	58.9 •44	6.0 •76	1.9 •70	9 •37	74.0 •48
Portugal [5] (I3)	Lisbon	91.90 •112	10,366.9 •76	113 •82	12,167 •16	5,459 •21	n/a	2,105 •35	99,120 •27	109.30 •35	$10,904 •56	2.6 •127	4.07 •83	26.94 •50	2.69 •66	41.90 •41	81.94 •17	35.55 •25	45.1 •81	8.2 •29	2.1 •63	5 •17	76.4 •36
Puerto Rico (F5)	San Juan	8.90 •167	3,949.2 •125	444 •21	3,551 •40	2,728 •39	1,331 •56	1,004 •49	12,353 •84	42.10 •53	$10,964 •55	n/a	0.04 •143	10.59 •75	2.76 •64	34.64 •52	31.56 •59	15.63 •47	32.7 •118	n/a	M	16 •52	n/a
Qatar (L4)	Doha	11.40 •163	629.8 •162	55 •139	76 •161	n/a	n/a	20 •139	1,842 •159	16.45 •73	$27,515 •13	7.9 •7	72.06 •13	15.96 •65	26.70 •4	28.94 •59	43.72 •45	8.28 •69	5.8 •196	3.2 •164	10.0 •4	16 •52	72.5 •59
Réunion (L7)	Saint-Denis	2.50 •178	764.3 •160	306 •34	424 •109	244 •104	309 •77	449 •59	2,771 •142	8.25 •94	$11,666 •52	n/a	0.12 •129	1.04 •136	1.47 •92	n/a	n/a	n/a	20.0 •157	n/a	n/a	n/a	79.3 •9
Romania (K3)	Bucharest	236.40 •83	21,590.0 •50	91 •100	3,300 •42	362 •91	6,408 •22	449 •59	95,226 •29	38.60 •54	$1,723 •126	2.2 •140	30.06 •45	40.54 •39	1.81 •84	20.32 •85	17.17 •85	8.06 •72	62.6 •30	5.1 •172	2.1 •63	21 •70	71.2 •72
Russian Federation (M2)	Moscow	17,075.40 •1	141,364.2 •8	8.3 •206	21,169 •7	3,750 •30	18,371 •9	10,360 •11	188,255 •17	253.40 •19	$1,751 •125	2.5 •130	1110.98 •2	697.95 •3	4.82 •27	24.22 •71	12.05 •97	4.09 •100	12.7 •177	5.3 •96	4.0 •24	21 •70	65.6 •124
Rwanda (K6)	Kigali	26.30 •147	8,379.8 •87	319 •32	113 •150	9 •177	n/a	20 •139	1,754 •162	1.90 •153	$219 •210	11.1 •3	0.02 •147	0.31 •166	0.04 •197	0.27 •189	1.10 •153	0.25 •169	64.4 •26	5.2 •99	3.0 •42	183 •172	40.9 •188
St Helena (I7)	Jamestown	0.12 •218	7.0 •223	61 •127	n/a	n/a	n/a	n/a	n/a	0.01 •223	$1,492 •136	n/a	0.00 •164	0.01 •208	1.41 •95	n/a	0.00 •208	n/a	38.5 •98	n/a	M	n/a	n/a
St Kitts & Nevis (F5)	Basseterre	0.26 •207	38.5 •209	148 •68	71 •166	62 •140	n/a	9 •144	1,757 •161	0.30 •199	$6,644 •70	3.3 •96	0.00 •164	0.04 •199	0.81 •123	50.00 •25	10.64 •58	10.64 •58	38.5 •98	5.2 •99	M	24 •76	70.9 •79
St Lucia (F5)	Castries	0.62 •190	158.4 •189	255 •47	250 •129	232 •106	n/a	33 •131	4,428 •131	0.62 •184	$3,943 •89	1.5 •153	0.00 •164	0.12 •184	0.77 •127	n/a	n/a	n/a	30.6 •122	4.3 •123	M	19 •59	71.3 •69
St Pierre et Miquelon (G3)	St Pierre	0.24 •208	7.0 •224	29 •169	n/a	n/a	n/a	n/a	n/a	0.07 •214	$10,343 •57	n/a	0.00 •164	0.03 •203	4.46 •31	n/a	n/a	n/a	12.5 •178	n/a	T	n/a	n/a
St Vincent & the Gren. (F5)	Kingstown	0.39 •199	121.1 •192	311 •33	88 •158	39 •154	80 •132	9 •144	817 •177	0.32 •198	$2,733 •112	2.9 •112	0.01 •156	0.07 •193	0.60 •136	22.68 •75	n/a	4.78 •88	33.3 •115	6.3 •70	M	25 •80	70.1 •88
Samoa (S6)	Apia	2.80 •173	171.0 •186	61 •127	49 •182	n/a	n/a	4 •155	660 •182	0.26 •200	$1,494 •135	4.2 •64	0.01 •153	0.06 •194	0.36 •155	5.70 •130	1.78 •143	2.22 •118	43.9 •88	6.6 •64	M	25 •80	68.5 •109
San Marino (J3)	San Marino	0.06 •220	28.4 •213	473 •19	n/a	n/a	n/a	n/a	n/a	0.58 •186	$19,233 •29	n/a	n/a	n/a	n/a	n/a	n/a	n/a	16.7 •162	11.7 •3	T	6 •17	80.8 •2

•: Ranking (top 10 in **bold**). n/a: Not available, not relevant or not reliable. T: See note on page 33. M: See note on page 33. For more information, see pages 184 & 192.

Country (Map Ref pg10-11)	Capital	Life Expectancy (Years)	Infant Mortality (Deaths <5yrs/'000)	Military Spending (% of GNI)	Total Health Spending (% of GNI)	Agricultural Land (% of national area)	Internet Subscribers (Users/100)	Mobile Subscribers (Users/100)	Fixed Tel Lines (Lines/100)	Energy Consumption (Tonnes oil equiv/person)	Energy Consumption (Million tonnes oil equiv)	Energy Production (Million tonnes oil equiv)	GDP Growth (Av. annual % 1995-2004)	GNI per Person (US$)	Gross Nat'l Income (US$ million)	Hotel Bedrooms	Visitor Expenditure (US$ million)	International Depart's ('000)	Visitor Receipts (US$ million)	International Arrivals ('000)	Population Density (People/sq km)	Population ('000)	Area ('000 sq km)
São Tomé e Príncipe (J6)	São Tomé	64.0 •130	74 •129	0.8 •141	2.3 •182	48.0 •73	6.00 •82	n/a –	3.63 •142	0.26 •161	0.04 •199	0.00 •160	3.2 •102	$285 •199	0.04 •216	259 •189	4 •155	n/a –	8 •180	8 •199	137 •71	137.3 •191	1.00 •182
Saudi Arabia (L4)	Riyadh	71.0 •77	28 •85	11.6 •3	5.3 •96	1.8 •206	6.94 •77	11.33 •99	14.48 •92	5.68 •22	121.65 •18	504.14 •4	2.2 •140	$8,459 •65	181.10 •23	95,473 •28	n/a –	14,540 •12	3,320 •36	6,296 •25	10 •199	22,735.9 •48	2,200.00 •13
Senegal (I5)	Dakar	55.8 •156	138 •159	1.4 •97	4.6 •116	41.0 •92	1.07 •142	5.65 •121	2.29 •152	0.17 •170	1.64 •125	0.04 •145	5.2 •31	$481 •178	4.70 •119	9,835 •88	54 •119	n/a –	140 •114	396 •113	53 •140	10,317.1 •78	196.20 •87
Serbia & Montenegro (K3)	Belgrade	72.3 •60	16 •55	5.5 •10	5.6 •88	54.7 •57	5.97 •83	25.66 •67	23.26 •72	1.46 •93	15.57 •66	12.22 •61	1.3 •157	$929 •153	9.90 •88	37,782 •52	n/a –	n/a –	40 •153	351 •113	103 •91	10,494.4 •74	102.20 •106
Seychelles (L6)	Victoria	71.6 •67	17 •57	1.8 •74	6.2 •73	15.2 •170	10.99 •56	53.87 •40	26.11 •66	2.55 •70	0.21 •172	0.00 •164	1.0 •162	$6,561 •72	0.54 •189	2,444 •147	30 •133	41 •97	113 •122	130 •145	178 •61	82.0 •197	0.46 •195
Sierra Leone (I5)	Freetown	34.3 •196	316 •189	1.0 •130	4.3 •123	37.5 •103	0.14 •183	0.55 •172	0.46 •184	0.08 •187	0.35 •164	0.00 •164	-3.1 •178	$169 •217	0.78 •187	312 •187	4 •155	n/a –	8 •180	24 •190	66 •120	4,850.8 •113	73.30 •119
Singapore (O5)	Singapore	78.8 •17	4 •2	4.9 •15	3.5 •154	1.5 •207	53.97 •4	79.14 •18	46.36 •35	9.87 •12	40.78 •38	0.00 •164	4.6 •45	$21,496 •25	88.80 •39	35,674 •56	4,647 •22	4,363 •29	5,081 •23	6,726 •21	6,500 •3	4,225.0 •119	0.65 •189
Slovak Republic (K3)	Bratislava	73.4 •52	9 •37	1.8 •74	5.9 •82	49.8 •70	16.04 •44	54.36 •39	26.08 •67	4.68 •28	20.60 •61	7.38 •77	4.6 •45	$4,609 •82	20.30 •62	31,655 •60	287 •67	373 •72	639 •74	1,219 •69	110 •85	5,381.2 •108	49.00 •129
Slovenia (J3)	Ljubljana	75.8 •39	6 •6	1.2 •116	8.6 •20	25.5 •142	40.08 •20	83.52 •13	40.65 •42	3.80 •40	7.56 •82	3.39 •90	4.4 •52	$9,739 •59	19.40 •67	14,970 •80	519 •56	2,055 •45	996 •63	1,219 •70	96 •94	1,951.5 •144	20.30 •153
Solomon Is. (R6)	Honiara	66.6 •117	24 •76	M	5.9 •82	3.5 •198	0.50 •151	0.22 •178	1.49 •160	0.15 •173	0.06 •194	0.00 •164	-0.2 •173	$587 •169	0.25 •202	860 •176	7 •153	n/a –	6 •184	21 •192	17 •185	496.2 •164	28.40 •143
Somalia (L5)	Mogadishu	43.2 •183	225 •183	0.9 •137	1.3 •190	69.1 •22	n/a –	n/a –	n/a –	0.02 •206	0.21 •172	0.00 •164	n/a –	$183 •214	1.66 •156	n/a –	n/a –	n/a –	n/a –	n/a –	18 •184	11,326.8 •72	637.70 •42
South Africa (K7)	note 17	49.0 •169	71 •126	1.5 •90	8.8 •16	81.4 •4	6.82 •78	26.58 •65	10.77 •108	2.63 •69	113.87 •20	138.44 •17	2.8 •114	$2,819 •103	121.90 •31	51,874 •45	1,917 •37	3,733 •34	2,501 •44	5,908 •26	37 •158	45,919.2 •24	1,224.70 •24
Spain[6] (I4)	Madrid	79.0 •15	6 •17	1.3 •102	7.7 •44	58.8 •45	19.31 •40	82.28 •16	45.98 •36	3.43 •49	141.07 •15	35.95 •41	3.2 •100	$14,301 •43	588.00 •9	676,672 •6	5,974 •6	4,139 •32	32,873 •2	50,093 •2	82 •106	41,547.4 •32	504.80 •51
Sri Lanka (N5)	note 18	70.4 •85	19 •59	4.5 •18	3.6 •151	35.8 •110	1.06 •144	4.92 •125	4.66 •136	0.25 •163	4.70 •93	0.79 •109	4.5 •51	$876 •157	16.40 •74	15,637 •77	245 •76	505 •70	211 •108	337 •116	299 •39	19,615.3 •53	65.60 •122
Sudan (K5)	Khartoum	56.0 •155	107 •144	3.0 •42	4.7 •112	53.3 •63	0.26 •166	0.59 •169	2.06 •154	0.09 •185	2.90 •109	9.90 •70	6.0 •19	$338 •194	10.70 •84	4,545 •127	74 •113	n/a –	56 •143	50 •181	15 •187	37,985.9 •31	2,505.80 •10
Surinam (G5)	Paramaribo	67.5 •113	32 •95	n/a –	9.8 •10	0.5 •209	3.30 •106	19.77 •81	17.58 •87	2.15 •78	0.90 •138	0.95 •107	4.4 •52	$1,812 •124	0.76 •175	1,276 •165	29 •134	n/a –	14 •171	58 •173	2.8 •218	456.9 •166	163.80 •91
Swaziland (K7)	Mbabane	40.2 •190	149 •163	1.6 •84	4.2 •129	79.9 •5	1.94 •121	6.10 •120	3.40 •144	0.52 •141	0.56 •154	0.22 •124	2.7 •121	$1,311 •142	1.40 •161	1,276 •165	44 •121	n/a –	28 •160	283 •125	61 •127	1,068.6 •154	17.40 •157
Sweden (J2)	Stockholm	80.0 •5	3 •1	2.1 •63	8.4 •23	7.0 •193	57.31 •2	88.50 •7	72.02 •6	6.18 •20	54.98 •31	37.28 •39	2.7 •121	$25,399 •15	225.90 •21	99,267 •26	6,803 •14	10,500 •18	4,162 •25	2,894 •45	20 •182	8,872.6 •84	450.00 •56
Switzerland[3] (J3)	Bern	80.1 •4	6 •17	1.1 •124	10.7 •7	38.5 •98	32.62 •27	78.75 •20	73.27 •4	4.47 •30	32.29 •45	17.37 •56	1.3 •157	$38,335 •4	277.20 •17	141,171 •20	6,180 •17	12,110 •15	7,309 •15	10,700 •18	179 •60	7,376.0 •93	41.10 •135
Syria (K4)	Damascus	71.0 •77	19 •59	5.5 •10	2.5 •179	74.0 •15	0.36 •156	1.20 •151	10.30 •111	1.29 •100	21.36 •58	36.44 •40	3.8 •76	$1,043 •150	17.30 •72	15,705 •75	610 •52	3,492 •37	1,082 •37	1,318 •66	100 •93	18,444.4 •54	185.20 •88
Taiwan (P4)	Taipei	71.0 •77	28 •85	2.8 •47	n/a –	n/a –	38.25 •21	106.45 •1	58.33 •17	4.51 •29	100.67 •22	11.39 •65	4.3 •57	$12,640 •48	281.87 •16	20,789 •65	6,379 •16	7,189 •21	3,991 •26	2,617 •50	652 •12	23,614.2 •47	36.20 •136
Tajikistan (M4)	Dushanbe	63.4 •135	72 •127	1.2 •116	2.3 •182	30.5 •123	0.05 •189	0.21 •179	3.65 •141	0.98 •115	6.14 •84	3.65 •87	3.3 •93	$176 •216	1.10 •166	345 •186	n/a –	n/a –	n/a –	n/a –	45 •144	6,435.3 •100	143.10 •94
Tanzania (K6)	Dodoma	46.5 •175	165 •167	1.3 •102	5.9 •82	42.3 •90	0.30 •161	1.27 •149	0.44 •185	0.04 •197	1.52 •128	0.61 •113	4.7 •43	$273 •202	9.40 •90	10,325 •87	330 •65	330 •108	725 •70	501 •101	37 •161	34,827.6 •33	945.00 •31
Thailand (O5)	Bangkok	69.0 •101	28 •85	1.8 •74	3.7 •147	36.6 •105	7.76 •73	26.04 •66	9.87 •113	1.17 •105	71.88 •25	32.90 •43	2.8 •119	$1,937 •122	118.50 •33	320,565 •11	2,179 •33	2,044 •46	6,731 •17	10,133 •19	124 •79	63,393.6 •19	513.10 •50
Togo (J5)	Lomé	51.7 •164	141 •161	1.8 •74	2.8 •174	63.9 •27	2.58 •98	2.58 •139	1.09 •167	0.14 •175	0.64 •147	0.00 •163	3.3 •92	$279 •201	1.30 •163	2,888 •140	5 •154	n/a –	11 •175	57 •174	90 •101	5,097.4 •112	56.80 •125
Tonga (S6)	Nuku'alofa	69.5 •95	20 •65	M	7.5 •49	69.3 •17	2.93 •110	3.39 •136	11.31 •102	0.50 •143	0.05 •196	0.00 •164	2.7 •121	$1,525 •134	0.15 •208	642 •183	3 •158	n/a –	7 •182	32 •188	132 •73	99.2 •194	0.75 •185

•: Ranking (top 10 in bold). n/a: Not available, not relevant or not reliable. T: See note on page 33. M: See note on page 33. For more information, see pages 184 & 192.

Country / Map Ref	Capital	Area '000 sq km	Population '000	Pop. Density people/sq km	Int'l Arrivals '000	Visitor Receipts US$m	Int'l Departs '000	Visitor Expenditure US$m	Hotel Bedrooms	Gross Nat'l Income US$m	GNI per Person US$	GDP Growth Av. ann. % 1995-2004	Energy Production Mt oil equiv.	Energy Consumption Mt oil equiv.	Energy Consumption t oil equiv./person	Fixed Tel. Lines /100	Mobile Subscribers /100	Internet Subscribers /100	Agricultural Land %	Total Health Spending % GNI	Military Spending % GNI	Infant Mortality <5yrs/'000	Life Expectancy years
Trinidad & Tobago F5	Port of Spain	5.10 •170	1,362.0 •149	267 •45	383 •111	201 •109	n/a •—	67 •115	4,850 •123	7.80 •98	$5,954 •74	4.8 •41	20.52 •55	11.75 •73	8.97 •13	24.98 •70	27.81 •64	10.60 •59	26.1 •140	5.2 •99	1.4 •97	20 •65	70.0 •89
Tunisia J4	Tunis	154.50 •92	9,879.6 •82	64 •123	5,387 •29	1,605 •54	1,669 •50	273 •70	102,800 •25	20.00 •64	$2,067 •116	4.9 •37	6.01 •79	8.31 •80	0.86 •122	12.23 •98	4.01 •133	5.15 •86	58.7 •46	7.0 •58	1.7 •81	27 •84	71.3 •69
Turkey K4	Ankara	779.50 •15	73,197.2 •15	94 •98	10,783 •17	8,932 •11	4,856 •26	1,738 •40	176,635 •18	167.30 •25	$2,526 •106	3.7 •80	22.47 •52	71.58 •26	1.08 •110	28.12 •60	34.75 •57	7.28 •76	50.1 •68	5.0 •104	4.9 •15	43 •112	69.1 •100
Turkmenistan L4	Ashgabat	488.10 •52	5,650.4 •104	12 •197	300 •122	192 •110	357 •74	125 •100	2,153 •154	5.10 •117	$1,150 •146	4.1 •71	52.56 •37	11.81 •72	2.66 •67	8.02 •119	0.17 •181	0.17 •178	66.4 •22	5.4 •93	3.8 •28	99 •140	62.7 •137
Turks & Caicos Is. F4	Cockburn Town	0.50 •193	18.7 •216	37 •159	165 •142	311 •96	n/a •—	244 •77	2,210 •153	0.11 •212	$6,666 •69	n/a •—	0.00 •164	0.00 •211	0.00 •212	n/a •—	n/a •—	n/a •—	2.0 •205	n/a •—	T •—	n/a •—	n/a •—
Tuvalu R6	Funafuti	0.02 •224	11.4 •221	570 •16	1 •207	0 •—	n/a •—	n/a •—	59 •194	0.01 •222	$1,091 •147	n/a •—	0.00 •164	0.00 •211	0.00 •212	n/a •—	n/a •—	n/a •—	n/a •—	7.8 •41	T •—	52 •118	63.7 •133
Uganda K5	Kampala	241.00 •80	25,474.7 •42	106 •90	205 •133	158 •111	152 •89	95 •105	17,837 •70	5.90 •105	$259 •207	6.8 •13	0.49 •115	0.89 •139	0.04 •197	0.22 •192	1.59 •146	0.25 •169	36.3 •107	3.8 •144	1.8 •74	124 •153	46.5 •175
Ukraine K3	Kyiv (Kiev)	603.70 •44	47,637.3 •25	79 •109	5,791 •28	2,725 •40	9,410 •19	2,179 •34	43,487 •49	35.20 •57	$717 •160	0.1 •172	87.08 •26	150.40 •13	3.06 •58	21.21 •79	4.42 •129	1.19 •140	68.6 •20	4.1 •132	3.6 •32	20 •65	67.8 •112
United Arab Emirates L4	Abu Dhabi	83.70 •116	3,219.0 •132	38 •155	4,134 •39	1,064 •62	n/a •—	n/a •—	31,786 •58	43.30 •52	$14,548 •40	3.5 •89	172.05 •14	50.87 •34	17.09 •5	34.18 •53	75.88 •22	36.74 •23	6.6 •194	3.2 •164	3.1 •39	9 •37	72.7 •58
United Kingdom [7] I3	London	243.50 •79	59,040.3 •21	242 •50	22,835 •6	16,283 •7	58,281 •2	36,483 •3	575,663 •8	1,476.80 •4	$25,116 •17	2.5 •130	276.18 •11	242.82 •9	4.13 •36	58.74 •15	84.49 •10	40.62 •19	69.7 •16	7.3 •52	2.5 •52	7 •31	77.5 •29
United States of America D3	Washington DC	9,372.60 •4	291,639.9 •3	31 •168	45,491 •3	73,119 •1	57,963 •3	60,117 •1	4,200,000 •1	9,780.80 •1	$34,280 •8	3.1 •103	1771.55 •3	2402.23 •1	8.42 •14	65.89 •9	48.81 •42	53.75 •1	44.6 •83	13.0 •1	3.1 •39	8 •34	76.9 •33
US Virgin Is. F5	Charlotte Amalie	0.35 •201	119.0 •193	340 •27	592 •93	1,196 •60	n/a •—	n/a •—	5,049 •120	1.51 •159	$13,844 •44	0.00 •164	0.00 •164	3.43 •103	31.43 •3	63.49 •12	37.51 •12	15.55 •48	n/a •—	n/a •—	T •—	n/a •—	n/a •—
Uruguay G7	Montevideo	176.20 •90	3,452.6 •129	20 •182	1,892 •56	561 •80	531 •69	252 •74	18,057 •69	19.20 •68	$5,713 •76	-0.2 •173	2.04 •97	3.90 •98	1.16 •106	27.96 •61	15.47 •89	11.90 •52	84.5 •2	10.9 •5	1.1 •124	16 •52	75.1 •42
Uzbekistan M3	Tashkent	447.40 •57	26,599.2 •39	59 •134	345 •115	72 •137	183 •86	n/a •—	7,332 •104	13.80 •78	$551 •172	2.9 •113	64.92 •35	51.36 •33	2.05 •80	6.66 •126	0.74 •166	1.09 •141	61.8 •32	3.7 •147	1.7 •81	68 •124	65.6 •124
Vanuatu R6	Port Vila	12.20 •161	188.7 •183	15 •187	46 •179	46 •149	12 •104	8 •149	1,060 •172	0.21 •206	$1,055 •149	1.8 •149	0.00 •164	0.03 •203	0.15 •173	3.36 •145	0.17 •181	2.74 •111	13.3 •174	3.9 •139	M •—	42 •110	65.8 •123
Venezuela F5	Caracas	916.50 •33	23,865.8 •46	26 •172	584 •95	643 •73	933 •61	1,801 •39	78,212 •32	117.20 •34	$4,758 •81	-0.2 •173	221.36 •12	73.11 •24	2.97 •60	11.23 •103	25.55 •68	5.04 •87	23.6 •150	4.7 •112	1.2 •116	22 •74	73.6 •51
Vietnam O5	Hanoi	331.70 •65	81,660.4 •13	246 •48	1,599 •61	n/a •—	n/a •—	n/a •—	74,000 •34	32.80 •60	$412 •185	6.4 •15	30.68 •44	18.82 •63	0.24 •165	6.85 •124	2.34 •140	1.85 •124	24.1 •148	5.2 •99	2.5 •52	38 •101	69.4 •97
Wallis & Futuna S6	Matu Utu	0.24 •209	15.2 •218	63 •124	n/a •—	n/a •—	n/a •—	n/a •—	n/a •—	0.03 •218	$2,040 •117	n/a •—	0.00 •164	0.00 •211	n/a •—	n/a •—	n/a •—	n/a •—	20.8 •155	n/a •—	T •—	n/a •—	n/a •—
Western Sahara I4	Laâyoune	252.10 •77	347.1 •174	1.4 •224	n/a •—	n/a •—	n/a •—	n/a •—	n/a •—	0.15 •209	$605 •168	n/a •—	0.00 •164	0.10 •188	0.38 •154	n/a •—	n/a •—	n/a •—	19.8 •158	n/a •—	T •—	n/a •—	n/a •—
Yemen L5	San'a	555.00 •48	22,605.4 •49	41 •150	76 •161	38 •157	n/a •—	70 •114	13,151 •83	8.20 •95	$454 •182	5.6 •25	22.68 •51	3.61 •101	0.20 •168	2.24 •153	0.81 •164	0.09 •185	32.0 •119	5.0 •104	5.2 •13	107 •144	59.9 •147
Zambia K6	Lusaka	752.60 •38	11,193.9 •72	15 •187	492 •103	117 •120	n/a •—	44 •124	4,822 •124	3.30 •135	$321 •195	2.7 •121	2.10 •96	0.96 •137	0.09 •185	0.83 •172	1.30 •148	0.49 •152	46.9 •77	5.6 •88	0.6 •154	202 •180	36.9 •192
Zimbabwe K6	Harare	390.70 •60	14,300.7 •61	37 •162	2,068 •53	81 •131	331 •75	131 •99	5,590 •115	6.20 •107	$484 •177	-2.6 •177	3.91 •84	6.00 •86	0.47 •147	2.47 •151	3.03 •138	4.30 •96	52.6 •64	7.3 •52	4.8 •17	n/a •—	36.8 •193
• Lowest rank		•226	•226	•226	•207	•188	•108	•160	•194	•224	•224	•178	•164	•211	•212	•195	•187	•193	•211	•191	•159	•189	•196

Some country names have been shortened for reasons of space. For more information on sources and dates, see the pages referred to below. Every attempt has been made to obtain the most recent reliable figures. In some cases, however, these are estimates (official or otherwise). See also the notes below and at the top of the chart. Maps relating to many of the areas covered in this chart may be found on the following pages:

Countries & Capitals: pages 10-11.
Area, Population & Population Density: page 16.
Travel: pages 20-1; also the regional introductions.
GNI & GDP Growth: page 18.
Energy: pages 22-3.
Telecom & Internet: pages 28-9.
Health: page 30.
Agricultural Land: page 15.
Military: page 33.

NOTES:

1 Special Administrative Region (of China).
2 Figures exclude Northern Cyprus.
3 All figures exclude overseas Départements and other dependencies listed separately here.
4 National Autonomous Region.
5 All figures include Madeira and the Azores.
6 All figures include Balearic and Canary Islands.
7 All figures exclude the Channel Islands and the Isle of Man.
8 La Paz (seat of government); Sucre (judicial).
9 St Peter Port (Guernsey) & St Helier (Jersey).
10 Yamoussoukro (official); Abidjan (administrative & commercial).
11 Basse-Terre (administrative) & Pointe-à-Pitre (commercial).
12 Astana (Almaty until December 1998).
13 Plymouth was largely destroyed in 1997 by volcanic eruption. A temporary administrative centre has been established at Brades.
14 Formerly called Rangoon.
15 Amsterdam (capital); The Hague (seat of government).
16 Jerusalem, as declared by the Palestinian Authority.
17 Pretoria (administrative); Cape Town (legislative), Bloemfontein (judicial). This arrangement is currently under review.
18 Colombo (administrative & commercial); Sri Jayewardenepura Kotte (legislative).
19 Population and area figures exclude the disputed territory of Jammu & Kashmir.
20 Includes the Golan Heights and East Jerusalem.
21 Excludes Western Sahara.

Index

COMPREHENSIVE INDEX TO THE COMPLETE ATLAS

The index lists all locations and features which appear throughout this atlas, with the exception of the following special-subject map pages:

- World climate
- World time
- World statistical maps
- World health risks
- World sport
- World airports*
- World flight times
- World cruising
- Europe climate
- Europe empires
- European Union
- Europe airports & high-speed rail
- Europe rail & ferries
- Europe museums & art galleries*
- London airports and connections
- UK attractions
- The Netherlands attractions
- Germany attractions
- France attractions
- Spain & Portugal attractions
- Italy attractions
- Africa climate
- Asia climate
- Asia empires
- Asia museums & art galleries*
- North America climate
- USA & Canada airports & railways
- USA & Canada museums & art galleries*
- South America climate

Maps marked * include a list of locations on the page itself

GENERAL ABBREVIATIONS

(for Australian, Canadian and US state/province abbreviations, see appendices)

Arch.	Archaeological
Hist.	Historic/Historical
I.	Island, Ile and equivalents
Int.	International
Is.	Islands, Iles and equivalents
Mem.	Memorial
Mon.	Monument
Mt	Mount/Mont
Mtn	Mountain/Montagne
Mtns	Mountains/Monts
Nac.	Nacional
Nat.	National
Naz.	Nazionale
Prov.	Provincial
St	Saint/Sankt/Sint

(All 'St' entries are treated as if spelt 'Saint' and are located in the index accordingly)

Ste	Sainte
Vdkhr.	Vodokhranilishche

Countries and significant dependencies and possessions are shown in CAPITALS

Hyphens and some accents have been removed in certain cases for consistency and ease of viewing. The correct form appears on the map pages.

The following names, which appear in bold, indicate the entry is a featured location on one of the special subject maps:

Beach	Beach map
Dive	Diving site map
Hill Sta	Hill station map (India)
Ind Res	Indian Reservation map (USA)
Park L	Leisure/Theme park map
Park N	National Park map
Ski	Ski map
Heritage C	UNESCO cultural heritage map
Heritage N	UNESCO natural heritage map

The following abbreviations appear occasionally to distinguish features with the same name:

[Adm]	Administrative region
[Apt]	Airport
[Riv]	River

Amathus • Cyprus 96 C4
Amatuku • Tuvalu .... 139 R
Amazon • S. America 171 C3
Amazon Basin • S. America 173 C3
Amazon, Mouths of the • Brazil 174 B2
Amazonas • S. America 171 C3
Amazonas [Adm] • Brazil 173 C3
Ambala • India 122 B2
Ambassador Bridge •
  Canada/United States 161 C3
Ambato • Ecuador 173 B3
Ambatosoratra • Madagascar 110 D2
Amber • India 122 D4
Amber Coast • Dominican Rep. 165 G5
Amberg • Germany 72 D4
Ambergris Caye • Belize 170 K8
Ambérieu-en-Bugey • France 78 C3
Ambleside • United Kingdom 65 D4
Amblève • Belgium 70 C4
Ambo Channel • Marshall Is. .... 139 E
Ambohimanga Heritage C •
  Madagascar .... 43 [126]
Amboise • France 77 F5
Amboise [Château] • France 77 F5
Amboin • Indonesia 131 G4
Amboseli Nat. Park • Kenya 109 C5
Amboseli Nat. Park Park • Kenya .... 112 [79]
Ambre, I. d' • Mauritius 113 F5
Ambrym • Vanuatu .... 138 V
Ambunten • Indonesia 131 R11
Amchitka • I. AK, United States 157 C4
Amcho • China 125 D3
Ameca • Mexico 169 H7
Ameixal • Portugal 84 J7
Ameland • Netherlands 70 C1
Amélia • Italy 87 E4
America, North • 142
America, South • 171
America's Stonehenge •
  NH, United States 156 D1
American Adventure World Park L •
  United Kingdom .... 59 [27]
American Falls • NY, United States 161 A1
American Fork • UT, United States 148 D2
AMERICAN SAMOA • Pacific Ocean .... 139 H
American Samoa, Nat. Park of •
  American Samoa .... 139 H
Americus • GA, United States 151 D4
Amersfoort • Netherlands 70 H7
Amery Ice Shelf • Antarctica 176 R4
Ames • IA, United States 150 B2
Amfilohia • Greece 93 B2
Amherst • MA, United States 156 C1
Amherst • NS, Canada 160 B2
Amherst • NY, United States 161 A1
Amherst, Fort • PE, Canada 160 B2
Amiens • France 76 E2
Amiens Heritage C • France .... 44 [70]
Amik Gölü • Turkey 95 J10
Amini I. • India 124 A3
Amirantes, Les • Seychelles 113 B1
Amistad Nat. Recreation Area Park N •
  TX, United States .... 152 [136]
Amitie Estate • Seychelles 113 B2
Amlapura • Bali, Indonesia 131 L7
Amli • Norway 98 G9
Amman • Jordan 120 B3
Ammersee • Germany 74 F7
Ammochostos • Cyprus 96 C4
Amol • Iran 120 G6
Amorbach • Germany 74 B2
Amorgós • Greece 93 D3
Amorosa, Fontana • Cyprus 96 C4
Amot • Buskerud, Norway 98 D5
Amot • Telemark, Norway 98 G9
Amoy • China 125 F4
Amposta, Nevado de • Peru 173 F7
Amper • Germany 74 E7
Ampezzo, Valle d' • Italy 86 D4
Amposta • Spain 80 F3
Amravati • India 122 B3
Amritsar • India 122 B2
Amroha • India 123 F7
Amroth Beach • United Kingdom .... 64 [51]
Amrum • Germany 99 E8
Amstelland • Netherlands 70 H7
Amstelveen • Netherlands 70 H7
Amsterdam • Netherlands 70 H7
Amsterdam Heritage C • Netherlands .... 44 [35]
Amsterdam • NY, United States 156 C1
Amsterdam, Fort • St Maarten .... 166 C
Amsterdam-Rijnkanaal • Netherlands 70 H7
Amsterdamse Waterleiding Duinen •
  Netherlands 70 H7
Amstetten • Austria 91 G1
Amu Darya • Asia 121 D4
Amundsen Gulf • NT, Canada 158 D1
Amundsen-Scott [Base] • Antarctica .... 176 [24]
Amur • Russian Fed. 101 N5
Amrakikós Kólpos • Greece .... 94 J
An Loc • Vietnam 129 B5
An Nabi Samu'il • Palestine NAR. 120 A3
An Nafud • Saudi Arabia 120 E7
An Najaf • Iraq 120 E7
An Uaimh • Ireland 69 E6
Ana Maria, Golfo de • Cuba 164 G5
Anabar • Nauru .... 138 X
Anacapri • Italy 87 G7
Anaconda • MT, United States 148 C2
Anacortes • WA, United States 154 C5
Anacostia Park Park N •
  DC, United States .... 153 [264]
Anadolu • Turkey 95 B2
Anadolu Daglari • Turkey 95 C1
Anadyr' • Russian Fed. 101 R3
Anafi • Greece 93 D3
Anafiotiria • Zante, Greece .... 94 J
Anagarapa Aboriginal Land •
  NT, Australia 136 B1
Anagni • Italy 87 F5
Anaheim • CA, United States 149 C4
Anai Mudi • India 124 B3
Anakena • Easter I. .... 139 M
Anamaur • Turkey 95 I10
Anambas, Kepulauan • Indonesia 131 C3
Anamur Burun • Turkey 95 I10
Anangu-Pitjantjatjara Aboriginal Land •
  SA, Australia 136 A2
Ananindeua • Brazil 174 B3
Anantapur • India 124 B2
Anapa • Russian Fed. 100 E4
Anardara • Afghanistan 121 D5
Anascaul • Ireland 69 G10
Añasco • Puerto Rico 165 I7
Añasco, Río Grande de •
  Puerto Rico 165 I7
Anatahan • N. Mariana Is. 138 AA2
Anatolia • Turkey 95 B2
Anatolian Macedonia kai Thráki •
  Greece 94 CC1
Anatom • Vanuatu .... 138 V
Anávatos • Chios, Greece .... 94 D
Ancão, I. do • Portugal 84 J8
Ancenis • France 77 E5
Anchorage • AK, United States 157 E3
Anchor Keys • FL, United States 155 C2
Ancona • Italy 87 D3
Andalo Ski • Italy .... 61 [133]
Andalo • Italy 86 C4
Andalsnes • Norway 98 C2
Andalucia • Spain .... 82 I-I-
Andalucia • Spain 80 C5
Andaman I. • India 122 D4
Andaman Sea • Asia 124 D2
Andelys, les • France 78 A1
Anderdalen Nat. Park Park N • Norway .... 58 [9]
Andermatt • Switzerland 90 K5
Andernach • Germany 74 C5
Andersen Air Force Base • Guam .... 138 Z
Anderson • IN, United States 150 C3
Anderson • SC, United States 151 D4
Andersonville Nat. Hist. Site Park N •
  GA, United States .... 153 [209]
Andes • S. America 171 B4

Andhra Pradesh • India 124 C1
Andijon • Uzbekistan 121 F4
Andikíthira • Greece .... 94 H
Andípáros • Greece .... 93 H
Andípáros [I.] • Greece .... 94 H
Andípaxi • Greece 94 AA2
Andóros [I.] • Greece 82 E5
Andorra la Vella • Andorra 82 E6
Andover • United Kingdom 63 E9
Andøya • Norway 97 D2
Andrátx • Majorca, Spain 83 N11
Andreanof Is. • AK, United States 157 C4
Andreas, Cape • Cyprus 96 D3
Andrelândia • Brazil 174 E7
Andrew Johnson Nat. Hist. Site Park N •
  TN, United States .... 153 [227]
Andreys • TX, United States 149 F4
Andria • Italy 85 F4
Andriake • Turkey 95 G8
Andromeda Gardens • Barbados .... 167 M
Andros • Andros, Greece .... 94 I
Andros • Bahamas 164 A1
Andros [I.] • Greece .... 94 I
Andros Town • Bahamas 164 A1
Andrott I. • India 124 A3
Aneby • Sweden 99 G6
Anegada • British Virgin Is. .... 166 A
Aneto, Pico de • Spain 78 K10
Aneto, Pico de • Spain 80 F2
Ang Mo Moi • Singapore 129 I11
Angaga • Maldives 124 C7
Angara • Russian Fed. 101 J4
Angarsk • Russian Fed. 101 K4
Angaur • Palau .... 138 Y
Ange • Sweden 97 D3
Angel de la Guarda, I. • Mexico 168 H5
Angel Falls • Venezuela 173 C2
Angel, Salto de • Venezuela 173 C2
Angeles • Philippines 128 G3
Angelholm • Sweden 99 G7
Angerman älv • Sweden 97 D3
Angers • France 77 E5
Angers [Château] • France 77 E5
Angkor • Cambodia 128 C4
Angkor Heritage C • Cambodia .... 43 [203]
Anglesberg • Sweden 99 A1
Anglesey • United Kingdom 63 C7
Anglesey [County] • United Kingdom 64 A4
Angleton • TX, United States 155 F6
ANGOLA • Africa 110 A2
Angostura, Presa de la • Mexico 168 F4
Angoulême • France 78 E5
Angra do Heroísmo • Azores 84 C4
Angra do Heroísmo Heritage C •
  Terceira, Azores .... 42 [83]
Angren • Uzbekistan 121 F4
ANGUILLA • West Indies .... 166 B
Anguilla Cays • Bahamas 164 A2
Anguilla Channel • West Indies .... 166 B
Anguillita I. • Anguilla .... 166 B
Angus • United Kingdom 65 B1
Anholt • Denmark 99 F6
Anhui • China 126 D2
Aniakchak Nat. Mon. & Preserve •
  AK, United States 157 D4
Aniakchak Nat. Mon. & Preserve Park N •
  AK, United States .... 152 [11]
Anibare Bay • Nauru .... 138 X
Anjar Heritage C • Lebanon .... 44 [304]
Anji • China 126 G7
Anji • Tajikistan 121 E4
Anjou • France 77 E5
Anjuna Beach • Goa, India 123 C5
Ankara • Turkey 95 B2
Ankarsrum • Sweden 99 H6
Anklam • Germany 72 E2
Ann Arbor • MI, United States 150 C3
Ann, Cape • MA, United States 156 D1
Anna Point • Nauru .... 138 X
Annaba • Algeria 106 C1
Annaberg im Lammertal Ski • Austria .... 61 [112]
Annam • Vietnam 129 A2
Annandale Falls • Grenada .... 166 Q
Annapolis • MD, United States 151 E4
Annapolis Royal • NS, Canada 160 B2
Annapurna • Nepal 123 G7
Anne, Fort • NS, Canada 160 B2
Annecy • France 78 C3
Annevoie • Belgium 70 C4
Anniston • AL, United States 151 C4
Annonay • France 77 A2
Annotto Bay • Jamaica 165 C3
Annweiler • Germany 74 B3
Ano Mera • Mikonos, Greece .... 94 I
Ano Viános • Crete, Greece 93 I6
Anógia • Crete, Greece 93 H6
Anqing • China 125 F3
Ansbach • Germany 72 D4
Anse au Loup, L' • NF, Canada 160 D1
Anse aux Meadows, L' •
  NF, Canada 160 D1
Anse Boileau Bay • Seychelles 113 A1
Anse Courtois • Mauritius 113 E5
Anse d'Hainault • Haiti 165 E6
Anse La Raye • St Lucia .... 167 N
Anse Lavoute • St Lucia .... 167 N
Anse Royale • Seychelles 113 A1
Anse Royale Bay • Seychelles 113 A1
Anse Volbert Village • Seychelles 113 B2
Anse-Bertrand • Guadeloupe .... 167 J
Anses-d'Arlets, les • Martinique .... 167 L
Anshan • China 125 G2
Anshun • China 125 E4
Ansongo • Mali 106 C3
Anta • Peru 173 F6
Antabamba • Peru 173 F6
Antagnod Ski • Italy .... 61 [125]
Antakya • Turkey 95 J10
Antalaha • Madagascar 110 D2
Antalya • Turkey 95 G8
Antalya [Adm] • Turkey 95 G8
Antalya Körfezi • Turkey 95 H8
Antananarivo • Madagascar 110 D2
Antarctic Peninsula • Antarctica 176 M4
Antarctica • .... 176 M-X
Antarctica • .... 176 M-X
Antequera • Spain 82 J7
Anthony • NM, United States 155 H8
Anthony I. Heritage C • BC, Canada .... 42 [1]
Anti Atlas • Morocco 107 A3
Antibes • France 78 H8
Antibes, Cap d' • France 78 H8
Anticosti, I. d' • QU, Canada 160 B1
Anticosti, Réserve faunique de l. d' •
  QU, Canada 160 B1
Antietam Nat. Battlefield •
  MD, United States 156 A3
Antietam Nat. Battlefield Park N •
  MD, United States .... 153 [254]
Antigua • Antigua & Barbuda .... 167 I
Antigua •
  Fuerteventura, Canary Is. 83 H5
Antigua • Guatemala 170 H5
Antigua Heritage C • Guatemala .... 42 [22]
ANTIGUA & BARBUDA • West Indies .... 167 H-I
Antigua • Aruba .... 166 W
Antilla • Cuba 164 H5
Antilles • St Vincent & Gren. .... 167 P
Antilles, Greater • West Indies 142 F7
Antilles, Lesser • West Indies 142 F7
Antimahia • Cos, Greece .... 94 J
Antioch • Turkey 95 J10
Antiphonitis Monastery • Cyprus 96 C4
Antivari • Fed. Rep. of Yugoslavia 50 D3
Antofagasta • Chile 175 A2
Antonine Wall • United Kingdom 50 B1
Antonio B. Won Pat [Apt] • Guam .... 138 Z
Antrim • United Kingdom 62 B6
Antrim [County] • United Kingdom 64 A3
Antrim Hills • United Kingdom 65 F5
Antrol • Bonaire .... 166 U
Antsirabe • Madagascar 110 D3
Antsiranana • Madagascar 110 D2
Antseb, Jazirat • Yemen 109 E11

Antwerp • Belgium 70 B3
Antwerpen • Belgium 70 B3
Antwerpen [Adm] • Belgium 70 C4
Anupgarh • India 123 D7
Anuradhapura • Sri Lanka 124 C4
Anuradhapura Heritage C • Sri Lanka .... 43 [167]
Anvers I. • Antarctica 176 M4
Anxi • China 121 I7
Anyang • China 125 F3
Anyer • Java, Indonesia 131 O11
Anza-Borrego Desert State Park •
  CA, United States 154 J9
Anzère • Switzerland 90 J6
Anzio • Italy 87 E5
Ao To Nong • Ko Phuket, Thailand 130 F9
Aoba • Vanuatu .... 138 V
Aokigahara • Japan 127 H8
Aomori • Japan 127 D2
Aoraki • New Zealand 137 B3
Aosta • Italy 87 A1
Aotea Harbour • New Zealand 137 D5
Aotou • China 126 F3
Aoulef • Algeria 106 C2
Ap Lei Chau • Hong Kong, China 126 E5
Apalachee Bay • FL, United States 151 D5
Apalachicola • FL, United States 155 B1
Apalachicola [Riv] •
  FL, United States 155 B1
Aparri • Philippines 128 G3
Apatzingán • Mexico 169 I7
Apeldoorn • Netherlands 70 D2
Apennines • Italy 85 E4
Apex Ski • BC, Canada .... 146 [3]
Aphrodisias • Turkey 95 F5
Aphrodite, Temple of •
  Lesbos, Greece .... 94 C
Apia • Samoa .... 139 G
Apizaco • Mexico 169 J7
Aplau • Peru 173 F7
Apo, Mt • Philippines 128 H5
Apolima Strait • Samoa .... 139 G
Apóllo • Náxos, Greece .... 94 H
Apollo Bay • VI, Australia 136 G9
Apopka, Lake • FL, United States 155 C2
Apostle Is. • WI, United States 150 A1
Apostle Is. Nat. Lakeshore •
  MI, United States 161 A1
Apostle Is. Nat. Lakeshore Park N •
  WI, United States .... 153 [155]
Apóstoli • Crete, Greece 93 H6
Apoteri • Guyana 173 D2
Appalachian Mtns • United States 147 J3
Appennino • Italy 85 C2
Appennino Abruzzese • Italy 87 F4
Appennino Lucano • Italy 85 E4
Appenzell • Switzerland 74 E8
Appenzell-Ausser Rhoden •
  Switzerland 91 R9
Appenzell-Inner Rhoden • Switzerland 91 R9
Appleton • Jamaica 165 C3
Appleton • WI, United States 150 B2
Appomattox Court House Nat. Hist. Park •
  VA, United States 156 A4
Appomattox Court House Nat. Hist. Park N •
  VA, United States .... 153 [244]
Appomattox Court House Nat. Hist. Site •
  VA, United States 156 A4
Apra Harbour • Guam .... 138 Z
Apra Heights • Guam .... 138 Z
Aprica • Italy 87 B1
Aprilia • Italy 87 E5
Apt • France 78 G7
Aptera • Crete, Greece 93 G5
Apucarana • Brazil 175 C2
Apure • Venezuela 173 C2
Apurímac • Peru 173 H6
Apuseni, Muntii • Romania 92 C2
Aqaba • Jordan 120 D8
Aqaba, Gulf of •
  Egypt/Saudi Arabia 109 B1
Aqköl • Kazakstan 121 F1
Aqsay • Kazakstan 121 B1
Aqsu • Kazakstan 121 F1
Aqtau • Kazakstan 121 B3
Aqtöbe • Kazakstan 121 C1
Aqua Fantasy Park L • Turkey .... 59 [89]
Aqua Fantasy • Turkey 95 E5
Aquila, L' • Italy 87 F4
Aquila, L' • Italy 87 F4
Aquileia • Italy 87 D1
Aquileia Heritage C • Italy .... 44 [155]
Aquin • Haiti 165 E6
Aquitaine • France 77 A2
Ar Ramadi • Iraq 120 E7
Ar Raqqah • Syria 120 D6
Ar Riyad • Saudi Arabia 120 F9
Ar Rub' al Khali • Saudi Arabia 120 F9
Ar Rustaq • Oman 120 H9
Ara • India 123 G8
Ara-kawa • Japan 127 I8
Arabba Ski • Italy .... 61 [142]
Arabba • Italy 86 D4
Arabian Oryx Sanctuary Heritage N •
  Oman .... 41 [121]
Arabian Peninsula • Asia 120 E8
Arabian Sea • Asia 116 F5
Arabuko Sokoke Nat. Park • Kenya 109 C6
Aracaju • Brazil 174 C4
Aracati • Brazil 174 C3
Araçatuba • Brazil 175 C2
Aracena • Spain 82 H7
Arad • Romania 92 C2
Arafura Sea • Australia/Indonesia 131 H5
Aragón • Spain 80 E3
Aragón Heritage C • Spain .... 44 [102]
Araguaia • Brazil 174 B3
Araguaina • Brazil 174 B3
Araguari • Brazil 174 B4
Arak • Iran 120 F7
Arakan Yoma • Myanmar 128 A3
Aral • Kazakstan 121 D2
Aral Sea • Kazakstan/Uzbekistan 121 C2
Aramac • QL, Australia 136 C4
Arambol • Goa, India 123 C5
Arambol Beach • Goa, India 123 C5
Aran I. • Ireland 69 B1
Aran Is. • Ireland 69 G9
Aranda de Duero • Spain 80 D3
Aranjuez • Spain 80 D3
Aranjuez Heritage C • Spain .... 44 [117]
Arao • Japan 127 B4
Araouane • Mali 106 B3
Arapahoe Basin Ski •
  CO, United States .... 146 [57]
Arapiraca • Brazil 174 C3
Arapkir • Turkey 95 C2
Arapuni Dam • New Zealand 137 E5
Arar • Saudi Arabia 120 E7
Araraquara • Brazil 175 D2
Ararat • VI, Australia 136 G9
Ararat • Turkey 95 D1
Araruama, Lago de • Brazil 174 F7
Aras • Turkey 95 D1
Arasaki • Okinawa, Japan .... 138 A
Arashiyama • Japan 127 C3
Arauca • Colombia 173 B1
Aravalli Range • India 123 D8
Arawale Nat. Reserve • Kenya 109 D5
Arawua Bay • New Zealand 137 G7
Arbanasi • Bulgaria 92 H8
Arbatax • Sardinia, Italy 86 F6
Arbil • Iraq 120 E6
Arboga • Sweden 99 A2
Arbon • Switzerland 90 D2
Arbroath • United Kingdom 65 B1
Arc • France 78 D4
Arc-et-Senans Heritage C • France .... 44 [83]
Arcachon • France 78 E6
Arcachon, Bassin de • France 78 E6
Arcadins, Côte des • Haiti 165 F5
Arcadis • Andorra 82 E6
Arcata • CA, United States 148 B2
Arches Nat. Park Park N •
  UT, United States .... 152 [84]

Arco • ID, United States 148 D2
Arcola • SA, Canada 158 F4
Arcs, les Ski • France .... 61 [23]
Arcs, Coves d' Majorca, Spain 83 O11
Artesia • NM, United States 149 F4
Arthur • TS, Australia 136 E6
Arthur's Town • Bahamas 164 B1
Atchison • KS, United States 150 A3
Atengo • Mexico 169 H6
Aterno • Italy 87 F4
Ath • Belgium 70 B4
Athabasca • AL, Canada 160 J6
Athabasca, Lake • AL/SA, Canada 158 F3
Athabasca [Riv] • AL, Canada 158 E3
Athboy • Ireland 69 E6
Athenry • Ireland 69 H9
Athens • AL, United States 151 C4
Athens • GA, United States 151 D4
Athens • Greece 93 C2
Athens Heritage C • Greece .... 44 [241]
Athens • TN, United States 151 D3
Atherton Tableland • QL, Australia 136 C3
Athi • Kenya 109 D5
Athina • Greece 93 C2
Athina Heritage C • Greece .... 44 [241]
Athinios • Thira, Greece .... 94 G
Athlone • Ireland 69 C3
Athol I. • Bahamas 164 A2
Athos • Greece .... 94 B
Athos Heritage N • Greece .... 41 [79]
Athos Heritage C • Greece .... 44 [231]
Athy • Ireland 69 E7
Atikokan • Brazil 174 E7
Atico • Peru 173 E7
Atiki • Greece 94 BB3
Atitlán, Lago de • Guatemala 170 J9
Atka • AK, United States 157 C4
Atka I. • AK, United States 157 C4
Atlanta • GA, United States 151 C4
Atlanta • TX, United States 155 F4
Atlantic City • NJ, United States 156 C3
Atlantic Ocean • 8 G4
Atlántida • Uruguay 175 G6
Atlas Mtns • Algeria/Morocco 106 B1
Atløy • Norway 98 F8
Atneye Aboriginal Land •
  NT, Australia 136 B1
Atokos • Greece .... 94 J
Atoyac • Mexico 169 J7
Atran • Sweden 99 G6
Atran [Riv] • Sweden 99 G6
Atsugi • Japan 127 H8
Attawapiskat • OT, Canada 159 H3
Attersee • Austria 91 P7
Attnash-Bear Peak Ski •
  NH, United States .... 146 [116]
Attre • Belgium 70 B4
Atuona • French Polynesia .... 139 J
Atvidaberg • Sweden 99 H5
Atyrau • Kazakstan 121 B2
Au • Austria 91 M7
Au Vent • Réunion 113 D3
Aubagne • France 78 G8
Auburn • CA, United States 154 I8
Auburn • ME, United States 150 F2
Auburn • NY, United States 156 B1
Aubusson • France 78 F5
Auch • France 78 F6
Auckland • New Zealand 137 B2
Auckland [Adm] • New Zealand 137 B2
Aude [Adm] • France 78 L10
Aude [Riv] • France 78 L10
Audierne, Baie d' • France 77 C4
Audincourt • France 76 G3
Aue • Germany 89 D6
Auer • Italy 86 C4
Auerbacher Schloss • Germany 74 D6
Aufkirch • Austria 91 O7
Augathella • QL, Australia 136 C5
Aughrim • Ireland 69 F7
Aughty, Slieve • Ireland 69 H9
Augsburg • Germany 74 F7
Augusta • GA, United States 151 D4
Augusta • ME, United States 150 G2
Augusta • Sicily, Italy 86 H8
Augusta • WA, Australia 135 B6
Augustenborg • Denmark 99 E8
Augustow • Poland 89 C2
Auki • Solomon Is. .... 138 W
Aukstaitija Nat. Park Park N •
  Lithuania .... 58 [151]
Aukstaitija Nat. Park • Lithuania 100 K8
Aulavik Nat. Park Park N •
  NT, Canada .... 161 [6]
Aulendorf • Germany 74 E7
Aulnay • France 78 E5
Aulne • France 77 C3
Auluptagel • Palau .... 138 Y
Aunu'u • American Samoa .... 139 H
Aupaluk • QU, Canada 159 J3
Aurangabad • India 122 B4
Auray • France 77 D4
Aurina • Italy 86 D3
Aurina, Val • Italy 86 D3
Auris • France 78 C4
Auris-en-Oisans Ski • France .... 61 [41]
Aurlandsvangen • Norway 98 G8
Auron Ski • France .... 61 [52]
Aurora • France 78 H7
Aurora • CO, United States 148 F3
Aurora • IL, United States 150 C2
Auroville • India 124 C2
Aurunci, Monti • Italy 87 F5
Auschwitz • Poland 89 F8
Auschwitz Heritage C • Poland .... 44 [186]
Auschwitz-Birkenau • Poland 89 F8
Ausonm, Monti • Italy 87 F5
Auster-Agder • Norway 98 A3
Austad • Norway 98 G9
Austin • MN, United States 150 B2
Austin • NV, United States 154 J8
Austin • TX, United States 155 E5
Austnes • Norway 98 F7
Austral Is. • 134
Australes, la • French Polynesia 139 DD4
AUSTRALIA • Australasia 135
Australia's Wonderland •
  NS, Australia 136 H8
Australian Alps • NS/VI, Australia 136 H9
Australian Capital Territory •
  Australia 136 H8
AUSTRIA • Europe 91 G2
Austria, Lower • Austria 91 T11
Austria, Upper • Austria 91 P7
Austvagøy • Norway 97 C2
Autazes • Brazil 173 D3
Autieul • France 78 A2
Autlán • Mexico 169 H7
Autun • France 78 C3
Auvergne • France 77 A2
Auvernier • Switzerland 90 I5
Auxerre • France 76 E3
Auxi • France 76 E3
Auyuittuq Nat. Park Park N •
  NU, Canada .... 161 [9]
Auzangate, Nudo • Peru 173 F6
Avallon • France 78 B3
Avaldsnes • Norway 98 G8
Avalon Peninsula • NF, Canada 160 D1
Avarua • Cook Is. .... 139 N
Avatele • Niue .... 139 O
Avatele Bay • Niue .... 139 O
Avatoru • Cook Is. .... 139 P
Avebury • United Kingdom 65 K9
Avebury Heritage C • United Kingdom .... 44 [28]
Aveiro • Portugal 80 A3
Aveiro [Adm] • Portugal 84 A1
Avellino • Italy 87 H6
Averøya • Norway 98 F2
Avers • Switzerland 90 K6
Aves, Islas de • Venezuela 167 DD4
Avesnes • France 76 D2
Aveyron • France 78 F6
Aveyron, Gorges de l' • France 78 F6
Avezzano • Italy 87 F4

Aviano • Italy 86 D4
Aviemore • United Kingdom 62 D3
Avignon • France 76 F5
Avignon Heritage C • France .... 44 [86]
Avila • Spain 80 C3
Avila Heritage C • Spain .... 44 [113]
Avilés • Spain 80 C2
Avirons, les • Réunion 113 C4
Avisio • Italy 86 C4
Avoca • Ireland 69 F7
Avoca, Vale of • Ireland 69 F7
Avola • Sicily, Italy 86 H8
Avon • United Kingdom 65 F5
Avon • United Kingdom 65 K9
Avon Gorge • United Kingdom 65 K9
Avondale • AZ, United States 149 D4
Avoriaz Ski • France .... 61 [10]
Avoriaz • France 78 D3
Avranches • France 76 C2
Awaji • Japan 127 F7
Awaji-shima • Japan 127 F7
Awakino Gorge • New Zealand 137 D5
Awanui • New Zealand 137 B2
Awash lower valley Heritage C •
  Ethiopia .... 43 [101]
Awash Nat. Park • Ethiopia .... 112 [59]
Awbari • Libya 106 D2
Awjilah • Libya 108 B2
Ax-les-Thermes • France 78 K10
Axamer Lizum • Austria 91 N8
Axios • Greece 93 C1
Axminster • United Kingdom 65 K9
Axós • Crete, Greece 93 H6
Ayacucho • Argentina 175 F7
Ayacucho • Peru 173 E6
Ayaköz • Kazakstan 121 H2
Ayamonte • Spain 80 F1
Ayancik • Turkey 95 E1
Ayaviri • Peru 173 F6
Aydin • Turkey 95 F5
Aydin [Adm] • Turkey 95 F5
Aydinkent • Turkey 95 F4
Ayer Hitam • Malaysia 129 G10
Ayers Rock • NT, Australia 136 A2
Ayers Rock Resort • NT, Australia . 136 A2
Ayia Napa • Cyprus 96 D4
Aylesbury • United Kingdom 63 E9
Aylmer Lake • NT, Canada 158 F2
Aynunah • Saudi Arabia 109 E7
Ayodhya • India 123 G8
Ayoûn el Atroûs • Mauritania 106 B3
Ayr • QL, Australia 136 C3
Ayr • United Kingdom 62 C5
Ayr, Point of • Isle of Man 63 C6
Ayrshire • United Kingdom 64 A3
Aytos • Bulgaria 92 H8
Ayutthaya • Thailand 130 D7
Ayutthaya Heritage C • Thailand . 43 [206]
Ayvacik • Turkey 95 E4
Ayvalik • Turkey 95 E4
Az Zarqa • Jordan 120 D7
Az Zawiyah • Libya 106 D1
Az Zubayr, Jazaïr • Yemen 109 E11
Azahar, Costa del • Spain 80 F3
Azamgarh • India 123 G8
Azangaro • Peru 173 F7
Azay-le-Ferron [Château] • France . 77 F6
Azay-le-Rideau [Château] • France . 77 F5
Azemmour • Morocco 107 A1
Azenhas do Mar • Portugal 84 A7
AZERBAIJAN • Asia 120 F5
Azinhal • Portugal 84 K7
Azores • Atlantic Ocean .... 84 B-C
Azov • Russian Fed. 100 E4
Azov, Sea of •
  Russian Fed./Ukraine 100 E1
Azrou • Morocco 107 B1
Aztec Ruins Nat. Mon. •
  NM, United States 155 H7
Aztec Ruins Nat. Mon. Park N •
  NM, United States .... 152 [121]
Azua de Compostela • Dominican Rep. 165 G6
Azuaga • Spain 80 G4
Azuchi-Castle • Japan 127 G6
Azuero, Peninsula de • Panama 170 G7
Azul • Argentina 175 F7
Azul, Cerro • Galápagos Is. 171 G10
Azulcocha, Cerro • Peru 173 E6
Azur, Côte d' • France .... 78 G-H
Azure Window • Malta 96 A1
Azzurra, Grotta • Italy 87 G7

B

Ba • Fiji Is. .... 138 T
Ba'qubah • Iraq 120 E7
Baalbek Heritage C • Lebanon ... 44 [304]
Baarn • Netherlands 74 B6
Bab al Mandab • Djibouti/Yemen . 109 E11
Babadag • Romania 92 I7
Babaeski • Turkey 95 E3
Babahoyo • Ecuador 173 B3
Babanango • South Africa 111 C4
Rabayevo • Russian Fed. 100 M9
Babbacombe Bay • United Kingdom . 65 J10
Babeldaob • Palau .... 138 Y
Babenhausen • Germany 74 F7
Babiogórski Nat. Park Park N •
  Poland .... 58 [106]
Babiogórski Nat. Park • Poland 89 F9
Babruysk • Belarus 100 C3
Babuyan Is. • Philippines 128 G3
Bac Lieu • Vietnam 129 B6
Bac Ninh • Vietnam 128 D2
Bacabal • Brazil 174 B3
Bacau • Romania 92 D2
Bacharach • Germany 74 D6
Bäckefors • Sweden 99 F5
Bacolod • Philippines 128 E5
Bactra • Afghanistan 121 K7
Bad Aibling • Germany 74 G7
Bad Aussee • Austria 91 P7
Bad Bayersoien • Germany 74 F8
Bad Bergzabern • Germany 74 B3
Bad Birnbach • Germany 74 H7
Bad Breisig • Germany 74 C5
Bad Buchau • Germany 74 F7
Bad Doberan • Germany 72 D1
Bad Dürkheim • Germany 74 D5
Bad Ems • Germany 74 D5
Bad Endorf • Germany 74 H7
Bad Feilnbach • Germany 74 G8
Bad Godesberg • Germany 74 C5
Bad Goisern • Austria 91 P7
Bad Hall • Austria 91 P7
Bad Heilbrunn • Germany 74 F8
Bad Hersfeld • Germany 74 E5
Bad Hofgastein Ski • Austria ..... 61 [108]
Bad Hofgastein • Austria 91 N8
Bad Homburg vor der Höhe • Germany . 74 D5
Bad Honnef • Germany 74 C5
Bad Hönningen • Germany 74 C5
Bad Ischl • Austria 91 P7
Bad Kissingen • Germany 72 D3
Bad Kleinkirchheim Ski • Austria . 61 [115]
Bad Kohlgrub • Germany 74 F8
Bad Kreuznach • Germany 74 D6
Bad Mergentheim • Germany 74 E6
Bad Münstereifel • Germany 74 C5
Bad Neuenahr-Ahrweiler • Germany . 74 C5
Bad Reichenhall • Germany 74 H8
Bad River Ind Res •
  WI, United States .... 155 [63]
Bad Schussenried • Germany 74 F7
Bad Schwalbach • Germany 74 D6
Bad Tölz • Germany 74 F8
Bad Urach • Germany 74 F7
Bad Waldsee • Germany 74 F7
Bad Wiessee • Germany 74 F8
Bad Wildbad • Germany 74 E7
Bad Wimpfen • Germany 74 E6

Bad Windsheim • Germany 72 D4
Bad Wörishofen • Germany 74 F7
Bad Wurzach • Germany 74 F7
Badajoz • Spain 80 B4
Badalona • Spain 83 D4
Badami • India 124 B1
Baden • Austria 91 H1
Baden • Switzerland 90 D2
Baden-Baden • Germany 74 B3
Baden-Württemberg • Germany ..... 64 [74]
Badenweiler • Germany 74 A4
Badgastein Ski • Austria .... 61 [107]
Badgastein • Austria 91 P8
Badia, Val • Italy 86 D3
Badlands • ND/SD, United States . 154 B1
Badlands Nat. Park •
  SD, United States 148 F2
Badlands Nat. Park Park N •
  SD, United States .... 152 [150]
Badrinath • India 122 B2
Badulla • Sri Lanka 124 C4
Badung, Bukit • Bali, Indonesia ... 131 L8
Badung, Selat • Indonesia 131 L8
Badwater Basin • CA, United States 154 J8
Baena • Spain 80 G4
Baffin Bay • TX, United States 155 E6
Baffin I. • NU, Canada 159 I2
Bafoussam • Cameroon 106 D4
Bafra • Turkey 95 C1
Bafra Burun • Turkey 95 C1
Baga • Goa, India 123 C5
Baga Beach • Goa, India 123 C5
Bagamoyo • Tanzania 110 H7
Bagan Datuk • Malaysia 129 F9
Bagansiapiapi • Indonesia 131 N10
Bagé • Brazil 175 C3
Bagenkop • Denmark 99 F8
Bagerhat Heritage C • Bangladesh . 43 [166]
Baggs • WY, United States 148 E2
Baghdad • Iraq 120 E7
Baghelkhand Plateau • India 123 G8
Bagheria • Sicily, Italy 86 G7
Baghlan • Afghanistan 121 K4
Baghwan Mahaveer Wildlife Sanctuary •
  Goa, India 123 C6
Bagnrin [Apt] • United Kingdom 65 F5
Baguio • Philippines 128 G3
Bahama Sea • West Indies 164 G4
BAHAMAS • West Indies .... 164 A-B
Bahamas Nat. Trust Park • Bahamas 164 B2
Baharampur • India 122 C3
Bahariya Oasis • Egypt 109 A2
Bahau • Malaysia 129 G10
Bahawalpur • Pakistan 122 B3
Bahçe • Turkey 95 J9
Bahdur I. • Sudan 109 E10
Bahia • Brazil 174 C4
Bahia [Adm] • Brazil 174 B4
Bahia Blanca • Argentina 175 B3
Bahia de los Angeles • Mexico 168 H5
Bahia Grande • Majorca, Spain 83 N12
Bahia Honda • Cuba 164 E4
Bahia Honda State Recreation Area •
  FL, United States 155 D3
Bahía, Is. de la • Honduras 170 D2
Bahía Kino • Mexico 168 I5
Bahía Tortugas • Mexico 168 H6
Bahir Dar • Ethiopia 108 C3
Bahla Heritage C • Oman .... 43 [131]
Bahoruco, Sierra de •
  Dominican Rep. 165 F6
Bahr el Ghazal • Sudan 108 B4
Bahraich • India 123 F7
BAHRAIN • Asia 120 G8
Bâlu Buruhilu • Burundi, Italy 86 F3
Baicheng • China 125 N3
Baie Comeau • QU, Canada 160 A1
Baie Lazare Village • Seychelles .. 113 A2
Baie Verte • NF, Canada 160 C1
Baiersbronn • Germany 74 B3
Baikal, Lake Heritage N •
  Russian Fed. .... 41 [85]
Baile Átha Cliath • Ireland 69 F7
Daire Beach • Goa, India 123 C5
Bainbridge • FL, United States 155 B1
Bairiki • Kiribati .... 139 F
Bairnsdale • VI, Australia 136 G9
Bais • Philippines 128 G5
Baishan • China 125 G2
Baitenghu Resort • China 126 E4
Baixo, I. de •
  Porto Santo, Madeira 84 E5
Baiyun [Apt] • China 126 E3
Baja • Hungary 92 B2
Baja California • Mexico .... 168 H-I
Baja California [Adm] • Mexico 169 A2
Bajos de Haina • Dominican Rep. . 165 G6
Bakauheni • Indonesia 131 O11
Baker • OR, United States 154 H6
Baker I. • Pacific Ocean 138 CC3
Baker Lake • NU, Canada 158 G2
Bakersfield • CA, United States ... 154 J9
Baki • Azerbaijan 120 F5
Baki Heritage C • Azerbaijan ... 43 [138]
Bakirköy • Turkey 92 L5
Bakken Park I. • Denmark .... 59 [19]
Baku • Azerbaijan 120 F5
Baku Heritage C • Azerbaijan ... 43 [138]
Bakungan • Indonesia 131 M9
Balabac Strait •
  Malaysia/Philippines 128 F5
Balagne • Corsica, France 78 M11
Balakovo • Russian Fed. 100 G3
Balanacha • Mexico 169 F4
Balashov • Russian Fed. 100 F3
Balassagyarmat • Hungary 92 J7
Balaton • Hungary 92 B2
Balboa • Panama 170 M11
Balbriggan • Ireland 69 F6
Balcarce • Argentina 175 G7
Balchik • Bulgaria 92 I8
Balclutha • New Zealand 137 G8
Balderschwang • Germany 74 E8
Baldoyle • Ireland 69 F7
Baldwin • FL, United States 155 C1
Baldy Peak • AZ, United States .. 155 H8
Balé Gong Palace • Bali, Indonesia 131 L8
Bale Mtns Nat. Park Park • Ethiopia 112 [60]
Balearics • Spain 80 G4
Balearic Is. • Spain 80 G4
Baleine, Falls of •
  St Vincent & Gren. .... 167 O
Baleshwar • India 122 C3
Balestrand • Norway 98 G8
Balfour Town • Turks & Caicos Is. 164 D3
Balguerie, Cap • French Polynesia 139 J
Bali, Crete, Greece 93 H5
Bali • Indonesia .... 131 K-L
Bali Aga • Bali, Indonesia 131 L7
Bali Aga • Bali, Indonesia 131 L8
Bali Barat Nat. Park •
  Bali, Indonesia 131 K7
Bali Handara • Bali, Indonesia 131 L7
Bali Sea • Indonesia 131 L7
Bali, Selat • Indonesia 131 K7
Balice John Paul II [Apt] • Poland . 89 F9
Ballance • St Vincent & Gren. ...... 167 P
Baligill • Bali, Indonesia 131 L8
Balikesir • Turkey 95 F4
Balikesir [Adm] • Turkey 95 F4
Balikpapan • Indonesia 131 E4
Balkan • Germany 74 B3
Balkan Mtns • Bulgaria/Yugoslavia 92 C3
Balkh • Afghanistan 121 K4
Ballaghaderreen • Ireland 69 F6
Ballarat • VI, Australia 136 G9
Ballestas, Is. • Peru 173 E6
Ballia • India 123 G8
Ballina • Ireland 69 F6
Ballina • NS, Australia 136 D5

Ballinasloe • Ireland 69 H9
Ballinrobe • Ireland 69 H9
Ballinskelligs • Ireland 69 G11
Ballintober Abbey • Ireland 69 H8
Ballitore • Ireland 69 E7
Ballivor • Ireland 69 G6
Ballybunion • Ireland 69 G10
Ballycastle • Ireland 69 H10
Ballycastle • United Kingdom 62 B5
Ballycastle Beach • United Kingdom 64 [74]
Ballyclare • Ireland 69 G11
Ballyhaunis • Ireland 69 H8
Ballyheige • Ireland 69 G10
Ballyliffin • Ireland 69 E7
Ballymena • United Kingdom 62 B6
Ballymore Eustace • Ireland 69 E7
Ballymore • Ireland 69 H9
Ballyvaughan • Ireland 69 H9
Balonne • QL, Australia 136 C5
Balotra • India 124 A2
Balqash • Kazakstan 121 F2
Balqash Köli • Kazakstan 121 F12
Balranald • NS, Australia 136 G8
Balsams, The Ski •
  NH, United States .... 146 [117]
Balsas • Mexico 169 I8
Bålsta • Sweden 99 B1
Balta • Moldova 92 D2
Baltic Sea • Europe 97 D4
Baltim • Egypt 109 A1
Baltimore • Ireland 69 H11
Baltimore • MD, United States 156 B3
Baltiysk • Russian Fed. 100 J8
Baltra I. • Galápagos Is. 171 H10
Bam • Iran 120 H8
Bamako • Mali 106 B3
Bambari • Central African Rep. 108 B4
Bamberg • Germany 72 D4
Bamberg Heritage C • Germany .. 44 [64]
Bambolim Beach • Goa, India 123 C5
Bambous • Mauritius 113 E6
Bambui • Brazil 174 E6
Bamburi Beach • Kenya 106 C4
Bamenda • Cameroon 106 C4
Bamian • Afghanistan 121 E5
Bamingui-Bangoran, Parc nat. du Park •
  Central African Rep. .... 112 [39]
Bamovskoye • Russian Fed. 101 M4
Ban Bang Po • Ko Samui, Thailand 130 G11
Ban Bophut • Ko Samui, Thailand . 130 G11
Ban Chaweng • Ko Samui, Thailand 130 G11
Ban Chaweng Noi •
  Ko Samui, Thailand 130 G12
Ban Chiang • Thailand 130 A1
Ban Chiang Heritage C • Thailand . 43 [204]
Ban Hong • Thailand 130 B6
Ban Houayxay • Laos 130 G5
Ban Chaweng Noi •
  Ko Samui, Thailand 130 G12
Ban Hua Thanon •
  Ko Samui, Thailand 130 G12
Ban Klaeng • Thailand 130 E8
Ban Laem • Thailand 130 D8
Ban Lamai • Ko Samui, Thailand .. 130 G12
Ban Lipa Noi • Ko Samui, Thailand 130 G12
Ban Maenam • Ko Samui, Thailand 130 G11
Ban Pae • Thailand 130 E8
Ban Phang Ka • Ko Samui, Thailand 130 G12
Ban Pong • Thailand 130 D7
Ban Sa Ket • Ko Samui, Thailand . 130 G12
Ban So Sra Kret • Ko Samui, Thailand 130 G12
Ban Tah • Thailand 130 D8
Ban Tai • Ko Samui, Thailand 130 G11
Ban Taling Ngam •
  Ko Samui, Thailand 130 G12
Bäñ Thäle • Kó Sämui, Thailand .. 130 G12
Ban Thong Krut •
  Ko Samui, Thailand 130 G12
Ban Thong Tanot •
  Ko Samui, Thailand 130 G12
Ban Thurian • Ko Samui, Thailand 130 G12
Ban Tong Yang • Ko Samui, Thailand 130 G12
Banaba • Kiribati 138 CC3
Banaba • Kiribati .... 139 I
Banana, Ilha de • Brazil 174 A4
Banaba, Rás • Egypt 109 B3
Banaz • Turkey 95 F4
Bancroft • United Kingdom 62 B3
Banda Aceh • Indonesia 131 M9
Banda Sea • Indonesia 131 G5
Bandak • Norway 98 G9
Bandar Seri Begawan • Brunei 128 E6
Bandar-e Abbas • Iran 120 G8
Bandar-e Bushehr • Iran 120 G8
Bandar-e Lengeh • Iran 120 G8
Bandaranayake [Apt] • Sri Lanka . 124 C4
Bandarawela • Sri Lanka 124 C4
Bandeira, Pico da • Brazil 174 F6
Bandelier Nat. Mon. •
  NM, United States 155 H7
Bandelier Nat. Mon. Park N •
  NM, United States .... 152 [126]
Banderas, Bahía de • Mexico 169 H7
Bandiagara Cliffs Heritage N • Mali 41 [90]
Bandiagara Cliffs Heritage C • Mali 43 [107]
Bandirma Nat. Park • India 124 B2
Bandirma • Turkey 95 F4
Bandol • France 78 G8
Bandon • Ireland 69 H11
Bandon • OR, United States 154 G6
Bandos • Maldives 124 H8
Bandundu • Dem. Rep. of Congo . 107 O
Bandung • Java, Indonesia 131 P11
Bandung • Java, Indonesia 131 Q12
Baneasa [Apt] • Romania 92 H7
Baneasa • Cuba 164 H5
Banff • AT, Canada 160 J7
Banff Nat. Park Park N •
  AL, Canada .... 161 [19]
Banff Nat. Park • AL, Canada 160 J7
Banff • United Kingdom 65 K9
Bang Kao Bay • Ko Samui, Thailand 130 G12
Bang Kaong Beach •
  Ko Phuket, Thailand 130 F9
Bang Pa-In • Thailand 130 D7
Bang Saen • Thailand 130 E8
Bang Thao • Ko Phuket, Thailand . 130 F9
Bang Thao Beach •
  Ko Phuket, Thailand 130 F9
Bángalore • India 124 B2
Banganapalle • India 124 B3
Bangaram I. • India 124 A3
Bangassou • Central African Rep. . 108 B4
Bánghazi • Libya 106 D1
Bangka • Indonesia 131 R12
Bangkalan • Indonesia 131 R12
Bangkok • Thailand 130 D7
Bangkok, Bight of • Thailand 130 D8
BANGLADESH • Asia 123 L8
Bangli • Bali, Indonesia 131 L8
Bangor • ME, United States 156 G2
Bangor •
  N. Ireland, United Kingdom 63 C6
Bangor • Wales, United Kingdom . 63 C7
Bangui • Central African Rep. 108 D4
Bangweulu, Lake • Zambia 110 G8
Bani • Ko Phuket, Thailand 130 F9
Bani • Dominican Rep. 165 G6
Bani • Mali 106 B3
Baniyas • Syria 120 B1
Banja Luka • Bosnia-Herz. 92 G6
Banjar • Bali, Indonesia 131 P12

Banjarmasin • Indonesia 131 D4
Banjul • Gambia 106 A3
Bankberg • South Africa 111 G6
Bankgard • Sweden 99 G6
Banks I. • NT, Canada 158 D1
Banks Is. • Vanuatu .... 138 V
Banks Peninsula • New Zealand . 137 B3
Banks Strait • TS, Australia 136 F6
Bann • United Kingdom 62 B6
Bannockburn • United Kingdom 65 A2
Bannu • Pakistan 122 B2
Bansang • The Gambia 89 B4
Banská Bystrica • Slovak Rep. ..... 44 [188]
Banská Štiavnica Heritage C •
  Slovak Rep. .... 44 [188]
Banten • Java, Indonesia 131 O11
Bantry • Ireland 69 G11
Bantry Bay • Ireland 69 G11
Banyak, Kepulauan • Indonesia . 131 M10
Banyalbufar • Majorca, Spain 83 N11
Banyuls • France 78 L9
Banyumas • Java, Indonesia 131 P12
Banyuwangi • Java, Indonesia ... 131 R12
Banyuwedang • Bali, Indonesia .. 131 K7
Bao Loc • Vietnam 129 C5
Bao Nhai • China 126 A1
Baoding • China 125 F3
Baoji • China 125 E3
Baoshan • China 126 H6
Baotou • China 125 E2
Bar • Serbia & Montenegro 92 D2
Bar • QN • Israel 120 B1
Bar Harbor • ME, United States ... 156 G2
Bar-le-Duc • France 76 F2
Baracoa • Cuba 164 H5
Baradères, Presqu'île des • Haiti . 165 E6
Barahona • Dominican Rep. 165 G6
Barakaldo • Spain 80 D2
Barak Barak • Afghanistan 121 L5
Baranavichy • Belarus 100 C3
Barano d'Ischia • Italy 87 G7
Baranof I. • AK, United States 157 F4
Barbacena • Brazil 174 E6
BARBADOS • West Indies .... 167 M
Barbaresco • Italy 87 A2
Bárbaro, Villa • Italy 87 C1
Barbate de Franco • Spain 80 F2
Barbezieux • France 78 E5
Barbuda • Antigua & Barbuda ..... 167 H
Barcaldine • QL, Australia 136 C4
Barcelona • Spain 83 D4
Barcelona Heritage C • Spain .... 44 [96]
Barcelonnette • France 78 H7
Barcs • Hungary 92 G5
Bardejov Heritage C • Slovak Rep. . 44 [201]
Bardolino • Italy 86 C2
Bardonécchia Ski • Italy .... 61 [120]
Bardonécchia • Italy 87 A2
Bardsey I. • United Kingdom 63 C8
Barèges • France 78 J9
Bareilly • India 123 F7
Barentin • France 76 D2
Barents Sea • Norway/Russian Fed. 98 A
Barim • Yemen 109 E11
Barinas • Venezuela 173 B2
Baringo, Lake • Kenya 109 C4
Bârîs • Egypt 109 A3
Barisal • Bangladesh 122 D3
Barkerville • BC, Canada 160 I6
Barkly Tableland • NT, Australia . 135 F3
Barlad • Romania 92 D2
Barlee, Lake • WA, Australia 135 B5
Barletta • Italy 85 F4
Barlinek • Poland 89 A2
Barlovento de landía, Playa de •
  Fuerteventura, Canary Is. 83 H5
Barmer • India 123 D8
Barmouth • United Kingdom 63 C8
Barmouth Beach • United Kingdom 64 [61]
Barnaul • Russian Fed. 101 I4
Barnes Bay • Anguilla .... 166 B
Barnet • United Kingdom 65 G7
Barnsley • United Kingdom 63 E7
Barnstaple • United Kingdom 65 J9
Barnstaple Bay • United Kingdom . 65 J9
Baroda • India 122 B3
Barolo • Italy 87 A2
Baronia • Sardinia, Italy 86 F5
Barotse • Maldives 124 H8
Barques, Pointe Aux •
  MI, United States 161 C2
Barquisimeto • Venezuela 173 C1
Barr • United Kingdom 62 B4
Barra de Navidad • Mexico 169 H7
Barra de Tijuca • Brazil 174 E7
Barra do Corda • Brazil 174 B3
Barra do Garças • Brazil 174 A4
Barra Mansa • Brazil 174 E7
Barranca del Cobre, Parque Natural •
  Mexico 168 I6
Barrancabermeja • Colombia 173 B2
Barranco del Velho • Portugal 84 J7
Barranquilla • Colombia 173 B1
Barre de l'Isle • St Lucia .... 167 N
Barre des Ecrins • France 78 D4
Barreiras • Brazil 174 B4
Barreiro • Portugal 84 G6
Barra, I. da • Portugal 84 J6
Barretos • Brazil 174 B5
Barrie • OT, Canada 160 E4
Barrier Reef • Belize 170 E4
Barrier Reef Reserve System Heritage N •
  Belize .... 40 [22]
Barrington, Fort •
  Antigua & Barbuda .... 167 I
Barrington, Fort • Montserrat ...... 166 D
Barrington I. • Galápagos Is. 171 H10
Barro Colorado, Parque Nac. •
  Panama 170 L11
Barrouallie • St Vincent & Gren. .. 167 O
Barranco do Velho • Portugal 84 J7
Barrow • AK, United States 157 E2
Barrow I. • WA, Australia 135 C4
Barrow Creek • NT, Australia 136 B1
Barrow, Point •
  AK, United States 157 E2
Barrow-in-Furness • United Kingdom 65 C4
Barry • United Kingdom 65 J9
Barry's Amusement Park Park L •
  United Kingdom .... 59 [22]
Barrys Bay • OT, Canada 160 F4
Barsac • France 76 F3
Barstow • CA, United States 154 J9
Bartin • Turkey 95 B1
Bartle Frith • QL, Australia 136 C3
Bartlet Town • Bahamas 164 B1
Bartoszyce • Poland 89 C1
Barû, Volcán • Panama 170 F6
Barúmini • Sardinia, Italy 86 F6
Barung • Indonesia 131 R12
Baruun Urt • Mongolia 125 F2
Barysaw • Belarus 100 C3
Bas Médoc • France 76 E4
Basak • Cambodia 129 B5
Basavrutcha • Mexico 168 I5
Basdorf • Germany 73 F7
Basel • Switzerland 90 C2
Basel-Stadt [Adm] • Switzerland .. 91 Q9
Bashaw • AT, Canada 160 J6
Bashkortostan Russ Adm •
  Russian Fed. .... 101 [14]
Basilan • Philippines 128 G5
Basildon • United Kingdom 63 F7
Basilicata • Italy 86 B2
Basingstoke • United Kingdom 63 E9
Baskatong, Réservoir •
  QU, Canada 160 G3
Basle • Switzerland 90 C2
Basle • Switzerland 90 C2
Basque Coast • Spain 82 B2

Basque, Côte • France 78 I9
Basque Country • Spain 82 B1
Basque, Pays • France 78 I9
Basra • Iraq 120 F7
Bass, Ilots de • French Polynesia 139 EE4
Bass Is. • OH, United States 161 A3
Bass Lake • CA, United States ... 154 I8
Bass Strait • TS/VI, Australia 135 H7
Bassae • Greece 93 B3
Bassae Heritage C • Greece ..... 44 [237]
Bassano del Grappa • Italy 87 C1
Basse-Casamance, Parc nat. de Park •
  Senegal .... 112 [8]
Basse-Normandie • France 77 A1
Basse-Pointe • Martinique .... 166 J
Basse-Terre • Guadeloupe .... 167 J
Bassein • Myanmar 128 A3
Bassenthwaite • United Kingdom . 65 C3
Bassenthwaite Lake • United Kingdom 65 C3
Basseterre • St Kitts & Nevis ...... 167 F
Bassikounou • Mauritania 106 B3
Bassins Bleus • Haiti 165 F6
Bassum • Germany 72 C2
Basti • India 123 G7
Bastia • Corsica, France 78 M11
Bastogne • Belgium 70 C5
Bastrop • LA, United States 156 E5
Bastrop • TX, United States 156 D5
Bat Heritage C • Oman .... 43 [132]
Bat Yam • Israel 120 L7
Bata • Equat. Guinea 106 C4
Batabanó, Golfo de • Cuba 164 E4
Batalik Gölü • Turkey 95 I9
Batalha Heritage C • Portugal ... 44 [131]
Batan Is. • Philippines 128 G2
Batangas • Philippines 128 G4
Batavia • NY, United States 156 A1
Batchelor, Mt •
  OR, United States 154 G6
Batemans Bay • NS, Australia ... 136 H8
Bath • Jamaica 165 D4
Bath • United Kingdom 65 K9
Bath Heritage C • United Kingdom 44 [27]
Bathaway Beach • Grenada .... 166 Q
Bathgate • United Kingdom 65 B2
Bathinda • India 122 B2
Baths, The • British Virgin Is. ..... 166 A
Bathsheba • Barbados .... 167 M
Bathurst • NB, Canada 160 B1
Bathurst • NS, Australia 136 H8
Bathurst I. • NT, Australia 135 E2
Bathurst, Cape • NT, Canada 135 G2
Bathurst I. • NT, Australia 158 G1
Batman • Turkey 95 D2
Batna • Algeria 106 C1
Baton Rouge • LA, United States . 156 E5
Batroûn • Lebanon 120 D7
Bats Cave Beach • Cayman Is. .. 165 A2
Batsi • Andros, Greece 93 C3
Battambang • Cambodia 128 C4
Batticaloa • Sri Lanka 124 D4
Battipáglia • Italy 87 H7
Battle • United Kingdom 65 H8
Battle Creek • MI, United States . 150 C2
Battle Harbour • NF, Canada 159 K3
Battle Mtn • NV, United States ... 154 J7
Battonya • Hungary 92 C2
Battowia • St Vincent & Gren. ..... 167 P
Batu Berinchang, Gunung • Malaysia 129 F9
Batu Caves • Malaysia 129 G10
Batu Gajah • Malaysia 129 F9
Batu, Kepulauan • Indonesia ... 131 M10
Batu Pahat • Malaysia 128 C5
Batu Putih, Gunung • Malaysia ... 129 F9
Batukau, Gunung •
  Bali, Indonesia 131 L7
Batumi • Georgia 120 E5
Batur, Danau • Bali, Indonesia ... 131 L7
Batur, Gunung • Bali, Indonesia . 131 L7
Batur Temple • Bali, Indonesia .. 131 L7
Baturaja • Indonesia 131 B4
Batusangkar • Indonesia 131 N10
Baubau • Indonesia 131 F5
Baucau • MN, United States 150 B1
Baud, Cape • NF, Canada 160 D1
Baudry [Château] • France 77 F5
Baudry • Switzerland 90 I5
Bauerfield [Apt] • Vanuatu .... 138 V
Bauld, Cape • NF, Canada 160 D1
Baule-Escoublac, la • France 77 D4
Bauru • Brazil 175 D2
Bausen • Latvia 100 K7
Bavaria • Germany .... 64 [74]
Bávaro • Dominican Rep. 165 H6
Bavella, Col de •
  Corsica, France 78 N12
Bâven • Sweden 99 A2
Baw Sang • Thailand 130 B5
Bawamataluo • Indonesia 131 N11
Bawean • Indonesia 131 R11
Bawiti • Egypt 109 A2
Bay City • MI, United States 150 D2
Bay City • TX, United States 155 F6
Bay Is. • Honduras 170 D2
Bay of Plenty • New Zealand 137 E5
Bay View • New Zealand 137 E5
Bayahibe • Dominican Rep. 165 H6
Bayamo • Cuba 164 H5
Bayamón • Puerto Rico 165 J7
Bayan Lepas • Penang, Malaysia 129 D8
Bayan Lepas [Apt] •
  Penang, Malaysia 129 D8
Bayana • India 123 C2
Bayanhongor • Mongolia 125 E2
Bayano, Lago • Panama 170 H6
Bayburt • Turkey 95 D1
Baydhabo • Somalia 108 C4
Bayerische Alpen • Germany 74 G8
Bayern • Germany 72 D4
Bayeux • France 76 C2
Bayfield • MI, United States 161 A1
Bayfield • NY, United States 161 A4
Bayonne • France 78 I9
Bayramaly • Turkmenistan 121 D4
Bayramic • Turkey 95 E4
Bayreuth • Germany 72 D4
Bayrischer Wald, Nationalpark Park N •
  Germany .... 58 [70]
Bayrischzell Ski • Germany ..... 61 [4]
Baysyaltau • Russian Fed. 101 M4
Baytown • TX, United States 155 F5
Baza • Spain 82 K7
Bazas • France 78 E6
Be'er Sheva • Israel 120 C7
Beachy Head • United Kingdom ... 65 H8
Beachy Head Heritage C • United Kingdom 44 [27]
Béar, Cap • France 78 L10
Bear Creek Ski • MI, United States 146 [77]
Bear I. • Ireland 69 G11
Bear Peninsula • Ireland 69 G11
Bear, Cabo • Portugal 84 K6
Beata, I. • Dominican Rep. 165 F6
Beata, Cabo • Dominican Rep. ... 165 F6
Beatrice • NE, United States 150 A4
Beatty • NV, United States 154 J8
Beaucaire • France 78 F7
Beauceville • QU, Canada 160 H3
Beaufort • France 78 G4
Beaufort Sea • Canada/United States 142 C2
Beaufort West • South Africa 111 F6
Beaugency • France 77 F5
Beaujolais • France 78 I9
Beaulieu-sur-Mer • France 78 F7
Beaulieu • United Kingdom 63 E9
Beaumont • TX, United States 155 F5
Beaune • France 76 F3
Beauregard [Château] • France ... 77 F5
Beauséjour, Fort • NB, Canada ... 160 B2
Beauté, I. de • France 78 N12
Beauty Point • TS, Australia 136 F6

Beauvais • France 78 A1
Beaver • UT, United States 148 D3
Beaver Creek Ski •
  CO, United States .... 146 [60]
Beawar • India 123 E8
Becal • Mexico 169 F5
Becan • Mexico 169 F5
Béchar • Algeria 106 B1
Bechyne • Czech Rep. 89 E7
Becin Kalesi • Turkey 95 F5
Beckem • Germany 72 C3
Beckley • WV, United States 150 D3
Bective Abbey • Ireland 69 E6
Bedarra I. • QL, Australia 136 C3
Bedburg • Germany 73 C6
Bedford • IN, United States 150 C3
Bedford • PA, United States 156 A2
Bedford • United Kingdom 63 E8
Bedfordshire • United Kingdom 64 B5
Bedok • Singapore 129 I11
Bedulu • Bali, Indonesia 131 L8
Beechey I. • NU, Canada 158 G1
Beef I. [Apt] • British Virgin Is. ... 166 A
Beek [Apt] • Netherlands 70 C3
Beekse Bergen • Netherlands 70 C3
Beemster, Droogmakerij de Heritage C •
  Netherlands .... 44 [34]
Beersheba • Israel 120 A4
Beeville • TX, United States 155 E6
Bega • NS, Australia 136 H9
Begur • Spain 83 D3
Beherobie • France 78 I9
Bei'an • China 125 G2
Beijing • China 125 F3
Beijing Heritage C • China ...... 43 [175]
Beilstein • Germany 74 D6
Beira • Mozambique 110 C2
Beira • Portugal 84 I6
Beirut • Lebanon 120 D7
Beitbridge • Zimbabwe 110 C3
Beja • Portugal 80 B4
Béja • Tunisia 107 C4
Beja • NS, Australia 136 H9
Begur • Spain 83 D3
Béjaïa • Algeria 106 C1
Beji Temple • Bali, Indonesia 131 L7
Bekal • India 124 B2
Bekasi • Java, Indonesia 131 O11
Békéscsaba • Hungary 92 C2
Bel Air • Mauritius 113 F6
Bélabo • France 122 A3
Bela • Costa • Portugal 84 G6
Bela, Costa • Portugal 123 G8
Belalanta Park I. • Germany ...... 59 [59]
Belampung • India 124 B2
BELARUS • Europe 100 C3
Belawan • Indonesia 131 N9
Belchatów • Poland 89 B2
Belcher Is. • NU, Canada 159 I3
Beldibi • Turkey 95 G8
Beledweyne • Somalia 108 C4
Belek • Turkey 95 H8
Belém • Brazil 84 F6
Belém • Portugal 84 F6
Belém • NM, United States 155 H7
Belen • NM, United States 155 H7
Bélep, Is. • New Caledonia .... 138 U
Belfast • United Kingdom 63 C6
Belfield • United Kingdom 76 C3
Belford • United Kingdom 62 D5
Belfort • France 76 G3
Belfry, The • United Kingdom 65 F5
Belgaum • India 124 B1
BELGIUM • Europe 70
Belgorod • Russian Fed. 100 E3
Belgrade • Serbia & Montenegro . 92 C2
Belgrano II [Base] • Antarctica ... 176 [10]
Bélice • Sicily, Italy 86 G7
Beliche • Portugal 84 K7
Belisirma • Turkey 95 I9
Belitung • Indonesia 131 C4
BELIZE • C. America 170 C4
Belize City • Belize 170 K9
Belle Cuolia • BC, Canada 160 I7
Bellac • France 77 F6
Bellagio • Italy 87 B1
Bellaire • TX, United States 155 F5
Bellamonte Ski • Italy .... 61 [139]
Bellamonte • Italy 86 C4
Bellary • India 124 B2
Belle Fourche • SD, United States 148 F2
Belle Glade • FL, United States .. 155 D2
Belle Isle • France 77 D4
Belle Isle • NF, Canada 157 B1
Belle Isle, Strait of •
  NF, Canada 160 D1
Belle Mare Beach • Mauritius 113 F5
Belle-Anse • Haiti 165 F6
Belle-Île • France 77 D4
Belleayre Ski • NY, United States 146 [100]
Belleayre • NY, United States 156 C1
Bellegarde-sur-Valserine • France 78 C3
Bellegarde • France 77 F6
Bellegarde Abbey • Cyprus 96 D3
Bellemaine • Barbados .... 167 M
Belleville • TS, Australia 136 F7
Belleville • IL, United States 150 B3
Bellevue • WA, United States 154 G5
Bellevue, Col • Réunion 113 D4
Bellevue, Grotte de • France 78 F6
Bellwaerde Park Park L • Belgium 59 [41]
Bellingham • WA, United States . 154 G5
Bellingshausen [Base] • Antarctica 176 [2]
Bellingshausen Sea • Antarctica . 176 M5
Bellinzona • Switzerland 90 K6
Bellinzona Heritage C • Switzerland 44 [137]
Bellona • Solomon Is. .... 138 W
Belluno • Italy 86 D4
Bellville • South Africa 111 F6
Bellwald • Switzerland 90 J6
Belmont • NS, Australia 136 H8
Belmopan • Belize 170 K9
Belmullet • Ireland 69 B6
Belo • Colombia 173 B2
Belo Horizonte • Brazil 174 E6
Beloeil, Château de • Belgium 70 B4
Beloretsk • Russian Fed. 101 M4
Belorussian • Russian Fed. 100 D1
Belovezhskaya Pushcha Heritage N •
  Belarus .... 41 [69]
Beloye More • Russian Fed. 101 D3
Beloye, Ozero • Russian Fed. 100 E1
Belp [Apt] • Switzerland 90 J5
Belp • Switzerland 90 I5
Beltinci • Slovenia 91 S8
Belukha, Gora • Russian Fed. 101 I5
Belur • India 124 B2
Belvoir • Israel 120 B2
Bemaraha Park L •
  Madagascar .... 112 [56]
Bembibre • Spain 80 C2
Bemidji • MN, United States 150 A1
Ben Gardane • Tunisia 107 D6
Ben Lomond Nat. Park •
  TS, Australia 136 F6
Ben Tre • Vietnam 129 B6
Benago Beach • Grenada .... 166 Q
Benalla • VI, Australia 136 G9
Benalmádena Costa • Spain 82 J8
Benalup • Spain 80 G2
Benares • India 123 G8
Benavente • Spain 80 C2
Benavente • Portugal 84 G6
Bend • OR, United States 154 G6
Bendery • Moldova 92 D2
Bendigo • VI, Australia 136 G9
Bendinat, Castell de •
  Majorca, Spain 83 N12
Benenden Prinsen • St Maarten .. 166 C

Benesov • Severocesky, Czech Rep. 89 E6
Benesov • Stredocesky, Czech Rep. 89 E6
Benevento • Italy 87 H6
Bengal, Bay of • Asia 122 C4
Bengbu • China 125 F3
Benghazi • Libya 108 B1
Bengkulu • Indonesia 131 B4
Bengtsfors • Sweden 99 F5
Benguela • Angola 110 A2
Benguirir • Morocco 107 A2
Beni • Bolivia 173 C4
Beni Abbès • Algeria 107 B3
Benî Hammâd **Heritage C** • Algeria 44 [283]
Beni Hasan • Egypt 109 A2
Beni Suef • Egypt 109 A1
Benidorm • Spain 83 B1
BENIN • Africa 106 C4
Benin, Bight of • Benin/Nigeria 106 C4
Benin City • Nigeria 106 C4
Benissa • Spain 83 B1
Bénitiers, I. aux • Mauritius 113 E6
Benito Juárez [Apt] • Mexico 169 J7
Benito Juárez, Parque Nac. • Mexico 169 K8
Benítses • Corfu, Greece 94 A
Benjamin Constant • Brazil 173 B3
Benjamin Hill • Mexico 168 I5
Benllech **Beach** • United Kingdom 64 [70]
Bennington • VT, United States 156 C1
Benoa Port • Bali, Indonesia 131 L8
Benom • Malaysia 129 G9
Bénoué • Cameroon 106 D4
Bénoué, Parc nat. de la **Park** • Cameroon 112 [34]
Benrath, Schloss • Germany 73 C6
Bensafrim • Portugal 84 H8
Bensberg (Bergisch Gladbach) • Germany 73 D6
Bensheim • Germany 74 D6
Benson • AZ, United States 155 H8
Bent's Old Fort Nat. Hist. Site **Park N** • CO, United States 152 [95]
Benta Sebarang • Malaysia 129 G9
Benton • AR, United States 151 B4
Benton Harbor • MI, United States 150 C2
Bentong • Malaysia 129 G9
Bentota • Sri Lanka 124 C4
Benue • Nigeria 106 D4
Benwee Head • Ireland 69 G8
Benxi • China 125 G2
Benzou • Ceuta 82 D4
Beograd • Serbia & Montenegro 92 C2
Beppu • Japan 127 B4
Beqa • Fiji Is. 138 T
Beqa Lagoon • Fiji Is. 138 T
Bequia • St Vincent & Gren. 167 P
Berach • India 123 E8
Berat • Albania 92 B3
Berbera • Somalia 108 D3
Berbérati • Central Africa Rep. 106 D4
Berchtesgaden • Germany 74 H8
Berchtesgaden, Nationalpark **Park N** • Germany 58 [71]
Berchtesgaden, Nationalpark • Germany 74 H8
Berck • France 76 D1
Berdyans'k • Ukraine 100 E4
Bereeda • Somalia 108 E3
Berenice • Egypt 109 B3
Berenty, Réserve de **Park** • Madagascar 112 [151]
Berg • Germany 74 G7
Berga • Spain 83 C3
Berga • Sweden 99 G6
Bergama • Turkey 95 E5
Bérgamo • Italy 87 B2
Bergen • Norway 98 F8
Bergen **Heritage C** • Norway 44 [1]
Bergen op Zoom • Netherlands 70 B3
Bergerac • France 78 F5
Bergheim • Germany 73 C6
Bergisch Gladbach • Germany 73 D6
Bergischer Dom • Germany 73 D6
Bergkamen • Germany 73 D5
Bergkvara • Sweden 99 H7
Bergnaustadt • Germany 73 D6
Bergshamra • Sweden 99 B1
Bergstrom [Apt] • TX, United States 155 E5
Bergün • Switzerland 90 L5
Bergville • South Africa 111 B4
Bering Land Bridge Nat. Preserve • AK, United States 157 D2
Bering Land Bridge Nat. Preserve **Park N** • AK, United States 152 [2]
Bering Sea • Russian Fed./United States 101 S3
Bering Sea • Russian Fed./United States 142 K10
Bering Strait • Russian Fed./United States 157 D2
Berkakit • Russian Fed. 101 M4
Berkeley • CA, United States 154 I8
Berkner I. • Antarctica 176 N5
Berkshire • United Kingdom 64 B6
Berkshire East • MA, United States 156 C1
Berlin • Germany 73 F7
Berlin **Heritage C** • Germany 44 [47]
Berlin • NH, United States 150 F2
Berlin [Adm] • Germany 73 F7
BERMUDA • Atlantic Ocean 165 K-L
Bermuda Aquarium, Museum & Zoo • Bermuda 165 L9
Bermuda Beach • Bermuda 165 K10
Bermuda I. • Bermuda 165 K10
Bermuda Maritime Museum • Bermuda 165 K9
Bern • Switzerland 90 J5
Bern **Heritage C** • Switzerland 44 [136]
Bern [Adm] • Switzerland 91 Q9
Bernam • Malaysia 129 F9
Bernau bei Berlin • Germany 73 F7
Bernau Hof • Germany 74 B4
Berne • Switzerland 90 J5
Berne **Heritage C** • Switzerland 44 [136]
Berner Alpen • Switzerland 90 J6
Berner Oberland • Switzerland 90 J5
Berneray • United Kingdom 62 B3
Bernina, Passo del • Switzerland 90 L6
Bernina, Piz • Italy/Switzerland 90 L6
Bernkastel-Kues • Germany 74 C6
Berounka • Czech Rep. 89 D6
Berrechid • Morocco 107 A1
Berry • France 77 A1
Berry Is. • Bahamas 164 A1
Bertioga • Brazil 174 E7
Beruas • Malaysia 129 F9
Beruwala • Sri Lanka 124 C4
Berwick-upon-Tweed • United Kingdom 62 D5
Berwickshire • United Kingdom 64 B3
Berwyn, Cadair • United Kingdom 63 D8
Besakih Temple • Bali, Indonesia 131 L7
Besalú • Spain 83 D3
Besançon • France 76 G3
Beskonak • Turkey 95 H7
Bessemer • AL, United States 151 C4
Bestensee • Germany 73 F8
Bet Guvrin • Israel 120 A4
Bet She'an • Israel 120 B2
Bet She'arim • Israel 120 A2
Betalbatim Beach • Goa, India 123 C6
Betancuria • Fuerteventura, Canary Is. 83 H5
Beth Horon • Palestine NAR 120 A3
Beth-zur • Palestine NAR 120 A4
Bethany • MO, United States 150 B2
Bethany • OK, United States 149 G3
Bethany • Palestine NAR 120 B4
Bethany Beach • DE, United States 156 B3
Bethel • AK, United States 157 D3
Bethel • Palestine NAR 120 B3
Bethesda • MD, United States 150 E3
Bethesdaweg • South Africa 111 G6
Bethlehem • PA, United States 156 B2
Bethlehem • Palestine NAR 120 A4
Béthune • France 76 E1
Betia Nat. Park • India 123 G8
Béticos, Sistemas • Spain 80 C5
Betio • Kiribati 139 F
Betong • Malaysia 129 D8
Bettendorf • IA, United States 150 B2
Bettmeralp **Ski** • Switzerland 61 [67]
Bettmeralp • Switzerland 90 J6
Bettna • Sweden 99 A2
Betul • Goa, India 123 C6
Betul Beach • Goa, India 123 C6
Betwa • India 123 F8
Betws-y-Coed • United Kingdom 63 D7
Beuil-les-Launes **Ski** • France 61 [53]
Beuren, Kloster • Germany 74 B4
Beverwijk • Netherlands 70 G7
Bexhill • United Kingdom 65 H8
Bey Daglari • Turkey 95 G8
Beyneu • Kazakstan 121 C2
Beypore • India 124 B3
Beysehir • Turkey 95 H7
Beysehir Gölü • Turkey 95 H7
Bezhetsk • Russian Fed. 100 M9
Béziers • France 76 E5
Bhadohi • India 123 G8
Bhadravati • India 124 B2
Bhagalpur • India 122 C3
Bhaktapur • Nepal 123 G7
Bhamo • Myanmar 128 B2
Bharatpur • India 123 E7
Bharuch • India 122 B3
Bhatpara • India 122 C3
Bhavnagar • India 122 B3
Bheemunipatnam **Beach** • India 124 F6
Bhekuzulu • South Africa 111 B3
Bhijolia • India 123 E8
Bhilai • India 122 C3
Bhilwara • India 123 E8
Bhima • India 122 B4
Bhimavaram • India 124 D1
Bhind • India 123 F8
Bhiwani • India 123 E7
Bhopal • India 122 B3
Bhubaneswar • India 122 C3
Bhuj • India 122 A3
Bhumiphol Reservoir • Thailand 130 B6
Bhusawal • India 122 B3
BHUTAN • Asia 122 D3
Bia Nat. Park **Park** • Ghana 112 [22]
Biabou • St Vincent & Gren. 167 O
Biak • Indonesia 131 I4
Biala Podlaska • Poland 89 C2
Bialowieski Nat. Park **Park N** • Poland 58 [104]
Bialowieza Forest **Heritage N** • Poland 41 [69]
Bialystok • Poland 89 C2
Biaora • India 123 E8
Biarritz • France 78 I9
Biasca • Switzerland 90 K6
Biberach • Germany 74 E7
Bibione • Italy 87 D2
Bicester • United Kingdom 65 F6
Bicheno • TS, Australia 136 F7
Bicholim • Goa, India 123 C5
Bida • Nigeria 106 C4
Biddeford • ME, United States 150 F2
Bideford • United Kingdom 65 J9
Bideford Bay • United Kingdom 65 J9
Bidur • Malaysia 129 F9
Bidwell Mansion State Hist. Park • CA, United States 154 I7
Bié Plateau • Angola 110 A2
Biebrzanski Nat. Park **Park N** • Poland 58 [103]
Biel • Switzerland 90 J5
Bielefeld • Germany 72 C2
Bieler See • Switzerland 90 J5
Biella • Italy 87 A2
Bielsk Podlaski • Poland 89 C2
Bielsko-Biala • Poland 89 F9
Bien Hoa • Vietnam 129 B5
Bierset [Apt] • Belgium 70 C4
Biertan **Heritage C** • Romania 44 [220]
Biervliet • Netherlands 70 B3
Biesbosch, Nat. Park **Park N** • Netherlands 58 [60]
Biesbosch, Nat. Park • Netherlands 70 H8
Biesenthal • Germany 73 F7
Bieszczadzki Nat. Park **Park N** • Poland 58 [105]
Big Ambergris Cay • Turks & Caicos Is. 164 D3
Big Bear Lake • CA, United States 154 J9
Big Bend • Swaziland 111 C3
Big Bend Nat. Park • TX, United States 149 F5
Big Bend Nat. Park **Park N** • TX, United States 152 [135]
Big Boulder **Ski** • PA, United States 146 [93]
Big Boulder • PA, United States 156 B2
Big Cypress **Ind Res** • FL, United States 155 [70]
Big Cypress Nat. Preserve • FL, United States 155 D3
Big Cypress Nat. Preserve **Park N** • FL, United States 153 [219]
Big Cypress Swamp • FL, United States 155 D3
Big Hole Nat. Battlefield **Park N** • MT, United States 152 [67]
Big Mtn **Ski** • MT, United States 146 [41]
Big Pine Key • FL, United States 155 D3
Big Powderhorn Mtn **Ski** • MI, United States 146 [77]
Big Rapids • MI, United States 150 C2
Big Sand Cay • Turks & Caicos Is. 164 D3
Big Sioux • SD, United States 150 A2
Big Sky **Ski** • MT, United States 146 [42]
Big Smoky Valley • NV, United States 154 J8
Big Spring • TX, United States 149 F4
Big Springs • NE, United States 148 F2
Big Sur • CA, United States 154 I8
Big Thicket Nat. Preserve • TX, United States 155 F5
Big Thicket Nat. Preserve **Park N** • TX, United States 153 [141]
Big Timber • MT, United States 148 E1
Big White **Ski** • BC, Canada 146 [6]
Biga • Turkey 95 E4
Bigadic • Turkey 95 F4
Bigbury Bay • United Kingdom 65 J10
Bigbury-on-Sea **Beach** • United Kingdom 64 [42]
Bigej • Marshall Is. 139 E
Biggar • SA, Canada 158 F3
Biggar • United Kingdom 65 B2
Biggin Hill • United Kingdom 65 G7
Bighorn • MT/WY, United States 148 E2
Bighorn Canyon Nat. Recreation Area **Park N** • MT/WY, United States 152 [69]
Bighorn Mtns • WY, United States 148 E2
Bigi • Marshall Is. 139 E
Bigorre • France 78 J9
Biguglia, Etang de • Corsica, France 78 N11
Bihac • Bosnia-Herz. 92 G5
Bihar • India 123 B2
Bihar Sharif • India 122 C3
Bijapur • India 124 B1
Bijawar • India 123 F8
Bijelo Polje • Serbia & Montenegro 92 B3
Bijoutier • Seychelles 113 B2
Bikaner • India 123 D7
Bikin • Russian Fed. 101 N5
Bikini • Marshall Is. 138 BB2
Bila Tserkva • Ukraine 100 D4
Bilaspur • India 122 C3
Bilbao • Spain 80 D2
Bilharamulo • Tanzania 110 G7
Bilin • Myanmar 130 B6
Bill Baggs Cape Florida State Recreation Area • FL, United States 155 D3
Billings • MT, United States 148 E1
Billund • Denmark 99 E7
Biloela • QL, Australia 136 D4
Biloku • Guyana 173 D2
Biloxi • MS, United States 156 F6
Bilthoven • Netherlands 70 H7
Bimini Is. • Bahamas 164 A1
Bina-Etawa • India 123 F8
Binbirkilise • Turkey 95 I9
Bindloe I. • Galápagos Is. 171 H9
Bingen • Germany 74 D6
Bingham Channel • Kiribati 139 F
Binghamton • NY, United States 156 B1
Bingöl • Turkey 95 D2
Biniancolla • Minorca, Spain 83 K8
Binibequer Vell • Minorca, Spain 83 K8
Binissafúller • Minorca, Spain 83 K8
Binjai • Indonesia 131 N9
Bintulu • Sarawak, Malaysia 128 E6
Binzhou • China 125 F3
Biograd na Moru • Croatia 92 F6
Biogradska Gora Nat. Park **Park N** • Serbia & Montenegro 58 [127]
Bioko • Equat. Guinea 106 C4
Bioux, Les • Switzerland 90 I5
Bir Mogreïn • Mauritania 106 A2
Bira Int. Racing Circuit • Thailand 130 E8
Birak • Libya 106 D2
Birao • Central African Rep. 108 B3
Birch I. • BC, Canada 158 E3
Birch Mtns • AL, Canada 158 E3
Birchington **Beach** • United Kingdom 64 [26]
Birchwood • AK, United States 157 E3
Bird I. • Seychelles 113 B1
Bird of Paradise I. • Trinidad & Tobago 166 R
Birdsville • QL, Australia 135 F5
Bireuen • Indonesia 131 M9
Birganj • Nepal 123 G7
Birhet el Bibane • Tunisia 107 D6
Birjand • Iran 120 H7
Birka **Heritage C** • Sweden 44 [7]
Birkeland • Norway 99 E5
Birkenwerder bei Berlin • Germany 73 E7
Birkirkara • Malta 96 B2
Birmingham • AL, United States 151 C4
Birmingham • United Kingdom 65 F5
Birobidzhan • Russian Fed. 101 N5
Birstonas • Lithuania 100 J8
Birzai • Lithuania 100 K7
Birzebbuga • Malta 96 B2
Bisanadi Game Reserve • Kenya 109 D4
Bisau • India 123 E7
Biscarosse • France 78 E6
Biscay, Bay of • Europe 76 B4
Biscayne Nat. Park • FL, United States 155 D3
Biscayne Nat. Park **Park N** • FL, United States 153 [221]
Biserta • Tunisia 50 C4
Bisevo • Croatia 92 F6
Bishkek • Kyrgyzstan 121 F3
Bisho • South Africa 110 B4
Bishop • CA, United States 154 J8
Bishop's Stortford • United Kingdom 65 G7
Biskra • Algeria 106 C1
Biskupiec • Poland 89 C2
Bismarck • ND, United States 148 F1
Bismarck Archipelago • Papua New Guinea 138 BB3
Bismarck Sea • Papua New Guinea 134 C5
Bismo • Norway 98 G7
Bissau • Guinea-Bissau 106 A3
Bistrita • Romania 92 D2
Bitburg • Germany 74 C6
Bithia • Sardinia, Italy 86 F6
Bitola • FYR of Macedonia 92 C3
Bitonto • Italy 85 F4
Bitra I. • India 124 A3
Bitterfontein • South Africa 110 A4
Bitterroot Range • ID/MT, United States 154 H5
Biwa-ko • Japan 127 G6
Biyadoo • Maldives 124 H8
Biysk • Russian Fed. 101 I4
Bizana • South Africa 111 B5
Bizerta • Tunisia 107 D4
Bizerte • Tunisia 107 D4
Bjarehalvön • Sweden 99 G7
Bjelovar • Croatia 92 G5
Bjerringbro • Denmark 99 E7
Bjørkelangen • Norway 98 E5
Björklinge • Sweden 99 B1
Björko • Sweden 99 B1
Björkvik • Sweden 99 A2
Bjørnafjorden • Norway 98 F8
Björneborg • Finland 99 C3
Björnlunda • Sweden 99 A2
Black • Vietnam 128 C2
Black Bay Peninsula • OT, Canada 161 B1
Black Canyon • AZ/NV, United States 155 G7
Black Canyon of the Gunnison Nat. Park **Park N** • CO, United States 152 [89]
Black Country • United Kingdom 65 F5
Black Forest • Germany 74 B4
Black Head • United Kingdom 65 I10
Black I. • United Kingdom 62 C3
Black Lady Mtn • Vietnam 129 B5
Black Mtns • United Kingdom 65 E6
Black River • Jamaica 165 C4
Black Rock Desert • NV, United States 154 J7
Black Sea • Asia/Europe 100 D5
Black Umfolozi • South Africa 111 C3
Blackall • QL, Australia 136 C4
Blackbeard's Grave • Bahamas 164 A2
Blackburn • United Kingdom 63 D7
Blackcomb **Ski** • BC, Canada 146 [2]
Blackdown Hills • United Kingdom 65 J9
Blackfeet **Ind Res** • MT, United States 155 [15]
Blackmount • New Zealand 137 F8
Blackness Castle • United Kingdom 65 B2
Blackpool • United Kingdom 63 D7
Blackpool Pleasure Beach **Park L** • United Kingdom 59 [24]
Blackpool Sands **Beach** • United Kingdom 64 [41]
Blacksod Bay • Ireland 69 G8
Blackstairs Mtns • Ireland 69 C4
Blackstone River Valley Nat. Heritage Corridor • MA, United States 156 D1
Blackwater • Cork, Ireland 69 H11
Blackwater • Neath, Ireland 69 E6
Bladworth • SA, Canada 158 F3
Blaenavon • United Kingdom 65 E6
Blaenavon **Heritage C** • United Kingdom 44 [20]
Blagnac [Apt] • France 78 F6
Blagoevgrad • Bulgaria 92 C3
Blagoveshchensk • Russian Fed. 101 M4
Blaine • WA, United States 154 G5
Blair Athol • QL, Australia 136 C4
Blair Drummond Safari Park • United Kingdom 65 A2
Blairgowrie • United Kingdom 65 B1
Blambangan, Semenanjung • Java, Indonesia 131 R12
Blanc, Cap • Tunisia 107 D4
Blanc, Mont • France/Italy 78 D3
Blanc Sablon • QU, Canada 160 D1
Blanca, Bahía • Argentina 175 B3
Blanca, Costa • Spain 83 A-B
Blanca, I. • Mexico 169 G4
Blanche, Lake • SA, Australia 135 F5
Blanco, Cabo • Costa Rica 170 E6
Blanco, Cape • OR, United States 154 G6
Blandford Forum • United Kingdom 65 K9
Blanes • Spain 83 D4
Blangkerejen • Indonesia 131 M9
Blankaholm • Sweden 99 H6
Blankenberge • Belgium 70 F6
Blankenfelde • Germany 73 F8
Blankenheim • Germany 74 C5
Blantyre • Malawi 110 C2
Blarney • Ireland 69 H11
Blåsjøen • Norway 98 G9
Blatna • Czech Rep. 89 D7
Blatnik Bridge • MI/MN, United States 161 A1
Blaubeuren • Germany 74 E7
Blåvands Huk • Denmark 99 E7
Blavet • France 77 D4
Blaye • France 78 E5
Bled • Slovenia 92 F5
Bledes, Is. • Ibiza, Spain 83 L9
Blefjell • Norway 98 D5
Blekinge • Sweden 99 H7
Blenheim • New Zealand 137 B3
Blenheim Palace • United Kingdom 65 F6
Blenheim Palace **Heritage C** • United Kingdom 44 [29]
Blessington • Ireland 69 E7
Blidö • Sweden 99 B1
Blieskastel • Germany 74 A2
Bligh Sound • New Zealand 137 F7
Bligh Water • Fiji Is. 138 T
Bliss • ID, United States 154 H6
Blitar • Java, Indonesia 131 Q12
Blitta • Togo 106 C4
Blizzard Beach • FL, United States 157 A1
Block I. • RI, United States 156 D2
Bloemfontein • South Africa 110 B3
Blois • France 77 F5
Blois [Château] • France 77 F5
Blönduós • Iceland 97 H6
Blood River • South Africa 111 B3
Bloody Bay • Cayman Is. 165 A1
Bloomington • IL, United States 150 C2
Bloomington • IN, United States 150 C3
Bloomington • MN, United States 150 B2
Bloukrans River Bridge • South Africa 111 F7
Blowing Point • Anguilla 166 B
Blowing Point Beach • Anguilla 166 B
Bludenz • Austria 91 M8
Blue Bay • Mauritius 113 F6
Blue Belt **Dive** • Sudan 109 E9
Blue Caves • Zante, Greece 94 J
Blue Grotto • Malta 96 B2
Blue Hole • Jamaica 165 D3
Blue Lagoon • Malta 96 A1
Blue Mtn **Ski** • OT, Canada 146 [16]
Blue Mtn • PA, United States 156 B2
Blue Mtn Peak • Jamaica 165 D4
Blue Mtns **Heritage N** • Australia 41 [156]
Blue Mtns • Jamaica 165 D4
Blue Mtns • NS, Australia 136 H8
Blue Mtns • OR, United States 154 H6
Blue Nile • Ethiopia/Sudan 108 C3
Blue Ridge • United States 151 D3
Blue Ridge Parkway **Park N** • NC/VA, United States 153 [237]
Blue Stack Mtns • Ireland 69 B2
Blue Water Bridges • Canada/United States 161 C3
Bluebell Railway • United Kingdom 65 G8
Bluefield • WV, United States 150 D3
Bluefields • Jamaica 165 C3
Bluefields • Nicaragua 170 F4
Bluefields Bay • Jamaica 165 C4
Bluff • New Zealand 137 G8
Bluff Point Wreck **Dive** • Egypt 109 E7
Bluff, The • Cayman Is. 165 B1
Blumberg • Germany 73 F7
Blumenau • Brazil 175 D2
Blytheville • AR, United States 151 C3
Bø • Norway 98 D6
Bo • Sierra Leone 106 A4
Bo Hai • China 125 F3
Bo Sai • Ko Phuket, Thailand 130 F9
Boa Vista • Brazil 173 C2
Boa Vista • Cape Verde 106 E7
Boaco • Nicaragua 170 E4
Boaventura • Madeira 84 D5
Boaz I. • Bermuda 165 K10
Bobadilla • Spain 82 I7
Bobbejaanland **Park L** • Belgium 59 [42]
Bobbejaanland • Belgium 70 C3
Bobingen • Germany 74 F7
Böblingen • Germany 74 B3
Bobo-Dioulasso • Burkina 106 B3
Boca Chica • Dominican Rep. 165 H6
Boca del Río • Mexico 169 K7
Boca Grande • FL, United States 155 C2
Boca Onima Caves • Bonaire 166 U
Boca Raton • FL, United States 155 D3
Boca Tabla • Curaçao 166 V
Bocas del Toro • Panama 170 F6
Bochnia • Poland 89 G9
Bocholt • Germany 72 B3
Bochum • Germany 73 D5
Bocognano • Corsica, France 78 N12
Bodafors • Sweden 99 G6
Bodden Bay • Cayman Is. 165 B2
Bodden Town • Cayman Is. 165 B2
Bodegraven • Netherlands 70 H8
Boden • Sweden 97 E2
Bodensee • Germany 74 E8
Bodhgaya • India 123 G8
Bodhgaya **Heritage C** • India 43 [163]
Bodiam Castle • United Kingdom 65 H8
Bodmin • United Kingdom 65 I10
Bodmin Moor • United Kingdom 65 I10
Bodø • Norway 97 C2
Bodrum • Turkey 95 E6
Bodufinolhu • Maldives 124 H8
Boduhithi Coral Isle • Maldives 124 H7
Bœuf, Nez de • Réunion 113 D4
Bogalusa • LA, United States 156 F6
Bogen • Norway 97 D2
Bogense • Denmark 99 F7
Boggeragh Mtns • Ireland 69 H11
Boggy Peak • Antigua & Barbuda 167 I
Bogmalo Beach • Goa, India 123 C5
Bognor Regis • United Kingdom 65 G8
Bogolyubovo • Russian Fed. 100 M10
Bogor • Java, Indonesia 131 O11
Bogotá • Colombia 173 B2
Bogue Forts Museum • China 126 F3
Bogus Basin **Ski** • ID, United States 146 [39]
Bohan • Belgium 70 C5
Bohemia • Czech Rep. 89 D-E
Bohemia, Garden of • Czech Rep. 89 E6
Bohemian Forest • Czech Rep./Germany 72 E4
Bohemian Switzerland • Czech Rep. 89 D6
Bohol • Philippines 128 G5
Boí, Vall de **Heritage C** • Spain 44 [95]
Bois Blanc • Réunion 113 D4
Bois Blanc I. • MI, United States 161 B2
Bois d'Attilly, Parc zoologique du • France 78 B2
Bois Forte **Ind Res** • MN, United States 155 [59]
Boise • ID, United States 154 H6
Boise City • OK, United States 149 F3
Bojnurd • Iran 120 H6
Bojonegoro • Java, Indonesia 131 Q12
Bok Tower Gardens • FL, United States 155 C2
Boknafjorden • Norway 98 F9
Bokspits • Botswana 110 I10
Bol • Chad 106 D3
Bol'shevik, Ostrov • Russian Fed. 101 K2
Bolans • Antigua & Barbuda 167 I
Bole • China 125 C2
Boleslawiek • Poland 89 A3
Bolgatanga • Ghana 106 B3
Bolhrad • Ukraine 100 C4
Bolifushi • Maldives 124 H8
Boliqueime • Portugal 84 J8
Bolívar, Pico • Venezuela 173 B2
BOLIVIA • S. America 173 C4
Bolkesjø • Norway 98 D5
Bollebygd • Sweden 99 G6
Bollens • France 76 F4
Bollnäs • Sweden 97 D3
Bollon • QL, Australia 136 C5
Bolmen • Sweden 99 G6
Bologna • Italy 87 C2
Bologoye • Russian Fed. 100 L9
Bolovens Plateau • Laos 128 D3
Bolsena • Italy 87 E4
Bolsena, Lago di • Italy 87 E4
Bolsward • Netherlands 70 C1
Bolton • United Kingdom 63 D7
Bolu • Turkey 95 B1
Bolzano • Italy 86 C4
Bom Despacho • Brazil 174 E6
Bom Jesus de Lapa • Brazil 174 B4
Bombay • India 122 B4
Bømlafjorden • Norway 98 F9
Bømlo • Norway 98 F9
Bommelerwaard • Netherlands 70 H8
Bon Acceuil • Mauritius 113 F5
Bon, Cap • Tunisia 107 D4
Bon Echo Prov. Park • OT, Canada 160 F4
Bona • Algeria 50 C4
Bonaire • West Indies 166 U
Bonanza • Nicaragua 170 E3
Bonao • Dominican Rep. 165 G5
Bonasse • Trinidad & Tobago 166 S
Bonavista • NF, Canada 160 D1
Bonavista Bay • NF, Canada 160 D1
Bondla Wildlife Sanctuary • Goa, India 123 C5
Bondo • Dem. Rep. of Congo 108 B4
Bondokodi • Indonesia 131 E5
Bondowoso • Java, Indonesia 131 R12
Bong Bridge • MI/MN, United States 161 A1
Bongor • Chad 106 D3
Boni Nat. Reserve • Kenya 109 D5
Bonifacio • Corsica, France 78 N12
Bonifacio, Strait of • France/Italy 85 B4
Bonifica del Volturno • Italy 87 G6
Bonin Is. • Japan 138 AA1
Bonita, Playa • Cuba 164 G5
Bonita Springs • FL, United States 155 C3
Bonn • Germany 74 A1
Bonners Ferry • ID, United States 154 H5
Bonnerup Strand • Denmark 99 F7
Bonneval • France 77 F5
Bonneville • France 90 I6
Bonneville Salt Flats • UT, United States 154 J7
Bonnyville • AL, Canada 158 E3
Bonriki • Kiribati 139 F
Bontebok Nat. Park • South Africa 111 E7
Bontebok Nat. Park **Park** • South Africa 112 [128]
Booby Cay • Cayman Is. 165 A2
Booker T. Washington Nat. Mon. **Park N** • VA, United States 153 [243]
Booligal • NS, Australia 136 G8
Boone • IA, United States 150 B2
Boone • NC, United States 151 D3
Boosaaso • Somalia 108 D3
Boot • United Kingdom 65 C4
Boothia, Gulf of • NU, Canada 158 G1
Boothia Peninsula • NU, Canada 158 G1
Bophut Beach • Ko Samui, Thailand 130 G11
Boppard • Germany 74 D5
Boquerón • Puerto Rico 165 I8
Boquerón, Bahía de • Puerto Rico 165 I8
Boquete • Panama 170 F6
Boquillas del Carmen • Mexico 168 D2
Bor • Czech Rep. 89 D7
Bor • Russian Fed. 101 J3
Bor • Sudan 108 C4
Bor • Turkey 95 J9
Bora Bora • French Polynesia 139 DD4
Borås • Sweden 99 G6
Borca di Cadore • Italy 86 D4
Bordeaux • France 78 E6
Bordeaux Mtn • US Virgin Is. 166 X
Bordeira • Portugal 84 H8
Bordeira • Portugal 84 J8
Borden Peninsula • NU, Canada 159 H1
Bordighera • Italy 87 A3
Boreal **Ski** • CA, United States 146 [29]
Borensberg • Sweden 99 H5
Boréon, le • France 78 H7
Borgå • Finland 99 D4
Børgefjell • Norway 97 C2
Børgefjell Nat. Park **Park N** • Norway 58 [11]
Borger • TX, United States 149 F3
Borgholm • Sweden 99 H6
Borglund stavkirke • Norway 98 G8
Borgne, Le • Haiti 165 F5
Borgo • Corsica, France 78 N11
Borisoglebsk • Russian Fed. 100 F3
Borj Bourguiba • Tunisia 107 D6
Børkop • Denmark 99 E7
Borlänge • Sweden 97 D3
Bormio **Ski** • Italy 61 [129]
Bormio • Italy 87 C1
Borneo • Asia 131 D3
Bornholm [Adm] • Denmark 98 B4
Bornholm [I.] • Denmark 99 H8
Bornholmsgattet • Denmark/Sweden 99 G8
Börnicke • Germany 73 E7
Bornova • Turkey 95 E5
Borobodur **Heritage C** • Indonesia 43 [209]
Borobodur • Java, Indonesia 131 Q12
Borovichi • Russian Fed. 100 L9
Borrowdale • United Kingdom 65 D3
Borujerd • Iran 120 F7
Bosa • Sardinia, Italy 86 E5
Bosanski Dubica • Bosnia-Herz. 92 G5
Bosanski Gradiska • Bosnia-Herz. 92 G5
Bosanski Novi • Bosnia-Herz. 92 G5
Bosanski Petrovac • Bosnia-Herz. 92 G6
Boscastle • United Kingdom 65 I10
Boscobel • NY, United States 156 C2
Boscobel House • United Kingdom 65 E5
Boscobelle • Barbados 167 M
Boscomp • Surinam 174 A2
Bose • China 125 E4
Boskoop • Netherlands 70 G8
Bosna • Bosnia-Herz. 92 G5
BOSNIA-HERZEGOVINA • Europe 92 B2
Boso-hanto • Japan 127 I9
Bosporus • Turkey 95 F3
Bosra **Heritage C** • Syria 44 [303]
Bossangoa • Central African Rep. 108 A4
Bossier City • LA, United States 156 E5
Bosten Hu • China 126 B1
Boston • MA, United States 156 D1
Boston • United Kingdom 63 E8
Boston African American Nat. Hist. Site **Park N** • MA, United States 153 [289]
Boston Harbor Is. Nat. Recreation Area **Park N** • MA, United States 153 [289]
Boston Mills **Ski** • OH, United States 146 [86]
Boston Nat. Hist. Park **Park N** • MA, United States 153 [289]
Boswachterij Wassenaar • Netherlands 70 G7
Bosworth Field • United Kingdom 65 F5
Botany Bay • NS, Australia 136 H8
Boteti • Botswana 110 I9
Bothnia, Gulf of • Finland/Sweden 97 E3
Bothwell • TS, Australia 136 F7
Bothwell Castle • United Kingdom 65 A2
Botlek • Netherlands 70 G8
Botosani • Romania 92 D2
BOTSWANA • Africa 110 I-J
Bottle Creek • Turks & Caicos Is. 164 C3
Bottrop • Germany 73 C5
Botwood • NF, Canada 160 C1
Bötzow • Germany 73 E7
Bou Grara, Golfe de • Tunisia 107 D6
Bouaké • Côte d'Ivoire 106 B4
Bouar • Central African Rep. 108 A4
Bouârfa • Morocco 107 B2
Bouba Ndjida, Parc nat. de **Park** • Cameroon 112 [35]
Bouches-du-Rhône • France 78 G8
Bouchet, le [Château] • France 77 F6
Boudeuse • Seychelles 113 B1
Boudewijnpark **Park L** • Belgium 59 [41]
Boudewijnpark • Belgium 70 F6
Bougainville I. • Papua New Guinea 138 BB3
Bouillon • Belgium 70 C5
Boulanger, I. le • St Barthélemy 166 D
Boulder • CO, United States 148 E2
Boulder • WA, Australia 135 C6
Boulia • QL, Australia 135 F4
Boulogne-sur-Mer • France 76 D1
Bouma • Fiji Is. 138 S
Boumois [Château] • France 77 E5
Bountiful • UT, United States 148 D2
Bounty Bay • Pitcairn Is. 139 L
Bourail • New Caledonia 138 U
Bourdeilles • France 78 F5
Bourg • France 76 K9
Bourg-en-Bresse • France 78 C3
Bourg-St Maurice • France 78 D3
Bourges • France 76 E3
Bourges **Heritage C** • France 44 [79]
Bourget, le [Apt] • France 78 B1
Bourgogne • France 77 B1
Bourgueil • France 76 K8
Bourke • NS, Australia 135 H6
Bournemouth • United Kingdom 65 K9
Bournemouth **Beach** • United Kingdom 64 [33]
Bourscheid • Luxembourg 70 D5
Bourtange • Netherlands 70 D1
Bourton-on-the-Water • United Kingdom 65 F6
Boussay [Château] • France 77 F6
Bouvines • France 50 B2
Bovallstrand • Sweden 99 F5
Bovec • Slovenia 92 F5
Boven • St Eustatius 167 E
Boven Bolivia • Bonaire 166 U
Boven Prinsen • St Maarten 166 C
Bovey Tracey • United Kingdom 65 J10
Bow • AL, Canada 158 E4
Bowen • QL, Australia 136 C3
Bowie • TX, United States 155 E4
Bowling Green • KY, United States 151 C3
Bowness-on-Windermere • United Kingdom 65 D4
Bowral • NS, Australia 136 H8
Bowron Lake Prov. Park • BC, Canada 160 I6
Boxholm • Sweden 99 H5
Boyabat • Turkey 95 B1
Boyana **Heritage C** • Bulgaria 44 [224]
Boyle • Ireland 69 H8
Boyne • Ireland 69 E6
Boyne Highlands **Ski** • MI, United States 146 [78]
Boyne Mtn **Ski** • MI, United States 146 [78]
Boynton Beach • FL, United States 155 D3
Bozcaada • Turkey 95 E4
Bozeman • MT, United States 148 D1
Bozen • Italy 86 C4
Bozkir • Turkey 95 I9
Bozova • Turkey 95 G7
Bozüyük • Turkey 95 B2
Bozyazi • Turkey 95 I10
Brabant Wallon • Belgium 70 C4
Brac • Croatia 92 G6
Bracalândia **Park L** • Portugal 59 [76]
Bracciano • Italy 87 E4
Bracciano, Lago di • Italy 87 E4
Bracelona • Venezuela 173 C1
Brackenheim • Germany 74 B3
Bracknell • United Kingdom 63 E9
Bradenton • FL, United States 155 C2
Bradford • OT, Canada 160 E4
Bradford • PA, United States 156 A1
Bradford • United Kingdom 63 E7
Bradley [Apt] • CT, United States 156 C2
Braemar • United Kingdom 62 D3
Braga • Portugal 80 A3
Braga [Adm] • Portugal 84 A1
Bragado • Argentina 175 F6
Bragança • Brazil 174 B3
Bragança • Portugal 80 B3
Bragança [Adm] • Portugal 84 A1
Bragança Paulista • Brazil 174 E7
Brahmapur • India 122 C4
Brahmaputra • Bangladesh/India 122 D3
Braila • Romania 92 I7
Brainerd • MN, United States 150 B1
Braintree • United Kingdom 65 H7
Braithwaite • United Kingdom 65 C3
Braj • India 123 E7
Brålanda • Sweden 99 G5
Bramadero, Bahía • Puerto Rico 165 I8
Bramming • Denmark 99 E7
Brampton • OT, Canada 160 E5
Brampton I. • QL, Australia 136 C4
Branco • Brazil 173 C2
Brand • Austria 91 M8
Brandaris • Bonaire 166 U
Brandbu • Norway 98 E5
Brande • Denmark 99 E7
Brandenburg • Germany 72 E2
Brandenburg [Adm] • Germany 72 E2
Brandenburger Tor • Germany 73 F7
Brandon • MN, Canada 158 G4
Brandon Mtn • Ireland 69 G10
Brands Hatch • United Kingdom 65 G7
Brandval • Norway 98 E5
Brandywine **Ski** • OH, United States 146 [86]
Brandywine Battlefield State Hist. Park • PA, United States 156 B3
Branesti • Romania 92 H7
Branféré, Parc zoologique de • France 77 D4
Brani • Singapore 129 I12
Braniewo • Poland 89 B1
Bransby Point • Montserrat 167 G
Branson • MO, United States 151 B3
Brantas • Java, Indonesia 131 R12
Brantford • OT, Canada 160 E5
Brantôme • France 78 F5
Bras d'Or Lake • NS, Canada 160 C2
Bras-Panon • Réunion 113 D3
Brasileia • Brazil 173 C4
Brasília • Brazil 174 B4
Brasília **Heritage C** • Brazil 42 [69]
Braslaw • Belarus 100 K7
Brasov • Romania 92 D2
Brassus, Le • Switzerland 90 I5
Brastagi • Indonesia 131 N9
Bratan, Danau • Bali, Indonesia 131 L7
Bratislava • Slovak Rep. 89 B4
Bratsk • Russian Fed. 101 K4
Brattleboro • VT, United States 156 C1
Brattvåg • Norway 98 G7
Braubach • Germany 74 D5
Braunau am Inn • Austria 91 F1
Braunfels • Germany 74 D5
Braunschweig • Germany 72 D2
Braunwald • Switzerland 90 K5
Brauweiler • Germany 73 C6
Brava • Cape Verde 106 E7
Brava, Costa • Spain 83 C-D
Brawley • CA, United States 149 C4
Bray • Ireland 69 F7
Bray Head • Ireland 69 F7
BRAZIL • S. America 171 D3
Brazilian Highlands • Brazil 171 E4
Brazos • TX, United States 149 G4
Brazzaville • Congo 106 D5
Breadalbane • United Kingdom 65 A1
Breakers • Cayman Is. 165 B2
Breaksea Sound • New Zealand 137 F8
Brebes • Java, Indonesia 131 P11
Breckenridge **Ski** • CO, United States 146 [58]
Breckerfeld • Germany 73 D6
Breclav • Czech Rep. 89 B4
Brecon Beacons Nat. Park **Park N** • United Kingdom 58 [55]
Brecon Beacons Nat. Park • United Kingdom 63 D9

Breconshire • United Kingdom 64 A5
Breda • Netherlands 70 C3
Bredasdorp • South Africa 111 E7
Bredebro • Denmark 99 E8
Bredene-aan-Zee • Belgium 70 E6
Bree • Belgium 70 C3
Breede • South Africa 111 E7
Bregenz • Austria 91 M7
Bréhat, I. • France 77 D3
Breheimen • Norway 98 G7
Breidhafjördhur • Iceland 97 H6
Breimsvatnet • Norway 98 F7
Breisach • Germany 74 A4
Breitachklamm • Germany 74 F8
Breitenfeld • Germany 50 C2
Brejeira, Serra da • Portugal 84 I7
Brekke • Norway 98 F8
Bremangerlandet • Norway 98 F7
Bremen • Germany 72 C2
Bremen [Adm] • Germany 72 C2
Bremerhaven • Germany 72 C2
Bremerton • WA, United States 154 G5
Bremervörde • Germany 72 C2
Bremnes • Norway 98 F9
Brendon Hills • United Kingdom 65 J9
Brenham • TX, United States 155 E5
Brenner Pass • Austria/Italy 91 O8
Brenta • Italy 87 C1
Brenta [Riv] • Italy 86 C4
Brentwood • United Kingdom 65 G7
Bréscia • Italy 87 B2
Breskens • Netherlands 70 B3
Breslau • Poland 50 D2
Bressanone • Italy 86 C3
Bresse-Hohneck, la **Ski** • France 61 [6]
Bressuire • France 77 E6
Brest • Belarus 100 B3
Brest • France 77 C3
Bretagne • France 77 A1
Bretagne, Point de • Réunion 113 C4
Breton Sound • LA, United States 156 F6
Bretonne Corniche • France 77 C3
Bretton Woods **Ski** • NH, United States 146 [115]
Breueh • Indonesia 131 M9
Breuil-Cervínia **Ski** • Italy 61 [123]
Breuil-Cervínia • Italy 87 A1
Brewster • WA, United States 148 C1
Brian Head **Ski** • UT, United States 146 [52]
Briançon **Ski** • France 61 [45]
Briançon • France 78 D4
Bribie I. • QL, Australia 136 D5
Bribri • Costa Rica 170 F6
Briceni • Moldova 92 D1
Brices Cross Roads Nat. Battlefield Site **Park N** • MS, United States 153 [199]
Bridge of Orchy • United Kingdom 65 A1
Bridgend • United Kingdom 63 D9
Bridgeport • CT, United States 156 C2
Bridgeton • NJ, United States 156 B3
Bridgetown • Barbados 167 M
Bridgewater • NS, Canada 160 B2
Bridgnorth • United Kingdom 65 E5
Bridgwater • United Kingdom 65 K9
Bridgwater Bay • United Kingdom 65 J9
Bridlington • United Kingdom 63 E6
Bridlington **Beach** • United Kingdom 64 [9]
Bridport • TS, Australia 136 F6
Bridport • United Kingdom 65 K9
Brie • France 78 B2
Brielle • Netherlands 70 G8
Brienzer See • Switzerland 90 J5
Brieselang • Germany 73 E7
Brievengat • Curaçao 166 V
Brig • Switzerland 90 J6
Brigham City • UT, United States 148 D2
Brighouse • United Kingdom 63 E7
Brighton **Ind Res** • FL, United States 155 [69]
Brighton • United Kingdom 65 G8
Brignoles • France 78 G8
Brijuni Nat. Park • Croatia 92 F5
Brilon • Germany 72 C3
Brimstone Hill Fortress • St Kitts & Nevis 167 F
Brimstone Hill Fortress Nat. Park **Heritage C** • St Kitts & Nevis 42 [46]
Bríndisi • Italy 85 F4
Brisbane • QL, Australia 136 D5
Brissac [Château] • France 77 E5
Brissago • Switzerland 90 K6
Bristol • PA, United States 156 B2
Bristol • RI, United States 156 D2
Bristol • TN/VA, United States 151 D3
Bristol • United Kingdom 65 K9
Bristol Bay • AK, United States 157 D4
Bristol Channel • United Kingdom 65 J9
Bristol Mtn **Ski** • NY, United States 146 [97]
Bristol Mtn • NY, United States 156 A1
British Columbia • Canada 158 D3
British Isles • Europe 48 C2
BRITISH VIRGIN IS. • West Indies 166 A
Brittany • France 77 C-D
Brittas Bay • Ireland 69 F7
Brive-la-Gaillarde • France 78 F5
Brixen • Italy 86 C3
Brixham • United Kingdom 65 J10
Brixham **Beach** • United Kingdom 64 [40]
Brize Norton [Apt] • United Kingdom 65 F6
Brnik [Apt] • Slovenia 92 F5
Brno • Czech Rep. 89 B4
Brno **Heritage C** • Czech Rep. 44 [195]
Broad Law • United Kingdom 62 D5
Broad Sound • QL, Australia 136 C4
Broadsands **Beach** • United Kingdom 64 [40]
Broadstairs • United Kingdom 65 H7
Broadway • United Kingdom 65 F6
Broby • Sweden 99 G7
Brochet • MN, Canada 158 F3
Brockhole Visitor Centre • United Kingdom 65 D4
Brockton • MA, United States 156 D1
Brockville • OT, Canada 160 G4
Brodeur Peninsula • NU, Canada 159 H1
Brodick • United Kingdom 62 C5
Brodie • MA, United States 156 C1
Broek in Waterland • Netherlands 70 H7
Broek op Langedijk • Netherlands 70 C2
Broich, Schloss • Germany 73 C5
Broken Arrow • OK, United States 151 A3
Broken Hill • NS, Australia 135 G6
Brokopondo • Surinam 174 A2
Bromley Mtn • VT, United States 156 C1
Bromma [Apt] • Sweden 99 B2
Bromo, Gunung • Java, Indonesia 131 R12
Bromolla • Sweden 99 G7
Bromont **Ski** • QU, Canada 146 [18]
Brønderslev • Denmark 99 F6
Bronx • NY, United States 156 C2
Brookhaven • MS, United States 156 F5
Brooklyn • NY, United States 156 C2
Brooks • AL, Canada 158 E3
Brooks Range • AK, United States 157 E2
Broome • WA, Australia 135 C3
Brothers Is. **Dive** • Egypt 109 E8
Brouage • France 78 E5
Brougham Castle • United Kingdom 65 D3
Broughton in Furness • United Kingdom 65 C4
Broughty Ferry • United Kingdom 65 B1
Brovst • Denmark 99 E6
Brown v. Board of Education Nat. Hist. Site **Park N** • KS, United States 153 [170]
Browning • MT, United States 148 D1
Brownsea I. • United Kingdom 65 K9
Brownsville • TX, United States 149 G5
Brownwood • TX, United States 155 E5
Brú Na Bóinne • Ireland 69 F6
Brú Na Bóinne **Heritage C** • Ireland 44 [15]
Bruce Peninsula Nat. Park **Park N** • OT, Canada 161 [26]
Bruce Peninsula Nat. Park • OT, Canada 161 C2
Bruchsal • Germany 74 B3
Bruck an der Mur • Austria 91 G2
Bruckmühl • Germany 74 G7
Bruges • Belgium 70 F6
Bruges **Heritage C** • Belgium 44 [38]
Brugge • Belgium 70 F6
Brugge **Heritage C** • Belgium 44 [38]
Brühl • Germany 74 A1
Brühl **Heritage C** • Germany 44 [56]
Brûlé, le • Réunion 113 C3
Bruneck • Italy 86 D3
BRUNEI • Asia 128 E6
Brunico • Italy 86 D3
Brunnen • Switzerland 90 K5
Brunsbüttel • Germany 72 C2
Brunswick • GA, United States 155 C1
Brunswick • Germany 50 C2
Brunswick • ME, United States 150 F2
Bruny I. • TS, Australia 136 F7
Brusa • Turkey 50 E4
Brush • CO, United States 148 F2
Bruson • Switzerland 90 J6
Brussel • Belgium 70 B4
Brussel **Heritage C** • Belgium 44 [42]
Brussels • Belgium 70 B4
Brussels **Heritage C** • Belgium 44 [42]
Bruxelles • Belgium 70 B4
Bruxelles **Heritage C** • Belgium 44 [42]
Bryan • TX, United States 151 A4
Bryansk • Russian Fed. 100 D3
Bryce Canyon Nat. Park **Park N** • UT, United States 152 [79]
Bryrup • Denmark 99 E7
Brzeg • Poland 89 B3
Bua • Fiji Is. 138 S
Bua • Sweden 99 F6
Bua Chum • Thailand 128 C3
Bua Yai • Thailand 128 C3
Buada Lagoon • Nauru 138 X
Buala • Solomon Is. 138 W
Buariki • Kiribati 139 F
Buca • Fiji Is. 138 S
Buca • Turkey 95 E5
Bucak • Turkey 95 G7
Bucaramanga • Colombia 173 B2
Buccoo • Trinidad & Tobago 166 R
Buccoo Reef • Trinidad & Tobago 166 R
Buch (Berlin) • Germany 73 F7
Buchanan • Liberia 106 B4
Bucharest • Romania 92 H7
Buchloe • Germany 74 F7
Buchow (Berlin) • Germany 73 F8
Buck Hill **Ski** • MN, United States 146 [70]
Buck I. • US Virgin Is. 166 X
Buck I. Reef Nat. Mon. • US Virgin Is. 166 X
Buckeye • AZ, United States 155 G8
Buckfastleigh • United Kingdom 65 J10
Buckinghamshire • United Kingdom 64 B5
Buckland Abbey • United Kingdom 65 J10
Buckland Tableland • QL, Australia 136 C4
Bucovice • Czech Rep. 89 B4
Bucuresti • Romania 92 H7
Buda • Hungary 50 D3
Buda, I. de • Spain 80 F3
Budapest • Hungary 92 B2
Budapest **Heritage C** • Hungary 44 [205]
Budaun • India 123 F7
Bude • United Kingdom 65 I9
Bude Bay • United Kingdom 65 I9
Budennovsk • Russian Fed. 100 F5
Budhardalur • Iceland 97 H6
Büdingen • Germany 74 B1
Budleigh Salterton • United Kingdom 65 J10
Buena Vista • CO, United States 148 E3
Buena Vista • Panama 170 M10
Buenaventura • Colombia 173 B2
Buenaventura • Mexico 168 I5
Buenos Aires • Argentina 175 F6
Buenos Aires • Panama 170 M11
Buer (Gelsenkirchen) • Germany 73 D5
Buff Bay • Jamaica 165 D3
Buffalo • NY, United States 161 D1
Buffalo • SD, United States 148 F1
Buffalo • TX, United States 155 F5
Buffalo • WY, United States 148 E2
Buffalo Narrows • SA, Canada 158 F3
Buffalo Springs Nat. Reserve • Kenya 109 D4
Buffavento Castle • Cyprus 96 D3
Buffels • South Africa 111 B3
Buffels Bay • South Africa 111 F7
Buftea • Romania 92 H7
Bug • Poland/Ukraine 89 C2
Buga • Colombia 173 B2
Bugia • Algeria 50 B4
Bugibba • Malta 96 B1
Bugojno • Bosnia-Herz. 92 G6
Bui Nat. Park **Park** • Ghana 112 [19]
Builth Wells • United Kingdom 63 D8
Bujanovac • Serbia & Montenegro 92 C3
Bujumbura • Burundi 108 B5
Bukavu • Dem. Rep. of Congo 108 B5
Bukhara • Uzbekistan 121 D4
Bukhara **Heritage C** • Uzbekistan 43 [141]
Bukhoro • Uzbekistan 121 D4
Bukhoro **Heritage C** • Uzbekistan 43 [141]
Bukit Ferringhi • Penang, Malaysia 129 D7
Bukit Gemuruh Forest Reserve • Penang, Malaysia 129 D8
Bukit Genting Forest Reserve • Penang, Malaysia 129 D8
Bukit Juru Forest Reserve • Penang, Malaysia 129 E8
Bukit Kerajaan Forest Reserve • Penang, Malaysia 129 D7
Bukit Pulau • Penang, Malaysia 129 D8
Bukit Relau Forest Reserve • Penang, Malaysia 129 D8
Bukit Tengah • Penang, Malaysia 129 E8
Bukit Timah Nature Reserve • Singapore 129 H11
Bukittinggi • Indonesia 131 N10
Bukk Nat. Park **Park N** • Hungary 58 [114]
Bukoba • Tanzania 110 G7
Bukum • Singapore 129 H12
Bulan • Philippines 128 G4
Bulandshahr • India 123 F7
Bulawayo • Zimbabwe 110 B3
Buldan • Turkey 95 F5
Bulgan • Mongolia 125 E2
BULGARIA • Europe 92 D3
Bulguksa Temple **Heritage C** • Rep. of Korea 43 [192]
Bulla Regia • Tunisia 107 C4
Bullenbaai • Curaçao 166 V
Bullhead City • AZ, United States 149 D3
Bulukumba • Indonesia 131 F5
Bumba • Dem. Rep. of Congo 108 B4
Bunbury • WA, Australia 135 B6
Bundaberg • QL, Australia 136 D4
Bundelkhand Riva • India 123 F8
Bundi • India 123 E8
Bundoran • Ireland 69 H8
Bungle Bungle • WA, Australia 135 D3
Bungo-suido • Japan 127 B4
Bunratty Castle • Ireland 69 H10
Bünyan • Turkey 95 C2
Buon Me Thuot • Vietnam 129 C5
Bûr Sa'id • Egypt 109 B1
Bûr Safâga • Egypt 109 B2
Bur Sudan • Sudan 108 C3
Bura • Kenya 109 D5
Burao • Somalia 108 C4
Buraydah • Saudi Arabia 120 E8
Burdekin • QL, Australia 136 C3
Burdur • Turkey 95 G7
Burdur [Adm] • Turkey 95 G7
Burdur Gölü • Turkey 95 G7
Burg, Schloss • Germany 73 D6
Burgas • Bulgaria 92 H8
Burgau • Germany 74 F7
Burgau • Portugal 84 H8
Burgdorf • Switzerland 90 J5
Burgenland • Austria 91 T11
Burgeo • NF, Canada 160 C1
Burghausen • Germany 74 H7
Burgkirchen • Germany 74 H7
Burgos • Spain 80 D2
Burgos **Heritage C** • Spain 44 [105]
Burgundy • France 77 B1
Burhaniye • Turkey 95 E4
Burica, Punta • Panama 170 F6
Burin Peninsula • NF, Canada 160 D1
Buriram • Thailand 128 C4
BURKINA • Africa 106 B3
Burlington • CO, United States 148 F3
Burlington • IA, United States 150 B2
Burlington • NJ, United States 156 B2
Burlington • OT, Canada 160 E5
Burlington • VT, United States 150 F2
BURMA • Asia 128 B2
Burnham-on-Sea • United Kingdom 65 K9
Burnie • TS, Australia 136 E6
Burnley • United Kingdom 63 D7
Burns • OR, United States 154 H6
Burns Lake • BC, Canada 160 I6
Burntisland **Beach** • United Kingdom 64 [3]
Burren, The • Ireland 69 H9
Burrow Head • United Kingdom 63 C6
Bursa • Turkey 95 F4
Bursa [Adm] • Turkey 95 F4
Burscheid • Germany 73 D6
Bürserberg • Austria 91 M8
Burton upon Trent • United Kingdom 63 E8
Buru • Indonesia 131 G4
BURUNDI • Africa 108 C5
Burwick • United Kingdom 66 C2
Bury • United Kingdom 63 D7
Bury St Edmunds • United Kingdom 63 F8
Buryatia **Russ Adm** • Russian Fed. 101 [27]
Busan • Rep. of Korea 125 G3
Busch Gardens Tampa Bay • FL, United States 155 C2
Busch Gardens Tampa Bay **Park L** • FL, United States 157 [25]
Busch Gardens the Old Country • VA, United States 156 B4
Busch Gardens the Old Country **Park L** • VA, United States 157 [27]
Bushkill • PA, United States 156 B2
Busing • Singapore 129 H12
Buskerud • Norway 98 A3
Busko-Zdrój • Poland 89 G8
Bussana • Italy 87 A3
Busselton • WA, Australia 135 B6
Bussum • Netherlands 70 H7
Busto Arsízio • Italy 87 B2
Buta • Dem. Rep. of Congo 108 B4
Bute • United Kingdom 62 C5
Buteshire • United Kingdom 64 A3
Buthrotum • Albania 94 A
Buthrotum **Heritage C** • Albania 44 [217]
Butler, Lake • FL, United States 157 A1
Buton • Indonesia 131 F4
Butrint • Albania 94 A
Butrint **Heritage C** • Albania 44 [217]
Butte • MT, United States 148 D1
Butterfly Valley • Páros, Greece 94 H
Butterfly Valley • Rhodes, Greece 94 F
Buttermere • United Kingdom 65 C3
Buttermere [Lake] • United Kingdom 65 C3
Butternut Basin **Ski** • MA, United States 146 [103]
Butternut Basin • MA, United States 156 C1
Butterworth • Penang, Malaysia 129 E7
Buttevant • Ireland 69 H10
Butuan • Philippines 128 H5
Butzbach • Germany 74 D5
Buur Gaabo • Somalia 108 D4
Buxar • India 123 G8
Buyan, Danau • Bali, Indonesia 131 L7
Buynaksk • Russian Fed. 100 G5
Büyükmenderes • Turkey 95 F5
Buzau • Romania 92 H7
Buzau [Riv] • Romania 92 H7
Buzet • France 76 K9
Búzios • Brazil 174 F7
Bwindi Impenetrable Forest Nat. Park **Park** • Uganda 112 [65]
Bwindi Impenetrable Forest Nat. Park **Heritage N** • Uganda 41 [106]
Byala • Bulgaria 92 I8
Byblos **Heritage C** • Lebanon 44 [306]
Bydgoszcz • Poland 89 B2
Bygdin • Norway 98 G8
Bygland • Norway 98 G9
Byglandsfjord • Norway 99 E5
Bykle • Norway 98 G9
Bykovo [Apt] • Russian Fed. 100 M10
Bylot I. • NU, Canada 159 I1
Byodo-in • Japan 127 G6
Byramgore Reef • India 124 A2
Byrkjelo • Norway 98 G7
Byrock • NS, Australia 135 H6
Byron, Cape • NS, Australia 136 D5
Bytca • Slovak Rep. 89 F9
Bytom • Poland 89 F8
Bytow • Poland 89 B1
Byxelkrok • Sweden 99 H6

C

Ca Mau • Vietnam 129 B6
Ca Mau, Mui • Vietnam 129 B6
Caballas • Peru 173 E7
Caballo Reservoir • NM, United States 155 H8
Cabana • Peru 173 E6
Cabanas • Portugal 84 K8
Cabanatuan • Philippines 128 G3
Cabarete • Dominican Rep. 165 G5
Caberfae Peaks **Ski** • MI, United States 146 [81]
Cabinda • Angola 106 D5
Cabinet Mtns • MT, United States 154 H5
Cable Beach • Bahamas 164 A2
Cabo de Rama Fort • Goa, India 123 C6
Cabo Negro • Morocco 107 B1
Cabo San Lucas • Mexico 168 I6
Cabo San Lucas [Cape] • Mexico 168 I6
Caborca • Mexico 168 H5
Cabot Strait • NF/NS, Canada 160 C1
Cabral • Dominican Rep. 165 G6
Cabrera, I. de • Spain 83 O12
Cabrillo Nat. Mon. **Park N** • CA, United States 152 [55]
Cabritos, I. • Dominican Rep. 165 F6
Cabrits Nat. Park • Dominica 167 K
Cabrón, Cabo • Dominican Rep. 165 H5
Cacahuamilpa • Mexico 169 J7
Cacak • Serbia & Montenegro 92 C3
Cacém • Portugal 84 F6
Cáceres • Brazil 174 A4
Cáceres • Spain 80 B4
Cáceres **Heritage C** • Spain 44 [120]
Cachoeiro de Itapemirim • Brazil 174 F6
Cachopo • Portugal 84 J7
Cacoctin Mtn Park • MD, United States 156 A3
Cacocúm • Cuba 164 H5
Caconda • Angola 110 A2
Cadaqués • Spain 83 D3
Cadca • Slovak Rep. 89 F9
Cadenábbia • Italy 87 B1
Cades Reef • Antigua & Barbuda 167 I
Cadillac • MI, United States 150 C2
Cadillac • SA, Canada 158 F4
Cadiz • Philippines 128 G4
Cádiz • Spain 82 H8
Cádiz, Bahía de • Spain 82 H8
Cádiz, Golfo de • Spain 80 B5
Cadore • Italy 86 D3
Cadouin • France 78 F6
Caen • France 76 C2
Caernarfon • United Kingdom 63 C7
Caernarfon Bay • United Kingdom 63 C7
Caernarfonshire • United Kingdom 64 A4
Caesarea • Israel 120 A2
Caesarea Philippi • Syria 120 B1
Cafres, Plaine des • Réunion 113 D4
Cagayan de Oro • Philippines 128 G5
Cágliari • Sardinia, Italy 86 F6
Cágliari, Golfo di • Sardinia, Italy 86 F6
Cagnes-sur-Mer • France 78 H8
Caguas • Puerto Rico 165 J8
Caherciveen • Ireland 69 G11
Caherdaniel • Ireland 69 G11
Cahokia Mounds State Hist. Site **Heritage C** • IL, United States 42 [9]
Cahora Bassa, Lago de • Mozambique 110 C2
Cahors • France 78 F6
Caibarién • Cuba 164 G4
Caicos Bank • Turks & Caicos Is. 164 C3
Caicos Passage • West Indies 164 C3
Caille I. • Grenada 167 P
Caimancita • Venezuela 166 T
Caimanera • Cuba 164 H5
Caimito, Playa del • Cuba 164 F4
Cairngorm Mtns • United Kingdom 62 D3
Cairngorms Nat. Park **Park N** • United Kingdom 58 [46]
Cairngorms Nat. Park • United Kingdom 62 D3
Cairnryan • United Kingdom 62 C6
Cairns • QL, Australia 136 C3
Cairo • Egypt 109 A1
Cairo **Heritage C** • Egypt 44 [299]
Caithness • United Kingdom 64 A1
Cajamarca • Peru 173 B3
Cajones, Cayos • Honduras 166 BB3
Cajun Country • LA, United States 156 E6
Çakirlar • Turkey 95 G8
Cakovec • Croatia 92 G5
Cal • Turkey 95 F5
Cala Antena • Majorca, Spain 83 O12
Cala Bassa • Ibiza, Spain 83 L9
Cala Blanca • Minorca, Spain 83 J7
Cala Blanes • Minorca, Spain 83 J7
Cala Blava • Majorca, Spain 83 N12
Cala Bona • Majorca, Spain 83 O11
Cala Conta • Ibiza, Spain 83 L9
Cala d'Or • Majorca, Spain 83 O12
Cala de Sant Vicenç • Ibiza, Spain 83 M9
Cala de Sant Vicenç • Majorca, Spain 83 O11
Cala de Santandria • Minorca, Spain 83 J7
Cala Egos • Majorca, Spain 83 N12
Cala Egos • Majorca, Spain 83 O12
Cala En Bosc • Minorca, Spain 83 J8
Cala En Porter • Minorca, Spain 83 K8
Cala Estany • Majorca, Spain 83 O11
Cala Figuera • Majorca, Spain 83 O12
Cala Figuera, Cap de • Majorca, Spain 83 N12
Cala Forcat • Minorca, Spain 83 J7
Cala Fornells • Majorca, Spain 83 N12
Cala Gració • Ibiza, Spain 83 L9
Cala Liberotto • Sardinia, Italy 86 F5
Cala Llenya • Ibiza, Spain 83 M9
Cala Llombarts • Majorca, Spain 83 O12
Cala Llonga • Ibiza, Spain 83 M9
Cala Llonga • Majorca, Spain 83 O12
Cala Llonga • Minorca, Spain 83 K8
Cala Major • Majorca, Spain 83 N12
Cala Marçal • Majorca, Spain 83 O12
Cala Millor • Majorca, Spain 83 O11
Cala Mondragó • Majorca, Spain 83 O12
Cala Morell • Minorca, Spain 83 J7
Cala Murada • Majorca, Spain 83 O12
Cala Pi • Majorca, Spain 83 N12
Cala Ratjada • Majorca, Spain 83 O11
Cala Sahona • Formentera, Spain 83 L10
Cala Salada • Ibiza, Spain 83 L9
Cala Santanyí • Majorca, Spain 83 O12
Cala Tarida • Ibiza, Spain 83 L9
Cala Tirant • Minorca, Spain 83 K7
Cala Torret • Minorca, Spain 83 K8
Cala Vadella • Ibiza, Spain 83 L9
Cala Vinyes • Majorca, Spain 83 N12
Calabar • Nigeria 106 C4
Calábria • Italy 86 B2
Calábria, Parco Naz. della **Park N** • Italy 58 [98]
Calacuccia • Corsica, France 78 M11
Calafat • Romania 92 C3
Calafate • Argentina 175 A5
Calafell • Spain 83 C4
Calahonda • Spain 82 J8
Calais • France 76 D1
Calakmul • Mexico 169 F5
Calakmul **Heritage C** • Mexico 42 [30]
Calalin Channel • Marshall Is. 139 E
Calama • Chile 175 B2
Calamian Group • Philippines 128 G4
Calanche, les • Corsica, France 78 M11
Calang • Indonesia 131 M9
Calangute • Goa, India 123 C5
Calangute Beach • Goa, India 123 C5
Calanques, Côte des • France 78 G8
Calapan • Philippines 128 G4
Calarasi • Romania 92 H7
Calatayud • Spain 80 E3
Calbayog • Philippines 128 G4
Calcare, Cava di • Italy 87 G6
Calcasieu Lake • LA, United States 156 E6
Calcatoggio • Corsica, France 78 M12
Calçoene • Brazil 174 A2
Calcutta • India 122 C3
Caldbeck • United Kingdom 65 D3
Caldeirão, Serra do • Portugal 84 J7
Calder Hall • United Kingdom 65 C4
Caldera de Taburiente, Parque Nac. de **Park N** • La Palma, Canary Is. 58 [83]
Caldera de Taburiente, Parque Nac. de • La Palma, Canary Is. 83 H6
Caldonazzo, Lago di • Italy 86 C4
Caldwell • ID, United States 154 H6
Caledon • South Africa 111 D7
Caledon [Riv] • Lesotho/South Africa 110 B3
Calella • Spain 83 D4
Calenzana • Corsica, France 78 M11
Cales Coves • Minorca, Spain 83 K8
Cales de Mallorca • Majorca, Spain 83 O12
Caleta de Fustes • Fuerteventura, Canary Is. 83 H5
Caleton Blanc • Cuba 164 H5
Caletta, la • Sardinia, Italy 86 F5
Calf of Man • Isle of Man 63 C6
Calgary • AL, Canada 160 J7
Calheta • Madeira 84 D5
Cali • Colombia 173 B2
Calibishie • Dominica 167 K
Calico Ghost Town • CA, United States 154 J9
Calicut • India 124 B3
Cálida, Costa • Spain 83 A2
Caliente • NV, United States 154 J8
California • United States 154 I-J
California, Golfo de • Mexico 168 H-I
California Lighthouse • Aruba 166 W
Calis • Turkey 95 F6
Calitzdorp • South Africa 111 E7
Calivigny I. • Grenada 166 Q
Callahan • FL, United States 151 D4
Callanish • United Kingdom 62 B2
Callao • Peru 173 E6
Calma, Costa • Fuerteventura, Canary Is. 83 H5
Calma, Costa de la • Majorca, Spain 83 N12
Calore • Italy 87 H6
Caloundra • QL, Australia 136 D5
Calpe • Spain 83 B1
Caltagirone • Sicily, Italy 86 H8
Caltagirone **Heritage C** • Sicily, Italy 44 [175]
Caltanissetta • Sicily, Italy 86 H8
Calvi • Corsica, France 78 M11
Calvià • Majorca, Spain 83 N11
Calvinia • South Africa 111 E6
Calw • Germany 74 B3
Calzada Larga • Panama 170 M11
Cam • United Kingdom 63 E8
Cam Pha • Vietnam 128 D2
Cam Ranh • Vietnam 129 C5
Cam Ranh Bay • Vietnam 129 C5
Camaçari • Brazil 174 C4
Camacha • Porto Santo, Madeira 84 E5
Camagüey • Cuba 164 G5
Camagüey, Archipiélago de • Cuba 164 G4
Camaná • Peru 173 F7
Câmara de Lobos • Madeira 84 D5
Camarat, Cap • France 78 H8
Çamardi • Turkey 95 J9
Camargue • France 76 F5
Camber **Beach** • United Kingdom 64 [29]
Camberley • United Kingdom 63 E9
Cambo-les-Bains • France 78 I9
CAMBODIA • Asia 120 D4
Camborne • United Kingdom 65 I10
Cambrai • France 76 E1
Cambrian Mtns • United Kingdom 63 D8
Cambridge • MA, United States 156 D1
Cambridge • MD, United States 156 B3
Cambridge • New Zealand 137 D5
Cambridge • OH, United States 150 D2
Cambridge • United Kingdom 63 F8
Cambridge Bay • NU, Canada 158 F1
Cambridgeshire • United Kingdom 64 B5
Cambrils de Mar • Spain 83 C4
Camden • AR, United States 151 B4
Camden • NJ, United States 156 B3
Camelback **Ski** • PA, United States 146 [93]
Camelback • PA, United States 156 B2
Camelford • United Kingdom 65 I10
Cameli • Turkey 95 F6
Camelot Theme Park **Park L** • United Kingdom 59 [24]
Cameron Highlands • Malaysia 129 F9
Cameron Mtns • New Zealand 137 F8
CAMEROON • Africa 106 D4
Cametá • Brazil 174 B3
Camino de Santiago **Heritage C** • Spain 44 [107]
Çamlikköyü • Turkey 95 H7
Camooweal • QL, Australia 135 F4
Camp David • MD, United States 156 A3
Camp de Mar • Majorca, Spain 83 N12
Camp Snoopy **Park L** • MN, United States 157 [14]
Campagna • Italy 87 H7
Campal Beach • Goa, India 123 C5
Campana, I. • Chile 175 A4
Campanella, Punta • Italy 87 G7
Campania • Italy 87 H6
Campbell River • BC, Canada 160 I7
Campbell Town • TS, Australia 136 F7
Campbellton • NB, Canada 160 B1
Campbelltown • NS, Australia 136 H8
Campbeltown • United Kingdom 62 C5
Campeche • Mexico 169 E4
Campeche **Heritage C** • Mexico 42 [27]
Campeche [Adm] • Mexico 169 D3
Campechuela • Cuba 164 G5
Campello • Spain 83 B1
Campina Grande • Brazil 174 C3
Campinas • Brazil 175 D2
Campitello di Fassa **Ski** • Italy 61 [143]
Campitello di Fassa • Italy 86 C4
Campo del Oro [Apt] • Corsica, France 78 M12
Campo Felice • Italy 87 F4
Campo Formoso • Brazil 174 B4
Campo Grande • Brazil 175 C2
Campo Tures • Italy 86 D3
Campoamor • Spain 83 A2
Campobasso • Italy 85 E4
Campos • Brazil 174 F7
Campos • Majorca, Spain 83 O12
Campos do Jordão • Brazil 174 E7
Campotosto, Lago di • Italy 87 F4
Campsie Fells • United Kingdom 65 A2
Camrose • AL, Canada 160 J6
Camyuva • Turkey 95 G8
Can • Turkey 95 E4
Can Pastilla • Majorca, Spain 83 N12
Can Picafort • Majorca, Spain 83 O11
Can Tho • Vietnam 129 B6
Cana of Galilee • Israel 120 B2
Canaan • Trinidad & Tobago 166 R
Canaan Valley **Ski** • WV, United States 146 [90]
CANADA • N. America 158-159
Cañadas del Teide, Parque Nac. de las **Park N** • Tenerife, Canary Is. 58 [85]
Cañades del Teide, Parque Nac. de las • Tenerife, Canary Is. 82 G5
Canadian • United States 149 F3
Canadian Falls • OT, Canada 161 D1
Canadian Rocky Mtns Parks **Heritage N** • AL/BC, Canada 40 [4]
Canadian Shield • Canada 142 E3
Canaguinim Beach • Goa, India 123 C6
Canaima, Parque Nac. • Venezuela 173 C2
Canaima, Parque Nac. **Heritage N** • Venezuela 40 [32]
Canakkale • Turkey 95 E4
Canakkale [Adm] • Turkey 95 E4
Canakkale Bogazi • Turkey 95 E4
Canala • New Caledonia 138 U
Canandaigua Lake • NY, United States 156 A1
Cananea • Mexico 168 I5
Canaria, Costa • Gran Canaria, Canary Is. 82 G6
Canaries • St Lucia 167 N
Canarreros, Archipiélago de los • Cuba 164 F4
Canary Is. • Atlantic Ocean 83 G-I
Canaveral Nat. Seashore • FL, United States 155 D2
Canaveral Nat. Seashore **Park N** • FL, United States 153 [217]
Canazei **Ski** • Italy 61 [143]
Canazei • Italy 86 C4
Canberra • AC, Australia 136 H8
Canby • CA, United States 148 B2
Cancale • France 77 D3
Cancún • Mexico 169 G4
Cancún, I. • Mexico 169 G4
Candelaria • Mexico 169 E5
Candelaria • Tenerife, Canary Is. 82 G5
Candi Kuning Temple • Bali, Indonesia 131 L7
Candi Sukuh Temple • Java, Indonesia 131 Q12
Candidasa Beach • Bali, Indonesia 131 L8
Candolim Beach • Goa, India 123 C5
Cane Field • Dominica 167 K
Cane River Creole Nat. Hist. Park **Park N** • LA, United States 153 [192]
Canea • Crete, Greece 93 G5
Canelones • Uruguay 175 G6
Canet Plage • France 78 L10
Canggu Beach • Bali, Indonesia 131 L8
Cango Caves • South Africa 111 F7
Cangzhou • China 125 F3
Caniapiscau, Réservoir • QU, Canada 159 J3
Caniçal • Madeira 84 E5
Canicatti • Sicily, Italy 86 G8
Caniço • Madeira 84 E5
Canillo • Andorra 82 E5
Cankiri • Turkey 95 B1
Canna • United Kingdom 62 B3
Cannanore • India 124 B2
Cannanore **Beach** • India 124 E6
Cannes • France 78 H8
Cannock Chase • United Kingdom 65 F5
Cannon **Ski** • NH, United States 146 [114]
Cannon [Apt] • NV, United States 154 I8
Cannon Beach • OR, United States 154 G5
Canoas • Brazil 175 C2
Canoe Passage • Kiribati 139 I
Cañon City • CO, United States 148 E3
Canonica, la • Corsica, France 78 N11
Canonniers Point • Mauritius 113 E5
Canouan • St Vincent & Gren. 167 P
Canove **Ski** • Italy 61 [136]
Cansaulim Beach • Goa, India 123 C6
Canso, Strait of • NS, Canada 160 C2
Cantabria • Spain 80 C2
Cantabrica, Cordillera • Spain 80 C2
Canterbury • New Zealand 137 B3
Canterbury • United Kingdom 65 H8
Canterbury **Heritage C** • United Kingdom 44 [31]
Canterbury Bight • New Zealand 137 B3
Canterbury Plains • New Zealand 137 B3
Canton • China 126 E3
Canton • IL, United States 150 C2
Canton • MS, United States 156 F5
Canton • OH, United States 150 D2
Canvey I. • United Kingdom 65 H7
Canyon • TX, United States 149 F3
Canyon City • OR, United States 148 C2
Canyon de Chelly Nat. Mon. • AZ, United States 155 H7
Canyon de Chelly Nat. Mon. **Park N** • AZ, United States 152 [101]
Canyonlands Nat. Park • UT, United States 148 E3
Canyonlands Nat. Park **Park N** • UT, United States 152 [83]
Canyons, The **Ski** • UT, United States 146 [47]
Cao Banh • Vietnam 128 D2
Caorle • Italy 87 D2
Cap aux Meules • QU, Canada 160 B1
Cap de la Madeleine • QU, Canada 160 H3
Cap Malheureux • Mauritius 113 F5
Cap, Pointe du • St Lucia 167 N
Cap-Haïtien • Haiti 165 F5
Caparaó, Serra do • Brazil 174 F6
Caparra • Puerto Rico 165 J7
Capbreton • France 78 E6
Capdepera • Majorca, Spain 83 O11
Cape Barren I. • TS, Australia 136 F6
Cape Breton Highlands Nat. Park **Park N** • NS, Canada 161 [38]
Cape Breton Highlands Nat. Park • NS, Canada 160 C2
Cape Breton I. • NS, Canada 160 C2
Cape Canaveral • FL, United States 155 D2
Cape Cod Bay • MA, United States 156 D1
Cape Cod Nat. Seashore • MA, United States 156 D1
Cape Cod Nat. Seashore **Park N** • MA, United States 153 [287]
Cape Coral • FL, United States 155 C3
Cape Cross Reserve **Park** • Namibia 112 [125]
Cape Dorset • NU, Canada 159 I2
Cape Fear [Riv] • NC, United States 151 E4
Cape Hatteras Nat. Seashore **Park N** • NC, United States 153 [241]
Cape Krusenstern Nat. Mon. • AK, United States 157 D2
Cape Krusenstern Nat. Mon. **Park N** • AK, United States 152 [3]
Cape Lookout Nat. Seashore **Park N** • NC, United States 153 [240]
Cape of Good Hope Nature Reserve • South Africa 111 D7
Cape of Good Hope Nature Reserve **Park** • South Africa 112 [127]
Cape Parry • NT, Canada 158 D1
Cape Peninsula • South Africa 111 D7
Cape Region • Mexico 168 I6
Cape Town • South Africa 111 D7
CAPE VERDE • Atlantic Ocean 106 E7
Cape York Peninsula • QL, Australia 135 G2
Capella I. • US Virgin Is. 166 X
Capelle aan den IJssel • Netherlands 70 G8
Capernaum • Israel 120 B1
Capesterre-Belle-Eau • Guadeloupe 167 J
Capileira • Spain 82 J7
Capitán Arturo Prat [Base] • Antarctica 176 [2]
Capitol Hill • N. Mariana Is. 138 B
Capitol Hill parks **Park N** • DC, United States 153 [264]
Capitol Reef Nat. Park **Park N** • UT, United States 152 [80]
Capo Boi • Sardinia, Italy 86 F6
Capo d'Orlando • Sicily, Italy 86 H7
Capodichino [Apt] • Italy 87 G6
Capodimonte • Italy 87 E4
Cappadocia • Turkey 95 J9
Cappadocia **Heritage C** • Turkey 44 [253]
Cappadocia rock sites **Heritage N** • Turkey 41 [81]
Cappenberg, Schloss • Germany 73 D5
Capráia, I. di • Italy 87 B3
Caprera, I. • Sardinia, Italy 86 F5
Capri • Italy 87 G7
Capri, I. di • Italy 87 G7
Capriate San Gervasio • Italy 87 B2
Capricorn Channel • QL, Australia 136 D4
Capricorn Group • QL, Australia 136 D4
Caprivi Strip • Namibia 110 B2
Capt. Keith Roberts, MV • Cayman Is. 165 B1
Captain Cook • HI, United States 157 J6
Captiva I. • FL, United States 155 C3
Cápua • Italy 87 G6
Capucin, Cape • Dominica 167 K
Capulin Volcano Nat. Mon. **Park N** • NM, United States 152 [129]
Caputh • Germany 73 E8
Caquetá • Colombia 173 B3
Car Nicobar • India 122 D5
Caracarai • Brazil 173 C2
Caracas • Venezuela 173 C1
Caracas **Heritage C** • Venezuela 42 [49]
Caracol • Belize 170 K9
Caraguatatuba • Brazil 174 E7
Carajás • Brazil 174 A3
Caranzalem Beach • Goa, India 123 C5
Caraquet • NB, Canada 160 B1
Carasova • Romania 92 C2
Caratasca, Laguna de • Honduras 170 F3
Caratinga • Brazil 174 F6
Caravelle, Presqu'île la • Martinique 167 L
Carbet, la • Martinique 167 L
Carbo • Mexico 168 I5
Carbonara, Capo • Sardinia, Italy 86 F6
Carbondale • IL, United States 150 C3
Carbondale • PA, United States 156 B2
Carboneras • Spain 82 K7
Carbónia • Sardinia, Italy 86 E6
Carbury • Ireland 69 E6
Carcans • France 78 E5
Carcassonne • France 76 E5
Carcassonne **Heritage C** • France 44 [89]
Carcross • YT, Canada 158 C2
Cardamom Hills • India 124 B3
Cárdenas • Cuba 164 F4
Cárdenas • San Luis Potosí, Mexico 169 J6
Cárdenas • Tabasco, Mexico 168 F4
Cardiff • United Kingdom 65 J9
Cardigan • United Kingdom 63 C8
Cardigan **Beach** • United Kingdom 64 [56]
Cardigan Bay • United Kingdom 63 C8
Cardiganshire • United Kingdom 64 A5
Cardona • Spain 83 D3
Cardona • Uruguay 175 G6
Cardrona • New Zealand 137 G7
Carey, Lake • WA, Australia 135 C5
Carezza, Lago di • Italy 86 C4
Cargèse • Corsica, France 78 M12

Carhaix-Plouguer • France 77 C3
Caria • Turkey 95 F6
Cariacica • Brazil 174 B5
Carib Reserve • Dominica .... 167 K
Caribbean Sea • N. America 166-167
Caribou Mtns • AL, Canada 158 E3
Carinthia • Austria 91 T11
Carinthia Ski • VT, United States 156 B3
Carita • Java, Indonesia 131 O11
Carl Sandburg Home Nat. Hist. Site
  Park N • NC, United States .... 153 [236]
Carless Reef Dive • Egypt 109 E8
Carleton Place • OT, Canada 160 F4
Carlisle • PA, United States 156 A2
Carlisle • United Kingdom 62 D6
Carlow • Ireland 69 E7
Carlow [Adm] • Ireland 69 E7
Carlsbad • NM, United States 149 F4
Carlsbad Caverns Nat. Park Park N •
  NM, United States .... 152 [119]
Carlsbad Caverns Nat. Park Heritage N •
  NM, United States .... 40 [14]
Carmacks • YT, Canada 158 C2
Carmarthen • United Kingdom 63 C9
Carmarthen Bay • United Kingdom 63 C9
Carmarthenshire • United Kingdom 64 A5
Carmel • CA, United States 154 I8
Carmel, Mt • Israel 120 A2
Carmelo • Uruguay 175 G6
Carmen, I. • Mexico 168 I6
Carmen, I. del • Mexico 169 E5
Carmona • Spain 82 I7
Carna • Ireland 69 G9
Carnac • France 77 D4
Carnarvon • South Africa 110 B4
Carnarvon • WA, Australia 135 A4
Carnati • India 124 C3
Carnatic Dive • Egypt 109 E7
Carnegie, Lake • WA, Australia 135 C5
Carney I. • Antarctica 176 W5
Carnoustie • United Kingdom 65 B1
Carol City • FL, United States 155 D3
Carolina • Brazil 174 B3
Carolina • Puerto Rico 165 J7
Carolina, Puntan • N. Mariana Is. .... 138 B
Carolina I. • Kiribati 139 DD3
Caroline I. • Pacific Ocean 138 AA2
Caroni Bird Sanctuary •
  Trinidad & Tobago .... 166 S
Carpathians • Europe 92 D2
Carpatii Meridionali • Romania 92 D2
Carpentaria, Gulf of •
  NT/QL, Australia 135 F2
Carpi • Italy 87 C2
Carra, Lough • Ireland 69 H9
Carrantuohill • Ireland 69 G11
Carrapateira • Portugal 84 H8
Carrara • Italy 87 B3
Carraroe • Ireland 69 G9
Carrasco [Apt] • Uruguay 175 G6
Carreta, Punta • Peru 173 E6
Carriacou • Grenada .... 167 P
Carrick-on-Shannon • Ireland 69 C2
Carrigadrohid Reservoir • Ireland 69 H11
Carrizozo • NM, United States 155 H8
Carrollton • GA, United States 151 C4
Carroz, les Ski • France .... 61 [16]
Carroz, les • France 78 D3
Carson City • NV, United States 154 I8
Carson Sink • NV, United States 154 J7
Cartagena • Colombia 173 B1
Cartagena Heritage C • Colombia .... 42 [51]
Cartagena • Spain 83 A2
Cartago • Costa Rica 170 F6
Cartaya • Spain 82 H7
Carteret • France 63 J14
Cartersville • GA, United States 151 D4
Carthage • MO, United States 151 B3
Carthage • Tunisia 107 D4
Carthage Heritage C • Tunisia .... 44 [288]
Carthage [Apt] • Tunisia 107 D4
Caruaru • Brazil 174 C3
Carvoeiro • Portugal 84 I8
Cas Concos • Majorca, Spain 83 O12
Casa de Campo, Parque de Atracciones
  Park L • Spain .... 59 [73]
Casa Grande • AZ, United States 155 G8
Casa Grande Ruins Nat. Mon. •
  AZ, United States 155 G8
Casa Grande Ruins Nat. Mon. Park N •
  AZ, United States .... 152 [110]
Casablanca • Morocco 107 A1
Casale Monferrato • Italy 87 B2
Casamari, Abbazia di • Italy 87 F5
Casares • Spain 82 I8
Cascada de Basaseachic, Parque Natural •
  Mexico 168 I5
Cascade • ID, United States 148 C2
Cascade Mtn Ski •
  WI, United States .... 146 [75]
Cascade Point • New Zealand 137 A3
Cascade Range •
  OR/WA, United States .... 154 G
Cascais • Portugal 84 F6
Cascavel • Brazil 175 C2
Caserta [Apt] • Italy 87 A2
Caserta • Italy 87 F5
Caserta Heritage C • Italy .... 44 [168]
Casey [Base] • Antarctica .... 176 [21]
Cashel • Ireland 69 C4
Casilda • Argentina 175 F6
Casino • NS, Australia 136 D5
Casino Pier Park L •
  NJ, United States .... 157 [33]
Cáslav • Czech Rep. 89 E6
Casper • WY, United States 148 E2
Caspian Depression •
  Kazakhstan/Russian Fed. 121 A2
Caspian Sea • Asia/Europe 121 B3
Cassiar Mtns • BC, Canada 158 D3
Cassinga • Angola 110 A2
Cassino • Italy 87 F5
Castagneto Carducci • Italy 87 C3
Castanhal • Brazil 174 B3
Castel del Monte Heritage C • Italy .... 44 [172]
Castel Gandolfo • Italy 87 E5
Casteljaloux • France 78 E6
Castellammare del Golfo •
  Sicily, Italy 86 G7
Castellammare di Stábia • Italy 87 G7
Castellammare, Golfo di •
  Sicily, Italy 86 G7
Castellane • France 78 H7
Castelldefels • Spain 83 C4
Castelli Romani • Italy 87 F5
Castelló de la Plana • Spain 80 E3
Castelnaudary • France 76 D5
Castelnou • France 78 L10
Castelo Branco • Portugal 80 B4
Castelo Branco [Adm] • Portugal 84 D4
Castelo, Ponto do • Madeira 84 E5
Castelrotto • Italy 86 C3
Castelsardo • Sardinia, Italy 86 E5
Castelsarrasin • France 78 F6
Castelvetrano • Sicily, Italy 86 G7
Castiglioncello • Italy 87 C3
Castiglione • Trinidad & Tobago .... 166 R
Castiglione del Lago • Italy 87 D3
Castiglione della Pescáia • Italy 87 C3
Castilla, Playa de • Spain 82 H7
Castilla y León • Spain 80 C3
Castillo de Jagua • Cuba 164 F1
Castillo de San Marcos Nat. Mon. •
  FL, United States 155 D1
Castillo de San Marcos Nat. Mon. Park N •
  FL, United States .... 153 [216]
Castle Bruce • Dominica .... 167 K
Castle Clinton Nat. Mon. Park N •
  NY, United States .... 153 [278]
Castle Drogo • United Kingdom 65 C10
Castle Harbour • Bermuda 165 L9
Castle Hill • NF, United States 160 D1
Castle Matrix • Ireland 69 H10

Castle Peak • Hong Kong, China 126 E5
Castlebar • Ireland 69 H8
Castleblaney • United Kingdom 69 G7
Castleconnell • Ireland 69 H10
Castledermot • Ireland 69 E7
Castlegregory • Ireland 69 E6
Castleford • United Kingdom 63 E7
Castlegregory • Ireland 69 G10
Castleisland • Ireland 69 G10
Castlerea • Ireland 69 H8
Castlerigg Stone Circle •
  United Kingdom 65 C3
Castleton • Jamaica 165 D3
Castletownbere • Ireland 69 G11
Castricum • Netherlands 70 C2
Castries • St Lucia .... 167 N
Castro Marim • Portugal 84 K7
Castrop-Rauxel • Germany 73 D5
Castrovillari • Italy 85 F5
Caswell Sound • New Zealand 137 F2
Cat Head Point • MI, United States 161 B2
Cat I. • Bahamas 164 B1
Catalina, I. • Dominican Rep. 165 H6
Catalonia • Spain 80 F3
Catalunya • Spain 72 G6
Catamarca • Argentina 175 B2
Catanduanes • Philippines 128 G4
Catánia • Sicily, Italy 86 H8
Catánia Heritage C • Sicily, Italy .... 44 [175]
Catánia, Golfo di •
  Sicily, Italy 86 H8
Cataño • Puerto Rico 165 J7
Catanzaro • Italy 85 F5
Cataraman • Philippines 128 G4
Cataway Park • AL, Canada 160 J7
Catbalogan • Philippines 128 G4
Catena dei Lagorai • Italy 86 C4
Catholic I. • St Vincent & Gren. .... 167 P
Catináccio • Italy 86 C3
Catingas • Brazil 171 E3
Catlins, The • New Zealand 137 G8
Catoche, Cabo • Mexico 169 G4
Catoctin Mtn Park Park N •
  MD, United States .... 153 [255]
Catskill Mtns • NY, United States 156 C1
Cattólica • Italy 87 D3
Caubvik, Mt • NF/QU, Canada 159 J3
Coucaia • Brazil 174 C3
Caucasus • Asia/Europe 100 F5
Caucasus, Western Heritage N •
  Russian Fed. .... 41 [82]
Caulnes • France 77 D3
Causeway Bay • Hong Kong, China 126 F5
Cauterets • France 78 J9
Cauto • Cuba 164 H5
Cauvery • India 124 B2
Cauvery Delta • India 124 C3
Cava de' Tirreni • Italy 87 H7
Cavalaire-sur-Mer • France 78 H8
Cavalese Ski • Italy .... 61 [137]
Cavalese • Italy 86 C4
Cavalleria, Cap de •
  Minorca, Spain 83 K7
Cavallo, I. • Corsica, France 78 N12
Cavan • Ireland 69 C3
Çavdir • Turkey 95 G7
Cavelossim Beach • Goa, India 123 C6
Caviana, I. • Brazil 174 B2
Cavtat • Croatia 92 G6
Çavus Burun • Turkey 95 G8
Cawnpore • India 123 F8
Caxambu • Brazil 174 E7
Caxias • Brazil 174 B3
Caxias do Sul • Brazil 175 C2
Caxinas, Punta • Honduras 170 D2
Cay Sal Bank • Bahamas 166 BB1
Cayes, Baie des • Haiti 165 E6
Cayes, Les • Haiti 165 G6
Cayey • Puerto Rico 165 J8
Cayman Brac • Cayman Is. 165 B1
CAYMAN IS. • West Indies 166 CC2
Cayman Trench • West Indies 166 CC2
Cayman Turtle Farm • Cayman Is. 165 A2
Cayo Coco • Cuba 164 H5
Cayon • St Kitts & Nevis .... 167 F
Cayonne • Haiti 165 F5
Cayuga Lake • NY, United States 156 B1
Cazombo • Angola 110 B2
Ceanannas Mór • Ireland 69 E6
Ceará • Brazil 174 C3
Ceará [Adm] • Brazil 174 C3
Cebu • Philippines 128 G4
Cebu [I.] • Philippines 128 G4
Ceccano • Italy 87 F5
Cécina • Italy 87 C3
Cecis • Latvia 100 K7
Cedar • IA, United States 150 B2
Cedar Breaks Nat. Mon. Park N •
  UT, United States .... 152 [78]
Cedar City • UT, United States 148 D3
Cedar Falls • IA, United States 150 B2
Cedar Grove • Antigua & Barbuda .... 167 I
Cedar Key Nat. Wildlife Refuge •
  FL, United States 155 C1
Cedar Point • OH, United States .... 157 [18]
Cedar Point Park L •
  OH, United States .... 157 [18]
Cedar Pride Dive • Jordan 109 E7
Cedar Rapids • IA, United States 150 B2
Cedar Tree Point • Antigua & Barbuda .... 167 H
Cederberg • South Africa 111 D6
Cedros, I. • Mexico 168 H5
Ceduna • SA, Australia 135 E6
Cefalù • Sicily, Italy 86 H7
Cegar Perah • Malaysia 129 G9
Ceiba • Puerto Rico 165 J7
Céide Fields • Ireland 69 H8
Cekik • Bali, Indonesia 131 K7
Celano • Italy 87 E5
Celaque • Honduras 170 X9
Celaya • Mexico 169 I7
Celebes • Indonesia 131 F4
Celebes Sea • Indonesia 131 F3
Celerina Ski • Switzerland .... 61 [81]
Celerina • Switzerland 90 L5
Celestún • Mexico 169 E4
Celje • Slovenia 92 E5
Celle • Germany 72 D2
Celuk • Bali, Indonesia 131 L8
Cennet ve Cehennem • Turkey 95 I10
Cenouras, I. das •
  Porto Santo, Madeira 84 E5
Cento • Italy 87 C2
CENTRAL AFRICAN REPUBLIC •
  Africa 108 B4
Central Balkan Nat. Park Park N •
  Bulgaria .... 58 [134]
Central eastern rainforest reserves
  Heritage N • Australia .... 41 [151]
Central Forest Reserve • Dominica .... 167 K
Central High School Nat. Hist. Site Park N •
  AR, United States .... 153 [189]
Central Highlands • Kenya 109 H5
Central I. Nat. Park • Kenya 109 C4
Central I. Nat. Park Park • Kenya .... 112 [69]
Central Kalahari Game Reserve •
  Botswana 110 I9
Central Kalahari Game Reserve Park •
  Botswana .... 112 [122]
Central Plains • Thailand 130 A2
Central Plateau • New Zealand 137 E6
Central, Sistema • Spain 80 C3
Central Suriname Nature Reserve
  Heritage N • Surinam .... 40 [31]
Central-Leatherstocking •
  NY, United States 156 B1
Centralia • IL, United States 150 C3
Centralia • WA, United States 154 G5
Centre • France 77 A1
Centre, Canal du Heritage C •
  Belgium .... 44 [43]
Centre du Flaq • Mauritius 113 F6

Centre Hills • Montserrat .... 167 G
Centreville • OT, Canada 160 E5
Cephalonia • Greece .... 94 J
Cepu • Java, Indonesia 131 Q12
Cerbère • France 78 L10
Cerbicale, Is. • Corsica, France 78 N12
Cereal • AL, Canada 158 E3
Ceres • South Africa 111 D7
Cerf I. • Seychelles 113 A2
Cerf, I. au • Seychelles 113 A1
Cerfs, I. aux • Mauritius 113 F6
Cergy-Pontoise • France 78 A1
Cerignola • Italy 85 E6
Cerigo • Greece 93 C3
Cernavoda • Romania 92 I7
Cernay • France 76 G3
Cernóbbio • Italy 87 B1
Cerralvo, I. • Mexico 168 I6
Cerrillos • Mexico 169 J6
Cerritos, I. • Mexico 169 I4
Cerro Azul • Mexico 169 J6
Cerro de las Mesas • Mexico 169 K7
Cervená Lhota • Czech Rep. 89 E7
Cervéteri • Italy 87 E4
Cérvia • Italy 87 D2
Cerviatto, Monte • Italy 87 H7
Cesena • Italy 87 D3
Cesenático • Italy 87 D2
Ceská Lipa • Czech Rep. 89 E6
Ceske Budejovice • Czech Rep. 89 E7
Ceské Svycarsko • Czech Rep. 89 D6
Cesky Krumlov • Czech Rep. 89 E7
Cesky Krumlov Heritage C •
  Czech Rep. .... 44 [192]
Cesky Les • Czech Rep. 89 D7
Cesky Sternberk • Czech Rep. 89 E6
Cesme • Turkey 95 E5
Cessnock • NS, Australia 136 H8
Cetraro • Italy 85 F5
Ceuta • Spain 82 D4
Cévennes • France 76 E5
Cévennes, Parc nat. des Park N •
  France .... 58 [76]
Cevizli • Turkey 95 H7
Ceyhan • Turkey 95 J10
Ceyhan [Riv] • Turkey 95 J9
CEYLON see SRI LANKA
Cha-Am • Thailand 130 D8
Chaâlis, Abbaye de • France 78 B1
Chabahar • Iran 120 I8
Chablais • France 78 D3
Chablis • France 76 L3
Chabacuco • Argentina 175 D9
Chacachacare I. • Trinidad & Tobago .... 166 S
Chachoengsao • Thailand 130 E7
Chacultún • Mexico 169 F4
Chaco Culture Nat. Hist. Park •
  NM, United States .... 155 [122]
Chaco Culture Nat. Hist. Park Park N •
  NM, United States .... 152 [122]
Chaco Culture Nat. Hist. Park Heritage N •
  NM, United States .... 42 [17]
CHAD • Africa 108 A3
Chad, Lake • Africa 106 D3
Chadileuvú • Argentina 175 B3
Chaghcharan • Afghanistan 121 C5
Chagos Archipelago • Indian Ocean 116 G7
Chagres • Panama 170 M10
Chagres, Parque Nac. • Panama 170 M10
Chaguanas • Trinidad & Tobago .... 166 S
Chainat • Thailand 128 C3
Chake Chake • Tanzania 110 H7
Chala • Peru 173 E7
Chalan Kanoa • N. Mariana Is. .... 138 B
Chalbi Desert • Kenya 109 C4
Chaleur Bay • NB/QU, Canada 160 B1
Chalky Inlet • New Zealand 137 F8
Challans • France 76 C3
Chalon-sur-Saône • France 78 F3
Chalong • Ko Phuket, Thailand 130 F10
Chalong Bay • Ko Phuket, Thailand 130 F10
Chalong, Wat •
  Ko Phuket, Thailand 130 F10
Châlons-en-Champagne • France 76 F2
Chalusset, Château de • France 78 F5
Chaman • Pakistan 123 A2
Chamarel • Mauritius 113 F6
Chamba Hill Sta • India 124 E5
Chamba • Tanzania 110 H8
Chambal • India 123 E8
Chamberlain • SD, United States 148 G2
Chambers • AZ, United States 155 H7
Chambers Pillar • NT, Australia 136 B2
Chambersburg • PA, United States 156 A3
Chambéry • France 78 C3
Chambi, Jebel • Tunisia 107 C5
Chambly • France 78 A1
Chambly, Fort • QU, Canada 160 G4
Chambord Heritage C • France .... 44 [81]
Chambord [Château] • France 77 F5
Chamizal Nat. Mem. Park N •
  TX, United States .... 152 [132]
Chamois • Italy 87 A1
Chamonix-Mont-Blanc Ski • France .... 61 [21]
Chamonix-Mont-Blanc • France 78 D3
Champagne Castle • South Africa 111 B4
Champagne-Ardenne • France 77 B1
Champagny-en-Vanoise Ski • France .... 61 [28]
Champaign • IL, United States 150 C2
Champawat • India 124 E5
Champasak Heritage C • Laos .... 43 [202]
Champawat • India 123 F7
Champéry • Switzerland 90 I6
Champéry-Planachaux Ski •
  Switzerland .... 61 [55]
Champex • Switzerland 90 J6
Champigny-sur-Marne • France 78 B2
Champlain, Lake •
  NY/VT, United States 150 F2
Champoluc Ski • Italy .... 61 [125]
Champotón • Mexico 169 E5
Champoussin • Switzerland 90 I6
Champs, Château de • France 78 B2
Chan Chan Heritage C • Peru .... 42 [b/]
Chan Santa Cruz • Mexico 169 G5
Chañaral • Chile 175 A1
Chancay • Peru 173 D6
Chandannagar • India 124 C3
Chandeleur Sound •
  LA, United States 156 F6
Chanderi • India 123 F8
Chandigarh • India 122 B2
Chandler • AZ, United States 149 D4
Chandler • QU, Canada 160 B1
Chandor • Goa, India 123 C6
Chandragiri • India 124 C2
Chandraprabha Wildlife Sanctuary •
  India 123 G8
Chandrapur • India 122 B4
Chang Jiang • China 125 G3
Chang, Ko • Thailand 130 A3
Changchun • China 125 G2
Changde • China 125 F3
Changhua • Taiwan 125 G4
Changi • Singapore 129 I11
Changi [Apt] • Singapore 129 I11
Changping • China 126 H6
Changsha • China 125 F3
Changshu • China 126 H6
Changuinola • Panama 170 F6
Changxing • China 126 G2
Changzhi • China 125 F2
Channel Is. • Europe 77 C3
Channel Is. • CA, United States 154 I9
CHANNEL IS. • Europe 77 C3
Channel Is. Nat. Park •
  CA, United States 154 I9
Channel Is. Nat. Park Park N •
  CA, United States .... 152 [53]
Channel-Port aux-Basques •
  NF, Canada 160 C1
Channel Tunnel •
  France/United Kingdom 65 H8
Chanthaburi • Thailand 128 C3
Chantilly • France 78 A1
Chantilly, Forêt de • France 78 B1

Chao Phraya • Thailand 130 D7
Chaouèn • Morocco 107 B1
Chaoyang • China 125 G2
Chaozhou • China 125 F4
Chapada dos Veadeiros, Parque Nac. da
  Heritage N • Brazil .... 40 [44]
Chapayev • Kazakstan 121 B1
Chapala, Laguna de • Mexico 169 I7
Chapecó • Brazil 175 C2
Chapelle d'Abondance, La Ski •
  France .... 61 [8]
Chapleau • OT, Canada 159 H4
Chapora • Goa, India 123 C5
Chapora Fort • Goa, India 123 C5
Chapra • India 123 G8
Charcas • Mexico 169 I6
Chard • United Kingdom 65 K9
Charentais • France 76 K9
Charente [Adm] • France 78 E5
Charente • France 78 E5
Charente-Maritime • France 78 E5
Chari • Chad 108 A3
Charity • Guyana 173 D2
Charlecote Park • United Kingdom 65 F5
Charleroi • Belgium 70 B4
Charles, Cape •
  VA, United States 156 B4
Charles de Gaulle [Apt] • France 78 B1
Charles I. • Galápagos Is. 171 H10
Charles Pinckney Nat. Hist. Site Park N •
  SC, United States .... 153 [231]
Charles Sound • New Zealand 137 F7
Charleston • SC, United States 151 D4
Charleston • WV, United States 150 D3
Charlestown • Ireland 69 H8
Charlestown • St Kitts & Nevis .... 167 F
Charlestown • St Vincent & Gren. .... 167 P
Charleville Ql, Australia 136 C5
Charlevoix • MI, United States 161 B2
Charlotte • NC, United States 151 D3
Charlotte Amalie • US Virgin Is. .... 166 X
Charlotte, Fort • Bahamas 164 A2
Charlotte, Fort • St Lucia .... 167 N
Charlotte, Fort •
  St Vincent & Gren. .... 167 O
Charlotte Harbour •
  FL, United States 155 C2
Charlottenburg, Schloss • Germany 73 E7
Charlottesville •
  VA, United States 156 A4
Charlottesville Heritage C •
  VA, United States .... 42 [10]
Charlotteville • Trinidad & Tobago .... 166 R
Charlton • VI, Australia 136 G6
Charnwood Forest • United Kingdom 65 F5
Charters Towers • QL, Australia 136 C3
Chartres • France 78 A2
Chartres Heritage C • France .... 44 [72]
Chartwell • United Kingdom 65 G8
Chascomús • Argentina 175 G7
Château-d'Oex • Switzerland .... 61 [60]
Château-d'Oex • Switzerland 90 J6
Château-Thierry • France 78 B1
Châteaubelair • St Vincent & Gren. .... 167 O
Chateaubelair I. •
  St Vincent & Gren. .... 167 O
Châteaubriant • France 77 E5
Châteaudun • France 77 F5
Châteauneuf-du-Pape • France 76 L9
Châteauroux • France 77 F6
Châteaux, Pointe des • Guadeloupe .... 167 I
Châtel Ski • France .... 61 [9]
Châtel • France 78 D3
Châtellerault • France 77 F6
Chatham • NB, Canada 160 B1
Chatham • OT, Canada 161 A3
Chatham • United Kingdom 65 H7
Chatham I. • Galápagos Is. 171 H10
Chatham Is. • Pacific Ocean 134 G9
Chattahoochee River Nat. Recreation Area
  Park N • GA, United States .... 153 [206]
Chattanooga • TN, United States 151 C3
Chau Doc • Vietnam 129 B5
Chaudi • Goa, India 123 C6
Chaudiere • QU, Canada 160 H3
Chauka • India 123 F7
Chaumont • France 76 F2
Chaumont [Château] • France 77 F5
Chautauqua-Allegheny •
  NY, United States 156 A1
Chautauqua • NY, United States 156 A1
Chauvin • LA, United States 156 F6
Chaux-de-Fonds, La • Switzerland 90 I5
Chávez, Jorge [Apt] • Peru 173 E6
Chavin Heritage C • Peru .... 42 [58]
Chaweng Beach • Ko Samui, Thailand 130 G11
Chayamangkalaram, Wat •
  Penang, Malaysia 129 E7
Chbika • Tunisia 107 C5
Cheb • Czech Rep. 89 D6
Cheboksary • Russian Fed. 100 G2
Chech, Erg • Algeria/Mali 106 B2
Cheddar • United Kingdom 65 K9
Cheddar Gorge • United Kingdom 65 K9
Chedworth Roman Villa •
  United Kingdom 65 F6
Cheektowaga • NY, United States 161 D1
Chek Lap Kok • Hong Kong, China 126 E5
Chelm • Poland 89 C3
Chelmno • Poland 89 B2
Chelmsford • United Kingdom 65 H7
Chelmsford Nature Reserve •
  South Africa 111 B3
Chelsea • United Kingdom 65 G7
Cheltenham • United Kingdom 65 F6
Chelyabinsk • Russian Fed. 101 G3
Chemillé • France 77 E6
Chemin Grenier • Mauritius 113 E6
Chemnitz • Germany 72 E3
Chenab • India/Pakistan 122 B2
Chengde • China 125 F2
Chengde Heritage C • China .... 43 [174]
Chengdu • China 125 E3
Chenini • Tunisia 107 D6
Chennai • India 124 C2
Chenonceau [Château] • France 77 F5
Chenzhou • China 125 F3
Cheongjong Bay •
  Ko Samui, Thailand 130 G11
Chépénéhé • New Caledonia .... 138 U
Chepkitale Nat. Reserve • Kenya 109 C4
Chepstow • United Kingdom 65 E6
Cher • France 76 E3
Cherbaniani Reef • India 124 E2
Cherbourg • France 76 C2
Cheremkhovo • Russian Fed. 100 M9
Cheriyam I. • India 124 A3
Cherkasy • Ukraine 100 D4
Cherkessk • Russian Fed. 100 F5
Cherleville-Mézières • France 78 L5
Chernihiv • Ukraine 100 D3
Chernomorets • Bulgaria 92 H6
Chernyakhovsk • Russian Fed. 100 J8
Cherokee • NC, United States .... 155 [68]
Cherokee Ind Res •
  NC, United States .... 155 [68]
Cherskogo, Khrebet • Russian Fed. 101 O3
Chesapeake • VA, United States 156 B4
Chesapeake Bay • VA, United States 156 B4
Chesapeake Bay Bridge •
  VA, United States 156 B4
Chesapeake & Ohio Canal Nat. Hist. Park
  Park N • MD, United States .... 153 [257]
Cheshire • United Kingdom 64 B4
Chesil Beach • United Kingdom 65 K10
Chessington World of Adventures Park L •
  United Kingdom .... 59 [34]
Chessington World of Adventures •
  United Kingdom 65 G7

Chester • PA, United States 156 B3
Chester • United Kingdom 63 D7
Chester-le-Street • United Kingdom 62 E6
Chesterfield • United Kingdom 63 E7
Chesterfield I. • New Caledonia 138 BB4
Chettiatt I. • India 124 A2
Chetumal • Mexico 169 F5
Cheung Chau • Hong Kong, China 126 E5
Cheverny • France 76 K8
Cheverny [Château] • France 77 F5
Cheviot Hills • United Kingdom 62 D5
Chevreau, L. • St Barthélemy .... 166 D
Chewore safari area Heritage N •
  Zimbabwe .... 41 [113]
Cheyenne • WY, United States 148 F2
Cheyenne [Riv] •
  SD/WY, United States 148 F2
Cheyenne Rock Ind Res •
  SD, United States .... 155 [47]
Cheyenne Wells • CO, United States 148 F3
Chhattisgarh • India 123 B3
Chi • Thailand 130 A2
Chia • Sardinia, Italy 86 F6
Chiai • Taiwan 125 G4
Chiang Dao • Thailand 130 B5
Chiang Kham • Thailand 130 C5
Chiang Khan • Thailand 130 C6
Chiang Khong • Thailand 130 C5
Chiang Mai • Thailand 130 B5
Chiang Rai • Thailand 130 B5
Chiang Saen • Thailand 130 C5
Chianti • Italy 87 C3
Chiapas • Mexico 169 D3
Chiávari • Italy 87 B2
Chiba • Japan 127 I8
Chiba [Adm] • Japan 127 H8
Chibougamau • QU, Canada 159 I4
Chic-Chocs, Réserves des •
  QU, Canada 160 B1
Chicago • IL, United States 150 C2
Chicanná • Mexico 169 F5
Chichagof I. • AK, United States 157 F4
Chiclana de la Frontera • Spain 82 H8
Chiclayo • Peru 173 B3
Chico • CA, United States 154 I7
Chicopee • MA, United States 156 F2
Chicoutimi • QU, Canada 160 A1
Chidambaram • India 124 C3
Chidley, Cape • NF/QU, Canada 159 J2
Chiemsee • Germany 73 F7
Chiesa • Italy 87 B1
Chieti • Italy 85 E3
Chifeng • China 125 F2
Chigach Mtns • AK, United States 157 E3
Chignik • AK, United States 157 D4
Chihuahua • Mexico 168 C2
Chihuahua [Adm] • Mexico 169 I5
Chikitu, Playa • Bonaire .... 166 U
Chilaw • Sri Lanka 124 C4
Chilca • Peru 173 E6
Childers • QL, Australia 136 D5
Chile • S. America 170 M11
CHILE • S. America 170 M11
Chilibre • France 170 M11
Chilkoot Pass • Canada/United States 157 F4
Chilkan • Chile 175 A3
Chillagoe • QL, Australia 136 B2
Chillicothe • MO, United States 150 B3
Chillicothe • OH, United States 150 D3
Chillon, Château de • Switzerland 90 I6
Chiloé, I. de • Chile 175 A4
Chiloé, I. de Heritage C • Chile .... 42 [81]
Chilpancingo • Mexico 169 J8
Chiltern Hills • United Kingdom 63 E9
Chimborazo • Ecuador 173 B2
Chimbote • Peru 173 B3
Chimney Rock Nat. Hist. Site Park N •
  NE, United States .... 152 [163]
China Folk Culture Villages • China 126 E4
CHINA, PEOPLE'S REPUBLIC OF • Asia 125-126
Chinandega • Nicaragua 170 D4
Chincha Alta • Peru 173 E6
Chincheros • Peru 173 E6
Chinchilla • QL, Australia 136 D5
Chinchorro, Banco • Mexico 169 G5
Chincoteague • VA, United States 156 B4
Chindwin • Myanmar 128 A2
Chinese & Japanese Garden •
  Singapore 129 H11
Chingola • Zambia 110 B2
Chinguetti • Mauritania 106 A2
Chinguetti Heritage C • Mauritania .... 43 [105]
Chiniot • Pakistan 122 B2
Chinle • AZ, United States 155 H7
Chinon • France 76 K8
Chinon [Château] • France 77 F6
Chioggia • Italy 87 C2
Chios • Chios, Greece .... 94 D
Chios [I.] • Greece .... 94 D
Chipata • Zambia 110 C2
Chipiona • Spain 82 H8
Chipman • NB, Canada 160 B2
Chippawa • OT, Canada 161 D1
Chippenham • United Kingdom 65 K9
Chippewa Falls • WI, United States 150 B1
Chiquitos Jesuit missions Heritage C •
  Bolivia .... 42 [66]
Chirala • India 124 C1
Chirchiq • Uzbekistan 121 D3
Chiricahua Nat. Mon. •
  AZ, United States 155 H8
Chiricahua Nat. Mon. Park N •
  AZ, United States .... 152 [116]
Chiriquí, Golfo de • Panama 170 F6
Chiriquí, Laguna de • Panama 170 F6
Chirpan • Bulgaria 92 H8
Chirripó Grande • Costa Rica 170 F6
Chirskiy • Russian Fed. 101 Q3
Chisasibi • QU, Canada 159 I3
Chisinau • Moldova 92 D3
Chistopol' • Russian Fed. 100 H2
Chita • Russian Fed. 101 L4
Chitose • Japan 127 D2
Chitradurga • India 124 B2
Chitrakut • India 123 F8
Chitré • Panama 170 M10
Chittagong • Bangladesh 122 D3
Chittaurgarh • India 123 E8
Chittoor • India 124 C2
Chitungwiza • Zimbabwe 110 C2
Chiunzi, Válico di • Italy 87 H7
Chiusa • Italy 86 C3
Chiusi • Italy 87 D3
Chivasso • Italy 87 A2
Chivilcoy • Argentina 175 G6
Chiwan • China 126 E5
Chobe Nat. Park • Botswana 110 I9
Chobe Nat. Park Park • Botswana .... 112 [118]
Choele Choel • Argentina 175 B3
Choirokoitia • Cyprus 96 G6
Choirokoitia Heritage C • Cyprus .... 44 [260]
Choiseul • Solomon Is. .... 138 W
Choiseul • St Lucia .... 167 N
Choisy Beach • Mauritius 113 E5
Choix • Mexico 168 C2
Chojna • Poland 89 A2
Cholet • France 77 E6
Cholula • Mexico 169 J7
Choluteca • Honduras 170 D4
Chom Thong • Thailand 130 B6
Chomutov • Czech Rep. 89 D6

Chon Buri • Thailand 130 E8
Chongjin • D.P.R. of Korea 125 G2
Chongkrum, Laem •
  Ko Samui, Thailand 130 G12
Chongming • China 126 H6
Chongming Dao • China 126 H6
Chongqing • China 125 E4
Chongqing [Adm] • China 126 C2
Chora • Náxos, Greece .... 94 H
Chorao I. • Goa, India 123 C5
Chorwad Beach • India 124 E6
Choshi • Japan 127 D3
Chos Malal • Argentina 175 A3
Choshi • Japan 127 D3
Chota Nagpur • India 122 C3
Choybalsan • Mongolia 125 F2
Chrisoskalitissas, Moni •
  Crete, Greece 93 G6
Chrisoula K Dive • Egypt 109 E8
Christchurch • New Zealand 137 B3
Christian, Point • Pitcairn Is. .... 139 X
Christiana • Jamaica 165 C3
Christiana • Norway 50 C1
Christiansfeld • Denmark 99 E8
Christianso • US Virgin Is. .... 166 X
Christmas I. • Kiribati .... 139 I
Chrysorroyiatissa Monastery • Cyprus .... 96 CA
Chrzanów • Poland 89 F8
Chu Yang Sin • Vietnam 129 C5
Chuang, Ko • Thailand 130 E8
Chuansha • China 126 H6
Chubu • Japan 127 C3
Chubut • Argentina 175 B4
Chudovo • Russian Fed. 100 L9
Chugoku • Japan 127 B3
Chukai • Malaysia 128 C6
Chukchi Sea •
  Russian Fed/United States 101 S2
Chukot Russ Adm • Russian Fed. .... 101 [31]
Chumphon • Thailand 128 B4
Chunar • India 123 G8
Chunyacache • Mexico 169 G4
Chuquibamba • Peru 173 F7
Chur • Switzerland 90 L5
Church Bay • Bermuda 165 K10
Churchill • MN, Canada 158 G3
Churchill, Cape • MN, Canada 158 G3
Churchill Falls • NF, Canada 159 J3
Churchill [Riv] • MN, Canada 158 G3
Churchill [Riv] • NF, Canada 159 J3
Churchs Ferry • ND, United States 148 G1
Churu • India 123 E7
Chute-Montmorency • QU, Canada 160 A1
Chuuk • Fed. States of Micronesia .... 138 C
Chuuk Lagoon •
  Fed. States of Micronesia .... 138 C
Chuvashia Russ Adm • Russian Fed. .... 101 [11]
Chuzhou • China 126 G6
Chynovska jeskyne • Czech Rep. 89 E7
Chyulu Nat. Park • Kenya 109 D5
Ciamis • Java, Indonesia 131 P12
Cianjur • Java, Indonesia 131 O11
Cibao • Dominican Rep. 165 G5
Cicia • Fiji .... 138 G
Ciechanów • Poland 89 C2
Ciego de Avila • Cuba 164 G4
Cienfuegos • Cuba 164 F1
Cieszyn • Poland 89 F9
Cieza • Spain 83 A1
Çiftehan • Turkey 95 J9
Çiftlik • Turkey 95 J9
Cijara, Embalse de • Spain 80 C4
Cijulang • Java, Indonesia 131 P12
Cilacap • Java, Indonesia 131 P12
Cilaos • Réunion 113 C4
Cilaos, Bras de la • Réunion 113 C4
Cilaos, Cirque de • Réunion 113 C4
Cilédug • Java, Indonesia 131 P11
Cilento • Italy 87 H7
Cilento Heritage C • Italy .... 44 [171]
Cilicia • Turkey 95 I10
Cilician Gates • Turkey 95 J9
Cima, I. de •
  Porto Santo, Madeira 84 E5
Cimahi • Java, Indonesia 131 P11
Cimarron • KS/OK, United States 149 G3
Cimini, Monti • Italy 87 E4
Cincinnati • OH, United States 150 D3
Cine • Turkey 95 F5
Cinque Terre • Italy 87 B3
Cinque Terre Heritage C • Italy .... 44 [159]
Cintalapa • Mexico 169 F4
Cinto, Monte • Corsica, France 78 M11
Ciotat, la • France 78 G8
Circeo, Parco Naz. del Park N •
  Italy .... 58 [97]
Circeo, Parco Naz. del • Italy 87 F5
Circle • AK, United States 157 E3
Circle • UT, United States 148 E1
Circleville • OH, United States 150 D3
Cirebon • Java, Indonesia 131 P11
Cirema, Gunung • Java, Indonesia 131 P11
Cirencester • United Kingdom 65 F6
Ciro Marina • Italy 85 F5
Cisco • TX, United States 155 E4
Citadelle, La • Haiti 165 F5
Città di Castello • Italy 87 D3
Cittadella • Italy 87 C2
City of Rocks Nat. Reserve •
  ID, United States 154 H6
City of Rocks Nat. Reserve Park N •
  ID, United States .... 152 [60]
Ciudad Acuña • Mexico 168 C2
Ciudad Altamirano • Mexico 169 I7
Ciudad Bolívar • Venezuela 173 C2
Ciudad Camargo • Mexico 168 C2
Ciudad Constitución • Mexico 168 I6
Ciudad de Guatemala • Guatemala 170 B3
Ciudad de México Heritage C • Mexico .... 42 [22]
Ciudad de Panamá • Panama 170 M11
Ciudad de Panamá Heritage C • Panama .... 42 [38]
Ciudad del Carmen • Mexico 169 E5
Ciudad del Este • Paraguay 175 C2
Ciudad Guayana • Venezuela 173 C2
Ciudad Guzmán • Mexico 169 H7
Ciudad Juárez • Mexico 168 C1
Ciudad Madero • Mexico 169 J6
Ciudad Mante • Mexico 169 J7
Ciudad Mendoza • Mexico 169 K7
Ciudad Obregón • Mexico 168 I6
Ciudad Real • Spain 80 D4
Ciudad Rodrigo • Spain 80 B3
Ciudad Valles • Mexico 169 J6
Ciudad Victoria • Mexico 169 J6
Ciutadella • Minorca, Spain 83 J7
Civa Lara Fun Park Park L • Ireland .... 153 [258]
Ciavraville • NF, Canada 160 C1
Clare Abbey • Ireland 69 H10
Clare [Adm] • Ireland 69 H10
Clare Glens • Ireland 69 H10
Clare I. • Ireland 69 H8
Claregalway Abbey • Ireland 69 H9
Claremont • NH, United States 150 F2
Claremorris • Ireland 69 H8
Clarence • New Zealand 137 B3
Clarence Town • Bahamas 164 B2
Clara Barton Nat. Hist. Site Park N •
  MD, United States .... 153 [256]

Clarion • PA, United States 156 A2
Clarión, I. • Mexico 168 B4
Clarke I. • TS, Australia 136 F6
Clarksburg • WV, United States 150 D3
Clarksdale • MS, United States 151 B4
Clarksville • TN, United States 151 C3
Clatsop, Fort, Nat. Mem. •
    OR, United States 154 G5
Clausholm • Denmark 99 F7
Clavière Ski • Italy . . . . 61 [117]
Clavière • Italy 87 A2
Clayton • NM, United States 149 F3
Clayton, Fuerte • Panama 170 M11
Clear, Cape • Ireland 69 G11
Clear I. • Ireland 69 G11
Clear Water Bay • Hong Kong, China . 126 F5
Clearfield • PA, United States 156 A2
Clearwater • FL, United States 155 C2
Cleator Moor • United Kingdom 65 C3
Cleburne • TX, United States 155 E4
Cleethorpes • United Kingdom 63 E7
Cleethorpes Beach • United Kingdom . 64 [10]
Clermont • FL, United States 157 A1
Clermont • France 78 B1
Clermont • QL, Australia 136 C4
Clermont-Ferrand • France 76 E4
Clervaux • Luxembourg 70 D5
Clevedon • United Kingdom 65 K9
Cleveland • MS, United States 151 B4
Cleveland • OH, United States 161 A3
Cleveland • TN, United States 151 D3
Cleveland • TX, United States 155 F5
Clew Bay • Ireland 69 G8
Clewiston • FL, United States 155 D2
Clifden • Ireland 69 G9
Clifden • New Zealand 137 F8
Clifton • AZ, United States 148 E2
Clifton Harbour • St Vincent & Gren. . 167 P
Clinton • BC, Canada 160 I7
Clinton • IA, United States 150 B2
Cloghane • Ireland 69 G10
Clogher Head • Ireland 69 F6
Clonakilty • Ireland 69 H11
Clonakilty Bay • Ireland 69 H11
Cloncurry • QL, Australia 135 G4
Clonmel • Ireland 69 G6
Clonmellon • Ireland 69 E6
Clontarf • Ireland 50 A2
Cloquet • MN, United States 150 B1
Cloudy Bay • New Zealand 137 B3
Clovelly • United Kingdom 65 J9
Clovis • NM, United States 149 F4
Cluff Lake Mine • SA, Canada 158 F3
Cluj-Napoca • Romania 92 C2
Clun Forest • United Kingdom 65 E5
Clusaz, la Ski • France . . . . 61 [17]
Clusaz, la • France 78 D3
Clutha • New Zealand 137 G8
Clutha District • New Zealand 137 G8
Clyde • United Kingdom 65 A2
Clyde, Firth of • United Kingdom . . . 62 C5
Clyde River • NU, Canada 159 J1
Clydebank • United Kingdom 65 A2
Côa, Vale do Heritage C • Portugal . . 44 [129]
Coachella • CA, United States 149 C4
Coahuila • Mexico 169 B2
Coal I. • New Zealand 137 F8
Coaldale • NV, United States 148 C3
Coalville • United Kingdom 65 F5
Coamo • Puerto Rico 165 J8
Coari • Brazil 173 C3
Coast Mtns • Canada/United States . . 158 D3
Coastal Plain • United States 142 E5
Coates I. • NU, Canada 159 H2
Coats Land • Antarctica 176 O5
Coatzacoalcos • Mexico 169 K8
Coatzacoalcos [Riv] • Mexico 169 K8
Cobán • Mexico 169 G4
Cobán • Guatemala 170 K9
Çobanısa • Turkey 95 G8
Cobblers Reef • Barbados . . . . 167 M
Cóbh • Ireland 69 H11
Coburg • Germany 72 D3
Cochabamba • Bolivia 173 C4
Coche, I. de • Venezuela . . . . 166 T
Cochem • Germany 74 C5
Coches, les Ski • France . . . . . . 61 [27]
Cochin • India 124 B3
Cochin China • Vietnam 129 B6
Cochinos, Bahía de • Cuba 164 F4
Cochrane • OT, Canada 159 H4
Cockburn Harbour •
    Turks & Caicos Is. 164 D3
Cockburn I. • OT, Canada 161 C2
Cockburn Town • Bahamas 164 B2
Cockburn Town • Turks & Caicos Is. . 164 D3
Cockermouth • United Kingdom 65 C3
Cockpit Country • Jamaica 165 C3
Coco • Honduras/Nicaragua 170 K3
Coco, Cayo • Cuba 164 G4
Coco, I. • St Barthélemy . . . . 166 D
Cocoa Beach • FL, United States . . . 155 D2
Cocoa I. • Maldives 124 H8
Cocoa Point • Antigua & Barbuda . . . 167 H
Coconut Point • American Samoa . . . 139 H
Cocos Bay • Trinidad & Tobago . . . . 166 S
Cocos I. • Guam . . . . 130 Z
Cocos Lagoon • Guam . . . . 130 Z
Cocula • Mexico 169 H7
Cod, Cape • MA, United States 156 D1
Codó • Brazil 174 B3
Codrington • Antigua & Barbuda . . . 167 H
Codrington College • Barbados . . . . 167 M
Codrington Lagoon •
    Antigua & Barbuda . . . . 167 H
Cody • WY, United States 148 E2
Coesfeld • Germany 72 B3
Coëtivy • Seychelles 113 B2
Coeur d'Alene • ID, United States . . 154 H5
Coeur d'Alene Ind Res •
    ID, United States . . . . 155 [13]
Coevorden • Netherlands 70 D2
Coffs Harbour • NS, Australia 135 I6
Cofresí • Dominican Rep. 165 G5
Coglians, Monte • Austria/Italy. 87 D1
Cognac • France 78 E5
Cogolin • France 78 H8
Coiba, I. de • Panama 170 G7
Coihaique • Chile 175 A4
Coimar • Cuba 164 F4
Coimbatore • India 124 B3
Coimbra • Portugal 80 A3
Coimbra [Adm] • Portugal 84 A2
Colac • New Zealand 137 G8
Colac • VI, Australia 136 G9
Colares • Portugal 84 F6
Colatina • Brazil 174 F6
Colbeck Castle • Jamaica 165 C3
Colby • KS, United States 148 F3
Colca • Peru 173 F7
Colca, Cañon del • Peru 173 F7
Colchester • United Kingdom 65 H7
Cold Bay • AK, United States 157 D4
Coleford Nature Reserve •
    South Africa 111 B5
Colenso • South Africa 111 B4
Coleraine • United Kingdom 62 B5
Coles, Punta • Peru 173 F7
Colfosco Ski • Italy . . . . 61 [146]
Colfosco • Italy 86 D3
Colihaut • Dominica . . . . 167 Y
Colima • Mexico 169 H7
Colima [Adm] • Mexico 169 B3
Colima, Nevado de • Mexico 169 H7
Coll • United Kingdom 62 B4
College Park & GA, United States . . 151 D4
College Station •
    TX, United States 155 E5
Colliers • Cayman Is. 165 B2
Collingwood • New Zealand 137 B3
Collingwood • OT, Canada 160 E4
Collins • MS, United States 156 F5
Collinsville • QL, Australia 136 C3
Collioure • France 78 L10
Collonges-la-Rouge • France 78 F5
Collooney • Ireland 69 H8
Colmar • France 76 G2
Colmenar • France 74 E8
Colóane • Macau, China 126 E4
Colóane Village • Macau, China 126 E4
Cologne • Germany 73 C6
Cologne Heritage C • Germany . . . . 44 [56]
Colom, l. d'En • Minorca, Spain 83 K8
Coloma • CA, United States 154 I8
Coloma Beach • Goa, India 123 C6
COLOMBIA • S. America 173 B2
Colombian Basin • West Indies 166 CC4
Colombier • St Barthélemy . . . . 166 D
Colombier • St Martin . . . . 166 C
Colombier • Switzerland 90 I5
Colombier, Pointe à •
    St Barthélemy . . . . 166 D
Colombo • Sri Lanka 124 C4
Colombo, Cristofo [Apt] • Italy. 87 B2
Colón • Cuba 164 F4
Colón • Panama 170 L10
Colón, Archipiélago de •
    Pacific Ocean . . . . 171 G-H
Colón [Adm] • Panama 170 M10
Colón, Cos, Greece . . . . 94 E
Colonia Suiza • Uruguay 175 G6
Colonia del Sacramento • Uruguay . . 175 B4
Colonia del Sacramento Heritage C •
    Uruguay . . . . 42 [78]
Colonia del Sacramento • Uruguay . . 175 G6
Colonial Nat. Hist. Park •
    VA, United States 156 B4
Colonial Nat. Hist. Park Park N •
    VA, United States . . . . 153 [246]
Colonna, Capo • Italy 88 G5
Colonsay • United Kingdom 62 B4
Colorado • Argentina 175 B3
Colorado [Adm] • United States 148 E3
Colorado Desert •
    CA, United States 154 J9
Colorado Nat. Mon. Park N •
    CO, United States . . . . 152 [88]
Colorado Plateau • United States . . . 155 G7
Colorado Point Lighthouse • Aruba . . 166 W
Colorado [Riv] • TX, United States . . 149 G4
Colorado River • United States 148 E3
Colorado River Ind Res •
    AZ, United States . . . . 155 [27]
Colorado Springs •
    CO, United States 148 E3
Colossae • Turkey 95 F5
Columbia • LA, United States 156 E5
Columbia • MO, United States 150 B3
Columbia • MS, United States 151 C4
Columbia • SC, United States 151 D4
Columbia • TN, United States 151 C3
Columbia Basin • WA, United States . 154 H5
Columbia Gorge •
    OR/WA, United States 154 G5
Columbia Icefield • AL, Canada 160 J7
Columbia, Mt • AL/BC, Canada 160 J7
Columbia Plateau • United States . . . 154 H6
Columbine, Cape • South Africa 111 D6
Columbus • GA, United States 151 D4
Columbus • MS, United States 151 C4
Columbus • MT, United States 148 E1
Columbus • NE, United States 148 G2
Columbus • OH, United States 150 D3
Columbus • TX, United States 155 E5
Columbus Mon. • Bahamas 164 B2
Columbus Park • Jamaica 165 C2
Colva • Goa, India 123 C6
Colva Beach • Goa, India 123 C6
Colville • AK, United States 157 F2
Colville Ind Res •
    WA, United States . . . . 155 [3]
Colwyn Bay • United Kingdom 63 D7
Colwyn Bay [Bay] • United Kingdom . 63 D7
Coma Pedrosa • Andorra 82 E5
Comácchio, Lido di • Italy 87 D2
Comácchio, Valli di • Italy 87 C2
Comalapa [Apt] • El Salvador 170 K9
Comandante Ferraz [Base] •
    Antarctica . . . . 176 [2]
Comarapa • Bolivia 173 C4
Comayagua • Honduras 170 K9
Combarelles, Grotte des • France . . . 78 F5
Combarro • Dominican Rep. 165 F5
Comeragh Mtns • Ireland 69 C4
Comerío • Puerto Rico 165 J8
Cometa, Punta • Mexico 169 K8
Comino • Malta 96 A1
Comino • Malta 96 H8
Comiso • Sicily, Italy 88 H8
Comitán de Domínguez • Mexico . . . 168 F4
Commandersbaai • Aruba . . . . 166 W
Commingers • France 78 K10
Commissioner's Point • Bermuda . . . 165 K9
Committee Bay • NU, Canada 159 H2
Como • Italy 87 B1
Como, Lago di • Italy 87 B1
Comodoro Rivadavia • Argentina . . . 175 B4
Comoé, Parc nat. de la Park •
    Côte d'Ivoire . . . . 112 [17]
Comoé, Parc nat. de la Heritage N •
    Côte d'Ivoire . . . . 41 [95]
Comorin, Cape • India 110 D2
Compiègne • France 78 B1
Compiègne, Forêt de • France 78 B1
Comrat • Moldova 92 D3
Comté Tolosan • France 76 K9
Comtés Rhodaniens • France 76 L9
Con Dao • Vietnam 129 B6
Conakry • Guinea 106 A4
Concarneau • France 77 C4
Conceição • Portugal 84 K9
Conceição do Araguaia • Brazil 174 B3
Concepción • Chile 175 A3
Concepción • Paraguay 175 C2
Concepción • Peru 173 E6
Concepción • Seychelles 113 A1
Concepción • Bahamas 164 B2
Concepción, Point •
    CA, United States 154 I9
Conch Bar • Turks & Caicos Is. 164 C3
Conchos • Mexico 168 C2
Concord • CA, United States 148 B3
Concord • MA, United States 156 D1
Concord • NH, United States 156 C1
Concórdia • Argentina 175 C3
Concordia Baai • St Eustatius . . . . . 167 E
Condobolin • NS, Australia 136 G8
Condrieu • France 76 L9
Conero, Costa • Italy 87 D3
Coney I. • Bermuda 165 L9
Conflens • France 78 F5
Cóng • Ireland 69 H9
Congaree Swamp Nat. Mem. Park N •
    SC, United States . . . . 153 [232]
CONGO • Africa 106 D5
Congo Basin • Dem. Rep. of Congo . 108 B5
CONGO, DEMOCRATIC REPUBLIC OF •
    Africa 108 B5
Congo [Riv] •
    Congo/Dem. Rep. of Congo . . . 108 A4
Congonhas • Brazil 174 E6
Congonhas Heritage C • Brazil . . . . . 42 [76]
Coni de la Frontera • Spain 83 012
Conillera, I. • Spain 83 K8
Conni • Panama 170 M11
Conn, Lough • Ireland 69 H8
Connacht • Ireland 69 B3
Connaught • Ireland 69 B3
Connecticut [Adm] • United States . . 156 C1
Connecticut [Riv] • United States . . . 156 C1
Connellan [Apt] • NT, Australia 136 A2
Connemara • Ireland 69 B3
Connemara Nat. Park Park N • Ireland 58 [43]
Connemara Nat. Park • Ireland 69 G9
Conny-Land Park L • Switzerland . . . 59 [79]
Conroe • TX, United States 155 F5
Conselheiro Lafaiete • Brazil 174 E6
Constance • Germany 74 B4
Constance, Lake • Germany 74 E8
Constanţa • Romania 92 I7
Constantina • Spain 82 I7
Constantine • Algeria 106 C1
Constantinople • Turkey 50 E3
Constitution of 1857, Parque Nac. •
    Mexico 168 H5
Constitution Gardens Park N •
    DC, United States . . . . 153 [264]
Contact • NV, United States 148 D2
Contamines-Montjoie, les Ski •
    France . . . . 61 [22]
Contamines-Montjoie, les • France . . 78 D3
Contitución • Chile 175 A3
Contoy, I. • Mexico 169 G4
Contwoy • AR, United States 151 B3
Conway • FL, United States 157 B1
Coober Pedy • SA, Australia 135 E5
Cook, Grand Récif de •
    New Caledonia . . . . 138 U
Cook Inlet • AK, United States 157 E3
Cook IS. • Pacific Ocean 139 DD4
Cook, Mt • New Zealand 137 B3
Cook Strait • New Zealand 137 B3
Cookeville • TN, United States 151 C3
Cookhouse • South Africa 111 G6
Cooktown • United Kingdom 63 B6
Cooktown • QL, Australia 135 H3
Coolangatta • QL, Australia 136 D5
Coolgardie • WA, Australia 135 C6
Cooma • NS, Australia 136 H9
Coon Rapids • MN, United States . . . 150 B1
Coonabarabran • NS, Australia 135 H6
Coonamble • NS, Australia 135 H6
Coonoor • India 124 B3
Coonoor Hill Sta • India 124 C6
Cooper Creek • SA, Australia 135 F5
Cooper I. • British Virgin Is. . . . . . . 166 A
Cooper I. • New Zealand 137 F8
Cooperstown • NY, United States . . . 156 B1
Coorg • India 124 B2
Coorow • WA, Australia 135 B5
Coos Bay • OR, United States 154 G6
Cootamundra • NS, Australia 136 H8
Copacabana • Bolivia 173 F7
Copacabana • Brazil 174 F7
Copala • Mexico 169 J8
Copán • Honduras 170 K9
Copán Heritage C • Honduras . . . . . 42 [34]
Copang Bay • TX, United States 156 F5
Copeland Forest • United Kingdom . . 65 C3
Copenhagen • Denmark 99 G7
Copiapó • Chile 175 A2
Copper Harbor • MI, United States . . 161 B1
Copper Mtn Ski • CO, United States . 146 [59]
Copperas Cove • TX, United States . . 155 E5
Coppermine • NU, Canada 158 E2
Coquelles • France 66 D5
Coquimbo • Chile 175 A2
Coral Bay • Cyprus 96 C4
Coral Bay • US Virgin Is. . . . . 166 X
Coral Coast • Tunisia 107 O4
Coral Gables • FL, United States . . . 155 D3
Coral Harbour • NU, Canada 159 H2
Coral Heights • Bahamas 164 A2
Coral Sea • Pacific Ocean 134 D6
Coral Sea Is. Territory • Australia . . . 136 C2
Coral Springs • FL, United States . . . 155 D3
Coralarium • Singapore 129 I17
Corallo, Riviera del •
    Sardinia, Italy 86 E5
Corbeil-Essonnes • France 78 B1
Corbett Nat. Park • India 123 F7
Corbie Ski • France . . . . 61 [35]
Corbières • France 78 L10
Corby • United Kingdom 65 H11
Corcaigh • Ireland 69 H11
Córcega • Puerto Rico 165 I7
Corcovado, Golfo de • Chile 175 A4
Corcovado • SR, United States 151 D4
Cordèvole • Italy 86 D4
Cordillera Central • Dominican Rep. . 165 G5
Cordillera Central • Panama 170 L10
Cordillera Central • Puerto Rico 165 I8
Cordillera Occidental • Colombia . . . 173 B2
Cordillera Occidental • Peru 173 E6
Cordillera Oriental • Colombia 173 B2
Cordillera Oriental • Dominican Rep. . 165 H6
Cordillera Oriental • Peru 173 F6
Cordillera Real • Ecuador 173 B3
Cordilleras Central Heritage C •
    Philippines . . . . 43 [207]
Córdoba • Argentina 175 B3
Córdoba Heritage C • Argentina . . . . 42 [79]
Córdoba • Mexico 169 K7
Córdoba • Spain 82 I7
Córdoba Heritage C • Spain . . . . . 44 [123]
Cordova • AK, United States 157 E3
Corfe Castle • United Kingdom 65 K10
Corfu • Corfu, Greece . . . . 94 A
Corfu [I.] • Greece . . . . 94 A
Corigliano Cálabro • Italy. 85 F5
Corinaldo • Italy 87 D3
Corinna • TS, Australia 136 E6
Corinth • Greece 93 C3
Corinth • MS, United States 151 C4
Corinth, Gulf of • Greece 94 BB3
Corjuem Fort • Goa, India 123 C5
Cork • Ireland 69 H11
Cork [I.] • Ireland 69 H11
Corn Is. • Nicaragua 170 F4
Cornas • France 76 L9
Corner Brook • NF, Canada 160 C1
Corner Point • Saba . . . . 167 F
Corniche, la • France 78 H7
Corníglia Heritage C • Italy . . . . . . 44 [159]
Corning • NY, United States 156 B1
Corno Grande • Italy 87 F4
Cornouaille • France 77 C4
Cornwall • OT, Canada 160 G4
Cornwall • United Kingdom 65 I10
Cornwall, Cape • United Kingdom . . . 65 I10
Cornwallis I. • NU, Canada 158 G1
Coro • Venezuela 173 C1
Coro Heritage C • Venezuela . . . . . . 42 [50]
Coroatín • Ireland 69 H9
Coromandel • New Zealand 137 C2
Coromandel Coast • India 124 C2
Coromandel Peninsula • New Zealand 137 C2
Coronado, Bahía de • Costa Rica . . . 170 F7
Coronado Nat. Mem. •
    AZ, United States . . . . 152 [113]
Coronado Nat. Mem. Park N •
    AZ, United States . . . . 152 [113]
Coronation Gulf • NU, Canada 158 E2
Coronel Fabriciano • Brazil 174 F6
Coronel Oviedo • Paraguay 175 B3
Coronel Pringles • Argentina 175 B3
Coronel Suárez • Argentina 175 F7
Coronel Peak • New Zealand 137 G7
Coropuna, Nudo • Peru 173 F7
Corossol • St Barthélemy . . . . 166 D
Corozal • Panama 170 M11
Corozal • Belize 170 K8
Corpus Christi • TX, United States . . 155 E6
Corpus Christi Bay •
    TX, United States 155 E6
Corralejo •
    Fuerteventura, Canary Is. 83 H5
Corralejo, Playas de •
    Fuerteventura, Canary Is. 83 H5
Correggio • Italy 87 B2
Corregidor-en-Vercors Ski • France . 61 [38]
Correze • France 78 F5
Corrib, Lough • Ireland 69 H9
Corrientes • Argentina 175 B3
Corrientes, Cabo • Cuba 164 E4
Corrientes, Cabo • Mexico 169 H7
Corrigan • TX, United States 155 F5
Corse • France . . . . 76 I-J
Corse, Cap • Corsica, France 78 N11
Corse-du-Sud • Corsica, France . . . 78 N12
Corsham Court • United Kingdom . . . 65 K9
Corsica • France . . . . 78 M-N
Corsicana • TX, United States 155 E4
Corte • Corsica, France 78 N11
Cortés, Laguna de • Cuba 164 E4
Cortina • Italy . . . . 61 [147]
Cortina d'Ampezzo • Italy 86 D3
Cortona • Italy 87 C3
Coruche • Portugal 84 G6
Corum • Turkey 95 B1
Corumbá • Brazil 174 A4
Coruña, A • Spain 80 A2
Corunna • Spain 50 A3
Corvallis • OR, United States 154 G6
Corvara Ski • Italy . . . . 61 [146]
Corvara in Badia • Italy 86 D3
Corvo • Azores 84 B4
Çorycus • Turkey 95 I10
Cos • Cos, Greece . . . . 94 E
Cos [I.] • Greece . . . . 91 E
Cosenza • Italy 85 F5
Cosigüina, Punta • Nicaragua 170 D4
Cosmoledo, Atoll de • Seychelles . . 113 A2
Cosne-Cours-sur-Loire • France 76 E3
Costa d'en Blanes • Majorca, Spain . 83 N12
Costa da Caparica • Portugal 84 F6
COSTA RICA • C. America 170 E5
Costa Smeralda [Apt] •
    Sardinia, Italy 86 F5
Costa Teguise •
    Lanzarote, Canary Is. 83 I5
Costanza • Dominican Rep. 165 G6
Costières de Nîmes • France 76 L9
Costinesti • Romania 92 I7
Cotabato • Philippines 128 G5
Cotahuasi • Peru 173 F7
Cotahuasi, Cañon del • Peru 173 F7
Cote 2000 Ski • France . . . . 61 [37]
Côte Chalonnaise • France 76 L8
Côte d'Azur • France . . . . 78 G-H
CÔTE D'IVOIRE • Africa 106 B4
Côte de Beaune • France 76 L8
Côte de Nuits • France 76 L8
Côte Rotie • France 76 L9
Coteaux de Vendômois • France . . . 76 K8
Coteaux du Tricastin • France 76 K9
Coteaux les Baux-de-Provence •
    France 76 L9
Cotehele • United Kingdom 65 J10
Côtes d'Armor • France 77 D3
Côtes du Frontonnais • France 76 K9
Côtes du Lubéron • France 76 L9
Côtes du Marmandais • France 76 K9
Côtes du Rhône • France 76 L9
Côtes du Roussillon • France 76 L9
Côtes de Ventoux • France 76 L9
Côtes du Vivarais • France 76 L9
Cotigao Wildlife Sanctuary •
    Goa, India 123 C6
Cotswold • United Kingdom . . . . . . 146 [24]
Csorna • Hungary 92 B2
Ctesiphon • Iraq 121 J7
Cu Chi Tunnels • Vietnam 129 B5
Cu Lao Hon • Vietnam 129 C6
Cuamba • Mozambique 110 C2
Cuando • Angola 110 B2
Cuango • Angola 110 A2
Cuauhtémoc • Mexico 168 C2
Cuautla • Mexico 169 J7
CUBA • West Indies . . . . 164 E-H
Cubagua, I. de • Venezuela . . . . . . 166 T
Cubango • Angola 110 A2
Cubells • Ibiza, Spain 83 L10
Cuchilla Grande • Uruguay 175 G6
Cuchillas de Toa • Cuba 164 H4
Cucuí • Brazil 173 C2
Cúcuta • Colombia 173 B2
Cuddalore • India 124 C2
Cuddapah • India 124 C2
Cuenca • Ecuador 173 B3
Cuenca Heritage C • Ecuador . . . . . 42 [55]
Cuenca • Spain 80 D3
Cuenca Heritage C • Spain . . . . . . 44 [103]
Cuernavaca • Mexico 169 J7
Cueto • Cuba 164 H5
Cueva de Bellamar • Cuba 164 F4
Cueva de las Manos Heritage C •
    Argentina . . . . 42 [80]
Cuevas de Camuy • Puerto Rico . . . 165 I7
Cuevas del Drach • Majorca, Spain . 83 N12
Cugir • Romania 92 C2
Cuiabá • Brazil 174 A4
Cuidado, Punta • Easter I. . . . . 139 M
Cuiheng • China 126 F3
Cuillin Hills • United Kingdom 62 B3
Cuito • Angola 110 I9
Cuitzeo • Mexico 169 I7
Cuitzeo, Laguna de • Mexico 169 I7
Cul-de-Sac • St Martin . . . . 166 C
Culatra, I. da • Portugal 84 J8
Culbone Church • United Kingdom . . 65 J9
Culcairn • NS, Australia 136 H8
Culebra Cut • Panama 170 M11
Culebra [I.] • Puerto Rico 165 J8
Culebrón • Netherlands 70 H8
Culemborg • Netherlands 70 H8
Culiacán • Mexico 168 C3
Culik • Bali, Indonesia 131 L7
Culpeper • VA, United States 156 A3
Culpepper I. • Galápagos Is. 171 G9
Culross • United Kingdom 65 B2
Culuba • Mexico 169 G4
Cuma • Italy 87 G7
Cumaná • Venezuela 173 C1
Cumberland • KY/TN, United States . 151 C3
Cumberland • MD, United States . . . 156 A3
Cumberland • MD, United States . . . 156 A3
Cumberland Gap Nat. Hist. Park Park N •
    United States . . . . 153 [228]
Cumberland I. Nat. Seashore Park N •
    GA, United States . . . . 153 [213]
Cumberland Peninsula • NU, Canada . 159 J2
Cumberland Sound • NU, Canada . . 159 J2
Cumberland • United Kingdom 63 D6
Cumbrian Mtns • United Kingdom . . 63 D6
Cummings • CA, United States 148 B3
Cumnock • United Kingdom 65 B6
Cupar • United Kingdom 65 B2
Cupra Marittima • Italy 87 D3
Curaçao • West Indies . . . . 166 V
Curaçao Seaquarium • Curaçao . . . . 166 V
Curaçao Underwater Park • Curaçao . 166 V
Curecanti Nat. Recreation Area Park N •
    CO, United States . . . . 152 [90]
Curicó • Chile 113 C6
Curieuse • Seychelles 113 B2
Curitiba • Brazil 175 D2
Curium • Cyprus 96 C4
Curonian Spit •
    Lithuania/Russian Fed. 100 J3
Curonian Spit Heritage C •
    Lithuania/Russian Fed. . . . . . 44 [263]
Currah, The • Ireland 69 B4
Curral das Freiras • Madeira 84 D5
Currane, Lough • Ireland 69 G11
Currie • TS, Australia 136 E6
Curtea de Argeş • Romania 92 C2
Curtis I. • QL, Australia 136 D4
Cusco • Peru 173 F6
Cusco Heritage C • Peru . . . . 42 [60]
Cusset • France 76 E3
Custer • MT, United States 148 E1
Cuttack • India 122 C2
Cuxhaven • Germany 72 C2
Cuyabeno Valley Nat. Park Park N •
    OH, United States . . . . 153 [185]
Cwmbran • United Kingdom 65 E6
Cyclades • Greece 93 D3
Cypress Hills • SA, Canada 158 F4
CYPRUS • Europe . . . . 96 C-D

Cyrenaica • Libya 108 B2
Cyrene Heritage C • Libya . . . . 44 [296]
Cyril E. King [Apt] • US Virgin Is. . . . 166 X
CZECH REPUBLIC • Europe 89 A4
Czechowice-Dziedzice • Poland 89 F9
Czestochowa • Poland 89 F8
Czluchów • Poland 89 B2

D

D.F. Wouda steam pumping station
    Heritage C • Netherlands. . . . . 44 [32]
D.F. Woudagemaal • Netherlands . . . 70 C1
D'Arros • Seychelles 113 B1
D'Entrecasteaux Channel •
    TS, Australia 136 F7
D'Entrecasteaux Is. •
    Papua New Guinea 138 BB3
D'Urville I. • New Zealand 137 B3
Da Lat • Vietnam 129 C5
Da Lat Plateau • Vietnam 129 C5
Ua Nang • Vietnam 128 D3
Da Yang • Vietnam 129 A1
Da Yunhe • China 125 F3
Dabolim [Apt] • Goa, India 123 C5
Dabrowa Górnicza • Poland 89 F8
Dabuleni • Romania 92 D3
Dachang • China 126 G6
Dachau • Germany 74 G7
Dachstein • Austria 91 F7
Dachstein Heritage C • Austria . . . 44 [141]
Dadès, Gorges du • Morocco 107 B2
Dädesjö • Sweden 99 H6
Dadra & Nagar Haveli • India 123 A3
Daedalus Reef Dive • Egypt 109 E8
Daegu • Rep. of Korea 125 G3
Daejeon • Rep. of Korea 125 G3
Daer • Romania 92 I7
Dáfni • Greece . . . . 94 B
Dafnoúdi, Akra •
    Cephalonia, Greece . . . . 94 J
Dagali • Norway 98 G8
Dagg Sound • New Zealand 137 F7
Dagupan • Philippines 128 G3
Dahab • Egypt 109 D2
Dahlak Archipelago • Eritrea 109 E10
Dahlak Kebir • Eritrea 109 E10
Dahlem (Berlin) • Germany 73 E8
Dahshur • Egypt 109 A1
Dai I. • Solomon Is. . . . . 138 W
Dai Shan • China 126 H7
Dailekh • Nepal 123 E2
Daimiel, Parque Nac. de las Tablas de
    Park N • Spain . . . . 58 [81]
Daishan • China 126 H7
Daito-shoto • Japan 138 AA1
Daitō Heritage C • Dominican Rep. . 165 G6
Dakar • Senegal 106 A3
Dakhla Oasis • Egypt 109 A2
Dakovica • Serbia & Montenegro . . . 92 C3
Dala • Austria 91 K8
Dalälven • Sweden 97 C3
Dalaman • Turkey 95 F6
Dalaman [Riv] • Turkey 95 F6
Dalarnas • Sweden 98 B3
Dalarö • Sweden 99 B2
DEbossjön • Sweden 99 G5
Dalby • QL, Australia 136 T6
Dalby • Sweden 98 G7
Dale • Hordaland, Norway 98 F8
Dale • Sogn og Fjordane, Norway . . 98 F8
Dalem Temple • Bali, Indonesia . . . 131 L8
Dalen • Norway 98 G9
Dalhart • TX, United States 149 F3
Dalslands kanal • Sweden 99 F5
Dalton • South Africa 111 B4
Dalton-in-Furness • United Kingdom . 63 D6
Daltonganj • India 123 G8
Daluis, Gorges de • France 78 D4
Daly Waters • NT, Australia 135 C3
Dalyan • Turkey 95 F6
Dama • Fiji Is. . . . . 138 S
Daman Beach • India 124 E6
Daman & Diu • India 123 A3
Damaraland • Namibia 110 A3
Damascus • Syria 120 D7
Damascus Heritage C • Syria . . . . . 44 [302]
Damawand, Dolleh-ye • Iran 120 G6
Dambulla Golden Rock Temple •
    Sri Lanka 124 C4
Dambulla Golden Rock Temple Heritage N •
    Sri Lanka . . . . 41 [127]
Dambulla Golden Rock Temple Heritage C •
    Sri Lanka . . . . 43 [167]
Dame-Marie, Cap • Haiti 165 E6
Damietta • Egypt 109 B1
Damietta Mouth • Egypt 109 B1
Damnoan Saduak floating market •
    Thailand 130 D7
Damoh • India 123 F8
Dampier • WA, Australia 135 B4
Dampir • Russian Fed. 91 M7
Danakil • Eritrea/Ethiopia 109 E11
Danbury • CT, United States 156 C1
Dancheng • China 126 H7
Dandeldhura • Nepal 123 F7
Dandenong • VI, Australia 136 G9
Dandong • China 125 G2
Dangan Liedao • China 126 F4
Danger Point • South Africa 111 E7
Dani • China 170 K9
Dania • FL, United States 155 D3
Daniel • WY, United States 148 D2
Danilov • Russian Fed. 100 M9
Danish Riviera • Denmark 99 G7
Dankov • Russian Fed. 100 E3
Danlí • Honduras 170 K9
Dannemora • Sweden 99 B1
Dannenberg • Germany 72 D2
Dannevirke • New Zealand 137 C2
Dansville • NY, United States 156 A1
Danube • Europe 92 I7
Danube Delta • Romania 92 I7
Danube Delta Heritage N • Romania . 41 [125]
Danube • IL, United States 150 C2
Danyang • China 126 G6
Daphne I. • Galápagos Is. 171 H10
Daphni Heritage C • Greece . . . . . . 44 [243]
Dar es Salaam • Tanzania 110 H8
Dar Bouâzza • Morocco 107 A2
Darbhanga • India 122 C3
Dardanelles • Turkey 95 E4
Darfur • Sudan 108 B3
Darién •
    Colombia/Panama. 170 I6
Darién, Istmo de • Panama 170 H6
Darién, Parque Nac. del • Panama . 170 I7

Darién, Parque Nac. del Heritage N •
   Panama .... 40 [27]
Darjiling Hill Sta • India 124 F5
Darjiling • India 122 C3
Darjiling Heritage C • India .... 43 [164]
Darling • NS, Australia 135 G6
Darling Downs • QL, Australia 136 C5
Darlington • United Kingdom 64 B6
Darmstadt • Germany 74 D6
Darnah • Libya 108 B1
Darnley, Cape • Antarctica 176 R4
Daroca • Spain 80 E3
Darrah Wildlife Sanctuary • India 123 E8
Darsser Ort • Germany 72 E1
Dart • United Kingdom 65 J10
Dartmoor • United Kingdom 65 J10
Dartmoor Nat. Park Park N •
   United Kingdom .... 58 [57]
Dartmoor Nat. Park • United Kingdom . 65 J10
Dartmoor Wildlife Centre •
   United Kingdom 65 J10
Dartmouth • NS, Canada 160 B2
Dartmouth • United Kingdom 65 J10
Daru • Papua New Guinea 134 C5
Daruvar • Croatia 92 G5
Darvishan • Afghanistan 121 D5
Darwen • United Kingdom 63 D7
Darwin • NT, Australia 135 E2
Darwin, I. • Galápagos Is. 171 G9
Darwin Research Station •
   Galápagos Is. 171 H10
Dashhowuz • Turkmenistan 121 C3
Dasht-e Kavir • Iran 120 G7
Dasht-e Lut • Iran 120 H7
Dasht-i-Margow • Afghanistan 121 D5
Daskalopetra • Chios, Greece .... 94 D
Dassen I. • South Africa 111 D7
Datca • Turkey 95 F6
Datia • India 123 F8
Datong • China 125 F2
Daugava • Latvia 100 K7
Daugavpils • Latvia 100 K7
Daun • Germany 74 C5
Dauphin • MN, Canada 158 F3
Dausa • India 123 E8
Davangere • India 124 B2
Davao • Philippines 128 H5
Davenport • IA, United States 150 B2
David • Panama 170 F6
David Point • Grenada .... 166 Q
Davis [Base] • Antarctica .... 176 [19]
Davis Bay • US Virgin Is. .... 166 X
Davis Dam • AZ/NV, United States ... 154 J8
Davis, Fuerte • Panama 170 L10
Davis Sea • Antarctica 176 S4
Davis Strait • Canada/Greenland 159 K2
Davos • NY, United States 156 B2
Davos Ski • Switzerland .... 61 [79]
Davos • Switzerland 90 L5
Dawa • Ethiopia 109 D4
Dawlish Warren Beach •
   United Kingdom .... 64 [38]
Dawson • QL, Australia 136 C5
Dawson • YT, Canada 158 C2
Dawson Creek • BC, Canada 160 I6
Dax • France 76 C5
Daxian • China 125 E3
Daydream I. • QL, Australia 136 C3
Daylesford • VI, Australia 136 G9
Dayr az Zawr • Syria 120 E6
Dayton • OH, United States 150 D3
Dayton Aviation Nat. Hist. Park N •
   OH, United States .... 153 [181]
Daytona Beach • FL, United States ... 155 D1
Dazu Heritage C • China .... 43 [187]
De Aar • South Africa 110 B4
De Efteling Park L • Netherlands .... 58 [40]
De Efteling • Netherlands 70 C3
De Funiak Springs •
   FL, United States 155 B1
De Haan • Belgium 70 F6
De Haar • Netherlands 70 H7
De Hoge Veluwe, Nat. Park Park N •
   Netherlands .... 58 [59]
De Hoge Veluwe, Nat. Park •
   Netherlands 70 C2
De Hoop Nature Reserve •
   South Africa 111 E7
De Kalb • TX, United States 155 F4
De Land • FL, United States 155 D1
De Panne • Belgium 70 E6
De Quincy Village • Seychelles 113 A1
De Rust • South Africa 111 F7
De Soto Nat. Mem. •
   FL, United States 155 C2
De Soto Nat. Mem. Park N •
   FL, United States .... 153 [218]
De Zijpe • Netherlands 70 C1
Dead Sea • Asia 120 B4
Deal • United Kingdom 65 H8
Dean, Forest of • United Kingdom 65 E6
Deán Funes • Argentina 175 B3
Dearborn • MI, United States 150 D2
Dearg, Beinn • United Kingdom 62 C3
Dease Lake • BC, Canada 158 D3
Death Valley Nat. Park •
   CA, United States 154 J8
Death Valley Nat. Park Park N •
   CA/NV, United States .... 152 [52]
Debar • FYR of Macedonia 92 C3
Debre Markos • Ethiopia 109 C3
Debrecen • Hungary 92 C2
Decapolis • Asia 120 B2
Decatur • AL, United States 151 C4
Decatur • IL, United States 150 C3
Decatur • TX, United States 155 E4
Deccan • India 124 B1
Decin • Czech Rep. 89 E6
Dedeagac • Guam .... 138 Z
Dedegöl Dag • Turkey 95 H7
Dee • United Kingdom 62 D3
Dee • United Kingdom 63 D7
Deep Bay • China 126 E4
Deep Cove • New Zealand 137 F7
Deep Sea World • United Kingdom ... 65 B1
Deer I. • NB, Canada 160 A2
Deer Lake • NF, Canada 160 C1
Deer Lake [Lake] • NF, Canada 160 C1
Deer Valley Ski •
   UT, United States .... 146 [48]
Defiance • OH, United States 150 D2
Degebarga • Sweden 99 G7
Degerhamn • Sweden 99 H7
Deggendorf • Germany 72 E4
Degirmenlik • Cyprus 96 D3
Deh Shu • Afghanistan 121 D5
Dehiba • Tunisia 107 D6
Dehiwala • Sri Lanka 124 C4
Dehpehk • Fed. States of Micronesia . 138 D
Dehra Dun Hill Sta • India 124 E5
Dehra Dun • India 123 E8
Dehri • India 123 G8
Deià • Majorca, Spain 83 N11
Deir Mar Saba • Palestine NAR 120 B4
Del Rio • TX, United States 149 F5
Delano • CA, United States 154 I8
Delap-Uliga-Djarrit • Marshall Is. .... 139 E
Delaware [Adm] • United States 156 B3
Delaware Bay •
   DE/NJ, United States 156 B3
Delaware, Fort •
   NY, United States 156 B2
Delaware [Riv] • United States 156 B2
Delaware Water Gap Nat. Recreation Area •
   PA, United States 156 B2
Delaware Water Gap Nat. Recreation Area
   Park N • PA, United States .... 153 [270]
Delcevo • FYR of Macedonia 92 C3
Delegate • NS, Australia 136 H9
Delémont • Switzerland 90 C2
Delft • Greece 93 C2
Delfi Heritage C • Greece .... 44 [235]
Delfland • Netherlands 70 G8
Delft • Netherlands 70 G8
Delfzijl • Netherlands 70 D1

Delhi • CO, United States 148 F3
Delhi • India 123 E7
Delhi Heritage C • India .... 43 [149]
Del • Indonesia 131 Q11
Delicias • Mexico 168 C2
Delimara Point • Malta 96 B2
Delmenhorst • Germany 72 C2
Delnice • Croatia 92 F5
Deloraine • TS, Australia 136 F6
Delos • Greece .... 94 I
Delos Heritage C • Greece .... 44 [242]
Delphi • Greece 93 C2
Delphi Heritage C • Greece ...... 44 [235]
Delray Beach • FL, United States ... 155 D3
Delta • UT, United States 148 D3
Delta Country • MS, United States .. 156 F5
Delta du Saloum, Parc nat. du Park •
   Senegal .... 112 [7]
Delta Junction • AK, United States .. 157 E3
Deltona • FL, United States 155 D2
Delvin • Ireland 69 E6
Demak • Java, Indonesia 131 Q11
Demidov • Russian Fed. 100 L10
Deming • NM, United States 155 H8
Demirkazik Tepe • Turkey 95 F5
Demirköprü Baraji • Turkey 95 F5
Demirtas • Turkey 95 H8
Demone, Val • Sicily, Italy 86 H7
Demopolis • AL, United States 151 C4
Den Chai • Thailand 130 C6
Den Haag • Netherlands 70 G7
Den Helder • Netherlands 70 C1
Denali • AK, United States 157 E3
Denali Nat. Park & Preserve •
   AK, United States 157 E3
Denali Nat. Park & Preserve Park N •
   AK, United States .... 152 [8]
Denau • Uzbekistan 121 E4
Denbigh • United Kingdom 63 D7
Denbighshire • United Kingdom 64 A4
Dendera • Egypt 108 B2
Denia • Spain 83 B1
Denig • Nauru .... 138 X
Deniliquin • NS, Australia 136 G8
Denio • NV, United States 148 C2
Denis, I. • Seychelles 113 B1
Denison • TX, United States 155 E4
Denison Dam • OK/TX, United States 155 E4
Denizli • Turkey 95 F5
Denizli [Adm] • Turkey 95 F5
DENMARK • Europe 99 F7
Dennery • St Lucia .... 167 N
Denpasar • Bali, Indonesia 131 L8
Denton • TX, United States 155 E4
Denver • CO, United States 148 E3
Deoli • India 123 E8
Deoria • India 123 G8
Deqing • China 126 E7
Dera Ghazi Khan • Pakistan 122 B2
Dera Ismail Khan • Pakistan 122 B2
Derbent • Russian Fed. 100 G5
Derbent • Uzbekistan 121 E4
Derby • KS, United States 149 G3
Derby • United Kingdom 63 E8
Derby • WA, Australia 135 C3
Derbyshire • United Kingdom 64 B4
Derg, Lough • Ireland 69 H9
Derinkuyu • Turkey 95 J9
Derrynasaggart Mtns • Ireland 69 H11
Derventa • Bosnia-Herz. 92 G5
Derwent • TS, Australia 136 F7
Derwent • United Kingdom 64 B4
Derwent • United Kingdom 63 E6
Derwent Valley mills Heritage C •
   United Kingdom .... 44 [24]
Derwent Water • United Kingdom ... 65 D3
Derzhavinsk • Kazakhstan 121 E1
Des Moines • IA, United States 150 B2
Des Moines [Riv] •
   IA, United States 150 B2
Des Plains • IL, United States 150 C2
Desaguadero • Peru 173 F7
Désappointement, Is. du •
   French Polynesia 139 EE4
Desaru • Malaysia 130 F6
Descartes • France 77 F6
Deschutes • OR, United States 154 G6
Dese • Ethiopia 108 C3
Desembarco del Granma, Parque Nac.
   Heritage N • Cuba .... 40 [28]
Desenzano • Italy 87 C2
Deshnoke • India 123 D7
Desierto Central de Baja California, Parque
   Natural del • Mexico 168 C1
Désirade, la • Guadeloupe .... 167 J
Desna • Ukraine 100 D3
Desnœfs • Seychelles 113 B1
Desolación, I. • Chile 175 A5
Desolation, Valley of •
   South Africa 111 F6
Despotikó • Greece 94 CC3
Desroches • Seychelles 113 B1
Dessau • Germany 72 E3
Dessau Heritage C • Germany .... 44 [49]
Dessau-Wörlitz Heritage C • Germany 44 [49]
Destin • FL, United States 155 B1
Detmold • Germany 72 C2
Detroi-Windsor Tunnel •
   MI, United States 161 C3
Detroit • MI, United States 161 A3
Detroit [Riv] • Canada/United States . 161 A3
Deurne [Apt] • Belgium 70 B3
Deutsche Bucht • Germany 72 B1
Deux Alpes, les Ski • France .... 61 [42]
Deux Alpes • France 78 C4
Deux Sèvres • France 77 E6
Deva • Romania 92 C2
Develi • Turkey 95 J9
Deventer • Netherlands 70 D2
Devil's Bridge • Antigua & Barbuda . 167 I
Devil's Woodyard • Trinidad & Tobago 166 S
Devils Head Ski •
   WI, United States .... 146 [75]
Devils Lake • ND, United States 148 G1
Devils Lake Ind Res •
   ND, United States .... 155 [44]
Devils Postpile Nat. Mon. •
   CA, United States 154 J8
Devils Postpile Nat. Mon. Park N •
   CA, United States .... 152 [70]
Devils Tower Nat. Mon. Park N •
   WY, United States .... 152 [70]
Devin • Bulgaria 92 D3
Devizes • United Kingdom 65 K9
Devon • United Kingdom 65 J9
Devon I. • Canada 142 E1
Devonport • TS, Australia 136 F6
Dewas • India 123 E8
Deyang • China 125 E3
Dezful • Iran 120 G7
Dezhou • China 125 F3
Dhahran • Saudi Arabia 120 D4
Dhaka • Bangladesh 122 D3
Dhali • Cyprus 96 C4
Dhamar • Yemen 120 E11
Dhanbad • India 122 C3
Dharamsala Hill Sta • India 124 E5
Dharwad • India 124 B1
Dhaulagiri • Nepal 122 C3
Dheftera • Cyprus 96 C4
Dhekelia • Cyprus 96 D4
Dhiban • Jordan 120 B4
Dhidhufi • Maldives 124 H7
Dhigufinolhu • Maldives 124 H8
Dhofar • Oman 120 G10
Dhule • India 122 B3
Dhundar • India 123 E8
Dia • Greece 93 I5
Diable, Pointe du • Mauritius 113 F6
Diablerets Ski • Switzerland .... 61 [59]
Diablerets, Les • Switzerland 90 J6
Diablo, Picacho del • Mexico 168 H5
Diablo Range • CA, United States .. 154 I8
Diamant, Ile • Martinique .... 167 L

Diamant, Rocher du • Martinique ... 167 L
Diamantina Heritage C • Brazil .... 42 [74]
Diamantina • QL, Australia 135 G4
Diamantina Gates Nat. Park •
   QL, Australia 135 G4
Diamond Head State Mon. •
   HI, United States 157 H6
Diamond Is. • CL, Australia 136 D3
Diamond Peak Ski •
   NV, United States .... 146 [36]
Diani Beach • Kenya 109 C6
Diano Marina • Italy 87 A3
Dibrugarh • India 122 D3
Dickenson Bay • Antigua & Barbuda . 167 I
Dickinson • ND, United States 148 F1
Didge City • KS, United States 148 F3
Didyma • Turkey 95 E6
Die • France 78 C4
Diefenbaker, Lake • SA, Canada .. 158 F3
Diekirch • Luxembourg 70 D5
Diélette • France 63 J14
Dien Bien Phu • Vietnam 128 C2
Dieng Plateau • Java, Indonesia ... 131 P12
Diepholz • Germany 72 C2
Dieppe • France 76 D2
Dieppe Bay • St Kitts & Nevis ..... 167 F
Diessen-Rieden • Germany 74 F7
Diest • Belgium 70 C4
Diez • Germany 74 D5
Difnein I. Dive • Eritrea 109 E10
Digby • NS, Canada 160 B2
Digha Beach • India 124 F6
Digne • France 78 C4
Digoin • France 76 E3
Digue, la • Seychelles 113 B2
Dijon • France 76 E3
Dikili • Turkey 95 E5
Diksmuide • Belgium 70 E6
Diktéon Antron • Crete, Greece 93 I6
Dikti Oros • Crete, Greece 93 I6
Diktinéon • Crete, Greece 93 G5
Dili • East Timor 131 G5
Dillenburg • Germany 74 D5
Dilling • Sudan 108 B3
Dillingen • Germany 50 C2
Dillon • MT, United States 148 D1
Dilolo • Dem. Rep. of Congo 108 B6
Dilos • Greece .... 94 I
Dimashq • Syria 120 D7
Dimashq Heritage C • Syria ...... 44 [302]
Dimbovita • Romania 92 H7
Dimitrovgrad • Bulgaria 92 H8
Dimitrovgrad • Russian Fed. 100 G3
Dinajpur • Bangladesh 122 D3
Dinan • France 77 D3
Dinant • Belgium 70 C5
Dinara • Bosnia-Herz./Croatia 92 G6
Dinard • France 77 D3
Dinaric Alps • Europe 48 E3
Dinas Dinlle Beach • United Kingdom 64 [65]
Dinder Nat. Park Park • Sudan .... 112 [57]
Dindigul • India 124 C3
Dingle • Ireland 69 G10
Dingle Bay • Ireland 69 G11
Dingle Peninsula • Ireland 69 G10
Dingli Cliffs • Malta 96 E2
Dingwall • United Kingdom 62 C3
Dinosaur • CO, United States 148 E2
Dinosaur Nat. Mon. Park N •
   CO/UT, United States .... 152 [86]
Dinosaur Prov. Park Heritage N •
   AL, Canada .... 40 [6]
Dinosaurier Park Münchehagen Park L •
   Germany .... 59 [48]
Dinotown • BC, Canada 160 I7
Dinslaken • Germany 73 C5
Dionisiádes • Greece 93 J5
Dionysos, Temple of •
   Lesbos, Greece .... 94 C
Diourbel • Senegal 106 A3
Dipkarpaz • Cyprus 96 D3
Dire Dawa • Ethiopia 108 D4
Dirk Hartog I. • WA, Australia 135 A5
Dirranbandi • QL, Australia 135 H5
Disappointment, Lake •
   WA, Australia 135 C4
Discovery Bay • Jamaica 165 C3
Discovery Coast Atlantic forest reserves
   Heritage N • Brazil .... 40 [45]
Discovery I. • FL, United States ... 155 D2
Disentis • Switzerland 90 K5
Disko • Greenland 159 K2
Disney Institute •
   FL, United States 155 D2
Disney Village Park L • France ... 59 [63]
Disney's Animal Kingdom •
   FL, United States 157 A1
Disney's Animal Kingdom Park L •
   FL, United States .... 157 [24]
Disney's California Adventure Park L •
   CA, United States .... 157 [5]
Disney-MGM Studios •
   FL, United States 157 A1
Disney-MGM Studios Park L •
   FL, United States .... 157 [24]
Disneyland Park L •
   CA, United States .... 157 [5]
Disneyland Resort •
   France 154 J9
Disneyland Paris Park L • France . 59 [63]
Disneyland Resort Paris •
   France .... 59 [63]
Disneyland Resort Paris Park L •
   France 78 B2
Distington • United Kingdom 65 C3
Distrito Federal • Brazil 174 B4
Distrito Federal • Mexico 169 C3
Diu Beach • India 124 E6
Divar I. • Goa, India 123 C5
Divinópolis • Brazil 174 E6
Divjaka Nat. Park N • Albania .... 58 [131]
Divrigi Heritage C • Turkey ...... 44 [264]
Diyarbakir • Turkey 95 D2
Dja, Réserve du Park • Cameroon . 112 [33]
Dja, Réserve du Heritage N •
   Cameroon .... 41 [101]
Djanet • Algeria 106 C2
Djelfa • Algeria 106 C1
Djemila Heritage C • Algeria ..... 44 [284]
Djenné Heritage C • Mali .... 43 [108]
Djerdap Nat. Park Park N •
   Serbia & Montenegro .... 58 [125]
Djibouti Africa 108 D3
Djibouti [City] • Djibouti 108 D3
Djoudi Nat. Bird Sanctuary Heritage N •
   Senegal .... 41 [92]
Djoudj, Parc nat. des Oiseaux du Park •
   Senegal .... 112 [5]
Djoudj, Parc nat. des Oiseaux du
   Heritage N • Senegal .... 41 [92]
Djurs Sommerland Park L • Denmark 59 [17]
Djurs Sommerland • Denmark 99 F7
Djursdala • Sweden 99 H6
Djursland • Denmark 99 F7
Dmitrov • Russian Fed. 100 M10
Dniester • Moldova/Ukraine 92 E1
Dnipro • Ukraine 100 D4
Dniprodzerzhyns'k • Ukraine 100 D4
Dnipropetrovs'k • Ukraine 100 D4
Dnister • Ukraine 100 C2
Don • Russian Fed. 100 C2
Doaktown • NB, Canada 160 B2
Dobbiaco • Italy 80 B3
Dobele • Latvia 100 J7
Dobiegi, Jazirah • Indonesia 131 H4
Doboj • Bosnia-Herz. 92 G6
Dobrich • Bulgaria 92 I7
Dobrodsja • Romania 92 I7
Docker River • NT, Australia 136 A2
Dover, Strait of •
   France/United Kingdom 65 H8
Doda Betta • India 124 B3
Dodecanese • Greece 93 E3
Dodekánissa • Greece 93 E3

Dodge Ridge Ski •
   CA, United States .... 146 [32]
Dodoma • Tanzania 110 H7
Dodori Nat. Reserve • Kenya 109 C6
Doe Mtn Ski • PA, United States .. 146 [92]
Doe Mtn • PA, United States 156 B2
Dog I. • Anguilla .... 166 B
Dog I. • FL, United States 155 B1
Doganbey • Turkey 95 H7
Dogashima • Japan 127 H9
Dogo • Japan 127 B3
Dogondoutchi • Niger 106 C3
Dogs, The • British Virgin Is. ..... 166 A
Dogubayazit • Turkey 95 D2
Doha • Qatar 120 G8
Doi Inthanon • Thailand 130 B6
Doi Inthanon Nat. Park • Thailand . 130 B6
Doi Khun Tan Nat. Park • Thailand . 130 B6
Doi Suthep Nat. Park • Thailand .. 130 B5
Dokkum • Netherlands 70 C1
Dokos • Greece 94 BB3
Dol-de-Bretagne • France 77 D3
Dolak • Indonesia 131 I5
Dole • France 76 F3
Dolent, Mt • Europe 90 I6
Dolfinarium Harderwijk Park L •
   Netherlands .... 59 [38]
Dolfinarium Harderwijk • Netherlands 70 C2
Dolgellau • United Kingdom 63 D8
Dollywood Park L •
   TN, United States .... 151 [21]
Dolny Vakuf • Bosnia-Herz. 89 F9
Dolomites • Italy .... 86 C-D
Dolomiti • Italy .... 86 C-D
Dolores • Argentina 175 B3
Dolores • Uruguay 175 G6
Dolphin Coast • South Africa 111 C4
Dolphin Reef Dive • Egypt 109 E8
Dolphin Reef Dive • Israel 109 E7
Dom • Switzerland 90 J6
Domâs • Norway 98 G7
Dome Creek • BC, Canada 160 I6
Dome Fuji [Base] • Antarctica .... 176 [25]
DOMINICA • West Indies .... 167 K
DOMINICAN REPUBLIC
   • West Indies .... 165 G-H
Domme • France 78 F6
Dommel • Netherlands 70 C2
Domodedovo [Apt] • Russian Fed. 100 M10
Domodóssola • Italy 87 B1
Don • Mexico 168 I6
Don • Russian Fed. 100 F4
Don • Russian Fed. 80 C4
Dona Paula Beach • Goa, India ... 123 C5
Donabate • Ireland 69 F6
Donau • Austria/Germany 72 E4
Donau-auen, Nationalpark Park N •
   Austria .... 58 [91]
Donaueschingen • Germany 74 B4
Donauwörth • Germany 72 D4
Doncaster • United Kingdom 63 E7
Dondo • Angola 110 A2
Dondra Head • Sri Lanka 124 C4
Donegal • Ireland 69 B2
Donegal Bay • Ireland 69 B2
Donets'k • Ukraine 100 E4
Dong Hoi • Vietnam 128 D3
Dong Jiang • China 126 F3
Dong Nai • Vietnam 129 C5
Dongara • WA, Australia 135 A5
Dongchuan • China 125 E4
Dongguan • China 126 F3
Donghae • Rep. of Korea 125 G3
Dongola • Sudan 108 C3
Dongsha Qundao • China 126 D2
Dongsheng • China 125 F3
Dongyang • China 125 F3
Donji Vakuf • Bosnia-Herz. 92 G6
Donnelly • AL, Canada 160 J6
Donner Pass • CA, United States . 154 I8
Donner Ski Ranch Ski •
   CA, United States .... 146 [29]
Donore • Ireland 69 F6
Donostia-San Sebastián • Spain .. 80 D2
Donoússa • Greece 94 CC3
Doon • Ireland 69 H9
Doon, Loch • United Kingdom 62 C4
Doonass, Falls of • Ireland 69 H10
Door Peninsula • WI, United States 161 B2
Doorn • Netherlands 70 H8
Dor • Israel 120 B4
Dora • NM, United States 149 F4
Dora Baltea • Italy 87 A2
Dorada, Costa • Spain 83 C4
Dorado • Puerto Rico 165 J7
Dorchester • United Kingdom 65 K9
Dordabis • Namibia 110 J9
Dordogne • France 78 E5
Dordogne [Apt] • VA, United States . 156 A3
Dordogne, Gorges de la • France . 78 F5
Dordrecht • Netherlands 70 G8
Dore, Mt • New Caledonia .... 138 U
Dores do Indaiá • Brazil 174 E6
Dorf • Germany 74 H7
Dorfgastein • Austria 91 P7
Doring • South Africa 111 E6
Dormagen • Germany 73 C6
Dornbirn • Austria 91 M7
Dorney Park • PA, United States .. 156 A3
Dornoch • United Kingdom 62 C3
Dorog • Hungary 89 G9
Dorotea • Sweden 97 D3
Dorset • United Kingdom 65 J9
Dorset & East Devon coast Heritage N •
   United Kingdom .... 41 [57]
Dorsten • Germany 73 C5
Dortmund • Germany 73 D5
Dortmund: Florianturm • Germany 73 D5
Dortmund: Tierpark • Germany 73 D5
Dortmund-Ems Kanal • Germany .. 73 D5
Dörtyol • Turkey 95 J10
Dorval [Apt] • QU, Canada 160 G4
Dos Hermanos • Spain 82 H7
Dösmeath • Turkey 95 G7
Dossor • Kazakhstan 121 B2
Dosuoth • Kazakhstan 121 H2
Douai • France 76 E1
Douala • Cameroon 106 C4
Douarnenez • France 77 C4
Double, Fôret de la • France 78 E5
Double • Hong Kong, China 98 B2
Doubtful Sound • New Zealand ... 137 F7
Dougga Heritage C • Tunisia ..... 44 [287]
Dougga • Tunisia 107 C4
Douglas • AZ, United States 155 H8
Douglas • GA, United States 151 D4
Douglas • Isle of Man 63 C6
Douglas • WY, United States 148 E2
Doukáto, Akra • Levkas, Greece .. 94 J
Doumen • China 126 E3
Dourada, Costa da • Portugal 84 A3
Dourados • Brazil 175 C2
Douro • Portugal 84 B2
Douro • Tunisia 107 C6
Dove Cottage • United Kingdom ... 65 D3
Dove Holes • United Kingdom 65 B1
Dover • DE, United States 156 B3
Dover • TS, Australia 136 F7
Dover • United Kingdom 65 H8
Dover, Strait of •
   France/United Kingdom 65 H8
Dovercourt Beach • United Kingdom 64 [22]
Dovrefjell • Norway 97 B3
Dovrefjell Nat. Park Park N • Norway 58 [130]
Dovrefjell Nat. Park • Norway 98 G7

Down • United Kingdom 64 A3
Downunderland • NS, Australia 136 H8
Dowth • Ireland 69 F6
Dozen • Japan 127 B3
Dràa • Algeria/Morocco 107 A3
Dràa, Cap • Morocco 107 A3
Dràa, Vallée du • Morocco 107 B3
Drac • France 78 C4
Drac, Coves del • Majorca, Spain . 83 O11
Drachenfels • Germany 74 C5
Dragonda • Greece 93 J5
Dragon's Mouth • Trinidad & Tobago 166 C
Dragonera I. • Majorca, Spain 83 N11
Draguignan • France 78 H8
Drakensberg • Lesotho/South Africa 110 B4
Drakensberg Nat. Park & Africa .. 111 B4
Dráma • Greece 93 D1
Drammen • Norway 98 D6
Drangedal • Norway 98 D6
Dràpano, Akra • Crete, Greece 93 H5
Drau • Austria 91 P8
Drava • Croatia/Hungary 92 B2
Drava • Hungary 92 G5
Drayton Manor Park L •
   United Kingdom .... 59 [29]
Drayton Manor Park • United Kingdom 65 F5
Dreamworld • QL, Australia 136 H8
Drehermozpite • Austria/Italy 86 D3
Drenthe • Netherlands 70 D1
Dresden • Germany 72 E3
Dreux • France 78 A2
Drievliet Park L • Netherlands .... 59 [39]
Drin • Albania 93 B1
Drina • Bosnia-Herz./Yugoslavia .. 92 B2
Drobeta-Turnu Severin • Romania . 92 C2
Drogheda • Ireland 69 F6
Droichead Atha • Ireland 69 F6
Droichead Nua • Ireland 69 E7
Dröme • France 78 C4
Drottningholm • Sweden 99 B2
Drottningholms Slott Heritage C •
   Sweden .... 44 [8]
Druif Beach • Aruba .... 166 W
Drumcliff • Ireland 69 H8
Drumheller • AL, Canada 160 J7
Drummond • MT, United States ... 148 D1
Drummond I. • MI, United States .. 161 A2
Drummondville • QU, Canada 160 H3
Drusillas Park • United Kingdom .. 65 G8
Druskininkai • Lithuania 97 E5
Drvar • Bosnia-Herz. 92 G6
Drvenik • Croatia 92 G6
Dry Falls • WA, United States 154 H5
Dry Harbour Mtns • Jamaica 165 C3
Dry Tortugas • United States 166 BB1
Dry Tortugas Nat. Park •
   FL, United States 155 C3
Dry Tortugas Nat. Park Park N •
   FL, United States .... 153 [222]
Dryden • CT, United States 158 G4
Duarte, Pico • Dominican Rep. 165 G5
Duba • Saudi Arabia 120 C8
Dubai • United Arab Emirates 120 H8
Dubawnt Lake • NU, Canada 158 F2
Dubayy • United Arab Emirates ... 120 H8
Dubbo • NS, Australia 135 H6
Dublin • GA, United States 151 D4
Dublin • Ireland 69 F6
Dublin [Adm] • Ireland 69 F6
Dublin Bay • Ireland 69 F6
Dubno • Russian Fed. 100 M10
Dubno • Ukraine 100 C3
Dubois • PA, United States 156 A2
Dubois • WY, United States 148 E2
Dubrovnik • Croatia 92 G6
Dubrovnik Heritage C • Croatia ... 44 [212]
Dubuc, Château • Martinique ..... 167 L
Dubuque • IA, United States 150 B2
Duc de Gloucester, Is. du •
   French Polynesia 139 EE4
Duchess • QL, Australia 135 F4
Ducie I. • Pitcairn Is. 139 FF4
Duck Valley Ind Res •
   ID/NV, United States .... 155 [10]
Duderstadt • Germany 65 C4
Dudden • Turkey 95 G8
Düdenbasi • Turkey 95 H7
Düdensuyu • Turkey 95 H7
Dudhsagar Falls • Goa, India 123 C6
Dudhwa Nat. Park • India 123 F7
Dudinka • Russian Fed. 101 I3
Dudley • United Kingdom 65 F5
Duero • Spain 80 D3
Duff Is. • Solomon Is. .... 138 W
Dufourspitze • Italy/Switzerland .. 90 J6
Dugi Otok • Croatia 92 F6
Duino • Italy 87 D1
Duinrell Park L • Netherlands .... 59 [39]
Duinrell • Netherlands 70 G7
Duisburg • Germany 73 C5
Duitama • Colombia 172 B2
Duiveland • Netherlands 70 B3
Dujiangyan Heritage C • China ... 43 [188]
Dukwe • Botswana 110 J9
Duleek • Ireland 69 F6
Dulles [Apt] • VA, United States .. 156 A3
Duluth • MN, United States 150 B1
Dumaguete • Philippines 128 G5
Dumai • Indonesia 131 N10
Dumas Beach • India 124 E6
Dumas • TX, United States 149 F3
Dumbarton • United Kingdom 65 A1
Dumbéa • New Caledonia .... 138 U
Dumfries • United Kingdom 62 D5
Dumfriesshire • United Kingdom .. 64 A3
Dumont d'Urville [Base] • Antarctica 176 [22]
Dumont d'Urville Sea • Antarctica . 176 T1
Dumyat [Apt] • Egypt 109 B1
Dún Aengus • Ireland 69 G9
Dún Dealgan • Ireland 69 C2
Dún Laoghaire • Ireland 69 F6
Duna • Hungary 92 B2
Dunaj • Slovak Rep. 89 B5
Dunany • Ireland 69 H8
Dunärea • Romania 89 D2
Dunav • Bulgaria/Yugoslavia 92 D2
Dunbartonshire • United Kingdom . 65 A2
Dunblane • United Kingdom 65 A1
Dunboyne • Ireland 69 F6
Duncan • BC, Canada 160 I8
Duncan • OK, United States 149 G4
Duncan I. • Galápagos Is. 171 G10
Duncansby Head • United Kingdom 62 C2
Dundalk • Ireland 69 C2
Dundee • South Africa 111 B3
Dundee • United Kingdom 62 D4
Dundee • United Kingdom 65 B2
Dundonald • New Zealand 137 B4
Dundrum • United Kingdom 65 B2
Dungarvan • Ireland 69 D8
Dungeness • United Kingdom 65 H8
Dungun • Malaysia 130 C6
Dunhua • China 125 G2
Dunhuang • China 125 D2
Dunkeld • United Kingdom 65 A1
Dunkerque • France 76 E1
Dunkery Beacon • United Kingdom . 65 J9
Dunkirk • France 76 E1
Dunkirk • NY, United States 156 A1
Dunlavin • Ireland 69 H9
Dunloe, Gap of • Ireland 69 H10
Dunmanus Bay • Ireland 69 H11
Dunmore • Ireland 69 H9
Dunmore Town • Bahamas 164 A1
Dunn's River Falls • Jamaica 165 D3
Dunnet Head • United Kingdom ... 62 D2
Dunnville • OT, Canada 160 E5
Dunoon • United Kingdom 65 A1
Dunquin • Ireland 69 G10
Dunraven Bay • United Kingdom .. 64 [37]
Dunraven Dive • Egypt 109 E7
Dunsandel • New Zealand 137 B3
Dunshaughlin • Ireland 69 F6
Dunstan Mtns • New Zealand 137 G7

Dunster • United Kingdom 65 J9
Duque de Caxias • Brazil 174 F7
Durance • France 76 F4
Durango • CO, United States 155 H7
Durango • Mexico 168 D3
Durango [Adm] • Mexico 169 B2
Durango Mtn Resort Ski •
   CO, United States .... 146 [64]
Durankulak • Bulgaria 92 I7
Durant • MS, United States 156 F5
Durant • OK, United States 155 E4
Durazno • Uruguay 175 G6
Durazzo • Albania 50 C4
Durban • South Africa 111 B5
Düren • Germany 74 A1
Durg • India 122 C3
Durham • NC, United States 156 E3
Durham • United Kingdom 76 F4
Durham [County] • United Kingdom 64 B3
Durham Downs • QL, Australia 135 G5
Durham Heritage C • United Kingdom 44 [22]
Durmitor Nat. Park Park N •
   Serbia & Montenegro .... 58 [127]
Durmitor Nat. Park Heritage N •
   Serbia & Montenegro .... 41 [73]
Durrës • Albania 92 B3
Dursey I. • Ireland 69 G11
Dursunbey • Turkey 95 F4
Dushanbe • Tajikistan 121 E4
Dusky Sound • New Zealand 137 F8
Düsseldorf • Germany 73 C6
Dutch Country • PA, United States . 156 B2
Dutch Harbor • AK, United States . 157 C4
Duvergé • Dominican Rep. 165 F6
Duvernette, Fort •
   St Vincent & Gren. .... 167 O
Duyun • China 125 E4
Dvarka Beach • India 124 E5
Dwingelderveld, Nat. Park Park N •
   Netherlands .... 58 [58]
Dwingelderveld, Nat. Park •
   Netherlands 70 D1
Dyersburg • TN, United States 151 C3
Dyje • Czech Rep. 91 H1
Dymchurch • United Kingdom 65 H8
Dyrehavsbakken Park L • Denmark 59 [19]
Dytiki Eláda • Greece 94 AA2
Dytiki Macedonia • Greece 94 AA1
Dzanga-Sangha, Réserve du Park •
   Central African Rep. .... 112 [40]
Dzerzhinsk • Russian Fed. 100 F2
Dzhankoy • Ukraine 100 D4
Dzhalovzer • Poland 89 G8
Dzibilchaltún • Mexico 169 F4
Dzibilnocac • Mexico 169 F5
Dzukija Nat. Park Park N • Lithuania 58 [154]
Dzukija Nat. Park • Lithuania 100 K8

E

E.T. Joshua [Apt] •
   St Vincent & Gren. .... 167 O
Eagle • CO, United States 148 E3
Eagle Beach • Aruba .... 166 W
Eagle Farm [Apt] • QL, Australia . 136 D5
Eagle Pass • TX, United States 149 F5
Earn • United Kingdom 65 A1
Earn, Loch • United Kingdom 65 A1
Earnslaw, Mt • New Zealand 137 G7
Easley • SC, United States 151 D4
East Anglia • United Kingdom 63 F8
East Antarctica • Antarctica 176 R5
East Aurora • NY, United States .. 156 A1
East Branch Delaware •
   NY, United States 156 B1
East Caicos • Turks & Caicos Is. .. 164 D3
East Cape • New Zealand 137 C2
East China Sea • China/Japan ... 125 G4
East Coast Park • Singapore 129 I12
East Cowes • United Kingdom 64 D6
East End • Cayman Is. 165 B2
East Falkland • Falkland Is. 175 C5
East Grinstead • United Kingdom . 65 G8
East Hampton • NY, United States 156 C2
East Kilbride • United Kingdom ... 65 A2
East Lake Tohopekaliga •
   FL, United States 157 B1
East London • South Africa 110 B4
East Lothian • United Kingdom ... 65 B2
East Midlands [Apt] • United Kingdom 66 C5
East Neuk • United Kingdom 65 B2
East of England • United Kingdom . 64 B5
East Pacific Ridge • Pacific Ocean . 8 D6
East Point • Cayman Is. 165 A1
East Point • GA, United States 151 D4
East Point • US Virgin Is. .... 166 X
East Rennell Heritage N •
   Solomon Is. .... 41 [165]
East Riding of Yorkshire •
   United Kingdom 64 B4
East Siberian Sea • Russian Fed. 101 Q2
East St Louis • IL, United States . 150 B3
EAST TIMOR • Asia 131 G5
Eastbourne • United Kingdom 65 H8
Easter I. • Pacific Ocean .... 139 M
Easter Ross • United Kingdom 62 C3
Eastern Cape • South Africa 111 A2
Eastern Desert • Egypt .... 95 I-J
Eastern Mediterranean Coast • Turkey . 95 I-J
Eastern Valleys • Norway 98 A3
Eastern • QU, Canada 159 I3
Eastmain [Riv] • QU, Canada 159 I3
Eau Claire • WI, United States ... 150 B2
Ebadon • Marshall Is. .... 139 E
Ebano • Mexico 169 E5
Ebbw Vale • United Kingdom 65 E6
Ebeltoft • Denmark 99 F7
Eberbach • Germany 74 D6
Eberbach, Kloster • Germany 74 D6
Ebersberg • Germany 89 D3
Eberswalde-Finow • Germany 72 E2
Ebetsu • Japan 127 D2
Ebey's Landing Nat. Hist. Reserve Park N •
   WA, United States .... 152 [16]
Eboli • Italy 87 H7
Ebon • Marshall Is. 138 BB2
Ebony Showroom • Germany 74 D6
Ebro • Spain 80 D2
Ecab • Mexico 169 G4
Eceabat • Turkey 95 E4
Ech Chélif • Algeria 106 C1
Echmiatsin Heritage C • Armenia . 43 [137]
Echo Bay • NT, Canada 158 E2
Echterdingen [Apt] • Germany 70 D5
Echternach • Luxembourg 70 D5
Echuca • VI, Australia 136 G9
Ecija • Spain 82 H7
Eckernförde • Germany 72 C1
Eckerö • Finland 99 B2
Ecouen, Château d' • France 78 A1
Ecrins, Parc nat. des • France ... 58 [73]
Ecrins, Parc nat. des • France ... 78 D4
ECUADOR • S. America 172 C4
Ed • Sweden 99 F5
Ed Damazin • Sudan 108 C3
Edam • Netherlands 70 C2
Eday • United Kingdom 65 B1
Eddystone Point • TS, Australia .. 136 F6
Eddystone Rocks • United Kingdom 65 J10
Ede • Netherlands 70 C2
Eden • NS, Australia 136 H9
Eden • United Kingdom 65 D3
Eden Project • United Kingdom ... 65 J10
Edendale • South Africa 111 B4
Edenderry • Ireland 69 E6
Edenlandia Park L • Italy .... 59 [86]
Edessa • Greece 93 C1
Edfu • Egypt 109 B3

Edgar Allen Poe Nat. Hist. Site **Park N** •
   PA, United States . . . . 153 [269]
Edgigen • Marshall Is. . . . . 139 E
Edinburgh • United Kingdom 65 B2
Edinburgh **Heritage C** •
   United Kingdom . . . . 44 [17]
Edirne • Turkey 95 E3
Edirne [Adm] • Turkey 95 E3
Edison Nat. Hist. Site **Park N** •
   NJ, United States . . . . 153 [281]
Edmonds • WA, United States 154 G5
Edmonton • AL, Canada 160 J6
Edmunston • NB, Canada 160 A1
Edremit • Turkey 95 E4
Edremit Körfezi • Turkey . . . . 94 C
Edsbro • Sweden 99 B1
Edson • AL, Canada 160 J6
Edward, Lake •
   Dem. Rep. of Congo/Uganda 108 B5
Edwards Plateau •
   TX, United States 149 G4
Edwardsville • IL, United States 150 B3
Eeklo • Belgium 169 F5
Ee • Cook Is. . . . . 139 N
Eelde [Apt] • Netherlands 70 D1
Eemshaven • Netherlands 70 D1
Efaté • Vanuatu . . . . 138 V
Effigy Mounds Nat. Mon. **Park N** •
   IA, United States . . . . 153 [165]
Effingham • IL, United States 150 C3
Eforie Nord • Romania 92 I7
Eforie Sud • Romania 92 I7
Ega, Val d' • Italy 86 C4
Egadi, Is. • Italy 86 G7
Eger • Hungary 92 C2
Egersund • Norway 97 B4
Egeskov • Denmark 99 F8
Eggenfelden • Germany 74 H7
Egina • Greece 94 BB3
Egina • Greece 93 C2
Egirdir • Turkey 95 H7
Egirdir Gölü • Turkey 95 H7
Egmont, Cape • New Zealand 137 D6
Egmont, Mt • New Zealand 137 D6
Egmont Nat. Park • New Zealand 137 D6
Egmont • United Kingdom 65 C3
EGYPT • Africa . . . . 109 A-D
Ehingen • Germany 74 E7
Ehrenbreitstein • Germany 74 D5
Ehrwald Ski • Austria . . . . 01 [92]
Ehrwald • Austria 91 N7
Eichwalde • Germany 73 F8
Eidanger • Norway 98 G8
Eidfjord • Norway 98 G8
Eidfjorden • Norway 98 G8
Eidsdal • Norway 98 G7
Eidsfoss • Norway 98 D5
Eidsvåg • Norway 98 G7
Eidsvoll • Norway 98 E5
Eifel • Germany 74 C5
Eifelpark **Park L** • Germany . . . . 59 [55]
Eifelpark • Germany 74 C5
Eiger • Switzerland 90 J5
Eigg • United Kingdom 62 B4
Eighe, Carn • United Kingdom 62 C3
Eight Degree Channel • Indian Ocean . . 124 A4
Eighty Mile Beach • WA, Australia 135 C3
Eikeren • Norway 98 D5
Eikesdalsvatnet • Norway 98 G7
Eil Malik • Palau . . . . 138 V
Eilat • Israel 120 C7
Eileithyia • Crete, Greece 93 I6
Eindhoven • Netherlands 70 C3
Einsiedeln • Switzerland 90 K5
EIRE see **IRELAND**
Eisenhower Birthplace State Hist. Site •
   TX, United States 155 E4
Eisenhower Nat. Hist. Site **Park N** •
   PA, United States . . . . 153 [267]
Eisenstadt • Austria 91 H2
Eisleben **Heritage C** • Germany . . . . . 44 [48]
Eivissa • Ibiza, Spain 83 M9
Eivissa **Heritage C** • Spain . . . . 44 [99]
Eivissa [I.] • Spain . . . . 83 L-M
Ejido, El • Spain 82 K8
Ejin • China 125 E2
Ek Balam • Mexico 169 G4
Ekenäs • Finland 99 D4
Eketorpsborg • Sweden 99 H7
Ekibastuz • Kazakstan 121 G1
Eklingji • India 123 D8
Ekoln • Sweden 99 H6
Eksjö • Sweden 99 H6
El Abrigo • Tenerife, Canary Is. 82 G5
El Alamein • Egypt 109 A1
El Arco • Mexico 168 H5
El Arish • Egypt 109 B1
El Ashmûnein • Egypt 109 A2
El Cabo de Gata • Spain 82 K8
El Campo • TX, United States 151 D4
El Cañuelo • Puerto Rico 165 J7
El Centro • CA, United States 149 C4
El Cerro del Aripo •
   Trinidad & Tobago . . . . 166 S
El Chico, Parque Nac. • Mexico 169 J7
El Cuyo • Mexico 169 G4
El Dorado • AR, United States 151 D4
El Dorado • KS, United States 150 B3
El Escorial **Heritage C** • Spain . . . . . 44 [115]
El Faiyûm • Egypt 109 A1
El Fasher • Sudan 108 B3
El Fuerte de Samaipata **Heritage C** •
   Bolivia . . . . 42 [66]
El Geneina • Sudan 108 B3
El Giza • Egypt 109 A1
El Gogorrón, Parque Nac. • Mexico 169 I6
El Golea • Algeria 106 C1
El Iskandariya • Egypt 109 A1
El Jadida • Morocco 107 A1
El Jem • Tunisia 107 D5
El Jem **Heritage C** • Tunisia . . . . 44 [292]
El Khârga • Egypt 109 A2
El Limón • Panama 170 L10
El Llobregat • Spain 83 C3
El Macao • Dominican Rep. 165 H6
El Malhalla el Kubra • Egypt 109 A1
El Malpais Nat. Mon. •
   NM, United States 155 H7
El Malpais Nat. Mon. **Park N** •
   NM, United States . . . . 152 [124]
El Mansûra • Egypt 109 B1
El Masnou • Spain 83 D4
El Meco • Mexico 169 G4
El Medano • Tenerife, Canary Is. 82 G5
El Mina **Dive** • Egypt 109 E8
El Minya • Egypt 109 A2
El Mirador • Guatemala 170 K8
El Moharraq • Egypt 109 A2
El Muliñar • Majorca, Spain 83 N11
El Morro • Cuba 164 H5
El Morro, Castillo • Puerto Rico 165 J7
El Morro Nat. Mon. •
   NM, United States 155 H7
El Morro Nat. Mon. **Park N** •
   NM, United States . . . . 152 [123]
El Nouzha [Apt] • Egypt 109 A1
El Oasis • Mexico 168 I5
El Obeid • Sudan 108 B3
El Palo • Spain 82 J8
El Paso • TX, United States 155 H8
El Pilar • Venezuela, Spain 83 M10
El Porvenir • Mexico 168 C1
El Porvenir • Panama 170 H6
El Prat de Llobregat [Apt] • Spain 83 C4
El Progreso • Galápagos Is. 171 H10
El Progreso • Guatemala 170 K9
El Progreso • Honduras 170 K9
El Puerto de Santa Maria • Spain 82 H8
El Qâhira • Egypt 109 A1
El Qâhira **Heritage C** • Egypt . . . . . . 44 [299]
El Qasr • Egypt 109 A2
El Reno • OK, United States 149 G3
El Rey • Mexico 169 G4
El Rompido • Spain 82 H7

El Rosario • Mexico 168 H5
El Salto • Mexico 169 H6
EL SALVADOR • C. America 170 C4
El Sebúca • Egypt 109 B3
El Seibo • Dominican Rep. 165 H6
El Serrat • Andorra 82 E5
El Socorro • Mexico 168 H5
El Sueco • Mexico 168 C2
El Suweis • Egypt 109 B1
El Tajín • Mexico 169 J7
El Tajín **Heritage C** • Mexico . . . . . . 42 [70]
El Tarter • Andorra 82 E5
El Tigre • Venezuela 173 C2
El Tigre, Parque Nac. • Guatemala 170 J9
El Torro • Minorca, Spain 83 K7
El Tûr • Egypt 109 B2
El Veladero, Parque Nac. • Mexico 169 J8
El Vendrell • Spain 83 C4
El Vizcaíno whale sanctuary **Heritage N** •
   Mexico . . . . 40 [19]
El Yunque • Puerto Rico 165 J7
Elafonísi • Crete, Greece 93 G6
Elafónissi • Greece 94 BB3
Elat • Israel 120 C7
Elati • Levkas, Greece . . . . 94 I
Elazig • Turkey 95 C2
Elba, Cape • Egypt/Sudan 109 E9
Elba, I. d' • Italy 87 B3
Elbasan • Albania 92 B3
Elbe • Germany 72 D2
Elbert, Mt • CO, United States 148 E3
Elbistan • Turkey 95 C2
Elblag • Poland 89 B1
Elbrus • Russian Fed. 100 F5
Elburz • Iran 120 G6
Elche **Heritage C** • Spain . . . . 44 [100]
Elda • Spain 83 A1
Elde • Germany 72 D2
Eldora Mtn **Ski** • CO, United States . . 146 [55]
Eldorado • TX, United States 149 F4
Eldoret • Kenya 109 C4
Eleanor Roosevelt Nat. Hist. Site **Park N** •
   NY, United States . . . . 153 [277]
Elephant Butte Reservoir •
   NM, United States 155 H8
Elephant Village •
   Pattaya, Thailand 130 E8
Eleuphanta Caves **Heritage C** • India . . 43 [156]
Elephantine I. • Egypt 109 B3
Eleuthera • Bahamas 164 A1
Elgin • IL, United States 150 C2
Elgin • United Kingdom 62 D3
Elgon, Mt • Kenya/Uganda 109 C4
Elias Piña • Dominican Rep. 165 F5
Elie • United Kingdom 65 B1
Elie **Beach** • United Kingdom . . . . . . 64 [2]
Elista • Russian Fed. 100 F4
Elizabeth • NJ, United States 156 C2
Elizabeth City • NC, United States 150 E3
Elizabethton • TN, United States 151 D3
Elizabethtown • KY, United States 150 C3
Elk • Poland 89 C2
Elk City • OK, United States 149 F3
Elk I. Nat. Park **Park N** •
   AL, Canada . . . . 161 [17]
Elk I. Nat. Park • AL, Canada 160 J6
Elk River • MN, United States 150 B1
Elkhovo • Bulgaria 92 H8
Elko • NV, United States 154 J7
Ellendale • ND, United States 148 G1
Ellensburg • WA, United States 154 G5
Eller • Marshall Is. . . . . 139 E
Ellertrin, Plains of • Ireland 69 H9
Ellesmere I. • Canada 142 E1
Ellesmere I. Nat. Park **Park N** •
   NU, Canada . . . . 161 [7]
Ellesmere, Lake • New Zealand 137 B3
Ellesmere Port • United Kingdom 63 D7
Ellice Is. • Tuvalu 138 CC3
Elliot, Mt • QL, Australia 136 C3
Ellis • ID, United States 148 D2
Elliston • SA, Australia 135 E6
Ellmau • Austria 91 07
Ellora Temple Caves **Heritage C** •
   India . . . . 43 [155]
Ellsworth Land • Antarctica 176 M5
Elmali • Turkey 95 G8
Elmas [Apt] • Sardinia, Italy 86 F6
Elmira • NY, United States 156 B1
Elmshorn • Germany 72 C2
Elora • OT, Canada 160 E5
Elounda • Crete, Greece 93 J6
Eloy • AZ, United States 155 G8
Elphinstone **Dive** • Egypt 109 E8
Elsdorf • Germany 73 C6
Elsinore **Heritage C** • Denmark . . . . . 44 [11]
Elstal • Germany 73 E7
Eltham • New Zealand 137 D6
Eltville • Germany 74 D6
Eltz, Burg • Germany 74 C5
Eluru • India 124 C1
Elvas • Portugal 84 A2
Elx • Spain 83 A1
Elx **Heritage C** • Spain . . . . 44 [100]
Ely • NV, United States 154 J8
Ely • United Kingdom 63 F8
Ely's Harbour • Bermuda 165 K10
Elyria • OH, United States 150 D2
Emamrud • Iran 120 H6
Emån • Sweden 99 H6
Emangusi • South Africa 111 C4
Emas, Parque Nac. das **Heritage N** •
   Brazil . . . . 40 [44]
Emba • Kazakstan 121 C2
Embonas • Rhodes, Greece . . . . 94 F
Embório • Thira, Greece . . . . 94 G
Embrun • France 78 D4
Embudhu • Maldives 124 H8
Embudhu Finolhu • Maldives 124 H8
Emden • Germany 72 D2
Emei Sham • China . . . . 126 [9]
Emei Shan **Heritage N** • China . . . . . . 41 [131]
Emei Shan **Heritage C** • China . . . . . . 43 [189]
Emerald • QL, Australia 130 C4
Emerald Coast • FL, United States 155 B1
Emerald Pool • Dominica . . . . 167 K
Emeraude, Côte d' • France 77 D3
Emet • Turkey 95 J9
Emilia-Romagna • Italy 87 C2
Emiliano Zapata • Mexico 169 E5
Emita • TS, Australia 136 F6
Emmaboda • Sweden 99 H7
Emmaste • Estonia 100 J6
Emmeloord • Netherlands 70 C2
Emmen • Netherlands 70 D2
Empangeni • South Africa 111 C4
Empoli • Italy 87 C3
Emporia • KS, United States 150 A3
Emporia • VA, United States 156 A4
Empty Quarter • Saudi Arabia 120 F10
Empúries • Spain 83 D3
Ems • Germany 72 B2
Emsland • Germany 73 A2
En Gedi • Israel 120 B3
En Nahud • Sudan 108 B3
Encamp • Andorra 82 E6
Encarnación • Mexico 169 I6
Encarnación • Paraguay 175 C2
Encinada • Indonesia 131 F5
Endelave • Denmark 99 F7
Enderby Land • Antarctica 176 Q4
Enewetak • Marshall Is. 138 BB2
Enfer, Pointe d' • Martinique . . . . 167 L
Engaño, Cabo • Dominican Rep. 165 G7
Engaño, Cabo • Dominican Rep. 165 G7
Engel's • Russian Fed. 100 G3
Engelberg **Ski** • Switzerland . . . . . . 61 [73]
Engelberg • Switzerland 90 K5
Engelsberg **Heritage C** • Sweden . . . . 44 [6]
Enggano • Indonesia 131 B5
England • United Kingdom 63 E10

England, Southeast •
   United Kingdom . . . . 65 G-H
Englee • Nf, Canada 160 D1
English Channel •
   France/United Kingdom 63 E10
English Harbour • Antigua & Barbuda . . . 167 I
English Harbour Town •
   Antigua & Barbuda . . . . 167 I
English Riviera • United Kingdom 65 J10
Enid • OK, United States 149 G3
Enkhuizen • Netherlands 70 C2
Enkirch • Germany 74 C6
Enna • Sicily, Italy 86 H8
Enköping • Sweden 99 A1
Ennepetal • Germany 73 D6
Ennepetal Water • United Kingdom 65 C3
Ennis • Ireland 69 C4
Enniscorthy • Ireland 69 C4
Enniskerry • Ireland 69 F7
Enniskillen • United Kingdom 63 B6
Ennistymon • Ireland 69 H9
Ennswetak • Marshall Is. . . . . 139 E
Enns • Austria 91 P7
Enns • Austria 91 G2
Ennylabagan • Marshall Is. . . . . 139 E
Eno • Cephalonia, Greece . . . . 94 J
Enoshima • Japan 127 I9
Enriquillo • Dominican Rep. 165 G6
Enriquillo, Lago • Dominican Rep. 165 F6
Enryaku-ji • Japan 127 G6
Enschede • Netherlands 70 D2
Ensenada • Argentina 175 G6
Ensenada • Mexico 168 H4
Ensenada de los Muertos • Mexico 168 I6
Ensheim [Apt] • Germany 74 A3
Enshi • China 125 E3
Enstone • Uganda 108 C4
Enterprise • AL, United States 151 C4
Enterprise • MS, United States 156 F5
Enterprise • NT, Canada 158 E2
Entrance, The • NS, Australia 136 H8
Entre-Deux • Réunion 113 C4
Entre-Deux-Mers • France 76 K9
Enugu • Nigeria 108 A2
Envigado • Colombia 173 B2
Enzan • Japan 127 H8
Éolie, I. **Heritage N** • Italy . . . . 41 [68]
Éolie, Is. • Sicily, Italy 86 H7
Epcot • FL, United States 157 A1
Epcot **Park L** • FL, United States . . . . 157 [24]
Ephesus • Turkey 95 E5
Ephraim • WI, United States 161 B2
Ephraim, Mt • Palestine NAR 120 B3
Epi • Vanuatu . . . . 138 V
Epidaurus • Greece 93 C3
Epidaurus **Heritage C** • Greece . . . . . 44 [240]
Epidavros • Greece 93 C3
Epidavros **Heritage C** • Greece . . . . . 44 [240]
Epinal • France 76 G2
Episkopí • Crete, Greece 93 H6
Episkopí • Cyprus 96 C4
Episkopí Bay • Cyprus 96 C4
Epping • United Kingdom 65 G7
Epsom • United Kingdom 63 E9
Epsom Downs • United Kingdom 65 G8
Equatorial Channel • Maldives 124 G8
EQUATORIAL GUINEA • Africa 106 C4
Er Rachidia • Morocco 107 B2
Eraclea Minoa • Sicily, Italy 86 G8
Erbach • Germany 74 E7
Erbalunga • Corsica, France 78 N11
Ercis • Turkey 95 D2
Erciyes Dag • Turkey 95 J9
Erculano • Italy 87 G7
Erdek • Turkey 95 F4
Erdemli • Turkey 95 I10
Erdenet • Mongolia 125 E2
Erdeven • France 77 D4
Erding • Germany 74 G7
Erebus, Mt • Antarctica 176 J8
Erenhot • China 125 F2
Erenköy • Cyprus 96 C4
Eressós • Lesbos, Greece . . . . 94 C
Eressós, Skála • Lesbos, Greece . . . . . . 94 C
Erfoud • Morocco 107 B3
Erfurt • Germany 73 C6
Erftstadt • Germany 74 A1
Erfurt • Germany 72 D3
Erg Abu Ramada **Dive** • Egypt 109 E8
Ergani • Turkey 95 E3
Ergun He • China 125 G1
Erice • Sicily, Italy 84 F6
Ericeira • Portugal 84 F6
Ericht, Loch • United Kingdom 62 C3
Erie • PA, United States 156 A1
Erie Canal • NY, United States 161 D1
Erie, Fort • OT, Canada 160 E5
Erie, Lake • Canada/United States 156 E6
Erimo-misaki • Japan 127 D2
Erinngarbha • Sweden 99 H7
ERITREA • Africa 108 C3
Eriyadu • Maldives 124 H8
Erken • Sweden 99 B1
Erkner • Germany 73 F8
Erkrath • Germany 73 C6
Erl • Austria 91 07
Erlangen • Germany 72 D4
Erldunda • NT, Australia 136 B2
Ermelo • Netherlands 70 C2
Ermenek • Turkey 95 I10
Ermiónes • Corfu, Greece . . . . 94 A
Ermoúpoli • Síros, Greece 136 F6
Ernabella • SA, Australia 136 B2
Ernakulam • India 124 B3
Erode • India 124 B3
Ergeler Ley • Germany 77 D3
Erquy • France 77 D3
Erritsoe • Denmark 99 E7
Erromango • Vanuatu . . . . 138 V
Erskine • MN, United States 150 A1
Ertis • Kazakstan 121 G1
Erzgebirge • Germany 72 E3
Erzincan • Turkey 95 C2
Erzurum • Turkey 95 D2
Es Canar • Ibiza, Spain 83 K8
Es Canyar • Ibiza, Spain 83 M9
Es Delfins • Minorca, Spain 83 J7
Es Grau • Minorca, Spain 83 K8
Es Mercadal • Minorca, Spain 83 J7
Es Migjorn Retorns Gran Sant Cristóbal •
   Minorca, Spain 83 J8
Es Pinar, Cap d' •
   Majorca, Spain 83 011
Es Pla • Majorca, Spain 83 011
Es Pujols • Formentera, Spain 83 M10
Es Semara • Western Sahara 106 A2
Es Tudóns, Naveta d' •
   Minorca, Spain 83 J7
Es Vedra, I. • Ibiza, Spain 83 L10
Esbjerg • Denmark 99 E7
Escala, I' • Spain 83 D3
Escaldes • Andorra 82 E6
Escalier, I' • Mauritius 113 C4
Escambia • AL/FL, United States 155 A1
Escambray, Sierra del • Cuba 164 F4
Escanaba • MI, United States 150 C1
Escárcega • Mexico 169 E5
Escaut • France 76 B4
Esch-sur-Alzette • Luxembourg 70 D5
Esch-sur-Sûre • Luxembourg 70 D5
Escobedo • Mexico 169 I7
Escocesa, Bahía • Dominican Rep. 165 G6
Escondido • CA, United States 154 J9
Escuinapa • Mexico 169 H6
Escuintla • Guatemala 170 J9

Esenguly • Turkmenistan 121 B4
Esfahan • Iran 120 G7
Esfahan **Heritage C** • Iran . . . . 43 [134]
Eskasham • Tajikistan 121 F4
Eshowe • South Africa 111 C4
Eshtemoa • Palestine NAR 120 A4
Esikhawini • South Africa 111 C4
Esil • Kazakstan . . . . 136 C
Esil [Riv] • Kazakstan 121 E1
Esk • TS, Australia 136 F6
Esk • United Kingdom 65 C4
Esker • Nf, Canada 159 J3
Eskilstuna • Sweden 99 A2
Eskilstuna, Parken Zoo I **Park L** •
   Sweden . . . . 59 [6]
Eskimo Point • NU, Canada 158 G2
Eskisehir • Turkey 95 J9
Esler Dagi • Turkey 95 F5
Eslöv • Sweden 99 G7
Esme • Turkey 95 F5
Esmeraldas • Ecuador 173 B2
Esna • Egypt 109 B2
Espace Killy **Ski** • France . . . . 61 [25-26]
Espalmador, I. • Ibiza, Spain 83 M10
Espanola • NM, United States 155 I7
Española, I. • Galápagos Is. 171 H10
Espardell, I. • Ibiza, Spain 83 M10
Esperance • WA, Australia 135 C6
Espérance [Apt] • St Martin . . . . 166 C
Esperanza [Base] • Antarctica . . . . 176 [4]
Espichel, Cabo • Portugal 84 F6
Espinho • Portugal 84 H7
Espírito Santo • Brazil 174 B4
Espíritu Santo • Vanuatu . . . . 138 V
Espíritu Santo, Bahía del • Mexico 169 G5
Espíritu Santo, I. • Mexico 168 I6
Espoo • Finland 99 D4
Espool • Argentina 173 B3
Essaouira • Morocco 107 A2
Essaouira **Heritage C** • Morocco . . . . 44 [278]
Essen • Germany 73 C5
Essen **Heritage C** • Germany . . . . . . 44 [54]
Essex • CT, United States 156 C2
Essex • United Kingdom 65 G7
Esslingen am Neckar • Germany 74 B3
Essonne • France 78 A2
Est, I. de I' • Mauritius 113 F6
Est, Pointe de l' • QU, Canada 160 B1
Est, Rivière de l' • Réunion 113 D4
Estaca de Bares, Punta • Spain 80 B2
Estartit, I' • Spain 83 D3
Estcourt • South Africa 111 B4
Este, Parque Nac. del •
   Dominican Rep. 165 H6
Este, Playas del • Cuba 164 F4
Este, Villa d' **Heritage C** • Italy . . . . . 44 [166]
Esteli • Nicaragua 170 D4
Estellencs • Majorca, Spain 83 N11
Estepa • Spain 82 I7
Estepona • Spain 82 I8
Esterel, I' • France 78 D4
Estevan • SA, Canada 158 F4
Estói • Spain 84 G7
ESTONIA • Europe 100 K6
Estoril • Portugal 84 F6
Estoril, Costa do • Portugal 84 F6
Estrela, Serra da • Portugal 84 A2
Estuario do Tejo, Reserva Natural •
   Portugal 84 G6
Esztergom • Hungary 92 B2
Et Tleta de Oued Laou • Morocco 107 B1
Étables-sur-Mer • France 77 D3
Étampes • France 78 A2
Étang-Salé • Réunion 113 C4
Étampel • India 123 F8
Etawah • India 123 F7
ETHIOPIA • Africa 108 C4
Ethiopian Highlands • Ethiopia 108 C3
Etna, Monte • Sicily, Italy 86 H7
Etne • Norway 98 F9
Etoile • Seychelles 113 B1
Eton • United Kingdom 65 G7
Etorofu-to • Russian Fed. 127 E2
Etosha Nat. Park **Park N** • Namibia . . 112 [124]
Etrier [Apt] • South Africa 74 F6
Etten • Fed. States of Micronesia . . . . . 138 C
Euaiki • Tonga . . . . 139 P
Euboea • Greece 93 D2
Euclid • OH, United States 150 D2
Eucumbene, Lake • NS, Australia 136 H9
Eugene • OR, United States 154 G6
Eugene O'Neill Nat. Hist. Site **Park N** •
   CA, United States . . . . 152 [46]
Eugenia, Punta • Mexico 168 H5
Eugmo • Finland 97 E3
Eungella Nat. Park • QL, Australia 136 C4
Eunice • LA, United States 156 E6
Euphrates • Iraq/Syria 120 E7
Eura • Finland 99 C3
Eurajoki • Finland 99 C3
Eure [Adm] • France 78 A1
Eure [Riv] • France 78 A1
Eure-ei-Loir • France 78 A2
Eureka • CA, United States 154 I7
Eureka • NV, United States 154 J7
Euromast • Rotterdam, Netherlands 70 G8
Euromos • Turkey 95 F6
Europa Park • Germany 74 B3
Europa, Point • Gibraltar 82 G3
Europa-Park **Park L** • Germany . . . . . 59 [62]
Europapark • Germany 74 A4
Europe • 48
Europoort • Netherlands 70 G8
Euskadi • Spain 82 B1
Euskirchen • Germany 74 C5
Evandale • TS, Australia 136 F6
Evanger • Norway 98 G8
Evans Strait • NU, Canada 159 H2
Evanston • IL, United States 150 C2
Evanston • WY, United States 148 D7
Evansville • IN, United States 150 C3
Evaton • South Africa 111 B4
Everard, Lake • SA, Australia 135 F6
Everest, Mt • China/Nepal 122 C3
Everett • WA, United States 154 F5
Everglades • FL, United States 155 D3
Everglades Nat. Park •
   FL, United States 155 C2
Everglades Nat. Park **Park N** •
   FL, United States . . . . 153 [220]
Evergreen • AL, United States 151 C4
Evesham • United Kingdom 65 F6
Evesham, Vale of • United Kingdom 65 F6
Évia • Greece 93 D2
Évian-les-Bains • France 78 C3
Evje • Norway 97 B4
Evora • Portugal 84 B2
Evora **Heritage C** • Portugal . . . . 44 [151]
Evora [Adm] • Portugal 84 A3
Evreux • France 76 D2
Évros • Greece 93 E1
Évry • France 78 B2
Ewa Beach • HI, United States 157 G6
Ewaso Ngiro • Kenya 109 C4
Excelsior Springs •
   MO, United States 150 B3
Exe • United Kingdom 65 J9
Exeter • NH, United States 156 D1
Exeter • United Kingdom 65 J9
Exeter • United Kingdom 63 D9
Exmoor Nat. Park **Park N** •
   United Kingdom . . . . 58 [56]
Exmoor Nat. Park • United Kingdom 65 J9
Exmouth • United Kingdom 65 J10
Exmouth Gulf • WA, Australia 135 A4
Exmouth **Beach** • United Kingdom . . . 64 [43]
Exombúrgo • Tínos, Greece . . . . 94 I
Expoland • Japan 127 G6

Exposition, Parc des (Paris) •
   France 78 B1
Express [Apt] • OH, United States 161 A3
Extremadura • Spain 80 B4
Exuma Cays • Bahamas 164 A2
Exuma Cays Land & Sea Park •
   Bahamas 164 A1
Eyasi, Lake • Tanzania 110 H7
Eymoutiers • France 76 F4
Eyre Mtns • New Zealand 137 G7
Eyre North, Lake • SA, Australia 135 F5
Eyre Peninsula • SA, Australia 135 F6
Eyre South, Lake • SA, Australia 135 F5
Ezakheni • South Africa 111 B4
Eze • France 78 H7
Ezeiza [Apt] • Argentina 175 F6
Ezine • Turkey 95 E4

F

Faaa • French Polynesia . . . . 139 K
Faan, Ko • Thailand 130 B11
Fåborg • Denmark 99 F8
Facho, Pico do •
   Porto Santo, Madeira 84 E5
Fadiffolu Atoll • Maldives 124 G7
Faenza • Italy 87 C2
Fagamalo • Samoa . . . . 139 G
Fagaras • Romania 92 D2
Fagasa • American Samoa . . . . 139 H
Fagatogo • American Samoa . . . . 139 H
Fagerhult • Sweden 99 H6
Fagersta • Sweden 99 A1
Faguibine, Lac **Park** • Mali . . . . 112 [2]
Fahrland • Germany 73 E8
Fahrlander See • Germany 73 E8
Fai di Paganella • Italy 86 C4
Faial • Azores 84 B4
Faial • Madeira 84 E5
Faichuk • Fed. States of Micronesia . . . 138 C
Fair I. • United Kingdom 62 H13
Fairbanks • AK, United States 157 E3
Faiadourno **Beach** • United Kingdom . . 65 F6
Fairford • United Kingdom 65 F6
Fairmont • MN, United States 150 B2
Fairmont • WV, United States 150 D3
Fairmount Hot Springs • BC, Canada . . . 160 J7
Fairview Park • Hong Kong, China 126 E4
Fairview Shores •
   FL, United States 157 B1
Fairweather, Mt •
   Canada/United States 157 F4
Fairyhouse • Ireland 69 F6
Faisalabad • Pakistan 122 B2
Faizabad • India 123 G8
Fakaofo • Tokelau 138 CC3
Fakfak • Indonesia 131 H4
Fakse Bugt • Denmark 99 F8
Fakse Ladeplads • Denmark 99 F8
Falaise, Gorges de la • Martinique . . . . . 167 L
Falam • Myanmar 128 A2
Fálasama • Crete, Greece 93 G5
Falcade • Italy 86 D4
Falconara Marittima • Italy 87 D3
Falcone, Capo del •
   Sardinia, Italy 86 E5
Faleapuna • Samoa . . . . 139 G
Falefatu • Tuvalu . . . . 139 G
Falelatai • Samoa . . . . 139 G
Faleolo [Apt] • Samoa . . . . 139 G
Falfurrias • TX, United States 155 C6
Foliráki • Rhodes, Greece . . . . 94 F
Falkenberg • Sweden 99 G6
Falkensee • Germany 73 E8
Falkirk • United Kingdom 65 A2
Falkland • United Kingdom 65 B1
FALKLAND IS. • Atlantic Ocean 175 C5
Falköping • Sweden 99 G5
Fall River • MA, United States 156 D2
Fallon • NV, United States 154 J8
Falls Creek • VI, Australia 136 G9
Falmouth • Antigua & Barbuda . . . . 167 I
Falmouth • Jamaica . . . . 164 C
Falmouth • United Kingdom 65 I10
Falmouth **Beach** • United Kingdom . . . 64 [43]
False Bay • South Africa 111 D7
Falso, Cabo • Dominican Rep. 165 F6
Falster • Denmark 99 F8
Falsterbo • Sweden 99 D3
Falun • Sweden 97 D3
Falun **Heritage C** • Sweden . . . . 44 [5]
Famagusta • Cyprus 96 C4
Famagusta Bay • Cyprus 96 D3
Fana • Norway 98 F8
Fanchang • China 126 G7
Fancy • St Vincent & Gren. . . . . 167 O
Fang • Thailand 130 B5
Fanling • Hong Kong, China 126 E4
Fanning I. • Kiribati . . . . 139 I
Fanø • Denmark 99 E7
Fano • Italy 87 D3
Fanø Bugt • Denmark 99 E8
Fantasylandia • Ibiza, Spain 83 M9
Faoia, I. • Wallis & Futuna . . . . 139 G
Farafra Oasis • Egypt 109 A2
Farah • Afghanistan 121 D5
Faralón • Margarita . . . . 166 T
Farasan, Jaza'ir • Saudi Arabia 109 E10
Farbairn Reservoir • QL, Australia 136 C4
Farewell, Cape • Greenland 158 L3
Farewell, Cape • New Zealand 137 B3
Farghona • Uzbekistan 121 F4
Fársala • Greece 93 C2
Farnham • United Kingdom 65 G8
Faro • Portugal 84 A3
Faro • YT, Canada 158 C2
Faro [Adm] • Portugal 84 J8
FAROE IS. • Atlantic Ocean 48 C1
Farquhar, Atoll de • Seychelles 113 A2
Fársala • Greece 93 C2
Farúkolhufushi • Maldives 124 H8
Fårup • Denmark 99 E7
Fårup Aquapark & Sommerland **Park L** •
   Denmark . . . . 59 [15]
Fårup Aquapark & Sommerland •
   Denmark . . . . 99 Eb
Fasil Ghebbi **Heritage C** • Ethiopia . . . 43 [99]
Fasillar • Turkey . . . . 139 O
Fastiv • Ukraine 100 D3
Fatato • Tuvalu . . . . 139 G
Fatehgarh • India 123 F7
Fatehpur • Rajasthan, India 123 E7
Fatehpur • Uttar Pradesh, India 123 F8
Fatehpur Sikri • India 123 E7
Fatehpur Sikri **Heritage C** • India . . . . 43 [151]
Father Marquette Nat. •
   MI, United States 161 B2
Father Marquette Nat. Mem. **Park N** •
   MI, United States . . . . 153 [159]
Fathom Five Nat. Marine Park **Park N** •
   OT, Canada . . . . 161 [26]
Fathom Five Nat. Marine Park •
   OT, Canada 161 C2
Fatiau Tuai • Niue . . . . 139 O
Fátima • Portugal 84 A2
Fatrade Beach • Goa, India 124 G7
Fatu Hiva • French Polynesia 139 EE3
Fatua, Pointe • Wallis & Futuna . . . . . . 139 G
Faucigny • France 78 D3
Faugères • France 76 I9
Faurei • Romania 92 E2
Fauske • Norway 97 D2

Favàritx, Cap de •
   Minorca, Spain 83 K7
Fawgnana, I. • Italy 86 G7
Fawdaw, Aran • United Kingdom 63 D8
Faxaflói • Iceland 97 H6
Faya • Chad 108 A3
Fayaoué • New Caledonia . . . . 138 U
Faye, Pas de la • France 78 H7
Fayette • NF, United States 161 B2
Fayetteville • AR, United States 151 B3
Fayetteville • NC, United States 151 E3
Fazao-Malfakassa, Parc nat. de **Park** •
   Togo . . . . 112 [76]
Feale • Ireland 69 H10
Fear, Cape • NC, United States 151 E4
Fécamp • France 76 D2
Federal Hall Nat. Mem. **Park N** •
   NY, United States . . . . 153 [278]
Fedje • Norway 98 F8
Fefan • Fed. States of Micronesia . . . . . 138 C
Fohmarn • Germany 72 D1
Foia • Lago • Brazil 174 F7
Feilding • New Zealand 137 C4
Feira de Santa • Brazil 174 C4
Foke • Turkey 95 J9
Felanitx • Majorca, Spain 83 012
Feldafing • Germany 74 G7
Feldberg **Ski** • Germany . . . . 61 [1]
Feldberg • Germany 73 B3
Feldkirch • Austria 91 M8
Feliceto • Corsica, France 78 M11
Félicité • Seychelles 113 B2
Felidu Atoll • Maldives 124 G7
Felipe Carillo Puerto • Mexico 169 G5
Felixstowe • United Kingdom 65 H7
Felixstowe **Beach** • United Kingdom . . 64 [21]
Fell Foot Park • United Kingdom 65 C4
Feltre • Italy 86 D4
Femer Bælt • Denmark/Germany 99 F8
Fenghua • China 126 H7
Fengxian • China 126 H7
Fenit • Ireland 69 G10
Fens, The • United Kingdom 78 L10
Fens, The • United Kingdom 63 E8
Fensfjorden • Norway 98 F8
Foodosiya • Ukraine 100 C4
Feolin Ferry • United Kingdom 66 A2
Ferapontov Monastery **Heritage C** •
   Russian Fed. . . . . 44 [273]
Féres • Greece 93 E1
Fergus Falls • MN, United States 150 A1
Ferienzentrum Schloss Dankern **Park L** •
   Germany . . . . 59 [46]
Ferkessédougou • Côte d'Ivoire 106 B4
Fermanagh • United Kingdom 64 A3
Fermo • Italy 87 D3
Fermont • QU, Canada 159 J3
Fermoy • Ireland 69 H11
Fern Gully • Jamaica 165 D3
Fernandina Beach •
   FL, United States 155 C1
Fernandina, I. • Galápagos Is. 171 G10
Fernando de Noronha **Heritage N** •
   Brazil . . . . 40 [42]
Fernie Snow Valley **Ski** •
   BC, Canada . . . . 146 [10]
Fernmeldeturm • Germany 73 C6
Ferragudo • Portugal 84 I8
Ferrara • Italy 87 C2
Ferrara **Heritage C** • Italy . . . . 44 [156]
Ferraria, Ponta da • Azores 84 B4
Ferreiras • Portugal 84 I8
Ferreries • Minorca, Spain 83 J7
Ferret, Cap • France 78 E6
Ferro, I. do •
   Porto Santo, Madeira 84 E5
Ferrol • Spain 80 A2
Ferru, Monte • Sardinia, Italy 86 E5
Ferté-Bernard, la • France 77 F5
Fertília [Apt] • Sardinia, Italy 86 E5
Fertö **Heritage C** • Hungary . . . . 44 [146]
Fès • Morocco 107 B1
Fès **Heritage C** • Morocco . . . . 44 [275]
Festu I. • Maldives 124 G7
Festós • Crete, Greece 93 H6
Fetesti • Romania 92 I7
Fethiye • Turkey 95 F6
Fetlar • United Kingdom 62 H12
Fetsund • Norway 98 E5
Fevzipasa • Turkey 95 J9
Feyzabad • Afghanistan 121 F4
Fezzan • Libya 106 D2
Fiabilandia **Park L** • Italy . . . . 59 [84]
Fianarantsoa • Madagascar 110 D3
Fichtelgebirge • Germany 73 B3
Fichtenwalde • Germany 73 E8
Fidenza • Italy 87 B2
Fideris **Ski** • Switzerland . . . . 61 [60]
Fieberbrunn **Ski** • Austria . . . . 61 [102]
Fieberbrunn • Austria 91 07
Fiemme, Val di • Italy 86 C4
Fier • Albania 92 B3
Fiesch **Ski** • Switzerland . . . . 61 [67]
Fiesch • Switzerland 90 J6
Fiésole • Italy 87 C3
Fife • United Kingdom 66 B1
Figari • Corsica, France 78 F6
Figeac • France 78 F6
Figeholm • Sweden 99 H6
Figuera da Foz • Portugal 84 A2
Figueres • Spain 83 D3
Figuig • Morocco 107 B2
Fihalhohi • Maldives 124 H8
FIJI IS. • Pacific Ocean 139 CC4
Filadelfia • Paraguay 176 N5
Filderstadt • Germany 74 B3
Filfla • Malta 96 B2
Filicudi, I. • Italy 86 H7
Filipiáka • Greece 93 B2
Filipstad • Sweden 97 C4
Fillefjell • Norway 98 E4
Fillmore • UT, United States 148 D3
Filmpark Babelsberg • Germany 73 E8
Filosorma • Corsica, France 78 M11
Filóti • Náxos, Greece . . . . 94 H
Filzmoos • Austria 91 P7
Fimbul Ice Shelf • Antarctica 176 D5
Findel [Apt] • Luxembourg 70 D5
Fínikas • Greece . . . . 94 G
Finger Lakes • NY, United States 156 B1
Finhaut • Switzerland 90 I6
Finikás • Síros, Greece . . . . 94 I
Finike • Turkey 95 G8
Finike Körfezi • Turkey 95 G8
Finisterre • France 77 C3
Finke • N. Australia 136 B2
Finke Gorge Nat. Park •
   NT, Australia 136 B2
Finke [Riv] • NT/SA, Australia 136 B2
FINLAND • Europe 97
Finland, Gulf of • Europe 97 E4
Finnemarka • Norway 98 D5
Finnish Archipelago • Finland 98 D5
Finnish Lakeland • Finland 98 C1
Finnmark • Finland 98 C1
Finnsnes • Norway 97 C1
Finse • Norway 98 G8
Finspång • Sweden 99 A2
Finsteraarhorn • Switzerland 90 J6
Fiordland • New Zealand 137 F7
Fiordland Nat. Park • New Zealand 137 F7
Firat • Turkey 95 C3
Firatin • Turkey 95 J9
Fire I. Nat. Seashore •
   NY, United States 156 C2
Fire I. Nat. Seashore **Park N** •
   NY, United States . . . . 153 [280]

Firefly • Jamaica ... 165 D3
Firenze • Italy ... 87 E2
Firenze Heritage C • Italy ... 44 [160]
Firmat • Argentina ... 175 F6
Firozabad • India ... 123 F7
Fischen • Germany ... 74 F8
Fishbourne • United Kingdom ... 66 D6
Fisher Strait • NU, Canada ... 159 H2
Fishers I. • NY, United States ... 156 D2
Fishguard • United Kingdom ... 63 C9
Fishnish • United Kingdom ... 66 A2
Fiskárdo • Cephalonia, Greece ... 94 J
Fiskebäckskil • Sweden ... 99 F5
Fisterra, Cabo • Spain ... 80 A2
Fito, Mt • Samoa ... 139 G
Fitzroy • France ... 76 L9
Fitz Roy • Argentina ... 175 B4
Fitzcarrald • Peru ... 173 F6
Fitzroy • QL, Australia ... 136 D4
Fitzroy Crossing • WA, Australia ... 135 D3
Fitzroy I. • QL, Australia ... 136 C3
Fiumicino • Italy ... 87 E5
Fiumicino [Apt] • Italy ... 87 E5
Fiumorbo • Corsica, France ... 78 N12
Five Cays • Turks & Caicos Is. ... 164 C3
Five Is. Harbour • Antigua & Barbuda ... 167 I
Fjällbacka • Sweden ... 99 F5
Fjäråsbräcka • Sweden ... 99 F6
Fjerritslev • Denmark ... 99 E6
Flå • Norway ... 98 D5
Flachau Ski • Austria ... 61 [110]
Flachau • Austria ... 91 P7
Flagstaff • AZ, United States ... 155 G7
Flagstaff • South Africa ... 111 B5
Flagstaff, Mt •
  St Martin, West Indies ... 166 C
Flaine Ski • France ... 61 [15]
Flaine • France ... 78 D3
Flåm • Norway ... 98 G8
Flamants, I. • Mauritius ... 113 F6
Flambards Victorian Village •
  United Kingdom ... 65 I10
Flamborough Head • United Kingdom ... 63 E6
Flamingo [Apt] • Bonaire ... 166 U
Flamingo Land Park L •
  United Kingdom ... 59 [25]
Flamingo Sanctuary • Bonaire ... 166 U
Flanders Heritage C • Belgium ... 44 [40-41]
Flanders • Europe ... 70 A4
Flannan Is. • United Kingdom ... 62 B2
Flat I. • Mauritius ... 113 F5
Flateby • Norway ... 98 E5
Flathead Ind Res •
  MT, United States ... 155 [14]
Flathead Lake • MT, United States ... 154 H5
Flattery, Cape •
  WA, United States ... 154 G5
Flatts Village • Bermuda ... 165 L9
Flåvatn • Norway ... 98 D6
Flèche, la • France ... 77 E5
Flen • Sweden ... 99 A2
Flensburg • Germany ... 72 C1
Flesberg • Norway ... 98 D5
Flesland [Apt] • Norway ... 98 F8
Flevoland • Netherlands ... 70 C2
Flevoland [Adm] • Netherlands ... 70 C2
Flims Ski • Switzerland ... 61 [75]
Flims • Switzerland ... 90 K5
Flin Flon • MN, Canada ... 158 J3
Flinders • QL, Australia ... 135 G3
Flinders I. • TS, Australia ... 136 F6
Flinders Passage • QL, Australia ... 136 C3
Flinders Ranges • SA, Australia ... 135 F6
Flinders Reefs • QL, Australia ... 136 C3
Flint • MI, United States ... 161 A2
Flint I. • Kiribati ... 139 DD3
Flintshire • United Kingdom ... 64 A4
Floating Garden Is. • Palau ... 137 A
Floreana, I. • Galápagos Is. ... 171 H10
Florence • AL, United States ... 151 C4
Florence • Italy ... 87 C3
Florence Heritage C • Italy ... 44 [160]
Florence • OR, United States ... 154 G6
Florence • SC, United States ... 151 E4
Florencia • Colombia ... 172 B2
Florenville • Belgium ... 70 C5
Flores • Argentina ... 175 F7
Flores • Azores ... 84 B4
Flores • Guatemala ... 170 K9
Flores • Indonesia ... 131 F5
Flores, I. de • Uruguay ... 175 G6
Flores Sea • Indonesia ... 131 F5
Floresta • Brazil ... 174 C3
Floresville • TX, United States ... 155 E6
Floriana • Malta ... 96 B2
Floriano • Brazil ... 174 B3
Florianópolis • Brazil ... 175 D2
Florida • Cuba ... 164 G5
Florida • United States ... 155 A-D
Florida • Uruguay ... 175 G6
Florida Caverns State Park •
  FL, United States ... 155 B1
Florida Citrus Bowl •
  FL, United States ... 157 B1
Florida Citrus Tower •
  FL, United States ... 157 A1
Florida City • FL, United States ... 155 D3
Florida Keys • FL, United States ... 155 D3
Florida's Cypress Gardens •
  FL, United States ... 155 C2
Florida's Silver Springs •
  FL, United States ... 155 C1
Flórina • Greece ... 93 B1
Florissant Fossil Beds Nat. Mon. Park N •
  CO, United States ... 152 [94]
Florø • Norway ... 98 F7
Flumendosa • Sardinia, Italy ... 86 F5
Flumserberg Ski • Switzerland ... 61 [76]
Flumserberg • Switzerland ... 90 K5
Flushing • Netherlands ... 70 B3
Flying Tigers Warbird Air Museum •
  FL, United States ... 157 B1
Foca • Bosnia-Herz. ... 92 B3
Foca • Turkey ... 95 E5
Focsani • Romania ... 92 D2
Fogdön • Sweden ... 99 A2
Fóggia • Italy ... 85 E4
Fogo • Cape Verde ... 106 E7
Fogo • NF, Canada ... 160 D1
Fogo [I.] • NF, Canada ... 160 D1
Föhr • Germany ... 72 C1
Fóia • Portugal ... 84 I7
Foix • France ... 78 K10
Foix [Region] • France ... 78 K10
Folégandros • Greece ... 93 D3
Folelli • Corsica, France ... 78 N11
Folgaria Ski • Italy ... 61 [134]
Folgária Ski • Italy ... 61 [130]
Folgefonn • Norway ... 98 F8
Folgoët, le • France ... 77 C3
Foligno • Italy ... 87 D3
Folkestone • United Kingdom ... 65 H8
Folkestone Underwater Park •
  Barbados ... 167 M
Follónica • Italy ... 87 C3
Fomento • Cuba ... 164 F4
Fond d'Or Bay • St Lucia ... 167 N
Fond du Lac Ind Res •
  MN, United States ... 155 [61]
Fondi • Italy ... 87 F5
Fongafale • Tuvalu ... 139 R
Fonseca • Mexico ... 168 I5
Fonseca, Golfo de • C. America ... 170 D4
Font • Switzerland ... 90 I5
Font-Romeu • France ... 78 L10
Fontainebleau • France ... 78 B2
Fontainebleau Heritage C • France ... 44 [75]
Fontainebleau, Forêt de • France ... 78 B2
Fontana Rossa [Apt] •
  Sicily, Italy ... 86 H8
Fonte alla Róccia • Italy ... 86 D3
Fonte Boa • Brazil ... 173 C3
Fontein Cave • Aruba ... 166 W
Fontenay Heritage C • France ... 44 [77]

Fontenay-le-Comte • France ... 77 E6
Fontevraud • France ... 77 E6
Fonyód • Hungary ... 92 B2
Fópolo • Italy ... 87 B1
Fóra • Sweden ... 99 H6
Fora, I. de • Madeira ... 84 E5
Foral de Navarra, Comunidad •
  Spain ... 80 E2
Forbes • NS, Australia ... 136 H8
Ford's Theatre Nat. Hist. Site Park N •
  DC, United States ... 153 [264]
Førde • Rogaland, Norway ... 98 F9
Førde • Sogn og Fjordane, Norway ... 98 F7
Fordefjorden • Norway ... 98 F7
Fore Abbey • Ireland ... 69 E6
Forest Finland • Finland ... 98 C2
Forest of the Cedars of God Heritage C •
  Lebanon ... 44 [305]
Forestier Peninsula •
  TS, Australia ... 136 F7
Forestville • QU, Canada ... 160 A1
Forez • United Kingdom ... 65 B1
Forggensee • Germany ... 74 F8
Forillon, Parc nat. de •
  QU, Canada ... 160 B1
Forillon, Parc national de Park N •
  QU, Canada ... 161 [33]
Forio • Italy ... 87 G7
Forks • WA, United States ... 154 G5
Forlì • Italy ... 87 C2
Formentera • Spain ... 83 M10
Formentor • Majorca, Spain ... 83 O11
Formentor, Cap de •
  Majorca, Spain ... 83 O11
Fórmia • Italy ... 87 F5
Formiga • Brazil ... 174 E6
Formigas • Azores ... 84 C4
FORMOSA see TAIWAN
Formosa • Argentina ... 175 C2
Formosa • Brazil ... 174 B4
Fornells • Minorca, Spain ... 83 K7
Forrest City • AR, United States ... 151 B3
Fors • Sweden ... 99 A1
Forsayth • QL, Australia ... 135 G3
Forssa • Finland ... 99 D4
Forsyth • MT, United States ... 148 E1
Fort Albany • OT, Canada ... 159 H3
Fort Apache Ind Res •
  AZ, United States ... 155 [31]
Fort Apache Indian Reservation •
  AZ, United States ... 155 G8
Fort Bay • Saba ... 167 E
Fort Beaufort • South Africa ... 111 G6
Fort Belknap Ind Res •
  MT, United States ... 155 [17]
Fort Benton • MT, United States ... 148 D1
Fort Berthold Ind Res •
  ND, United States ... 155 [42]
Fort Bowie Nat. Hist. Site •
  AZ, United States ... 155 H8
Fort Bowie Nat. Hist. Site Park N •
  AZ, United States ... 152 [115]
Fort Bragg • CA, United States ... 154 I7
Fort Caroline Nat. Mem. •
  FL, United States ... 155 C1
Fort Caroline Nat. Mem. Park N •
  FL, United States ... 153 [215]
Fort Chimo • QU, Canada ... 159 J3
Fort Chipewyan • AL, Canada ... 158 E3
Fort Clatsop Nat. Mem. Park N •
  OR, United States ... 152 [34]
Fort Collins • CO, United States ... 148 F2
Fort Davis Nat. Hist. Site Park N •
  TX, United States ... 152 [134]
Fort de France • Martinique ... 167 L
Fort de France, Baie de •
  Martinique ... 167 L
Fort Delaware State Park •
  DE, United States ... 156 B3
Fort Dodge • IA, United States ... 150 B2
Fort Donelson Nat. Battlefield Park N •
  TN, United States ... 153 [224]
Fort Erie • OT, Canada ... 161 D1
Fort Frances • OT, Canada ... 158 G4
Fort Frederica Nat. Mon. Park N •
  GA, United States ... 153 [212]
Fort Fun Abenteuerland Park L •
  Germany ... 59 [52]
Fort Gadsden State Hist. Site •
  FL, United States ... 155 B1
Fort George • QU, Canada ... 159 I3
Fort Good Hope • NT, Canada ... 158 D2
Fort Hall Ind Res •
  ID, United States ... 155 [11]
Fort Laramie Nat. Hist. Site Park N •
  WY, United States ... 152 [71]
Fort Larned Nat. Hist. Site Park N •
  KS, United States ... 152 [168]
Fort Lauderdale •
  FL, United States ... 155 D3
Fort Liard • NT, Canada ... 158 D2
Fort Liberté • Haiti ... 165 F5
Fort Macleod • AL, Canada ... 160 J7
Fort Madison • IA, United States ... 150 B2
Fort Matanzas Nat. Mon. Park N •
  FL, United States ... 153 [216]
Fort McDermitt Ind Res •
  NV/OR, United States ... 155 [9]
Fort McHenry Nat. Mon. & Hist. Shrine
  Park N • MD, United States ... 153 [263]
Fort McMurray • AL, Canada ... 158 E3
Fort McPherson • YT, Canada ... 158 C2
Fort Médoc • France ... 78 H7
Fort Moultrie Nat. Mon. Park N •
  SC, United States ... 153 [231]
Fort Myers • FL, United States ... 155 C3
Fort Necessity Nat. Battlefield Park N •
  PA, United States ... 153 [265]
Fort Nelson • BC, Canada ... 158 D3
Fort Norman • NT, Canada ... 158 D2
Fort Pearson • South Africa ... 111 C4
Fort Peck • MT, United States ... 148 E1
Fort Peck Ind Res •
  MT, United States ... 155 [18]
Fort Peck Lake • MT, United States ... 148 E1
Fort Pierce • FL, United States ... 155 D2
Fort Point Nat. Hist. Site Park N •
  CA, United States ... 152 [43]
Fort Providence • NT, Canada ... 158 E2
Fort Pulaski Nat. Mon. Park N •
  GA, United States ... 153 [211]
Fort Raleigh Nat. Hist. Site Park N •
  NC, United States ... 153 [242]
Fort Ross State Hist. Park •
  CA, United States ... 154 I8
Fort Saskatchewan • AL, Canada ... 160 J6
Fort Scott Nat. Hist. Site Park N •
  KS, United States ... 153 [171]
Fort Shevchenko • Kazakhstan ... 121 B3
Fort Simpson • NT, Canada ... 158 D2
Fort Smith • AR, United States ... 151 B3
Fort Smith • NT, Canada ... 158 E2
Fort Smith Nat. Hist. Site Park N •
  AR, United States ... 153 [187]
Fort St John • BC, Canada ... 160 I5
Fort Stanwix Nat. Mon. •
  ... 156 B1
Fort Stanwix Nat. Mon. Park N •
  NY, United States ... 153 [274]
Fort Steele • BC, Canada ... 160 J7
Fort Stockton • TX, United States ... 149 F4
Fort Sumner • NM, United States ... 149 F4
Fort Sumter Nat. Mon. Park N •
  SC, United States ... 153 [231]
Fort Union Nat. Mon. Park N •
  NM, United States ... 152 [128]
Fort Union Trading Post Nat. Hist. Site
  Park N • ND, United States ... 152 [145]
Fort Vancouver Nat. Hist. Site Park N •
  WA, United States ... 152 [33]
Fort Walton Beach •
  FL, United States ... 155 B1
Fort Washington Park •
  MD, United States ... 156 A3
Fort Washington Park Park N •
  MD, United States ... 153 [260]

Fort Wayne • IN, United States ... 150 C2
Fort Wilderness •
  FL, United States ... 157 A1
Fort William • United Kingdom ... 62 C4
Fort Worth • TX, United States ... 155 E4
Fort Yukon • AK, United States ... 157 E2
Fortaleza • Brazil ... 174 C3
Forte dei Marmi • Italy ... 87 B3
Forte Village Resort •
  Sardinia, Italy ... 86 F6
Forth • United Kingdom ... 65 A2
Forth, Firth of • United Kingdom ... 65 B2
Fortín Madrejón • Paraguay ... 175 C2
Fortress Mtn Ski • AL, Canada ... 146 [13]
Fortune • NF, Canada ... 160 C1
Fortune Bay • NF, Canada ... 160 C1
Fortuneswell • United Kingdom ... 65 K10
Foscári, Villa • Italy ... 87 D1
Fosforescente, Bahía • Puerto Rico ... 165 I8
Foshan • China ... 126 H7
Fosnavåg • Norway ... 98 F7
Fossanova, Abbazia di • Italy ... 87 F5
Fossil Butte Nat. Mon. Park N •
  WY, United States ... 152 [74]
Foster • VT, Australia ... 136 G9
Fougères • France ... 76 C2
Foul Bay • Egypt ... 109 E8
Foula • United Kingdom ... 62 G12
Foulness I. • United Kingdom ... 65 H7
Foulwind, Cape • New Zealand ... 137 B3
Fountain Cameroon ... 106 D4
Fountain Nat. Park • Anguilla ... 166 B
Fouras • France ... 78 E5
Fourchue, I. • St Barthélemy ... 166 D
Fourourás • Crete, Greece ... 93 H6
Fourka • Greece ... 94 B
Fournaise, Piton de la • Réunion ... 113 D4
Fourneau, I. • Mauritius ... 113 E6
Foúrni • Greece ... 94 CC3
Foúrni • Greece ... 94 E
Foux, Cap-à • Haiti ... 165 E5
Foux, la Ski • France ... 61 [51]
Foveaux Strait • New Zealand ... 137 G8
Fox Glacier • New Zealand ... 137 B3
Fox Is. • AK, United States ... 157 C4
Fox Is. • MI, United States ... 161 B2
Fox's Bay • Montserrat ... 167 G
Foxe Basin • NU, Canada ... 159 H1
Foxe Channel • NU, Canada ... 159 I2
Foxe Peninsula • NU, Canada ... 159 I2
Foxen • Sweden ... 98 E6
Foxford • Ireland ... 69 H8
Foyle, Lough • United Kingdom ... 62 B5
Foynes • Ireland ... 69 H10
Foz do Iguaçu • Brazil ... 175 C2
Frabosa • Italy ... 87 A2
Frailes, Los • Venezuela ... 166 T
Franca • Brazil ... 174 B4
FRANCE • Europe ... 76
Francés, Punta • Cuba ... 164 E4
Franceville • Gabon ... 106 D5
Franche-Comté • France ... 77 B1
Francistown • Botswana ... 110 J9
Frangokástelo • Crete, Greece ... 93 H6
Frank Sound • Cayman Is. ... 165 B2
Frankenthal, Burg • Germany ... 74 D6
Frankenwald • Germany ... 72 D3
Frankfort • MI, United States ... 150 D3
Frankfurt • KY, United States ... 150 D3
Frankfurt am Main • Germany ... 74 D6
Frankfurt an der Oder • Germany ... 72 F2
Frankincense Trail Heritage C •
  Oman ... 43 [130]
Fränkische Alb • Germany ... 72 D4
Franklin • TN, United States ... 151 C3
Franklin • VA, United States ... 156 A4
Franklin Bay • NT, Canada ... 158 D1
Franklin D. Roosevelt [Apt] •
  St Eustatius ... 167 E
Franklin Delano Roosevelt Mem. Park N •
  DC, United States ... 153 [264]
Franklin-Gordon Wild Rivers Nat. Park •
  TS, Australia ... 136 E7
Frankston • VI, Australia ... 136 G9
Frans, Playa • Bonaire ... 166 U
Frantsa-Iosifa, Zemlya •
  Russian Fed. ... 101 F1
Franz Josef Land • Russian Fed. ... 101 F1
Franz Josef Strauss [Apt] • Germany ... 74 G7
Frasassi, Grotta di • Italy ... 87 D3
Frascati • Italy ... 87 E5
Fraser • BC, Canada ... 160 I5
Fraser, Represa de • Brazil ... 174 E6
Fraser Hill • Malaysia ... 129 G9
Fraser I. • QL, Australia ... 136 D5
Fraser Lake • BC, Canada ... 160 I6
Fraserburg • South Africa ... 111 E6
Fraserburgh • United Kingdom ... 62 D3
Fraserdale • OT, Canada ... 159 H4
Fray Bentos • Uruguay ... 175 G6
Fredericia • Denmark ... 99 E7
Frederick • MD, United States ... 156 A3
Frederick Douglass Nat. Hist. Site Park N •
  DC, United States ... 153 [264]
Frederick, Fort • Grenada ... 166 Q
Frederick Law Olmsted Nat. Hist. Site
  Park N • MA, United States ... 153 [289]
Fredericksburg • TX, United States ... 155 E6
Fredericksburg • VA, United States ... 156 A3
Fredericksburg & Spotsylvania County
  Battlefields Mem. Nat. Military Park
  Park N • VA, United States ... 153 [250]
Fredericksburg & Spotsylvania Nat. Military
  Park • VA, United States ... 156 A3
Fredericton • NB, Canada ... 160 B2
Frederiksberg • Denmark ... 99 F7
Frederikshåb • Greenland ... 159 L2
Frederikshavn • Denmark ... 99 F6
Frederikssund • Denmark ... 99 F7
Frederiksted • US Virgin Is. ... 166 X
Frederiksværk • Denmark ... 99 F7
Fredrikstad • Norway ... 98 E6
Free State • South Africa ... 111 A1
Freels, Cape • NF, Canada ... 160 D1
Freeport • Bahamas ... 164 B1
Freeport • TX, United States ... 155 F6
Freer • TX, United States ... 155 E6
Freetown • Antigua & Barbuda ... 167 I
Freetown • Sierra Leone ... 106 A4
Frégate, I. • St Barthélemy ... 166 D
Frégate • Seychelles ... 113 B1
Freiberg • Germany ... 72 E3
Freiburg im Breisgau • Germany ... 74 B4
Freilassing • Germany ... 74 H8
Freising • Germany ... 74 G7
Freistadt • Austria ... 89 E7
Freizeit-Land Park L • Germany ... 59 [58]
Freizeitpark Lochmühle • Germany ... 74 D5
Fréjus • Hautes-Alpes, France ... 78 H8
Fréjus • Var, France ... 78 D4
Fréjus, Tunnel du • France/Italy ... 78 G6
Fremantle • WA, Australia ... 135 D6
Fremont • CA, United States ... 154 I8
Fremont • NE, United States ... 150 A2
Fremont Mtns • OR, United States ... 154 G6
French Cay • Turks & Caicos Is. ... 164 C3
French Frigate Shoals •
  HI, United States ... 139 DD1
FRENCH GUIANA • S. America ... 174 A2
French I. • VI, Australia ... 136 G9
FRENCH POLYNESIA • Pacific Ocean ... 139 EE4
Frere • South Africa ... 111 B4
Fresh Water Lagoons • Kiribati ... 139 I
Fresnillo • Mexico ... 169 I6
Fresno • CA, United States ... 154 I8
Freudenstadt • Germany ... 74 C7
Freycinet Peninsula •
  TS, Australia ... 136 F7
Fribourg • Switzerland ... 90 I5
Fribourg [Adm] • Switzerland ... 91 Q10

Fridlevstad • Sweden ... 99 H7
Friedberg • Bavaria, Germany ... 74 F7
Friedberg • Hesse, Germany ... 74 D5
Friedrichshafen • Germany ... 74 E8
Friendship Hill Nat. Site Park N •
  PA, United States ... 153 [265]
Friesland [Adm] • Netherlands ... 70 C1
Frigate Bay • St Kitts & Nevis ... 167 F
Frigate I. • Grenada ... 166 P
Frijoles • Panama ... 170 L11
Frikes • Greece ... 94 J
Frio, Cabo • Brazil ... 174 F7
Frisian Is. • Germany/Netherlands ... 72 B2
Frisian Is., East • Germany ... 73 A1
Frisian Is., North • Germany ... 73 A1
Frisian Is., West • Netherlands ... 70 C1
Fristad • Sweden ... 99 G6
Friuli • Romania ... 92 I7
Friuli-Venezia Giulia • Italy ... 87 D1
Frobisher Bay • NU, Canada ... 159 J2
Frobisher Bay [Bay] • NU, Canada ... 159 J2
Frohnau (Berlin) • Germany ... 73 E7
Frome • United Kingdom ... 65 K9
Frome, Lake • SA, Australia ... 135 F5
Fronsac • France ... 76 K9
Front Royal • VA, United States ... 156 A3
Frontenac, Parc de • QU, Canada ... 160 H3
Frontera • Hierro, Canary Is. ... 83 H6
Frontera • Mexico ... 168 F4
Frontignan • France ... 76 E5
Frosinone • Italy ... 87 F5
Frøya • Norway ... 97 B3
Fruska Gora Nat. Park Park N •
  Serbia & Montenegro ... 58 [124]
Frydek-Místek • Czech Rep. ... 89 F9
Frýdlant • Czech Rep. ... 89 E6
Fua'amotu • Tonga ... 139 P
Fuafatu • Tuvalu ... 139 R
Fuagea • Tuvalu ... 139 R
Fuah Mulah Atoll • Maldives ... 124 G8
Fualifeke • Tuvalu ... 139 R
Fualopa • Tuvalu ... 139 R
Fuchu • Japan ... 127 I8
Fuchun Jiang • China ... 126 G7
Fucino, Piana del • Italy ... 82 I8
Fuengirola • Spain ... 80 E4
Fuente • Mexico ... 168 I6
Fuerteventura • Canary Is. ... 83 H5
Fuga • Japan ... 91 O7
Fuggerschloss • Germany ... 74 F7
Fujairah • United Arab Emirates ... 120 H8
Fuji • Japan ... 127 H9
Fuji Five Lakes • Japan ... 127 H8
Fuji-Hakone-Izu Nat. Park • Japan ... 127 H9
Fuji-kawa • Japan ... 127 H9
Fuji-san • Japan ... 127 H9
Fujian • China ... 126 D2
Fujieda • Japan ... 127 C4
Fujinomiya • Japan ... 127 H8
Fujiyoshida • Japan ... 127 H8
Fukue-jima • Japan ... 127 A4
Fukui • Japan ... 127 C3
Fukuoka • Japan ... 127 B4
Fukusaki • Japan ... 127 F6
Fukushima • Japan ... 127 D3
Fukuyama • Japan ... 127 B4
Fulda • Germany ... 72 C3
Fulda • Germany ... 72 C3
Full Moon • Maldives ... 124 H8
Fulpen • Austria ... 91 N8
Fulton • AR, United States ... 155 F4
Fulton • KY, United States ... 150 B3
Fulton • MO, United States ... 150 B3
Fulton • NY, United States ... 156 B1
Furi • Maldives ... 124 H7
Funabashi • Japan ... 127 I8
Funafara • Tuvalu ... 139 R
Funafuti • Tuvalu ... 139 R
Funafuti Lagoon • Tuvalu ... 139 R
Funamanu • Tuvalu ... 139 R
Funangongo • Tuvalu ... 139 R
Funchal • Madeira ... 84 E5
Fundy, Bay of • NB/NS, Canada ... 160 B2
Fundy Nat. Park Park N •
  NB, Canada ... 161 [35]
Fundy Nat. Park • NB, Canada ... 160 B2
Fünen • Denmark ... 99 F8
Fünfkirchen • Hungary ... 92 B2
Fungus Rock • Malta ... 96 A1
Fur • Denmark ... 99 E6
Furano • Maldives ... 124 H8
Furkapass • Switzerland ... 90 K5
Furnas • Azores ... 84 B4
Furnas Dam • Brazil ... 174 E6
Furnas, Reprêsa de • Brazil ... 174 E6
Furneaux Group • TS, Australia ... 136 F6
Furness Abbey • United Kingdom ... 65 C4
Furness Fells • United Kingdom ... 64 G7
Fürstenfeldbruck • Germany ... 74 G7
Fürth • Germany ... 72 D4
Furtwangen • Germany ... 74 B4
Furukawa • Japan ... 127 D3
Furuviksparken Park L • Sweden ... 59 [8]
Fusa • Norway ... 98 F8
Fushun • China ... 126 G2
Füssen • Germany ... 74 F8
Futog • Serbia & Montenegro ... 92 B2
Futtsu • Japan ... 127 I9
Futuna, I. • Wallis & Futuna ... 139 Q
Futuroscope Park L • France ... 59 [66]
Futuroscope • France ... 77 F6
Fuxin • China ... 126 G2
Fuyang • China ... 126 F6
Fuzhou • China ... 125 F4
Fyn [Apt] • Denmark ... 99 F8
Fyn [Adm] • Denmark ... 99 F8
Fyn [I.] • Denmark ... 99 F8
Fyne, Loch • United Kingdom ... 62 C4
Fynshav • Denmark ... 99 E8
Fyresdal • Norway ... 98 G9
Fyresvatn • Norway ... 98 G9

G

Gaafaru Atoll • Maldives ... 124 H7
Gabbs • NV, United States ... 154 J8
Gabès • Tunisia ... 107 D5
Gabès, Golfe de • Tunisia ... 107 D5
Gaberones • Botswana ... 110 J9
Gabone • Botswana ... 110 J9
Gabriel I. • Mauritius ... 113 F5
GABON • Africa ... 106 D5
Gaborone • Botswana ... 110 J9
Gabrovo • Bulgaria ... 92 H8
Gadag • India ... 124 B1
Gádara • Jordan ... 120 C4
Gadsden • AL, United States ... 151 C4
Gaesti • Romania ... 92 H7
Gaeta • Italy ... 87 F5
Gaeta, Golfo di • Italy ... 85 D4
Gafsa • Tunisia ... 107 C5
Gagarin • Russian Fed. ... 100 L10
Gagil-Tamil •
  Fed. States of Micronesia ... 138 C
Gagnoa • Côte d'Ivoire ... 106 B4
Gagnon • QU, Canada ... 159 J3
Gaillac • France ... 78 F6
Gaillimh • Ireland ... 69 H9
Gailtaler Alpen • Austria ... 91 P8
Gainer Wildlife Sanctuary • India ... 123 D7
Gainesville • FL, United States ... 155 C1
Gainesville • GA, United States ... 151 D4
Gainesville • TX, United States ... 155 E4
Gainsborough • United Kingdom ... 63 E7
Gal Oya Nat. Park • Sri Lanka ... 124 D4
Gala • Java, Indonesia ... 131 P12
Galana • Kenya ... 109 D5
Galápagos, Parque Nac. Heritage N •
  Pacific Ocean ... 40 [35]
Galashiels • United Kingdom ... 65 B2

Galata • Bulgaria ... 92 I8
Galata • Cyprus ... 96 C4
Galați • Romania ... 92 I7
Galdhøpiggen • Norway ... 98 G7
Galé, Costa da • Portugal ... 84 A3
Galeão [Apt] • Brazil ... 174 F7
Galena • AK, United States ... 157 D3
Galeota Point • Trinidad & Tobago ... 166 S
Galera • Trinidad & Tobago ... 166 S
Galera Point • Trinidad & Tobago ... 166 S
Galesburg • IL, United States ... 150 B2
Galets, Pointe des • Réunion ... 113 C3
Galgibaga Beach • Goa, India ... 123 C6
Galicia • Spain ... 80 B2
Galicica Nat. Park Park N •
  F.Y.R. of Macedonia ... 58 [130]
Galilee • Israel ... 120 B1
Galilee • Israel ... 120 B2
Galilei, Galileo [Apt] • Italy ... 87 C3
Galina Point • Jamaica ... 165 D3
Galissas • Síros, Greece ... 94 I
Galite, La • Tunisia ... 107 C4
Gallarus Oratory • Ireland ... 69 G10
Gallatin • TX, United States ... 151 C3
Galle • Sri Lanka ... 124 C4
Galle Heritage C • Sri Lanka ... 43 [168]
Gállipoli • Italy ... 85 F4
Gallipoli • Turkey ... 95 E4
Gallipoli Peninsula • Turkey ... 95 E4
Gállivare • Sweden ... 97 E2
Galloway, Mull of • United Kingdom ... 63 C6
Gallup • NM, United States ... 155 H7
Gáltür • Austria ... 91 M8
Galty Mtns • Ireland ... 69 H10
Galu Beach • Kenya ... 109 C6
Galveston • TX, United States ... 155 F6
Galveston Bay • TX, United States ... 155 F6
Galveston I. • TX, United States ... 155 F6
Galway • Ireland ... 69 H9
Galway [Adm] • Ireland ... 69 H9
Galway Bay • Ireland ... 69 H9
Galway's Soufrière • Montserrat ... 167 G
Gamasa • Egypt ... 109 B1
GAMBIA, THE • Africa ... 106 A3
Gambie • Guinea/Senegal ... 106 A3
Gambier • Bahamas ... 164 A2
Gambier Is. • French Polynesia ... 139 EE4
Gamboa • Panama ... 170 M11
Gamla Uppsala • Sweden ... 99 B1
Gamleby • Sweden ... 99 H5
Gammarth • Tunisia ... 107 D4
Gammertingen • Germany ... 74 E7
Gamph, Slieve • Ireland ... 69 H8
Gan • Maldives ... 124 G8
Gáncaĭ • Azerbaijan ... 120 F5
Gandak • India ... 123 G8
Gander • NF, Canada ... 160 D1
Gandhi Dam • India ... 123 D8
Gandhi Sagar • India ... 123 E8
Gandia • Spain ... 80 E4
Gandria • Switzerland ... 90 K6
Ganga • Bangladesh/India ... 124 C3
Gangakondacholapuram • India ... 124 D3
Ganganagar • India ... 122 B3
Gangapur • India ... 123 E8
Gandhar • India ... 123 E8
Ganges • Bangladesh/India ... 122 C3
Ganges, Mouths of the •
  Bangladesh/India ... 122 C3
Gangneung • Rep. of Korea ... 125 G3
Gangtok • India ... 122 C3
Gangtok Hill Sta • India ... 124 F5
Gannett Peak • WY, United States ... 148 E2
Gansbaai • South Africa ... 111 D7
Gansu • China ... 126 C1
Ganteng • China ... 126 H7
Ganyushkino • Kazakstan ... 121 A2
Ganzano di Roma • Italy ... 87 E5
Ganzhou • China ... 125 F4
Gao • Mali ... 106 B3
Gaochun • China ... 126 H7
Gaolan • China ... 126 E4
Gaolan Dao • China ... 126 E4
Gap • France ... 78 C4
Gar • China ... 125 B3
Gara, Lough • Ireland ... 69 H8
Garabogaz Aylagy • Turkmenistan ... 121 B3
Garachico • Tenerife, Canary Is. ... 82 G5
Garagum • Turkmenistan ... 121 D4
Garagum Canal • Turkmenistan ... 121 C4
Garajonay, Parque Nac. de Park N •
  Gomera, Canary Is. ... 58 [84]
Garajonay, Parque Nac. de •
  Gomera, Canary Is. ... 83 H6
Garajonay, Parque Nac. de Heritage N •
  Gomera, Canary Is. ... 41 [66]
Garamba, Parc nat. de la Park N •
  Dem. Rep. of Congo ... 112 [50]
Garamba, Parc nat. de la Heritage N •
  Dem. Rep. of Congo ... 41 [103]
Garapan • N. Mariana Is. ... 138 B
Garberville • CA, United States ... 148 B2
Garching bei München • Germany ... 74 G7
Garda, Lago di • Italy ... 87 C1
Gardaland Park L • Italy ... 59 [82]
Gardaland • Italy ... 87 C2
Gardelegen • Germany ... 72 D2
Garden City • KS, United States ... 148 F3
Garden Peninsula •
  MI, United States ... 161 B2
Garden Route • South Africa ... 111 F7
Gardez • Afghanistan ... 121 E5
Gardíki • Corfu, Greece ... 94 A
Gardone Riviera • Italy ... 87 C2
Gárdsjö • Sweden ... 99 G5
Gárdslösa • Sweden ... 99 H6
Gargano, Promontório del • Italy ... 85 E4
Gargellen • Austria ... 91 M8
Gargždai • Lithuania ... 100 J7
Garibaldi Prov. Park • BC, Canada ... 160 J6
Garigliano • Italy ... 87 F5
Garissa • Kenya ... 109 D5
Garmisch-Partenkirchen Ski • Germany ... 61 [3]
Garmisch-Partenkirchen • Germany ... 74 F8
Garmo, Qullai • Tajikistan ... 121 F4
Garmsar • Iran ... 120 G6
Garoowe • Somalia ... 108 C4
Garoua • Cameroon ... 106 D4
Garphyttan Nat. Park Park N • Sweden ... 58 [26]
Garrison • Barbados ... 167 M
Garsa, Chott el • Tunisia ... 107 C5
Garut • Java, Indonesia ... 131 P12
Garve Mtns • New Zealand ... 137 B3
Garwa • India ... 123 G8
Garwolin • Poland ... 89 C3
Gary • IN, United States ... 150 C2
Gaschurn • Austria ... 91 M8
Gascoigne • France ... 78 E6
Gascony • France ... 77 A2
Gascony, Gulf of • France/Spain ... 78 B4
Gasfinolhu • Maldives ... 124 [47]
Gashaka Game Reserve Park • Nigeria ... 112 [29]
Gaspar Hernández • Dominican Rep. ... 165 I5
Gaspé • QU, Canada ... 160 B1
Gaspé, Cap de • QU, Canada ... 160 B1
Gaspésie, Péninsule de •
  QU, Canada ... 160 B1
Gaston, Lake • VA, United States ... 156 A4
Gastonia • NC, United States ... 151 D3
Gastoúni • Greece ... 93 B3
Gata, Cabo de • Spain ... 82 K8
Gata, Cape • Cyprus ... 96 C4
Gateway Bay Is. Nat. Park Park N •
  OT, Canada ... 161 [27]

Gateshead • United Kingdom ... 62 E6
Gatesville • TX, United States ... 155 E5
Gateway Nat. Recreation Area Park N •
  NJ/NY, United States ... 153 [278]
Gatineau • QU, Canada ... 160 G4
Gatineau Park • QU, Canada ... 160 F3
Gatineau [Riv] • QU, Canada ... 160 F3
Gatorland • FL, United States ... 157 B1
Gatún • Panama ... 170 L10
Gatún, Esclusas de • Panama ... 170 L10
Gatún, Lago • Panama ... 170 L11
Gatún, Represa • Panama ... 170 L10
Gatwick [Apt] • United Kingdom ... 65 G8
Gauja • Latvia ... 100 K7
Gauja Nat. Park Heritage N • Latvia ... 58 [148]
Gauja Nat. Park • Latvia ... 100 K7
Gateway River Nat. Recreation Area Park N •
  WV, United States ... 153 [252]
Gaume, Fonte de • France ... 78 F5
Gausta • Norway ... 98 G8
Gaustablikk • Norway ... 98 D5
Gauteng • South Africa ... 111 A1
Gavarnie • France ... 78 J9
Gavdopoúla • Greece ... 93 G6
Gávdos • Greece ... 93 G6
Gävleborg • Sweden ... 98 B3
Gávrio • Ándros, Greece ... 94 I
Gawler • SA, Australia ... 135 F6
Gaya • India ... 123 G8
Gayndah • QL, Australia ... 136 D5
Gaza • Palestine NAR ... 120 C7
Gazanjyk • Turkmenistan ... 121 C4
Gazelle, Récif de la •
  New Caledonia ... 138 U
Gazi Beach • Kenya ... 109 C6
Gaziantep • Turkey ... 95 C2
Gazimagusa • Cyprus ... 96 C4
Gazipasa • Turkey ... 95 I10
Gazojak • Turkmenistan ... 121 D3
Gcwihaba Caverns • Botswana ... 110 I9
Gdansk • Poland ... 89 B1
Gdansk, Gulf of • Poland ... 89 B1
Gdynia • Poland ... 95 H7
Gebze • Turkey ... 95 H7
Gecitkale [Apt] • Cyprus ... 96 C3
Gedaref • Sudan ... 108 C3
Gedi Nat. Mon. • Kenya ... 109 C5
Gediz • Turkey ... 95 F5
Gediz [Riv] • Turkey ... 95 F5
Gedser • Denmark ... 99 F8
Geelong • Malaysia ... 129 E8
Geelong • VI, Australia ... 136 G9
Geevston • TS, Australia ... 136 F7
Geghard Heritage C • Armenia ... 43 [137]
Geilo • Norway ... 98 G8
Geiranger • Norway ... 98 G7
Geirangerfjorden • Norway ... 98 G7
Geishügelhof • Germany ... 74 C5
Geíte • Tanzania ... 110 G7
Geíthus • Norway ... 98 D5
Gejiu • China ... 125 E4
Gela • Sicily, Italy ... 86 H8
Gela, Golfo di • Sicily, Italy ... 86 H8
Gelderland • Netherlands ... 70 H8
Geldermalsen • Netherlands ... 70 H8
Geleen • Netherlands ... 70 D4
Gelibolu • Turkey ... 95 E4
Gelibolu Yarimdasi • Turkey ... 95 E4
Gellinam • Marshall Is. ... 139 E
Gelnhausen • Germany ... 74 D5
Gelsenkirchen • Germany ... 73 D5
Gelugor • Penang, Malaysia ... 129 E8
Gemas • Malaysia ... 129 G10
Gembloux • Belgium ... 70 B4
Gemena • Dem. Rep. of Congo ... 108 A4
Gemlik • Turkey ... 95 F4
Gemlik Körfezi • Turkey ... 95 F4
Gemona del Friuli • Italy ... 87 E5
Gen. G. Luperón [Apt] •
  Dominican Rep. ... 165 G5
Gen. Santiago Mariño [Apt] •
  ... 166 T
Genádio • Rhodes, Greece ... 94 F
Gencek • Turkey ... 95 H7
General Bernardo O'Higgins [Base] •
  Antarctica ... 176 [3]
General Grant Nat. Mem. Park N •
  ... 153 [278]
General Juan N. Alvarez [Apt] •
  Mexico ... 169 J8
General Lavalle • Argentina ... 175 G7
General Mitchell [Apt] •
  WI, United States ... 161 B3
General Roca • Argentina ... 175 B3
General Santos • Philippines ... 128 H5
Genesee • NY, United States ... 156 A1
Geneva • NY, United States ... 156 B1
Geneva • Switzerland ... 90 I6
Geneva, Lake of •
  Switzerland/France ... 90 I6
Genève • Switzerland ... 90 I6
Genève [Adm] • Switzerland ... 91 Q10
Gengenbach • Germany ... 82 J7
Genil • Spain ... 70 C4
Genk • Belgium ... 70 C4
Gennargentu, Monte del •
  Sardinia, Italy ... 86 F5
Genoa • Italy ... 87 B2
Génova • Italy ... 87 B2
Génova, Golfo di • France/Italy ... 87 B2
Genovesa, I. • Galápagos Is. ... 171 H9
Gent • Belgium ... 70 B4
Gent naar Oostende, Kanaal van •
  Belgium ... 70 F6
Genteng • Indonesia ... 131 O12
Genteng [I.] • Indonesia ... 131 R12
Genting Highlands • Malaysia ... 129 G10
Geok-Tepe • Turkmenistan ... 121 C4
George • South Africa ... 111 F7
George Bush [Apt] •
  TX, United States ... 155 F5
George F.L. Charles [Apt] • St Lucia ... 167 N
George, Fort • Grenada ... 166 Q
George, Lake • NS, Australia ... 136 H8
George Rogers Clark Nat. Hist. Park
  Park N • IN, United States ... 153 [178]
George Sound • New Zealand ... 137 F7
George Town • Bahamas ... 164 B2
George Town • Cayman Is. ... 165 A2
George Town • Penang, Malaysia ... 129 E7
George V Land • Antarctica ... 176 U5
George Washington Birthplace Nat. Mon. •
  VA, United States ... 156 B4
George Washington Birthplace Nat. Mon.
  Park N • VA, United States ... 153 [248]
George Washington Carver Nat. Mon.
  Park N • MO, United States ... 153 [173]
George Washington Mem. Parkway
  Park N • ... 153 [251]
Georgetown • Guyana ... 173 D2
Georgetown • KY, United States ... 150 D3
Georgetown • SC, United States ... 151 E4
Georgetown • St Vincent & Gren. ... 167 N
Georgetown • TX, United States ... 155 E5
GEORGIA • Asia ... 120 E5
Georgia • United States ... 151 D4
Georgian Bay Is. Nat. Park Park N •
  OT, Canada ... 161 [27]
Georgian Bay Is. Nat. Park •
  OT, Canada ... 160 E4
Georgina • NT/QL, Australia ... 135 F4
Georgioúpoli • Crete, Greece ... 93 H5
Gera • Germany ... 94 B
Gerald's • Montserrat ... 167 G
Geraldton • WA, Australia ... 135 A5
Gérardmer • France ... 77 C2
Gerasa • Jordan ... 120 C4
Gêres, Serra do • Portugal ... 84 A1

Gereshk • Afghanistan 121 D5
Geretsried • Germany 74 G7
Gergeri • Crete, Greece 93 I6
Gerizim, Mt • Palestine NAR 120 B3
Gerlachovsky štit • Slovak Rep. 89 G9
Gerlos • Austria 91 O8
GERMANY • Europe 72
Gernsheim • Germany 74 D6
Gerolstein • Germany 74 C5
Gerrard Smith [Apt] • Cayman Is. ..165 B1
Gers [Adm] • France 78 F6
Gers [Riv] • France 78 F6
Gersau • Switzerland 90 K5
Gersthofen • Germany 74 F7
Gertak Sanggul • Penang, Malaysia .129 D8
Gertak Sanggul, Tanjong •
   Penang, Malaysia 129 D8
Geta • Finland 99 C4
Getafe • Spain 80 D3
Gets, les Ski • France ....61 [11]
Gets, les • France 78 D3
Gettysburg Nat. Military Park •
   PA, United States 156 A3
Gettysburg Nat. Military Park Park N •
   PA, United States 156 A3
Geuroudong, Gunung • Indonesia ..131 M0
Gevelsberg • Germany 73 D5
Gevgelija • FYR of Macedonia 92 C3
Gevne Çayı • Turkey 95 I10
Gezer • Israel 120 A3
Ggantija • Malta 96 A1
Ggantija Heritage C • Malta ....44 [256]
Ghadamis • Libya 106 C2
Ghadamis Heritage C • Libya ....44 [293]
Ghaghara • India 123 G8
Ghajn Tuffieha Bay • Malta 96 A2
GHANA • Africa 106 B4
Ghanzi • Botswana 110 I9
Ghar Dalam • Malta 96 B2
Gharb • Malta 96 A1
Gharbi • Tunisia 107 D5
Ghardaïa • Algeria 106 C1
Ghats, Eastern • India 122 B4
Ghats, Western • India 123 E7
Ghaziabad • India 123 G4
Ghazipur • India 123 G8
Ghazni • Afghanistan 121 E5
Ghent • Belgium 70 B4
Gheorgheni • Romania 92 D2
Ghisonaccia • Corsica, France 78 N12
Ghisoni • Corsica, France 78 N12
Ghoumrassen • Tunisia 107 D6
Giali • Greece 94 DD3
Gianisáda • Greece 93 J6
Gianissá • Greece 93 C1
Giannis D Dive • Egypt 109 E7
Giannutri, I. di • Italy 85 C3
Giant's Castle • South Africa 111 B4
Giant's Castle Game Reserve Park •
   South Africa ....112 [141]
Giant's Causeway • United Kingdom ..62 B5
Giant's Causeway Heritage N •
   United Kingdom ....41 [56]
Giants Ridge Ski •
   MN, United States ....146 [67]
Gianyar • Bali, Indonesia 131 L8
Giardini-Naxos • Sicily, Italy 85 G8
Giarre • Sicily, Italy ....94 I
Gibara • Cuba 164 H5
Gibb's Hill Lighthouse • Bermuda ..165 K10
Gibbes Beach • Barbados ....167 M
Gibeon • Palestine NAR 120 A3
GIBRALTAR • Europe 82
Gibraltar, Strait of •
   Africa/Europe ....82 C-D
Gibson Desert • WA, Australia 135 C4
Giens • France 78 G8
Giessen • Germany 74 B1
Giethoorn • Netherlands 70 D2
Gifhorn • Germany 72 D2
Giftun Seghir Dive • Egypt 109 E8
Gifu • Japan 127 C6
Gigha • United Kingdom 62 C5
Giglio, I. del • Italy 85 C3
Gijón • Spain 80 C2
Gila Bend • AZ, United States 155 G8
Gila Cliff Dwellings Nat. Mon. •
   NM, United States 155 H8
Gila Cliff Dwellings Nat. Mon. Park N •
   NM, United States ....152 [117]
Gila [Riv] • AZ/NM, United States ..155 H8
Gila River Ind Res •
   AZ, United States ....155 [29]
Gilbert Is. • Kiribati 138 CC3
Gilboa, Mt • Israel/Palestine NAR ..120 B2
Gilimanuk • Bali, Indonesia 131 K7
Gili, Lough • Ireland 69 H8
Gillam • MN, Canada 158 G3
Gilleleje • Denmark 99 F7
Gillette • WY, United States 148 E2
Gillingham • United Kingdom 65 K9
Gimie, Mt • St Lucia ....167 N
Gin Gin • QL, Australia 136 D5
Ginger I. • British Virgin Is. 111 C4
Gingindlovu • South Africa 111 C4
Gióia del Colle • Italy 85 F4
Gioúra • Greece 94 BB2
Gippsland • VI, Australia 136 E9
Gippsland Lakes • VI, Australia 136 G9
Giraglia, I. de la •
   Corsica, France 78 N11
Girão, Cabo • Madeira 84 D5
Giravaru • Maldives 124 H8
Giresun • Turkey 95 C1
Girne • Cyprus 96 C3
Girolata, Golfe de •
   Corsica, France 78 M11
Girolata, Golfe de Heritage N •
   Corsica, France ....41 [61]
Girona • Spain 83 D3
Gironde • France 78 E5
Gironde [Adm] • France 78 E6
Girvan • United Kingdom 62 C5
Gisborne • New Zealand 137 C2
Gisborne [Adm] • New Zealand 137 C2
Gislaved • Sweden 99 G6
Gisors • France 78 A1
Gistel • Belgium 70 E6
Gitgit Waterfall • Bali, Indonesia ...131 L7
Githio • Greece 93 C3
Giulianova • Italy 87 D3
Giurgeni • Romania 92 I7
Giurgiu • Romania 92 I7
Give • Denmark 99 E7
Givorny • France 78 A1
Givors • France 78 C3
Giza Pyramids • Egypt 109 A1
Gizo • Solomon Is. ....138 W
Gizycko • Poland 89 C1
Gjerstad • Norway 98 H7
Gjøvik • Norway 91 C3
Glace Bay • NS, Canada 160 C2
Glacier Bay • AK, United States 157 F4
Glacier Bay Nat. Park •
   AK, United States 157 F4
Glacier Bay Nat. Park & Preserve Park N •
   AK, United States ....152 [15]
Glacier Bay Nat. Park & Preserve Heritage N •
   AK, United States ....40 [1]
Glacier Nat. Park Park N •
   BC, Canada ....161 [13]
Glacier Nat. Park • BC, Canada 160 J7
Glacier Nat. Park •
   MT, United States 154 H5
Glacier Nat. Park Park N •
   MT, United States ....152 [65]
Gladbeck • Germany 73 C5
Gladstone • QL, Australia 136 D5
Glamis Castle • United Kingdom 65 B1
Glamorgan • United Kingdom 64 A5
Glan • Sweden 99 H5
Gland • Switzerland 90 I6
Glarner Alpen • Switzerland 90 K5
Glarus • Switzerland 91 R9
Glasgow • KY, United States 151 C3

Glasgow • MT, United States 148 E1
Glasgow • United Kingdom 65 A2
Glasriket • Sweden 99 H6
Glass Country • Sweden 93 I5
Glass Window Bridge • Bahamas ...164 A1
Glasshouse Mtns Nat. Park •
   QL, Australia 136 D5
Glastonbury • United Kingdom 65 K9
Glastonbury Tor • United Kingdom ..65 K9
Glazov • Russian Fed. 100 H2
Glen Canyon • UT, United States ...148 D3
Glen Canyon Dam •
   AZ, United States 155 G7
Glen Canyon Nat. Recreation Area •
   AZ/UT, United States 155 G7
Glen Canyon Nat. Recreation Area Park N •
   AZ/UT, United States ....152 [99]
Glen Helen • NT, Australia 136 A1
Glen Shee • United Kingdom 65 B1
Glenallen • AK, United States 157 E3
Glenbeigh • Ireland 69 G11
Glencoe • South Africa 111 B3
Glencree • Ireland 69 J2
Glendale • AZ, United States 155 G8
Glendale • CA, United States 149 C4
Glendalough • Ireland 69 I7
Glendive • MT, United States 148 F1
Gleneagles • United Kingdom 65 A1
Glenorchy • New Zealand 137 G7
Glenorchy • TS, Australia 136 F7
Glenridding • United Kingdom 65 D3
Glenrothes • United Kingdom 65 B1
Glens Falls • NY, United States 150 F2
Glenveagh Nat. Park Park N • Ireland ..58 [42]
Glenwood Springs •
   CO, United States 148 E3
Gletsch • Switzerland 90 K5
Glifáda • Corfu, Greece ....94 A
Glindow • Germany 73 E8
Glittertind • Norway 98 G7
Gliwice • Poland 89 F8
Globe • AZ, United States 155 G8
Gloggov • Poland 89 B3
Glomma • Norway 97 C3
Glorenza • Italy 87 C1
Gloucester • MA, United States 156 D1
Gloucester • United Kingdom 65 E6
Gloucester • VA, United States 156 B4
Gloucestershire • United Kingdom ..65 F6
Glover Reef • Belize 166 AA3
Gloversville • NY, United States 156 C1
Glurns • Italy 87 C1
Glyngøre • Denmark 99 E6
Gmünd • Germany 74 G8
Gmünd • Kärnten, Austria 91 P8
Gmünd • Niederösterreich, Austria ..91 G1
Gmunden • Austria 91 P7
Gnesen • Poland 50 D2
Gnesta • Sweden 99 H4
Gniezno • Poland 89 B2
Gnosjö • Sweden 99 G6
Goa • India ....123 C
Goa Beach • India 124 E6
Goa Heritage C • India ....43 [157]
Goa Lawah Cave • Bali, Indonesia ..131 L8
Goalpara • India 62 H7
Goat I. • Antigua & Barbuda 167 A1
Goat I. • NT, Australia 161 A1
Goat I. • Trinidad & Tobago ....166 R
Goat Point • Antigua & Barbuda ....167 H
Gobabis • Namibia 110 A3
Gobernador Gregores • Argentina ..175 A4
Gobi • China/Mongolia 125 E2
Goch • Germany 73 C5
Cashang Heritage 0 • Rep. of Korea ..43 [131]
Godavari • India 122 C4
Godavari, Mouths of the • India 124 D1
Godbout • QL, Canada 160 A1
Gödene • Turkey 95 G8
Goderich • OT, Canada 161 C3
Godhavn • Greenland 159 K2
Godinne • Belgium 70 C4
Gods Lake • MN, Canada 158 G2
Godthåb • Greenland 159 K2
Goelo, Côte du • France 77 D3
Goeree • Netherlands 70 B3
Gogama • OT, Canada 159 H4
Goiânia • Brazil 174 B4
Goiás • Brazil 174 B4
Goiás Heritage C • Brazil ....42 [16]
Goiás [Adm] • Brazil 174 E4
Golfuha Fehendhu Atoll • Maldives ..124 G7
Göinge • Sweden 99 G7
Gojo • Japan 127 C7
Gokarn • India 122 C4
Gokayama Heritage C • Japan ...43 [196]
Gökceada • Turkey 95 E4
Gökova Körfezi • Turkey 95 I10
Göksun • Turkey 95 C1
Göksun • Turkey 95 J9
Gol • Norway 98 G8
Gölcük • Turkey 95 F3
Gold Beach • OR, United States 154 G6
Gold Coast • FL, United States 155 D3
Gold Coast • Ghana 106 C4
Gold Coast • HI, United States 157 J6
Gold Coast • QL, Australia 136 D5
Goldau • Switzerland 90 K5
Golden • BC, Canada 160 J7
Golden Bay • Malta 96 A2
Golden Bay • New Zealand 137 B3
Golden Coast • Sweden 99 F6
Golden Gate Nat. Recreation Area Park N •
   CA, United States ....152 [43]
Golden Horseshoe • OT, Canada ...160 E5
Golden Is. • GA, United States 155 C1
Golden Mile • South Africa 111 C5
Golden Ring • Russian Fed. 100 M10
Golden Sands • Bulgaria 92 I8
Golden Spike Nat. Hist. Site Park N •
   UT, United States ....152 [75]
Golden Triangle • Asia 129 A1
Golden Triangle • India 123 E7
Golden Valley • United Kingdom 65 E6
Goldsboro • NC, United States 151 E3
Goldthwaite • TX, United States 155 E5
Goleniów • Poland 89 A2
Golfe-Juan • France 78 H8
Golfo Aranci • Sardinia, Italy 86 F5
Golfo de Santa Clara • Mexico ......168 Q
Golßen • Germany 73 E8
Gölmarmara • Turkey 95 F4
Golmud • China 125 D3
Golo • Corsica, France 78 N11
Goma • Dem. Rep. of Congo 108 B5
Gombe • Nigeria 106 O3
Gombe Nat. Park • Tanzania 108 G2
Gombe Nat. Park Park • Tanzania ..112 [91]
Gomera • Canary Is. 84 H6
Gómez Palacio • Mexico 168 D2
Gonáïves • Haiti 165 F5
Gonarezhou Nat. Park Park •
   Zimbabwe ....112 [117]
Gonâve, Golfe de la • Haiti 165 E5
Gonâve, I. de la • Haiti 165 F6
Gonder • Ethiopia 108 C3
Gonder Heritage C • Ethiopia ......43 [99]
Gondia • India 122 C3
Gönen • Turkey 95 E4
Gongbai • China 92 G8
Gonzales • Mexico 169 J6
Good Hope, Cape of • South Africa ..111 D7
Goodlands • Mauritius 113 F5
Goodrich • United Kingdom 65 E6
Goodwood • United Kingdom 65 F6
Goondiwindi • QL, Australia 135 I5
Goonolly Downs • United Kingdom ..65 E6
Goose Lake • CA/OR, United States ..154 G6
Gooty • India 124 B1
Gopalpur-on-Sea Beach • India 124 F6
Göppingen • Germany 72 C4
Gorakhpur • India 123 E7
Gorazde • Bosnia-Herz. 92 B3

Gorczanski Nat. Park Park N • Poland ..58 [106]
Gorczanski Nat. Park • Poland 89 G9
Gorda, Punta • CA, United States ..154 I7
Gordon, Lake • TS, Australia 136 F7
Gordon Reef Dive • Egypt 109 E7
Gore • New Zealand 137 G8
Gorée, I. de Heritage C • Senegal ..43 [110]
Göreme • Turkey 95 J9
Göreme Nat. Park • Turkey 95 J9
Göreme Nat. Park Heritage N • Turkey ..41 [81]
Göreme National Park Heritage C •
   Turkey ....44 [253]
Gorey • Channel Is. 66 A6
Gorgona, I. di • Italy 87 B3
Gorinchem • Netherlands 70 H8
Goris • Italy 87 D1
Gorlice • Poland 89 G9
Gorling Bluff Lighthouse •
   Cayman Is. 165 B2
Görlitz • Germany 72 F3
Gorna Orjahovica • Bulgaria 92 H8
Gorongosa, Parque Nac. da Park •
   Mozambique ....112 [147]
Gorontalo • Indonesia 131 K3
Gorriti, I. de • Uruguay 175 G6
Gort • Ireland 69 H9
Gortis • Crete, Greece 93 I6
Gortyna • Crete, Greece 93 I6
Gorumna I. • Ireland 69 H9
Gory Stolowe Nat. Park Park N •
   Poland ....58 [108]
Gorzów Wielkopolski • Poland 89 A2
Gosainthan • China 125 C4
Gosau • Austria 91 P8
Gosford • NS, Australia 136 H8
Goshen • Jamaica 165 D3
Goshen • NY, United States 156 C2
Goshute Ind Res •
   NV/UT, United States ....155 [22]
Gosier • Guadeloupe ....167 J
Gosier • Germany 72 D3
Goslar Heritage C • Germany .....44 [52]
Gospic • Croatia 92 B3
Gossies • FYR of Macedonia 92 C3
Gostivar • FYR of Macedonia 92 C3
Göta älv • Sweden 99 F5
Göta kanal • Sweden 99 H5
Göteborg • Sweden 99 F6
Göteborg och Bohus • Sweden 99 F5
Gotemba • Japan 127 H9
Götene • Sweden 99 G5
Gotha • Germany 72 D3
Gothenburg • NE, United States 148 F2
Gothenburg • Sweden 99 F6
Gotland • Sweden 97 D4
Gotland [Adm] • Sweden 98 B4
Goto Meer • Bonaire ....166 U
Goto-retto • Japan 127 A4
Gotska Sandön Park N • Sweden ..58 [29]
Göttingen • Germany 72 C3
Gouda • Netherlands 70 G8
Gough I. • Atlantic Ocean 10 I8
Gough I. Wildlife Reserve Heritage N •
   Atlantic Ocean ....41 [120]
Goulburn • NS, Australia 136 H8
Goulburn [Riv] • VI, Australia 136 G9
Goulimine • Morocco 107 A3
Gouritsmond • South Africa 111 E7
Gournay-en-Bray • France 78 A1
Gournia • Crete, Greece 93 J6
Gourock • United Kingdom 66 A2
Gourock Range • NS, Australia 136 H8
Goussainville, Apt, du •
   St Barthélemy ....166 D
Gouves • Crete, Greece 93 I6
Gouviá • Corfu, Greece ....94 A
Gouyave • Grenada ....166 Q
Governador Valadares • Brazil 174 F6
Govind Ballabh Pant Sagar • India ..123 G8
Gower Peninsula • United Kingdom ..63 C6
Goya • Argentina 175 C2
Gøynük • Turkey 95 I9
Gozo • Malta 96 A1
Graaff-Reinet • South Africa 111 G6
Grächen • Switzerland 90 J6
Gracias • Honduras 170 K9
Gracias a Dios, Cabo de •
   Honduras/Nicaragua 170 F3
Graciosa • Azores 84 A5
Graciosa • Canary Is. 83 I5
Grado • Italy 87 D2
Grafton • NS, Australia 135 I5
Graham • TX, United States 155 E4
Graham I. • BC, Canada 160 F6
Grahamstown • South Africa 111 G6
Grain Coast • Liberia 106 A4
Grainau • Germany 74 F8
Grajewo • Poland 99 E8
Gram • Denmark 99 E7
Gramat, Causse de • France 78 F6
Grampian Mtns • United Kingdom ..62 C4
Grampians Nat. Park •
   VI, Australia 135 G7
Gramvoúsa • Crete, Greece 93 G5
Gramvoúsa, Akria • Crete, Greece ..93 H5
Gran • Hungary 50 D3
Gran Cairo • Mexico 169 G4
Gran Canaria • Canary Is. 84 G6
Gran Chaco • Argentina/Paraguay ..175 B2
Gran Desierto del Pinacate,
   Parque Natural del • Mexico 168 H5
Gran Paradiso • Italy 87 A2
Gran Paradiso, Parco Nac. del Park N •
   Italy ....58 [93]
Gran Paradiso, Parco Nac. del •
   Italy 87 A2
Gran Piedra • Cuba 164 H5
Gran Pilastro • Austria/Italy 86 C3
Gran Sasso d'Italia • Italy 87 F4
Gran Sasso e Monti della Laga, Parco Naz. •
   Italy 87 F4
Gran Sasso e Monti della Laga, Parco Naz. del
   Park N • Italy ....58 [95]
Gran Tarajal •
   Fuerteventura, Canary Is. 83 H5
Granada • Nicaragua 170 D5
Granada • Spain 82 J7
Granada Heritage C • Spain ....44 [124]
Granby • QU, Canada 160 H4
Grand • MI, United States 161 B3
Grand • OT, Canada 161 C3
Grand Anse Bay • Grenada ....166 Q
Grand Anse Bay • Grenada ....166 Q
Grand Bahama I. • Bahamas ....164 T
Grand Baie • Mauritius 113 F5
Grand Bank • NF Canada 160 C2
Grand Bassin • Mauritius 113 G5
Grand Bay • Dominica ....167 K
Grand Bay • Réunion 113 C4
Grand Bourg • Guadeloupe ....167 J
Grand Brière • France 77 D3
Grand Caicos • Turks & Caicos Is. ..164 C3
Grand Canal • Ireland 69 I6
Grand Canyon • AZ, United States ..155 G7
Grand Canyon Nat. Park •
   AZ, United States 155 G7
Grand Canyon Nat. Park Heritage N •
   AZ, United States ....40 [13]
Grand Canyon of Pennsylvania •
   PA, United States 150 B5
Grand Canyon of the East •
   NY, United States 156 A1
Grand Canyon Village •
   AZ, United States 155 G7
Grand Case • St Martin ....166 C
Grand Cayman • Cayman Is. 165 A2
Grand Coulee Dam •
   WA, United States 154 H5

Grand Domaine Ski • France ....61 [23-24]
Grand Erg Oriental • Tunisia 107 C6
Grand Etang • Grenada 166 I7
Grand Etang • Réunion 113 D3
Grand Etang Nat. Park • Grenada ..166 Q
Grand Falls • NB, Canada 160 C1
Grand Fond • St Barthélemy ....166 D
Grand Forks • ND, United States ...148 G1
Grand Gaube • Mauritius 113 F5
Grand Harbour • Malta 96 B2
Grand Haven • MI, United States ...150 C2
Grand I. • MI, United States 161 B2
Grand I. • NY, United States 161 A1
Grand Island • NE, United States ..148 G2
Grand Junction • CO, United States ..148 E3
Grand Lake • LA, United States 156 E6
Grand Lake • NB, Canada 160 C1
Grand Lake • NF, Canada 160 C1
Grand Manan I. • NB, Canada 161 B1
Grand Marais • MN, United States ..161 A1
Grand Massif Ski • France ....61 [12-15]
Grand Morin, Vallée du • France 78 B2
Grand Parc du Puy du Fou • France ..77 E6
Grand Port • Mauritius 113 F6
Grand Portage • MN, United States ..161 A1
Grand Portage Nat. Mon. Park N •
   MN, United States ....153 [154]
Grand Prairie • TX, United States ..155 E4
Grand Pré NS, Canada 160 C1
Grand Pressigny, le [Château] •
   France 77 F6
Grand Rapids • MI, United States ..150 C2
Grand Rivière • Martinique ....167 L
Grand' Rivière • France 78 B2
Grand Rivière Noire • Mauritius 113 E6
Grand Rivière SE • Mauritius 113 F6
Grand Roy • Grenada ....166 Q
Grand Serre-Chevalier Ski • France ..61 [45]
Grand St-Bernard, Col du •
   Italy/Switzerland 90 J6
Grand Teton Nat. Park Park N •
   WY, United States ....152 [73]
Grand Turk • Turks & Caicos Is. 164 D3
Grand Turk Wall • Turks & Caicos Is. ..164 D3
Grand-Bay • VM, United States 161 A1
Grand-Terre • Guadeloupe ....167 J
Grande • Nicaragua 170 E4
Grande, Bahía • Argentina 175 B5
Grande, Baia de I. • Portugal 80 A5
Grande Cache • AL, Canada 160 J6
Grande Cayemite • Haiti 165 E6
Grande I. • Brazil 174 E7
Grande Lande, Ecomusée de la •
   France 78 E6
Grande Pointe • St Barthélemy ......166 D
Grande Prairie • AL, Canada 160 J6
Grande, Rio • Brazil 174 B5
Grande, Rio • Jamaica 165 D4
Grande Vigie, Pointe de la •
   Guadeloupe ....167 J
Grandi, Playa • Curaçao ....166 V
Grands-Jardins, Réserve de •
   QU, Canada 160 A1
Grange-over-Sands • United Kingdom ..65 D4
Grangemouth • United Kingdom 65 B2
Granhult • Sweden 99 H6
Grant Rose, Côte de • France 77 D3
Granite Peak • NV, United States ...154 J7
Grankulla • Finland 99 D4
Granma, Parque Desembarco del •
   Cuba 164 G5
Gränna • Sweden 99 G5
Granollers • Spain 83 D4
Grantham • United Kingdom 72 E2
Grant-Kohrs Ranch Nat. Hist. Site Park N •
   MT, United States ....152 [66]
Grantown • United Kingdom 63 E8
Grantley Adams [Apt] • Barbados ..167 M
Grants Pass • OR, United States ...154 G6
Granville • France 77 D3
Grasmere • United Kingdom 65 D3
Grasmoor • United Kingdom 65 C3
Grass I. • Hong Kong, China 126 F4
Grass Valley • CA, United States 154 I7
Grasse • France 78 H8
Grasslands Nat. Park Park N •
   SA, Canada ....161 [22]
Grassy • TS, Australia 136 E6
Gråsten • Denmark 99 E8
Grasstadir • Iceland 97 I6
Grau Roig • Andorra 82 E5
Graubünden • Switzerland 91 R10
Grave [Battlefield] • Netherlands 70 C3
Grave, la Ski • France ....61 [43]
Grave, la • France 78 D4
Grave, Pointe de • France 78 E5
Gravenhurst • OT, Canada 160 E4
Gravesend • United Kingdom 65 G7
Gravdal • Norway 96 K9
Gravina • Corsica, France 78 M12
Grayling • MI, United States 150 D2
Grays Harbor • WA, United States ..154 H5
Graz • Austria 91 G2
Grazalema Heritage C • Spain ...44 [142]
Great Abaco • Bahamas 164 A1
Great Australian Bight •
   SA/WA, Australia 135 D6
Great Bahama Bank • Bahamas 166 BB1
Great Barrier I. • New Zealand 137 C2
Great Barrier Reef Heritage N •
   Australia ....41 [152]
Great Barrier Reef •
   CL/QL, Australia ....135 H-I
Great Barrier Reef Marine Park •
   Australia ....136 C-D
Great Basin • NV, United States 154 J7
Great Basin Nat. Park •
   NV, United States 154 J8
Great Basin Nat. Park Park N •
   NV, United States ....152 [59]
Great Bear Lake • NT, Canada 158 D2
Great Bend • KS, United States 148 G3
Great Bird I. • Antigua & Barbuda ..167 I
Great Blasket I. • Ireland 69 G11
Great Camanoe • British Virgin Is. ..166 A1
Great Coxwell Barn • United Kingdom ..65 F6
Great Cumbrae I. • United Kingdom ..66 A2
Great Dismal Swamp •
   VA, United States 156 B4
Great Dividing Range • Australia ...135 H-I
Great Exhibition Bay • New Zealand ..137 B1
Great Exuma • Bahamas 164 B2
Great Falls • MT, United States 148 D1
Great Falls of the Potomac •
   MD/VA, United States 156 A4
Great Fish • South Africa 111 G6
Great Gable • United Kingdom 65 C3
Great Gorge Resort Action Park •
   NJ, United States 156 C2
Great Harbour Cay • Bahamas 164 A1
Great Harbour Deep • NF, Canada ..160 D1
Great Inagua • Bahamas 164 B2
Great Karoo • South Africa 111 F6
Great Keppel I. • QL, Australia 136 D4
Great Lakes • Canada/United States ..161 A-D
Great Malvern • United Kingdom 65 E6
Great Nicobar • India 122 D5
Great Oasis, The • Egypt 109 A2
Great Ouse • United Kingdom 63 F8
Great Pedro Bluff • Jamaica 165 C3
Great Plains • Canada/United States ..142 D3
Great Rift Valley • Africa 108 B5
Great [Riv] • Grenada ....166 Q
Great [Riv] • Jamaica 165 C3
Great Ruaha • Tanzania 110 H8
Great Sacandaga Lake •
   NY, United States 156 C1
Great Salt Lake •
   UT, United States 148 D2
Great Salt Lake Desert •
   UT, United States 148 D2

Great Salt Pond • St Kitts & Nevis ..167 F
Great Salt Pond • St Maarten ....166 C
Great Sand Dunes Nat. Mon. Park N •
   CO, United States ....152 [93]
Great Sandy Desert •
   OR, United States 154 H6
Great Sandy Desert • WA, Australia ..135 C4
Great Sea Reef • Fiji Is. ....138 S
Great Skellig • Ireland 69 G11
Great Slave Lake • NT, Canada 158 E2
Great Smoky Mtns Nat. Park •
   NC/TN, United States 151 D3
Great Smoky Mtns Nat. Park Park N •
   NC/TN, United States ....153 [226]
Great Smoky Mtns Nat. Park Heritage N •
   NC/TN, United States ....40 [17]
Great Sound • Bermuda 165 K10
Great St James I. • US Virgin Is. ....166 X
Great Tobago • British Virgin Is. .....166 A
Great Torrington • United Kingdom ..65 J9
Great Victoria Desert •
   SA/WA, Australia 135 D5
Great Wall • China ....43 [173]
Great Wall [Base] • Antarctica ....176 [2]
Great Western Tiers •
   TS, Australia 136 H6
Great White Heron Nat. Wildlife Refuge •
   FL, United States 155 C3
Great Yarmouth • United Kingdom ..63 F8
Great Yarmouth Beach •
   United Kingdom ....64 [18]
Great Zimbabwe • Zimbabwe 65 J9
Great Zimbabwe Nat. Mon. Heritage C •
   Zimbabwe ....43 [120]
Greater St Lucia Wetland Park •
   South Africa 111 C3
Greater St Lucia Wetland Park Park •
   South Africa ....112 [139]
Greater St Lucia Wetland Park Heritage N •
   South Africa ....41 [115]
Grebbestad • Sweden 99 F5
Greco, Cape • Cyprus 96 D4
GREECE • Europe 93
Greece • Greece 93
Greek Peak Ski • NY, United States ..146 [98]
Greek Peak • NY, United States 156 B1
Greeley • CO, United States 148 F2
Green Bay • WI, United States 150 C2
Green I. • Antigua & Barbuda ....167 I
Green I. • Grenada ....166 Q
Green I. • QL, Australia 136 C3
Green Line • Cyprus 96 C4
Green Meadows Petting Farm •
   FL, United States 157 B1
Green [Riv] • UT/WY, United States ..148 E2
Green River • UT, United States 148 D3
Green River • WY, United States 148 E2
Green Turtle Cay • Bahamas 164 A1
Green Valley • AZ, United States 155 G8
Greenbelt Park Park N •
   MD, United States ....153 [259]
Greeneville • TN, United States 151 D3
GREENLAND • N. America 142 G1
Greenland Sea • Antarctica 142 G1
Greenock • United Kingdom 65 A2
Greensboro • NC, United States 151 E3
Greensburg • IN, United States 150 C3
Greenville • MS, United States 156 F5
Greenville • NC, United States 151 E3
Greenville • SC, United States 151 D4
Greenville • TX, United States 155 F4
Greenwich • United Kingdom 65 G7
Greenwood • MS, United States 156 F5
Greenwood Great House • Jamaica ..165 C3
Gregory Nat. Park • NT, Australia ..135 E3
Greifswald • Germany 73 E1
Greiz • Germany 99 F7
Greiz • Germany 99 F7
Grenaa • Denmark 99 F6
Grenada • MS, United States 151 C4
GRENADA • West Indies ....166 Q
Grenchen • Switzerland 90 J5
Grenen • Denmark 99 F6
Grenoble • France 78 C4
Grenville • Grenada ....166 Q
Grenville Bay • Grenada ....166 Q
Grésivaudan, Val du • France 78 H7
Gresham • OR, United States 154 G5
Gresik • Java, Indonesia 131 R12
Gressåmoen Nat. Park Park N •
   Norway ....58 [12]
Gressoney-la-Trinité Ski • Italy .....61 [126]
Gressoney-la-Trinité • Italy 87 A2
Gressoney-St Jean Ski • Italy ....61 [126]
Gréswrd • Greece 93 B1
Grevená • France 78 C3
Grevenbroich • Germany 73 C6
Grey Is. • NF, Canada 160 D1
Grey Range • QL, Australia 135 G5
Greymouth • New Zealand 137 B3
Greystones • Ireland 69 F7
Greytown • South Africa 111 C4
Grieskirchen • Germany 74 D6
Griffen • GA, United States 151 D4
Griffith • NS, Australia 136 G8
Grim, Cape • TS, Australia 136 E6
Grímey • Iceland 90 J6
Grimma • Germany 73 E8
Grimsby • United Kingdom 63 F7
Grimselpass • Switzerland 90 K5
Grímsstadhir • Iceland 97 I6
Grimstad • Norway 99 B3
Grindelwald Ski • Switzerland .....61 [72]
Grindelwald • Switzerland 90 J5
Grindsted • Denmark 99 E7
Gripsholm • Sweden 99 A2
Gris Gris • Mauritius 113 E6
Grisons • Switzerland 90 L5
Grisslehamn • Sweden 99 B2
Grytviken • South Georgia 175 J8
Grisheim • Germany 74 D6
Griffin • GA, United States 151 D4
Grnc-Néz, Cap • France 65 H8
Grizedale Forest • United Kingdom ..65 D4
Groix • France 77 C4
Gróljer • Poland 89 C3
Gromel • Germany 72 E3
Grønnedal • Greenland 159 L3
Groningen [Adm] • Netherlands 70 D1
Groot • South Africa 111 F6
Groot Bak • St Maarten ....166 C
Groote Eylandt • NT, Australia 135 F2
Groote Peel, Nat. Park de •
   Netherlands 70 C3
Gros Islet • St Lucia ....167 N
Gros Morne • Haiti 165 F5
Gros Morne • NF, Canada 160 D1
Gros Morne Nat. Park Park N •
   NF, Canada ....161 [39]
Gros Morne Nat. Park Heritage N •
   NF, Canada ....40 [8]
Gros Piton • St Lucia ....167 N
Gross-Gerau • Germany 74 D6
Grossarl • Austria ....61 [109]
Grosseto • Italy 85 E3
Grosser Feldberg • Germany 74 D5
Grossbeeren • Germany 73 E8
Grosse Cays • Antigua & Barbuda ..167 I
Grosser Zernsee • Germany 73 E8
Grosserdhütte Stausee • Germany ..73 D6
Grossglockner • Austria 91 P8
Grossrotte • Austria 91 O8
Grossvenediger • Austria 91 O7
Grosti • Morocco 107 A1
Grover Beach • CA, United States ..148 B3
Grozny • Russian Fed. 100 G5
Grudovo • Bulgaria 92 H8
Grudziadz • Poland 89 B2
Grums • Sweden 99 H4
Grünstadt • Germany 74 C6
Gründberg • Germany 74 B7
Grundy Lake Prov. Park •
   OT, Canada 160 E3

Grünthal • Germany 73 F7
Grüsch • Switzerland 90 L5
Gruyères • Switzerland 90 J5
Gryazovets • Russian Fed. 100 M9
Gryon Ski • Switzerland ....61 [58]
Gryon • Switzerland 90 J6
Gryt • Sweden 99 H5
Grytviken • South Georgia 175 J8
Gstaad-Saanenland Ski • Switzerland ..61 [61]
Guacanayabo, Golfo de • Cuba 164 G5
Guadalajara Heritage C • Mexico ..42 [16]
Guadalajara • Mexico 169 I7
Guadalajara • Spain 80 D3
Guadalcanal • Solomon Is. ....138 W
Guadalest • Spain 83 B1
Guadalete • Spain 80 D5
Guadalquivir • Spain 80 D5
Guadalupe • Nuevo León, Mexico ..168 D2
Guadalupe Heritage C • Spain ...44 [119]
Guadalupe • TX, United States 155 E6
Guadalupe • Zacatecas, Mexico 169 I7
Guadalupe • Mexico 149 C5
Guadalupe Mtns Nat. Park Park N •
   TX, United States ....152 [133]
Guadalupe Victoria • Mexico 168 D3
GUADELOUPE • West Indies ....167 J
Guadiana • Portugal/Spain 80 C4
Guadiana, Bahía de • Cuba 164 E4
Gudirikiri Caves • Aruba ....166 W
Guaíra • Brazil 82 K7
Guáimaro • Cuba 164 G5
Guajaba, Cayo • Cuba 164 G4
Guajataca • Puerto Rico 165 I7
Guajira, Península de • Colombia ..173 B1
Guakolak, Tanjung •
   Java, Indonesia 131 O11
Gualdo Tadino • Italy 50 C3
Gualeguay • Argentina 175 F6
Gualeguaychú • Argentina 175 F6
GUAM • Pacific Ocean ....138 Z
Guamá Indian Village • Cuba 164 F4
Guamúchil • Mexico 168 I6
Guana I. • British Virgin Is. ....166 A
Guanacaste, Área de Conservación
   Heritage N • Costa Rica ....40 [24]
Guanaja, I. de • Honduras 170 E2
Guanajay • Cuba 164 E4
Guanajuato • Mexico 169 I7
Guanajuato Heritage C • Mexico ..42 [17]
Guanajuato [Adm] • Mexico 169 C3
Guane • Cuba 164 E4
Guangde • China 126 C2
Guangdong • China 126 G7
Guangming Ding • China 126 G7
Guangxi Zhuangzu Zizhiqu • China ..125 E4
Guangyuan • China 126 C1
Guangzhou • China 126 F7
Guangzhou East • China 126 F7
Guánica • Puerto Rico 165 I8
Guanimar, Playa • Cuba 164 E4
Guantánamo • Cuba 164 H5
Guantánamo Bay • Cuba 164 H5
Guaporé • Bolivia/Brazil 173 C4
Guaqui • Bolivia 173 F7
Guaraparí • Brazil 174 F6
Guarapuava • Brazil 175 C2
Guaratinguetá • Brazil 174 E7
Guarda • Portugal 80 B3
Guarda [Adm] • Portugal 80 A3
Guardalavaca Playa • Cuba 164 H5
Guardalavaca • Cuba 164 H5
Guardamar del Segura • Spain 83 A2
Guárdia, A • Spain 80 A3
Guárdia Sanframondi • Italy 87 H6
Guaruja • Brazil 174 C7
Guarulhos • Brazil 174 E7
Guarulhos [Apt] • Brazil 174 E7
Guasave • Mexico 168 I6
GUATEMALA • C. America 170 B3
Guatemala City • Guatemala 170 J9
Guaviare • Colombia/Venezuela 173 C2
Guavle • Sweden 97 D3
Guaxupé • Brazil 174 E6
Guayama • Puerto Rico 165 J8
Guayanilla, Bahía de • Puerto Rico ..165 I8
Guayaquil • Ecuador 173 B3
Guayaquil, Golfo de • Ecuador 173 A3
Guaymas • Mexico 168 I5
Guaynabo • Puerto Rico 165 J7
Gúbbio • Italy 87 D3
Gudgeon Bay • Pitcairn Is. ....139 L
Gudhjem • Denmark 99 H8
Gudi • India 124 C2
Gudvangen • Norway 98 G8
Guéllala • Tunisia 107 D6
Guelph • OT, Canada 160 E5
Guérande • France 77 D4
Guéret • France 78 F5
Guernsey • Channel Is. 63 I14
Guernsey • Mexico 169 C3
Guerrero Negro • Mexico 168 H5
Guerrero, Parque Natural de •
   Mexico 169 J8
Guiana Highlands • S. America 173 C2
Guiana I. • Antigua & Barbuda ....167 I
Guildel • France 77 C1
Guignes • France 78 B2
Guildford • United Kingdom 65 F7
Guildford Courthouse Nat. Military Park
   Park N • NC, United States ....153 [238]
Guilin • China 125 E4
Gümar • Tenerife, Canary Is. 82 G5
Guimarães Heritage C • Portugal ..44 [126]
Guinchos Cay • Bahamas 164 G4
GUINEA • Africa 106 A3
Guinea, Gulf of • Africa 106 C4
Guinea, Lower • Africa 104 B4
Guinea, Upper • Africa 104 B4
GUINEA-BISSAU • Africa 106 A3
Güines • Cuba 164 F4
Guingamp • France 77 D3
Guipavas [Apt] • France 77 C3
Guiyang • China 126 D2
Guizhou • China 126 C2
Gujarat • India 123 A2
Gujranwala • Pakistan 122 B2
Gulbarga • India 124 B1
Gulbene • Latvia 100 K7
Gulen • Norway 98 F8
Gulf Coast • FL, United States 155 B4
Gulf Is. Nat. Reserve Park N •
   BC, Canada ....161 [12]
Gulf Is. Nat. Seashore Park N •
   FL/MS, United States 155 A1
Gulf Is. Nat. Seashore Park N •
   FL/MS, United States ....153 [214]
Gulf, The • Asia 120 G8
Gulfport • MS, United States 150 F0
Gulfstream Park •
   FL, United States 155 D3
Gulhi • Maldives 124 H8
Gulistan • Uzbekistan 121 E3
Gullivers Kingdom Park L •
   United Kingdom ....59 [26]
Gulispång • Sweden 99 G5
Güllük • Turkey 95 F4
Gulmarg Hill Sta • India 95 I10
Gülnar • France 95 I10
Gulu • Uganda 108 B4
Gumbet • Turkey 95 F4
Gun Bay • Cayman Is. 165 B2
Gun Hill Tower • Barbados ....167 M
Guna • India 123 E8
Gündogmus • Turkey 95 I9
Gunnbjørn Fjeld • Greenland 142 H2
Gunner's Quoin • Mauritius 113 F5
Gunnislake • United Kingdom 65 J10
Gunnison • CO, United States 148 E3
Guntakal • India 124 B1
Guntur • India 124 C1
Gunung Kawi • Bali, Indonesia 131 L7

Gunung Mulu Nat. Park **Heritage N** • Malaysia ... 41 [141]
Gunungsitoli • Indonesia ... 131 M10
Günzburg • Germany ... 74 F7
Gunzenhausen • Germany ... 72 D4
Gur, Lough • Ireland ... 69 H10
Guradu • Maldives ... 124 H8
Gurha • India ... 123 D8
Guri, Embalse de • Venezuela ... 173 C2
Gurskøy • Norway ... 98 F7
Gurupi • Brazil ... 174 B4
Guruvayur • India ... 124 B3
Gusau • Nigeria ... 106 C3
Gush Halav • Israel ... 120 B1
Gushgy • Turkmenistan ... 121 D4
Gushikawa • Okinawa, Japan ... 138 A
Güspini • Sardinia, Italy ... 86 E6
Gustavia • St Barthélemy ... 166 D
Gusum • Sweden ... 99 H5
Gutach • Germany ... 74 B4
Güterfelde • Germany ... 73 E8
Gütersloh • Germany ... 72 C3
Guthega • NS, Australia ... 136 H9
Guthrie • OK, United States ... 149 G3
Guttenberg, Burg • Germany ... 74 E2
Guwahati • India ... 122 D3
GUYANA • S. America ... 173 D2
Guyenne • France ... 78 F6
Güzelcamli • Turkey ... 95 E5
Güzelsu • Turkey ... 95 H8
Guzelyürt • Cyprus ... 96 C4
Gvarv • Norway ... 98 D6
Gwaii Haanas Nat. Park Reserve **Park N** • BC, Canada ... 161 [10]
Gwalior • India ... 123 F8
Gwangju • Rep. of Korea ... 125 G3
Gweru • Zimbabwe ... 110 B2
Gweta • Botswana ... 110 J9
Gyangze • China ... 125 C4
Gydanskiy Poluostrov • Russian Fed. ... 101 H2
Gyeongju **Heritage C** • Rep. of Korea ... 43 [192]
Gympie • QL, Australia ... 127 I8
Gyoda • Japan ... 127 I8
Gyokusendo Okoku mura • Okinawa, Japan ... 138 A
Györ • Hungary ... 92 B2
Gyumri • Armenia ... 120 E5
Gyzylarbat • Turkmenistan ... 121 C4

H

H.P. Leu Botanical Gardens • FL, United States ... 157 B1
Ha Dong • Vietnam ... 128 D2
Ha Giang • Vietnam ... 128 C2
Ha Long Bay • Vietnam ... 128 C2
Ha Long Bay **Heritage N** • Vietnam ... 41 [138]
Ha Tien • Vietnam ... 129 B6
Ha'amonga • Tonga ... 139 P
Ha'apai Group • Tonga ... 138 CC4
Ha-ad Chao Samran • Thailand ... 130 D8
Haag • Germany ... 74 H7
Haan • Germany ... 73 C6
Haapiti • French Polynesia ... 139 K
Haapsalu • Estonia ... 100 J6
Haarlem • Netherlands ... 70 G7
Haarlemmermeer Polder • Netherlands ... 70 G7
Haast • New Zealand ... 137 A3
Haast Bluff • NT, Australia ... 136 A1
Haasts Bluff Aboriginal Land • NT, Australia ... 136 A1
Habarana • Sri Lanka ... 124 C4
Habomai-shoto • Russian Fed. ... 127 E2
Hachinohe • Japan ... 127 D2
Hachioji • Japan ... 127 H8
Hacho, Monte • Ceuta ... 82 D4
Hacilar • Turkey ... 95 J6
Hadamar • Germany ... 74 D5
Hadano • Japan ... 127 H9
Hadarba, Ras • Egypt/Sudan ... 109 E9
Haddington • United Kingdom ... 65 B2
Haddumatti Atoll • Maldives ... 124 G8
Hadeland • Norway ... 98 E5
Haderslev • Denmark ... 99 C4
Hadim • Turkey ... 95 I10
Hadramawt • Yemen ... 120 F10
Hadrian, Villa • Italy ... 87 E4
Hadrian's Wall • United Kingdom ... 62 D5
Hadrian's Wall **Heritage C** • United Kingdom ... 44 [21]
Hadsund • Denmark ... 99 F6
Hae, Ko • Thailand ... 130 F10
Haeinsa Temple **Heritage C** • Rep. of Korea ... 43 [192]
Haeju • D.P.R. of Korea ... 125 G3
Hafar al Batin • Saudi Arabia ... 120 F8
Hafik • Turkey ... 95 C2
Hagar Qim • Malta ... 96 B2
Hagby • Sweden ... 99 H6
Hagen • Germany ... 73 D5
Hagerman Fossil Beds Nat. Mon. • ID, United States ... 154 H6
Hagerman Fossil Beds Nat. Mon. **Park N** • ID, United States ... 152 [62]
Hagerstown • MD, United States ... 156 A3
Haghpat **Heritage C** • Armenia ... 43 [137]
Hagi • Japan ... 127 A8
Hagman, Puntan • N. Mariana Is. ... 138 B
Hague, Cap de la • France ... 76 C2
Hague, The • Netherlands ... 70 G7
Haguenau • France ... 76 G2
Hahn [Apt] • Germany ... 74 C6
Hai'an • China ... 126 H6
Haicheng • China ... 125 G2
Haida Heritage Site **Park N** • BC, Canada ... 161 [10]
Haïfa • Israel ... 120 A2
Haikou • China ... 125 F5
Hail • Saudi Arabia ... 120 E8
Hailar • China ... 125 F2
Hailuoto • Finland ... 97 E2
Haimen • China ... 126 H6
Hainan • China ... 125 E5
Hainan Dao • China ... 125 E5
Hainaut • Belgium ... 70 B4
Haines • AK, United States ... 157 F4
Haines Junction • YT, Canada ... 158 C2
Haining • China ... 126 H7
Haiphong • Vietnam ... 128 D2
HAITI • West Indies ... 165 E-F
Haiyan • China ... 126 H7
Hajira Beach • India ... 124 E6
Hakai • French Polynesia ... 139 J
Hakken-zen • Japan ... 127 G7
Hakodate • Japan ... 127 D2
Hakone • Japan ... 127 H9
Hakone-yama • Japan ... 127 H9
Hakupu • Niue ... 139 O
Hal Saflieni Hypogeum • Malta ... 96 B2
Hal Saflieni Hypogeum **Heritage C** • Malta ... 44 [257]
Hala Sultan Tekke • Cyprus ... 96 C4
Halab • Syria ... 120 D6
Halab **Heritage C** • Syria ... 44 [300]
Halab • Saudi Arabia ... 120 D8
Halaib • Egypt/Sudan ... 109 E9
Halalo • Wallis & Futuna ... 139 U
Hälaveden • Sweden ... 99 G5
Halban • Mongolia ... 125 D2
Halberstadt • Germany ... 72 D3
Halden • Norway ... 98 E6
Haleakala Crater • HI, United States ... 157 I10
Haleakala Nat. Park • HI, United States ... 157 I5
Haleakala Nat. Park **Park N** • HI, United States ... 152 [19]
Halebid • India ... 124 B2
Haleiwa • HI, United States ... 157 G5

Halfmoon Bay • New Zealand ... 137 A4
Haliburton Highlands • OT, Canada ... 160 F4
Halicarnassus • Turkey ... 95 E6
Halifax • NS, Canada ... 160 B4
Halifax • United Kingdom ... 63 E7
Halifax Bay • QL, Australia ... 136 C3
Halifax, Mt • QL, Australia ... 136 C3
Halim Perdana Kusuma [Apt] • Java, Indonesia ... 131 O11
Hálki • Greece ... 94 F
Halkida • Greece ... 93 C3
Halkidiki • Greece ... 93 C1
Hall • Canada ... 159 H2
Hall in Tirol • Austria ... 91 N7
Hall Is. • Fed. States of Micronesia ... 138 BB2
Hall Peninsula • NU, Canada ... 159 J2
Halland • Sweden ... 99 G6
Hallandsås • Sweden ... 99 G6
Halle • Germany ... 72 D3
Halle-Neustadt • Germany ... 72 D3
Halleberg • Sweden ... 99 G5
Hälleforsnäs • Sweden ... 99 A2
Hallein • Austria ... 91 P7
Hallett, Cape • Antarctica ... 176 U5
Halley [Base] • Antarctica ... 176 [11]
Hallingdalselva • Norway ... 98 G8
Hallingskarvet • Norway ... 98 G8
Halls Creek • WA, Australia ... 135 D3
Hallstahammar • Sweden ... 99 A1
Hallstatt **Heritage C** • Austria ... 44 [140]
Hallstatt • Austria ... 99 B1
Hallstavik • Sweden ... 99 A2
Hals • Denmark ... 99 F6
Halsskov • Denmark ... 99 F8
Halstatt • Austria ... 91 P7
Haltwhistle • United Kingdom ... 62 D6
Halver • Germany ... 73 D6
Hamada • Japan ... 127 A8
Hamadan • Iran ... 120 F7
Hamah • Syria ... 120 D6
Hamamatsu • Japan ... 127 C4
Hamar • Norway ... 97 C3
Hamat Gader • Israel ... 120 B2
Hambantota • Sri Lanka ... 124 C4
Hamber Prov. Park • BC, Canada ... 160 J7
Hamborn (Duisburg) • Germany ... 73 C6
Hamburg • AR, United States ... 156 E5
Hamburg • Germany ... 72 D2
Hamburg • NY, United States ... 156 A1
Hamburg [Adm] • Germany ... 72 D2
Hamburgisches Wattenmeer, Nationalpark **Park N** • Germany ... 58 [62]
Häme • Finland ... 99 D3
Hämeenlinna • Finland ... 99 D4
Hameln • Germany ... 72 C2
Hamersley Range • WA, Australia ... 135 B4
Hamhung • D.P.R. of Korea ... 125 G3
Hami • China ... 125 D2
Hamilton • Bermuda ... 165 K10
Hamilton • MT, United States ... 148 D1
Hamilton • New Zealand ... 137 D5
Hamilton • OH, United States ... 150 D2
Hamilton • OT, Canada ... 160 E5
Hamilton • United Kingdom ... 65 A2
Hamilton • VI, Australia ... 135 G7
Hamilton, Fort • Bermuda ... 165 K10
Hamilton Grange Nat. Mem. **Park N** • NY, United States ... 153 [278]
Hamilton I. • QL, Australia ... 136 C3
Hamina • Finland ... 99 E3
Hammam Lif • Tunisia ... 107 D4
Hammamet • Tunisia ... 107 D4
Hammamet, Golfe de • Tunisia ... 107 D4
Hammarsjön • Sweden ... 99 G7
Hammel • Denmark ... 99 F7
Hammerfest • Norway ... 97 E1
Hammershus • Denmark ... 99 B3
Hammond • IL, United States ... 150 C2
Hammond • LA, United States ... 156 F6
Hammondsport • NY, United States ... 156 A1
Hampi • India ... 124 B1
Hampi **Heritage C** • India ... 43 [159]
Hampshire • United Kingdom ... 64 B6
Hampstead • United Kingdom ... 65 G7
Hampton • VA, United States ... 156 B4
Hampton Beach • NH, United States ... 156 D1
Hampton Court • United Kingdom ... 65 G7
Hampton Nat. Hist. Site • MD, United States ...
Hampton Nat. Hist. Site **Park N** • MD, United States ... 153 [263]
Hamra Nat. Park **Park N** • Sweden ... 58 [25]
Han Shui • China ... 125 F3
Han-sur-Lesse • Belgium ... 70 C5
Hana • HI, United States ... 157 J5
Hanaiapa • French Polynesia ... 139 J
Hanamenu • French Polynesia ... 139 J
Hanan [Apt] • Niue ... 139 O
Hanang • Tanzania ... 110 H7
Hanau • Germany ... 74 B2
Hancheng • China ... 125 F3
Hancock [Apt] • MI, United States ... 161 A1
Hancock [Apt] • NY, United States ... 156 B1
Handan • China ... 125 F3
Handen • Sweden ... 99 B2
Haneda [Apt] • Japan ... 127 H8
Hanford • CA, United States ... 154 I8
Hanga Piko • Easter I. ... 139 M
Hanga Roa • Easter I. ... 139 M
Hangklip, Cape • South Africa ... 111 D7
Hangö • Finland ... 99 D4
Hangzhou • China ... 126 H7
Hangzhou Wan • China ... 126 H7
Haniá • Crete, Greece ... 93 G5
Haniá [Adm] • Crete, Greece ... 93 G5
Hanión, Kólpos • Crete, Greece ... 94 S
Haniótis • Greece ... 94 B
Hanish al Kabir • Yemen ... 109 E11
Hanita • Israel ... 120 A1
Hankey • South Africa ... 111 E7
Hanko • Finland ... 99 D4
Hannibal • MO, United States ... 150 B3
Hanno • Japan ... 127 H8
Hannover • Germany ... 72 C2
Hannøbukten • Sweden ... 99 H7
Hanoi • Vietnam ... 128 D2
Hanover • Germany ... 72 C2
Hans Lollik I. • US Virgin Is. ... 166 X
Hansapark **Park L** • Germany ... 59 [45]
Hansted • Denmark ... 99 F6
Hanstholm • Denmark ... 99 F6
Hantu • Singapore ... 129 H12
Hanumangarh • India ... 123 E7
Hanyu • Japan ... 127 I8
Hanzhong • China ... 125 E3
Haouaria, El • Tunisia ... 107 D4
Haparanda • Sweden ... 97 E2
Happy Valley-Goose Bay • NF, Canada ... 159 J3
Haradh • Saudi Arabia ... 120 F9
Harare • Zimbabwe ... 110 C2
Harat • Eritrea ... 109 E10
Harbel • Liberia ... 106 A4
Harbin • China ... 125 G2
Harbo • Sweden ... 99 A1
Harbo • Denmark ... 99 F7
Harbour Breton • NF, Canada ... 160 D1
Harbour Park **Park L** • United Kingdom ... 59 [35]
Harby • United Kingdom ... 65 G8
Hardangerfjorden • Norway ... 98 F8
Hardangerjøkulen • Norway ... 98 F8
Hardangervidda • Norway ... 98 G8
Hardangervidda Nat. Park **Park N** • Norway ... 58 [16]
Hardangervidda Nat. Park • Norway ... 98 G8
Harderwijk • Netherlands ... 70 C2
Hardin • MT, United States ... 148 E1
Hardknott Pass • United Kingdom ... 65 C4
Hardoi • India ... 123 F8
Hareid • Norway ... 98 F7
Harestua • Norway ... 98 E5

Hargeysa • Somalia ... 108 C4
Hari Rud • Afghanistan/Iran ... 121 D5
Haridwar • India ... 123 F7
Harima-nada • Japan ... 127 F7
Haringvliet • Netherlands ... 70 G8
Haringvlietdam • Netherlands ... 70 G8
Harjavalta • Finland ... 99 C3
Harlingen • Netherlands ... 70 C1
Harlow • United Kingdom ... 65 G7
Harlowtown • MT, United States ... 148 D1
Harmal • Goa, India ... 123 C5
Harmil • Eritrea ... 109 E10
Harney Basin • OR, United States ... 154 H5
Harney Lake • OR, United States ... 154 H6
Härnösand • Sweden ... 97 D3
Harold Johnson Nature Reserve • South Africa ... 111 C4
Harpalpur • India ... 123 F8
Harplinge • Sweden ... 99 G6
Harpers Ferry Nat. Hist. Park • WV, United States ... 156 A3
Harpers Ferry Nat. Hist. Park **Park N** • WV, United States ... 153 [253]
Harrachov • Czech Rep. ... 89 E6
Harrington Harbour • QU, Canada ... 159 K3
Harrington Sound • Bermuda ... 165 L10
Harris • United Kingdom ... 62 E3
Harrisburg • PA, United States ... 156 B2
Harrison • AR, United States ... 151 B3
Harrison, Cape • NF, Canada ... 159 K3
Harrison's Cave • Barbados ... 167 M
Harrisonburg • VA, United States ... 156 A3
Harrogate • United Kingdom ... 63 E7
Harrow • United Kingdom ... 65 G7
Harry S. Truman Nat. Hist. Site **Park N** • MO, United States ... 153 [172]
Harstad • Norway ... 97 D2
Hart, Lake • FL, United States ... 157 B1
Harteigen • Norway ... 98 G8
Hartford • CT, United States ... 156 C2
Hartland Covered Bridge • NB, Canada ... 160 A2
Hartland Point • United Kingdom ... 65 I9
Hartlepool • United Kingdom ... 63 E6
Hartola • Finland ... 99 D3
Harwich • United Kingdom ... 65 H7
Haryana • India ... 123 E7
Harz • Germany ... 72 D3
Hasbaya • Lebanon ... 120 B1
Hashimoto • Japan ... 127 G7
Haslev • Denmark ... 99 F8
Hasle • Denmark ... 99 B3
Hassel I. • US Virgin Is. ... 166 X
Hasselt • Belgium ... 70 C4
Hässleholm • Sweden ... 99 G7
Hastière-Lavaux • Belgium ... 70 B5
Hastings • MN, United States ... 150 B2
Hastings • NE, United States ... 148 G2
Hastings • New Zealand ... 137 E6
Hastings • United Kingdom ... 65 H8
Hat Yai • Thailand ... 130 F10
Hatay • Turkey ... 95 J10
Hatfield • United Kingdom ... 65 G7
Hathras • India ... 123 F7
Hatibah, Ra's • Saudi Arabia ... 109 E9
Hatiheu • French Polynesia ... 139 J
Hatillo • Puerto Rico ... 165 I7
Hato [Apt] • Curaçao ... 166 V
Hato Cave • Curaçao ... 166 V
Hato Mayor • Dominican Rep. ... 165 H6
Hatra **Heritage C** • Iraq ... 44 [313]
Hatsu-shima • Japan ... 127 H9
Hatteras, Cape • NC, United States ... 151 E3
Hattiesburg • MS, United States ... 156 F5
Hattingen • Germany ... 73 D5
Hattula • Finland ... 99 D3
Hattusha • Turkey ... 95 B1
Hattusha **Heritage C** • Turkey ... 44 [252]
Haugesund • Norway ... 98 F9
Hauhungaroa Range • New Zealand ... 137 E6
Haukeligrend • Norway ... 98 D6
Hauraki Gulf • New Zealand ... 137 C2
Hauroko, Lake • New Zealand ... 137 F8
Haut Atlas • Morocco ... 107 B2
Haut-Médoc • France ... 76 K9
Haute-Corse • Corsica, France ... 78 H8
Haute-Garonne • France ... 78 J9
Haute-Loire • France ... 78 F5
Haute-Marne • France ... 77 A1
Haute-Normandie • France ... 77 A1
Haute-Saône • France ... 78 D3
Haute-Savoie • France ... 78 D3
Haute-Vienne • France ... 78 F5
Hautefort • France ... 78 F5
Hautes-Alpes • France ... 78 D3
Hautes-Pyrénées • France ... 78 J9
Hauula • HI, United States ... 157 G5
Havana • Cuba ... 164 E4
Havana **Heritage C** • Cuba ... 42 [40]
Havant • United Kingdom ... 63 E10
Havasu, Lake • AZ/NV, United States ... 155 G7
Havasupai **Ind Res** • AZ, United States ... 155 [25]
Havel • Germany ... 72 E2
Havelkanal • Germany ... 73 E7
Havelock • NC, United States ... 151 E4
Havelock North • New Zealand ... 137 F6
Havelte • Netherlands ... 70 D2
Haverfordwest • United Kingdom ... 63 C9
Haverhill • MA, United States ... 156 C1
Haverthwaite • United Kingdom ... 65 D4
Havírov • Czech Rep. ... 89 F7
Havlíckuv Brod • Czech Rep. ... 89 E7
Havnsø • Denmark ... 99 F7
Havre • MT, United States ... 148 E1
Havre, le • France ... 76 D2
Havre-Aubert • QU, Canada ... 160 B1
Havre-St Pierre • QU, Canada ... 160 B1
Havza • Turkey ... 95 C1
Haw Par Villa • Singapore ... 129 H12
Hawaii • Pacific Ocean ... 157 G-J
Hawaii [I.] • HI, United States ... 157 J6
Hawaii Volcanoes Nat. Park • HI, United States ... 157 J6
Hawaii Volcanoes Nat. Park **Park N** • HI, United States ... 152 [23]
Hawaii Volcanoes Nat. Park **Heritage N** • HI, United States ... 40 [9]
Hawaiian Is. • Pacific Ocean ... 139 DD1
Hawea • New Zealand ... 137 G3
Hawea, Lake • New Zealand ... 137 G7
Hawera • New Zealand ... 137 D6
Haweswater Reservoir • United Kingdom ... 65 D3
Hawi • HI, United States ... 157 I5
Hawick • United Kingdom ... 62 D5
Hawke Bay • New Zealand ... 137 E6
Hawke's Bay [Adm] • New Zealand ... 137 E6
Hawksbill • VA, United States ... 156 A3
Hawkshead • United Kingdom ... 65 D4
Hawra • Yemen ... 120 F10
Hawthorne • NV, United States ... 154 H7
Hay • AL/NT, Canada ... 158 E3
Hay • NS, Australia ... 136 B4
Hay River • NT, Canada ... 158 E2
Hay-on-Wye • United Kingdom ... 65 E6
Hayange • France ... 76 G2
Hayle • United Kingdom ... 65 I10
Hayling I. **Beach** • United Kingdom ... 64 [32]
Hayma • Oman ... 120 H10
Hayman I. • QL, Australia ... 136 C3
Haynesville • LA, United States ... 156 E5
Hays • KS, United States ... 148 G3
Haystack **Ski** • VT, United States ... 146 [105]
Hayward • CA, United States ... 154 B3
Haywards Heath • United Kingdom ... 65 G8
Hazleton • BC, Canada ... 160 I6
Hazleton • PA, United States ... 156 B2
Hazor • Israel ... 120 B1

Healdsburg • CA, United States ... 154 I8
Heard & McDonald Is. • Indian Ocean ... 11 M8
Heard & McDonald Is. **Heritage N** • Southern Ocean ... 41 [160]
Hearne • TX, United States ... 155 H4
Hearst • OT, Canada ... 158 I8
Hearst San Simeon State Hist. Mon. • CA, United States ... 154 I8
Heart of England • United Kingdom ... 65 E-F
Heathrow [Apt] • United Kingdom ... 65 G7
Heavenly **Ski** • NV, United States ... 146 [37]
Hebbronville • TX, United States ... 155 E6
Hebei • China ... 126 C1
Hebrides, Sea of the •
Hebron • NF, Canada ... 159 J3
Hebron • Palestine NAR ... 120 A4
Heby • Sweden ... 99 A1
Hecate Strait • BC, Canada ... 157 F4
Hecelchakán • Mexico ... 169 F4
Hed • Sweden ... 99 A1
Heddal stavkirke • Norway ... 98 D5
Hedemora • Sweden ... 99 A1
Hedensted • Denmark ... 99 F7
Hedesunda • Sweden ... 99 A1
Hedmark • Norway ... 98 D5
Hedo • Okinawa, Japan ... 138 A
Hedo-misaki • Okinawa, Japan ... 138 A
Heemstede • Netherlands ... 70 G7
Heerenlogement Cave • South Africa ... 111 D6
Heerenveen • Netherlands ... 70 C1
Heerlen • Netherlands ... 70 C4
Hefa • Israel ... 120 A2
Hefei • China ... 125 F3
Hegang • China ... 125 H2
Hei Ling Chau • Hong Kong, China ... 126 E5
Heide • Germany ... 72 C2
Heide-Park **Park L** • Germany ... 59 [47]
Heidelberg • Germany ... 74 B2
Heidenheim an der Brenz • Germany ... 90 E1
Heihe • China ... 125 G1
Heilbronn • Germany ... 74 E1
Heiligenberg, Schloss • Germany ... 74 E8
Heiligenblut • Austria ... 91 P8
Heiligenhaus • Germany ... 73 C5
Heiligenstadt • Germany ... 72 D3
Heilong Jiang • China ... 125 G1
Heilongjiang • China ... 126 D1
Heimdal • Norway ... 97 B3
Heinola • Finland ... 99 D3
Hekeani • French Polynesia ... 139 J
Hekou • China ... 125 E4
Helen Reef • Palau ... 138 AA3
Helena, Mt • MT, United States ... 148 D1
Helengeli • Maldives ... 124 H7
Helensburgh • United Kingdom ... 65 A2
Helgasjön • Sweden ... 99 G6
Helgeland • Norway ... 97 C2
Helgoländer Bucht • Germany ... 72 C1
Heligan, Lost Gardens of • United Kingdom ... 65 I10
Heliopolis • Egypt ... 109 B1
Hell • Cayman Is. ... 165 A2
Hell • Norway ... 97 C3
Hell's Gate • Saba ... 167 E
Hell-Bourg • Réunion ... 113 C3
Hellendoorn, Avonturenpark **Park L** • Netherlands ... 59 [37]
Hellendoorn, Avonturenpark • Netherlands ... 70 D2
Hellesylt • Norway ... 98 G7
Hellevoetsluis • Netherlands ... 70 G8
Hellín • Spain ... 83 H6
Hells Canyon Nat. Recreation Area • ID/OR, United States ... 154 H6
Hells Gate Nat. Park • Kenya ... 109 C5
Hellshire Hills • Jamaica ... 165 D4
Helmand • Afghanistan ... 121 D5
Helmond • Netherlands ... 70 C3
Helmsley • United Kingdom ... 63 E6
Helsingborg • Sweden ... 99 G7
Helsingfors • Finland ... 99 D4
Helsingør • Denmark ... 99 G7
Helsingør **Heritage C** • Denmark ... 44 [11]
Helsinki • Finland ... 99 D4
Helsinki **Heritage C** • Finland ... 44 [10]
Helston • United Kingdom ... 65 I10
Helvellyn • United Kingdom ... 65 D3
Helwân • Egypt ... 109 B1
Hembadoo • Maldives ... 124 H7
Hemel Hempstead • United Kingdom ... 63 E9
Hemnes • Norway ... 98 E5
Hempstead • TX, United States ... 155 H5
Hemsedal • Norway ... 98 G8
Hemse • Sweden ... 99 B2
Henan • China ... 126 C2
Henbury • NT, Australia ... 136 B2
Henbury meteorite craters • NT, Australia ... 136 B2
Hendala • Sri Lanka ... 124 C4
Hendaye • France ... 78 I9
Henderson • NC, United States ... 150 E3
Henderson • NV, United States ... 155 G6
Henderson • TX, United States ... 155 F4
Henderson [Apt] • Solomon Is. ... 138 W
Henderson I. • Pitcairn Is. ... 139 EE4
Henderson I. **Heritage N** • Pitcairn Is. ... 41 [166]
Heng Shan • Hunan, China ... 126 [5]
Heng Shan • Shanxi, China ... 126 [1]
Hengelo • Netherlands ... 70 D2
Hengoed • United Kingdom ... 65 E6
Hengqin [I.] • China ... 126 E4
Hengyang • China ... 125 F4
Henne Strand • Denmark ... 99 E7
Hennebont • France ... 77 D4
Hennigsdorf • Germany ... 73 E7
Henrietta Maria, Cape • OT, Canada ... 159 H3
Henry, Cape • VA, United States ... 156 B4
Henry E. Rohlsen [Apt] • US Virgin Is. ... 166 X
Henry Ice Rise • Antarctica ... 176 M6
Henzada • Myanmar ... 128 B3
Heptagon • Israel ... 120 B2
Heraíon • Sámos, Greece ... 94 E
Heraklea • Turkey ... 95 H8
Herakleion • Crete, Greece ... 93 I6
Herald Cays • CL, Australia ... 136 C3
Herat • Afghanistan ... 121 D5
Herbert Hoover Nat. Hist. Site **Park N** • IA, United States ... 153 [166]
Herbertville • New Zealand ... 137 C3
Herculaneum • Italy ... 87 G7
Herculaneum **Heritage C** • Italy ... 44 [169]
Herdecke • Germany ... 73 D5
Heredia • Costa Rica ... 170 E5
Hereford • TX, United States ... 149 F4
Hereford • United Kingdom ... 65 E6
Herentals • Belgium ... 70 C3
Hergiswil • Switzerland ... 90 K5
Herisau • Tunisia ... 107 D4
Hergozenbuchsee • Switzerland ... 90 J5
Herkimer • NY, United States ... 156 B1
Herm • Channel Is. ... 63 I14
Hermannsburg • NT, Australia ... 136 B2
Hermansverk • Norway ... 98 G8
Hermanus • South Africa ... 111 D7
Hermiston • OR, United States ... 148 C1
Hermitage • France ... 76 L9
Hermitage, The • Bahamas ... 164 B1
Hermon, Mt • Lebanon/Syria ... 120 B1
Hermosillo • Mexico ... 168 I5
Hernals • Austria ... 91 I15
Herne • Germany ... 73 D5
Herne Bay • United Kingdom ... 64 [25]
Herne Bay **Beach** • United Kingdom ... 64 [25]
Herning • Denmark ... 99 F7
Herodium • Palestine NAR ... 120 B4
Heroine's monument • Ko Phuket, Thailand ... 130 F9
Herolds Bay • South Africa ... 111 F7
Heron I. • QL, Australia ... 136 D4

Herouval, le Bois • France ... 78 A1
Herräng • Sweden ... 99 B1
Herrenchiemsee, Schloss • Germany ... 74 H7
Herrljunga • Sweden ... 99 G5
Herrnsheim • Germany ... 74 G7
Herrsching • Germany ... 74 G7
Herschel I. • YT, Canada ... 158 C2
Hershey • PA, United States ... 156 B2
Hersheypark **Park L** • PA, United States ... 157 [31]
Herten • Germany ... 73 D5
Hertford • United Kingdom ... 65 G7
Hertfordshire • United Kingdom ... 65 G7
Hervey Bay • QL, Australia ... 136 D4
Herzberg • Germany ... 72 E3
Herzliyya • Israel ... 120 B4
Heshbon • Jordan ... 120 B3
Hesperia • CA, United States ... 149 C4
Hesse • Germany ... 72 C3
Hessen • Germany ... 72 C3
Hetauda • Nepal ... 123 C7
Hettstedt • Germany ... 72 D3
Hever Castle • United Kingdom ... 65 G8
Hewanorra [Apt] • St Lucia ... 167 N
Hexrivierberge • South Africa ... 111 E7
Heywoods Beach • Barbados ... 167 M
Heze • China ... 125 F3
Hialeah • FL, United States ... 155 C3
Hibberdene • South Africa ... 111 B5
Hibbing • MN, United States ... 150 B1
Hibiscus Coast • South Africa ... 111 B5
Hicacos, Peninsula • Cuba ... 164 F4
Hickory • NC, United States ... 151 D3
Hicks Bay • New Zealand ... 137 C2
Hidaka • Japan ... 127 I8
Hidalgo • Mexico ... 169 C2
Hidalgo del Parral • Mexico ... 168 C2
Hidcote Manor • United Kingdom ... 65 F6
Hidden Valley **Ski** • PA, United States ... 146 [91]
Hidden Valley • PA, United States ... 156 A2
Hierakonpolis • Egypt ... 109 B3
Hierapolis • Turkey ... 95 F5
Hierapolis-Pamukkale **Heritage N** • Turkey ... 41 [80]
Hierapolis-Pamukkale **Heritage C** • Turkey ... 44 [248]
Hierro • Canary Is. ... 83 H6
Higashi-matsuyama • Japan ... 127 H8
Higashi-suido • Japan ... 127 A8
High Coast • Sweden ... 98 B3
High Coast **Heritage N** • Sweden ... 41 [53]
High I. Reservoir • Hong Kong, China ... 126 F5
High Island • TX, United States ... 155 F5
High Plains • OK/TX, United States ... 149 F3
High Point • NC, United States ... 151 D3
High Rock • Bahamas ... 164 B1
High Street • United Kingdom ... 65 D3
High Willhays • United Kingdom ... 65 I10
High Wycombe • United Kingdom ... 63 E9
Highgate • Jamaica ... 165 D3
Highland Park • Ko Samui, Thailand ... 130 G12
Highlands Forest Reserve • Penang, Malaysia ... 129 D7
Highlands Hammock State Recreation Area • FL, United States ... 155 C2
Highlands, The • Antigua & Barbuda ... 167 H
Higüero, Punta • Puerto Rico ... 165 I7
Higüey • Dominican Rep. ... 165 H6
Hiiumaa • Estonia ... 100 J6
Hikkaduwa • Sri Lanka ... 124 C4
Hiko • NV, United States ... 148 C3
Hikutavake • Niue ... 139 O
Hilden • Germany ... 73 C6
Hildesheim • Germany ... 72 C2
Hildesheim **Heritage C** • Germany ... 44 [53]
Hilisimaetano • Indonesia ... 131 M10
Hill End • NS, Australia ... 136 H8
Hillaby, Mt • Barbados ... 167 M
Hillegom • Netherlands ... 70 G7
Hillerød • Denmark ... 99 F7
Hillsboro • TX, United States ... 155 E4
Hillsborough • Grenada ... 167 P
Hillsborough • United Kingdom ... 62 H12
Hilvarenbeek • Netherlands ... 70 C3
Hilversum • Netherlands ... 70 H7
Himachal Pradesh • India ... 123 A1
Himalaya • Asia ... 122 C3
Himeji • Japan ... 127 F7
Himeji **Heritage C** • Japan ... 43 [194]
Himeville Nature Reserve • South Africa ... 111 B4
Himmafushi • Maldives ... 124 H7
Himmerland • Denmark ... 99 F6
Himos • Finland ... 99 D3
Hims • Syria ... 120 D7
Hin Khom, Laem • Ko Samui, Thailand ... 130 G12
Hinche • Haiti ... 165 F5
Hinchinbrook I. • QL, Australia ... 136 C3
Hindelang • Germany ... 74 F8
Hindsholm • Denmark ... 99 F7
Hindu Kush • Afghanistan/Pakistan ... 121 F4
Hindupur • India ... 124 B2
Hinesville • GA, United States ... 151 D4
Hinlad Falls • Ko Samui, Thailand ... 130 G11
Hinnøya • Norway ... 97 D2
Hinterglemm • Austria ... 91 O7
Hintertux • Austria ... 91 O8
Hinton • AL, Canada ... 160 J6
Hios • Chios, Greece ... 94 D
Hios [I.] • Greece ... 93 E2
Hippos • Israel ... 120 B2
Hirakata • Japan ... 127 G6
Hirakud Reservoir • India ... 122 C3
Hiratsuka • Japan ... 127 H9
Hirebhasgar Reservoir • India ... 124 B2
Hirosaki • Japan ... 127 D2
Hiroshima • Japan ... 127 B4
Hiroshima **Heritage C** • Japan ... 43 [193]
Hirschegg **Ski** • Austria ... 61 [88]
Hirson • France ... 76 F2
Hîrsova • Romania ... 92 I7
Hirtshals • Denmark ... 99 F6
Hisar • India ... 123 E7
Hispaniola • West Indies ... 165 E-H
Hitra • Romania ... 92 I7
Hitachi • Japan ... 127 D3
Hitchin • United Kingdom ... 63 E9
Hitra • Norway ... 97 B3
Hiva Oa • French Polynesia ... 139 J
Hjallerup • Denmark ... 99 F6
Hjälmaren • Sweden ... 99 A2
Hjelmeland • Norway ... 98 F9
Hjo • Sweden ... 99 G5
Hjørring • Denmark ... 99 F6
Hkakabo Razi • Myanmar ... 128 B1
Hlane Royal Nat. Park **Park** • Swaziland ... 112 [143]
Hlemoútsi • Greece ... 94 J
Hluboká • Czech Rep. ... 89 E7
Hluhluwe-Umfolozi Game Reserve • South Africa ... 111 C4
Hluhluwe-Umfolozi Game Reserve **Park** • South Africa ... 112 [140]
Hlybokaye • Belarus ... 100 D3
Ho Chi Minh City • Vietnam ... 129 B5
Hoa Da • Vietnam ... 129 B5
Hobart • TS, Australia ... 136 F7
Hobbs • NM, United States ... 149 E4
Hobe Sound • FL, United States ... 155 D2
Hobro • Denmark ... 99 F6
Hoch Harz, Nationalpark **Park N** • Germany ... 58 [69]
Hochberg • Switzerland ... 90 K5
Hochfeiler • Austria/Italy ... 86 C3

Hochgurgl **Ski** • Austria ... 61 [93]
Hochgurgl • Austria ... 91 N8
Höchneukirch • Germany ... 73 C6
Hochob • Mexico ... 169 F5
Hockenheim • Germany ... 91 N8
Hockenheim • Germany ... 74 N8
Hodeida • Yemen ... 120 E11
Hoedspruit • South Africa ... 110 C3
Hoek van Holland • Netherlands ... 70 G8
Hoekse Waard • Netherlands ... 70 G8
Hof • Germany ... 72 D3
Höfn • Iceland ... 97 I6
Hofsjökull • Iceland ... 97 16
Hög • Norway ... 127 B4
Hog I. • Grenada ... 166 Q
Höganäs • Sweden ... 99 G6
Högby • Sweden ... 99 H6
Höglwörth • Germany ... 74 H8
Högsby • Sweden ... 99 H6
Hogneker • Norway ... 98 F9
Hohe Acht • Germany ... 74 C5
Hohe Tauern, Nationalpark **Park N** • Austria ... 58 [89]
Hohe Tauern, Nationalpark • Austria ... 91 P8
Hohe Wilde • Austria/Italy ... 86 C3
Hohen Neuendorf • Germany ... 73 E7
Hohen-Limburg (Hagen) • Germany ... 73 D5
Hohenschwangau • Germany ... 74 F8
Hohentwiel • Germany ... 74 B4
Hohenzollern, Schloss • Germany ... 74 B3
Hohhot • China ... 125 F2
Hohneck, Burg • Germany ... 74 H6
Hohokam Pima Nat. Mon. **Park N** • AZ, United States ... 152 [109]
Hoi An **Heritage C** • Vietnam ... 43 [200]
Højer • Denmark ... 99 E8
Hokksås • Sweden ... 99 G5
Hokitika • New Zealand ... 137 B3
Hokkaido • Japan ... 127 D2
Hokksund • Norway ... 98 D5
Hol • Norway ... 98 G8
Holasovice • Czech Rep. ... 89 E7
Holasovice **Heritage C** • Czech Rep. ... 44 [191]
Holbæk • Denmark ... 99 F7
Holbox, I. • Mexico ... 169 G4
Holbrooks • AZ, United States ... 155 G7
Holden • AL, Canada ... 158 E3
Holden • UT, United States ... 148 D3
Holen • Norway ... 98 E6
Holetown • Barbados ... 167 M
Holguín • Cuba ... 164 H5
Holiday Mtn • NY, United States ... 156 B2
Holiday Park • Germany ... 74 B2
Holiday Valley **Ski** • NY, United States ... 146 [96]
Holiday Valley • NY, United States ... 156 A1
Holiday-Park **Park L** • Germany ... 59 [56]
Hollabrunn • Austria ... 91 H1
Holland • MI, United States ... 150 C2
Holland • United Kingdom ... 64 B5
Hollandse IJssel • Netherlands ... 70 H8
Hollant Beach • Goa, India ... 123 C6
Hollei • Norway ... 98 D5
Hollíkó **Heritage C** • Hungary ... 44 [204]
Hollywood • CA, United States ... 154 J9
Hollywood • FL, United States ... 155 D3
Holman • NT, Canada ... 158 E1
Holmestrand • Norway ... 98 D6
Holmsland Klit • Denmark ... 99 E7
Holmsund • Sweden ... 97 E3
Hölö • Sweden ... 99 B2
Holsnøy • Norway ... 98 F8
Holstebro • Denmark ... 99 E7
Holsworthy • United Kingdom ... 65 J9
Holt • United Kingdom ... 65 G8
Holwerd • Netherlands ... 70 C1
Holy I. • England, United Kingdom ... 62 E5
Holy I. **Beach** • United Kingdom ... 64 [69]
Holy I. • Wales, United Kingdom ... 63 C7
Holy Land Experience • FL, United States ... 157 B1
Holy Valley **Heritage C** • Lebanon ... 44 [305]
Holyhead • United Kingdom ... 63 C7
Holzgau • Austria ... 91 N7
Holzkirchen • Germany ... 74 G7
Homa Bay • Kenya ... 109 C5
Homberg (Duisburg) • Germany ... 73 C5
Home Hill • QL, Australia ... 136 C3
Home of Franklin Delano Roosevelt Nat. Hist. Site **Park N** • NY, United States ... 153 [277]
Homer • AK, United States ... 157 E4
Homestead • FL, United States ... 155 D3
Homestead Nat. Mon. of America **Park N** • NE, United States ... 153 [164]
Homewood • AL, United States ... 151 C4
Homosassa Springs State Wildlife Park • FL, United States ... 155 C2
Homs • Syria ... 120 D7
Homyel' • Belarus ... 100 D3
Hon Chong • Vietnam ... 129 B6
Hon Quan • Vietnam ... 129 B5
Honakaa • HI, United States ... 157 J6
Honavar • India ... 124 A2
Hondo • Belize/Mexico ... 169 F5
HONDURAS • C. America ... 170 D3
Honduras, Gulf of • C. America ... 170 K9
Hanefoss • Norway ... 98 D5
Honey Lake Resort • China ... 126 E4
Hong Kong • Hong Kong, China ... 126 F5
HONG KONG SPECIAL ADMIN. REGION • China ... 126 E-F
Hong, Song • Vietnam ... 129 A1
Hongcun **Heritage C** • China ... 43 [184]
Hongqiao [Apt] • China ... 126 H6
Honguedo, Détroit d' • QU, Canada ... 160 B1
Honiara • Solomon Is. ... 138 W
Honister Pass • United Kingdom ... 65 D3
Honiton • United Kingdom ... 65 J9
Honkajoki • Finland ... 99 C3
Honolulu • HI, United States ... 157 H6
Honshu • Japan ... 127 C3
Hood, I. • Galápagos Is. ... 171 H10
Hood, Mt • OR, United States ... 154 G6
Hoofddorp • Netherlands ... 70 G7
Hoogeveen • Netherlands ... 70 D2
Hoogezand • Netherlands ... 70 D1
Hoogvliet • Netherlands ... 70 G8
Hook I. • QL, Australia ... 136 C3
Hook of Holland • Netherlands ... 70 G8
Hoopa Valley **Ind Res** • CA, United States ... 155 [6]
Hoopers Bay • AK, United States ... 157 D3
Höör • Sweden ... 99 G7
Hoorn • Netherlands ... 70 G7
Hoorn Is. • Wallis & Futuna ... 139 U
Hoover Dam • AZ/NV, United States ... 155 G7
Hopa • Turkey ... 95 D1
Hope • BC, Canada ... 160 I7
Hope Bay • Jamaica ... 165 D3
Hope I. • Jamaica ... 165 G3
Hope, Point • AK, United States ... 157 D2
Hope Town • Bahamas ... 164 B1
Hopetoun House • United Kingdom ... 65 B1
Hopewell Culture Nat. Hist. Park **Park N** • OH, United States ... 153 [182]
Hopewell Furnace Nat. Hist. Site **Park N** • PA, United States ... 156 B2
Hopfgarten im Brixental **Ski** • Austria ... 61 [99]
Hopi **Ind Res** • AZ, United States ... 155 [32]
Hopi Indian Reservation • AZ, United States ... 155 G7
Hopkins [Apt] • OH, United States ... 161 A3
Hopkins, Lake • WA, Australia ... 136 A2
Hopkinsville • KY, United States ... 151 C3

Hóra • Sámos, Greece .... 94 E
Horain • Turkey 95 G8
Horbat Ashdod Yam • Israel 120 A3
Hörby • Sweden 99 G7
Hordaland • Norway 98 F8
Horezu Heritage C • Romania .... 44 [218]
Horlivka • Ukraine 100 E4
Hormiguero • Mexico 169 F5
Hormigueros • Puerto Rico 165 I8
Hormuz, Strait of • Iran/Oman 120 H8
Horn, Cape • Chile 175 B5
Horn of Africa • Africa 104 G4
Hornberg, Burg • Germany 74 B2
Hornell • NY, United States 150 A1
Hornindalsvatn • Norway 98 F7
Hornisgrinde • Germany 74 B3
Hornos, Cabo de • Chile 175 B5
Horovice • Czech Rep. 89 D6
Horred • Sweden 99 G6
Horse Is. • NF, Canada 160 C1
Horse Shoe Reef • Antigua & Barbuda .... 167 I
Horseley Hills • India 124 C2
Horseley Hills Hill Sta • India 124 E6
Horsens • Denmark 99 E7
Horseshoe Bay • Bermuda 165 K10
Horseshoe Bend Nat. Military Park
   Park N • AL, United States .... 153 [201]
Horseshoe Falls • OT, Canada 161 D1
Horseshoe Reef • British Virgin Is. .... 166 A
Horsham • United Kingdom 65 G8
Horten, VI, Australia 135 G7
Horst, Schloss • Germany 73 D5
Horta • Azores 84 B4
Hortas do Tabual • Portugal 84 H8
Horten • Norway 98 E6
Hortobágyi Nat. Park Park N •
   Hungary .... 58 [115]
Hortobágyi National Park Heritage C •
   Hungary .... 44 [203]
Horyu-ji • Japan 127 G7
Horyu-ji Heritage C • Japan .... 43 [195]
Hospet • India 124 B1
Hospitalet Près-l'Andorre, l' •
   France 82 F5
Hossegor • France 78 E6
Hossios Luckas Heritage C • Greece .... 44 [243]
Hóssmo • Sweden 99 H6
Hoste, I. • Chile 175 B5
Hot • Thailand 130 B6
Hot Springs • AR, United States 151 B4
Hot Springs • SD, United States 148 F2
Hot Springs Nat. Park Park N •
   AR, United States .... 153 [188]
Hotan • China 125 B3
Hoting • Sweden 97 D3
Hotte, Massif de la • Haiti 165 E6
Hottentots Holland Nature Reserve •
   South Africa 111 D7
Hotton • Belgium 70 C4
Hotuiti, Caleta • Easter I. .... 139 M
Houaïlou • New Caledonia .... 138 U
Houdan • France 78 A2
Hougang • Singapore 129 I11
Houghton • MI, United States 161 A1
Houghton-le-Spring • United Kingdom 62 E6
Houlton • ME, United States 150 G1
Houma • China 125 F3
Houma • LA, United States 156 F6
Houma • Tonga .... 139 P
Houma Toloa • Tonga .... 139 P
Houmt-Souk • Tunisia 107 D5
Houmt-Souq • Tunisia 107 D5
Houssaye, Cap la • Réunion 113 C3
Houston • BC, Canada 160 I6
Houston • TX, United States 155 F5
Hov • Denmark 99 F7
Høvd • Mongolia 125 D2
Hovdehytta • Norway 98 G9
Hove • United Kingdom 65 G8
Hovenweep Nat. Mon. Park N •
   CO/UT, United States .... 152 [85]
Hovgården Heritage C • Sweden .... 44 [7]
Hövsgöl Nuur • Mongolia 125 E1
Howe, Cape • NS/VI, Australia 136 H9
Howe Caverns • NY, United States 156 C1
Howick • South Africa 111 B4
Howland I. • Pacific Ocean 138 CC3
Howletts Park • United Kingdom 65 H8
Howth • Ireland 69 F6
Höxter • Germany 72 C3
Hoy • United Kingdom 62 D2
Høyanger • Norway 98 F8
Hoyerswerda • Germany 72 F3
Hozu-gawa • Japan 127 G6
Hpakant • Myanmar 128 B1
Hradec Králové • Czech Rep. 89 E6
Hranice • Czech Rep. 89 B4
Hrebinka • Ukraine 100 D3
Hrissi • Greece 93 J6
Hristan • Greece 94 CC4
Hristoú Dásous • Páros, Greece .... 94 H
Hsipaw • Myanmar 128 B2
Hua Hin • Thailand 130 D8
Hua Shan • China .... 126 [4]
Huacho • Peru 173 B4
Huahine • French Polynesia 139 DD4
Huailai • China 125 E4
Huainan • China 125 F3
Huaiyin • China 125 F3
Huajuápan de León • Mexico 169 J8
Hualapai Ind Res •
   AZ, United States .... 155 [26]
Hualapai Indian Reservation •
   AZ, United States 155 G7
Hualien • Taiwan 125 G4
Huallaga • Peru 173 B3
Huambo • Angola 110 A2
Huancapi • Peru 173 E6
Huancavelica • Peru 173 E6
Huancayo • Peru 173 E6
Huang He • China 125 E3
Huang Shan • China 126 E3
Huang Shan Heritage N • China .... 41 [134]
Huang Shan Heritage C • China .... 44 [108]
Huanglong Heritage N • China .... 41 [130]
Huangpu • China 126 G7
Huangshan • China 126 G7
Huangshi • China 125 F3
Huangtian [Apt] • China 126 E4
Huanta • Peru 173 E6
Huanuco • Peru 173 B4
Huapá • Peru 173 E6
Huaráz • Peru 173 B3
Huarmey • Peru 173 B4
Huascarán • Peru 173 B3
Huascarán, Parque Nac. • Peru 173 B3
Huascarán, Parque Nac. de Heritage C •
   Peru .... 40 [37]
Huatabampo • Mexico 168 I6
Huatulco • Mexico 169 K8
Huauchinango • Mexico 169 J7
Hubbell Trading Post Nat. Hist. Site •
   AZ, United States 155 H7
Hubbell Trading Post Nat. Hist. Site Park N •
   AZ, United States .... 152 [102]
Hubei • China 126 C2
Hubli • India 124 B1
Hückeswagen • Germany 73 D6
Huddersfield • United Kingdom 63 E7
Huddinge • Sweden 99 B2
Hudiksvall • Sweden 99 D2
Hudhwali [I.] • Maldives 124 H8
Hudiksvall • Sweden 97 D3
Hudson • NY, United States 156 C1
Hudson Bay • SA, Canada 158 F3
Hudson Bay [Bay] • Canada 159 H3
Hudson [Riv] • NY, United States 156 C1
Hudson Strait • NU/QU, Canada 159 I2
Hue • Vietnam 130 D5
Hue Heritage C • Vietnam .... 43 [199]
Huehuetenango • Guatemala 170 J9
Huejutla • Mexico 169 J7
Huelgoat • France 77 C3
Huelva • Spain 82 H7

Huercal-Overa • Spain 82 K7
Huesca • Spain 80 E2
Huéscar • Spain 82 K7
Huftarøy • Norway 98 F8
Hügel, Villa • Germany 73 C5
Hugh Town • United Kingdom 63 B11
Hughenden • QL, Australia 135 G4
Hugo • OK, United States 155 F4
Huiarau Range • New Zealand 137 E5
Huicheong • China 126 E6
Huila • Colombia 173 B2
Humangullo • Mexico 168 F4
Huiñamarca, Lago de • Bolivia/Peru 173 F7
Huittinen • Finland 99 D3
Huixtla • Mexico 168 F4
Huizen • Netherlands 70 H7
Huka Falls • New Zealand 137 E5
Hula Valley • Israel 120 B1
Huliba Cave • Aruba .... 166 W
Hull • QU, Canada 160 G4
Hultsfred • Sweden 99 H6
Huludao • China 125 G2
Hulun Nur • China 125 F2
Humacao • Puerto Rico 165 J8
Humaitá • Brazil 173 C3
Humber • United Kingdom 63 E7
Humberside [Apt] • United Kingdom 66 C4
Humboldt • NV, United States 154 J7
Hume, Lake • NS, Australia 136 E9
Humen • China 126 F3
Humphreys Peak • AZ, United States ... 155 G7
Humppila • Finland 99 D4
Húnaflói • Iceland 97 H6
Hunan • China 126 C2
Hundested • Denmark 99 F7
Hunedoara • Romania 92 B2
HUNGARY • Europe 92 G5
Hunneberg • Sweden 99 G5
Hunnebostrand • Sweden 99 F5
Hunsrück • Germany 74 C6
Hunstanton • United Kingdom 63 F8
Hunter • NS, Australia 136 H8
Hunter I. • TS, Australia 136 E6
Hunter Is. • TS, Australia 136 E6
Hunter Mtn Ski • NY, United States .... 146 [101]
Hunter Mtn • NY, United States 156 C1
Hunter Mtns • New Zealand 137 F8
Huntingdon • IN, United States 150 C2
Huntingdon • NY, United States 156 C2
Huntingdon • PA, United States 156 A2
Huntingdon • United Kingdom 63 E8
Huntington • WV, United States 150 D3
Huntington Beach •
   CA, United States 154 J9
Huntingdonshire • United Kingdom 64 B5
Huntly • New Zealand 137 D5
Huntly • United Kingdom 62 D3
Huntsville • AL, United States 151 C4
Huntsville • OT, Canada 160 E4
Huntsville • TX, United States 155 F5
Hünxe • Germany 73 C5
Huonville • TS, Australia 136 F7
Hura • Maldives 124 H7
Hurdalsjøen • Norway 98 E5
Hurghada • Egypt 109 B2
Huron • SD, United States 148 G2
Huron, Lake • Canada/United States ... 161 C2
Huskvarna • Sweden 99 G6
Husum • Germany 72 C1
Hutanopan • Indonesia 131 N10
Hutchinson • KS, United States 148 G3
Hutchinson • South Africa 111 F6
Huy • Belgium 70 C4
Huzhou • China 126 G7
Hvaler • Norway 98 E6
Hvannadalshnúkur • Iceland 97 I6
Hvar • Croatia 92 G6
Hvar [I.] • Croatia 92 G6
Hvidbjerg • Denmark 99 E6
Hvitsten • Norway 98 E5
Hvittingfoss • Norway 98 E5
Hwange • Zimbabwe 110 B2
Hwange Nat. Park Park • Zimbabwe .. 112 [115]
Hwasun Heritage C • Rep. of Korea .... 43 [191]
Hyannis • MA, United States 156 D2
Hycklinge • Sweden 99 H5
Hyde • United Kingdom 63 D7
Hyde Park • NY, United States 156 C2
Hyderabad • India 124 C1
Hyderabad • Pakistan 122 A3
Hydra • Greece 93 C3
Hyères • France 78 G8
Hyères, Is. d' • France 78 G8
Hyères-Plage • France 78 G8
Hyesan • D.P.R. of Korea 125 G2
Hylestad • Norway 98 G9
Hyltebruk • Sweden 99 G6
Hyogo • Japan 127 F6
Hythe • United Kingdom 65 H8
Hyvinkää • Finland 99 D4

I

I Naftan, Puntan • N. Mariana Is. .... 138 B
I te Lape, Te Ava • Tuvalu .... 139 R
Ialisos • Rhodes, Greece .... 94 F
Iao Valley State Mon. •
   HI, United States 157 I5
Iar-Chonnacht • Ireland 69 H9
Iasi • Romania 92 D2
Ibadan • Nigeria 106 C4
Ibagué • Colombia 173 B2
Ibaraki • Japan 127 G6
Ibaraki [Adm] • Japan 127 I8
Ibarra • Ecuador 173 B2
Ibb • Yemen 120 E11
Iberia • 80
Iberian Peninsula • Portugal/Spain 48 C3
Ibérico, Sistema • Spain 80 E3
Iberville, Mt d' • NF/QU, Canada 159 J3
Ibiza • Ibiza, Spain 83 M9
Ibiza Heritage N • Spain .... 41 [63]
Ibiza Heritage C • Spain .... 44 [99]
Ibiza [I.] • Spain .... 83 L-M
Ibri • Oman 120 H9
Içá • Brazil 173 C3
Içana • Brazil 173 C3
Icacos Point • Trinidad & Tobago .... 166 S
Içel • Turkey 95 J10
Içel [Adm] • Turkey 95 I10
ICELAND • Atlantic Ocean .... 97 H-I
Içericumra • Turkey 95 I9
Ichalkaranji • India 124 B1
Ichihara • Japan 127 I8
Ichikawa • Japan 127 I8
Ichkeul Nat. Park • Tunisia 107 D4
Ichkoul Nat. Park Heritage N •
   Tunisia .... 41 [88]
Ichpatun • Mexico 169 F5
Icmeler • Turkey .... 94 C
Ico de los Vinos •
   Tenerife, Canary Is. 82 G5
Idaho • United States 148 D2
Idaho City • ID, United States 154 H6
Idaho Falls • ID, United States 148 D2
Idar-Oberstein • Germany 74 C6
Idéon Antron • Crete, Greece 93 H6
Idhra [I.] • Greece 93 H6
Idi Oros • Crete, Greece 93 H6
Idlib • Syria 120 D6
Idlib • Syria 95 J10
Idra • Greece 93 C3
Idre • Sweden 97 C3
Idris, Cadair • United Kingdom 63 D8
Ie-jima • Okinawa, Japan .... 138 A
Iejper • Belgium 70 A4
Ierápetra • Crete, Greece 93 J6
Ierissós • Greece .... 94 B
Ieshima-shoto • Japan 127 F6
Ifach, Peñon de • Spain 83 L7

Ifakara • Tanzania 110 H8
Ifrane • Morocco 107 B1
Iglesias • Sardinia, Italy 91 N8
Igls • Austria 91 N8
Ignace • OT, Canada 159 G4
Ignalina Nat. Park Park N •
   Lithuania .... 58 [152]
Igoumenitsa • Greece 93 B2
Igra • Russian Fed. 100 H2
Igtham Mote • United Kingdom 65 G8
Iguaçu, Parque Nac. do • Brazil 175 C2
Iguaçu, Parque Nac. do Heritage N •
   Brazil .... 40 [48]
Iguala • Mexico 169 J7
Igualada • Spain 83 C4
Iguazú, Parque Nac. de • Argentina 175 C2
Iguazú, Parque Nac. de Heritage N •
   Argentina .... 40 [49]
Iguidi, Erg • Algeria/Mauritania 106 B2
Ihavandiffulu Atoll • Maldives 124 G7
Ihlara • Turkey 95 I9
Ihuru • Maldives 124 H7
Iisalmi • Finland 97 F3
IJ-meer • Netherlands 70 H7
IJmuiden • Netherlands 65 G8
IJssel • Netherlands 70 D2
IJsselmeer • Netherlands 70 C2
Ijuw • Nauru .... 138 X
IJzendijke • Netherlands 70 B4
Ikaalinen • Finland 99 D3
Ikaria • Greece 93 E3
Ikast • Denmark 99 E7
Ikeda • Japan 127 G6
Ipatinga • Brazil 174 F7
Ikhtiman • Bulgaria 92 C3
Ikil • Mexico 169 F4
Ikoli • Dem. Rep. of Congo 108 B5
Il'men', Ozero • Russian Fed. 100 L9
Ilagan • Philippines 128 G3
Ilanz • Switzerland 90 K5
Ilawa • Poland 89 B2
Ile • Kazakstan 121 G2
Ilebo • Dem. Rep. of Congo 108 B5
Ilfracombe • United Kingdom 65 J9
Ilhabela • Brazil 174 C4
Ilhéus • Brazil 174 C4
Iliamna Lake • AK, United States 157 D4
Iligan • Philippines 128 G4
Iráklio • Crete, Greece 93 I6
Ille-et-Vilaine • France 77 D3
Iller • Germany 74 E7
Illertissen • Germany 74 E7
Illescas • Majorca, Spain 83 N12
Illichivs'k • Ukraine 100 D4
Illinois [Adm] • United States 151 B4
Illinois [Riv] • IL, United States 150 B2
Ilo • Peru 173 F7
Iloilo • Philippines 128 G4
Ilorin • Nigeria 106 C4
Ilovya • Russian Fed. 100 F4
Imatra • Finland 97 F3
Imbert • Dominican Rep. 165 G5
Immenstadt • Germany 74 F8
Imogiri • Java, Indonesia 131 Q12
Imola • Italy 87 C2
Imotski • Croatia 92 G6
Imperatriz • Brazil 174 B3
Impéria • Italy 87 A3
Imphal • India 128 A2
Imrali Adasi • Turkey 95 F4
Imroz • Turkey 95 E4
İmst • Austria 91 N8
İmuris • Mexico 168 I5
In Amenas • Algeria 106 C2
In Salah • Algeria 106 C2
Inambari • Peru 173 F6
Inarajan • Guam .... 138 Z
Inarijärvi • Finland 97 F2
Inatori Spa • Japan 127 H9
Inca • Majorca, Spain 83 N11
Ince Burun • Turkey 95 B1
Inchinnan • Turkey 95 F4
Incekum Burun • Turkey 95 I10
Incheon • Rep. of Korea 125 G3
Incir Han • Turkey 95 G7
Indefatigable I. • Galápagos Is. 171 H10
Independence • CA, United States 154 L8
Independence • MO, United States 150 B3
Independence Nat. Hist. Park Park N •
   PA, United States .... 153 [269]
Independencia, I. • Peru 173 E6
INDIA • Asia 122 B3
Indian Ocean • 9 N6
Indian Springs • NV, United States 148 C3
Indian Town Point •
   Antigua & Barbuda .... 167 I
Indiana • PA, United States 156 A2
Indianola • MS, United States 156 F5
Indija • Serbia & Montenegro 92 C2
Indio • CA, United States 149 C4
Indira Gandhi [Apt] • India 123 E7
Indira Gandhi Nahar • India 123 D7
Indira Gandhi Wildlife Sanctury •
   India 124 B3
Indonesia • Asia 131
INDONESIA • Asia 122 B3
Indramayu • Java, Indonesia 131 P11
Indre • France 77 E6
Indre [Adm] • France 77 F6
Indre [Riv] • France 77 F5
Indre-et-Loire • France 77 F5
Indurawe • Sri Lanka 124 C4
Indus • Asia 122 A3
Indus, Mouths of the • Pakistan 122 A3
Inegöl • Turkey 95 F4
Ineu • Romania 92 C2
Infangan [Apt] • Morocco 107 A3
Infanta, Cape • South Africa 111 E7
Infantado • Portugal 84 G6
Infiernillo, Presa del • Mexico 169 I7
Ingenio • Gran Canaria, Canary Is. 82 G6
Ingenio, Valley de los Heritage C •
   Cuba .... 42 [41]
Ingham • QL, Australia 136 C3
Inglewood • New Zealand 137 D6
Inglewood • QL, Australia 136 D5
Ingolstadt • Germany 72 D4
Ingushetia Russ Adm • Russian Fed. ... 101 [5]
Inhambane • Mozambique 110 C3
Inis • Ireland 69 H10
Inishbofin • Ireland 69 H8
Inishcrone • Ireland 69 H8
Inishkea North Is. Park N •
   MI, United States 161 A1
Inishkea South • Ireland 69 G8
Inishmaan • Ireland 69 G9
Inishmore • Ireland 69 G9
Inishmurray • Ireland 69 H8
Inishowen Peninsula • Ireland 69 C1
Inishturk • Ireland 69 G8
Inland Sea • Malta 96 A1
Inn • Europe 90 F2
Innaanganeq • Greenland 142 F1
Innamincka • Australia 135 H5
Inner Hebrides • United Kingdom 62 I5
Inner Mongolia • China 125 F2
Innfield • Ireland 69 F6
Innichen • Italy 91 N8
Innisfail • QL, Australia 136 C3
Innsbruck • Austria 91 N8
Innvikfjorden • Norway 98 F8
Inonú • Greece .... 94 D
Inowroclaw • Poland 89 B2

Insein • Myanmar 128 B3
Insurgente J.M. Morelos y Pavón,
   Parque Nac. • Mexico 169 I7
Insuyu • Turkey 95 G7
Inta • Russian Fed. 101 F3
Intepe • Turkey 95 E4
Inveraray • United Kingdom 62 C3
Intercourse • PA, United States 156 B3
Interlaken Ski • Switzerland .... 61 [71]
Interlaken • Switzerland 90 J5
Internacional de las Americas [Apt] •
   Dominican Rep. 165 H6
International Drive •
   FL, United States 157 B1
International Falls •
   MN, United States 150 B1
Intracoastal Waterway •
   United States 156 F6
Inukjuak • QU, Canada 159 I3
Inuvik • YT, Canada 158 C2
Invercargill • New Zealand 137 G8
Invergordon • United Kingdom 62 C3
Inverness • NS, Canada 160 B2
Inverness • United Kingdom 62 C3
Inverness-shire • United Kingdom 64 A2
Inza • Russian Fed. 100 G3
Ioánina • Greece 93 B2
Ioánina [Adm] • Greece 93 B2
Ion Corvin • Romania 92 I7
Iona • United Kingdom 62 B4
Ionian Is. • Greece 93 B2
Ionian Sea • Mediterranean Sea 48 E4
Ios • Greece 93 D3
Iowa • United States 150 B2
Iowa City • IA, United States 150 B2
Ipanema • Brazil 174 F7
Ipatinga • Brazil 174 C4
Ipek • Fed. Rep. of Yugoslavia 92 B3
Ipil • Slovak Rep. 89 B4
Ipiros • Greece 94 AA2
Ipoh • Malaysia 129 F9
Ipsos • Corfu, Greece .... 94 A
Ipswich • Jamaica 165 C3
Ipswich • QL, Australia 136 D5
Ipswich • United Kingdom 63 F8
Iqaluit • NU, Canada 159 J2
Iquique • Chile 173 F7
Iquitos • Peru 173 B3
Iráklia • Greece .... 94 H
Iráklio • Crete, Greece 93 I6
Iráklio [Adm] • Crete, Greece 93 I6
IRAN • Asia 120 G7
Iranian Plateau • Iran 120 H7
Iranshahr • Iran 120 I8
Irapuato • Mexico 169 I7
IRAQ • Asia 120 E7
Irbid • Jordan 120 C6
Irbil • Iraq 120 E6
IRELAND • Europe 69
Ireland I. North • Bermuda 165 K9
Ireland I. South • Bermuda 165 K10
Iringa • Tanzania 110 H8
Iriona • Honduras 165 E6
Iriri • Brazil 174 A3
Irkutsk • Russian Fed. 101 K4
Iro-zaki • Japan 127 H9
Iron Mtn • MI, United States 150 C1
Ironbridge • United Kingdom 65 E5
Ironbridge Gorge Heritage C •
   United Kingdom .... 44 [26]
Irondequoit • NY, United States 156 B1
Ironton • OH, United States 150 D3
Ironwood • MI, United States 150 B1
Irouléguy • France 76 K9
Irrawaddy • Myanmar 128 B1
Irrawaddy, Mouths of the • Myanmar .. 128 A3
Irrsdorf • Austria 91 P7
Irtysh • Russian Fed. 101 H4
Irtyshsk • Kazakstan 121 G1
Iruma • Japan 127 H8
Irún • France 78 I9
Irvine • CA, United States 149 C4
Irvine • United Kingdom 62 C5
Isa, Ra's • Yemen 109 E11
Isabel de Torres, Pico •
   Dominican Rep. 165 G5
Isabela • Puerto Rico 165 G5
Isabela, Cabo • Dominican Rep. 165 G5
Isabela • la Sagua • Cuba 164 F4
Isabela, I. • Galápagos Is. 171 G10
Isabela, Cordillera • Nicaragua 170 E4
Isafjörthur • Iceland 97 H5
Isandlwana • South Africa 111 B4
Isar • Germany 72 E4
Isarco • Italy 86 C3
Isarkanal • Germany 74 G7
Ischgl Ski • Austria .... 61 [91]
Ischia • Italy 91 N8
Ischia • TN, United States 151 C3
Ischia Hole Ski •
   WY, United States .... 146 [44]
Ischia, I. d' • Italy 87 G7
Ischigualasto Natural Park Heritage C •
   Argentina .... 40 [50]
Ise • Japan 127 C4
Ise-wan • Japan 127 C4
Isel • Austria 86 D3
Iseltwald • Austria 91 N8
Iseo, Lago d' • Italy 87 B1
Isère • France 78 C4
Isère [Adm] • France 78 C4
Iserlohn • Germany 73 D5
Isernia • Italy 85 E4
Isfahan • Iran 120 G7
Isfahan Heritage C • Iran .... 43 [134]
Isfjorden • Norway 98 G7
Ishikawa • Okinawa, Japan .... 138 A
Ishim • Russian Fed. 101 G3
Ishinomaki • Japan 127 D4
Isinlón • Kenya 109 D4
Isipingo • South Africa 111 B5
Isiro • Dem. Rep. of Congo 108 B4
Iskandar • Turkey 95 J10
Iskenderun • Turkey 95 J10
Iskenderun Körfezi • Turkey 95 J10
Iskur • Bulgaria 92 C3
Isla Cristina • Spain 82 H7
Isla del Coco, Parque Nac. Heritage N •
   Costa Rica .... 40 [25]
Isla Magica, Parque Park L • Spain ..... 59 [74]
Islamabad • Pakistan 122 A2
Islahiye • Turkey 95 J10
Islamorada • FL, United States 155 D3
Island Harbour • Anguilla .... 166 B
Islands, Bay of • NF, Canada 160 C1
Islands of Adventure Park L •
   FL, United States .... 157 [24]
Islay • United Kingdom 62 B5
Islaz • Romania 92 H6
Isle • France 78 E5
Isle Royale Nat. Park •
   MI, United States 161 A1
Isle Royale Nat. Park Park N •
   MI, United States .... 153 [156]
Isles Lagoon, The • Kiribati .... 139 I
Isleta Ind Res • NM, United States ... 155 [39]
Islote de Hilario •
   Lanzarote, Canary Is. 83 I5
Ismâ'îlîya • Egypt 109 B1
Isna • Egypt 109 B2
Isny • Germany 131 B4
Isoka • Zambia 110 G8
Isola 2000 • France 78 I7
Isonzo • Italy 87 D1
Isparta • Turkey 95 H7
Isparta [Adm] • Turkey 95 H7
Isparta [Riv] • Turkey 95 H7
Ispica, Cava d' • Sicily, Italy 86 H8
ISRAEL • Asia 120 C7
Issia • Eritrea 109 E10
Issoire • France 76 K4
Issosire • France 76 E5
Issum • Germany 73 C5
Ist • Croatia 92 F6

Istanbul • Turkey 95 F3
Istanbul Heritage C • Turkey .... 44 [250]
Istanbul [Adm] • Turkey 95 F3
Istanbul Bozagi • Turkey 95 F3
Istra • Croatia 92 F5
Itabapoana • Brazil 174 F6
Itaberaba • Brazil 174 B4
Itabira • Brazil 174 C4
Itabuna • Brazil 174 C4
Itaituba • Brazil 174 A3
Itajaí • Brazil 174 E7
Itala Nature Reserve • South Africa 111 C3
Italian Lake District • Italy 86 A1
ITALY • Europe 85
Itami [Apt] • Japan 127 G6
Itanagar • India 122 D3
Itanós • Crete, Greece 93 J6
Itaperuna • Brazil 174 F6
Itatiaia • Brazil 174 E7
Itchan Kala Heritage C • Uzbekistan 43 [140]
Itéa • Greece 93 C2
Ithaca • Greece .... 94 J
Ithaca • NY, United States 156 B1
Ithaki • Greece .... 94 J
Itháki [I.] • Greece .... 94 J
Iti Oros Nat. Park Park N • Greece .... 58 [161]
Ito • Japan 127 H9
Itocoatiara • Brazil 173 D3
Itoman • Okinawa, Japan .... 138 A
Itsukushima Shrine Heritage C •
   Japan .... 43 [193]
Itter • Austria 91 O7
Ituiutaba • Brazil 174 B4
Itzehoe • Germany 72 C2
Ivalo • Finland 174 F6
Ivanhoe • NS, Australia 136 G8
Ivano-Frankivs'k • Ukraine 100 B4
Ivanovo • Bulgaria 92 H8
Ivanovo Heritage C • Bulgaria .... 44 [226]
Ivanovo • Russian Fed. 100 M10
Iveragh Peninsula • Ireland 69 G11
Ivindo, Parc nat. de l' Park •
   Gabon .... 112 [43]
IVORY COAST see CÔTE D'IVOIRE
Ivory Coast • Côte d'Ivoire 106 B4
Ivösjön • Sweden 99 G7
Ivrea • Italy 87 A2
Ivujivik • QU, Canada 159 I2
Ivvavik Nat. Park Park N •
   YT, Canada .... 161 [1]
Iwaki • Japan 127 D3
Iwakuni • Japan 127 B4
Iwanai • Japan 127 D2
Iwatsuki • Japan 127 I8
Ixmiquilpan • Mexico 169 J7
Ixopo • South Africa 111 B5
Ixtapa-Zihuatanejo • Mexico 169 I8
Izabal • Lago de • Guatemala 170 K9
Izamal • Mexico 169 F4
Izhevsk • Russian Fed. 100 H2
Izmayil • Ukraine 100 C4
Izmir • Turkey 95 E5
Izmir [Adm] • Turkey 95 E5
Izmir [Riv] • Turkey 95 F3
Iznik • Turkey 95 F4
Iznik Gölü • Turkey 95 F4
Izu-hanto • Japan 127 H9
Izu-shoto • Japan 127 C4
Izúcar de Matamoros • Mexico 169 J7
Izumi-sanmakyu • Japan 127 G7
Izumiotsu • Japan 127 G7
Izumisano • Japan 127 F7

J

J.F. Mitchell [Apt] •
   St Vincent & Gren. .... 167 P
J.N. 'Ding' Darling Nat. Wildlife Refuge •
   FL, United States 155 C3
Jabal al Qarantal • Palestine NAR 120 B3
Jabal Zuqar • Yemen 109 E11
Jabalpur • India 122 B3
Jabbeke • Belgium 70 F6
Jablanica • Bosnia-Herz. 92 G6
Jablonné v Podjestedi • Czech Rep. 89 E6
Jabridge Wilderness Area •
   NV, United States 154 J7
Jaca • Spain 80 E2
Jacareacanga • Brazil 174 A3
Jáchymov • Czech Rep. 89 D6
Jack Frost • PA, United States 156 B2
Jackson • MS, United States 156 F5
Jackson • TN, United States 151 C3
Jackson Hole Ski •
   WY, United States .... 146 [44]
Jackson Prairie •
   MS, United States 156 F5
Jackson Reef Dive • Egypt 109 E7
Jacksonville • AR, United States 151 B4
Jacksonville • FL, United States 155 C1
Jacksonville • IL, United States 150 B3
Jacksonville • NC, United States 151 E4
Jacksonville • TX, United States 155 F4
Jacmel • Haiti 165 F6
Jacob's Well • Palestine NAR 120 B3
Jacobabad • Pakistan 122 A3
Jacques-Cartier, Détroit de •
   QU, Canada 160 B1
Jacques-Cartier, Mt • QU, Canada 160 B1
Jacques-Cartier, Parc de la •
   QU, Canada 160 A1
Jade Gates Pass • China 121 L7
Jade Sea • Ethiopia/Kenya 109 C4
Jaén • Peru 173 B3
Jaén • Spain 82 J7
Jaffa • Israel 120 A3
Jaffar, Cirque de • Morocco 107 B2
Jaffna • Sri Lanka 124 C3
Jagarage Temple • Bali, Indonesia 131 L7
Jagdalpur • India 122 C4
Jagüey Grande • Cuba 164 F4
Jahrom • North • Grenada .... 166 U
Jaicós • Brazil 174 B4
Jaipur • India 123 E8
Jaisalmer • India 123 D7
Jajce • Bosnia-Herz. 92 F6
Jakarta • Java, Indonesia 131 O11
Jakobstad • Finland 97 E3
Jalal Abad • Kyrgyzstan 121 F3
Jalalabad • Afghanistan 121 F5
Jalandhar • India 123 E7
Jalapa • Guatemala 170 K9
Jalapa • Mexico 169 K7
Jalgaon • India 122 B3
Jalisco • Mexico 169 B3
Jalna • India 122 B3
Jalpa • Mexico 169 I6
Jalpaiguri • India 122 D3
Jaluit • Marshall Is. .... 138 V
Jam Heritage C • Afghanistan .... 43 [143]
Jamaame • Somalia 109 D5
JAMAICA • West Indies .... 165 C-D
Jambi • Indonesia 131 B4
Jameos del Agua •
   Lanzarote, Canary Is. 83 I5
James • ND/SD, United States 148 G2
James • VA, United States 156 A4
James A. Garfield Nat. Hist. Site •
   OH, United States 161 D3
James A. Garfield Nat. Hist. Site Park N •
   OH, United States .... 153 [184]
James Bay • Canada 159 H3
James Fort • Antigua & Barbuda .... 167 I
James Ross I. • Antarctica 176 N4

Jamestown • ND, United States 148 G1
Jamestown • NY, United States 156 A1
Jamestown • VA, United States 156 B4
Jammerbugten • Denmark 99 E6
Jammu • India 122 B2
Jammu & Kashmir • Asia 123 A1
Jamnagar • India 122 B3
Jämsä • Finland 99 D3
Jämsänkoski • Finland 99 D3
Jamshedpur • India 122 C3
Jämtland • Sweden 98 B2
Jamtli Historieland Park L • Sweden ... 59 [9]
Jan Mayen • Arctic Ocean 176 J2
Jandía • Fuerteventura, Canary Is. 83 H5
Jandía Playa •
   Fuerteventura, Canary Is. 83 H5
Jandía, Punta de •
   Fuerteventura, Canary Is. 83 H5
Jane Peak • New Zealand 137 G7
Janesville • WI, United States 150 C3
Janos • Mexico 168 I5
Janské Lázne • Czech Rep. 89 E6
JAPAN • Asia 127
Japan, Sea of • Asia 116 M3
Japanoo Gordons Dive • Israel 109 C7
Japurá • Brazil 173 C3
Jarabacoa • Dominican Rep. 165 G5
Jaraguá, Parque Nac. •
   Dominican Rep. 165 F6
Jard-sur-Mer • France 77 E6
Jardin d'Acclimation, Le Park L •
   France .... 59 [64]
Jardin de la France • France 76 K8
Jardines de la Reina, Archipiélago de los •
   Cuba ....
Jären • Norway 98 E5
Järläsa • Sweden 99 A1
Järna • Sweden 99 B2
Järnlunden • Sweden 99 H5
Jarocin • Poland 89 B3
Jaromer • Czech Rep. 89 E6
Jaroslaw • Poland 89 B3
Jaru • Brazil 173 C4
Järvenpää • Finland 99 D4
Jarvis I. • Pacific Ocean 139 DD3
Jask • Iran 120 H8
Jaslo • Poland 89 C4
Jasmund, Nationalpark Park N •
   Germany .... 58 [65]
Jasper • AL, Canada 160 J6
Jasper • IN, United States 150 C3
Jasper • TX, United States 155 F5
Jasper Nat. Park Park N •
   AL, Canada .... 161 [18]
Jasper Nat. Park • AL, Canada 160 J6
Jassy • Romania 50 E3
Jastrowie • Poland 89 B2
Jastrzebie Zdroj • Poland 89 F9
Jatai • Brazil 174 A4
Jatibarang • Java, Indonesia 131 P11
Jatibonico • Cuba 164 G4
Jatijajar Caves • Java, Indonesia 131 P12
Jatiwangi • Java, Indonesia 131 P11
Jaú • Brazil 175 D2
Jaú, Parque Nac. • Brazil 173 C3
Jaú, Parque Nac. Heritage N •
   Brazil .... 40 [41]
Jauja • Peru 173 E6
Jaunpur • India 123 E8
Java • Indonesia .... 131 O-R
Java Sea • Indonesia 131 D5
Java Trench • Indian Ocean 9 D6
Jávea • Spain 83 B1
Jawa • Indonesia 131 C5
Jawa Barat • Java, Indonesia 131 Q11
Jawa Tengah • Java, Indonesia 131 Q11
Jawa Timur • Java, Indonesia 131 Q12
Jawi • Penang, Malaysia 129 E8
Jawor Heritage C • Poland .... 44 [187]
Jaworzno • Poland 89 F8
Jay Peak Ski • VT, United States .... 146 [111]
Jaya Ancol Dreamland •
   Indonesia 131 O11
Jaya, Puncak • Indonesia 131 I4
Jayaprana Grave • Bali, Indonesia 131 K7
Jayapura • Indonesia 131 J4
Jaypur • India 122 C4
Jeanerette • LA, United States 156 F6
Jean Lafitte Nat. Hist. Park •
   LA, United States 156 F6
Jean Lafitte Nat. Hist. Park & Preserve Park N •
   LA, United States .... 153 [194]
Jebaldar Musa Heritage C • Egypt ... 43 [96]
Jeddah • Saudi Arabia 120 D9
Jeddore Lake • NF, Canada 160 C1
Jedrzejow • Poland 89 G8
Jefferson • TX, United States 155 F4
Jefferson City • MO, United States 150 B3
Jefferson, Fort •
   FL, United States 155 C3
Jefferson Nat. Expansion Mem. Park N •
   MO, United States .... 153 [175]
Jeffrey's Bay • South Africa 111 G7
Jeju-do • Rep. of Korea 125 G3
Jekabpils • Latvia 100 K7
Jelai • Malaysia 129 O9
Jelenia Góra • Poland 89 A3
Jelgava • Latvia 100 J7
Jelling Heritage C • Denmark .... 44 [13]
Jeløy • Norway 98 E6
Jels • Denmark 99 E8
Jelutong • Penang, Malaysia 129 E7
Jember • Java, Indonesia 131 R12
Jemnice • Czech Rep. 89 E6
Jena • Germany 72 D3
Jenner • Germany 74 H8
Jennings • LA, United States 156 E6
Jenolan Caves • NS, Australia 136 H8
Jeonju • Rep. of Korea 125 G3
Jepara • Java, Indonesia 131 Q11
Jequié • Brazil 174 B4
Jerada • Morocco 107 B2
Jerantut • Malaysia 129 G9
Jerba • Tunisia 107 D6
Jerejak • Malaysia 129 E8
Jérémie • Haiti 165 E6
Jerez • Mexico 169 I6
Jeréz de la Frontera • Spain 82 H8
Jericho • Palestine NAR 120 B3
Jericho • QL, Australia 136 C4
Jerid, Chott el • Tunisia 107 C6
Jerome • ID, United States 148 D2
Jersey • Channel Is. 63 I14
Jersey City • NJ, United States 156 C2
Jerusalem • Israel/Palestine NAR 120 A3
Jerusalem Heritage C •
   Israel/Palestine NAH .... 44 [308]
Jervis Bay • AC, Australia 136 H8
Jervis I. • Galápagos Is. 171 G10
Jesenice • Slovenia 92 F5
Jesi • Italy 87 D3
Jesperhus Blomsterpark • Denmark 99 E6
Jesperhus Blomsterpark Park L •
   Denmark .... 59 [14]
Jessheim • Norway 98 E5
Jessore • Bangladesh 122 D3
Jesup, Fort • LA, United States 155 F5
Jesús Heritage C • Paraguay .... 42 [67]
Jeumont • France 70 A5
Jevnaker • Norway 98 E5
Jewel Cave Nat. Mon. Park N •
   SD, United States .... 152 [148]
Jewish Autonomous Region Russ Adm •
   Russian Fed. .... 101 [29]
Jezersel, Valley of • Israel 120 B2
Jhajjar • India 123 E7
Jhalarapatan • India 123 E8
Jhalawar • India 123 E8
Jhansi • India 122 B2
Jharkhand • India 123 B2
Jhelum • Pakistan 122 B2
Jhelum [Riv] • India/Pakistan 121 F5

Jhunjhunun • India 123 E7
Ji'an • China 125 F4
Jiading • China 126 H6
Jiamusi • China 125 H2
Ji'an • China 125 F4
Jiangmen • China 126 E3
Jiangshan • China 126 H7
Jiangsu • China 126 D1
Jiangsu [Adm] • China 126 D2
Jiangxi • China 126 G6
Jiangyin • China 126 G6
Jiashan • China 126 H7
Jiaxing • China 126 H7
Jiayuguan • China 125 D3
Jibacoa • Cuba 164 F4
Jicarilla Apache Ind Res •
  NM, United States . . . . 155 [36]
Jicin • Czech Rep. 89 E6
Jida • China 125 F4
Jiddah • Saudi Arabia 120 D9
Jihlava • Czech Rep. 89 E7
Jilin • China 125 G2
Jilin [Adm] • China 126 D1
Jima • Ethiopia 108 C4
Jimani • Dominican Rep. 165 H6
Jimbaran Beach • Bali, Indonesia 131 L8
Jiménez • Mexico 168 D2
Jimenoa, Salto de • Dominican Rep. . . . 165 G5
Jiminy Peak Ski •
  MA, United States . . . . 146 [104]
Jiminy Peak • MA, United States 156 C1
Jimmy Carter Nat. Hist. Site Park N •
  GA, United States . . . . 153 [210]
Jin I. • Hong Kong, China 126 F5
Jinan • China 125 F3
Jinchang • China 125 E3
Jincheng • China 125 F3
Jindrichuv Hradec • Czech Rep. 89 E7
Jing Xian • China 126 G7
Jingde • China 126 G7
Jinghong • China 125 E4
Jingjiang • China 126 H6
Jinhua • China 125 F4
Jining • Inner Mongolia, China 125 F2
Jining • Shandong, China 125 F3
Jinja • Uganda 109 C4
Jinju • Rep. of Korea 125 K3
Jinotega • Nicaragua 170 D4
Jinotepe • Nicaragua 170 D5
Jinsha • China 126 H6
Jinsha Jiang • China 125 D3
Jintan • China 126 H7
Jinzhou • China 125 G2
Jishou • China 125 E4
Jiuhua Shan • China . . . . 126 [8]
Jiujiang • China 126 F7
Jiuzhaigou Heritage N • China . . . . 41 [130]
Jizhou • China 126 E3
Jixi • China 126 G7
Jixi • China 125 H2
Jizan • Saudi Arabia 120 E10
Jizzakh • Uzbekistan 121 E3
João Pessoa • Brazil 174 C3
Jochgrimm • Italy 86 C4
Jodhpur • India 123 D8
Joensuu • Finland 97 F3
Joetsu • Japan 127 C3
Jog Falls • India 124 B2
Joga-shima • Japan 127 I9
Jõgeva • Estonia 100 K6
Johannesburg • South Africa 111 I10
John D. Rockefeller Jr. Mem. Parkway
  Park N • WY, United States . . . . . . 152 [73]
John Day • OR, United States 154 H6
John Day Fossil Beds Nat. Mon. •
  OR, United States 154 G6
John Day Fossil Beds Nat. Mon. Park N •
  OR, United States . . . . 152 [35]
John F. Kennedy [Apt] •
  NY, United States 156 C2
John F. Kennedy Nat. Hist. Site Park N •
  MA, United States . . . . 153 [289]
John Muir Nat. Hist. Site Park N •
  CA, United States . . . . 152 [45]
John o'Groats • United Kingdom 62 D2
John Pennekamp Coral Reef State Park •
  FL, United States 155 D3
John Wayne [Apt] •
  CA, United States 154 J9
John Day • OR, United States 154 H6
Johns Lake • FL, United States 157 A1
Johnson Space Center •
  TX, United States 155 F6
Johnson's Crossing • YT, Canada 158 C2
Johnston Atoll • Pacific Ocean 139 DD2
Johnstone • United Kingdom 65 A4
Johnstown • PA, United States 156 A2
Johnstown Flood Nat. Mem. •
  PA, United States 156 A2
Johnstown Flood Nat. Mem. Park N •
  PA, United States . . . . 153 [266]
Johor Bahru • Malaysia 129 H11
Johor Strait • Malaysia/Singapore 129 H11
Joinville • Brazil 175 D2
Jokkmokk • Sweden 97 D2
Jökulsárgljúfur Nat. Park Park N •
  Iceland . . . . 58 [1]
Joliet • IL, United States 150 C2
Joliette • QU, Canada 160 G3
Jolo • Philippines 128 G5
Jolo [I.] • Philippines 128 G5
Jalstravatnet • Norway 98 F7
Jombang • Java, Indonesia 131 Q12
Jondhal • Norway 98 D6
Jomsom • Nepal 123 G7
Jomtien • Thailand 130 E8
Jonava • Lithuania 100 K8
Jonesboro • AR, United States 151 B3
Jonesville • LA, United States 156 C5
Jönköping • Sweden 99 G6
Jönköping [Adm] • Sweden 95 J9
Jonquière • QU, Canada 160 A1
Joplin • MO, United States 151 B3
Joppa • Israel 120 A3
JORDAN • Asia 120 D7
Jordan • MT, United States 148 E1
Jordan [Riv] • Asia 120 B3
Jørpeland • Norway 98 F9
Jos • Nigeria 106 C3
José Cardel • Mexico 169 K7
José Martí [Apt] • Cuba 164 F4
José Miguel, Cuevas de • Cuba 164 E4
Joseph Bonaparte Gulf •
  NT/WA, Australia 135 D2
Joshua Tree Nat. Park •
  CA, United States 154 J9
Joshua Tree Nat. Park Park N •
  CA, United States . . . . 152 [56]
Josselin • France 77 D4
Jost van Dyke • British Virgin Is. . . . . . . 166 A
Jostedalsbreen • Norway 98 G7
Jostedalsbreen • Norway 98 G7
Jotunheimen Nat. Park Park N •
  Norway . . . . 58 [15]
Jotunheimen Nat. Park • Norway 98 G7
Joubertina • South Africa 111 F7
Joumâa • Tunisia 107 D6
Joutsa • Finland 99 D3
Jovellanos • Cuba 164 F4
Joya de Cerén Heritage C •
  El Salvador . . . . 42 [35]
Joyce's Country • Ireland 69 G9
Jozani Reserve Park • Tanzania . . . . . 112 [90]
Juan de Fuca, Strait of •
  Canada/United States 160 I7
Juan Díaz • Panama 170 M11
Juan Dolio • Dominican Rep. 165 H6
Juan Fernández, Is. •
  Pacific Ocean 171 B6
Juan Francisco, Playa • Cuba 164 F4
Juan les Pins • France 78 H4
Juancho Yrausquin [Apt] • Saba . . . . . . 167 E
Juárez, Sierra • Mexico 169 K8
Juàzeiro • Brazil 174 B3

Juàzeiro do Norte • Brazil 174 C3
Juba • Sudan 108 C4
Jubany [Base] • Antarctica . . . . 176 [2]
Júcar • Spain 80 E4
Júcaro • Cuba 164 G4
Jüchen • Germany 73 C6
Juchipila • Mexico 169 I6
Juchitán • Mexico 169 K6
Judaberg • Norway 98 F9
Judaea • Israel/Palestine NAR 120 A4
Judaea, Wilderness of •
  Israel/Palestine NAR 120 B4
Judenburg • Austria 91 G2
Juegang • China 126 H6
Juelsminde • Denmark 99 F7
Juhu Beach Beach • India 124 E6
Juigalpa • Nicaragua 170 E4
Juiz de Fora • Brazil 98 G8
Juklevegga • Norway 98 G8
Juli • Peru 173 F7
Juliaca • Peru 173 F7
Julianadorp • Curaçao . . . . 166 V
Julianehâb • Greenland 159 L2
Julita • Sweden 99 A2
Jumba • Kenya 109 C6
Jumilla • Spain 83 A1
Junagadh • India 122 B3
Junction • TX, United States 149 G4
Junction City • KS, United States 150 A3
June Mtn Ski • CA, United States . . . . . 146 [32]
Juneau • AK, United States 157 F4
Junee • NS, Australia 136 G8
Jungfrau • Switzerland 90 J5
Jungfrau-Aletsch-Bietschhorn Heritage N •
  Switzerland . . . . 41 [67]
Junggar Basin • China 126 A1
Junggar Pendi • China 125 C2
Jungholz • Austria 91 N7
Jungutbatu • Indonesia 131 K8
Junín • PA, United States 156 C2
Junín • Argentina 175 F6
Juntura • OR, United States 148 C2
Jupiter • Romania 92 I7
Jura • France/Switzerland 90 C2
Jura [Adm] • France 78 C3
Jura [Adm] • Switzerland 91 Q9
Jurançon • France 76 K9
Jurbarkas • Lithuania 100 J8
Jurilovca • Romania 92 I7
Jurmala • Latvia 100 J7
Jurong • China 126 G6
Jurong • Singapore 129 H11
Jurong Bird Park • Singapore 129 H11
Jurong I. • Singapore 129 H12
Juru • Penang, Malaysia 129 E8
Juruá • Brazil 173 B3
Juruena • Brazil 173 D4
Jutiapa • Guatemala 170 K9
Juticalpa • Honduras 170 K9
Jutland • Denmark 99 F7
Juventud, I. de la • Cuba 164 E4
Juymand • Iran 120 H7
Juzur al Halaniyat • Oman 120 H10
Jwaneng • Botswana 110 J10
Jyderup • Denmark 99 F7
Jylland • Denmark 99 F7
Jyväskylä • Finland 99 D3

K

K2 • China/Pakistan 122 B2
Ka Lae • HI, United States 157 J6
Ka, Laem • Ko Phuket, Thailand 130 F10
Kaa-Iya, Parque Nac. • Bolivia 173 C4
Kaala • HI, United States 157 G6
Kaamanen • Finland 97 F2
Kaarst • Germany 73 C6
Kaatsheuvel • Netherlands 70 C3
Kabáh • Mexico 169 F4
Kabale • Uganda 108 B5
Kabalo • Dem. Rep. of Congo 108 B5
Kabanjahe • Indonesia 131 M9
Kabardino-Balkaria Russ Adm •
  Russian Fed. . . . . 101 [3]
Kabelvåg • Norway 130 E7
Kabinda • Dem. Rep. of Congo 108 B5
Kablow-Ziegelei • Germany 73 F8
Kabul • Afghanistan 121 E5
Kabwe • Zambia 110 B2
Kachchh, Gulf of • India 122 A3
Kachchh, Rann of • India 122 A3
Kácina • Czech Rep. 89 E6
Kadanatst • India 124 A3
Kadan • Czech Rep. 89 D6
Kadavu • Fiji Is. 138 CC4
Kadavu • Fiji Is. . . . . 138 T
Kadena • Okinawa, Japan . . . . 138 A
Kadíköy • Turkey 95 F3
Kadirli • Turkey 95 J9
Kadugli • Sudan 108 B3
Kaduna • Nigeria 106 C3
Kaduy • Russian Fed. 100 M9
Kaédi • Mauritania 106 A3
Kaena Point • HI, United States 157 G6
Kaew Noi, Ko • Thailand 130 F9
Kaew Yai, Ko • Thailand 130 F10
Kafue Nat. Park Park • Zambia . . . . . . 112 [108]
Kagaznagar • India 122 B4
Kagera • Rwanda/Tanzania 110 H2
Kagoshima • Japan 127 B4
Kahalu'u • HI, United States 157 H6
Kahama • Tanzania 110 G2
Kahana Valley State Park •
  HI, United States 157 G6
Kahoolawe • HI, United States 157 I6
Kahramanmaras [Adm] • Turkey 95 J9
Kahuku Point • HI, United States 157 G5
Kahului • HI, United States 157 I5
Kahuzi-Biega, Parc nat. du Park •
  Dem. Rep. of Congo . . . . 112 [54]
Kahuzi-Biega, Parc nat. du Heritage N •
  Dem. Rep. of Congo . . . . 41 [105]
Kai, Kepulauan • Indonesia 131 H5
Kaibab Ind Res • AZ, United States . . . 155 [24]
Kaibara • Japan 127 F6
Kaifeng • China 125 F3
Kaikoura • New Zealand 137 B3
Kaili • China 125 E4
Kailua • HI, United States 157 J6
Kailua-Kona • HI, United States 157 J6
Kaimanawa Mtns • New Zealand 137 E6
Kainaba • Kiribati . . . . 139 F
Kainuu • Finland 98 C2
Kaipara Harbour • New Zealand 137 E5
Kairouan Heritage C • Tunisia . . . . . . 44 [291]
Kaiser-Gebirge • Austria 91 O7
Kaiserslautern • Germany 74 B2
Kaiserstuhl • Germany 74 A4
Kaiserswerth (Düsseldorf) • Germany . . . 73 C5
Kaiwi Channel • HI, United States 157 I5
Kaiyuan • China 125 E4
Kaizuka • Japan 127 F7
Kajaani • Finland 97 F3
Kajang • Malaysia 129 G10
Kakadu Nat. Park Heritage N •
  Australia . . . . 41 [149]
Kakadu Nat. Park Park •
  Australia . . . . 43 [210]
Kakadu Nat. Park • NT, Australia 135 E2
Kakamega • Kenya 108 C4
Kakamega Forest Game Reserve • Kenya 109 C4
Kakinada • India 124 D1
Kakisa • NT, Canada 158 E2
Kako-gawa • Japan 127 F6
Kakogawa • Japan 127 I8
Kakonko • Tanzania 110 H2
Kaktovik • AK, United States 157 E2
Kakum Nature Park Park • Ghana . . . . 112 [23]

Kala • Ko Phuket, Thailand 130 F9
Kalaâ Kasbah • Tunisia 107 C5
Kalabsha • Egypt 99 B3
Kalacha Beach • Goa, India 123 C5
Kaladar • OT, Canada 164 G4
Kalahari Desert • Africa 110 B3
Kalai Mor • Turkmenistan 121 D4
Kalalau Lookout •
  HI, United States 157 H5
Kalamaki • Greece 93 C1
Kalamáta • Greece 93 C3
Kalamazoo • MI, United States 150 C2
Kalambáka • Greece 93 B2
Kalambo Falls • Tanzania 110 G8
Kalámi • Crete, Greece 93 G5
Kálimnos • Greece 93 E3
Kalimnos • Greece . . . . 94 B
Kalapana • HI, United States 157 J6
Kalasin • Thailand 130 D7
Kalauppapa Nat. Hist. Park •
  HI, United States 157 I5
Kalávdrda • Rhodes, Greece . . . . 94 F
Kale • Alanya, Turkey 95 G8
Kale • Antalya, Turkey 95 H8
Kale • Denizli, Turkey 95 F6
Kalémié • Dem. Rep. of Congo 108 B5
Kalemyo • Myanmar 128 A2
Kalgoorlie • WA, Australia 135 C6
Kali Liménes • Crete, Greece 93 H6
Kalimantan • Indonesia 131 D4
Kálimnos • Greece 93 E3
Kálimnos • Greece . . . . 94 B
Kalimpong Hill Sta • India 124 F5
Kaliningrad • Russian Fed. 100 J8
Kalinjar • India 123 F8
Kalispell • MT, United States 154 H5
Kaliste • Czech Rep. 89 E7
Kalisz • Poland 89 B3
Kaliua • Tanzania 110 G7
Kaliurang • Java, Indonesia 131 Q12
Kalithéa • Halkidikí, Greece . . . . 94 B
Kalithéa • Rhodes, Greece . . . . 94 F
Kaliua • Tanzania 110 G7
Kalix • Sweden 97 E2
Kalix älv • Sweden 97 E2
Kalkudah • Sri Lanka 124 D4
Kálándoš • Sweden 99 G5
Kallirhoe • Jordan 120 B4
Kalloní • Lesbos, Greece . . . . 94 C
Kallonís, Kólpos •
  Lesbos, Greece . . . . 94 C
Kaltsjön • Sweden 97 C3
Kaluga • Russian Fed. 99 H6
Kalmar • Sweden 99 H6
Kalmar [Adm] • Sweden 99 H6
Kalmarsund • Sweden 99 H6
Kalmykia Russ Adm • Russian Fed. . . . 101 [8]
Kaló Horió • Crete, Greece 93 J6
Kalolímnos • Greece 94 DD3
Kalopanayiotis • Cyprus 96 C4
Kalpeni I. • India 124 A3
Kaltene • Latvia 100 J7
Kaluga • Russian Fed. 100 E3
Kalundborg • Denmark 99 F7
Kalutara • Sri Lanka 124 C4
Kalvåg • Norway 98 F7
Kalwaria Zebrzydowska • Poland 89 F9
Kalwaria Zebrzydowska Park N •
  Poland . . . . 58 [108]
Kalwaria Zebrzydowska Heritage C •
  Poland . . . . 44 [185]
Kalyan • India 122 B4
Kalyazin • Russian Fed. 100 M10
Kam Shan Country Park •
  Hong Kong, China 126 E5
Kama • Russian Fed. 100 H2
Kamaina • Indonesia 131 H4
Kamakura • Japan 127 I9
Kamaran • Yemen 109 E11
Kamchatka, Poluostrov •
  Russian Fed. 101 P4
Kamchatka volcanoes Heritage N •
  Russian Fed. . . . . 41 [87]
Kamchiya • Bulgaria 92 I8
Kámen • Czech Rep. 89 E7
Kámen • Germany 73 D5
Kamenjak, Rt • Croatia 92 F5
Kameoka • Japan 127 G6
Kamina • Dem. Rep. of Congo 108 B5
Kámiros • Rhodes, Greece . . . . 94 F
Kamloops • BC, Canada 160 I7
Kammam • India 124 C1
Kamnik Nat. Reserve • Kenya 127 I9
Kamogawa • Japan 127 I9
Kamp-Lintfort • Germany 73 C5
Kampala • Uganda 108 C4
Kampen • Netherlands 70 C2
Kampenwand • Germany 74 H8
Kampiá • Chios, Greece . . . . 94 D
Kampinoski Nat. Park Park N •
  Poland . . . . 58 [101]
Kamskoye Vdkhr. • Russian Fed. 100 I2
Kamuela • HI, United States 157 J6
Kamui, L. • AK, United States 157 C4
Kanagawa • Japan 127 H8
Kananga • Dem. Rep. of Congo 108 B5
Kanash • Russian Fed. 100 G2
Kanazawa • Japan 127 H8
Kanbalu • Myanmar 128 B2
Kanchanaburi • Thailand 130 D7
Kanchipuram • India 124 C2
Kandahar • Afghanistan 121 E5
Kandalaksha • Russian Fed. 101 D3
Kandanghaur • Java, Indonesia 131 P11
Kandanos • Crete, Greece 93 G6
Kandel • Germany 74 B4
Kandersteg • Switzerland 91 R11
Kandi • Benin 106 C3
Kandooma • Maldives 124 H8
Kandy • Sri Lanka 124 C4
Kandy Heritage C • Sri Lanka . . . . . . 43 [167]
Kane • PA, United States 156 A1
Kaneohe • HI, United States 157 H6
Kaneohe Bay • HI, United States 157 H6
Kang • Botswana 110 I10
Kang Kra Chan Nat. Park • Thailand . . . 130 D8
Kangar • Malaysia 128 C5
Kangaroo I. • SA, Australia 135 F7
Kangchenjunga • India/Nepal 122 C3
Kangerlussuaq • Greenland 159 K2
Kanggye • D.P.R. of Korea 125 G2
Kangra Hill Sta • India 123 E7
Kaniflushu • Maldives 124 G8
Kanin, Poluostrov • Russian Fed. 101 E3
Kaniranpää • Finland 97 E2
Kanikakee • IL, United States 150 C2
Kankroli • India 123 D8
Kannauj • India 123 F7
Kanniyakumari • India 124 B4
Kanniyakumari Beach • India 124 E6
Kano • Nigeria 106 C3
Kansai [Apt] • Japan 127 F7
Kansas [Adm] • United States 148 G3
Kansas City • KS, United States 150 B3
Kansas City • MO, United States 150 B3
Kansk • Russian Fed. 101 J4
Kantara Castle • Cyprus 96 C3
Kanto • Japan 127 I8
Kanton • Kiribati 138 CC3
Kanturk Castle • Ireland 69 H10
Kanye • Botswana 110 J10
Kanazaki • Japan 127 F6
Kaohsiung • Taiwan 125 G4
Kaolack • Senegal 106 A3

Kaole • Tanzania 110 H8
Kapaa • HI, United States 157 H5
Kapellskär • Sweden 99 B1
Kapenguria • Kenya 109 C4
Kapingamarangi • Micronesia 138 BB3
Kapingamarangi Atoll •
  Fed. States of Micronesia 138 BB2
Kaposvar • Hungary 92 B2
Kappeln • Germany 72 C1
Kaprun Ski • Austria . . . . 61 [105]
Kaprun • Austria 91 P7
Kapuas • Indonesia 131 D3
Kapuskasing • OT, Canada 159 H4
Kara Sea • Russian Fed. 101 G2
Kara-Balta • Kyrgyzstan 121 F3
Kara-Köl • Kyrgyzstan 121 F3
Kará-Köl • Kyrgyzstan 121 F3
Karabük • Turkey 95 B1
Karabiga • Turkey 95 E1
Karachay-Cherkessia Russ Adm •
  Russian Fed. . . . . 101 [2]
Karachi • Pakistan 122 A3
Karaginskiy, Ostrov • Russian Fed. 101 Q4
Karaikal • India 124 C3
Karaikal Beach • India 124 E6
Karaisali • Turkey 95 J9
Karaj • Iran 120 G6
Karakol • Kyrgyzstan 121 G3
Karakoram • Asia 122 B2
Karaman • Turkey 95 I9
Karaman [Adm] • Turkey 95 I10
Karaman Turkey 95 B1
Karamay • China 125 C2
Karamea Bight • New Zealand 137 B3
Karangsari Cave • Indonesia 131 L8
Karapinar • Turkey 95 I9
Karasburg • Namibia 110 A3
Karasjok • Norway 97 F2
Karataş • Turkey 95 J10
Karatau • Kazakhstan 121 E3
Karatep • Rang • Easter I. . . . . 139 M
Karauli • India 123 E8
Karawang • Java, Indonesia 131 O11
Karbala • Iraq 120 E7
Kardam • Bulgaria 92 I7
Kardámena • Cos, Greece . . . . 94 E
Kardamili • Tinos, Greece . . . . 94 I
Karditsa • Greece 93 B2
Kardla • Estonia 100 J6
Kareedouw • South Africa 111 F7
Karelia Russ Adm • Russian Fed. . . . . 101 [9]
Karelia, Northern • Finland 98 C2
Karesuando • Sweden 97 E2
Karfás • Chios, Greece . . . . 94 D
Kari • Park • Kenya 109 C5
Kariba Dam • Zambia/Zimbabwe 110 B2
Kariba, Lake • Zambia/Zimbabwe 110 B2
Karidu Atoll • Maldives 124 G7
Karidu • South Africa 111 F6
Karijini Nat. Park • WA, Australia 135 B4
Karimata • Indonesia 131 C4
Karimskoye • Russian Fed. 101 O11
Karimunjawa, Kepulauan • Indonesia . 131 D11
Karis • Finland 99 D4
Káristos • Greece 93 D2
Karkonosze Nat. Park Park N •
  Poland . . . . 58 [108]
Karleby • Finland 97 E3
Karlovac • Croatia 92 F5
Karlovássi • Sámos, Greece . . . . 94 E
Karlovo • Bulgaria 92 G3
Karlovy Vary • Czech Rep. 89 D6
Karlsbad • Czech Rep. 89 D6
Karlsborg • Sweden 99 G5
Karlshamn • Sweden 99 H7
Karlskrona • Sweden 99 H7
Karlskrona Heritage C • Sweden . . . . . 43 [170]
Karlslunde • Denmark 99 F7
Karlsruhe • Germany 74 B3
Karlstad • Sweden 97 C4
Karlstejn • Czech Rep. 89 E6
Karmøy • Norway 98 F9
Karnal • India 123 E7
Karnataka • India 124 B1
Karnataka Plateau • India 124 B1
Karnische Alpen • Austria/Italy 91 Q8
Karnobat • Bulgaria 92 I8
Kärnten • Austria 91 T11
Karo Batak Villages • Indonesia 131 M9
Karon • Ko Phuket, Thailand 130 F10
Karon Beach • Ko Phuket, Thailand . . . 130 F10
Karonga • Malawi 110 A3
Karoo, Great • South Africa 111 F6
Karoo, Little • South Africa 111 E7
Karoo Nat. Park • South Africa 111 F6
Karoo Nat. Park Park • South Africa . . 112 [129]
Karpas Peninsula • Cyprus 96 C3
Kárpathos • Greece 93 E4
Kárpathos [I.] • Greece 93 E4
Karratha • WA, Australia 135 B4
Karsava • Latvia 100 K7
Karsiyaka • Turkey 95 E5
Kartal • Turkey 95 F3
Karula Nat. Park Park N • Estonia . . . . 58 [147]
Karula Nat. Park • Estonia 100 K6
Karun • Iran 120 G7
Karup • Denmark 99 F7
Karur • India 124 C3
Karvina • Czech Rep. 89 F9
Karwar • India 124 A1
Karwendel • Austria 91 N7
Kas • Turkey 95 G8
Kasai • Dem. Rep. of Congo 108 A5
Kasai • Japan 127 F6
Kasama • Zambia 110 G8
Kasane Nat. Park Park • Zambia . . . . 112 [107]
Kasar, Ras • Sudan 109 E10
Kasaragod • India 124 B2
Kasba Lake • NT/NU, Canada 158 F2
Kashan • Iran 120 G7
Kashgar • China 125 B3
Kashi • China 125 B3
Kashihara • Japan 127 F6
Kashin • Russian Fed. 100 M10
Kashiwa • Japan 127 I8
Kasikinen • Finland 99 C3
Kaskö • Finland 99 C3
Kasongo • Dem. Rep. of Congo 108 B5
Kaspiysk • Russian Fed. 100 G5
Kassala • Sudan 108 C3
Kassándra • Greece . . . . 94 B
Kassándras, Kólpos • Greece . . . . 94 B
Kasselburg • Germany 74 C5
Kassandra • Greece . . . . 94 B
Kassel • Germany 74 D5
Kasserine • Tunisia 107 C5
Kastamonu • Turkey 95 I8
Kastelruth • Italy 86 C3
Kaštel • Belgium 71 G7
Kastélli • Crete, Greece 93 J6
Kastoría • Greece 93 B1
Kassós • Greece 93 E4
Kastráki • Tínos, Greece . . . . 94 I
Kastrup [Apt] • Denmark 99 G7
Kasubi Heritage C • Uganda . . . . 43 [115]
Kasukabe • Japan 127 I8
Kasumiga-ura • Japan 127 I8
Kata • Ko Phuket, Thailand 130 F10
Kata Noi Beach •
  Ko Phuket, Thailand 130 F10
Kata Tjuta • NT, Australia 136 A2

Kata Yai Beach •
  Ko Phuket, Thailand 130 F10
Katanga • Dem. Rep. of Congo 108 B6
Katavi Nat. Park • Tanzania 110 G8
Katelios • Cephalonia, Greece . . . . 94 J
Katerini • Greece 93 C1
Katherine • NT, Australia 135 E2
Kathiawar • India 123 A2
Kathmandu • Nepal 122 C3
Kathmandu valley Heritage C • Nepal 43 [170]
Katikati • New Zealand 137 E5
Katima Mulilo • Namibia 110 B2
Katiola • Côte d'Ivoire 106 B4
Katiti Aboriginal Land •
  NT, Australia 136 A2
Katlehong • South Africa 110 J10
Katmai Nat. Park & Preserve •
  AK, United States 157 D4
Katmai Nat. Park & Preserve Park N •
  AK, United States . . . . 152 [110]
Káto Ahaía • Greece 93 B2
Kato Koufonísi • Greece . . . . 94 H
Kato Tithorea • Greece 93 C2
Káto Zákros • Crete, Greece 93 J6
Katong • Singapore 129 H11
Katoomba • NS, Australia 136 H8
Katowice • Poland 89 F8
Katrine, Loch • United Kingdom 65 A1
Katrineholm • Sweden 99 A2
Katsina • Nigeria 106 C3
Katsura • Japan 127 G6
Katsuren-zaki • Okinawa, Japan . . . . . 138 A
Katsuura • Japan 127 I9
Kattavía • Rhodes, Greece . . . . 94 F
Kattegat • Denmark/Sweden 99 F6
Katu • Ko Phuket, Thailand 130 F10
Katwijk • Netherlands 70 C2
Katwijks Duinen • Netherlands 70 C2
Katy Hill • Montserrat . . . . 167 G
Katzenbuckel • Germany 74 D5
Kau, Ranø • Easter I. . . . . 139 M
Kau Sai Chau • Hong Kong, China 126 F5
Kauai • HI, United States 157 H5
Kauai Channel • HI, United States 157 I5
Kaub • Germany 74 D6
Kaufbeuren • Germany 74 F7
Kaukiainen • Finland 99 D4
Kaula I. • HI, United States 157 G5
Kaunakakai • HI, United States 157 I5
Kaunos • Turkey 95 F6
Kaunas • Lithuania 100 J8
Kaupanger • Norway 98 G8
Kausambi • India 123 F8
Kavak • Turkey 95 E4
Kavála • Greece 93 D1
Kaválla • Greece 93 D1
Kavaratti • India 124 A3
Kavaratti I. • India 124 A3
Kavárna • Bulgaria 92 I8
Kavieng • Papua New Guinea 134 D5
Kávos • Corfu, Greece . . . . 94 A
Kavoúsi • Crete, Greece 93 J6
Kawachi-nagano • Japan 127 G7
Kawaguchi • Japan 127 I8
Kawaguchi • Japan 127 I8
Kawaikini • HI, United States 157 H5
Kawasaki • Japan 127 I8
Kaweka Range • New Zealand 137 E6
Kawerau • New Zealand 137 E5
Kawhia • New Zealand 137 D5
Kawhia Harbour • New Zealand 137 D5
Kawm Umbu • Egypt 99 B3
Kaxgar • Burkina 106 C3
Kayenta • AZ, United States 149 D3
Kayes • Mali 106 A3
Kaymaklı • Turkey 95 J9
Kaynar • Kazakhstan 121 G2
Kayseri • Turkey 95 J9
Kayseri [Adm] • Turkey 95 J9
Kazak Uplands • Kazakhstan 121 F2
Kazakhstan • Asia 121 E2
KAZAKHSTAN • Asia 121 E2
Kazalinsk • Kazakhstan 121 D2
Kazan' • Russian Fed. 100 G2
Kazan Heritage C • Russian Fed. . . . . 43 [95]
Kazan-shoto • Japan 138 AA1
Kazanluk • Bulgaria 92 H3
Kazanluk Heritage C • Bulgaria . . . . . 44 [229]
Kazbek • Georgia/Russian Fed. 120 E5
Kazerun • Iran 120 G8
Kâzim Karabekir • Turkey 95 I9
Kaziranga Nat. Park Heritage N •
  India . . . . 41 [125]
Kéa • Greece 93 D3
Kearney • NE, United States 148 G2
Keban Baraji • Turkey 95 C2
Kebili • Tunisia 107 C6
Kebnekaise • Sweden 97 D2
Kebumen • Java, Indonesia 131 P12
Kecskemét • Hungary 92 B2
Kedainiai • Lithuania 100 J8
Kediri • Java, Indonesia 131 Q12
Kedzierzyn-Kozle • Poland 89 F8
Keekorok Lodge • Kenya 109 C5
Keel • Ireland 69 H8
Keene • NH, United States 156 C1
Keetmanshoop • Namibia 110 A3
Keeweenaw Peninsula •
  MI, United States 161 B1
Kefaloniá • Greece . . . . 94 J
Kefaloniá Nat. Park •
  Cephalonia, Greece . . . . 94 E
Kefalvík • Iceland 97 H6
Kehlstein • Germany 74 H8
Keighley • United Kingdom 63 E7
Keihoku • Japan 127 G6
Keilah • Palestine NAR 120 A4
Keilor • VI, Australia 136 G9
Keitele • Finland 97 F3
Keith • SA, Australia 135 G7
Kejimkujik Nat. Park Park N •
  NS, Canada . . . . 161 [37]
Kejimkujik Nat. Park • NS, Canada . . . 160 B2
Kek Lok Si Temple •
  Penang, Malaysia 129 D7
Kekaha • HI, United States 157 H5
Kekova • Turkey 95 G8
Kelang • Malaysia 129 F10
Kelang [I.] • Malaysia 129 F10
Keld Chapel • United Kingdom 65 D3
Kelibia • Tunisia 107 D4
Kelkit • Turkey 95 C1
Kellerwand • Austria/Italy 91 R8
Kells, Cape • NT, Canada 158 D1
Kelleys I. • OH, United States 161 A3
Kellie Castle • United Kingdom 65 B1
Kellie's Castle • Malaysia 129 F9
Kellogg • MT, United States 154 H5
Kells • Ireland 69 E6
Kelme • Lithuania 100 K7
Kelowna • BC, Canada 160 J7
Kelso • WA, United States 148 B1
Kem • Russian Fed. 101 D3
Kemaman • Malaysia 129 F10
Kemer • Turkey 95 G8
Kemerovo • Russian Fed. 101 I4
Kemi • Finland 97 E2
Kemijärvi • Finland 97 F2
Kemijoki • Finland 99 C4
Kemiö • Finland 99 C4
Kemp Land • Antarctica 176 A4
Kempele • Finland 97 F3
Kempen • Germany 73 C5
Kempten • Germany 74 F8
Kempton Park • South Africa 110 J10
Kenai • AK, United States 157 E3
Kenai Fjords Nat. Park Park N •
  AK, United States . . . . 152 [112]
Kendal • Java, Indonesia 131 Q12
Kendal • United Kingdom 65 D3
Kendari • Indonesia 131 F4
Kenema • Sierra Leone 106 A4
Kengtung • Myanmar 128 B2
Kenitra • Morocco 107 A1

Kenmare • Ireland 69 G11
Kenmare [Riv] • Ireland 69 G11
Kenncraig • United Kingdom 62 C5
Kennedy Space Center •
  FL, United States 155 D2
Kennemerduinen, Nat. Park de •
  Netherlands 70 G7
Kenner • LA, United States 151 B5
Kennesaw Mtn Nat. Battlefield Park
  Park N • GA, United States . . . . . 153 [205]
Kennet • United Kingdom 63 E9
Kennewick • WA, United States 154 H5
Kennywood Park L •
  PA, United States . . . . 157 [30]
Keno Hill • YT, Canada 158 C2
Kenosha • WI, United States 150 C2
Kenosha • WI, United States 150 C2
Kensington • Haiti . . . . 65 [2]
Kent • United Kingdom 65 H8
Kent Peninsula • NU, Canada 158 F1
Kentau • Kazakhstan 121 E3
Kentríkí Macedonía • Greece 94 BB1
Kentucky [Adm] • United States 150 C3
Kentucky [Riv] • KY, United States 150 D3
Kentwood • LA, United States 156 F6
KENYA • Africa . . . . 109 C-D
Kenya, Mt • Kenya 109 C5
Kenyatta, Jomo [Apt] • Kenya 109 C5
Keokuk • IA, United States 150 B2
Keoladeo Nat. Park • India 123 E7
Keoladeo Nat. Park Heritage N •
  India . . . . 41 [123]
Kepler Mtns • New Zealand 137 F7
Kepno • Poland 89 B3
Kepsut • Turkey 95 F4
Kerala • India 124 B3
Keramos • Turkey 95 F6
Keran, Parc nat. de la Park • Togo . . . 112 [25]
Kerang • VI, Australia 136 G8
Kerava • Finland 99 D4
Kerch • Ukraine 100 E4
Kerguelen Is. • Indian Ocean 11 M8
Keri • Zante, Greece . . . . 94 J
Kerinci, Gunung • Indonesia 131 B4
Kerio Valley Nat. Reserve • Kenya 109 C4
Kerken • Germany 73 C5
Kerkenah, Is. • Tunisia 107 D5
Kerki • Turkmenistan 121 E4
Kérkira • Corfu, Greece . . . . 94 A
Kérkira [I.] • Greece 93 A2
Kerkouane • Tunisia 107 D4
Kerkouane Heritage C • Tunisia . . . . . 44 [289]
Kerkrade • Netherlands 70 C4
Kermadec Is. • Pacific Ocean 134 G8
Kerman • Iran 120 H7
Kermanshah • Iran 120 F7
Kernwasser Wunderland Park L •
  Germany . . . . 59 [49]
Kernwasser Wunderland • Germany . . . 73 C5
Kéros • Greece 94 CC3
Kerrobert • SA, Canada 158 F3
Kerrville • TX, United States 149 G4
Kerry • Ireland 69 G10
Kerry [Apt] • Ireland 69 G10
Kerry Head • Ireland 69 G10
Kerry, Ring of • Ireland 69 G11
Kerteminde • Denmark 99 F8
Kertosono • Java, Indonesia 131 Q12
Kervansaray • Turkey 95 I9
Kesamuna • Japan 127 D3
Keski-Suomi • Finland 98 C3
Kesteven • United Kingdom 64 B4
Keswick • United Kingdom 65 D3
Keszthely • Hungary 92 B2
Ketapang • Java, Indonesia 131 R12
Ketchikan • AK, United States 157 F4
Ketrzyn • Poland 89 C2
Kettering • OH, United States 150 D3
Kettering • TS, Australia 136 I9
Kettering • United Kingdom 63 E8
Ketzin • Germany 73 E8
Keuka Lake • NY, United States 156 A1
Keukenhof • Netherlands 70 G7
Keurusselka • Finland 99 D3
Keuruu • Finland 98 C3
Kevelaer • Germany 73 C5
Kew • Turks & Caicos Is. 164 C3
Kew Gardens • United Kingdom 65 G7
Keweenaw Ind Res •
  MI, United States . . . . 155 [67]
Keweenaw Nat. Hist. Park •
  MI, United States 161 A1
Keweenaw Nat. Hist. Park Park N •
  MI, United States . . . . 153 [157]
Keweenaw Point • MI, United States . . . 161 B1
Key Biscayne • FL, United States 155 D3
Key Deer Nat. Wildlife Refuge •
  FL, United States 155 D3
Key Largo • FL, United States 155 D3
Key, Lough • Ireland 69 H8
Key West • FL, United States 155 C3
Keylong Hill Sta • India 124 E5
Keynes Country Park Beach •
  United Kingdom . . . . 64 [13]
Keystone Ski • CO, United States . . . 146 [56]
Kgalagadi Transfrontier Park •
  Botswana/South Africa 110 I10
Kgalagadi Transfrontier Park Park •
  Botswana/South Africa . . . . . . 112 [123]
Khabarovsk • Russian Fed. 101 N5
Khajuraho • India 123 F8
Khajuraho Heritage C • India . . . . . . 43 [152]
Khakassia Russ Adm • Russian Fed. . . 101 [24]
Khama Rhino Sanctuary • Botswana . . 110 J9
Khambhat, Gulf of • India 122 B3
Khami Ruins Nat. Mon. Heritage C •
  Zimbabwe . . . . 43 [121]
Khan al Ahmar • Palestine NAR 120 B3
Khandwa • India 122 B3
Khanewal • Pakistan 122 B3
Khanka, Lake • China/Russian Fed. . . . 125 H2
Khanty-Mansi Russ Adm • Russian Fed. 101 [20]
Khanty-Mansiysk • Russian Fed. 101 G3
Khao Chamao Nat. Park • Thailand . . . 130 E8
Khao Kheow Zoo • Thailand 130 E8
Khao Laem • Thailand 130 D7
Khao Yai Nat. Park • Thailand 130 E7
Kharagpur • India 123 G8
Kharavoddo Beach • Goa, India 123 C5
Kharkiv • Ukraine 100 E3
Kharmanli • Bulgaria 92 H3
Khartoum • Sudan 108 C3
Khasav'yurt • Russian Fed. 100 G5
Khaskovo • Bulgaria 92 H3
Khayelitsha • South Africa 111 K7
Khenifra • Morocco 107 A1
Kherson • Ukraine 100 D4
Khilok • Russian Fed. 101 L4
Khimki • Russian Fed. 100 M10
Khizi Pogost Heritage C •
  Russian Fed. . . . . 43 [94]
Khmel'nyts'kyy • Ukraine 100 C3
Khoai, Hon • Vietnam 128 E6
Khok Pip • Thailand 130 E7
Kholm • Russian Fed. 100 L10
Khram, Ko • Thailand 130 E8
Khrysokhou Bay • Cyprus 96 C4
Khujand • Tajikistan 121 E3
Khŭjayli • Uzbekistan 121 D3
Khulna • Bangladesh 122 C3
Khunti • India 123 G8
Khun Yuam • Thailand 130 B5
Khutse Game Reserve • Botswana . . . 110 I10
Khuzdar • Pakistan 122 A3

Khyber Pass • Afghanistan/Pakistan . . 121 F5
Kiang West Nat. Park Park • Gambia . 112 [11]
Kibondo • Tanzania 110 G7
Kicevo • FYR of Macedonia 92 G4
Kicking Horse Pass • AL/BC, Canada . 160 J7
Kid I. • Antigua & Barbuda . . . . 167 H
Kidderminster • United Kingdom 65 E5
Kidnappers, Cape • New Zealand . . . 137 E6
Kiedrich • Germany 74 D6
Kiel • Germany 72 D1
Kielce • Poland 89 G8
Kielder Water • United Kingdom 62 D5
Kieler Bucht • Denmark/Germany 72 D1
Kierspe • Germany 73 U6
Kiev • Ukraine 100 D3
Kiev Heritage C • Ukraine . . . . . . 44 [267]
Kifissos • Greece 93 C2
Kigali • Rwanda 110 B5
Kigoma • Tanzania 110 G7
Kihei • HI, United States 157 I5
Kii-sanchi • Japan 127 G7
Kii-suido • Japan 127 C4
Kiikoinen • Finland 99 C3
Kikambala • Kenya 109 C6
Kikládes • Greece 93 D3
Kikwit • Dem. Rep. of Congo 108 A5
Kilauea Caldera •
    HI, United States 157 J6
Kilchoan • United Kingdom 66 A2
Kilcock • Ireland 69 E6
Kilconnell Friary • Ireland 69 H3
Kilcrea Abbey • Ireland 69 H11
Kilcreggan • United Kingdom 66 A2
Kilcullen • Ireland 69 E7
Kildare • Ireland 69 E7
Kildare [Adm] • Ireland 69 E7
Kilfenora • Ireland 69 H9
Kilgore • TX, United States 155 F4
Kilifi • Kenya 109 C6
Kilimanjaro, Mt • Tanzania 110 H7
Kilimanjaro Nat. Park • Tanzania . . . 110 H7
Kilimanjaro Nat. Park Park •
    Tanzania . . . . 112 [87]
Kilimanjaro Nat. Park Heritage N •
    Tanzania . . . . 41 [110]
Kilindoni • Tanzania 110 H8
Kilini • Greece . . . . 94 J
Kilis • Turkey 95 C2
Kiliya • Ukraine 92 I7
Kilkee • Ireland 69 G10
Kilkenny • Ireland 69 C4
Kilkenny [Adm] • Ireland 69 E7
Kilkis • Greece 93 C1
Killala • Ireland 69 H8
Killala Bay • Ireland 69 H8
Killala • Ireland 69 H10
Killam • AL, Canada 158 G3
Killarney • Ireland 69 G11
Killarney, Lake • Bahamas 164 A2
Killarney, Lakes of • Ireland 69 G11
Killarney Nat. Park Park N • Ireland . 58 [44]
Killarney Nat. Park • Ireland 69 G9
Killary Harbour • Ireland 69 C3
Killeen • TX, United States 155 E5
Killerton House • United Kingdom . . . 65 J9
Killiecrankie, Pass of •
    United Kingdom 65 A1
Killiney • Ireland 69 F7
Killington Ski • VT, United States . 146 [107]
Killorglin • Ireland 69 G11
Kilmacduagh • Ireland 69 H9
Kilmallock • Ireland 69 H10
Kilmarnock • United Kingdom 62 C5
Kilmichael Point • Ireland 69 F7
Kilosa • Tanzania 110 H8
Kilronan • Ireland 69 G9
Kilrush • Ireland 69 H10
Kittan I. • India 124 A3
Kilwa Kisiwani • Tanzania 110 H8
Kilwa Kisiwani Heritage C • Tanzania . 43 [136]
Kilwa Kivinje • Tanzania 110 H8
Kilwa Masoko • Tanzania 110 H8
Kilyos • Turkey 95 F3
Kimball • NE, United States 148 F2
Kimberley Ski • BC, Canada 156 A9
Kimberley • South Africa 110 B3
Kimberley Plateau • WA, Australia . . 135 D3
Kimchaek • D.P.R. of Korea 125 G2
Kimi • Greece 93 D2
Kimito • Finland 99 C4
Kimitsu • Japan 127 I9
Kimolos • Greece 94 CC3
Kimon M Dive • Egypt 109 E7
Kimovsk • Russian Fed. 100 N2
Kimry • Russian Fed. 100 M10
Kin • Okinawa, Japan . . . . 138 A
Kin-wan • Okinawa, Japan . . . . 138 A
Kinabalu, Gunung •
    Sabah, Malaysia 128 F5
Kinabalu Park Heritage N • Malaysia . 41 [142]
Kinaros • Greece . . . . 94 [9]
Kinbasket Lake • BC, Canada 160 J7
Kincardine • United Kingdom 65 B2
Kincardineshire • United Kingdom . . . 64 B2
Kind • Sweden 99 G6
Kinda • Sweden 99 H5
Kinder • LA, United States 156 E6
Kinderdijk • Netherlands 70 G8
Kinderdijk-Elshout Heritage C •
    Netherlands . . . . 44 [37]
Kindersley • SA, Canada 158 F3
Kindia • Guinea 106 A3
Kindu • Dem. Rep. of Congo 108 B5
Kineshima • Russian Fed. 100 F2
King City • CA, United States 148 B3
King Country, The • New Zealand . . 137 D5
King I. • TS, Australia 136 J6
King Salmon • AK, United States . . . 157 D4
King Sejong [Base] • Antarctica . . . 176 [2]
King Sound • WA, Australia 135 C3
King William I. • NU, Canada 158 G2
King's Bay Falls • Trinidad & Tobago . 166 R
King's Lynn • United Kingdom 63 F8
King's Canyon • QL, Australia 136 C5
Kingman • AZ, United States 150 E5
Kingman Reef • Pacific Ocean . . . 139 DD2
Kings Canyon • NT, Australia 136 A2
Kings Canyon Nat. Park •
    CA, United States 154 J8
Kings Canyon Nat. Park Park N •
    CA, United States . . . . 152 [50]
Kings Landing • NB, Canada 160 A2
Kings Mtn Nat. Military Park Park N •
    SC, United States . . . . 153 [234]
Kings, Valley of the • Egypt 109 E2
Kingsbridge • United Kingdom 65 J10
Kingsburgh • South Africa 111 B5
Kingsford Smith [Apt] •
    NS, Australia 136 H8
Kingsmill Group • Kiribati 138 CC3
Kingsport • TN, United States 151 D3
Kingston Dive • Egypt 109 E7
Kingston • Jamaica 165 D4
Kingston • New Zealand 137 J6
Kingston Bay • St Vincent & Gren. . . 167 O
Kingston • NY, United States 156 C1
Kingston • OT, Canada 160 F4
Kingston • TS, Australia 136 F7
Kingston upon Hull • United Kingdom . 63 E7
Kingston-upon-Thames •
    United Kingdom 65 G7
Kingstown • St Vincent & Gren. . . . . 167 O
Kingstown Bay • St Vincent & Gren. . 167 O
Kingsville • OT, Canada 161 A3
Kingsville • TX, United States 155 E6
Kinki • Japan 127 C4
Kinloch • United Kingdom 66 A2
Kinna • Sweden 99 G6
Kinnaird Head • United Kingdom . . . 68 E6
Kinnegad • Ireland 69 E6
Kinnekulle • Sweden 99 G5
Kino-kawa • Japan 127 G7
Kinoosao • SA, Canada 158 F3
Kinpu-san • Japan 127 H8
Kinross • United Kingdom 65 B1

Kinross-shire • United Kingdom 65 B1
Kinsale • Ireland 69 H11
Kinsarvik • Norway 98 G8
Kinshasa • Dem. Rep. of Congo . . . 106 C6
Kinston • NC, United States 151 E3
Kintyre • United Kingdom 62 C5
Kintyre, Mull of • United Kingdom . . . 62 C5
Kinvarra • Ireland 69 H9
Kinzua Dam • PA, United States . . . 156 A1
Kiónia • Tinos, Greece . . . . 94 I
Kiparissiakós Kólpos • Greece 93 B3
Kipembawe • Tanzania 110 G8
Kipengere Range • Tanzania 110 G8
Kipili • Tanzania 110 G8
Kirakira • Solomon Is. . . . . 138 W
Kirbyville • TX, United States 155 F5
Kirchdorf • Austria 91 O7
Kirchhain • Germany 74 B1
Kirchheim bei München • Germany . . 74 G7
Kirchheim-Bolanden • Germany 74 D6
Kireli • Turkey 95 H7
Kirgöz Hani • Turkey 95 G7
Kırıkhan • Turkey 96 B2
Kırıkkale • Turkey 95 G5
Kirishi • Russian Fed. 100 L9
Kiritimati • Kiribati . . . . 139 I
Kirkagaç • Turkey 95 E5
Kirkby Stephen • United Kingdom . . . 63 D6
Kirkcaldy • United Kingdom 65 B2
Kirkcudbright • United Kingdom 62 C6
Kirkcudbrightshire • United Kingdom . . 64 A2
Kirkenær • Norway 98 E5
Kirkenes • Norway 97 F2
Kirkintilloch • United Kingdom 65 A2
Kirkkonummi • Finland 99 D4
Kirkland Lake • OT, Canada 159 H4
Kırklareli • Turkey 95 E3
Kırklareli [Adm] • Turkey 95 E3
Kirkstone Pass • United Kingdom 65 D6
Kirksville • MO, United States 150 B2
Kirkuk • Iraq 120 E6
Kirkwall • United Kingdom 62 D2
Kirkwood Ski • CA, United States . . 146 [31]
Kirkwood • MO, United States 150 B3
Kirkwood • South Africa 111 G7
Kirov • Russian Fed. 100 G2
Kirovohrad • Ukraine 100 D3
Kirriemuir • United Kingdom 65 B1
Kirsehir • Turkey 95 B2
Kiruna • Sweden 97 E2
Kisa • Sweden 99 H5
Kisangani • Dem. Rep. of Congo . . . 108 B4
Kisarazu • Japan 127 I9
Kishangarh • India 123 E8
Kishiwada • Japan 127 G7
Kisii • Kenya 109 C5
Kiskinörad Nat. Park Park N •
    Hungary . . . . 58 [116]
Kislovodsk • Russian Fed. 100 F5
Kismaayo • Somalia 108 D4
Kissámou Kastéli • Crete, Greece . . . 93 G5
Kissámou, Kólpos • Crete, Greece . . 93 G5
Kissimmee • FL, United States 157 B1
Kissing Bridge • NY, United States . 156 A1
Kisumu • Kenya 109 C5
Kitakyushu • Japan 127 B4
Kitale • Kenya 109 C4
Kitami • Japan 127 D2
Kitayama-gawa • Japan 127 G7
Kitchener • OT, Canada 160 E5
Kithira • Greece 93 C3
Kithnos • Greece 93 D3
Kiti, Cape • Cyprus 96 C4
Kitimat • BC, Canada 158 D3
Kitunda • Tanzania 110 G8
Kitwanga • BC, Canada 160 I6
Kitwe • Zambia 110 B2
Kitzbühel Ski • Austria . . . . 61 [101]
Kitzbühel • Austria 91 O7
Kitzbüheler Alpen • Austria 91 O7
Kiu Tsui Chau • Hong Kong, China . . 126 F5
Kiukiu, Pointe • French Polynesia . . . 139 J
Kiunga Marine Nat. Reserve • Kenya . 109 D5
Kivik • Sweden 99 G7
Kiviöli • Estonia 100 K6
Kivu, Lac •
    Rwanda/Dem. Rep. of Congo . . . 110 G7
Kiwayu • Kenya 109 D5
Kizikkaya • Turkey 95 G7
Kizil Adalar • Turkey 95 F3
Kizil Irmak • Turkey 95 B1
Kizilkadag • Turkey 95 G7
Kizkalesi • Turkey 95 I10
Kjellerup • Denmark 99 F7
Kjevik [Apt] • Norway 99 E5
Kladno • Czech Rep. 89 E6
Kladruby • Czech Rep. 89 D7
Klaeng • Thailand 130 E8
Klagenfurt • Austria 91 G2
Klaipéda • Lithuania 100 J7
Klamath • CA/OR, United States . . . 154 I7
Klamath Falls • OR, United States . . 154 G6
Klamath Mtns • CA, United States . 154 I/J7
Klarälven • Sweden 97 D3
Klating Beach • Bali, Indonesia . . . 131 L8
Klatovy • Czech Rep. 89 D7
Klausen • Italy 86 C3
Klawer • South Africa 111 D6
Klein Bonaire • Bonaire . . . . 166 U
Kleinmachnow • Germany 73 E8
Kleinwalsertal Ski • Austria . . . . . 61 [88]
Klenci pod Čerchovem • Czech Rep. . 89 D7
Klerksdorp • South Africa 110 B3
Klin • Russian Fed. 100 M10
Klingenberg • Germany 74 B2
Klingenthal • Germany 89 D6
Klínovec • Czech Rep. 89 D6
Klippan • Sweden 99 G7
Klipplaat • South Africa 111 F6
Klitmøller • Denmark 99 E6
Klodzko • Poland 89 B3
Klofta • Norway 98 E5
Klondike Gold Rush Nat. Hist. Park •
    AK, United States 157 F4
Klondike Gold Rush Nat. Hist. Park Park N •
    AK, United States . . . . 152 [14]
Klos • Albania 92 G3
Klosters Ski • Switzerland . . . . 61 [80]
Klosters • Switzerland 90 L5
Kluane Nat. Park & Reserve Park N •
    YT, Canada . . . . 161 [3]
Kluane Nat. Park & Reserve Heritage N •
    YT, Canada . . . . 40 [1]
Kluczbork • Poland 89 B3
Klungkung • Bali, Indonesia 131 L8
Klyuchevskaya, Sopka •
    Russian Fed. 101 Q4
Knäred • Sweden 99 G7
Knarvik • Norway 98 F8
Knebworth House • United Kingdom . . 65 G7
Knechtsteden • Germany 73 C6
Knidos • Turkey 95 E6
Knife River Indian Villages Nat. Hist. Site
    Park N • ND, United States . . . 152 [147]
Knightshayes Court • United Kingdom . 65 J9
Knin • Croatia 92 G6
Knislinge • Sweden 99 G7
Knittelfeld • Austria 91 B3
Knivsta • Sweden 99 B1
Knob Hill • Cayman Is. . . . . 164 R
Knobbe, Fuerte • Panama 170 M11
Knock • Ireland 69 H8
Knock [Apt] • Ireland 69 H8
Knoebels Amusement Resort •
    PA, United States 156 B2
Knoebels Amusement Resort Park L •
    PA, United States . . . . 157 [31]
Knokke-Heist • Belgium 70 F6
Knole • United Kingdom 65 G8
Knossós • Crete, Greece 93 G6

Knott's Berry Farm Park L •
    CA, United States . . . . 157 [5]
Knowth • Ireland 69 E6
Knox, Cape • BC, Canada 158 C3
Knoxville • TN, United States 151 D3
Knutby • Sweden 99 B1
Knuthenborg Park • Denmark 99 F8
Knysna • South Africa 107 D4
Knysna Nat. Lake Area • South Africa . 111 F7
Koanaka Hills • Botswana 110 I9
Koba • Cape H • India 127 F6
Kobe • Japan 127 F6
Kobe Portopia Land • Japan 127 F6
København • Denmark 99 G7
Kobe Bay • China/D.P.R. of Korea . 125 G3
Kobern-Gondorf • Germany 74 C5
Koblenz • Germany 74 D5
Kobryn • Belarus 100 B3
Kobuk Valley Nat. Park •
    AK, United States 157 D2
Kobuk Valley Nat. Park Park N •
    AK, United States . . . . 152 [4]
Kocaeli • Turkey 95 F3
Kocani • FYR of Macedonia 92 C3
Koceviç • Slovenia 92 F5
Kniyama • Japan 127 D3
Kochelsee • Germany 74 G8
Kochi • India 124 B3
Kochi • Japan 127 B4
Kochkor • Kyrgyzstan 121 G3
Kodagu • India 124 B3
Kodaikanal • India 124 B3
Kodaikanal Hill Sta • India 124 E6
Kodiak • AK, United States 157 E4
Kodiak I. • AK, United States 157 E4
Kodikkarai Bird Sanctuary • India . . 124 C3
Kodungallur • India 124 B3
Koforidua • Ghana 106 B3
Koflach • Austria 91 G2
Koga • Japan 127 H8
Koga • Japan 127 I8
Kogalniceanu, Mihail [Apt] •
    Romania 92 I7
Køge • Denmark 99 F8
Køge Bugt • Denmark 99 G8
Kohima • India 122 D3
Kohtla-Järve • Estonia 100 K6
Kohunlich • Mexico 169 F5
Koinaa • Kiribati . . . . 139 F
Kok • Thailand 130 C5
Kokand • Uzbekistan 121 K7
Kokemäenjoki • Finland 99 C3
Kokemäki • Finland 99 C3
Kokenau • Indonesia 131 I4
Kokini Hani • Crete, Greece 93 I6
Kokkári • Sámos, Greece . . . . 94 E
Kokkína • Cyprus 96 C4
Kokkola • Finland 97 E3
Koko Head Natural Park •
    HI, United States 157 H6
Koko Nur • China 125 C3
Kokorin • Czech Rep. 89 E6
Koksijde-Bad • Belgium 70 E6
Koksoak • QU, Canada 159 J3
Kokstad • South Africa 111 B5
Kol'skiy Poluostrov • Russian Fed. . 101 D3
Kolar • India 124 C2
Kolar Gold Fields • India 123 D7
Kosta • Sweden 99 A1
Kolbermoor • Germany 74 G8
Kolding • Denmark 99 E7
Kölen • Sweden 97 D2
Kolguyev, Ostrov • Russian Fed. . . . 101 E3
Kolhapur • India 124 A1
Kolimbia • Rhodes, Greece . . . . 94 F
Kolimvári • Crete, Greece 93 G5
Kolín • Czech Rep. 89 E6
Kolka • Latvia 100 J7
Kolkata • India 122 C3
Kollam • India 124 B3
Kollfuschg • Italy 86 D3
Kolmården • Sweden 99 A2
Kolmårdens Djurpark • Sweden 99 A2
Köln • Germany 73 C6
Köln Heritage C • Germany . . . . . 44 [56]
Köln-Bonn [Apt] • Germany 74 A1
Kolobrzeg • Poland 89 A1
Kolofau, Mt • Wallis & Futuna . . . . . 139 Q
Kolombangara • Solomon Is. . . . . . 138 W
Kolomna • Russian Fed. 100 M10
Kolonga • Tonga . . . . 139 P
Kolonia • Fed. States of Micronesia . 138 D
Kolonos • Tonga . . . . 139 S
Kolpino • Russian Fed. 100 L9
Kolsva • Sweden 99 A1
Kolumadulu Atoll • Maldives 124 G8
Kolwezi • Dem. Rep. of Congo 108 B6
Kolyma • Russian Fed. 101 P3
Kolymskiy, Khrebet • Russian Fed. . 101 Q3
Kom Ombo • Egypt 109 D8
Koma tou Gialou • Cyprus 96 D3
Komárno • Slovak Rep. 89 B5
Komatipoort • South Africa 111 A1
Komatsu • Japan 127 C3
Komatsushima • Japan 127 C4
Komebail Lagoon • Palau . . . . 138 Y
Komi Russ Adm • Russian Fed. 101 G4
Komi virgin forests Heritage N •
    Russian Fed. . . . . 41 [83]
Komi-Permyak Russ Adm •
    Russian Fed. . . . . 101 [16]
Komodo Nat. Park Heritage N •
    Indonesia . . . . 41 [146]
Kompasberg • South Africa 111 G6
Kompong Cham • Cambodia 129 B5
Kompong Chhnang • Cambodia . . . 129 A4
Kompong Som • Cambodia 128 C4
Kompong Thom • Cambodia 129 A4
Komsomol'sk na-Amure • Russian Fed. 101 N4
Komsomolets, Ostrov • Russian Fed. . 101 J1
Kon Tum • Vietnam 129 B5
Kona [Apt] • HI, United States 157 J6
Kona Coast • HI, United States 157 J6
Konakovo • Russian Fed. 100 M10
Konarak Heritage C • India . . . . . 43 [162]
Kondoa • Tanzania 110 H7
Kondopoga • Russian Fed. . . . . 138 U
Kongolo • Dem. Rep. of Congo 108 B5
Kongoni • Tonga 98 D5
Kongsvinger • Norway 98 E5
Konigs Wusterhausen • Germany . . . 73 F8
Königsberg • Russian Fed. 50 D1
Königsbrunn • Germany 74 H8
Königssee • Germany 74 H8
Königstein im Taunus • Germany . . . 74 C5
Konin • Poland 89 B2
Konispol • Albania 93 B1
Konjic • Bosnia-Herz. 92 F6
Konosha • Russian Fed. 100 F2
Konrei • Palau . . . . 138 Y
Konstanz • Germany 74 F9
Kontiomäki • Finland 97 F3
Kontum Plateau • Vietnam 129 B5
Konya • Turkey 95 I9
Konya [Adm] • Turkey 95 H8
Konya Ovasi • Turkey 95 I9
Konyaaltı • Turkey 95 G8
Konz • Germany 74 C6
Koolau Range • HI, United States . . 157 G6
Kootenay • Canada/United States . . 160 J7
Kootenay Nat. Park Park N •
    BC, Canada . . . . 161 [15]
Kootenay Nat. Park • BC, Canada . . 160 J7
Köpenick (Berlin) • Germany 73 F7
Koper • Slovenia 92 B2
Kopervik • Norway 98 F9
Kopet Dag • Iran/Turkmenistan 121 J2
Köping • Sweden 99 A1

Koprivnica • Croatia 92 G5
Köprülü • Turkey 95 H8
Kora Nat. Park • Kenya 109 D5
Korab • Albania/Macedonia 92 C3
Korakia • Crete, Greece 93 H6
Korat • Thailand 127 I8
Korat Plateau • Thailand 130 A2
Korbous • Tunisia 107 D4
Korçë • Albania 92 C3
Korcula [I.] • Croatia 92 G6
Korday • Kazakstan 121 F3
Kordofan • Sudan 108 B3
Korea Bay • China/D.P.R. of Korea . 125 G3
KOREA, DEMOCRATIC PEOPLE'S
    REPUBLIC OF • Asia 125 G2
KOREA, NORTH • Asia 125 G2
KOREA, REPUBLIC OF • Asia . . . 125 G3
KOREA, SOUTH • Asia 125 G3
Korean War Veterans Memorial Park N •
    DC, United States . . . . 153 [264]
Korff Ice Rise • Antarctica 176 M5
Korhogo • Côte d'Ivoire 106 B4
Korinthiakós Kólpos • Greece 93 C2
Kórinthos • Greece 93 C3
Kóriyama • Japan 127 D3
Korkuteli • Turkey 95 G7
Korla • China 125 B2
Kormakiti, Cape • Cyprus 96 C3
Körmend • Hungary 92 B2
Kornat • Croatia 92 F6
Kornati Nat. Park Park N • Croatia . 58 [120]
Kornati Nat. Park • Croatia 92 F6
Kornelimünster • Germany 74 A1
Koror • Cyprus 96 C4
Kornsjø • Norway 98 E6
Koro • Fiji Is. . . . . 138 S
Koro Sea • Fiji Is. . . . . 138 S
Korogwe • Tanzania 110 H8
Koror • Palau . . . . 138 Y
Körös • Hungary 92 C2
Korosten' • Ukraine 100 C3
Korotogo • Fiji Is. . . . . 138 T
Korpilahti • Finland 99 D3
Korpo • Finland 99 C4
Korschenbroich • Germany 73 C6
Korsør • Denmark 99 F8
Kortrijk • Belgium 70 A4
Korup, Parc nat. du Park •
    Cameroon . . . . 112 [32]
Koryak Russ Adm • Russian Fed. . . 101 [32]
Kós • Cos, Greece . . . . 94 E
Kos [I.] • Greece 93 E3
Kosciol drewniany • Poland 89 G9
Kosciusko • MS, United States 156 F5
Kosciuszko, Mt • NS, Australia 136 H9
Koshigaya • Japan 127 I8
Kosi Bay • South Africa 111 C3
Kosi Bay Nature Reserve •
    South Africa 111 C3
Kosice • Slovak Rep. 89 C4
Koski • Finland 99 D4
Ko-Ring-Gai Chase Nat. Park •
    NS, Australia 136 H8
Kosovska Mitrovica •
    Serbia & Montenegro 92 C3
Kosrae • Fed. States of Micronesia . 138 D
Kosta • Sweden 100 M9
Kostomuksha Vdkhr. • Russian Fed. . 100 M9
Kostrzyn • Poland 89 A2
Koszalin • Poland 89 B1
Koszeg • Hungary 91 H2
Kota • India 123 E8
Kota Bharu • Malaysia 128 C5
Kota Kinabalu • Sabah, Malaysia . . 128 F5
Kotabaru • Indonesia 131 B4
Kotabumi • Indonesia 131 C4
Kotagiri Hill Sta • India 124 E6
Kotare Gorge • New Zealand 137 D6
Kotel'nyy, Ostrov • Russian Fed. . . 101 N2
Kotka • Finland 97 F3
Kotlas • Russian Fed. 100 G1
Kotlin, Ostrov • Russian Fed. 100 L9
Kotor • Serbia & Montenegro 92 B3
Kotor Heritage C •
    Serbia & Montenegro . . . . 44 [213]
Kotisfoú, Farági • Crete, Greece . . . 93 H6
Kottaguden • India 122 C4
Kottayam • India 124 B3
Kotuy • Russian Fed. 101 K2
Kotzebue • AK, United States 157 D2
Kotzebue Sound • AK, United States . 157 D2
Kouchibouguac Nat. Park Park N •
    NB, Canada . . . . 161 [34]
Kouchibouguac Nat. Park •
    NB, Canada 160 A2
Koudougou • Burkina 106 B3
Koufonisi, Crete, Greece . . . . 94 H
Koufonisia • Cyclades, Greece . . . . . 94 H
Koufonisi • Greece 93 J6
Kougaberge • South Africa 111 F7
Koulikoro • Mali 106 C4
Koumac • New Caledonia . . . . 138 U
Kourim • Czech Rep. 89 E6
Kourtaliótiko Farági •
    Crete, Greece 93 H6
Koutsounari • Crete, Greece 93 J6
Kouvola • Finland 97 F3
Kovalam • India 124 B3
Kovalam Beach • India 124 E6
Kovel' • Ukraine 100 B3
Kovrov • Russian Fed. 100 F2
Kowloon • Hong Kong, China 126 F5
Kowloon City • Hong Kong, China . . 126 F5
Koza • Okinawa, Japan . . . . 138 A
Kozagaci • Turkey 95 G8
Kozani • Greece 93 B1
Kozani • Turkey 95 G8
Kozhikode • India 124 B3
Kozyatyn • Ukraine 100 C4
Kra, Isthmus of • Thailand 130 A3
Kraalfontein • South Africa 111 D7
Krabbfjärden • Sweden 99 A2
Kragerø • Norway 98 D6
Kragujevac • Serbia & Montenegro . . 92 C3
Krakatau • Java, Indonesia 131 O11
Krakatau Nature Reserve Heritage N •
    Indonesia . . . . 41 [145]
Kraków • Poland 89 G8
Kraków Heritage C • Poland . . . . 44 [184]
Krakowska, Jura • Poland 89 G8
Kraljevic • Bonaire . . . . 166 U
Kraljevo • Serbia & Montenegro . . . 92 C3
Kramfors • Sweden 97 D3
Kramsach • Austria 91 O7
Kranebitten [Apt] • Austria 91 N7
Kranj • Slovenia 92 F5
Kranjska Gora • Slovenia 92 F5
Kranskloof Nature Reserve •
    South Africa 111 B5
Kranskop • South Africa 111 B4
Krapina • Croatia 92 F5
Kraslava • Latvia 100 K7
Krasnik • Poland 89 C3
Krasnodar • Russian Fed. 100 E4
Krasnoyarsk • Russian Fed. 100 J4
Krasnyy Luch • Ukraine 100 E4
Kratiê • Cambodia 127 C3
Kratovo • Serbia & Montenegro 92 C3
Krefeld • Germany 73 C5
Kremenchuk • Ukraine 100 D4
Kremnica • Slovak Rep. 89 E7
Krems an der Donau • Austria 91 G1
Kreuzberg (Berlin) • Germany 73 F8
Kreuzlingen • Switzerland 90 K4
Kreuztal • Germany 74 B1
Kribi • Cameroon 106 C4
Krimml • Austria 91 N7
Krimpen • Netherlands 70 H8
Kriós, Akra • Crete, Greece 93 G6

Krishna • India 124 C1
Krishna, Mouths of the • India 124 C1
Kristdala • Sweden 99 H6
Kristianopel • Sweden 99 H7
Kristiansand • Norway 99 E5
Kristiansand Dyrepark Park L •
    Norway . . . . 59 [1]
Kristiansand Dyrepark • Norway 99 E5
Kristianstad • Sweden 99 G7
Kristiansund • Norway 97 B3
Kristiinankaupunki • Finland 99 C3
Kristinestad • Finland 99 C3
Kriti [Adm] • Greece 94 CC4
Kritinia • Rhodes, Greece . . . . 94 F
Kritsá • Crete, Greece 93 I6
Krivoklát • Czech Rep. 89 D6
Krivolátska Vrchovina • Czech Rep. . 89 D6
Krivyy Rih • Ukraine 100 D4
Krk • Croatia 92 F5
Krk [I.] • Croatia 92 F5
Krka Nat. Park Park N • Croatia . . . 58 [121]
Krka Nat. Park • Slovenia 92 F5
Krkonose Nat. Park Park N •
    Czech Rep. . . . . 68 [100]
Krkonose Nat. Park • Czech Rep. . . . 89 E6
Krøderen • Norway 98 D5
Krøderen [Lake] • Norway 98 D5
Krokek • Sweden 99 A2
Kromdraai Heritage C • South Africa . 43 [123]
Kromeriz Heritage C • Czech Rep. . 44 [196]
Kronberg • Germany 74 D5
Kronoberg • Sweden 99 G6
Kronstadt • Russian Fed. 100 L9
Kroonstad • South Africa 110 B3
Kropotkin • Russian Fed. 100 F4
Kroppefjäll • Sweden 99 F5
Krosno • Poland 89 G9
Kroussónas • Crete, Greece 93 I6
Kröv • Germany 74 C6
Kroya • Java, Indonesia 131 P12
Krsko • Slovenia 92 F5
Kruger • South Africa 111 A1
Kruger Nat. Park • South Africa . . 112 [136]
Kruje • Albania 92 B3
Krumbach • Germany 74 F7
Krung Thep • Thailand 130 D7
Krüpelsee • Germany 73 F8
Krusevac • Serbia & Montenegro . . . 92 C3
Krusne Hory • Czech Rep. 89 D6
Kryksläitt • Finland 99 D4
Krym • Ukraine 100 D4
Krymsk • Russian Fed. 100 E4
Krynica • Poland 89 G9
Krzyz • Poland 89 B2
Ksar el Kebir • Morocco 107 A1
Ksar Hadada • Tunisia 107 D6
Ksar Hellal • Tunisia 107 D5
Ksar Ouled Soltane • Tunisia 107 D6
Ksar Sghir • Morocco 107 A1
Kuala Belait • Brunei 128 E5
Kuala Dungun • Malaysia 129 G10
Kuala Kubu Baharu • Malaysia . . . 129 G9
Kuala Lipis • Malaysia 129 G9
Kuala Lumpur • Malaysia 129 G10
Kuala Selangor • Malaysia 129 F10
Kuala Terengganu • Malaysia 128 C5
Kuandang • Indonesia 131 F3
Kuantan • Malaysia 128 C6
Kubenskoye, Ozero • Russian Fed. . 100 M9
Kubutambahan • Bali, Indonesia . . . 131 L7
Kuching • Sarawak, Malaysia 128 E6
Kücükkuyu • Turkey 95 C4
Kudahithi • Maldives 124 H7
Kudarebe • Aruba . . . . 166 W
Kudat • Sabah, Malaysia 128 F5
Kudus • Java, Indonesia 131 O11
Kufri Hill Sta • India 124 E5
Kufstein • Austria 91 O7
Kugluktuk • NU, Canada 158 E2
Kuhmo • Finland 97 F3
Kuito • Angola 110 A2
Kuji • L • AK, United States 157 F4
Kujani Game Reserve Park • Ghana . 112 [20]
Kuju-san • Japan 127 B4
Kukës • Albania 92 C3
Kuki • Japan 127 I8
Kula • Turkey 95 F5
Kulagino • Kazakstan 121 B2
Kuldiga • Latvia 100 J7
Kulgera • NT, Australia 136 B2
Kulmbach • Germany 72 D3
Kulu Hill Sta • India 124 E5
Kulu • Turkey 95 B2
Kumagaya • Japan 127 H8
Kumamoto • Japan 127 B4
Kumanovo • FYR of Macedonia 92 C3
Kumasi • Ghana 106 B4
Kumba • Cameroon 106 C4
Kumbakonam • India 124 C3
Kumbhalgarh • India 123 D8
Kumla • Sweden 99 A1
Kumluca • Turkey 95 G8
Kumo • Nigeria 106 D4
Kumo älv • Finland 99 C3
Kumrokhali, Cape •
    HI, United States 157 J6
Kumul • China 125 C2
Kumyali • Cyprus 96 D3
Kunashiri-to • Russian Fed. 127 E2
Kundapura • India 124 B2
Kundelungu, Parc nat. de Park •
    Dem. Rep. of Congo . . . . 112 [56]
Kunduchi • Tanzania 110 H8
Kung Bay • Ko Phuket, Thailand . . 130 F9
Kungagraven • Sweden 99 G7
Kungälv • Sweden 99 F6
Kungsbacka • Sweden 99 F6
Kungshamn • Sweden 99 A2
Kungsör • Sweden 99 A1
Kunlun Shan • China 125 A2
Kunming • China 125 E4
Kunshan • China 126 H6
Kuopio • Finland 97 F3
Kuopio [Adm] • Finland 98 C2
Kup'yans'k • Ukraine 100 E4
Kupa • Croatia/Slovenia 92 G5
Kupang • Indonesia 130 K7
Kupiskis • Lithuania 100 K7
Kuprianof I. • AK, United States . . . 157 F4
Kuqa • China 125 C2
Kuramathi • Maldives 124 H7
Kuranda • QL, Australia 136 C3
Kurashiki • Japan 127 B4
Kurchum • Kazakstan 121 H2
Kurdistan • Asia 120 E6
Kurdzhali • Bulgaria 92 D3
Kure • Japan 127 B4
Kure Atoll • HI, United States 138 CC1
Kurukshetra • India 123 E7
Kuruman • South Africa 110 B3
Kurumba • Maldives 124 H8
Kurunegala • Sri Lanka 124 C4

Kurzeme • Latvia 100 J7
Kus Gölü • Turkey 95 F5
Kusadasi • Turkey 95 E5
Kusamba • Bali, Indonesia 131 L8
Kusatsu • Japan 127 G6
Kuscenneti Nat. Park • Turkey 95 F4
Kushinagar • India 123 G7
Kushiro • Japan 127 D2
Kuskowim • AK, United States 157 D3
Kuskowim-ko • Japan 127 D2
Kussnacht • Switzerland 90 K5
Kut, Ko • Thailand 130 A3
Kuta • Bali, Indonesia 131 L8
Kuta Beach • Bali, Indonesia 131 L8
Kütahya • Turkey 95 F4
Kütahya [Adm] • Turkey 95 F4
Kutaisi • Georgia 120 F4
Kutaisi Heritage C • Georgia . . . . 44 [315]
Kutina • Croatia 92 G5
Kutná Hora • Czech Rep. 89 E6
Kutná Hora Heritage C • Czech Rep. . 44 [189]
Kutno • Poland 89 B2
Kuttanad • India 124 B3
Kuujjuarapik • QU, Canada 159 I3
Kuujjuaq • QU, Canada 159 J3
Kuusamo • Finland 97 F2
KUWAIT • Asia 120 F8
Kuwait [City] • Kuwait 120 F8
Kuybyshev • Russian Fed. 101 H4
Kuybyshevskoye Vdkhr. • Russian Fed. . 100 G2
Kuytun • China 125 C2
Kuznetsk • Russian Fed. 100 G3
Kvalaya • Norway 97 C2
Kvalvaya • Norway 97 E1
Kvarner • Croatia 92 F5
Kvarneric • Croatia 92 F6
Kvicksund • Sweden 99 A2
Kvinesdal • Norway 97 E4
Kviteseid • Norway 98 G9
Kwai Chung Port • Hong Kong, China . 126 E5
Kwajalein • Marshall Is. . . . . 139 E
Kwajalein Lagoon • Marshall Is. . . . 139 E
Kwakoegron • Surinam 174 A2
Kwale • Kenya 109 C6
KwaMashu • South Africa 111 B4
Kwambonambi • South Africa 111 C4
Kwango • Dem. Rep. of Congo 108 A5
Kwango • Dem. Rep. of Congo 108 A5
KwaNobuhle • South Africa 111 G7
KwaZulu-Natal • South Africa . . . . 111 B-C
Kyancutta • SA, Australia 135 F6
Kyiv • Ukraine 100 D3
Kyiv Heritage C • Ukraine . . . . . 44 [267]
Kykkos Monastery • Cyprus 96 C4
Kyle of Lochalsh • United Kingdom . . 62 C3
Kyll • Germany 74 C6
Kymi • Finland 98 C3
Kynnefjäll • Sweden 99 F5
Kyoga, Lake • Uganda 109 C4
Kyorara • Turkey 95 F5
Kyoto • Japan 127 G6
Kyoto Heritage C • Japan . . . . . . 43 [194]
Kyoto [Adm] • Japan 127 G6
Kyrenia • Cyprus 96 C4
Kyrenia • Cyprus 96 C3
Kyrenia Mtns • Cyprus 96 C3
Kyrgyz Range • Kazakstan/Kyrgyzstan . 121 F3
KYRGYZSTAN • Asia 121 F3
Kyrkhult • Sweden 99 G7
Kyrosjärvi • Finland 99 D3
Kythera • Cyprus 96 D3
Kythira • Greece 127 B4
Kyushu • Japan 127 B4
Kyustendil • Bulgaria 92 C3
Kyzyl • Russian Fed. 101 J4

L

L'Aire, I. de • Minorca, Spain 83 K8
L'Anse aux Meadows Hist. Park
    Heritage C • NF, Canada . . . . 42 [5]
L'Hospitalet de Llobregat • Spain . . 83 C4
L'Île Rousse • Corsica, France . . . 78 M11
L'viv • Ukraine 100 B4
L'vov • Ukraine 100 B4
La Amistad, Parque Int. •
    Costa Rica/Panama 170 F6
La Amistad, Parque Int. Heritage N •
    Costa Rica/Panama . . . . 40 [26]
La Angostura, Presa de • Mexico . . 168 F4
La Antilla • Spain 82 H7
La Arenosa • Panama 170 L11
La Ascension, Bahia de • Mexico . . 169 F5
La Asunción • Margarita . . . . 166 T
La Aurora [Apt] • Guatemala 170 K9
La Blanquilla • Venezuela 167 EE4
La Cadena • Puerto Rico 165 I7
La Caleta • Tenerife, Canary Is. . . . 82 G5
La Canal • Ibiza, Spain 83 L10
La Cantera, I. de • Spain 83 A1
La Ceiba • Honduras 170 K9
La Chorrera • Panama 170 L11
La Citadelle Heritage C • Haiti . . . 42 [43]
La Concepción • Panama 170 F6
La Crosse • VA, United States 156 A4
La Crosse • WI, United States 150 B2
La Cumbre, Volcán • Galápagos Is. . 171 G10
La Esmeralda • Venezuela 173 C2
La Esperanza • Cuba 164 E4
La Esperanza • Honduras 170 K9
La Fé • Cuba 164 E4
La Fortaleza • Puerto Rico 165 J7
La Fortaleza Heritage C •
    Puerto Rico . . . . 42 [45]
La Goulette • Tunisia 107 D4
La Grande 4, Réservoir • QU, Canada . 154 H6
La Grande 2, Réservoir •
    QU, Canada 159 I3
La Grande 3, Réservoir •
    QU, Canada 159 I3
La Grange • GA, United States 151 D4
La Guardia, Ensenada • Margarita . . 166 T
La Habana • Cuba 164 E4
La Habana Heritage C • Cuba . . . 42 [34]
La Isabela • Dominican Rep. 165 G5
La Isleta • Lanzarote, Canary Is. . . . 83 I5
La Joyanca • Spain 83 D3
La Junta • CO, United States 148 F3
La Junta • Mexico 168 C2
La Laguna, Picacho de • Mexico . . . 168 I6
La Línea de la Concepción • Spain . 82 D3
La Loche • SA, Canada 158 F3
La Louvière • Belgium 70 B4
La Luz, Costa de • Spain 82 I8
La Manga del Mar Menor • Spain . . . 83 A2
La Marsa • Tunisia 107 D4
La Montaña • Peru 173 B3
La Mora • Mont. Costa de • Spain . . 83 A3
La Nao, Cabo de • Spain 83 B1
La Oliva •
    Fuerteventura, Canary Is. 83 H5
La Orchila • Venezuela 167 EE4
La Orotava • Tenerife, Canary Is. . . . 82 G5
La Oroya • Peru 173 E6
La Palma • Canary Is. 83 D5
La Palma • Panama 170 L11
La Palmita • Cuba 164 F4
La Panchita • Cuba 164 F4
La Parad, Istmo de •
    Fuerteventura, Canary Is. 83 H5
La Paz • Bolivia 173 C4
La Paz • Honduras 170 D3
La Paz • Mexico 168 I6
La Pérouse Strait •
    Japan/Russian Fed. 127 D1
La Piedad • Mexico 169 I7
La Pineda • Spain 83 C4
La Plaine • Dominica 175 G4
La Plata, Río de •
    Argentina/Uruguay 175 G6
La Playa de Mogán •
    Gran Canaria, Canary Is. 82 G6
La Point Beach • St Lucia . . . . 167 N

La Pointe • MI, United States 161 A1
La Purisma • Mexico 168 H6
La Purisma Mission State Hist. Park •
  CA, United States 154 I9
La Rapita • Majorca, Spain 83 Q12
La Restinga, Laguna • Margarita .... 166 T
La Rioja • Argentina 175 B2
La Rioja • Spain 80 D2
La Rochelle • France 77 E6
La Roda • Spain 80 D4
La Romana • Dominican Rep. 165 H6
La Ronde Amusement Park •
  QU, Canada 160 G3
La Ronge • SA, Canada 158 F3
La Ronge, Lake • SA, Canada 158 F3
La Serena • Chile 175 A2
La Seu d'Urgell • Spain 83 C3
La Spézia • Italy 87 B3
La Unión • El Salvador 170 D4
La Unión • Spain 83 A2
La Vega • Dominican Rep. 165 G5
La Veguita • Lanzarote, Canary Is. 83 I5
La Vila Joiosa • Spain 83 B1
Laarne • Belgium 70 B4
Laax Ski • Switzerland .... 61 [74]
Laax • Switzerland 90 K5
Laâyoune • Western Sahara 106 A2
Labasa • Fiji Is. .... 138 S
Labe • Czech Rep. 89 E6
Labé • Guinea 106 A3
Labná • Mexico 169 F4
Laborie • St Lucia .... 167 N
Labouheyre • France 78 E6
Labrador • NF, Canada 159 J3
Labrador City • NF, Canada 159 J3
Labrador Mtn Ski •
  NY, United States .... 146 [99]
Labrador Mtn • NY, United States 156 B1
Labrador Sea • Canada/Greenland 159 K2
Labuan • Malaysia 128 F5
Labuhan • Java, Indonesia 131 O11
Labuhanbilik • Indonesia 131 N9
Lac • Bonaire .... 166 U
Lac Court Oreilles Ind Res •
  WI, United States .... 155 [62]
Lac du Flambeau Ind Res •
  WI, United States .... 155 [64]
Lac La Biche • AL, Canada 158 E3
Lac Mégantic • QU, Canada 160 H3
Lacanau • France 78 E5
Lacandón, Parque Nac. • Guatemala 170 J9
Lachi • Cyprus 96 C4
Lachlan • NS, Australia 136 G8
Lachute • QU, Canada 160 G3
Lacken Reservoir • Ireland 69 F7
Läckö • Sweden 99 G5
Lacre Punt • Bonaire .... 166 U
Ladakh • Asia 123 A1
Ladispoli • Italy 87 E4
Ladoga, Lake • Russian Fed. 100 D1
Ladozhskoye Ozero • Russian Fed. 100 D1
Ladrone Is. • Pacific Ocean 9 O5
Lady Barron • TS, Australia 136 F6
Lady Elliot I. • QL, Australia 136 D4
Ladysmith • South Africa 111 B4
Lae • Papua New Guinea 134 C5
Laem Chabang • Thailand 130 E8
Laem So Pagoda •
  Ko Samui, Thailand 130 G12
Lærdalsøyri • Norway 98 G3
Læsø • Denmark 99 F6
Læsø Rende • Denmark 99 F6
Lafayette • IN, United States 150 C2
Lafayette • LA, United States 156 E6
Lafite, Château • France 78 E5
Lagan • Sweden 99 G6
Lagan • United Kingdom 63 B6
Lagana, Kólpos • Zante, Greece .... 94 J
Laganas • Zante, Greece .... 94 J
Lågen • Norway 97 C3
Lago de Camécuaro, Parque Nac. •
  Mexico 169 I7
Lagoa • Azores 84 B3
Lagoa • Portugal 84 I8
Lagoon Park L • UT, United States .... 157 [9]
Lagos • Greece 93 D1
Lagos • Nigeria 106 C4
Lagos • Portugal 84 I8
Lagos, Baía de • Portugal 84 I8
Lagos de Moreno • Mexico 169 I6
Lagoa • Tanzania 110 G7
LaGuardia [Apt] •
  NY, United States 156 C2
Lagun, Playa • Curaçao .... 166 V
Laguna Ind Res • NM, United States .... 155 [39]
Laguna de Chapala • Mexico 168 H5
Laguna Quays • QL, Australia 136 D4
Lagunas de Chacahua, Parque Nac. •
  Mexico 169 J8
Lahaina • HI, United States 157 I5
Lahat • Indonesia 131 N4
Lahemaa Nat. Park Park N • Estonia .... 58 [144]
Lahemaa Nat. Park • Estonia 100 K6
Lahewa • Indonesia 131 M10
Lahi Passage • Tonga .... 139 P
Lahn • Germany 74 B1
Lahnstein • Germany 74 D5
Laholm • Sweden 99 G7
Laholmsbukten • Sweden 99 G7
Lahore • Pakistan 122 B2
Lahore Heritage C • Pakistan .... 43 [148]
Lahr • Germany 74 B3
Lahti • Finland 99 D4
Lai'an • China 126 G6
Laie • HI, United States 157 G5
Laiguéglia • Italy 87 A3
Laikipia Nat. Reserve • Kenya 109 C4
Laingsburg • South Africa 111 E6
Lairg • United Kingdom 62 C2
Laitila • Finland 99 C4
Lajes • Brazil 175 C2
Lajes do Pico • Azores 84 B4
Lake Bogoria Nat. Reserve • Kenya 109 C4
Lake Buena Vista •
  FL, United States 157 B1
Lake Charles • LA, United States 156 E6
Lake Chelan Nat. Recreation Area •
  WA, United States 154 G5
Lake Chelan Nat. Recreation Area Park N •
  WA, United States .... 152 [29]
Lake City • FL, United States 155 C1
Lake Clark Nat. Park & Preserve •
  AK, United States 157 D3
Lake Clark Nat. Park & Preserve Park N •
  AK, United States .... 152 [9]
Lake District • United Kingdom .... 65 C-D
Lake District Nat. Park Park N •
  United Kingdom .... 58 [40]
Lake District Nat. Park •
  United Kingdom 65 C3-D4
Lake Eyre Nat. Park •
  SA, Australia 135 F5
Lake Gairdner Nat. Park •
  SA, Australia 135 F6
Lake Havasu City •
  AZ, United States 155 G7
Lake King • WA, Australia 135 B6
Lake Louise Ski • AL, Canada .... 146 [12]
Lake Louise • AL, Canada 160 J7
Lake Mackay Aboriginal Land •
  NT, Australia 136 A1
Lake Malawi Nat. Park •
  Malawi .... 112 [99]
Lake Malawi Nat. Park Heritage N •
  Malawi .... 41 [112]
Lake Manyara Nat. Park • Tanzania 110 H7
Lake Manyara Nat. Park •
  Tanzania .... 112 [86]
Lake Mead Nat. Recreation Area •
  AZ/NV, United States 155 G7
Lake Mead Nat. Recreation Area Park N •
  AZ/NV, United States .... 152 [58]
Lake Meredith Nat. Recreation Area
  Park N • TX, United States .... 152 [130]

Lake Monroe • FL, United States 155 D2
Lake Nakuru Nat. Park • Kenya 109 C5
Lake Nakuru Nat. Park Park N • Kenya .... 112 [76]
Lake Roosevelt Nat. Recreation Area •
  WA, United States 154 H5
Lake Roosevelt Nat. Recreation Area
  Park N • WA, United States .... 152 [30]
Lake Torrens Nat. Park •
  SA, Australia 135 F6
Lake Traverse Ind Res •
  SD, United States .... 155 [45]
Lake Wales • FL, United States 155 C2
Lake Wood • OH, United States 150 D2
Lakefield Nat. Park •
  QL, Australia 135 G2
Lakeland • FL, United States 155 C2
Lakepa • Niue .... 139 Q
Lakes Entrance • VI, Australia 136 G9
Lakes Entrance • VI, Australia 136 G9
Lakeview • OR, United States 154 G6
Lakewood • CO, United States 148 E3
Lakhpat • India 122 A3
Lakonikós Kólpos • Greece 93 C3
Laksamana Forest Reserve •
  Penang, Malaysia 129 D7
Lakselv • Norway 97 E1
Lakshadweep • India 124 A3
Lakshadweep Sea • India 124 B3
Lakshar Gah • Afghanistan 121 D5
Lalibela Heritage C • Ethiopia .... 43 [100]
Lalitpur • India 123 F8
Lalolalo, Lac • Wallis & Futuna .... 139 Q
Lalomanu • Samoa .... 139 G
Lam Po Reservoir • Thailand 130 A2
Lam Tseun Country Park •
  Hong Kong, China 126 E4
Lamai Beach • Ko Samui, Thailand 130 G12
Lambale • Belize 170 K8
Lamar • CO, United States 148 F3
Lambari • Brazil 174 E7
Lambay I. • Ireland 69 F6
Lambert's Bay • South Africa 111 D6
Lambi • Cos, Greece .... 94 E
Lamen • Vanuatu .... 138 V
Lameth [Apt] • Martinique .... 167 L
Lameque, I. • NB, Canada 160 B1
Lamesa • TX, United States 149 F4
Lamézia Terme • Italy 85 F5
Lamía • Greece 93 C2
Lamington Nat. Park •
  QL, Australia 136 D5
Lamlam, Mt • Guam .... 138 Z
Lamma I. • Hong Kong, China 126 E5
Lammermuir Hills • United Kingdom 65 B2
Lammhult • Sweden 99 G6
Lamongan • Java, Indonesia 131 R11
Lamoni • IA, United States 150 B2
Lamont • WA, United States 148 C2
Lampang • Thailand 130 D6
Lampasas • TX, United States 155 C5
Lampedusa, I. di • Italy 85 D7
Lampeter • United Kingdom 63 C8
Lamphun • Thailand 130 B6
Lamu • Kenya 109 D5
Lamu Heritage C • Kenya .... 43 [116]
Lamu I. • Kenya 109 D5
Lanai City • HI, United States 157 I5
Lanark • United Kingdom 65 A2
Lanarkshire • United Kingdom 65 A2
Lancang Jiang • China 125 D3
Lancashire • United Kingdom 64 B4
Lancaster • PA, United States 156 B2
Lancaster • United Kingdom 63 D6
Lancaster Sound • NU, Canada 159 H1
Lance aux Epines • Grenada .... 166 Q
Lancieno • Italy 85 E3
Landau an der Isar • Germany 91 F1
Landau in der Pfalz • Germany 74 B3
Landeck • Austria 91 N8
Lander • WY, United States 148 E2
Landes • France 78 F6
Landes, Côte des • France 78 E5
Landes • France 165 E4
Landing, The • Pitcairn Is. .... 139 L
Lands End • United Kingdom 65 I10
Landsberg am Lech • Germany 74 F7
Landshut • Germany 72 E4
Landskrona • Sweden 99 G2
Landvetter [Apt] • Sweden 99 F6
Lanersbach • Austria 91 O8
Landstort • Sweden 99 J2
Lang Son • Vietnam 128 D2
Langdale Fell • United Kingdom 65 D3
Langkais [Château] • France 77 F5
Langeberg • South Africa 111 E7
Langeland • Denmark 99 F8
Långelmävesi • Finland 99 D3
Langenfeld • Germany 73 G6
Langer See • Germany 73 F8
Langesund • Norway 98 D6
Langi tombis • Tonga .... 139 P
Langkawi • Malaysia 128 S5
Langkloof • South Africa 111 F7
Langon • France 78 E6
Langøya • Norway 97 C2
Langreo • Spain 80 C2
Langres • France 79 A4
Langsa • Indonesia 131 M9
Langue de Barbarie, Parc nat. de la
  Park • Senegal .... 112 [6]
Languedoc-Roussillon • France 77 B2
Langxi • China 126 G6
Lanhydrock House • United Kingdom 65 I10
Lankanfinolhu • Maldives 124 H8
Lannemezan • France 79 F5
Lannion • France 77 C3
Lano • Wallis & Futuna .... 139 O
Lansdowne Hill Sta • India 124 E5
Lansing • MI, United States 150 D2
Lanta, Ko • Thailand 130 A4
Lantau Country Parks •
  Hong Kong, China 126 E5
Lantau I. • Hong Kong, China 126 E5
Lantau Peak • Hong Kong, China 148 B2
Lante, Villa • Italy 87 E4
Lanzarote • Canary Is. 83 I5
Lanzhou • China 125 C2
Lao • Thailand 130 C5
Lao Cai • Vietnam 128 C2
Laoag • Philippines 128 G3
Laodicaia • Turkey 95 F5
Laoha He • China 125 F2
Laohukou • China 126 F6
Laois • Ireland 69 E7
Laon • France 76 E2
Laos • Asia 128 C3
LAOS • Asia 128 C3
Lapaich, Sgurr na • United Kingdom 62 C3
Lapithos • Cyprus 96 C3
Ledbury • United Kingdom 65 E6
Lapland • Finland/Sweden 97 E2
Lappeenranta • Finland 97 F3
Lappi • Finland 97 E2
Lapponian area Heritage N • Sweden .. 41 [54]
Lapponian area Heritage N • Sweden .. 40 [8]
Laptev Sea • Russian Fed. 101 M2
Lápseki • Turkey 95 E4
Lapta • Cyprus 96 C3
Laptev Sea • Russian Fed. 101 M2
Lapua • Finland 97 E3
Lar, Plaj • Turkey 95 G8
Larache • Morocco 107 A1
Laramie • WY, United States 148 E2
Laramie Mtns • WY, United States 148 E2
Laredo • TX, United States 149 G5
Laren • Netherlands 70 H8
Largi I. • Grenada .... 167 P
Largo • FL, United States 151 D5
Largo, Cayo • Cuba 164 F4

Largs • United Kingdom 65 A2
Lárissa • Greece 93 C2
Larnaca • Cyprus 122 A3
Larnaca • Cyprus 96 D4
Larnaca Bay • Cyprus 96 D4
Larnaca [Apt] • Cyprus 62 C6
Larochette • Luxembourg 70 D5
Laroquebrou • France 78 I9
Larsen Ice Shelf • Antarctica 176 M4
Larsen Sound • NU, Canada 158 G1
Larvik • Norway 98 D6
Las Cruces • NM, United States 155 H8
Las Cumbres • Panama 170 M11
Las Flores • Argentina 175 F7
Las Galletas •
  Tenerife, Canary Is. 82 G5
Las Hadas • Mexico 169 H7
Las Heras • Argentina 175 B3
Las Marismas • Spain 82 H7
Las Marites, Laguna de • Margarita .... 166 T
Las Médulas Heritage C • Spain .. 44 [106]
Las Nieves, Pico de •
  Gran Canaria, Canary Is. 82 G6
Las Palmas de Gran Canaria •
  Gran Canaria, Canary Is. 82 G6
Las Perlas, Archipiélago de •
  Panama 170 H6
Las Piedras • Uruguay 175 C3
Las Pipinas • Argentina 175 G7
Las Salinas • Dominican Rep. 165 G6
Las Tablas • Panama 170 G7
Las Terrenas • Dominican Rep. 165 H5
Las Tunas • Cuba 164 G5
Las Vegas • NM, United States 149 E3
Las Vegas • NV, United States 154 J8
Lascaux Heritage C • France .. 44 [91]
Lascaux, Grotte de • France 78 F5
Lassen Volcanic Nat. Park •
  CA, United States 154 I7
Lassen Volcanic Nat. Park Park N •
  CA, United States .... 152 [41]
Lassi • Cephalonia, Greece .... 94 J
Lassithi • Crete, Greece 93 I6
Lassithi [Adm] • Crete, Greece 93 J6
Lastovo • Croatia 92 G6
Lata • Solomon Is. .... 138 W
Lata Mtn • American Samoa .... 139 H
Latacunga • Ecuador 173 B3
Latakia • Syria 120 D6
Lâtemar • Italy 86 C4
Latgale • Latvia 100 K7
Latina • Italy 87 F5
Latmos • Turkey 95 E6
Lató • Crete, Greece 93 J6
Latrobe • PA, United States 156 A2
Latrobe • TS, Australia 136 F6
Latrobe Valley • VI, Australia 136 G9
Lattari, Monti • Italy 87 G7
Latur • India 122 B4
Latvia • Europe 100 K7
Lau Group • Fiji Is. 138 CC4
Lauenburg • Germany 72 D2
Laufen • Germany 74 H7
Laughlin • NV, United States 154 J9
Laukaa • Finland 99 D3
Laulau, Bahia • N. Mariana Is. .... 138 B
Launceston • TS, Australia 136 F6
Launceston • United Kingdom 65 J10
Laupheim • Germany 74 E7
Laura • Marshall Is. .... 138 E
Laurel • MS, United States 156 F5
Laurentides • QU, Canada 160 F3
Laurentides, Réserve faunique des •
  QU, Canada 160 A1
Lauria • Italy 85 E4
Laurinburg • NC, United States 151 E4
Lausanne • Switzerland 90 I6
Laut • Indonesia 131 E4
Lauterbach • Germany 74 B1
Lauterbrunnen • Switzerland 90 J5
Lautoka • Fiji Is. .... 138 T
Lauttawar, Danau • Indonesia 131 M9
Lava Beds Nat. Mon. •
  CA, United States 154 I7
Lava Beds Nat. Mon. Park N •
  CA, United States .... 152 [39]
Lavagna • Italy 87 B2
Laval • France 77 E5
Lavandou, le • France 78 G8
Lavarai, Ko • Thailand 130 F9
Laverton • WA, Australia 135 C5
Lavezzi, I. • Corsica, France 78 N12
Lavik • Norway 98 F8
Lavon Lake • TX, United States 155 F4
Lavras • Brazil 174 E6
Lávrio • Greece 93 D3
Lavumisa • Swaziland 111 C3
Lawang • Java, Indonesia 131 R12
Lawdar • Yemen 120 F11
Lawrence • KS, United States 150 A3
Lawrence • MA, United States 156 D1
Lawrenceburg • TN, United States 151 C3
Lawton • OK, United States 149 G4
Lawu, Gunung • Java, Indonesia 131 Q12
Laxá • Sweden 99 G5
Laycock Abbey • United Kingdom 65 K9
Layla • Saudi Arabia 129 F9
Layou • St Vincent & Gren. .... 167 O
Laysan I. • HI, United States 138 CC1
Lázaro Cárdenas •
  Baja California, Mexico 168 H5
Lázaro Cárdenas •
  Michoacán, Mexico 169 I7
Lazio • Italy 87 E4
Le Bourget [Apt] • France 76 D2
Le Havre • France 76 D2
Le Kef • Tunisia 107 C4
Le Mans • France 77 F5
Le Phang Bay • Ko Phuket, Thailand .. 130 F9
Leamington • OT, Canada 161 A3
Leamington Caves • Bermuda 165 L9
Leap • Ireland 69 H11
Leatherhead • United Kingdom 65 G8
Leavenworth • WA, United States 154 H5
Leba • Poland 89 B1
Lebanon • NH, United States 150 D7
Lebanon • OR, United States 148 B2
Lebanon • PA, United States 156 B2
Lebanon • TN, United States 151 C3
Lebap • Turkmenistan 121 D3
Leblon • Brazil 174 F7
Lebork • Poland 89 B1
Lebu • Chile 175 A3
Lecce • Italy 85 G4
Lecco • Italy 87 B1
Lech Ski • Austria .... 61 [89]
Lech • Austria 91 M8
Lechang • China 126 E8
Lechi, Playa • Bonaire .... 166 U
Lechtaler Alpen • Austria 91 N7
Ledbury • United Kingdom 65 E6
Ledesma • France 78 I10
Leducate, Etang de • France 78 I10
Leek • Netherlands 70 J6
Leen • Guyana 173 D2
Leeuwarden • Netherlands 70 H6
Leesburg • FL, United States 155 D1
Leeuwin, Cape • WA, Australia 135 B6
Leeward Is. • West Indies 167 EE3
Lefaga • Samoa .... 139 G
Lefka • Cyprus 96 C4
Lefka Ori • Crete, Greece 93 G6

Lefka Ori Nat. Park •
  Crete, Greece 93 G6
Lefkáda • Levkas, Greece .... 94 J
Lefkáda [I.] • Greece .... 94 J
Lefkara • Cyprus 96 C4
Lefke • Cyprus 96 C4
Lefkimi • Corfu, Greece .... 94 A
Lefkosa • Cyprus 96 D4
Leganes • Spain 80 D3
Legaspi • Philippines 128 G4
Legendes, Côte des • France 77 C3
Legges Tor • TS, Australia 136 F6
Leghorn • Italy 87 D3
Legian Beach • Bali, Indonesia 131 L8
Legnago • Lombardy, Italy 87 B2
Legnano • Véneto, Italy 89 D3
Legnica • Poland 89 D3
Legoland Billund Park L • Denmark .. 59 [18]
Legoland Billund • Denmark 99 E7
Legoland California •
  CA, United States 154 J9
Legoland California Park L •
  CA, United States .... 157 [6]
Legoland Deutschland Park L •
  Germany .... 59 [60]
Legoland Deutschland • Germany 74 F7
Legoland Windsor Park L •
  United Kingdom .... 59 [33]
Legoland Windsor • United Kingdom .. 131 O11
Legundi • Indonesia 131 O11
Leh Hill Sta • India 124 E5
Leh • India 122 B2
Lehigh Valley [Apt] •
  PA, United States 156 B2
Lehinch • Ireland 69 H9
Leibnitz • Austria 91 G3
Leicester • United Kingdom 65 F5
Leicestershire • United Kingdom 65 F5
Leichlingen • Germany 73 C6
Leiden • Netherlands 70 G7
Leighton Buzzard • United Kingdom .. 63 E9
Leipzig • Poland 50 D2
Leikanger • Norway 98 G8
Leinster • Ireland 69 F6
Leipnitzsee • Germany 73 F7
Leipzig • Germany 72 E3
Leiria • Portugal 80 A4
Leiria [Adm] • Portugal 84 A2
Leirvik • Norway 98 F9
Leisure I. • Maldives 124 H7
Leith • United Kingdom 65 B2
Leitrim • Ireland 69 H5
Leixlip • Ireland 69 F6
Leka • Norway 97 C2
Leksand • Sweden 97 C3
Leland • MI, United States 161 B2
Lelång • Sweden 98 E6
Lelystad • Netherlands 70 H7
Léman, Lac • Switzerland 90 I6
Lemba Harau Reserve • Indonesia 131 N10
Lemland • Finland 99 J4
Lemmenjoki Nat. Park Park N •
  Finland .... 58 [31]
Lemnos • Greece 93 D2
Lempa • El Salvador/Honduras 170 C3
Lemvig • Denmark 99 E7
Lena • Russian Fed. 101 K4
Léndas • Crete, Greece 93 I6
Lenggries • Germany 74 G8
Lengwe Nat. Park Park N • Malawi .. 112 [102]
Lenk Ski • Switzerland .... 61 [63]
Lenk • Switzerland 90 J6
Lenne • Germany 73 D5
Lennestadt • Germany 72 C3
Leno • Fond du Lac, QU, Canada 160 H4
Lens • France 76 E1
Lenzerheide • Switzerland 90 L5
Lenzerheide-Valbella Ski •
  Switzerland .... 61 [77]
Léogâne • Haiti 165 G6
Leogang Ski • Austria .... 61 [104]
Leominster • MA, United States 156 D1
Leominster • United Kingdom 65 E5
León • Mexico 169 I6
León • Nicaragua 170 D4
León • Spain 80 C2
Leon, Pays de • France 77 C3
Leonardo Da Vinci [Apt] • Italy 87 E5
Leonberg • Germany 74 D6
Leone • American Samoa .... 139 H
Leone Bay • American Samoa .... 139 H
Leone, Monte • Italy/Switzerland 90 J6
Leonídio • Greece 93 C3
Leonora • WA, Australia 135 C5
Leontes • Lebanon 120 B1
Leopardstown • Ireland 69 F6
Leópoldina • Brazil 174 E6
Léova • Moldova 92 D3
Lepanto • Greece 50 E4
Lepe • Spain 80 H6
Lephepe • Botswana 110 J10
Lepini, Monti • Italy 87 F5
Lepsi • Kazakhstan 121 G2
Leptis Magna Heritage C • Libya .. 44 [295]
Lérici • Italy 81 B3
Lérida • Spain 80 F3
Lérins, Is. de • France 78 H8
Lerma • Mexico 169 I7
Lermoos Ski • Austria .... 61 [92]
Lermoos • Austria 91 N7
Lerum • Sweden 99 F6
Lerwick • United Kingdom 62 H12
Lesbos • Greece .... 94 C
Lesbos • China 125 E4
Leshan Giant Buddha Heritage N •
  China .... 41 [131]
Leshan giant buddha Heritage C •
  China .... 43 [189]
Lesina, Lago di • Italy 85 E4
Lesjaskog • Norway 98 G7
Lesjaskogsvatnet • Norway 98 F7
Lesko • Poland 89 C4
Leskovac • Serbia & Montenegro 92 C3
Lesleen M • St Lucia .... 167 N
Lesnevern • France 77 C3
LESOTHO • Africa 110 B3
Lester B. Pearson [Apt] •
  OT, Canada 160 E5
Lésvos • Greece 93 E2
Leszno • Poland 89 B3
Letchworth • United Kingdom 63 E9
Letchworth State Park •
  NY, United States 156 A1
Leticia • Colombia 173 C3
Lethakeng • Botswana 110 J10
Lethbridge • AL, Canada 158 E3
Lethmathe • Germany 73 D5
Letoon • Turkey 95 F6
Letterfrack • Ireland 69 G9
Letterkenny • Ireland 69 C2
Leucate • France 78 I10
Leucate, Etang de • France 78 I10
Leuk • Switzerland 90 J6
Leukerbad • Switzerland 90 A2
Leuser • Gunung • Indonesia 131 M9
Leutkirch • Germany 74 E8
Leuven • Belgium 70 C3
Levant, I. du • France 78 G8
Levanto • Italy 87 B2
Levante, Cayo • Dominican Rep. 165 H5
Lévanzo, I. de • Italy 86 G7
Leven, Loch • United Kingdom 65 B1
Levens Hall • United Kingdom 65 C3
Levens Pond Nat. Park • Grenada .... 166 Q
Leverkusen • Germany 73 C6
Levice • Slovak Rep. 89 B4
Lévico Terme • Italy 86 C4

Levin • New Zealand 137 C3
Lévis • QU, Canada 160 H3
Levítha • Greece 94 CC3
Levoca • Slovak Rep. 89 C4
Levski • Bulgaria 92 H8
Levuka • Fiji Is. .... 138 T
Lewes • DE, United States 156 B3
Lewes • United Kingdom 65 G8
Lewis • United Kingdom 62 B2
Lewis, Butt of • United Kingdom 62 B2
Lewis Hills • NF, Canada 160 C1
Lewisburg • PA, United States 156 B2
Lewiston • ID, United States 154 H5
Lewiston • ME, United States 150 F2
Lewiston • NY, United States 161 A1
Lewistown • PA, United States 156 A2
Lexington • KY, United States 151 C3
Lexington • MA, United States 150 D3
Lexington • NE, United States 148 G2
Leyritz, Plantation • Martinique .... 167 L
Leysin • Switzerland 90 I6
Leyte • Philippines 128 H4
Lezhë • Albania 92 B3
Lhasa • China 125 C3
Lhasa Heritage C • China .... 43 [171]
Lho-Nga Beach • Indonesia 131 M9
Lhohifushi • Maldives 124 H7
Lhokseumawe • Indonesia 131 M9
Liamuiga, Mt • St Kitts & Nevis .... 167 F
Lianhuashan • China 126 F3
Lianyungang • China 126 G1
Liaoning • China 126 D1
Liaoyang • China 125 G2
Liaoyuan • China 125 G2
Liard • BC/NT, Canada 158 D3
Liard River • BC, Canada 158 D3
Libáchov • Czech Rep. 89 E6
Liberal • KS, United States 149 F3
Liberec • Czech Rep. 89 E6
LIBERIA • Africa 106 B4
Liberia • Costa Rica 170 E5
Liberty • MO, United States 150 B3
Liberty • TX, United States 155 F5
Liberty [Apt] • NJ, United States 156 C2
Libournais • France 76 K9
Libourne • France 78 E5
Libreville • Gabon 106 C4
LIBYA • Africa 106 D2
Libyan Desert • Africa 108 B2
Licata • Sicily, Italy 86 G8
Lichfield • United Kingdom 65 E5
Lichinga • Mozambique 110 C2
Lichnice • Czech Rep. 89 E6
Lichtenberg (Berlin) • Germany 73 F7
Lichtenrade (Berlin) • Germany 73 F8
Lida • Belarus 100 C3
Lidice • Czech Rep. 89 E6
Lidingö • Sweden 99 B2
Lidköping • Sweden 99 G5
Lido • Italy 87 D2
Lido de Camaiore • Italy 87 B3
Lido de Jésolo • Italy 87 C2
Lido di Ostia • Italy 87 E5
Lidzbark Warmiński • Poland 100 J8
Liebeneck, Burg • Germany 74 D5
Liebenstein, Burg • Germany 74 D5
Liebig, Mt • NT, Australia 136 A1
LIECHTENSTEIN • Europe 91 M8
Liège • Belgium 70 C4
Liège [Adm] • Belgium 70 C4
Lienz • Austria 91 P8
Liepaja • Latvia 100 J7
Lier • Belgium 70 C3
Lierbyen • Norway 98 D5
Liesjärvi Nat. Park Park N • Finland .. 58 [39]
Liesjärvi Nat. Park • Finland 99 D4
Liffey • Ireland 69 F6
Lifford • Ireland 69 C2
Lifjell • Norway 98 D6
Lifou • New Caledonia .... 138 U
Lightbourne Cay • Bahamas 164 B1
Lighthouse Reef • Belize 166 AA3
Lightwater Valley Park L •
  United Kingdom .... 59 [25]
Ligonier • PA, United States 156 A2
Ligórtinos • Crete, Greece 93 I6
Liguria • Italy 87 B2
Ligurian Sea • Mediterranean Sea 85 B3
Liha Point • Niue .... 139 O
Lihou Reef & Cays • CL, Australia 136 D3
Lihue • HI, United States 157 H5
Lijiang Heritage C • China .... 43 [190]
Likasi • Dem. Rep. of Congo 108 B6
Likoni • Kenya 109 C6
Liku • Niue .... 139 Q
Lilla Edet • Sweden 99 F5
Lille • Belgium 70 C3
Lille • France 76 E1
Lille Bælt • Denmark 99 E8
Lillehammer • Norway 97 C3
Lillesand • Norway 99 E5
Lillestrøm • Norway 98 D5
Lillooet • BC, Canada 160 I7
Lilongwe • Malawi 110 C2
Lima • OH, United States 150 D2
Lima • Peru 173 E6
Lima Heritage C • Peru .... 42 [59]
Limassol • Cyprus 96 C4
Limbé • Haiti 165 F5
Limburg • Belgium 70 C4
Limburg • Netherlands 70 D3
Limburg an der Lahn • Germany 74 D5
Limenas Hersonissou •
  Crete, Greece 93 I6
Limerick • Ireland 69 H10
Limerick [Adm] • Ireland 69 H9
Limes • Germany 50 C2
Limfjorden • Denmark 99 E6
Limni Vólvi • Greece .... 78 B
Limni • Chios, Greece .... 94 C
Limnos • Greece 93 D2
Limnos • Greece .... 94 C
Limoges • France 78 F5
Limoilou, Causse de • France 78 I6
Limon • Colorado 148 F3
Limón • CO, United States 148 F3
Limon • Honduras 170 E3
Limone Piemonte Ski • Italy .... 61 [116]
Limone Piemonte • Italy 87 A2
Limousin • France 77 A2
Limoux • France 76 K9
Lin'an • China 126 G7
Linares • Mexico 168 E3
Linares • Spain 80 D4
Linaro, Capo • Italy 87 E4
Linate [Apt] • Italy 87 B1
Lincoln • ME, United States 156 G1
Lincoln • NE, United States 150 A2
Lincoln • United Kingdom 63 E7
Lincoln Boyhood Nat. Mem. Park N •
  IN, United States .... 153 [179]
Lincoln City • OR, United States 148 I10
Lincoln Home Nat. Hist. Site Park N •
  IL, United States .... 153 [176]
Lincoln Mem. Park N •
  DC, United States .... 153 [264]
Lincolnshire • United Kingdom 64 B4
Lincolnshire Wolds • United Kingdom .. 63 E7
Lindås • Norway 98 F8
Lindau • Germany 74 E8
Lindbergh Field [Apt] •
  CA, United States 154 J9
Lindeman I. • QL, Australia 136 C3
Lindenberg • Germany 73 F7
Lindenholt, Schloss • Germany 74 F8
Linderödsåsen • Sweden 99 G7
Lindi • Tanzania 110 H8
Lindis Pass • New Zealand 137 G7

Lindisfarne • United Kingdom 62 E5
Lindlar • Germany 73 D6
Lindos, Rhodes, Greece .... 94 F
Lindsay • OT, Canada 160 E4
Lindsdal • Sweden 99 H6
Lindsey • United Kingdom 64 B4
Line Is. • Kiribati 139 DD3
Linfen • China 125 F3
Lingding I. • China 126 F4
Lingen • Germany 72 B2
Lingga • Indonesia 131 B4
Lingsugur • India 124 B1
Linhares • Brazil 174 B4
Linhe • China 125 E2
Linköping • Sweden 99 H5
Linlithgow Palace • United Kingdom .. 65 B2
Linn, Burg • Germany 73 C5
Linnanmäki Park L • Finland .... 59 [12]
Linnansaari Nat. Park Park N • Finland
  .... 58 [36]
Linne, loch • United Kingdom 62 C4
Linru • China 125 F3
Linz • Austria 91 G1
Linz • Germany 74 C5
Lion, Golfe du • Mediterranean Sea .. 76 F5
Lion Rock Country Park •
  Hong Kong, China 126 F5
Lipari, I. • Italy 86 H7
Lipari, I. Heritage N • Italy .... 41 [68]
Lipari, Is. • Italy 86 H7
Lipcani • Moldova 92 D1
Lipenská Prehradní Nádrz •
  Czech Rep. 89 E7
Lipetsk • Russian Fed. 100 E3
Lipnice nad Sázavou • Czech Rep. 89 E7
Lippe • Germany 72 C3
Lipsí • Greece 94 CC3
Lira • Uganda 108 C4
Lisboa • Portugal 84 G6
Lisboa Heritage C • Portugal .. 44 [134]
Lisboa [Adm] • Portugal 84 A2
Lisboa, Costa de • Portugal 84 F6
Lisbon • Portugal 84 G6
Lisbon Heritage C • Portugal .. 44 [134]
Lisburn • United Kingdom 63 B6
Lisdoonvarna • Ireland 69 H8
Liseberg Park L • Sweden .... 59 [5]
Liseux • France 76 D2
Lishui • China 126 G6
Lisianski I. • HI, United States 138 CC1
Liskeard • United Kingdom 65 J10
Lismore • NS, Australia 136 D5
Lismore • United Kingdom 62 C4
Lissadell House • Ireland 69 H8
Lisse • Netherlands 70 G7
Listowel • Ireland 69 G10
Lit-et-Mixe, Fôret de • France 78 E6
Litani • Lebanon 120 B1
Litani • Suriname 87 G6
Lithgow • NS, Australia 136 H8
Lithino, Akra • Crete, Greece 93 H6
LITHUANIA • Europe 100 J8
Litomerice • Czech Rep. 89 E6
Litomysl Castle Heritage C •
  Czech Rep. .... 44 [190]
Little • TX, United States 155 E5
Little Abaco • Bahamas 164 A1
Little Ambergris Cay •
  Turks & Caicos Is. 164 D3
Little Andaman • India 122 D4
Little Bighorn Battlefield Nat. Mon.
  Park N • MT, United States .... 152 [68]
Little Cayman • Cayman Is. 165 A1
Little Colorado •
  AZ, United States 149 D3
Little Exuma • Bahamas 164 D2
Little Hura • Maldives 124 H7
Little Inagua • Bahamas 164 B2
Little Karoo • South Africa 111 E7
Little Minch • United Kingdom 62 B3
Little Missouri • United States 148 F1
Little River Canyon Nat. Preserve
  Park N • AL, United States .... 153 [202]
Little Rock • AR, United States 151 B4
Little Scrub I. • Anguilla .... 166 B
Little Skellig • Ireland 69 G11
Little Sound • Bermuda 165 K10
Little Sound • Cayman Is. 165 A2
Little Tobago • Trinidad & Tobago .... 166 R
Littlehampton Beach •
  United Kingdom .... 64 [30]
Litvinov • Czech Rep. 89 D6
Liuzhou • China 125 E4
Livadiá • Greece 93 C2
Liverpool • NS, Canada 160 B2
Liverpool • United Kingdom 63 D7
Liverpool Bay • United Kingdom 63 D7
Livigno Ski • Italy .... 61 [128]
Livigno • Italy 87 B1
Livingston • Guatemala 170 K9
Livingston • MT, United States 148 D1
Livingston • TX, United States 155 F5
Livingston, Lake •
  TX, United States 155 F5
Livingstone • Zambia 110 B2
Livingstone Mtns • New Zealand 137 G7
Livland • Estonia/Latvia 100 K7
Livno • Bosnia-Herz. 92 G6
Livojoki • Finland 97 F2
Livonia • Estonia/Latvia 100 K7
Livonia • MI, United States 150 D2
Livorno • MI, United States 161 A3
Livorno • Italy 87 C3
Liwale • Tanzania 110 H8
Liwonde Nat. Park Park • Malawi .. 112 [100]
Lixoúri • Cephalonia, Greece .... 94 J
Liyang • China 126 G6
Lize • China 126 H6
Lizard Point • United Kingdom 65 I10
Ljubljana • Slovenia 92 F5
Ljugarn • Sweden 99 H5
Ljungsbro • Sweden 99 H5
Ljusdal • Sweden 97 D3
Ljusnan • Sweden 97 D3
Ljusterö [I.] • Sweden 99 B1
Llafranc • Spain 83 D3
Llançá • Spain 83 D3
Llanddona Beach • United Kingdom .. 64 [71]
Llandovery • United Kingdom 65 D6
Llandudno Beach • United Kingdom .. 64 [66]
Llanelli • United Kingdom 65 D6
Llano • TX, United States 155 E5
Llano Estacado •
  NM/TX, United States 149 F4
Llano [Riv] • TX, United States 155 E5
Llanos • Colombia/Venezuela 173 B2
Llanos de Concepcion •
  Fuerteventura, Canary Is. 83 J5
Llantwit Major • United Kingdom 65 E6
Lleida • Spain 80 F3
Llevant, Costa de • Spain 83 D3
Lleyn Peninsula • United Kingdom .. 63 C8
Llíria • Spain 82 F6
Lloret de Mar • Spain 83 D3
Lloydminster • SA, Canada 158 E3
Lluc Alcari • Majorca, Spain 83 N11
Lluc, Monestir de •
  Majorca, Spain 83 N11
Llucmajor • Majorca, Spain 83 N12
Llywyn, Carnedd • United Kingdom .. 63 C7
Lo Wu • Hong Kong, China 126 F4
Loango, Parc nat. de Park • Gabon .. 112 [44]
Lobatse • Botswana 110 J10
Lobería • Argentina 175 F7

Lobito • Angola 110 A2
Lobos • Argentina 175 F6
Lobos • Canary Is. 83 H5
Lobos, I. de • Uruguay 175 G6
Locarno • Switzerland 90 K6
Loch Lomond & the Trossachs **Park N** •
 United Kingdom ....58 [47]
Loch Lomond & the Trossachs Nat. Park •
 United Kingdom 65 A1
Lochaline • United Kingdom 65 A2
Lochboisdale • United Kingdom 62 B3
Loches [Château] • France 77 F6
Lochinvar Nat. Park **Park** • Zambia ..112 [109]
Lochmaddy • United Kingdom 62 R3
Lochnagar • United Kingdom 62 D4
Lochranza • United Kingdom 66 A2
Lockerbie • United Kingdom 62 D5
Lockhart • TX, United States 155 E5
Lockport • NY, United States 161 D1
Locle, Le • Switzerland 90 I5
Locmariaquer • France 77 C4
Locronan • France 77 C4
Lod • Israel 120 A3
Lodeynoye Pole • Russian Fed. 100 D1
Lodi • CA, United States 148 B3
Ludi • Italy 87 B2
Lodore Falls • United Kingdom 65 D3
Lodwar • Kenya 109 C4
Łódź • Poland 89 B3
Loei • Thailand 130 C6
Loerie • South Africa 111 G7
Lofoten • Norway 97 C2
Loftahammar • Sweden 99 H5
Lofthus • Norway 98 G8
Log • Russian Fed. 100 F4
Logan [Apt] • MA, United States 156 D1
Logan, Mt • YT, Canada 158 C2
Logansport • IN, United States 156 E5
Logansport • LA, United States 156 F5
Logroño • Spain 80 D2
Løgstør • Denmark 99 E6
Løgumkloster • Denmark 99 E8
Lohausen [Apt] • Germany 73 C6
Lohja • Finland 99 C4
Lohria • Crete, Greece 93 H6
Loikaw • Myanmar 128 B3
Loimaa • Finland 99 D4
Loir • France 77 F5
Loir-et-Cher • France 77 F5
Loire [Adm] • France 78 C3
Loire [Riv] • France 76 E3
Loire Valley **Heritage C** • France ......44 [80]
Loire-Atlantique • France 77 E4
Loita Aldea • Puerto Rico 165 J7
Loíza, Río Grande de • Puerto Rico 165 J8
Loja • Ecuador 173 B3
Loja • Spain 82 J7
Løken • Norway 98 E5
Loket • Czech Rep. 89 D6
Løkken • Denmark 99 E6
Lokwe Kangole • Kenya 109 C4
Lolland • Denmark 99 H8
Lolo Pass • MT, United States 154 H5
Lom • Bulgaria 92 C3
Lom • Norway 98 G7
Lom Sak • Thailand 130 C6
Lomas de Zamora • Argentina 175 F6
Lombardia • Italy 87 B1
Lombardsijde-Bad • Belgium 70 E6
Lombardy • Italy 86 A1
Lomblen • Indonesia 131 F5
Lombok • Indonesia 131 E5
Lomé • Togo 106 C4
Lomond, Loch • United Kingdom 65 A2
Lompoc • CA, United States 149 B4
Łomża • Poland 89 C2
Lon, Hon • Vietnam 129 C5
Lon, Ko • Thailand 130 F10
Lonavala **Hill Sta** • India 124 E6
Londerzeel • Belgium 70 B4
London • Kiribati ....139 I
London • OT, Canada 159 H4
London • United Kingdom 65 G7
London **Heritage C** • United Kingdom ..44 [30]
London City [Apt] • United Kingdom 65 G7
Londonderry, Cape •
 WA, Australia 135 D2
Londonderry [County] •
 United Kingdom 64 A3
Londrina • Brazil 175 C2
Long Ashton • United Kingdom 65 K9
Long Bay • Anguilla ....166 J
Long Bay • Jamaica 165 D4
Long Bay [Bay] • Jamaica 165 C4
Long Beach • CA, United States 154 J9
Long Branch • NJ, United States 156 C2
Long Cay • Bahamas 164 B2
Long Cay • Turks & Caicos Is. 164 D3
Long Ground • Montserrat ....167 G
Long Hai • Vietnam 129 C5
Long I. • Antigua & Barbuda ....167 I
Long I. • Bahamas 164 B2
Long I. • New Zealand 137 F8
Long I. • NY, United States 156 C2
Long I. • QL, Australia 136 C3
Long I. Sound • NY, United States 156 C2
Long Mynd, The • United Kingdom 65 E5
Long Point • New Zealand 137 F8
Long Point • OT, Canada 160 E5
Long Range Mtns • NF, Canada 160 C1
Long Xuyen • Vietnam 129 B6
Longarone • Italy 86 A4
Longboat Key • FL, United States 155 C2
Longchamp • France 78 E3
Longfellow Nat. Hist. Site **Park N** •
 MA, United States ....153 [289]
Longford • Ireland 69 C3
Longford • TS, Australia 136 F6
Longgang • China 126 F3
Longleat House & Safari Park •
 United Kingdom 65 K9
Longmen Grottoes **Heritage C** •
 China ....43 [180]
Longmont • CO, United States 148 E2
Longovárdas • Páros, Greece ....94 H
Longreach • QL, Australia 135 G4
Longue, I. • Seychelles 113 A1
Longview • TX, United States 155 F4
Longview • WA, United States 154 G5
Longwood Gardens •
 PA, United States 156 B3
Longyearbyen • Arctic Ocean 176 I2
Löningen • Germany 72 B2
Lons-le-Saunier • France 76 F3
Looe • United Kingdom 65 J10
Looe Key Nat. Marine Sanctuary •
 FL, United States 155 D3
Lookout, Cape •
 NC, United States 151 E4
Loon **Ski** • NH, United States ....146 [114]
Loop Head • Ireland 69 G10
Loosdrechtse Plassen • Netherlands 70 H7
Lop Nur • China 125 D2
Lopé, Parc nat. de **Park** • Gabon .....112 [42]
Lopez • Philippines 128 G4
Lopikerwaard • Netherlands 70 H6
Loppem • Belgium 70 F6
Lorain • OH, United States 161 A3
Lorca • Spain 80 E5
Lorch • Germany 74 D6
Lord Howe I. • Tasman Sea 134 D8
Lord Howe island group **Heritage N** •
 Australia ....41 [159]
Lordsburg • NM, United States 155 H8
Loreley • Germany 74 D6
Lorentz Nat. Park **Heritage N** •
 Indonesia ....41 [147]
Loreto **Heritage C** • Argentina ....42 [77]
Loreto •
 Baja California Sur, Mexico 168 A6
Loreto • Italy 87 D3
Loreto • Zacatecas, Mexico 169 H6
Lorian Swamp • Kenya 109 D4

Lorient • France 77 C4
Lorient • St Barthélemy ....166 D
Lorimers • Turks & Caicos Is. 164 D3
Lorn, Firth of • United Kingdom 62 C4
Lörrach • Germany 74 A4
Lorraine • France 76 K8
Lorsch • Germany 74 D6
Lorsch **Heritage C** • Germany ....44 [60]
Los Alamos • NM, United States 155 H7
Los Alcázares • Spain 83 A2
Los Andes • Chile 175 A3
Los Arenales del Sol • Spain 83 A1
Los Ayala • Mexico 169 H7
Los Barrios • Spain 82 D3
Los Chiles • Costa Rica 170 E5
Los Chonos, Archipiélago de •
 Chile 175 A4
Los Cristianos •
 Tenerife, Canary Is. 82 G5
Los Dosvenurados, Is. de •
 Pacific Ocean 171 A5
Los Estados, I. de • Argentina 175 B5
Los Gigantes •
 Tonorife, Canary Is. 82 G6
Los Glaciares, Parque Nac. •
 Argentina 175 A4
Los Glaciares, Parque Nac. **Heritage N** •
 Argentina ....40 [52]
Los Haítises, Parque Nac. •
 Dominican Rep. 165 H5
Los Hermanos • Venezuela 167 EE4
Los Hernández • Venezuela ....166 T
Los Katios, Parque Nac. • Colombia ...173 B2
Los Katios, Parque Nac. **Heritage N** •
 Colombia ....40 [33]
Los Llanos de Aridane •
 La Palma, Canary Is. 83 H6
Los Mármoles, Parque Nac. • Mexico ..169 J7
Los Mochis • Mexico 168 I6
Los Monos • Mexico 169 I8
Los Padres, Laguna de • Argentina 175 G7
Los Palacios • Cuba 164 E4
Los Pinos, Costa de •
 Majorca, Spain 83 O11
Los Pocillos •
 Lanzarote, Canary Is. 83 I5
Los Rodeos [Apt] •
 Tenerife, Canary Is. 82 G5
Los Roques, Is. • Venezuela 167 EE4
Los Testigos • Venezuela 167 EE4
Losai Nat. Reserve • Kenya 109 C4
Losinj • Croatia 92 F6
Lost Trail Pass •
 MT, United States 154 H5
Lostwithiel • United Kingdom 65 I10
Lot • Fed. States of Micronesia ....138 D
Lot [Adm] • France 78 E4
Lot [Riv] • France 76 E4
Lot-et-Garonne • France 78 E4
Lotkipi Plain • Kenya 109 C4
Lotus Mtn • China 128 F3
Louangphrabang • Laos 128 C3
Louangphrabang **Heritage C** • Laos ..43 [201]
Loubomo • Congo 106 D5
Loudéac • France 77 D3
Loudi • China 125 F4
Loudun • France 77 E6
Loughborough • United Kingdom 65 F5
Loughrea • Ireland 69 H9
Loughwood Meeting House •
 United Kingdom 65 K9
Louis Armstrong [Apt] •
 LA, United States 156 F6
Louisa, Lake • FL, United States 157 A1
Lóusa, Lake, State Park •
 FL, United States 157 A1
Louisbourg, Fortress of •
 NS, Canada 160 C2
Louisburgh • Ireland 69 G8
Louisiade Archipelago •
 Papua New Guinea 138 BB3
Louisiana • United States ....156 E-F
Louisville • GA, United States 151 D4
Louisville • KY, United States 150 C3
Louisville • MS, United States 156 F5
Loulan • China 121 L7
Loulé • Portugal 84 J8
Louny • Czech Rep. 89 D6
Loup • France 78 H7
Loup, Le • NE, United States 148 G2
Loup, Gorges du • France 78 J9
Lourdes • France 78 I9
Lourinhã • Portugal 69 F6
Loutrá • Greece ....94 B
Loutra Edipsoú • Greece 93 C2
Louviers • France 76 D2
Lovat • Russian Fed. 100 L10
Lovcen Nat. Park **Park N** •
 Serbia & Montenegro ....58 [128]
Lovech • Bulgaria 92 D3
Loveland **Ski** • CO, United States ....146 [56]
Lovelock • NV, United States 154 J7
Lover's Leap • Jamaica 165 C4
Lovina Beach • Bali, Indonesia 131 L7
Lovosice • Czech Rep. 89 D6
Løvstad • Sweden 99 H5
Low Head • TS, Australia 136 F6
Lowell • MA, United States 156 D1
Lowell Nat. Hist. Park **Park N** •
 MA, United States ....153 [291]
Lower Brule **Ind Res** •
 SD, United States ....155 [50]
Lower Egypt • Egypt 109 A1
Lower Hutt • New Zealand 137 B3
Lower Lough Erne • United Kingdom ...63 B6
Lower Post • BC, Canada 158 A3
Lower Saxony • Germany 72 C2
Lower Zambezi Nat. Park **Park** •
 Zambia ....112 [110]
Lowestoft • United Kingdom 65 F8
Lowestoft **Beach** • United Kingdom ..64 [19]
Loweswater • United Kingdom 65 C3
Łowicz • Poland 89 B2
Loxton • South Africa 111 F6
Loyangalani • Kenya 109 C4
Loyauté, Is. • New Caledonia ....138 U
Lozenets • Bulgaria 92 I8
Loznica • Serbia & Montenegro 92 B2
Lü Shan **Heritage C** • China ....43 [185]
Luacano • Angola 110 B2
Luahasibuka • Indonesia 131 M10
Lualaba • Dem. Rep. of Congo 108 B5
Luana Point • Jamaica 165 C4
Luanda • Angola 110 A1
Luang Pra Bang • Thailand 130 D8
Luang Prabang • Laos 128 C3
Luang Prabang **Heritage C** • Laos ....43 [201]
Luang Prabang Range • Laos/Thailand ..130 C5
Luanshya • Zambia 110 B2
Lubanas Ezers • Latvia 100 K7
Lubango • Angola 110 A2
Lübbecke • Germany 72 E3
Lübbenau • Germany 72 E3
Lubbock • TX, United States 149 F4
Lübeck • Germany 72 D2
Lübeck **Heritage C** • Germany ....44 [45]
Lubin • Poland 89 C3
Lublin • Poland 89 F8
Lubukllinggau • Indonesia 131 B4
Lubumbashi • Dem. Rep. of Congo 108 B6
Luc, le • France 78 C4
Luc-en-Diois • France 78 C4
Lucan • France 69 F6
Lucaya • Bahamas 164 B1
Lucaya Estates • Bahamas 164 B1
Lucca • Italy 86 B2
Lucea • Jamaica 165 C3
Lucena • Philippines 128 G4
Lučenec • Slovak Rep. 89 B4
Lucerne • Switzerland 90 K6

Lucerne, Lake of • Switzerland 90 K5
Lucknow • India 123 F7
Luçon • France 77 E6
Lucrecia, Cabo • Cuba 164 H5
Luda • China 125 G3
Lude, le • France 77 F5
Lüdenscheid • Germany 73 D6
Lüderitz • Namibia 110 A3
Ludhiana • India 122 B2
Ludington • MI, United States 150 C2
Ludlow • CA, United States 149 C4
Ludvika • Sweden 97 D3
Ludwigsburg • Germany 74 B2
Ludwigsfelde • Germany 73 E8
Ludwigshafen • Germany 74 B4
Ludwigshafen am Rhein • Germany ...74 B2
Ludwigslust • Germany 72 D2
Ludza • Latvia 100 K7
Luleå • TX, United States 155 F5
Luga • Russian Fed. 100 C2
Luga [Riv] • Russian Fed. 100 C2
Lugano • Switzerland 90 K6
Lugano, Lago di •
 Italy/Switzerland 90 K6
Lugansk • Ukraine 100 K6
Lugazi • Latvia 100 K6
Lugnaquilla • Ireland 69 F7
Lugo • Italy 87 C2
Lugo • Spain 80 B2
Lugo **Heritage C** • Spain ....44 [110]
Lugovoy • Kazakstan 121 F3
Luhans'k • Ukraine 100 E4
Luhe • China 126 G6
Luhur Batukau Temple •
 Bali, Indonesia 131 L7
Luimneach • Ireland 69 H10
Luing • United Kingdom 62 C4
Luis Muñoz Marín [Apt] • Puerto Rico ..165 J7
Luján • Argentina 175 F6
Lukeville • AZ, United States 155 G8
Lule älv • Sweden 97 E2
Luleå • Sweden 97 E2
Luleå **Heritage C** • Sweden ....43 [89]
Lüleburgaz • Turkey 95 E3
Lulu Fakahega, Mt •
 Wallis & Futuna ....139 Q
Luma • American Samoa ....139 H
Lumajang • Java, Indonesia 131 R12
Lumberton • NC, United States 151 E4
Lumbini • Nepal 123 G7
Lumbini **Heritage C** • Nepal ....43 [169]
Lumjiag, Laem •
 Ko Phuket, Thailand 130 F10
Lumphat • Cambodia 128 D4
Lumsden • New Zealand 137 G8
Lumut • Malaysia 129 F9
Lumut [I.] • Malaysia 129 F10
Lün • Mongolia 124 A1
Luna Park 'Ta Aidonakia' **Park L** •
 Greece ....59 [87]
Lunar Crater • NV, United States 154 J8
Lund • Sweden 99 G7
Lunde • Norway 98 D6
Lunds Tivoli **Park L** • Norway ....59 [3]
Lundy • United Kingdom 65 I9
Lüneburg • Germany 72 D2
Lüneburger Heide • Germany 73 D5
Lünen • Germany 73 D5
Lunenburg • NS, Canada 160 B2
Lunenburg **Heritage C** • NS, Canada ..42 [4]
Luneur **Park L** • Italy ....59 [85]
Lung Kwu Chau • Hong Kong, China ..126 E5
Luni • India 123 D8
Luoyang • China 125 F3
Luperón • Dominican Rep. 165 G5
Luqa [Apt] • Malta 91 B8
Luquillo • Puerto Rico 165 J7
Luquillo, Sierra de • Puerto Rico 165 J7
Luray Caverns • VA, United States .....84 D-E
Lure • France 90 C2
Lurin, Mt • St Barthélemy ....166 C
Lusaka • Zambia 110 B2
Lusanne **Ski** • Italy ....61 [135]
Lushoto • Tanzania 110 H7
Lussac-les-Châteaux • France 77 F6
Lütilim • Goa, India 123 C6
Luton • United Kingdom 65 G7
Luts'k • Ukraine 100 C3
Luvuka • Fiji Is. ....138 T
Luxembourg • Europe 70 D5
Luxembourg [Adm] • Belgium 70 C5
Luxembourg-Ville • Luxembourg 70 D5
Luxembourg-Ville **Heritage C** •
 Luxembourg ....44 [44]
Luxolweni • South Africa 111 G6
Luxor • Egypt 109 B2
Luxus • Morocco 107 C2
Luz • France 78 J9
Luze • Switzerland 90 K5
Luzern [Adm] • Switzerland 91 Q9
Luzern **Heritage C** • Switzerland 91 Q9
Luzhou • China 124 F6
Luziânia • Brazil 174 B4
Luznice • Czech Rep. 89 E7
Luzon • Philippines 128 G2
Luzon Strait • Philippines 128 G1
Lviv • Ukraine 100 B4
Lviv **Heritage C** • Ukraine ....44 [266]
Lvov • Ukraine 100 B4
Lvov **Heritage C** • Ukraine ....44 [266]
Lyakhovskiye Ostrova • Russian Fed. ..101 D2
Lyall, Mt • New Zealand 137 F7
Lycaonia • Turkey 95 I9
Lycia • Turkey 95 G8
Lycksele • Sweden 97 D3
Lydd [Apt] • United Kingdom 65 H8
Lydford Cay • Bahamas 164 A2
Lydia • Turkey 95 F5
Lydstep **Beach** • United Kingdom ...65 K10
Lyme Bay • United Kingdom 65 K10
Lyme Regis • United Kingdom 65 K9
Lymington • United Kingdom 66 D6
Lympne • United Kingdom 65 H8
Lynchburg • VA, United States 156 A4
Lyndon B. Johnson Mem. Grove on the Potomac
 Park N • DC, United States ....153 [264]
Lyndon B. Johnson Nat. Hist. Park •
 TX, United States 155 E5
Lyndon B. Johnson Nat. Hist. Park **Park N** •
 TX, United States ....152 [137]
Lyntupy • Apurie Aboriginal Land •
 NT, Australia 136 B1
Lyon • France 78 C3
Lyon • United Kingdom 65 J9
Lyon • France 78 C3
Lyon **Heritage C** • France ....44 [84]
Lyons • France 78 C3
Lyons **Heritage C** • France ....44 [84]
Lysebotn • Norway 98 F9
Lysefjorden • Norway 98 F9
Lysekil • Sweden 99 G5
Lytham St Annes • United Kingdom ...65 D7
Lytton • BC, Canada 158 C3
Lyubertsy • Russian Fed. 100 M10

M

Ma On Shan Country Park •
 Hong Kong, China 126 F5
Ma Wan • Hong Kong, China 126 F5
Ma'an • Jordan 120 D7
Ma'anshan • China 126 G6
Ma'aza Plateau • Egypt 109 B2
Maafushi • Maldives 124 H7
Maara • Fed. States of Micronesia .....138 C
Maardu • Estonia 100 K6
Maarianhamina • Finland 99 C4
Maarssen • Netherlands 70 H5
Maas • Netherlands 70 H7
Maas en Waal, Land van •
 Netherlands 70 H8
Maasai Mara Nat. Reserve • Kenya ...109 C5

Maasai Mara Nat. Reserve **Park** •
 Kenya ....112 [77]
Maasin • Philippines 128 H4
Maassluis • Netherlands 70 G8
Maastricht • Netherlands 70 C4
Maasvlakte • Netherlands 70 F8
Mablethorpe **Beach** • United Kingdom ..64 [11]
Mabuasehube Game Reserve •
 Botswana 110 I10
Macaé • Brazil 174 F7
Macanao, Peninsula de • Margarita ....166 T
Maçanet • Spain 83 D3
Macapá • Brazil 174 A2
MacArthur [Apt] •
 NY, United States 156 C2
MACAU SPECIAL ADMIN. REGION •
 China 126 E3
Macaya • Parque Nac. • Haiti 165 E6
Macclesfield • United Kingdom 63 D7
Macclesfield Bank • South China Sea ..126 D2
Macdhui, Ben • United Kingdom 62 D3
Macdonald, Lake •
 NT/WA, Australia 136 A1
Macedonia • Greece 93 C1
MACEDONIA, FORMER YUGOSLAV
 REPUBLIC OF • Europe 92 C3
Maceió • Brazil 174 F7
Macgillicuddy's Reeks • Ireland 69 G11
Machachi • Ecuador 173 B3
Machaerus • Jordan 120 B4
Machakos • Kenya 109 C5
Machala • Ecuador 173 B3
Mácher • Lanzarote, Canary Is. 83 I5
Machico • Madeira 84 E5
Machida • Japan 127 I8
Machilipatnam • India 124 C1
Machilipatnam **Beach** • India 124 E6
Machu Picchu • Peru 173 F6
Machu Picchu, Santuario histórico
 Heritage N • Peru ....40 [38]
Machu Picchu, Santuario Histórico
 Heritage C • Peru ....42 [60]
Macia • Mozambique 110 C3
Macinaggio • Corsica, France 78 N11
Mackay • QL, Australia 136 C4
Mackay, Lake • NT/WA, Australia 136 A1
Mackenzie • Guyana 160 I6
Mackenzie Bay • YT, Canada 158 C2
Mackenzie Delta • YT, Canada 158 C2
Mackenzie Mtns • NT/YT, Canada 158 D2
Mackenzie [Riv] • Canada 158 D2
Mackerricher State Park •
 CA, United States 154 I7
Mackinac I. • MI, United States 161 B2
Mackinac, Straits of •
 MI, United States 161 B2
Mackinaw Bridge •
 MI, United States 161 B2
Mackinaw City • MI, United States 150 D1
Mackinnon Road • Kenya 109 C6
MacLeod, Lake • WA, Australia 135 A4
Macomb • IL, United States 156 E5
Mâcon • France 78 C3
Macon • GA, United States 151 D4
Macon • MO, United States 150 B3
Mâconnais • France 76 L8
Macquarie Harbour • TS, Australia 136 F7
Macquarie I. **Heritage N** •
 Southern Ocean ....41 [161]
Macroom • Ireland 69 H11
Macugnaga • Italy 87 A1
Macusani • Peru 173 F6
Macuspana • Mexico 168 F4
Madaba • Jordan 120 B4
Madadeni • South Africa 111 B3
MADAGASCAR • Africa 110 D2
Madara • Bulgaria 92 H8
Madara **Heritage C** • Bulgaria ....44 [227]
Maddalena, Arcipelago de la •
 Sardinia, Italy 86 F5
Maddalena, I. • Sardinia, Italy 86 F5
Madden, Represa • Panama 170 M10
Madeira • Atlantic Ocean ....84 D-E
Madeira, Lauraselva of **Heritage N** •
 Madeira ....41 [65]
Mädelegabel • Austria/Germany 74 F8
Madeleine, Is. de la •
 QU, Canada 160 B1
Madera • CA, United States 148 B3
Madera • Mexico 168 D2
Madère • Brazil 173 C3
Madeira • Brazil 173 C3
Madésimo • Italy 87 B1
Madgaon • Goa, India 123 C6
Madhya Pradesh • India 123 A2
Madidi, Parque Nac. • Peru 173 F6
Madikeri • India 124 B2
Madikwe Nat. Park **Park** •
 South Africa ....112 [134]
Madiran • France 76 K9
Madison • WI, United States 150 C2
Madisonville • KY, United States 150 C3
Madiun • Java, Indonesia 131 Q12
Madona • Latvia 100 K7
Madone d'Utelle • France 78 H7
Madonie • Sicily, Italy 86 H7
Madonna di Campiglio **Ski** • Italy ...61 [132]
Madonna di Campiglio • Italy 87 C1
Madras • India 124 C2
Madre de Dios • Bolivia 173 C4
Madre de Dios • Peru 173 F6
Madre del Sur, Sierra • Mexico 169 J8
Madre, Laguna • Mexico 168 E2
Madre Occidental, Sierra • Mexico 168 C2
Madre Oriental, Sierra • Mexico 168 F4
Madre Sierra • Guatemala/Mexico 169 J8
Madrid • Spain 80 D3
Madrid, Comunidad de • Spain 80 D3
Madura • Indonesia 131 R11
Madura, Selat • Java, Indonesia 131 R12
Madurai • India 124 C3
Madurodam • Netherlands 70 G8
Mae Hong Son • Thailand 130 D7
Mae Klong • Thailand 130 D7
Mae La Noi • Thailand 130 B6
Mae Ping Nat. Park • Thailand 130 B6
Mae Rim • Thailand 130 C5
Mae Sai • Thailand 130 D6
Mae Sariang • Thailand 130 B6
Mae Suai • Thailand 130 D5
Mae Taeng • Thailand 130 B5
Mae-jima • Okinawa, Japan ....138 A
Maebashi • Japan 127 C3
Mæl • Norway 98 D5
Maenam Beach •
 Ko Samui, Thailand 130 G11
Maestra, Sierra • Cuba 164 H5
Maewo • Vanuatu ....138 V
Mafate, Cirque de • Réunion 113 C3
Mafia • Tanzania 110 H8
Mafikeng • South Africa 111 B3
Mafra • Portugal 84 F6
Magadan • Russian Fed. 101 P4
Magadi • Kenya 109 C5
Magadi, Lake • Kenya 109 C5
Magallanes, Estrecho de •
 Argentina/Chile 175 B5
Magaluf • Majorca, Spain 83 N12
Magdalena • Argentina 175 G6
Magdalena, I. • Mexico 168 H6
Magdeburg • Germany 72 D3
Magelang • Java, Indonesia 131 Q12
Magens Bay • US Virgin Is. ....166 X
Magenta [Apt] • New Caledonia ....138 U
Magerøya • Norway 98 A1
Maggiore, Lago • Italy 90 A2
Maghaghah • Egypt 109 A2
Magic Hill Farm • FL, United States ...160 E4
Magic Kingdom • FL, United States ...157 A1
Magic Valley • NS, Canada 160 B2
Magilligan **Beach** • United Kingdom ..64 [72]

Malegaon • India 122 B3
Maléme • Crete, Greece 93 G5
Mälerås • Crete, Greece 99 H6
Malgrat de Mar • Spain 83 D4
Malheur Lake • OR, United States 154 H6
MALI • Africa 106 B3
Mália • Crete, Greece 93 C1
Mália [Hist.] • Crete, Greece 93 I6
Mália • CA, United States 154 J9
Malin Head • Ireland 69 C1
Malindi • Kenya 109 D5
Malindi Marine Nat. Park • Kenya 109 C5
Malindi Marine Nat. Reserve • Kenya ..109 C6
Malion, Kólpos • Crete, Greece 93 I6
Malka Mari Nat. Park • Kenya 109 C4
Malkara • Turkey 95 E3
Mallacoota • VI, Australia 136 E6
Mallaig • United Kingdom 62 C4
MALLORCA • Spain 80 G4
Mallorca • Spain 80 G4
Mallow • Ireland 69 H11
Malmberget • Sweden 97 E2
Malmesbury • South Africa 111 D7
Malmköping • Sweden 99 F7
Malmö • Sweden 99 G7
Malmok • Bonaire ....166 U
Malmok • Aruba ....166 W
Maloelap • Marshall Is. 138 CC2
Malolo **Ski** • Switzerland ....61 [34]
Malolo Barrier Reef • Fiji Is. ....138 T
Malolo Lailai • Fiji Is. ....138 T
Malosmadulu Atoll North • Maldives ..124 G7
Malosmadulu Atoll South • Maldives ..124 G7
Måløy • Norway 98 F7
Malpensa [Apt] • Italy 87 B2
Malsch • Germany 74 B3
MALTA • Europe ....96 A-B
Malta • Latvia 100 K7
Malta • MT, United States 148 E1
Malton • United Kingdom 65 C5
Maluku • Indonesia 131 G4
Malunda • Indonesia 131 E4
Malung • Sweden 97 C3
Malvasia • Greece 50 E4
Malveira da Serra • Portugal 84 F6
Malvern Hills • United Kingdom 65 E6
Malvinas, Is • Atlantic Ocean 175 C5
Malwan • India 124 A1
Mamaia-Bai • Romania 92 I7
Mamaia-Sat • Romania 92 I7
Mamallapuram • India 124 C2
Mamallapuram **Beach** • India 124 E6
Mamanuca Group • Fiji Is. ....43 [161]
Mamberamo • Indonesia 131 I4
Mambrui • Kenya 109 C5
Mamelodi • South Africa **Park** • 110 J10
Mammoth Cave Nat. Park **Park N** •
 KY, United States ....153 [229]
Mammoth Cave Nat. Park **Heritage N** •
 KY, United States ....40 [16]
Mammoth Lakes • CA, United States ..154 J8
Mammoth Mtn **Ski** •
 CA, United States ....146 [33]
Mamoré • Bolivia 173 C4
Mamou • Guinea 106 A3
Mamoudzou • Mayotte 113 E4
Mamoutzou • Botswana 110 I10
Mamuno • Botswana 110 B3
Mamure Kalesi • Turkey 95 I10
MAN, I. OF • Europe ....138 T
Man o' War Bay • Trinidad & Tobago ..166 R
Mana • Fiji Is. ....138 T
Mana Pools Nat. Park **Park** •
 Zimbabwe ....112 [112]
Mana Pools Nat. Park **Heritage N** •
 Zimbabwe ....41 [113]
Manacapuru • Brazil 173 C3
Manacor • Majorca, Spain 83 O11
Manage • Belgium 70 A4
Managua • Nicaragua 170 D4
Managua, Lago de • Nicaragua 170 D4
Manakara • Madagascar 110 D3
Manali **Hill Sta** • India 124 E5
Manali • India 122 B2
Mananjary • Madagascar 137 F8
Manapouri • New Zealand 137 F8
Manapouri, Lake • New Zealand 137 F8
Manarola **Heritage C** • Italy ....44 [159]
Manas Wildlife Sanctuary **Heritage N** •
 India ....41 [124]
Manassas Nat. Battlefield Park •
 VA, United States 156 A3
Manassas Nat. Battlefield Park **Park N** •
 VA, United States ....153 [251]
Manati • Puerto Rico 165 I7
Manati, Río Grande de •
 Puerto Rico 165 J7
Manaus • Brazil 173 C3
Manavgat • Turkey 95 H8
Manawatu-Wanganui • New Zealand ..137 C2
Manchester • CT, United States 156 C2
Manchester • NH, United States 156 D1
Manchester • United Kingdom 63 D7
Manchester • United Kingdom 63 D7
Mancheras Monastery • Cyprus 96 C4
Manda • Tanzania 110 G8
Manda • Kenya 110 H7
Mandai Orchid Gardens • Singapore ..129 H11
Mandal • Norway 99 E5
Mandalay • Myanmar 128 B2
Mandalgovi • Mongolia 124 A1
Mandalselva • Norway 98 F9
Mandan • ND, United States 148 F1
Mandera • Kenya 109 D4
Mandera [Region] • Kenya 109 D4
Manderscheid • Germany 74 C6
Mandeville • Jamaica 165 C4
Mandore • India 123 D8
Mandrem Beach • Goa, India 123 C5
Mandu • India 123 E8
Mandurah • WA, Australia 135 B6
Mandvi • India 122 A3
Manfredónia • Italy 85 E4
Manfrédonia, Golfo di • Italy 85 F4
Mangaia • Cook Is. 139 DD4
Mangalia • Romania 92 I7
Mangalore • India 124 B2
Mangalore **Beach** • India 124 E6
Mangaratiba • Brazil 174 E7
Mangaweka • New Zealand 137 E6
Mangfall • Germany 74 G8
Manggaualu • Solomon Is. ....138 W
Manginipudi **Beach** • India 124 E6
Mangle, Punta • Margarita ....166 T
Manhattan • KS, United States 150 A3
Manhattan • NY, United States 156 C2
Manhuaçan • Brazil 174 E6
Manicougan, Réservoir •
 QU, Canada 159 J3
Manihi • French Polynesia 139 DD3
Manika • Indonesia 131 G4
Manila **Heritage C** • Philippines .....43 [208]
Manila • UT, United States 148 E2
Manila • Spain 82 E3
Maninjau, Danau • Indonesia 131 N10
Manisa • Turkey 95 F5
Manisa [Adm] • Turkey 95 F5
Manistee • MI, United States 161 B2
Manitoba • Canada 158 G3
Manitoba, Lake • MN, Canada 158 G3
Manitou Is. • MI, United States 161 B2
Manitoulin I. • OT, Canada 159 J4
Manitowoc • WI, United States 161 B2
Manizales • Colombia 173 B2
Mânkarbo • Sweden 99 A1
Mankato • MN, United States 150 B2
Mann Ranges • NT/SA, Australia 136 C5
Mannar • Sri Lanka 124 C3

Mannar, Gulf of • India/Sri Lanka 124 C4
Mannheim • Germany 74 B2
Manoa • Bolivia 173 C3
Manokwari • Indonesia 131 H4
Manono • Samoa .... 139 G
Manori Beach • India 124 E6
Manosque • France 78 G7
Manovo-Gounda-St-Floris, Parc nat. Park • Central African Rep. .... 112 [38]
Manovo-Gounda-St-Floris, Parc nat. du Heritage N • Central African Rep. 41 [100]
Manresa • Spain 83 C4
Mans, le • France 77 F5
Mansa • Zambia 110 B2
Mansel I. • NU, Canada 159 I2
Mansfield • LA, United States 156 E5
Mansfield • OH, United States 150 D2
Mansfield • United Kingdom 63 E7
Mansura • LA, United States 156 E6
Manta • Ecuador 173 A3
Manta Rota • Portugal 84 K8
Mantamados • Lesbos, Greece .... 94 C
Mantaro • Peru 173 E6
Mantes-la-Jolie • France 78 A1
Mantiqueira, Serra da • Brazil 174 E7
Mantova • Italy 87 C2
Mäntsälä • Finland 99 D4
Mänttä • Finland 99 D3
Mantua • Italy 87 C2
Manú • Peru 173 F6
Manu Bay • New Zealand 137 D5
Manú, Parque Nac. del • Peru 173 F6
Manú, Parque Nac. del Heritage N • Peru .... 40 [39]
Manu'a Group • American Samoa .... 139 H
Manukau • New Zealand 137 B2
Manuoha, Mt • New Zealand 137 E5
Many • LA, United States 156 E5
Manyas-Kuscenneti Nat. Park Park N • Turkey .... 58 [143]
Manyoni • Tanzania 110 G7
Manzanar Nat. Hist. Site Park N • CA, United States .... 152 [51]
Manzanares • Spain 80 D4
Manzanillo • Cuba 164 G5
Manzanillo • Margarita .... 166 T
Manzanillo • Mexico 169 H7
Manzhouli • China 125 F2
Mao • Dominican Rep. 165 G5
Maó • Minorca, Spain 83 K8
Mao Shan • China 126 G6
Maoke, Penunungan • Indonesia 131 I4
Maoming • China 125 F4
Mapelane Nat. Park • South Africa 111 C4
Mapou, Ko • Thailand 130 F10
Mapuca • Goa, India 123 C5
Maputaland • South Africa 111 C3
Maputo • Mozambique 110 C3
Maputo, Baía de • Mozambique 110 C3
Maputo Elephant Reserve Park • Mozambique .... 112 [146]
Maqaman Nabi Musá • Palestine NAR .. 120 B4
Maqat • Kazakstan 121 B2
Maquan He • China 125 C4
Mar Chiquita, Lago • Argentina 175 B3
Mar Chiquita, Laguna • Argentina 175 B3
Mar del Plata • Argentina 175 G7
Mar del Tuyú • Argentina 175 G7
Mar, Serra do • Brazil 174 E7
Maraba • French Guiana .... 139 K
Maraba • Brazil 174 B3
Maracaibo • Venezuela 173 B1
Maracaibo, Lago de • Venezuela 173 B2
Maracas Bay • Trinidad & Tobago .... 166 T
Maracay • Venezuela 173 C1
Maradi • Niger 106 C3
Maragheh • Iran 120 F6
Marahoué, Parc nat. de la Park • Côte d'Ivoire .... 112 [16]
Marajó, Baia de • Brazil 174 B3
Marajó, Ilha de • Brazil 174 B3
Marakele Nat. Park Park • South Africa .... 112 [135]
Maralal Nat. Reserve • Kenya 109 C4
Maramasike • Solomon Is. .... 138 W
Marambio [Base] • Antarctica .... 176 [51]
Maramures Heritage C • Romania .. 44 [222]
Maranhão • Brazil 174 B3
Marañón • Peru 173 B3
Maratea • Italy 85 E5
Marathia, Akra • Zante, Greece .... 94 J
Marathókambos • Sámos, Greece .... 94 E
Marathon • FL, United States 155 D3
Marathon • OT, Canada 161 B1
Márathópolis • Crete, Greece 93 H6
Marbella • Spain 82 I8
Marble Canyon • AZ, United States 155 G7
Marburg an der Lahn • Germany 74 B1
Marche • Italy 87 D3
Marche-en-Famenne • Belgium 70 C5
Marchena, I. • Galápagos Is. 171 H9
Märchenwald im Isartal • Germany 74 G7
Marches, The • United Kingdom 65 C5
Marcianise • Italy 87 G6
Marco I. • FL, United States 155 C3
Marconi, G [Apt] • Italy 87 C2
Marcoussis • France 78 A2
Marcus • Japan 138 BB1
Maré • New Caledonia .... 138 U
Mare aux Vacoas Reservoir • Mauritius 113 E6
Marécottes, Les • Switzerland 90 I6
Maree, Loch • United Kingdom 62 C3
Mareeba • QL, Australia 136 C3
Maremma • Italy 87 C3
Marennes • France 78 E5
Maresme, Costa del • Spain 83 D4
Marehti • Tunisia 107 D6
Marettimo, I. • Italy 86 G7
Marfa • TX, United States 149 F4
Marfa Point • Malta 96 A1
Margarita • Panama 170 L10
Margarita, I. de • Venezuela .... 166 T
Margate • South Africa 111 B5
Margate • United Kingdom 65 H7
Margate Beach • United Kingdom .... 64 [27]
Margaux • France 78 E5
Mari-El Russ Adm • Russian Fed. .... 101 [12]
Maria • French Polynesia 139 DD4
Maria Chiquita • Panama 170 L10
Maria I. • TS, Australia 136 F7
Maria Is. • St Lucia .... 167 N
Maria Laach • Germany 74 C6
Maria Madre, I. • Mexico 169 H6
Maria Magdalena, I. • Mexico 169 H6
Mariana • Brazil 174 F6
Mariana Trench • Pacific Ocean 9 G5
Marianao • Cuba 164 E4
Mariankani • Kenya 109 C6
Marianna • FL, United States 155 B1
Marianne • Seychelles 113 B1
Mariannelund • Sweden 99 H6
Mariánské Lázne • Czech Rep. 75 F6
Marías, Is. • Mexico 169 H6
Mariato, Punta • Panama 170 G7
Maribo • Denmark 99 F8
Maribor • Slovenia 92 F5
Marie Byrd Land • Antarctica 176 W5
Marie Louise • Seychelles 113 B1
Marie-Galante • Guadeloupe .... 167 J
Mariedamm • Sweden 99 H5
Mariefred • Sweden 99 A2
Mariehamn • Finland 99 C4
Mariel • Cuba 164 E4
Marienbad • Czech Rep. 75 F6
Marienheide • Germany 73 D6
Mariental • Namibia 110 A3
Mariestad • Sweden 99 G5
Marietta • GA, United States 151 D4
Marietta • OH, United States 150 D3
Marigot • Dominica .... 167 K
Marigot • St Martin .... 166 C

Marigot Bay • St Lucia .... 167 N
Marijampole • Lithuania 100 J8
Marikostinovo • Bulgaria 92 C3
Marilia • Brazil 175 C2
Marilléva • Italy 87 C1
Marina Bay • Singapore 129 I12
Marina del Rey • CA, United States 154 J9
Marina Real del Oeste • Bermuda 165 K9
Marineland of Florida • FL, United States 155 D1
Marinella, Golfo di • Sardinia, Italy 86 F5
Marinette • WI, United States 150 C1
Maringá • Brazil 175 C2
Marion • IL, United States 150 C3
Marion • OH, United States 150 D2
Marion Reef • CL, Australia 136 D3
Mariposa • CA, United States 154 I8
Marir • Egypt 109 E9
Maritime Museum • Singapore 129 I12
Maritsa • Bulgaria 92 D3
Mariupol' • Ukraine 100 G8
Marka • Somalia 108 C4
Markaryd • Sweden 99 G7
Marken • Netherlands 70 H7
Markermeer • Netherlands 70 H7
Markerwaardijk • Netherlands 70 C2
Märkisch Wilmersdorf • Germany 73 E8
Marksburg • Germany 74 D5
Marktoberdorf • Germany 74 F8
Marl • Germany 73 D5
Marlborough • VT, United States 156 C1
Marlborough • New Zealand 137 B3
Marlborough • QL, Australia 136 D4
Marley Beach • Bermuda 165 K10
Marlin • TX, United States 155 E5
Marlin Coast • QL, Australia 136 C3
Marlow • United Kingdom 65 G7
Marmagao • Goa, India 123 C5
Marmande • Portugal 84 H7
Marmande • France 78 E6
Marmara • Chios, Greece .... 94 D
Marmara, Gruppo delle • Italy 86 D4
Marmolada • Italy 86 D4
Mármora, Punta La • Sardinia, Italy 86 F6
Marmot Basin Ski • AL, Canada .... 146 [11]
Marne • France 76 F2
Maroantsetra • Madagascar 110 D2
Maroochydore • QL, Australia 136 D5
Maróstica • Italy 87 C1
Maroua • Cameroon 106 D3
Marquette • MI, United States 150 C1
Marquis I. • Grenada .... 166 Q
Marquises, Is. • French Polynesia 139 EE3
Marrakech • Morocco 107 A2
Marrakech Heritage C • Morocco .. 44 [279]
Marrakesh Medina • Morocco .... 44 [279]
Marrawah • TS, Australia 136 E6
Marree • SA, Australia 135 F5
Marrero • LA, United States 151 B5
Marroquí, Punta de • Spain 82 J3
Marsa Alam • Egypt 109 B3
Marsabit • Kenya 109 C4
Marsabit Nat. Park • Kenya 109 C4
Marsabit Nat. Reserve • Kenya 109 C4
Marsabit Nat. Reserve Park • Kenya .112 [70]
Marsala • Sicily, Italy 86 G7
Marsalforn • Malta 96 A1
Marsalforn Bay • Malta 96 A1
Marsaskala • Malta 96 B2
Marsaxlokk • Malta 96 B2
Marsaxlokk Bay • Malta 96 B2
Marseille • France 78 G8
Marseilles • France 78 G8
Marsh Harbour • Bahamas 164 A1
Marsh I. • LA, United States 156 E6
Marsh-Billings-Rockefeller Nat. Hist. Park Park N • VT, United States .153 [293]
Marshall • TX, United States 155 F4
MARSHALL IS. • Pacific Ocean 138 CC2
Marshfield • WI, United States 150 B2
Marssum • Netherlands 70 C2
Mårsta • Sweden 99 B1
Marstal • Denmark 99 F8
Marston Moor • United Kingdom 50 B2
Marstrand • Sweden 99 F6
Martaban, Gulf of • Myanmar 128 B3
Martapura • Indonesia 131 D4
Martha Brae • Jamaica 165 C3
Martha's Vineyard • MA, United States 156 D2
Marthaville • LA, United States 156 E5
Marti • Cuba 164 G5
Martigny • Switzerland 90 J6
Martigues • France 76 F5
Martil • Morocco 107 B1
Martim Longo • Portugal 84 K7
Martin • Slovak Rep. 89 F9
Martin Luther King Jr. Nat. Historic Site Park N • GA, United States .. 153 [207]
Martin Van Buren Nat. Hist. Site • NY, United States 156 A4
Martin Van Buren Nat. Hist. Site Park N • NY, United States .... 153 [276]
Martinez • Mexico 169 J7
MARTINIQUE • West Indies .... 167 L
Martins Bay • New Zealand 137 G7
Martinsburg • WV, United States 156 A3
Martok • Kazakstan 121 C1
Martorell • Spain 83 C4
Marve Beach • India 124 E6
Marwar • India 123 D8
Mary • Turkmenistan 121 D4
Mary Heritage C • Turkmenistan .... 43 [139]
Mary Jane Ski • CO, United States .. 146 [56]
Mary McLeod Bethune Council House Nat. Hist. Site Park N • DC, United States .. 153 [264]
Maryborough • QL, Australia 136 D5
Maryborough • VI, Australia 136 G9
Maryland • United States 156 B3
Maryport • United Kingdom 65 C3
Marysville • CA, United States 148 B3
Marysville • KS, United States 150 B2
Maryville • TN, United States 151 D3
Marzahn (Berlin) • Germany 73 F7
Masada • Israel 120 B4
Masada Nat. Park Heritage C • Israel .44 [310]
Masai • Malaysia 129 I11
Masai Steppe • Tanzania 110 H7
Masalembo, Kepulauan • Indonesia . 131 R11
Masan • Rep. of Korea 125 G3
Masasi • Tanzania 110 H8
Masaya • Nicaragua 170 D5
Masbate • Philippines 128 G4
Mascarene Is. • Indian Ocean 9 M7
Maseru • Lesotho 110 B3
Mashabih • Saudi Arabia 109 E8
Mashatu Game Reserve • Botswana .110 J10
Mashhad • Iran 120 H6
Masindi • Uganda 108 C4
Masirah • Oman 120 I8
Masirah, Khalij • Oman 120 H10
Mask, Lough • Ireland 69 H9
Mason City • IA, United States 150 B2
Mason's Limestone Valley • New Zealand 137 D5
Maspalomas • Gran Canaria, Canary Is. 82 G6
Masqat • Oman 120 H9
Massa • Italy 87 B3
Massa Lubrense • Italy 87 G7
Massa Marittima • Italy 87 C3
Massachusetts • United States 156 C1
Massachusetts Bay • United States .. 156 D1
Massanutten VA, United States 156 A3
Massawa • Eritrea 108 C3
Massena • NY, United States 150 F2
Massif Central • France 76 E4

Massif des Bongo • Central African Rep. 108 B4
Massy • France 78 A2
Masterton • New Zealand 137 C3
Mastigouche, Réserve faunique de • QU, Canada 160 G3
Mastihári • Cos, Greece .... 94 E
Masuda • Japan 127 B4
Masuguru • Tanzania 110 H8
Masuho • Japan 127 H8
Masuko • Zimbabwe 110 C2
Mat Lang, Ko • Thailand 130 G11
Mât, Rivière du • Réunion 113 D3
Mata'utu • Wallis & Futuna .... 139 G
Matadi • Dem. Rep. of Congo 106 D5
Matagalpa • Nicaragua 170 E4
Matagami • QU, Canada 159 I4
Matagorda • Lanzarote, Canary Is. 83 I5
Matagorda Bay • TX, United States .. 155 F6
Matagorda I. • TX, United States 155 E6
Matagorda Peninsula • TX, United States 155 F6
Mataiea • French Polynesia .... 139 K
Matakana I. • New Zealand 137 E5
Matala • Crete, Greece 93 H6
Matala'a, Pointe • Wallis & Futuna ... 139 G
Matalascanas, Playa de • Spain 82 H8
Matale • Sri Lanka 124 C5
Matam • Senegal 106 A3
Matamanoa • Fiji Is. .... 138 T
Matamata • New Zealand 137 E5
Matamoros • Mexico 168 E2
Matane • QU, Canada 160 A1
Matanzas • Cuba 164 F4
Matanzas, Fort, Nat. Mon. • FL, United States 155 D1
Matapédia • QU, Canada 160 B1
Matara • Sri Lanka 124 C4
Mataram • Indonesia 131 E5
Matarani • Peru 173 F7
Mataranka • NT, Australia 135 C2
Mataró • Spain 83 D4
Matatula, Cape • American Samoa ... 139 H
Mataura • New Zealand 137 G8
Mataura [Riv] • New Zealand 137 G8
Matautoa, Cap • French Polynesia ... 139 J
Matavera • Cook Is. .... 139 N
Mataveri • Easter I. .... 139 M
Mateka • Tuvalu .... 139 L
Mateka, Te Ava • Tuvalu .... 139 L
Matelica • Italy 87 D3
Matelot • Trinidad & Tobago .... 166 S
Matera • Italy 85 F4
Matera Heritage C • Italy .... 44 [173]
Matese, Monti del • Italy 87 G6
Mateur • Tunisia 107 D4
Matheran Hill Sta • India 124 E6
Mathráki • Greece .... 94 A
Mathura • India 123 E7
Mati • Philippines 128 H5
Matias Romero • Mexico 169 K8
Matmata • Tunisia 107 D6
Mato Grosso • Brazil 174 A4
Mato Grosso do Sul • Brazil 175 C1
Mato Grosso, Planalto de • Brazil ... 174 A4
Matobo Nat. Park • Zimbabwe .112 [116]
Matosinhos • Portugal 80 A3
Matre • Norway 98 F8
Matrei • Austria 91 I8
Matrûh • Egypt 109 A1
Matsu Tao • Taiwan 125 F3
Matsubara-ko • Japan 127 H8
Matsudo • Japan 127 I8
Matsue • Japan 127 B3
Matsumoto • Japan 127 C3
Matsumoto-ko • Japan 127 C3
Matsusaka • Japan 127 H9
Mattancheri • India 124 B3
Matterdale • United Kingdom 65 D3
Matterhorn • Italy/Switzerland 90 J6
Matthew Town • Bahamas 164 B2
Matto • Japan 127 C3
Mattoon • IL, United States 150 C3
Matucana • Peru 173 E6
Maturín • Venezuela 173 D6
Matusadona Nat. Park Park • Zimbabwe .... 112 [113]
Mau • India 123 G8
Maubeuge • France 76 E1
Maubuisson • France 78 E5
Mauganj • India 123 G8
Maui • HI, United States 157 I5
Mauke • Cook Is. 139 DD4
Maulbronn Heritage C • Germany .. 44 [62]
Mauléon-Licharre • France 78 I9
Maumee • OH, United States 161 C3
Maumturk Mftns • Ireland 69 G9
Maun • Botswana 110 I9
Mauna Kea • HI, United States 157 J6
Mauna Lani • HI, United States 157 J6
Mauna Loa • HI, United States 157 J6
Maunganui • Cook Is. .... 139 N
Maurepas, Lake • LA, United States 156 F6
Maures, Massif des • France 78 G8
Mauricie, Parc nat. de la • QU, Canada 160 H3
Mauricie, Parc national de la Park N • QU, Canada .... 161 [30]
Maurienne • France 78 D4
MAURITANIA • Africa 106 A3
MAURITIUS • Indian Ocean .... 113 E-F
Maus, Burg • Germany 74 D5
Mäuseturm • Germany 74 D6
Mav • Turkey 95 J10
Mavrovo Nat. Park Park N • F.Y.R. of Macedonia .... 58 [129]
Mawan • China 126 E4
Mawkmai • Myanmar 130 B5
Mawson [Base] • Antarctica .... 176 [17]
Maxglan [Apt] • Austria 91 F7
Máximo Gómez • Cuba 164 G4
Maxwell • Barbados .... 167 M
May Day Mtns • Jamaica 165 C4
May Pen • Jamaica 165 D4
May Point, Cape • NJ, United States 156 B3
Maya • Indonesia 131 C4
Maya, La Ruta • C. America .... 170 J-K
Maya Mtns • Belize 170 K9
Mayaguana • Bahamas .... 164 [310]
Mayagüez • Puerto Rico 165 I8
Mayagüez, Bahía de • Puerto Rico .. 165 I8
Mayo Route • C. America .... 170 J-K
Mayapán • Mexico 169 F4
Mayari • Cuba 164 G5
Mayda Shahr • Afghanistan 121 E5
Mayen • Germany 74 C6
Mayenne [Adm] • France 77 E5
Mayenne [Riv] • France 77 E5
Mayenne-de-Riddes Ski • Switzerland . 91 [57]
Maykop • Russian Fed. 100 F5
Maymyo • Myanmar 130 B4
Mayo • Ireland 69 H8
Mayo • Oman 158 C2
Mayo, Plains of • Ireland 69 H8
Mayor I. • New Zealand 137 E5
MAYOTTE • Indian Ocean 110 D2
Mayrhofen • Austria 91 I8
Mayshos • Germany 74 E7
Mayumba, Parc nat. de Park • Gabon .112 [47]
Mazagón • Spain 82 H8
Mazar-e Sharif • Afghanistan 121 E4
Mazara del Vallo • Sicily, Italy 86 G7
Mazara, Val di • Sicily, Italy 86 G7
Mazarrón • Spain 83 A2
Mazatlán • Mexico 169 H6
Mazeikiai • Lithuania 100 J7
Mazinga • St Eustatius .... 167 E
Mazocahui • Mexico 168 I5

Mazuria • Poland 89 D2
Mazurski Nat. Park Park N • Poland . 58 [102]
Mazyr • Belarus 100 C3
Mazzarò • Sicily, Italy 86 H7
Mbabane • Swaziland 110 C3
Mbala • Zambia 110 G8
Mbale • Uganda 108 C4
Mbamba Bay • Tanzania 110 G8
Mbandaka • Dem. Rep. of Congo 108 A4
Mbarabara • Uganda 108 C5
Mbarara • Uganda 108 C5
Mbaswana • South Africa 111 C3
Mbeya • Tanzania 110 G8
Mbuji-Mayi • Dem. Rep. of Congo .. 108 B5
Mbulu • Tanzania 110 H7
McAlester • OK, United States 151 A4
McAllen • TX, United States 149 G5
McCall • ID, United States 154 H6
McCarran [Apt] • NV, United States .. 154 J8
McClintock Channel • NU, Canada .. 158 F1
McComb • MS, United States 156 F5
McCook • NE, United States 148 C2
McDermitt • NV, United States 154 I8
McGrath • AK, United States 157 D3
Mchinga • Tanzania 110 H8
McIntosh • SD, United States 148 F1
McKerrow, Lake • New Zealand 137 G7
McKinley, Mt • AK, United States 157 E3
McKinney • TX, United States 155 E4
McLean's Town • Bahamas 164 B1
McLeod Lake • BC, Canada 160 I6
McMinnville • OR, United States 154 G6
McMurdo [Base] • Antarctica .... 176 [23]
McPherson • KS, United States 148 G3
Mdantsane, Fort, Nat. Mon. • FL, United States 155 D1
Mdina • Malta 96 B2
Mdiq • Morocco 107 B1
Me'arot Hever • Israel 120 B4
Mead, Lake • AZ/NV, United States 155 G7
Mead's Bay • Anguilla .... 166 B
Meadow Lake • SA, Canada 158 F3
Meagaidh, Creag • United Kingdom .. 62 C4
Meander River • AL, Canada 158 E3
Meath • Ireland 69 E6
Meaux • France 78 B1
Mecca • Saudi Arabia 120 E9
Mechelen • Belgium 70 B4
Mermaid Beach • Bermuda 165 K10
Meckenheim • Germany 74 C5
Mecklenburg-Vorpommern • Germany . 72 E2
Mecklenburger Bucht • Germany .. 72 D1
Medan • Indonesia 131 N9
Mededsiz Tepe • Turkey 95 J9
Medellin • Colombia 173 B2
Medenine • Tunisia 107 D6
Medewi Beach • Bali, Indonesia 131 K7
Medford • OR, United States 154 G6
Medgidia • Romania 92 I7
Media Luna • Cuba 164 G5
Media Luna, Arrecife de la • Honduras/Nicaragua 166 BB3
Medias • Romania 92 D2
Medias Aguas • Mexico 169 K8
Medicine Hat • AL, Canada 158 E3
Medina • Saudi Arabia 120 D9
Medina del Campo • Spain 80 C3
Medinipur • India 122 C3
Mediterranean Sea • Africa/Europe 96
Mediterranean seaboard prehistoric rock-art sites Heritage C • Spain .... 44 [125]
Médoc • France 78 E5
Meekatharra • WA, Australia 135 B5
Meelpaeg lake • NF, Canada 160 C1
Meenambakkam • India 124 C2
Meerbusch • Germany 73 C6
Meersburg • Germany 74 E8
Meeufenbrunn • Maldives 124 B8
Meerut • India 123 F7
Megalonissos • Greece 94 B83
Megalópoli • Greece 93 C3
Meganissi • Greece .... 94 J
Megève Ski • France .... 61 [20]
Megève • France 78 D3
Meghalaya • India 123 B2
Megisti • Greece 95 G8
Megísti • Greece 95 G8
Mehdia-Plage • Morocco 107 A1
Mei Yuan • China 126 G6
Meijinomori-Mino Quasi Nat. Park • Japan 127 G6
Meiktila • Myanmar 128 B2
Meinershagen • Germany 73 D6
Meiningen • Germany 86 H7
Meiningen • Switzerland 90 J5
Meiringspoort • South Africa 111 F7
Meisenheim • Germany 74 D6
Meizhou • China 125 F4
Mejez el Bab • Tunisia 107 D4
Mek'ele • Ethiopia 108 C3
Mekele Gölü • Turkey 95 I9
Meknassy • Tunisia 107 C5
Meknès • Morocco 107 A1
Meknès Heritage C • Morocco .... 44 [277]
Mekong • Asia 128 C5
Mekong, Mouths of the • Vietnam .. 129 B6
Melaka • Malaysia 128 C6
Mélanes • Náxos, Greece .... 94 H
Melanesia • Pacific Ocean 138 SB2
Melapua • Mexico 169 H7
Melbourne • FL, United States 155 D2
Melbourne • VI, Australia 136 G9
Melchsee-Frutt • Switzerland 90 K5
Melekeiok • Palau .... 138 Y
Melfort • SA, Canada 158 F3
Melidoni • Crete, Greece 93 H5
Melilla • Africa 107 B1
Melincué • Argentina 175 F6
Melissani • Cephalonia, Greece .... 94 J
Melita [Apt] • Tunisia 107 D5
Melitopol' • Ukraine 100 E4
Mellègue • Algeria/Tunisia 107 C4
Mellerud • Sweden 99 G5
Mellieha • Malta 96 A1
Mellieha Bay • Malta 96 A1
Mellifont Abbey • Ireland 69 E6
Melmoth • South Africa 111 C4
Melnik • Czech Rep. 89 E6
Melo • Uruguay 175 C3
Melos • Greece 93 D3
Melun • France 78 B2
Melville • SA, Canada 158 F3
Melville Hall [Apt] • Dominica .... 167 K
Melville I. • Canada 142 D1
Melville I. • NT, Australia 135 E2
Melville Is. • Trinidad & Tobago .... 166 R
Melville Peninsula • NU, Canada 159 H2
Memel • South Africa 111 B3
Memmingen • Germany 74 F7
Memphis • Egypt 109 A1
Memphis Heritage C • Egypt .... 44 [298]
Memphis • TN, United States 151 C3
Ménaka • Mali 106 C3
Menang • Nauru .... 138 X
Menang Point • Nauru .... 138 X
Menawali • Bali, Indonesia 131 K7
Mende • France 76 E4
Mendip Hills • United Kingdom 65 K9
Mendocino • CA, United States 154 I8
Mendocino, Cape • CA, United States 148 B2
Mendrisio • Switzerland 90 B3
Menemen • Turkey 95 E5
Menen • Belgium 70 B5
Menfi • Sicily, Italy 86 G8
Mengen • Germany 74 E7
Menjangan • Bali, Indonesia 131 K7
Menominee I. • MI, United States 161 B2
Menominee River • OT, Canada 161 B1
Menomonie • WI, United States 150 B2
Menominee Ind Res • MI, United States .... 155 [65]
Menongue • Angola 110 A2
Menonurk • Russian Fed. 169 B3
Menor, Mar • Spain 83 A2
Menorca • Spain 80 H3
Mentakab • Malaysia 129 G10
Mentana • Italy 87 E4
Mentawai, Kepulauan • Indonesia .. 131 A4
Mentigi • Indonesia 131 L8

Menton • France 78 H7
Menuires, les Ski • France .... 61 [32]
Menuires, les • France 78 D4
Menzies • WA, Australia 135 C5
Meppel • Netherlands 70 G2
Meppen • Germany 72 B2
Mequinenza, Embalse de • Spain 80 E3
Mer de Sable • Java, Indonesia 131 O11
Mer de Sable, la Park L • France .. 59 [63]
Mer de Sable, La • France 78 B1
Merak • Java, Indonesia 131 O11
Mérano • Italy 86 C3
Merano • Italy 86 C3
Merapi, Gunung • Indonesia 131 N10
Merauke • Indonesia 131 J5
Merbabu, Gunung • Java, Indonesia 131 Q12
Mercantour, Parc nat. du Park N • France .... 58 [74]
Mercantour, Parc nat. du • France 78 H7
Mercara Hill Sta • India 124 E6
Mercato • Italy 87 H7
Merced • CA, United States 154 I8
Mercedes • Argentina 175 G5
Mercedes • Uruguay 175 G6
Mercedes • Argentina 175 B3
Mercier Dam • QU, Canada 160 F3
Mergui • Myanmar 128 B4
Mergui Archipelago • Myanmar 128 B4
Méribel Ski • France .... 61 [30]
Méribel • France 78 D4
Meric • Turkey 95 E3
Mérida • Mexico 169 F4
Mérida • Spain 80 B4
Mérida Heritage C • Spain .... 44 [121]
Mérida • Venezuela 173 B2
Meridian • MS, United States 156 F5
Mérignac [Apt] • France 78 E6
Merikarvia • Finland 99 C3
Merimbula • NS, Australia 136 H9
Mering • Germany 74 F7
Merioneth • United Kingdom 64 A5
Merizo • Guam .... 138 Z
Merke • Kazakstan 121 F3
Merktredwitz • Germany 72 E3
Merlette • France 78 D4
Mermaid Beach • Bermuda 165 K10
Meron • Israel 120 B1
Merredin • WA, Australia 135 B6
Merrick • United Kingdom 62 C5
Merrimack • MA/NH, United States .. 156 D1
Merritt I. Nat. Wildlife Refuge • FL, United States 155 D2
Merryville • LA, United States 156 E6
Mersa Fatma • Eritrea 109 E11
Mersa Tek'lay • Eritrea 109 E10
Mersch • Luxembourg 70 D5
Mersea I. • United Kingdom 65 H7
Mersey • United Kingdom 63 D7
Mersin • Turkey 95 J10
Mersing • Malaysia 128 C6
Merthyr Tydfil • United Kingdom 63 D9
Méru • France 78 A1
Meru • Kenya 109 D4
Meru, Mt • Tanzania 110 H7
Meru Nat. Park • Kenya .... 112 [73]
Merv • Turkmenistan .... 121 [J7]
Merv State Hist. & Cultural Park Heritage C • Turkmenistan .... 43 [139]
Meryemana • Turkey .... 95 [95]
Mesa • AZ, United States 155 G8
Mesa Verde Nat. Park • CO, United States 155 H7
Mesa Verde Nat. Park Park N • CO, United States .... 152 [92]
Mesa Verde Nat. Park Heritage C • United States .... 42 [6]
Mescalero Ind Res • NM, United States .... 155 [41]
Meski • Morocco 107 B2
Meskiá • Crete, Greece 93 G5
Mesquer • France 78 E5
Messalonghi • Greece .... 94 A
Mesté • Chios, Greece .... 94 D
Messancy • France 78 E5
Messaoria Plain • Cyprus 96 C4
Messarás, Ormos • Crete, Greece .. 93 H6
Messel • Germany 74 B2
Messel Pit fossil site Heritage N • Germany .... 41 [58]
Messina • Sicily, Italy 86 H7
Messina, Stretto di • Italy 86 H7
Messiniakós Kólpos • Greece 93 C3
Messlingen • Sweden 99 H4
Messonghi • Corfu, Greece .... 94 A
Mestre • Italy 87 D2
Meta • Colombia/Venezuela 173 B2
Meta • Italy 87 G7
Meta Incognita Peninsula • NU, Canada 159 J2
Métabief Ski • France .... 61 [7]
Metairie • LA, United States 156 F6
Metán • Argentina 175 B2
Metéora • Greece 93 B2
Metéora Heritage N • Greece .... 41 [78]
Metéora Heritage C • Greece .... 44 [234]
Methana • Greece 93 C3
Méthana • Greece 94 BB3
Methoni • Greece .... 94 A
Methil • United Kingdom 65 B1
Methven • New Zealand 137 C3
Metkovic • Croatia 92 G6
Metro Toronto Zoo • OT, Canada 160 E5
Mettlach • Germany 74 A2
Mettmann • Germany 73 C6
Metz • France 77 F6
Meulaboh • Indonesia 131 M9
Meureudu • Indonesia 131 M9
Meuse • Belgium/France 70 C4
Meuse • France 76 F2
Meuse Valley • Belgium 70 C4
Mevagissey • United Kingdom 65 I10
Mexborough • United Kingdom 65 E7
Mexicali • Mexico 168 I5
Mexican Hat • UT, United States 148 E3
Mexican Water • AZ, United States .. 150 B3
MEXICO • N. America 168
México [Adm] • Mexico 169 C3
Mexico City • Mexico 169 J8
Mexico City Heritage C • Mexico .. 42 [22]
Mexico, Gulf of • N. America 142 E6
Meymaneh • Afghanistan 121 D4
Mfanganu I. • Uganda 109 C5
Mgahlongu • United Kingdom 109 C5
Mgunguindlovu • South Africa 111 C4
Mhamid • Morocco 107 B3
Miahuatlán • Mexico 169 K8
Miahuatlán, Sierra de • Mexico 169 K8
Miami • FL, United States 155 D3
Miami Beach • FL, United States 155 D3
Miami Seaquarium • FL, United States 155 D3
Miamisburg • United States .... 42 [20]
Mianwali • Pakistan 122 C3
Mianyang • China 125 E3
Miass • Russian Fed. 101 F4
Miastko • Poland 89 B2
Miccosukee Ind Res • FL, United States .... 155 [70]
Michalovce • Slovak Rep. 89 G9
Michelson, Mt • AK, United States 157 E2
Michelstadt • Germany 74 B2
Michendorf • Germany 73 E8
Michigan • United States 161 B3
Michigan, Lake • United States 161 B3
Michigan Is. Nat. Wildlife Refuge • MI, United States 161 B-C2
Michipicoten I. • OT, Canada 161 B1
Michipicoten River • OT, Canada 161 B1
Michoacán • Mexico 169 B3
Michurinsk • Russian Fed. 100 F3
Micoud • St Lucia .... 167 N
MICRONESIA • Pacific Ocean 138 BB2
MICRONESIA, FEDERATED STATES OF • Pacific Ocean 138 BB2
Mid-Atlantic Ridge • Atlantic Ocean . 8 H5

Mid-Indian Ridge • Indian Ocean 9 M6
Middelburg • Netherlands 70 B3
Middelburg • South Africa 111 G6
Middelfart • Denmark 99 E7
Middelharnis • Netherlands 70 G8
Middelkirke-Bad • Belgium 70 E6
Middle Andaman • India 122 D4
Middle Caoicos • Turks & Caicos Is. .. 164 C3
Middlesboro • KY, United States 151 D3
Middlesbrough • United Kingdom 63 E6
Middlesex • United Kingdom 65 G7
Middleton • NS, Canada 160 B2
Middletown • NY, United States 156 B2
Midès • Tunisia 107 C5
Midi • France 76 L9
Midi, Canal du • France 76 D5
Midi, Canal du Heritage C • France .. 44 [90]
Midi-Pyrénées • France 77 A2
Midland • MI, United States 161 C2
Midland • OT, Canada 160 E4
Midland • TX, United States 149 F4
Midleton • Ireland 69 H11
Midlothian • United Kingdom 65 B2
Midmar Nature Reserve • South Africa 111 B4
Midnight Sun Coast • Sweden 98 B2
Midway [Apt] • IL, United States 161 B3
Midway Is. • Pacific Ocean 138 CC1
Midwest City • OK, United States 149 G3
Miechów • Poland 89 G8
Mielán • France 78 J9
Miercurea Ciuc • Romania 92 C2
Miesbach • Germany 74 G8
Migjorn, Platja de • Formentera, Spain 83 M10
Migori • Kenya 109 C5
Miguasha Prov. Park Heritage N • QU, Canada .... 40 [7]
Miguel Alemán • Mexico 169 K8
Miguel Alemán, Presa • Mexico 169 K8
Miguel Alemán, Presa • Mexico 168 D3
Miguel Hidalgo [Apt] • Mexico 169 I7
Mihara-yama • Japan 127 I9
Miho • Japan 127 H9
Mijas Costa • Spain 82 I8
Mijdrecht • Netherlands 70 H7
Mikhaylovka • Russian Fed. 100 F3
Miki • Japan 127 F6
Mikkeli • Finland 97 F3
Mikkeli [Adm] • Finland 98 C3
Mikonos • Mikonos, Greece .... 94 I
Mikonos [I.] • Greece .... 94 I
Mikumi • Tanzania 110 H8
Mikumi Nat. Park • Tanzania 110 H8
Mikun' • Russian Fed. 100 C1
Milan • Italy 87 B2
Milan Heritage C • Italy .... 44 [148]
Milano • Italy 87 B2
Milano Heritage C • Italy .... 44 [148]
Milano Marittima • Italy 87 D2
Milas • Turkey 95 F6
Milatos • Crete, Greece 93 I6
Milazzo • Sicily, Italy 86 H7
Mildura • VI, Australia 135 G6
Miles • QL, Australia 136 D5
Miles City • MT, United States 148 E1
Miletus • Turkey 95 E6
Milevsko • Czech Rep. 89 E7
Milford Haven • United Kingdom 63 C9
Milford Sound • New Zealand 137 G7
Milford Sound [Fiord] • New Zealand . 137 F7
Milford Track • New Zealand 137 G7
Milh, Wadi al • Iraq 120 C3
Milltown Malbay • Ireland 69 H10
Milnthorpe • United Kingdom 65 D3
Milos • Greece 93 D3
Miltenberg • Germany 74 B2
Milton • FL, United States 155 A1
Milton • New Zealand 137 B4
Milton Keynes • United Kingdom 63 E8
Milwane Game Reserve Park • Swaziland .... 112 [145]
Milwaukee • WI, United States 150 C2
Milyas • Turkey 95 G7
Mimaland • Malaysia 129 G10
Mimizan • France 78 E6
Mimizan, Fôret de • France 78 E6
Minami Tori Shima • Japan 138 BB1
Minamiashigara • Japan 127 H9
Minas • Uruguay 175 G6
Minas Gerais • Brazil 174 B4
Minatitlán • Mexico 169 K8
Minbu • Myanmar 128 A2
Minch, The • United Kingdom 62 C2
Mincio • Italy 87 C2
Mindanao • Philippines 128 H5
Mindelheim • Germany 74 F7
Mindelo • Cape Verde 106 E7
Minden • Germany 72 C2
Minden • LA, United States 156 E5
Mindoro • Philippines 128 G4
Minehead • United Kingdom 65 J9
Mineola • TX, United States 155 F4
Mineral Wells • TX, United States 155 E4
Mineral'nye Vody • Russian Fed. 100 F5
Minervois • France 78 J9
Ming Village • Singapore 129 H12
Mingan • QU, Canada 160 B1
Mingan Archipelago • QU, Canada .. 160 B1
Mingan, Réserve du Parc national de l'Archipel-de- Park N • QU, Canada . 161 [32]
Minidoka Internment Nat. Mon. Park N • ID, United States .... 152 [61]
Minneapolis • MN, United States 150 B2
Minnedosa • Lake • FL, United States 157 A1
Minnesota [Adm] • United States 150 B1
Minnesota [Riv] • MN, United States 150 A2
Minorca • Spain .... 83 J-K
Minot • ND, United States 148 F1
Minquiers, Les • Channel Is. 64 A6
Minsk • Belarus 100 C2
Minute Man Nat. Hist. Park Park N • MA, United States .... 153 [292]
Minuteman Missile Nat. Hist. Site Park N • SD, United States .... 152 [151]
Minupan • QU, Canada 159 I4
Mira • Portugal 84 I7
Mirabel [Apt] • QU, Canada 160 G3
Mirabilandia Park L • Italy .... 59 [83]
Miraflores • Italy 87 D2
Miracema • Brazil 174 F6
Mirador dos Lagunas Rio Azul, Parque Nac. • Guatemala 170 K8
Miraflores, Esclusas de • Panama .. 170 M11
Miragoâne • Haiti 165 F6
Miraj • India 124 B1
Miramar • Argentina 175 G7
Miramar [Apt] • Italy 87 D3
Miramar Beach • Goa, India 123 C5
Mirambeau • France 78 E6
Mirambello, Kólpos • Crete, Greece 93 I6
Mirándola • Italy 87 C2
Mirbat • Oman 109 E9
Mirebalais • Haiti 165 F6
Mirear • Egypt 109 E9
Miri • Sarawak, Malaysia 128 E6

Mirik **Hill Sta** • India 124 F5
Mirim, Lagoa • Brazil/Uruguay 175 C3
Mirina • Greece 93 D2
Mirny [Base] • Antarctica .... 176 [20]
Mirny • Russian Fed. 101 L3
Mirpur Khas • Pakistan 122 A3
Mirs Bay • China 126 F4
Mirtiotissa • Corfu, Greece .... 94 A
Mirtoan Sea • Greece 94 BB3
Mirtóo Pélagos • Greece 93 C3
Mirtos • Crete, Greece 93 I6
Mirzapur • India 123 G8
Misaki • Japan 127 F7
Micano Adriático • Italy 87 D3
Miscou I. • NB, Canada 160 B1
Miseno, Capo • Italy 87 G7
Mish, Slieve • Ireland 69 G10
Mishima • Japan 127 H9
Miskitos, Cayos • Nicaragua 170 F3
Miskitos, Costa de • Nicaragua 170 F4
Miskolc • Hungary 92 C1
Misoöl • Indonesia 131 H4
Misratah • Libya 106 D1
Misrikh • India 123 F7
Mission Beach • QL, Australia 136 C3
Mission San Javier • Mexico 168 I6
Mississauga • OT, Canada 160 E5
Mississippi [Adm] • United States .. 151 C4
Mississippi [Riv] • United States ... 147 H2
Mississippi River Delta •
   LA, United States 156 F6
Missoula • MT, United States 154 H5
Missouri [Adm] • United States 150 B3
Missouri Breaks •
   MT, United States 154 B1
Missouri [Riv] • United States 148 L1
Mistassini, Lake • QU, Canada 159 I3
Mistelbach • Austria 91 H1
Misterhult • Sweden 99 H6
Mistrás • Greece 93 C3
Mistrás **Heritage C** • Greece ..... 44 [238]
Misty Fjords • AK, United States 157 F4
Mitchell • QL, Australia 136 C5
Mitchell • SD, United States 148 G2
Mitchell, Mt • NC, United States ... 151 D3
Mitchell [Riv] • QL, Australia 135 G3
Mitchelstown • Ireland 69 H10
Mithimna • Lesbos, Greece .... 94 C
Mitikas • Greece .... 94 J
Mitilíni • Lesbos, Greece .... 94 C
Mito • Japan 127 D3
Mitohama • Japan 127 H9
Mitte (Berlin) • Germany 73 F7
Mittelberg **Ski** • Austria .... 61 [88]
Mittelberg • Austria 91 M7
Mittelland • Switzerland 90 J5
Mittellandkanal • Germany 72 C2
Mittenwald • Germany 74 G8
Mittenwalde • Germany 73 F8
Mitú • Colombia 173 C2
Miura • Japan 127 I9
Miura-hanto • Japan 127 I9
Mixteco • Mexico 169 J8
Miyagusuku-jima • Okinawa, Japan . 138 A
Miyako • Japan 127 D3
Miyakonojo • Japan 127 B4
Miyazaki • Japan 127 B4
Mizen Head • Cork, Ireland 69 G11
Mizen Head • Wicklow, Ireland 69 F7
Mizoram • India 123 B2
Mjölby • Sweden 99 H5
Mjøndalen • Norway 98 D5
Mjörn • Sweden 99 G5
Mjøsa • Norway 97 C3
Mkhondvo • Swaziland 111 C3
Mkuze • South Africa 111 C3
Mkuzi Game Reserve • South Africa . 111 C3
Mkuzi Game Reserve **Park** •
   South Africa .... 112 [138]
Mladá Boleslav • Czech Rep. 89 E6
Mlawula Nature Reserve **Park** •
   Swaziland .... 112 [144]
Mljet • Croatia 92 G6
Mljet Nat. Park **Park N** • Croatia . 58 [122]
Mljet Nat. Park • Croatia 92 G6
Mmabatho • South Africa 110 B3
Mnajdra • Malta 96 B2
Mnarani • Kenya 109 C6
Mnichovo Hradiste • Czech Rep. 89 E6
Mo i Rana • Norway 97 C3
Moa • Cuba 164 H5
Moab • Jordan 120 B4
Moanda • Gabon 106 D5
Moba • Dem. Rep. of Congo 110 G8
Mobara • Japan 127 I8
Moberly • MO, United States 150 B3
Mobile • AL, United States 155 A1
Mobile Bay • AL, United States 155 A1
Mobor Beach • Goa, India 123 C4
Mobridge • SD, United States 148 F1
Moca • Dominican Rep. 165 G5
Moçambique, I. de **Heritage C** •
   Mozambique .... 43 [199]
Mocha • Yemen 120 E11
Mochudi • Botswana 110 J10
Mocímboa da Praia • Mozambique . 110 H8
Moëkoln • Sweden 99 C7
Moctezuma • Mexico 168 I5
Modane • France 78 D4
Modane • Belgium 70 C4
Modena • Italy 87 C2
Modena **Heritage C** • Italy .... 44 [198]
Modesto • CA, United States 154 I8
Módi • Greece .... 94 B
Módica • Sicily, Italy 86 H8
Módica **Heritage C** • Sicily, Italy . 44 [175]
Mödling • Austria 91 H1
Moea • Italy 86 C4
Moengo • Surinam 174 A2
Moers • Germany 73 C5
Moga • India 122 B2
Mogadishu • Somalia 108 C4
Mogán • Gran Canaria, Canary Is. .. 82 G6
Mogao Caves • China 125 D4
Mogao Caves **Heritage C** • China . 43 [172]
Mogaung • Myanmar 128 C1
Moguer • Spain 82 H7
Mohammed V [Apt] • Morocco 107 A1
Mohammedia • Morocco 107 A1
Mohave, Lake •
   AZ/NV, United States 155 G7
Mohawk • NY, United States 156 B1
Mohawk Mtn • CT, United States ... 156 C1
Mohenjodaro **Heritage C** • Pakistan 43 [165]
Moher, Cliffs of • Ireland 69 H9
Moi • Myanmar/Thailand 130 B6
Moi [Apt] • Kenya 109 C6
Moisdale • France 78 H1
Moita • Corsica, France 78 N11
Möja • Sweden 99 B2
Mojácar • Spain 82 K7
Mojave • CA, United States 149 C3
Mojave Desert • CA, United States .. 154 J9
Mojave Nat. Preserve •
   CA, United States 154 J9
Mojave Nat. Preserve **Park N** •
   CA, United States .... 152 [57]
Mojeidi I. **Dive** • Indonesia 109 E10
Mojokerto • Java, Indonesia 131 R12
Mokapu Peninsula •
   HI, United States 157 H6
Mokau • New Zealand 137 D6
Mokau [Riv] • New Zealand 137 D5
Mokgware Hills • Botswana 110 J10
Moknine • Tunisia 107 D5
Mokpo • Rep. of Korea 125 G3
Mokuleia Beach • HI, United States . 157 I5
Molara, I. • Sardinia, Italy 86 F5
Moldat • Croatia 92 F6
Moldavia • Moldova/Romania 92 D2
Moldavian churches **Heritage C** •
   Romania .... 44 [223]
Molde • Norway 98 C7

MOLDOVA • Europe 92 E2
Moldova Noua • Romania 92 C2
Moldovita • Romania 92 D2
Môle, Cap du • Haiti 165 E5
Mole Creek • TAS, Australia 136 F6
Mole Nat. Park **Park** • Ghana ... 112 [18]
Môle St Nicolas • Haiti 165 E5
Molepole • Botswana 110 J10
Molfetta • Italy 85 F4
Moline • IL, United States 150 B2
Molise • Italy 86 B2
Molivos • Lesbos, Greece .... 94 C
Mölle • Sweden 99 G7
Mollendo • Peru 173 F7
Mollerussa • Spain 83 C3
Molnabo • Sweden 99 F5
Mollösund • Sweden 99 F6
Molodezhnaya [Base] • Antarctica .. 176 [16]
Molokai • HI, United States 157 I5
Molong • NS, Australia 135 H6
Molopo • Botswana/South Africa .. 110 I10
Molteno • South Africa 111 G6
Molucca Sea • Indonesia 131 G3
Moluccas • Indonesia 131 G4
Mombasa • Kenya 109 C6
Mombasa Marine Nat. Park • Kenya 109 C6
Mombasa Marine Nat. Reserve •
   Kenya 109 C6
Mombetsu • Japan 127 D2
Mompós **Heritage C** • Colombia . 42 [52]
Man • Denmark 99 G8
Mona, I. • West Indies 167 DD3
Mona Passage •
   Dominican Rep./Puerto Rico 167 DD3
Monach Is. • United Kingdom 62 B3
MONACO • Europe 79 H7
Monadliath Mtns • United Kingdom . 62 C3
Monaghan • Ireland 69 C2
Monahans • TX, United States 149 F4
Monasterevin • Ireland 69 E7
Monastir • Tunisia 107 D5
Moncalieri • Italy 87 A2
Monção • Portugal 84 A1
Moncarapacho • Portugal 84 K8
Mönchengladbach • Germany 73 C6
Mönchique • Portugal 84 I7
Monchique, Serra de • Portugal 84 I7
Monclova • Mexico 168 D2
Moncton • NB, Canada 160 B2
Mondello • Sicily, Italy 86 G7
Mondlo • South Africa 111 B3
Mondorf-les-Bains • Luxembourg ... 70 D5
Mondovì • Italy 87 A2
Mondragone • Italy 87 P7
Mondsee • Austria 91 P7
Mondsee [Lake] • Austria 91 P7
Monéglia • Italy 87 B2
Monemvassía • Greece 93 C3
Monforte de Lemos • Spain 80 B2
Mong Gai • Vietnam 128 D2
Mong Hang • Myanmar 130 B5
Mong Kok • Hong Kong, China 126 E5
Mong Pan • Myanmar 128 C2
Mong Un • Myanmar 128 C2
Mongia, la • France 78 J9
MONGOLIA • Asia 125 E2
Mongora • Pakistan 122 B2
Mongstad • Norway 98 F8
Mongu • Zambia 110 B2
Monheim • Germany 73 C6
Monmouth • United Kingdom 65 E6
Monmouthshire • United Kingdom . 65 E6
Monnickendam • Netherlands 70 H7
Mono Lake • CA, United States 154 J8
Monocacy Nat. Battlefield •
   MU, United States 156 A3
Monocacy Nat. Battlefield **Park N** •
   MD, United States .... 153 [256]
Monolithos • Rhodes, Greece .... 94 F
Monos • Trinidad & Tobago .... 166 S
Monowai, Lake • New Zealand 137 F8
Monpazier • France 78 F6
Monreale • Sicily, Italy 86 G7
Monroe • LA, United States 156 E5
Monroe • NC, United States 151 D4
Monroe • WI, United States 150 C2
Monrovia • Liberia 106 A4
Mons • Belgium 70 B4
Mons **Heritage C** • Belgium ..... 44 [43]
Mons Klint • Denmark 99 G8
Monschau • Germany 74 A1
Monsélice • Italy 87 C2
Monsheim • Germany 74 D6
Monster • Netherlands 70 H6
Mönsterás • Sweden 99 H6
Mont Blanc • France/Italy 78 D3
Mont Blanc **Ski** • QU, Canada .. 146 [17]
Mont Blanc, Tunnel du •
   France/Italy 78 D3
Mont Cenis, Col du • France 78 D4
Mont d'Or, le **Ski** • France ...... 61 [7]
Mont de Marsan • France 78 E6
Mont Gabriel **Ski** • QU, Canada . 146 [17]
Mont Joli • QU, Canada 160 A1
Mont Laurier • QU, Canada 160 G3
Mont Mégantic, Parc du •
   QU, Canada 160 I14
Mont Orford **Ski** • QU, Canada . 146 [20]
Mont Orford, Parc du •
   QU, Canada 160 H4
Mont St-Bruno, Parc du •
   QU, Canada 160 H4
Mont-St-Michel • France 77 D3
Mont-St-Michel **Heritage N** • France 41 [60]
Mont-St-Michel **Heritage C** • France 44 [71]
Mont-Ste-Anne **Ski** • QU, Canada 146 [21]
Mont-Ste-Sauveur **Ski** • QU, Canada 146 [17]
Mont Tremblant, Parc du •
   QU, Canada 160 G3
Montabaur • Germany 74 D5
Montacute House • United Kingdom 65 K9
Montagnana • Italy 87 C2
Montagne Blanche • Mauritius 113 F6
Montagne, la • Réunion 113 P6
Montagnes Noires • France 77 C4
Montagnes Noires • Haiti 165 F5
Montagu • South Africa 111 E7
Montana • Bulgaria 92 C3
Montana • United States 148 E1
Montaña Blanca •
   Lanzarote, Canary Is. 83 I5
Montaña Clara • Canary Is. 83 I5
Montañas de Anaga •
   Tenerife, Canary Is. 84 A1
Montargis • France 78 F6
Montauban • France 78 F6
Montauk • NY, United States 156 D2
Montbard • France 90 B2
Montbéliard • France 78 D3
Montblanc • Spain 83 B3
Montchavin **Ski** • France .... 61 [27]
Monte Carlo • Monaco 78 H7
Monte Cristi • Dominican Rep. 165 F5
Monte Cristi, Parque Nac. •
   Dominican Rep. 165 F5
Monte Fogo, Serra de • Portugal ... 84 J8
Monte Gordo • Portugal 84 K8
Monte Jata • Sicily, Italy 86 G7
Monte Oliveto Maggiore, Abbazia di •
   Italy 87 C3
Monte Plata • Dominican Rep. 165 G6
Montebelluna • Italy 87 F1
Montecastini • Italy 87 F1
Montechoro • Portugal 84 I8
Montecorvino • Italy 87 H7
Montefalco • Italy 87 D3
Montefiascone • Italy 87 D3
Montego Bay • Jamaica 165 G2
Montegrotto • Italy 87 C2

Montélimar • France 78 C4
Montélimar • Nicaragua 170 D5
Montella • Italy 87 H6
Montemorelos • Mexico 168 E2
Montenegro • Serbia & Montenegro . 92 E3
Montepulciano • Italy 87 C3
Montereau-Faut-Yonne • France ... 78 B2
Monterey • CA, United States 154 I8
Monterey Bay • CA, United States .. 154 I8
Montería • Colombia 173 B2
Monteriggioni • Italy 87 C3
Monterotondo • Italy 87 D3
Monterosso **Heritage C** • Italy ... 44 [159]
Monterrey • Mexico 168 D2
Montes Claros • Brazil 174 B4
Montesárchio • Italy 87 H6
Montevideo • Uruguay 175 G6
Montezuma Castle Nat. Mon. •
   AZ, United States 155 G7
Montezuma Castle Nat. Mon. **Park N** •
   AZ, United States .... 152 [107]
Montfort • Israel 120 A1
Montgenèvre **Ski** • France .... 61 [46]
Montgenèvre • France 78 D4
Montgeoffroy [Château] • France ... 77 E5
Montgomery • AL, United States ... 151 C4
Montgomery • United Kingdom 65 E5
Montgomeryshire • United Kingdom 64 A5
Monthey • Switzerland 90 I6
Monti Sibillini, Parco Naz. del **Park N** •
   Italy .... 58 [94]
Monti Sibillini, Parco Naz. dei •
   Italy 87 D3
Monticello • Corsica, France 78 M11
Monticello • FL, United States 155 C1
Monticello • UT, United States 148 E3
Monticello • VA, United States 156 A4
Montignac • France 78 F5
Montijo • Portugal 84 G6
Montilla • Spain 82 I7
Montluis • France 76 K8
Montluçon • France 76 E3
Montmagny • QU, Canada 160 A1
Montmélian • France 78 C3
Monto • QL, Australia 136 D4
Montpelier • VT, United States 156 C1
Montpellier • France 78 G6
Montpoupon [Château] • France ... 77 F5
Montréal • QU, Canada 160 G4
Montreux • Switzerland 90 I6
Montrose • CO, United States 148 E3
Montrose • United Kingdom 62 D4
Montserrat • Spain 83 C4
MONTSERRAT • West Indies .... 167 G
Monu • Fiji Is. .... 138 T
Monu [Apt] • Fiji Is. .... 138 T
Monyva • Myanmar 128 B2
Monza • Italy 87 B2
Monzón • Spain 83 C3
Mooi • South Africa 111 B4
Mooi River • South Africa 111 B4
Moon Beach • Okinawa, Japan ..... 138 A
Moone • Ireland 69 E7
Moonta • SA, Australia 135 G6
Moonstone **Ski** • OT, Canada ... 146 [15]
Moor Abbey • Ireland 69 H10
Moore, Lake • WA, Australia 135 B6
Moorea • French Polynesia .... 139 K
Moores Creek Nat. Battlefield **Park N** •
   NC, United States .... 153 [239]
Moorfoot Hills • United Kingdom .. 70 F2
Moorhead • MN, United States 150 A1
Moosburg • Germany 74 G7
Moose Jaw • SA, Canada 158 F3
Moosoonee • OT, Canada 159 H3
Mupil • Mali 106 B3
Moquegua • Peru 173 F7
Mor, Glen • United Kingdom 62 C3
Mora • Sweden 97 C3
Moradabad • India 123 F7
Moraira • Spain 83 B1
Moràltika • Corfu, Greece .... 94 A
Moran • WY, United States 148 D2
Morant Bay • Jamaica 165 D4
Morant Point • Jamaica 165 D4
Moratuwa • Sri Lanka 124 C4
Morava • Czech Rep. 89 B4
Morawhanna • Guyana 173 D2
Moray Firth • United Kingdom 62 D3
Morayshire • United Kingdom 64 A1
Morbach • Germany 74 C6
Morbegno • Italy 87 B1
Morbihan • France 77 C4
Morbihan, Golfe du • France 77 D4
Mörbylånga • Sweden 99 H7
Morcenx • France 78 E6
Morcote • Switzerland 90 K6
Morden • MN, Canada 158 F3
Mordovia **Russ Adm** • Russian Fed. 101 [10]
Möre • Sweden 99 H7
More of Romsdal • Norway 98 C7
Morecambe • United Kingdom 63 D6
Moree • NS, Australia 135 H5
Morehead City • NC, United States . 151 D4
Morel-Breiten **Ski** • Switzerland . 61 [67]
Mória • Lesbos, Greece .... 94 C
Morelia **Heritage C** • Mexico .... 42 [21]
Morelos • Mexico 169 C3
Moremi Game Reserve • Botswana . 110 I9
Moremi Game Reserve **Park** • Botswana 112 [119]
Morena • India 123 F8
Moreni • Romania 92 H7
Moreton I. • QL, Australia 136 D5
Moreton-in-Marsh • United Kingdom 65 F6
Morey's Piers **Park L** •
   NJ, United States .... 157 [32]
Morgan City • LA, United States ... 156 F6
Morgan Lewis Mill • Barbados ..... 167 M
Morgantina • Sicily, Italy 86 H8
Morgantown • WV, United States .. 150 E3
Morges • Switzerland 90 I6
Morgins • Switzerland 90 I6
Morhange • Malaysia 129 F10
Morillon les Essert **Ski** • France . 61 [7]
Morioka • Japan 127 D3
Moriyama • Japan 127 G6
Morjim Beach • Goa, India 123 C5
Mörkö • Sweden 99 B2
Morlaix • France 77 C3
Mörlunda • Sweden 99 H6
Morne des Sauteurs • Grenada ..... 166 Q
Morne Diablotins • Dominica ...... 167 K
Morne Garu Mtns • St Vincent & Gren. 167 O
Morne Seychellois • Seychelles 113 A1
Morne Seychellois Nat. Park •
   Seychelles 113 A1
Morne Trois Pitons • Dominica ..... 167 K
Morne Trois Pitons Nat. Park •
   Dominica .... 167 K
Morne Trois Pitons Nat. Park **Heritage N** •
   Dominica .... 40 [30]
Mornington I. • QL, Australia 135 G3
Moro Gulf • Philippines 128 G5
MOROCCO • Africa 107 A-9
Morogoro • Tanzania 110 H8
Morón • Cuba 164 G4
Mörön • Mongolia 125 D2
Morondava • Madagascar 110 D3
Moroni • Comoros 110 D3
Morotai • Indonesia 131 G3
Morphou • Cyprus .... 94 C
Morphou Bay • Cyprus 96 C3
Morrinsville • New Zealand 137 E5
Morris • Montserrat .... 167 G
Morrisburg • QU, Canada 160 G4
Morristown • TN, United States 151 D3
Morristown Nat. Hist. Park **Park N** •
   NJ, United States .... 153 [281]
Morro Bay State Park •
   CA, United States 154 I9
Mörrum • Sweden 99 H7
Mors • Denmark 99 E6

Morshansk • Russian Fed. 100 F3
Mortes, Rio das • Brazil 174 A4
Mortlock Is. •
   Fed. States of Micronesia 138 BB2
Morton • WA, United States 154 G5
Moruga • Trinidad & Tobago .... 166 S
Morvan • France 76 E3
Morven • QL, Australia 136 C5
Morwell • VI, Australia 136 F6
Morzine **Ski** • France .... 61 [11]
Morzine • France 78 D3
Mosbach • Germany 74 B2
Moscow • ID, United States 154 H5
Moscow • Russian Fed. 100 M10
Moscow **Heritage C** • Russian Fed. 44 [270]
Mosel • Germany 74 C6
Mosel Valley • Germany 74 C6
Moselle • Germany 74 B2
Moses Lake • WA, United States ... 154 G5
Moses Rock **Dive** • Israel 109 E7
Moshi • Tanzania 110 H7
Mosi-oa-Tunya **Heritage N** •
   Zambia/Zimbabwe .... 41 [114]
Mosi-oa-Tunya Nat. Park **Park** •
   Zambia .... 112 [111]
Moskenes • Norway 97 C3
Moskenscy • Norway 97 C2
Moskva • Russian Fed. 100 M10
Moskva **Heritage C** • Russian Fed. 44 [270]
Moskva [Riv] • Russian Fed. 100 M10
Moskvy, Kanal im • Russian Fed. .. 100 M10
Mosonmagyaróvár • Hungary 92 B2
Mosquitos, Golfo de los • Panama . 170 G6
Moss • Norway 98 E6
Moss Park • FL, United States 157 B1
Mossburn • New Zealand 137 G8
Mossel Bay • South Africa 111 F7
Mosses, Les • Switzerland 90 J6
Mossoró • Brazil 174 C3
Most • Czech Rep. 89 D6
Mosta • Malta 96 B2
Mostar • Bosnia-Herz. 92 G6
Móstoles • Spain 80 D3
Mostrim • Ireland 69 C3
Mosul • Iraq 120 E6
Mosvatn • Norway 98 G9
Motala • Sweden 99 H5
Motherwell • United Kingdom 65 A2
Mothari • India 123 G8
Motiti I. • New Zealand 137 E5
Moto Nui • Easter I. .... 139 M
Motobu • Okinawa, Japan .... 138 A
Motril • Spain 82 J9
Motu Nui • Easter I. .... 139 M
Motu Tautara • Easter I. .... 139 M
Motueka • New Zealand 137 B3
Motuhora I. • New Zealand 137 E5
Moturiki • Fiji Is. .... 138 T
Mouche, Anse a la • Seychelles 113 A1
Mouila • Gabon 106 D5
Moukalaba-Doudou, Parc nat. de **Park** •
   Gabon .... 112 [46]
Moulay Bousselham • Morocco 107 A1
Moulay Idriss • Morocco 107 A1
Moule a Chique, Cap • St Lucia ... 167 N
Moulin [Château] • France 77 F5
Moulins • France 76 E3
Moulmein • Myanmar 128 B3
Moulouya • Morocco 107 B1
Moultrie • GA, United States 155 C1
Mounda, Akra •
   Cephalonia, Greece .... 94 J
Moundou • Chad 106 D4
Moundsville • WV, United States ... 150 D3
Mount Abu • India 123 D8
Mount Abu **Hill Sta** • India 124 D7
Mount Aspiring Nat. Park •
   New Zealand 137 G7
Mount Ayliff • South Africa 111 B5
Mount Bachelor **Ski** •
   OR, United States .... 146 [28]
Mount Buffalo • VI, Australia 136 G9
Mount Buller • VI, Australia 136 G9
Mount Carleton Prov. Park •
   NB, Canada 160 B1
Mount Currie Nature Reserve •
   South Africa 111 B5
Mount Douglas • QL, Australia 136 C4
Mount Elgon Nat. Park • Kenya 109 C4
Mount Elgon Nat. Park **Park** • Kenya 112 [71]
Mount Gambier • SA, Australia 135 G7
Mount Hood Meadows **Ski** •
   OR, United States .... 146 [26]
Mount Isa • QL, Australia 135 F4
Mount Kenya • Kenya 109 C5
Mount Kenya Nat. Park • Kenya ... 109 C5
Mount Kenya Nat. Park **Park** • Kenya 112 [74]
Mount Kenya Nat. Park **Heritage N** •
   Kenya .... 41 [108]
Mount Kenya Nat. Reserve • Kenya . 109 C5
Mount Lavinia • Sri Lanka 124 C4
Mount Longonot Nat. Park • Kenya 109 C5
Mount Magnet • WA, Australia 135 B5
Mount Mansfield **Ski** •
   VT, United States .... 146 [109]
Mount Maunganui • New Zealand . 137 E5
Mount Nimba Strict Nature Reserve
   Heritage N • Guinea/Côte d'Ivoire 41 [94]
Mount Pleasant • Jamaica 165 A2
Mount Pleasant • MI, United States 150 D2
Mount Pleasant • SC, United States . 151 E4
Mount Pleasant • TX, United States 155 F4
Mount Rainier Nat. Park •
   WA, United States 154 G5
Mount Rainier Nat. Park **Park N** •
   WA, United States .... 152 [32]
Mount Revelstoke Nat. Park **Park N** •
   BC, Canada .... 161 [13]
Mount Revelstoke Nat. Park •
   BC, Canada 160 J7
Mount Robson Prov. Park •
   AL, Canada 160 J6
Mount Rose **Ski** • NV, United States 146 [36]
Mount Rushmore Nat. Mem. **Park N** •
   SD, United States .... 152 [148]
Mount Rushmore Nat. Mon. •
   SD, United States 148 F2
Mount Snow **Ski** • VT, United States 146 [105]
Mount Snow • VT, United States ... 156 C1
Mount St George • Trinidad & Tobago 166 R
Mount St Helens Nat. Volcanic Mon. •
   WA, United States 154 G5
Mount St Louis **Ski** • OT, Canada 146 [15]
Mount Sunapee **Ski** •
   NH, United States .... 146 [112]
Mount Tom • MA, United States ... 156 C1
Mount Vernon • IL, United States .. 150 C3
Mount Vernon • WA, United States 154 A3
Mount Washington **Ski** • BC, Canada 146 [1]
Mount William Nat. Park •
   TS, Australia 136 F6
Mount's Bay • United Kingdom 65 I10
Mountain Creek **Ski** •
   NJ, United States .... 146 [95]
Mountain High **Ski** •
   CA, United States .... 146 [34]
Mountain Zebra Nat. Park •
   South Africa 111 G6
Mountain Zebra Nat. Park **Park** •
   South Africa .... 112 [130]
Mountsandel • Ireland 69 H9
Moura • Portugal 84 H6
Moura • QL, Australia 136 D4
Mourne Mtns • United Kingdom ... 63 B6
Mouscron • Belgium 70 A4
Moussoro • Chad 106 D3
Moutiers • France 78 D3
Mouton, Château • France 78 E5
Moutsouna • Náxos, Greece .... 94 L
Moxey Town • Bahamas 164 A1
Moy • Ireland 69 H8
Moyale • Kenya 109 D4
Moyen Atlas • Morocco 107 B1

Moyne Abbey • Ireland 69 H8
Moyynqum • Kazakstan 121 F3
Mutare • Zimbabwe 110 C2
MOZAMBIQUE • Africa 110 C2
Mozambique Channel •
   Madagascar/Mozambique 110 D3
Mpanda • Tanzania 110 G7
Mpumalanga • South Africa 111 B5
Mpumalanga [Adm] • South Africa . 111 C4
Mpunguti Marine Reserve • Kenya . 109 C6
Msasani • Tanzania 110 H8
Msta • Russian Fed. 100 L9
Mtskheta **Heritage C** • Georgia .. 43 [36]
Mtunzini • South Africa 111 C4
Mtwara • Tanzania 110 H8
Mu'a • Tonga .... 139 P
Muang Mai • Ko Phuket, Thailand . 130 F9
Muar • Malaysia 128 C6
Muaro Takus • Indonesia 131 N10
Muck • United Kingdom 62 B4
Muckross Abbey • Ireland 69 G11
Mudanjiang • China 125 G2
Mudanya • Turkey 95 F4
Muddus Nat. Park **Park N** • Sweden 58 [19]
Mudgee • NS, Australia 136 H8
Mudumalai Wildlife Sanctuary • India 124 B3
Mueros, I. Caja de • Puerto Rico ... 165 I8
Mugdock Country Park •
   United Kingdom 65 A2
Mughalzhar Tauy • Kazakstan 121 C2
Mughshin • Oman 120 G10
Mugla • Turkey 95 F6
Mugla [Adm] • Turkey 95 F6
Muhammad Qol • Sudan 109 B2
Muhammad, Râs **Dive** • Egypt ... 109 E7
Muhlberg • Germany 50 C2
Mühldorf am Inn • Germany 74 H7
Mühlenbeck • Germany 73 F7
Muhu • Estonia 100 J6
Mui Hopohoponga • Tonga .... 139 P
Mui Wo • Hong Kong, China 126 E5
Muiden • Netherlands 70 H7
Muiderslot • Netherlands 70 H7
Muir Woods Nat. Mon. **Park N** •
   CA, United States .... 152 [43]
Muirfield • United Kingdom 65 B2
Muka Head • Penang, Malaysia 129 D7
Mukah • Sarawak, Malaysia 128 E6
Mukawwar I. • Sudan 109 E9
Mukdahan • Thailand 130 A2
Mukeru • Palau .... 138 Y
Mukogaoka Yuen • Japan 127 I8
Mulaku Atoll • Maldives 124 G8
Mule Creek • WY, United States 148 F2
Mulegé • Mexico 168 I6
Mülhacén • Spain 82 J7
Mülheim an der Ruhr • Germany .. 73 C5
Mulhouse • France 76 G3
Mulifanua • Samoa .... 139 G
Mull • United Kingdom 62 C4
Mullaghareirk Mtns • Ireland 69 H10
Mullativu • Sri Lanka 124 C3
Mullet Peninsula • Ireland 69 G8
Mullingar • Ireland 69 C3
Mullsjö • Sweden 99 G5
Mulranny • Ireland 69 G8
Multan • Pakistan 122 B2
Mumbai • India 122 B4
Mumford • NY, United States 156 A1
Mummelsee • Germany 74 B3
Mun • Thailand 130 A2
Mun, Ko • Thailand 130 F10
Muna • Mexico 169 F4
München • Germany 74 G7
Muncie • IN, United States 150 C2
Mundelsey **Beach** • United Kingdom 64 [16]
Mungbere • Dem. Rep. of Congo ... 108 B4
Mungindi • NS, Australia 136 H8
Munich • Germany 74 G7
Müningen • NJ, United States 161 B2
Munkedal • Sweden 99 F5
Munku-Sardyk, Gora • Russian Fed. 101 K4
Munnar • India 124 B3
Munro, Mt • TS, Australia 136 F6
Münster • Germany 72 B3
Munster • Ireland 69 A2
Münsterland • Germany 73 A2
Munster • Romania 92 H7
Münzenberg • Germany 74 B1
Muonio • Finland 97 E2
Muonionjoki • Finland 97 E2
Muqdisho • Somalia 108 C4
Mur • Austria 91 G2
Muranga • Kenya 109 C5
Muratli • Turkey 95 E3
Murchison Falls Nat. Park **Park** •
   Uganda .... 112 [62]
Murcia • Spain 83 A2
Murcia, Región de • Spain 80 E5
Murdo • SD, United States 148 F2
Mures • Romania 92 C2
Murfreesboro • TN, United States .. 151 C3
Murgon • QL, Australia 136 D5
Müritz • Germany 72 E2
Müritz, Nationalpark **Park N** •
   Germany .... 58 [86]
Murlaé • Brazil 174 F6
Murmansk • Russian Fed. 101 D3
Murnau • Germany 74 G8
Muro • Majorca, Spain 83 D11
Muro • Spain 80 F2
Mörotan • Japan 127 B4
Muroto-zaki • Japan 127 B4
Murray • Australia 135 G2
Murray's Anchorage • Bermuda 165 U9
Murraysburg • South Africa 111 F6
Murren **Ski** • Switzerland .... 61 [69]
Mürren • Switzerland 90 J5
Murrisk • Ireland 69 G8
Murrumbidgee • NS, Australia 136 G8
Murter • Croatia 91 H2
Murtle Lake • BC, Canada 160 J7
Murtoa • VI, Australia 135 G6
Murud **Beach** • India 124 E6
Murupara • New Zealand 137 E5
Murwara • India 123 A1
Murwillumbah • NS, Australia 136 D5
Mürzzuschlag • Austria 91 H2
Mus • Turkey 95 H5
Musala • Bulgaria 92 C3
Musandam, Ra's • Oman 120 G8
Musashi Hills Forest Park • Japan .. 127 H8
Musashino • Japan 127 I8
Muscadet • France 76 K8
Muscat • Oman 120 H9
Musgrave Ranges • SA, Australia ... 135 B4
Musi • Indonesia 131 B4
Musina • South Africa 110 C3
Muskegon • MI, United States 161 B3
Muskegon [Riv] • MI, United States 161 B3
Muskö • Sweden 99 B2
Muskö [I.] • Sweden 99 B2
Muskogee • OK, United States 151 A3
Musoma • Tanzania 110 G7
Mussoorie **Hill Sta** • India 124 C6
Mustafakemalpasa • Turkey 95 F4
Müstair • Switzerland 90 K6
Müstair **Heritage C** • Switzerland 44 [139]
Mustique • St Vincent & Gren. ..... 167 O
Mustvee • Estonia 100 K6
Mut • Egypt 107 A4
Mut • Turkey 95 G7

Mutalau • Niue .... 139 O
Mutare • Zimbabwe 110 C2
Mutsu-wan • Japan 127 D2
Mutters • Austria 91 M4
Muyil • Mexico 169 G4
Muzaffarnagar • India 123 F7
Muzaffarpur • India 123 G8
Múzquiz • Mexico 168 D2
Mwabvi Wildlife Reserve **Park** •
   Malawi .... 112 [103]
Mwanza • Tanzania 110 G7
Mwaya • Tanzania 110 G8
Mwea Nat. Reserve • Kenya 109 D5
Mweelrea • Ireland 69 G9
Mwene-Ditu • Dem. Rep. of Congo . 108 B5
Mweru, Lake •
   Dem. Rep. of Congo/Zambia 110 B2
My San sanctuary **Heritage C** •
   Vietnam .... 43 [200]
My Tho • Vietnam 129 N6
Myakka River State Park •
   FL, United States 155 C2
MYANMAR • Asia 128 B2
Mycenae • Greece 93 C3
Mycenae **Heritage C** • Greece ... 44 [239a]
Myingyan • Myanmar 128 B2
Myitkyina • Myanmar 128 B1
Mykolayiv • Ukraine 100 D4
Mymensingh • Bangladesh 122 D3
Myra • Turkey 95 G8
Myrdal • Norway 98 H8
Myrtle Beach • SC, United States ... 151 E4
Myrstuen • Norway 98 E6
Mysia • Turkey 95 E4
Myslenice • Poland 89 G9
Myslibórz • Poland 89 A2
Mysore • India 124 B2
Mystery Park **Park L** • Switzerland 59 [78]
Mystery Park • Switzerland 90 J5
Mystic • CT, United States 156 D2
Myszków • Poland 89 F8
Mytishchi • Russian Fed. 100 M10
Mzab Valley **Heritage C** • Algeria . 44 [286]
Mze • Czech Rep. 89 D6
Mzuzu • Malawi 110 C2

N

N'dalatando • Angola 110 A1
N'djamena • Chad 106 D3
Na Caillighe, Sliabh • Ireland 69 E6
Na Pali Coast State Park •
   HI, United States 157 H5
Na Phra Lan, Laem •
   Ko Samui, Thailand 130 G11
Naalehu • HI, United States 157 J6
Naantali • Finland 99 C4
Naarden • Netherlands 70 H7
Naas • Ireland 69 E7
Nabari • Japan 127 G6
Nabari • Kiribati .... 139 I
Naberezhnye Chelny • Russian Fed. 100 H2
Nabeul • Tunisia 107 D4
Nablus • Palestine NAR 120 B3
Nacala • Mozambique 110 K9
Nacaome • Honduras 170 K9
Nachingwea • Tanzania 110 H8
Nacka • Sweden 99 B2
Nacogdoches • TX, United States ... 155 F5
Nädendal • Finland 99 C4
Nadi • Fiji Is. .... 138 T
Nadiad • India 122 B3
Nadòr • Morocco 107 B1
Nadur • Malta 96 A1
Naduri • Fiji Is. .... 138 S
Nærøyfjord • Norway 98 H8
Næstved • Denmark 99 F8
Nafpaktos • Greece 93 B2
Nafplio • Greece 93 C3
Nag's Head • St Kitts & Nevis ...... 167 F
Naga • Philippines 128 G4
Naga Hills • India/Myanmar 122 D3
Nagano • Japan 127 H8
Nagano [Adm] • Japan 127 H8
Nagaoka • Japan 127 C3
Nagapattinam • India 124 C3
Nagarhole Nat. Park • India 124 C1
Nagarjuna Sagar • India 124 C1
Nagarjunakonda • India 124 C1
Nagasaki • Japan 127 B4
Nagato • Japan 127 H9
Nagaur • India 123 D7
Nagda • India 123 D8
Nagercoil • India 124 C4
Nagina • India 123 F7
Nagleabend Nature Reserve •
   South Africa 111 B4
Nago • Okinawa, Japan .... 138 A
Nago-wan • Okinawa, Japan .... 138 A
Nagold • Germany 74 B3
Nagpur • India 123 A1
Nagpur • India 122 B3
Nagruawalia • New Zealand 137 D5
Nagua • Dominican Rep. 165 G5
Nagyatád • Hungary 92 C2
Nagykanizsa • Hungary 92 B2
Naha • Okinawa, Japan .... 138 A
Nahan **Hill Sta** • India 124 C5
Nahanni Nat. Park **Park N** •
   NT, Canada .... 161 [4]
Nahanni Nat. Park **Heritage N** •
   NT, Canada .... 40 [2]
Nahariyya • Israel 120 A1
Nahe • Germany 74 D6
Nai Ham Beach •
   Ko Phuket, Thailand 130 F10
Nai Yang • Ko Phuket, Thailand 130 F9
Nai Yang **Beach** •
   Ko Phuket, Thailand 130 F9
Nailsworth • United Kingdom 65 E6
Nain • NF, Canada 159 J3
Nainital **Hill Sta** • India 124 C5
Nainital • India 123 F7
Nairnshire • United Kingdom 64 A1
Nairobi • Kenya 109 C5
Nairobi Nat. Park • Kenya 109 C5
Nairobi Nat. Park **Park** • Kenya . 112 [78]
Naivasha • Kenya 109 C5
Najran • Saudi Arabia 120 E10
Naka Noi, Ko • Thailand 130 F9
Naka Yai, Ko • Thailand 130 F9
Nakadomari • Okinawa, Japan ..... 138 A
Nakagusuku-wan • Okinawa, Japan 138 A
Nakamura • Japan 127 B4
Nakanai Range • Japan 127 D3
Nakanoshima • Japan .... 138 C
Nakhodka • Russian Fed. 101 G5
Nakhon Phanom • Thailand 130 A2
Nakhon Nayok • Thailand 130 D7
Nakhon Pathom • Thailand 128 C3
Nakhon Ratchasima • Thailand 128 C3
Nakhon Sawan • Thailand 128 C2
Nakhon Si Thammarat • Thailand . 128 C4
Nakina • OT, Canada 159 H3
Nakiska **Ski** • AL, Canada .... 146 [13]
Naksov • Denmark 99 F8
Naktong • Rep. of Korea 125 G3
Nal'chik • Russian Fed. 100 F5
Nalaikh • Mongolia 125 E2
Nalla malla Range • India 124 C1
Nallihan • Turkey 95 B1
Nam Cat Tien Nat. Park • Vietnam . 129 N5
Nam Dinh • Vietnam 128 D2
Nam Tok Surin Nat. Park • Thailand 130 F9
Nam Wu Wu • Ko Phuket, Thailand 130 F9
Namangan • Uzbekistan 121 F4
Namasagali • Uganda 108 C4
Nambour • QL, Australia 136 D5
Nambucca • Sweden 99 D4
Namib Desert • Namibia 110 A3

Namib-Naukluft Nat. Park **Park** •
Namibia..............................112 [126]
Namibe • Angola..........................110 A2
NAMIBIA • Africa........................110 A3
Namlea • Indonesia.....................131 G4
Namotu • Fiji Is.............................138 T
Nampa • ID, United States..........154 H6
Nampo • D.P.R. of Korea.............125 G3
Nampula • Mozambique..............110 C2
Namrud • Syria..............................91 G2
Namsen • Norway............................97 C3
Namsos • Norway.............................97 C3
Namu • Marshall Is.....................138 BB2
Namuang Falls • Ko Samui, Thailand..130 G12
Namukulu • Niue..............................139 O
Namur • Belgium..............................70 C4
Namur [Adm] • Belgium..................70 C4
Nan • Thailand...............................130 C5
Nan [Riv] • Thailand.....................130 C5
Nanaimo • BC, Canada..................160 I7
Nanango • QL, Australia...............136 D5
Nanbo Paradise • Japan................127 I9
Nanbu • Okinawa, Japan...............138 A
Nanchang • China...........................125 F4
Nanchong • China.........................125 E3
Nancroix-Vallandry **Ski** • France....61 [24]
Nancy • France..................................76 G2
Nancy **Heritage C** • France............44 [68]
Nancy Sound • New Zealand.........137 F7
Nanda Devi Nat. Park **Heritage N** •
India..................................41 [122]
Nandan • Japan...............................127 F7
Nanded • India..............................122 B4
Nandikanima Pass • India.............124 C1
Nandyal • India.............................124 C1
Nanga Parbat • Pakistan...............122 B2
Nangis • France................................78 B2
Nanhua • France.............................126 H7
Ninikirata • Kiribati.......................139 L5
Nanjing • China.............................126 G6
Nanlaud • Fed. States of Micronesia..138 D
Nanling • China..............................126 G7
Nanning • China............................125 E4
Nanping • China............................125 F4
Nanpo-shoto • Japan...................138 AA1
Nanqiao • China.............................126 H7
Nansei-shoto • Japan.....................125 G4
Nansha • China...............................126 F3
Nantes • France.................................77 E5
Nanticoke • OT, Canada................161 C3
Nanton • AL, Canada......................160 J7
Nantong • China...........................126 H6
Nantou • China...............................126 E4
Nantucket I. • MA, United States....156 D2
Nantucket Sound •
MA, United States.....................156 D2
Nanumea • Tuvalu........................138 CC3
Nanus Fort • Goa, India................123 C5
Nanyang • China............................125 F3
Nanyuki • Kenya.............................109 C4
Náousa • Páros, Greece.....................94 H
Napa • CA, United States..............148 B3
Napa Valley • CA, United States....154 I8
Napier • New Zealand...................137 E6
Naples • FL, United States............155 C3
Naples • Italy....................................87 G7
Naples **Heritage C** • Italy..............44 [169]
Napo • Ecuador/Peru....................173 B3
Napoléon, Route • France...............78 C7
Nápoli • Italy....................................87 G7
Nápoli **Heritage C** • Italy...........44 [169]
Nápoli, Golfo di • Italy....................87 G7
Napoule, la • France........................78 H8
Nara • Japan...................................127 G6
Nara **Heritage C** • Japan.............43 [195]
Nara [Adm] • Japan........................127 G7
Nara Dreamland • Japan...............127 G6
Naracoorte **Heritage N** • Australia..41 [154]
Naracoorte • SA, Australia.............135 C7
Naranjos • Mexico........................169 J6
Narbonne • France...........................76 E5
Narborough I. • Galápagos Is........171 G10
Nardò • Italy......................................85 F4
Narew • Poland..................................89 C2
Narita • Japan.................................127 I8
Narita [Apt] • Japan.......................127 I8
Narithiwat • Thailand...................128 C5
Nariva Swamp • Trinidad & Tobago..166 S
Narmada • India............................122 B3
Narnaul • India..............................123 C2
Naro • Sicily, Italy...........................86 G8
Narodnaya, Gora • Russian Fed...101 G3
Närpes • Finland...............................97 E3
Narrabeen **NS**, Australia...............136 B6
Narrangansett • RI, United States...156 D2
Narsarsuaq • Greenland................159 L2
Naruto • Japan...............................127 F7
Naruto-kaikyo • Japan...................127 F7
Narva • Estonia...............................100 K6
Narvik • Norway................................97 D2
Naryn • Kyrgyzstan........................121 G3
Naryn [Riv] • Kyrgyzstan...............121 F3
Nasau • Fiji Is..................................138 S
Nasca • Peru....................................173 E6
Nasca Lines • Peru..........................173 E6
Naseby • United Kingdom.................50 B2
Nash Point • United Kingdom..........65 J9
Nashik • India.................................122 B3
Nashoba Valley • MA, United States..156 D1
Nashua • NH, United States..........156 D1
Nashville • TN, United States.........151 C3
Näsijärvi • Finland............................99 D3
Našice • Croatia................................92 G5
Nasorolevu • Fiji Is.........................138 S
Nassau • Bahamas........................164 A2
Nassau • Cook Is..........................139 DD3
Nasser, Lake • Egypt......................109 B3
Nässjö • Sweden...............................99 G3
Nata • Botswana............................110 J9
Natal • Brazil..................................174 L6
Natal • Indonesia...........................131 N10
Natal Midlands • South Africa.......111 B4
Natashquan • QU, Canada............160 B1
Natchez • MS, United States........155 E5
Natchez Nat. Hist. Park **Park N** •
MS, United States....................153 [195]
Natchez Trace Parkway •
United States...........................156 F5
Natchez Trace Parkway **Park N** •
United States...........................153 [197]
Natchitoches • LA, United States...156 E5
Natewa Bay • Fiji Is........................138 S
Nathdwara • India.........................123 D8
Nathon • Ko Samui, Thailand.......130 G11
National Agricultural Centre •
United Kingdom.........................65 F5
National Birds of Prey Centre •
United Kingdom.........................65 E6
National Capital parks **Park N** •
DC, United States....................153 [264]
National Exhibition Centre •
United Kingdom.........................65 F5
National Mall **Park N** •
DC, United States....................153 [264]
National Park • New Zealand.........137 D6
Natinngoo • Benin........................106 C3
Natron, Lake • Tanzania...............110 H7
Nattawasaga Bay • OT, Canada....160 E4
Natua • Fiji Is...................................138 S
Natuna Besar • Indonesia.............131 C3
Natuna Sea • Indonesia................128 D6
Natural Bridges Nat. Mon. **Park N** •
UT, United States....................152 [82]
Nature's Valley • South Africa.......111 F7
Nauders • Austria.............................91 N8
Nauen • Germany.............................73 E7
Naul • Ireland...................................69 F6
Nauplia • Greece..............................50 E4
NAURU • Pacific Ocean..................138 T
Nausori • Fiji Is...............................138 S
Nautla • Mexico.............................169 K7
Navajo **Ind Res** •
AZ/NM/UT, United States........155 [33]

Navajo Indian Reservation •
AZ/NM, United States.............155 H7
Navajo Nat. Mon. •
AZ, United States.....................155 G7
Navajo Nat. Mon. **Park N** •
AZ, United States....................152 [100]
Navajo Reservoir •
CO/NM, United States..............69 E6
Navan • Ireland.................................69 F6
Navapolack • Belarus....................100 C2
Navarino • Greece............................50 E4
Navarino, I. • Chile........................175 B5
Navarre Beach • FL, United States..155 A1
Navas de Tolosa, Las • Spain..........50 A4
Navasota • TX, United States........155 F5
Navassa I. • West Indies..............166 CC3
Navini • Fiji Is..................................138 T
Naviti • Fiji Is....................................138 T
Navojoa • Mexico..........................168 I6
Navolato • Mexico.........................168 I6
Navsari • India..............................122 B3
Navua • Fiji Is..................................138 T
Navy I. • OT, Canada.......................161 D1
Nawabshah • Pakistan..................122 A3
Nawalgarh • India..........................123 E7
Nawiliwili • HI, United States........157 H5
Nawoiy • Uzbekistan.....................121 E3
Naxçivan • Azerbaijan...................120 F6
Náxos • Náxos, Greece....................94 H
Náxos [I.] • Greece............................94 H
Nayarit • Mexico............................169 B2
Nayoro • Japan...............................127 D2
Nazaré • Portugal............................84 A2
Nazareth • Israel............................120 B2
Nazario Sauro **Dive** • Eritrea......109 E10
Nazca **Heritage C** • Peru...............42 [61]
Nazilli • Turkey................................95 F5
Nazran' • Russian Fed...................100 G5
Nazret • Ethiopia...........................108 C4
Nazwa • Oman..............................120 H9
Ndendé, Réserve de **Park** • Gabon..112 [48]
Ndeni • Solomon Is........................138 W
Ndere I. Nat. Park • Kenya............109 C5
Ndjolé • Gabon..............................106 D5
Ndola • Zambia..............................110 B2
Ndumo Game Reserve • South Africa..111 C3
Ndumo Game Reserve **Park** •
South Africa..............................112 [137]
Nea Kaméni • Thira, Greece............94 G
Néa Moni • Chios, Greece................94 D
Néa Moni **Heritage C** • Greece.....44 [243]
Néa Stíra • Greece...........................94 H
Neagh, Lough • United Kingdom......63 B6
Neale, Lake • NT, Australia............136 A2
Neanderthal • Germany...................73 C6
Neapean • OT, Canada...................160 G4
Neápoli • Crete, Greece...................93 I6
Neápoli • Macedonia, Greece..........93 B1
Neápoli • Peloponnese, Greece.......93 C3
Neapolitan Riviera • Italy................87 H7
Neath • United Kingdom.................63 D9
Nebbio • Corsica, France.................78 N11
Nebitdag • Turkmenistan...............121 B4
Nebo • QL, Australia......................136 C4
Nebo, Mt • Jordan.........................120 B4
Nebraska • United States...............148 F2
Nechako • BC, Canada...................160 I6
Neches • TX, United States............155 F5
Neckar • Germany............................74 B3
Necker I. • HI, United States........139 DD1
Necochea • Argentina....................175 F7
Nedstrand • Norway.........................98 F9
Needles • CA, United States..........154 J9
Neepawa • MN, Canada................158 G3
Nefta • Tunisia...............................107 C5
Neftekamsk • Russian Fed............100 H2
Negara • Bali, Indonesia...............131 K7
Negele • Ethiopia...........................108 C4
Negeri Sembilan • Malaysia.........129 G10
Negombo • Sri Lanka....................124 C4
Negotin • Serbia & Montenegro......92 C2
Negra, Punta • Peru......................173 A3
Negril • Jamaica............................165 C3
Negro • Uruguay...........................175 G6
Negro, Cabo • Margarita...............166 T
Negro, Rio • Argentina..................175 B4
Negro, Rio • Brazil.........................173 C3
Negroponte • Greece........................50 E4
Negros • Philippines.....................128 G5
Negru Vodă • Romania....................92 I7
Nei Mongol Zizhiqu • China.........125 F2
Neiba • Dominican Rep.................165 F6
Neiba, Sierra de • Dominican Rep...165 F6
Neidpath Castle • United Kingdom..62 B2
Neijiang • China............................125 E4
Neisse • Germany.............................72 F3
Nekhen • Egypt..............................109 B3
Nekse • Denmark..............................99 H8
Nelidovo • Russian Fed................100 L10
Nell • Marshall Is............................139 E
Nell Passage • Marshall Is..............139 E
Nellore • India...............................124 C2
Nelson • MN, Canada....................158 G3
Nelson • New Zealand...................137 B3
Nelson • United Kingdom................63 D7
Nelson [Adm] • New Zealand........137 B3
Nelson Forks • BC, Canada............158 D3
Nelson Museum • St Kitts & Nevis..167 F
Nelson's Dockyard •
Antigua & Barbuda.....................167 I
Nelspoort • South Africa................111 F6
Nelspruit • South Africa................110 C3
Néma • Mauritania........................106 B3
Neman • Russian Fed....................100 J8
Nemi, Lagi di • Italy........................87 E5
Nemours • France............................78 B2
Nemrut Dağı **Heritage C** • Turkey..44 [255]
Nemunas • Lithuania....................100 J8
Nemuro • Japan.............................127 E2
Nen Jiang • China..........................125 G2
Nenagh • Ireland.............................69 H10
Nenana • AK, United States..........157 E3
Nene • United Kingdom.................64 G7
Nenets **Russ Adm** • Russian Fed...101 [18]
Neoch • Fed. States of Micronesia...138 C
Néos Marmarás • Greece..................94 B
Neosho • KS/OK, United States....151 A3
NEPAL • Asia..................................122 C3
Nepalganj • Nepal........................123 G7
Nephin Beg Range • Ireland............69 G8
Neptun-Olimp • Romania................92 I7
Nera • Italy..87 E4
Neretva • Bosnia-Herz....................92 G6
Neris • Lithuania............................100 K8
Nerja • Spain....................................82 J8
Nesbyen • Norway...........................98 G8
Nesebur • Bulgaria..........................92 H8
Nesebur **Heritage C** • Bulgaria....44 [228]
Nesjahraun • Iceland.......................97 I6
Neslandsvatn • Norway..................98 D6
Ness, Loch • United Kingdom..........62 C3
Nessebar • Bulgaria.........................92 H8
Nessebar **Heritage C** • Bulgaria..44 [228]
Nesselwang • Germany...................74 F8
Nestos • Greece...............................93 D1
Nesttun • Norway.............................98 F8
Netanya • Israel.............................110 I9
Netarhat **Hill Sta** • India............124 F2
NETHERLANDS • Europe..................70
NETHERLANDS ANTILLES •
West Indies.............................167 FF2
Nette • Germany..............................74 C5
Nettlé, Baie • St Martin...................166 C
Nettuno • Italy.................................87 E5
Nettuno, Grotta di •
Sardinia, Italy............................86 E5
Neu-Anspach • Germany................74 D5
Neu-Ulm • Germany........................74 E7
Neubrandenburg • Germany...........72 E2
Neuburg an der Donau • Germany..74 F7
Neuchâtel • Switzerland...................90 I5
Neuchâtel [Adm] • Switzerland........91 J1
Neuchâtel, Lac de • Switzerland.......90 I5
Neuenhagen bei Berlin • Germany...73 F7
Neues Palais (Potsdam) • Germany...73 F7
Neufchâteau • Belgium...................70 C5

Neufchâteau • France........................76 F2
Neukirchen • Germany.....................73 C5
Neukölln (Berlin) • Germany............73 F8
Neuleiningen • Germany.................74 B2
Neultin Lake • NU, Canada...........158 G2
Neumagen-Dhron • Germany..........74 C6
Neumarkt-St Veit • Germany............74 H7
Neumayer [Base] • Antarctica.......176 [12]
Neumünster • Germany...................72 D1
Neunkirchen • Austria......................91 G2
Neunkirchen • Germany...................74 A2
Neuquén • Argentina....................175 B3
Neuruppin • Germany.......................72 E2
Neusiedl am See • Austria................91 H2
Neusiedler See, Nationalpark **Park N** •
Austria.....................................58 [91]
Neusiedlersee **Heritage C** • Austria..44 [146]
Neuss • Germany..............................73 C6
Neustadt an der Weinstrasse •
Germany....................................74 B2
Neustadt in Holstein • Germany......72 D1
Neustift • Austria.............................91 N8
Neustrelitz • Germany......................72 E2
Neuveville, La • Switzerland...........90 J5
Neuwied • Germany.........................74 C5
Neuwiller • Germany.......................74 D5
Nevada • United States..................154 J
Nevada, Sierra •
CA, United States....................154 I8
Nevada, Sierra • Spain....................82 J7
Nevers • France................................76 E3
Nevesinje • Bosnia-Herz..................92 G6
Neviges • Germany...........................73 D5
Nevinnomyssk • Russian Fed.........100 F5
Nevis • St Kitts & Nevis.................167 F
Nevis, Ben • United Kingdom...........62 C4
Nevis Peak • St Kitts & Nevis.........167 F
Newark • Turkey...............................95 F5
New Bedford • MA, United States...156 D2
New Bedford Whaling Nat. Hist. Park
Park N • MA, United States....153 [286]
New Bern • NC, United States.......151 E3
New Braunfels • TX, United States..155 E5
New Britain • Papua New Guinea..138 BB3
New Brunswick • Canada...............160 B1
New Brunswick • NJ, United States..156 C2
NEW CALEDONIA • Pacific Ocean....138 B3
New Castle • DE, United States......156 B3
New Delhi • India..........................123 E7
New England • United States.........150 F2
New Georgia • Solomon Is..............138 W
New Georgia S. • Solomon Is..........138 W
New Georgia Sound • Solomon Is...138 W
New Glasgow • NS, Canada...........160 B2
New Guinea •
Indonesia/Papua New Guinea..131 J4
New Hampshire • United States.....150 F2
New Hanover • Papua New Guinea..138 BB3
New Haven • CT, United States......156 C2
New Iberia • LA, United States.......156 E6
New Ireland • Papua New Guinea..138 BB3
New Jersey • United States............156 C3
New Lanark • United Kingdom........65 A2
New Lanark **Heritage C** •
United Kingdom.........................44 [18]
New Liskeard • OT, Canada...........159 I4
New London • CT, United States.....156 C2
New Market • VA, United States.....156 A3
New Metroland **Park L** •
United Kingdom.........................59 [23]
New Mexico • United States..........149 E4
New Norfolk • TS, Australia...........135 C8
New Orleans • LA, United States....155 F6
New Orleans Jazz Nat. Hist. Park **Park N** •
LA, United States....................153 [193]
New Paltz • NY, United States........156 C2
New Plymouth • New Zealand.......137 D6
New Providence • Bahamas..........164 A2
New Quay **Beach** • United Kingdom..64 [58]
New [Riv] • WV, United States.......150 D3
New Siberian Is. • Russian Fed......101 O2
New Smyrna Beach •
FL, United States....................155 D1
New South Wales • Australia.........135 H6
New Territories • Hong Kong, China..126 E5
New Ulm • MN, United States.......150 B2
New Valley, The • Egypt................109 A2
New York • NY, United States........150 F2
New York [Adm] • United States.....150 F2
NEW ZEALAND • Australasia............137
New Zealand sub-antarctic islands
Heritage N • Southern Ocean....41 [162]
Newark • DE, United States...........150 E3
Newark • NJ, United States............156 C2
Newark • OH, United States..........150 D2
Newark-on-Trent • United Kingdom..63 F7
Newberg • OR, United States.........148 B1
Newborough **Beach** • United Kingdom..64 [68]
Newburgh • NY, United States.......156 C2
Newbury • United Kingdom.............63 E9
Newcastle • Jamaica.....................165 D4
Newcastle • NB, Canada................160 B1
Newcastle • NS, Australia..............136 H8
Newcastle • South Africa................111 B3
Newcastle • St Kitts & Nevis..........167 F
Newcastle upon Tyne • United Kingdom..62 E6
Newcastle West • Ireland................69 H10
Newcastle-under-Lyme •
United Kingdom.........................63 D7
Newfoundland [I.] • NF, Canada....160 C1
Newfoundland & Labrador • Canada..159 K3
Newgale **Beach** • United Kingdom..64 [54]
Newgrange • Ireland........................69 F6
Newhalen • AK, United States.......157 D4
Newhaven • United Kingdom..........65 G8
Newman • WA, Australia...............135 B4
Newmarket • Ireland.......................69 H10
Newmarket • OT, Canada..............160 E4
Newmarket on Fergus • Ireland......69 H10
Newport • Ireland.............................69 G8
Newport • OR, United States.........154 G6
Newport • RI, United States...........156 D2
Newport • United Kingdom.............63 D9
Newport • VT, United States.........160 H4
Newport News • VA, United States..156 B3
Newquay • United Kingdom.............63 B6
Newry • United Kingdom.................63 B6
Newton • KS, United States...........148 G3
Newton Abbot • United Kingdom....65 J10
Newton Stewart • United Kingdom..62 C6
Newtown • MA, United States.......150 F2
Newtown • United Kingdom............65 C7
Newtownabbey • United Kingdom...63 C6
Neyagawa • Japan.........................127 G6
Neyshabur • Iran...........................120 H7
Neyveli • India...............................124 C3
Nez Perce **Ind Res** •
ID, United States...................155 [12]
Nez Perce Nat. Hist. Park •
ID, United States....................154 H5
Nez Perce Nat. Hist. Park **Park N** •
ID, United States....................152 [64]
Nezahualcóyotl • Mexico..............169 J7
Nga, Laem • Ko Phuket, Thailand..130 D1
Ngamegei Passage • Palau.............138 V
Ngami, Lake • Botswana...............110 I9
Ngamring • China..........................124 F1
Ngaoundéré • Cameroon..............106 D4
Ngaruroro • New Zealand.............137 E6
Ngauruhoe, Mt • New Zealand.....137 E6
Nggatokae • Solomon Is................138 W
Nggela • Solomon Is......................138 W
Ngoan Muc Pass • Vietnam...........129 C5
Ngorongoro Conservation Area •
Tanzania..................................110 H7
Ngorongoro Conservation Area **Park** •
Tanzania..................................112 [85]
Ngorongoro Conservation Area **Heritage N** •
Tanzania..................................41 [110]
Ngorongoro Crater • Tanzania......110 H7
Ngulu Atoll •
Fed. States of Micronesia........138 AA2
Ngum, Ko • Thailand....................130 F9
Ngunut • Java, Indonesia..............131 Q13

Ngurah Rai [Apt] • Bali, Indonesia..131 L8
Nha Trang • Vietnam.....................129 C5
Nhabuddin (Berlin) • Germany.........73 F8
Nhandoewe • Namibia...................110 A3
Noordoostpolder • Netherlands.......70 C2
Niagara • Canada/United States...161 A1
Niagara Falls • NY, United States..161 D1
Niagara Falls • OT, Canada...........161 D1
Niagara Falls [Falls] •
Canada/United States..............161 D1
Niagara, Fort •
NY, United States....................161 A1
Niagara-on-the-Lake • OT, Canada..161 D1
Niamey • Niger..............................106 C3
Nias • Indonesia...........................131 M10
Nibe • Denmark................................99 E6
Nicaragua • C. America.................170 E4
Nicaragua, Lago de • Nicaragua...170 E5
Nice • France....................................78 H7
Nicholls Town • Bahamas.............164 A1
Nicobar Is. • India.........................122 D5
Nicodemus Nat. Hist. Site **Park N** •
KS, United States...................152 [167]
Nicosia • Cyprus..............................96 D4
Nicoya • Costa Rica......................170 E5
Nicoya, Golfo de • Costa Rica.......170 E6
Nicoya, Peninsula de • Costa Rica..170 E6
Nida • Lithuania............................100 J8
Nida • Poland...................................89 C3
Nidderau • Germany........................74 A1
Nidersachsen • Germany.................72 C2
Nidersächsisches Wattenmeer, Nationalpark
Park N • Germany....................58 [61]
Nidri • Levkas, Greece.....................94 B
Nidwalden • Switzerland.................91 R9
Nidzica • Poland..............................89 C2
Niederau • Austria..........................91 O7
Niederbayern • Germany.................74 G7
Niederlausitz • Germany.................73 B2
Niederösterreich • Austria.............91 T11
Niederrhein [Apt] • Germany.........73 C5
Nienburg • Germany........................72 C2
Nieuwegein • Netherlands..............70 H8
Nieuwpoort • Belgium.....................70 E6
Nieuwpoort • Curaçao.................166 V
Nieuwpoort-aan-Zee • Belgium.......70 E6
Niğde • Turkey.................................95 J9
Nigde [Adm] • Turkey......................95 J9
NIGER • Africa................................106 C2
Niger Delta • Nigeria.....................106 C4
Niger [Riv] • Africa........................106 B3
NIGERIA • Africa............................106 C4
Nihoa • HI, United States.............139 DD1
Niigata • Japan..............................127 C3
Niihama • Japan............................127 B4
Niihau • HI, United States............157 H5
Nijar • Spain....................................82 K7
Nijmegen • Netherlands..................70 C3
Nika • Cook Is.................................139 N
Nika • Maldives.............................124 G7
Nikaupara • Cook Is......................139 N
Nikolayevsk • Russian Fed...........100 G3
Nikkō **Heritage C** • Japan...........43 [197]
Nikkō-Yuwaki • Russian Fed.........100 O3
Nikopol' • Ukraine........................100 E4
Niksic • Serbia & Montenegro.........92 B3
Nilandu Atoll North • Maldives.....124 C7
Nilandu Atoll South • Maldives.....124 G8
Nilaveli • Sri Lanka.......................124 C3
Nile • Africa....................................108 C3
Nile Delta • Egypt..........................109 A1
Nilgiri Hills • India........................124 B3
Nilometer • Egypt..........................109 N8
Nîmes • France................................76 F5
Nin • Croatia.....................................92 F6
Nine Degree Channel • Indian Ocean..124 A3
Ninety Mile Beach • VI, Australia...136 G9
Ninety Six Nat. Hist. Site **Park N** •
SC, United States....................153 [233]
Ning Zhen Shan • China...............126 G6
Ningbo • China..............................126 H7
Ningguo • China.............................126 G7
Ninghai • China.............................126 H7
Ningxia Huizu Zizhiqu • China.....125 E3
Ninh Hoa • Vietnam......................129 C5
Ninigo Group • Papua New Guinea..138 AA3
Niobrara • NE, United States........150 A1
Niokolo Koba, Parc nat. de **Park** •
Senegal....................................112 [9]
Niolo • Corsica, France....................78 M11
Nioro • Mali..................................106 B3
Niort • France...................................77 E6
Nipigon, Lake • OT, Canada..........159 H4
Nipissing, Lake • OT, Canada.......160 E4
Niquero • Cuba.............................164 G5
Nirasaki • Japan............................127 H8
Niš • Serbia & Montenegro.............92 C3
Nishi-Akashi • Japan.....................127 F6
Nishinomiya • Japan.....................127 F6
Nishiwaki • Japan.........................127 F6
Nishtun • Yemen..........................120 G10
Nissedal • Norway............................98 G9
Nissiros • Greece.............................93 E3
Nissum Bredning • Denmark...........99 E6
Nissum Fjord • Denmark..................99 E7
Nistru • Moldova.............................92 E1
Niterói • Brazil...............................174 F7
Nith • United Kingdom.....................62 D5
Nithavris • Crete, Greece..................93 H6
Nitra • Slovak Rep...........................89 B4
Nitray [Château] • France................77 F5
Niterland • Norway..........................98 E5
Niu Aunofo • Tonga......................139 O
Nivelles • Belgium...........................70 B4
Nizamabad • India.........................122 B4
Nizhnekamsk • Russian Fed.........100 H2
Nizhnevartovsk • Russian Fed......101 H3
Nizhniy Novgorod • Russian Fed...100 F2
Nizhniy Tagil • Russian Fed..........101 G3
Nizhnyaya Tunguska • Russian Fed..101 J3
Nizke Tatry Nat. Park **Park N** •
Slovak Rep...............................58 [111]
Njombe • Tanzania.......................110 G8
Njunjulp • Sweden.........................99 F6
Nkhotakota Wildlife Reserve **Park** •
Malawi.....................................112 [97]
Nkongsamba • Cameroon.............106 C4
No Name City • Germany................74 G7
Noatak Nat. Preserve •
AK, United States....................157 D2
Noatak Nat. Preserve **Park N** •
AK, United States....................152 [5]
Nobeoka • Japan...........................127 B4
Noce • Italy.......................................86 C4
Nockberge, Nationalpark **Park N** •
Austria.....................................58 [90]
Noda • Japan................................127 I8
Noel Kempff Mercado, Parque Nac. •
Bolivia.....................................173 C4
Noel Kempff Mercado, Parque Nac.
Heritage N • Bolivia.................40 [40]
Nogales • AZ, United States.........155 G8
Nogales • Mexico...........................168 I5
Nogent-le-Rotrou • France..............77 F5
Noginsk • Russian Fed..................100 M10
Nogliki • Russian Fed....................101 L3
Nogoa • QL, Australia...................136 C4
Nohcacab • Mexico......................169 F4
Noirmoutier, I. de • France..............76 B3
Nojima-zaki • Japan......................127 I9
Nokhra • India...............................123 D7
Nokhu Hills • Thailand..................130 I3
Nola • Chad...................................106 D4
Nola • Italy.......................................87 G6
Nolia • Italy......................................87 A2
Nome • AK, United States.............157 D3
Nong'an • China............................126 H2
Nongkhai • Fed. States of Micronesia..138 C
Non, Val di • Italy...........................86 C4
Nong Khai • Thailand...................130 A1
Nong Nooch Garden • Thailand.....130 E8
Nonsuch • South Africa.................111 C3
Nonthaburi • Thailand..................130 D7
Noord • Aruba...............................166 W
Noord-Beveland • Netherlands.......70 B3

Noord-Brabant • Netherlands.........70 C3
Noord-Holland • Netherlands..........70 C2
Noordoewer • Namibia..................110 A3
Noordzee Kanaal • Netherlands......70 H7
Noordpunt • Curaçao..................166 V
Noordwijk • Netherlands................70 G7
Noordzee Kanaal • Netherlands......70 H7
Noormarkku • Finland......................99 C3
Noosa Heads • QL, Australia.........136 D5
Nora • Eritrea................................109 E10
Nora • Sardinia, Italy......................86 F6
Nora • Sweden..................................99 A1
Noranda • QU, Canada..................159 I4
Norberg • Sweden............................99 A1
Nordaustlandet • Svalbard..............96 J7
Nord, I. du • Seychelles................113 B1
Nord-Ostsee Kanal • Germany........72 C1
Nord-Ouest, Presqu'île de • Haiti..165 F5
Nord-Pas de Calais • France..........76 D2
Nord-Trøndelag • Norway...............98 B2
Nordagutu • Norway........................98 D6
Nordborg • Denmark........................99 E8
Nordby • Denmark............................99 F7
Norden • Germany...........................72 B2
Norderstedt • Germany....................72 D2
Nordeste • Azores..........................84 C4
Nordfjord • Norway..........................98 F7
Nordfjordeid • Norway.....................98 F7
Nordfriesische Inseln • Germany....72 C1
Nordhausen • Germany...................72 D3
Nordhorn • Germany.......................72 B2
Nordic Mtn Ski • WI, United States..146 [74]
Nordjylland • Denmark....................99 E6
Nordkapp • Norway..........................97 F1
Nordland • Norway..........................98 B2
Nordrhein-Westfalen • Germany.....72 C3
Nordstrand • Germany.....................99 E8
Nore • Norway..................................98 D5
Nore og Uvdal • Norway..................98 D5
Norefjell • Norway............................98 D5
Noresund • Norway.........................98 D5
Norfolk • NE, United States...........148 G2
Norfolk • United Kingdom.................64 B5
Norfolk • VA, United States...........156 B4
Norfolk I. • Pacific Ocean..............134 E7
Norheimsund • Norway....................98 F8
Noril'sk • Russian Fed...................101 I3
Norman • OK, United States..........148 G3
Norman I. • British Virgin Is...........166 A
Norman Manley [Apt] • Jamaica...165 D4
Norman Mineta [Apt] •
CA, United States....................154 I8
Norman Wells • NT, Canada.........158 D2
Normans Lagoon • Kiribati............139 I
Normanton • QL, Australia............135 G3
Normanville • South Africa............111 A4
Norrbotten • Sweden.......................98 B2
Narre Nebel • Denmark....................99 E7
Narre Snede • Denmark...................99 E7
Narre Vorupør • Denmark...............99 E6
Narresundby • Denmark..................99 E6
Norrhult • Sweden............................99 H6
Norristown • PA, United States......156 B2
Norrköping • Sweden.......................99 H5
Norrland Riviera • Sweden..............98 B2
Norrtälje • Sweden...........................99 B1
Norseman • WA, Australia.............135 C6
Norsjø • Norway...............................98 D5
Norsup • Vanuatu............................138 V
Norte, Cabo • Easter I....................139 M
Norte, Punta • Argentina...............175 G7
North America •.............................142
North Andaman • India.................122 D4
North Augusta • SC, United States..151 D4
North Battleford • SA, Canada.......158 F3
North Bay • OT, Canada................160 E3
North Berwick • United Kingdom.....65 B2
North Branch Potomac •
MD/WV, United States.............156 A3
North Caicos • Turks & Caicos Is..164 C3
North Cape • Kiribati......................139 I
North Cape • New Zealand...........137 B1
North Carolina • United States......151 E3
North Cascades Nat. Park •
WA, United States...................154 G5
North Cascades Nat. Park **Park N** •
WA, United States...................152 [27]
North Channel • OT, Canada.........161 C2
North Channel • United Kingdom....62 C5
North Dakota • United States........148 F1
North Dorset Downs • United Kingdom..65 K9
North Downs • United Kingdom......65 G8
North East Point • Cayman Is.......165 B1
North Frigate Bay • St Kitts & Nevis..167 F
North I. • New Zealand..................137 C2
North Kitui Nat. Reserve • Kenya...109 D5
North Little Rock •
AR, United States...................151 B4
North Luangwa Nat. Park **Park** •
Zambia...................................112 [105]
North Magnetic Pole • Arctic Ocean..176 A3
North Negril Point • Jamaica........165 C3
North Ossetia **Russ Adm** •
Russian Fed............................101 [4]
North Platte • NE, United States...148 F2
North Platte [Riv] • United States..148 F2
North Point • Barbados.................167 M
North Point • MI, United States.....161 C2
North Point • Seychelles...............113 A1
North Pole • Arctic Ocean.............176
North Rhine-Westphalia • Germany..72 C3
North Riding of Yorkshire •
United Kingdom.........................64 B4
North Rona • United Kingdom........62 C1
North Ronaldsay • United Kingdom..62 C1
North Saskatchewan • AL/SA, Canada..158 E3
North Sea • Europe.........................48 D3
North Shields • United Kingdom.....62 E5
North Side • Cayman Is.................165 B2
North Slope • AK, United States....157 E2
North Sound • Cayman Is..............165 A2
North Stradbroke I. •
QL, Australia............................136 D5
North Sydney • NS, Canada..........160 C2
North Tonawanda •
NY, United States....................161 A1
North Top • United Kingdom..........63 B6
North Uist • United Kingdom..........62 C2
North West • South Africa.............111 A1
North West • United Kingdom........64 B4
North West Bluff • Montserrat.......167 G
North West Cape • WA, Australia...135 A4
North West Moors Nat. Park **Park N** •
United Kingdom.........................58 [51]
North West Moors Nat. Park •
United Kingdom.........................63 E6
North-East Point • Kiribati.............139 I
Northallerton • United Kingdom.....64 B4
Northam • WA, Australia...............135 B6
Northampton • MA, United States..156 C1
Northampton • United Kingdom......63 E8
Northamptonshire • United Kingdom..64 B5
Northampton Nat. Park • South Africa..111 A2
Northern Cape • South Africa........111 A2
Northern Cheyenne **Ind Res** •
MT, United States...................155 [19]
Northern Forest Reserve • Dominica..167 K
Northern Hills • Thailand..............130 A1
Northern Ireland • United Kingdom..63 B6
NORTHERN MARIANA IS. •
Pacific Ocean..........................138 AA2
Northern Territory • Australia........135 E4
Northfield • MN, United States......150 B2
Northland • New Zealand..............137 B2
Northwest Territories • Canada......158 E3
Northumberland Is. • QL, Australia..136 D4
Northumberland Nat. Park **Park N** •
United Kingdom.........................58 [48]
Northumberland Nat. Park •
United Kingdom.........................62 E5
Northumbria • United Kingdom......64 B3

Northwest Highlands • United Kingdom..62 C3
Northwest Territories • Canada......158 E2
Northwest Wales castles **Heritage C** •
United Kingdom.........................44 [19]
Norton Sound • AK, United States..157 D3
NORWAY • Europe............................97
Norwegian Sea • Europe..................48 D1
Norwich • CT, United States..........156 D2
Norwich • United Kingdom..............63 F8
Norwood • OH, United States.......150 D3
Noshiro • Japan.............................127 D2
Nosivka • Ukraine.........................100 E2
Noss Head • United Kingdom.........62 C2
Nossebro • Sweden..........................99 G5
Nostalgia Town • QL, Australia......136 D5
Nostra Senyora de Cura, Santuari de •
Majorca, Spain...........................83 O12
Nostra Señora de Guadelupe •
Portugal....................................84 H8
Notec • Poland.................................89 CC3
Nótio Egéo • Greece.......................94 CC3
Noto **Heritage C** • Sicily, Italy....44 [175]
Noto, Golfo di • Sicily, Italy.............86 H8
Noto, Val di • Sicily, Italy................86 H8
Noto, Val di **Heritage C** •
Sicily, Italy..............................44 [175]
Noto-hanto • Japan.......................127 C3
Notodden • Norway.........................98 D6
Notoue • Kiribati............................139 F
Notre-Dame Bay • NF, Canada.....160 C1
Notre-Dame, Mts • QU, Canada....160 A1
Notre-Dame-de-Bellecombe **Ski** •
France.......................................61 [18]
Nottekanal • Germany.....................73 F8
Nottingham • United Kingdom........63 E8
Nottingham I. • NU, Canada..........159 I2
Nottingham Road • South Africa...111 B4
Nottinghamshire • United Kingdom..64 B4
Noudhibou • Mauritania................106 A2
Nouakchott • Mauritania...............106 A3
Nouméa • New Caledonia..............138 U
Nouvelle Calédonie [I.] •
New Caledonia.........................138 U
Nouvelle Decouverte • Mauritius..113 F5
Nova Friburgo • Brazil..................174 F7
Nova Gradiska • Croatia..................92 G5
Nova Iguaçu • Brazil.....................174 E7
Nova Levante • Italy........................86 C4
Nova Lima • Brazil.........................174 E6
Nova Scotia • Canada...................160 B2
Nová Ves • Slovak Rep....................89 C4
Nova Zagora • Bulgaria...................92 H8
Novara • Italy...................................87 B2
Novaya Sibir', Ostrov •
Russian Fed............................101 O2
Novaya Zemlya • Russian Fed......101 F2
Novelda • Spain...............................83 A1
Novgorod, Velikiy • Russian Fed...100 L9
Novi Iskur • Bulgaria.......................92 C3
Novi Pazar • Bulgaria......................92 H8
Novi Sad • Serbia & Montenegro....92 B2
Novigrad • Croatia...........................92 F5
Novo Hamburgo • Brazil................174 E7
Novo Mesto • Slovenia...................92 F5
Novo Orjahovo • Bulgaria...............92 I8
Novoaleksseyevka • Kazakhstan..121 C1
Novocherkassk • Russian Fed......100 G3
Novokuybyshev • Russian Fed......100 G3
Novomoskovsk • Russian Fed......100 I4
Novoleksiyivka • Ukraine..............100 E4
Novorossiysk • Russian Fed.........100 E5
Novoshakhtinsk • Russian Fed......100 I4
Novosibirsk • Russian Fed............101 I4
Novosibirskiye Ostrova •
Russian Fed............................101 O2
Novyy Urengoy • Russian Fed......101 H3
Nowgong • India............................123 F8
Nowra • NS, Australia...................136 H8
Nowy Sacz • Poland........................89 G9
Nowy Targ • Poland........................89 G9
Nowy Wisnicz • Poland..................89 G9
Noyon • France................................76 E2
Nsumbu Nat. Park **Park** • Zambia..112 [104]
Nu Jiang • China............................125 D3
Nub's Nob **Ski** • MI, United States..146 [78]
Nube Flan • Mexico.......................169 K8
Nubian Desert • Sudan..................108 C2
Nubu • Fiji Is....................................138 S
Nudow • Germany............................73 F8
Nueva • TS, United States.............155 E6
Nueva Cádiz • Venezuela..............166 T
Nueva Gerona • Cuba...................164 E4
Nueva Italia • Mexico....................169 I7
Nueva Lubecka • Argentina...........175 A4
Nueva Ocotepeque • Honduras.....170 K9
Nueva Palmira • Uruguay..............175 F6
Nueva Rosita • Mexico..................168 D2
Nueva San Salvador • El Salvador..170 C4
Nueve (9) de Julio • Argentina......175 F7
Nuevitas • Cuba.............................164 G4
Nuevo Casas Grandes • Mexico....168 I5
Nuevo Emperador • Panama.........170 L11
Nuevo Laredo • Mexico.................168 E2
Nuevo León • Mexico.....................169 C2
Nui Ba Den • Vietnam...................129 B6
Nuku • Fiji Is...................................138 S
Nuku • Wallis & Futuna.................139 Q
Nuku Hiva • French Polynesia.......139 J
Nuku'alofa • Tonga.......................139 P
Nukuatea • Wallis & Futuna..........139 Q
Nukufetau • Solomon Is................138 W
Nukulaelae • Wallis & Futuna.......139 Q
Nukunono • Tokelau.....................138 CC3
Nukus • Uzbekistan......................121 C3
Nullagine • WA, Australia.............135 B4
Nullarbor Nat. Park •
SA, Australia...........................135 D6
Nullarbor Plain • SA/WA, Australia..135 D6
Numazu • Japan............................127 H9
Numedal • Norway...........................98 D5
Numedalslågen • Norway................98 D6
Numfor • Indonesia......................131 H3
Nunap Isua • Greenland...............159 L3
Nunavut • Canada.........................159 H3
Nuneaton • United Kingdom..........65 F5
Nunivak I. • AK, United States......157 D3
Nuoro • Sardinia, Italy....................86 F5
Nuotaea • Kiribati..........................139 F
Nuqui • Solomon Is.......................138 W
Nürburg • Germany.........................74 C5
Nürburgring • Germany...................74 C5
Nuremberg • Germany....................72 D4
Nurmes • Finland.............................97 F3
Nürnberg • Germany.......................72 D4
Nurra, la • Sardinia, Italy................86 E5
Nusa Dua • Bali, Indonesia..........131 L8
Nusa Penida • Indonesia..............131 L8
Nushima • Japan...........................127 F7
Nushki • Pakistan..........................122 A3
Nuthe • Germany.............................73 F8
Nuuk • Greenland.........................159 K2
Nuwara Eliya • Sri Lanka..............124 C3
Nuweiba • Egypt............................109 B1
Nuwerveldberge • South Africa.....111 A4
Nxai Pan Nat. Park • Botswana.....110 J9
Nyala • Sudan...............................108 B3
Nyali • Kenya.................................109 C6
Nyali Beach • Kenya......................109 C6
Nyborg • Denmark...........................99 F8
Nybro • Sweden...............................99 H6
Nydala • Sweden.............................99 G6
Nyeri • Kenya.................................109 C5
Nyika Nat. Park **Park** • Malawi....112 [95]
Nyíregyháza • Hungary..................92 C1
Nykøbing • Falster, Denmark..........99 F8
Nykøbing • Mors, Denmark............99 F6
Nykøbing • Sjælland, Denmark.......99 F7
Nyköping • Sweden.........................99 A2
Nymphs, Cave of the • Greece........94 J
Nynäshamn • Sweden.....................99 B2
Nyon • Switzerland..........................90 I6

Nysa • Turkey 95 F5
Nysa Luzycka • Poland 89 A3
Nystad • Finland 99 C4
Nysted • Denmark 99 F8
Nzega • Tanzania 110 G7
Nzérékoré • Guinea 106 B4

O

O'Hare [Apt] • IL, United States 161 A3
Oahe, Lake • SD, United States 148 F1
Oahu • HI, United States 157 G6
Oak Lawn • IL, United States 150 C2
Oak Ridge • TN, United States 151 D3
Oakland • CA, United States 154 I8
Oakridge • OR, United States 154 G6
Oakura • New Zealand 137 D6
Oakwood Adventure Park L •
   United Kingdom .... 59 [32]
Oamaru • New Zealand 137 B4
Oasis • NV, United States 148 D2
Oasis de Nazaret •
   Lanzarote, Canary Is. 83 I5
Oates Land • Antarctica 176 U5
Oatlands • TS, Australia 136 F7
Oaxaca • Mexico 169 K8
Oaxaca Heritage C • Mexico .... 42 [25]
Oaxaca [Adm] • Mexico 169 C3
Ob' • Russian Fed. 101 I4
Oban • United Kingdom 62 C4
Ober Engadin • Switzerland 90 L6
Oberammergau • Germany 74 F8
Oberau • Austria 91 O7
Oberaudorf • Germany 74 H8
Oberbayern • Germany 74 G7
Obereggen Ski • Italy .... 61 [138]
Obereggen • Italy 86 D2
Obergurgl Ski • Austria .... 61 [93]
Obergurgl • Austria 91 N8
Oberhausen • Germany 73 C5
Oberinntal • Austria 91 N8
Oberjoch • Germany 74 F8
Oberkirch • Germany 74 B3
Oberlausitz • Germany 73 B2
Oberlech Ski • Austria .... 61 [89]
Oberlin • KS, United States 148 F3
Oberndorf • Austria 91 P7
Oberösterreich • Austria 91 T11
Obersaxen • Switzerland 90 K5
Oberschleissheim • Germany 74 G7
Oberstaufen • Germany 74 E8
Oberstdorf Ski • Germany .... 61 [2]
Oberstdorf • Germany 74 F8
Obertauern • Austria 91 P8
Obertraun • Austria 91 P7
Obervellach • Austria 91 P8
Oberwald • Switzerland 90 K6
Oberwesel • Germany 74 D6
Obi • Indonesia 131 G4
Obidos • Brazil 174 A3
Obihiro • Japan 100 M10
Obo • Central African Rep. 108 B4
Oborniki • Poland 89 B2
Obruk • Turkey 95 I9
Obwalden • Switzerland 91 R9
Obzor • Bulgaria 92 I8
Oc, d' • France 76 L9
Ocala • FL, United States 155 C1
Ocean City • MD, United States 156 B3
Ocean City • NJ, United States 156 C3
Ocean Expn Park • Okinawa, Japan .... 138 A
Ocean Hole • Bahamas 164 A1
Ocean I. • HI, United States 138 CC1
Ocean I. • Kiribati 138 CC3
Ocean Park • Hong Kong, China 126 F5
Ocean World Water Park • Thailand 130 E8
Oceania • 134
Oceanside • CA, United States 154 J9
Ochils, The • United Kingdom 65 B1
Ocho Rios • Jamaica 165 D3
Ochrid • F.Y.R. of Macedonia 50 C4
Ochsenhausen • Germany 74 E7
Oclini • Italy 86 C4
Ocmulgee Nat. Mon. Park N •
   GA, United States .... 153 [208]
Ocoee • FL, United States 157 A1
Ocotal • Nicaragua 170 D4
Ocotlán • Mexico 169 I7
Odawara • Japan 127 H9
Odda • Norway 98 G7
Odder • Denmark 99 F5
Odeborg • Sweden 99 F5
Odeceixe • Portugal 84 H7
Odelette • Portugal 84 K7
Odeleuca • Portugal 84 I7
Odemira • Portugal 80 A5
Odemis • Turkey 95 F5
Odense • Denmark 99 D6
Odenthal • Germany 73 D8
Odenwald • Germany 74 B2
Oder • Germany 74 F2
Oderhaff • Germany/Poland 72 F2
Odesa • Ukraine 100 D4
Odeshög • Sweden 99 G5
Odessa • DE, United States 156 B3
Odessa • TX, United States 154 H4
Odessa • Ukraine 100 D4
Odie • Botswana 110 J10
Odiáxere • Portugal 84 I8
Odienné • Côte d'Ivoire 106 B4
Odle, Le • Italy 86 C3
Odra • Poland 89 B3
Oeiras • Brazil 174 B3
Oeiras • Portugal 84 F6
Oeno I. • Pitcairn Is. 139 EE4
Oer-Erkenschwick • Germany 73 D5
Ofanto • Italy 87 H6
Offaly • Ireland 69 E7
Offenbach am Main • Germany 74 B2
Offenburg • Germany 74 B3
Ofidoússa • Greece 94 CC3
Ofu • American Samoa .... 139 H
Oga • Japan 127 C3
Ogaden • Ethiopia 108 D4
Ogaki • Japan 127 C3
Ogano • Japan 127 G3
Ogasawara-shoto • Japan 138 AA4
Ogbomoso • Nigeria 106 C4
Ogden • UT, United States 148 D2
Ogdensburg • NY, United States 150 E2
Ogimi • Okinawa, Japan .... 138 A
Oglio • Italy 87 B1
Ogoto Spa • Japan 127 G6
Ogre • Latvia 100 K7
Oqulin • Croatia 91 G3
Ohakune • New Zealand 137 D6
Ohau • New Zealand 137 B4
Ohio [Riv] • United States 150 D2
Ohio • United States 150 D3
Ohlstadt • Germany 74 G7
Ohope • New Zealand 137 E6
Ohre • Czech Rep. 88 B2
Ohrid • F.Y.R. of Macedonia 92 C3
Ohrid, Lake •
   Albania/FYR of Macedonia 92 C3
Ohrid, Lake Heritage N •
   Albania/FYR of Macedonia .... 41 [74]
Ohrid, Lake Heritage C •
   Albania/FYR of Macedonia .... 44 [216]
Ohura • New Zealand 137 D6
Oía • Thíra, Greece .... 94 G
Oiapoque • Brazil 174 A2
Oinoanda • Turkey 95 G8
Oise • France 76 E2
Oise [Adm] • France 78 B1
Oiseaux, Parc des • France 77 A5
Oistins • Barbados .... 167 M
Oita • Japan 127 B4
Ojców Nat. Park N • Poland .... 58 [107]
Ojcówski Nat. Park • Poland 89 G8

Ojinaga • Mexico 168 D2
Ojiwarongo • Namibia 110 A3
Ojo de Liebre, Parque Natural •
   Mexico 168 H6
Oka • Russian Fed. 100 E3
Okahandja • Namibia 110 A3
Okaihau • New Zealand 137 B2
Okanagan • Canada/United States 160 J7
Okapi, Réserve du Park •
   Dem. Rep. of Congo .... 112 [51]
Okapi, Réserve du Heritage N •
   Dem. Rep. of Congo .... 41 [104]
Okara • Pakistan 122 B2
Okavango Delta • Botswana 110 I9
Okayama • Japan 127 B4
Okazaki • Japan 127 C4
Okeechobee • FL, United States 155 D2
Okeechobee, Lake •
   FL, United States 155 D2
Okefenokee Swamp •
   GA, United States 155 C1
Okehampton • United Kingdom 65 J9
Okhotsk, Sea of • Russian Fed. 101 O4
Okhyrka • Ukraine 100 E4
Oki-shoto • Japan 127 B3
Okinawa • Japan .... 138 A
Okinawa City • Okinawa, Japan .... 138 A
Okino Tori Shima • Japan 138 AA2
Oklahoma • United States 147 G3
Oklahoma City • OK, United States 149 G3
Oklahoma City Nat. Mem. Park N •
   OK, United States .... 153 [143]
Oklan • Myanmar 128 B3
Okmulgee • OK, United States 151 A3
Okomo Sanctuary Park • Nigeria .... 112 [30]
Oksbøl • Denmark 99 E7
Okso' Takpochao • N. Mariana Is. ...... 138 B
Oktyabr'sk • Kazakstan 121 C2
Oktyabr'skoy, Ostrov •
   Russian Fed. 101 J2
Okulovka • Russian Fed. 100 L9
Okuma • Okinawa, Japan .... 138 A
Okushiri-to • Japan 127 C2
Ol-Doinyo Sabuk Nat. Park • Kenya ... 109 C5
Olaine • Latvia 100 J7
Olanchito • Honduras 170 K9
Öland • Sweden 99 H6
Öland Heritage C • Sweden .... 44 [4]
Öland • Italy 86 D3
Olathe • KS, United States 150 B3
Olavarría • Argentina 175 F7
Olbia • Sardinia, Italy. 86 F5
Old Bedford Village •
   PA, United States 156 A2
Old Crow • YT, Canada 158 C2
Old Devonshire Church • Bermuda 165 L10
Old Fort Point • Montserrat .... 167 G
Old Goa • Goa, India 123 C5
Old Harbour • Jamaica 165 D4
Old Head of Kinsale • Ireland 69 H11
Old Kilcullen • Ireland 69 F7
Old Man Bay • Cayman Is. 165 B2
Old Man of Coniston • United Kingdom .. 65 C4
Old Road Bay • Montserrat .... 167 G
Old Road Town • St Kitts & Nevis ...... 167 F
Old Sarum • United Kingdom 65 K9
Olden • Norway 98 G7
Oldenburg • Germany 72 C2
Oldham • United Kingdom 63 D7
Olduvai Gorge • Tanzania 110 H7
Olean • NY, United States 156 A1
Olekma • Russian Fed. 101 M4
Olen • Norway 98 F9
Olenek • Russian Fed. 101 M2
Oléron, I. de • France 78 E5
Olesnica • Poland 89 B3
Oletta • Corsica, France 78 N11
Olga, Mt • NT, Australia 136 A2
Olgod • Denmark 99 E7
Olhão • Portugal 84 J8
Olhos de Agua • Portugal 84 J8
Olhuveli • Maldives 124 H8
Olib • Croatia 92 F6
Oliena • Sardinia, Italy. 86 F5
Olifants •
   Mpumalanga/Limpopo, South Africa .. 111 A1
Olifants •
   Western Cape, South Africa 111 D6
Olifants •
   Western Cape, South Africa 111 F7
Olimbi • Chios, Greece .... 94 D
Olimbía • Greece 93 B3
Olimbía Heritage C • Greece .... 44 [236]
Olimbos • Greece 93 G1
Olimbos Nat. Park Park N • Greece .... 58 [138]
Olinda • Brazil 174 C3
Olinda Heritage C • Brazil .... 42 [72]
Olkusz • Poland 89 F8
Ollagüe • Chile 175 B2
Ollantaytambo • Peru 173 F6
Olmaliq • Uzbekistan 121 E3
Olmeto • Corsica, France 78 M12
Olmütz • Czech Rep. 50 D2
Olney • TX, United States 155 E4
Olofstrom • Sweden 99 G7
Olomouc • Czech Rep. 89 B4
Olomouc Heritage C • Czech Rep. ..... 44 [197]
Olongapo • Philippines 128 G4
Oloron-Ste Marie • France 78 H9
Olosega • American Samoa .... 139 H
Olot • Spain 83 D3
Oloús • Crete, Greece 93 D3
Oluvvannaya • Russian Fed. 101 L4
Olsztyn • Czestochowa, Poland 89 F8
Olsztyn • Olsztyn, Poland 89 C2
Olsztynek • Poland 89 C2
Olt • Romania 92 C2
Olten • Switzerland 90 C2
Oltenita • Romania 92 C2
Oltu • Turkey 95 D1
Olüdeniz • Turkey 95 H6
Olveston • Montserrat .... 167 G
Olympia • Greece 93 B3
Olympia Heritage C • Greece .... 44 [236]
Olympia • WA, United States 154 G5
Olympiastadion (Berlin) • Germany 73 E7
Olympic Nat. Park •
   WA, United States 154 G5
Olympic Nat. Park Park N •
   WA, United States .... 152 [25]
Olympic Nat. Park Heritage N •
   WA, United States .... 40 [10]
Olympos • Turkey 95 G8
Olympos • Cyprus 96 C4
Olympos • Cyprus 93 C1
Olympus, Mt • WA, United States 154 G5
Olympus Nat. Park Park N • Greece .... 58 [138]
Omagh • United Kingdom 63 B6
Omaha • NE, United States 150 A2
Umaha Ind Res • NE, United States ... 155 [66]
OMAN • Asia 120 H9
Omama • Iran/Oman 120 H9
Omarama • New Zealand 137 A3
Ombo • Norway 98 F9
Omdurman • Sudan 108 C3
Omeath • Ireland 69 D6
Omeo • VI, Australia 136 G9
Ometepe, I. de • Nicaragua 170 E5
Omis • Croatia 92 G6
Omiya • Japan 127 I8
Ommen • Netherlands 70 D2
Omo Lower valley, Ethiopia Heritage C •
   Ethiopia .... 43 [102]
Omo Nat. Park • Ethiopia .... 112 [61]
Omo Wenz • Ethiopia 108 C4
Omokoroa • New Zealand 137 E5
Omsk • Russian Fed. 101 H4
Onalaska • WI, United States 150 B2
Onamue • NE, United States 150 A2
Onancock • VA, United States 156 B3
Ondangwa • Namibia 110 A2
Ondjiva • Angola 110 A2
Öndörhaan • Mongolia 125 F2
Onega, Lake • Russian Fed. 100 E1

Oneida Ind Res • WI, United States ... 155 [66]
Oneida Indian Reservation •
   NY, United States 156 B1
Oneida Lake • NY, United States 156 B1
Oneonta • NY, United States 156 B1
Onerca • Cook Is. .... 139 N
Onesti • Romania 92 D2
Onezhskoye Ozero • Russian Fed. 100 E1
Ongole • India 124 C1
Onishi • Japan 127 H8
Onitsha • Nigeria 106 C4
Onna • Okinawa, Japan .... 138 A
Ono • Japan 127 F6
Onsala • Sweden 99 F6
Onsalalandet • Sweden 99 F6
Ontario • Canada 159 H3
Ontario • OR, United States 154 H6
Ontario, Lake •
   Canada/United States 160 F5
Oodnadatta • SA, Australia 135 F5
Ontong Java Atoll • Solomon Is. 138 BB3
Oost-Vlaanderen • Belgium 70 B4
Oostduinkerke-Bad • Belgium 70 E6
Oostende • Belgium 70 E6
Oosterbeek (Battlefield) •
   Netherlands 70 C2
Oosterhuit • Netherlands 70 C3
Oostpunt • Curaçao .... 166 V
Oostvaardersplassen • Netherlands ... 70 H7
Ootacamund • India 124 B3
Ootacamund Hill Sta • India 124 E6
Ooty Hill Sta • India 124 E6
Opatija • Croatia 92 F5
Opatów • Poland 89 C3
Opava • Czech Rep. 89 B4
Opelika • AL, United States 151 C4
Opelousas • LA, United States 156 E6
Opochka • Russian Fed. 100 K7
Opole • Poland 89 B3
Oporto • Portugal 80 A3
Oporto Heritage C • Portugal .... 44 [127]
Opotiki • New Zealand 137 E5
Opp • AL, United States 151 C4
Oppdal • Norway 98 A3
Oppenheim • Germany 74 D6
Opua • New Zealand 137 D6
Ora • Italy 86 C4
Oracabessa • Jamaica 165 D3
Oradea • Romania 92 C2
Oradour-sur-Glane • France 78 F5
Orai • India 123 F8
Orakei Korako • New Zealand 137 E5
Oral • Kazakstan 121 B1
Orán • Argentina 175 B2
Orange • France 76 F4
Orange Heritage C • France .... 44 [85]
Orange • Namibia/South Africa 110 A3
Orange • NS, Australia 136 H8
Orange • TX, United States 155 F5
Orange County FL, United States 157 A1
Orange County [Apt] •
   CA, United States 154 J9
Orange Walk • Belize 170 K8
Orangeburg • SC, United States 151 D4
Orangeville • OT, Canada 160 E5
Oranienburg • Germany 73 E7
Oranje Baai • St Eustatius .... 167 E
Oranjestad • Aruba .... 166 W
Oranjestad • St Eustatius .... 167 E
Orapa • Botswana 110 J9
Orastie Monts Heritage C • Romania .. 44 [219]
Orava • Slovak Rep. 89 F9
Orbe • Switzerland 90 I5
Orbost • VI, Australia 136 H9
Urcadas (Base) • Antarctica .... 176 [I]
Orchha • India 123 F8
Ordesa, Parque Nac. de Park N •
   Spain .... 58 [79]
Ordino • Andorra 82 E5
Ordos • China 126 C1
Ordu • Turkey 95 C1
Orebro • Sweden 97 D4
Örebro [Adm] • Sweden 98 B3
Oregon • United States 154 G6
Oregon Caves Nat. Mon. •
   OR, United States 154 G6
Oregon Caves Nat. Mon. Park N •
   OR, United States .... 152 [37]
Oregon City • OR, United States 154 G6
Oregon Dunes Nat. Recreation Area •
   OR, United States 154 G6
Oregrund • Sweden 99 B1
Orekhovo-Zuyevo • Russian Fed. 100 M10
Orenburg [Apt] • Romania 137 D5
Orel • Russian Fed. 100 E3
Oren • UT, United States 148 D2
Oren • Turkey 95 E4
Orenburg • Russian Fed. 101 F4
Orepuki • New Zealand 137 F8
Oresund • Denmark/Sweden 99 G7
Oresund • Denmark/Sweden 137 G8
Organ Pipe Cactus Nat. Mon. •
   AZ, United States 155 G8
Organ Pipe Cactus Nat. Mon. Park N •
   AZ, United States .... 152 [111]
Organos, Sierra de los • Cuba 164 E4
Órgãos, Serra dos • Brazil 174 F7
Orhangazi • Turkey 95 F4
Orient • Majorca, Spain 83 N11
Orientale, Plaine •
   Corsica, France 78 N12
Orihuela • Spain 83 A2
Orillia • OT, Canada 160 F5
Orimattila • Finland 99 D4
Orinoco • Colombia/Venezuela 173 C2
Orinoco Delta • Venezuela 173 C2
Orio [Apt] • Italy 86 I9
Orissa • India 123 B3
Oristano • Sardinia, Italy 86 E6
Cristano, Golfo di •
   Sardinia, Italy 86 E6
Orivesi • Finland 99 D3
Orivesi [Lake] • Finland 99 C4
Orizaba • Mexico 169 J7
Orizaba, Pico de • Mexico 169 J7
Orkanger • Norway 98 A3
Orkelljunga • Sweden 99 G7
Orkney Heritage C • United Kingdom .. 44 [16]
Orkney Is. • United Kingdom 62 D1
Orlando • FL, United States 157 B1
Orlando Arena • FL, United States 157 B1
Orlando Museum of Art •
   FL, United States 157 B1
Orlando Science Center •
   FL, United States 157 B1
Orléans • France 77 F5
Orléans • St Martin .... 167 E
Orléans, I. d' • QU, Canada 160 H3
Orléck • Czech Rep. 88 B2
Orlovista • FL, United States 157 B1
Orly [Apt] • France 78 A2
Orlyata • Italy 87 A2
Ormiston Gorge Nat. Park •
   NT, Australia 136 A1
Ormoc • Philippines 128 G4
Ormond Beach • FL, United States 155 D1
Ormos Korthiou • Andros, Greece ..... 94 I
Örnö • Sweden 99 B2
Örnö [I.] • Sweden 99 B2
Örnsköldsvik • Sweden 97 D3
Oro Verde • San Marino 86 B2
Orohena, Mt • French Polynesia .... 139 K
Orongo • Easter I. .... 139 M
Orontes • Syria/Turkey 95 C3
Oroqen Zizhiqi • China 125 G1
Orosei • Sardinia, Italy 86 F5
Orosei, Golfo di •
   Sardinia, Italy 86 F5
Oroto Peninsula • Guam .... 138 Z
Oroville • CA, United States 148 B3
Orpheus I. • QL, Australia 136 C3
Orrefors • Sweden 99 H6

Orres, les Ski • France .... 61 [49]
Orres, les • France 78 D4
Orsa • Belarus 100 D3
Orsk • Russian Fed. 101 F4
Orsoy • Germany 73 C5
Ørsta • Norway 98 F7
Orsundsbro • Sweden 99 A1
Orta • Italy 87 B1
Orta • Turkey 95 F6
Ortaköy • Turkey 95 I9
Orte • Italy 87 F7
Orthez • France 78 I9
Ortisei Ski • Italy .... 61 [145]
Ortisei • Italy 86 C3
Ortles • Italy 87 C1
Orumiyeh • Iran 120 F6
Orumiyeh, Daryacheh-ye • Iran 120 F6
Oruro • Bolivia 173 C4
Orust • Sweden 99 F5
Orval, Abbaye-d' • Belgium 70 C5
Orvieto • Italy 87 E4
Orzola • Lanzarote, Canary Is. 83 I5
Osa, Península de • Costa Rica 170 F6
Osage • KS/MO, United States 150 B3
Osage Ind Res • OK, United States ... 155 [55]
Osaka • Japan 127 G6
Osaka [Adm] • Japan 127 G7
Osaka-wan • Japan 127 F7
Osan • Sweden 99 G5
Osby • Sweden 99 G7
Osceola • IA, United States 150 B2
Osceola County, FL, United States 157 A1
Oscoda • MI, United States 161 C2
Osh • Kyrgyzstan 121 F3
Oshawa • OT, Canada 160 E5
Oshima • Japan 127 H9
Oshima [I.] • Japan 127 I9
Oshima-hanto • Japan 127 E8
Oshkosh • WI, United States 150 C2
Oshogbo • Nigeria 106 C4
Osijek • Croatia 92 G5
Osiyan • India 123 D8
Osizweni • South Africa 111 B3
Oskarshamn • Sweden 99 H6
Oskemen • Kazakstan 121 G2
Oskerström • Sweden 99 G6
Oslo • Norway 98 E5
Oslofjorden • Norway 98 E6
Osmaniye • Turkey 95 J10
Osmo • Sweden 99 B2
Osnabrück • Germany 72 C2
Osorno • Chile 175 A4
Osorno • Spain 80 C2
Osøyro • Norway 98 F8
Ospedaletti • Italy 87 A3
Oss • Netherlands 70 C3
Ossa, Mt • TS, Australia 136 F7
Ossun [Apt] • France 78 J9
Ost-Friesland • Germany 72 B1
Ostashkov • Russian Fed. 100 L10
Ostend • Belgium 70 E6
Oster Hurup • Denmark 99 F6
Osterbymo • Sweden 99 H5
Ostergötland • Sweden 99 A1
Osteroya • Norway 98 F8
Ostersund • Sweden 97 C3
Östervåla • Sweden 99 A1
Ostfold • Norway 98 E6
Ostfriesische Inseln • Germany 72 B2
Osthammar • Sweden 99 B1
Ostia Antica • Italy 87 E5
Ostrava • Czech Rep. 89 F9
Ostrava • Czech Rep. 89 F9
Ostrobothnia • Finland 98 C2
Ostroda • Poland 89 B2
Ostroleka • Poland 89 C2
Ostrov • Czech Rep. 88 B2
Ostrov • Russian Fed. 100 C2
Ostrów Wielkopolski • Poland 89 B3
Ostuni • Italy 85 F4
Osumi-hanto • Japan 127 B4
Osumi-shoto • Japan 127 B4
Osumi-shoto • Japan 138 AA1
Oswego • NY, United States 156 B1
Oswego [Riv] • NY, United States 160 F5
Oswiecim • Poland 89 F8
Oswiecim Heritage C • Poland .... 44 [186]
Otago • New Zealand 137 A4
Otago Peninsula • New Zealand 137 B4
Otaru • Japan 127 D2
Otautau • New Zealand 137 F8
Oti • Africa 106 B4
Otisco Lake • NY, United States 156 B1
Otjinim [Apt] • Romania 137 D5
Otorohanga • New Zealand 137 D5
Otra • Norway 97 B4
Otranto • Italy 85 G4
Otranto, Strait of • Albania/Italy 92 B3
Otrey • Norway 98 G7
Otrey • Norway 137 G8
Otsuki • Japan 127 H8
Otstadalen • Norway 98 G7
Ottaviano • Italy 87 G7
Ottawa • IL, United States 150 C2
Ottawa • KS, United States 150 A3
Ottawa • OT, Canada 160 G4
Otterup • Denmark 99 F7
Ottobeuren • Germany 74 F7
Ottumwa • IA, United States 150 B2
Otway, Cape • VI, Australia 136 G9
Otztal • Austria 91 N8
Otztaler Alpen • Austria/Italy 91 N8
Ouachita • AR/LA, United States 151 C3
Ouachita Mtns •
   AR/OK, United States 151 B4
Ouadane Heritage C • Mauritania ..... 43 [105]
Ouagadougou • Burkina 106 B3
Oualata • Mauritania 106 C3
Oualata Heritage C • Mauritania ...... 43 [105]
Ouarga • Algeria 106 C1
Ouarzazate • Morocco 107 B3
Oubangui • Central African Rep. 108 B4
Oud-Beijerland • Netherlands 70 G8
Oudenaarde • Belgium 70 B4
Oudewater • Netherlands 70 H8
Oudna • Tunisia 107 D4
Oudong • Cambodia 129 B5
Oudref • Tunisia 107 D5
Oudtshoorn • South Africa 111 F7
Ouémé • Benin 106 C4
Ouerrha • Morocco 107 B1
Ouessant, I. d' • France 77 C3
Ouesso • Congo 106 D4
Ouezzane • Morocco 107 A1
Oughterard • Ireland 69 H9
Ouistreham • France 66 C6
Oujda • Morocco 107 A3
Oulainen • Morocco 107 A1
Oulanka Nat. Park Park N • Finland ... 58 [34]
Oulmès • Morocco 107 A1
Oulu • Finland 97 F2
Oulu [Adm] • Finland 98 C2
Oulujoki • Finland 97 F3
Oulujärvi • Finland 98 C2
Ounasjoki • Finland 97 F2
Ouranópoli • Greece .... 94 B
Ourense • Spain 80 B2
Ourinhos • Brazil 175 C2
Ouro Prêto • Brazil 174 E6
Ouro Prêto Heritage C • Brazil .... 42 [75]
Ourthe • Belgium 70 C4
Ouse • United Kingdom 63 E6
Outamba-Kilimi Nat. Park Park •
   Sierra Leone .... 112 [12]
Outão • Portugal 84 G6
Outeniqua Mtns • South Africa 111 F7
Outeniqua Pass • South Africa 111 F7
Outer Hebrides • United Kingdom 62 B3
Outjo • Namibia 110 A3
Ouvéa • New Caledonia .... 138 U
Ovahe • Easter I. .... 139 M

Ovahe, Caleta • Easter I. .... 139 M
Ovalau • Fiji Is. .... 138 T
Ovalle • Chile 175 A3
Overberg • United Kingdom 110 A2
Overbeck • United Kingdom 65 J10
Overberg • South Africa 111 E7
Overflakkee • Netherlands 70 G8
OverIJssel • Netherlands 70 D2
Overlida • Sweden 99 G6
Overloon • Netherlands 70 C3
Overton • NV, United States 154 J8
Overum • Sweden 99 H5
Oviedo • Spain 80 C2
Oviedo Heritage C • Spain .... 44 [109]
Ovre Anarjokka Nat. Park Park N •
   Norway .... 58 [6]
Ovre Ardal • Norway 98 G8
Ovre Dividal Nat. Park Park N •
   Norway .... 58 [8]
Ovre Pasvik Nat. Park Park N •
   Norway .... 58 [4]
Ovre Sirdal • Norway 98 G9
Owabi Wildlife Sanctuary Park •
   Ghana .... 112 [21]
Owaka • New Zealand 137 G8
Uwasco Lake • NY, United States 156 B1
Owen I. • Cayman Is. 165 A1
Owen River • New Zealand 137 B3
Owen Roberts [Apt] • Cayman Is. 165 A2
Owen Sound • OT, Canada 159 H4
Owensboro • KY, United States 151 C3
Owl's Head Ski • QU, Canada .... 146 [19]
Owyhee • NV, United States 148 C2
Owyhee [Riv] • United States 154 H6
Ox Mtns • Ireland 69 H8
Oxcutzcab • Mexico 169 F4
Oxelösund • Sweden 99 A2
Oxford • United Kingdom 65 F6
Oxfordshire • United Kingdom 65 F6
Oxkintok • Mexico 169 F4
Oxnard • CA, United States 154 I9
Oy Mittelberg • Germany 74 F8
Oyama • Japan 127 C3
Oyem • Gabon 106 D4
Oyeren • Norway 98 A3
Oyster Bay • South Africa 111 G7
Oz-en-Oisans Ski • France .... 61 [40]
Ozark Plateau • MO, United States ... 151 B3
Ozieri • Sardinia, Italy 86 F5
Ozona • TX, United States 149 F4

P

Pa Sang • Thailand 130 B6
Paamiut • Greenland 159 L2
Paarl • South Africa 111 D7
Pabbay • United Kingdom 62 B3
Pabna • Bangladesh 122 C3
Pacaraima, Serra • Venezuela 173 C2
Pachino • Sicily, Italy 86 H8
Pachmarhi Hill Sta • India 124 E5
Pachuca • Mexico 169 J7
Pacific Ocean • 138-139
Pacific Palisades •
   HI, United States 157 G6
Pacific Rim Nat. Park Reserve Park N •
   BC, Canada .... 161 [11]
Pacific Rim Nat. Park Reserve •
   BC, Canada 160 I7
Pacitan • Java, Indonesia 131 Q12
Padang • Indonesia 131 L8
Padangbai • Bali, Indonesia 131 L8
Padanglawas • Indonesia 131 N10
Padangpanjang • Indonesia 131 N10
Padangsidempuan • Indonesia 131 N10
Padasjoki • Finland 99 D3
Paddock • South Africa 111 B5
Paderborn • Germany 72 C3
Paderne • Portugal 84 J8
Padirac, Gouffre de • France 78 F6
Padjelanta Nat. Park Park N • Sweden .. 58 [20]
Padmanabhapuram • India 124 B4
Pádova • Italy 87 C2
Pádova Heritage C • Italy .... 44 [153]
Padre I. • TX, United States 155 E6
Padre I. Nat. Seashore •
   TX, United States 155 E6
Padre I. Nat. Seashore Park N •
   TX, United States .... 153 [140]
Padstow • United Kingdom 65 I10
Padstow Bay • United Kingdom 65 I10
Padua • Italy 87 C2
Padua Heritage C • Italy .... 44 [153]
Paducah • KY, United States 151 C3
Paelau • Kiribati .... 139 I
Paestum • Italy 87 H7
Paestum Heritage C • Italy .... 44 [171]
Pag • Croatia 92 F6
Pag [I.] • Croatia 92 F6
Pagadian • Philippines 128 G5
Pagan • Myanmar 128 A2
Pagan • N. Mariana Is. 138 AA2
Page • AZ, United States 155 G7
Payel I. • Denmark 99 F7
Pago Pago • American Samoa .... 139 H
Pago Pago Harbor • American Samoa .. 139 H
Pagwa River • OT, Canada 159 H4
Pahalgam Hill Sta • India 124 E5
Pahang [Adm] • Malaysia 129 G9
Pahang [Riv] • Malaysia 129 G9
Paharpur Heritage C • Bangladesh .... 43 [165]
Pãhnes • Crete, Greece 93 G6
Pai • Thailand 130 B5
Paide • Estonia 100 K6
Paignton • United Kingdom 65 J10
Päijänne • Finland 99 D3
Paimpol • France 77 D3
Painted Desert • AZ, United States ... 155 G7
País Vasco • Spain 80 D2
Paisley • United Kingdom 65 A2
Paitilla [Apt] • Panama 170 M11
Pakanbaru • Indonesia 131 N10
Pakaraima Mtns • Guyana .... 173 K
Pakistan • Asia 122 A2
Pakleniça Nat. Park Park N • Croatia .. 58 [119]
Pakleniça Nat. Park • Croatia 92 F6
Pakokku • Myanmar 128 A2
Pakokku • Myanmar 128 A2
Pakrac • Croatia 92 G5
Pakse • Laos 129 A2
Pakxan • Laos 128 D3
Pakxe • Laos 129 B4
Pal • Andorra 82 E5
Pal, Le Park L • France .... 59 [67]
Palafrugell • Spain 83 D3
Palagruza • Croatia 92 B3
Palamau Nat. Park • India 123 G4
Palamós • Spain 83 D3
Palana • Russian Fed. 101 O4
Palanan • Philippines 128 G4
Palander • Lithuania 100 J7
Palangkaraya • Indonesia 131 D4
Palani • India 124 E6
Palanka • Serbia & Montenegro 92 B3
Palanpur • India 123 D8
Palapye • Botswana 110 J10
Palatka • FL, United States 155 C1
Palau • Philippines 128 G5
Palauli Bay • Samoa .... 139 G
Palawan • Philippines 128 G5
Palazzolo • Sicily, Italy 86 H8
Palazzolo Heritage C •
   Sicily, Italy .... 44 [175]
Paldiski • Estonia 100 K6
Palea Paphos • Cyprus 96 C4
Palékastro • Crete, Greece 93 J6
Palembang • Indonesia 131 B4
Palencia • Spain 80 C2
Palendria • Cyprus 96 C4
Palenque • Mexico 169 E5
Palenque Heritage C • Mexico .... 42 [14]
Paleohóri • Crete, Greece 93 B4
Paleokastritsa • Corfu, Greece .... 94 A
Paleópolis • Andros, Greece .... 94 I
Palermo • Sicily, Italy 86 G7

Páleros • Greece .... 94 J
Palestine • TX, United States 155 F5
PALESTINE NATIONAL AUTHORITY
   REGION • Asia 120 B3
Palestrina • Italy 87 F5
Palestrina • Italy 124 B3
Pali • India 123 D8
Palia Kaméni • Thíra, Greece .... 94 G
Palikir • Fed. States of Micronesia ..... 138 D
Palioúri • Greece .... 94 B
Palisades • NJ/NY, United States 165 D4
Palisadoes • Jamaica 165 D4
Palk Bay • Sri Lanka 124 C3
Palk Strait • India/Sri Lanka 124 C3
Pallkäne • Finland 99 D3
Pallas-Ounastunturi Nat. Park Park N •
   Finland .... 58 [30]
Palliser, Cape • New Zealand 137 D3
Palm Beach • FL, United States 155 D2
Palm Beach • FL, Australia .... 166 W
Palm I. • St Vincent & Gren. .... 167 P
Palm Springs • CA, United States 154 J9
Palm Valley • NT, Australia 136 B2
Palma, Badia de • Majorca, Spain 83 N11
Palma del Rio • Spain 82 I7
Palma de Mallorca • Majorca, Spain .. 83 N11
Palma Nova • Majorca, Spain 83 N12
Palma, Playa de • Majorca, Spain 83 N12
Palma Soriana • Cuba 164 H5
Palmanova • Italy 87 D1
Palmar Beach • Mauritius 113 F6
Palmária, I. Heritage C • Italy .... 44 [159]
Pálmas • Brazil 174 B4
Pálmas, Golfo di •
   Sardinia, Italy 86 E6
Palmdale • CA, United States 149 C4
Palmeira • Portugal 84 G6
Palmer • AK, United States 157 E3
Palmer [Base] • Antarctica .... 176 [6]
Palmer Land • Antarctica 176 M5
Palmerston • Cook Is. 139 DD4
Palmerston • Cook Is. 137 B4
Palmerston North • New Zealand 137 C3
Palmetto Point • Antigua & Barbuda ... 167 H
Palmetto Point • Cayman Is. 165 A2
Palmira • Colombia 173 B2
Palmyra • NY, United States 156 A1
Palmyra Heritage C • Syria .... 44 [301]
Palmyra Atoll • Pacific Ocean 139 DD2
Palo Alto Battlefield Nat. Hist. Site Park N •
   TX, United States .... 153 [139]
Palolem Beach • Goa, India 123 C6
Palomani, Nevado • Bolivia/Peru 173 F6
Palombara • Italy 169 K8
Palos, Cabo de • Spain 83 A2
Palos, Cabo de • Spain 173 E6
Palu • Indonesia 131 E4
Pals • Spain 83 D3
Palu • Indonesia 131 E4
Pamekasan • Indonesia 131 R12
Pameungpeuk • Java, Indonesia 131 P12
Pamiers • France 76 D5
Pamir • Asia 121 F4
Pamlico Sound • NC, United States ... 151 E3
Pampa • TX, United States 149 F3
Pampa Húmida • Argentina 175 F7
Pampas • Argentina 175 B3
Pampas • Peru 173 E6
Pampatar • Margarita .... 166 T
Pamphylia • Turkey 95 H7
Pamplemousses • Mauritius 113 F5
Pamplona • Spain 80 E2
Pamporovo • Bulgaria 92 D3
Pamporovo Ski • Bulgaria 90 H7
Pampus • Netherlands 70 H7
Pamukkale • Turkey 95 F5
Panaca • NV, United States 148 D3
Panaitan • Indonesia 131 O11
Panaji • Goa, India 123 C5
Panajia Kerá • Crete, Greece 93 J6
PANAMA • C. America 170 G6
Panamá [Adm] • Panama 170 L11
Panama Canal • Panama .... 170 L-M
Panama City • FL, United States 155 B1
Panama City • Panama 170 M11
Panama City Heritage C • Panama ... 42 [38]
Panama Viejo • Panama 170 M11
Panará, I. • Italy 86 H7
Panaro • Italy 87 C2
Panay • Philippines 128 G4
Pančevo • Serbia & Montenegro 92 C3
Panchgani Hill Sta • India 124 E6
Pandan • Philippines 128 G4
Pandharpur • Goa, India 124 C6
Panevezys • Lithuania 100 K7
Pangandaran • Java, Indonesia 131 P12
Pangkalanbrandan • Indonesia 131 M9
Pangkalpinang • Indonesia 131 N10
Pangkor • Malaysia 129 F9
Pangnirtung • NU, Canada 159 J2
Pangrango, Gunung •
   Java, Indonesia 131 O11
Panhala • India 124 A1
Panhala Hill Sta • India 124 E6
Panié, Mt • New Caledonia .... 138 U
Panipat • India 123 E7
Pankow (Berlin) • Germany 73 F7
Pankwo • Indonesia 131 U11
Panna • India 123 F8
Pannonhalma Heritage C • Hungary .. 44 [206]
Panorama Ski • BC, Canada .... 146 [8]
Panorama • Brazil 175 C2
Panoramapark Sauerland Park L •
   Germany .... 59 [53]
Pánormos • Crete, Greece 93 H5
Pantai Acheh Forest Reserve •
   Penang, Malaysia 129 D7
Pantai Sahib Hill Sta • India 124 E5
Pantai • Indonesia 131 L8
Pantal • Indonesia 131 A4
Pantanal conservation area Heritage N •
   Brazil .... 40 [4?]
Pantar • Indonesia 131 F15
Pantelleria, I. di • Italy 85 D6
Pánuco • Mexico 169 A2
Panuco [Riv] • Mexico 169 A2
Panyu • China 126 E3
Panzhihua • China 125 E4
Paola • Malta 96 B2
Paoli Peaks Ski •
   IN, United States .... 146 [85]
Papa Westray • United Kingdom 62 D1
Papagayo, Golfo de • Costa Rica 170 E5
Papago Ind Res • AZ, United States ... 155 [28]
Papago Indian Reservation •
   AZ, United States 155 G8
Papakura • New Zealand 137 B2
Papaloapan • Mexico 169 K8
Papanikolis Cave • Greece .... 94 J
Papantla • Mexico 169 J7
Papara • French Polynesia .... 139 K
Papeete • French Polynesia .... 139 K
Papendrecht • Netherlands 70 G8
Papenoo • French Polynesia .... 139 K
Paphos • Cyprus 96 C4
Paphos Heritage C • Cyprus .... 44 [258]
Papineau-Labelle, Réserve faunique de •
   QU, Canada 160 G3
PAPUA NEW GUINEA • Australasia ... 134 F3
Papuk • Croatia 92 G5
Papun • Myanmar 130 B3
Papunya • NT, Australia 136 A1
Paquimé Casas Grandes Heritage C •
   Mexico .... 42 [14]
Pará • Brazil 174 A3
Paraburdoo • WA, Australia 135 B4
Paracel Is. • South China Sea 128 E3
Paracin • Serbia & Montenegro 92 C3

Paradise • CA, United States 148 B3
Paradise Bay • Malta 96 A1
Paradise I. • Bahamas 164 A2
Paradise Sea-Side Resort •
   BC, Canada 160 I7
Paradisi [Apt] • Rhodes, Greece .... 94 F
Paragould • AR, United States 151 B3
PARAGUAY • S. America 175 C2
Paraguay [Riv] • S. America 175 C2
Paraíba • Brazil 174 C3
Paraíba do Sul • Brazil 174 F7
Parainen • Finland 99 C4
Parakou • Benin 106 C4
Paralimni • Cyprus 96 C4
Paramaribo • Surinam 174 A2
Paramount Canada's Wonderland •
   OT, Canada 160 E5
Paramount's Carowinds Park L •
   NC, United States .... 157 [26]
Paramount's Great America •
   CA, United States 154 I8
Paramount's Great America Park L •
   CA, United States .... 157 [2]
Paramount's Kings Dominion •
   VA, United States 156 A4
Paramount's Kings Dominion Park L •
   VA, United States .... 157 [28]
Paramount's Kings Island Park L •
   OH, United States .... 157 [20]
Paraná • Argentina 175 C2
Paraná [Adm] • Brazil 175 C2
Paraná, Delta del • Argentina 175 F6
Paraná [Riv] • S. America 175 C2
Paranaguá • Brazil 175 C2
Paranaíba • Brazil 175 C2
Paranaíba [Riv] • Brazil 174 A4
Parangtritis • Java, Indonesia 131 Q12
Parashant Nat. Mon. Park N •
   AZ, United States .... 152 [96]
Paratí • Brazil 174 E7
Parbhani • India 122 B4
Parc Astérix Park L • France .... 59 [63]
Parc Astérix • France 78 B1
Parc des Princes (Paris) • France 78 A2
Parc nat. du Niokolo Koba Heritage N •
   Senegal .... 41 [93]
Pardubice • Czech Rep. 89 E6
Parece Vela • Japan 138 AA2
Parempei • Fed. States of Micronesia .. 138 D
Parepare • Indonesia 131 E4
Párga • Greece 93 B2
Pargas • Finland 99 C4
Pargo, Ponta do • Madeira 84 D5
Parguera • Puerto Rico 165 I8
Parham • Antigua & Barbuda .... 167 I
Parham Harbour • Antigua & Barbuda .. 167 I
Paria, Gulf of •
   Trin. & Tob./Venezuela .... 166 S
Paria, Península de • Venezuela 173 C1
Pariaman • Indonesia 131 N10
Parikía • Páros, Greece .... 94 H
Parikkala • Finland 97 F3
Parima-Tapirapecó, Parque Nac. •
   Venezuela 173 C2
Parintins • Brazil 173 D3
Paris • France 78 A2
Paris Heritage N • France .... 41 [59]
Paris Heritage C • France .... 41 [59]
Paris • Kiribati .... 139 I
Paris • TX, United States 155 F4
Paris Expo • France 78 A2
Parish Closes • France 77 C3
Parita, Bahía de • Panama 170 G6
Park City Ski • UT, United States .... 146 [48]
Parkano • Finland 99 D3
Parker • AZ, United States 155 G8
Parker Dam • AZ/NV, United States .. 155 G8
Parkersburg • WV, United States 150 D3
Parkes • NS, Australia 136 H8
Parlatuvier • Trinidad & Tobago .... 166 R
Parma • Italy 87 C2
Parnaíba • Brazil 174 B3
Parnaíba [Riv] • Brazil 174 B3
Parnassós Nat. Park Park N • Greece .58 [141]
Parnassus • New Zealand 137 B3
Pärnitha Nat. Park Park N • Greece ... 58 [142]
Pärnu • Estonia 100 K6
Páros • Páros, Greece .... 94 H
Páros [I.] • Greece .... 94 H
Parpan Ski • Switzerland .... 61 [77]
Parramatta • NS, Australia 136 H8
Parrett • United Kingdom 65 K9
Parry Is. • Canada 142 D1
Parry Sound • OT, Canada 160 E4
Parsons • KS, United States 151 A3
Partenen • Austria 91 M8
Parthenay • France 77 E6
Partinico • Sicily, Italy 86 G7
Partry Mtns • Ireland 69 H9
Pas de la Casa • Andorra 82 E5
Pas, The • MN, Canada 158 F3
Pasadena • CA, United States 154 J9
Pasadena • TX, United States 155 F5
Pascagoula • MS, United States 155 A1
Pasco • WA, United States 154 H5
Pascua, I. de • Pacific Ocean .... 139 M
Pasewalk • Germany 72 E2
Pasir Panjang • Penang, Malaysia .. 129 D8
Pasir Ras • Singapore 129 I11
Pasirputih • Java, Indonesia 131 R12
Påskallavik • Sweden 99 H6
Pasley, Cape • WA, Australia 135 C6
Pasman • Croatia 92 F6
Paso de los Toros • Uruguay 175 G6
Paso Robles • CA, United States 148 B3
Pasos-Limáni • Chios, Greece .... 94 D
Pássaro, Capo • Sicily, Italy 86 H8
Passau • Germany 72 E4
Passendale [Battlefield] • Belgium .. 70 A4
Passer • Italy 86 C3
Passo Fundo • Brazil 175 C2
Passo Tonale Ski • Italy .... 61 [131]
Passos • Brazil 174 E6
Pastavy • Belarus 100 K8
Pasto • Colombia 173 B2
Pasuruan • Java, Indonesia 131 R12
Pasut Beach • Bali, Indonesia 131 L8
Pat Sin Leng Country Park •
   Hong Kong, China 126 F4
Patagonia • Argentina 175 A4
Patan • Nepal 122 C3
Patara • Turkey 95 F6
Pate I. • Kenya 109 D5
Patea • New Zealand 137 D6
Paterno • Sicily, Italy 86 H8
Paterson • NJ, United States 156 C2
Paterson • South Africa 111 G7
Pathankot • India 122 B2
Pati Point • Guam .... 138 Z
Patiala • India 122 B2
Patillas, Puerto • Puerto Rico 165 J8
Pátmos • Greece 93 B3
Pátmos Heritage C • Greece .... 44 [245]
Patna • India 123 G8
Patnem Beach • Goa, India 123 C6
Patnos • Turkey 95 D2
Patong • Ko Phuket, Thailand 130 F10
Patong Bay • Ko Phuket, Thailand .. 130 F10
Patong Beach • Ko Phuket, Thailand .. 130 F10
Patos de Minas • Brazil 174 B4
Patos, Lagoa dos • Brazil 175 C3
Patras • Greece 93 B2
Patras • Greece 93 B2
Pats Peak • NH, United States 156 D1
Pattadakal • India 124 B1
Pattadakal Heritage C • India .... 43 [158]
Pattani • Thailand 128 C5
Pattaya • Thailand 130 E8
Patterdale • United Kingdom 65 C3
Patuca • Honduras 170 H9
Patuca, Punta • Honduras 170 E3
Pátzcuaro • Mexico 169 I7

Pau • France 78 J9
Pau [Riv] • France 78 I9
Pauillac • France 78 E5
Paul de Serra • Madeira 84 D5
Paulo Afonso • Brazil 174 C3
Paulpietersburg • South Africa 111 B3
Pavia • Italy 87 B2
Pavia, Certosa di • Italy 87 B2
Pavilosta • Latvia 100 J3
Pavlodar • Kazakstan 121 G1
Pavlohrad • Ukraine 100 E4
Pavlovsk • Russian Fed. 100 M8
Pavullo nel Frignano • Italy 87 C2
Pawai • Singapore 129 H12
Pawnee • Russian Fed. 92 F5
Pawtucket • RI, United States 156 D1
Pawu Aboriginal Land •
   NT, Australia 136 A1
Paxí • Greece 93 B2
Paximadia • Greece 93 J5
Paximadia • Greece 93 H6
Paya Lebar • Singapore 129 I11
Payakumbuh • Indonesia 131 N10
Payangan • Bali, Indonesia 131 L7
Payerne • Switzerland 90 I5
Paynes Find • WA, Australia 135 B5
Paynesville • VI, Australia 136 G9
Pays de la Loire • France 77 A1
Paysandú • Uruguay 175 C3
Pazar • Turkey 95 D1
Pazardzhik • Bulgaria 92 D3
Pazin • Croatia 92 F5
Pea • Tonga .... 139 P
Pea Ridge Nat. Military Park Park N •
   AR, United States .... 153 [186]
Peace • AL/BC, Canada 158 D3
Peace Bridge • Canada/United States .. 161 D3
Peace River • AL, Canada 160 J6
Peach Springs • AZ, United States .. 149 D3
Peak District Nat. Park Park N •
   United Kingdom .... 58 [52]
Peak District Nat. Park •
   United Kingdom 63 E7
Pearl • MS, United States 156 F5
Pearl City • HI, United States 157 G6
Pearl Harbor • HI, United States 157 G6
Pearl & Hermes Atoll •
   HI, United States 138 CC1
Pearl Land • China 126 F3
Pearl River Delta • China .... 126 E-F
Pearsall • TX, United States 149 G5
Pearston • South Africa 111 G6
Peatland World • Ireland 69 E6
Peatra Neamt • Romania 92 D2
Peauges, Safari de • France 78 A2
Pec • Serbia & Montenegro 92 C3
Peche-Merle, Grotte du • France 78 F6
Pechora • Russian Fed. 101 F3
Pechora [Riv] • Russian Fed. 101 F3
Pecos • TX, United States 149 F4
Pecos Nat. Hist. Park •
   NM, United States 155 H7
Pecos Nat. Hist. Park Park N •
   NM, United States .... 152 [127]
Pecos [Riv] • NM/TX, United States .. 149 F4
Pécs • Hungary 92 B2
Pécs Heritage C • Hungary .... 44 [207]
Pedde Beach • Goa, India 123 C6
Pedder, Lake • TS, Australia 136 H9
Pedernales • Dominican Rep. 165 F6
Pedracàs Ski • Italy .... 61 [146]
Pedràces • Italy 86 D3
Pedraisches • Italy 86 D3
Pedregal • Panama 170 M11
Pedro Castle • Cayman Is. 165 A2
Pedro Juan Caballero • Paraguay .. 175 C2
Pedro Miguel, Esclusas de • Panama 170 M11
Peebinga • United Kingdom 65 B2
Peeblesshire • United Kingdom 65 B2
Peel's Grave, John •
   United Kingdom 65 D3
Péfki • Crete, Greece 93 J6
Péfkos • Crete, Greece 93 I6
Pefkos • Rhodes, Greece .... 94 F
Pegasus Bay • New Zealand 137 B3
Peggys Cove • NS, Canada 160 B2
Pegnitz • Germany 72 C4
Pegu • Myanmar 128 B3
Peguera • Majorca, Spain 83 N12
Pehlivanköy • Turkey 95 E3
Pehuajó • Argentina 175 F7
Peillon • France 78 H7
Peipus, Lake •
   Estonia/Russian Fed. 100 K6
Peisey Ski • France .... 61 [24]
Peissenberg • Germany 74 F8
Peixoto de Azevedo • Brazil 174 A4
Pekalongan • Java, Indonesia 131 P11
Pekanbaru • Indonesia 131 N10
Pekelmeer • Bonaire .... 166 U
Peking • China 125 F3
Peking Heritage C • China .... 43 [175]
Pelabuhan Kelang • Malaysia 129 F10
Pelabuhanratu • Java, Indonesia 131 O11
Pelagie, Is. • Italy 85 D7
Pélagos • Greece 94 BB2
Pelat, Mont • France 78 H7
Pelée, Mont • Martinique .... 167 J
Pelékas • Corfu, Greece .... 94 A
Peleliu • Palau .... 138 Y
Pelhrimov • Czech Rep. 89 E7
Pelican Cay Nat. Park • Bahamas .. 164 A1
Pelineó • Chios, Greece .... 94 D
Pelister Nat. Park Park N •
   F.Y.R. of Macedonia .... 58 [130]
Peljesac • Croatia 92 A2
Pella • Jordan 120 B2
Pellston [Apt] • WI, United States .. 161 B2
Pellworm • Germany 99 E8
Pelly Bay • NU, Canada 159 H2
Pelopónissos [Adm] • Greece 94 BB3
Peloponnese • Greece 93 C3
Peloponnisos • Greece 93 C3
Peloritani • CA, United States 154 I8
Petare • Venezuela 173 C1
Pelotas • Brazil 175 C3
Pelusium • Egypt 109 B1
Pemalang • Java, Indonesia 131 P11
Pematangsiantar • Indonesia 131 N9
Pemba • Mozambique 110 D2
Pemba I. • Tanzania 110 H7
Pembrey Country Park Beach •
   United Kingdom .... 64 [50]
Pembroke • OT, Canada 160 F3
Pembroke • United Kingdom 63 C9
Pembrokeshire • United Kingdom 64 A5
Pembrokeshire Coast Nat. Park •
   United Kingdom 63 C9
Pembrokeshire Nat. Park Park N •
   United Kingdom .... 58 [54]
Pembury • United Kingdom 65 H8
Peña Blanca • Mexico 168 I5
Penambo Range • Indonesia/Malaysia .131 E4
Penang • Malaysia .... 129 D-E
Penang Bird Park •
   Penang, Malaysia 129 E7
Penang Botanic Gardens •
   Penang, Malaysia 129 D7
Penang Hill • Penang, Malaysia 129 D7
Penang I. Bridge •
   Penang, Malaysia 129 E8
Penang Snake Forest Reserve •
   Penang, Malaysia 129 D8
Peñas, Cabo de • Spain 80 C2
Peñas, Golfo de • Chile 175 A4
Pend Oreille Lake •
   ID, United States 154 H5
Pendennis Castle • United Kingdom .. 65 I10
Pendjari, Parc nat. de la Park •
   Benin .... 112 [27]
Pendleton • OR, United States 154 H6
Penebel • Bali, Indonesia 131 L7
Peneda, Serra da • Portugal 84 A1
Peneda-Gerês, Parque Nac. da Park •
   Portugal .... 58 [37]
Penelokan • Bali, Indonesia 131 L7
Penemei • OT, Canada 160 E4
Peng Chau • Hong Kong, China .. 126 E5

Pengambengan • Bali, Indonesia .. 131 K7
Pengastulan • Bali, Indonesia 131 K7
Penghu • Taiwan 126 D2
Peniche • Portugal 80 A4
Peninsula [Apt] •
   CA, United States 154 I8
Penjakent • Tajikistan 121 E4
Penjat, I. des •
   Formentera, Pointe de • France .. 83 M10
Penmarc'h, Pointe de • France 77 C4
Penn's Cave • PA, United States 156 A2
Pennant • India 124 C1
Pennine Alps • Italy/Switzerland 90 J6
Pennines • United Kingdom 63 D6
Pennsylvania • United States 156 A2
Pennsylvania Avenue Nat. Hist. Site
   Park N • DC, United States .... 153 [264]
Pennsylvania • Panama 170 G6
Penonomé • Panama 170 G6
Penrhyn • Cook Is. 139 DD3
Penrith • United Kingdom 65 D3
Penrith • United Kingdom 155 A1
Penshurst Place • United Kingdom .. 65 G8
Pentecost I. • Vanuatu .... 138 V
Penticton • BC, Canada 160 J7
Pentland Firth • United Kingdom 62 D2
Pentland Hills • United Kingdom 65 B2
Penukonda • India 124 B2
Penza • Russian Fed. 100 F3
Penzance • United Kingdom 65 I10
Penzberg • Germany 74 G8
Peoria • IL, United States 151 G6
Pequeno I. • Goa, India 123 C5
Peraea • Jordan 120 B3
Perai • Penang, Malaysia 129 E7
Perak • Malaysia 129 F9
Perak [Riv] • Malaysia 129 F9
Pérama • Corfu, Greece .... 94 A
Pérama • Crete, Greece 93 H5
Percé • QU, Canada 160 B1
Perdido, Monte Heritage N •
   France/Spain .... 41 [62]
Perdido, Monte Heritage C •
   France/Spain .... 44 [94]
Perdu, Mont Heritage N •
   France/Spain .... 41 [62]
Perdu, Mont Heritage C •
   France/Spain .... 44 [94]
Pereira • Colombia 173 B2
Pereiro • Portugal 84 K7
Perejil, I. del • Spain 82 D4
Perétola [Apt] • Italy 87 C3
Pereyaslav • Ukraine 50 E2
Pérèybère Beach • Mauritius 113 F5
Pergamino • Argentina 175 F6
Pergamum • Turkey 95 E4
Perge • Turkey 95 G7
Périgord Blanc • France 78 F5
Périgord Noir • France 78 F5
Périgord Vert • France 78 F5
Périgueux • France 78 F5
Périm • Yemen 109 E11
Perinet-Mantadia, Réserve de Park •
   Madagascar .... 112 [148]
Perisher Blue • NS, Australia 136 H9
Périssa • Thíra, Greece .... 94 G
Peristéra • Greece 94 BB2
Peristério • Greece 93 C2
Perpar Wildlife Sanctuary • India 124 B3
Perks Pleasure Park Park L • Ireland .. 59 [20]
Perl • Germany 74 A2
Perlak, Kuala • Malaysia 129 F9
Perlas, Laguna de • Nicaragua 170 F4
Perleberg • Germany 72 D2
Perm' • Russian Fed. 100 I2
Pernambuco • Brazil 174 C3
Pernambuco [Adm] • Brazil 174 C3
Pernem • Goa, India 123 C5
Pernik • Bulgaria 92 C3
Perník • Finland 99 D4
Pernis • Netherlands 70 G8
Perote, Cofre de • Mexico 169 K7
Perpignan • France 78 L10
Perranporth • United Kingdom 65 I10
Perros-Guirec • France 77 C3
Perry • FL, United States 155 C1
Perry's Victory & Int. Peace Mem. •
   OH, United States 161 A3
Perry's Victory & Int. Peace Mem. Park N •
   OH, United States .... 153 [183]
Persepolis Heritage C • Iran .... 43 [130]
Perstorp • Sweden 99 G7
Perth • United Kingdom 65 B1
Perth • WA, Australia 135 B6
Perthshire • United Kingdom 65 A1
Pertuis • France 78 G7
Pertusato, Capo •
   Corsica, France 78 N12
PERU • S. America 173 B3
Peru, Altiplano del • Peru 173 F6
Peru-Chile Trench • Pacific Ocean .. 8 F7
Perúgia • Italy 87 D3
Perumal Par I. • India 124 A3
Pervomays'k • Ukraine 100 D4
Pésaro • Italy 87 D3
Pescadores • Taiwan 126 D2
Pescara • Italy 85 E3
Peshawar • Pakistan 122 B2
Peshkopi • Albania 92 C3
Pesnica • Slovenia 91 G2
Pessac-Léognan • France 76 K9
Pessada • Cephalonia, Greece .... 94 J
Pessel • Haiti 165 F6
Pestovo • Russian Fed. 100 M9
Petäjävesi • Finland 99 D3
Petäjävesi Heritage C • Finland .... 43 [91]
Petaling Jaya • Malaysia 129 G10
Petaloúdes • Páros, Greece .... 94 H
Petaloúdes • Rhodes, Greece .... 94 F
Petaluma • CA, United States 154 I8
Petare • Venezuela 173 C1
Petatlán • Mexico 169 I8
Petén • Guatemala 170 K9
Peter I. • British Virgin Is. .... 166 A
Peterborough • NH, United States .. 156 D1
Peterborough • OT, Canada 160 E4
Peterborough • United Kingdom 65 F7
Peterhead • United Kingdom 62 E3
Petermann Aboriginal Land •
   NT, Australia 136 A2
Petermann Ranges •
   NT/WA, Australia 136 A2
Petersburg • VA, United States 156 A4
Petersburg Nat. Battlefield •
   VA, United States 156 A4
Petersburg Nat. Battlefield Park N •
   VA, United States .... 153 [245]
Petersfield • United Kingdom 63 E9
Petersville • AK, United States 157 E3
Pétionville • Haiti 165 F6
Petit Canouan • St Vincent & Gren. .. 167 P
Petit Goâve • Haiti 165 F6
Petit Jean, I. • St Barthélemy .... 166 F
Petit Nevis • St Vincent & Gren. .... 167 P
Petit Piton • St Lucia .... 167 J
Petit St Bernard, Col du •
   France/Italy 78 D3
Petit St Vincent ('PSV') •
   St Vincent & Gren. .... 167 P
Petit-Loango, Réserve de faune du Park •
   Gabon .... 112 [45]
Petite Ile • Réunion 113 D4
Petite Martinique • Grenada .... 167 P
Petite Rivière de l'Artibonite •
   Haiti 165 F5
Petite Rivière Noire, Piton de la •
   Mauritius 113 E6
Petite Terre, Is. de la •
   Guadeloupe .... 167 J
Petkeljärvi Nat. Park Park N •
   Finland .... 58 [35]

Peto • Mexico 169 F4
Petoskey • MI, United States 161 B2
Petra • Jordan 120 D7
Petra Heritage C • Jordan .... 44 [312]
Petra • Lesbos, Greece .... 94 C
Petre, Point • OT, Canada 160 F5
Petreto-Bicchisano •
   Corsica, France 78 M12
Petrified Forest Nat. Park •
   AZ, United States 155 H7
Petrified Forest Nat. Park Park N •
   AZ, United States .... 152 [107]
Petrolyph Nat. Mon. Park N •
   NM, United States .... 152 [125]
Petrolina • Brazil 174 B3
Petropavl • Kazakstan 121 E1
Petropavlovsk-Kamchatskiy •
   Russian Fed. 101 P4
Petrópolis • Brazil 174 F7
Petrovac • Romania 92 C2
Petrovsk • Russian Fed. 100 G3
Petrozavodsk • Russian Fed. 100 D1
Petworth House • United Kingdom .. 65 G8
Peuetsagoe, Gunung • Indonesia .. 131 M9
Pevek • Russian Fed. 101 R3
Peyia Basilica • Cyprus 96 C4
Pfälzer Wald • Germany 74 B2
Pfalzgrafenstein • Germany 74 D6
Pfarrkirchen • Germany 74 H7
Pfeiffer Big Sur State Park •
   CA, United States 154 I8
Pforzheim • Germany 74 B5
Pfronten • Germany 74 F8
Pfullendorf • Germany 74 E7
Phaestos • Crete, Greece 93 H6
Phai Hong Wua, Wat • Thailand .. 130 D7
Phalodi • India 122 B3
Phan Rang • Vietnam 130 C5
Phan Thiet • Vietnam 129 C5
Phanat Nikhom • Thailand 130 E8
Phang Nga Bay • Thailand 130 F9
Phangan, Ko • Thailand 130 A3
Phangnga • Thailand 128 B5
Pharaoh • France 130 A2
Phatthalung • Thailand 130 B5
Phattasalamd Park L • Germany .. 59 [54]
Phaulkon's Residence • Thailand 74 A1
Phayao • Thailand 130 D5
Phelan • CA, United States 155 G8
Phenix City • AL, United States 151 C4
Phet Buri • Thailand 130 D8
Phi Phi, Ko • Thailand 130 F10
Philadelphia • Jordan 120 B2
Philadelphia • MS, United States 156 F5
Philadelphia • PA, United States 156 B3
Philadelphia Heritage C •
   PA, United States .... 42 [11]
Philae • Egypt 109 B2
Philip S.W. Goldson [Apt] • Belize .. 170 K8
Philippine Sea • Pacific Ocean 138 A3
PHILIPPINES • Asia 128 G4
Philippopolis • Bulgaria 50 E3
Philipsburg • St Maarten .... 166 C
Philistia • Israel 120 A4
Phillip I. • VI, Australia 136 G9
Phimai • Thailand 130 A2
Phitsanulok • Thailand 130 C6
Phitshane • Botswana 110 J10
Phlu, Khao • Ko Samui, Thailand .. 130 G12
Phnom Penh • Cambodia 129 B5
Phoenicia • Israel/Lebanon 120 A1
Phoenicia • NY, United States 156 C2
Phoenix • AZ, United States 155 G8
Phoenix Is. • Kiribati 138 CC3
Phoenix Park • Ireland 69 F6
Phoi, Ko • Thailand 130 E9
Phongsali • Laos 128 C2
Phra Buddha Sothorp • Thailand .. 130 E7
Phra Pathom Chedi • Thailand 130 D7
Phra Phutthabat • Thailand 130 D7
Phra Sriratana Mahathat, Wat •
   Thailand 130 D6
Phra Thong, Ko • Thailand 130 A4
Phrae • Thailand 130 D5
Phu, Khao •
   Ko Phuket, Thailand 130 F9
Phu Hin Rongkla Nat. Park • Thailand .. 130 C6
Phu Luang Nat. Park • Thailand 130 C6
Phu Quoc • Vietnam 129 A3
Phu Rua Nat. Park • Thailand 130 C6
Phuket, Ko • Thailand 130 F9
Piacenza • Italy 87 B2
Piamafua Mtn • American Samoa .. 139 M
Piana • Corsica, France 78 M11
Piana Calanches Heritage N •
   Corsica, France .... 41 [61]
Piancavallo • Italy 91 G2
Pianosa, I. • Italy 85 C3
Piarco [Apt] • Trinidad & Tobago .. 166 S
Piau-Engaly • France 78 J9
Piauí • Brazil 174 B3
Piave • Italy 87 C1
Piazza Armerina • Sicily, Italy 86 H8
Picardy • France 77 B1
Picayune • MS, United States 151 C4
Picentini, Monti • Italy 87 H7
Pichanal • Argentina 175 B2
Pichilemu • Chile 175 A3
Pichilingue • Mexico 168 I6
Pickens, Fort •
   FL, United States 155 A1
Pickle Lake • OT, Canada 159 G3
Pico • Azores 84 B4
Pico de Neblina, Parque Nac. do •
   Brazil 173 C2
Pico dei Tre Signori • Austria/Italy .. 86 B1
Picos • Brazil 174 B3
Picton • New Zealand 137 B3
Picton • OT, Canada 160 F5
Picton, Mt • TS, Australia 136 H9
Pictured Rocks Nat. Lakeshore •
   MI, United States 161 B1
Pictured Rocks Nat. Lakeshore Park N •
   MI, United States .... 153 [158]
Piduratalagala • Sri Lanka 124 C4
Pie de la Cuesta • Mexico 169 J8
Piedade, Ponta da • Portugal 84 I8
Piedmont • Italy 86 A1
Piedmont Matese • Italy 87 F6
Piedra, I. • Mexico 169 E4
Piedras Negras • Coahuila, Mexico .. 168 J7
Piedras Negras • Guatemala 170 J9
Piedras Punta • Argentina 175 F7
Piekary Slaskie • Poland 89 F9
Pielavesi • Finland 97 F3
Pielinen • Finland 97 F3
Pielisjärvi Nat. Park Park N •
   Sweden .... 58 [21]
Piemonte • Italy 86 A1
Pieninski Nat. Park Park N • Poland .58 [106]
Pieninski Nat. Park • Poland 89 G9
Pieniński Nat. Park Park N •
   Slovak Rep. .... 58 [112]
Pienza • Italy 87 C3
Pienza Heritage C • Italy .... 44 [163]
Pierce Reservoirs • Singapore 129 H11
Pierre • SD, United States 148 F2
Pierrefonds • France 78 B1
Pierreville • Trinidad & Tobago .... 166 S
Pieskowa Skala • Poland 89 G8
Piest'any • Slovak Rep. 89 B4
Piet Retief • South Africa 111 B3
Pietarsaari • Finland 97 F3
Pietermaritzburg • South Africa 111 B4
Pietersaari • Finland 97 F3
Pietersburg • South Africa 110 B3
Pietra Ligure • Italy 87 A3

Pietrasanta • Italy 87 B3
Pieve di Cadore • Italy 86 D4
Pigeon I. Nat. Park • St Lucia .... 167 N
Pigeon Point Beach •
   Trinidad & Tobago .... 166 R
Pigi • Crete, Greece 93 H5
Pigs, Bay of • Cuba 164 F4
Piha Passage • Tonga .... 139 P
Piilanihale Heiau Temple •
   HI, United States 157 J5
Piketberg • South Africa 111 D6
Pila • Italy 87 A1
Pila • Poland 89 B2
Pilanesberg Nat. Park Park •
   South Africa .... 112 [133]
Pilar de la Horadada • Spain 83 A2
Pilbara • WA, Australia 135 B4
Pilcomayo • Argentina/Paraguay .. 175 C3
Pili • Cos, Greece .... 94 E
Pilibhit • India 123 F7
Pillories, The •
   St Vincent & Gren. .... 167 P
Pillsbury Sound • US Virgin Is. .... 166 X
Pilón • Cuba 164 G5
Pílos • Greece 93 B3
Pittstown • VA, United States 156 F6
Pilsrundale • Latvia 100 J7
Pimenta Bueno • Brazil 173 C4
Pinamar • Argentina 175 G7
Pinar del Rio • Cuba 164 E4
Pinarbasi • Turkey 95 J9
Pinarello • Corsica, France 95 E3
Pinarhisar • Turkey 128 G3
Pinatubo, Mt • Philippines .... 58 [139]
Pindos Nat. Park Park N • Greece .. 93 B2
Pindos Oros • Greece 151 B4
Pine Bluff • AR, United States 157 B1
Pine Castle • FL, United States 164 C3
Pine Cay • Turks & Caicos Is. 158 D3
Pine Falls • MN, Canada 157 B1
Pine Hills • FL, United States 155 C3
Pine I. • FL, United States 155 C3
Pine Ridge • SD, United States 148 F2
Pine Ridge Ind Res •
   SD, United States .... 155 [48]
Pinega • Russian Fed. 100 D1
Pinehurst • NC, United States 155 H1
Pinel, Ilet • St Martin .... 166 C
Pinerolo • Italy 86 A1
Pineta • Sardinia, Italy 86 F6
Pineville • LA, United States 151 B4
Ping • Thailand 130 B6
Ping Chau • Hong Kong, China .. 126 F4
Pingdingshan • China 125 F3
Pinghu • China 126 H7
Pingxiang • China 125 C4
Pingyao Heritage C • China .... 43 [177]
Pini • Indonesia 131 N10
Piniós • Greece 93 B2
Pink Beach • Bonaire .... 166 U
Pink Mtn • BC, Canada 158 C3
Pinnacles Nat. Mon. Park N •
   CA, United States .... 152 [47]
Pinney's Beach • St Kitts & Nevis .. 167 F
Pino • Corsica, France 78 N11
Pinos, I. de • Cuba 164 E4
Pinotepa Nacional • Mexico 169 J8
Pins, Anse aux • Seychelles 113 A1
Pins, I. des • New Caledonia .... 138 U
Pins, Point aux • OT, Canada 161 A3
Pinsk • Belarus 100 C3
Pinta, I. • Galápagos Is. 171 G10
Pinto • Argentina 175 B2
Pintu Gedong • Malaysia 129 F10
Pinzón, I. • Galápagos Is. 171 G10
Piombino • Italy 87 C3
Pioneer Territory •
   NV, United States 154 J8
Piopio • New Zealand 137 D6
Piotrków Trybunalski • Poland 89 B3
Pipalyatjara • SA, Australia 136 A2
Pipamuanan, Réservoir •
   QU, Canada 160 A1
Pipe Spring Nat. Mon. •
   AZ, United States 155 G7
Pipe Spring Nat. Mon. Park N •
   AZ, United States .... 152 [97]
Pipestone Nat. Mon. Park N •
   MN, United States .... 153 [152]
Pipiriki • New Zealand 137 D6
Piqua • OH, United States 150 D2
Piran • Slovenia 92 F5
Pireás • Greece 93 C3
Piraeus • Greece 93 C3
Pirgaki • Náxos, Greece .... 94 H
Pirgi • Chios, Greece .... 94 D
Pirgi • Corfu, Greece .... 94 A
Pirgi Thermis • Lesbos, Greece .... 94 C
Pirgos • Crete, Greece 93 I6
Pirgos • Peloponnese, Greece 93 B3
Pirgos • Tínos, Greece .... 94 I
Piriac-sur-Mer • France 77 D4
Piráópolis • Uruguay 175 G6
Pirin Nat. Park Park N • Bulgaria .. 58 [136]
Pirin Nat. Park Heritage N •
   Bulgaria .... 41 [77]
Pirmasens • Germany 74 A3
Pirongia, Mt • New Zealand 137 D5
Pirot • Serbia & Montenegro 92 C3
Pisa • Italy 87 B3
Pisa Heritage C • Italy .... 44 [161]
Pisa Range • New Zealand 137 G7
Pisac • Peru 173 F6
Pisagua • Fed. States of Micronesia .. 138 C
Pisar • Fed. States of Micronesia .. 138 C
Piscataway Park •
   MD, United States 156 A3
Piscataway Park Park N •
   MD, United States .... 153 [260]
Pisco • Peru 173 E6
Písek • Czech Rep. 89 E7
Pisidia • Turkey 95 H7
Piso Livadi • Páros, Greece .... 94 H
Pissouri • Cyprus 96 C4
Pisté • Mexico 169 F4
Pistóia • Italy 87 C3
Pisz • Poland 89 C2
Pita, I. • CA, United States 154 I7
Pitcairn I. • Pitcairn Is. .... 139 L
PITCAIRN IS. • Pacific Ocean 139 EE4
Pitch Lake • Trinidad & Tobago .... 166 S
Piti • Guam .... 138 Z
Pitești • Romania 92 F7
Pithágorio • Sámos, Greece .... 94 E
Piti • Guam .... 138 Z
Pitkas Point • AK, United States 157 D3
Pitlochry • United Kingdom 65 A1
Pitr I. • India 124 A3
Pitsburg • KS, United States 151 B3
Pittsfield • MA, United States 156 D1
Piura • Peru 173 A3
Pla I. • India 124 A3
Placentia • Belize 170 K9
Placentia Bay • NF, Canada 160 F2
Placeres • Cuba 164 F4
Plage de la Corniche • Tunisia 107 D4
Plage des Nations • Morocco 107 A1
Plagne, la Ski • France .... 61 [27]
Plagne, la • France 78 D3
Plagne Montalbert Ski • France .... 61 [27]
Plaine, Bras de la • Réunion 113 C4
Plaine Champagne • Mauritius 113 E6
Plaine des Palmistes, la • Réunion .. 113 D4
Plaine du Nord • Haiti 165 F5
Plaine-Verte Ski • France .... 61 [27]
Plaisance • Haiti 165 F5
Plakiás • Crete, Greece 93 H5
Plana Cays • Bahamas 164 B2
Planachaux • Switzerland 90 I6
Planícies • Portugal 84 A3
Plano • TX, United States 155 E4
Plános • Zante, Greece .... 94 J

Platanés • Crete, Greece 93 H5
Plátani • Sicily, Italy 86 G8
Platanias • Crete, Greece 93 G5
Plátanos • Crete, Greece 93 G5
Plátanos • Lesbos, Greece .... 94 I
Plate, River • Argentina/Uruguay .. 175 G6
Platí Giali • Mikonos, Greece .... 94 I
Platja d'Aro • Spain 83 D3
Platja d'En Bossa • Ibiza, Spain .. 83 L10
Platja de Muro • Majorca, Spain .. 83 O11
Platja dels Dols • Majorca, Spain .. 83 O12
Platja Talamanca • Ibiza, Spain .. 83 M9
Platres • Cyprus 96 C4
Platte • NE, United States 148 G2
Plattsburgh • NY, United States 150 F2
Plauen • Germany 72 E3
Plauer See • Germany 72 E2
Plavsk • Russian Fed. 100 E3
Play Cu • Vietnam 128 D4
Playa Ancón • Cuba 164 F4
Playa Azul • Mexico 169 I8
Playa Blanca •
   Lanzarote, Canary Is. 83 I5
Playa de Fajardo • Puerto Rico 165 J7
Playa de Guayanés • Puerto Rico .. 165 J8
Playa de Guyanilla • Puerto Rico .. 165 I8
Playa de la Arena •
   Tenerife, Canary Is. 82 G5
Playa de la Balita •
   Gran Canaria, Canary Is. .. 82 G6
Playa de las Americas •
   Tenerife, Canary Is. 82 G5
Playa del Carmen • Mexico 169 G4
Playa del Inglés •
   Gran Canaria, Canary Is. .. 82 G6
Playa de Curo •
   Gran Canaria, Canary Is. .. 82 G6
Playa Dorada • Dominican Rep. .. 165 G5
Playa Grande • Dominican Rep. .. 164 F4
Playa Guacuco • Margarita .... 166 T
Playa Larga • Cuba 164 F4
Playa Paraíso •
   Tenerife, Canary Is. 82 G5
Pleasure I. • FL, United States 157 B1
Pleasurewood Hills Park L •
   United Kingdom .... 59 [31]
Plechy • Czech Rep. 89 D7
Pleiney, le Ski • France .... 61 [39]
Plenty • NT, Australia 136 B1
Plenty, Bay of • New Zealand 137 C2
Plérin • France 77 D3
Plesetsk • Russian Fed. 100 F1
Pleso [Apt] • Croatia 92 F5
Plessis-Bourré, le [Château] •
   France 77 E5
Plettenberg Bay • South Africa 111 F7
Pleurtuit [Apt] • France 77 D3
Pleven • Bulgaria 92 D3
Plimoth Plantation •
   MA, United States 156 D1
Pliska • Bulgaria 92 H8
Plitvice • Croatia 92 F5
Plitvice Lakes Nat. Park Park N •
   Croatia .... 58 [119]
Plitvice Lakes Nat. Park • Croatia .. 92 F5
Plitvice Lakes Nat. Park Heritage N •
   Croatia .... 41 [72]
Pljevlja • Serbia & Montenegro 92 B3
Ploce • Croatia 92 A2
Plock • Poland 89 B2
Ploërmel • France 77 D4
Ploiesti • Romania 92 H7
Plomári • Lesbos, Greece .... 94 C
Plonsk • Poland 89 C2
Plopsaland Park L • Belgium .... 59 [41]
Plopsaland • Belgium 70 E6
Plouay • France 77 D4
Plötzin • Germany 73 E8
Plouha • France 77 D3
Ploumanac'h • France 77 C3
Plovdiv • Bulgaria 92 D3
Plover Cove Country Park •
   Hong Kong, China 126 F4
Plover Cove Reservoir •
   Hong Kong, China 126 F4
Plummer • ID, United States 148 C1
Plunge • Lithuania 100 J7
Plymouth • IN, United States 150 C2
Plymouth • MA, United States 156 D1
Plymouth • Montserrat .... 166 E
Plymouth • Trinidad & Tobago .... 166 R
Plymouth • United Kingdom 65 J10
Plynlimon • United Kingdom 63 D8
Pizen • Czech Rep. 89 D6
Pmere Nyente Aboriginal Land •
   NT, Australia 136 B2
Po • Italy 86 A1
Po Basin • Italy 87 A2
Po, Colline del • Italy 87 A2
Po, Foci del • Italy 87 D2
Po Lin Monastery •
   Hong Kong, China 126 E5
Po Toi • Hong Kong, China 126 F5
Pobeda, Gora • Russian Fed. 101 O3
Pobedy, Pik • China/Kyrgyzstan .. 121 G3
Poblet Heritage C • Spain .... 44 [98]
Poblet, Reial Monestir de • Spain .. 83 C4
Pocahontas • AR, United States 151 B3
Pocatello • ID, United States 148 D2
Pochentong [Apt] • Cambodia 129 B5
Pocking • Germany 91 F1
Poço das Antas, Reserva Biológica •
   Brazil 174 F7
Pocono Mtns • PA, United States .. 156 B2
Poços de Caldas • Brazil 174 E7
Podebrady • Czech Rep. 89 E6
Podgorica • Serbia & Montenegro .. 92 B3
Podhale • Poland 89 G9
Podkamennaya Tunguska •
   Russian Fed. 101 J3
Podol'sk • Russian Fed. 100 M10
Podravina • Croatia 92 G5
Podujevo • Serbia & Montenegro .. 92 C3
Pogradec • Albania 92 C3
Pohjois-Karjala • Finland 98 C2
Pohnpei • Fed. States of Micronesia .. 138 D
Poi • Wallis & Futuna .... 139 Q
Poike • Easter I. .... 139 M
Poindimié • New Caledonia .... 138 U
Poinsett, Cape • Antarctica 176 S4
Point au Fer I. •
   LA, United States 155 B1
Point Fortin • Trinidad & Tobago .. 166 S
Point Lisas • Trinidad & Tobago .. 166 S
Point Pelee Nat. Park Park N •
   OT, Canada .... 161 [28]
Point Pelee Nat. Park • OT, Canada .. 161 A3
Point Pleasant • NJ, United States .. 156 C2
Point Reyes Nat. Seashore Park N •
   CA, United States .... 152 [42]
Point Salines [Apt] • Grenada .... 166 O
Pointe au Sel • Seychelles 113 B1
Pointe aux Piments Beach • Mauritius .113 C5
Pointe d'Esny Beach • Mauritius .. 113 F6
Pointe du Bout • Martinique .... 167 I
Pointe-Noire • Guadeloupe .... 167 J
Pointe-Noire • Congo 106 D5
Pointe-Taillon, Parc de la •
   QU, Canada 160 A1
Poitevin, Marais • France 77 E6
Poitiers • France 77 F6
Poitou • France 77 A2
Poitou-Charentes • France 77 A2
Poivre • Seychelles 113 B1
Pok Fu Lam Country Park •
   Hong Kong, China 126 E5
Pokaran • India 123 D7
Pokhara • Nepal 123 C3
Pol-e-Khomri • Afghanistan 121 E4
Pola de Siero • Spain 80 C2
POLAND • Europe 89 B2

Poland • Kiribati ... 139 I
Polati • Turkey ... 95 B2
Polatsk • Belarus ... 100 C2
Pole • México ... 169 G4
Polem Beach • Goa, India ... 123 C6
Polesine • Italy ... 87 C2
Police, Pointe • Seychelles ... 113 A2
Policoro • Italy ... 85 B2
Poliégos • Greece ... 94 CC3
Polígiros • Greece ... 94 B
Polihnitos • Lesbos, Greece ... 94 C
Polírnila • Crete, Greece ... 93 G5
Polis • Cyprus ... 96 C4
Polk, Fort • LA, United States ... 156 E6
Pollachi • India ... 124 B3
Pollença • Majorca, Spain ... 83 O11
Polo, Marco [Apt] • Italy ... 87 D2
Polokwane • South Africa ... 110 B3
Polonia [Apt] • Indonesia ... 131 N9
Polonnaruwa • Sri Lanka ... 124 C4
Polonnaruwa Heritage C • Sri Lanka ... 43 [167]
Polson • MT, United States ... 154 H5
Poltava • Ukraine ... 100 D4
Polva • Estonia ... 100 K6
Polyhnron • Greece ... 94 B
Polzeath Beach • United Kingdom ... 64 [46]
Pomarkku • Finland ... 99 C3
Pombal • Brazil ... 174 C3
Pomerania • Germany/Poland ... 89 A2
Pomeranian Bay • Germany/Poland ... 72 F1
Pomerol • France ... 76 K9
Pomorie • Bulgaria ... 92 H8
Pompadour, Château de • France ... 78 F5
Pompano Beach • FL, United States ... 155 D3
Pompei • Italy ... 87 G7
Pompeii Heritage C • Italy ... 44 [169]
Pomposa Abbazia • Italy ... 87 D2
Ponca City • OK, United States ... 149 G3
Ponce • Puerto Rico ... 165 I8
Poncha Springs • CO, United States ... 148 E3
Pond Inlet • NU, Canada ... 159 I1
Ponda • Goa, India ... 123 C5
Pondicherry • India ... 124 C2
Pondicherry Beach • India ... 124 E6
Ponferrada • Spain ... 80 B2
Pongola • South Africa ... 111 C3
Pongola Bush Nature Reserve • South Africa ... 111 B3
Pongola [Riv] • South Africa ... 111 C3
Pongolapoort Dam • South Africa ... 111 C3
Pongolapoort Nature Reserve • South Africa ... 111 C3
Ponmudi • India ... 124 B3
Ponmudi Hill Sta • India ... 124 E6
Pont-Aven • France ... 77 C4
Pont-l'Abbé • France ... 77 C4
Ponta Delgada • Azores ... 84 B4
Ponta do Sol • Madeira ... 84 C3
Ponta Grossa • Brazil ... 175 C2
Pontal • Portugal ... 84 H8
Pontarlier • France ... 76 G3
Pontarlier • France ... 90 I5
Pontchartrain, Lake • LA, United States ... 156 F6
Ponte di Legno • Italy ... 87 C1
Ponte Leccia • Corsica, France ... 78 N11
Ponte Nova • Brazil ... 174 F6
Pontecagnano • Italy ... 87 H7
Pontevedre • Spain ... 80 A2
Pontiac • IL, United States ... 150 C2
Pontiac • MI, United States ... 161 A3
Pontianak • Indonesia ... 131 C4
Pontivy • France ... 77 D4
Pontrémoli • Italy ... 87 B2
Pontresina Ski • Switzerland ... 61 [85]
Pontresina • Switzerland ... 90 L6
Pony Express Territory • NV, United States ... 154 J7
Ponziane, Is. • Italy ... 85 D4
Poole • United Kingdom ... 65 K9
Poole Beach • United Kingdom ... 64 [34]
Poole Bay • United Kingdom ... 65 K10
Poopó Lago • Bolivia ... 173 C4
Popayan • Colombia ... 173 B2
Popeye • Belgium ... 70 A4
Popeye Village • Malta ... 96 A1
Poplar Bluff • MO, United States ... 151 B3
Popocatépetl • Mexico ... 169 J7
Popocatépetl Heritage C • Mexico ... 42 [23]
Pópoli • Italy ... 87 F4
Popomanasay, Mt • Solomon Is. ... 138 W
Popovo • Bulgaria ... 92 H8
Poprad • Slovak Rep. ... 89 C3
Poptún • Guatemala ... 170 K9
Porangatu • Brazil ... 174 B4
Porbandar Beach • India ... 124 E6
Porbandar • India ... 122 A3
Porcupine • Canada/United States ... 157 E2
Pordenone • Italy ... 86 D4
Porec Heritage C • Croatia ... 44 [208]
Poretta [Apt] • Corsica, France ... 78 N11
Pori • Finland ... 99 C3
Porirua • New Zealand ... 137 B3
Porkkala • Finland ... 99 D4
Porlamar • Margarita ... 166 T
Porlock • United Kingdom ... 65 J9
Pornichet • France ... 77 D4
Póros • Cephalonia, Greece ... 94 J
Póros • Peloponnese, Greece ... 93 C3
Porpoise Bay • Antarctica ... 176 T4
Porpoise Bay • New Zealand ... 137 G8
Porquerolles, I. de • France ... 78 J8
Porsangen • Norway ... 97 F1
Porsgrunn • Norway ... 98 D6
Port a Piment • Haiti ... 165 E6
Port Alberni • BC, Canada ... 158 H7
Port Angeles • WA, United States ... 154 G5
Port Antonio • Jamaica ... 165 D3
Port Aransas • TX, United States ... 155 E6
Port Arthur • TS, Australia ... 136 F7
Port Arthur • TX, United States ... 155 F5
Port Askaig • United Kingdom ... 66 A2
Port aux Choix • NF, Canada ... 160 D1
Port au Prince • Haiti ... 165 F6
Port Augusta • SA, Australia ... 135 F6
Port Barcarès • France ... 78 L10
Port Blair • India ... 122 D4
Port Campbell Nat. Park • VI, Australia ... 136 G9
Port Canaveral • FL, United States ... 155 D2
Port Charlotte • FL, United States ... 155 C2
Port Chicago Naval Magazine Nat. Mem. Park N • CA, United States ... 152 [45]
Port Clinton • OH, United States ... 161 A3
Port Colborne • OT, Canada ... 161 D1
Port Cros, I. de • France ... 78 J8
Port Cros, Parc nat. de Park N • France ... 58 [75]
Port Cros, Parc nat. de • France ... 78 G8
Port d'Addaia • Minorca, Spain ... 83 K7
Port d'es Torrent • Ibiza, Spain ... 83 L9
Port Daniel, Réserve faunique de • QU, Canada ... 160 B1
Port de Alcúdia • Majorca, Spain ... 83 O11
Port de Andratx • Majorca, Spain ... 83 N12
Port de Paix • Haiti ... 165 F5
Port de Pollença • Majorca, Spain ... 83 O11
Port de Prince, Baie de • Haiti ... 165 F6
Port de Sóller • Majorca, Spain ... 83 N11
Port de St Miquel • Ibiza, Spain ... 83 M9
Port Dickson • Malaysia ... 129 G10
Port Edward • South Africa ... 111 B5
Port el Kantaoui • Tunisia ... 107 D4
Port Elgin • OT, Canada ... 161 C2
Port Elizabeth • South Africa ... 111 G7
Port Elizabeth • St Vincent & Gren. ... 167 P
Port Ellen • United Kingdom ... 62 B5
Port Eynon Beach • United Kingdom ... 64 [49]
Port Gentil • Gabon ... 106 C5
Port Gibson • MS, United States ... 156 F5
Port Grimaud • France ... 78 H8
Port Harcourt • Nigeria ... 106 C4
Port Hardy • BC, Canada ... 160 I7

Port Harrison • QU, Canada ... 159 I3
Port Hawkesbury • NS, Canada ... 160 B2
Port Hedland • WA, Australia ... 135 B4
Port Hope • KT, Canada ... 160 B2
Port Hope Simpson • NF, Canada ... 159 K3
Port Huron • MI, United States ... 161 A2
Port I. • Hong Kong, China ... 126 F4
Port Jackson • NS, Australia ... 136 H8
Port Jervis • NY, United States ... 156 B2
Port Kelang • Malaysia ... 129 F10
Port Kembla • NS, Australia ... 136 H8
Port Lairge • Ireland ... 69 C4
Port Lavaca • TX, United States ... 155 E6
Port, le • Réunion ... 113 C3
Port Leucate • France ... 78 L10
Port Lincoln • SA, Australia ... 135 F6
Port Louis • Guadeloupe ... 167 J
Port Louis • Mauritius ... 113 E5
Port Lympne Wildlife Park • United Kingdom ... 65 H8
Port Macquarie • NS, Australia ... 135 I6
Port Maria • Jamaica ... 165 D3
Port Menier • QU, Canada ... 160 B1
Port Morant • Jamaica ... 165 D4
Port Moresby • Papua New Guinea ... 138 BB3
Port O'Connor • TX, United States ... 155 E6
Port of Spain • Trinidad & Tobago ... 166 S
Port Phillip Bay • VI, Australia ... 136 G9
Port Pirie • SA, Australia ... 135 F6
Port Radium • NT, Canada ... 158 E2
Port Royal • Jamaica ... 165 D4
Port Royal des Champs, Abbaye de • France ... 78 A2
Port Safaga • Egypt ... 109 E8
Port Said • Egypt ... 109 B1
Port Salut • Haiti ... 165 E6
Port Sanilac • MI, United States ... 161 C3
Port Saunders • NF, Canada ... 160 D1
Port Shelter • Hong Kong, China ... 126 F5
Port Shepstone • South Africa ... 111 B5
Port St Lucie City • FL, United States ... 155 D2
Port Sudan • Sudan ... 108 C3
Port Talbot • United Kingdom ... 63 D9
Port Vila • Vanuatu ... 138 V
Port Washington • WI, United States ... 161 B3
Porta, la • Corsica, France ... 78 N11
Portadown • United Kingdom ... 63 B6
Portage • WI, United States ... 150 C2
Portage la Prairie • MN, Canada ... 158 G3
Portalegre • Portugal ... 80 B4
Portalegre [Adm] • Portugal ... 84 A2
Portales • NM, United States ... 149 F4
Portals Nous • Majorca, Spain ... 83 N12
Portals Vells • Majorca, Spain ... 83 N12
Portarlington • Ireland ... 69 E7
Portavadie • United Kingdom ... 66 A2
Portbou • Spain ... 83 D3
Porté Puymorens • France ... 78 K10
Portela • Madeira ... 84 E5
Porterville • CA, United States ... 154 I8
Portes du Soleil Ski • France ... 61 [9-11]
Portes du Soleil • France ... 78 G8
Portes du Soleil • Switzerland ... 61 [54-55]
Porthcawl • United Kingdom ... 65 J9
Porthmadog • United Kingdom ... 63 C8
Porticcio • Corsica, France ... 78 M12
Portici • Italy ... 87 G7
Portigliolo • Corsica, France ... 78 M12
Portimão • Portugal ... 84 I8
Portinho da Arrábida • Portugal ... 84 G6
Portinatx • Ibiza, Spain ... 83 M9
Portland • ME, United States ... 150 F2
Portland • OR, United States ... 154 G6
Portland • VI, Australia ... 136 G9
Portland Bight • Jamaica ... 165 D4
Portland Bill • United Kingdom ... 65 K10
Portland, I. of • United Kingdom ... 65 K10
Portland Point • Jamaica ... 165 D4
Portlaoise • Ireland ... 69 C3
Portmarnock • Ireland ... 69 D3
Portmore • Jamaica ... 165 D4
Porto • Corsica, France ... 78 M11
Porto • Portugal ... 80 A3
Porto Heritage C • Portugal ... 44 [127]
Porto [Adm] • Portugal ... 84 A1
Pôrto Alegre • Brazil ... 175 C2
Porto Azzurro • Italy ... 87 C3
Pôrto Carras • Greece ... 94 B
Pôrto Cervo • Sardinia, Italy ... 86 F5
Pôrto Colom • Majorca, Spain ... 83 O12
Pôrto Conte • Sardinia, Italy ... 86 E5
Pôrto Cristo • Majorca, Spain ... 83 O11
Porto da Cruz • Madeira ... 84 E5
Porto Empédocle • Sicily, Italy ... 86 G8
Pôrto Franco • Brazil ... 174 B3
Porto Garibaldi • Italy ... 87 D2
Porto, Golfe de • Corsica, France ... 78 M11
Porto, Golfe de Heritage N • Corsica, France ... 41 [61]
Pôrto Grande • Brazil ... 174 A2
Pôrto Katsiki • Levkas, Greece ... 94 J
Pôrto Koufós • Greece ... 94 B
Porto Moniz • Madeira ... 84 D5
Pôrto Novo • Benin ... 106 C4
Pôrto Petro • Majorca, Spain ... 83 O12
Pôrto Potenza Picena • Italy ... 87 D3
Pôrto Rafael • Sardinia, Italy ... 86 F5
Pôrto Recanati • Italy ... 87 D3
Pôrto Rotondo • Sardinia, Italy ... 86 F5
Pôrto Santo [I.] • Atlantic Ocean ... 84 E5
Pôrto Seguro • Brazil ... 174 C4
Porto Tolle • Italy ... 87 D2
Pôrto Tôrres • Sardinia, Italy ... 86 E5
Porto Vecchio • Corsica, France ... 78 N12
Pôrto Velho • Brazil ... 173 C3
Portobelo • Panama ... 170 M10
Portobelo Heritage C • Panama ... 42 [37]
Portobelo, Parque Nac. • Panama ... 170 M10
Portoferráio • Italy ... 87 B3
Portofino • Italy ... 87 B2
Portogruaro • Italy ... 87 D1
Portoroz • Slovenia ... 92 F5
Portoscuso • Sardinia, Italy ... 86 E6
Portovénere • Italy ... 87 B3
Portovénere Heritage C • Italy ... 44 [159]
Portoviejo • Ecuador ... 173 A3
Portree • United Kingdom ... 62 B3
Portrush Beach • United Kingdom ... 64 [73]
Portsea • United Kingdom ... 66 D6
Portsmouth • Dominica ... 167 K
Portsmouth • NH, United States ... 156 D1
Portsmouth • OH, United States ... 150 D3
Portsmouth • United Kingdom ... 63 E10
Portsmouth • VA, United States ... 156 B4
PORTUGAL • Europe ... 80
Portumna • Ireland ... 69 H9
Porvoo • Finland ... 99 D4
Posada • Sardinia, Italy ... 86 F5
Posavina • Croatia ... 92 G5
Poschiavo • Switzerland ... 90 L6
Positano • Italy ... 87 G7
Poso • Indonesia ... 131 F4
Possession, la • Réunion ... 113 C3
Poste de la Baleine • QU, Canada ... 159 I3
Poste Lafayette • Mauritius ... 113 F5
Postojna • Slovenia ... 92 F5
Postojna Cave • Slovenia ... 92 I6
Potamiás • Crete, Greece ... 93 I6
Potawatomi Ind Res • KS, United States ... 155 [54]
Potenza • Italy ... 85 B4
Poteriteri, Lake • New Zealand ... 137 F8
Potídaia • Greece ... 94 B
Potnarvon • Vanuatu ... 138 V
Potó • Peru ... 173 F6
Potomac • United States ... 156 A3
Potosina Cave • Slovenia ... 92 I6
Potosí • Bolivia ... 173 C4
Potosí Heritage C • Bolivia ... 42 [64]
Potsdam • Germany ... 73 E8

Potsdam Heritage C • Germany ... 44 [47]
Potsdam • NY, United States ... 150 F2
Pottsville • PA, United States ... 156 A2
Pottuvil • Sri Lanka ... 124 D4
Potwoots Dam • Antigua & Barbuda ... 167 I
Pouébo • New Caledonia ... 138 U
Poughkeepsie • NY, United States ... 156 C2
Pouilly-Fumé • France ... 76 L8
Poule et les Poussins, la • St Barthélemy ... 166 D
Pouso • New Caledonia ... 138 U
Poúncia • Páros, Greece ... 94 H
Pouso Alegre • Brazil ... 174 E7
Poverty Point Nat. Mon. • LA, United States ... 156 E5
Poverty Point Nat. Mon. Park N • LA, United States ... 153 [191]
Povoa de Varzim • Portugal ... 84 A1
Povoação • Azores ... 84 B4
Powder Mtn Ski • UT, United States ... 146 [45]
Powell, Lake • UT, United States ... 148 D3
Powell River • BC, Canada ... 160 I7
Powerscourt House • Ireland ... 69 F7
Poyang Hu • China ... 125 F4
Pöytyä • Finland ... 99 C4
Poza Rica • México ... 169 J7
Pozantı • Turkey ... 95 J9
Pozega • Serbia & Montenegro ... 92 C3
Poznan • Poland ... 89 B2
Pozza di Fassa • Italy ... 86 C4
Pozzallo • Sicily, Italy ... 86 H8
Pozzuoli • Italy ... 87 G7
Pra-Loup Ski • France ... 61 [50]
Pra-Loup • France ... 78 H7
Prachatice • Czech Rep. ... 89 D7
Prachin Buri • Thailand ... 130 E7
Prachuap Khiri Khan • Thailand ... 128 B4
Prado • France ... 78 L10
Præstø • Denmark ... 99 F8
Prague • Czech Rep. ... 89 E6
Prague Heritage C • Czech Rep. ... 44 [188]
Praha • Czech Rep. ... 89 E6
Praha Heritage C • Czech Rep. ... 44 [188]
Praia • Cape Verde ... 106 E7
Praia da Barra • Portugal ... 84 B1
Praia da Bengali • Portugal ... 84 I9
Praia da Falésia • Portugal ... 84 H8
Praia da Luz • Portugal ... 84 H8
Praia da Oura • Portugal ... 84 J8
Praia da Rocha • Portugal ... 84 J8
Praia das Maças • Portugal ... 84 J8
Praia de Balaia • Portugal ... 84 J8
Praia de Castelo • Portugal ... 84 J8
Praia de Galé • Portugal ... 84 J8
Praia do Guincho • Portugal ... 84 F6
Praia Grande • Portugal ... 84 F6
Praia Parede • Portugal ... 84 F6
Praia Verde • Portugal ... 84 K8
Prainha • Brazil ... 174 A3
Prainha • Madeira ... 84 E5
Pralognan • France ... 154 C1
Prambanan Heritage C • Indonesia ... 43 [209]
Prambanan • Java, Indonesia ... 131 Q12
Pranauron Ski • Italy ... 61 [144]
Prapat • Indonesia ... 131 N9
Prapoutel Ski • France ... 61 [39]
Praslin • Seychelles ... 113 B2
Praslin • St Lucia ... 167 N
Prassonisi, Akra • Rhodes, Greece ... 94 F
Prat Mataou • France ... 78 K10
Prata, Costa de • Portugal ... 84 A2
Pratas Is. • China ... 126 D2
Prato • Italy ... 87 C3
Prats-de-Mollo • France ... 78 L10
Prattville • AL, United States ... 151 C4
Prawl Point • United Kingdom ... 65 J10
Praz-sur-Arly Ski • France ... 61 [19]
Prazeres • Madeira ... 84 D5
Prêcheur, le • Martinique ... 167 L
Predazzo • Italy ... 86 C4
Pregolya • Russian Fed. ... 100 J8
Pregolya • Russian Fed. ... 100 J8
Prehistoire, Musée de • France ... 78 M11
Premuda • Croatia ... 92 F6
Prenn Falls • Vietnam ... 129 C5
Prenzlau • Germany ... 72 E2
Prenzlauer Berg (Berlin) • Germany ... 73 F7
Prerov • Czech Rep. ... 89 B4
Prerov nad Labem • Czech Rep. ... 89 E6
Prescott • AZ, United States ... 155 G1
Prescott • OT, Canada ... 160 G4
Preseli, Mynydd • United Kingdom ... 63 C9
Preservation Inlet • New Zealand ... 137 F8
Presidencia Roque Sáenz Peña • Argentina ... 175 B2
Presidente Eduardo Frei [Base] • Antarctica ... 176 [2]
Presidente Prudente • Brazil ... 174 E7
Prešov • Slovak Rep. ... 89 H8
Prespa • Bulgaria ... 92 H8
Prespa, Lake • Greece/FYR of Macedonia ... 93 B1
Préspa Nat. Park Park N • Greece ... 58 [137]
Presque Isle • ME, United States ... 150 G1
Pressburg • Slovak Rep. ... 89 D7
Preston • United Kingdom ... 63 D7
Prestwick • United Kingdom ... 62 C5
Pretoria • South Africa ... 110 B3
Prevel, Fort • QU, Canada ... 160 B1
Préveza • Greece ... 94 A
Pribilof Is. • AK, United States ... 157 C4
Priboj • Serbia & Montenegro ... 92 B3
Pribram • Czech Rep. ... 89 E7
Pribyslav • Czech Rep. ... 89 E7
Prichard • AL, United States ... 155 A1
Prickly Pear Cays • Anguilla ... 166 B
Prickly Pear I. • British Virgin Is. ... 166 A
Prickly Point • Grenada ... 166 Q
Prien • Germany ... 74 H7
Priene • Turkey ... 95 E5
Prieros • Germany ... 73 F8
Prijedor • Bosnia-Herz. ... 92 G5
Prijepolje • Serbia & Montenegro ... 92 B3
Prilep • FYR of Macedonia ... 92 C3
Primorsko • Bulgaria ... 92 H8
Primosten • Croatia ... 92 F6
Prince Albert • SA, Canada ... 158 F3
Prince Albert • South Africa ... 111 H10
Prince Albert Nat. Park Park N • SA, Canada ... 161 [21]
Prince Albert Road • South Africa ... 111 E6
Prince Alfreds Pass • South Africa ... 111 F7
Prince Charles I. • NU, Canada ... 159 I2
Prince Edward I. • Canada ... 160 B2
Prince Edward I. Nat. Park Park N • PE, Canada ... 161 [36]
Prince Edward Is. • Indian Ocean ... 11 K8
Prince George • BC, Canada ... 160 I6
Prince of Wales, Cape • AK, United States ... 157 F4
Prince of Wales I. • AK, United States ... 157 F4
Prince of Wales I. • NU, Canada ... 158 G2
Prince of Wales I. • QL, Australia ... 135 G2
Prince Rupert • BC, Canada ... 158 C3
Prince Rupert Bay • Dominica ... 167 K
Prince William Forest Park Park N • VA, United States ... 153 [250]
Prince William Sound • AK, United States ... 157 E3
Princes Is. • Turkey ... 95 F3
Princess Charlotte Bay • QL, Australia ... 135 G2
Princess Elizabeth Land • Antarctica ... 176 R5
Princess Juliana [Apt] • St Maarten ... 166 C
Princeton • BC, Canada ... 160 I7
Princeton • IL, United States ... 150 B2
Princeton • NJ, United States ... 156 B2
Príncipe • São Tomé & Príncipe ... 106 C4

Prínos • Crete, Greece ... 93 H5
Prinzapolka • Nicaragua ... 170 F4
Pristina • Serbia & Montenegro ... 92 C3
Privas • France ... 76 F4
Priverno • Italy ... 87 F5
Prizren • Serbia & Montenegro ... 92 C3
Probolinggo • Java, Indonesia ... 131 R12
Prócida, I. di • Italy ... 87 G7
Prochhomos • Cyprus ... 96 C4
Profitis Ilías • Thíra, Greece ... 94 G
Profondeville • Belgium ... 70 C4
Progreso • México ... 169 F4
Prokhladnyy • Russian Fed. ... 100 F5
Prokuplje • Serbia & Montenegro ... 92 C3
Promthep, Laem • Ko Phuket, Thailand ... 130 F10
Propriano • Corsica, France ... 78 M12
Proserpine • QL, Australia ... 136 A3
Prosna • Poland ... 89 B2
Prospect Beach • Cayman Is. ... 165 A2
Prospect, Fort • Bermuda ... 165 L10
Prospect Park • Cayman Is. ... 165 A2
Prostejov • Czech Rep. ... 89 B4
Protaras • Cyprus ... 96 C4
Protea Banks • South Africa ... 111 B5
Provadiya • Bulgaria ... 92 H8
Provence • France ... 78 G7
Provence-Alpes-Côte d'Azur • France ... 77 B2
Providence • RI, United States ... 156 D1
Providence • Seychelles ... 113 A2
Providence, Banca • Seychelles ... 113 A2
Providencia, I. de • Caribbean Sea ... 170 G4
Providencia • Turks & Caicos Is. ... 164 C3
Provins • France ... 78 B2
Provins Heritage C • France ... 44 [76]
Provo • UT, United States ... 156 D1
Prozor • Bosnia-Herz. ... 92 G6
Prudhoe Bay • AK, United States ... 157 E2
Prüm • Germany ... 74 A1
Prune I. • St Vincent & Gren. ... 167 P
Pruszków • Poland ... 89 C2
Prut • Moldova/Romania ... 92 D2
Pruské • Czech Rep. ... 89 B4
Pryluky • Ukraine ... 100 D3
Prypyats • Belarus ... 100 C3
Przemysl • Poland ... 89 C3
Psará • Greece ... 93 D2
Psérimos • Greece ... 94 CD3
Psilorítis • Crete, Greece ... 93 H6
Pskov • Russian Fed. ... 100 C2
Pskov, Lake • Estonia/Russian Fed. ... 100 K6
Ptolemais • Israel ... 120 A1
Ptuj • Slovenia ... 92 F5
Pu'uhonua o Honaunau Nat. Hist. Park • HI, United States ... 157 J6
Pu'uhonua o Honaunau Nat. Hist. Park Park N • HI, United States ... 152 [22]
Pu'ukoholā Heiau Nat. Hist. Site • HI, United States ... 157 J6
Pua Pua, Te Ava • Tuvalu ... 139 R
Pua'pua • Samoa ... 139 G
Puakakiti • Easter I. ... 139 M
Puamau • French Polynesia ... 139 J
Pucallpa • Peru ... 173 B3
Pucón • Chile ... 175 A4
Pudent, Estany • Formentera, Spain ... 83 M10
Pudong • China ... 125 F4
Pudozh • Russian Fed. ... 100 E1
Pudukkottai • India ... 124 C3
Puebla • Mexico ... 169 J7
Puebla Heritage C • Mexico ... 42 [33]
Puebla [Adm] • Mexico ... 169 C3
Pueblo • CO, United States ... 148 F3
Pueblo de Taos Heritage C • NM, United States ... 42 [8]
Pueblo Viejo • Dominican Rep. ... 165 G6
Puente Alto • Chile ... 175 A3
Puerto Acosta • Bolivia ... 173 C4
Puerto Aisén • Chile ... 175 A4
Puerto Angel • Mexico ... 169 K8
Puerto Armuelles • Panama ... 170 F6
Puerto Ayacucho • Venezuela ... 173 C2
Puerto Ayora • Galápagos Is. ... 171 H10
Puerto Banús • Spain ... 82 I8
Puerto Baquerizo Moreno • Galápagos Is. ... 171 H10
Puerto Barrios • Guatemala ... 170 K9
Puerto Cabezas • Nicaragua ... 170 F3
Puerto Caimito • Panama ... 170 L11
Puerto Caldera • Costa Rica ... 170 E6
Puerto Cortés • Honduras ... 170 K9
Puerto Cortés • Mexico ... 168 I6
Puerto de la Cruz • Tenerife, Canary Is. ... 82 G5
Puerto de la Peña • Fuerteventura, Canary Is. ... 83 H5
Puerto de Los Angeles, Parque Natural • Mexico ... 169 H6
Puerto de Mazarrón • Spain ... 83 A2
Puerto de Santiago • Tenerife, Canary Is. ... 82 G5
Puerto del Carmen • Lanzarote, Canary Is. ... 83 I5
Puerto del Rosario • Fuerteventura, Canary Is. ... 83 H5
Puerto Deseado • Argentina ... 175 B4
Puerto Escondido • Baja California Sur, Mexico ... 168 I6
Puerto Escondido • Oaxaca, Mexico ... 169 K8
Puerto Inca • Peru ... 173 E7
Puerto Inírida • Colombia ... 173 C2
Puerto Juárez • Mexico ... 169 F3
Puerto Lempira • Honduras ... 170 F3
Puerto Libertad • Mexico ... 168 H5
Puerto Limón • Costa Rica ... 170 F6
Puerto Maldonado • Peru ... 173 C4
Puerto Maunabo • Puerto Rico ... 165 J8
Puerto Montt • Chile ... 175 A4
Puerto Morelos • Mexico ... 169 G4
Puerto Obaldía • Panama ... 170 L6
Puerto Padre • Cuba ... 164 H5
Puerto Páez • Venezuela ... 173 C2
Puerto Palawan • Philippines ... 128 F5
Puerto Peñasco • Mexico ... 168 H5
Puerto Pilón • Panama ... 170 L10
Puerto Plata • Dominican Rep. ... 165 G5
Puerto Real • Majorca, Spain ... 83 N12
Puerto Rico • Gran Canaria, Canary Is. ... 82 G6
PUERTO RICO • West Indies ... 165 I-J
Puerto Santa Cruz • Argentina ... 175 B4
Puerto Suárez • Bolivia ... 173 D4
Puerto Vallarta • Mexico ... 169 H7
Puerto Velasco Ibarra • Galápagos Is. ... 171 H10
Puerto Villamil • Galápagos Is. ... 171 G10
Puerto-Princesa Subterranean River Nat. Park Heritage N • Philippines ... 41 [143]
Puertollano • Spain ... 80 C4
Puglia • Italy ... 86 B2
Puigcerdà • Spain ... 83 C2
Pukaki, Lake • New Zealand ... 137 Q4
Pukapuka Atoll • Cook Is. ... 139 DD3
Pukaskwa Nat. Park Park N • OT, Canada ... 161 [31]
Pukaskwa Nat. Park • OT, Canada ... 161 B1
Puke, Mt • Wallis & Futuna ... 139 Q
Pukekohe • New Zealand ... 137 B2
Pula • Croatia ... 92 F6
Pulau Langkawi • Malaysia ... 129 D-E
Pulau Pinang • Penang, Malaysia ... 129 E7
Pulawy • Poland ... 89 C3
Pulheim • Germany ... 73 C6
Pulicat Lake • India ... 124 C2
Pulkovo [Apt] • Russian Fed. ... 100 E1
Pullman • WA, United States ... 154 H5
Pultusk • Poland ... 89 C2
Puluwat Atoll • Fed. States of Micronesia ... 138 BB2
Pump Bay • St Kitts & Nevis ... 167 F
Puna Pau quarry • Easter I. ... 139 M
Puná, I. • Ecuador ... 173 A3
Punakaiki • New Zealand ... 137 H7
Punaauia • French Polynesia ... 139 H
Punchestown • Ireland ... 69 E7
Pune • India ... 122 B4
Pune [Apt] • India ... 124 B1
Punggol • Singapore ... 129 I11
Punjab • India ... 123 A1
Puno • Peru ... 173 F7
Punta Alta • Argentina ... 175 B3

Punta Arenas • Chile ... 175 A5
Punta Arenas • Margarita ... 166 T
Punta Cana • Dominican Rep. ... 165 H6
Punta, Cerro de • Puerto Rico ... 165 I8
Punta de Piedra • Margarita ... 166 T
Punta del Este • Uruguay ... 175 G6
Punta Gorda • Belize ... 170 K9
Punta Gorda • Nicaragua ... 170 F5
Punta Prieta • Mexico ... 168 H5
Punta Prima • Minorca, Spain ... 83 K8
Punta Räsi [Apt] • Sicily, Italy ... 86 G7
Punta Umbria • Spain ... 82 H7
Puntarenas • Costa Rica ... 170 E6
Punto Fijo • Venezuela ... 173 B1
Puolanka • Finland ... 99 H12
Puqi • China ... 125 E4
Puquio • Peru ... 173 E6
Purbeck, I. of • United Kingdom ... 65 K10
Purbolinggo • Java, Indonesia ... 131 P12
Pureora Forest Park • New Zealand ... 137 E5
Puri Beach • India ... 124 F6
Puri • India ... 122 C4
Purmerend • Netherlands ... 70 H7
Purnia • India ... 122 C3
Puru'aon Nat. Park • WA, Australia ... 135 D3
Purus • Brazil/Peru ... 173 C3
Purwakarta • Java, Indonesia ... 131 U11
Purwodadi • Java, Indonesia ... 131 P12
Purwokerto • Java, Indonesia ... 131 P12
Pushkar • India ... 123 E8
Püspökladány • Hungary ... 92 C2
Pusteria, Val • Italy ... 86 D3
Pustertal • Austria/Italy ... 86 D3
Putao • Myanmar ... 128 B3
Putaruru • New Zealand ... 137 R11
Puteran • Indonesia ... 131 R11
Putian • China ... 125 G10
Putignano • Italy ... 85 B4
Putrajaya • Malaysia ... 129 G10
Puttalam • Sri Lanka ... 124 C4
Puttaparthy • India ... 124 B2
Putten • Netherlands ... 70 G8
Puttgarden • Germany ... 72 D1
Putumayo • Colombia/Peru ... 173 B2
Putuo Shan • China ... 126 H7
Puuc • Mexico ... 169 F4
Puukoholā Heiau Nat. Hist. Site Park N • HI, United States ... 152 [20]
Puuwai • HI, United States ... 157 H5
Puy du Fou, Grand Parc du Park • France ... 59 [65]
Puy-en-Velay, le • France ... 76 K8
Puy-l'Evêque • France ... 78 F6
Puyallup • WA, United States ... 154 G5
Puymorens, Col de • France ... 82 F5
Puysegur Point • New Zealand ... 137 F8
Pwel Weite • Fed. States of Micronesia ... 138 D
Pwllheli • Wales ... 63 C8
Pwllheli Beach • United Kingdom ... 64 [63]
Pwnk • Fed. States of Micronesia ... 138 D
Pyatogorsk • Russian Fed. ... 100 F5
Pyè • Myanmar ... 128 B3
Pyhä-Häkki Nat. Park Park N • Finland ... 58 [37]
Pyhäjärvi • Finland ... 99 C4
Pyhäjoki • Finland ... 97 E3
Pyhätunturi Nat. Park Park N • Finland ... 58 [33]
Pyinmana • Myanmar ... 128 B3
Pyongyang • D.P.R. of Korea ... 125 G3
Pyramid Canyon • AZ/NV, United States ... 155 G3
Pyramid Lake • NV, United States ... 154 I7
Pyrenees • France/Spain ... 76 D5
Pyrénées Occidentales, Parc nat. des Park N • France ... 58 [77]
Pyrénées-Atlantiques • France ... 78 I9
Pyrénées-Occidentales • France ... 78 I-J
Pyrénées-Occidentales, Parc nat. des • France ... 78 J9
Pyrénées-Orientales • France ... 78 K-L
Pyrénées-Orientales [Adm] • France ... 78 L10

Q

Qaidam Pendi • China ... 125 D3
Qal'at al Jundi • Egypt ... 109 B1
Qal'eh-ye Now • Afghanistan ... 121 D4
Qala • Malta ... 96 A1
Qalaikhum • Tajikistan ... 121 F4
Qalat • Afghanistan ... 121 E5
Qalito • Fiji Is. ... 138 T
Qapshaghay • Kazakstan ... 121 G2
Qaqortoq • Greenland ... 159 O3
Qaraghandy • Kazakstan ... 121 F2
Qaraghayly • Kazakstan ... 121 G2
Qarokul • Tajikistan ... 121 F4
Qarqan He • China ... 125 D3
Qarshi • Uzbekistan ... 121 E3
Qasr Amra Heritage C • Jordan ... 44 [311]
Qasr Ibrim • Egypt ... 109 B1
Qasr es Sagha • Egypt ... 109 B1
QATAR • Asia ... 120 G9
Qattāra Depression • Egypt ... 109 A1
Qawra • Malta ... 96 B1
Qazimämmäd • Azerbaijan ... 120 F5
Qazrin • Syria ... 120 B1
Qazvin • Iran ... 120 H5
Qena • Egypt ... 109 B2
Qeqertarsuaq • Greenland ... 159 K2
Qeqertarsuaq [I.] • Greenland ... 159 K2
Qeshm • Iran ... 120 H8
Qianshan • China ... 125 F4
Qiao Dao • China ... 126 F4
Qidong • China ... 125 F4
Qiemo • China ... 121 H3
Qikiqtaluk • NU, Canada ... 159 I2
Qilian Shan • China ... 125 D3
Qin Shihuangdi Tomb • China ... 125 E3
Qincheng Shan Heritage C • China ... 43 [188]
Qingdao • China ... 125 F3
Qinghai • China ... 125 D3
Qinghai Hu • China ... 125 C3
Qingpu • China ... 126 H6
Qingyi Jiang • China ... 125 E4
Qinhuangdao • China ... 125 F3
Qinzhou • China ... 125 E5
Qiqihar • China ... 125 G2
Qixiashan • China ... 126 H6
Qizilqum • Uzbekistan ... 121 D3
Qom • Iran ... 120 H6
Qomisheh • Iran ... 120 H6
Qornet es Sauda • Lebanon ... 120 B1
Qorni • Malta ... 96 B2
Qostanay • Kazakstan ... 121 E1
Qu'App Long • Vietnam ... 129 C6
Quang Nam • Vietnam ... 128 C3
Quang Ngai • Vietnam ... 128 C4
Quang Tri • Vietnam ... 128 C3
Quannapowitt, L. • United Kingdom ... 65 J9
Quanzhou • China ... 125 F5
Quaqtaq • QU, Canada ... 159 J2
Quarry Bay • Hong Kong, China ... 84 J8
Quartier Militaire • Mauritius ... 113 F5
Quartu Sant'Elena • Sardinia, Italy ... 86 F6
Quartzite • AZ, United States ... 155 G8
Quatre Bornes • Mauritius ... 113 B3
Quatre Bornes • Seychelles ... 113 A2
Quatro, I. á • St Vincent & Gren. ... 167 P
Quba • Azerbaijan ... 120 F5
Queanbeyan • NS, Australia ... 136 F9
Québec Heritage C • QU, Canada ... 42 [9]
Québec [Adm] • Canada ... 159 J3
Quedlinburg Heritage C • Germany ... 44 [51]
Queen Beatrix [Apt] • Aruba ... 166 W
Queen Charlotte Is. • BC, Canada ... 158 C3

Queen Elizabeth Is. • Canada ... 142 E1
Queen Elizabeth Nat. Park Park • Uganda ... 112 [64]
Queen Mary Land • Antarctica ... 176 S4
Queen Maud Gulf • NU, Canada ... 158 F1
Queen Maud Land • Antarctica ... 176 P5
Queen of Spains Valley • Jamaica ... 165 C3
Queens • NY, United States ... 156 C2
Queensland • Australia ... 135 G4
Queensland wet tropics Heritage N • Australia ... 41 [150]
Queenston • OT, Canada ... 161 D1
Queenston-Lewiston Bridge • Canada/United States ... 161 D1
Queenstown • New Zealand ... 137 G7
Queenstown • Singapore ... 129 H12
Queenstown • South Africa ... 111 G6
Queenstown • TS, Australia ... 136 E7
Queets • WA, United States ... 154 G5
Quelimane • Mozambique ... 110 C2
Queluz • Portugal ... 84 J8
Quemado Beach • Goa, India ... 123 C6
Quenza • Corsica, France ... 78 N12
Quepem • Goa, India ... 123 C6
Queqén • Argentina ... 175 F7
Quercianella • Italy ... 87 C3
Querétaro • Mexico ... 169 I7
Querétaro Heritage C • Mexico ... 42 [18]
Querétaro [Adm] • Mexico ... 169 C3
Querim Beach • Goa, India ... 123 C5
Quesnel • BC, Canada ... 160 I6
Quesnel, Lake • BC, Canada ... 160 I6
Quetta • Pakistan ... 122 A2
Quetzaltenango • Guatemala ... 170 J9
Queyras • France ... 78 D4
Quezon City • Philippines ... 128 G4
Qufu Heritage C • China ... 43 [182]
Qui Nhon • Vietnam ... 128 C4
Quibdó • Colombia ... 173 B2
Quiberon • France ... 77 C4
Quill, The • St Eustatius ... 167 E
Quillabamba • Peru ... 173 F6
Quillan • France ... 78 L10
Quilmes • Argentina ... 175 F6
Quilon Beach • India ... 124 E6
Quilon • India ... 124 B3
Quimper • France ... 77 C4
Quimperlé • France ... 77 C4
Quinault Ind Res • WA, United States ... 155 [1]
Quincy • France ... 76 K8
Quincy • CA, United States ... 154 I7
Quincy • IL, United States ... 150 B3
Quincy • MA, United States ... 156 D1
Quinta do Lago • Portugal ... 84 J8
Quinta do Palheiro Ferreiro • Madeira ... 84 E5
Quintana Roo • Mexico ... 169 D3
Quinze, Lac • QU, Canada ... 161 C1
Quiriguá Heritage C • Guatemala ... 42 [63]
Quita Sueño Bank • Caribbean Sea ... 166 BB4
Quito • Ecuador ... 173 B3
Quito Heritage C • Ecuador ... 42 [54]
Qujing • China ... 125 E4
Qulsary • Kazakstan ... 121 B2
Qumran • Palestine NAR ... 120 B4
Qunghirot • Uzbekistan ... 121 C2
Quoin I. • QL, Australia ... 136 A3
Quran • Uzbekistan ... 121 E4
Qurghonteppa • Tajikistan ... 121 E4
Quseir • Egypt ... 109 B2
Quttinirpaaq Nat. Park Park N • NU, Canada ... 161 [7]
Quzhou • China ... 125 F4
Qyzylorda • Kazakstan ... 121 E3

R

Råå • Sweden ... 99 G7
Raab • Austria ... 91 G2
Raabs • Austria ... 89 E7
Raahe • Finland ... 97 E3
Raas • Indonesia ... 131 R12
Raasay • United Kingdom ... 62 B3
Rab • Croatia ... 92 F6
Rab [I.] • Croatia ... 92 F5
Raba • Hungary ... 91 H2
Raba • Indonesia ... 131 E5
Rabat • Malta ... 96 B2
Rabat • Morocco ... 107 A1
Rabaul • Papua New Guinea ... 134 D5
Rabbah • Jordan ... 120 B3
Rabbit I. • Antigua & Barbuda ... 167 H
Rabbit I. • Fiji Is. ... 138 S
Rabida • I. • Galápagos Is. ... 171 G10
Rabigh • Saudi Arabia ... 108 C4
Rabka • Poland ... 89 G9
Rábnitsa • Moldova ... 92 D2
Race, Cape • NF, Canada ... 160 D1
Rach Gia • Vietnam ... 129 B6
Racibórz • Poland ... 89 F8
Racine • WI, United States ... 150 C2
Rad, Ko • Thailand ... 130 P5
Radauti • Romania ... 92 C2
Radeberg • Germany ... 73 D6
Radisson • QU, Canada ... 159 I3
Radium Hot Springs • BC, Canada ... 160 J7
Radnor Forest • United Kingdom ... 65 C9
Radnorshire • United Kingdom ... 65 C9
Radom • Poland ... 89 C3
Radovis • FYR of Macedonia ... 92 C3
Radøy • Norway ... 98 F8
Radviliskis • Lithuania ... 100 J7
Radyn Podlaski • Poland ... 89 C3
Rae Bareli • India ... 123 F8
Rae-Edzo • NT, Canada ... 158 E2
Raetihi • New Zealand ... 137 D6
Raf-Raf • Tunisia ... 107 D4
Rafaela • Argentina ... 175 B3
Raffles • Singapore ... 129 I12
Raffles Lighthouse • Singapore ... 129 H12
Rafha • Saudi Arabia ... 108 D4
Ragged I. • Bahamas ... 165 A2
Ragged I. Range • Bahamas ... 164 A2
Ragged Point • Barbados ... 166 V
Raglan • New Zealand ... 137 D5
Raglan Castle • United Kingdom ... 65 E6
Raglan Harbour • New Zealand ... 137 D5
Ragley Hall • United Kingdom ... 65 F5
Ragusa • Croatia ... 50 D3
Ragusa • Sicily, Italy ... 86 H8
Ragusa Heritage C • Sicily, Italy ... 44 [175]
Rahimyar Khan • Pakistan ... 122 B3
Rahole Nat. Reserve • Kenya ... 139 DD4
Raiatea • French Polynesia ... 139 D
Raichur • India ... 124 B2
Rainbow Beach • US Virgin Is. ... 166 X
Rainbow Beach • QL, Australia ... 155 G7
Rainbow Bridge Nat. Mon. Park N • UT, United States ... 152 [81]
Rainbow Bridge Nat. Mon. • UT, United States ... 148 D3
Rainbow Int. Bridge • Canada/United States ... 161 D1
Rainbow Springs • New Zealand ... 137 E5
Rainier, Mt • WA, United States ... 154 G5
Rainy Lake • Canada/United States ... 150 B1
Raippaluoto • Finland ... 97 E3
Raipur • India ... 122 C3
Raja • Indonesia ... 131 Q12
Raja Ampat • Indonesia ... 131 R12
Raja Noi, Ko • Thailand ... 130 F10
Rajahmundry • India ... 124 D1
Rajang • Malaysia ... 124 B3
Rajasthan • India ... 123 D8

Rajasthan Canal • India 123 D7
Rajbag Beach • Goa, India 123 C6
Rajkot • India 122 B3
Rajshahi • Bangladesh 122 C3
Rakahanga • Cook Is. 139 DD3
Rakiraki • Fiji Is. ....138 T
Rakit • Indonesia 131 P11
Rakkestad • Norway 98 E6
Rakops • Botswana 110 I9
Rakvere • Estonia 100 K6
Raleigh • NC, United States 151 E3
Ralik Chain • Marshall Is. 138 BB2
Ramah Navajo Ind Res •
NM, United States ....155 [38]
Ramatuelle • France 78 H8
Rambouillet • France 78 A2
Rambouillet, Forêt de • France 78 A2
Rambut Siwi Temple •
Bali, Indonesia 131 K7
Rameswaram • India 124 C3
Rameswaram Beach • India 124 E6
Ramgarh • India 123 D7
Ramiers Heritage C • Haiti ....42 [43]
Ramisi • Kenya 109 C6
Ramla • Israel 120 A3
Ramla Bay • Malta 96 A1
Ramnagar • India 123 G8
Ramnäs • Sweden 99 A1
Râmnicu Vâlcea • Romania 92 D2
Ramokgwebane • Botswana 110 J9
Ramonal • Mexico 169 F5
Ramotswa • Botswana 110 J10
Rampur • India 123 F7
Ramsau • Germany ....61 [70]
Ramsau am Dachstein Ski • Austria ....61 [113]
Ramsgate Beach • United Kingdom ....64 [28]
Ranakpur • India 123 D8
Rånäsfoss • Norway 98 E5
Ranau • Sabah, Malaysia 128 F5
Rancagua • Chile 175 A3
Rance • France 77 D3
Ranchi • India 122 C3
Rancho Luna, Playa • Cuba 164 F4
Randa • Majorca, Spain 83 O12
Randaberg • Norway 98 F9
Randers • Denmark 99 F7
Randolph, Fuerte • Panama 170 L10
Random I. • NT, Canada 160 D1
Randstad • Netherlands ....70 G-H
Rangiora • New Zealand 137 B3
Rangiroa • French Polynesia 139 DD4
Rangitaiki • Bay of Plenty, NZ 137 E5
Rangitikei • Manawatu-Wanganui, NZ 137 E6
Rangkasbitung • Java, Indonesia 131 O11
Rangoon • Myanmar 128 B3
Rangpur • Bangladesh 122 C3
Rangsdorf • Germany 73 F8
Rangsdorfer See • Germany 73 F8
Ranikhet • India 123 F7
Ranikhet Hill Sta • India 124 E5
Rankin Inlet • NU, Canada 158 G2
Rannalhi • Maldives 124 H8
Rannoch, Loch • United Kingdom 65 A1
Rano, Mt • Solomon Is. ....138 W
Rano Raraku quarry • Easter I. ....139 M
Ranomafana, Parc nat. de Park •
Madagascar ....112 [149]
Ranongga • Solomon Is. ....138 W
Ransdfjorden • Norway 98 E5
Rantauprapat • Indonesia 131 N10
Rantemario, Gunung • Indonesia 131 I4
Ranthambhor Nat. Park • India 123 E8
Rantoul • IL, United States 150 C2
Rapa Nui • Pacific Ocean ....139 M
Rapa Nui, Parque Nac. Heritage C •
Pacific Ocean ....42 [82]
Rapa Passage • Kiribati ....139 I
Rapallo • Italy 86 F1
Rapid City • SD, United States 148 F2
Rapla • Estonia 100 K6
Raposeira • Portugal 84 H8
Rapperswil • Switzerland 90 K5
Rarotonga • Cook Is. ....139 N
Ras Dashen • Ethiopia 108 C3
Râs el Bar • Egypt 109 B1
Râs Ghârib • Egypt 109 B2
Rasa, Punta • Argentina 175 B4
Rasdhu Atoll • Maldives 124 G7
Rashîd • Egypt 109 A1
Rasht • Iran 120 F6
Raso, Cabo • Portugal 84 F6
Rastatt • Germany 74 B3
Rat Buri • Thailand 130 D7
Ratak Chain • Marshall Is. 138 CC2
Ratan • Sweden 97 C3
Ratangarh • India 123 E7
Ráth Luirc • Ireland 69 H10
Rathangan • Ireland 69 E7
Rathcoole • Ireland 69 F6
Rathdrum • Ireland 69 F7
Rathkeale • Ireland 69 H10
Rathlin I. • United Kingdom 62 B5
Rathvilly • Ireland 69 E7
Ratiborice • Czech Rep. 89 E6
Ratingen • Germany 73 C6
Ratnagiri • India 124 A1
Raton • NM, United States 149 F3
Rattenberg • Austria 91 O7
Rattlesnake Nat. Recreation Area •
MT, United States 154 H5
Rattray Head • United Kingdom 62 E3
Rättvik • Sweden 97 D3
Raub • Malaysia 129 G9
Rauch • Argentina 175 F7
Rauland • Norway 98 G9
Rauma • Finland 100 J5
Rauma Heritage C • Finland ....43 [90]
Raume • Norway 98 G7
Raung, Gunung • Java, Indonesia 131 N12
Raurkela • India 122 C3
Ravascletto • Italy 87 D1
Ravello • Italy 87 H7
Ravenglass • United Kingdom 65 C4
Ravenglass & Eskdale Railway •
United Kingdom 65 C4
Ravenglass Estuary • United Kingdom 65 C4
Ravenna • Italy 87 D2
Ravenna Heritage C • Italy ....44 [157]
Ravensberger Spieleland Park L •
Germany ....59 [61]
Ravensburg • Germany 74 E8
Ravensburger Spieleland • Germany 74 E8
Ravenshoe • QL, Australia 136 C3
Rawa • India/Pakistan 121 F5
Rawai • Ko Phuket, Thailand 130 F10
Rawai Beach • Ko Phuket, Thailand 130 F10
Rawalpindi • Pakistan 122 B2
Rawicz • Poland 89 B3
Rawlins • WY, United States 148 E2
Rawson • Argentina 175 B4
Raxaul • India 123 G7
Ray, Cape • NF, Canada 160 C1
Rayong • Thailand 130 E8
Raysut • Oman 120 G10
Raz, Pointe de • France 77 C4
Razelm, Lacul • Romania 92 I7
Razgrad • Bulgaria 92 H8
Razlog • Bulgaria 92 F6
Ré, I. de • France 77 E6
Reach Falls • Jamaica 165 D4
Reading • PA, United States 156 B2
Reading • United Kingdom 63 E9
Rebild Bakker • Denmark 99 E6
Rebild Bakker Nat. Park Park N •
Denmark ....58 [41]
Rebun-to • Japan 127 D1
Rechytsa • Belarus 100 D3
Recife • Brazil 174 C3
Recife, Cape • South Africa 111 G7
Recklinghausen • Germany 73 D5
Reconquista • Argentina 175 C2
Red • United States 149 G4
Red • Vietnam 128 C2
Red Basin • China 126 C2
Red Bluff • CA, United States 154 I7
Red Centre, The • NT, Australia ....136 A-B
Red Deer • AL, Canada 160 J7
Red Deer [Riv] • AL, Canada 160 E3
Red Hill Patrick Henry Nat. Mem. •
VA, United States 156 A4
Red Lake • MN, United States 150 A1
Red Lake Ind Res •
MN, United States ....155 [57-58]
Red Lodge Mtn Ski •
MT, United States ....146 [43]
Red Mountain Ski • BC, Canada ....146 [7]
Red River of the North •
NM, United States 150 A1
Red Rock • OT, Canada 159 H4
Red Rock • OT, Canada 161 B1
Red Sea • Africa/Asia ....109 E-F
Redcar • United Kingdom 63 D7
Redding • CA, United States 154 I7
Redditch • United Kingdom 65 F5
Redeyef • Tunisia 107 C5
Redon • France 77 D4
Redonda, Roca • Galápagos Is. 171 G9
Redondo, Monte • Corsica, France 78 N11
Redruth • United Kingdom 65 I10
Redstone • BC, Canada 160 I7
Redwood Nat. Park •
CA, United States 154 I7
Redwood Nat. Park Park N •
CA, United States ....152 [38]
Redwood Nat. Park Heritage N •
CA, United States ....40 [11]
Ree, Lough • Ireland 69 C3
Reeds, Plain of • Vietnam 129 B6
Reedsport • OR, United States 148 B2
Reedville • WA, United States 150 E3
Reefton • New Zealand 137 B3
Reethi Rah • Maldives 124 H7
Refugio • TX, United States 155 E6
Regen • Germany 91 F1
Regensburg • Germany 72 E4
Reggane • Algeria 106 C2
Réggio di Calabria • Italy 86 H7
Réggio nell' Emilia • Italy 87 C2
Régina • French Guiana 174 A2
Regina • SK, Canada 158 F3
Rehoboth • Namibia 110 A3
Rehoboth Beach • DE, United States 156 B3
Rei, Costa • Sardinia, Italy 86 F6
Reichenau • Germany 74 B4
Reichenau Heritage C • Germany ....44 [66]
Reichstag • Germany 73 F7
Reigate • United Kingdom 65 G8
Reims • France 76 F2
Reims Heritage C • France ....44 [69]
Reina Adelaida, Archipiélago de •
Chile 175 A5
Reina Sofia [Apt] •
Tenerife, Canary Is. 82 G5
Reindeer Lake • MN/SA, Canada 158 F3
Reiner's Beach • Goa, India 123 C6
Reinhardstein, Château de •
Belgium 70 D4
Reinickendorf (Berlin) • Germany 73 F7
Reis Magos Fort • Goa, India 123 C5
Reisa Nat. Park Park N • Norway ....58 [7]
Reischach • Italy 86 D3
Reislern • Switzerland 74 F8
Reit im Winkl Ski • Germany ....61 [70]
Reit im Winkl • Germany 74 H8
Rejmyre • Sweden 99 A2
Rekarne • Sweden 99 A2
Reliance • NT, Canada 158 F2
Remada • Tunisia 107 D6
Remagen • Germany 74 C5
Remarkables, The • New Zealand 137 G7
Rembang • Java, Indonesia 131 O11
Rembau • Malaysia 129 G10
Remich • Luxembourg 70 D5
Rémire • Seychelles 113 B1
Remoulins Heritage C • France ....44 [88]
Rempart, Rivière du • Mauritius 113 F5
Remparts, Rivière des • Réunion 113 C4
Remscheid • Germany 73 D6
Rendezvous Bay • Montserrat 166 F2
Rendova • Solomon Is. ....138 W
Rendsburg • Germany 72 C1
Renfrewshire • United Kingdom 65 A2
Rennell • Solomon Is. ....138 W
Rennes • France 77 D4
Rennesøy • Norway 98 F9
Reno • Italy 87 C2
Reno • NV, United States 154 I7
Renon • Italy 86 C3
Réole, la • France 78 E6
Reposaari • Finland 99 C3
Republican • United States 148 G2
Repulse Bay • Hong Kong, China 126 F5
Repulse Bay • NU, Canada 159 H2
Repulse Bay • QL, Australia 136 C4
Resistencia • Argentina 175 C2
Resita • Romania 92 C2
Resolute • NU, Canada 158 G1
Resolution I. • New Zealand 137 F8
Resolution I. • NU, Canada 159 J2
Restonica, Gorges de la •
Corsica, France 78 N11
Retalhuleu • Guatemala 170 J9
Retezat Nat. Park Park N • Romania ....58 [132]
Rethal • France 76 F2
Réthimno • Crete, Greece 93 H5
Réthimno [Adm] • Crete, Greece 93 H6
Rétság • Hungary 92 B2
Rettenberg • Germany 74 F8
Retz • Austria 89 E7
Reuilly • France 76 K8
REUNION • Indian Ocean ....113 C-D
Réunion, la • Seychelles 113 B2
Reus • Spain 83 C4
Reuss • Switzerland 90 K5
Reutlingen • Germany 74 B3
Reval • Estonia 50 D1
Revelstoke • BC, Canada 160 J7
Revillagigedo I. •
AK, United States 157 F4
Revillagigedo, Is. • Mexico 168 B4
Rewa • India 123 F8
Rewari • India 123 E7
Rexburg • ID, United States 148 D2
Rey, I. del • Panama 170 H6
Reyes, Point • CA, United States 154 I8
Reykjavik • Iceland 97 H8
Reynolds Range • NT, Australia 136 B1
Reynosa • Mexico 168 E2
Reyy • Iran 121 J7
Rezekne • Latvia 100 K7
Reznas Ezers • Latvia 100 K7
Reznok • Slovak Rep. 89 B4
Rezovo • Bulgaria 92 G6
Rhaetian Alps • Italy/Switzerland 90 L5
Rhayader • United Kingdom 63 D8
Rhein • Germany/Switzerland 72 C4
Rhein-Main [Apt] • Germany 74 D6
Rheinbach • Germany 74 C5
Rheinberg • Germany 73 C5
Rheine • Germany 72 C3
Rheineck • Burg • Germany 74 C5
Rheinfelden • Germany 74 B4
Rheinfels, Burg • Germany 74 C5
Rheingau • Germany 74 D6
Rheinhausen (Duisburg) • Germany 73 C5
Rheinhessen • Germany 74 D6
Rheinland-Pfalz • Germany 74 C5
Rheinstein, Burg • Germany 74 D6
Rheinturm • Germany 73 C6
Rhenen • Netherlands 70 C3
Rhens • Germany 74 D5
Rheurdt • Germany 73 C5
Rheydt, Schloss • Germany 73 C6
Rhin • France 76 G2
Rhine Gorge • Germany 74 D5
Rhine Valley Heritage C • Germany ....44 [57]
Rhinelander • WI, United States 149 C4
Rhir, Cap • Morocco 107 A3
Rhode I. • RI, United States 156 D2
Rhode I. [Adm] • United States 156 D2
Rhodes Heritage C • Greece ....44 [246]
Rhodes • Rhodes, Greece ....94 F
Rhodes [I.] • Greece ....94 F
Rhodope • Bulgaria 92 C3
Rhön • Germany 72 C3
Rhône • France/Switzerland 76 F4
Rhône, RMS • British Virgin Is. ....166 A
Rhône-Alpes • France 77 B2
Rhos-on-Sea Beach • United Kingdom ....64 [67]
Rhyl • United Kingdom 63 D7
Rias Altas • Spain 82 A1
Rias Bajas • Spain 82 A1
Riau • Indonesia 131 N10
Riau, Kepulauan • Indonesia 131 B3
Ribatejo • Portugal 84 A2
Ribble • United Kingdom 63 D7
Ribe • Denmark 99 E8
Ribe [Adm] • Denmark 99 E8
Ribeira Grande • Azores 84 B4
Ribeirão das Neves • Brazil 174 B4
Ribeirão Prêto • Brazil 174 B5
Ribnica • Slovenia 91 G3
Ricard, Circuit Paul • France 78 G8
Riccione • Italy 87 D3
Richards Bay • South Africa 111 C4
Richards Bay Nature Reserve •
South Africa 111 C4
Richardson Mtns • New Zealand 137 G7
Richborough Castle • United Kingdom 65 G9
Richelieu • QU, Canada 160 H4
Richfield • UT, United States 148 D3
Richland • WA, United States 154 H5
Richmond •
KwaZulu-Natal, South Africa 111 B5
Richmond • IN, United States 150 C3
Richmond • TS, Australia 135 G4
Richmond • VA, United States 156 A4
Richmond •
Northern Cape, South Africa 111 F6
Richmond Nat. Battlefield Park Park N •
VA, United States ....153 [247]
Ricobayo, Embalse de • Spain 80 C3
Ridderkerk • Netherlands 70 G8
Ridge Park • KY, United States 150 C3
Ridgecrest • CA, United States 148 C3
Riding Mtn Nat. Park Park N •
MN, United States ....161 [24]
Ried im Innkreis • Austria 91 F1
Riederalp Ski • Switzerland ....61 [70]
Riederalp • Switzerland 90 J6
Riedlingen • Germany 74 E7
Riesa • Italy 86 C3
Rieti • Italy 87 F4
Rietini, Monti • Italy 87 F4
Riezlern Ski • Austria ....61 [88]
Riezlern • Austria 91 M7
Rif • Morocco 107 B1
Rifle • CO, United States 148 E3
Riga • Latvia 100 K7
Riga Heritage C • Latvia ....44 [262]
Riga, Gulf of • Estonia/Latvia 100 J6
Riggins • ID, United States 148 C1
Rigolet • NF, Canada 159 K3
Rihand Dam • India 123 G8
Rihiveli Beach • Maldives 124 H8
Riihimäki • Finland 99 C3
Riiser-Larsen Ice Shelf • Antarctica 176 O5
Riiser-Larsen Peninsula • Antarctica 176 O4
Rijeka • Croatia 92 B2
Rijnsburg • Netherlands 70 G7
Rijswijk • Netherlands 70 G7
Rila • Bulgaria 92 C3
Rila Heritage C • Bulgaria ....44 [230]
Rila Nat. Park Park N • Bulgaria ....58 [136]
Riley • OR, United States 154 H6
Rimatara • French Polynesia 139 DD4
Rimau • Malaysia 129 D8
Rimavská Sobota • Slovak Rep. 89 B4
Rimbo • Sweden 99 B1
Rimbo Panti Reserve • Indonesia 131 N10
Rimforsa • Sweden 99 H5
Rimini • Italy 87 D3
Rimouski • QU, Canada 160 A1
Rimouski, Réserve faunique de •
QU, Canada 160 A1
Rincon • Bonaire ....166 U
Rincón • Costa Rica 170 F6
Rincón, Bahía de • Puerto Rico 165 J8
Rincón de Romos • Mexico 169 I6
Rincon del Bonete, Lago Artificial de •
Uruguay 175 G6
Ringe • Denmark 99 F8
Ringebu • Norway 97 C3
Ringerike • Norway 98 E5
Ringkøbing • Denmark 99 E7
Ringkøbing [Adm] • Denmark 99 E7
Ringkøbing Fjord • Denmark 99 E7
Ringsjön • Sweden 99 G7
Ringsted • Denmark 99 F8
Ringvassøy • Norway 97 D1
Rinia • Greece ....94 I
Rinteln • Germany 72 C2
Río Abiseo, Parque Nac. • Peru 171 N11
Río Abiseo, Parque Nac. Heritage N •
Peru ....40 [36]
Río Abiseo, Parque Nac. Heritage C •
Peru ....42 [56]
Río Azul • Guatemala 170 K8
Río Bec • Mexico 169 F5
Río Branco • Brazil 173 C3
Río Bravo del Norte • Mexico 168 C1
Río Bueno • Jamaica 165 C3
Río Claro • Trinidad & Tobago ....166 S
Río Colorado • Argentina 175 B3
Río Cuarto • Argentina 175 B3
Río das Ostras • Brazil 174 F7
Río de Janeiro • Brazil 174 B5
Río de Janeiro [Adm] • Brazil 174 F7
Río de la Plata • Argentina 175 J7
Río Formosa, Reserva Natural da •
Portugal 84 J8
Río Gallegos • Argentina 175 B6
Río Grande • Argentina 175 B5
Río Grande • Argentina 123 E7
Río Grande • Mexico 169 I6
Río Grande • United States 149 F4
Río Grande do Norte • Brazil 174 C3
Río Grande do Sul • Brazil 175 C2
Río Lagartos • Mexico 169 F4
Río Marina • Italy 87 C3
Río Negro • Honduras 170 E3
Río Plátano • Honduras 170 E3
Río Plátano, Reserva de la Biósfera
Heritage N • Honduras ....40 [23]
Río Rancho • NM, United States 155 H7
Rio Rita • Panama 170 L10
Río San Juan • Dominican Rep. 165 I5
Rio Verde • Brazil 174 A4
Río Verde • Mexico 169 I6
Riohacha • Colombia 173 B1
Riom • France 76 E4
Riomaggiore Heritage C • Italy ....44 [159]
Rionero in Vulture • Italy 87 G5
Ripoll • Spain 83 D3
Riscone • Italy 86 D3
Rishiri-to • Japan 127 D1
Risnjak Nat. Park Park N • Croatia ....58 [118]
Risnjak Nat. Park • Croatia 91 G3
Riser • Norway 99 F5
Risoul Ski • France ....61 [47]
Risoul • France 78 D4
Ristidian Point • Guam ....138 Z
Ritzville • WA, United States 154 H5
Riva del Garda • Italy 87 C1
Rivas • Nicaragua 170 J10
River Kwai Bridge • Thailand 130 D7
Rivera • Uruguay 175 C2
Riverina • NS, Australia 136 G8
Riverside • CA, United States 148 C4
Riverside [Apt] • United States 149 C4
Riverside [Apt] • United States 65 H5
Riverside • Australia ....41 [154]
Riverton • New Zealand 137 G8
Riverton • ND, United States 160 B2
Riverview • South Africa 111 C4
Rivesaltes [Apt] • France ....78 [10]
Riviera di Levante • Italy 87 B3
Riviera di Ponente • Italy 87 A3
Rivière du Loup • QU, Canada 160 A1
Rivière-Pilote • Martinique ....167 L
Rivne • Ukraine 100 C3
Rivoli • Italy 87 A2
Rixensart • Belgium 70 B4
Riyadh • Saudi Arabia 120 F9
Rize • Turkey 95 D1
Rizokarpaso • Cyprus 96 D3
Rjukan • Norway 98 F5
Roa • Norway 98 E5
Road Bay • Anguilla ....166 P
Road Town • British Virgin Is. ....166 A
Roanne • France 76 F3
Roanoke Rapids • NC, United States 150 E3
Roatán, I. de • Honduras 170 K9
Rob Roy's Grave • United Kingdom 65 A1
Robben I. • South Africa 111 D7
Robben I. Heritage C • South Africa ....43 [125]
Robbins I. • TS, Australia 136 E6
Robe • Ireland 69 H9
Robert L. Bradshaw [Apt] •
St Kitts & Nevis ....167 F
Roberts, Mt • QL, Australia 136 D5
Robertsganj • India 123 G8
Robertson • South Africa 111 E7
Robertstown • Ireland 69 E7
Roberval • QU, Canada 160 A1
Robledal • Margarita ....166 T
Robson, Mt • AL, Canada 160 J6
Robson • TX, United States 155 E6
Roca, Cabo da • Portugal 84 F6
Rocamadour • France 76 D4
Rocas, Atol das Heritage N •
Brazil ....40 [42]
Rocca di Cambio • Italy 87 F4
Rocca di Papa • Italy 87 F5
Rochdale • United Kingdom 63 D7
Roche-Ecrite, la • Réunion 113 C3
Roche-en-Ardenne, La • Belgium 70 C5
Roche-Guyon, la • France 78 A1
Roche-Racan [Château] • France 77 F5
Roche-sur-Yon, la • France 77 E6
Rochefort • Belgium 70 C5
Rochefort • France 78 E5
Rochefoucauld, la • France 78 E5
Rochehaut • Belgium 70 C5
Rochelle, la • France 77 E6
Roches Noire • Mauritius 113 F5
Roches, Plaine des • Mauritius 113 F5
Rochester • MN, United States 150 B2
Rochester • NY, United States 156 A1
Rochester • United Kingdom 65 H7
Rochester Falls • Mauritius 113 F5
Rock Creek Park Park N •
DC, United States ....153 [264]
Rock Harbor Lodge •
MI, United States 161 A1
Rock Hill • SC, United States 151 E3
Rock I. • WI, United States 161 B2
Rock Sound • Bahamas 164 F3
Rock Springs • WY, United States 148 E2
Rockford • IL, United States 150 C2
Rockhampton • QL, Australia 136 D4
Rockingham • WA, Australia 135 B6
Rockley • Barbados ....167 M
Rockport • TX, United States 155 E6
Rocky Boy's Ind Res •
MT, United States ....155 [16]
Rocky I. Dive • Egypt 109 E8
Rocky Mount • NC, United States 151 E3
Rocky Mtn Nat. Park Park N •
CO, United States 148 E2
Rocky Mtn Nat. Park Park N •
CO, United States ....152 [87]
Rocky Mtns • Canada/United States 142 D4
Rocky Point • Jamaica 165 D4
Rocque-Gageac, la • France 78 F6
Rocquefort • France 78 E6
Rod Hill, Fort • BC, Canada 160 L7
Rodeo • NM, United States 155 I7
Rodrigo M. Quevedo • Mexico 168 D1
Roermond • Netherlands 70 D3
Roes Welcome Sound • NU, Canada 159 H2
Rogaland • Norway 98 F9
Rogaška Slatina • Slovenia 91 G3
Roger Williams Nat. Mem. Park N •
RI, United States ....153 [283]
Rogers • AR, United States 151 B3
Roggeveen, Cabo • Easter I. ....139 M
Rogliano • Corsica, France 78 N11
Rogaland • Norway ....139 E
Rohtak • India 123 E7
Rohtas • India 123 G8
Rohtas Heritage C • Pakistan ....43 [147]
Roi • Thailand 128 C3
Roi-Namur • Marshall Is. ....139 E
Roissy-Charles de Gaulle [Apt] •
France 78 B1
Roja, Cabo • Mexico 169 J6
Rojo, Cabo • Puerto Rico 165 I8
Rokan • Indonesia 131 N10
Rokiskis • Lithuania 100 K7
Rokko-san • Japan 127 F6
Rokycany • Czech Rep. 89 D6
Roland-Garros [Apt] • Réunion 113 C3
Rolandsbogen • Germany 74 C5
Rolde • Netherlands 70 B2
Rolla • MO, United States 150 B3
Rollag • Norway 98 E5
Rolle, Passo di • Italy 86 C4
Rolvsøya • Norway 97 C5
Roma • Italy 87 F5
Roma Heritage C • Italy ....44 [167]
Roma • QL, Australia 136 C5
Romainmôtier • Switzerland 90 I5
Roman • Romania 92 D2
Romana del Casale, Villa •
Sicily, Italy 86 H8
Romana del Casale, Villa Heritage C •
Sicily, Italy ....44 [176]
ROMANIA • Europe 92 D2
Romano, Cayo • Cuba 164 G4
Romanshorn • Switzerland 91 M7
Romanshorn • Switzerland 91 M7
Romantische Strasse • Germany 74 D8
Rombo Pass • Austria/Italy 86 D3
Rome • GA, United States 151 C4
Rome • Italy 87 F5
Rome Heritage C • Italy ....44 [167]
Rome • NY, United States 156 B1
Romeleåsen • Sweden 99 G7
Romerike • Norway 98 E5
Romford • United Kingdom 65 G7
Romilly-sur-Seine • France 76 F2
Rommerskirchen • Germany 73 C6
Romney, Hythe & Dymchurch Light Railway •
United Kingdom 65 H8
Rømø • Denmark 99 E8
Romoranthin-Lanthenay • France 77 F5
Romsdalfjorden • Norway 98 G7
Ronaldsay, North • United Kingdom 62 G2
Ronald Reagan [Apt] •
VA, United States 156 A3
Roncador, Cayo de • Caribbean Sea 166 BB4
Roncesvalles • France 78 I9
Ronda • Spain 82 I8
Ronda, Serranía de • Spain 82 I8
Rondane Nat. Park Park N • Norway ....58 [14]
Rondane Nat. Park • Norway 99 F7
Rande • Denmark 99 F7
Ronde I. • Grenada ....167 P
Ronde, I. • Seychelles 113 B2
Rondônia • Brazil 173 C4
Rondonópolis • Brazil 174 A4
Ronge, Lac la • SK, Canada 158 F3
Rong • China 126 E3
Rønne • Denmark 99 H8
Ronne Ice Shelf • Antarctica 176 M5
Ronneby • Sweden 99 H7
Roosboom • South Africa 111 B4
Roosendaal • Netherlands 70 B3
Roosevelt Campobello Int. Park •
NB, Canada 160 A2
Roosevelt, Franklin D., Lake •
WA, United States 154 H5
Roosevelt I. • Antarctica 176 V5
Rope, The • Pitcairn Is. ....139 L
Roquetas de Mar • Spain 82 K8
Roraima • S. America 173 C2
Roraima [Adm] • Brazil 173 C2
Rorke's Drift • South Africa 111 B4
Rəros • Norway 97 C3
Rəros Heritage C • Norway ....43 [86]
Rørvig • Denmark 99 F7
Rosa, Lake • Bahamas 164 B2
Rosa, Monte • Italy/Switzerland 90 J6
Rosalie Moller Dive • Egypt 109 E7
Rosario • Argentina 175 F6
Rosario • Mexico 169 H6
Rosario • Uruguay 175 G6
Rosario [Adm] • Brazil 173 C2
Rosário do Sul • Brazil 175 C3
Rosario, Sierra del • Cuba 164 E4
Rosarito • Baja California, Mexico 168 K5
Rosario •
Baja California Sur, Mexico 168 I6
Rosarno • Italy 86 E5
Roscoff • France 77 C3
Roscommon • Ireland 69 H9
Roscommon [Adm] • Ireland 69 H8
Roscrea • Ireland 69 C4
Rose Belle • Mauritius 113 F6
Rose Hall • Jamaica 165 C3
Rose Hill • Mauritius 113 E6
Roseau • Dominica ....167 K
Rosebery • TS, Australia 136 E7
Rosebud Ind Res •
SD, United States ....155 [49]
Roseburg • OR, United States 148 B2
Rosenberg • TX, United States 155 F6
Rosenheim • Germany 74 G7
Rosenholm • Denmark 99 F7
Roses • Spain 83 D3
Roses, Golfo de • Spain 83 D3
Roses, Valley of • Bulgaria 92 H8
Rosetown • SA, Canada 158 F3
Rosetta • Egypt 109 A1
Rosetto Mouth • Egypt 109 A1
Rosie the Riveter WWII Home Front Nat. Hist.
Park Park N • CA, United States ....152 [44]
Rosière, la • France 78 D4
Rosignano Marittimo • Italy 87 C3
Rosiori de Vede • Romania 92 H7
Roskilde • Denmark 99 F7
Roskilde Heritage C • Denmark ....44 [12]
Roslagen • Sweden 99 B1
Roslavl' • Russian Fed. 100 D3
Rosmead • South Africa 111 G6
Ross • TS, Australia 136 F7
Ross Abbey • Ireland 69 H9
Ross Carbery • Ireland 69 H11
Ross Ice Shelf • Antarctica 176 U5
Ross Lake Nat. Recreation Area •
WA, United States 154 G5
Ross Lake Nat. Recreation Area Park N •
WA, United States ....152 [28]
Ross River • NT, Australia 136 B1
Ross River • YT, Canada 158 C2
Ross Sea • Antarctica 176 V5
Ross-on-Wye • United Kingdom 65 E6
Ross-shire & Cromartyshire •
United Kingdom 64 A1
Rossan Point • Ireland 69 B2
Rossano • Italy 85 F5
Rossens Point • Ireland 69 H8
Rossignol, Lake • NS, Canada 160 B2
Rosslare • Ireland 69 C4
Rosslyn Chapel • United Kingdom 65 B2
Rossosh • Russian Fed. 100 E3
Rostock • Germany 72 E1
Rostov • Russian Fed. 100 M10
Rostov-na-Donu • Russian Fed. 100 E4
Rostrenen • France 77 C3
Roswell • GA, United States 151 D4
Roswell • NM, United States 149 F4
Rot • Germany 74 E7
Rota • N. Mariana Is. 138 AA2
Rota • Spain 82 H8
Rotenburg • Germany 72 C2
Rothenburg ob der Tauber • Germany 72 D4
Rothera [Base] • Antarctica ....176 [8]
Rotherham • South Africa 111 B4
Rotherham • United Kingdom 63 E7
Rothesay • United Kingdom 65 A2
Rotoehu, Lake • New Zealand 137 E5
Rototiti, Lake • New Zealand 137 E5
Rotoma, Lake • New Zealand 137 E5
Rotorua • New Zealand 137 E5
Rotorua, Lake • New Zealand 137 E5
Rott • Germany 74 G8
Rottach-Egern • Germany 74 G8
Rottal • Germany 74 F8
Rottenbuch • Germany 74 F8
Rottenburg am Neckar • Germany 74 B3
Rottenmann • Austria 91 G2
Rotterdam • Netherlands 70 B3
Rottnen • Sweden 99 H6
Rottne • Sweden 99 H6
Rottweil • Germany 74 B3
Rotuma • Fiji Is. ....138 T
Roubaix • France 76 E1
Rouen • France 76 D2
Rouergue • France 78 F6
Rouge-Matawan, Réserve faunique •
QU, Canada 160 G3
Rougemont • Switzerland 90 J6
Rouhuma • Mozambique 110 C2
Rouméa • Mauritius 113 F5
Roxas • Mindanao, Philippines 128 G5
Roxas • Panay, Philippines 128 G5
Roxborough • Trinidad & Tobago ....166 R
Roxburgh • New Zealand 137 G8
Roxburgh, Lake • New Zealand 137 G7
Roxburghshire • United Kingdom 64 B3
Roxen • Sweden 99 H5
Roya • France 78 H7
Royal & Ancient, The •
United Kingdom 65 B1
Royal Canal • Ireland 69 E6
Royal Chitwan Nat. Park Heritage N •
Nepal ....41 [128]
Royal Highland Showground •
United Kingdom 65 B2
Royal Leamington Spa •
United Kingdom 65 E5
Royal Nat. Park • NS, Australia 136 H8
Royal St George's • United Kingdom 65 H8
Royal Tunbridge Wells •
United Kingdom 65 G8
Royale, I. • MI, United States 161 A1
Royan • France 78 E5
Royaumont, Abbaye de • France 78 A1
Røyrheim • Norway 98 G7
Rozmberk • Czech Rep. 89 F7
Roznava • Slovak Rep. 89 C4
Rtishchevo • Russian Fed. 100 F3
Ruacana • Namibia 110 A2
Ruaha Nat. Park • Tanzania 110 G8
Ruaha Nat. Park Heritage N • Tanzania ....112 [93]
Ruahine Range • New Zealand 137 E6
Ruapehu, Mt • New Zealand 137 E6
Rubondo I. Nat. Park • Tanzania 110 G7
Rubondo I. Nat. Park Heritage N • Tanzania ....112 [83]
Rubtsovsk • Russian Fed. 101 I4
Ruby Mtns • NV, United States 154 I7
Rucava • Latvia 99 F8
Ruda Slaska • Poland 89 F8
Rudall River Nat. Park •
WA, United States 135 C4
Rüdersdorf • Germany 73 F8
Rüdesheim • Germany 74 D6
Rudkøbing • Denmark 99 F8
Rüdnitz • Germany 73 F7
Rudnyy • Kazakhstan 121 D1
Rudolstadt • Germany 72 D3
Rudong • China 126 H6
Rueil-Malmaison • France 78 A2
Ruffec • France 78 E5
Rufiji • Tanzania 110 H8
Rufino • Argentina 175 B3
Rugao • China 126 H6
Rugby • ND, United States 148 F1
Rugby • United Kingdom 65 F5
Rügen • Germany 72 E1
Ruhnu • Estonia 100 J6
Ruhpolding • Germany 74 H8
Ruhr • Germany 73 D5
Ruhrgebiet • Germany ....73 C-D
Ruivo, Pico • Madeira 84 D5
Ruiz • Mexico 169 H6
Rukwa, Lake • Tanzania 110 G8
Rum • United Kingdom 62 B4
Rum Cay • Bahamas 165 B2
Rum Point • Cayman Is. 165 A2
Ruma Nat. Park • Kenya 109 C5
Rumbek • South Sudan 89 E6
Rumford • ME, United States 150 F2
Rumoi • Japan 127 D2
Rumung • Fed. States of Micronesia ....138 C
Runaway Bay • Jamaica 165 C3
Runcorn • United Kingdom 110 A2
Rungwa • Tanzania 110 G8
Runhällen • Sweden 99 A1
Runkel • Germany 74 D5
Runmarö • Sweden 99 B2
Runnymede • United Kingdom 65 G7
Ruo • Fed. States of Micronesia ....138 C
Ruoqiang • China 125 C3
Ruovesi • Finland 99 C3
Rupat • Indonesia 131 N10
Rupert • ID, United States 148 D2
Rupert • QU, Canada 159 I3
Rupurta • French Polynesia 139 DD4
Rusalka • Bulgaria 92 I8
Rusape • Zimbabwe 92 H7
Rusenski Lom Nat. Park Park N •
Bulgaria ....58 [133]
Rusenski Lom Nat. Park • Romania 69 F6
Rush • Ireland 69 F6
Rusk • TX, United States 155 F5
Russborough House • Ireland 69 E7
Russell Cave Nat. Mon. Park N •
AL, United States ....153 [203]
Russell Is. • Solomon Is. ....138 W
Russellville • AR, United States 151 B3
Russelsheim • Germany 74 D6
RUSSIAN FEDERATION • Asia/Europe 101
Rustavi • Georgia 121 G3
Ruston • LA, United States 156 C5
Ruta Maya, La • C. America ....170 J-K
Rutland • VT, United States 150 F2
Rutland Water • United Kingdom 63 E8
Ruvu • Tanzania 110 H7
Ruvuma • Tanzania 110 H8
Ruwenzori Mtns Nat. Park Park •
Uganda ....112 [63]
Ruwenzori Mtns Nat. Park Heritage N •
Uganda ....41 [106]
Ruzayevka • Russian Fed. 100 F3
Ruzomberok • Slovak Rep. 89 F9
Ruzyne [Apt] • Czech Rep. 89 B5
RWANDA • Africa 108 B5
Ry • Denmark 99 E7
Ryan Field [Apt] •
AZ, United States 156 F6
Ryazan' • Russian Fed. 100 E3
Rybinsk • Russian Fed. 100 M9
Rybinskoye Vdkhr. • Russian Fed. 100 M9
Rybnik • Poland 89 F8
Rycroft • AL, Canada 160 J6
Rydaholm • Sweden 99 G6
Ryde • Isle of Wight • United Kingdom 65 G3
Ryde • United Kingdom 63 E10
Ryde Beach • United Kingdom ....64 [36]
Rye • United Kingdom 65 H8
Ryfylke • Norway 98 G9
Rygge • Norway 98 E5
Ryki • Poland 89 C3
Ryotsu • Japan 127 E2
Rypin • Poland 89 B2
Rysy • Poland/Slovak Rep. 89 G9
Ryugasaki • Japan 127 I8
Ryujin Spa • Japan 127 G7
Ryukyu Is. Heritage C • Japan ....43 [198]
Ryukyu-mura • Okinawa, Japan ....138 A
Rzeszów • Poland 89 G9
Rzhev • Russian Fed. 100 L10

S

S'Albufeira • Majorca, Spain 83 O11
S'Algar • Minorca, Spain 83 K8
S'Arenal • Majorca, Spain 83 O11
S'Argamassa • Majorca, Spain 83 L9
S'Horta • Majorca, Spain 83 O11
S'Illot • Majorca, Spain 83 O11
s-Gravenhage • Netherlands 70 C3
s-Hertogenbosch • Netherlands 70 C3
Sa Calobra • Majorca, Spain 83 O11
Sa Coma • Majorca, Spain 83 O11
Sa Conillera • Ibiza, Spain 83 L9
Sa Keo • Thailand 130 E7
Sa Pobla • Majorca, Spain 83 O11
Sa Talaiassa de Sant Josep •
Ibiza, Spain 83 L9
Saalach • Austria/Germany 74 H8
Saalbach • Austria 91 F2
Saalbach Hintermglemm Ski • Austria ....61 [103]
Saale • Germany 72 D3
Saalfeld • Germany 72 D3
Saalfelden • Austria 91 F7
Saanen • Switzerland 90 J6
Saanenmöser • Switzerland 90 J6
Saar • Germany 74 A2
Saarbrücken • Germany 74 A2
Saaremaa • Estonia 100 J6
Saaristomeri Nat. Park Park N •
Finland ....58 [40]
Saaristomeri Nat. Park • Finland 99 C4
Saarland • Germany 74 A2
Saarlouis • Germany 74 A2
Saas Fee Ski • Switzerland ....61 [66]
Saas Fee • Switzerland 90 J6

Saba • West Indies .... 167 E
Sabac • Serbia & Montenegro 92 B2
Sabadell • Spain 83 C4
Sabah • Malaysia 128 F5
Sabaki • Kenya 109 C6
Saban, Archipiélago de • Cuba 164 F4
Sabana de la Mar • Dominican Rep. 165 H5
Sabaneta, Puntan • N. Mariana Is. .. 138 B3
Sabang • Indonesia 131 M9
Sabará • Brazil 174 E6
Sabaudia • Italy 87 F5
Sabáudia, Lago di • Italy 106 D2
Sabha • Libya 87 C4
Sabinal, Cayo • Cuba 164 G4
Sabinas • Mexico 168 D2
Sabinas Hidalgo • Mexico 168 D2
Sabine LA/TX, United States 155 F4
Sabine • LA/TX, United States 155 E6
Sable, Cape • FL, United States 155 D3
Sable, Cape • NS, Canada 160 B2
Sable I. • NS, Canada 160 C2
Sablé-sur-Sarthe • France 77 E5
Sables-d'Olonne, les • France 76 C3
Sabratha Heritage C • Libya ..... 44 [294]
Sabzevar • Iran 120 H6
Saché [Château] • France 77 F5
Sachs Harbour • NT, Canada 158 D1
Sachsen • Germany 72 E3
Sachsen-Anhalt • Germany 72 D2
Sächsische Schweiz, Nationalpark Park N •
  Germany .... 58 [68]
Saco • MT, United States 148 E1
Sacramento • CA, United States ... 154 I8
Sacramento [Riv] •
  CA, United States 154 I7
Sacred Falls State Park •
  HI, United States 157 G6
Sada Temple • Bali, Indonesia 131 L8
Sadani • Tanzania 110 H7
Sadao • Thailand 130 A4
Sadiklar • Turkey 95 H8
Sado • Portugal 84 G6
Sado-shima • Japan 127 C3
Sæby • Denmark 99 F6
Safad • Israel 120 B1
Safari & Hollywood-Park Park L •
  Germany .... 59 [51]
Safari- und Abenteuerpark Park L •
  Austrie .... 59 [80]
Säffle • Sweden 97 C4
Safi • Morocco 107 A2
Safonovo • Russian Fed. 100 D2
Safranbolu • Turkey 95 B1
Safranbolu Heritage C • Turkey .. 44 [251]
Sag Harbor • NY, United States 156 C2
Saga • Japan 127 B4
Sagalassos • Turkey 95 G7
Sagami-nada • Japan 127 I9
Sagami-wan • Japan 127 H9
Sagamihara • Japan 127 H8
Sagamore Hill Nat. Hist. Site Park N •
  NY, United States .... 153 [279]
Sagar • India 123 F8
Sagarmatha Nat. Park Heritage N •
  Nepal .... 41 [129]
Sage, Mt • British Virgin Is. .... 166 A
Saginaw • MI, United States 150 D2
Saginaw Bay • MI, United States .. 150 D2
Sagone • Corsica, France 78 M12
Sagone, Golfe de •
  Corsica, France 78 M12
Sagres • Portugal 84 H8
Sagres, Ponta de • Portugal 84 H8
Saguache • CO, United States 154 H5
Saguaro Nat. Park •
  AZ, United States 155 G8
Saguaro Nat. Park Park N •
  AZ, United States .... 152 [114]
Saguenay, Parc du • QU, Canada .. 160 A1
Saguenay-St-Laurent, Parc marin du Park N •
  QU, Canada .... 161 [31]
Sagunto • Spain 80 E4
Sahara • Africa 106 C2
Sahel • Africa 106 C3
Sahel • Tunisia 107 D5
Sahiwal • Pakistan 122 B2
Sahri-i-Bahlol Heritage C • Pakistan 43 [146]
Sahuayo • Mexico 169 I7
Sai Gon [Riv] • Vietnam 129 B5
Sai Kung • Hong Kong, China 126 F5
Sai Kung Country Park •
  Hong Kong, China 126 F5
Sai, Laem • Ko Samui, Thailand . 130 G11
Saïdia • Morocco 107 B1
Saidpur • Bangladesh 122 C3
Saigon • Vietnam 129 B5
Sailla-Gouset • France 82 F6
Saimaa • Finland 97 F3
St Agnes • United Kingdom 65 I10
St Alban's Head • United Kingdom 65 K10
St Albans • United Kingdom 65 G7
St Albans • VT, United States 150 F2
St Albans • WV, United States 150 D3
St Albert • AL, Canada 160 A6
St Aldhelm's Head • United Kingdom 65 K10
St André • Réunion 113 D3
St Andrews • NB, Canada 160 A2
St Andrews • United Kingdom 65 B1
St Andrews Beach • United Kingdom 64 [1]
St Andrews Bay • United Kingdom . 62 D4
St Ann's Bay • Jamaica 165 D3
St Anne • Channel Is. 63 I14
St Anthony • NF, Canada 160 D1
St' Antioco • Sardinia, Italy 86 E6
St' Antioco, I. di •
  Sardinia, Italy 86 E6
St Anton am Arlberg Ski • Austria .. 61 [90]
St Anton am Arlberg • Austria 91 N8
St Arnaud • VI, Australia 136 G9
St Augustine • FL, United States .. 155 D1
St Austell • United Kingdom 65 I10
St Barbe • NF, Canada 160 D1
St Barthélemy • West Indies .... 166 D
St Barts • West Indies .... 166 D
St Bee's Head • United Kingdom ... 65 C3
St Benoît • Réunion 113 D3
St Blaise • Switzerland 90 I5
St Blasien • Germany 74 B4
St Brevin • France 77 D4
St Bride's Bay • United Kingdom ... 63 C9
St Brieuc • France 77 D3
St Brieuc, Baie de • France 63 I15
St Calais • France 77 F5
St Cast • France 77 D3
St Catharines • OT, Canada 161 D1
St Catherine area Heritage C • Egypt 43 [96]
St Catherine, Fort • Bermuda 165 L9
St Catherine, Monastery of • Egypt 109 B2
St Catherine, Mt • Grenada .... 166 Q
St Catherine Point • Bermuda 165 L9
St Chamond • France 76 F4
St Charles • MO, United States ... 150 B3
St Chinian • France 76 L9
St Christina in Gröden • Italy 86 C3
St Christoffelberg • Curaçao .... 166 V
St Christoph am Arlberg Ski •
  Austria .... 61 [90]
St Christoph am Arlberg • Austria .. 91 M8
St Christopher • St Kitts & Nevis .. 167 F
St Christopher, Rocque • France ... 78 F6
St Cirq-Lapopie • France 78 F6
St Clair • Canada/United States ... 161 A3
St Clair, Lake •
  Canada/United States 161 A3
St Claude • France 78 C3
St Claude • Guadeloupe .... 167 J
St Cloud • MN, United States 150 B1
St Croix • US Virgin Is. .... 166 X
St Croix I. Int. Hist. Site •
  United States 160 A2
St Croix I. Int. Hist. Site Park N •
  ME, United States .... 153 [296]
St Cyr-sur-Mer • France 78 G8

St David's • United Kingdom 63 C9
St David's Beach • United Kingdom 64 [55]
St David's Head • United Kingdom 63 C9
St David's I. • Bermuda 165 L9
St Denis • France 78 A1
St Denis • Réunion 113 C3
St Dié • France 76 G2
St Dizier • France 76 F2
St Egrève • France 78 C4
St Elias, Cape •
  AK, United States 157 E4
St Elias Mtns • YT, Canada 158 C2
St Emilion • France 78 E5
St Émilion Heritage C • France ... 44 [92]
St Estephe • France 76 K9
St Etienne • France 76 F4
St Étienne-de-Tinée Ski • France .. 61 [52]
St Eustatius • West Indies .... 167 E
St Exupéry [Apt] • France 78 C3
St Florent • Corsica, France 78 N11
St Florent, Golfe de •
  Corsica, France 78 N11
St Florentin • France 78 B3
St Flour • France 76 E4
St Francis Bay • South Africa 111 G7
St Francis, Cape • South Africa 111 G7
St Francisville •
  LA, United States 156 F6
St François • Guadeloupe .... 167 J
St François • QU, Canada 160 H3
St François • Seychelles 113 B2
St Gall • Switzerland 90 D2
St Gall Heritage C • Switzerland .. 44 [138]
St Gallen • Switzerland 90 D2
St Gallen Heritage C • Switzerland 44 [138]
St Gallen [Adm] • Switzerland 91 R9
St Gallenkirch Ski • Austria .... 61 [87]
St Gaudens France 78 E6
St Genis Nat. Hist. Site Park N •
  NH, United States .... 153 [294]
St Geoirs [Apt] • France 78 C4
St George • Bermuda 165 L9
St George Heritage C • Bermuda 42 [39]
St George • QL, Australia 136 C5
St George • UT, United States 155 G2
St George • FL, United States 157 C4
St George I. • FL, United States .. 155 B1
St George, Monastery of •
  Palestine NAR 120 B3
St George's • Grenada .... 166 Q
St George's Bay • NF, Canada 160 C1
St George's Channel •
  Ireland/United Kingdom 63 C8
St George Harbour • Bermuda 165 L9
St George's I. • Bermuda 165 L9
St Georges • QU, Canada 160 A2
St Germain • France 78 A1
St Germain-en-Laye • France 78 A1
St Gervais-les-Bains • France 78 D3
St Giles Is. • Trinidad & Tobago .. 166 R
St Gilgen • Austria 91 P7
St Gilles-Croix-de-Vie • France 76 C3
St Gilles-les-Bains • Réunion 113 C3
St Girons • France 78 K10
St Goar • Germany 74 D5
St Gotthard, Passo del •
  Switzerland 90 K5
ST HELENA • Atlantic Ocean 104 B6
St Helena Bay • South Africa 111 D6
St Helens • TS, Australia 136 F6
St Helens • United Kingdom 63 D7
St Helens, Mt •
  WA, United States 154 G5
St Helier • Channel Is. 63 I14
St Hilarion Castle • Cyprus 96 C3
St Hyacinthe • QU, Canada 160 H3
St Idlesbald • Belgium 70 D4
St Ignace • MI, United States 150 D1
St Ignace I. • OT, Canada 161 B1
St Ives • United Kingdom 65 I10
St Ives Beach • United Kingdom .. 64 [45]
St Ives Bay • United Kingdom 65 I10
St Jacques [Apt] • France 77 D4
St Jacut • France 77 D3
St Jakob am Arlberg Ski • Austria .. 61 [90]
St James • MI, United States 161 B2
St Jean • QU, Canada 160 H4
St Jean [Apt] • St Barthélemy .... 166 D
St Jean, Baie de • St Barthélemy . 166 D
St Jean d'Arves Ski • France .... 61 [36]
St Jean, Lac • QU, Canada 160 A1
St Jean-Cap-Ferrat • France 78 H7
St Jean-d'Angély • France 78 E5
St Jean-de-Luz • France 78 I9
St Jean-Pied-de-Port • France 78 J9
St Johann im Pongau • Austria 91 P7
St Johann in Tirol • Austria 91 O7
St John • NB, Canada 160 B2
St John • US Virgin Is. .... 166 X
St John [Riv] • Canada/United States 160 A2
St John's • Antigua & Barbuda ...... 167 I
St John's • Montserrat .... 167 G
St John's • NF, Canada 160 D1
St John's Church • Barbados .... 167 M
St John's Point • United Kingdom .. 63 C6
St Johns • AZ, United States 155 G3
St Jorisbaai • Curaçao .... 166 V
St Joseph • Dominica .... 167 K
St Joseph • France 76 L9
St Joseph • MI, United States 161 B3
St Joseph • MO, United States ... 150 B3
St Joseph • Réunion 113 D4
St Joseph • Seychelles 113 B1
St Joseph I. • OT, Canada 161 B2
St Joseph [Riv] •
  IN/MI, United States 161 B3
St Julian's • Malta 96 B2
St Julien's Beach • Malta 76 K9
St Just • United Kingdom 65 I10
St Kassian Ski • Italy .... 61 [146]
St Kassien • Italy 86 D3
St Kilda • United Kingdom 62 A3
St Kilda Heritage N • United Kingdom 41 [55]
St Kitts • St Kitts & Nevis .... 167 F
ST KITTS & NEVIS • West Indies .. 167 F
St Lary Soulan • France 78 J9
St Laurent • OT/QU, Canada 160 A1
St Lawrence • OT/QU, Canada ... 160 A1
St Lawrence, Gulf of •
  QU, Canada 160 B1
St Lawrence I. • AK, United States 157 D3
St Lawrence Is. Nat. Park Park N •
  OT, Canada .... 161 [29]
St Lawrence Is. Nat. Park •
  OT, Canada 160 F4
St Léonard-de-Noblat • France 78 F5
St Leonhard Ski • Italy .... 61 [146]
St Leonhard in Passeier • Italy 86 C3
St Leu • Réunion 113 L4
St Liz • France 78 K10
St Lô • France 76 C2
St Louis • MO, United States 150 B3
St Louis • Réunion 113 C4
St Louis • Senegal 106 A3
St Louis du Nord • Haiti 165 F5
St Louis, I. de Heritage C •
  Senegal .... 43 [109]
St Lucia • South Africa 111 C4
St LUCIA • West Indies .... 167 N
St Lucia Lake • South Africa 111 C4
St Lucie, Lake • United States ...... 166 C
St Maarten • West Indies .... 166 C
St Malo • France 77 D3
St Malo, Golfe de • France 63 I15
St Marc • Haiti 165 F5
St Marc, Canal de • Haiti 165 F5
St Märgen • Germany 74 B4
St Martin • West Indies .... 166 C
St Martin-de-Belleville Ski • France 61 [33]
St Martinville • LA, United States 156 E6
St Mary's • United Kingdom 63 B11
St Mary's, Cape • NF, Canada 160 D1
St Marys • PA, United States 156 A2
St Marys • TS, Australia 136 F6

St Marys City • MD, United States 156 B4
St Marys [Riv] •
  Canada/United States 161 B2
Salem Maritime Nat. Hist. Site Park N •
  MA, United States .... 153 [290]
St Mathieu, Point de • France 77 C3
St Matthias Group •
  Papua New Guinea 138 BB3
St Maurice, Réserve faunique du •
  QU, Canada 160 H3
St Mawes • United Kingdom 65 I10
St Maximin la Ste Baume • France 78 G8
St Michael im Lungau Ski • Austria . 61 [114]
St Michael im Lungau • Austria 91 P8
St Michael's Mount • United Kingdom 65 I10
St Miohol • Finland 97 F2
St Michel de l'Atalaye • Haiti 165 F5
St Moritz Ski • Switzerland .... 61 [82]
St Moritz • Switzerland 90 L6
St Nazaire • France 77 D4
St Nicholas' Abbey • Barbados .... 167 M
St Nicolas-de-Véroce Ski • France 61 [22]
St Niklaas • Belgium 70 B3
St Omer • France 76 E1
St Paul • France 78 H7
St Paul • MN, United States 150 B2
St Paul • Réunion 113 C3
St Paul, Baie de • Réunion 113 C3
St Paul I. • AK, United States 157 C4
St Paul I. • NS, Canada 160 C1
St Paul, Monastery of • Egypt 109 B2
St Paul's • St Kitts & Nevis .... 167 F
St Paul's Bay • Malta 96 B1
St Paul's Church Nat. Hist. Site Park N •
  NY, United States .... 153 [278]
St Paul's Is. • Malta 96 B1
St Paul's Point • Pitcairn Is. .... 139 L
St Pé, Parc zoologique • France ... 78 J9
St Peter Germany 74 B4
St Peter Port • Channel Is. 63 I14
St Petersburg • Russian Fed. 100 L9
St Petersburg • FL, United States 155 C2
St Petersburg • Russian Fed. 100 L9
St Petersburg Heritage C •
  Russian Fed. .... 44 [268]
St Philippe • Réunion 113 D4
St Pôlten • Austria 91 G1
St Quay-Portrieux • France 77 D3
St Quentin • France 76 E2
St Raphaël • France 78 H8
St Sauveur-des-Monts • QU, Canada 160 G3
St Savin • France 77 F6
St Savin-sur-Gartempe Heritage C •
  France .... 44 [82]
St Siméon • QU, Canada 160 A1
St Stephen • NB, Canada 160 A2
St Thegonnec • France 77 C3
St Thomas • US Virgin Is. .... 166 X
St Thomas Bay • Malta 96 B2
St Tropez • France 78 H8
St Ulrich Ski • Italy .... 61 [145]
St Ulrich • Italy 86 C3
St Veit an der Glan • Austria 91 G2
St Vigil in Enneberg • Italy 86 D3
St Vincent • MN, United States ... 150 A1
St Vincent, Gulf • SA, Australia ... 136 H8
St Vincent I. • FL, United States .. 155 B1
ST VINCENT & THE GRENADINES •
  West Indies .... 167 O-P
St Vith • Belgium 70 D4
St Wilfibaldsau • Germany 72 I8
St Wolfgang • Austria 91 P7
Ste Agathe-des-Monts • QU, Canada 160 G3
Ste Anne • Guadeloupe .... 167 J
Ste Anne • Martinique .... 167 L
Ste Anne • Réunion 113 D4
Ste Anne Marine Nat. Park •
  Seychelles 113 A1
Ste Anne-de-Beaupré • QU, Canada 160 A1
Ste Anne-des-Monts • QU, Canada 160 B1
Ste Croix • Switzerland 90 I5
Ste Croix, Lac de • France 78 G7
Ste Engrâce • France 78 I9
Ste Foy • QU, Canada 160 A1
Ste Foy-la-Grande • France 78 E6
Ste Marie • Martinique .... 167 L
Ste Marie • Réunion 113 D3
Ste Maxime • France 78 H8
Ste Rose • Guadeloupe .... 167 J
Ste Rose • Réunion 113 D4
Ste Suzanne • Réunion 113 D3
Saintes • France 78 E5
Saintes, les • Guadeloupe .... 167 J
Saintonge • France 78 E5
Saipan • N. Mariana Is. .... 138 B
Saipan • Palau .... 138 Y
Saipan Channel • N. Mariana Is. .. 138 B
Saïs [Apt] • Morocco 107 B1
Saitama • Japan 127 H8
Saiwa Swamp Nat. Park • Kenya . 109 C4
Sajama, Nevado • Bolivia 173 C4
Sakai • Japan 127 G7
Sakakawea, Lake •
  ND, United States 148 F1
Sakami • QU, Canada 159 I3
Sakarya • Turkey 95 B1
Sakarya [Riv] • Turkey 95 B2
Sakenan Temple • Bali, Indonesia 127 C3
Sakha Russ Adm • Russian Fed. . 101 [30]
Sakhalin • Russian Fed. 101 O5
Sakhira • Tunisia 107 D5
Sakon Nakhon • Thailand 130 A1
Saksköbing • Denmark 99 F8
Sakti • Tanzania 110 H7
Sakura • Japan 127 H8
Sakura • Japan 127 G7
Sal • Cape Verde 106 E7
Sala • Slovak Rep. 89 B9
Sala • Sweden 99 A1
Sala 'ilua • Samoa .... 139 G
Sala-y-Gómez • Pacific Ocean ... 139 FF4
Salacgrva • Latvia 100 K6
Saladillo • Argentina 175 F7
Salado • Argentina 175 B2
Salado • Cuba 164 E4
Salado, Ojos de • Argentina/Chile 175 B2
Salalah • Oman 120 G10
Salamá • Guatemala 170 K9
Salamanca • Mexico 169 I7
Salamanca • NY, United States .. 156 A1
Salamanca • Panama 170 M10
Salamanca • Spain 80 C3
Salamanca Heritage C • Spain ... 44 [112]
Salamina • Greece 94 BB3
Salamis • Cyprus 96 C3
Salani • Samoa .... 139 G
Salatiga • Java, Indonesia 131 Q12
Salazie • Réunion 113 D3
Salazie, Cirque de • Réunion 113 C3
Salcantay, Nevado de • Peru 173 F6
Saldae • United Kingdom 65 J10
Salda Gölü • Turkey 95 C7
Saldanha • South Africa 111 D6
Saldanha Bay • South Africa 111 D6
Saldus • Latvia 100 J7
Salé • Morocco 107 A1
Salé • United Kingdom 63 D7
Salé [Apt] • Morocco 107 A1
Salekhard • Russian Fed. 101 G3
Salelologa • Samoa .... 139 G
Salém • India 124 C3
Salem • MA, United States 156 D1
Salem • Montserrat .... 167 G

Salem • OR, United States 154 G6
Salem Express Dive • Egypt 109 E8
Salem Maritime Nat. Hist. Site Park N •
  MA, United States .... 153 [290]
Salema • Portugal 84 H8
Salerno • Italy 87 H7
Salerno, Golfo di • Italy 87 H7
Salgótarján • Hungary 92 B1
Salgueiro • Brazil 174 C3
Salihli • Turkey 95 F5
Salihorsk • Belarus 100 C3
Salima • KS, United States 148 G3
Salina • UT, United States 155 F5
Salina Bay • Malta 96 B1
Salina Cruz • Mexico 169 K8
Salina, I. • Italy 86 H7
Salina • Mexico 169 I6
Salinas • Mexico 169 I6
Salinas • Puerto Rico 165 I8
Salinas, Bahía • Puerto Rico 165 I8
Salinas Pueblo Missions Nat. Mon. •
  NM, United States 155 H8
Salinas Pueblo Missions Nat. Mon. Park N •
  NM, United States .... 152 [120]
Saline I. • Grenada .... 166 P
Salir • Portugal 84 J7
Salisbury • MD, United States 156 B3
Salisbury • United Kingdom 65 K9
Salisbury I. • NU, Canada 159 I2
Salisbury Plain • United Kingdom . 65 K9
Sallins • Ireland 69 E7
Salliut • QU, Canada 159 I2
Sallyana • Nepal 123 G7
Salmon • ID, United States 148 D1
Salmon Arm • BC, Canada 158 E3
Salmon • Cabo • Negros, Philippines 128 G3
Salmon Falls • ID, United States . 154 H6
Salmon • ID, United States 154 H6
Salmon River Mtns •
  ID, United States 154 H6
Salmonsdam Nature Reserve •
  South Africa 111 E7
Salo • Finland 99 D4
Saló • Italy 87 C2
Salobreña • Spain 82 J8
Salon-de-Provence • France 76 F5
Salonga, Parc nat. de la Park •
  Dem. Rep. of Congo .... 112 [49]
Salonga, Parc nat. de la Heritage N •
  Dem. Rep. of Congo .... 41 [102]
Salonika • Greece 93 C1
Salonika Heritage C • Greece ... 44 [232]
Salou • Spain 83 C4
Salsa • Sicily, Italy 86 H8
Salsomaggiore • Italy 87 B2
Salt • AZ, United States 155 G8
Salt Cay • Bahamas 164 A2
Salt Cay • Turks & Caicos Is. 164 D3
Salt I. • British Virgin Is. .... 166 A
Salt Lake City • UT, United States 155 F5
Salta • Argentina 175 B2
Saltaire Heritage C • United Kingdom 44 [25]
Saltash • United Kingdom 65 J10
Saltfjellet-Svartisen Nat. Park Park N •
  Norway .... 58 [10]
Saltholm • Denmark 99 G7
Saltillo • Mexico 168 D2
Salto • Italy 87 F4
Salto • Uruguay 175 C3
Salton Sea • CA, United States ... 154 J9
Saltrum • United Kingdom 65 J10
Saltsjöbaden • Sweden 99 B2
Saluafata • Samoa .... 139 G
Saluda • SC, United States 155 B1
Saluzzo • Italy 87 A1
Salvador • Brazil 174 C4
Salvador de Bahia Heritage C •
  Brazil .... 42 [73]
Salween • Myanmar 128 B2
Salzach • Austria 91 P7
Salzburg • Austria 91 P7
Salzburg Heritage C • Austria .... 44 [140]
Salzburg [Adm] • Austria 91 G7
Salzburger Alpen • Austria/Germany 91 H8
Salzgitter • Germany 72 D2
Salzkammergut • Austria 91 P7
Salzkammergut Heritage C • Austria 44 [141]
Salzwedel • Germany 72 D2
Sam • India 123 D7
Sam Lord's Castle • Barbados ..... 167 M
Sam Ngao • Thailand 130 B6
Sam Rayburn Reservoir •
  TX, United States 155 F5
Samae San • Thailand 130 E8
Samae San, Ko • Thailand 130 E8
Samak • Dominican Rep. 165 H5
Samaná, Bahía de • Dominican Rep. 165 H5
Samana, Cabo • Dominican Rep. . 165 H5
Samana Cay • Bahamas 164 B2
Samaná, Península de •
  Dominican Rep. 165 H5
Samandag • Turkey 95 J10
Samar • Philippines 128 G4
Samar • Russian Fed. 100 H3
Samar • Mindoro, Philippines 128 G4
Samar • N. Mariana Is. .... 138 B
Samar • Spain 82 K8
Samara • Palestine NAR 120 A3
Samaria [Region] •
  Israel/Palestine NAR 120 A3
Samariás, Faraġi • Crete, Greece . 93 G6
Samarinda • Indonesia 131 E4
Samarkand • Uzbekistan 121 E4
Samarkand Heritage C • Uzbekistan 43 [142]
Samarra • Iraq 120 E7
Sambalpur • India 124 C2
Sambasekikyo • Japan 127 H8
Sambhal • India 123 F7
Sambhar • India 123 E7
Sambor • Cambodia 129 C5
Sambor, Bahia • Argentina 175 G7
Sambre • Belgium 70 B4
Samburu-Shaba-Buffalo Springs Nat. Park •
  Kenya 109 D4
Samburu-Shaba-Buffalo Springs Nat. Park
  Park • Kenya .... 112 [72]
Same • Tanzania 110 H7
Samedan Ski • Switzerland .... 61 [81]
Samedan • Switzerland 90 L6
Samet, Ko • Thailand 130 E8
Sámi • Cephalonia, Greece .... 94 J
Sammallahdenmäki •
  Heritage C • Finland .... 43 [90]
Sammallahdenmäki Heritage C •
  Finland .... 43 [90]
Samnaun • Austria 91 N8
Samnaun • Switzerland .... 91 [86]
Samo • India 123 E7
Samoa • Pacific Ocean .... 139 G
Samoëns Ski • France .... 61 [13]
Samoëns • France 78 D3
Samora • Portugal 84 G6
Samorin • Slovak Rep. 91 H1
Sámos • Greece .... 94 E
Sámos Heritage C • Greece ..... 44 [244]
Sámos • Sámos, Greece .... 94 E
Sámos [I.] • Greece .... 94 E
Samosir • Indonesia 131 N9
Samothráki [I.] • Greece 93 D1
Samothráki • Greece 93 D1
Sampang • Java, Indonesia 131 D4
Samrong, Laem •
  Ko Samui, Thailand 130 G11
Samsø • Denmark 99 F7
Samsø Bælt • Denmark 99 F7
Samui, Ko • Thailand 130 G11
Samut Prakan • Thailand 130 E7
Samut Sakhon • Thailand 130 D7
Samut Songkhram • Thailand 130 D8
San • Poland 89 C3
San Agustín •
  Gran Canaria, Canary Is. 82 G6
San Agustín, Parque Arqueológico
  Heritage C • Colombia .... 42 [53]
San Andreas • CA, United States . 148 B3
San Andrés, I. de • Caribbean Sea 170 G4
San Andrés • Mexico 170 K9
San Angelo • TX, United States .. 149 F4
San Antonio • Ibiza, Spain 83 L9

San Miguel I. • CA, United States 154 I9
San Miguelito • Panama 170 M11
San Millán Heritage C • Spain ... 44 [104]
San Nicolas • Aruba .... 166 W
San Nicolás de los Arroyos •
  Argentina 175 F6
San Nicolás de Tolentino •
  Gran Canaria, Canary Is. 82 G6
San Nicolas I. • CA, United States 154 I9
San Pablo • Philippines 128 G4
San Pawl il-Bahar • Malta 96 B1
San Pedro • AZ, United States ... 149 D4
San Pedro •
  Buenos Aires, Argentina 175 F6
San Pedro • Côte d'Ivoire 106 B4
San Pedro • Salta, Argentina 175 B2
San Pedro Alcántara • Spain 82 I8
San Pedro de Coche • Venezuela 166 T
San Pedro de Macorís •
  Dominican Rep. 165 H4
San Pedro del Pinatar • Spain 83 A2
San Pedro Sula • Honduras 170 K9
San Philippe, Cayo de • Cuba 164 E4
San Pietro, I. di •
  Sardinia, Italy 86 E6
San Quintín • Mexico 168 H5
San Rafael • Argentina 175 B3
San Rafael • Dominican Rep. 165 G6
San Rafael del Yuma • Dominican Rep. 165 H6
San Remo • Italy 87 A3
San Roque • Spain 82 D3
San Saba • TX, United States 155 E5
San Salvador • El Salvador 170 K9
San Salvador de Jujuy • Argentina 175 B2
San Salvador I. • Bahamas 164 B2
San Sebastián • Argentina 175 B5
San Sebastián • Puerto Rico 165 I7
San Sebastián • Spain 80 D2
San Sebastián de la Gomera •
  Gomera, Canary Is. 83 H6
San Severo • Italy 85 E4
San Sicário Ski • Italy .... 61 [117]
San Tin • Hong Kong, China 126 F4
San Vicente • Mexico 168 H5
San Vicente de Cañete • Peru 173 E6
San Vigilio di Marebbe Ski • Italy .. 61 [148]
San Vigilio in Marebbe • Italy 86 D3
San Vincenzo • Italy 87 C3
San Vito Lo Capo • Sicily, Italy 86 G7
San Xoriguer • Minorca, Spain 83 J8
Sana • Yemen 120 E10
Sana'a [Apt] • Yemen .... 43 [128]
Sana'a • Yemen 120 E10
Sana'a Heritage C • Yemen ...... 43 [128]
SANAE [Base] • Antarctica .... 176 [13]
Sanahin Heritage C • Armenia ... 43 [137]
Sanandaj • Iran 120 F6
Sanarate • Guatemala 170 K9
Sanary-sur-Mer • France 78 G8
Sánchez • Dominican Rep. 165 H5
Sancti Heritage C • India .... 43 [153]
Sancti-Spíritus • Cuba 164 G4
Sancy, Puy de • France 76 E4
Sand • Rogaland, Norway 98 E5
Sand Cay • Seychelles 113 B1
Sand Hills • NE, United States ... 148 F2
Sand Key • FL, United States 155 C2
Sanda • Japan 127 F6
Sandakan • Sabah, Malaysia 128 F5
Sandane • Norway 98 F7
Sandaré • Mali 106 B3
Sandbach • United Kingdom 62 D1
Sande • Norway 98 D6
Sandefjord • Norway 98 D6
San Francisco Maritime Nat. Hist. Park
  Park N • CA, United States ..... 152 [43]
San Francisco, Sierra • Mexico ... 168 H6
San Francisco, Sierra de la Heritage C •
  Mexico .... 42 [13]
Sandnessjøen • Norway 98 F9
Sandness • United Kingdom 62 H12
Sandover • NT, Australia 136 B1
Sandoway • Myanmar 128 A3
Sandown Beach • United Kingdom 64 [37]
Sandown Park • United Kingdom .. 65 G7
Sandpoint • ID, United States 154 E6
Sandur • India 124 B1
Sandvig-Allinge • Denmark 99 H8
Sandviken • Sweden 97 D3
Sandwich • United Kingdom 50 B2
Sandy Bay • Jamaica 165 C3
Sandy Bay • St Vincent & Gren. .. 167 O
Sandy Cape • QL, Australia 136 C4
Sandy Cape • TS, Australia 136 E6
Sandy Ground • Anguilla .... 166 B
Sandy Ground Beach • Anguilla ... 166 B
Sandy Hook • NJ, United States .. 156 C2
Sandy I. • Anguilla .... 166 B
Sandy I. • Grenada .... 166 Q
Sandy Point • St Kitts & Nevis .... 167 F
Sandy Point • US Virgin Is. .... 166 X
Sandy Point Beach • Cayman Is. . 165 A1
Sandycove • Ireland 69 F8
Sandykgachy • Turkmenistan 121 D4
Sänfjället Nat. Park Park N • Sweden 58 [24]
Sanford • FL, United States 155 C2
Sanganeb Dive • Sudan 109 E9
Sanganer • India 123 E7
Sangatte • France/United Kingdom 76 D6
Sangeang • India 124 C1
Sangay, Parque Nac. • Ecuador .. 173 B3
Sangay, Parque Nac. Heritage N •
  Ecuador .... 40 [34]
Sangir • Indonesia 131 G3
Sangiran Heritage C • Indonesia 43 [209]
Sangir-e Java, Indonesia 131 Q12
Sangre de Cristo Range •
  CO/NM, United States 148 E3
Sangre Grande • Trinidad & Tobago 166 S
Sanguem • Goa, India 123 C6
Sanguinaires, Is. •
  Corsica, France 78 M12
Sani Greece .... 94 B
Sani Pass • South Africa 111 B4
Sanibel I. • FL, United States 155 C3
Sankasia • India 123 F7
Sankt-Petersburg Heritage C •
  Russian Fed. .... 44 [268]
Sanlíurfa • Turkey 95 C2
Sanlúcar de Barrameda • Spain ... 82 H8
Sanming • China 125 F4
Sanok • Poland 89 C4
Sans Souci • Haiti 165 F5
Sans Souci Heritage C • Haiti ... 42 [43]
Sanski Most • Bosnia-Herz. 92 G6
Sanssouci, Schloss • Germany ... 73 E8
Sant' Agnello • Italy 87 G7
Sant' Andria Priu, Necropoli di •
  Sardinia, Italy 86 F5
Sant' Angelo dei Lombardi • Italy .. 87 H6
Sant' Angelo in Fórmis • Italy 87 G6
Sant Carles de Peralta •
  Ibiza, Spain 83 L9
Sant Climent • Minorca, Spain 83 K8
Sant Feliu de Guíxols • Spain 83 I2
Sant Fransesc de Formentera •
  Formentera, Spain 83 M10
Sant Joan de Labritja •
  Ibiza, Spain 83 M9
Sant Josep de sa Talaia •
  Ibiza, Spain 83 L9
Sant Julia de Lória • Andorra 82 E6
Sant Lluís • Minorca, Spain 83 K8
Sant Miquel de Balansat •
  Ibiza, Spain 83 M9
Sant Pere de Rodes • Spain 83 D3
Sant Pere Pescador • Spain 83 D3

Sant Rafael de Forca •
  Ibiza, Spain 83 L9
Sant Salvador, Santuari de •
  Majorca, Spain 83 O12
Sant Telm • Majorca, Spain 83 N11
Sant Tomás • Majorca, Spain 83 J8
Santa Ana **Heritage C** • Argentina . . 42 [77]
Santa Ana • CA, United States 154 J9
Santa Ana • El Salvador 170 K9
Santa Ana • Mexico 168 I5
Santa Barbara • CA, United States . . 154 I9
Santa Barbara • Honduras 170 K9
Santa Barbara I. •
  CA, United States 154 I9
Santa Catalina I. •
  CA, United States 149 C4
Santa Catarina • Brazil 175 C2
Santa Catarina • Mexico 168 D2
Santa Catarina • Curaçao . . . . 166 V
Santa Caterina di Pittinuri •
  Sardinia, Italy 86 E5
Santa Caterina Valfurva • Italy 87 C1
Santa Clara • Cuba 164 F4
Santa Clara, Barragem de •
  Portugal 84 I7
Santa Clara Peak •
  NM, United States 155 H7
Santa Clara-a-Velha • Portugal 84 I7
Santa Clarita • CA, United States . . 149 C4
Santa Cristina **Ski** • Italy . . . . 61 [144]
Santa Cruz de Tenerife •
  Tenerife, Canary Is. 82 G5
Santa Cruz Valgardena • Italy 86 C3
Santa Croce, Lago di • Italy 86 D4
Santa Cruz • Aruba . . . . 166 W
Santa Cruz • Bolivia 173 C4
Santa Cruz • CA, United States 154 I8
Santa Cruz • Galápagos Is. 171 H10
Santa Cruz • Madeira 84 E5
Santa Cruz Barillas • Guatemala . . . 170 J9
Santa Cruz Beach Boardwalk **Park L** •
  CA, United States . . . . 157 [3]
Santa Cruz da Graciosa • Azores 84 C4
Santa Cruz das Flores • Azores 84 B4
Santa Cruz de la Palma •
  La Palma, Canary Is. 83 H6
Santa Cruz de Tenerife •
  Tenerife, Canary Is. 82 G5
Santa Cruz del Quiché • Guatemala . 170 J9
Santa Cruz del Sur • Cuba 164 G5
Santa Cruz I. • CA, United States . . . 154 I9
Santa Cruz I. •, L. - Galápagos Is. . . 171 H10
Santa Cruz Is. • Solomon Is. . . . . . . 138 W
Santa Cruz Mtns • Jamaica 165 C4
Santa Elena, Cabo • Costa Rica 170 E5
Santa Eufemia, Faro di • Italy 87 F5
Santa Eulalia del Río •
  Ibiza, Spain 83 M9
Santa Fé • Argentina 175 B3
Santa Fé • Cuba 164 E4
Santa Fe • NM, United States 155 H7
Santa Fe, I. • Galápagos Is. 171 H10
Santa Galdana • Minorca, Spain 83 J8
Santa Inés, I. • Chile 175 A5
Santa Isabel • Solomon Is. . . . . 138 W
Santa Lucía, Playa • Cuba 164 G4
Santa Margalida • Majorca, Spain . . 83 O11
Santa Margarita, I. • Mexico 168 I6
Santa Margherita di Pula •
  Sardinia, Italy 86 F6
Santa Margherita Ligure • Italy 87 B2
Santa María • Azores 84 C4
Santa Maria • Brazil 175 C2
Santa Maria • CA, United States . . . 154 I9
Santa Maria • Greece 50 D4
Santa Maria • Mexico 168 E3
Santa María • Páros, Greece . . . . 94 H
Santa Maria, Cabo de • Portugal 84 J8
Santa María di Capua Vetere • Italy . . 87 G6
Santa Maria di Leuca, Capo • Italy . . 85 G5
Santa Maria I. • Vanuatu . . . . 138 V
Santa Maria Mayor **Heritage C** •
  Argentina . . . . 42 [77]
Santa Marinella • Italy 87 E4
Santa Marta • Colombia 173 B1
Santa Monica Mtns Nat. Recreation Area
  Park N • CA, United States . . . . 152 [54]
Santa Pola • Spain 83 A1
Santa Ponça • Majorca, Spain 83 N12
Santa Rita • Belize 170 K8
Santa Rita • Guam . . . . 138 Z
Santa Rosa • Mexico 168 E4
Santa Rosa • Argentina 175 B3
Santa Rosa • CA, United States 154 I8
Santa Rosa • Mexico 168 I5
Santa Rosa • NM, United States . . . 149 F4
Santa Rosa de Copán • Honduras . . 170 K9
Santa Rosa I. • CA, United States . . 155 I1
Santa Rosa I. • FL, United States . . . 155 A1
Santa Rosa Xtampak • Mexico 169 F4
Santa Rosalía • Mexico 168 H6
Santa Severina • Italy 50 D4
Santa Susanna • Spain 83 D4
Santa Teresa • NT, Australia 136 B2
Santa Teresa di Gallura •
  Sardinia, Italy 86 F5
Santa's Village • OT, Canada 160 E4
Santana • Madeira 84 E5
Santana da Serra • Portugal 84 I7
Santander • Spain 80 D2
Santanilla, Is. • Honduras 170 F2
Santanyí • Majorca, Spain 83 O12
Santarém • Brazil 174 A3
Santarém • Portugal 80 A4
Santarém [Adm] • Portugal 84 A2
Santee Sioux **Ind Res** •
  NE, United States . . . . 155 [52]
Santes Creus, Monestir de • Spain . . 83 C4
Santiago • Chile 175 A3
Santiago • Mexico 168 I6
Santiago • Panama 170 G6
Santiago de Compostela • Spain 80 A2
Santiago de Compostela **Heritage C** •
  Spain . . . . 44 [111]
Santiago de Cuba • Cuba 164 H5
Santiago de Cuba **Heritage C** • Cuba . . 42 [42]
Santiago de la Ribera • Spain 83 A2
Santiago de los Caballeros •
  Dominican Rep. 165 G5
Santiago del estero • Argentina 175 B2
Santiago, I. • Galápagos Is. 171 G10
Santiago Ixcuintla • Mexico 169 H6
Santiago [Riv] • Mexico 169 H6
Santiago Tuxtla • Mexico 169 K7
Santíssima Trinità di Saccargia •
  Sardinia, Italy 86 E5
Santo André • Brazil 174 E7
Santo Antão • Cape Verde 106 C7
Santo António de Pádua • Brazil . . . 174 F6
Santo da Serra • Madeira 84 E5
Santo Domingo • Cuba 164 F4
Santo Domingo • Dominican Rep. . . 165 G5
Santo Domingo **Heritage C** •
  Dominican Rep. . . . . 42 [44]
Santo Domingo • Mexico 168 H5
Santo Domingo • NM, United States . 155 H7
Santo Domingo Tehuantepec • Mexico 169 K8
Santo Estêvão • Portugal 84 G6
Santorini • Greece 93 D3
Santos • Brazil 174 E7
Santos Dumont • Brazil 174 F6
Santpoort • Netherlands 70 G7
Sanur • Bali, Indonesia 131 L8
Sanur Beach • Bali, Indonesia 131 L8
Sanya • China 125 E5
Sanzao • China 126 E4
Sanzao Dao • China 126 E4
São Bartolomeu de Messines •
  Portugal 84 I7
São Borja • Brazil 175 C2
São Brás de Alportel • Portugal 84 J8
São Carlos • Brazil 175 D2
São Félix • Brazil 174 A3
São Francisco • Brazil 174 B4
São Gonçalo • Brazil 174 F7
São Gotardo • Brazil 174 E6
São João da Barra • Brazil 174 F7

São João del Rei • Brazil 174 E6
São Jorge • Azores 84 C4
São Jorge • Madeira 84 E5
São Jorge I. • Goa, India 123 C6
São Jose de Rio Prêto • Brazil 175 D2
São José do Campos • Brazil 174 E7
São Lourenço • Brazil 174 E7
São Luís • Brazil 174 B3
São Luís **Heritage C** • Brazil . . . . . 42 [71]
São Marcos, Baia de • Brazil 174 B3
São Marcos da Serra • Portugal 84 I7
São Miguel • Azores 84 C4
São Paulo • Brazil **Heritage C** • . . . . 42 [77]
São Nicolau • Cape Verde 106 E7
São Paulo • Brazil 174 E7
São Paulo [Adm] • Brazil 175 D2
São Raimundo Nonato • Brazil 174 B3
São Roque, Cabo de • Brazil 174 C3
São Sebastião, I. de • Brazil 174 E7
São Teotónio • Portugal 84 H7
São Tiago • Cape Verde 106 E7
São Tomé • São Tomé e Príncipe . . . 106 C4
São Tomé, Cabo de • Brazil 174 F7
SÃO TOMÉ E PRÍNCIPE • Africa . . 106 C4
SÃO TOMÉ [Island] •
  São Tomé e Príncipe 106 C4
São Vicente • Cape Verde 106 E7
São Vicente • Madeira 84 D5
São Vicente, Cabo de • Portugal 84 H8
Saon Beach • Ko Phuket, Thailand . . 130 V9
Saona, I. • Dominican Rep. 165 H6
Saône • France 76 F3
São Vicente • Ko Phuket, Thailand . . 130 F9
Sapi safari area **Heritage N** •
  Zimbabwe . . . . 41 [113]
Sapiéndza • Greece 94 AA3
Sapo Nat. Park **Park** • Liberia . . . 112 [14]
Sappada • Italy 86 D3
Sapporo • Japan 127 D2
Sapudi • Indonesia 131 R12
Sapulpa • OK, United States 124 E6
Saputara **Hill Sta** • India 123 D6
Saqqara • Egypt 109 A1
Saquarema • Brazil 174 F7
Sara Buri • Thailand 130 E7
Saragossa • Spain 50 B3
Saragossa • Spain 80 E3
Saragt • Turkmenistan 121 L10
Sarajevo • Bosnia-Herz. 92 G6
Saran • Kazakstan 121 F2
Sarandê • Albania 92 C4
Sarandi del Yí • Uruguay 175 G6
Saransk • Russian Fed. 100 G3
Sarapul • Russian Fed. 100 H2
Sarasin Bridge •
  Ko Phuket, Thailand 130 V9
Sarasota • FL, United States 155 C2
Saratoga Nat. Hist. Park •
  NY, United States 156 C1
Saratoga Nat. Hist. Park **Park N** •
  NY, United States . . . . 153 [275]
Saratoga Springs •
  NY, United States 156 C1
Saratovskoye Vdkhr. • Russian Fed. . 100 G3
Sarawak • Malaysia 128 E6
Saray • Iraq 120 F7
Sarayköy • Turkey 95 F5
Sardarshahar • India 123 E7
Sardegna • Italy . . . . 86 E-F
Sardinida Plain • Kenya 109 D4
Sardinia • Italy 50 D4
Sardis • Turkey 95 F5
Sarek Nat. Park **Park N** • Sweden . . 58 [20]
Sargodha • Pakistan 122 B2
Sarh • Chad 108 A4
Sari • Iran 120 D3
Sari d'Orcino • Corsica, France 78 M12
Sariá • Greece 94 DD4
Sarigerme • Turkey 95 F5
Sarina • QL, Australia 136 C4
Sariska Nat. Park • India 123 E7
Sariwon • D.P.R. of Korea 125 G3
Sariyer • Turkey 95 F3
Sark • Channel Is. 63 I14
Sarkisla • Turkey 95 C2
Sarköy • Turkey 95 E4
Sarlat-la-Canéda • France 77 F4
Sarnath • India 123 G8
Sarnen • Switzerland 90 K5
Sarnia • OT, Canada 161 A2
Saros Körfezi • Turkey 95 E4
Sarpsborg • Norway 98 E6
Sarqant • Kazakstan 121 G3
Sartène • Corsica, France 78 M12
Sarthe • France 77 E5
Sarthe [Adm] • France 77 F5
Sárti • Greece . . . . 94 B
Sárvár • Hungary 91 H2
Sary-Tash • Kyrgyzstan 121 F4
Saryözek • Kazakstan 121 G3
Saryshagan • Kazakstan 121 F2
Sarzana • Italy 87 B3
Sasaram • India 123 G8
Sasayama • Japan 127 F6
Sasebo • Japan 127 A4
Saskatchewan • Canada 158 F3
Saskatoon • SA, Canada 158 F3
Sasolburg • South Africa 110 B3
Sassandra • Côte d'Ivoire 106 B4
Sassari • Sardinia, Italy 86 E5
Sassnitz • Germany 72 E1
Sasso-misato • Japan 127 B4
Satna • India 123 F8
Satpayev • Kazakstan 121 E2
Satsuma-hantô • Japan 127 B4
Sattahip • Thailand 130 E8
Satu Mare • Romania 92 C2
Saturn • Romania 92 I7
Sauda • Norway 98 F9
SAUDI ARABIA • Asia 120 F9
Sauer • Germany 74 C6
Sauerland • Germany 73 A2
Saugatuck • MI, United States 161 B3
Saugus Iron Works Nat. Hist. Site •
  MA, United States 156 D1
Saugus Iron Works Nat. Hist. Site **Park N** •
  MA, United States . . . . 153 [290]
Sauland • Norway 98 G9
Saulgau • Germany 74 E7
Sault Ste Marie •
  MI, United States 150 D1
Sault Ste Marie • OT, Canada 159 H4
Sault Ste Marie Int. Bridge •
  Canada/United States 161 B2
Saum, Laem • Ko Phuket, Thailand . . 130 F9
Saumarez Reef • QL, Australia 136 D4
Saumâtre, Étang • Haiti 165 F6
Saumlaki • Indonesia 131 H5
Saumur • France 77 E5
Saumur [Château] • France 77 E5
Saundersfoot • United Kingdom . . . 64 [145]
Saurimo • Angola 110 B2
Sausalito • CA, United States 154 I8
Saut d'Eau • Haiti 165 F6
Sauternes • France 76 K9
Sauteurs • Grenada . . . . 166 Q
Sautron • Bay • Grenada . . . . 166 Q
Sauvage, Côte • France 77 D4
Sauve, la • France 78 E6
Sauveterre • France 78 E6
Sâuze d'Oulx **Ski** • Italy . . . . 61 [118]
Sâuze d'Oulx • Italy 87 A2
Sava • Europe 92 B2
Savage River • TS, Australia 136 E6
Savage River Nat. Park •
  TS, Australia 136 E6
Savai'i • Samoa . . . . 139 G
Savan I. • St Vincent & Gren. . . . . . 167 P
Savaneta • Aruba . . . . 166 W
Savanna-la-Mar • Jamaica 165 C4
Savannah • GA, United States 151 D4
Savannah [Riv] •
  GA/SC, United States 151 D4

Savannakhét • Laos 128 C3
Savant Lake • OT, Canada 159 G3
Savaré • India 124 B1
Savastepe • Turkey 95 E4
Saverne • France 76 G2
Savina, Es • Formentera, Spain 83 M10
Savognin • Switzerland 90 L5
Savoie • France 78 D4
Savona • Italy 87 B2
Savoy • France 77 B2
Savusavu • Fiji Is. . . . . 138 S
Savusavu Bay • Fiji Is. . . . . 138 S
Sawai Madhopur • India 123 E8
Sawankhalok • Thailand 130 C6
Sawantwadi • India 124 A1
Sawara • Japan 127 I8
Sawtooth Mtns • MN, United States . 161 A1
Sawtooth Nat. Recreation Area •
  ID, United States 154 H6
Saxony • Germany 72 E3
Sayak • Kazakstan 121 G2
Sayama • Japan 127 I8
Sayaxché • Guatemala 170 K9
Sayhut • Yemen 120 G10
Sayil • Mexico 169 F4
Saynshand • Mongolia 125 F2
Sázava • Czech Rep. 89 E6
Sázava [Riv] • Czech Rep. 89 E6
Sbeïtla • Tunisia 107 C5
Scafell Pike • United Kingdom 65 C3
Scalloway • United Kingdom 62 H12
Scalpay • United Kingdom 62 B3
Scalpay • Skye, United Kingdom 62 C3
Scandicci • Italy 87 C3
Scandola, Réserve naturelle •
  Corsica, France 78 M11
Scandola, Réserve naturelle **Heritage N** •
  Corsica, France . . . . 41 [61]
Scarba • United Kingdom 62 C4
Scarborough • Trinidad & Tobago . . 166 R
Scarborough • United Kingdom 63 E6
Scarborough **Beach** • United Kingdom . 64 [8]
Scariff, I. • Ireland 69 G11
Scarinish • United Kingdom 66 A2
Scarnjokki • Finland 97 E3
Scarp • United Kingdom 62 B2
Scaur, Fort • Bermuda 165 K10
Sciacca • Sicily, Italy 58 E7
Scie, Baie de la • France 76 E2
Seine • France 76 E2
Seine, Val de • France 78 B2
Seine-et-Marne • France 78 B2
Seitseminen Nat. Park **Park N** •
  Finland . . . . 58 [38]
Seitseminen Nat. Park • Finland 99 D3
Seixal • Madeira 84 D5
Seixal • Portugal 84 G6
Sejerø Bugt • Denmark 99 F7
Sekeren • Japan 127 I8
Sekinchan • Malaysia 129 F10
Sekoma • Botswana 110 I10
Sekondi-Takoradi • Ghana 106 B4
Sekseuil • Kazakstan 121 D2
Selah • WA, United States 148 B1
Selangor • Malaysia 129 F10
Selatan • Sumbawa • Sea 99 A2
Selatan, Selat •
  Penang, Malaysia 129 E8
Selawik • AK, United States 157 D2
Selçuk • Turkey 95 E5
Sele • Italy 87 H7
Sele, Piana dei • Italy 87 H7
Selebi-Phikwe • Botswana 110 J9
Selemdga • Mongolia 125 E2
Selemnk • Gabon 65 E5
Seletar • Singapore 129 I11
Seletar Reservoir • Singapore 129 I11
Seleuca • Iraq 121 J7
Seleucia Pierie • Turkey 95 J10
Seleucia Trachectis • Turkey 95 H7
Selibaby • Mauritania 106 E1
Seliger, Ozero • Russian Fed. 100 L10
Selingan • AZ, United States 149 D3
Selimiye • Antalya, Turkey 95 H8
Selimiye • Mugla, Turkey 95 F6
Selinunte • Sicily, Italy 86 G7
Selje • Norway 98 F7
Seljord • Norway 98 D6
Seljord stavkirke • Norway 98 D6
Seljordsvatnet • Norway 98 G9
Selkirk • MN, Canada 158 G3
Selkirkshire • United Kingdom 64 A3
Sella Nevea • Italy 87 D1
Sella, Passo di • Italy 86 C4
Sella Ronda **Ski** • Italy . . . . . . 61 [142-146]
Sellafield • United Kingdom 65 C3
Sellin • Germany 165 F6
Selma, Massif de La • Haiti 165 F6
Selma • AL, United States 151 C4
Selous Game Reserve • Tanzania . . 110 M8
Selous Game Reserve **Park** •
  Tanzania . . . . 112 [94]
Selous Game Reserve **Heritage N** •
  Tanzania . . . . 41 [111]
Selva di Cadore • Italy 86 C4
Selva di Val Gardena • Italy 86 C3
Selva Gardena **Ski** • Italy . . . . . . 61 [144]
Selvas • Brazil 173 C3
Selwyn Mtns • NT/YT, Canada 158 D2
Semakau • Singapore 129 H12
Semarang • Java, Indonesia 131 Q11
Semani, Gunung • Java, Indonesia . 131 R12
Semey • Kazakstan 121 H2
Semmering Railway **Heritage C** •
  Austria . . . . 44 [143]
Semnan • Iran 120 D3
Semois • Belgium/France 70 C5
Sempu • Indonesia 131 R12
Senang • Singapore 129 H12
Senanga • Zambia 110 B2
Sénart, Forêt de • France 78 B2
Sendai • Kyushu, Japan 127 B4
Sendai • Tohoku, Japan 127 D3
Sendai-wan • Japan 127 D3
Senden • Germany 74 E7
Senec • Slovak Rep. 89 B4
Seneca Lake • NY, United States . . . 156 B1
Senefe, Château de • Belgium 70 B4
Senegal • Africa 106 A3
SENEGAL • Africa 106 A3
Sénégal [Riv] • Africa 106 A3
Senftenberg • Germany 72 F3
Senica • Slovak Rep. 89 B4
Senigállia • Italy 87 D3
Senj • Croatia 92 D5
Senja • Norway 97 D2
Senlis • France 78 B1
Sennar • Sudan 108 C3
Sennen Cove **Beach** • United Kingdom . 64 [44]
Senneterre • QU, Canada 159 I4
Sens • France 76 E2
Sentosa • Singapore 129 H12
Seokguram Grotto **Heritage C** •
  Rep. of Korea . . . . 43 [192]
Seoul • Rep. of Korea 125 G3
Seoul **Heritage C** • Rep. of Korea . 43 [191]
Seoul [Adm] • Rep. of Korea 125 G3
Sepang • Malaysia 129 F10
Sepetiba, Baía de • Brazil 174 E7
Sephoris • Israel 120 C2
Sept Laux, les **Ski** • France . . . . . 61 [39]
Sept-Îles • France 76 D2
Sept-Îles-Port-Cartier, Réserve faunique des •
  QU, Canada 160 A1
Sequoia Nat. Park •
  CA, United States 154 J8
Sequoia Nat. Park **Park N** •
  CA, United States . . . . 152 [50]
Shap • United Kingdom 65 D3
Shap Abbey • United Kingdom 65 D3
Shap Fells • United Kingdom 65 D3
Shapinsay • United Kingdom 62 E2
Sharjah • United Arab Emirates 120 H8
Shark Bay **Heritage N** • Australia . 41 [146]
Shark Bay • WA, Australia 136 A5
Sharm el Sheikh • Egypt 109 B2
Sharon • Israel 120 A2
Sharp I. • Hong Kong, China 126 F5
Serbia • Serbia & Montenegro 92 C3
SERBIA & MONTENEGRO • Europe . 92 C3
Serebryansk • Kazakstan 121 H2
Shashi • China 125 F3

Seremban • Malaysia 129 G10
Serengeti Nat. Park • Tanzania 110 H7
Serengeti Nat. Park **Park** • Tanzania . 112 [84]
Serengeti Nat. Park **Heritage N** •
  Tanzania . . . . 41 [109]
Serengeti Plain • Tanzania 110 G7
SeaWorld California **Park L** •
  CA, United States . . . . 157 [7]
SeaWorld Florida •
  FL, United States 157 B1
SeaWorld Florida **Park L** •
  FL, United States . . . . 157 [24]
SeaWorld Texas • TX, United States . 155 E6
SeaWorld Texas **Park L** •
  TX, United States . . . . 157 [12]
Sérifos • Greece 129 H12
Sérifos • Greece 93 D3
Serik • Turkey 95 H8
Serov • Russian Fed. 100 J2
Serowe • Botswana 110 J10
Serpent I. • Mauritius 113 E5
Serpukhov • Russian Fed. 100 M10
Serra • Brazil 174 F6
Serra da Capivara, Parque Nac. **Heritage C** •
  Brazil . . . . 42 [70]
Serra da Capivara, Parque Nac. da •
  Brazil 174 B3
Serra da Capivara, Parque Nac. da •
  Heritage N • Brazil . . . . 40 [43]
Serra do Navio • Brazil 174 A2
Serra Orrios, Villaggio nuragico di •
  Sardinia, Italy 86 F5
Serrana Bank • Caribbean Sea 166 BB4
Serrant [Château] • France 77 E5
Serre-Chevalier **Ski** • France . . . . 61 [45]
Serre-Chevalier • France 78 D4
Serule • Botswana 110 J9
Servion • Switzerland 90 I5
Ses Animas, Mirador de •
  Majorca, Spain 83 N11
Ses Figueretes • Ibiza, Spain 83 M9
Ses Portes, Punta de •
  Ibiza, Spain 83 L10
Ses Salines • Majorca, Spain 83 O12
Ses Salines, Cap de •
  Majorca, Spain 83 O12
Seseh Beach • Bali, Indonesia 131 L8
Sesimbra • Portugal 84 G6
Sessa Aurunca • Italy 87 G6
Sesto • Italy 86 D3
Sestri Levante • Italy 87 B2
Sestriere **Ski** • Italy . . . . 61 [118]
Sestriere • Italy 87 A2
Sete Cidades, Caldeira das •
  Azores 84 B4
Sete Lagoas • Brazil 174 E6
Sete • France 77 A3
Sétif • Algeria 106 C1
Seto-naikai • Japan 127 B4
Setonaikai Nat. Park • Japan 127 F6
Settat • Morocco 107 A1
Settle • United Kingdom 63 D6
Setúbal • Portugal 84 G6
Setúbal [Adm] • Portugal 84 A3
Seul, Lac • OT, Canada 158 G4
Sevastopol' • Ukraine 100 D5
Sevelen • Switzerland 75 C5
Seven Mile Beach • Cayman Is. . . . 165 A2
Seven Springs **Ski** •
  PA, United States . . . . 146 [91]
Seven Springs • PA, United States . . 156 A2
Severn • OT, Canada 159 G3
Severn • United Kingdom 65 E6
Severn Gorge • United Kingdom 65 E5
Severn Valley Railway •
  United Kingdom 65 F6
Severnaya Dvina • Russian Fed. . . . 100 F1
Severnaya Zemlya • Russian Fed. . . 101 J2
Severobaykal'sk • Russian Fed. . . . 101 K4
Severodvinsk • Russian Fed. 100 F1
Sevilla • Spain 80 D4
Seville **Heritage C** • Spain . . . . 44 [122]
Seville • Spain 82 H7
Seville **Heritage C** • Spain . . . . 44 [122]
Seville Nueva • Jamaica 165 D3
Sevlievo • Bulgaria 92 H8
Sèvre Nantaise • France 77 E5
Sewall-Belmont Nat. Hist. Site **Park N** •
  DC, United States . . . . 153 [264]
Seward • AK, United States 157 E4
Seward Peninsula •
  AK, United States 157 D3
Sexten • Italy 86 D3
SEYCHELLES • Indian Ocean . . . 113 A-B
Seydhisfjördhur • Iceland 97 I6
Seymchan • Russian Fed. 101 Q3
Seyhan • Turkey 95 J9
Seymour • IN, United States 150 C3
Seymour • TX, United States 149 G4
Seymour • VI, Australia 136 G5
Seymour, I. • Galápagos Is. 171 H10
Sfakiá • Crete, Greece 93 G6
Sfânte Gheorghe • Covasna, Romania . 92 D2
Sfântu Gheorghe • Tulcea, Romania . 92 I7
Sfax • Tunisia 107 D5
Sfinári • Crete, Greece 93 G5
Sha Tin • Hong Kong, China 126 E5
Sha'ab Mahal **Dive** • Egypt 109 E8
Sha'ab Rumi **Dive** • Sudan 109 E9
Shaanxi • China 126 C1
Shaba Nat. Reserve • Kenya 109 D4
Shabeelle • Somalia 108 I4
Shable • Bulgaria 92 I8
Shache • China 121 K7
Shackleton Ice Shelf • Antarctica . . 176 S14
Shaeridan • WY, United States 148 E2
Shaftesbury • United Kingdom 65 K9
Shah Alam • Malaysia 129 G10
Shahdol • India 123 F7
Shahjahanpur • India 123 E8
Shahpura • India 123 E8
Shakaland • South Africa 111 C4
Shakawe • Botswana 110 I9
Shakhrisabz • Uzbekistan 121 E4
Shakhrisyabz **Heritage C** •
  Uzbekistan . . . . 43 [142]
Shakhty • Russian Fed. 100 F4
Shalqar • Kazakstan 121 C2
Shamattawa • MN, Canada 158 G3
Shan Plateau • Myanmar 128 B2
Shandan • China 125 E3
Shandong • China 126 D1
Shandong Bandao • China 126 D1
Shandong Peninsula • China 126 E2
Shangani • Zimbabwe 110 J9
Shanghai • China 126 H6
Shanghai [Adm] • China 125 G3
Shangqiu • China 125 F3
Shangrao • China 125 F4
Shangri-La • Minorca, Spain 83 K8
Shanguan Cave • China 126 E5
Shanklin **Beach** • United Kingdom . 64 [37]
Shannon [Apt] • Ireland 69 H10
Shannon, Mouth of the • Ireland 69 G10
Shannon • Ireland 69 G10
Shantou • China 125 F4
Shanty Creek **Ski** •
  MI, United States . . . . 146 [90]
Shanxi • China 126 C1
Shanzu Becah • Kenya 109 C6
Shaoguan • China 125 F4
Shaoxing • China 126 H7

Shasta, Mt • CA, United States 154 I7
Shatoujiao • China 126 F4
Shau Tau Kok • Hong Kong, China . 126 F4
Shawnee Mtn **Ski** •
  PA, United States . . . . 146 [94]
Shawnigan • QU, Canada 160 H3
Shaybara • Saudi Arabia 109 E8
Sheboygan • WI, United States 150 C2
Sheep's Head • Ireland 69 G11
Sheerness • United Kingdom 65 H7
Sheerness **Beach** • United Kingdom . 64 [24]
Sheet Harbour • NS, Canada 151 C4
Sheffield • AL, United States 151 C4
Sheffield • New Zealand 137 B3
Sheffield • United Kingdom 63 E6
Shek Kwu Chau • Hong Kong, China . 126 E5
Shek O • Hong Kong, China 126 F5
Shek O Country Park •
  Hong Kong, China 126 F5
Shekerley Mtns • Antigua & Barbuda . 123 E7
Shekhawati • India 123 E7
Shekou • China 126 E4
Sheksna • Russian Fed. 100 M9
Shelburne • NS, Canada 160 B2
Shelby • MT, United States 148 D1
Shelbyville • TN, United States 151 C3
Shelikof Strait •
  AK, United States 157 D4
Shelley Beach • Kenya 109 C6
Shellharbour • NS, Australia 136 H8
Shenandoah • VA, United States . . . 156 A3
Shenandoah Mtns •
  VA/WV, United States 156 A3
Shenandoah Nat. Park •
  VA, United States 156 A3
Shenandoah Nat. Park **Park N** •
  VA, United States . . . . 153 [249]
Shendi • Sudan 108 C3
Shengsi Liedao • China 126 H7
Shenghou • China 126 H7
Shenyang • China 125 G2
Shenzhen • China 126 E4
Shenzhen Special Economic Zone •
  China 126 E4
Shepherd Is. • Vanuatu . . . . 138 V
Shepparton • VI, Australia 136 G9
Sheppey, Isle of • United Kingdom . . 65 H7
Sherborne • United Kingdom 65 K9
Sherbrooke • QU, Canada 160 H4
Sherbrooke Village • NS, Canada . . 160 B2
Sheremetyevo [Apt] • Russian Fed. . 100 M10
Shergui • Tunisia 107 D5
Sheringham • United Kingdom 63 F8
Sheringham **Beach** • United Kingdom . 64 [14]
Sherkin I. • Ireland 69 H11
Sherman • TX, United States 155 E4
Sherman, Fuerte • Panama 170 L10
Sherwood • Botswana 110 J10
Shetland Is. • United Kingdom 62 H12
Sheung Shui • Hong Kong, China . . 126 F4
Sheung Wan • Hong Kong, China . . 126 E5
Shexian • China 126 G7
Sheyenne • ND, United States 148 G1
Shiant Is. • United Kingdom 62 B3
Shibam • Yemen 120 F10
Shibam **Heritage C** • Yemen . . . 43 [129]
Shibetsu • Japan 127 E2
Shibata • Kazakstan 121 E3
Shiga • Japan 127 G6
Shiga [Adm] • Japan 127 G6
Shigaraki • Japan 125 G2
Shiizhuang • China 125 F3
Shikarpur • Pakistan 122 A3
Shikohabad • India 123 F7
Shikoku • Japan 127 C4
Shikoku-tan • Russian Fed. 127 E2
Shiliguri • India 122 C3
Shillong **Hill Sta** • India 124 F5
Shimla • India 122 D3
Shilong • China 126 E4
Shimba Hills Nat. Reserve • Kenya . 109 C6
Shimba Hills Nat. Reserve **Park** •
  Kenya . . . . 112 [82]
Shimizu • Chubu, Japan 127 H9
Shimizu • Kinki, Japan 127 G7
Shimla **Hill Sta** • India 124 C5
Shimla • India 122 B2
Shimoda • Japan 124 B2
Shimoga • India 127 I9
Shimokama Spa • Japan 127 D2
Shimokita-hantô • Japan 127 D2
Shimonita • Kenya 109 C6
Shimonita • Japan 127 H8
Shimonoseki • Japan 127 B4
Shimotsuma • Japan 127 I8
Shin, Lough • United Kingdom 62 C2
Shing Mun Country Park •
  Hong Kong, China 126 E5
Shinjo • Japan 127 D3
Shinkansen • Japan 127 G6
Shinoisaka • Japan . . . . 94 H
Shintuya • Peru 173 F6
Shinyanga • Tanzania 110 G7
Shiono-misaki • Japan 127 C4
Shipai • China 126 E4
Shipka Pass • Bulgaria 92 H8
Shipley • United Kingdom 63 E6
Shiraito Falls • Japan 127 H9
Shirajganj Ghat • Bangladesh 122 C3
Shirakami-Sanchi **Heritage N** •
  Japan . . . . 41 [137]
Shirakawa-go **Heritage C** • Japan . 43 [196]
Shiraz • Iran 120 G8
Shiretoko-misaki • Japan 127 E2
Shirley, Cape • Antigua & Barbuda . 167 I
Shirley, Fort • Dominica . . . . 167 K
Shirley Heights • Antigua & Barbuda . 167 I
Shishaldin Volcano •
  AK, United States 157 D4
Shivpuri • India 123 E8
Shivpuri Nat. Park • India 123 E8
Shiyan Lake Hot Springs Resort •
  China 126 F3
Shíza • Greece 94 AA3
Shizuishan • China 125 E3
Shizuoka • Japan 127 H9
Shizuoka [Adm] • Japan 127 H9
Shkodër • Albania 92 B3
Shoalhaven • NS, Australia 136 H8
Shodoury Common **Beach** •
  United Kingdom . . . . 64 [23]
Shoebuyrness **Beach** • United Kingdom . 64 [23]
Shortland Is. • Solomon Is. . . . . 138 W
Shosenkyo Gorge • Japan 127 H8
Shoshone • ID, United States 154 H6
Shoshone Falls • ID, United States . 154 H6
Shoshone Mtns • NV, United States . 154 H6
Shreveport • LA, United States 156 E5
Shrewsbury • United Kingdom 65 E6
Shri Mahalsa Temple • Goa, India . . 123 C6
Shri Mallikarjun Temple •
  Goa, India 123 C6
Shri Mangesh Temple • Goa, India . 123 C6
Shropshire • United Kingdom 65 E5
Shropshire Hills • United Kingdom . . 65 E5
Shuangbai • China 125 E4
Shuangyashan • China 121 C2
Shubarkuduk • Kazakstan 121 C2
Shumen • Bulgaria 92 H8
Shunde • China 126 E4
Shungnak • AK, United States 157 D2
Shuri • Okinawa, Japan . . . . 138 A
Shute Harbour • QL, Australia 136 C3
Shymkent • Kazakstan 121 E3
Si Racha • Thailand 130 E8
Si Satchanalai • Thailand 130 C6
Si Satchanalai Nat. Park • Thailand . 130 C6
Si'umu • Samoa . . . . 139 G
Siak Kecil Reserve • Indonesia 131 N10
Sian Ka'an, Reserva de la Biósfera •
  Mexico 169 G5

Sian Ka'an, Reserva de la Biósfera **Heritage N** • Mexico 40 [20]
Siauliai • Lithuania 100 J7
Sibaya, Lake • South Africa 111 C3
Sibenik • Croatia 92 F6
Sibenik **Heritage C** • Croatia 44 [209]
Siberia • Russian Fed. 101 M3
Siberut • Indonesia 131 A4
Sibigo • Indonesia 131 M9
Sibiloi Nat. Park • Kenya 109 C4
Sibiloi Nat. Park **Park** • Kenya 112 [68]
Sibiu • Romania 92 D2
Sibolga • Indonesia 131 N10
Siboney, Playa • Cuba 164 H5
Sibu • Sarawak, Malaysia 128 E6
Sichang, Ko • Thailand 130 E8
Sichuan • China 126 C2
Sichuan Pendi • China 126 C2
Sicié, Cap • France 78 G8
Sicilia • Italy 86 G-H
Sicilia, Canale di • Italy/Tunisia 85 D6
Sicily • Italy 86 G-H
Sicuani • Peru 173 F6
Sidári • Corfu, Greece 94 A
Side • Turkey 95 H8
Sideby • Finland 99 C3
Síderos, Akra • Crete, Greece 93 J6
Sidi Barrani • Egypt 108 B1
Sidi Bel Abbès • Algeria 106 B1
Sidi Bou Saïd • Tunisia 107 D4
Sidi Daoud • Tunisia 107 D4
Sidi Ifni • Morocco 107 A3
Sidi Kacem • Morocco 107 A1
Sidi Moussa • Morocco 107 A1
Sidlaw Hills • United Kingdom 65 B1
Sidmouth • United Kingdom 65 J10
Sidney • MT, United States 148 F1
Sidney • OH, United States 150 D2
Siebengebirge • Germany 74 A1
Siedlce • Poland 89 C2
Siegburg • Germany 74 A1
Siegen • Germany 74 B1
Siem Reap • Cambodia 128 C4
Siena • Italy 87 C3
Siena **Heritage C** • Italy 44 [162]
Sieradz • Poland 89 B3
Sierra Blanca • TX, United States 149 E4
SIERRA LEONE • Africa 106 A4
Sierra Nevada • Spain 82 J7
Sierra San Pedro Martír, Parque Nac. • Mexico 168 H5
Sierra Vista • AZ, United States 149 D4
Sierra-at-Tahoe **Ski** • CA, United States 146 [31]
Sierre • Switzerland 90 J6
Siesta Key • FL, United States 155 C2
Siete Hermanos, Cayos • Dominican Rep. 165 F5
Sífnos • Greece 93 D3
Sigatoka • Fiji Is. 138 T
Sigdal • Norway 98 D5
Sigean, Réserve africaine de • France 78 L10
Sighisoara **Heritage C** • Romania 44 [221]
Sigiriya • Sri Lanka 124 C4
Sigiriya **Heritage C** • Sri Lanka 43 [167]
Siglufjördhur • Iceland 97 I6
Sigmaringen • Germany 74 E7
Sígri • Lesbos, Greece 94 C
Sigtuna • Sweden 99 B1
Siguanea • Cuba 164 E4
Siguenza • Spain 50 B4
Siguiri • Guinea 106 B3
Sigulda • Latvia 100 K7
Sihanoukville • Cambodia 128 C4
Siilinjärvi • Finland 97 F3
Siipyy • Finland 99 C3
Siirt • Turkey 95 D2
Sijunjung • Indonesia 131 N10
Sikar • India 123 E7
Sikeston • MO, United States 151 C3
Sikhote-Alin **Heritage N** • Russian Fed. 41 [86]
Síkinos • Greece 93 D3
Sikkim • India 123 B2
Silale • Lithuania 100 J8
Silandro • Italy 87 C1
Silao • Mexico 169 I7
Silba • Croatia 92 F6
Silchar • India 122 D3
Sile • Turkey 95 F3
Silencio, Costa del • Tenerife, Canary Is. 82 G5
Silesia • Czech Rep./Poland 89 A3
Silhouette • Seychelles 113 B1
Silicon Valley • CA, United States 154 I8
Silifke • Turkey 95 I10
Silisili, Mt • Samoa 139 G
Silistra • Bulgaria 92 H7
Siljan • Norway 98 D6
Siljan • Sweden 97 C3
Silk Road • Asia 121 J-L
Silkeborg • Denmark 99 E7
Sillé-le-Guillaume [Château] • France 77 E5
Sillyon • Turkey 95 H7
Siloso, Fort • Singapore 129 H12
Sils-Maria **Ski** • Switzerland 61 [83]
Sils-Maria • Switzerland 90 L6
Siluatan, Gunung • Indonesia 131 M9
Silute • Lithuania 100 J8
Silvan • Turkey 95 D2
Silvaplana • Switzerland 90 L6
Silvassa • India 122 B3
Silver City • NM, United States 155 H8
Silver Dollar City **Park L** • MO, United States 157 [17]
Silver Hill • Montserrat 167 G
Silver Lake Resort • China 126 E4
Silver Mtn **Ski** • ID, United States 146 [38]
Silver Spring • MD, United States 156 A3
Silver Star **Ski** • BC, Canada 146 [5]
Silverwood • ID, United States 154 H5
Silves • Portugal 84 I8
Silvretta **Ski** • Austria 61 [91]
Silvretta • Austria 91 M8
Simav • Turkey 95 F4
Simbach • Germany 74 H7
Simbruini, Monti • Italy 87 F4
Simcoe, Lake • OT, Canada 160 E4
Siméto • Sicily, Italy 86 H8
Simeuluë • Indonesia 131 M9
Simferopol' • Ukraine 100 D5
Sími • Greece 93 E3
Simien Mtns Nat. Park **Park** • Ethiopia 112 [58]
Simien Mtns Nat. Park **Heritage N** • Ethiopia 41 [99]
Simlångsdalen • Sweden 99 G6
Simmer • Germany 74 C6
Simmern • Germany 74 C6
Simon's Town • South Africa 111 D7
Simonstorp • Sweden 99 A2
Simplon Tunnel • Italy/Switzerland 90 J6
Simplonpass • Switzerland 90 J6
Simpson Bay Lagoon • St Martin, West Indies 166 C
Simpson Desert • NT/QL, Australia 135 F5
Simpson Desert Nat. Park • QL, Australia 135 F5
Simpson I. • OT, Canada 161 B1
Simrishamn • Sweden 99 G7
Simson Baai • St Maarten 166 C
Simssee • Germany 74 H7
Sinabang • Indonesia 131 M10
Sinai • Egypt 109 B1
Sinai, Mt • Egypt 109 B2
Sinaia • Romania 92 D2
Sinaloa • Mexico 169 B2
Sincelejo • Colombia 173 B2
Sindal • Denmark 99 F6
Sindangan • Philippines 128 G5
Sindangbarang • Java, Indonesia 131 O12
Sines • Portugal 80 A5
Sinéu • Majorca, Spain 83 O11
SINGAPORE • Asia 129 H-I
Singapore City • Singapore 129 I12
Singapore Crocadilarium • Singapore 129 I12
Singapore Science Centre • Singapore 129 H11
Singapore, Straits of • Asia 129 I12
Singapore Zoological Gardens • Singapore 129 H11
Singaraja • Bali, Indonesia 131 L7
Singen • Germany 74 B4
Singh Beach • Ko Phuket, Thailand 130 F10
Singida • Tanzania 110 G7
Singkarak, Danau • Indonesia 131 N10
Singkawang • Indonesia 131 C3
Singkep • Indonesia 131 B4
Singkil • Indonesia 131 M10
Singleton • NS, Australia 136 H8
Singö • Sweden 99 B1
Singö [I.] • Sweden 99 B1
Singos • Greece 94 B
Sinharaja Forest Reserve • Sri Lanka 124 C4
Sinharaja Forest Reserve **Heritage N** • Sri Lanka 41 [127]
Sinis • Sardinia, Italy 86 E6
Siniscóla • Sardinia, Italy 86 F5
Sinj • Croatia 92 G6
Sinoe, Lacul • Romania 92 I7
Sinop • Turkey 95 C1
Sinquerim Beach • Goa, India 123 C5
Sintang • Indonesia 131 D4
Sintra • Portugal 84 F6
Sintra **Heritage C** • Portugal 44 [133]
Sintra, Serra de • Portugal 84 F6
Sinzig • Germany 74 C5
Sion • Switzerland 90 J6
Sioux City **Park L** • Gran Canaria, Canary Is. 59 [75]
Sioux City • Gran Canaria, Canary Is. 82 G6
Sioux City • IA, United States 150 A2
Sioux Falls • SD, United States 150 A2
Sioux Lookout • OT, Canada 159 G3
Sipacate • Guatemala 170 J9
Sipalay • Philippines 128 G5
Sipan • Croatia 92 G6
Sipcenski prohod • Bulgaria 92 H8
Siping • China 125 G2
Siple I. • Antarctica 176 W5
Siponto • Italy 50 D4
Sir Donald Sangster [Apt] • Jamaica 165 C3
Sir Edward Pellow Group • NT, Australia 135 F3
Sir Francis Drake Channel • British Virgin Is. 166 A
Sir Sam's **Ski** • OT, Canada 146 [14]
Sir Seewoosagur Ramgoolam [Apt] • Mauritius 113 F6
Sir Seretse Khama [Apt] • Botswana 110 J10
Siracusa • Sicily, Italy 86 H8
Sirat • Romania 92 D2
Sire, Ko • Thailand 130 F10
Siridao Beach • Goa, India 123 C5
Sirikit Reservoir • Thailand 130 C6
Sirjan • Iran 120 H8
Sirmilik Nat. Park **Park N** • NU, Canada 161 [8]
Sirmione • Italy 87 C2
Sírna • Greece 94 CC4
Sirnak • Turkey 95 D2
Sirohi • India 123 D8
Sirolo • Italy 87 D3
Síros • Greece 94 I
Sirsa • India 123 E7
Sirsi • India 124 B1
Sirte • Libya 100 A1
Sirte, Gulf of • Libya 108 A1
Sisak • Croatia 92 G5
Sisimiut • Greenland 159 K2
Sisophon • Cambodia 128 C4
Sissi • Crete, Greece 93 I6
Sistan • Iran 120 I7
Sisteron • France 78 G7
Sisters, The • Trinidad & Tobago 166 R
Sistiana • Italy 87 D1
Sitakunda • Bangladesh 122 D3
Sitapur • India 123 F7
Sitges • Spain 83 C4
Sithonía • Greece 94 B
Sitía • Crete, Greece 93 J6
Sitka • AK, United States 157 F4
Sitka Nat. Hist. Park **Park N** • AK, United States 152 [16]
Sittard • Netherlands 70 D4
Sittingbourne • United Kingdom 65 H7
Sittwe • Myanmar 128 A2
Situbondo • Java, Indonesia 131 R12
Siufaalele Point • American Samoa 139 H
Siuna • Nicaragua 170 E4
Siv. Donets • Ukraine 100 E4
Sivas • Turkey 95 C2
Sivrisihar • Turkey 95 B2
Siwan • India 123 G8
Six Flags America • MD, United States 156 B3
Six Flags America **Park L** • MD, United States 157 [29]
Six Flags AstroWorld • TX, United States 155 F5
Six Flags AstroWorld **Park L** • TX, United States 157 [13]
Six Flags Belgium **Park L** • Belgium 59 [43]
Six Flags Belgium • Belgium 70 C4
Six Flags Darien Lake **Park L** • NJ, United States 157 [35]
Six Flags Darien Lake • NY, United States 156 A1
Six Flags Elitch Gardens **Park L** • CO, United States 157 [10]
Six Flags Fiesta Texas • TX, United States 155 E5
Six Flags Fiesta Texas **Park L** • TX, United States 157 [12]
Six Flags Great Adventure • NJ, United States 156 C2
Six Flags Great Adventure **Park L** • NJ, United States 157 [34]
Six Flags Great America • IL, United States 161 A3
Six Flags Great America **Park L** • IL, United States 157 [15]
Six Flags Holland **Park L** • Netherlands 59 [38]
Six Flags Holland • Netherlands 70 C2
Six Flags Magic Mtn • CA, United States 154 J9
Six Flags Magic Mtn **Park L** • CA, United States 157 [4]
Six Flags Marine World **Park L** • CA, United States 157 [1]
Six Flags New England • MA, United States 156 C1
Six Flags New England **Park L** • MA, United States 157 [36]
Six Flags over Georgia **Park L** • GA, United States 157 [22]
Six Flags over Texas • TX, United States 155 E4
Six Flags over Texas **Park L** • TX, United States 157 [11]
Six Flags St Louis **Park L** • MO, United States 157 [16]
Six Flags WaterWorld • TX, United States 155 F5
Six Flags WaterWorld **Park L** • TX, United States 157 [13]
Six Flags Worlds of Adventure **Park L** • OH, United States 157 [19]
Sixt **Ski** • France 61 [14]
Siyal Is. • Egypt/Sudan 109 E9
Sizergh Castle • United Kingdom 65 D4
Sjælland • Denmark 99 F7
Sjöbo • Sweden 99 G7
Skadarsko jezero Nat. Park **Park N** • Serbia & Montenegro 58 [128]
Skælsør • Denmark 99 F8
Skærbæk • Denmark 99 E7
Skaftafell Nat. Park **Park N** • Iceland 58 [2]
Skäfthammar • Sweden 99 B1
Skagen • Denmark 99 F6
Skagern • Sweden 99 G5
Skaggerak • Europe 99 E6
Skagway • AK, United States 157 F4
Skála • Cephalonia, Greece 94 J
Skála • Peloponnese, Greece 93 C3
Skälderviken • Sweden 99 G7
Skanderborg • Denmark 99 E7
Skándzoura • Greece 94 BB2
Skåne • Sweden 99 G7
Skaneateles Lake • NY, United States 156 B1
Skanès [Apt] • Tunisia 107 D5
Skånevik • Norway 98 F9
Skänninge • Sweden 99 H5
Skanör • Sweden 99 G8
Skara • Sweden 99 G5
Skaraborg • Sweden 99 G5
Skaralid • Sweden 99 G7
Skarnes • Norway 98 E5
Skavsta [Apt] • Sweden 99 A2
Skawina • Poland 89 G9
Skeena • BC, Canada 160 I6
Skegness • United Kingdom 63 F7
Skegness **Beach** • United Kingdom 64 [12]
Skei • Norway 98 G7
Skeleton Coast • Namibia 110 A2
Skellefte älv • Sweden 97 D2
Skellefteå • Sweden 97 E3
Skellig Michael • Ireland 69 G11
Skellig Michael **Heritage C** • Ireland 44 [14]
Skelmersdale • United Kingdom 63 D7
Skerries • Ireland 69 F6
Skhirat Plage • Morocco 107 A1
Ski • Norway 98 E5
Ski Apache **Ski** • NM, United States 146 [66]
Ski Beech Mtn **Ski** • NC, United States 146 [87]
Ski Liberty • PA, United States 156 A3
Ski Morin Heights **Ski** • QU, Canada 146 [17]
Ski Roundtop • PA, United States 156 B2
Ski Sundown • CT, United States 156 C1
Ski Windham • NY, United States 156 C1
Skíathos • Greece 93 C2
Skibbereen • Ireland 69 H11
Skibotn • Norway 97 E2
Skiddaw • United Kingdom 65 D3
Skiddaw Forest • United Kingdom 65 D3
Skien • Norway 98 D6
Skierniewice • Poland 89 C3
Skiftet Kihti • Finland 99 C4
Skikda • Algeria 106 C1
Skilingaryd • Sweden 99 G6
Skinári • Zante, Greece 94 J
Skinári, Akra • Zante, Greece 94 J
Skinnskatteberg • Sweden 99 A1
Skíros • Greece 93 D2
Skive • Denmark 99 E7
Skjærhalden • Norway 98 E6
Skjeberg • Norway 98 E6
Skjern • Denmark 99 E7
Skjolden • Norway 98 G7
Sklavopoúla • Crete, Greece 93 G6
Skocjan Caves • Slovenia 92 F5
Skocjan Caves **Heritage N** • Slovenia 41 [71]
Skomer I. • United Kingdom 63 C9
Skópelos • Greece 93 C2
Skopje • FYR of Macedonia 92 C3
Skorba • Malta 96 A2
Skørping • Denmark 99 E6
Skotfoss • Norway 98 D6
Skotselv • Norway 98 D5
Skotterud • Norway 98 E5
Skövde • Sweden 99 G5
Skrimfjella • Norway 98 D6
Skudeneshavn • Norway 98 F9
Skuleskogen Nat. Park **Park N** • Sweden 58 [22]
Sky Harbor [Apt] • AZ, United States 155 G8
Sky Lake • FL, United States 157 B1
Skye • United Kingdom 62 B3
Skylands • NJ, United States 156 C2
Slagbaai, Boca • Bonaire 166 U
Slagelse • Denmark 99 F8
Slagharen, Attractiepark **Park L** • Netherlands 59 [37]
Slagharen, Attractiepark • Netherlands 70 D2
Slamet, Gunung • Java, Indonesia 131 P12
Slane • Ireland 69 E6
Slaney • Ireland 69 E7
Slantsy • Russian Fed. 100 K6
Slaski • Poland 89 F9
Slate Is. • OT, Canada 161 B1
Slave • AL/NT, Canada 158 E3
Slave Coast • Benin/Nigeria 106 C4
Slave Lake • AL, Canada 160 J6
Slave Lake, Lesser • AL, Canada 160 J6
Slavonia • Croatia 92 G5
Slavonice • Czech Rep. 89 E7
Slavonski Brod • Croatia 92 G5
Slavskovsky Les • Czech Rep. 89 D6
Slea Head • Ireland 69 G11
Sleeping Bear Dunes Nat. Lakeshore • MI, United States 161 B2
Sleeping Bear Dunes Nat. Lakeshore **Park N** • MI, United States 153 [160]
Slemmestad • Norway 98 E5
Slidell • LA, United States 156 F6
Slidre • Norway 98 G8
Sliedrecht • Netherlands 70 H8
Sliema • Malta 96 B2
Slieve Aughty Mtns • Ireland 69 H9
Slieve Bloom Mtns • Ireland 69 C3
Slieve Mish Mtns • Ireland 69 G10
Sligo • Ireland 69 H8
Sligo [Adm] • Ireland 69 H8
Sligo Bay • Ireland 69 H8
Slimbridge • United Kingdom 65 E6
Sliven • Bulgaria 92 H8
Slobozia • Ialomita, Romania 92 H7
Slobozia • Pitesti, Romania 92 H7
Slough • United Kingdom 65 G7
Slov'yans'k • Ukraine 100 E4
Slovak karst **Heritage N** • Slovak Rep. 41 [70]
SLOVAK REPUBLIC • Europe 89 B4
SLOVENIA • Europe 91 G3
Slovenská raj Nat. Park **Park N** • Slovak Rep. 58 [113]
Slowinski Nat. Park **Park N** • Poland 58 [100]
Slubice • Poland 89 A2
Slunchev Bryag • Bulgaria 92 H8
Slunj • Croatia 92 F5
Slupsk • Poland 89 B1
Slutsk • Belarus 100 C3
Sluys • North Sea 50 B2
Slyne Head • Ireland 69 G9
Småland • Sweden 99 H6
Smålandsfarvandet • Denmark 99 F8
Smålandsstenar • Sweden 99 G6
Smallwood Reservoir • NF, Canada 159 J3
Smarhon • Belarus 100 K8
Smeralda, Costa • Sardinia, Italy 86 F5
Smeraldo, Grotta di • Italy 87 H7
Smir-Restinga • Morocco 107 B1
Smith • AL, Canada 160 J6
Smith I. • MD, United States 156 B4
Smith's I. • Bermuda 165 L9
Smiths Falls • OT, Canada 160 F4
Smithton • TS, Australia 136 E6
Smögen • Sweden 99 F5
Smoky Hill • KS, United States 148 F3
Smøla • Norway 97 B3
Smolensk • Russian Fed. 100 D3
Smólikas • Greece 93 B1
Smolyan • Bulgaria 92 D3
Smuggler's Cove • Zante, Greece 94 J
Smugglers' Notch **Ski** • VT, United States 146 [110]
Smyadovo • Bulgaria 92 H8
Smyrna • DE, United States 156 B3
Smyrna • GA, United States 151 D4
Smyrna • Turkey 95 E5
Snaefell • Isle of Man 63 C6
Snake • United States 148 C2
Snake River Plain • ID, United States 154 H6
Snake Temple, Penang • Penang, Malaysia 129 D8
Sneek • Netherlands 70 C1
Sneem • Ireland 69 G11
Sneeuberg • South Africa 111 G6
Snezka • Czech Rep./Poland 89 E6
Snøhetta • Norway 98 G7
Snow Summit **Ski** • CA, United States 146 [35]
Snowbasin **Ski** • UT, United States 146 [46]
Snowbird **Ski** • UT, United States 146 [51]
Snowdon • United Kingdom 63 C7
Snowdonia Nat. Park **Park N** • United Kingdom 58 [53]
Snowdonia Nat. Park • United Kingdom 63 D7
Snowmass **Ski** • CO, United States 146 [61]
Snowshill Manor • United Kingdom 65 F6
Snowshoe **Ski** • WV, United States 146 [89]
Snowy Mtns • NS/VI, Australia 136 H9
Snowy [Riv] • NS/VI, Australia 136 H9
Snug Corner • Bahamas 164 B2
Snuol • Cambodia 129 B5
Snyder • TX, United States 149 F4
So, Laem • Ko Samui, Thailand 130 G12
Soave • Italy 87 C2
Soay • United Kingdom 62 B3
Soberanía, Parque Nac. • Panama 170 L11
Sobotka • Czech Rep. 89 E6
Sobradinho, Barragem de • Brazil 174 B4
Sobral • Brazil 174 B3
Soc Trang • Vietnam 129 B6
Sochaczew • Poland 89 C2
Sochi • Russian Fed. 100 E5
Societé, Archipel de la • French Polynesia 139 DD4
Socompa • Argentina 175 B2
Socorro • NM, United States 155 H8
Socorro, I. • Mexico 168 B4
Socotra • Yemen 120 G11
Sodankylä • Finland 97 F2
Sodegaura • Japan 127 I8
Söderåsen • Sweden 99 G7
Söderhamn • Sweden 97 D3
Söderköping • Sweden 99 H5
Södermanland • Sweden 99 A2
Södertälje • Sweden 99 B2
Södertörn • Sweden 99 B2
Sodwana Bay Nat. Park • South Africa 111 C3
Soekarno-Hatta [Apt] • Java, Indonesia 131 O11
Soest • Germany 50 C2
Soest • Netherlands 70 H7
Sœurs, les • Seychelles 113 B2
Sofades • Greece 93 C2
Sofala • NS, Australia 136 H8
Sofala, Baía de • Mozambique 110 C3
Sofia • Bulgaria 92 C3
Sofiya • Bulgaria 92 C3
Sofrino • Russian Fed. 100 M10
Sogamoso • Colombia 173 B2
Sogn og Fjordane • Norway 98 F7
Sogndal • Norway 98 G8
Sognefjorden • Norway 98 F8
Sohâg • Egypt 109 B2
Sohna • India 123 E7
Soissons • France 78 B1
Soka Beach • Bali, Indonesia 131 K8
Söke • Turkey 95 E5
Sokhumi • Georgia 120 E5
Sokna • Norway 98 D5
Soko Is. • Hong Kong, China 126 E5
Sokodé • Togo 106 C4
Sokol • Russian Fed. 100 M9
Sokolov • Czech Rep. 89 D6
Sokoto • Nigeria 106 C3
Sol, Costa del • Spain 82 H-K
Sol, Costa do • Portugal 84 F6
Sol y Nieve • Spain 82 J7
Sola [Apt] • Norway 98 F9
Solapur • India 122 B4
Solda • Italy 87 C1
Sölden **Ski** • Austria 61 [94]
Sölden • Austria 91 N8
Soldeu • Andorra 82 E5
Soldotna • AK, United States 157 E4
Solenzara • Corsica, France 78 N12
Solignac • France 78 F5
Solingen • Germany 73 D6
Solitude **Ski** • UT, United States 146 [49]
Söll **Ski** • Austria 61 [100]
Söll • Austria 91 O7
Sollentuna • Sweden 99 B2
Sóller • Majorca, Spain 83 N11
Solna • Sweden 99 B2
Solo • Java, Indonesia 131 Q12
Solo [Riv] • Java, Indonesia 131 Q11
Solok • Indonesia 131 N10
Sololá • Guatemala 170 J9
SOLOMON IS. • Pacific Ocean 138 W
Solomon Sea • Papua New Guinea/Solomon Is. 134 D5
Solothurn • Switzerland 90 J5
Solothurn [Adm] • Switzerland 91 Q9
Solovetskiye Ostrova **Heritage C** • Russian Fed. 43 [93]
Solsvik • Norway 98 F8
Solta • Croatia 92 G6
Soltau • Germany 72 C2
Solund • Norway 98 F8
Solvang • CA, United States 154 I9
Sølvegruvene • Norway 98 D5
Sölvesborg • Sweden 99 G7
Solway Firth • United Kingdom 62 D6
Solwezi • Zambia 110 B2
Som, Ko • Thailand 130 G11
Soma • Turkey 95 E4
Somali Peninsula • Somalia 106 D4
SOMALIA • Africa 108 D4
Sombor • Serbia & Montenegro 92 B2
Sombrerete • Mexico 169 H6
Sombrero • Anguilla 166 B
Somerset • KY, United States 150 D3
Somerset • United Kingdom 65 K9
Somerset Bridge • Bermuda 165 K10
Somerset East • South Africa 111 G6
Somerset I. • Bermuda 165 K10
Somerset I. • NU, Canada 158 G1
Somerset Village • Bermuda 165 K10
Somerset West • South Africa 111 D7
Somerton • United Kingdom 65 K9
Somme • France 76 D1
Sommen • Sweden 99 H5
Somnath **Beach** • India 124 E6
Somnathpur • India 124 B2
Somosomo • Fiji Is. 138 S
Somoto • Nicaragua 170 D4
Son • India 123 G8
Son • Norway 98 E6
Son Bou de Baix • Minorca, Spain 83 K8
Son Bou, Platja de • Minorca, Spain 83 J8
Son La • Vietnam 128 C2
Son Moll • Majorca, Spain 83 O11
Son Parc • Minorca, Spain 83 K7
Son Sant Joan [Apt] • Majorca, Spain 83 N11
Sonagiri • India 123 F8
Sonamarg **Hill Sta** • India 124 E5
Sonderborg • Denmark 99 E8
Sønderjylland • Denmark 99 E8
Søndervig • Denmark 99 E7
Søndre-Strømfjord • Greenland 159 K2
Sondrio • Italy 87 B1
Song Shan • China 126 [3]
Songea • Tanzania 110 H8
Songhua Jiang • China 125 G2
Songjiang • China 126 H7
Songkhla • Thailand 128 C5
Songo Mnara • Tanzania 110 H8
Songo Mnara **Heritage C** • Tanzania 43 [118]
Sonipat • India 123 E7
Sonneburg • Germany 72 D3
Sonobe • Japan 127 G6
Sonoma • CA, United States 154 I8
Sonora • CA, United States 154 I8
Sonora • TX, United States 149 F4
Sonora [Adm] • Mexico 169 A1
Sonora [Riv] • Mexico 168 I5
Sonoran Desert • AZ, United States 155 G8
Sonoyta • Mexico 168 H5
Sonsbeck • Germany 73 C5
Sonsonate • El Salvador 170 K9
Sonsorol Is. • Palau 138 AA2
Sonthofen • Germany 74 F8
Soo Locks • Canada/United States 161 B2
Soomaa Nat. Park **Park N** • Estonia 58 [146]
Soomaa Nat. Park • Estonia 100 K6
Sooneck, Burg • Germany 74 D6
Soontornpoo Mon. • Thailand 130 E8
Sopocani Monastery **Heritage C** • Serbia & Montenegro 44 [215]
Sopot • Poland 89 B1
Sopweru • Fed. States of Micronesia 138 C
Sør-Trøndelag • Norway 98 B2
Sora • Italy 87 F5
Sorel • QU, Canada 160 H3
Sorell • TS, Australia 136 F7
Sorell, Cape • TS, Australia 136 E7
Sörenberg **Ski** • Switzerland 61 [68]
Sörenberg • Switzerland 90 J5
Sorfjorden • Norway 98 G8
Soria • Spain 80 D3
Sorø • Denmark 99 F8
Soroa • Cuba 164 E4
Soroca • Moldova 92 E1
Sorocaba • Brazil 175 D2
Sorong • Indonesia 131 H4
Soroti • Uganda 109 C4
Sørøya • Norway 97 E1
Sorraia • Portugal 84 G6
Sorrento • Italy 87 G7
Sorsele • Sweden 97 D2
Sortavala • Russian Fed. 100 D1
Sösdala • Sweden 99 G7
Sosnowiec • Poland 89 F8
Sospel • France 78 H7
Sosúa • Dominican Rep. 165 G5
Sotavento de Jandía, Playa de • Fuerteventura, Canary Is. 83 H5
Sotkamo • Finland 97 F3
Soto • Curaçao 166 V
Soto la Marina • Mexico 169 J6
Sotra • Norway 98 F8
Sottern • Sweden 99 H5
Souahel, Boukhalef [Apt] • Morocco 107 A1
Soúda • Crete, Greece 93 G5
Soúda, Ormos • Crete, Greece 93 H5
Souflí • Greece 93 E1
Soufrière • Dominica 167 K
Soufrière • Guadeloupe 167 J
Soufrière • St Lucia 167 N
Soufrière Bay • Dominica 167 K
Soufrière Bay • St Lucia 167 N
Soufrière Hills • Montserrat 167 G
Soufrière, La • St Vincent & Gren. 167 O
Soúgia • Crete, Greece 93 G6
Souillac • France 78 F5
Souillac • Mauritius 113 E6
Souk el Arba du Rharb • Morocco 107 A1
Soulac-sur-Mer • France 78 E5
Soúnion Nat. Park **Park N** • Greece 58 [142]
Soûr **Heritage C** • Lebanon 44 [307]
Souris • Canada/United States 148 F1
Souris • PE, Canada 160 B2
Sous le Vent • Réunion 113 C4
Sousse • Tunisia 107 D4
Sousse **Heritage C** • Tunisia 44 [290]
Souterraine, la • France 77 F6
SOUTH AFRICA • Africa 110 B3
South America • 171
South Andaman • India 122 D4
South Australia • Australia 135 E5
South Baymouth • OT, Canada 161 C2
South Beach • Bahamas 164 A2
South Bend • IN, United States 150 C2
South Boston • VA, United States 156 A4
South Branch Potomac • WV, United States 156 A3
South Caicos • Turks & Caicos Is. 164 D3
South Cape • HI, United States 157 J6
South Carolina • United States 151 D4
South China Sea • Asia 128 E4
South Dakota • United States 148 F2
South Downs • United Kingdom 63 E10
South East Cape • TS, Australia 136 F7
South East Point • VI, Australia 136 G9
South Frigate Bay • St Kitts & Nevis 167 F
South Georgia • Atlantic Ocean 175 E5
South Haven • MI, United States 161 B3
South Hole Sound • Cayman Is. 165 A1
South I. • New Zealand 137 B3
South I. Nat. Park • Kenya 109 C4
South Kitui Nat. Reserve • Kenya 109 D5
South Lake Tahoe • CA, United States 148 C3
South Luangwa Nat. Park **Park** • Zambia 112 [106]
South Magnetic Pole • Antarctica 176 T4
South Molle I. • QL, Australia 136 C3
South Negril Point • Jamaica 165 C3
South Passage • Marshall Is. 139 E
South Platte • CO, United States 148 F2
South Pole • Antarctica 176
South Rock • Turks & Caicos Is. 164 D3
South Ronaldsay • United Kingdom 62 D2
South Sandwich Is. • Atlantic Ocean 10 H8
South Saskatchewan • AL/SA, Canada 158 E3
South Seymour [Apt] • Galápagos Is. 171 H10
South Shetland Is. • Antarctica 176 N4
South Shields • United Kingdom 62 E6
South Shields **Beach** • United Kingdom 64 [6]
South Sound • Cayman Is. 165 A2
South Town • Cayman Is. 165 A1
South Turkana Nat. Reserve • Kenya 109 C4
South Uist • United Kingdom 62 B3
South West • United Kingdom 64 A6
South West Cape • New Zealand 137 A4
South West Cape • TS, Australia 136 E7
Southampton • United Kingdom 63 E10
Southampton I. • NU, Canada 159 H2
Southaven • MS, United States 151 C4
Southbroom • South Africa 111 B5
Southeast Atlantic forest reserves **Heritage N** • Brazil 40 [46]
Southeast Cuba coffee plantations **Heritage C** • Cuba 42 [42]
Southeast Indian Ridge • Indian Ocean 9 O8
Southend-on-Sea • United Kingdom 65 H7
Southend-on-Sea **Beach** • United Kingdom 64 [23]
Southern • United Kingdom 64 B5
Southern Alps • New Zealand 137 A3
Southern Cross • WA, Australia 135 B6
Southern Indian Lake • MN, Canada 158 G3
Southern Ocean • 9 K8
Southern Uplands • United Kingdom 62 D5
Southern Ute **Ind Res** • CO, United States 155 [35]
Southland • New Zealand 137 G8
Southport • QL, Australia 136 D5
Southport • TS, Australia 136 F7
Southport • United Kingdom 63 D7
Southsea • United Kingdom 66 D6
Southwest Florida [Apt] • FL, United States 155 C3
Southwest Indian Ridge • Indian Ocean 9 L7
Southwest Nat. Park • TS, Australia 136 E7
Southwest New Zealand parks **Heritage N** • New Zealand 41 [163]
Southwold • United Kingdom 63 F8
Southwold **Beach** • United Kingdom 64 [20]
Sovetsk • Russian Fed. 100 J8
Sovetskaya Gavan • Russian Fed. 101 N5
Soweto • South Africa 110 B3
Soya-misaki • Japan 127 D1
Sozopol • Bulgaria 92 H8
Spa • Belgium 70 D4
Spa-Francorchamps • Belgium 70 D4
Spaandem • Netherlands 70 G7
Spaans Lagoen • Aruba 166 W
Spaanswater • Curaçao 166 V
Space Coast • FL, United States 155 D2
SPAIN • Europe 80
Spalato • Croatia 50 D3
Spánda, Akra • Crete, Greece 93 G5
Spandau (Berlin) • Germany 73 E7
Spanish Fork • UT, United States 148 D2
Spanish Point • Antigua & Barbuda 167 H
Spanish Point • Bermuda 165 K10
Spanish Town • British Virgin Is. 166 A
Spanish Town • Jamaica 165 D4
Spanish Wells • Bahamas 164 A1
Sparks • NV, United States 154 I7
Sparreholm • Sweden 99 A2
Sparta • Greece 93 C3
Spartanburg • SC, United States 151 D4
Spartel, Cap • Morocco 107 A1
Spárti • Greece 93 C3
Spartivento, Capo • Calábria, Italy 85 F6
Spartivento, Capo • Sardinia, Italy 86 F6
Speichersee • Germany 74 G7
Speightstown • Barbados 167 M
Spello • Italy 87 D3
Spencer • IA, United States 150 A2
Spencer • ID, United States 148 D2
Spencer Gulf • SA, Australia 135 F6
Sperillen • Norway 98 D5
Sperlonga • Italy 87 F5
Sperrin Mtns • United Kingdom 62 B6
Spessart • Germany 73 A3
Spetsai • Greece 93 C3
Spétses • Greece 93 C3
Spey • United Kingdom 62 D3
Speyer • Germany 74 B2
Speyer **Heritage C** • Germany 44 [61]
Speyside • Trinidad & Tobago 166 R
Spézia, La • Italy 87 B3
Spézia, La • Italy 87 B3
Sphinx • Egypt 109 A1
Spice Is. • Indonesia 131 G4
Spiddal • Ireland 69 H9
Spiennes **Heritage C** • Belgium 44 [43]
Spiez • Switzerland 90 J5
Spijkenisse • Netherlands 70 G8
Spíli • Crete, Greece 93 H6
Spílion Kamarón • Crete, Greece 93 H6
Spilva [Apt] • Latvia 100 J7
Spin Buldak • Afghanistan 121 E5
Spinalónga, Herson • Crete, Greece 93 J6
Spingdale • NF, Canada 160 C1
Spion Kop Nature Reserve • South Africa 111 B4
Spirit Mtn **Ski** • MN, United States 146 [68]
Spisské Pohradie **Heritage C** • Slovak Rep. 44 [200]
Spitsbergen • Arctic Ocean 176 I2
Spittal an der Drau • Austria 91 P8
Spitzingsee • Germany 74 G8
Spjelkavik • Norway 98 G7
Splendid China • China 126 E4
Splendid China • FL, United States 157 A1
Split • Croatia 92 G6
Split **Heritage C** • Croatia 44 [211]
Splügen • Switzerland 90 K5
Spodsbjerg • Denmark 99 F8
Spokane • WA, United States 154 H5
Spokane **Ind Res** • WA, United States 155 [3]
Spoleto • Italy 87 E4
Spongeorama • FL, United States 155 C2
Spontin • Belgium 70 C4
Sporades, Northern • Greece 94 BB2
Sporades, Southern • Greece 94 DD4
Sporádes, Vóries • Greece 93 D2
Sportgastein • Austria 91 P8
Spot Bay • Cayman Is. 165 B1
Spotorno • Italy 87 B2
Spotted Horse • WY, United States 148 E2
Spratly Is. • South China Sea 128 E5
Spray • OR, United States 148 C2
Spree • Germany 72 F3
Spreepark (Berlin) • Germany 73 F8
Spring Bay • Saba 167 E
Spring Hill • FL, United States 155 C2
Springdale • AR, United States 151 B3
Springer • NM, United States 149 F3
Springfield • CO, United States 149 F3
Springfield • IL, United States 150 C3
Springfield • MA, United States 156 C1
Springfield • MO, United States 151 B3
Springfield • OH, United States 150 D3
Springfield • OR, United States 154 G6
Springfield Armory Nat. Hist. Site **Park N** • MA, United States 153 [285]
Springhill • NS, Canada 160 B2
Springsure • QL, Australia 136 C4
Sprockhövel • Germany 73 D5
Spruce Grove • AL, Canada 160 J6
Spui • Netherlands 70 G8
Spurn Head • United Kingdom 63 F7
Spurr, Mt • AK, United States 157 E3
Squaw Valley **Ski** • CA, United States 146 [30]
Squillace, Golfo di • Italy 85 F5
Sravanabelgola • India 124 B2
Sravasti • India 123 G7
Srebarna • Bulgaria 92 H7
Srebarna Nature Reserve **Heritage N** • Bulgaria 41 [76]
Sredne-Sibirskoye Ploskorgor'ye • Russian Fed. 101 K3
Sremska Mitrovica • Serbia & Montenegro 92 B2
Sri Aman • Sarawak, Malaysia 128 E6
Sri Jayewardenepura Kotte • Sri Lanka 124 C4
SRI LANKA • Asia 124 C4
Srikalahasti • India 124 C2
Srinagar **Hill Sta** • India 124 E5
Srinagar • India 122 D2
Srirangam • India 124 C3
Srirangapatnam • India 124 B2
Srisailam • India 124 C1
Stabbursdalen Nat. Park **Park N** • Norway 58 [5]
Stack Skerry • United Kingdom 62 C1
Stade • Germany 72 C2
Stade de France (Paris) • France 78 A1
Stadtlohn • Germany 72 B3
Staffelsee • Germany 74 G8
Stafford • United Kingdom 63 D8
Staffordshire • United Kingdom 64 B4
Stagnone, I. della • Italy 86 G7
Stahnsdorf • Germany 73 E8
Staigue Fort • Ireland 69 G11
Staines • United Kingdom 63 E9
Stake Bay • Cayman Is. 165 B1
Stalheim • Norway 98 G8
Stalís • Crete, Greece 93 I6
Stalowa Wola • Poland 89 C3
Stamford • CT, United States 156 C2
Stamford Bridge • United Kingdom 50 B2
Stamnes • Norway 98 F8
Stampalia • Greece 93 E3

Standing Rock Ind Res • SD, United States....155 [46]
Standley Chasm • NT, Australia....136 B1
Stanger • South Africa....111 C4
Stanley • Falkland Is.....175 C5
Stanley • Hong Kong, China....126 E5
Stanley • ID, United States....148 D2
Stanley • TS, Australia....136 E6
Stanovoy Khrebet • Russian Fed.....101 M4
Stansted [Apt] • United Kingdom....65 G7
Stara Planina • Bulgaria/Yugoslavia....92 D3
Stara Zagora • Bulgaria....92 H8
Starachowice • Poland....89 C3
Staraya Russa • Russian Fed.....100 L9
Starbuck I. • Kiribati....139 DD3
Stargard Szczecinski • Poland....89 A2
Stari Ras Heritage C • Serbia & Montenegro....44 [215]
Starkenburg • Germany....74 C6
Starkville • MS, United States....156 F5
Starnberg • Germany....74 G7
Starnberger See • Germany....74 G7
Starogard Gdanski • Poland....89 B2
Start Bay • United Kingdom....65 J10
Start Point • United Kingdom....65 J10
Staryy Oskol • Russian Fed.....100 F2
Staszów • Poland....89 G8
State College • PA, United States....156 A2
Staten I. • NY, United States....156 C2
Statesboro • GA, United States....151 D3
Statesville • NC, United States....151 D3
Stathelle • Norway....98 D6
Statia • West Indies....167 E
Statue of Liberty Heritage C • NY, United States....42 [12]
Statue of Liberty Nat. Mon. • NY, United States....156 C2
Statue of Liberty Nat. Mon. Park N • NY, United States....153 [278]
Staunton • VA, United States....156 A4
Staurt • FL, United States....155 D2
Stavanger • Norway....98 F9
Stavern • Norway....98 D6
Stavoren • Netherlands....70 C1
Stavronikita, SS • Barbados....167 M
Stavropol • Russian Fed.....100 F4
Stavrós • Crete, Greece....93 G5
Stavrós • Halkidiki, Greece....94 B
Stavrós, Akra • Crete, Greece....93 I5
Stavrovouni Monastery • Cyprus....96 D4
Steamboat Ski • CO, United States....146 [54]
Steamtown Nat. Hist. Site Park N • PA, United States....153 [271]
Stebbins • AK, United States....157 D3
Stechelberg Ski • Switzerland....61 [69]
Stefansson I. • NU, Canada....158 F1
Stege • Denmark....99 F8
Steglitz (Berlin) • Germany....73 F8
Steiermark • Austria....91 T11
Steinach • Austria....91 N8
Steinau an der Strasse • Germany....74 F8
Steingaden • Germany....74 F8
Steinkjer • Norway....97 C3
Steinsel • Luxembourg....70 D5
Stella Maris • Bahamas....164 B2
Stellenbosch • South Africa....111 D7
Stelvio • Italy....87 C1
Stelvio, Parco Naz. dello Park N • Italy....58 [92]
Stelvio, Parco Naz. dello • Italy....87 C1
Stenbrohult • Sweden....99 G7
Stendal • Germany....72 D2
Stenungsund • Sweden....99 F5
Stephens Point • WI, United States....150 C2
Stephenville • NF, Canada....160 C1
Stephenville • TX, United States....155 E14
Steps Point • American Samoa....139 H
Stereá Eláda • Greece....94 BB2
Sterkfontein Heritage C • South Africa....43 [123]
Sterkrade (Oberhausen) • Germany....73 C5
Sterkstroom • South Africa....111 G6
Sterling • CO, United States....148 F2
Sterling • IL, United States....150 C2
Sterling Heights • MI, United States....161 A3
Stern Ski • Italy....61 [146]
Stern • Italy....86 D3
Sterrenberg, Burg • Germany....74 D5
Sterzing • Italy....86 C3
Stettin • Poland....89 A2
Stevenage • United Kingdom....65 F7
Stevens Pass Ski • WA, United States....146 [23]
Stevens Village • AK, United States....157 E3
Stewart I. • New Zealand....137 A4
Stewart Is. • Solomon Is.....138 W
Steynsburg • South Africa....111 G6
Steyr • Austria....91 G1
Steytlerville • South Africa....111 F7
Stilfs • Italy....87 C1
Still Bay • South Africa....111 E7
Stillwater • MN, United States....150 B1
Stillwater • OK, United States....151 A3
Stirling • United Kingdom....65 A2
Stirlingshire • United Kingdom....65 A2
Stjernøya • Norway....97 C1
Sto Paláti • Náxos, Greece....94 H
Stockholm • Sweden....99 B2
Stockholm Heritage C • Sweden....44 [8]
Stockholm [Adm] • Sweden....99 B1
Stockport • United Kingdom....63 D7
Stockton • CA, United States....154 I8
Stockton-on-Tees • United Kingdom....63 E6
Stoke-on-Trent • United Kingdom....63 D7
Stoke-sub-Hamdon Priory • United Kingdom....65 K9
Stolzenfels, Schloss • Germany....74 C5
Stonehaven • United Kingdom....62 D4
Stonehenge • United Kingdom....65 K9
Stonehenge Heritage C • United Kingdom....44 [28]
Stones River Nat. Battlefield Park N • TN, United States....153 [225]
Stony Rapids • SA, Canada....158 F3
Stora Le • Norway/Sweden....98 E6
Stora Sjöfallet Nat. Park Park N • Sweden....58 [20]
Stord • Norway....98 F9
Stordal • Norway....98 G2
Store • Norway....98 F8
Store Bælt • Denmark....99 F7
Store Heddinge • Denmark....99 G8
Store Mosse Nat. Park Park N • Sweden....58 [28]
Store Mosse Nat. Park • Sweden....99 G6
Støren • Norway....97 C3
Storfjorden • Norway....98 G2
Storm Bay • TS, Australia....136 F7
Stornoway • United Kingdom....62 B2
Storsjøen • Norway....98 E5
Storsjön • Sweden....97 C3
Storstrøm • Denmark....99 F8
Storuman • Sweden....97 D2
Storvreta • Sweden....99 B1
Storybook Land • NJ, United States....156 K5
Stour • United Kingdom....65 K9
Stour • United Kingdom....63 F9
Stourbridge • United Kingdom....65 F5
Stourport • United Kingdom....65 E5
Stow-on-the-Wold • United Kingdom....65 F6
Stowmarket • United Kingdom....65 H8
Strá • Italy....87 C2
Strabane • United Kingdom....62 B6
Stradbally • Ireland....69 E7
Strahan • TS, Australia....136 E7
Straits of Florida • Cuba/United States....166 BB1
Strakonice • Czech Rep.....89 D7
Stralsund • Germany....72 E1

Stralsund Heritage C • Germany....44 [46]
Stranda • Norway....98 G7
Strangford Lough • United Kingdom....63 C6
Strängnäs • Sweden....99 A2
Strängsjö • Sweden....99 A2
Stranraer • United Kingdom....62 C6
Strasbourg • France....76 G2
Strasbourg Heritage C • France....44 [67]
Strasburg • PA, United States....156 B3
Strassburg • France....50 C2
Stratford • New Zealand....137 D6
Stratford-upon-Avon • United Kingdom....65 F5
Strath Earn • United Kingdom....65 A1
Strathclyde Country Park • United Kingdom....65 A2
Strathcona Prov. Park • BC, Canada....160 I7
Strathgordon • TS, Australia....136 F7
Strathmore • United Kingdom....65 B1
Strathy • Greece....94 B
Stratton Ski • VT, United States....146 [106]
Stratton • VT, United States....156 C1
Straubing • Germany....91 F1
Streaky Bay • SA, Australia....135 E6
Streator • IL, United States....150 C2
Strelitza Coast • South Africa....111 B5
Stresa • Italy....87 B1
Strib • Denmark....99 E7
Strigno • Italy....86 C4
Strímónas • Greece....93 C1
Strómboli, I. • Italy....86 H7
Stromness • United Kingdom....62 D2
Strömsnäsbruk • Sweden....99 G7
Strömstad • Sweden....99 F5
Strömsund • Sweden....97 D3
Stronsay • United Kingdom....62 D1
Stroud • United Kingdom....65 E6
Stroudsburg • PA, United States....156 B2
Struer • Denmark....99 E7
Struga • FYR of Macedonia....92 C3
Struisbaai • South Africa....111 E7
Strumica • FYR of Macedonia....92 C3
Stryn • Norway....98 G2
Strynsvatn • Norway....98 G7
Strzelecki Peaks • TS, Australia....136 F6
Stuart Mem. • NT, Australia....136 B1
Stuart Mtns • New Zealand....137 F7
Stubaier Alpen • Austria....91 N8
Stubbekøbing • Denmark....99 F8
Stubbs • St Vincent & Gren.....167 O
Studen • Switzerland....91 M8
Studen • Switzerland....90 J5
Studenica Heritage C • Serbia & Montenegro....44 [214]
Studley Royal Park Heritage C • United Kingdom....44 [23]
Stung Treng • Cambodia....128 C4
Sturgeon Bay • WI, United States....161 B2
Sturgeon Falls • OT, Canada....160 E3
Sturgis • MI, United States....150 C2
Sturt Nat. Park • NS, Australia....135 G5
Sturt Stony Desert • QL/SA, Australia....135 G5
Sturup [Apt] • Sweden....99 G7
Stuttgart • Germany....74 B3
Stykkishólmur • Iceland....97 H6
Styria • Austria....91 T11
Su Nuraxi di Barúmini • Sardinia, Italy....86 F6
Su Nuraxi di Barúmini Heritage C • Sardinia, Italy....44 [178]
Suakin • Sudan....109 E10
Suakin Archipelago • Sudan....109 E10
Suavanao • Solomon Is.....138 V
Subang • Java, Indonesia....131 P11
Subotica • Serbia & Montenegro....92 B2
Suceava • Romania....92 D2
Sucia, Bahía • Puerto Rico....165 I8
Suck • Ireland....69 H9
Sucre • Bolivia....173 C6
Sucre Heritage C • Bolivia....42 [65]
Sud, Canal du • Haiti....165 E6
Sud, Costa del • Sardinia, Italy....86 E6
Sud, Grand Récif du • New Caledonia....138 U
Sud Ouest, Point • Mauritius....113 E6
Sudama • Japan....127 H8
SUDAN • Africa....108 C4
Sudbury • OT, Canada....159 H4
Sudbury • United Kingdom....63 F8
Sudd • Sudan....108 C4
Sudety • Czech Rep./Poland....89 B3
Sudong • Singapore....129 H12
Suez • Egypt....109 B1
Suez Canal • Egypt....109 B1
Suez, Gulf of • Egypt....109 B2
Suffolk • United Kingdom....64 B5
Suffolk • VA, United States....156 B4
Sugar Loaf Ski • MI, United States....146 [82]
Sugar Mtn Ski • NC, United States....146 [87]
Sugarbush Ski • VT, United States....146 [108]
Sugarloaf USA Ski • ME, United States....146 [119]
Sugla Gölü • Turkey....95 E5
Suhar • Oman....120 H9
Sühbaatar • Mongolia....125 E1
Suheli I. • India....124 A3
Suhl • Germany....72 D3
Suir • Ireland....69 C4
Suizhou • China....125 F3
Sukabumi • Java, Indonesia....131 Q11
Sukhona • Russian Fed.....100 M9
Sukhothai • Thailand....130 C6
Sukhothai Heritage N • Thailand....41 [139]
Sukhothai Heritage C • Thailand....43 [205]
Sukkur • Pakistan....122 A3
Sukumo • Japan....127 B4
Sukur Heritage C • Nigeria....43 [114]
Sula • Norway....98 F8
Sula, Kepulauan • Indonesia....131 I4
Sula Sgeir • United Kingdom....62 B1
Sulawesi • Indonesia....131 F4
Suldalsvatn • Norway....98 G9
Sulden • Italy....87 C1
Sule Skerry • United Kingdom....62 C1
Suleskar • Norway....98 G9
Sulina • Romania....92 I7
Sulitjelma • Peru....173 A3
Sulmona • Italy....87 F4
Sulphur • LA, United States....151 B4
Sulphur [Riv] • AR/TX, United States....155 F4
Sulphur Springs • TX, United States....155 F4
Sultanhani • Turkey....95 I9
Sultanpur • India....123 G8
Sulu Archipelago • Philippines....128 G5
Sulu Sea • Philippines....128 F5
Sulz am Neckar • Germany....74 B3
Sulzbach-Rosenberg • Germany....72 D4
Sumatera Barat • Indonesia....131 B4
Sumatera Utara • Indonesia....131 N10
Sumatra • Indonesia....131 B4
Sumava • Czech Rep.....89 A4
Sumava Nat. Park Park N • Czech Rep.....58 [110]
Sumba • Indonesia....131 E5
Sumba • Indonesia....131 E5
Sumbawa • Indonesia....110 G8
Sumbe • Angola....110 A2
Sumbing, Gunung • Java, Indonesia....131 Q12
Sumbu • Zambia....110 H2
Sumburgh • United Kingdom....62 H13
Sumedang • Java, Indonesia....131 P11
Sumenep • Indonesia....131 R11
Sumiseh • Sudan....108 B4
Summel • Iraq....120 E6
Summerside • PE, Canada....160 B2
Summit • Panama....170 M11
Sumoto • Japan....127 F7
Sumqayit • Azerbaijan....120 F5
Sumter • SC, United States....151 D4

Sumy • Ukraine....100 D3
Sun City • South Africa....110 B3
Sun Peaks Ski • BC, Canada....146 [4]
Sun Prairie • WI, United States....150 C2
Sun Valley Ski • ID, United States....146 [40]
Sun Valley • ID, United States....154 H6
Sun Valley ski resort • China....126 F3
Sunbaran Roads • N. Mariana Is.....138 A5
Sunda Is., Lesser • Indonesia....131 F5
Sunda, Selat • Java, Indonesia....131 O11
Sundarbans Heritage N • Bangladesh....41 [126]
Sundarbans • Bangladesh/India....123 B2
Sundarbans Nat. Park Heritage N • India....41 [126]
Sunday River Ski • ME, United States....146 [118]
Sunde • Norway....98 F9
Sunderland • United Kingdom....62 E6
Sundsval Sound • New Zealand....137 F7
Sundsli • Norway....98 G9
Sundsvall • Sweden....97 D3
Sundybyberg • Sweden....99 B2
Sunderland • China....126 D1
Sungei Buloh Nature Park • Singapore....129 H11
Sunndalsøra • Norway....98 G7
Sunnerbo • Sweden....99 G6
Sunnersta • Sweden....99 B1
Sunny Beach • Bulgaria....92 H8
Sunnyside • WA, United States....148 C1
Sunnyvale • CA, United States....148 B3
Sunport [Apt] • NM, United States....155 H7
Sunrise Park Ski • AZ, United States....146 [53]
Sunset Beach • HI, United States....146 A
Sunset Crater Volcano Nat. Mon. • AZ, United States....155 G7
Sunset Crater Volcano Nat. Mon. Park N • AZ, United States....152 [104]
Sunshine Coast • QL, Australia....136 D5
Sunshine Village Ski • AL, Canada....146 [12]
Suolahti • Finland....99 D3
Suomenlinna • Finland....99 D4
Suomussalmi • Finland....97 F3
Super-Sauze • France....78 H7
Super-St-Bernard • Switzerland....90 J6
Superbagnères • France....78 K10
Superior • WI, United States....150 B1
Superior, Lake • Canada/United States....161 B1
Suphan Buri • Thailand....130 D7
Sur • Lebanon....120 A1
Sur • Oman....120 H9
Sur, Cabo • Easter I.....139 M
Surabaya • Java, Indonesia....131 R12
Surahammar • Sweden....99 A1
Surakarta • Java, Indonesia....131 Q12
Surat • India....122 B3
Surat • QL, Australia....136 C5
Surat Thani • Thailand....128 B5
Suratgarh • India....123 E7
Süre • Luxembourg....70 D5
Surendranagar • India....122 B3
Surfers Paradise • QL, Australia....136 D5
Surgidero de Batabano • Cuba....164 F4
Surgut • Russian Fed.....101 H3
Surigao • Philippines....128 H5
Surin Beach • Ko Phuket, Thailand....130 F9
Surin, Ko • Thailand....130 A3
Surinam • Mauritius....113 E6
SURINAM • S. America....174 A2
Surinam Quarters • Jamaica....165 C4
Surrey • United Kingdom....65 G8
Surt • Libya....108 A1
Suruga-wan • Japan....127 H9
Sušac • Croatia....92 G6
Susanville • CA, United States....154 I7
Susehri • Turkey....95 C1
Susice • Czech Rep.....89 D7
Suso Heritage C • Spain....44 [104]
Susoh • Indonesia....131 M9
Susquehanna • United States....156 B2
Sussex • United Kingdom....65 G8
Susuga, Hagoi • N. Mariana Is.....138 B
Susurluk • Turkey....95 H7
Sütçüler • Turkey....95 H7
Sutherland • South Africa....111 E6
Sutherland • United Kingdom....64 A1
Sutjeska Nat. Park Park N • Bosnia-Herz.....58 [123]
Sutlej • India/Pakistan....122 B3
Sutton Coldfield • United Kingdom....65 F5
Sutton Hoo • United Kingdom....63 F8
Sutton in Ashfield • United Kingdom....63 E7
Sutton on Sea Beach • United Kingdom....64 [11]
Suva • Fiji Is.....138 T
Suvadiva Atoll • Maldives....124 G8
Suwalki • Poland....89 C1
Suwannee [Riv] • FL/GA, United States....155 C1
Suwarrow • Cook Is.....139 DD3
Suwon • Rep. of Korea....125 G3
Suwon Heritage C • Rep. of Korea....43 [191]
Suzhou • Anhui, China....125 F3
Suzhou Heritage C • China....43 [183]
Suzhou • Jiangsu, China....126 H6
Suzu Han • Turkey....95 H9
Svalbard • Arctic Ocean....176 I2
Svaneti area Heritage C • Georgia....44 [314]
Svarstad • Norway....98 D6
Svärtinge • Sweden....99 A2
Svartisen • Norway....97 C2
Sveg • Sweden....97 C3
Svelvik • Norway....98 E5
Svendborg • Denmark....99 F8
Svene • Norway....98 D5
Svenstavik • Sweden....97 C3
Sveshtari Heritage C • Bulgaria....44 [225]
Svetac • Croatia....92 F6
Svidník • Slovak Rep.....89 C4
Svihov • Czech Rep.....89 D7
Svilengrad • Bulgaria....92 D3
Svishtov • Bulgaria....92 C3
Svobodnyy • Russian Fed.....101 M4
Svyetlahorsk • Belarus....100 C3
Swabia • Germany....73 A4
Swain Reefs • QL, Australia....136 D4
Swains I. • American Samoa....138 CC3
Swakopmund • Namibia....110 A3
Swallow Is. • Solomon Is.....138 W
Swan Hill • VI, Australia....136 G8
Swan Is. • Honduras....170 F7
Swan River • MN, Canada....158 F3
Swanage • United Kingdom....65 K10
Swanage Beach • United Kingdom....64 [35]
Swansea • TS, Australia....136 F7
Swansea • United Kingdom....63 F9
Swansea Beach • United Kingdom....64 [29]
Swartberg Pass • South Africa....111 F7
Swartkrans Heritage C • South Africa....43 [123]
SWAZILAND • Africa....110 C3
SWEDEN • Europe....97
Swedish Lakeland • Sweden....99 G5
Sweetwater • TX, United States....155 E13
Swellendam • South Africa....111 E7
Swidnica Heritage C • Poland....44 [187]
Swiebodzin • Poland....89 A2
Swietokrzyski Nat. Park • Poland....89 G8
Swift Current • SA, Canada....158 F3
Swinden • United Kingdom....63 E9
Swinoujscie • Poland....89 A2
Swiss Nat. Park Park N • Switzerland....58 [88]

Swiss Nat. Park • Switzerland....90 L5
SWITZERLAND • Europe....90 D2
Syburg (Dortmund) • Germany....73 D5
Sydney • NS, Australia....136 B4
Sydney • NS, Canada....160 C2
Sydney Mines • NS, Canada....160 C2
Syeverodonets'k • Ukraine....100 E4
Sykkylven • Norway....98 G7
Syktyvakr • Russian Fed.....100 H1
Sylhet • Bangladesh....122 D3
Sylling • Norway....98 D5
Sylt • Germany....72 C1
Sylvan Ski • MI, United States....146 [79]
Sylvania • OH, United States....150 D2
Sylvensteinsee • Germany....74 G8
Symond's Yat • United Kingdom....65 E6
Syowa [Base] • Antarctica....176 [15]
Syr Darya • Asia....121 F4
Syracuse • NY, United States....156 B1
Syracuse • Sicily, Italy....86 H8
SYRIA • Asia....120 D6
Syvde • Norway....98 F7
Szczawnica • Poland....89 G9
Szczecin • Poland....89 A2
Szczecinek • Poland....89 B2
Szeged • Hungary....92 C2
Székesfehérvár • Hungary....92 B2
Szekszárd • Hungary....92 B2
Szolnok • Hungary....92 C2
Szombathely • Hungary....92 B2

T

Ta'izz • Yemen....120 E11
Ta'u • American Samoa....139 H
Taaoa • French Polynesia....139 J
Taaoa, Baie • French Polynesia....139 J
Taapuna • French Polynesia....139 K
Tab • Egypt....109 B1
Tabarka • Tunisia....107 C4
Tabas • Iran....120 H7
Tabasco • Mexico....169 D3
Tabasqueño • Mexico....169 F5
Tabatinga • Brazil....173 C3
Tabelbala • Algeria....107 B3
Tabernas • Spain....81 D7
Tabik Channel • Marshall Is.....139 E
Tabik • Marshall Is.....139 E
Table Bay • South Africa....111 D7
Table Mtn • South Africa....111 D7
Table, Pointe de la • Réunion....113 D4
Taboga, I. • Panama....170 M11
Tabontebike • Kiribati....139 F
Tábor • Czech Rep.....89 D7
Tabor, Mt • Israel....120 B2
Tabora • Tanzania....110 G7
Tabriz • Iran....120 F6
Tabuaeran • Kiribati....139 I
Tabuk • Saudi Arabia....120 D8
Tabwémasana, Mt • Vanuatu....138 V
Täby • Sweden....99 B1
Tacheng • China....125 C1
Tachikawa • Japan....127 H8
Tachilek • Myanmar....130 C5
Tacloban • Philippines....128 G4
Tacna • Peru....173 F7
Taco Pozo • Argentina....175 C5
Tacoma • WA, United States....154 G5
Tacoronte • Tenerife, Canary Is.....82 G5
Tadine • New Caledonia....138 U
Tadmur Heritage C • Syria....44 [301]
Tadrart Acacus Heritage C • Libya....43 [103]
Tafers • Switzerland....90 J5
Tafí Viejo • Argentina....175 B2
Tafilalt • Morocco....107 B3
Tafraout • Morocco....107 A3
Tafunsak • Fed. States of Micronesia....138 D
Tagajo • Japan....127 C3
Tagomago, I. de • Ibiza, Spain....83 M9
Tagus • Portugal/Spain....80 C4
Tahan, Gunung • Malaysia....128 C6
Tahcob • Mexico....169 F4
Tahcok • Mexico....169 F4
Tahiti • French Polynesia....139 K
Tahlequah • OK, United States....151 B3
Tahoe, Lake • CA/NV, United States....154 I8
Tahoua • Niger....106 C3
Tahtlith • Saudi Arabia....120 D10
Tai • Fiji Is.....138 T
Tai Hu • China....126 G6
Tai Lam Country Park • Hong Kong, China....126 E5
Tai Mo Shan • Hong Kong, China....126 E5
Tai Mo Shan Country Park • Hong Kong, China....126 E5
Tai O • Hong Kong, China....126 E5
Tai Po • Hong Kong, China....126 E5
Tai Po Kau Country Park • Hong Kong, China....126 F5
Tai Shan • China....126 F3
Tai Shan Heritage N • China....41 [135]
Tai Shan Heritage C • China....43 [181]
Tai Tam Country Park • Hong Kong, China....126 F5
Taiarapu, Presqu'île de • French Polynesia....139 K
Taicang • China....126 H6
Taichung • Taiwan....126 G6
Taihape • New Zealand....137 E6
Tainan • Taiwan....125 G4
Taiohae • French Polynesia....139 J
Taipa • Macau, China....126 E3
Taipa Village • Macau, China....126 E3
Taipei • Taiwan....125 G4
Taiping • Anhui, China....126 F3
Taiping • Guangdong, China....126 E6
Taisetsu-zan • Japan....127 D2
Taitao, Península de • Chile....175 A4
Taitung • Taiwan....86 H7
TAIWAN • Asia....125 G4
Taiwan Strait • China/Taiwan....126 G6
Taixing • China....125 G4
Taiyuan • China....125 F3
Taizhou • Jiangsu, China....126 G6
Taizhou • Zhejiang, China....125 G4
Taj Mahal Heritage C • India....43 [146]
Tajumulco, Volcán de • Guatemala....170 F7
TAJIKISTAN • Asia....121 F4
Tajo • Spain....80 B4
Tak • Thailand....130 C6
Takamatsu • Japan....127 B3
Takaoka • Japan....127 C3
Takapoto • French Polynesia....139 F
Takarano • Kiribati....139 F
Takaroa • French Polynesia....139 F
Takarazuka Family Land • Japan....127 F6
Takasago • Japan....127 F6
Takasaki • Japan....127 C3
Takayama • Japan....127 C3
Takeo • Cambodia....129 B5
Taranaki Bight, North • New Zealand....137 D6
Takikawa • Japan....127 D2
Takimu Mtns • New Zealand....137 G8
Taklimakan Desert • China....126 A1
Taklimakan Shamo • China....125 C3
Talaion • Crete, Greece....93 H5
Talamanca, Cordillera de • Costa Rica/Panama....170 F6
Talamanca, Cordillera de Heritage C • Costa Rica/Panama....40 [26]

Talampaya Natural Park Heritage N • Argentina....40 [50]
Talas • Kyrgyzstan....121 F3
Talaud, Kepulauan • Indonesia....131 G3
Talavera de la Reina • Spain....80 C4
Talca • Chile....175 A3
Talcahuano • Chile....175 A3
Talcy [Château] • France....77 F5
Taldyqorghan • Kazakhstan....121 G2
Taling Ngam Beach • Ko Samui, Thailand....130 G12
Tallahassee • FL, United States....155 C1
Tallgrass Prairie Nat. Preserve Park N • KS, United States....153 [169]
Tallinn • Estonia....100 K6
Tallinn Heritage C • Estonia....44 [261]
Talofofo • Guam....138 Z
Taloqan • Afghanistan....121 E4
Talpona Beach • Goa, India....123 C6
Talsi • Latvia....100 J7
Talwood • QL, Australia....135 H5
Tama • Japan....127 I8
Tama-gawa • Japan....127 H8
Tamakautoga • Niue....139 O
Tamale • Ghana....106 B4
Taman Ayun Temple • Bali, Indonesia....131 L8
Taman Negara Nat. Park • Malaysia....129 A4
Tamanrasset • Algeria....106 C2
Tamar • TS, Australia....136 F6
Tamar • United Kingdom....65 J10
Tamarin • Mauritius....113 C6
Tamarin Beach • Mauritius....113 E6
Tamarin Falls • Mauritius....113 E6
Tamarinda • Minorca, Spain....83 J8
Tamaulipas • Mexico....169 C2
Tamazunchale • Mexico....169 J6
Tambacounda • Senegal....106 A3
Tamblingan, Danau • Bali, Indonesia....131 L7
Tambo • Peru....173 F7
Tambo • QL, Australia....136 C4
Tambo Colorado • Peru....173 E6
Tambov • Russian Fed.....100 F3
Tambura • Sudan....108 B4
Tamdi Surla Temple • Goa, India....123 C5
Tamegroute • Morocco....107 B3
Tamerza • Tunisia....107 C5
Tamiahua, Laguna de • Mexico....169 J6
Tamil Nadu • India....124 C2
Tammerfors • Finland....99 D3
Tammisaari • Finland....99 D4
Tämnaren • Sweden....99 A1
Tampa • FL, United States....155 C2
Tampa Bay • FL, United States....155 C2
Tampere • Finland....99 D3
Tampereen Sarkanniemi Oy Park L • Finland....59 [11]
Tampico • Mexico....169 J6
Tampin • Malaysia....129 G10
Tampines • Singapore....129 I11
Tampon, le • Réunion....113 C4
Tamuda • Morocco....107 B1
Tamuning • Guam....138 Z
Tamworth • United Kingdom....65 F5
Tan An • Vietnam....129 B6
Tan Son Nhat [Apt] • Vietnam....129 B5
Tan-Tan • Morocco....107 A3
Tana • Kenya....109 D5
Tana • Norway....97 F1
Tana, Lake • Ethiopia....108 C3
Tana [Riv] • Norway....97 F1
Tana River Primate Nat. Reserve • Kenya....109 D5
Tana River Primate Nat. Reserve Park • Kenya....112 [81]
Tanabe • Japan....127 C4
Tanaga I. • AK, United States....157 C4
Tanah Lot Temple • Bali, Indonesia....131 L8
Tanah Rata • Malaysia....129 F9
Tanahbala • Indonesia....131 M10
Tanahmasa • Indonesia....131 M10
Tanami Desert • NT, Australia....135 E3
Tanami Desert Wildlife Sanctuary • NT, Australia....136 A1
Tanana • AK, United States....157 E3
Tanapag • N. Mariana Is.....138 B
Tanaro • Italy....87 A2
Tancitaro • Mexico....169 I7
Tancredo Neves [Apt] • Brazil....174 E6
Tanda • India....123 G8
Tandil • Argentina....175 F7
Tanega-shima • Japan....127 B4
Tang Kem Bay • Ko Phuket, Thailand....130 F10
Tanga • Tanzania....110 H7
Tangalle • Sri Lanka....124 C4
Tanganyika, Lake • Dem. Rep. of Congo/Tanzania....110 G8
Tanger • Morocco....107 A1
Tangier • Morocco....107 A1
Tangier I. • VA, United States....156 B4
Tangkuban Perahu, Gunung • Java, Indonesia....131 P11
Tanglin • Singapore....129 I12
Tangshan • China....125 F3
Tania, la Ski • France....61 [29]
Tanimbar, Kepulauan • Indonesia....131 H5
Tanjung • Indonesia....131 E4
Tanjung Bunga • Penang, Malaysia....129 F9
Tanjung Malim • Malaysia....129 F9
Tanjung Tokong • Penang, Malaysia....129 F9
Tanjungbalai • Indonesia....131 N9
Tanjungkarang-Telukbetung • Indonesia....131 O11
Tanjungpandan • Indonesia....131 C4
Tanjungredeb • Indonesia....131 E3
Tankwa-Karoo Nat. Park • South Africa....111 E6
Tanna • Vanuatu....138 V
Tannenberg • Poland....50 D2
Tannis Bugt • Denmark....99 F6
Tantå • Egypt....109 A1
Tantallon Castle • United Kingdom....65 B2
Tanum • Sweden....99 F5
Tanum Heritage C • Sweden....44 [9]
TANZANIA • Africa....110 G-H
Tao, Ko • Thailand....130 A3
Tao e Wallis & Futuna....139 Q
Taongi • Marshall Is.....138 CC2
Taormina • Sicily, Italy....86 H7
Taos Ski • NM, United States....146 [65]
Taos • NM, United States....155 [37]
Taounate • Morocco....107 B1
Taoudenni • Mali....106 B2
Taourirt • Morocco....107 B2
Tapa • Estonia....100 K6
Tapachula • Mexico....168 F5
Tapah • Malaysia....129 F9
Tapajós • Brazil....174 A3
Tapaktuan • Indonesia....131 M9
Tapauá • Brazil....174 A3
Tara • Morocco....107 B1

Tarapoto • Peru....173 B3
Tarascon • France....76 F5
Tarascon-sur-Ariège • France....78 K10
Tarasp-Vulpera • Switzerland....90 L5
Tarata • Peru....173 F7
Taravao • French Polynesia....139 K
Taravao, Isthme de • French Polynesia....139 K
Taravo • Corsica, France....78 M12
Tarawa • Kiribati....139 F
Tarawera, Lake • New Zealand....137 E5
Taraz • Kazakhstan....121 F3
Tarbert • Harris, United Kingdom....62 B3
Tarbert • Kintyre, United Kingdom....66 A2
Tarbes • France....78 J9
Tarboro • NC, United States....151 E3
Tarcoola • SA, Australia....135 E6
Tarentais • France....78 D3
Tarfa, Ra's at • Saudi Arabia....109 F10
Tarifa • Morocco....107 A3
Târgu Jiu • Romania....92 H7
Târgoviste • Romania....92 H7
Târgu Mures • Romania....92 D2
Tarija • Bolivia....173 C5
Tarim Basin • China....125 A1
Tarim He • China....125 C2
Tarim Kowt • Afghanistan....121 E5
Tarlac • Philippines....128 ...
Tarn • Denmark....99 E7
Tarn [Adm] • France....78 F6
Tarn Hows • United Kingdom....65 D4
Tarn [Riv] • France....76 F4
Tarn-et-Garonne • France....78 F5
Tarnobrzeg • Poland....89 C3
Tarnów • Poland....89 C3
Tarnowskie Góry • Poland....89 F8
Tärnsjö • Sweden....99 A1
Taroom • QL, Australia....136 C5
Taroudannt • Morocco....107 A3
Tarpon Springs • FL, United States....155 C2
Tarquínia • Italy....87 E4
Tárraco Heritage C • Spain....44 [97]
Tarragona • Spain....83 C4
Tarragona Heritage C • Spain....44 [97]
Tarraleah • TS, Australia....136 F7
Tarrytown • NY, United States....156 C2
Tartu • Estonia....100 K6
Tartus • Syria....120 D7
Tarutung • Indonesia....131 N10
Tarxien Temples • Malta....96 B2
Tasagil • Turkey....95 H8
Tash-Kömür • Kyrgyzstan....121 F3
Tashkent • Uzbekistan....121 E3
Tashkent Heritage C • Uzbekistan....121 P12
Täsinge • Denmark....99 F8
Tasikmalaya • Java, Indonesia....131 Q12
Taskent • Turkey....137 B3
Tasman Bay • New Zealand....137 B3
Tasman Sea • Australia/New Zealand....134 E8
Tasmania • Australia....135 E-F
Tasmanian wilderness Heritage N • Australia....41 [158]
Tasmanian wilderness Heritage C • Australia....43 [213]
Tassili n'Ajjer • Algeria....106 C2
Tassili n'Ajjer Heritage N • Algeria....41 [89]
Tassili n'Ajjer Heritage C • Algeria....43 [104]
Tatabánya • Hungary....92 B2
Tataouine • Tunisia....107 D6
Tatarstan Russ Adm • Russian Fed.....101 [13]
Tatebayashi • Japan....127 I8
Tateyama • Japan....127 I9
Tatila Turizm Park L • Turkey....59 [88]
Tatila Turizm • Turkey....95 F3
Tatlisu • Cyprus....96 D3
Tatry • Poland/Slovak Rep.....89 G9
Tatry Heritage C • Poland/Slovak Rep.....89 G9
Tatranski Nat. Park Park N • Poland....58 [106]
Tatranski Nat. Park • Poland....89 G9
Tatshenshini-Alsek Prov. Wilderness Park Heritage N • YT, Canada....40 [1]
Tatsuno • Japan....127 F6
Tau • Norway....98 F9
Tauak Passage • Fed. States of Micronesia....138 D
Taubaté • Brazil....174 E7
Tauern, Hohe • Austria....91 O8
Tauern, Niedere • Austria....91 P8
Taufkirchen • Germany....74 G7
Taumarunui • New Zealand....137 D6
Taungup • Myanmar....128 B2
Taunus • Germany....74 D5
Taunus-Wunderland • Germany....74 D6
Taupo • New Zealand....137 E6
Taupo, Lake • New Zealand....137 E6
Tauranga • Lithuania....100 J8
Tautama Mtns • Turkey....139 E
Tautira • French Polynesia....139 K
Tautu • Cook Is.....139 N
Tavarua • Fiji Is.....138 T
Taveuni • Fiji Is.....138 S
Tavignano • Corsica, France....78 N11
Tavira • Portugal....84 K8
Tavira, l. de • Portugal....84 K8
Tavistock • United Kingdom....65 J10
Tavolara, I. • Sardinia, Italy....86 F5
Tavoy • Myanmar....128 B4
Tavsanli • Turkey....95 F4
Tavua • Fiji Is.....138 T
Taw • United Kingdom....65 J9
Tawakoni, Lake • TX, United States....155 F4
Tawangmangu • Java, Indonesia....131 Q12
Tawau • Sabah, Malaysia....128 E6
Tawitawi • Philippines....128 G5
Taxco • Mexico....169 J7
Taxila Heritage C • Pakistan....43 [146]
Tay • United Kingdom....65 B1
Tay, Firth of • United Kingdom....65 B1
Tay, Loch • United Kingdom....65 A1
Tay Ninh • Vietnam....129 B5
Tayinloan • United Kingdom....66 A2
Taylor • TX, United States....155 C5
Taylorville • IL, United States....150 C3
Taymyr Russ Adm • Russian Fed.....101 [21]
Taymyr, Poluostrov • Russian Fed.....101 K2
Tayshet • Russian Fed.....101 J4
Tayu • Java, Indonesia....131 R11
Taza • Morocco....107 B1
Tbilisi • Georgia....120 E5
Tchogha Zanbil Heritage C • Iran....43 [135]
Tczew • Poland....89 B1
Te Ana-Au Caves • New Zealand....137 F7
Te Anau • New Zealand....137 F7
Te Anau, Lake • New Zealand....137 F7
Te Araroa • New Zealand....137 D5
Te Awamutu • New Zealand....137 D5
Te Kaha • New Zealand....137 D5
Te Kuiti • New Zealand....137 D6
Te Manga • Cook Is.....139 N
Te Ngaio • Solomon Is.....138 W
Te Pito Kura • Easter I.....139 M
Te Puke • New Zealand....137 D5
Te Urewera Nat. Park • New Zealand....137 E5
Te Weewee Bay • New Zealand....137 F8
Teahitia, Point • French Polynesia....139 K
Teafuafou • Tuvalu....139 R
Teano • Italy....87 G6
Teaoraereke • Kiribati....139 F
Teapa • Mexico....168 F4
Tebang • Kiribati....139 F
Tebay • United Kingdom....65 D4
Tébessa • Algeria....107 C5

Tebingtinggi • Indonesia 131 N9
Techirghiol • Romania 92 I7
Tecomán • Mexico 169 H7
Técpan • Mexico 169 I8
Tecuala • Mexico 169 H6
Tecuci • Romania 92 D2
Tees • United Kingdom 63 D6
Teesside [Apt] • United Kingdom 66 C4
Tefala • Tuvalu .... 139 R
Tefenni • Turkey 95 G7
Tegal • Java, Indonesia 131 P11
Tegeh Koripan Temple •
     Bali, Indonesia 131 L7
Tegel [Apt] • Germany 73 E7
Tegel (Berlin) • Germany 73 E7
Tegeler See • Germany 73 E7
Tegernsee • Germany 74 G8
Tegernsee [Lake] • Germany 74 G8
Tegucigalpa • Honduras 170 K9
Teguise • Lanzarote, Canary Is. 83 I5
Tehran • Iran 120 G6
Tehuacán • Mexico 169 J7
Tehuantepec • Mexico 169 K8
Tehuantepec, Golfo de • Mexico 168 F4
Tehuantepec, Istmo de • Mexico 168 F4
Teicha, Ia • France 78 E6
Teide, Pico de •
     Tenerife, Canary Is. 82 G5
Teifi • United Kingdom 63 C8
Teignmouth • United Kingdom 65 J10
Teirio • Kiribati .... 139 F
Teisendorf • Germany 74 H7
Teith • United Kingdom 65 A1
Tejakula • Bali, Indonesia 131 L7
Tejeda • Gran Canaria, Canary Is. ... 82 G6
Tejen • Turkmenistan 121 D4
Tejo • Portugal 80 A4
Tejupan, Punta • Mexico 169 H8
Tekao, Mt • French Polynesia .... 139 J
Tekapo, Lake • New Zealand 137 B3
Tekirdağ • Turkey 95 E3
Tekirdağ [Adm] • Turkey 95 E3
Tekirova • Turkey 95 G8
Tekojärvi, Lokan • Finland 97 F2
Tekojärvi, Porttipahdan • Finland ... 97 F2
Tekopua • Cook Is. .... 139 N
Tel Arad • Israel 120 A4
Tel Ashqelon • Israel 120 A4
Tel Aviv • Israel 120 A3
Tel Bet Shemesh • Israel 120 A4
Tel Dan • Israel 120 B1
Tel Lakhish • Israel 120 A4
Tel Meggido • Israel 120 A2
Tela • Honduras 170 K9
Telangana Plateau • India 124 C1
Telc • Czech Rep. 89 E7
Telc Heritage C • Czech Rep. ... 44 [193]
Telde • Gran Canaria, Canary Is. 82 G6
Telele • Tuvalu .... 139 R
Telemark • Norway 98 A3
Telemark Sommerland Park L • Norway . 59 [2]
Telemark Sommerland • Norway 98 D6
Teles Pires • Brazil 174 A3
Telford • United Kingdom 65 E6
Telfs • Austria 91 N7
Telkwa • BC, Canada 160 I6
Tell Deir 'Alla • Jordan 120 B3
Tell el Amarna • Egypt 109 A2
Telluride Ski • CO, United States .. 146 [63]
Telmessos • Turkey 95 F6
Telšiai • Lithuania 100 J7
Teltow • Germany 73 E8
Teltowkanal • Germany 73 E8
Teluk Anson • Malaysia 129 F9
Teluk Bahang • Penang, Malaysia ... 129 D7
Teluk Bahang Forest Reserve •
     Penang, Malaysia 129 D7
Teluk Duyung • Penang, Malaysia ... 129 F9
Teluk Intan • Malaysia 129 F9
Teluk Kumbar • Penang, Malaysia ... 129 D8
Telukdalem • Indonesia 131 M10
Tema • Ghana 106 C4
Temanggung • Java, Indonesia 131 Q12
Témara Plage • Morocco 107 A1
Tembe Elephant Park • South Africa . 111 C3
Tembeling • Malaysia 129 G9
Tembeling [Riv] • Malaysia 129 G9
Teme Valley • United Kingdom 65 E5
Temerloh • Malaysia 129 G10
Temetiu, Mt • French Polynesia .... 139 J
Temirtau • Kazakhstan 121 F1
Temora • NS, Australia 136 G8
Témpio [Apt] • Germany 73 E9
Templar Park • Malaysia 129 G10
Temple • TX, United States 155 E5
Templi, Valle dei •
     Sicily, Italy 86 G8
Templin • Germany 72 E2
Templiner See • Germany 73 E8
Temuco • Chile 175 A3
Temwen • Fed. States of Micronesia . 138 D
Ten Thousand Is. •
     FL, United States 155 D3
Tenabo • Mexico 169 F4
Tenali • India 124 C1
Tenaro, Akra • Greece 93 C3
Tenby Beach • United Kingdom ...... 64 [52]
Tende • France 78 H7
Tendrara • Morocco 107 B1
Ténéré • Niger 106 D2
Ténéré Natural Reserve Park • Niger . 112 [4]
Ténéré Natural Reserve Heritage N •
     Niger .... 41 [98]
Tenerife • Canary Is. 82 G5
Ténès • Algeria 107 A4
Tengiz Köli • Kazakhstan 121 E1
Tennant Creek • NT, Australia 135 E3
Tennessee [Adm] • United States ... 151 C3
Tennessee [Riv] • United States ... 151 C3
Tenojoki • Finland 97 F2
Tenom • Sabah, Malaysia 128 F5
Tenosique • Mexico 169 E5
Tenri • Japan 127 G7
Teófilo Otôni • Brazil 174 B4
Teos • Turkey 95 F5
Teotihuacán • Mexico 169 J7
Teotihuacán Heritage C • Mexico ... 42 [19]
Tepalcatepec • Mexico 169 I7
Tepic • Mexico 169 H6
Teplá • Czech Rep. 89 D6
Teplice • Czech Rep. 89 D6
Tepuka • Tuvalu .... 139 R
Tepuka, Te Ava • Tuvalu .... 139 R
Tequila • Mexico 169 H7
Tequisquiapán • Mexico 169 J7
Ter • Spain 83 D3
Ter Heijde • Netherlands 70 G8
Teraina • Kiribati 139 D02
Téramo • Italy 87 A4
Torceira • Azores 84 C4
Teresina • Brazil 174 B3
Teresópolis • Brazil 174 F7
Terevaka • Easter I. .... 139 M
Terezín • Czech Rep. 89 E6
Tergnier • France 76 E2
Terme • Turkey 95 E4
Termessos • Turkey 95 G7
Términi Imerese, Golfo di •
     Sicily, Italy 86 G7
Términos, Laguna de • Mexico 169 E5
Termiz • Uzbekistan 121 E4
Termoli • Italy 85 E4
Ternate • Indonesia 131 G3
Terneuzen • Netherlands 70 B3
Terni • Italy 87 E4
Ternopil' • Ukraine 100 C4
Terra Mítica Park L • Spain .... 59 [71]
Terra Nova Nat. Park Park N •
     NF, Canada .... 161 [40]
Terrace • BC, Canada 160 D7
Terrace Bay • OT, Canada 159 H4

Terracina • Italy 87 F5
Terralba • Sardinia, Italy 86 E6
Terrassa • Spain 83 C4
Terre Déserte • French Polynesia ... 139 J
Terre Haute • IN, United States ... 150 C3
Terre Rouge, Ia • Mauritius 113 F6
Terre-de-Haut • Guadeloupe .... 167 J
Terreiro da Luta • Madeira 84 E5
Terrell • TX, United States 155 E4
Terres Basses • St Martin .... 166 C
Terry • MT, United States 148 E1
Terschelling • Netherlands 70 C1
Teruel • Spain 80 E3
Teruuau, Ku • Thailand 128 B5
Tervel • Bulgaria 92 H7
Tésero • Italy 86 C4
Teskraia • Tunisia 107 C4
Tesovo-Netyl'skiy • Russian Fed. ... 100 L13
Testa, Capo • Sardinia, Italy 86 F5
Testa-de-Buch, la • France 78 E6
Têt • France 78 U10
Tete • Mozambique 110 C2
Tetepare • Solomon Is. .... 138 W
Teterow • Germany 72 E2
Tétouan • Morocco 107 A1
Tétouan Heritage C • Morocco ... 44 [274]
Tetovo • FYR of Macedonia 93 B2
Tettnang • Germany 74 E8
Teulada • Spain 83 B1
Tévere • Italy 85 D3
Teviot • United Kingdom 62 D5
Tewkesbury • United Kingdom 65 F6
Texarkana • AR/TX, United States ... 155 F4
Texas • United States 147 G4
Texas City • TX, United States 155 F6
Texas Safari Wildlife Park •
     TX, United States 155 E5
Texcoco • Mexico 169 J7
Texel • Netherlands 70 C1
Texoma, Lake •
     OK/TX, United States 155 E4
Teykovo • Russian Fed. 100 M10
Tezuitlán • Mexico 169 J7
Tha Chin • Thailand 130 D7
Tha Rua • Ko Phuket, Thailand 130 F9
Thabankulu • South Africa 111 B3
Thaddeus Kosciuszko Nat. Mem. Park N •
     PA, United States .... 153 [269]
Thai Nguyen • Vietnam 128 C2
THAILAND • Asia 128 C3
Thailand, Gulf of •
     Cambodia/Thailand 128 C4
Thailand, Peninsular • Thailand 130 A4
Thalang • Ko Phuket, Thailand 130 F9
Thale Luang • Thailand 130 A4
Thames • New Zealand 137 C2
Thames • OT, Canada 161 A3
Thames • United Kingdom 63 E9
Thames Estuary • United Kingdom ... 65 H7
Thanet, Isle of • United Kingdom .. 65 H7
Thanh Hoa • Vietnam 128 C2
Thanjavur • India 124 C2
Thanjavur Heritage C • India .... 43 [160]
Thannhausen • Germany 74 F7
Thar Desert • India/Pakistan 123 D7
Thárros • Sardinia, Italy 86 E6
Thássos • Greece 93 C1
Thássos [I.] • Greece 93 C1
Thaton • Myanmar 128 B3
Thatta Heritage C • Pakistan .... 43 [144]
Thayetmyo • Myanmar 128 B3
The Bight • Turks & Caicos Is. 164 C3
The Bottom • Saba .... 167 E
The Dalles • OR, United States 154 G6
The Narrows • St Kitts & Nevis .... 167 F
The Quarter • Anguilla .... 166 B
The Settlement • British Virgin Is. . 166 A
The Valley • Anguilla .... 166 B
Thebes • Egypt 109 B2
Thebes Heritage C • Egypt ...... 43 [97]
Thedford • NE, United States 148 F2
Thelle • France 78 A1
Theodore • QL, Australia 136 D4
Theodore Roosevelt Birthplace Nat. Hist. Site
     Park N •
     NY, United States .... 153 [278]
Theodore Roosevelt Dam •
     AZ, United States 155 G8
Theodore Roosevelt I. Park N •
     DC, United States .... 153 [264]
Theodore Roosevelt Inaugural Nat. Hist. Site
     Park N • NY, United States .. 153 [272]
Theodore Roosevelt Lake •
     AZ, United States 155 G8
Theodore Roosevelt Nat. Park Park N •
     ND, United States .... 152 [146]
Theódori, Agii • Crete, Greece 93 G5
Thera • Thíra, Greece .... 94 G
Thérèse, I. • Seychelles 113 A1
Thermaïkós Kólpos • Greece 93 C1
Thermia • Greece 93 D3
Thermopolis • WY, United States ... 148 E2
Thessalía • Greece 94 BB2
Thessaloníki • Greece 93 C1
Thessaloníki Heritage C • Greece . 44 [232]
Thessaly • Greece 94 B1
Thetford • United Kingdom 63 F8
Thetford Mines • QU, Canada 160 A2
Thibodaux • LA, United States 156 F6
Thiers • France 76 E4
Thika • Kenya 109 C5
Thimphu • Bhutan 122 C3
Thingvellir Nat. Park Park N •
     Iceland .... 58 [3]
Thionville • France 76 G2
Thíra • Thíra, Greece .... 94 G
Thíra [I.] • Greece .... 94 G
Thirasia • Greece .... 94 G
Thirasía [I.] • Greece .... 94 G
Thirlmere • United Kingdom 65 D3
Thiruvarur • India 124 C3
Thisted • Denmark 99 E6
Thistlegorm Dive • Egypt 109 E7
Thíva • Greece 93 C2
Thiviers • France 76 B4
Thoams Stone Nat. Hist. Site Park N •
     MD, United States .... 153 [261]
Thoiry, Parc zoologique de •
     France 78 A2
Tholen • Netherlands 70 B3
Thomas Jefferson Mem. Park N •
     DC, United States .... 153 [264]
Thomas Reef Dive • Egypt 109 E7
Thomas Stone Nat. Hist. Site •
     MD, United States 156 A3
Thomas Stone Nat. Hist. Site •
     MD, United States 155 C1
Thomasville • GA, United States ... 155 C1
Thompson • MB, Canada 160 I1
Thomonde • Haiti 165 F5
Thompson • BC, Canada 160 I7
Thompson • MN, Canada 158 G3
Thompson Falls • MT, United States . 148 C1
Thompson Sound • New Zealand 137 F7
Thomson • QL, Australia 135 G5
Thon Buri • Thailand 130 D7
Thongwa • Myanmar 128 B3
Thong Krok, Laem •
     Ko Samui, Thailand 130 G12
Thonon-les-Bains • France 78 D3
Thorn • Poland 50 D2
Thoronet, Abbaye du • France 78 H7
Thorpe Park Park L • United Kingdom . 59 [34]
Thorpe Park • United Kingdom 65 K8
Thórshöfn • Iceland 97 I6
Thouars • France 77 E6
Thousand Is. Int. Bridge •
     Canada/United States 161 D2
Thrace Heritage C • Turkey 93 E1
Thráki Pélagos • Greece 93 D1
Thredbo • NS, Australia 136 H9
Three Hummock I. • TS, Australia ... 136 E6
Threlkeld • United Kingdom 65 D3
Thu Dau Mot • Vietnam 129 B5
Thurburo Majus • Tunisia 107 D4

Thugga • Tunisia 107 C4
Thugga Heritage C • Tunisia ... 44 [287]
Thuile, la Ski • Italy .... 61 [121]
Thuile, Ia • Italy 87 A1
Thulhagiri • Maldives 124 H7
Thulusdhu • Maldives 124 H7
Thun • Switzerland 90 J5
Thunder Bay • OT, Canada 159 H4
Thuner See • Switzerland 90 J5
Thung Salaeng Nat. Park •
     Thailand 130 C6
Thung Yai-Huai Kha Khaeng Wildlife Sanctuaries
     Heritage N • Thailand .... 41 [140]
Thur • Switzerland 91 R9
Thüringer Wald • Germany 72 D3
Thüringen • Germany 72 D3
Thurles • Ireland 69 C4
Thurso • United Kingdom 62 D2
Thurston I. • Antarctica 176 X5
Thusis • Switzerland 90 L5
Thuy Duong • Vietnam 129 C6
Thy • Denmark 99 E6
Thyborøn • Denmark 99 E6
Thyon 200 • Switzerland 90 J6
Thyrrheion • Greece 93 B2
Tia Tiare • NT, Australia 136 H1
Tianjin • China 125 F3
Tianjun • China 125 D3
Tianmu Shan • China 126 C7
Tianshui • China 125 E3
Tiarei • French Polynesia .... 139 K
Tias • Lanzarote, Canary Is. 83 I5
Tib, Ras el • Tunisia 107 D4
Tibbetts Turn • Cayman Is. 165 B1
Tiber • Italy 85 D3
Tiberias • Israel 120 B2
Tiberias, Lake • Israel 120 B2
Tibério, Villa di • Italy 87 F5
Tibesti • Chad 108 A2
Tibet • China 125 C3
Tibet, Lake • FL, United States ... 157 A1
Tibet, Plateau of • China 125 C3
Tibidabo • Spain 83 C4
Tibidabo, Parc d'Atraccions Park L •
     Spain .... 59 [69]
Tibro • Sweden 99 G5
Tiburón, I. • Mexico 168 H5
Tichurón Peninsula • Haiti 165 E6
Tichitt Heritage C • Mauritania ... 43 [105]
Ticino • Switzerland 90 K6
Ticino [Adm] • Switzerland 91 R10
Ticino [Riv] • Italy/Switzerland ... 87 B2
Ticul • Mexico 169 F4
Tidaholm • Sweden 99 G5
Tidjikja • Mauritania 106 A3
Tiefenbronn • Germany 74 B3
Tiefencastel • Switzerland 90 L5
Tieling • China 125 G2
Tielt • Belgium 70 F6
Tien Shan • China/Kyrgyzstan 125 B2
Tienen • Belgium 70 C4
Tienstin Dive • Egypt 109 E8
Tiergarten (Berlin) • Germany 73 F7
Tierp • Sweden 99 B1
Tierpark Friedrichsfelde (Berlin) •
     Germany 73 F7
Tierra Blanca • Mexico 169 K7
Tierra del Fuego, I. Grande de •
     Argentina/Chile 175 B5
Tierradentro, Parque Arqueológico Nac.
     Heritage C • Colombia ...... 42 [53]
Tiflet • Morocco 107 A1
Tifton • GA, United States 155 C1
Tigani, Hersónisos •
     Crete, Greece 93 G5
Tiger Balm Gardens • Singapore ... 129 H12
Tigina • Moldova 92 D2
Tignes Ski • France .... 61 [25]
Tignes • France 78 D3
Tigra, Punta de • Margarita .... 166 T
Tigre • Argentina 175 F6
Tigris • Iraq/Turkey 120 F7
Tijuana • Mexico 168 H5
Tikal • Guatemala 170 K9
Tikal, Parque Nac. • Guatemala 170 K9
Tikal, Parque Nac. Heritage C •
     Guatemala .... 40 [21]
Tikapo, Cap • French Polynesia .... 139 J
Tikhoretsk • Russian Fed. 100 F4
Tikhvin • Russian Fed. 100 L9
Tiktere • New Zealand 137 E5
Tikrit • Iraq 120 F7
Tiksi • Russian Fed. 101 M2
Tikus • Malaysia 129 F7
Tiladummati-Miladummadulu Atoll •
     Maldives 124 G7
Tilburg • Netherlands 70 C3
Till • United Kingdom 65 B1
Tilisos • Crete, Greece 93 I6
Tillberga • Sweden 99 A1
Tilos • Greece 93 E3
Timanfaya, Parque Nac. de Park N •
     Lanzarote, Canary Is. .... 50 [30]
Timanfaya, Parque Nac. de •
     Lanzarote, Canary Is. 83 I5
Timaru • New Zealand 137 B3
Timber Ridge Ski •
     MI, United States .... 146 [84]
Timberline Ski • OR, United States . 146 [27]
Timbuktu • Mali 106 B3
Timbuktu Heritage C • Mali ..... 43 [106]
Timgad Heritage C • Algeria .... 44 [285]
Timimoun • Algeria 107 B5
Timișoara • Romania 92 C2
Timiti's Crack • Pitcairn Is. ...... 139 L
Timmernabben • Sweden 99 H6
Timmins • OT, Canada 159 H4
Timon • Brazil 174 B3
Timor Bay • Guam .... 138 Z
Timor • East Timor/Indonesia 131 G5
Timor Sea • Indonesia/Australia ... 135 D2
Timpanogos Cave Nat. Mon. Park N •
     UT, United States .... 152 [76]
Timpson • TX, United States 155 F5
Timrå • Sweden 97 D3
Timucuan Ecological & Hist. Preserve •
     FL, United States 155 C1
Timucuan Ecological & Hist. Preserve
     Park N • FL, United States . 153 [215]
Tin Can Bay • QL, Australia 136 D5
Tin Shui Wai • Hong Kong, China ... 126 E5
Tinahely • Ireland 69 F7
Tinaztepe • Turkey 95 H7
Tindari • Sicily, Italy 86 H7
Tindouf • Algeria 106 B2
Tinerhir • Morocco 107 D2
Tinetto, I. del Heritage C • Italy . 44 [159]
Tíngáki • Cos, Greece .... 94 E
Tinglev • Denmark 99 E8
Tingsryd • Sweden 99 H7
Tinian • N. Mariana Is. .... 138 B
Tinian I. • N. Mariana Is. .... 138 B
Tinker Field • FL, United States .. 157 B1
Tinnsjø • Norway 98 D5
Tino, I. del Heritage C • Italy ... 44 [159]
Tinogasta • Argentina 175 B2
Tinos • Tínos, Greece .... 94 I
Tínos [I.] • Greece .... 94 I
Tinsukia • India 122 D3
Tintagel • United Kingdom 65 I10
Tintamarre, I. de • St Martin ..... 166 C
Tintern Abbey • United Kingdom 65 E6
Tintina Valley • YT, Canada 158 C2
Tioman • Malaysia 129 A4
Tipasa Heritage C • Algeria .... 44 [281]
Tipitapa • Nicaragua 170 D4
Tiracol Fort • Goa, India 123 C5
Tiradentes • Brazil 174 E6
Tirana • Albania 92 B3
Tirane • Albania 93 B2
Tiraně • Albania 93 B2

Tirano • Italy 87 B1
Tiraspol • Moldova 92 D3
Tire • Turkey 95 F5
Tiree • United Kingdom 62 B4
Tírnavos • Greece 93 C2
Tírnovo • Bulgaria 92 G3
Tirol • Austria 91 N8
Tirrénia • Italy 87 B3
Tirso • Sardinia, Italy 86 F5
Tirstrup [Apt] • Denmark 99 F7
Tirtha Empul Temple •
     Bali, Indonesia 131 L7
Tiruchchendur • India 124 C4
Tiruchirappalli • India 124 C2
Tirukalikundram • India 124 C2
Tirumala • India 124 C2
Tirunelveli • India 124 B3
Tirupati • India 124 C2
Tiruppur • India 124 B3
Tiruvanamalai • India 124 C2
Tiryns Heritage C • Greece ... 44 [239]
Tisnaren • Sweden 99 A2
Tisvilde • Denmark 99 F7
Tisza • Hungary 92 C2
Titisee • Germany 74 B4
Tittmoning • Germany 74 H7
Titusville • FL, United States 155 D2
Titz • Germany 74 G5
Tiveden • Sweden 99 G5
Tiveden Nat. Park Park N • Sweden . 58 [27]
Tiveden Nat. Park • Sweden 99 G5
Tiverton • United Kingdom 65 J9
Tivoli Park L • Denmark .... 59 [16]
Tivoli • Grenada .... 166 Q
Tivoli • Italy 87 F4
Tivoli Heritage C • Italy ...... 44 [166]
Tivoliland Park L • Denmark ..... 59 [16]
Tiwai I. Wildlife Sanctuary Park •
     Sierra Leone .... 112 [13]
Tiwanaku Heritage C • Bolivia ... 42 [63]
Tiwi Beach • Kenya 109 C6
Tiya Heritage C • Ethiopia ..... 43 [102]
Tizimin • Mexico 169 F4
Tiznit • Morocco 107 A3
Tjällmo • Sweden 99 A2
Tjolöholm • Sweden 99 F6
Tjøme • Norway 98 E6
Tjørn • Sweden 99 F5
Tjust • Sweden 99 H6
Tlacotalpán • Mexico 169 K7
Tlacotalpán Heritage C • Mexico ... 42 [24]
Tlapa • Mexico 169 J8
Tlaquepaque • Mexico 169 I7
Tlaxcala • Mexico 169 J7
Tlaxcala [Adm] • Mexico 169 J7
Tlaxco • Mexico 169 J7
Tlemcen • Algeria 106 B1
Tlokweng • Botswana 110 J10
Toa Payoh • Singapore 129 I11
Toamasina • Madagascar 110 D2
Toapoon, Ko • Thailand 130 G11
Toba • Indonesia 131 N9
Toba & Kakar Ranges • Pakistan 122 A2
Tobago • Trinidad & Tobago .... 166 R
Tobago Cays • St Vincent & Gren. .. 167 P
Tobago Forest Reserve •
     Trinidad & Tobago .... 166 R
Tobercurry • Ireland 69 H8
Tobermory • OT, Canada 161 C2
Tobermory • United Kingdom 62 B4
Tobol • Kazakhstan/Russian Fed. .. 121 D1
Tobol'sk • Russian Fed. 101 G3
Tobruk • Libya 108 B1
Toc Vers, I. • St Barthélemy ...... 166 C
Tocantins [Adm] • Brazil 174 B4
Tocantins [Riv] • Brazil 174 B3
Toco • Trinidad & Tobago .... 166 S
Tocopilla • Chile 175 A2
Tocumen • Panama 170 M11
Todd • NT, Australia 136 B2
Todi • Italy 87 E3
Todos Santos • Mexico 168 I6
Todra, Gorges du • Morocco 107 B2
Toetoes Bay • New Zealand 137 G8
Tofino • BC, Canada 160 I7
Tofol • Fed. States of Micronesia . 138 D
Tofsingdalen Nat. Park Park N •
     Sweden .... 58 [23]
Toft • United Kingdom 62 H12
Toftlund • Denmark 99 E8
Togane • Japan 127 I8
Toggenburg • Switzerland 90 K5
Togiak • AK, United States 158 F2
TOGO • Africa 106 C4
Togo Chasm • Niue .... 139 O
Tohatchi • NM, United States 149 E3
Tohiea, Mt • French Polynesia ..... 139 K
Toi • Niue .... 139 O
Toi-misaki • Japan 127 B4
Toijala • Finland 99 D3
Toisvesi • Finland 99 D3
Tojaki wine region Heritage C •
     Slovak Rep. .... 44 [202]
Tok • AK, United States 157 E3
Tok • Thailand 128 B4
Tokara-retto • Japan 127 A5
Tokat • Turkey 95 C1
TOKELAU • Pacific Ocean 138 CC3
Tokkevatn • Norway 98 A2
Tokoroa • New Zealand 137 E5
Tokoriki • Fiji Is. .... 138 T
Tokushima • Japan 127 C3
Tokyo • Japan 127 I8
Tokyo [Adm] • Japan 127 H8
Tokyo Bay • Japan 127 I8
Tokyo Disney Resort • Japan 127 I8
Tokyo-wan • Japan 127 I8
Tol • Fed. States of Micronesia ... 138 C
Tol'yatti • Russian Fed. 100 G3
Tolanaro • Madagascar 110 D3
Tolano • OH, United States 161 A3
Toledo • Spain 80 C4
Toledo Heritage C • Spain ...... 44 [118]
Toledo Bend Reservoir •
     LA/TX, United States 156 E5
Tolentino • Italy 87 D3
Tolfa • Italy 87 A4
Tolfa, Monti della • Italy 87 E4
Tolíara • Madagascar 110 D3
Tolk-Schau, Familíen-Freizeitpark Park L •
     Germany .... 59 [44]
Tollarp • Sweden 99 H7
Tølløse • Denmark 99 E7
Tolmin • Slovenia 92 F5
Tolo Harbour • Hong Kong, China ... 126 F5
Toluca • Mexico 169 J7
Tolú, Nevado de • Mexico 169 J7
Tomakomai • Japan 127 D2
Tomanivi • Fiji Is. .... 138 T
Tomar Heritage C • Portugal .... 44 [130]
Tomás de Berlanga • Galápagos Is. 171 G10
Tomaszów Mazowiecki • Poland 89 C7
Tomatlán • Mexico 169 H7
Tombouctou • Mali 106 B3
Tombouctou Heritage C • Mali ... 43 [106]
Tombstone • AZ, United States 155 H8
Tomelilla • Sweden 99 G7
Tomi-saki • Japan 127 I8
Tomlinson Ranges •
     SA/WA, Australia 136 A2
Tomogashima-suido • Japan 127 B3
Tomsk • Russian Fed. 101 I4
Tonale • Italy 87 B1
Tonale, Passo del • Italy 87 C1

Tonasket • WA, United States 148 C1
Tonawanda • NY, United States 161 A1
Tonbridge • United Kingdom 65 G8
Tonbridge [Apt] • Honduras 170 K9
Tondabayashi • Japan 127 G7
Tønder • Denmark 99 E8
Tone-gawa • Japan 127 I8
Tonesai Falls •
     Ko Phuket, Thailand 130 F9
Tonga • Pacific Ocean 138 CC4
Tonga Trench • Pacific Ocean 9 S7
Tongaat • South Africa 111 C4
Tongariki • Easter I. .... 139 M
Tongariro Nat. Park • New Zealand . 137 E6
Tongariro Nat. Park Heritage N •
     New Zealand .... 41 [164]
Tongatapu • Tonga .... 139 P
Tongatapu Group • Tonga 138 CC4
Tongchuan • China 125 E3
Tongliao • China 125 G2
Tongliao • China 125 D3
Tonglu • China 125 D3
Tongtian He • China 125 D3
Tongue • United Kingdom 62 C2
Tonini, Gulf of • China/Vietnam ... 128 C3
Tonle Sap • Cambodia 128 C4
Tonoas • Fed. States of Micronesia . 138 C
Tonopah • NV, United States 154 J8
Tønsberg • Norway 98 E6
Tonto Nat. Mon. Park N •
     AZ, United States 155 G8
Tontouta [Apt] • New Caledonia .... 138 U
Tonumea • Tonga .... 139 P
Toowoomba • QL, Australia 136 D5
Topcam Plaj • Turkey 95 G8
Topeka • KS, United States 150 A3
Töpliz • Germany 73 E8
Topolobampo • Mexico 168 I6
Topolovgrad • Bulgaria 92 H8
Torbali • Turkey 95 F5
Töreboda • Sweden 99 G5
Toresund • Sweden 99 A1
Torgau • Germany 72 E3
Torgon Ski • Switzerland .... 61 [34]
Torkanium • Sweden 99 H7
Tornarträsk • Sweden 97 D2
Tornio • Finland 97 D2
Tornionjoki • Finland 97 F2
Tornio • Italy 87 D2
Toro • Japan 127 H9
Toro Muerto • Peru 173 F7
Toronto • OT, Canada 160 E5
Toropets • Russian Fed. 100 L10
Tororo • Uganda 109 B4
Torpa [Apt] • Norway 98 D6
Torpa • Sweden 99 F6
Torquay • United Kingdom 65 J10
Torquay Beach • United Kingdom .... 64 [57]
Torralba • Portugal 84 I8
Torrance • CA, United States 154 J9
Torre Annunziata • Italy 87 G7
Torre Annunziata Heritage C • Italy . 44 [169]
Torre de la Higuera • Spain 82 B7
Torre del Greco • Italy 87 G7
Torre del Mar • Spain 82 J8
Torre Pedro • Spain 83 C4
Torredembarra • Spain 83 J7
Torredonjimeno • Spain 82 J7
Torrelavega • Spain 80 C2
Torremolinos • Spain 82 J8
Torrens Creek • QL, Australia 136 C4
Torrens Point • Saba .... 167 E
Torreón • Spain 80 E4
Torres de Alcala • Morocco 107 B1
Torres del Paine • Chile .... 138 V
Torres Strait • QL, Australia 135 G2
Torrevieja • Spain 83 A2
Torridge • United Kingdom 65 J9
Torrox • Spain 82 J8
Torshälla • Sweden 99 A1
Torsö • Sweden 99 G5
Tortoise Reserve • Galápagos Is. . 171 H10
Tortola • British Virgin Is. .... 166 A
Tortoli • Sardinia, Italy 86 F6
Tortona • Italy 87 B2
Tortue, I. de la • Haiti 165 F5
Tortue, la • St Barthélemy .... 166 D
Tortuga • Mexico 169 J7
Tortuga, I. • Galápagos Is. 171 G10
Tortuguero • Costa Rica 170 F5
Tortuguero • Costa Rica 170 F5
Torul • Turkey 95 D1
Torun Heritage C • Poland ...... 44 [180]
Torup • Sweden 99 G6
Torver • United Kingdom 65 D4
Tory I. • Ireland 69 B1
Torzhok • Russian Fed. 100 L10
Tosa • Japan 127 B4
Toscana • Italy 87 B2
Toshimaen • Japan 127 I8
Toshka Depression • Egypt 109 B3
Toshkent • Uzbekistan 121 E3
Tossa de Mar • Spain 83 D3
Tosterön • Sweden 99 A2
Tostón • Fuerteventura, Canary Is. . 83 H5
Tosya • Turkey 95 D1
Totak • Norway 98 D3
Totnes • United Kingdom 65 J10
Totness • Surinam 174 A2
Totsugawa • Japan 127 B3
Tottori • Japan 127 C3
Touggourt • Algeria 106 C1
Touhu • New Caledonia .... 138 U
Toul • France 76 G2
Toukkal, Jebel • Morocco 107 A3
Toulon • France 78 G8
Toulouse • France 78 F7
Tououga • Myanmar 128 B3
Tour • France 76 D4
Tourcoing • France 76 E1
Tourlaïe, Col du • France 78 F8
Tournai • Belgium 70 B4
Tournon • France 78 G6
Touros • Brazil 174 A2
Tours • France 76 D4
Toussuire, la • France 78 E6
Touwsrivier • South Africa 111 E7
Touws River • South Africa 111 E7
Tovdal • Norway 98 G9
Towanda • PA, United States 161 A1
Tower I. • Galápagos Is. 171 H9
Townshend, Cape • QL, Australia .. 136 D4
Townsville • QL, Australia 136 C4
Towson • United Kingdom 65 110
Toyama • Japan 127 C3
Toyapakeh • Indonesia 131 L8
Toyohashi • Japan 127 C3
Toyota • Japan 127 C3
Tozeur • Tunisia 107 C5
Tra Vinh • Vietnam 129 B6
Traben-Trarbach • Germany 74 C6

Trabzon • Turkey 95 C1
Trafalgar, Cabo • Spain 82 H8
Trafalgar Falls • Dominica .... 167 K
Traighli • Ireland 69 G10
Trail • BC, Canada 160 J7
Trakai Nat. Park Park N • Lithuania . 58 [153]
Trakai Nat. Park • Lithuania 100 K8
Tralee • Ireland 69 G10
Tralee Bay • Ireland 69 G10
Tramuntana, Serra de •
     Majorca, Spain 83 N11
Tranås • Sweden 99 H5
Tranebjerg • Denmark 99 F6
Tranemo • Sweden 99 G6
Trang • Thailand 130 A4
Trans World Radio • Bonaire .... 166 U
Transantarctic Mtns • Antarctica .. 176 M-X
Transylvanian Alps • Romania 92 D2
Tranum Strand • Denmark 99 F5
Trápani • Sicily, Italy 86 G7
Traralgon • VI, Australia 136 G9
Tras os Muntes • Portugal 84 A1
Trasimeno, Lago • Italy 87 C3
Trat • Thailand 128 C4
Traumland • Germany 74 B3
Trawniki • Martinique 74 H7
Trausnee • Austria 91 P7
Traunstein • Germany 74 H7
Travemünde • Germany 72 D2
Traverse City • MI, United States . 150 C2
Travnik • Bosnia-Herz. 92 G6
Travo • Corsica, France 78 N12
Trbovlje • Slovenia 91 G2
Tre, Hon • Vietnam 129 C5
Treasure Beach • Jamaica 165 C4
Treasure Cay • Bahamas 164 A1
Trebalugar • Minorca, Spain 83 K8
Trebbin • Germany 73 E8
Trébeurden • France 77 C3
Trebević Nat. Park • Bosnia-Herz. . 92 G6
Trebic • Czech Rep. 89 E7
Trebnje • Bosnia-Herz. 92 G6
Trebon • Czech Rep. 89 E7
Trédrez • France 77 C3
Treetops Ski • MI, United States . 146 [79]
Trégastel • France 77 C3
Tregosse Is. • CL, Australia 136 D3
Tréguier • France 77 C3
Treis-Karden • Germany 74 C5
Trelleborg • Sweden 99 G8
Tremblade, la • France 78 E5
Tremblant Ski • QU, Canada ...... 146 [17]
Tremblet, Pointe du • Réunion 113 D4
Tremezzo • Italy 87 B1
Trémiti, Is. • Italy 85 E3
Tremmen • Germany 72 E3
Trencín • Slovak Rep. 89 B4
Trento • United Kingdom 63 D8
Trentino-Südtirol • Italy 87 C1
Trento • Italy 86 C4
Trenton • NJ, United States 156 B2
Trenton • OT, Canada 160 F4
Trepassey • NF, Canada 160 D1
Tréport (Berlin) • Germany 73 F8
Très Corações • Brazil 174 E7
Tres Puntas, Cabo • Argentina 175 B4
Três Rios • Brazil 174 F7
Tres Zapotes • Mexico 169 K7
Tresaith Beach • United Kingdom ... 64 [57]
Treuchtlingen • Germany 74 G6
Treuer Range • NT, Australia 136 A1
Treviso • Italy 87 D2
Trevose Head • United Kingdom 65 I10
Triabunna • TS, Australia 136 F7
Triánda • Rhodes, Greece .... 94 F
Tilberg • Germany 74 B4
Tribhuvan [Apt] • Nepal 123 G7
Tribulation, Cape •
     QL, Australia 135 H3
Trichur • India 124 B3
Trier • Germany 74 C6
Trier Heritage C • Germany ..... 44 [58]
Trieste • Italy 87 D2
Trieste, Golfo di • Italy/Slovenia . 87 D2
Trifels, Burg • Germany 74 B3
Triglav Nat. Park Park N • Slovenia . 58 [117]
Triglav Nat. Park • Slovenia 92 B2
Trikala • Greece 93 B2
Trikomo • Cyprus 96 D3
Trim • Ireland 69 E6
Trincomalee • Sri Lanka 124 C4
Trinidad • Bolivia 173 C4
Trinidad & Tobago • West Indies .. 166 R-S
Trinidad • Cuba 164 F4
Trinidad Heritage C • Cuba ..... 42 [41]
Trinidad Heritage C • Paraguay .. 42 [67]
Trinidad • Uruguay 175 G6
TRINIDAD & TOBAGO • West Indies . 166 R-S
Trinidade • Brazil 174 B4
Trinité, la • Martinique .... 167 L
Trinity • TX, United States 155 F5
Trinity Bay • NF, Canada 160 D1
Trinity Is. • AK, United States .. 157 D4
Trinkstein • Italy 86 D3
Triolet • Mauritius 113 E5
Tripoli • Greece 93 C3
Tripoli • Libya 106 D1
Tripolitania • Libya 106 D1
Tripura • India 123 B2
Tristan da Cunha • Atlantic Ocean . 10 I7
Troarn • France 78 F5
Trobriand Is. • Papua New Guinea .. 138 BB3
Trogir • Croatia 92 G6
Trogir Heritage C • Croatia .... 44 [210]
Troglav • Bosnia-Herz./Croatia 92 G6
Tróia • Portugal 84 G6
Trois Fourches, Cap de • Morocco .. 107 B1
Trois Vallées Ski • France ..... 61 [23-25]
Trois-Bassins • Réunion 113 C4
Trois-Îlets, les • Martinique .... 167 L
Trois-Rivières • Guadeloupe ...... 167 J
Trois-Rivières • QU, Canada 160 H3
Troisdorf • Germany 74 A1
Trollhättan • Sweden 99 F5
Trou aux Biches Beach • Mauritius . 113 F6
Trou d'Eau Beach • Mauritius 113 F6
Troussay [Château] • France 77 F5
Troutbeck • United Kingdom 65 D4
Trowbridge • United Kingdom 65 K9
Trowulan • Java, Indonesia 131 R12
Troy • AL, United States 151 C4
Troy • MT, United States 148 C1
Troy • NY, United States 156 C1
Troy • Turkey 95 E4
Troy Heritage C • Turkey .... 44 [249]
Troyes • France 76 F2
Trujillo • Honduras 170 K9
Trujillo • Peru 173 E3
Truro • United Kingdom 65 K9
Truro • NS, Canada 160 B2
Truro • United Kingdom 65 I10
Truth or Consequences •
     NM, United States 155 H8
Truva • Turkey 95 E4
Truva Heritage C • Turkey ...... 44 [249]
Tryavna • Bulgaria 92 H8

Tsagaannuur • Mongolia 125 C2
Tsambika, Moni • Rhodes, Greece 94 F
Tsarevo • Bulgaria 92 I8
Tsarevo • Bulgaria 95 F3
Tsarkoye Selo • Russian Fed. 100 L9
Tsau • Botswana 110 I9
Tsavo East Nat. Park • Kenya 109 D5
Tsavo Nat. Park **Park** • Kenya 112 [80]
Tsavo West Nat. Park • Kenya 109 D5
Tsetserleg • Mongolia 125 E2
Tseung Kwan O • Hong Kong, China 126 F5
Tshabong • Botswana 110 I10
Tshane • Botswana 110 I10
Tshikapa • Dem. Rep. of Congo 108 B5
Tshootsa • Botswana 110 I9
Tshuapa • Dem. Rep. of Congo 108 B5
Tsiigehtchic • YT, Canada 158 C2
Tsim Sha Tsui • Hong Kong, China 126 F5
Tsimlyanskoye Vdkhr. • Russian Fed. 100 F4
Tsing Yi • Hong Kong, China 126 E5
Tsingy de Bemaraha, Réserve naturelle intégrale du **Park** • Madagascar 112 [150]
Tsingy de Bemaraha, Réserve naturelle intégrale du **Heritage N** • Madagascar 41 [117]
Tsitsikamma Mtns • South Africa 111 F7
Tsitsikamma Nat. Park • South Africa 111 F7
Tsodilo • Botswana 110 I9
Tsodilo **Heritage C** • Botswana 43 [122]
Tsodilo Hills • Botswana 110 I9
Tsu • Japan 127 C4
Tsuchiura • Japan 127 I8
Tsuen Wan • Hong Kong, China 126 E5
Tsugaru-kaikyo • Japan 127 D2
Tsukigase Garden • Japan 127 G6
Tsukuba Science City • Japan 127 I8
Tsumeb • Namibia 110 A2
Tsuna • Japan 127 F7
Tsuru • Japan 127 H8
Tsuruga • Japan 127 C3
Tsurugi-saki • Japan 127 I9
Tsushima • Japan 127 A4
Tswapong Hills • Botswana 110 J10
Tuam • Ireland 69 H9
Tuamotu, Archipel des • French Polynesia 139 EE4
Tuapa • Niue 139 O
Tuapse • Russian Fed. 100 E5
Tuarabu • Kiribati 139 F
Tuas • Singapore 129 H11
Tuasivi • Samoa 139 G
Tuatapere • New Zealand 137 F8
Tuba City • AZ, United States 155 G7
Tuban • Java, Indonesia 131 Q11
Tubbataha Reef Marine Park **Heritage N** • Philippines 41 [144]
Tübingen • Germany 74 B3
Tubruq • Libya 108 B1
Tubuai • French Polynesia 139 DD4
Tuchitua • YT, Canada 158 D2
Tucker's Town • Bermuda 165 L9
Tucson • AZ, United States 155 G8
Tucuarembó • Uruguay 175 C3
Tucumcari • NM, United States 149 F3
Tucupita • Venezuela 173 C2
Tucuruí • Brazil 174 B3
Tucuruí, Represa • Brazil 174 B3
Tuen Mun • Hong Kong, China 126 E5
Tugela • South Africa 111 C4
Tugela Ferry • South Africa 111 B4
Tuguegarao • Philippines 128 G3
Tuineje • Fuerteventura, Canary Is. 83 H5
Tuk Tuk • Indonesia 131 N9
Tuktoyaktuk • YT, Canada 158 C2
Tuktut Nogait Nat. Park **Park N** • NT/NU, Canada 161 [5]
Tukums • Latvia 100 J7
Tula • American Samoa 139 H
Tula • Hidalgo, Mexico 169 J7
Tula • Russian Fed. 100 E3
Tula • Tamaulipas, Mexico 169 J6
Tulamben • Bali, Indonesia 131 L7
Tulancingo • Mexico 169 J7
Tulayat al Ghassul • Jordan 120 B3
Tulbagh • South Africa 111 D6
Tulcán • Ecuador 173 B2
Tulcea • Romania 92 I7
Tule River **Ind Res** • CA, United States 155 [8]
Tuli Block • Botswana 110 J10
Tuli Block safari reserves **Park** • Botswana 112 [121]
Tulita • NT, Canada 158 D2
Tulla • Ireland 69 H10
Tullahoma • TN, United States 151 C3
Tullamarine [Apt] • VI, Australia 136 G9
Tulle • France 78 F5
Tulln • Austria 91 H1
Tullow • Ireland 69 E7
Tully • QL, Australia 136 C3
Tulovo • Bulgaria 92 H8
Tulsa • OK, United States 151 A3
Tulsk • Ireland 69 H8
Tulum • Mexico 169 G4
Tulungagung • Java, Indonesia 131 Q12
Tumacacori Nat. Hist. Park • AZ, United States 155 G8
Tumacacori Nat. Hist. Park **Park N** • AZ, United States 152 [112]
Tumaco • Colombia 173 B2
Tumba • Sweden 99 B2
Tumbes • Peru 173 A3
Tumkur • India 124 B2
Tummel • United Kingdom 65 A1
Tumu Mtn • American Samoa 139 H
Tumucumaque, Serra • S. America 174 A2
Tun • Sweden 99 G5
Tun Chung • Hong Kong, China 126 E5
Tunapuna • Trinidad & Tobago 166 S
Tunas de Zaza • Cuba 164 F4
Tuncurry • NS, Australia 135 I6
Tunduma • Tanzania 110 G8
Tunduru • Tanzania 110 H8
Tung Ling Chau • Hong Kong, China 126 F5
Tungabhadra • India 124 B1
Tungaru • Kiribati 138 CC3
Tungelsta • Sweden 99 B2
Tunis • Tunisia 107 D4
Tunis **Heritage C** • Tunisia 44 [288]
Tunis, Golfe de • Tunisia 107 D4
TUNISIA • Africa 107 C-D
Tunxi • China 126 G7
Tupelo • MS, United States 151 C4
Tupelo Nat. Battlefield **Park N** • MS, United States 153 [198]
Tupiza • Bolivia 173 C5
Tuque, La • QU, Canada 159 I4
Tuquerres • Colombia 173 B2
Tura • Russian Fed. 101 K3
Turangi • New Zealand 137 E6
Turayf • Saudi Arabia 120 D7
Turballe, la • France 77 D4
Turbat • Pakistan 122 A3
Turda • Romania 92 C2
Turenne • France 78 F5
Turgay Valley • Kazakstan 121 D1
Turgovishte • Bulgaria 92 H8
Turgutreis • Turkey 95 E6
Turhal • Turkey 95 C1
Turin • Italy 87 A2
Turin **Heritage C** • Italy 44 [147]
Turkana, Lake • Ethiopia/Kenya 109 C4
Turkana, Lake **Heritage N** • Kenya 41 [107]
TURKEY • Asia/Europe 95
Türkistan • Kazakstan 121 E3
Türkmenbashy • Turkmenistan 121 B4
TURKMENISTAN • Asia 121 C4
TURKS & CAICOS IS. • West Indies 164 C-D
Turks I. Passage • Turks & Caicos Is. 164 D3
Turku • Finland 99 C4
Turku Archipelago • Finland 99 C4
Turkwel • Kenya 109 C4
Turneffe Is. • Belize 170 K9
Turnhout • Belgium 70 C3
Turnov • Czech Rep. 89 E6
Turoa • New Zealand 137 E6
Turpan • China 125 C2
Turpan Pendi • China 125 C2
Turquino, Pico • Cuba 164 H5
Turquoise Coast • Turkey 95 G-H
Turrialba • Costa Rica 170 F6
Turtle I. • Bali, Indonesia 131 L8
Turtle I. • CL, Australia 136 D3
Turtle Mtn **Ind Res** • ND, United States 155 [43]
Turukhansk • Russian Fed. 101 I3
Turun Ja Pori • Finland 99 C4
Turunc • Turkey 95 F6
Tuscaloosa • AL, United States 151 C4
Tuscánia • Italy 87 E4
Tuscany • Italy 86 A1
TusenFryd **Park L** • Norway 59 [4]
TusenFryd • Norway 98 E5
Tuskegee Airman Nat. Hist. Site **Park N** • AL, United States 153 [200]
Tuskegee Institute Nat. Hist. Site **Park N** • AL, United States 153 [200]
Tuticorin • India 124 C3
Tuttlingen • Germany 74 B4
Tutuala • East Timor 131 G5
Tutuila • American Samoa 139 H
Tutupaca, Volcán • Peru 173 F7
Tuva **Russ Adm** • Russian Fed. 101 [25]
TUVALU • Pacific Ocean 138 CC3
Tuxpan • Nayarit, Mexico 169 H6
Tuxpan • Veracruz, Mexico 169 J7
Tuxtepec • Mexico 169 K8
Tuxtla Gutiérrez • Mexico 168 F4
Tuyen Quang • Vietnam 128 D2
Tuz Gölü • Turkey 95 B2
Tuzigoot Nat. Mon. • AZ, United States 155 G7
Tuzigoot Nat. Mon. **Park N** • AZ, United States 152 [106]
Tuzla • Bosnia-Herz. 92 G6
Tuzlata • Bulgaria 92 I8
Tvedestrand • Norway 99 E5
Tveitsund • Norway 98 G9
Tver' • Russian Fed. 100 M10
Tverfjellet • Norway 98 G7
Tvertsa • Russian Fed. 100 L10
Tweed • United Kingdom 62 D5
Tweedsmuir Prov. Park • BC, Canada 160 I6
Twelve Apostles, The • VI, Australia 136 G9
Twelve Bens • Ireland 69 G9
Twente [Apt] • Netherlands 70 D2
Twin Falls • ID, United States 154 H6
Twin Lakes • AL, Canada 158 E3
Two Rivers • WI, United States 150 C2
Twycross • United Kingdom 65 F5
Txiki Park **Park L** • Spain 59 [72]
Tyana • Turkey 95 J9
Tychy • Poland 89 F8
Tyin • Norway 98 G8
Tykkimäki **Park L** • Finland 59 [13]
Tyler • TX, United States 155 F4
Tylösand • Sweden 99 G7
Tylöskog • Sweden 99 H5
Tynda • Russian Fed. 101 M4
Tyndrum • United Kingdom 65 A1
Tynemouth **Beach** • United Kingdom 64 [5]
Typhoon Lagoon • FL, United States 157 A1
Tyre • Lebanon 120 A1
Tyre **Heritage C** • Lebanon 44 [307]
Tyrella **Beach** • United Kingdom 64 [75]
Tyrifjorden • Norway 98 D5
Tyrone • United Kingdom 64 A3
Tyrrhenian Sea • Mediterranean Sea 85 D5
Tysnesøy • Norway 98 F9
Tyssedal • Norway 98 G8
Tystberga • Sweden 99 A2
Tyulenovo • Bulgaria 92 I8
Tyumen' • Russian Fed. 101 G3
Tzermiádo • Crete, Greece 93 I6
Tzoumas, La **Ski** • Switzerland 61 [57]

U

Ua Huka • French Polynesia 139 EE3
Uaboe • Nauru 138 X
Uaupés • Brazil 173 C2
Ubá • Brazil 174 F6
Ubangi • Dem. Rep. of Congo 108 B4
Ubarat **Beach** • India 124 E6
Ubatuba • Brazil 174 E7
Ube • Japan 127 B4
Uberaba • Brazil 174 B4
Uberlândia • Brazil 174 B4
Uberlingen • Germany 74 E8
Ubin • Singapore 129 I11
Ubon Rat Reservoir • Thailand 130 A2
Ubon Ratchathani • Thailand 128 C3
Ubud • Bali, Indonesia 131 L8
Ucayali • Peru 173 B3
Uch Adzhi • Turkmenistan 121 D4
Uchiura-wan • Japan 127 D2
Uchquduq • Uzbekistan 121 D3
Uckermark • Germany 73 B1
Uçpinar • Turkey 95 H7
Udaipur • India 123 D8
Udayapur • India 123 F8
Uddevalla • Sweden 99 F5
Uddjaure • Sweden 97 D2
Udhagamandalam • India 124 B3
Udine • Italy 87 D1
Udmurtia **Russ Adm** • Russian Fed. 101 [15]
Udon Thani • Thailand 128 C3
Udot • Fed. States of Micronesia 138 C
Udupi • India 124 B2
Udupi **Beach** • India 124 E6
Ueda • Japan 127 C3
Uele • Dem. Rep. of Congo 108 B4
Uelen • Russian Fed. 157 D2
Uelzen • Germany 72 D2
Ueno • Japan 127 G6
Ufa • Russian Fed. 101 F4
Ugadamandalam **Hill Sta** • India 124 E6
UGANDA • Africa 108 C4
Ugine • France 78 D3
Uglich • Russian Fed. 100 M10
Ugljan • Croatia 92 F6
Uhlava • Czech Rep. 89 D7
Uig • United Kingdom 62 B3
Uíge • Angola 110 A1
Uinta Mtns • UT, United States 148 D2
Uintah & Ouray **Ind Res** • UT, United States 155 [23]
Uitenhage • South Africa 111 G7
Uithoorn • Netherlands 70 H7
Uithuizen • Netherlands 70 D1
Ujelang • Marshall Is. 138 BB2
Uji • Japan 127 G6
Ujjain • India 122 B3
Ujung • Bali, Indonesia 131 L8
Ujung Kulon Nat. Park **Heritage N** • Indonesia 41 [145]
Ujung Kulon Nat. Park • Java, Indonesia 131 O11
Ujung Pandang • Indonesia 131 E5
uKhahlamba-Drakensberg **Heritage C** • South Africa 43 [124]
uKhahlamba-Drakensberg Park **Heritage N** • South Africa 41 [116]
Ukhta • Russian Fed. 101 F3
Ukiah • CA, United States 148 B3
Ukimi-do • Japan 127 G6
Ukmerge • Lithuania 100 K8
UKRAINE • Europe 100 D4
Ukunda • Kenya 109 C6
Ul'yanovsk • Russian Fed. 100 G3
Ula • Turkey 95 F6
Ulaanbaatar • Mongolia 125 E2
Ulaangom • Mongolia 125 D2
Ulan Bator • Mongolia 125 E2
Ulan-Ude • Russian Fed. 101 K4
Ulanhot • China 125 G2
Ulássai • Sardinia, Italy 86 F6
Ulawa I. • Solomon Is. 138 W
Uleåborg • Finland 97 F2
Ulefoss • Norway 98 D6
Ulfborg • Denmark 99 E7
Uliastay • Mongolia 125 D2
Ulithi Atoll • Fed. States of Micronesia 138 AA2
Ullal **Beach** • India 124 E6
Ullapool • United Kingdom 62 C3
Ullared • Sweden 99 G6
Ulleungdo • Rep. of Korea 127 B3
Ullswater • United Kingdom 65 D3
Ulm • Germany 74 E7
Ulmen • Germany 74 C5
Ulricehamn • Sweden 99 G6
Ulsan • Rep. of Korea 125 G3
Ulsta • United Kingdom 62 H12
Ulsteinvik • Norway 98 F7
Ulster • Ireland 69 C2
Ultimatum Tree • South Africa 111 C4
Ulu Watu Temple • Bali, Indonesia 131 L8
Ulubat Gölü • Turkey 95 F4
Ulubey • Turkey 95 F5
Uludag • Turkey 95 F4
Ulukisla • Turkey 95 I9
Ulundi • South Africa 111 C4
Uluru • NT, Australia 136 A2
Uluru-Kata Tjuta Nat. Park **Heritage N** • Australia 41 [153]
Uluru-Kata Tjuta Nat. Park **Heritage C** • Australia 43 [211]
Uluru-Kata Tjuta Nat. Park • NT, Australia 136 A2
Ulva • United Kingdom 62 B4
Ulverston • United Kingdom 65 D4
Ulvik • Norway 98 G8
Ulysses **Dive** • Egypt 109 E7
Ulysses S. Grant Nat. Hist. Site **Park N** • MO, United States 153 [175]
Uman • Fed. States of Micronesia 138 C
Umán • Mexico 169 F4
Uman' • Ukraine 100 D4
Umatac • Guam 138 Z
Umatilla **Ind Res** • OR, United States 155 [4]
Umbargaon **Beach** • India 124 E6
Umbria • Italy 87 D3
Umbria **Dive** • Sudan 109 E9
Ume älv • Sweden 97 D3
Umeå • Sweden 97 E3
Umhlanga Rocks • South Africa 111 C4
Umlalazi Nature Reserve • South Africa 111 C4
Umlazi • South Africa 111 B5
Umm Sid, Râs **Dive** • Egypt 109 E7
Umm Urumah • Saudi Arabia 109 E8
Umnak I. • AK, United States 157 C4
Umtamvuna Nature Reserve • South Africa 111 B5
Umtata • South Africa 110 B4
Umzimkulu • South Africa 111 B5
Umzinto • South Africa 111 B5
Una • Bosnia-Herz./Croatia 92 G5
Unalakleet • AK, United States 157 D3
Unalaska I. • AK, United States 157 C4
Unapool • United Kingdom 62 C2
Unayzah • Saudi Arabia 120 E8
Undandita • NT, Australia 136 A1
Unden • Sweden 99 G5
Underberg • South Africa 111 B5
Undredal • Norway 98 G8
Ungava Bay • NU/QU, Canada 159 J3
Ungava, Péninsule d' • QU, Canada 159 I3
Ungheni • Moldova 92 D2
Ungwana Bay • Kenya 109 D5
Unije • Croatia 92 F6
Unimak I. • AK, United States 157 D4
Union I. • St Vincent & Gren. 167 P
Uniondale • South Africa 111 F7
UNITED ARAB EMIRATES • Asia 120 G9
UNITED KINGDOM • Europe 62-63
UNITED STATES OF AMERICA • N. America 147
UNITED STATES VIRGIN IS. • West Indies 166 X
Universal Mediterranea **Park L** • Spain 59 [70]
Universal Mediterranea • Spain 83 C4
Universal Orlando • FL, United States 157 B1
Universal Orlando **Park L** • FL, United States 157 [24]
Universal Studios Florida **Park L** • FL, United States 157 [24]
Universal Studios Hollywood **Park L** • CA, United States 157 [4]
Universal Studios Japan • Japan 127 G6
Unna • Germany 73 D5
Unst • United Kingdom 62 H12
Unter Engadin • Switzerland 90 L5
Unteres Odertal, Nationalpark **Park N** • Germany/Poland 58 [67]
Unterinntal • Austria 91 O7
Unterwasser • Switzerland 90 K5
Upemba, Parc nat. de l' **Park** • Dem. Rep. of Congo 112 [55]
Upington • South Africa 110 B3
Uplands [Apt] • OT, Canada 160 G4
Upolu • Samoa 139 G
Upper Arlington • OH, United States 150 D2
Upper Arrow Lake • BC, Canada 158 E3
Upper Canada Village • OT, Canada 160 G4
Upper Egypt • Egypt 109 B2
Upper Klamath Lake • OR, United States 154 G6
Upper Lough Erne • United Kingdom 63 B6
Uppsala • Sweden 99 B1
Uppsala [Adm] • Sweden 99 B1
Upua • New Zealand 137 B2
Urabá, Golfo de • Colombia 170 I6
Ural Mtns • Russian Fed. 101 G3
Ural [Riv] • Russian Fed. 101 F4
Ural'skiy Khrebet • Russian Fed. 101 G3
Urania **Dive** • Eritrea 109 E10
Uranium City • SA, Canada 158 F3
Urawa • Japan 127 I8
Urbana • IL, United States 150 C2
Urbino • Italy 87 D3
Urbino **Heritage C** • Italy 44 [164]
Uren' • Russian Fed. 100 G2
Urengoy • Russian Fed. 101 H3
Urenui • New Zealand 137 D6
Urganch • Uzbekistan 121 D3
Urgüp • Turkey 95 J9
Urhjo Kekkonen Nat. Park **Park N** • Finland 58 [32]
Uri • Switzerland 91 R10
Uritskiy • Kazakstan 121 E1
Urk • Netherlands 70 C2
Urla • Turkey 95 E5
Urnes **Heritage C** • Norway 43 [85]
Urnes stavkirke • Norway 98 G8
Urosevac • Serbia & Montenegro 92 C3
Uroteppa • Tajikistan 121 E4
Urshult • Sweden 99 H7
Uruapan • Mexico 169 I7
Urubamba • Peru 173 F6
Urubamba [Riv] • Peru 173 F6
Uruguai • Brazil 175 C2
Uruguaiana • Brazil 175 C2
URUGUAY • S. America 175 C3
Uruguay [Riv] • Argentina/Uruguay 175 C2
Urukthapel • Palau 138 Y
Urümqi • China 125 C2
Urziceni • Romania 92 H7
Urzig • Germany 74 C6
Usak • Turkey 95 F5
Usak [Adm] • Turkey 95 F5
Usambara Mtns • Tanzania 110 H7
Usedom • Germany 72 F2
Ushakova, Ostrov • Russian Fed. 101 H1
Ushant • France 77 C3
Ushi Point • N. Mariana Is. 138 B
Ushuaia • Argentina 175 B5
Uskedal • Norway 98 F9
Usküb • F.Y.R. of Macedonia 50 D3
Usküdar • Turkey 95 F3
USS Arizona Mem. • HI, United States 157 G6
USS Arizona Mem. **Park N** • HI, United States 152 [17]
Ussé [Château] • France 77 F5
Ussuri • Russian Fed. 125 H2
Ussuriysk • Russian Fed. 101 N5
Ust' Kamchatsk • Russian Fed. 101 Q4
Ust'-Ordyn-Buryat **Russ Adm** • Russian Fed. 101 [26]
Ust'Ilimsk • Russian Fed. 101 K4
Ustaoset • Norway 98 G8
Ustek • Czech Rep. 89 E6
Usti nad Labem • Czech Rep. 89 D6
Ustica, I. di • Italy 86 G7
Ustka • Poland 89 B1
Ustrzyki Dolne • Poland 89 C4
Ustyurt Plateau • Kazakstan/Uzbekistan 121 C3
Usulután • El Salvador 170 C4
Usumacinta • Guatemala/Mexico 168 F4
Utah • United States 148 D3
Utara, Selat • Penang, Malaysia 129 E7
Utatlán • Guatemala 170 J9
Ute Mtn **Ind Res** • CO, United States 155 [34]
Utena • Lithuania 100 K8
Utete • Tanzania 110 H8
Utica • NY, United States 156 B1
Utica • Tunisia 107 D4
Utiel • Spain 80 E4
Utila, I. de • Honduras 170 K9
Utlängen • Sweden 99 H7
Utne • Norway 98 G8
Utö • Sweden 99 B2
Utö [I.] • Sweden 99 B2
Utorda Beach • Goa, India 123 C6
Utrecht • Netherlands 70 H8
Utrecht **Heritage C** • Netherlands 44 [36]
Utrecht • South Africa 111 B3
Utrecht [Adm] • Netherlands 70 H8
Utsjoki • Finland 97 F2
Utsukushino-mori • Japan 127 H8
Utsunomiya • Japan 127 C3
Uttar Pradesh • India 123 F8
Uttaradit • Thailand 130 C6
Uttaranchal • India 123 A1
Utu Magalua • Wallis & Futuna 139 Q
Utuado • Puerto Rico 165 I7
Utulei • American Samoa 139 H
Utupua • Solomon Is. 138 W
Utvær • Norway 98 F8
Utwa Ma • Fed. States of Micronesia 138 D
Uudenmaa • Finland 99 D4
Uummannaq • Greenland 159 K1
Uusikaupunki • Finland 99 C4
Uvalde • TX, United States 149 G5
Uvdal • Norway 98 G8
Uvea, I. • Wallis & Futuna 139 Q
Uvinza • Tanzania 110 G7
Uvira • Dem. Rep. of Congo 110 G7
Uvongo • South Africa 111 B5
Uvs Nuur • Mongolia 125 D1
Uxmal • Mexico 169 F4
Uxmal **Heritage C** • Mexico 42 [28]
Uyuni • Bolivia 173 C5
UZBEKISTAN • Asia 121 D3
Uzerche • France 78 F5
Uzhhorod • Ukraine 100 B4
Uzice • Serbia & Montenegro 92 B3
Uzümlü • Turkey 95 H7
Uzuncaburç • Turkey 95 I10
Uzunköpru • Turkey 95 E3

V

V.C. Bird [Apt] • Antigua & Barbuda 167 I
Vaadhu Diving Paradise • Maldives 124 H8
Vaal • South Africa 110 B3
Vaasa • Finland 97 E3
Vaasa [Adm] • Finland 98 C2
Vabbinfaru • Maldives 124 H7
Vác • Hungary 92 B2
Vacaos • Mauritius 113 E6
Vacaville • CA, United States 148 B3
Vacca, Cape • South Africa 111 E7
Vache, I.-à- • Haiti 165 E6
Vaches, I. aux • Seychelles 113 B1
Vadheim • Norway 98 F8
Vadili • Cyprus 96 D4
Vadodara • India 122 B3
Vadsø • Norway 97 F1
Vadstena • Sweden 99 H5
Vaduz • Liechtenstein 91 M8
Vadvetjåkka Nat. Park **Park N** • Sweden 58 [17]
Vågåmo • Norway 98 G7
Vagator Beach • Goa, India 123 C5
Vågåvatn • Norway 98 G7
Vaggeryd • Sweden 99 G6
Vagnhärad • Sweden 99 A2
Vågslid • Norway 98 G9
Vågsøy • Norway 98 F7
Váh • Slovak Rep. 89 B4
Vai • Crete, Greece 93 J6
Vaiaku • Tuvalu 139 R
Vaiea • Niue 139 O
Vaihu • Easter I. 139 M
Vaikona Chasm • Niue 139 O
Vail **Ski** • CO, United States 146 [59]
Vail • CO, United States 148 E3
Vailala • Wallis & Futuna 139 Q
Vailoa • Samoa 139 G
Vainguinim Beach • Goa, India 123 C5
Vaini • Tonga 139 P
Vaishali • India 123 G8
Vaitogi • American Samoa 139 H
Vaitupu • Tuvalu 138 CC3
Vaksdal • Norway 98 F8
Val André, le • France 77 D3
Val Camónica • Italy 87 C1
Val Camónica **Heritage C** • Italy 44 [150]
Val d'Allos-la Foux **Ski** • France 61 [51]
Val d'Isère **Ski** • France 61 [26]
Val d'Isère • France 78 D3
Val d'Oise • France 78 A1
Val d'Or • QU, Canada 159 I4
Val Grande, Parco Naz. della • Italy 87 B1
Val Thorens **Ski** • France 61 [31]
Val Thorens • France 78 D4
Val-d'Illiez **Ski** • Switzerland 61 [55]
Val-Marie • SA, Canada 158 F4
Valais • Switzerland 90 J6
Valais [Adm] • Switzerland 91 Q10
Valbella • Switzerland 90 L5
Valberg **Ski** • France 61 [53]
Valcabrère • France 78 J9
Valdàora • Italy 86 D3
Valday • Russian Fed. 100 L9
Valdayskaya Vozvyshennost • Russian Fed. 100 L10
Valdecañas, Embalse de • Spain 80 C4
Valdemarsslot • Denmark 99 F8
Valdemarsvik • Sweden 99 H5
Valdepeñas • Spain 80 D4
Valderrama • Spain 82 D3
Valdés, Península • Argentina 175 B4
Valdés, Península **Heritage N** • Argentina 40 [51]
Valdez • AK, United States 157 E3
Valdivia • Chile 175 A3
Valdosta • GA, United States 155 C1
Vale de Bravo • Mexico 169 J7
Vale de Parra • Portugal 84 I8
Vale Navio • Portugal 84 J8
Vale of Trent • United Kingdom 65 F5
Valença • Brazil 174 C4
Valençay • France 76 K8
Valençay [Château] • France 77 F6
Valence • France 78 C4
Valencia • Spain 80 E4
Valencia **Heritage C** • Spain 44 [101]
Valencia • Venezuela 173 C1
Valencia, Costa de • Spain 80 E4
Valenciana, Comunidad • Spain 80 E4
Valenciennes • France 76 E1
Valentia I. • Ireland 69 G11
Valentine • NE, United States 148 F2
Valera • Venezuela 173 B2
Valga • Estonia 100 K6
Valinco, Golfe de • Corsica, France 78 M12
Valjevo • Serbia & Montenegro 92 B2
Valkeakoski • Finland 99 D3
Valkenburg • Netherlands 70 D4
Valladolid • Mexico 169 F4
Valladolid • Spain 80 C3
Valldal • Norway 98 G7
Valldemossa • Majorca, Spain 83 N11
Valle • Norway 98 G9
Valle d'Aosta • Italy 87 A1
Valledupar • Colombia 173 B1
Vallée de Mai Nature Reserve • Seychelles 113 B2
Vallée de Mai Nature Reserve **Heritage N** • Seychelles 41 [119]
Vallejo • CA, United States 154 I8
Vallenar • Chile 175 A2
Vallendar • Germany 74 D5
Vallentuna • Sweden 99 B1
Valletta • Malta 96 B2
Valletta **Heritage C** • Malta 44 [257]
Valley City • ND, United States 148 G1
Valley Forge Nat. Hist. Park • PA, United States 156 B2
Valley Forge Nat. Hist. Park **Park N** • PA, United States 153 [268]
Valley of 1000 Hills • South Africa 111 B4
Valley of Fire State Park • NV, United States 154 J8
Valleyfield • QU, Canada 160 G4
Valleyview • AL, Canada 160 J6
Valloire **Ski** • France 61 [44]
Valloire • France 78 D4
Vallorbe • Switzerland 90 I5
Valls • Spain 83 C4
Valmiera • Latvia 100 K7
Valmorel **Ski** • France 61 [34]
Valmorel • France 78 D3
Valois • France 78 B1
Valparaíso • Chile 175 A3
Valpoi • Goa, India 123 C5
Valpolicella • Italy 87 C2
Vals • Switzerland 90 K5
Vals, Tanjung • Indonesia 131 I5
Valsamonero, Moní • Crete, Greece 93 H6
Valtournenche **Ski** • Italy 61 [124]
Valtournenche • Italy 87 A1
Valverde • Hierro, Canary Is. 83 H6
Valverde del Camino • Spain 80 B5
Vammala • Finland 99 D3
Vámos • Crete, Greece 93 H5
Van • Turkey 95 D2
Van Buren • AR, United States 151 B3
Van Diemen Gulf • NT, Australia 135 E2
Van Gölü • Turkey 95 D2
Van Horn • TX, United States 149 F4
Van Reenen • South Africa 111 B4
Van Wert • OH, United States 150 D2
Vanadzor • Armenia 120 E2
Vanajanselka • Finland 99 D3
Vânatori • Romania 92 D2
Vancouver • BC, Canada 160 I7
Vancouver • WA, United States 154 G5
Vancouver I. • BC, Canada 160 I7
Vanda • Finland 99 D4
Vanderbilt Mansion Nat. Hist. Site **Park N** • NY, United States 153 [277]
Vanderhoof • BC, Canada 160 I6
Vänersborg • Sweden 99 F5
Vang • Norway 98 G8
Vangaindrano • Madagascar 110 D3
Vangsnes • Norway 98 G8
Vangunu • Solomon Is. 138 W
Vanikoro Is. • Solomon Is. 138 W
Vanille Crocodile Park, La • Mauritius 113 E6
Vanna • Norway 97 D1
Vannes • France 77 D4
Vannsjø • Norway 98 E6
Vanoise, Parc nat. de la **Park N** • France 58 [72]
Vanoise, Parc nat. de la • France 78 D4
Vanrhynsdorp • South Africa 110 A4
Vantaa • Finland 99 D4
Vanua Lava • Vanuatu 138 V
Vanua Levu • Fiji Is. 138 S
VANUATU • Pacific Ocean 138 V
Vao • New Caledonia 138 U
Vao, Ko • Thailand 130 F10
Var [Adm] • France 78 G8
Var [Riv] • France 78 H7
Vara • Sweden 99 G5
Vara, Pico da • Azores 84 B4
Varadero • Cuba 164 F4
Varanasi • India 123 G8
Varangerfjorden • Norway 97 G1
Varangerhalvøya • Norway 97 F1
Varano, Lago di • Italy 85 E4
Varazdin • Croatia 92 G5
Varberg • Sweden 99 F6
Varca • Goa, India 123 C6
Varca Beach • Goa, India 123 C6
Vardar • F.Y.R. of Macedonia 93 C1
Varde • Denmark 99 E7
Varese • Italy 87 B1
Vårgårda • Sweden 99 G5
Varginha • Brazil 174 E6
Varkala • India 124 B4
Varkala **Beach** • India 124 E6
Varkaus • Finland 97 F3
Värmdölandet • Sweden 99 B2
Värmland • Sweden 98 B3
Värmlandsnäs • Sweden 99 G5
Varna • Bulgaria 92 I8
Värnamo • Sweden 99 G6
Vars **Ski** • France 61 [48]
Vars • France 78 D4
Vasa • Finland 97 E3
Vasafua • Tuvalu 139 R
Vasca, Costa • Spain 82 B1
Vascao • Portugal 84 K7
Vasco da Gama • Goa, India 123 C5
Vasiliki • Crete, Greece 93 J6
Vaslui • Romania 92 D2
Vassdalsegga • Norway 98 G9
Vassilikí • Levkas, Greece 94 J
Vassilikós • Zante, Greece 94 J
Västerås • Sweden 99 A1
Våsterbotten • Sweden 98 B2
Västerhaninge • Sweden 99 B2
Västerlen • Sweden 99 G7
Västermo • Sweden 99 A2
Våsternorrland • Sweden 98 B2
Västervik • Sweden 99 H6
Västmanland • Sweden 99 A1
Vasto • Italy 85 E3
Vaterá • Lesbos, Greece 94 C
Váthi • Crete, Greece 93 G5
Vathí • Sámos, Greece 94 E
Vathípetro • Crete, Greece 93 I6
Vathy • Greece 94 J
Vatican City • Europe 87 E5
VATICAN CITY • Europe 87 E5
Vatican City **Heritage C** • Europe 44 [167]
Vatili • Cyprus 96 D4
Vatnajökull • Iceland 97 I6
Vatne • Norway 98 G7
Vatra Dornei • Romania 92 D2
Vättern • Sweden 99 G5
Vattholma • Sweden 99 B1
Vatu-i-Ra Channel • Fiji Is. 138 S
Vatukoula • Fiji Is. 138 T
Vatulele • Fiji Is. 138 T
Vauclin, le • Martinique 167 L
Vaucluse • France 78 G7
Vaud • Switzerland 91 Q10
Vaud, Le • Switzerland 90 I6
Vaughn • NM, United States 149 E4
Vaujany **Ski** • France 61 [40]
Vaux-le-Vicomte, Château de • France 78 B2
Vava'u Group • Tonga 138 CC4
Väversunda • Sweden 99 G5
Vavuniya • Sri Lanka 124 C3
Vaxholm • Sweden 99 B2
Växjö • Sweden 99 H6
Veckholm • Sweden 99 A1
Vedbæk • Denmark 99 G7
Veddige • Sweden 99 F6
Veenendaal • Netherlands 70 C2
Veere • Netherlands 70 B3
Vega • Norway 97 C2
Vega Baja • Puerto Rico 165 J7
Vegår • Norway 98 G9
Veggli • Norway 98 D5
Veinge • Sweden 99 G7
Vejbystrand • Sweden 99 G7
Vejen • Denmark 99 E7
Vejer de la Frontera • Spain 82 I8
Vejle • Denmark 99 E7
Vejle [Adm] • Denmark 99 E7
Vel Vaddo Beach • Goa, India 123 C6
Velas • Azores 84 B4
Velassaru • Maldives 124 H8
Velbert • Germany 73 D5
Velddrif • South Africa 111 D6
Veldenz, Schloss • Germany 74 C6
Velebit • Croatia 92 F6
Velenje • Slovenia 92 F5
Veleta, Pico de • Spain 82 J7
Vélez-Málaga • Spain 82 J8
Vélez-Rubio • Spain 82 K7
Velhas • Brazil 174 E6
Vélia **Heritage C** • Italy 44 [171]
Veligandu Huraa • Maldives 124 H8
Velikaya • Russian Fed. 100 K7
Velikiy Novgorod • Russian Fed. 100 L9
Velikiy Novgorod **Heritage C** • Russian Fed. 44 [269]
Velikiy Ustyug • Russian Fed. 100 G1
Velikiye-Luki • Russian Fed. 100 L10
Veliko Turnovo • Bulgaria 92 H8
Velino • Italy 87 F4
Vella Lavella • Solomon Is. 138 W
Velletri • Italy 87 E5
Vellinge • Sweden 99 G8
Vellore • India 124 C2
Velsao Beach • Goa, India 123 C6
Velten • Germany 73 E7
Veluwezoom, Nat. Park **Park N** • Netherlands 58 [59]
Veluwezoom, Nat. Park • Netherlands 70 D2
Ven • Sweden 99 G7
Venaco • Corsica, France 78 N11
Vence • France 78 H7
Vendays-Montalivet • France 78 E5
Vendée • France 77 E6
Vendôme • France 77 F5
Venegas • Mexico 169 I6
Véneta, Laguna • Italy 87 D2
Venetian Riviera • Italy 87 D2
Véneto • Italy 87 C2
Venézia • Italy 87 D2
Venézia **Heritage C** • Italy 44 [154]
VENEZUELA • S. America 173 C2
Venezuela, Golfo de • Venezuela 173 B1
Venice • FL, United States 155 C2
Venice • Italy 87 D2
Venice **Heritage C** • Italy 44 [154]
Venice, Gulf of • Croatia/Italy 87 D2
Venissieux • France 78 C3
Venlo • Netherlands 70 D3
Vennesla • Norway 99 E5
Vensyssel • Denmark 99 E6
Venta • Latvia 100 J7
Ventadour, Château de • France 78 F5
Ventimiglia • Italy 87 A3
Ventnor **Beach** • United Kingdom 64 [37]
Ventoténe, I. • Italy 85 D4
Ventry • Ireland 69 G10
Ventspils • Latvia 100 J7
Ventura • CA, United States 154 I9
Venus Baai • St Eustatius 167 E
Venus Bay • VI, Australia 136 G9
Vénus, Pointe • French Polynesia 139 K
Venus-Aurora • Romania 92 I7
Venzone • Italy 87 D1
Vera • Argentina 175 B2
Vera • Spain 82 K7
Veracruz • Mexico 169 K7
Veracruz • Panama 170 M11
Veracruz [Adm] • Mexico 169 C3
Veraval **Beach** • India 124 E6
Veraval • India 122 B3
Verbánia • Italy 87 B1
Verbier **Ski** • Switzerland 61 [56]
Verbier • Switzerland 90 J6
Vercelli • Italy 87 B2
Vercors • France 78 C4
Verdala Palace • Malta 96 B2
Verdalsøra • Norway 97 C3
Verde, Costa • Portugal 84 A1
Verde, Costa • Sardinia, Italy 86 E6
Verde, Costa • Spain 80 C2
Verden • Germany 72 C2
Verdon • France 78 H7
Verdon, Basses Gorges du • France 78 G7
Verdon, Grand Canyon du • France 78 G7
Verdon-sur-Mer, le • France 78 E5
Verdun • France 76 F2
Vereeniging • South Africa 111 A1
Vérendrye, Réserve faunique de la • QU, Canada 160 F3
Vergina **Heritage C** • Greece 44 [233]
Véria • Greece 93 C1
Veringenstadt • Germany 74 E7
Verkhoyanskiy Khrebet • Russian Fed. 101 M3
Verla **Heritage C** • Finland 43 [92]
Vermeille, Côte • France 78 L10
Vermilion • OH, United States 161 A3
Vermilion • SD, United States 148 G2
Vermont • United States 150 F2
Verna, Abbazia La • Italy 87 C3
Vernadsky [Base] • Antarctica 176 [7]
Vernazza **Heritage C** • Italy 44 [159]
Verneuil-sur-Avre • France 76 D2
Vernon • BC, Canada 158 E3
Vernon • France 78 A1
Vernon • TX, United States 149 G4
Vernon Crookes Nature Reserve • South Africa 111 B5
Vernon Valley • NJ, United States 156 C2
Vero Beach • FL, United States 155 D2
Verona • Italy 87 C2
Verona **Heritage C** • Italy 44 [151]
Verrettes • Haiti 165 F5
Versailles • France 78 A2
Versailles **Heritage C** • France 44 [73]
Versciaco **Ski** • Italy 61 [149]
Verte, Caye • St Martin 166 C
Vertientes • Cuba 164 G5
Verulam • South Africa 111 C4
Verviers • Belgium 70 D4
Vesijärvi • Finland 99 D4
Vesoul • France 76 G3
Vest Sjælland • Denmark 99 F7

Vest-Agder • Norway 98 A4
Vesterålen • Norway 97 C2
Vestera Havn • Denmark 99 F6
Vestfjorden • Norway 97 C2
Vestfold • Norway 98 D6
Vestmannaeyjar • Iceland 97 H6
Vestnes • Norway 98 G7
Vestvagøy • Norway 97 C2
Vesubie • France 78 H7
Vesuvio • Italy 87 G7
Vesuvius • Italy 87 G7
Veszprém • Hungary 92 B2
Vetlanda • Sweden 99 H6
Vetluzhskiy • Russian Fed. 100 G2
Vetralla • Italy 87 E4
Vette, le • Italy 86 D4
Veurne • Belgium 70 E6
Vevey • Switzerland 90 I6
Vexin • France 78 A1
Vézelay Heritage C • France ....44 [78]
Vézère • France 78 F5
Vézère, Gorges de la • France 78 F5
Vézère, Vallée du Heritage C •
France ....44 [91]
Vezzani • Corsica, France 78 N11
Viana do Castelo • Portugal 80 A3
Viana do Castelo [Adm] • Portugal ..84 A1
Vianden • Luxembourg 70 D5
Viangchan • Laos 128 C3
Viaréggio • Italy 87 B3
Vibo Valentia • Italy 85 F5
Viborg • Denmark 99 E7
Viborg [Adm] • Denmark 99 E7
Vic • Spain 83 D3
Vicam • Mexico 168 I6
Vicarstown • Ireland 69 E7
Vicdessos • France 78 K10
Vicenza • Italy 87 C2
Vicenza Heritage C • Italy ....44 [152]
Vichy • France 76 E3
Vicksburg • MS, United States 98 G8
Vicksburg Nat. Military Park Park N •
MS, United States ....153 [196]
Vico • Corsica, France 78 M11
Vico Equense • Italy 87 G7
Vico, Lago di • Italy 87 E4
Victoria • Australia 135 G7
Victoria • BC, Canada 160 I7
Victoria • Grenada ....166 Q
Victoria • Malta 96 A1
Victoria • Seychelles 113 A1
Victoria • TX, United States 155 E6
Victoria Falls • Zambia/Zimbabwe ..110 B2
Victoria Falls Heritage N •
Zambia/Zimbabwe ....41 [114]
Victoria Harbour •
Hong Kong, China 126 E5
Victoria I. • NT/NU, Canada 158 F1
Victoria, Lake • Africa 108 C5
Victoria Lake • NF, Canada 160 C1
Victoria Land • Antarctica 176 U5
Victoria Lines • Malta 96 B2
Victoria Peak • Hong Kong, China ...126 E5
Victoria River • NT, Australia 135 E3
Victoria West • South Africa 111 F6
Videle • Romania 92 H7
Vidin • Bulgaria 92 C2
Vidöstern • Sweden 99 G6
Viedma • Argentina 175 B4
Viella, Túnel de • Spain 78 K10
Vienna • Austria 91 H1
Vienna Heritage C • Austria ....44 [145]
Vienne • France 78 C3
Vienne [Adm] • France 77 F6
Vienne [Riv] • France 76 U3
Vientiane • Laos 128 C3
Vieques • Puerto Rico 165 J8
Vierschach Ski • Italy ....61 [149]
Viersen • Germany 73 C6
Vierwaldstätter See • Switzerland ...90 K5
Vierzon • France 76 E3
Vieste • Italy 85 F4
VIETNAM • Asia 128 C4
Vietnam Veterans Mem. Park N •
DC, United States ....153 [264]
Vieux Fort • St Lucia ....167 N
Vieux-Boucau-les-Bains • France 78 E6
Vigan Heritage C • Philippines .....43 [207]
Vigévano • Italy 87 B2
Vigie [Apt] • St Lucia ....167 N
Vigie Beach • St Lucia ....167 N
Vigo • Spain 80 A2
Vigo di Fassa • Italy 86 C4
Vigso Bugt • Denmark 99 E6
Viiala • Finland 99 I5
Vijayadurg • India 124 A1
Vijayapuri • India 124 C1
Vijayawada • India 124 C1
Vijterhof • Netherlands 70 H8
Vik • Iceland 97 I6
Vikbolandet • Sweden 99 H5
Vikedal • Norway 98 F9
Viken • Sweden 99 G7
Vikersund • Norway 98 D5
VikingLandet Park L • Norway ......59 [4]
VikingLandet • Norway 30 C5
Vikna • Norway 97 C3
Vikos-Aóos Nat. Park Park N •
Greece ....58 [139]
Viksøyri • Norway 98 G8
Vila Baleira •
Porto Santo, Madeira 84 E5
Vila do Bispo • Portugal 84 H8
Vila do Porto • Azores 84 E8
Vila Franca de Xira • Portugal 84 G6
Vila Franca do Campo • Azores 84 B4
Vila Nogueira de Azeitão • Portugal ..84 G6
Vila Nova de Gaia • Portugal 80 A3
Vila Real • Portugal 80 B3
Vila Real [Adm] • Portugal 84 A1
Vila Real de Santo António •
Portugal 84 K8
Vila Velha • Brazil 174 F6
Vilafranca del Penédes • Spain 83 C4
Vilaine • France 77 D4
Vilamoura • Portugal 84 J8
Vilanova i la Geltrú • Spain 173 E6
Vilcanota • Peru 173 F6
Vilhelmina • Sweden 97 D3
Vilhena • Brazil 173 C4
Viliya • Belarus 100 K8
Viljandi • Estonia 100 K6
Vilkaviskis • Lithuania 100 J6
Villa Altagracia • Dominican Rep. ..165 G6
Villa Carlos Menorca, Spain 83 K8
Villa Constitución • Argentina 175 B6
Villa Flores • Mexico 168 F4
Villa Gesell • Argentina 175 D7
Villa Insurgentes • Mexico 168 I6
Villa, La Ski • Italy ....61 [146]
Villa, la • Italy 86 D3
Villa Maria • Argentina 175 B6
Villa Unión • Durango, Mexico 168 D3
Villa Unión • Sinaloa, Mexico 169 H6
Villa Vásquez • Dominican Rep. 165 G5
Villach • Austria 91 P8
Villaggio Cóppola • Italy 168 F4
Villahérmosa • Mexico 168 F4
Villaines [Château] • France 77 E6
Villaputzu • Sardinia, Italy 86 F6
Villard-de-Lans Ski • France ....61 [37]
Villard-de-Lans • France 78 D4
Villard-Reculas Ski • France ....61 [41]
Villarrica • Paraguay 175 C2
Villarrobledo • Spain 80 D4
Villars-sur-Ollon Ski • Switzerland ..61 [58]
Villars-sur-Ollon • Switzerland 90 J6
Villasimius • Sardinia, Italy 86 F6
Villavicencio • Colombia 173 C3
Villazon • Bolivia 173 C5
Villefranche-de-Rouergue • France ..78 F6
Villefranche-sur-Mer • France 78 H7

Villefranche-sur-Sâone • France 78 C3
Villena • Spain 83 A1
Villeneuve • Switzerland 90 I6
Villeneuve-lez-Avignon • France 78 F6
Villeneuve-sur-Lot • France 78 F6
Villers-la-Ville, Abbaye de •
Belgium 70 B4
Villesavin [Château] • France 77 F5
Villeurbanne • France 78 C3
Villingen • Germany 74 B4
Villingili Beach • Maldives 124 H8
Villnarvu • Maldives 124 H8
Vilnius • Lithuania 100 K8
Vilnia Heritage C • Lithuania ....44 [264]
Vilppula • Finland 99 D3
Vilsandi Nat. Park Park N • Estonia ..58 [145]
Vilsandi Nat. Park • Estonia 100 J6
Vilsburg • Germany 74 H7
Vilshofen • Germany 91 F1
Vimmerby • Sweden 99 H6
Vimperk • Czech Rep. 89 D7
Viña del Mar • Chile 164 E4
Viñales • Cuba 164 E4
Viñales valley Heritage C • Cuba ...42 [40]
Vinapu • Easter I. ....139 M
Vinaròs • Spain 80 F3
Vinaroz • Spain 80 F3
Vincennes • IN, United States 150 C3
Vincennes Bay • Antarctica 176 S4
Vincovci • Croatia 92 B2
Vinderup • Denmark 99 E7
Vindhya Range • India 123 A2
Vindö • Sweden 99 B2
Vineland • NJ, United States 156 B3
Vingåker • Sweden 99 A2
Vinh • Vietnam 128 D3
Vinh Long • Vietnam 129 G6
Vinnytsya • Ukraine 100 C4
Vinslöv • Sweden 99 G7
Vinson Massif • Antarctica 176 M5
Vipiteno • Italy 86 C3
Vir • Croatia 92 F6
Viransehir • Turkey 95 C2
Virden • MN, Canada 158 F4
Virgin • NV/UT, United States 155 G7
Virgin Gorda • British Virgin Is. .....166 A
Virgin Is. Nat. Park • US Virgin Is. ..166 X
Virgin Islands • United States 156 A4
Virginia Beach • VA, United States ..156 B4
Virginia City • NV, United States 154 I8
Virovitica • Croatia 92 G5
Virrat • Finland 99 D3
Virsbo • Sweden 99 A1
Virton • Belgium 70 C5
Virtsu • Estonia 100 J6
Virunga, Parc nat. des Park •
Dem. Rep. of Congo ....112 [52]
Virunga, Parc nat. des Heritage N •
Dem. Rep. of Congo ....41 [104]
Vis • Croatia 92 G6
Visby • Sweden 97 D4
Visby Heritage C • Sweden ....44 [9]
Viscount Melville Sound •
NT/NU, Canada 158 F1
Viseu • Portugal 80 B3
Viseu [Adm] • Portugal 84 A1
Vishakhapatnam • India 122 C4
Vishnyi Volochek • Russian Fed. ...100 L10
Visingsö • Sweden 99 G5
Vislanda • Sweden 99 G6
Viso, Monte • Italy 87 A2
Visoko • Bosnia-Herz. 92 G6
Visp • Switzerland 90 J6
Vistula • Poland 89 C3
Viterbo • Italy 87 E4
Vitet, Mont du • St Barthélemy .....166 D
Viti Levu • Fiji Is. ....138 T
Vitim • Russian Fed. 101 L4
Vitória • Brazil 174 F6
Vitória da Conquista • Brazil 174 C3
Vitoria de Santa Antão • Brazil 174 C3
Vitoria-Gasteiz • Spain 80 D2
Vitorog • Bosnia-Herz. 92 G6
Vitosa Nat. Park Park N • Bulgaria ..58 [135]
Vitré • France 77 E5
Vitré [Château] • France 77 E5
Vitsyebsk • Belarus 100 D2
Vittangi • Sweden 97 E2
Vittinge • Sweden 99 A1
Vittória • Sicily, Italy 86 H8
Vittório Véneto • Italy 86 B6
Vittoriosa • Malta 96 B2
Vittsjö • Sweden 99 G7
Vitznau • Switzerland 90 K5
Vivian • LA, United States 155 E5
Vizcaino, Desierto del • Mexico 168 H6
Vizcaino, Sierra • Mexico 168 H6
Vizianagaram • India 122 C4
Vjosë • Albania 93 B1
Vlaams-Brabant • Belgium 70 C4
Vlaardingen • Netherlands 70 G8
Vladikavkaz • Russian Fed. 101 A8
Vladimir • Russian Fed. 100 M10
Vladimir Heritage C • Russian Fed. ..44 [272]
Vladivostok • Russian Fed. 101 N5
Vlaardinge • Estonia 100 J6
Vlemhere • Corfu, Greece ....94 A
Vlieland • Netherlands 70 G1
Vlihada, Paralia • Crete, Greece 93 J5
Vlihó • Levkas, Greece ....94 J
Vlissingen • Netherlands 70 B3
Vlkolinec Heritage C • Slovak Rep. ..44 [199]
Vlorë • Albania 92 B3
Vltava • Czech Rep. 89 E7
Vluyn • Germany 73 C5
Vnukovo [Apt] • Russian Fed. 100 M10
Vöcklabruck • Austria 91 F1
Vodice • Croatia 92 F6
Voerde • Germany 73 C5
Voergård • Denmark 99 F6
Voghera • Italy 87 B2
Voi • Kenya 109 D5
Voile de la Mairée, Cascade du •
Réunion 113 D3
Vojens • Denmark 99 E8
Vojvodina • Serbia & Montenegro ..92 B2
Vol'sk • Russian Fed. 100 G3
Volary • Czech Rep. 89 D7
Volcano • HI, United States 138 AA1
Volcano Is. • Japan 127 D5
Volcans, Parc des Park • Rwanda ...112 [66]
Volda • Norway 98 F7
Volendam • Netherlands 70 H7
Volga • Russian Fed. 100 G3
Volga Delta • Russian Fed. 121 A2
Volga, Ozero • Russian Fed. 100 L10
Vogodonsk • Russian Fed. 100 F4
Voigograd • Russian Fed. 100 F4
Volgugvardyskoye Vukhl. • Russian Fed. ..100 F4
Volimes • Zante, Greece ....94 J
Volissós • Chíos, Greece ....94 D
Völkermarkt • Austria 91 G2
Volkhov • Russian Fed. 100 L9
Volkhov [Riv] • Russian Fed. 100 L9
Volklingen • Germany 74 A2
Völklingen Heritage C • Germany ...44 [59]
Volksrust • South Africa 111 B3
Vologda • Russian Fed. 100 M9
Vólos • Greece 93 C2
Volta Heritage C • Ghana ....43 [112]
Volta, Black • Burkina/Ghana 106 B4
Volta, Lake • Ghana 106 B4
Volta Redonda • Brazil 174 E7
Volta, White • Burkina/Ghana 106 C3
Volterra • Italy 87 C3
Volturno • Italy 85 E4
Volubilis • Morocco 107 A1
Volubilis Heritage C • Morocco .....44 [276]
Vólzhskiy • Russian Fed. 100 F4
Vóni • Crete, Greece 93 I6
Vónitsa • Greece ....94 J
Voorburg • Netherlands 70 G8
Voorne • Netherlands 92 D2

Voorschoten • Netherlands 70 G7
Vorarlberg • Austria 91 M7
Vordingborg • Denmark 99 F8
Vóreio Egéo • Greece 94 CC2
Voreingdssaen • Norway 98 G8
Vorkuta • Russian Fed. 101 G3
Vorma • Norway 98 E5
Vormsi • Estonia 100 J6
Vormsund • Norway 98 E5
Voronezh • Russian Fed. 100 E3
Vorpommersche Boddenlandschaft,
Nationalpark Park N • Germany ..58 [64]
Vörts järv • Estonia 100 K6
Võru • Estonia 100 K6
Vosges • France 76 G2
Vosresensk • Russian Fed. 100 M10
Voss • Norway 98 G8
Vostochnyy Sayan • Russian Fed. ..101 J4
Vostok I. • Kiribati 139 DD3
Vostok • Russian Fed. 100 F2
Votkinsk • Russian Fed. 100 H2
Votkinskoye Vdkhr. • Russian Fed. ..100 H2
Votterey • Norway 98 E6
Votua • Fiji Is. ....138 S
Vouliés • Crete, Greece 93 G5
Voúla • Greece 93 G3
Vouvray • France 76 K8
Vouvray • France 77 F5
Voúxa, Akra • Crete, Greece 93 G5
Voyageurs Nat. Park Park N •
MN, United States ....153 [153]
Vozmesensk • Ukraine 100 D4
Vrå • Denmark 99 F6
Vrådal • Norway 98 D5
Vrahási • Crete, Greece 93 I6
Vrangelya, Ostrov • Russian Fed. ..101 S2
Vranje • Serbia & Montenegro 92 C3
Vratsa • Bulgaria 92 C3
Vrbas • Serbia & Montenegro 92 G5
Vredenburg • South Africa 111 D6
Vredendal • South Africa 111 D6
Vrindaban • India 123 E7
Vrontados • Chíos, Greece ....94 D
Vrontisiou, Moní • Crete, Greece 93 H6
Vryburg • South Africa 110 B3
Vryheid • South Africa 111 B3
Vuckovar • Croatia 92 B2
Vukuzakhe • South Africa 111 B3
Vulcanesti • Moldova 92 D2
Vulcano, l. • Italy 86 H7
Vulkaneifel • Germany 74 C5
Vung Tau • Vietnam 129 C6
Vuntut Nat. Park Park N •
YT, Canada ....161 [2]
Vuokatti • Finland 98 D3
Vvaza Marsh Wildlife Reserve Park •
Malawi ....112 [96]
Vyaz'ma • Russian Fed. 100 L10
Vyborg • Russian Fed. 100 C1
Vygozevo, Ozero • Russian Fed. ...100 L9
Vyritsa • Russian Fed. 100 L9
Vysehrad • Czech Rep. 89 E6
Vysoké Tatry Nat. Park Park N •
Slovak Rep. ....58 [111]
Vysoké Tatry Nat. Park • Slovak Rep. ..89 D7
Vyssi Brod • Czech Rep. 89 E7
Vytegra • Russian Fed. 100 E1

W

W.A.C. Bennett Dam • BC, Canada ..160 I6
W, Parc nat. du Park • Niger ....112 [3]
W, Parc nat. du Heritage N • Niger ..41 [97]
Waal • Netherlands 70 C3
Wabash • IN, United States 150 C2
Waccasassa Bay • FL, United States ..151 D5
Wachademia Plain • Kenya 109 D4
Wachau • Austria 91 H1
Wachau Heritage C • Austria ....44 [144]
Wachtendonk • Germany 73 C5
Wächtersbach • Germany 74 H1
Wachusett Mtn • MA, United States ..128 D1
Waco • TX, United States 155 E5
Wad Medani • Sudan 108 C2
Waddan • Libya 108 A2
Waddeneilanden • Netherlands 70 C1
Waddenzee • Netherlands 70 C1
Waddi Beach • Goa, India 123 C6
Waddington, Mt • BC, Canada 160 I7
Wadebridge • United Kingdom 65 I10
Wadi • India 124 B1
Wadi Dahab • Egypt 109 E8
Wadi Halfa • Sudan 108 C2
Wadowice • Poland 89 F9
Wagendrift Nature Reserve •
South Africa 111 B4
Wagga Wagga • NS, Australia 136 G8
Wagin • WA, Australia 135 B6
Wagner • Germany 74 H7
Waginger See • Germany 74 H7
Wagram • Austria 91 P7
Wah • Pakistan 122 B2
Wahpeton • ND, United States 150 A1
Wahiawa • HI, United States 157 I5
Wahiwa • HI, United States 157 G6
Waialua • HI, United States 157 G6
Waianae • HI, United States 157 G6
Waianae Range • HI, United States ..157 G6
Waiau • New Zealand 137 F8
Waidhofen an der Ybbs • Austria ..91 G2
Waigeo • Indonesia 131 H4
Waihi • New Zealand 137 E5
Waihi Beach • New Zealand 137 E5
Waikaremoana, Lake • New Zealand ..137 E5
Waikato • New Zealand 137 D5
Waikato [Riv] • New Zealand 137 D5
Waikawa • New Zealand 137 G8
Waikerie • SA, Australia 135 G6
Waikiki • HI, United States 157 I5
Waikkal • Sri Lanka 124 C4
Wailua Falls • HI, United States 157 I5
Wailuku • HI, United States 157 I5
Wailuku River State Park •
HI, United States 157 J6
Waimanalo Beach •
HI, United States 157 H6
Waimangu Volcanic Valley •
New Zealand 137 E5
Waimarie • New Zealand 137 B3
Waimea • Hawaii, HI, United States ..157 J6
Waimea • Kauai, HI, United States ..157 H5
Waimea Bay • HI, United States 157 G6
Waimea Canyon State Park •
HI, United States 157 H5
Waingapu • Indonesia 131 F4
Waingaro • New Zealand 137 D5
Wainiha • HI, United States 157 H5
Wainwright • AK, United States 157 D2
Waiogogradi • Russian Fed. 100 F4
Waipahu • HI, United States 157 A1
Waipara • New Zealand 137 E6
Waipawa • New Zealand 137 E6
Waipio Valley • HI, United States ..157 J6
Waipukurau • New Zealand 137 E6
Wairakei Thermal Valley •
New Zealand 137 E5
Wairoa • New Zealand 137 E5
Waitaki • New Zealand 137 B3
Waitara • New Zealand 137 D6
Waitomo Caves • New Zealand 137 D6
Wajir • Kenya 109 D4
Wakasa-wan • Japan 127 C4
Wakatipu, Lake • New Zealand 137 B3
Wakayama • Japan 127 G2
Wakayama [Adm] • Japan 127 C4
Wakefield • United Kingdom 65 D7
Wakefield Ski • United Kingdom ....64 [5]
Wakefield • United Kingdom 150 G2
Waki • Pacific Ocean 138 BB2
Wakkanai • Japan 127 D1
Wakkerstroom • South Africa 111 B3
Wakulla Springs •
FL, United States 151 D5
Walachia • Romania 92 D2

Walbrzych • Poland 89 B3
Walchensee • Germany 74 G8
Walchern • Germany 70 B3
Walchkirch • Germany 74 B4
Waldkraiburg • Germany 74 H7
Waldshut • Germany 74 B4
Walensee • Switzerland 90 K5
Wales • United Kingdom 63 D8
Walgett • NS, Australia 135 H6
Walibi Rhône-Alpes Park L • France ..59 [68]
Walibi Rhône-Alpes • France 78 C3
Walker Lake • NV, United States ...154 J8
Walkerston • QL, Australia 135 E4
Wall • SD, United States 148 F2
Walla Walla • WA, United States ...154 H5
Wallace • United Kingdom 63 D7
Wallasey • United Kingdom 63 D7
Wallblake [Apt] • Anguilla ....166 U
Wallibou Beach • St Vincent & Gren. ..167 D
Wallis • United Kingdom 66 C1
WALLIS & FUTUNA • Pacific Ocean ..138 CC4
Wallis & Futuna • Pacific Ocean ....138 G
Walls of Jerusalem Nat. Park •
TS, Australia 136 F7
Walls • United Kingdom 66 C1
Walnut Canyon Nat. Mon. •
AZ, United States ....152 [105]
Walnut Canyon Nat. Mon. Park N •
AZ, United States ....152 [105]
Walpole • WA, Australia 135 B6
Walsall • United Kingdom 65 F5
Walsertal, Grosser • Austria 91 M8
Walsertal, Kleiner • Austria 91 M7
Walt Disney Studios Park Park L •
France ....59 [63]
Walt Disney World Int. Sports Complex •
....................................157 A1
Walt Disney World Resort •
FL, United States 157 A1
Walt Disney World Resort Park L •
FL, United States ....157 [24]
Walton Heath • United Kingdom 65 G8
Waltrop • Germany 73 D5
Walvis Bay • Namibia 110 A3
Wan Chai • Hong Kong, China 126 F5
Wan Hsa-la • Myanmar 128 C3
Wanaka • New Zealand 137 B3
Wanaka, Lake • New Zealand 137 G7
Wanapa • Bonaire ....166 U
Wanci • China 126 E3
Wandlitz • Germany 73 F7
Wandlitzer See • Germany 73 F7
Wang Phetburi Mtn • Thailand 130 D8
Wang Takhai Gardens • Thailand ..130 E7
Wang Takhai Nat. Park • Thailand ..130 D7
Wanganui • New Zealand 137 D6
Wanganui [Riv] • New Zealand 137 D6
Wangaratta • VI, Australia 136 G9
Wangerin • Germany 74 E8
Wangan Yang • China 126 H7
Wangs-Pizol • Switzerland 90 L5
Wanne-Eickel (Herne) • Germany ...73 D5
Wanneperveen • Netherlands 70 D2
Wannsee (Berlin) • Germany 73 E8
Wanshan Qundao • China 126 F4
Wanxian • China 125 E3
Wanzai • China 126 E3
Wapusk Nat. Park Park N •
MN, Canada ....161 [23]
War in the Pacific Nat. Hist. Park •
Guam ....138 Z
Warakarna-Wingellina-Irrunytju Aboriginal
Land • NT, Australia 136 A2
Warangal • India 122 B4
Waratah Bay • VI, Australia 136 F9
Warburg • Germany 72 C3
Warburton • WA, Australia 135 D6
Wardha • India 122 B3
Wardija Point • Malta 96 A1
Wareham • United Kingdom 65 K10
Waren • Indonesia 131 I4
Warm Springs • NV, United States ..148 C3
Warm Springs Ind Res •
OR, United States ....155 [5]
Warminster • United Kingdom 65 K9
Warner Brothers Movie World Park L •
Germany ....59 [50]
Warner Brothers Movie World •
Germany 73 C5
Warner Brothers Movie World •
QL, Australia 136 D5
Warner Robins • GA, United States ..151 D4
Warner Valley • OR, United States ..154 G6
Warren • MI, United States 161 A3
Warren • OH, United States 156 A1
Warren • PA, United States 156 A1
Warrington • FL, United States 155 B3
Warrington • United Kingdom 63 D7
Warsaw • Poland 89 C2
Warsaw Heritage C • Poland ....44 [181]
Warszawa • Poland 89 C2
Warszawa Heritage C • Poland .....44 [181]
Warta • Poland 89 B3
Wartburg Heritage C • Germany ...44 [181]
Warth • Austria 91 M8
Warwick • QL, Australia 136 D5
Warwick • United Kingdom 65 F5
Warwick Long Bay • Bermuda 165 K10
Warwickshire • United Kingdom ...65 F5
Wasalandia Park L • Finland ....59 [10]
Wash, The • United Kingdom 63 F8
Washago • OT, Canada 160 E4
Washington • IN, United States 150 C3
Washington • MO, United States ...150 B3
Washington • NC, United States 151 D4
Washington [Adm] • United States ..154 G5
Washington Crossing State Hist. Site •
PA, United States 156 A3
Washington DC • United States 156 A3
Washington [Adm] • United States ..156 A3
Washington Mon. Park N •
DC, United States ....153 [264]
Washington/Slagbaai Nat. Park •
Bonaire ....166 U
Washita Battlefield Nat. Hist. Site Park N •
OK, United States ....152 [144]
Wassenaar • Netherlands 70 G7
Wasserburg • Germany 74 H7
West Water • United Kingdom 66 C1
Wat Phra That Doi Suthep • Thailand ..130 B5
Watampone • Indonesia 131 F4
Watamu • Kenya 109 C6
Watarrka Nat. Park • NT, Australia ..136 A2
Water Cay • Bahamas 164 B1
Water Cay • Turks & Caicos Is. 164 C3
Water I. • US Virgin Is. ....166 X
Water Manua • FL, United States ...155 D2
Waterbury • CT, United States 156 C2
Waterford • Ireland 70 H4
Waterford [Adm] • Ireland 69 D7
Waterland • Netherlands 70 H7
Waterloo • IA, United States 150 B2
Waterloo [Battlefield] • Belgium 70 B4
Watermouth Castle • United Kingdom ..65 J9
Waterport • NY, United States 156 A1
Waterton Lakes Nat. Park Park N •
AL, Canada ....161 [20]
Waterton Lakes Nat. Park •
AL, Canada 160 J7
Waterton-Glacier Int. Peace Park •
Canada/United States 160 J7
Waterton-Glacier Int. Peace Park Heritage N •
Canada/United States ....40 [5]
Watertown • SD, United States 148 G1
Waterville • ME, United States 156 D1
Waterville Valley Ski •
NY, United States ....146 [113]
Watford • United Kingdom 65 G9

Westland • Netherlands 70 G8
Westliche Karwendelspitze •
Austria/Germany 74 G8
Westmeath • Ireland 69 E6
Westminster • United Kingdom 65 D4
Westmorland • United Kingdom 65 K9
Weston-super-Mare • United Kingdom ..65 D4
Westport • Ireland 69 D4
Westport • New Zealand 137 B3
Westport House • Ireland 69 G8
Westpunt • Curaçao ....166 V
Westray • United Kingdom 62 D1
Westward Ho! • United Kingdom ...65 J9
Westwego • LA, United States 156 F6
Wet'n'Wild • FL, United States 157 B1
Wet'n'Wild • QL, Australia 136 D5
Wetar • Indonesia 131 G5
Wetaskiwin • AL, Canada 160 J6
Wethersfield • CT, United States ...156 C2
Wetter • Germany 73 D5
Wetterstein • Austria 91 N7
Wetzlar • Germany 74 C4
Wewak • Papua New Guinea 134 C5
Wewei • China 125 E3
Wexford • Ireland 69 C4
Wexford [Adm] • Ireland 69 F7
Weyburn • SA, Canada 158 F4
Weymouth • MA, United States 156 D1
Weymouth • United Kingdom 65 K10
Weymouth Bay • United Kingdom ..65 K10
Weza State Forest • South Africa ..111 B5
Whakapapa • New Zealand 137 E6
Whakatane • New Zealand 137 E5
Whale Coast • South Africa 111 D7
Whalsay • United Kingdom 62 H12
Whanganui Nat. Park • New Zealand ..137 D6
Whangarei • New Zealand 137 B2
Wheatland • WY, United States 148 E2
Wheeler Peak • NV, United States ..154 J8
Wheeling • WV, United States 150 D2
Whiddy I. • Ireland 69 G11
Whim Greathouse Museum •
US Virgin Is. ....166 X
Whipsnade Zoo • United Kingdom ..65 G7
Whirlpool Rapids Bridge •
Canada/United States 161 D3
Whiskytown-Shasta-Trinity Nat. Recreation
Area Park N • CA, United States ..152 [40]
Whistler • BC, Canada 160 I7
Whistler & Blackcomb Ski •
BC, Canada ....146 [2]
Whitburn Beach • United Kingdom ..64 [6]
Whitby • OT, Canada 160 E5
Whitby • Turks & Caicos Is. 164 C3
Whitby • United Kingdom ....64 [7]
Whitby Beach • United Kingdom ...64 [7]
White • AR/MO, United States 151 B3
White • SD, United States 148 F2
White Bay • NF, Canada 160 C1
White Earth Ind Res •
MN, United States ....155 [56]
White House, The, & Presidents Park N •
DC, United States ....153 [264]
White I. • New Zealand 137 E5
White Lake • LA, United States 156 E6
White Nile • Sudan 106 C3
White Pass Village Ski •
WA, United States ....146 [25]
White Plains • NY, United States ...156 C2
White River • OT, Canada 159 H4
White Sands Nat. Mon. •
NM, United States 155 H8
White Sands Nat. Mon. Park N •
NM, United States ....152 [118]
White Umfolozi • South Africa 111 C3
Whitecap Mtns Ski •
WI, United States ....146 [72]
Whitecourt • AL, Canada 160 J6
Whiteface Mtn Ski •
NY, United States ....146 [102]
Whitefish Point •
MI, United States 161 B1
Whitehaven • United Kingdom 65 J10
Whitehorse • YT, Canada 158 C2
Whitehouse • Jamaica 165 C4
Whitesand Bay • United Kingdom ..65 J10
Whiteitail • PA, United States 156 A3
Whitley Bay • United Kingdom .....64 [7]
Whitman Mission Nat. Hist. Site •
WA, United States 154 H5
Whitman Mission Nat. Hist. Site Park N •
WA, United States ....152 [31]
Whitmore Village •
HI, United States 157 G6
Whitney, Mt • CA, United States ...154 J8
Whitsunday Group • QL, Australia ..135 H4
Whitsunday • QL, Australia 136 C3
Whittier • AK, United States 157 E3
King Ko Sai Nat. Park • Thailand ..130 C6
Wichita • KS, United States 148 G3
Wichita Falls • TX, United States ..155 E4
Wick • United Kingdom 62 D2
Wickenburg • AZ, United States ...155 G8
Wicklow • Ireland 69 F7
Wicklow [Adm] • Ireland 69 F7
Wicklow Head • Ireland 69 F7
Wicklow Mtns • Ireland 69 F7
Wicklow Mtns Nat. Park Park N •
Ireland ....58 [45]
Wicksteed Park Park L •
United Kingdom ....59 [30]
Wied • Germany 74 D5
Wieliczka • Poland 89 G9
Wieliczka Heritage C • Poland .....44 [183]
Wien • Austria 91 H1
Wien Heritage C • Austria ....44 [145]
Wien [Adm] • Austria 91 T11
Wiener Neustadt • Austria 91 H2
Wiener Prater Park L • Austria .....59 [81]
Wieringermeer • Netherlands 70 C1
Wies Heritage C • Germany ....44 [65]
Wiesbaden • Germany 74 D6
Wieskirche • Germany 74 I8
Wigan • United Kingdom 63 D7
Wiggins • MS, United States 156 F6
Wight, I. of • United Kingdom 63 E10
Wigierski Nat. Park Park N • Poland ..58 [102]
Wigtownshire • United Kingdom ...64 A3
Wilcannia • NS, Australia 135 G6
Wild Adventures •
GA, United States 155 C1
Wild Adventures Park L •
GA, United States ....157 [23]
Wild Coast • South Africa 111 A2
Wildau • Germany 73 F8
Wildbad Kreuth • Germany 74 G8
Wildenbruch • Germany 73 F8
Wilderness Nat. Lake Area •
South Africa 111 F7
Wilderswil bei Interlaken Ski •
Switzerland ....61 [/1]
Wildhaus • Switzerland 90 K5
Wildon • Austria 91 G2
Wildspitze • Austria 91 N8
Wildwood • NJ, United States 156 B3
Wilhelm II Land • Antarctica 176 S4
Wilhelm, Mt • Papua New Guinea ..134 C5
Wilhelmina Gebergte • South Africa ..166 V
Wilhelmsdorf • Germany 74 E6
Wilhelmshaven • Germany 72 B1
Wilkes-Barre • PA, United States ..156 B2
Willamette • OR, United States 154 G6
Willandra Lakes Heritage N •
Australia ....41 [155]
Willandra Lakes Heritage C •
Australia ....43 [212]
Willandra Lakes • NS, Australia ...135 G6
Willapa Bay • WA, United States ..154 G5
Willcox • AZ, United States 155 H8
Willem Pretorius Game Reserve Park •
South Africa ....112 [132]
Willemstad • Curaçao ....166 V
Willemstad Heritage C • Curaçao ..42 [47]
William H. Bramble [Apt] •
Montserrat ....167 G

William Howard Taft Nat. Hist. Site **Park N** •
OH, United States . . . . 153 [180]
William P Hobby [Apt] •
TX, United States 155 F5
Williams • AZ, United States 155 G7
Williams Lake • BC, Canada 160 I7
Williamsburg • VA, United States 156 B4
Williamsport • PA, United States 156 A2
Willich • Germany 73 C6
Willis Group • Australia 138 BB4
Williston • ND, United States 148 F1
Williston • South Africa 111 E6
Williston Lake • BC, Canada 160 I6
Willmar • MN, United States 150 B1
Willowmore • South Africa 111 F6
Wilmersdorf (Berlin) • Germany 73 E8
Wilmington • DE, United States 156 B3
Wilmington • NC, United States 151 E4
Wilmot Mtn **Ski** • WI, United States . 146 [76]
Wilpattu Nat. Park • Sri Lanka 124 C4
Wilson, Mt • CO, United States 148 E3
Wilson's Creek Nat. Battlefield **Park N** •
MO, United States . . . . 153 [174]
Wilsons Promontory • VI, Australia . . . 136 G9
Wiltshire • United Kingdom 64 B6
Wiltz • Luxembourg 70 D5
Wiluna • WA, Australia 135 C5
Wincanton • United Kingdom 65 K9
Winchester • KY, United States 150 D3
Winchester • United Kingdom 63 E9
Wind Cave Nat. Park **Park N** •
SD, United States . . . . 152 [149]
Wind River **Ind Res** •
WY, United States . . . . 155 [21]
Windermere • United Kingdom 65 D4
Windermere [Lake] • United Kingdom . . 65 D4
Windhoek • Namibia 110 A3
Window on the World • China 126 E4
Window Rock • AZ, United States 155 H7
Windsor • NS, Canada 160 B2
Windsor • OT, Canada 161 A3
Windsor • United Kingdom 65 G7
Windward Is. • West Indies 167 FF4
Windward Passage • Cuba/Haiti 165 E1
Windwardside • Saba . . . . 167 E
Winfield • KS, United States 151 A3
Winisk • OT, Canada 159 H3
Winnebago **Ind Res** •
NE, United States . . . . 155 [53]
Winneconne [Lake] •
WI, United States 150 C2
Winnemucca • NV, United States 154 J7
Winnfield • LA, United States 156 E5
Winningen • Germany 74 C5
Winnipeg • MN, Canada 158 G4
Winnipeg, Lake • MN, Canada 158 G3
Winnipegosis, Lake • MN, Canada . . . 158 F3
Winona • MN, United States 150 C2
Winsen • Germany 72 D2
Winslow • AZ, United States 155 G7
Winston • OR, United States 154 G6
Winston-Salem • NC, United States . . 151 D3
Winter Garden • FL, United States . . . 157 A1
Winter Haven • FL, United States 155 C2
Winter Park **Ski** •
CO, United States . . . . 146 [56]
Winter Park • FL, United States 157 B1
Winterberge • South Africa 111 G6
Wintergreen **Ski** •
VA, United States . . . . 146 [88]
Wintergreen • VA, United States 156 A4
Winterswijk • Netherlands 70 D2
Winterthur • Switzerland 90 D2
Winton • New Zealand 137 G8
Winton • QL, Australia 135 G4
Winton Heights • Bahamas 164 A2
Wipperfürth • Germany 73 D6
Wirliyajarrayi Aboriginal Land •
NT, Australia 136 A1
Wisas • Fed. States of Micronesia . . . 138 C
Wisconsin [Adm] • United States 150 B1
Wisconsin Rapids •
WI, United States 150 C2
Wisconsin [Riv] •
WI, United States 150 B2
Wishaw • United Kingdom 65 A2
Wisła • Poland 89 F9
Wisła [Riv] • Poland 89 C3
Wiślica • Poland 89 G8
Wismar • Germany 72 D2
Wismar **Heritage C** • Germany . . . 44 [46]
Wison • NC, United States 151 E3
Witjira Nat. Park • SA, Australia 136 B2
Witsand • South Africa 111 E7
Witten • Germany 73 D5
Wittenberg • Germany 72 E3
Wittenberg **Heritage C** • Germany . 44 [48]
Wittenberge • Germany 72 D2
Wittlich • Germany 74 C6
Wittstock • Germany 72 E2
Władysławowo • Poland 89 B1
Wrocławek • Poland 89 B2
Włodowa • Poland 89 C3
Wodonga • VI, Australia 136 G9
Wodzisław Śląski • Poland 89 F8
Woerden • Netherlands 70 H8
Woking • United Kingdom 65 G8
Wolf, I. • Galápagos Is. 171 G9
Wolf Trap Nat. Park for the Performing Arts
Park N • VA, United States . . . . 153 [251]
Wolf, Volcán • Galápagos Is. 171 G10
Wolfegg • Germany 74 E8
Wolfratshausen • Germany 74 G7
Wolfsberg • Austria 91 G2
Wolfsburg • Germany 72 D2
Wolin • Poland 89 A2
Wolin [I.] • Poland 89 A2
Woliński Nat. Park **Park N** • Poland . . 58 [99]
Wolkenstein **Ski** • Italy . . . . 61 [144]
Wolkenstein in Gröden • Italy 86 C3
Wollaston Lake • SA, Canada 158 F3
Wollaston Lake [Lake] • SA, Canada . 158 F3
Wolverhampton • United Kingdom 65 F5
Wolwefontein • South Africa 111 G7
Women's Rights Nat. Hist. Park •
NY, United States 156 B1
Women's Rights Nat. Hist. Park **Park N** •
NY, United States . . . . 153 [273]
Wondsorejo • Indonesia 131 K7
Wonosobo • Java, Indonesia 131 Q12
Wonsan • D.P.R. of Korea 125 G3
Wonthaggi • VI, Australia 136 G9
Wood Buffalo Nat. Park **Park N** •
AL/NT, Canada . . . . 161 [16]
Wood Buffalo Nat. Park •
AL/NT, Canada 158 E3
Wood Buffalo Nat. Park **Heritage N** •
AL/NT, Canada . . . . 40 [3]
Woodbridge • United Kingdom 63 E8
Woodbridge Bay • Dominica . . . . 167 K
Woodhouse Reef **Dive** • Egypt . . . 109 E7
Woodhouse Reef • CA, United States . 148 B3
Woodlands • Singapore 129 H11
Woodlark I. • Papua New Guinea . . . 138 BB3
Woodroffe, Mt • SA, Australia 136 A2
Woods Hole • MA, United States 156 D2
Woods, Lake • NT, Australia 135 E3
Woods, Lake of the •
Canada/United States 150 B1
Woods, Lake of the •
Canada/United States 158 G4
Woodstock • IL, United States 150 C2
Woodstock • NY, United States 156 C1
Woodville • LA, United States 156 E5
Woodville • TX, United States 155 F5
Woodward • OK, United States 149 G3
Wookey Hole • United Kingdom 65 K9
Woolacombe **Beach** • United Kingdom 64 [47]
Woolloomgong • NS, Australia 136 H8
Woonsocket • RI, United States 156 C1
Worcester • MA, United States 156 D1
Worcester • South Africa 111 D7
Worcester • United Kingdom 65 F5
Worcestershire • United Kingdom 65 F5

Wordsworth House • United Kingdom . . 65 C3
Wörgl • Austria 91 O7
Workington • United Kingdom 65 C3
Worksop • United Kingdom 63 E7
Wormerveer • Netherlands 70 H7
Worms • Germany 74 D6
Worthing • United Kingdom 65 G8
Worthington • MN, United States 150 A2
Worthsee • Germany 74 F7
Wotje • Marshall Is. 138 CC2
Wotu • Indonesia 131 F4
Wrangel I. • Russian Fed. 101 S2
Wrangell • AK, United States 157 F4
Wrangell Mtns • AK, United States . . . 157 E3
Wrangell-St Elias Nat. Park & Preserve •
AK, United States 157 E3
Wrangell-St Elias Nat. Park & Preserve
Heritage N • AK, United States . . 40 [1]
Wrath, Cape • United Kingdom 58 F2
Wreck Reef • Australia 138 BB4
Wrecks, Bay of • Kiribati . . . . 139 I
Wrekin, The • United Kingdom 65 E5
Wrexham • United Kingdom 63 D7
Wright Brothers Nat. Mem. **Park N** •
NC, United States . . . . 153 [242]
Wrigley • NT, Canada 158 D2
Wrocław • Poland 89 B3
Września • Poland 89 B2
Wubin • WA, Australia 135 B6
Wudangshan **Heritage C** • China . 43 [179]
Wuhai • China 125 E3
Wuhan • China 125 F3
Wuhu • China 125 F3
Wuliang • China 126 H6
Wülfrath • Germany 73 C6
Wulingyuan **Heritage N** • China . . 41 [132]
Wunstorf • Germany 72 C2
Wuntho • Myanmar 128 B2
Wupatki Nat. Mon. •
AZ, United States 155 G7
Wupatki Nat. Mon. **Park N** •
AZ, United States . . . . 152 [104]
Wupper • Germany 73 D6
Wuppertal • Germany 73 D6
Würm • Germany 74 G7
Würzburg • Germany 72 C4
Würzburg **Heritage C** • Germany . . 44 [63]
Wüstenmark • Germany 73 D8
Wusuli Jiang • China 125 H2
Wutai Shan • China . . . . 126 [6]
Wutong Shan • China 126 F4
Wuxi • China 126 H6
Wuyi Shan **Heritage N** • China . . . 41 [133]
Wuyi Shan **Heritage C** • China . . . 43 [186]
Wuyuanzhen • China 125 H1
Wuzhou • China 125 F4
Wyandra • QL, Australia 135 H6
Wye • United Kingdom 65 E6
Wye Valley • United Kingdom 65 E6
Wyndham • New Zealand 137 G8
Wyndham • WA, Australia 135 D3
Wyndham-Werribee • VI, Australia . . . 136 G9
Wynyard • TS, Australia 136 E6
Wyoming • MI, United States 150 C2
Wyoming • United States 148 E2
Wyre Forest • United Kingdom 65 E5
Wyszków • Poland 89 C2

X

Xabia • Spain 83 B1
Xaghra • Malta 96 A1
Xai-Xai • Mozambique 110 C3
Xalandriani • Síros, Greece . . . . 94 I
Xalapa • Mexico 169 K7
Xam Hua • Laos 128 C2
Xanten • Germany 73 C5
Xánthi • Greece 93 D1
Xanthos • Turkey 95 F6
Xanthos-Letoon **Heritage C** • Turkey 44 [247]
Xay • Laos 128 C2
Xcalak • Mexico 169 G5
Xcaret • Mexico 169 G4
Xelha • Mexico 169 G4
Xewkija • Malta 96 A1
Xi Hu • China 126 G7
Xi Jiang • China 125 F4
Xi'an • China 125 E3
Xi'an **Heritage C** • China . . . . 43 [178]
Xiamen • China 125 F4
Xiangfan • China 125 F3
Xianggang • China 125 F4
Xiangkhoang • Laos 128 C3
Xiangshan • China 126 H7
Xiangtan • China 125 F4
Xiangzhou • China 126 E3
Xianyang • China 125 E3
Xiaomeisha Beach Resort • China . . . 126 F4
Xiaoshan • China 126 H7
Xichang • China 125 C4
Xidi **Heritage C** • China . . . . 43 [184]
Xigaze • China 125 C4
Xili Lake Resort • China 126 E4
Xilinhot • China 125 F2
Xingtai • China 125 F3
Xingu • Brazil 174 A3
Xining • China 125 D3
Xinjiang Uygur Zizhiqu • China 125 C2
Xinxiang • China 125 F3
Xinyang • China 125 F3
Xisha Qundao • South China Sea . . . 126 C2
Xitianmu Shan • China 126 G7
Xixabangma Feng • China 125 C4
Xizang Zizhiqu • China 125 C3
Xkichmook • Mexico 169 F4
Xlacah • Mexico 169 F3
Xlendi • Malta 96 A1
Xlendi Bay • Malta 96 A1
Xochicalco • Mexico 169 J7
Xochicalco **Heritage C** • Mexico . . 42 [22]
Xochimilco **Heritage C** • Mexico . . 42 [22]
Xpuhil • Mexico 169 F5
Xuan Loc • Vietnam 129 E5
Xuanzhou • China 126 G7
Xuwen • China 125 F4
Xuzhou • China 125 F3
Xylóskalo • Crete, Greece 93 G6

Y

Ya Men • China 126 E4
Yabelo • Ethiopia 108 C4
Yablonovyy Khrebet • Russian Fed. . . 101 L4
Yabu, Laem • Ko Phuket, Thailand . . . 130 F9
Yabula • QL, Australia 135 H4
Yacuiba • Bolivia 173 C5
Yadua • Fiji Is. . . . . 138 S
Yafo • Israel 120 A3
Yai, Khao • Ko Samui, Thailand 130 G11
Yai, Laem • Ko Samui, Thailand 130 G11
Yaiza • Lanzarote, Canary Is. 83 I5
Yaizu • Japan 127 C4
Yakacik • Turkey 95 J10
Yakima • WA, United States 154 G5
Yakima **Ind Res** • WA, United States 155 [2]
Yakmach • Pakistan 122 A3
Yaku-shima • Japan 127 B4
Yaku-shima **Heritage N** • Japan . . 41 [136]
Yakutat • AK, United States 157 E4
Yakutsk • Russian Fed. 101 M3
Yala Nat. Park • Sri Lanka 124 D4
Yalikavak • Turkey 95 E6
Yalong Jiang • China 125 C4
Yalova • Turkey 95 F3

Yalova [Adm] • Turkey 95 F4
Yalta • Ukraine 100 D5
Yalu • China/D.P.R. of Korea 125 G2
Yamagata • Japan 127 D3
Yamaguchi • Japan 127 B4
Yamal, Poluostrov • Russian Fed. . . . 101 H2
Yamalo-Nenets **Russ Adm** •
Russian Fed. . . . . 101 [19]
Yamanashi [Adm] • Japan 127 H8
Yamasá, Parc de la • QU, Canada . . . 160 H4
Yamato-Koriyama • Japan 127 G6
Yambacoona • TS, Australia 136 E6
Yambol • Bulgaria 92 H8
Yamoussoukro • Côte d'Ivoire 106 B4
Yamuna • India 123 F8
Yamunanagar • India 122 B2
Yana • India 124 D3
Yanam • India 124 D1
Yancheng • China 125 G3
Yandina • Solomon Is. . . . . 138 W
Yangambi • Dem. Rep. of Congo 108 B4
Yangon • Myanmar 128 B3
Yangquan • China 125 F3
Yangtze • China 125 E3
Yangzhou • China 125 G3
Yanji • China 125 G2
Yankari Nat. Park **Park** • Nigeria . . 112 [28]
Yankton • SD, United States 148 G2
Yankton **Ind Res** •
SD, United States . . . . 155 [51]
Yantai • China 125 G3
Yantian • China 126 F4
Yantra • Bulgaria 92 H8
Yanuya • Fiji Is. . . . . 138 T
Yao • Japan 127 G7
Yaoundé • Cameroon 106 D4
Yap • Fed. States of Micronesia . . . . . 138 C
Yap Is. • Fed. States of Micronesia . . 138 C
Yapen • Indonesia 131 I4
Yaqaga • Fiji Is. . . . . 138 S
Yaque del Norte • Dominican Rep. . . . 165 F5
Yaque del Sur • Dominican Rep. 165 G6
Yaqui • Mexico 168 I5
Yardimci Burun • Turkey 95 G8
Yaren • Nauru . . . . 138 X
Yariga-take • Japan 127 C3
Yarkant • China 121 K7
Yarmouth • NS, Canada 160 B2
Yarmouth • United Kingdom 66 D6
Yaroslavl' • Russian Fed. 100 M9
Yasawa Group • Fiji Is. . . . . 138 T
Yashio Maru • Niue . . . . 139 O
Yass • NS, Australia 136 H8
Yasur • Vanuatu . . . . 138 V
Yatagan • Turkey 95 F6
Yaté • New Caledonia . . . . 138 U
Yateritas • Cuba 164 H5
Yathkyed Lake • NU, Canada 158 G2
Yatsushiro • Japan 127 B4
Yatta Plateau • Kenya 109 D5
Yau Ma Tei • Hong Kong, China 126 F3
Yauca • Peru 173 E7
Yáuco • Puerto Rico 165 I8
Yauyos • Peru 173 E6
Yavatmál • India 122 B3
Yavero • Peru 173 F6
Yaviza • Panama 170 I6
Yaxchilán • Mexico 170 J9
Yazd • Iran 120 G7
Yazoo • MS, United States 156 F5
Yazoo City • MS, United States 156 F5
Ydstebøhavn • Norway 99 H6
Yebbenohr • Marshall Is. . . . . 139 E
Yecheng • China 125 B3
Yecla • Spain 83 A1
Yécora • Mexico 168 C2
Yefremov • Russian Fed. 100 E3
Yekaterinburg • Russian Fed. 101 G3
Yelapa • Mexico 169 H7
Yelets • Russian Fed. 100 E3
Yell • United Kingdom 62 H12
Yellow Mtns • China 126 G7
Yellow [Riv] • China 125 E2
Yellow Sea • China/Rep. of Korea . . . 125 G3
Yellowhead Pass • AL/BC, Canada . . 160 J6
Yellowknife • NT, Canada 158 E2
Yellowstone • MT, United States 148 E1
Yellowstone Nat. Park **Park N** •
MT/WY, United States . . . . 152 [72]
Yellowstone Nat. Park •
United States 148 D2
Yellowstone Nat. Park **Heritage N** •
WY, United States . . . . 40 [15]
YEMEN • Asia 120 F10
Yenierenköy • Cyprus 96 D3
Yenisehir • Turkey 95 F4
Yenisey • Russian Fed. 101 I3
Yeo I. • OT, Canada 161 C2
Yeosu • Rep. of Korea 125 G3
Yeovil • United Kingdom 65 K9
Yeppoon • QL, Australia 136 D4
Yercaud • India 124 C2
Yercaud **Hill Sta** • India 124 E6
Yerçómtos • Crete, Greece 93 I6
Yerevan • Armenia 120 E2
Yerköprü • Turkey 95 I10
Yerköy • Turkey 95 F4
Yermasoyia • Cyprus 96 C4
Yeroskipos • Cyprus 96 B4
Yesilbag • Turkey 95 H7
Yesilhisar • Turkey 95 J9
Yesilova • Turkey 95 G7
Yevpatoriya • Ukraine 100 D4
Yeysk • Russian Fed. 100 E4
Yí • Uruguay 175 G6
Yi Xian • China 126 G7
Yialousa • Cyprus 96 D3
Yibin • China 125 E4
Yichang • China 125 F3
Yichun • China 125 G2
Yigo • Guam . . . . 138 Z
Yilanli • Turkey 95 H7
Yilanlikale • Turkey 95 J10
Yinchuan • China 125 E3
Yingkou • China 125 G2
Yingtan • China 125 F4
Yining • China 125 C2
Yishun • Singapore 129 I11
Yitulihe • China 125 G1
Yixing • China 126 G6
Ylåne • Finland 99 C4
Yli-Kitka • Finland 97 F2
Ylöjärvi • Finland 99 D3
Yngaren • Sweden 99 A2
Yoakum • TX, United States 155 E6
Yodo-gawa • Japan 127 G6
Yogyakarta • Java, Indonesia 131 Q12
Yogyakarta [Adm] • Java, Indonesia . 131 Q12
Yoho Nat. Park **Park N** • BC, Canada 161 [4]
Yoho Nat. Park • BC, Canada 160 J7
Yokkaichi • Japan 127 C3
Yokohama • Japan 127 I8
Yokohama-Hakkeijima Sea Paradise •
Japan 127 I9
Yokosuka • Japan 127 I9
Yokote • Japan 127 D3
Yom • Thailand 130 C5
Yonago • Japan 127 B3
Yonaha-dake • Okinawa, Japan . . . . 138 A
Yonabaru • Okinawa, Japan . . . . 138 A
Yong'an • China 125 F4
Yonkers • NY, United States 156 F6
Yonne [Adm] • France 78 B2
Yonne [Riv] • France 78 E2
York • NE, United States 148 G2
York • PA, United States 156 A3
York • United Kingdom 63 E7
York, Cape • Greenland 142 F1
York, Cape • QL, Australia 135 G2
Yorke Peninsula • SA, Australia 135 F6
Yorkshire • United Kingdom 64 B4
Yorkshire [County] • United Kingdom . 64 B4

Yorkshire Dales Nat. Park **Park N** •
United Kingdom . . . . 58 [50]
Yorkshire Dales Nat. Park •
United Kingdom 63 D6
Yorkshire Wolds • United Kingdom . . . 63 E6
Yorkton • SA, Canada 158 F3
Yorktown • VA, United States 156 B4
Yoro Gorge • Japan 127 I9
Yosemite Nat. Park •
CA, United States 154 I8
Yosemite Nat. Park **Park N** •
CA, United States . . . . 152 [48]
Yosemite Nat. Park **Heritage N** •
CA, United States . . . . 40 [12]
Yoshino-Kumano Nat. Park • Japan . . 127 G7
Yoshinoyama • Japan 127 G7
Yoshkar-Ola • Russian Fed. 100 G2
Youghal • Ireland 69 C5
Young I. • St Vincent & Gren. . . . . . . 167 O
Young's Rock • Pitcairn Is. . . . . 139 L
Youngstown • NY, United States 161 D1
Youngstown • OH, United States 150 D2
Yow Beach • Ko Samui, Thailand . . . 130 G11
Yozgat • Turkey 95 B2
Ypres • Belgium 70 A4
Yquem, Château • France 78 E6
Yrghyz • Kazakstan 121 D2
Ystad • Sweden 99 G8
Ysyk-Köl [Lake] • Kyrgyzstan 121 G3
Ysyk-Köl • Kyrgyzstan 121 G3
Ytre Arna • Norway 98 F8
Ytre Sula • Norway 98 F8
Yuan Jiang • China 125 E4
Yuantouzhu • China 126 G6
Yuba City • CA, United States 148 B3
Yucatán [Adm] • Mexico 169 D2
Yucatan Basin • West Indies 166 AA2
Yucatan Channel • West Indies 166 AA2
Yucatán, Peninsula de • Mexico . . . . 169 E-G
Yucca House Nat. Mon. **Park N** •
CO, United States . . . . 152 [91]
Yucca Valley • CA, United States 149 C4
Yuen Long • Hong Kong, China 126 E5
Yuendumu • NT, Australia 136 A1
Yuendumu Aboriginal Land •
NT, Australia 136 A1
Yueyang • China 125 F4
YUGOSLAVIA see SERBIA & MONTENEGRO
Yuhang • China 126 H7
Yukon [Riv] • Canada/United States . . 157 E3
Yukon Territory • Canada 158 C2
Yukon-Charley Rivers Nat. Preserve •
AK, United States 157 E3
Yukon-Charley Rivers Nat. Preserve **Park N** •
AK, United States . . . . 152 [7]
Yulara • NT, Australia 136 A2
Yulin • China 125 F4
Yuma • AZ, United States 155 G8
Yumara Spa • Japan 127 H8
Yumen • China 125 D3
Yumurtalik • Turkey 95 J10
Yuna • Dominican Rep. 165 G5
Yunak • Turkey 95 B2
Yungang Grottoes **Heritage C** • China 43 [176]
Yungkanjini Aboriginal Land •
NT, Australia 136 A1
Yunnan • China 126 B2
Yuscarán • Honduras 170 K9
Yuxikou • China 126 G6
Yuyao • China 126 H7
Yuzhno-Sakhalinsk • Russian Fed. . . 101 O5
Yvelines • France 78 A2
Yverdon-les-Bains • Switzerland 90 I5
Yvoir • Belgium 70 C4

Z

Zaanse Schans • Netherlands 70 H7
Zaanstad • Netherlands 70 H7
Zabargad I. **Dive** • Egypt 109 E8
Zabid **Heritage C** • Yemen . . . . . . 43 [127]
Zabrze • Poland 89 F8
Zacapa • Guatemala 170 K9
Zacatecas • Mexico 169 I6
Zacatecas **Heritage C** • Mexico . . . 42 [15]
Zacatecas [Adm] • Mexico 169 B2
Zacatlán • Mexico 169 J7
Zacchodnie, Beskidy • Poland 89 G9
Zaculeu • Guatemala 170 J9
Zadar • Croatia 92 F6
Zafra • Spain 80 B4
Zagazig • Egypt 109 B1
Zaghouan • Tunisia 107 D4
Zagora • Croatia 92 G6
Zagora • Morocco 107 B3
Zagreb • Croatia 92 F5
Zagros, Kuhha-ye • Iran 120 G7
Zagros Mtns • Iran 120 G7
Zahara de los Atunes • Spain 82 C3
Zahedan • Iran 120 I8
Záhrada Čech • Czech Rep. 89 E6
Zaječar • Serbia & Montenegro 92 C3
Zakhmet • Turkmenistan 121 D4
Zákinthos • Zante, Greece . . . . 94 I
Zákinthos [I.] • Greece . . . . 94 I
Zakopane • Poland 89 G9
Zákoros • Crete, Greece 93 J6
Zalaegerszeg • Hungary 92 B2
Zalantun • China 125 G2
Zalau • Romania 92 C2
Zalim • Saudi Arabia 120 E9
Zamba • Malawi 110 C2
Zambeze • Angola/Mozambique 110 C2
Zambezi • Zambia/Zimbabwe 110 B2
Zambezi Nat. Park **Park** • Zimbabwe 112 [114]
ZAMBIA • Africa 110 B2
Zamboanga • Philippines 128 G5
Zambrów • Poland 89 C2
Zamek Boněřov • Poland 89 F8
Zamek Krzyztopor • Poland 89 G8
Zamek Lubomirskich • Poland 89 G9
Zamora • Spain 80 C3
Zamora de Hidalgo • Mexico 169 I7
Zamosc • Poland 89 C3
Zamosc **Heritage C** • Poland . . . . 44 [182]
Zandvoort • Netherlands 70 G7
Zandvoort, Auto Circuit •
Netherlands 70 G7
Zanjan • Iran 120 F6
Zante • Greece . . . . 94 J
Zanzibar • Botswana 110 J10
Zanzibar • Tanzania 110 H7
Zanzibar **Heritage C** • Tanzania . . 43 [117]
Zanzibar I. • Tanzania 110 H7
Zaozhuang • China 125 F3
Zapadno Dvina • Russian Fed. 100 L10
Zapadno-Sibirskaya Ravnina •
Russian Fed. 101 H3
Zapadnyy Sayan • Russian Fed. 101 J4
Zapata, Peninsula de • Cuba 164 F4
Zapicán • Uruguay 175 G6
Zapopan • Mexico 169 H7
Zara • Croatia 50 D3
Zarafshon • Uzbekistan 121 D3
Zaragoza • Spain 80 B3
Zaranj • Afghanistan 121 D5
Zárate • Argentina 175 F6
Zarco, Baia de • Madeira 84 E5
Zarghun Shahr • Afghanistan 121 E5
Zaria • Nigeria 106 C3
Zarinsk • Russian Fed. 101 I4
Zary • Poland 89 B2
Zarzis • Tunisia 107 D6
Zatec • Czech Rep. 89 D6
Zaventem [Apt] • Belgium 70 B4
Zawiercie • Poland 89 F8
Zaysan • Kazakstan 121 H2

Zaysan Köli • Kazakstan 121 H2
Zdúnska Wola • Poland 89 B3
Zealand • Denmark 99 F7
Zebbug • Malta 96 B2
Zeebrugge • Belgium 70 F6
Zeehan • TS, Australia 136 E7
Zeeland • Netherlands 70 B3
Zeelandia • St Eustatius . . . . 167 E
Zeesen • Germany 73 F8
Zehlendorf (Berlin) • Germany 73 E8
Zeil, Mt • NT, Australia 136 A1
Zeist • Netherlands 70 H8
Zelená Hora **Heritage C** • Czech Rep. 44 [196]
Zelezná Rudá • Czech Rep. 89 D7
Zell • Baden-Württemberg, Germany . . 74 C6
Zell • Rheinland-Pfalz, Germany 74 C6
Zell am See **Ski** • Austria . . . . . . 61 [106]
Zell am See • Austria 91 P7
Zell am Ziller **Ski** • Austria . . . . . 61 [97]
Zell am Ziller • Austria 91 O8
Zelonodol'sk • Russian Fed. 100 G2
Zelve • Turkey 95 J9
Zemaitija Nat. Park **Park N** •
Lithuania . . . . 58 [150]
Zemaitija Nat. Park • Lithuania 100 J7
Zembra • Tunisia 107 D4
Zembretta • Tunisia 107 D4
Zemgale • Latvia 100 K7
Zemst • Belgium 70 B4
Zemun • Serbia & Montenegro 92 C2
Zenica • Bosnia-Herz. 92 G6
Zennor • United Kingdom 65 I10
Zepce • Bosnia-Herz. 92 G6
Zepernick • Germany 73 F7
Zermatt **Ski** • Switzerland . . . . . . 61 [65]
Zermatt • Switzerland 90 J6
Zernabatim Beach • Goa, India 123 C6
Zernez • Switzerland 90 L5
Zernsdorf • Germany 73 F8
Zestienhoven [Apt] • Netherlands 70 G8
Zéus • Náxos, Greece . . . . 94 H
Zeuthen • Germany 73 F8
Zeven • Germany 72 C2
Zgierz • Poland 89 B3
Zgorzelec • Poland 89 A3
Zhagvay • Kazakstan 121 B3
Zhangadzen • Kazakstan 121 B3
Zhanggong Cave • China 126 G6
Zhangiztobe • Kazakstan 121 H2
Zhangjiagang • China 126 H6
Zhangjiakou • China 125 F2
Zhangmutou • China 126 F4
Zhangzhou • China 125 F4
Zhanjiang • China 125 F4
Zhaotong • China 125 E4
Zhejiang • China 126 H7
Zheleznogorsk • Russian Fed. 100 E3
Zhengzhou • China 125 F3
Zhenhai • China 126 H7
Zhenjiang • China 126 G6
Zhezqazghan • Kazakstan 121 E2
Zhlobin • Belarus 100 C3
Zhongsha Qundao • South China Sea 126 C3
Zhongshan • China 126 E4
Zhongshan [Base] • Antarctica . . . . . 176 [18]
Zhosaly • Kazakstan 121 D2
Zhoukoudian **Heritage C** • China . 43 [175]
Zhoushan • China 126 H7
Zhoushan Dao • China 126 H7
Zhoushan Qundao • China 126 H7
Zhu Jiang • China 126 E3
Zhuhai Holiday Resort • China 126 E5
Zhuhai Special Economic Zone • China 126 E4
Zhuji • China 126 H7
Zhujing • China 126 H7
Zhuzhou • China 125 F4
Zhytomyr • Ukraine 100 C3
Zibo • China 125 F3
Zicavo • Corsica, France 78 N12
Ziegenhals • Germany 73 F8
Zielona Góra • Poland 89 A3
Zigong • China 125 E4
Ziguinchor • Senegal 106 A3
Zijin Shan • China 126 G6
Zilina • Slovak Rep. 89 F8
Zillah • Libya 108 A2
Zillertal • Austria 91 O8
Zillertaler Alpen • Austria/Italy 91 O8
ZIMBABWE • Africa 110 B2
Zimnicea • Romania 92 H7
Zinal • Switzerland 90 J6
Zinjibar • Yemen 120 F11
Zinder • Niger 106 C3
Zingara **Dive** • Egypt 109 E7
Zingst • Germany 72 E1
Zion Nat. Park • UT, United States . . . 155 G7
Zion Nat. Park **Park N** •
UT, United States . . . . 152 [77]
Zippori • Israel 120 B2
Zirje • Croatia 92 F6
Zitácuaro • Mexico 169 J7
Ziyaaraifyushi • Maldives 124 H7
Zlatá Koruna • Czech Rep. 89 E7
Zlatni Pyasutsi • Bulgaria 92 I8
Zleby • Czech Rep. 89 E6
Zlin • Czech Rep. 89 E7
Znojmo • Czech Rep. 89 E7
Zoetermeer • Netherlands 70 G8
Zoldo Alto • Italy 86 D4
Zollverein **Heritage C** • Germany . 44 [54]
Zomba • Malawi 110 C2
Zongshan Hot Springs • China 126 E4
Zonguldak • Turkey 95 B1
Zonhoven • Belgium 70 C4
Zonnebeke [Battlefield] • Belgium . . . 70 A4
Zons • Germany 73 C6
Zoologischer Garten Berlin • Germany 73 F7
Zoomarine **Park L** • Portugal . . . . 59 [77]
Zoomarine • Portugal 84 J8
Zoorama • France 78 E5
Zossen • Germany 73 F8
Zouérat • Mauritania 106 A2
Zrenjanin • Serbia & Montenegro 92 C2
Zuari Estuary • Goa, India 123 C5
Zug • Switzerland 90 K5
Zug [Adm] • Switzerland 91 R9
Zuger See • Switzerland 90 K5
Zugspitze • Austria/Germany 74 F8
Zuid Holland • Netherlands 70 B3
Zuid-Beveland • Netherlands 70 B3
Zülpich • Germany 74 C6
Zululand • South Africa 111 B3/4
Zunyi • China 125 E4
Zuni **Ind Res** • NM, United States . 155 H7
Zuni • China 125 E4
Zuoz • Switzerland 90 L5
Zürich • Switzerland 90 D2
Zürich [Adm] • Switzerland 91 R9
Zürichsee • Switzerland 90 K5
Zurrieq • Malta 96 B2
Zürs **Ski** • Austria . . . . 61 [89]
Zürs • Austria 91 M8
Zusmarshausen • Germany 74 F7
Zut • Croatia 92 F6
Zutphen • Netherlands 70 D2
Zvartnots **Heritage C** • Armenia . . 43 [137]
Zvikov • Czech Rep. 89 E7
Zvolen • Slovak Rep. 89 B4
Zvornik • Bosnia-Herz. 92 B2
Zweibrücken • Germany 74 A2
Zweisimmen • Switzerland 90 B4
Zwickau • Germany 72 E3
Zwijndrecht • Netherlands 70 G8
Zwolle • Netherlands 70 D2
Zyryanovsk • Kazakstan 121 H2
Zywiec • Poland 89 F9

World

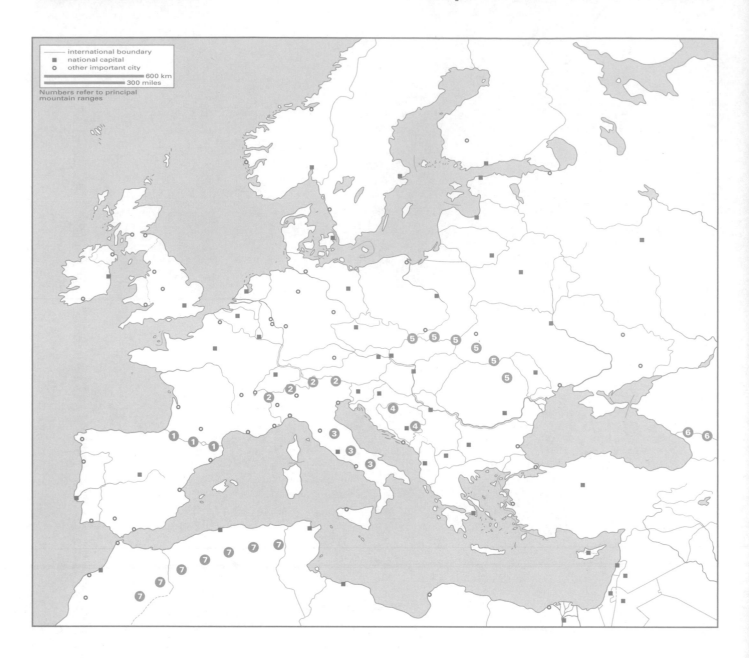

international boundary
national capital
other important city
600 km
300 miles
Numbers refer to principal
mountain ranges

international boundary
national capital
other important city

See Europe map

British Isles

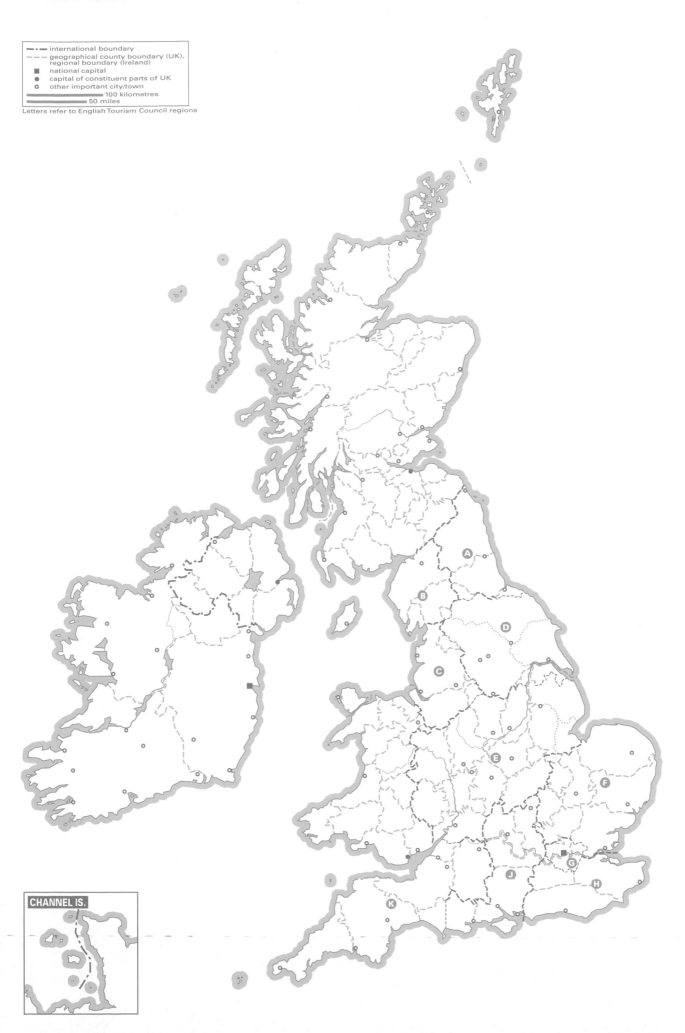

international boundary
geographical county boundary (UK),
regional boundary (Ireland)
national capital
capital of constituent parts of UK
other important city/town
100 kilometres
50 miles
Letters refer to English Tourism Council regions

CHANNEL IS.

—·—·—	international boundary
— — —	provincial boundary
■	national capital
●	provincial capital
○	other important city/town

80 km
40 miles

—·—·—	international boundary
— — —	provincial boundary
■	national capital
●	provincial capital
○	other important city/town

80 km
40 miles

Germany

60 kilometres
30 miles

Iberia

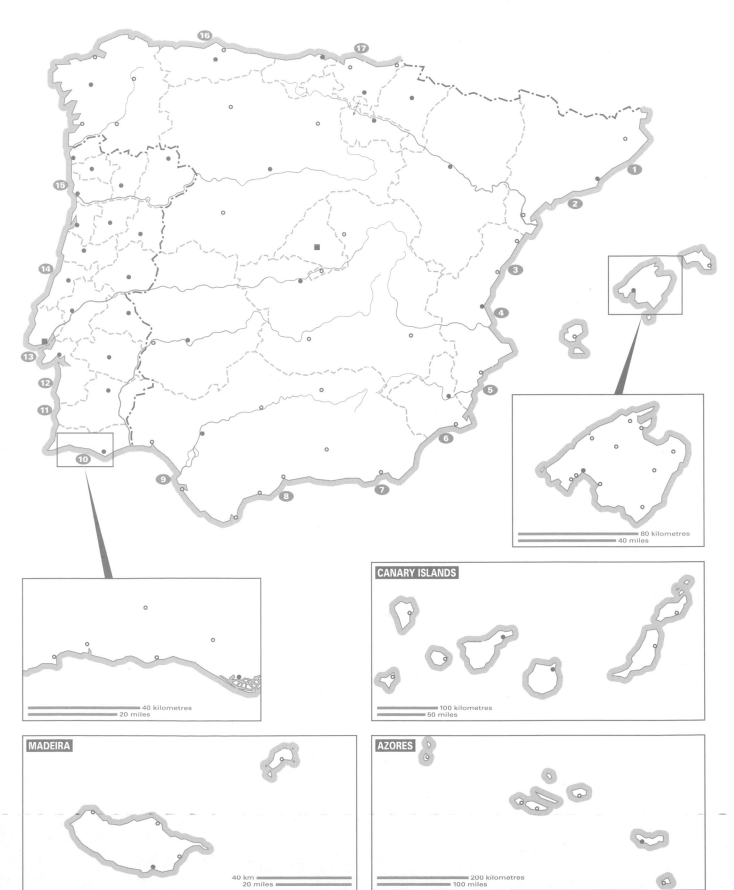

international boundary
autonomous community boundary (Spain)
district boundary (Portugal)
national capital
autonomous community capital (Spain)
district capital (Portugal)
other important city/town

200 km
100 miles

Numbers refer to Spanish and Portuguese 'Costas'

80 kilometres
40 miles

40 kilometres
20 miles

CANARY ISLANDS

100 kilometres
50 miles

MADEIRA

40 km
20 miles

AZORES

200 kilometres
100 miles

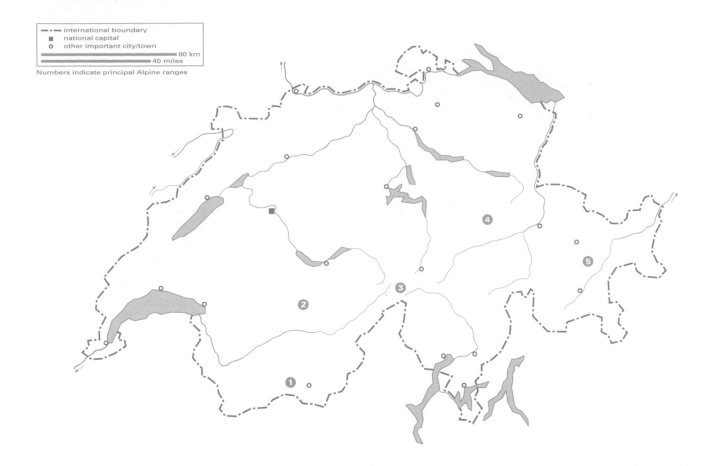

international boundary
national capital
other important city/town

80 km
40 miles

Numbers indicate principal Alpine ranges

international boundary
Land boundary
national capital
Land capital
other important city/town

100 km
50 miles

Numbers indicate principal Alpine ranges

Italy

international boundary
■ national capital
○ other important city/town

200 km
100 miles

international boundary
■ national capital
○ other important city/town

400 km
200 miles

Scandinavia, Malta & Cyprus

--- international boundary
--- regional boundary
■ national capital
○ other important city/town

400 km
200 miles

■ national capital
○ other important town

10 km
5 miles

■ national capital
○ other important town

60 km
30 miles

Africa

international boundary
national capital
other important city

international boundary
provincial boundary
national capital
provincial capital
other important city/town

600 km
300 miles